PHILOSOPHY FOR THE 21ST CENTURY

A Comprehensive Reader

Edited by

Steven M. Cahn
City University of New York Graduate Center

Associate Editors

Delia Graff   *Cornell University*

Robin Jeshion   *Yale University*

L. A. Paul   *University of Arizona*

Jesse J. Prinz   *University of North Carolina at Chapel Hill*

Stuart Rachels   *University of Alabama*

Gabriela Sakamoto   *Mount Saint Mary's College*

David Sosa   *University of Texas at Austin*

Cynthia A. Stark   *University of Utah*

New York   Oxford

OXFORD UNIVERSITY PRESS

2003

Oxford University Press

Oxford   New York
Auckland   Bangkok   Buenos Aires   Cape Town   Chennai
Dar es Salaam   Delhi   Hong Kong   Istanbul   Karachi   Kolkata
Kuala Lumpur   Madrid   Melbourne   Mexico City   Mumbai
Nairobi   São Paulo   Shanghai   Taipei   Tokyo   Toronto

Published by Oxford University Press, Inc.
198 Madison Avenue, New York, New York, 10016
http://www.oup-usa.org

Oxford is a registered trademark of Oxford University Press

Library of Congress Cataloging-in-Publication Data

Philosophy for the 21st century : a comprehensive reader / edited by Steven M. Cahn.
   p. cm.
   ISBN 0-19-514792-8 (pbk. : alk. paper)
   1. Philosophy—Introductions. I. Title: Philosophy for the twenty-first century. II.
Cahn, Steven M.

BD21 .P475 2002
100—dc21   2002029007

Printing number: 9 8 7 6 5 4 3 2 1

Printed in the United States of America
on acid-free paper

CONTENTS

~

3.   PHILOSOPHY OF SCIENCE

4.   METAPHYSICS

5.   PHILOSOPHY OF MIND

6.   PHILOSOPHY OF LANGUAGE

7.   ETHICS

8.   POLITICAL PHILOSOPHY

9.   PHILOSOPHY OF ART

PREFACE

~

Introductory anthologies typically reflect the philosophical viewpoints of one or more senior scholars, each of whom makes editorial decisions in a variety of fields. This collection draws on the judgments of a new generation of scholars, each of whom has chosen the selections and provided introductions in one area of expertise: David Sosa (epistemology), L. A. Paul (philosophy of science), Delia Graff (metaphysics), Jesse J. Prinz (philosophy of mind), Robin Jeshion (philosophy of language), Stuart Rachels (ethics), Cynthia A. Stark (political philosophy), and Gabriela Sakamoto (philosophy of art). While the choice of associate editors, the structure of the book, and the contents of the first section are the responsibility of the editor, the rest of the work has been done by the associate editors. These philosophers are in the vanguard of 21st-century philosophy, and the choices they have made reflect their views of the most important materials that should be mastered by 21st-century students.

Those who wish to learn more about a particular philosopher or a specific philosophical issue are urged to consult the *Encyclopedia of Philosophy* (Routledge, 1999), ed. Edward Craig. It contains detailed entries with bibliographies on every significant topic in the field. Shorter entries, but informative and reliable, are to be found in *The Oxford Dictionary of Philosophy* (Oxford and New York, 1994), ed. Simon Blackburn and *The Cambridge Dictionary of Philosophy, Second Edition* (Cambridge and New York, 1999), ed. Robert Audi.

I am grateful to Robert Miller, my editor at Oxford University Press, for his encouragement and advice; to David Shatz, with whom I consulted regarding the contents of the first section; to Maureen Eckert, my research assistant at the City University of New York Graduate Center, for her generous help in preparing the manuscript for publication; to Ian Gardiner, for his conscientious proofreading; and to the staff of Oxford University Press for its help at all stages of production. I especially thank the eight outstanding scholars who readily agreed to participate in this collaborative project.

ABOUT THE EDITORS

~

STEVEN M. CAHN (Ph.D., Columbia University) is professor of philosophy at City University of New York Graduate Center. He served as the school's provost and vice president for academic affairs and then acting president. He taught at Dartmouth College, Vassar College, the University of Rochester, New York University, and the University of Vermont, where he headed the Department of Philosophy. He is the author or editor of more than 25 books, including *Classics of Western Philosophy, Sixth Edition; Classics of Political and Moral Philosophy;* and *Classic and Contemporary Readings in the Philosophy of Education.*

DELIA GRAFF (Ph.D., Massachusetts Institute of Technology) is Assistant Professor in the Sage School of Philosophy, Cornell University, and taught previously at Princeton University. Her research interests are in metaphysics, epistemology, philosophical logic, and philosophy of language. Her articles have appeared in *Mind, Philosophical Studies, Philosophical Topics* and *Philosophy and Phenomenological Research.*

ROBIN JESHION (Ph.D., University of Chicago) is Associate Professor of Philosophy at Yale University. She previously taught at the University of Southern California. Her articles have appeared in *Mind, Philosophical Studies,* and *Philosophical and Phenomenological Research.*

L. A. PAUL (Ph.D., Princeton University) is Assistant Professor of Philosophy at the University of Arizona and a fellow at the Institute for Advanced Study Research at the Australian National University Research School of Social Science. She previously taught at Yale University. She has written articles that have appeared in *Noûs, The Journal of Philosophy, Analysis, Utilitas,* and *Synthese;* is a coeditor of *Causation and Counterfactuals,* forthcoming with MIT Press; and is advisory editor for an issue of *The Monist* on the metaphysics of objects.

JESSE J. PRINZ (Ph.D., University of Chicago) is Associate Professor of Philosophy at the University of North Carolina at Chapel Hill. Previously he taught in the Department of Philosophy and the Philosophy-Neuroscience-Psychology Program at Washington University in St. Louis. He is the author of *Furnishing the Mind: Concepts and Their Perceptual Basis* and *Emotional Perception.*

STUART RACHELS (Ph.D., Syracuse University) is Assistant Professor of Philosophy at the University of Alabama. He received undergraduate degrees from Emory University and Oxford University, where he was a Marshall Scholar. His articles on ethics have appeared in *Noûs, Philosophical Studies, Bioethics,* and *The Australasian Journal of Philosophy.* He became United States Chess Champion in 1989, at the age of 20.

GABRIELA SAKAMOTO (Ph.D., University of Chicago) is a lecturer in the Department of Philosophy at Mount Saint Mary's College. Previously, she taught at Howard University. She has contributed articles to *The Encyclopedia of Aesthetics* and the *Journal of Aesthetics and Art Criticism.*

DAVID SOSA (Ph.D., Princeton University) is Associate Professor of Philosophy at the University of Texas at Austin. He is the author of articles in *Mind, Philosophical Review*, and *Noûs*, among other publications, and is a coeditor of *A Companion to Analytic Philosophy* and *Analytic Philosophy: An Anthology,* both from Blackwell Publishers.

CYNTHIA A. STARK (Ph.D., University of North Carolina) is Associate Professor of Philosophy at the University of Utah. Her articles have appeared in the *Journal of the History of Philosophy, Noûs* and *The Journal of Philosophy,* among other publications.

Introduction

What Is Philosophy?

~

SIMON BLACKBURN

Simon Blackburn is professor of philosophy at the University of Cambridge. Previously he was Edna J. Koury Distinguished Professor of Philosophy at the University of North Carolina, Chapel Hill. He is the author of *The Oxford Dictionary of Philosophy.*

This book is for people who want to think about the big themes: knowledge, reason, truth, mind, freedom, destiny, identity, God, goodness, justice. These are not the hidden preserve of specialists. They are things that men and women wonder about naturally, for they structure the ways we think about the world and our place in it. . . .

The word "philosophy" carries unfortunate connotations: impractical, unworldly, weird. I suspect that all philosophers and philosophy students share that moment of silent embarrassment when someone innocently asks us what we do. I would prefer to introduce myself as doing conceptual engineering. For just as the engineer studies the structure of material things, so the philosopher studies the structure of thought. Understanding the structure involves seeing how parts function and how they interconnect. It means knowing what would happen for better or worse if changes were made. This is what we aim at

when we investigate the structures that shape our view of the world. Our concepts or ideas form the mental housing in which we live. We may end up proud of the structures we have built. Or we may believe that they need dismantling and starting afresh. But first, we have to know what they are. . . .

WHAT ARE WE TO THINK ABOUT?

Here are some questions any of us might ask about ourselves: What am I? What is consciousness? Could I survive my bodily death? Can I be sure that other people's experiences and sensations are like mine? If I can't share the experience of others, can I communicate with them? Do we always act out of self-interest? Might I be a kind of puppet, programmed to do the things that I believe I do out of my own free will?

Here are some questions about the world: Why is there something and not nothing? What is the difference between past and future? Why does causation run always from past to future, or does it make sense to think that the future might influence the past? Why does nature keep on in a regular way? Does the world presuppose a Creator? And if so, can we understand why he (or she or they) created it?

Finally, here are some questions about ourselves *and* the world: How can we be sure that the world is really like we take it to be? What is knowledge, and how much do we have? What makes a field of inquiry a science? (Is psychoanalysis a science? Is economics?) How do we know about abstract objects, like numbers? How do we know about values and duties? How are we to tell whether our opinions are objective, or just subjective?

The queer thing about these questions is that not only are they baffling at first sight, but they also defy simple processes of solution. If someone asks me when it is high tide, I know how to set about getting an answer. There are authoritative tide tables I can consult. I may know roughly how they are produced. And if all else fails, I could go and measure the rise and fall of the sea myself. A question like this is a matter of experience: an *empirical* question. It can be settled by means of agreed procedures, involving looking and seeing, making measurements, or applying rules that have been tested against experience and found to work. The questions of the last paragraphs are not like this. They seem to require more reflection. We don't immediately know where to look. Perhaps we feel we don't quite know what we mean when we ask them, or what would count as getting a solution. What would show me, for instance, whether I am not after all a puppet, programmed to do the things I believe I do freely? Should we ask scientists who specialize in the brain? But how would they know what to look for? How would they know when they had found it? Imagine the headline: "Neuroscientists discover human beings not puppets." How?

So what gives rise to such baffling questions?

In a word, self-reflection. Human beings are relentlessly capable of reflecting on themselves. We might do something out of habit, but then we can begin to reflect on the habit. We can habitually think things, and then reflect on what we are thinking. We can ask ourselves (or sometimes we get asked by

other people) whether we know what we are talking about. To answer that we need to reflect on our own positions, our own understanding of what we are saying, our own sources of authority. We might start to wonder whether we know what we mean. We might wonder whether what we say is "objectively" true, or merely the outcome of our own perspective, or our own "take" on a situation. Thinking about this we confront categories like knowledge, objectivity, truth, and we may want to think about them. At that point we are *reflecting* on concepts and procedures and beliefs that we normally just *use*. We are looking at the scaffolding of our thought, and doing conceptual engineering.

This point of reflection might arise in the course of quite normal discussion. A historian, for example, is more or less bound at some point to ask what is meant by "objectivity" or "evidence," or even "truth," in history. A cosmologist has to pause from solving equations with the letter t in them, and ask what is meant, for instance, by the flow of time or the direction of time or the beginning of time. But at that point, whether they recognize it or not, they become philosophers. And they are beginning to do something that can be done well or badly. The point is to do it well.

How is philosophy learned? A better question is: how can thinking skills be acquired? The thinking in question involves attending to basic structures of thought. This can be done well or badly, intelligently or ineptly. But doing it well is not primarily a matter of acquiring a body of knowledge. It is more like playing the piano well. It is a "knowing how" as much as a "knowing that." The most famous philosophical character of the classical world, the Socrates of Plato's dialogues, did not pride himself on how much he knew. On the contrary, he prided himself on being the only one who knew how little he knew (reflection, again). What he was good at—supposedly, for estimates of his success differ—was exposing the weaknesses of other peoples' claims to know. To process thoughts well is a matter of being able to avoid confusion, detect ambiguities, keep things in mind one at a time, make reliable arguments, become aware of alternatives, and so on.

To sum up: our ideas and concepts can be compared with the lenses through which we see the world. In philosophy the lens is itself the topic of study. Success will be a matter not of how much you know at the end, but of what you can do when the going gets tough: when the seas of argument rise, and confusion breaks out. Success will mean taking seriously the implications of ideas.

WHAT IS THE POINT?

It is all very well saying that, but why bother? What's the point? Reflection doesn't get the world's business done. It doesn't bake bread or fly aeroplanes. Why not just toss the reflective questions aside, and get on with other things? I shall sketch three kinds of answer: high ground, middle ground, and low ground.

The high ground questions the question—a typical philosophical strategy, because it involves going up one level of reflection. What do we mean when we ask what the point is? Reflection bakes no bread, but then neither does architecture, music, art, history, or literature. It is just that we want to understand ourselves. We want this for its own sake, just as a pure scientist or pure mathematician may want to understand the beginning of the universe, or the theory of sets, for its own sake, or just as a musician might want to solve some problem in harmony or counterpoint just for its own sake. There is no eye on any practical applications. A lot of life is indeed a matter of raising more hogs, to buy more land, so we can raise more hogs, so that we can buy more land. . . . The time we take out, whether it is to do mathematics or music, or to read Plato or Jane Austen, is time to be cherished. It is the time in which we cosset our mental health. And our mental health is just good in itself, like our physical health. Furthermore there is after all a payoff in terms of pleasure. When our physical health is good, we take pleasure in physical exercise, and when our mental health is good, we take pleasure in mental exercise.

This is a very pure-minded reply. The problem with it is not that it is wrong. It is just that it is only likely to appeal to people who are half-convinced already—people who didn't ask the original question in a very aggressive tone of voice.

So here is a middle-ground reply. Reflection matters because it is *continuous* with practice. How you think about what you are doing affects how you do it, or whether you do it at all. It may direct your research, or your attitude to people who do things differently, or indeed your whole life. To take a simple example, if your reflections lead you to believe in a life after death, you may be prepared to face persecutions that you would not face if you became convinced—as many philosophers are—that the notion makes no sense. Fatalism, or the belief that the future is fixed whatever we do, is a purely philosophical belief, but it is one that can paralyse action. Putting it more politically, it can also express an acquiescence with the low status accorded to some segments of society, and this may be a pay-off for people of higher status who encourage it.

Let us consider some examples more prevalent in the West. Many people reflecting on human nature think that we are at bottom entirely selfish. We only look out for our own advantage, never really caring about anyone else. Apparent concern disguises hope of future benefit. The leading paradigm in the social sciences is *homo economicus*—economic man. Economic man looks after himself, in competitive struggle with others. Now, if people come to think that we are all, always, like this, their relations with each other become different. They become less trusting, less cooperative, more suspicious. This changes the way they interact, and they will incur various costs. They will find it harder, and in some circumstances impossible, to get cooperative ventures going: they may get stuck in what the philosopher Thomas Hobbes (1588–1679) memorably called "the war of all against all." In the market-place, because they are always looking out to be cheated, they will incur heavy transaction costs. If my attitude is that "a verbal contract is not worth the paper it is written on," I will have to pay lawyers to design contracts with penalties, and if I will not trust the lawyers to do anything except just enough to pocket their fees, I will have to get the contracts checked by other lawyers, and so on. But all this may be based on a philosophical mistake—looking at human motivation through the wrong set of categories, and hence misunderstanding its nature. Maybe people can care for each other, or at least care for doing their bit or keeping their promises. Maybe if a more optimistic self-image is on the table, people can come to live up to it. Their lives then become better. So this bit of thinking, getting clear about the right categories with which to understand human motivation, is an important *practical* task. It is not confined to the study, but bursts out of it.

Here is a very different example. The Polish astronomer Nicholas Copernicus (1473–1543) reflected on how we *know* about motion. He realized that how we perceive motion is *perspectival:* that is, whether we see things as moving is the result of how we ourselves are placed and in particular whether we ourselves are moving. (We have mostly been subject to the illusion in trains or airports, where the next-door train or aeroplane seems to move off, and then we realize with a jolt that it is we who are moving. But there were fewer everyday examples in the time of Copernicus.) So the apparent motions of the stars and planets might arise because they are not moving as they appear to do, but we observers move. And this is how it turned out to be. Here reflection on the nature of knowledge—what philosophers call an *epistemological* inquiry, from the Greek *episteme,* meaning knowledge—generated the first spectacular leap of modern science. Einstein's reflections on how we know whether two events are simultaneous had the same structure. He realized that the results of our measurements would depend upon the way we are travelling compared to the events we are clocking. This led to the Special Theory of Relativity (and Einstein himself acknowledged the importance of preceding philosophers in sensitizing him to the epistemological complexities of such a measurement).

For a final example, we can consider a philosophical problem many people get into when they think about mind and body. Many people envisage a strict separation between mind, as one thing, and body, as a different thing. When this seems to be just good common sense, it can begin to infect practice in quite insidious ways. For instance, it begins to be difficult to see how these two different things interact. Doctors might then find it almost *inevitable* that treatments of physical conditions that address mental or psychological causes will fail. They might find it next to impossible to see how messing with someone's mind could possibly cause changes in the complex physical system that is their body. After all, good science tells

us that it takes physical and chemical causes to have physical and chemical effects. So we might get an a priori, armchair certainty that one kind of treatment (say, drugs and electric shocks) has to be "right" and others (such as treating patients humanely, counselling, analysis) are "wrong": unscientific, unsound, bound to fail. But this certainty is premised not on science but on a false *philosophy.* A better philosophical conception of the relation between mind and body changes it. A better conception should enable us to see how there is nothing *surprising* in the fact of mind-body interaction. It is the most commonplace fact, for instance, that thinking of some things (mental) can cause people to blush (physical). Thinking of a future danger can cause all kinds of bodily changes: hearts pound, fists clench, guts constrict. By extrapolation there should be nothing difficult to comprehend about a mental state such as cheerful optimism affecting a physical state like the disappearance of spots or even the remission of a cancer. It becomes a purely *empirical* fact whether such things happen. The armchair certainty that they could not happen is itself revealed as dependent on bad understanding of the structures of thought, or in other words bad philosophy, and is in that sense unscientific. And this realization can change medical attitudes and practice for the better.

So the middle-ground answer reminds us that reflection is continuous with practice, and our practice can go worse or better according to the value of our reflections. A system of thought is something we live in, just as much as a house, and if our intellectual house is cramped and confined, we need to know what better structures are possible.

The low-ground answer merely polishes this point up a bit, not in connection with nice clean subjects like economics or physics, but down in the basement where human life is a little less polite. One of the series of satires etched by the Spanish painter Goya is entitled "The Sleep of Reason Produces Monsters." Goya believed that many of the follies of mankind resulted from the "sleep of reason." There are always people telling us what we want, how they will provide it, and what we should believe. Convictions are infectious, and people can make others convinced of almost anything. We are typically ready to believe that *our* ways, *our* beliefs, *our* religion, *our* politics are better than theirs, or that *our* God-given rights trump theirs or that *our* interests require defensive or pre-emptive strikes against them. In the end, it is ideas for which people kill each other. It is because of ideas about what the others are like, or who we are, or what our interests or rights require, that we go to war, or oppress others with a good conscience, or even sometimes acquiesce in our own oppression by others. When these beliefs involve the sleep of reason, critical awakening is the antidote. Reflection enables us to step back, to see our perspective on a situation as perhaps distorted or blind, at the very least to see if there is argument for preferring our ways, or whether it is just subjective. Doing this properly is doing one more piece of conceptual engineering.

Since there is no telling in advance where it may lead, reflection can be seen as dangerous. There are always thoughts that stand opposed to it. Many people are discomfited, or even outraged, by philosophical questions. Some are fearful that their ideas may not stand up as well as they would like if they start to think about them. Others may want to stand upon the "politics of identity," or in other words the kind of identification with a particular tradition, or group, or national or ethnic identity that invites them to turn their back on outsiders who question the ways of the group. They will shrug off criticism: their values are "incommensurable" with the values of outsiders. They are to be understood only by brothers and sisters within the circle. People like to retreat to within a thick, comfortable, traditional set of folkways, and not to worry too much about their structure, or their origins, or even the criticisms that they may deserve. Reflection opens the avenue to criticism, and the folkways may not like criticism. In this way, ideologies become closed circles, primed to feel outraged by the questioning mind.

For the last two thousand years the philosophical tradition has been the enemy of this kind of cosy complacency. It has insisted that the unexamined life is not worth living. It has insisted on the power of rational reflection to winnow out bad elements in our practices, and to replace them with better ones. It has identified critical self-reflection with freedom, the idea being that only when we can see ourselves properly can we obtain control over the direction in which we would wish to move. It is only when we can see our situation steadily and see it whole that we can start to think what to do about it.

The Elements of Logic

SIMON BLACKBURN

Simon Blackburn, who also wrote the previous selection, is the author of *Spreading the Word, Ruling Passions,* and *Being Good.*

A LITTLE LOGIC

The working parts of an argument are, first, its *premises.* These are the starting point, or what is accepted or assumed, so far as the argument is concerned. An argument can have one premise, or several. From the premises an argument derives a *conclusion.* If we are reflecting on the argument, perhaps because we are reluctant to accept the conclusion, we have two options. First, we might reject one or more of the premises. But second, we might reject the way the conclusion is drawn from the premises. The first reaction is that one of the premises is *untrue.* The second is that the reasoning is *invalid.* Of course, an argument may be subject to both criticisms: its premises are untrue, and the reasoning from them is invalid. But the two criticisms are distinct (and the two words, untrue and invalid, are well kept for the distinction).

In everyday life, arguments are criticized on other grounds again. The premises may not be very sensible. It is silly to make an intricate argument from the premise that I will win next week's lottery, if it hasn't a dog's chance of happening. It is often inappropriate to help ourselves to premises that are themselves controversial. It is tactless and tasteless in some circumstances to argue some things. But "logical" is not a synonym for "sensible." Logic is interested in whether arguments are valid, not in whether it is sensible to put them forward. Conversely, many people called "illogical" may actually be propounding valid arguments, but be dotty in other ways.

Logic has only one concern. It is concerned whether there is *no way* that the premises could be true without the conclusion being true.

It was Aristotle (384–322 BC) who first tried to give a systematic taxonomy of valid and invalid arguments. Aristotle realized that any kind of theory would need to classify arguments by the patterns of reasoning they exhibit, or what is called their *form*. One of the most famous forms of argument, for instance, rejoicing in the title "modus ponendo ponens," or modus ponens for short, just goes:

p;
If p then q;
So, q.

Here p and q stand for any piece of information, or proposition, that you like. The form of the argument would remain the same whether you were talking of cows or philosophers. Logic then studies forms of information, not particular examples of it. Particular arguments are instances of the forms, but the logician is interested in the form or structure, just as a mathematician is interested in numerical forms and structure, but not interested in whether you are counting bananas or profits.

We want our reasonings to be valid. We said what this means: we want there to be *no way* that our conclusion could be false, if our premises are true. So we need to study whether there is "any way" that one set of things, the premises, can be true without another thing, the conclusion, also being true. To investigate this we need to produce a science of the *ways* things can be true. For some very simple ways of building up information, we can do this.

TRUTH-TABLES

The classical assumptions are first that every proposition ($p, q \ldots$) has just one of two *truth*-values. It must be either true or false, and it cannot be both. ("But suppose I don't grant that?" Patience.) The second assumption is that the terms the logic is dealing with—centrally, "and," "not," "or," and "If . . . then . . ."—can be characterized in terms of what they do to truth-values. ("But suppose I don't grant that?" Patience, again.)

Thus, consider "not-p." Not-p, which is often written $\neg p$, is the denial or negation of p: it is what you say when you disagree with p. Whatever it is talking about, p, according to our first assumption, is either true (T), or false (F). It is not both. What does "not" do? It simply reverses truth-value. If p is true, then $\neg p$ is false. If p is false, then $\neg p$ is true. That is what "not" does. We can summarize the result as a *truth-table:*

p	$\neg p$
T	F
F	T

The table gives the result, in terms of truth or falsity, for each assignment of truth-value to the components (such an assignment is called an *interpretation*). A similar table can be written for "and," only here there are more combinations to consider. We suppose that "and" conjoins two propositions, each of which can be true or false. So there are four situations or interpretations to consider:

p	q	$p \,\&\, q$
T	T	T
T	F	F
F	T	F
F	F	F

We are here given the truth-value for the overall combination, the conjunction, as a function of the combination of truth-values of the components: the four different interpretations of the formula.

The fact that we can give these tables is summed up by saying that conjunction, and negation, are *truth-functional*, or that they are truth-functional operators. Elementary propositional logic studies the truth-functions. Besides "not" and "and," they include "or" (*p* or *q*, regarded as true except when both *p* and *q* are false); and a version of "If *p* then *q*," regarded as true except in the case where *p* is true yet *q* false. If we write this latter as "*p* → *q*," its truth-table is:

p	*q*	*p* → *q*
T	T	T
T	F	F
F	T	T
F	F	T

These are also called Boolean operators. People familiar with databases and spreadsheets will know about Boolean searches, which implement exactly the same idea. A search for widgets over five years old held in the warehouse in York returns a hit when it finds a widget meeting *both* conditions. A search for customers *not* paid up on 1 December returns just the reverse hits from a search for customers paid up on 1 December. A search for customers who *either* bought a washing machine *or* a lawnmower turns up those who bought one and those who bought the other.

We can now see a rationale for some rules of inference. Consider the rule that from "*p* & *q*" we can derive *p* (or equally *q*). You cannot thereby get from truth to falsity, because the only interpretation (the top line) that has "*p* & *q*" true also has each ingredient true. So this is a good rule. We can also see why modus ponendo ponens, introduced above, is a good rule. It has two premises, "*p*," and "If *p* then *q*." Can we find an interpretation (a "way") in which both these are true without *q* being true? No. Because given that *p* is true, the only interpretation of *p* → *q* that allows it to be true also displays *q* as true.

There are some interesting animals in this jungle. One is that of a contradiction. Consider this formula:

$$p \ \& \ \neg p.$$

This expresses a contradiction—the ultimate no-no. And we now have a precise sense in which it is a no-

no. For it is easy to show from the two tables we have, that *whatever* the truth-value of *p*, the truth-value of this formula comes out as F. There is *no way* it could be true. Because when one of the conjuncts is true the other is false: there is always a false element. And the truth-table for conjunction shows that in that case the overall formula is false.

Now suppose we complicate things by negating it:

$$\neg(p \ \& \ \neg p).$$

The brackets here show that the outside ¬ negates the whole thing. They act like the brackets in $3 \times (4 + 2)$, which show that the result is to be 18, rather than what we would get if we had $(3 \times 4) + 2$, which is 14. This bracketing is extremely important in logic, as it is in arithmetic: many fallacies in formal and informal reasoning can be avoided by knowing where the brackets fall. This is called knowing the *scope* of operation of the negations and conjunctions and the rest. In this example the outside negation has the whole of the rest of the formula to operate upon. A quite different reading would be given by ¬*p* & ¬*p*, which simply conjoins ¬*p* to itself, and, incidentally, is false in the case in which *p* is true (saying something false twice does not make it any better). One of the terrific virtues of formal logic is that it sensitizes people to scope *ambiguities,* which arise when it is not clear where the brackets lie, or in other words what is governing what. Without knowing this, you do not know *in what ways* your premises and your conclusions might be true, and hence whether there is *any way* your premises might be true without your conclusion being so.

This new formula, ¬(*p* & ¬*p*), reverses the truth-value of the old contradiction. So it is true, whatever the truth-values of its components. It is called a *tautology.* This is an important notion. In propositional logic if we have premises blah-blah-blah and conclusion yadda-yadda, we want it to be true that 'If blah-blah-blah then yadda-yadda' is a tautology. There is no interpretation (no way of assigning truth-values) that is to make the premises true, while the conclusion is false. When this is so, the argument is valid in exactly the sense we have been talking about.

One way of discovering whether an argument is valid is common enough to deserve a name. You can find whether "If blah-blah-blah then yadda-yadda" is valid by adding "not yadda-yadda" to "blah-blah-blah" and seeing if you can get out a contradiction. If you can, the argument was valid. This corresponds directly to there being no way that the premises could be true and the conclusion false. There is no interpretation or no model for that state of affairs. Contradiction bars the way. This is called "assuming towards a contradiction" or "assuming towards a reductio," from the Latin name for this kind of procedure: the *reductio ad absurdum,* or reduction to absurdity. Anselm's ontological argument . . . had that form [see Section I].

In mathematics we can have not only 2 + 2, but also 3 × (2 + 2) and ((2 + 3) × (2 + 2)) − 5, and so on forever, and so it is with information. In so far as complex bits of information are produced by applying and reapplying truth-functional combinations, we can keep perfect control of the interpretations under which we have truth and falsity.

NOTHING TO BE AFRAID OF

So logic studies the structure of information. Its aim is to exhibit that structure, and thereby also exhibit what follows from what: what is sufficient to prove *p* and what follows from *p,* for *p* of any complexity. The connection between structure and proof is just this: the structure shows us if there is *no way* that the premises can be true without the conclusion being true. Because to understand the structure of information is to understand the ways it can be true.

So far, we have looked at complexity of information arising because propositions are negated or conjoined, or connected by implication. But we have not broken inside propositions. As far as the analysis so far goes, "Some persons are philosophers" and "All persons are philosophers" will come out looking alike. Each is just an example of a proposition, *p.* But we cannot get inside the proposition, and understand how these mean different things.

The breakthrough that cracked this problem created modern logic. It was made by the German mathematician and logician Gottlob Frege (1848–1925), in his seminal *Begriffsschrift* ("concept writing") of

1879. Consider this argument: every inquiry stops somewhere, so there is somewhere every inquiry stops. . . . Something must be wrong, for a parallel would be: everyone has a mother, so there is someone who is everyone's mother. Or, everyone ties his own laces, so someone ties everyone's laces. Until Frege, people could see that there was something wrong, but, lacking any understanding of how this kind of information is built, they could not say what it was.

The key to understanding Frege's achievement is to think in terms of two quite different kinds of information. The first is very familiar. It corresponds to attaching a term to a name or other expression that refers to a particular person or thing: Bill is rich, Tony grins, this is an orange. Here we have a subject term (the names "Bill" and "Tony," and the demonstrative "this"), and things are said of what they pick out: "is rich," "grins," or "is an orange." These terms stand for conditions that things might meet. They are called "predicates": the rich things satisfy the predicate "is rich," and other things do not. This is the basic subject–predicate form of information.

Now we can do something surprising. Suppose we delete the term that stands for the subject. We are left with only a gappy sentence, or predicate: "is rich," and so on. We can better signal the gap by the expression called a variable, usually written *x, y, z* . . . , as in algebra. So we have "*x* is rich." This is no longer a sentence carrying a piece of information, because nobody is being said to be rich. It is a sentence with a hole in it: a predicate, or an open sentence, in logicians' jargon.

Now, here comes the magic. Suppose I ask you to take an open sentence into a particular domain, such as a classroom, or New York City, and come back giving me some information. You *could* just reconstruct a piece of information like the one we started with, naming some particular individual, and saying that he or she is rich. But you don't have to do this. You can do a fundamentally different kind of thing. You can come back and tell me about the *quantity* of times the predicate is satisfied. And you can tell me this without telling me who satisfies it. It is as if you use the open sentence by pointing the "*x*" in it at all the different people in the domain in turn, and note how often you get a hit. Suppose we symbolize the predicate by ϕ

(the Greek letter "phi"). Then you ask: "Is *this* φ, is *this* φ?" of each of the members of the domain in succession. Then you can tell me what happened.

Perhaps the simplest kind of thing you could tell me is that at least once, somewhere, you got a hit. This is equivalent to "Something is φ." Or you might tell me that somewhere you got a miss: "Something is not-φ." Contrast this last with getting a hit nowhere: "Nothing is φ." Or it might be that everywhere you got a hit: "Everything is φ."

"Something is φ" is given by a new piece of symbolism: the *existential quantifier*. It is written as $(\exists x)\phi x$ (the fact that the variable comes after the predicate in "ϕx" whereas in English predicates usually finish sentences and things like names start them is irrelevant). If you never get a hit, you can enter $\neg(\exists x)\phi x$: nothing is φ. If, somewhere, you get a result that is not a hit, you have the very different $(\exists x)\neg(\phi x)$. If you nowhere get a result other than a hit, you have $\neg(\exists x)\neg\phi x$. This says that nowhere is there anything that is not φ. Or, in other words, as far as this domain goes, everything is φ. This last kind of information is sufficiently important to have its own symbol, the *universal quantifier*, written as $(\forall x)\phi x$: 'Everything is φ.'

Leibniz thought that if we had a sufficiently logical notation, dispute and confusion would cease, and men would sit together and resolve their disputes by calculation. The invention of the quantifier did not bring about this utopia, but it does an astonishing amount towards it. Its full power is exhibited when we get multiple quantifications. This is information built with more than one quantifier in play. When we have more than one quantifier, we use different variables $(x, y, z \ldots)$ to indicate the different gaps to which they correspond. To illustrate the idea, we can see how easily it dissects the invalid argument: everybody has a mother, so someone is everyone's mother. If we write "x is the mother of y" as "xMy" we symbolize the first by $(\forall y)(\exists x)\ xMy$. The second is $(\exists x)(\forall y)\ xMy$. How are these different?

Start with a sentence claiming motherhood between two different people: Beth is the mother of Albert. Knock out reference to Beth, and we have the open sentence xMa (where "a" abbreviates Albert). We know that this predicate is satisfied (it is satisfied by Beth), so we know $(\exists x)\ xMa$. Somebody is Albert's mother. Now knock out reference to Albert: $(\exists x)\ xMy$. We have a gappy, or open, sentence again, with y marking the gap. It corresponds to the predicate "having someone as a mother." We can take this into the domain and point the variable y at each in turn: does *this* person have a mother, does *this* ... ? If we get the answer "yes" on each occasion (which we do), we can universally quantify $(\forall y)(\exists x)\ xMy$. Everyone has a mother.

Now look at the second formula. To get this, we similarly start with Beth (b) being the mother of Albert. But now we knock out reference to Albert first: bMy. We take this round the domain. *If* we could (as in the real world we cannot) write $(\forall y)\ bMy$, this would be because Beth is the mother of everyone (whoever you point the variable y at, it turns out that Beth is their mother!). What has just been supposed of Beth, might be supposed true of someone (if not Beth): in that case you can knock out reference to Beth, take the predicate "being mother of everyone," or in other words $(\forall y)\ xMy$, round the domain, and find eventually someone giving the answer yes. In that case you would be able to write $(\exists x)(\forall y)\ xMy$. But the point to notice is that this is an *entirely* different procedure. It gives an entirely different kind of information (false of the domain of human beings). And the quantificational structure shows the difference on its face, because the stringing out of the quantifiers shows how the information is built.

In the real world, nobody is the mother of everybody. Before we understood quantification, that might have sounded weird, as if the human race sprung out of Nothing. This might have seemed a creepy metaphysical thesis. But now it is tamed. It just means that $\neg(\exists x)(\forall y)\ xMy$. And this is a simple truth. At least, unless you use the relation 'mother' to include more remote kinds of ancestry, in which case you might want to claim that there is someone, biological Eve, the first female *homo sapiens,* who is the mother of everyone. But I would regard that as an illegitimate or metaphorical usage. My grandmother is not literally my mother.

We can give more precise information about the quantity of times some condition is met in a domain. We might say that there is *exactly* one thing satisfying the condition. This means that any time you get a hit, if you go on pointing the variable at the rest of the things in the domain, whenever you get a hit it turns out to be the same one. There are no two distinct hits. This is the core of Russell's famous theory of definite descriptions [See Part Six.] For it to be true that the unique king of France has a beard, there would need to be someone who rules France and no other person who rules France, and it should be true of whoever does rule France that he has a beard. Otherwise, the claim is false.

Quantificational structure is just one thing, but a very important thing to be aware of. Ordinary language is good at generating ambiguities that it easily resolves. "All the nice girls love a sailor" said the song. There is some lucky sailor they all love? They all have one, but perhaps a different sailor that they love? Take any sailor, then all the nice girls love him (or her)? Very different things, true in very different circumstances. A related ambiguity is responsible for some thirty thousand deaths a year in the United States. "A well-regulated militia being necessary to the security of a free state, the right of the people to keep and bear arms shall not be infringed." Each person? Or the people as a collective, as in "The team can have a bus"? If the founding fathers had been able to think in terms of quantificational structure, a lot of blood might not have been spilt.

PART 1

~

Philosophy of Religion

Introduction

STEVEN M. CAHN

Philosophy of religion is an ancient branch of philosophical inquiry that attempts to clarify religious beliefs and subject them to critical scrutiny. Some thinkers have employed the methods of philosophy to support religion, while others have used these same methods with quite different aims. All philosophy of religion, however, is concerned with questions that arise when religious doctrines are tested by the canons of reason.

An early, influential work in this area is Plato's *Euthyphro*. While it contains many points of philosophical interest, the work is best known for its challenge to the view that morality rests on belief in God. Socrates asks: Are actions right just because God says they are right, or does God say actions are right just because they are right? If actions are right because of God's command, then the discomforting conclusion is that anything God commands is right, even if He should command torture or murder. Furthermore, note that accepting this view removes any significance from the claim that God issues good commands. For if the good is whatever God commands, then to say God commands rightly is simply to say that He commands as He commands, a statement that is uninformative.

To avoid these unwanted implications, we are led to the view that actions are not right because God commands them; on the contrary, God commands them because they are right. In other words, what God commands conforms to a standard that is independent of God's will. But then one can oneself intentionally act in accord with that standard, thereby doing what is right without necessarily believing in the existence of God.

The *Euthyphro* also challenges the view that we ought to serve the Divine. For how can the Divine benefit from such service?

Chief among the issues that philosophers of religion have examined throughout the centuries is the question: "Does God exist?" Theism is the belief that God does exist. Atheism is the belief that God does not exist. Agnosticism is the belief that sufficient evidence is not available to decide whether God exists. Which of these positions is correct?

To answer this question, we need to determine what we mean by "God," a term that has been used in many different ways. Let us adopt a view, shared by many theists, that the word refers to an all-good, all-knowing, all-powerful creator of the world. The question then is: Does a Being so described exist?

Several proofs have been offered to defend the claim that God does exist. In the selection by Saint Anselm, we are presented with the ontological argument for the existence of God. This argument makes no appeal to empirical evidence but purports to demonstrate that by His very nature God, the Being greater than which none can be conceived, must exist. A criticism of this argument is offered by the monk Gaunilo, who maintains that Anselm's reasoning could be used to prove the existence of the island greater than which none can be conceived, an absurd conclusion.

But if Anselm's argument is unsound, where does its mistake lie? Immanuel Kant identifies the crucial error as the assumption that existence is an attribute. In other words, Kant claims that the definition of anything remains the same regardless of whether that thing exists. For example, the definition of a unicorn would not be altered if we discovered a living unicorn, just as our definition of a whooping crane would not be altered if whooping cranes became extinct. In short, whether unicorns or whooping cranes exist does not affect the meaning of the terms "unicorn" and "whooping crane." A fuller discussion of Kant's claim is offered in a classic essay by G. E. Moore. Moore considers the statement "Tame tigers growl" and points out how it differs in surprising ways from the statement "Tame tigers exist." William Rowe continues the examination of the ontological argument. He argues that it is unsound, but his analysis reveals the many subtleties implicit in this deservedly famous and still-challenging piece of philosophical reasoning.

Several other arguments for the existence of God are offered in the selection by Saint Thomas Aquinas. They are called "cosmological arguments," for they are based on a variety of fundamental principles about the structure of the world, such as the thesis that nothing is uncaused, which is supposed to imply that the world itself is caused and that its cause is God. Criticisms of these sorts of arguments are presented in the selection by Michael Martin.

A third type of proof, the "teleological argument," or argument from design, proceeds from the premise of the world's magnificent order to the conclusion that the world is the work of a Supreme Mind responsible for that order. This argument is explored in detail in the selection from David Hume's classic book *Dialogues Concerning Natural Religion*.

"Natural religion" was the term used by 18th-century writers to refer to theological tenets provable by human reason alone, unaided by an appeal to divine revelation. The three characters in the *Dialogues* are distinguished by their views concerning the scope and limits of human reason. Cleanthes claims he can present arguments that demonstrate the truth of theism. Demea is deeply committed to theism but does not believe scientific evidence can provide any defense for his faith. Philo doubts that reason yields conclusive results in any field of inquiry, especially theology. By subtle and realistic interplay among these three characters, Hume suggests a surprising affinity between the skeptic and the person of faith, as well as the equally surprising lack of affinity between the person of faith and the philosophical theist.

To attack an argument supporting the existence of God, however, is not equivalent to offering an argument against the existence of God. Are there arguments not only against theism but in favor of atheism?

A well-known argument of this sort is the problem of evil, presented by Demea and supported by Philo in Hume's *Dialogues*. Why should there be evil in a world created by an all-good, all-powerful being? A being who is all-good would do everything possible to abolish evil. A being who is all powerful would be able to abolish evil. Therefore, if there were an all-good, all-powerful being, there would be no evil. But evil exists. Thus, it would seem there is no being who is all-good and all-powerful.

Numerous attempts have been made to find a solution to the problem of evil. A familiar strategy is to try to demonstrate how the goods of the world are made possible by the presence of evils. For instance, it has been argued that evil is necessary so that human beings can bear moral responsibility for their actions. This strategy for resolving the problem of evil is developed by Richard Swinburne.

Steven M. Cahn's essay asks whether those who believe in God have any different expectations about the events of this life than do those who believe that the world was created by an omnipotent, omniscient, omnimalevolent demon. Cahn argues that the more tenaciously we cling to one of these beliefs, the less it matters which one.

A different approach to belief in God is taken by William James, who maintains that the issue of whether God exists cannot be decided intellectually but is a matter for our passions. According to James, we should not allow the fear of holding a false belief to cause us to lose the benefits of holding a belief that may be true. James's position is criticized by Michael Martin.

If it is important that we believe in God, why does God remain hidden to us? Why does He not reveal Himself in a manner accessible to all? Robert McKim concludes that the evidence suggests that it doesn't matter much whether we believe in God, for if it did make an important difference, then the existence of God would be more apparent.

In studying all these issues, readers are advised to remember that some of the most renowned philosophers of the past and present have been committed to theism, while others of equal stature have been agnostics or atheists. All would have agreed, however, that whatever one's position, it is more clearly and fully understood in the light of philosophical inquiry.

Euthyphro

~

PLATO

Plato (c. 428–347 B.C.), the famed Athenian philosopher, wrote a series of dialogues, most of which feature his teacher Socrates (469–399 B.C.), who himself wrote nothing but, in conversation, was able to befuddle the most powerful minds of his day. Plato responded to Socratic teaching not, as one may suppose, by being intimidated, but by becoming the greatest of philosophical writers.

2a   *Euthyphro.* What trouble has arisen, Socrates, to make you leave your haunts in the Lyceum, and spend your time here today at the Porch of the King Archon? Surely you of all people don't have some sort of lawsuit before him, as I do?

Socrates. Well no; Athenians, at any rate, don't call it a lawsuit, Euthyphro—they call it an indictment.

b   *Euthyphro*. What's that you say? Somebody must have indicted you, since I can't imagine your doing that to anyone else.

Socrates. No, I haven't.

Euthyphro. But someone else has indicted you?

Socrates. Exactly.

Euthyphro. Who is he?

Socrates. I hardly even know the man myself, Euthyphro; I gather he's young and unknown—but I believe he's named Meletus. He belongs to the Pitthean deme—can you picture a Meletus from that deme, with straight hair, not much of a beard, and a rather aquiline nose?

c   *Euthyphro*. No, I can't picture him, Socrates. But tell me, what is this indictment he's brought against you?

Socrates. The indictment? I think it does him credit. To have made such a major discovery is no mean achievement for one so young: he claims to know how the young people are being corrupted, and who are corrupting them. He's probably a smart fellow; and noticing that in my ignorance I'm corrupting his contemporaries, he is going to denounce me to the city, as if to his mother.

d   Actually, he seems to me to be the only one who's making the right start in politics: it *is* right to make it one's first concern that the young should be as good as possible, just as a good farmer is likely to care first for the young plants, and only later for the others.

3a   And so Meletus is no doubt first weeding out those of us who are "ruining the shoots of youth," as he puts it. Next after this, he'll take care of the older people, and will obviously bring many great blessings to the city: at least that would be the natural outcome after such a start.

Euthyphro. So I could wish, Socrates, but I'm afraid the opposite may happen: in trying to injure you, I really think he's making a good start at damaging the city. Tell me, what does he claim you are actually doing to corrupt the young?

Socrates. Absurd things, by the sound of   b them, my admirable friend: he says that I'm an inventor of gods; and for inventing strange gods, while failing to recognize the gods of old, he's indicted me on their behalf, so he says.

Euthyphro. I see, Socrates; it's because you say that your spiritual sign visits you now and then. So he's brought this indictment against you as a religious innovator, and he's going to court to misrepresent you, knowing that such things are easily misrepresented before the public. Why, it's just the same with me: when-   c ever I speak in the Assembly on religious matters and predict the future for them, they laugh at me as if I were crazy; and yet not one of my predictions has failed to come true. Even so, they always envy people like ourselves. We mustn't worry about them, though—we must face up to them.

Socrates. Yes, my dear Euthyphro, being laughed at is probably not important. You know, Athenians don't much care, it seems to me, if they think someone clever, so long as he's not imparting his wisdom to others; but once they think he's making other people clever, then they get angry—whether from   d envy, as you say, or for some other reason.

Euthyphro. In that case I don't much want to test their feelings towards me.

Socrates. Well, they probably think you give sparingly of yourself, and aren't willing to impart your wisdom. But in my case, I fear my benevolence makes them think I give all that I have, by speaking without reserve to every comer; not only do I speak without charge, but I'd gladly be out of pocket if anyone cares to listen to me. So, as I was just saying, if they   e were only going to laugh at me, as you say they laugh at you, it wouldn't be bad sport if they passed the time joking and laughing in the courtroom. But if they're going to be serious, then there's no knowing how things will turn out—except for you prophets.

Euthyphro. Well, I dare say it will come to nothing, Socrates. No doubt you'll handle your case with intelligence, as I think I shall handle mine.

Socrates. And what is this case of yours, Euthyphro? Are you defending or prosecuting?

Euthyphro. Prosecuting.

Socrates. Whom?

4a *Euthyphro.* Once again, someone whom I'm thought crazy to be prosecuting.

Socrates. How's that? Are you chasing a bird on the wing?

Euthyphro. The bird is long past flying: in fact, he's now quite elderly.

Socrates. And who is he?

Euthyphro. My father.

Socrates. What? Your own *father!*

Euthyphro. Precisely.

Socrates. But what is the charge? What is the case about?

Euthyphro. It's a case of murder, Socrates.

Socrates. Good heavens above! Well, Eu-thyphro, most people are obviously ignorant of
b where the right lies in such a case, since I can't imagine any ordinary person taking that action. It must need someone pretty far advanced in wisdom.

Euthyphro. Goodness yes, Socrates. Far advanced indeed!

Socrates. And is your father's victim one of your relatives? Obviously, he must be—you'd hardly be prosecuting him for murder on behalf of a stranger.

Euthyphro. It's ridiculous, Socrates, that you should think it makes any difference whether the victim was a stranger or a relative, and not see that the sole consideration is whether or not the slaying was lawful. If it was, one should leave the slayer alone; but if
c it wasn't, one should prosecute, even if the slayer shares one's own hearth and board— because the pollution is just the same, if you knowingly associate with such a person, and

fail to cleanse yourself and him by taking legal action.

In point of fact, the victim was a day-labourer of mine: when we were farming in Naxos, he was working there on our estate. He had got drunk, flown into a rage with one of our servants, and butchered him. So my father had him bound hand and foot, and flung into a ditch; he then sent a messenger here to find out from the religious authority what should be done. In the mean time, he disregarded his cap-
d tive, and neglected him as a murderer, thinking it wouldn't much matter even if he died. And that was just what happened: the man died of hunger and cold, and from his bonds, before the messenger got back from the authority.

That's why my father and other relatives are now upset with me, because I'm prosecuting him for murder on a murderer's behalf. According to them, he didn't even kill him. And even if he was definitely a killer, they say that, since the victim was a murderer, I shouldn't be troubled on such a fellow's behalf—because it is unholy for a son to pros-
e ecute his father for murder. Little do they know, Socrates, of religious law about what is holy and unholy.

Socrates. But heavens above, Euthyphro, do you think *you* have such exact knowledge of religion, of things holy and unholy? Is it so exact that in the circumstances you describe, you aren't afraid that, by bringing your father to trial, you might prove guilty of unholy con-duct yourself?

Euthyphro. Yes it is, Socrates; in fact I'd be good for nothing, and Euthyphro wouldn't dif-   5a fer at all from the common run of men, unless I had exact knowledge of all such matters.

Socrates. Why then, my admirable Euthy-phro, my best course is to become your stu-dent, and to challenge Meletus on this very point before his indictment is heard. I could say that even in the past I always used to set a high value upon religious knowledge; and that now, because he says I've gone astray by free-thinking and religious innovation, I have become your student.

b   "Meletus," I could say: "If you agree that Euthyphro is an expert on such matters, then you should regard me as orthodox too, and drop the case. But if you don't admit that, then proceed against that teacher of mine, not me, for corrupting the elderly—namely, myself and his own father—myself by his teaching, and his father by admonition and punishment."

Then, if he didn't comply and drop the charge, or indict you in my place, couldn't I repeat in court the very points on which I'd already challenged him?

Euthyphro. By God, Socrates, if he tried
c   indicting me, I fancy I'd soon find his weak spots; and we'd have *him* being discussed in the courtroom long before I was.

Socrates. Why yes, dear friend, I realize that, and that's why I'm eager to become your student. I know that this Meletus, amongst others no doubt, doesn't even seem to notice you; it's me he's detected so keenly and so readily that he can charge me with impiety.

So now, for goodness' sake, tell me what you were just maintaining you knew for sure. What sort of thing would you say that the pious
d   and the impious are, whether in murder or in other matters? Isn't the holy itself the same as itself in every action? And conversely, isn't the unholy the exact opposite of the holy, in itself similar to itself, or possessed of a single character, in anything at all that is going to be unholy?

Euthyphro. Indeed it is, Socrates.

Socrates. Tell me, then, what do you say that the holy is? And the unholy?

Euthyphro. All right, I'd say that the holy is just what I'm doing now: prosecuting wrong-
e   doers, whether in cases of murder or temple-robbery, or those guilty of any other such offence, be they one's father or mother or anyone else whatever; and failing to prosecute is unholy.

See how strong my evidence is, Socrates, that this is the law—evidence I've already

given others that my conduct was correct: one must not tolerate an impious man, no matter who he may happen to be. The very people who recognize Zeus as best and most righteous   6a of the gods admit that he put his father in bonds for wrongfully gobbling up his children; and that that father in turn castrated *his* father for similar misdeeds. And yet they are angry with me, because I'm prosecuting *my* father as a wrongdoer. Thus, they contradict themselves in what they say about the gods and about me.

Socrates. Could this be the reason why I'm facing indictment, Euthyphro? Is it because when people tell such stories of the gods, I somehow find them hard to accept? That, I suppose, is why some will say that, I've gone astray. But now, if these stories convince you—   b with your great knowledge of such matters— then it seems that the rest of us must accept them as well. What can we possibly say, when by our own admission we know nothing of these matters? But tell me, in the name of friendship, do you really believe that those things happened as described?

Euthyphro. Yes, and even more remarkable things, Socrates, of which most people are ignorant.

Socrates. And do you believe that the gods actually make war upon one another? That they have terrible feuds and fights, and much more of the sort related by our poets, and depicted by   c our able painters, to adorn our temples—especially the robe which is covered with such adornments, and gets carried up to the Acropolis at the great Panathenaean festival? Are we to say that those stories are true, Euthyphro?

Euthyphro. Not only those, Socrates, but as I was just saying, I'll explain to you many further points about religion, if you'd like, which I'm sure you'll be astonished to hear.

Socrates. I shouldn't be surprised. But explain them to me at leisure some other time. For now, please try to tell me more clearly what   d I was just asking. You see, my friend, you didn't instruct me properly when I asked my earlier question: I asked what the holy might be, but you told me that the holy was what you are now doing, prosecuting your father for murder.

Euthyphro. Yes, and there I was right, Socrates.

Socrates. Maybe. Yet surely, Euthyphro, there are many other things you call holy as well.

Euthyphro. So there are.

Socrates. And do you recall that I wasn't urging you to teach me about one or two of those many things that are holy, but rather about the form itself whereby all holy things are holy? Because you said, I think, that it was by virtue of a single character that unholy things are unholy, and holy things are holy. Don't you remember?

Euthyphro. Yes, I do.

Socrates. Then teach me about that character, about what it might be, so that by fixing my eye upon it and using it as a model, I may call holy any action of yours or another's, which conforms to it, and may deny to be holy whatever does not.

Euthyphro. All right, if that's what you want, Socrates, that's what I'll tell you.

Socrates. Yes, that *is* what I want.

Euthyphro. In that case, *what is agreeable to the gods is holy,* and what is not agreeable to them is unholy.

Socrates. Splendid, Euthyphro!—You've given just the sort of answer I was looking for. Mind you, I don't yet know whether it's correct, but obviously you will go on to show that what you say is true.

Euthyphro. I certainly will.

Socrates. All right then, let's consider what it is we're saying. A thing or a person loved-by-the-gods is holy, whereas something or someone hated-by-the-gods is unholy; and the holy isn't the same as the unholy, but is the direct opposite of it. Isn't that what we're saying?

Euthyphro. Exactly.

Socrates. And does it seem well put?

Euthyphro. I think so, Socrates.

Socrates. And again, Euthyphro, the gods quarrel and have their differences, and there is mutual hostility amongst them. Hasn't that been said as well?

Euthyphro. Yes, it has.

Socrates. Well, on what matters do their differences produce hostility and anger, my good friend? Let's look at it this way. If we differed, you and I, about which of two things was more numerous, would our difference on these questions make us angry and hostile towards one another? Or would we resort to counting in such disputes, and soon be rid of them?

Euthyphro. We certainly would.

Socrates. Again, if we differed about which was larger and smaller, we'd soon put an end to our difference by resorting to measurement, wouldn't we?

Euthyphro. That's right.

Socrates. And we would decide a dispute about which was heavier and lighter, presumably, by resorting to weighing.

Euthyphro. Of course.

Socrates. Then what sorts of questions would make us angry and hostile towards one another, if we differed about them and were unable to reach a decision? Perhaps you can't say offhand. But consider my suggestion, that they are questions of what is just and unjust, honourable and dishonourable, good and bad. Aren't those the matters on which our disagreement and our inability to reach a satisfactory decision occasionally make enemies of us, of you and me, and of people in general?

Euthyphro. Those are the differences, Socrates, and that's what they're about.

Socrates. And what about the gods, Euthyphro? If they really do differ, mustn't they differ about those same things?

Euthyphro. They certainly must.

Socrates. Then, by your account, noble Euthyphro, different gods also regard different things as just, or as honourable and dishonourable, good and bad; because unless they differed on those matters, they wouldn't quarrel, would they?

Euthyphro. Correct.

Socrates. And again, the things each of them regards as honourable, good, or just, are also the things they love, while it's the opposites of those things that they hate.

Euthyphro. Indeed.

8a *Socrates.* And yet it's the same things, according to you, that some gods consider just, and others unjust, about which their disputes lead them to quarrel and make war upon one another. Isn't that right?

Euthyphro. It is.

Socrates. Then the same things, it appears, are both hated and loved by the gods, and thus the same things would be both hated-by-the-gods and loved-by-the-gods.

Euthyphro. It does appear so.

Socrates. So by this argument, Euthyphro, the same things would be both holy and unholy.

Euthyphro. It looks that way.

Socrates. So then you haven't answered my question, my admirable friend. You see, I wasn't asking what selfsame thing proves to be at once holy and unholy. And yet something which is loved-by-the-gods is apparently also b hated-by-the-gods. Hence, as regards your present action in punishing your father, Euthyphro, it wouldn't be at all surprising if you were thereby doing something agreeable to Zeus but odious to Cronus and Uranus, or pleasing to Hephaestus but odious to Hera; and likewise for any other gods who may differ from one another on the matter.

Euthyphro. Yes Socrates, but I don't think any of the gods do differ from one another on this point, at least: whoever has unjustly killed another should be punished.

Socrates. Really? Well, what about human c beings, Euthyphro? Have you never heard any of them arguing that someone who has killed unjustly, or acted unjustly in some other way, should not be punished?

Euthyphro. Why yes, they are constantly arguing that way, in the lawcourts as well as elsewhere: people who act unjustly in all sorts of ways will do or say anything to escape punishment.

Socrates. But do they admit acting unjustly, Euthyphro, yet still say, despite that admission, that they shouldn't be punished?

Euthyphro. No, they don't say that at all.

Socrates. So it isn't just anything that they will say or do. This much, I imagine, they don't dare to say or argue: if they act unjustly, they   d should not be punished. Rather, I imagine, they deny acting unjustly, don't they?

Euthyphro. True.

Socrates. Then they don't argue that one who acts unjustly should not be punished; but they do argue, maybe, about who it was that acted unjustly, and what he did, and when.

Euthyphro. True.

Socrates. Then doesn't the very same thing also apply to the gods—if they really do quarrel about just and unjust actions, as your account suggests, and if each party says that the other acts unjustly, while the other denies it? Because surely, my admirable friend, no one among gods or men dares to claim that   e anyone should go unpunished who *has* acted unjustly.

Euthyphro. Yes, what you say is true, Socrates, at least on the whole.

Socrates. Rather, Euthyphro, I think it is the individual act that causes arguments among gods as well as human beings—if gods really do argue: it is with regard to some particular action that they differ, some saying it was done justly, while others say it was unjust. Isn't that so?

Euthyphro. Indeed.

Socrates. Then please, my dear Euthyphro,   9a instruct me too, that I may grow wiser. When a hired man has committed murder, has been put in bonds by the master of his victim, and has died from those bonds before his captor can find out from the authorities what to do about him, what proof have you that all gods regard that man as having met an unjust death? Or that it is right for a son to prosecute his father and   b press a charge of murder on behalf of such a man? Please try to show me plainly that all gods undoubtedly regard that action in those circumstances as right. If you can show that to my satisfaction, I'll never stop singing the praises of your wisdom.

Euthyphro. Well, that may be no small task, Socrates, though I *could* of course prove it to you quite plainly.

Socrates. I see. You must think me a slower learner than the jury, because obviously you will show them that the acts in question were unjust, and that all the gods hate such things.

Euthyphro. I will show that very clearly, Socrates, provided they listen while I'm talking.

c   *Socrates.* They'll listen all right, so long as they approve of what you're saying.

But while you were talking, I reflected and put to myself this question: "Even suppose Euthyphro were to instruct me beyond any doubt that the gods all do regard such a death as unjust, what more have I learnt from him about what the holy and the unholy might be? This particular deed would be hated-by-the-gods, apparently; yet it became evident just now that the holy and unholy were not defined in that way, since what is hated-by-the-gods proved to be loved-by-the-gods as well."

So I'll let you off on that point; Euthyphro; d   let *all* the gods consider it unjust, if you like, and let *all* of them hate it. Is this the correction we are now making in our account: whatever *all* the gods hate is unholy, and whatever they *all* love is holy; and whatever some gods love but others hate is neither or both? Is that how you would now have us define the holy and the unholy?

Euthyphro. What objection could there be, Socrates?

Socrates. None on my part, Euthyphro. But consider your own view, and see whether, by making that suggestion, you will most easily teach me what you promised.

e   *Euthyphro.* Very well, I would say that the holy is whatever all the gods love; and its opposite, whatever all the gods hate, is unholy.

Socrates. Then shall we examine that in turn, Euthyphro, and see whether it is well put? Or shall we let it pass, and accept it from ourselves and others? Are we to agree with a posi-

tion merely on the strength of someone's say-so, or should we examine what the speaker is saying?

Euthyphro. We should examine it. Even so, for my part I believe that this time our account is well put.

Socrates. We shall soon be better able to   10a tell, sir. Just consider the following question: is the holy loved by the gods because it is holy? Or is it holy because it is loved?

Euthyphro. I don't know what you mean, Socrates.

Socrates. All right, I'll try to put it more clearly. We speak of a thing's "being carried" or "carrying," of its "being led" or "leading," of its "being seen" or "seeing." And you understand, don't you, that all such things are different from each other, and how they differ?

Euthyphro. Yes, I think I understand.

Socrates. And again, isn't there something that is "being loved," while that which loves is different from it?

Euthyphro. Of course.

Socrates. Then tell me whether something   b in a state of "being carried" is in that state because someone is carrying it, or for some other reason.

Euthyphro. No, that is the reason.

Socrates. And something in a state of "being led" is so because someone is leading it, and something in a state of "being seen" is so because someone is seeing it?

Euthyphro. Certainly.

Socrates. Then someone does not see a thing because it is in a state of "being seen," but on the contrary, it is in that state because someone is seeing it; nor does someone lead a thing because it is in a state of "being led," but rather it is in that state because someone is leading it; nor does someone carry a thing because it is in a state of "being carried," but it is in that state because someone is carrying it. Is my meaning   c quite clear, Euthyphro? What I mean is this: if something gets into a certain state or is affected in a certain way, it does not get into that state because it possesses it; rather, it possesses that state because it gets into it; nor is it thus affected because it is in that condition; rather, it is in that condition because it is thus affected. Don't you agree with that?

Euthyphro. Yes, I do.

Socrates. Again, "being loved" is a case of either being in a certain state or being in a certain condition because of some agent?

Euthyphro. Certainly.

Socrates. Then this case is similar to our previous examples: it is not because it is in a state of "being loved" that an object is loved by those who love it; rather, it is in that state because it is loved by them. Isn't that right?

Euthyphro. It must be.

d   *Socrates.* Now, what are we saying about the holy, Euthyphro? On your account, doesn't it consist in being loved by all the gods?

Euthyphro. Yes.

Socrates. Is that because it is holy, or for some other reason?

Euthyphro. No, that is the reason.

Socrates. So it is loved because it is holy, not holy because it is loved.

Euthyphro. So it seems.

Socrates. By contrast, what is loved-by-the-gods is in that state—namely, being loved-by-the-gods—because the gods love it.

Euthyphro. Of course.

Socrates. Then what is loved-by-the-gods is not the holy, Euthyphro, nor is the holy what is loved-by-the-gods, as you say, but they differ from each other.

e   *Euthyphro.* How so, Socrates?

Socrates. Because we are agreed, aren't we, that the holy is loved because it is holy, not holy because it is loved?

Euthyphro. Yes.

Socrates. Whereas what is loved-by-the-gods is so because the gods love it. It is loved-by-the-gods by virtue of their loving it; it is not because it is in that state that they love it.

Euthyphro. That's true.

Socrates. But if what is loved-by-the-gods and the holy were the same thing, Euthyphro,

11a   then if the holy were loved because it is holy, what is loved-by-the-gods would be loved because it is loved-by-the-gods; and again, if what is loved-by-the-gods were loved-by-the-gods because they love it, then the holy would be holy because they love it. In actual fact, however, you can see that the two of them are related in just the opposite way, as two entirely different things: one of them is lovable because they love it, whereas the other they love for the reason that it is lovable.

And so, Euthyphro, when you are asked what the holy might be, it looks as if you'd prefer not to explain its essence to me, but would rather tell me one of its properties—namely,   b
that the holy has the property of being loved by all the gods; but you still haven't told me what it *is*.

So please don't hide it from me, but start again and tell me what the holy might be—whether it is loved by the gods or possesses any other property, since we won't disagree about that. Out with it now, and tell me what the holy and the unholy are.

Euthyphro. The trouble is, Socrates, that I can't tell you what I have in mind, because whatever we suggest keeps moving around somehow, and refuses to stay put where we established it.

Socrates. My ancestor Daedalus seems to be the author of your words, Euthyphro.   c
Indeed, if they were my own words and suggestions, you might make fun of me, and say that it's because of my kinship with him that my works of art in conversation run away from me too, and won't stay where they're placed. But in fact those suggestions are your own; and so you need a different joke, because you're the one for whom they won't stay put—as you realize yourself.

Euthyphro. No, I think it's much the same joke that is called for by what we said, Socrates: I'm not the one who makes them move around and not stay put. I think you're   d
the Daedalus because, as far as I'm concerned, they would have kept still.

Socrates. It looks then, my friend, as if I've grown this much more accomplished at my craft than Daedalus himself: he made only his own works move around, whereas I do it, apparently, to those of others besides my own. And indeed the really remarkable feature of my craft is that I'm an expert at it without even wanting to be. You see, I'd prefer to have words stay put for me, immovably established, than to acquire the wealth of Tantalus and the skill of Daedalus combined.

e

But enough of this. Since I think you are being feeble, I'll join you myself in an effort to help you instruct me about the holy. Don't give up too soon, now. Just consider whether you think that everything that is holy must be just.

Euthyphro. Yes, I do.

Socrates. Well then, is everything that is just holy? Or is everything that is holy just, but not everything that is just holy? Is part of it holy, and part of it something else?

12a

Euthyphro. I can't follow what you're saying, Socrates.

Socrates. And yet you are as much my superior in youth as you are in wisdom. But as I say, your wealth of wisdom has enfeebled you. So pull yourself together, my dear sir—it really isn't hard to see what I mean: it's just the opposite of what the poet meant who composed these verses:

> *With Zeus, who wrought it and who generated all these things,*
> *You cannot quarrel, for where there is fear, there is also shame.*

b

I disagree with that poet. Shall I tell you where?

Euthyphro. By all means.

Socrates. I don't think that "where there is fear, there is also shame," because many people, I take it, dread illnesses, poverty, and many other such things. Yet although they dread them, they are not ashamed of what they fear. Don't you agree?

Euthyphro. Certainly.

Socrates. On the other hand, where there is shame, there is also fear: doesn't anyone who is ashamed and embarrassed by a certain action

c

both fear and dread a reputation for wickedness?

Euthyphro. Indeed he does.

Socrates. Then it isn't right to say that "where there is fear, there is also shame," nevertheless, where there is shame there is also fear, even though shame is not found everywhere there is fear. Fear is broader than shame, I think, since shame is one kind of fear, just as odd is one kind of number. Thus, it is not true that wherever there is number there is also odd, although it is true that where there is odd, there is also number. You follow me now, presumably?

Euthyphro. Perfectly.

Socrates. Well, that's the sort of thing I meant just now: I was asking, "Is it true that wherever a thing is just, it is also holy? Or is a thing just wherever it is holy, but not holy wherever it is just?" In other words, isn't the holy part of what is just? Is that what we're to say, or do you disagree?

d

Euthyphro. No, let's say that: your point strikes me as correct.

Socrates. Then consider the next point: if the holy is one part of what is just, it would seem that we need to find out which part it might be. Now, if you asked me about one of the things just mentioned, for example, which kind of number is even, and what sort of number it might be, I'd say that it's any number which is not scalene but isosceles. Would you agree?

Euthyphro. I would.

Socrates. Now you try to instruct me, likewise, which part of what is just is holy. Then we'll be able to tell Meletus not to treat us unjustly any longer, or indict us for impiety, because I've now had proper tuition from you about what things are pious or holy, and what are not.

e

Euthyphro. Well then, in my view, the part of what is just that is pious or holy has to do with ministering to the gods, while the rest of it has to do with ministering to human beings.

Socrates. Yes, I think you put that very well, Euthyphro. I am still missing one small

13a

detail, however. You see, I don't yet understand this "ministering" of which you speak. You surely don't mean "ministering" to the gods in the same sense as "ministering" to other things. That's how we talk, isn't it? We say, for example, that not everyone understands how to minister to horses, but only the horse-trainer. Isn't that right?

Euthyphro. Certainly.

Socrates. Because, surely, horse-training is ministering to horses.

Euthyphro. Yes.

Socrates. Nor, again, does everyone know how to minister to dogs, but only the dog-trainer.

Euthyphro. Just so.

Socrates. Because, of course, dog-training is ministering to dogs.

b   *Euthyphro.* Yes.

Socrates. And again, cattle-farming is ministering to cattle.

Euthyphro. Certainly.

Socrates. And holiness or piety is ministering to the gods, Euthyphro? Is that what you're saying?

Euthyphro. It is.

Socrates. Well, doesn't all ministering achieve the same thing? I mean something like this: it aims at some good or benefit for its object. Thus, you may see that horses, when they are being ministered to by horse-training, are benefited and improved. Or don't you think they are?

Euthyphro. Yes, I do.

Socrates. And dogs, of course, are bene-

c   fited by dog-training, and cattle by cattle-farming, and the rest likewise. Or do you suppose that ministering is for harming its objects?

Euthyphro. Goodness, no!

Socrates. So it's for their benefit?

Euthyphro. Of course.

Socrates. Then, if holiness is ministering to the gods, does it benefit the gods and make them better? And would you grant that whenever you do something holy, you're making some god better?

Euthyphro. Heavens, no!

Socrates. No, I didn't think you meant that, Euthyphro—far from it—but that was the rea-   d son why I asked what sort of ministering to the gods you did mean. I didn't think you meant that sort.

Euthyphro. Quite right, Socrates: that's not the sort of thing I mean.

Socrates. Very well, but then what sort of ministering to the gods would holiness be?

Euthyphro. The sort which slaves give to their masters, Socrates.

Socrates. I see. Then it would appear to be some sort of service to the gods.

Euthyphro. Exactly.

Socrates. Now could you tell me what result is achieved by service to doctors? It would be health, wouldn't it?

Euthyphro. It would.

Socrates. And what about service to ship-   e wrights? What result is achieved in their service?

Euthyphro. Obviously, Socrates, the construction of ships.

Socrates. And service to builders, of course, achieves the construction of houses.

Euthyphro. Yes.

Socrates. Then tell me, good fellow, what product would be achieved by service to the gods? You obviously know, since you claim religious knowledge superior to any man's.

Euthyphro. Yes, and there I'm right, Socrates.

Socrates. Then tell me, for goodness' sake, just what that splendid task is which the gods accomplish by using our services?

Euthyphro. They achieve many fine things, Socrates.

Socrates. Yes, and so do generals, my   14a friend. Yet you could easily sum up their achievement as the winning of victory in war, couldn't you?

Euthyphro. Of course.

Socrates. And farmers too. They achieve many fine things, I believe. Yet they can be summed up as the production of food from the earth.

Euthyphro. Certainly.

Socrates. And now how about the many fine achievements of the gods? How can their work be summed up?

Euthyphro. I've already told you a little
b while ago, Socrates, that it's a pretty big job to learn the exact truth on all these matters. But I will simply tell you this much: if one has expert knowledge of the words and deeds that gratify the gods through prayer and sacrifice, those are the ones that are holy: such practices are the salvation of individual families, along with the common good of cities; whereas practices that are the opposite of gratifying are impious ones, which of course upset and ruin everything.

Socrates. I'm sure you could have given a summary answer to my question far more
c briefly, Euthyphro, if you'd wanted to. But you're not eager to teach me—that's clear because you've turned aside just when you were on the very brink of the answer. If you'd given it, I would have learnt properly from you about holiness by now. But as it is, the questioner must follow wherever the person questioned may lead him. So, once again, what are you saying that the holy or holiness is? Didn't you say it was some sort of expertise in sacrifice and prayer?

Euthyphro. Yes, I did.

Socrates. And sacrifice is giving things to the gods, while prayer is asking things of them?

Euthyphro. Exactly, Socrates.

d *Socrates.* So, by that account, holiness will be expertise in asking from the gods and giving to them.

Euthyphro. You've gathered my meaning beautifully, Socrates.

Socrates. Yes, my friend, that's because I'm greedy for your wisdom, and apply my intelligence to it, so that what you say won't fall wasted to the ground. But tell me, what is this service to the gods? You say it is asking from them, and giving to them?

Euthyphro. I do.

Socrates. Well, would asking rightly be asking for things we need from them?

Euthyphro. Why, what else could it be?

Socrates. And conversely, giving rightly
e would be giving them in return things that they do, in fact, need from us. Surely it would be inept to give anybody things he didn't need, wouldn't it?

Euthyphro. True, Socrates.

Socrates. So then holiness would be a sort of skill in mutual trading between gods and mankind?

Euthyphro. Trading, yes, if that's what you prefer to call it.

Socrates. I don't prefer anything unless it is actually true. But tell me, what benefit do the gods derive from the gifts they receive from us? What they give, of course, is obvious to
15a anyone—since we possess nothing good which they don't give us. But how are they benefited by what they receive from us? Do we get so much the better bargain in our trade with them that we receive all the good things from them, while they receive none from us?

Euthyphro. Come, Socrates, do you really suppose that the gods are benefited by what they receive from us?

Socrates. Well if not, Euthyphro, what ever would they be, these gifts of ours to the gods?

Euthyphro. What else do you suppose but honour and reverence, and—as I said just now—what is gratifying to them?

Socrates. So the holy is gratifying, but not
b beneficial or loved by the gods?

Euthyphro. I imagine it is the most loved of all things.

Socrates. Then, once again, it seems that this is what the holy is: what is loved by the gods.

Euthyphro. Absolutely.

Socrates. Well now, if you say that, can you wonder if you find that words won't keep still for you, but walk about? And will you blame me as the Daedalus who makes them walk, when you're far more skilled than Daedalus yourself at making them go round in a circle? Don't you notice that our account has come full circle back to the same point? You recall, no doubt, how we found earlier that what is holy and what is loved-by-the-gods were not the same, but different from each other? Don't you remember?

c

Euthyphro. Yes, I do.

Socrates. Then don't you realize that now you're equating holy with what the gods love? But that makes it identical with loved-by-the-gods, doesn't it?

Euthyphro. Indeed.

Socrates. So either our recent agreement wasn't sound; or else, if it was, our present suggestion is wrong.

Euthyphro. So it appears.

Socrates. Then we must start over again, and consider what the holy is, since I shan't be willing to give up the search till I learn the answer. Please don't scorn me, but give the matter your very closest attention and tell me the truth—because you must know it, if any man does; and like Proteus you mustn't be let go until you tell it.

d

You see, if you didn't know for sure what is holy and what unholy, there's no way you'd ever have ventured to prosecute your elderly father for murder on behalf of a labourer. Instead, fear of the gods would have saved you from the risk of acting wrongly, and you'd have been embarrassed in front of human beings. But in fact I'm quite sure that you think you have certain knowledge of what is holy and what is not; so tell me what you believe it to be, excellent Euthyphro, and don't conceal it.

e

Euthyphro. Some other time, Socrates: I'm hurrying somewhere just now, and it's time for me to be off.

Socrates. What a way to behave, my friend, going off like this, and dashing the high hopes I held! I was hoping I'd learn from you what acts are holy and what are not, and so escape Meletus' indictment, by showing him that Euthyphro had made me an expert in religion, and that my ignorance no longer made me a free-thinker or innovator on that subject: and also, of course, that I would live better for what remains of my life.

16a

The Ontological Argument

SAINT ANSELM

Saint Anselm (1033–1109) was archbishop of Canterbury. The *Proslogion,* from which this selection is taken, is his most famous work.

2. THAT GOD TRULY EXISTS

Well then, Lord, You who give understanding to faith, grant me that I may understand, as much as You see fit, that You exist as we believe You to exist, and that You are what we believe You to be. Now we believe that You are something than which nothing greater can be thought. Or can it be that a thing of such a

Reprinted from *Anselm of Canterbury: The Major Works,* eds. Brian Davies and G. R. Evans (Oxford: Oxford University Press, 1998), by permission of the publisher.

nature does not exist, since "the Fool has said in his heart, there is no God" [Ps. 13: 1; 52: 1]? But surely, when this same Fool hears what I am speaking about, namely, "something-than-which-nothing-greater-can-be-thought," he understands what he hears, and what he understands is in his mind, even if he does not understand that it actually exists. For it is one thing for an object to exist in the mind, and another thing to understand that an object actually exists. Thus, when a painter plans beforehand what he is going to execute, he has [the picture] in his mind, but he does not yet think that it actually exists because he has not yet executed it. However, when he has actually painted it, then he both has it in his mind and understands that it exists because he has now made it. Even the Fool, then, is forced to agree that something-than-which-nothing-greater-can-be-thought exists in the mind, since he understands this when he hears it, and whatever is understood is in the mind. And surely that-than-which-a-greater-cannot-be-thought cannot exist in the mind alone. For if it exists solely in the mind, it can be thought to exist in reality also, which is greater. If then that-than-which-a-greater-cannot-be-thought exists in the mind alone, this same that-than-which-a-greater-*cannot*-be-thought is that-than-which-a-greater-*can*-be-thought. But this is obviously impossible. Therefore there is absolutely no doubt that something-than-which-a-greater-cannot-be-thought exists both in the mind and in reality.

3.   THAT GOD CANNOT BE THOUGHT NOT TO EXIST

And certainly this being so truly exists that it cannot be even thought not to exist. For something can be thought to exist that cannot be thought not to exist, and this is greater than that which can be thought not to exist. Hence, if that-than-which-a-greater-cannot-be-thought can be thought not to exist, then that-than-which-a-greater-cannot-be-thought is not the same as that-than-which-a-greater-cannot-be-thought, which is absurd. Something-than-which-a-greater-cannot-be-thought exists so truly then, that it cannot be even thought not to exist.

And You, Lord our God, are this being. You exist so truly, Lord my God, that You cannot even be thought not to exist. And this is as it should be, for if some intelligence could think of something better than You, the creature would be above its Creator and would judge its Creator—and that is completely absurd. In fact, everything else there is, except You alone, can be thought of as not existing. You alone, then, of all things most truly exist and therefore of all things possess existence to the highest degree; for anything else does not exist as truly, and so possesses existence to a lesser degree. Why then did "the Fool say in his heart, there is no God" [Ps. 13: 1; 52: 1] when it is so evident to any rational mind that You of all things exist to the highest degree? Why indeed, unless because he was stupid and a fool?

4.   HOW "THE FOOL SAID IN HIS HEART" WHAT CANNOT BE THOUGHT

How indeed has he "said in his heart" what he could not think; or how could he not think what he "said in his heart," since to "say in one's heart" and to "think" are the same? But if he really (indeed, since he really) both thought because he "said in his heart" and did not "say in his heart" because he could not think, there is not only one sense in which something is "said in one's heart" or thought. For in one sense a thing is thought when the word signifying it is thought; in another sense when the very object which the thing is is understood. In the first sense, then, God can be thought not to exist, but not at all in the second sense. No one, indeed, understanding what God is can think that God does not exist, even though he may say these words in his heart either without any [objective] signification or with some peculiar signification. For God is that-than-which-nothing-greater-can-be-thought. Whoever really understands this understands clearly that this same being so exists that not even in thought can it not exist. Thus whoever understands that God exists in such a way cannot think of Him as not existing.

I give thanks, good Lord, I give thanks to You, since what I believed before through Your free gift I now so understand through Your illumination, that if I did not want to *believe* that You existed, I should nevertheless be unable not to *understand* it.

In Behalf of the Fool

⌒

GAUNILO

Gaunilo was a monk of Marmoutier, France, about whom little is known apart from his being the author of this famous reply to his contemporary Saint Anselm.

1

To one doubting whether there is, or denying that there is, something of such a nature than which nothing greater can be thought, it is said here [in the *Proslogion*] that its existence is proved, first because the very one who denies or doubts it already has it in his mind, since when he hears it spoken of he understands what is said; and further, because what he understands is necessarily such that it exists not only in the mind but also in reality. And this is proved by the fact that it is greater to exist both in the mind and in reality than in the mind alone. For if this same being exists in the mind alone, anything that existed also in reality would be greater than this being, and thus that which is greater than everything would be less than some thing and would not be greater than everything, which is obviously contradictory. Therefore, it is necessarily the case that that which is greater than everything, being already proved to exist in the mind, should exist not only in the mind but also in reality, since otherwise it would not be greater than everything.

2

But he [the Fool] can perhaps reply that this thing is said already to exist in the mind only in the sense that I understand what is said. For could I not say that all kinds of unreal things, not existing in themselves in any way at all, are equally in the mind since if anyone speaks about them I understand whatever he says? . . .

6

For example: they say that there is in the ocean somewhere an island which, because of the difficulty (or rather the impossibility) of finding that which does not exist, some have called the "Lost Island." And the story goes that it is blessed with all manner of priceless riches and delights in abundance, much more even than the Happy Isles, and, having no owner or inhabitant, it is superior everywhere in abundance of riches to all those other lands that men inhabit. Now, if anyone tell me that it is like this, I shall easily understand what is said, since nothing is difficult about it. But if he should then go on to say, as though it were a logical consequence of this: You cannot any more doubt that this island that is more excellent than all other lands truly exists somewhere in reality than you can doubt that it is in your mind; and since it is more excellent to exist not only in the mind alone but also in reality, therefore it must needs be that it exists. For if it did not exist, any other land existing in reality would be more excellent than it, and so this island, already conceived by you to be more excellent than others, will not be more excellent. If, I say, someone wishes thus to persuade me that this island really

Reprinted from *Anselm of Canterbury: The Major Works,* eds. Brian Davies and G. R. Evans (Oxford: Oxford University Press, 1998), by permission of the publisher.

exists beyond all doubt, I should either think that he was joking, or I should find it hard to decide which of us I ought to judge the bigger fool—I, if I agreed with him, or he, if he thought that he had proved the existence of this island with any certainty, unless he had first convinced me that its very excellence exists in my mind precisely as a thing existing truly and indubitably and not just as something unreal or doubtfully real.

7

Thus first of all might the Fool reply to objections. And if then someone should assert that this greater [than everything] is such that it cannot be thought not to exist (again without any other proof than that otherwise it would not be greater than everything), then he could make this same reply and say: When have I said that there truly existed some being that is "greater than everything," such that from this it could be proved to me that this same being really existed to such a degree that it could not be thought not to exist? That is why it must first be conclusively proved by argument that there is some higher nature, namely that which is greater and better than all the things that are, so that from this we can also infer everything else which necessarily cannot be wanting to what is greater and better than everything.

Critique of the Ontological Argument

~

IMMANUEL KANT

Immanuel Kant (1724–1804), who lived his entire life in the Prussian town of Königsberg, is a preeminent figure in the history of philosophy. He made groundbreaking contributions in virtually every area of philosophical inquiry, and his most notable works are the three great critiques—*Critique of Pure Reason, Critique of Practical Reason,* and *Critique of Judgment.*

[W]e may be challenged with a case which is brought forward as proof . . . that there is one concept, and indeed only one, in reference to which the not-being or rejection of its object is in itself contradictory. . . . It is declared that it possesses all reality, and that we are justified in assuming that such a being is possible. . . . Now [the argument proceeds] "all reality" includes existence; existence is therefore contained in the concept of a thing that is possible. If, then, this thing is rejected, the internal possibility of the thing is rejected—which is self-contradictory. . . .

I should have hoped to put an end to these idle and fruitless disputations in a direct manner, by an accurate determination of the concept of existence, had I not found that the illusion which is caused by the confusion of a logical with a real predicate (that is, with a predicate which determines a thing) is almost beyond correction. Anything we please can be made to serve as a logical predicate; the subject can even be predicated of itself; for logic abstracts from all content. But a determining predicate is a predicate which is added to the concept of the subject and enlarges it.

From *The Critique of Pure Reason,* translated by Norman Kemp Smith, 1929.

Consequently, it must not be already contained in the concept.

"*Being*" is obviously not a real predicate; that is, it is not a concept of something which could be added to the concept of a thing. It is merely the positing of a thing, or of certain determinations, as existing in themselves. Logically, it is merely the copula of a judgment. The proposition, "God is omnipotent," contains two concepts, each of which has its object—God and omnipotence. The small word "is" adds no new predicate, but only serves to posit the predicate *in its relation* to the subject. If, now, we take the subject (God) with all its predicates (among which is omnipotence), and say "God is," or "There is a God," we attach no new predicate to the concept of God, but only posit the subject in itself with all its predicates, and indeed posit it as being an *object* that stands in relation to my *concept*. The content of both must be one and the same; nothing can have been added to the concept, which expresses merely what is possible, by my thinking its object (through the expression "it is") as given absolutely. Otherwise stated, the real contains no more than the merely possible. A hundred real thalers do not contain the least coin more than a hundred possible thalers. For as the latter signify the concept, and the former the object and the positing of the object, should the former contain more than the latter, my concept would not, in that case, express the whole object, and would not therefore be an adequate concept of it. My financial position is, however, affected very differently by a hundred real thalers than it is by the mere concept of them (that is, of their possibility) . . . and yet the conceived hundred thalers are not themselves in the least increased through thus acquiring existence outside my concept.

By whatever and by however many predicates we may think a thing—even if we completely determine it—we do not make the least addition to the thing when we further declare that this thing *is*. Otherwise, it would not be exactly the same thing that exists, but something more than we had thought in the concept; and we could not, therefore, say that the exact object of my concept exists. If we think in a thing every feature of reality except one, the missing reality is not added by my saying that this defective thing exists. On the contrary, it exists with the same defect with which I have thought it, since otherwise what exists would be something different from what I thought. When, therefore, I think a being as the supreme reality, without any defect, the question still remains whether it exists or not.

Is Existence a Predicate?

~

G. E. MOORE

G. E. Moore (1873–1958), who taught at the University of Cambridge, was one of the key figures in the development of analytic philosophy. His most famous book is *Principia Ethica*. His style of writing places extraordinary stress on clarity, even if that clarity requires a painstaking attention to detail.

I am not at all clear as to the meaning of this question. Mr. Kneale says that existence is not a predicate. But what does he mean by the words "Existence is not a predicate"?

This essay was the second paper in a symposium published in the *Proceedings of the Aristotelian Society*, Supplementary Volume XV, 1936, and is reprinted by permission of the Editor of the Aristotelian Society. The philosopher William Kneale wrote the first paper.

In this second paragraph, he says that the word "predicate" has two different senses, a logical sense and a grammatical one. If so, it would follow that the words "Existence is not a predicate" may have two different meanings, according as the person who uses them is using "predicate" in the logical or the grammatical sense. And I think it is clear that he means us to understand that when he says "Existence is not a predicate," he is using "predicate" in the logical sense, and not in the grammatical one. I think his view is that if anyone were to say "Existence is a predicate," using "predicate" in the grammatical sense, such a person would be perfectly right: I think he holds that existence really is a predicate in the grammatical sense. But, whether he holds this or not, I think it is clear that he does not wish to discuss the question whether it is or is not a predicate in the grammatical sense, but solely the question whether it is so in the logical one.

Now I think it is worth noticing that if we assert "Existence is a predicate," using "predicate" in the grammatical sense, our proposition is a proposition about certain *words,* to the effect that they are often used in a certain way; but not, curiously enough, about the word "existence" itself. It is a proposition to the effect that the word "exists" and other finite parts of the verb "to exist," such as "existed," "will exist," or "exist" (in the plural) are often the predicates (in some grammatical sense) of sentences in which they occur; but nobody means to say that the word "existence" itself is often the predicate of sentences in which it occurs. And I think Mr. Kneale implies that, similarly, the proposition which anyone would express, if he asserted "Existence is a predicate," using "predicate" in the logical sense, is again equivalent to a proposition, *not* about the word "existence" itself, but about the word "exists," and other finite parts of the verb "to exist." He implies that "Existence is a predicate," with this use of "predicate," is equivalent to the proposition that the word "exists," and other finite parts of the verb, often do "*stand for* a predicate in the logical sense." It would appear, therefore, that one difference between the two different meanings of "Existence is a predicate" is as follows: namely that, if a person who says these words is using "predicate" in the grammatical sense, he is *not* saying that the words, "exists," etc., ever "*stand for* a predicate in the logical sense;" whereas, if he is using "predicate" in the logical sense, he is saying that they do (often, at least) "*stand for* a predicate in the logical sense." What Mr. Kneale himself means by "Existence is not a predicate" is apparently some proposition which he would express by saying: "The words, "exists," etc., never stand for a predicate in the logical sense."

What I am not clear about is as to what is meant by saying of a particular word (or particular phrase) in a particular sentence that it "stands for a predicate in the logical sense;" nor, therefore, as to what is meant by saying of another particular word in another particular sentence that it does *not* "stand for a predicate in the logical sense." Mr. Kneale does, indeed, tell us that a "predicate in the logical sense" is the same as "an attribute;" but, though I think that the meaning of the word "attribute" is perhaps a little clearer than that of the phrase "predicate in the logical sense," it still seems to me far from clear: I do not clearly understand what he would mean by saying that "exists," etc., do not "stand for attributes." But, from examples which he gives, it is, I think, clear that he would say that in the sentence "This is red" the word "red," or the phrase "is red" (I am not clear which), does "stand for an attribute;" and also that in the sentence "Tame tigers growl," "growl" so stands, and in the sentence "Rajah growls," "growls" does. It is, therefore, presumably some difference between the way in which "exists," etc., are used in sentences in which they occur, and the way in which "is red" (or "red") and "growl" and "growls" are used in these sentences, that he wishes to express by saying that, whereas "exists," etc., do *not* "stand for attributes," these words in these sentences do. And if we can find what differences there are between the use of finite parts of the verb "to exist," and the use of "is red," "growl" and "growls," we may perhaps find what the difference is which he expresses in this way.

It will, I think, be best to begin with one particular use of "exist"—the one, namely, which Mr. Kneale illustrates by the example "Tame tigers exist." He clearly thinks that there is some very important difference between the way in which "exist" is used here, and the way in which "growl" is used in "Tame tigers growl;" and that it is a difference which does not hold, e.g. between the use of "scratch" in "Tame tigers scratch" and the use of "growl" in "Tame tigers growl." He would say that "scratch" and "growl" both "stand for attributes," whereas "exist" does not; and he would also say that "Tame tigers exist" is a proposition of a different *form* from "Tame tigers growl," whereas I think he would say that "Tame tigers growl" and "Tame tigers scratch" are *of the same form*. What difference between "Tame tigers exist" and "Tame tigers growl" can be the one he has in mind?

That there is a difference between the way in which we use "exist" in the former sentence and "growl" in the latter, of a different kind from the difference between our usages of "scratch" and "growl" in the two sentences "Tame tigers scratch" and "Tame tigers growl," can, I think, be brought out in the following way.

The sentence "Tame tigers growl" seems to me to be ambiguous. So far as I can see, it might mean "All tame tigers growl," or it might mean merely "Most tame tigers growl," or it might mean merely "Some tame tigers growl." Each of these three sentences has a clear meaning, and the meaning of each is clearly different from that of either of the two others. Of each of them, however, it is true that the proposition which it expresses is one which cannot possibly be true, unless some tame tigers do growl. And hence I think we can say of "Tame tigers growl" that, whichever sense it is used in, it means something which cannot possibly be true unless some tame tigers do growl. Similarly I think it is clear that "Tame tigers exist" means something which cannot possibly be true unless some tame tigers do exist. But I do not think that there is any ambiguity in "Tame tigers exist" corresponding to that which I have pointed out in "Tame tigers growl." So far as I can see "Tame tigers exist" and "Some tame tigers exist" are merely two different ways of expressing exactly the same proposition. That is to say, it is not true that "Tame tigers exist" might mean "All tame tigers exist," or "Most tame tigers exist," instead of merely "Some tame tigers exist." It always means just "Some tame tigers exist," and nothing else whatever. I have said it is never used to mean "All tame tigers exist," or "Most tame tigers exist;" but I hope it will strike everyone that there is something queer about this

proposition. It seems to imply that "All tame tigers exist" and "Most tame tigers exist" have a clear meaning, just as have "All tame tigers growl," and "Most tame tigers growl;" and that it is just an accident that we do not happen ever to use "Tame tigers exist" to express either of those two meanings instead of the meaning "Some tame tigers exist," whereas we do sometimes use "Tame tigers growl" to mean "All tame tigers growl" or "Most tame tigers growl," instead of merely "Some tame tigers growl." But is this in fact the case? Have "All tame tigers exist" and "Most tame tigers exist" any meaning at all? Certainly they have not a clear meaning, as have "All tame tigers growl" and "Most tame tigers growl." They are puzzling expressions, which certainly do not carry their meaning, if they have any, on the face of them. That this is so indicates, I think, that there is some important difference between the usage of "exist" with which we are concerned, and the usage of such words as "growl" or "scratch;" but it does not make clear just what the difference is.

I think this can be made clear by comparing the expressions "Some tame tigers don't growl" and "Some tame tigers don't exist." The former, whether true or false, has a perfectly clear meaning—a meaning just as clear as that of "Some tame tigers do growl;" and it is perfectly clear that both propositions might be true together. But with "Some tame tigers don't exist" the case is different. "Some tame tigers exist" has a perfectly clear meaning: it just means "There are some tame tigers." But the meaning of "Some tame tigers don't exist," if any, is certainly not equally clear. It is another queer and puzzling expression. Has it any meaning at all? and, if so, what meaning? If it has any, it would appear that it must mean the same as: "There are some tame tigers which don't exist." But has *this* any meaning? And if so, what? Is it possible that there should be any tame tigers which don't exist? I think the answer is that, if in the sentence "Some tame tigers don't exist," you are using "exist" with the same meaning as in "Some tame tigers exist," then the former sentence as a whole has no meaning at all—it is pure nonsense. A meaning can, of course, be given to "Some tame tigers don't exist;" but this can only be done if "exist" is used in a different way from that in which it is used in "Some tame tigers exist." And, if this is so, it will follow that "All tame tigers exist" and "Most tame tigers exist," also have no meaning at all, if you are using "exist" in the sense with which we are concerned. For "All tame tigers growl" is equivalent to the conjunction "Some tame tigers growl, and there is no tame tiger which does not growl;" and this has a meaning, because "There is at least one tame tiger which does not growl" has one. If, therefore, "There is at least one tame tiger which does not exist" has no meaning, it will follow that "All tame tigers exist" also has none; because "There is no tame tiger which does not exist" will have none, if "There is a tame tiger which does not exist" has none. Similarly "Most tame tigers growl" is equivalent to the conjunction "Some tame tigers growl, and the number of those (if any) which do not growl is smaller than that of those which do"—a statement which has a meaning only because "There are tame tigers which do not growl" has one. If, therefore, "There are tame tigers which don't exist" has no meaning, it will follow that "Most tame tigers exist" will also have none. I think, therefore, we can say that one important difference between the use of "growl" in "Some tame tigers growl" and the use of "exist" in "Some tame tigers exist," is that if in the former case we insert "do not" before "growl," without changing the meaning of "growl," we get a sentence which is significant, whereas if, in the latter, we insert "do not" before "exist" without changing the meaning of "exist," we get a sentence which has no meaning whatever; and I think we can also say that this fact explains why, with the given meaning of "growl," "All tame tigers growl" and "Most tame tigers growl" are both significant, whereas, with the given meaning of "exist," "All tame tigers exist" and "Most tame tigers exist" are utterly meaningless. And if by the statement that "growl," in this usage, "stands for an attribute," whereas "exist," in this usage, does not, part of what is meant is that there is this difference between them, then I should agree that "exist," in this usage, does not "stand for an attribute."

But is it really true that if, in the sentence "Some tame tigers exist," we insert "do not" before "exist," without changing the meaning of "exist," we get a sentence which has no meaning whatever? I have admitted that a meaning *can* be given to "Some tame tigers do not exist;" and it may, perhaps, be contended by some people that the meaning which

"exist" has in this sentence, where it is significant, *is* precisely the same as that which it has in "Some tame tigers exist." I cannot show the contrary as clearly as I should like to be able to do; but I will do my best.

The meaning which such an expression as "Some tame tigers do not exist" sometimes does have, is that which it has when it is used to mean the same as "Some tame tigers are imaginary" or "Some tame tigers are not real tigers." That "Some tame tigers are imaginary" may really express a proposition, whether true or false, cannot I think be denied. If, for instance, two different stories have been written, each of which is about a different imaginary tame tiger, it will follow that there are at least two imaginary tame tigers; and it cannot be denied that the sentence "Two different tame tigers occur in fiction" is significant, though I have not the least idea whether it is true or false. I know that at least one unicorn occurs in fiction, because one occurs in *Alice Through the Looking Glass;* and it follows that there is at least one imaginary unicorn, and therefore (in a sense) at least one unicorn which does not exist. Again, if it should happen that at the present moment two different people are each having an hallucination of a different tame tiger, it will follow that there are at the present moment two different imaginary tame tigers; and the statement that two such hallucinations are occurring now is certainly significant, though it may very likely be false. The sentence "There are some tame tigers which do not exist" is, therefore, certainly significant, if it means only that there are some imaginary tigers, in either of the two senses which I have tried to point out. But what it means is that either some real people have written stories about imaginary tigers, or are having or have recently had hallucinations of tame tigers, or, perhaps, are dreaming or have dreamed of particular tame tigers. If nothing of this sort has happened or is happening to anybody, then there are no imaginary tame tigers. But if "Some tame tigers do not exist" means all this, is it not clear that "exist" has not, in this sentence, the same comparatively simple meaning as it has in "Some tame tigers exist" or in "No tame tigers exist"? Is it not clear that "Some tame tigers do not exist," if it means all this, is not related to "Some tame tigers exist," in the same simple way in which "Some tame tigers do not growl" is related to "Some tame tigers growl"?

Why the Ontological Argument Fails

~

WILLIAM L. ROWE

William L. Rowe, who has written extensively in the philosophy of religion, is professor of philosophy at Purdue University.

I want to present a . . . critique of [Anselm's] argument, a critique suggested by the basic conviction . . . , that from the mere logical analysis of a certain idea or concept, we can never determine that there exists in reality anything answering to that idea or concept.

Suppose someone comes to us and says:

> I propose to define the term *God as an existing, wholly perfect being.* Now since it can't be true that an existing, wholly perfect being does not exist, it can't be true that God, as I've defined him, does not exist. Therefore, God must exist.

This argument appears to be a very simple Ontological Argument. It begins with a particular idea or concept of God and ends by concluding that God, so conceived, must exist. What can we say in response? We might start by objecting to this definition of *God*, claiming (1) that only predicates can be used to define a term, and (2) that existence is not a predicate. But suppose our friend is not impressed by this response—either because he thinks no one has fully explained what a predicate is or proved that existence isn't one, or because he thinks that anyone can define a word in whatever way he pleases. Can we allow our friend to define the word *God* in any way he pleases and still hope to show that it will not follow from that definition that there actually exists something to which this concept of God applies? I think we can.

Let's first invite him, however, to consider some concepts other than this peculiar concept of God. . . .

[T]he term *magician* may be applied both to Houdini and Merlin, even though the former existed whereas the latter did not. Noting that our friend has used *existing* as part of this definition of *God,* suppose we agree with him that we can define a word in any way we please, and, accordingly, introduce the following words with the following definitions:

> A *magican* is defined as an *existing magician.*
> A *magico* is defined as a *nonexisting magician.*

Here we have introduced two words and used *existing* or *nonexisting* in their definitions. Now something of interest follows from the fact that *existing* is part of our definition of a magican. For while it's true that Merlin was a *magician* it isn't true that Merlin was a *magican.* And something of interest follows from our including *nonexisting* in the definition of a magico. For while it's true that Houdini was a *magician* it isn't true that Houdini was a *magico.* Houdini was a *magician* and a *magican,* but not a *magico,* whereas Merlin was a *magician* and a *magico,* but not a *magican.*

What we have just seen is that introducing *existing* or *nonexisting* into the definition of a concept has a very important implication. If we introduce *existing* into the definition of a concept, it follows that no nonexisting thing can exemplify that concept. And if

Reprinted from *Philosophy of Religion: An Introduction* (2nd ed.) (Belmont, Calif.: Wadsworth Publishing Company, 1993) by permission of the publisher.

we introduce *nonexisting* into the definition of a concept, it follows that no existing thing can exemplify that concept. No nonexisting thing can be a *magican* and no existing thing can be a *magico*.

But must some existing thing exemplify the concept *magican?* No! From the fact that *existing* is included in the definition of *magican* it does not follow that some existing thing is a *magican*—all that follows is that no nonexisting thing is a *magican*. If there were no magicians in existence there would be nothing to which the term *magican* would apply. This being so, it clearly does not follow merely from our definition of *magican* that some existing thing is a *magican*. Only if magicians exist will it be true that some existing thing is a *magican*.

We are now in a position to help our friend see that, from the mere fact that *God* is defined as an existing, wholly perfect being, it will not follow that some existing being is God. Something of interest does follow from his definition: namely, that no nonexisting being can be God. But whether some existing thing is God will depend entirely on whether some existing thing is a wholly perfect being. If no wholly perfect being exists there will be nothing to which this concept of God can apply. This being so, it clearly does not follow merely from this definition of *God* that some existing thing is God. Only if a wholly perfect being exists will it be true that God, as our friend conceives of him, exists.

The implications of these considerations for Anselm's ingenious argument can now be traced. Anselm conceives of God as a being than which none greater is possible. He then claims that existence is a greatmaking quality, something that has it is greater than it would have been had it lacked existence. Clearly then, no nonexisting thing can exemplify Anselm's concept of God. For if we suppose that some nonexisting thing exemplifies Anselm's concept of God and also suppose that that nonexisting thing might have existed in reality (is a possible thing), then we are supposing that that nonexisting thing (1) might have been a greater thing, and (2) is, nevertheless, a thing than which a greater is not possible. Thus far Anselm's reasoning is, I believe, impeccable. But what follows from it? All that follows from it is that no nonexisting thing can be God

(as Anselm conceives of God). All that follows is that given Anselm's concept of God, the proposition "Some nonexisting thing is God" cannot be true. But, as we saw earlier, this is also the case with the proposition "Some nonexisting thing is a magican." What remains to be shown is that some existing thing exemplifies Anselm's concept of God. What really does follow from his reasoning is that the only thing that logically could exemplify his concept of God is something which actually exists. And this conclusion is not without interest. But from the mere fact that nothing but an existing thing could exemplify Anselm's concept of God, it does not follow that some existing thing actually does exemplify his concept of God—no more than it follows from the mere fact that no nonexisting thing can be a magican that some existing thing is a magican.[1]

There is, however, one major difficulty in this critique of Anselm's argument. This difficulty arises when we take into account Anselm's implicit claim that God is a possible thing. . . . Possible things . . . [are] all those things that, unlike the round square, are not impossible things. Suppose we concede to Anselm that God, as he conceives of him, is a possible thing. Now, of course, the mere knowledge that something is a possible thing doesn't enable us to conclude that that thing is an existing thing. For many possible things, like the Fountain of Youth, do not exist. But if something is a possible thing, then it is either an existing thing or a nonexisting thing. The set of possible things can be exhaustively divided into those possible things which actually exist and those possible things which do not exist. Therefore, if Anselm's God is a possible thing, it is either an existing thing or a nonexisting thing. We have concluded, however, that no nonexisting thing can be Anselm's God; therefore, it seems we must conclude with Anselm that some actually existing thing does exemplify his concept of God.

To see the solution to this major difficulty we need to return to an earlier example. Let's consider again the idea of a magican, an existing magician. It so happens that some magicians have existed—Houdini, The Great Blackstone, and others. But, of course, it might have been otherwise. Suppose, for the moment, that no magicians have ever existed. The concept "magician" would still have application, for it would still be true that Merlin was a magician. But what about the concept of a "magican?" Would any possible object be picked out by that concept? No! For no nonexisting thing could exemplify the concept "magican." And on the supposition that no magicians ever existed, no existing thing would exemplify the concept "magican."[2] We then would have a coherent concept "magican" which would not be exemplified by any possible object at all. For if all the possible objects which are magicians are nonexisting things, none of them would be a magican and, since no possible objects which exist are magicians, none of them would be a magican. We then would have a coherent, consistent concept "magican", which in fact is not exemplified by any possible object at all. Put in this way, our result seems paradoxical. For we are inclined to think that only contradictory concepts like "the round square" are not exemplified by any possible things. The truth is, however, that when *existing* is included in or implied by a certain concept, it may be the case that no possible object does in fact exemplify that concept. For no possible object that doesn't exist will exemplify a concept like "magican" in which *existing* is included; and if there are no existing things which exemplify the other features included in the concept—for example, "being a magician" in the case of the concept "magican"—then no possible object that exists will exemplify the concept. Put in its simplest terms, if we ask whether any possible thing is a magican, the answer will depend entirely on whether any existing thing is a magician. If no existing things are magicians, then no possible things are magicians. Some possible object is a magican just in case some actually existing thing is a magician.

Applying these considerations to Anselm's argument we can find the solution to our major difficulty. Given Anselm's concept of God and his principle that existence is a great-making quality, it really does follow that the only thing that logically could exemplify his concept of God is something which actually exists. But, we argued, it doesn't follow from these considerations alone that God actually exists, that some existing thing exemplifies Anselm's concept of God. The difficulty we fell into, however, is that when we add the premise that God is a possible thing, that some possible object exemplifies his concept of God, it

really does follow that God actually exists, that some actually existing thing exemplifies Anselm's concept of God. For if some possible object exemplifies his concept of God, that object is either an existing thing or a nonexisting thing. But since no nonexisting thing could exemplify Anselm's concept of God, it follows that the possible object which exemplifies his concept of God must be a possible object that actually exists. Therefore, given (1) Anselm's concept of God, (2) his principle that existence is a great-making quality, and (3) the premise that God, as conceived by Anselm, is a possible thing, it really does follow that Anselm's God actually exists.

I think we now can see that in granting Anselm the premise that God is a possible thing we have granted far more than we intended to grant. All we thought we were granting is that Anselm's concept of God, unlike the concept of a round square, is not contradictory or incoherent. But without realizing it we were in fact granting much more than this, as became apparent when we considered the idea of a "magican." There is nothing contradictory in the idea of a magican, an existing magician. But in asserting that a magican is a possible thing, we are, as we saw, directly implying that some existing thing is a magician. For if no existing thing is a magician, the concept of a magican will apply to no possible object whatever. The same point holds with respect to Anselm's God. Since Anselm's concept of God logically cannot apply to some nonexisting thing, the only possible objects to which it could apply are possible objects which actually exist. Therefore, in granting that Anselm's God is a possible thing, we are granting far more than that his idea of God isn't incoherent or contradictory. Suppose, for example, that every existing being has some defect which it might not have had. Without realizing it, we were denying this when we granted that Anselm's God is a possible being. For if every existing being has a defect it might not have had, then every existing being might have been greater. But if every existing being might have been greater, then Anselm's concept of God will apply to no possible object whatever. Therefore, if we allow Anselm his concept of God and his principle that existence is a great-making quality, then in granting that God, as Anselm conceives of him, is a possible being, we will be granting much more than that his concept of God is not contradictory. We will be granting, for example, that some existing thing is as perfect as it can be. For the plain fact is that Anselm's God is a possible thing only if some *existing* thing is as perfect as it can be.

Our final critique of Anselm's argument is simply this. In granting that Anselm's God is a possible thing, we are in fact granting that Anselm's God actually exists. But since the purpose of the argument is to prove to us that Anselm's God exists, we cannot be asked to grant as a premise a statement which is virtually equivalent to the conclusion that is to be proved. Anselm's concept of God may be coherent and his principle that existence is a great-making quality may be true. But all that follows from this is that no nonexisting thing can be Anselm's God. If we add to all of this the premise that God is a possible thing it will follow that God actually exists. But the additional premise claims more than that Anselm's concept of God isn't incoherent or contradictory. It amounts to the assertion that some existing being is

supremely great. And since this is, in part, the point the argument endeavors to prove, the argument begs the question: it assumes the point it is supposed to prove.

If the above critique is correct, Anselm's argument fails as a proof of the existence of God. This is not to say, however, that the argument isn't a work of genius. Perhaps no other argument in the history of thought has raised so many basic philosophical questions and stimulated so much hard thought. Even if it fails as a proof of the existence of God, it will remain as one of the high achievements of the human intellect.

NOTES

1. An argument along the lines just presented may be found in J. Shaffer's illuminating essay, "Existence, Predication and the Ontological Argument," *Mind* LXXI (1962), pp. 307–25.

2. I am indebted to Professor William Wainwright for bringing this point to my attention.

Five Ways to Prove the Existence of God

~

SAINT THOMAS AQUINAS

Saint Thomas Aquinas (1225–1274), born near Naples, was the most influential philosopher of the medieval period. Aquinas' synthesis of Aristotelianism and Christianity was considered so successful by the Church that six hundred years later in 1879 Pope Leo XIII declared Aquinas' system to be the official Catholic philosophy. Aquinas' greatest work was the *Summa Theologiae,* and its most famous passage, reprinted here, is the five ways to prove the existence of God. In the fourth way Aquinas cites "*Metaph.* ii.*"* The reference is to the second book of Aristotle's *Metaphysics* and serves as a reminder of Aristotle's central place in Aquinas' thought.

There are five ways of proving there is a God:

The first and most obvious way is based on change. For certainly some things are changing: this

we plainly see. Now anything changing is being changed by something else. (This is so because what makes things changeable is unrealized potentiality,

Reprinted from *Aquinas: Selected Philosophical Writings,* ed. Timothy McDermott (Oxford: Oxford University Press, 1993), by permission of the publisher.

but what makes them cause change is their already realized state: causing change brings into being what was previously only able to be, and can only be done by something which already is. For example, the actual heat of fire causes wood, able to be hot, to become actually hot, and so causes change in the wood; now what is actually hot can't at the same time be potentially hot but only potentially cold, can't at the same time be actual and potential in the same respect but only in different respects; so that what is changing can't be the very thing that is causing the same change, can't be changing itself, but must be being changed by something else.) Again this something else, if itself changing, must be being changed by yet another thing; and this last by another. But this can't go on for ever, since then there would be no first cause of the change, and as a result no subsequent causes. (Only when acted on by a first cause do intermediate causes produce a change; unless a hand moves the stick, the stick won't move anything else.) So we are forced eventually to come to a first cause of change not itself being changed by anything, and this is what everyone understands by *God*.

The second way is based on the very notion of agent cause. In the observable world causes are found ordered in series: we never observe, nor ever could, something causing itself, for this would mean it preceded itself, and this is not possible. But a series of causes can't go on for ever, for in any such series an earlier member causes an intermediate and the intermediate a last (whether the intermediate be one or many). Now eliminating a cause eliminates its effects, and unless there's a first cause there won't be a last or an intermediate. But if a series of causes goes on for ever it will have no first cause, and so no intermediate causes and no last effect, which is clearly false. So we are forced to postulate some first agent cause, to which everyone gives the name *God*.

The third way is based on what need not be and on what must be, and runs as follows. Some of the things we come across can be but need not be, for we find them being generated and destroyed, thus sometimes in being and sometimes not. Now everything cannot

be like this, for a thing that need not be was once not; and if everything need not be, once upon a time there was nothing. But if that were true there would be nothing even now, because something that does not exist can only begin to exist through something that already exists. If nothing was in being nothing could begin to be, and nothing would be in being now, which is clearly false. Not everything then is the sort that need not be; some things must be, and these may or may not owe this necessity to something else. But just as we proved that a series of agent causes can't go on for ever, so also a series of things which must be and owe this to other things. So we are forced to postulate something which of itself must be, owing this to nothing outside itself, but being itself the cause that other things must be.

The fourth way is based on the levels found in things. Some things are found to be better, truer, more excellent than others. Such comparative terms describe varying degrees of approximation to a superlative; for example, things are hotter the nearer they approach what is hottest. So there is something which is the truest and best and most excellent of things, and hence the most fully in being; for Aristotle says that the truest things are the things most fully in being. Now *when many things possess a property in common, the one most fully possessing it causes it in the others: fire,* as Aristotle says, *the hottest of all things, causes all other things to be hot.* So there is something that causes in all other things their being, their goodness, and whatever other perfections they have. And this is what we call *God*.

The fifth way is based on the guidedness of nature. Goal-directed behaviour is observed in all bodies in nature, even those lacking awareness; for we see their behaviour hardly ever varying and practically always turning out well, which shows they truly tend to goals and do not merely hit them by accident. But nothing lacking awareness can tend to a goal except it be directed by someone with awareness and understanding: arrows by archers, for example. So everything in nature is directed to its goal by someone with understanding, and this we call *God*.

The Cosmological Argument

~

MICHAEL MARTIN

Michael Martin, who has written books in philosophy of religion and philosophy of law, is professor of philosophy at Boston University.

THE SIMPLE VERSION

In its simplest form the cosmological argument is this: Everything we know has a cause. But there cannot be an infinite regress of causes, so there must be a first cause. This first cause is God.

It is well to state the problems with this simple version of the argument, since, as we shall see, they are found in some of the more sophisticated versions as well. Perhaps the major problem with this version of the argument is that even if it is successful in demonstrating a first cause, this first cause is not necessarily God. A first cause need not have the properties usually associated with God. For example, a first cause need not have great, let alone infinite, knowledge or goodness. A first cause could be an evil being or the universe itself. In itself this problem makes the argument quite useless as support for the view that God exists. However, it has at least one other equally serious problem.

The argument assumes that there cannot be an infinite sequence of causes, but it is unclear why this should be so. Experience does not reveal causal sequences that have a first cause, a cause that is not caused. So the idea that there can be no infinite sequences and that there must be a first cause, a cause without a cause, finds no support in experience. This is not to say that experience indicates an infinite sequence of causes. Rather, the presumption of the existence of a first cause seems to be a nonempirical assumption that some people see as obvious or self-evident. From a historical point of view, however, any appeal to obviousness or self-evidence must be regarded with suspicion, for many things that have been claimed to be self-evidently true—for example, the divine right of kings and the earth as the center of the universe—have turned out not to be true at all.

Further, we have no experience of infinite causal sequences, but we do know that there are infinite series, such as natural numbers. One wonders why, if there can be infinite sequences in mathematics, there could not be one in causality. No doubt there are crucial differences between causal and mathematical series; but without further arguments showing precisely what these are, there is no reason to think that there could not be an infinite regression of causes. Some recent defenders of the cosmological argument have offered just such arguments, and I examine these arguments later. But even if they are successful, in themselves they do not show that the first cause is God.

MORE COMPLEX VERSIONS

As I have said, major problems facing the simple version of the cosmological argument reemerge in more sophisticated versions as well. Consider, for example, Aquinas's belief that God's existence could be demonstrated by rational arguments. In the *Summa Theologiae* he presents five arguments—what he calls ways—that he believes demonstrate the existence of God. The first three of his five ways are sophisticated versions of the simple cosmological argument presented alone. I consider ways two and three. . . .

[In] the second way . . . Aquinas attempts to show that there could not be an infinite series of efficient causes and consequently there must be a first cause. Although this notion of efficient cause is perhaps closer to our modern view of causality than the other Aristotelian concepts of cause he used, there are some important differences. An efficient cause of something, for Aristotle and Aquinas, is not a prior event but a substantial agent that brings about change. The paradigm cases of causation for an Aristotelian are heating and wetting. For example, if A heats B, then A produces heat in B; if A wets B, then A produces wetness in B. In general, if A Φs B, then A produces Φness in B. The priority of a cause need not be temporal; a cause is prior to its effects in the sense that the cause can exist without the effect but not conversely.

It is important to realize that Aquinas's argument purports to establish a first cause that maintains the universe here and now. His second way is not concerned with establishing a first cause of the universe in the distant past. Indeed, he believed that one could not demonstrate by philosophical argument that the universe had a beginning in time, although he believed that it did. This belief was a matter of faith, something that was part of Christian dogma, not something that one could certify by reason. Thus he was not opposed on *philosophical* grounds to the universe's having no temporal beginning. As the above quotation makes clear, he believed that the here-and-now maintenance of the universe could not be understood in terms of an infinite causal series.

Two analogies can perhaps make the distinction between temporal and nontemporal causal sequences clear. Consider a series of falling dominos. It is analogous to a temporal causal sequence. Aquinas does not deny on philosophical grounds that infinite sequences of this sort can exist. But now consider a chain in which one link supports the next. There is no temporal sequence here. The sort of causal sequence that Aquinas says cannot go on forever but must end in a first cause is analogous to this.

The same problems that plagued the simple version of the argument plague this more sophisticated version. The first cause, even if established, need not be God; and Aquinas gives no non-question-begging reason why there could not be a nontemporal infinite regress of causes. This latter is an especially acute problem. Unless some relevant difference is shown between a temporal and a nontemporal infinite series, Aquinas's claim that an infinite temporal sequence cannot be shown to be impossible by philosophical argument seems indirectly to cast doubt on his claim that philosophical argument can show the impossibility of a nontemporal causal series. . . .

To critically evaluate Aquinas's [third way], it is useful to reformulate it in the following steps.

(1) Each existing thing is capable of not existing.
(2) What is true of each thing is true of everything (the totality).
(3) Therefore, everything could cease to exist.
(4) If everything could cease to exist, then it has already occurred.
(5) Therefore, everything has ceased to exist.
(6) If everything has already ceased to exist and there could not be something brought into existence by nothing, then nothing exists now.
(7) There could not be something brought into existence by nothing.
(8) Therefore, nothing exists now.
(9) But something does exist now.
(10) Therefore, premise (1) is false.
(11) Therefore, there must be some being that is not capable of not existing—that is, a necessary being.
(12) Every necessary being must have the cause of its necessity either outside itself or not.
(13) There cannot be an infinite series of necessary beings that have a cause of their necessity outside themselves.
(14) Therefore, there is a necessary being that does not have the cause of its own necessity outside itself and that is the cause of the necessity of other beings.
(15) Therefore, God exists.

Of the many problems with Aquinas's argument, the major one is similar to that facing the simple version of the cosmological argument considered above. Even if a necessary being is established, it need not be God, for the universe itself may be necessary. Thus the last step of the argument from (14) to (15) is unwarranted.

There are a number of particular problems with Aquinas's argument as well. In premise (2) the argument seems to commit the fallacy of composition. Just because each thing is capable of not existing, it is not obvious that the totality would be capable of not existing. Furthermore, premise (4) seems implausible in the extreme. There is no reason to suppose that just because something is capable of not existing, at some time this possibility has been realized.

In addition, the supposition in premise (7) that there could not be something brought into existence by nothing is by no means self-evident. At least, given the biblical authority of the book of Genesis, where God created the world out of nothing, it should

not have seemed so to Aquinas. For if God could create the world out of nothing, one might suppose that something could be spontaneously generated out of nothing without God's help. Surely this is all step (7) is denying by the words "there could not be something brought into existence by nothing." Furthermore, recently proposed cosmological theories suggest that the universe may indeed have been generated from nothing. Although a critical evaluation of these recent theories is beyond the scope of this book, it is important to realize that such theories are being seriously discussed and debated by physicists, astronomers, and philosophers of science in respectable publications. Moreover, step (13) has all the problems inherited from Aquinas's arguments that there could not be an infinite series of efficient causes.

I must conclude, then, that these two deductive versions of the cosmological argument are unsound and therefore cannot be used to support a belief in God.

Dialogues Concerning Natural Religion

DAVID HUME

The Scotsman David Hume (1711–1776), essayist, historian, and philosopher, developed one of the most influential of all philosophical systems. He presented it first in his monumental *Treatise of Human Nature,* published when he was 28 years old. His *Dialogues Concerning Natural Religion* was published posthumously because of its controversial content. It remains a landmark in the philosophy of religion.

PART II

I MUST OWN, Cleanthes, said Demea, that nothing can more surprise me than the light in which you have all along put this argument. By the whole tenor of your discourse, one would imagine that you were maintaining the Being of a God against the cavils of atheists and infidels, and were necessitated to become a champion for that fundamental principle of all religion. But this, I hope, is not by any means a question

David Hume, *Dialogues Concerning Natural Religion* (1779).

among us. No man, no man at least of common sense, I am persuaded, ever entertained a serious doubt with regard to a truth so certain and self-evident. The question is not concerning the *being* but the *nature* of God. This I affirm, from the infirmities of human understanding, to be altogether incomprehensible and unknown to us. The essence of that supreme Mind, his attributes, the manner of his existence, the very nature of his duration—these and every particular which regards so divine a Being are mysterious to men. Finite, weak, and blind creatures, we ought to humble ourselves in his august presence, and, conscious of our frailties, adore in silence his infinite perfections which eye hath not seen, ear hath not heard, neither hath it entered into the heart of man to conceive. They are covered in a deep cloud from human curiosity; it is profaneness to attempt penetrating through these sacred obscurities, and, next to the impiety of denying his existence, is the temerity of prying into his nature and essence, decrees and attributes.

But lest you should think that my *piety* has here got the better of my *philosophy,* I shall support my opinion, if it needs any support, by a very great authority. I might cite all the divines, almost from the foundation of Christianity, who have ever treated of this or any other theological subject; but I shall confine myself, at present, to one equally celebrated for piety and philosophy. It is Father Malebranche who, I remember, thus expresses himself. "One ought not so much," says he, "to call God a spirit in order to express positively what he is, as in order to signify that he is not matter. He is a Being infinitely perfect—of this we cannot doubt. But in the same manner as we ought not to imagine, even supposing him corporeal, that he is clothed with a human body, as the anthropomorphites asserted, under colour that that figure was the most perfect of any, so neither ought we to imagine that the spirit of God has human ideas or bears any resemblance to our spirit, under colour that we know nothing more perfect than a human mind. We ought rather to believe that as he comprehends the perfections of matter without being material . . . he comprehends also the perfections of created spirits without being spirit, in the manner we conceive spirit: that his true name is *He that is,* or, in other words, Being without restriction, All Being, the Being infinite and universal."

After so great an authority, Demea, replied Philo, as that which you have produced, and a thousand more which you might produce, it would appear ridiculous in me to add my sentiment or express my approbation of your doctrine. But surely, where reasonable men treat these subjects, the question can never be concerning the *being* but only the *nature* of the Deity. The former truth, as you well observe, is unquestionable and self-evident. Nothing exists without a cause; and the original cause of this universe (whatever it be) we call God, and piously ascribe to him every species of perfection. Whoever scruples this fundamental truth deserves every punishment which can be inflicted among philosophers, to wit, the greatest ridicule, contempt, and disapprobation. But as all perfection is entirely relative, we ought never to imagine that we comprehend the attributes of this divine Being, or to suppose that his perfections have any analogy or likeness to the perfections of a human creature. Wisdom, thought, design, knowledge—these we justly ascribe to him because these words are honourable among men, and we have no other language or other conceptions by which we can express our adoration of him. But let us beware lest we think that our ideas anywise correspond to his perfections, or that his attributes have any resemblance to these qualities among men. He is infinitely superior to our limited view and comprehension, and is more the object of worship in the temple than of disputation in the schools.

In reality, Cleanthes, continued he, there is no need of having recourse to that affected scepticism so displeasing to you in order to come at this determination. Our ideas reach no further than our experience. We have no experience of divine attributes and operations. I need not conclude my syllogism, you can draw the inference yourself. And it is a pleasure to me (and I hope to you, too) that just reasoning and sound piety here concur in the same conclusion, and both of them establish the adorably mysterious and incomprehensible nature of the Supreme Being.

Not to lose any time in circumlocutions, said Cleanthes, addressing himself to Demea, much less in replying to the pious declamations of Philo, I shall briefly explain how I conceive this matter. Look round the world, contemplate the whole and every part of it: you will find it to be nothing but one great machine, subdivided into an infinite number of lesser machines, which again admit of subdivisions to a degree beyond what human senses and faculties can trace and explain. All these various machines, and even their most minute parts, are adjusted to each other with an accuracy which ravishes into admiration all men who have ever contemplated them. The curious adapting of means to ends, throughout all nature, resembles exactly, though it much exceeds, the productions of human contrivance—of human design, thought, wisdom, and intelligence. Since therefore the effects resemble each other, we are led to infer, by all the rules of analogy, that the causes also resemble, and that the Author of nature is somewhat similar to the mind of man, though possessed of much larger faculties, proportioned to the grandeur of the work which he has executed. By this argument a posteriori, and by this argument alone, do we prove at once the existence of a Deity and his similarity to human mind and intelligence.

I shall be so free, Cleanthes, said Demea, as to tell you that from the beginning I could not approve of your conclusion concerning the similarity of the Deity to men, still less can I approve of the mediums by which you endeavour to establish it. What! No demonstration of the Being of God! No abstract arguments! No proofs a priori! Are these which have hitherto been so much insisted on by philosophers all fallacy, all sophism? Can we reach no farther in this subject than experience and probability? I will not say that this is betraying the cause of a Deity; but surely, by this affected candour, you give advantages to atheists which they never could obtain by the mere dint of argument and reasoning.

What I chiefly scruple in this subject, said Philo, is not so much that all religious arguments are by Cleanthes reduced to experience, as that they appear not to be even the most certain and irrefragable of that inferior kind. That a stone will fall, that fire will burn, that the earth has solidity, we have observed a thousand and a thousand times; and when any new instance of this nature is presented, we draw without hesitation the accustomed inference. The exact similarity of the cases gives us a perfect assurance of a similar event, and a stronger evidence is never desired nor sought after. But wherever you depart, in the least, from the similarity of the cases, you diminish proportionably the evidence, and may at last bring it to a very weak *analogy,* which is confessedly liable to error and uncertainty. After having experienced the circulation of the blood in human creatures, we make no doubt that it takes place in Titius and Maevius; but from its circulation in frogs and fishes it is only a presumption, though a strong one, from analogy that it takes place in men and other animals. The analogical reasoning is much weaker when we infer the circulation of the sap in vegetables from our experience that the blood circulates in animals; and those who hastily followed that imperfect analogy are found, by more accurate experiments, to have been mistaken.

If we see a house, Cleanthes, we conclude, with the greatest certainty, that it had an architect or builder because this is precisely that species of effect which we have experienced to proceed from that species of cause. But surely you will not affirm that the universe bears such a resemblance to a house that we can with the same certainty infer a similar cause, or that the analogy is here entire and perfect. The dissimilitude is so striking that the utmost you can here pretend to is a guess, conjecture, a presumption concerning a similar cause; and how that pretension will be received in the world, I leave you to consider.

It would surely be very ill received, replied Cleanthes; and I should be deservedly blamed and detested did I allow that the proofs of Deity amounted to no more than a guess or conjecture. But is the whole adjustment of means to ends in a house and in the universe so slight a resemblance? the economy of final causes? the order, proportion, and arrangement of every part? Steps of a stair are plainly contrived that human legs may use them in mounting; and this inference is certain and infallible. Human legs are also contrived for walking and mounting; and this inference, I allow, is not altogether so certain because of the dissimilarity which you remark; but does it, therefore, deserve the name only of presumption or conjecture?

Good God! cried Demea, interrupting him, where are we? Zealous defenders of religion allow that the proofs of a Deity fall short of perfect evidence! And you, Philo, on whose assistance I depended in proving the adorable mysteriousness of the Divine Nature, do you assent to all these extravagant opinions of Cleanthes? For what other name can I give them? or, why spare my censure when such principles are advanced, supported by such an authority, before so young a man as Pamphilus?

You seem not to apprehend, replied Philo, that I argue with Cleanthes in his own way, and, by showing him the dangerous consequences of his tenets, hope at last to reduce him to our opinion. But what sticks most with you, I observe, is the representation which Cleanthes has made of the argument a posteriori; and, finding that the argument is likely to escape your hold and vanish into air, you think it so disguised that you can scarcely believe it to be set in its true light. Now, however much I may dissent, in other respects, from the dangerous principle of Cleanthes, I must allow that he has fairly represented that argument, and I shall endeavour so to state the matter to you that you will entertain no further scruples with regard to it.

Were a man to abstract from everything which he knows or has seen, he would be altogether incapable, merely from his own ideas, to determine what kind of scene the universe must be, or to give the preference to one state or situation of things above another. For as nothing which he clearly conceives could be esteemed impossible or implying a contradiction, every chimera of his fancy would be upon an equal footing; nor could he assign any just reason why he adheres to one idea or system, and rejects the others which are equally possible.

Again, after he opens his eyes and contemplates the world as it really is, it would be impossible for him at first to assign the cause of any one event, much less of the whole of things, or of the universe. He might set his fancy a rambling, and she might bring him in an infinite variety of reports and representations. These would all be possible, but, being all equally possible, he would never of himself give a satisfactory account for his preferring one of them to the rest. Experience alone can point out to him the true cause of any phenomenon.

Now, according to this method of reasoning, Demea, it follows (and is, indeed, tacitly allowed by

Cleanthes himself) that order, arrangement, or the adjustment of final causes, is not of itself any proof of design, but only so far as it has been experienced to proceed from that principle. For aught we can know a priori, matter may contain the source or spring of order originally within itself, as well as mind does; and there is no more difficulty in conceiving that the several elements, from an internal unknown cause, may fall into the most exquisite arrangement, than to conceive that their ideas, in the great universal mind, from a like internal unknown cause, fall into that arrangement. The equal possibility of both these suppositions is allowed. But, by experience, we find (according to Cleanthes) that there is a difference between them. Throw several pieces of steel together, without shape or form, they will never arrange themselves so as to compose a watch. Stone and mortar and wood, without an architect, never erect a house. But the ideas in a human mind, we see, by an unknown, inexplicable economy, arrange themselves so as to form the plan of a watch or house. Experience, therefore, proves that there is an original principle of order in mind, not in matter. From similar effects we infer similar causes. The adjustment of means to ends is alike in the universe, as in a machine of human contrivance. The causes, therefore, must be resembling.

I was from the beginning scandalized, I must own, with this resemblance which is asserted between the Deity and human creatures, and must conceive it to imply such a degradation of the Supreme Being as no sound theist could endure. With your assistance, therefore, Demea, I shall endeavour to defend what you justly call the adorable mysteriousness of the Divine Nature, and shall refute this reasoning of Cleanthes, provided he allows that I have made a fair representation of it.

When Cleanthes had assented, Philo, after a short pause, proceeded in the following manner.

That all inferences, Cleanthes, concerning fact are founded on experience, and that all experimental reasonings are founded on the supposition that similar causes prove similar effects, and similar effects similar causes, I shall not at present much dispute with you. But observe, I entreat you, with what extreme caution all just reasoners proceed in the transferring of experiments to similar cases. Unless the cases be exactly similar, they repose no perfect confidence in applying their past observation to any particular phenomenon. Every alteration of circumstances occasions a doubt concerning the event; and it requires new experiments to prove certainly that the new circumstances are of no moment or importance. A change in bulk, situation, arrangement, age, disposition of the air, or surrounding bodies—any of these particulars may be attended with the most unexpected consequences. And unless the objects be quite familiar to us, it is the highest temerity to expect with assurance, after any of these changes, an event similar to that which before fell under our observation. The slow and deliberate steps of philosophers here, if anywhere, are distinguished from the precipitate march of the vulgar, who, hurried on by the smallest similitude, are incapable of all discernment or consideration.

But can you think, Cleanthes, that your usual phlegm and philosophy have been preserved in so wide a step as you have taken when you compared to the universe houses, ships, furniture, machines, and, from their similarity in some circumstances, inferred a similarity in their causes? Thought, design, intelligence, such as we discover in men and other animals, is no more than one of the springs and principles of the universe, as well as heat or cold, attraction or repulsion, and a hundred others which fall under daily observation. It is an active cause by which some particular parts of nature, we find, produce alterations on other parts. But can a conclusion, with any propriety, be transferred from parts to the whole? Does not the great disproportion bar all comparison and inference? From observing the growth of a hair, can we learn anything concerning the generation of a man? Would the manner of a leaf's blowing, even though perfectly known, afford us any instruction concerning the vegetation of a tree?

But allowing that we were to take the *operations* of one part of nature upon another for the foundation of our judgment concerning the *origin* of the whole (which never can be admitted), yet why select so minute, so weak, so bounded a principle as the reason and design of animals is found to be upon this planet? What peculiar privilege has this little agitation of the brain which we call *thought,* that we must thus make it the model of the whole universe? Our partiality in our own favour does indeed present it on all occasions, but sound philosophy ought carefully to guard against so natural an illusion.

So far from admitting, continued Philo, that the operations of a part can afford us any just conclusion concerning the origin of the whole, I will not allow any one part to form a rule for another part if the latter be very remote from the former. Is there any reasonable ground to conclude that the inhabitants of other planets possess thought, intelligence, reason, or anything similar to these faculties in men? When nature has so extremely diversified her manner of operation in this small globe, can we imagine that she incessantly copies herself throughout so immense a universe? And if thought, as we may well suppose, be confined merely to this narrow corner and has even there so limited a sphere of action, with what propriety can we assign it for the original cause of all things? The narrow views of a peasant who makes his domestic economy the rule for the government of kingdoms is in comparison a pardonable sophism.

But were we ever so much assured that a thought and reason resembling the human were to be found throughout the whole universe, and were its activity elsewhere vastly greater and more commanding than it appears in this globe, yet I cannot see why the operations of a world constituted, arranged, adjusted, can with any propriety be extended to a world which is in its embryo state, and is advancing towards that constitution and arrangement. By observation we know somewhat of the economy, action, and nourishment of a finished animal, but we must transfer with great caution that observation to the growth of a foetus in the womb, and still more to the formation of an animalcule in the loins of its male parent. Nature, we find, even from our limited experience, possesses an infinite number of springs and principles which incessantly discover themselves on every change of her position and situation. And what new and unknown principles would actuate her in so new and unknown a situation as that of the formation of a universe, we cannot, without the utmost temerity, pretend to determine.

A very small part of this great system, during a very short time, is very imperfectly discovered to us; and do we thence pronounce decisively concerning the origin of the whole?

Admirable conclusion! Stone, wood, brick, iron, brass, have not, at this time, in this minute globe of earth, an order or arrangement without human art and contrivance; therefore, the universe could not originally attain its order and arrangement without something similar to human art. But is a part of nature a rule for another part very wide of the former? Is it a rule for the whole? Is a very small part a rule for the universe? Is nature in one situation a certain rule for nature in another situation vastly different from the former?

And can you blame me, Cleanthes, if I here imitate the prudent reserve of Simonides, who, according to the noted story, being asked by Hiero, *What God was?* desired a day to think of it, and then two days more; and after that manner continually prolonged the term, without ever bringing in his definition or description? Could you even blame me if I had answered, at first, *that I did not know,* and was sensible that this subject lay vastly beyond the reach of my faculties? You might cry out sceptic and raillier, as much as you pleased; but, having found in so many other subjects much more familiar the imperfections and even contradictions of human reason, I never should expect any success from its feeble conjectures in a subject so sublime and so remote from the sphere of our observation. When two *species* of objects have always been observed to be conjoined together, I can *infer,* by custom, the existence of one wherever I *see* the existence of the other; and this I call an argument from experience. But how this argument can have place where the objects, as in the present case, are single, individual, without parallel or specific resemblance, may be difficult to explain. And will any man tell me with a serious countenance that an orderly universe must arise from some thought and art like the human because we have experience of it? To ascertain this reasoning it were requisite that we had experience of the origin of worlds; and it is not sufficient, surely, that we have seen ships and cities arise from human art and contrivance.

Philo was proceeding in this vehement manner, somewhat between jest and earnest, as it appeared to me, when he observed some signs of impatience in Cleanthes, and then immediately stopped short. What I had to suggest, said Cleanthes, is only that you would not abuse terms, or make use of popular expressions to subvert philosophical reasonings. You know that the vulgar often distinguish reason from experience, even where the question relates only to matter of fact and existence, though it is found, where that *reason* is properly analyzed, that it is nothing but a species of experience. To prove by experience the origin of the universe from mind is not more contrary to common speech than to prove the motion of the earth from the same principle. And a caviller might raise all the same objections to the Copernican system which you have urged against my reasonings. Have you other earths, might he say, which you have seen to move? Have . . .

Yes! cried Philo, interrupting him, we have other earths. Is not the moon another earth, which we see to turn around its centre? Is not Venus another earth, where we observe the same phenomenon? Are not the revolutions of the sun also a confirmation, from analogy, of the same theory? All the planets, are they not earths which revolve about the sun? Are not the satellites moons which move round Jupiter and Saturn, and along with these primary planets round the sun? These analogies and resemblances, with others which I have not mentioned, are the sole proofs of the Copernican system; and to you it belongs to consider whether you have any analogies of the same kind to support your theory.

In reality, Cleanthes, continued he, the modern system of astronomy is now so much received by all inquirers, and has become so essential a part even of our earliest education, that we are not commonly very scrupulous in examining the reasons upon which it is founded. It is now become a matter of mere curiosity to study the first writers of that subject who had the full force of prejudice to encounter, and were obliged to turn their arguments on every side in order to render them popular and convincing. But if we peruse Galileo's famous *Dialogues* concerning the system of the world, we shall find that that great genius, one of the sublimest that ever existed, first bent all his endeavours to prove that there was no foundation for the distinction commonly made between elementary and celestial substances. The schools, proceeding from the illusions of sense, had carried this distinction very far; and had established the latter substances to be ingenerable, incorruptible, unalterable, impassible; and had assigned all the opposite qualities to the former. But Galileo, beginning with the moon, proved its similarity in every particular to the earth: its convex figure, its natural darkness when not illuminated, its density, its distinction into solid and liquid, the variations of its phases, the mutual illuminations of the earth and moon, their mutual eclipses, the inequalities of the lunar surface, etc. After many instances of this kind, with regard to all the planets, men plainly saw that these bodies became proper objects of experience, and that the similarity of their nature enabled us to extend the same arguments and phenomena from one to the other.

In this cautious proceeding of the astronomers you may read your own condemnation, Cleanthes, or rather may see that the subject in which you are engaged exceeds all human reason and inquiry. Can you pretend to show any such similarity between the fabric of a house and the generation of a universe? Have you ever seen nature in any such situation as resembles the first arrangement of the elements? Have worlds ever been formed under your eye, and have you had leisure to observe the whole progress of the phenomenon, from the first appearance of order to its final consummation? If you have, then cite your experience and deliver your theory.

PART III

How the most absurd argument, replied Cleanthes, in the hands of a man of ingenuity and invention, may acquire an air of probability! Are you not aware, Philo, that it became necessary for Copernicus and his first disciples to prove the similarity of the terrestrial and celestial matter because several philosophers, blinded by old systems and supported by some sensible appearances, had denied this similarity? But that it is by no means necessary that theists should prove the similarity of the works of *nature* to those of *art* because this similarity is self-evident and undeniable? The same matter, a like form; what more is requisite to show an analogy between their causes, and to ascertain the origin of all things from a divine

purpose and intention? Your objections, I must freely tell you, are no better than the abstruse cavils of those philosophers who denied motion, and ought to be refuted in the same manner—by illustrations, examples, and instances rather than by serious argument and philosophy.

Suppose, therefore, that an articulate voice were heard in the clouds, much louder and more melodious than any which human art could ever reach; suppose that this voice were extended in the same instant over all nations and spoke to each nation in its own language and dialect; suppose that the words delivered not only contain a just sense and meaning, but convey some instruction altogether worthy of a benevolent Being superior to mankind—could you possibly hesitate a moment concerning the cause of this voice, and must you not instantly ascribe it to some design or purpose? Yet I cannot see but all the same objections (if they merit that appellation) which lie against the system of theism may also be produced against this inference.

Might you not say that all conclusions concerning fact were founded on experience; that, when we hear an articulate voice in the dark and thence infer a man, it is only the resemblance of the effects which leads us to conclude that there is a like resemblance in the cause; but that this extraordinary voice, by its loudness, extent, and flexibility to all languages, bears so little analogy to any human voice that we have no reason to suppose any analogy in their causes; and, consequently, that a rational, wise, coherent speech proceeded, you know not whence, from some accidental whistling of the winds, not from any divine reason or intelligence? You see clearly your own objections in these cavils, and I hope too you see clearly that they cannot possibly have more force in the one case than in the other.

But to bring the case still nearer the present one of the universe, I shall make two suppositions which imply not any absurdity or impossibility. Suppose that there is a natural, universal, invariable language, common to every individual of the human race, and that books are natural productions which perpetuate themselves in the same manner with animals and vegetables, by descent and propagation. Several expressions of our passions contain a universal language: all brute animals have a natural speech, which, however limited, is very intelligible to their own species. And as there are infinitely fewer parts and less contrivance in the finest composition of eloquence than in the coarsest organized body, the propagation of an *Iliad* or *Aeneid* is an easier supposition than that of any plant or animal.

Suppose, therefore, that you enter into your library thus peopled by natural volumes containing the most refined reason and most exquisite beauty; could you possibly open one of them and doubt that its original cause bore the strongest analogy to mind and intelligence? When it reasons and discourses; when it expostulates, argues, and enforces its views and topics; when it applies sometimes to the pure intellect, sometimes to the affections; when it collects, disposes, and adorns every consideration suited to the subject; could you persist in asserting that all this, at the bottom, had really no meaning, and that the first formation of this volume in the loins of its original parent proceeded not from thought and design? Your obstinacy, I know, reaches not that degree of firmness; even your sceptical play and wantonness would be abashed at so glaring an absurdity.

But if there be any difference, Philo, between this supposed case and the real one of the universe, it is all to the advantage of the latter. The anatomy of an animal affords many stronger instances of design than the perusal of Livy or Tacitus; and any objection which you start in the former case, by carrying me back to so unusual and extraordinary a scene as the first formation of worlds, the same objection has place on the supposition of our vegetating library. Choose, then, your party, Philo, without ambiguity or evasion; assert either that a rational volume is no proof of a rational cause or admit of a similar cause to all the works of nature.

Let me here observe, too, continued Cleanthes, that this religious argument, instead of being weakened by that scepticism so much affected by you, rather acquires force from it and becomes more firm and undisputed. To exclude all argument or reasoning of every kind is either affectation or madness. The declared profession of every reasonable sceptic is only to reject abstruse, remote, and refined arguments; to adhere to common sense and the plain

instincts of nature; and to assent, wherever any reasons strike him with so full a force that he cannot, without the greatest violence, prevent it. Now the arguments for natural religion are plainly of this kind; and nothing but the most perverse, obstinate metaphysics can reject them. Consider, anatomize the eye, survey its structure and contrivance, and tell me, from your own feeling, if the idea of a contriver does not immediately flow in upon you with a force like that of sensation. The most obvious conclusion, surely, is in favour of design; and it requires time, reflection, and study, to summon up those frivolous though abstruse objections which can support infidelity. Who can behold the male and female of each species, the correspondence of their parts and instincts, their passions and whole course of life before and after generation, but must be sensible that the propagation of the species is intended by nature? Millions and millions of such instances present themselves through every part of the universe, and no language can convey a more intelligible irresistible meaning than the curious adjustment of final causes. To what degree, therefore, of blind dogmatism must one have attained to reject such natural and such convincing arguments?

Some beauties in writing we may meet with which seem contrary to rules, and which gain the affections and animate the imagination in opposition to all the precepts of criticism and to the authority of the established masters of art. And if the argument for theism be, as you pretend, contradictory to the principles of logic, its universal, its irresistible influence proves clearly that there may be arguments of a like irregular nature. Whatever cavils may be urged, an orderly world, as well as a coherent, articulate speech, will still be received as an incontestable proof of design and intention.

It sometimes happens, I own, that the religious arguments have not their due influence on an ignorant savage and barbarian, not because they are obscure and difficult, but because he never asks himself any question with regard to them. Whence arises the curious structure of an animal? From the copulation of its parents. And these whence? From *their* parents? A few removes set the objects at such a distance that to him they are lost in darkness and confusion; nor is he actuated by any curiosity to trace them farther. But this is neither dogmatism nor scepticism, but stupidity: a state of mind very different from your sifting, inquisitive disposition, my ingenious friend. You can trace causes from effects; you can compare the most distant and remote objects; and your greatest errors proceed not from barrenness of thought and invention, but from too luxuriant a fertility which suppresses your natural good sense by a profusion of unnecessary scruples and objections.

Here I could observe, Hermippus, that Philo was a little embarrassed and confounded; but, while he hesitated in delivering an answer, luckily for him, Demea broke in upon the discourse and saved his countenance.

Your instance, Cleanthes, said he, drawn from books and language, being familiar, has, I confess, so much more force on that account; but is there not some danger, too, in this very circumstance, and may it not render us presumptuous, by making us imagine we comprehend the Deity and have some adequate idea of his nature and attributes? When I read a volume, I enter into the mind and intention of the author; I become him, in a manner, for the instant, and have an immediate feeling and conception of those ideas which revolved in his imagination while employed in that composition. But so near an approach we never surely can make to the Deity. His ways are not our ways, his attributes are perfect but incomprehensible. And this volume of nature contains a great and inexplicable riddle, more than any intelligible discourse or reasoning.

The ancient Platonists, you know, were the most religious and devout of all the pagan philosophers, yet many of them, particularly Plotinus, expressly declare that intellect or understanding is not to be ascribed to the Deity, and that our most perfect worship of him consists, not in acts of veneration, reverence, gratitude, or love, but in a certain mysterious self-annihilation or total extinction of all our faculties. These ideas are, perhaps, too far stretched, but still it must be acknowledged that, by representing the Deity as so intelligible and comprehensible, and so similar to a human mind, we are guilty of the grossest and most narrow partiality, and make ourselves the model of the whole universe.

All the *sentiments* of the human mind, gratitude, resentment, love, friendship, approbation, blame, pity, emulation, envy, have a plain reference to the state and situation of man, and are calculated for preserving the existence and promoting the activity of such a being in such circumstances. It seems, therefore, unreasonable to transfer such sentiments to a supreme existence or to suppose him actuated by them; and the phenomena, besides, of the universe will not support us in such a theory. All our *ideas* derived from the senses are confessedly false and illusive, and cannot therefore be supposed to have place in a supreme intelligence. And as the ideas of internal sentiment, added to those of the external senses, composed the whole furniture of human understanding, we may conclude that none of the *materials* of thought are in any respect similar in the human and in the divine intelligence. Now, as to the *manner* of thinking, how can we make any comparison between them or suppose them anywise resembling? Our thought is fluctuating, uncertain, fleeting, successive, and compounded; and were we to remove these circumstances, we absolutely annihilate its essence, and it would in such a case be an abuse of terms to apply to it the name of thought or reason. At least, if it appear more pious and respectful (as it really is) still to retain these terms when we mention the Supreme Being, we ought to acknowledge that their meaning, in that case, is totally incomprehensible, and that the infirmities of our nature do not permit us to reach any ideas which in the least correspond to the ineffable sublimity of the Divine attributes.

PART IV

It seems strange to me, said Cleanthes, that you, Demea, who are so sincere in the cause of religion, should still maintain the mysterious, incomprehensible nature of the Deity, and should insist so strenuously that he has no manner of likeness or resemblance to human creatures. The Deity, I can readily allow, possesses many powers and attributes of which we can have no comprehension; but, if our ideas, so far as they go, be not just and adequate and correspondent to his real nature, I know not what there is in this subject worth insisting on. Is the name, without any meaning, of such mighty importance? Or how do you mystics, who maintain the absolute incomprehensibility of the Deity, differ from sceptics or atheists, who assert that the first cause of all is unknown and unintelligible? Their temerity must be very great if, after rejecting the production by a mind—I mean a mind resembling the human (for I know of no other)—they pretend to assign, with certainty, any other specific intelligible cause; and their conscience must be very scrupulous, indeed, if they refuse to call the universal unknown cause a God or Deity, and to bestow on him as many sublime eulogies and unmeaning epithets as you shall please to require of them.

Who could imagine, replied Demea, that Cleanthes, the calm philosophical Cleanthes, would attempt to refute his antagonists by affixing a nickname to them, and, like the common bigots and inquisitors of the age, have recourse to invective and declamation instead of reasoning? Or does he not perceive that these topics are easily retorted, and that *anthropomorphite* is an appellation as invidious, and implies as dangerous consequences, as the epithet of *mystic* with which he has honoured us? In reality, Cleanthes, consider what it is you assert when you represent the Deity as similar to the human mind and understanding. What is the soul of man? A composition of various faculties, passions, sentiments, ideas—united, indeed, into one self or person, but still distinct from each other. When it reasons, the ideas which are the parts of its discourse arrange themselves in a certain form or order which is not preserved entire for a moment, immediately gives place to another arrangement. New opinions, new passions, new affections, new feelings arise which continually diversify the mental scene and produce in it the greatest variety and most rapid succession imaginable. How is this compatible with that perfect immutability and simplicity which all true theists ascribe to the Deity? By the same act, say they, he sees past, present, and future; his love and hatred, his mercy and justice, are one individual operation; he is entire in every point of space, and complete in every instant of duration. No succession, no change, no acquisition, no diminution. What he is implies not in it any shadow of distinction or diversity. And what he is this moment he ever has been and ever will be, without any new judgment, sentiment, or operation. He stands fixed in one simple, perfect state; nor can you ever say, with any propriety, that this act of his is different from that other, or that this judgment or idea has been lately formed and will give place, by succession, to any different judgment or idea.

I can readily allow, said Cleanthes, that those who maintain the perfect simplicity of the Supreme Being, to the extent in which you have explained it, are complete mystics, and chargeable with all the consequences which I have drawn from their opinion. They are, in a word, atheists, without knowing it. For though it be allowed that the Deity possesses attributes of which we have no comprehension, yet ought we never to ascribe to him any attributes which are absolutely incompatible with that intelligent nature essential to him. A mind whose acts and sentiments and ideas are not distinct and successive, one that is wholly simple and totally immutable, is a mind which has no thought, no reason, no will, no sentiment, no love, no hatred; or, in a word, is no mind at all. It is an abuse of terms to give it that appellation, and we may as well speak of limited extension without figure, or of number without composition.

Pray consider, said Philo, whom you are at present inveighing against. You are honouring with the appellation of *atheist* all the sound, orthodox divines, almost, who have treated of this subject; and you will at last be, yourself, found, according to your reckoning, the only sound theist in the world. But if idolaters be atheists, as, I think, may justly be asserted, and Christian theologians the same, what becomes of the argument, so much celebrated, derived from the universal consent of mankind?

But, because I know you are not much swayed by names and authorities, I shall endeavor to show you, a little more distinctly, the inconveniences of that anthropomorphism which you have embraced, and shall prove that there is no ground to suppose a plan of the world to be formed in the Divine mind, consisting of distinct ideas, differently arranged, in the same manner as an architect forms in his head the plan of a house which he intends to execute.

It is not easy, I own, to see what is gained by this supposition, whether we judge of the matter by *reason* or by *experience.* We are still obliged to mount higher in order to find the cause of this cause which you had assigned as satisfactory and conclusive.

If *reason* (I mean abstract reason derived from inquiries a priori) be not alike mute with regard to all questions concerning cause and effect, this sentence at least it will venture to pronounce: that a mental world or universe of ideas requires a cause as much as does a material world or universe of objects, and, if similar in its arrangement, must require a similar cause. For what is there in this subject which should occasion a different conclusion or inference? In an abstract view, they are entirely alike; and no difficulty attends the one supposition which is not common to both of them.

Again, when we will needs force *experience* to pronounce some sentence, even on these subjects which lie beyond her sphere, neither can she perceive any material difference in this particular between those two kinds of worlds, but finds them to be governed by similar principles, and to depend upon an equal variety of causes in their operations. We have specimens in miniature of both of them. Our own mind resembles the one; a vegetable or animal body the other. Let experience, therefore, judge from these samples. Nothing seems more delicate, with regard to its causes, than thought; and a these causes never operate in two persons after the same manner, so we never find two persons who think exactly alike. Nor indeed does the same person think exactly alike at any two different period of time. A difference of age, of the disposition of his body, of weather, of food, of company, of books, of passions—any of these particulars, or others more minute, are sufficient to alter the curious machinery of thought and communicate to it very different movements and operations. As far as we can judge, vegetables and animal bodies are not more delicate in their motions, nor depend upon a greater variety or more curious adjustment of springs and principles.

How, therefore, shall we satisfy ourselves concerning the cause of that Being whom you suppose the Author of nature, or, according to your system of anthropomorphism, the ideal world into which you trace the material? Have we not the same reason to trace that ideal world into another ideal world or new intelligent principle? But if we stop and go no farther, why go so far? Why not stop at the material world? How can we satisfy ourselves without going on in infinitum? And, after all, what satisfaction is there in that infinite progression? Let us remember the story of the Indian philosopher and his elephant. It was never more applicable than to the present subject. If the material world rests upon a similar ideal world, this ideal world must rest upon some other, and so on without end. It were better, therefore, never to look beyond the present material world. By supposing it to contain the principle of its order within itself, we really assert it to be God: and the sooner we arrive at that Divine Being, so much the better. When you go one step beyond the mundane system, you only excite an inquisitive humour which it is impossible ever to satisfy.

To say that the different ideas which compose the reason of the Supreme Being fall into order of themselves and by their own nature is really to talk without any precise meaning. If it has a meaning, I would fain know why it is not as good sense to say that the parts of the material world fall into order of themselves and by their own nature. Can the one opinion be intelligible, while the other is not so?

We have, indeed, experience of ideas which fall into order of themselves and without any *known* cause. But, I am sure, we have a much larger experience of matter which does the same, as in all instances of generation and vegetation where the accurate analysis of the cause exceeds all human comprehension. We have also experience of particular systems of thought and of matter which have no order; of the first in madness, of the second in corruption. Why, then, should we think that order is more essential to one than the other? And if it requires a cause in both, what do we gain by your system, in tracing the universe of objects into a similar universe of ideas? The first step which we make leads us on for ever. It were, therefore, wise in us to limit all our inquiries to the present world, without looking farther. No satisfaction can ever be attained by these speculations which so far exceed the narrow bounds of human understanding.

It was usual with the Peripatetics, you know, Cleanthes, when the cause of any phenomenon was demanded, to have recourse to their *faculties* or *occult qualities,* and to say, for instance, that bread nourished by its nutritive faculty, and senna purged by its purgative. But it has been discovered that this subterfuge was nothing but the disguise of ignorance, and that these philosophers, though less ingenuous, really said the same thing with the sceptics or the vulgar who fairly confessed that they knew not the cause of these phenomena. In like manner, when it is asked, what cause produced order in the ideas of the Supreme Being, can any other reason be assigned by you, anthropomorphites, than that it is a *rational* faculty, and that such is the nature of the Deity? But why a similar answer will not be equally satisfactory in accounting for the order of the world, without having recourse to any such intelligent creator as you insist on, may be difficult to determine. It is only to say that *such* is the nature of material objects, and that they are all originally possessed of a *faculty* of order and proportion. These are only more learned and elaborate ways of confessing our ignorance; nor has the one hypothesis any real advantage above the other, except in its greater conformity to vulgar prejudices.

You have displayed this argument with great emphasis, replied Cleanthes: You seem not sensible how easy it is to answer it. Even in common life, if I assign a cause for any event, is it any objection, Philo, that I cannot assign the cause of that cause, and answer every new question which may incessantly be started? And what philosophers could possibly submit to so rigid a rule?—philosophers who confess ultimate causes to be totally unknown, and are sensible that the most refined principles into which they trace the phenomena are still to them as inexplicable as these phenomena themselves are to the vulgar. The order and arrangement of nature, the curious adjustment of final causes, the plain use and intention of every part and organ—all these bespeak in the clearest language an intelligent cause or author. The heavens and the earth join in the same testimony: The whole chorus of nature raises one hymn to the praises of its Creator. You alone, or almost alone, disturb this general harmony. You start abstruse doubts, cavils, and objections; you ask me what is the cause of this cause? I know not; I care not; that concerns not me. I have found a Deity; and here I stop my inquiry. Let those go farther who are wiser or more enterprising.

I pretend to be neither, replied Philo; and for that very reason I should never, perhaps, have attempted to go so far, especially when I am sensible that I must at last be contented to sit down with the same answer which, without further trouble, might have satisfied me from the beginning. If I am still to remain in utter ignorance of causes and can absolutely give an explication of nothing, I shall never esteem it any advantage to shove off for a moment a difficulty which you acknowledge must immediately, in its full force, recur upon me. Naturalists indeed very justly explain particular effects by more general causes, though these general causes themselves should remain in the totally inexplicable, but they never surely thought it satisfactory to explain a particular effect by a particular cause which was no more to be accounted for than the effect itself. An ideal system, arranged of itself, without a precedent design, is not a whit more explicable than a material one which attains its order in a like manner; nor is there any more difficulty in the latter supposition than in the former.

PART V

But to show you still more inconveniences, continued Philo, in your anthropomorphism, please to take a new survey of your principles. *Like effects prove like causes.* This is the experimental argument; and this, you say too, is the sole theological argument. Now it is certain that the liker the effects are which are seen and the liker the causes which are inferred, the stronger is the argument. Every departure on either side diminishes the probability and renders the experiment less conclusive. You cannot doubt of the principle; neither ought you to reject its consequences.

All the new discoveries in astronomy which prove the immense grandeur and magnificence of the works of nature are so many additional arguments for a Deity, according to the true system of theism; but, according to your hypothesis of experimental theism, they become so many objections, by removing the effect still farther from all resemblance to the effects of human art and contrivance. . . .

If this argument, I say, had any force in former ages, how much greater must it have at present when the bounds of Nature are so infinitely enlarged and such a magnificent scene is opened to us? It is still more unreasonable to form our idea of so unlimited a cause from our experience of the narrow productions of human design and invention.

The discoveries by microscopes, as they open a new universe in miniature, are still objections, according to you, arguments, according to me. The further we push our researches of this kind, we are still led to infer the universal cause of all to be vastly different from mankind, or from any object of human experience and observation.

And what say you to the discoveries in anatomy, chemistry, botany? . . . These surely are no objections, replied Cleanthes; they only discover new instances of art and contrivance, it is still the image of mind reflected on us from innumerable objects. Add a mind *like the human,* said Philo. I know of no other, replied Cleanthes. And the liker, the better, insisted Philo. To be sure, said Cleanthes.

Now, Cleanthes, said Philo, with an air of alacrity and triumph, mark the consequences. *First,* by this method of reasoning you renounce all claim to infinity in any of the attributes of the Deity. For, as the cause ought only to be proportioned to the effect, and the effect, so far as it falls under our cognizance, is not infinite, what pretensions have we, upon your suppositions, to ascribe that attribute to the Divine Being? You will still insist that, by removing him so much from all similarity to human creatures, we give in to the most arbitrary hypothesis, and at the same time weaken all proofs of his existence.

Secondly, you have no reason, on your theory, for ascribing perfection to the Deity, even in his finite capacity, or for supposing him free from every error, mistake, or incoherence, in his undertakings. There are many inexplicable difficulties in the works of nature which, if we allow a perfect author to be proved a priori, are easily solved, and become only seeming difficulties from the narrow capacity of man, who cannot trace infinite relations. But according to your method of reasoning, these difficulties become all real, and, perhaps, will be insisted on as new instances of likeness to human art and contrivance. At least, you must acknowledge that it is impossible for us to tell, from our limited views, whether this system contains any great faults or

deserves any considerable praise if compared to other possible and even real systems. Could a peasant, if the *Aeneid* were read to him, pronounce that poem to be absolutely faultless, or even assign to it its proper rank among the productions of human wit, he who had never seen any other production?

But were this world ever so perfect a production, it must still remain uncertain whether all the excellences of the work can justly be ascribed to the workman. If we survey a ship, what an exalted idea must we form of the ingenuity of the carpenter who framed so complicated, useful, and beautiful a machine? And what surprise must we feel when we find him a stupid mechanic who imitated others, and copied an art which, through a long succession of ages, after multiplied trials, mistakes, corrections, deliberations, and controversies, had been gradually improving? Many worlds might have been botched and bungled, throughout an eternity, ere this system was struck out; much labour lost, many fruitless trials made, and a slow but continued improvement carried on during infinite ages in the art of world-making. In such subjects, who can determine where the truth, nay, who can conjecture where the probability lies, amidst a great number of hypotheses which may be proposed, and a still greater which may be imagined?

And what shadow of an argument, continued Philo, can you produce from your hypothesis to prove the unity of the Deity? A great number of men join in building a house or ship, in rearing a city, in framing a commonwealth; why may not several deities combine in contriving and framing a world? This is only so much greater similarity to human affairs. By sharing the work among several, we may so much further limit the attributes of each, and get rid of that extensive power and knowledge which must be supposed in one deity, and which, according to you, can only serve to weaken the proof of his existence. And if such foolish, such vicious creatures as man can yet often unite in framing and executing one plan, how much more those deities or demons, whom we may suppose several degrees more perfect!

To multiply causes without necessity is indeed contrary to true philosophy, but this principle applies not to the present case. Were one deity antecedently proved by your theory who were possessed of every attribute requisite to the production of the universe, it would be needless, I own (though not absurd) to suppose any other deity existent. But while it is still a question whether all these attributes are united in one subject or dispersed among several independent beings, by what phenomena in nature can we pretend to decide the controversy? Where we see a body raised in a scale, we are sure that there is in the opposite scale, however concealed from sight, some counterpoising weight equal to it; but it is still allowed to doubt whether that weight be an aggregate of several distinct bodies or one uniform united mass. And if the weight requisite very much exceeds anything which we have ever seen conjoined in any single body, the former supposition becomes still more probable and natural. An intelligent being of such vast power and capacity as is necessary to produce the universe, or, to speak in the language of ancient philosophy, so prodigious an animal exceeds all analogy and even comprehension.

But further, Cleanthes: Men are mortal, and renew their species by generation; and this is common to all living creatures. The two great sexes of male and female, says Milton, animate the world. Why must this circumstance, so universal, so essential, be excluded from those numerous and limited deities? Behold, then, the theogeny of ancient times brought back upon us.

And why not become a perfect anthropomorphite? Why not assert the deity or deities to be corporeal, and to have eyes, a nose, mouth, ears, etc.? Epicurus maintained that no man had ever seen reason but in a human figure; therefore, the gods must have a human figure. And this argument, which is deservedly so much ridiculed by Cicero, becomes, according to you, solid and philosophical.

In a word, Cleanthes, a man who follows your hypothesis is able, perhaps, to assert or conjecture that the universe sometime arose from something like design; but beyond that position he cannot ascertain one single circumstance, and is left afterwards to fix every point of his theology by the utmost license of fancy and hypothesis. This world, for aught he knows, is very faulty and imperfect, compared to a superior standard, and was only the first rude essay of some infant deity who afterwards abandoned it, ashamed of his lame performance; it is the work only of some

dependent, inferior deity, and is the object of derision to his superiors; it is the production of old age and dotage in some superannuated deity, and ever since his death has run on at adventures, from the first impulse and active force which it received from him. You justly give signs of horror, Demea, at these strange suppositions; but these, and a thousand more of the same kind, are Cleanthes' suppositions, not mine. From the moment the attributes of the Deity are supposed finite, all these have place. And I cannot, for my part, think that so wild and unsettled a system of theology is, in any respect, preferable to none at all.

These suppositions I absolutely disown, cried Cleanthes: they strike me, however, with no horror, especially when proposed in that rambling way in which they drop from you. On the contrary, they give me pleasure when I see that, by the utmost indulgence of your imagination, you never get rid of the hypothesis of design in the universe, but are obliged at every turn to have recourse to it. To this concession I adhere steadily; and this I regard as a sufficient foundation for religion.

PART VI

It must be a slight fabric, indeed, said Demea, which can be erected on so tottering a foundation. While we are uncertain whether there is one deity or many, whether the deity or deities, to whom we owe our existence, be perfect or imperfect, subordinate or supreme, dead or alive, what trust or confidence can we repose in them? What devotion or worship address to them? What veneration or obedience pay them? To all the purposes of life the theory of religion becomes altogether useless; and even with regard to speculative consequences its uncertainty, according to you, must render it totally precarious and unsatisfactory.

To render it still more unsatisfactory, said Philo, there occurs to me another hypothesis which must acquire an air of probability from the method of reasoning so much insisted on by Cleanthes. That like effects arise from like causes—this principle he supposes the foundation of all religion. But there is another principle of the same kind, no less certain and derived from the same source of experience, that, where several known circumstances are observed to be similar, the unknown will also be found similar. Thus, if we see the limbs of a human body, we conclude that it is also attended with a human head, though hid from us. Thus, if we see, through a chink in a wall, a small part of the sun, we conclude that were the wall removed we should see the whole body. In short, this method of reasoning is so obvious and familiar that no scruple can ever be made with regard to its solidity.

Now, if we survey the universe, so far as it falls under our knowledge, it bears a great resemblance to an animal or organized body, and seems actuated with a like principle of life and motion. A continual circulation of matter in it produces no disorder; a continual waste in every part is incessantly repaired; the closest sympathy is perceived throughout the entire system; and each part or member, in performing its proper offices, operates both to its own preservation and to that of the whole. The world, therefore, I infer, is an animal; and the Deity is the *soul* of the world, actuating it, and actuated by it.

You have too much learning, Cleanthes, to be at all surprised at this opinion which, you know, was maintained by almost all the theists of antiquity, and chiefly prevails in their discourses and reasonings. For though, sometimes, the ancient philosophers reason from final causes, as if they thought the world the workmanship of God, yet it appears rather their favourite notion to consider it as his body whose organization renders it subservient to him. And it must be confessed that, as the universe resembles more a human body than it does the works of human art and contrivance, if our limited analogy could ever, with any propriety, be extended to the whole of nature, the inference seems juster in favour of the ancient than the modern theory.

There are many other advantages, too, in the former theory which recommended it to the ancient theologians. Nothing more repugnant to all their notions because nothing more repugnant to common experience than mind without body, a mere spiritual substance which fell not under their senses nor comprehension, and of which they had not observed one single instance throughout all nature. Mind and body they knew because they felt both; an order, arrangement, organization, or internal machinery, in both they likewise knew, after the same manner; and it could not but seem reasonable to transfer this experience to the universe, and to suppose the divine mind and body to be also coeval and to have, both of them, order and arrangement naturally inherent in them and inseparable from them.

Here, therefore, is a new species of *anthropomorphism,* Cleanthes, on which you may deliberate, and a theory which seems not liable to any considerable difficulties. You are too much superior, surely, to *systematical prejudices* to find any more difficulty in supposing an animal body to be, originally, of itself or from unknown causes, possessed of order and organization, than in supposing a similar order to belong to mind. But the *vulgar prejudice* that body and mind ought always to accompany each other ought not, one should think, to be entirely neglected; since it is founded on *vulgar experience,* the only guide which you profess to follow in all these theological inquiries. And if you assert that our limited experience is an unequal standard by which to judge of the unlimited extent of nature, you entirely abandon your own hypothesis, and must thenceforward adopt our mysticism, as you call it, and admit of the absolute incomprehensibility of the Divine Nature.

This theory, I own, replied Cleanthes, has never before occurred to me, though a pretty natural one; and I cannot readily, upon so short an examination and reflection, deliver any opinion with regard to it. You are very scrupulous, indeed, said Philo. Were I to examine any system of yours, I should not have acted with half that caution and reserve in stating objections and difficulties to it. However, if anything occur to you, you will oblige us by proposing it.

Why then, replied Cleanthes, it seems to me that, though the world does, in many circumstances, resemble an animal body, yet is the analogy also defective in many circumstances the most material: no organs of sense; no seat of thought or reason; no one precise origin of motion and action. In short, it seems to bear a stronger resemblance to a vegetable than to an animal, and your inference would be so far inconclusive in favour of the soul of the world.

But, in the next place, your theory seems to imply the eternity of the world; and that is a principle which, I think, can be refuted by the strongest reasons and probabilities. I shall suggest an argument to this purpose which, I believe, has not been insisted on by any writer. Those who reason from the late origin of arts and sciences, though their inference wants not force, may perhaps be refuted by considerations derived from the nature of human society, which is in continual revolution between ignorance and knowledge, liberty and slavery, riches and poverty; so that it is impossible for us, from our limited experience, to foretell with assurance what events may or may not be expected. Ancient learning and history seem to have been in great danger of entirely perishing after the inundation of the barbarous nations; and had these convulsions continued a little longer or been a little more violent, we should not probably have now known what passed in the world a few centuries before us. Nay, were it not for the superstition of the popes, who preserved a little jargon of Latin in order to support the appearance of an ancient and universal church, that tongue must have been utterly lost; in which case the Western world, being totally barbarous, would not have been in a fit disposition for receiving the Greek language and learning, which was conveyed to them after the sacking of Constantinople. When learning and books had been extinguished, even the mechanical arts would have fallen considerably to decay; and it is easily imagined that fable or tradition might ascribe to them a much later origin than the true one. This vulgar argument, therefore, against the eternity of the world seems a little precarious.

But here appears to be the foundation of a better argument. Lucullus was the first that brought cherry-trees from Asia to Europe, though that tree thrives so well in many European climates that it grows in the woods without any culture. Is it possible that, throughout a whole eternity, no European had ever passed into Asia and thought of transplanting so delicious a fruit into his own country? Or if the tree was once transplanted and propagated, how could it ever afterwards perish? Empires may rise and fall, liberty and slavery succeed alternately, ignorance and knowledge give place to each other; but the cherry-tree will still remain in the woods of Greece, Spain, and Italy, and will never be affected by the revolutions of human society.

It is not two thousand years since vines were transplanted into France, though there is no climate in the world more favourable to them. It is not three centuries since horses, cows, sheep, swine, dogs, corn, were known in America. Is it possible that during the revolutions of a whole eternity there never arose a Columbus who might open the communication between Europe and that continent? We may as well imagine that all men would wear stockings for ten thousand years, and never have the sense to think of garters to tie them. All these seem convincing proofs of the youth or rather infancy of the world, as being founded on the operation of principles more constant and steady than those by which human society is governed and directed. Nothing less than a total convulsion of the elements will ever destroy all the European animals and vegetables which are now to be found in the Western world.

And what argument have you against such convulsions? replied Philo. Strong and almost incontestable proofs may be traced over the whole earth that every part of this globe has continued for many ages entirely covered with water. And though order were supposed inseparable from matter, and inherent in it, yet may matter be susceptible of many and great revolutions, through the endless periods of eternal duration. The incessant changes to which every part of it is subject seem to intimate some such general transformations; though, at the same time, it is observable that all the changes and corruptions of which we have ever had experience are but passages from one state of order to another; nor can matter ever rest in total deformity and confusion. What we see in the parts, we may infer in the whole; at least, that is the method of reasoning on which you rest your whole theory. And were I obliged to defend any particular system of this nature, which I never willingly should do, I esteem none more plausible than that which ascribes an eternal inherent principle of order to the world, though attended with great and continual revolutions and alterations. This at once solves all difficulties; and if the solution, by being so general, is not entirely complete and satisfactory, it is at least a theory that we must sooner or later have recourse to, whatever system we embrace. How could things have been as they are, were there not an original inherent principle of order somewhere, in thought or in matter? And it is very indifferent to which of these we give the preference. Chance has no place, on any hypothesis, sceptical or religious. Everything is surely governed by steady, inviolable laws. And were the inmost essence of things laid open to us, we should then discover a scene of which, at present, we can have no idea. Instead of admiring the order of natural beings, we should clearly see that it was absolutely impossible for them, in the smallest article, ever to admit of any other disposition.

Were anyone inclined to revive the ancient pagan theology which maintained, as we learned from Hesiod, that this globe was governed by 30,000 deities, who arose from the unknown powers of nature, you would naturally object, Cleanthes, that nothing is gained by this hypothesis; and that it is as easy to suppose all men animals, beings more numerous but less perfect, to have sprung immediately from a like origin. Push the same inference a step further, and you will find a numerous society of deities as explicable as one universal deity who possesses within himself the powers and perfections of the whole society. All these systems, then, of Scepticism, Polytheism, and Theism, you must allow, on your principles, to be on a like footing, and that no one of them has any advantage over the others. You may thence learn the fallacy of your principles.

PART VII

But here, continued Philo, in examining the ancient system on the soul of the world there strikes me, all of a sudden, a new idea which, if just, must go near to subvert all your reasoning, and destroy even your first inferences on which you repose such confidence. If the universe bears a greater likeness to animal bodies and to vegetables than to the works of human art, it is more probable that its cause resembles the cause of the former than that of the latter, and its origin ought rather to be ascribed to generation or vegetation than to reason or design. Your conclusion, even according to your own principles, is therefore lame and defective.

Pray open up this argument a little further, said Demea, for I do not rightly apprehend it in that concise manner in which you have expressed it.

Our friend Cleanthes, replied Philo, as you have heard, asserts that, since no question of fact can be proved otherwise than by experience, the existence of a Deity admits not of proof from any other medium. The world, says he, resembles the works of human contrivance; therefore its cause must also resemble that of the other. Here we may remark that the operation of one very small part of nature, to wit, man, upon another very small part, to wit, that inanimate matter lying within his reach, is the rule by which Cleanthes judges of the origin of the whole; and he measures objects, so widely disproportioned, by the same individual standard. But to waive all objections drawn from this topic, I affirm that there are other parts of the universe (besides the machines of human invention) which bear still a greater resemblance to the fabric of the world, and which, therefore, afford a better conjecture concerning the universal origin of this system. These parts are animals and vegetables. The world plainly resembles more an animal or a vegetable than it does a watch or a knitting-loom. Its cause, therefore, it is more probable, resembles the cause of the former. The cause of the former is generation or vegetation. The cause, therefore, of the world we may infer to be something similar or analogous to generation or vegetation.

But how is it conceivable, said Demea, that the world can arise from anything similar to vegetation or generation?

Very easily, replied Philo. In like manner as a tree sheds its seed into the neighboring fields and produces other trees, so the great vegetable, the world, or this planetary system, produces within itself certain seeds which, being scattered into the surrounding chaos, vegetate into new worlds. A comet, for instance, is the seed of a world; and after it has been fully ripened, by passing from sun to sun, and star to star, it is, at last, tossed into the unformed elements which everywhere surround this universe, and immediately sprouts up into a new system.

Or if, for the sake of variety (for I see no other advantage), we should suppose this world to be an animal: a comet is the egg of this animal; and in like manner as an ostrich lays its egg in the sand, which, without any further care, hatches the egg and produces a new animal, so . . . I understand you, says Demea. But what wild, arbitrary suppositions are these! What *data* have you for such extraordinary conclusions? And is the slight, imaginary resemblance of the world to a vegetable or an animal sufficient to establish the same inference with regard to both? Objects which are in general so widely different, ought they to be a standard for each other?

Right, cries Philo: This is the topic on which I have all along insisted. I have still asserted that we have no *data* to establish any system of cosmogony. Our experience, so imperfect in itself and so limited both in extent and duration, can afford us no probable conjecture concerning the whole of things. But if we must needs fix on some hypothesis, by what rule, pray, ought we to determine our choice? Is there any other rule than the greater similarity of the objects compared? And does not a plant or an animal, which springs from vegetation or generation, bear a stronger resemblance to the world than does any artificial machine, which arises from reason and design?

But what is this vegetation and generation of which you talk? said Demea. Can you explain their operations, and anatomize that fine internal structure on which they depend?

As much, at least, replied Philo, as Cleanthes can explain the operations of reason, or anatomize that internal structure on which it depends. But without any such elaborate disquisitions, when I see an animal, I infer that it sprang from generation; and that with as great certainty as you conclude a house to have been reared by design. These words *generation, reason* mark only certain powers and energies in nature whose effects are known, but whose essence is incomprehensible; and one of these principles, more than the other, has no privilege for being made a standard to the whole of nature.

In reality, Demea, it may reasonably be expected that the larger the views are which we take of things, the better will they conduct us in our conclusions concerning such extraordinary and such magnificent subjects. In this little corner of the world alone, there are four principles, *reason, instinct, generation, vegetation,* which are similar to each other, and are the causes of similar effects. What a number of other principles may we naturally suppose in the immense extent and variety of the universe could we travel from planet to planet, and from system to system, in order to examine each part of this mighty fabric? Any one of these four principles above mentioned (and a

hundred others which lie open to our conjecture) may afford us a theory by which to judge of the origin of the world; and it is a palpable and egregious partiality to confine our view entirely to that principle by which our own minds operate. Were this principle more intelligible on that account, such a partiality might be somewhat excusable; but reason, in its internal fabric and structure, is really as little known to us as instinct or vegetation; and, perhaps, even that vague, undeterminate word *nature,* to which the vulgar refer everything is not at the bottom more inexplicable. The effects of these principles are all known to us from experience; but the principles themselves and their manner of operation are totally unknown; nor is it less intelligible or less conformable to experience to say that the world arose by vegetation, from a seed shed by another world, than to say that it arose from a divine reason or contrivance, according to the sense in which Cleanthes understands it.

But methinks, said Demea, if the world had a vegetative quality and could sow the seeds of new worlds into the infinite chaos, this power would be still an additional argument for design in its author. For whence could arise so wonderful a faculty but from design? Or how can order spring from anything which perceives not that order which it bestows?

You need only look around you, replied Philo, to satisfy yourself with regard to this question. A tree bestows order and organization on that tree which springs from it, without knowing the order an animal in the same manner on its offspring; a bird on its nest; and instances of this kind are even more frequent in the world than those of order which arise from reason and contrivance. To say that all this order in animals and vegetables proceeds ultimately from design is begging the question; nor can that great point be ascertained otherwise than by proving, a priori, both that order is from its nature, inseparably attached to thought, and that it can never of itself or from original unknown principles belong to matter.

But further, Demea, this objection which you urge can never be made use of by Cleanthes, without renouncing a defense which he has already made against one of my objections. When I inquired concerning the cause of that supreme reason and intelligence into which he resolves everything he told me that the impossibility of satisfying such inquiries could never be admitted as an objection in any species of philosophy. *We must stop somewhere,* says he; *nor is it ever within the reach of human capacity to explain ultimate causes or show the last connections of any objects. It is sufficient if any steps, as far as we go, are supported by experience and observation.* Now that vegetation and generation, as well as reason, are experienced to be principles of order in nature is undeniable. If I rest my system of cosmogony on the former, preferably to the latter, it is at my choice. The matter seems entirely arbitrary. And when Cleanthes asks me what is the cause of my great vegetative or generative faculty, I am equally entitled to ask him the cause of his great reasoning principle. These questions we have agreed to forbear on both sides; and it is chiefly his interest on the present occasion to stick to this agreement. Judging by our limited and imperfect experience, generation has some privileges above reason; for we see every day the latter arise from the former, never the former from the latter.

Compare, I beseech you, the consequences on both sides. The world, say I, resembles an animal; therefore it is an animal, therefore it arose from generation. The steps, I confess, are wide, yet there is some small appearance of analogy in each step. The world, says Cleanthes, resembles a machine; therefore it is a machine, therefore it arose from design. The steps are here equally wide, and the analogy less striking. And if he pretends to carry on *my* hypothesis a step further, and to infer design or reason from the great principle of generation on which I insist, I may, with better authority, use the same freedom to push further *his* hypothesis, and infer a divine generation or theogony from his principle of reason. I have at least some faint shadow of experience, which is the utmost that can ever be attained in the present subject. Reason, in innumerable instances, is observed to arise from the principle of generation, and never to arise from any other principle.

Hesiod and all the ancient mythologists were so struck with this analogy that they universally explained the origin of nature from an animal birth, and copulation. Plato, too, so far as he is intelligible, seems to have adopted some such notion in his *Timaeus.*

The Brahmins assert that the world arose from an infinite spider, who spun this whole complicated mass from his bowels, and annihilates afterwards the whole or any part of it, by absorbing it again and resolving it into his own essence. Here is a species of cosmogony which appears to us ridiculous because a spider is a little contemptible animal whose operations we are never likely to take for a model of the whole universe. But still here is a new species of analogy, even in our globe. And were there a planet wholly inhabited by spiders (which is very possible), this inference would there appear as natural and irrefragable as that which in our planet ascribes the origin of all things to design and intelligence, as explained by Cleanthes. Why an orderly system may not be spun from the belly as well as from the brain, it will be difficult for him to give a satisfactory reason.

I must confess, Philo, replied Cleanthes, that, of all men living, the task which you have undertaken, of raising doubts and objections, suits you best and seems, in a manner, natural and unavoidable to you. So great is your fertility of invention than I am not ashamed to acknowledge myself unable, on a sudden, to solve regularly such out-of-the-way difficulties as you incessantly start upon me, though I clearly see, in general, their fallacy and error. And I question not, but you are yourself, at present, in the same case, and have not the solution so ready as the objection, while you must be sensible that common sense and reason are entirely against you, and that such whimsies as you have delivered may puzzle but never can convince us.

PART VIII

What you ascribe to the fertility of my invention, replied Philo, is entirely owing to the nature of the subject. In subjects adapted to the narrow compass of human reason there is commonly but one determination which carries probability or conviction with it; and to a man of sound judgment all other suppositions but that one appear entirely absurd and chimerical. But in such questions as the present, a hundred contradictory views may preserve a kind of imperfect analogy, and invention has here full scope to exert itself. Without any great effort of thought, I believe that I could, in an instant, propose other systems of cosmogony which would have some faint appearance of truth, though it is a thousand, a million to one if either yours or any one of mine be the true system.

For instance, what if I should revive the old Epicurean hypothesis? This is commonly, and I believe justly, esteemed the most absurd system that has yet been proposed; yet I know not whether, with a few alterations, it might not be brought to bear a faint appearance of probability. Instead of supposing matter infinite, as Epicurus did, let us suppose it finite. A finite number of particles is only susceptible of finite transpositions; and it must happen, in an eternal duration, that every possible order or position must be tried an infinite number of times. This world, therefore, with all its events, even the most minute, has before been produced and destroyed, and will again be produced and destroyed, without any bounds and limitations. No one who has a conception of the powers of infinite, in comparison of finite, will ever scruple this determination.

But this supposes, said Demea, that matter can acquire motion without any voluntary agent or first mover.

And where is the difficulty, replied Philo, of that supposition? Every event, before experience, is equally difficult and incomprehensible; and every event, after experience, is equally easy and intelligible. Motion, in many instances, from gravity, from elasticity, from electricity, begins in matter, without any known voluntary agent; and to suppose always, in these cases, an unknown voluntary agent is mere hypothesis and hypothesis attended with no advantages. The beginning of motion in matter itself is as conceivable a priori as its communication from mind and intelligence.

Besides, why may not motion have been propagated by impulse through all eternity, and the same stock of it, or nearly the same, be still upheld in the universe? As much is lost by the composition of motion, as much is gained by its resolution. And whatever the causes are, the fact is certain that matter is and always has been in continual agitation, as far as human experience or tradition reaches. There is not probably, at present, in the whole universe, one particle of matter at absolute rest.

And this very consideration, too, continued Philo, which we have stumbled on in the course of the argument, suggests a new hypothesis of cosmogony that is not absolutely absurd and improbable. Is there a system, an order, an economy of things, by which matter can preserve that perpetual agitation which seems essential to it, and yet maintain a constancy in the forms which it produces? There certainly is such an economy, for this is actually the case with the present world. The continual motion of matter, therefore, in less than infinite transpositions, must produce this economy or order, and by its very nature, that order, when once established, supports itself for many ages if not to eternity. But wherever matter is so poised, arranged, and adjusted, as to continue in perpetual motion, and yet preserve a constancy in the forms, its situation must, of necessity, have all the same appearance of art and contrivance which we observe at present. All the parts of each form must have a relation to each other and to the whole; and the whole itself must have a relation to the other parts of the universe, to the element in which the form subsists, to the materials with which it repairs its waste and decay, and to every other form which is hostile or friendly. A defect in any of these particulars destroys the form, and the matter of which it is composed is again set loose, and is thrown into irregular motions and fermentations till it unite itself to some other regular form. If no such form be prepared to receive it, and if there be a great quantity of this corrupted matter in the universe, the universe itself is entirely disordered, whether it be the feeble embryo of a world in its first beginnings that is thus destroyed or the rotten carcase of one languishing in old age and infirmity. In either case, a chaos ensues till finite though innumerable revolutions produce, at last, some forms whose parts and organs are so adjusted as to support the forms amidst a continued succession of matter.

Suppose (for we shall endeavour to vary the expression) that matter were thrown into any position by a blind, unguided force; it is evident that this first position must, in all probability, be the most confused and most disorderly imaginable, without any resemblance to those works of human contrivance which, along with a symmetry of parts, discover an adjustment of means to ends and a tendency to self-preservation. If the actuating force cease after this operation, matter must remain for ever in disorder and continue an immense chaos, without any proportion or activity. But suppose that the actuating force, whatever it be, still continues in matter, this first position will immediately give place to a second which will likewise, in all probability, be as disorderly as the first, and so on through many successions of changes and revolutions. No particular order or position ever continues a moment unaltered. The original force, still remaining in activity, gives a perpetual restlessness to matter. Every possible situation is produced and instantly destroyed. If a glimpse or dawn of order appears for a moment, it is instantly hurried away and confounded by that never-ceasing force which actuates every part of matter.

Thus the universe goes on for many ages in a continued succession of chaos and disorder. But is it not possible that it may settle at last, so as not to lose its motion and active force (for that we have supposed inherent in it), yet so as to preserve an uniformity of appearance, amidst the continual motion and fluctuation of its parts? This we find to be the case with the universe at present. Every individual is perpetually changing, and every part of every individual; and yet the whole remains, in appearance, the same. May we not hope for such a position or rather be assured of it from the eternal revolutions of unguided matter; and may not this account for all the appearing wisdom and contrivance which is in the universe? Let us contemplate the subject a little, and we shall find that this adjustment if attained by matter of a seeming stability in the forms, with a real and perpetual revolution or motion of parts, affords a plausible, if not a true, solution of the difficulty.

It is in vain, therefore, to insist upon the uses of the parts in animals or vegetables, and their curious adjustment to each other. I would fain know how an animal could subsist unless its parts were so adjusted? Do we not find that it immediately perishes whenever this adjustment ceases, and that its matter, corrupting, tries some new form? It happens indeed that the parts of the world are so well adjusted that some regular form immediately lays claim to this corrupted matter; and if it were not so, could the world subsist? Must it not dissolve, as well as the ani-

mal, and pass through new positions and situations till in great but finite succession it fall, at last, into the present or some such order?

It is well, replied Cleanthes, you told us that this hypothesis was suggested on a sudden, in the course of the argument. Had you had leisure to examine it, you would soon have perceived the insuperable objections to which it is exposed. No form, you say, can subsist unless it possess those powers and organs requisite for its subsistence; some new order or economy must be tried, and so on, without intermission, till at last some order which can support and maintain itself is fallen upon. But according to this hypothesis, whence arise the many conveniences and advantages which men and all animals possess? Two eyes, two ears are not absolutely necessary for the subsistence of the species. The human race might have been propagated and preserved without horses, dogs, cows, sheep, and those innumerable fruits and products which serve to our satisfaction and enjoyment. If no camels had been created for the use of man in the sandy deserts of Africa and Arabia, would the world have been dissolved? If no loadstone had been framed to give that wonderful and useful direction to the needle, would human society and the human kind have been immediately extinguished? Though the maxims of nature be in general very frugal, yet instances of this kind are far from being rare; and any one of them is a sufficient proof of design—and of a benevolent design—which gave rise to the order and arrangement of the universe.

At least, you may safely infer, said Philo, that the foregoing hypothesis is so far incomplete and imperfect, which I shall not scruple to allow. But can we ever reasonably expect greater success in any attempts of this nature? Or can we ever hope to erect a system of cosmogony that will be liable to no exceptions, and will contain no circumstance repugnant to our limited and imperfect experience of the analogy of nature? Your theory itself cannot surely pretend to any such advantage, even though you have run into *anthropomorphism,* the better to preserve a conformity to common experience. Let us once more put it to trial. In all instances which we have ever seen, ideas are copied from real objects, and are ectypal, not archetypal, to express myself in learned terms. You reverse this order and give thought the precedence. In all instances which we have ever seen, thought has no influence upon matter except where that matter is so conjoined with it as to have an equal reciprocal influence upon it. No animal can move immediately anything but the members of its own body; and, indeed, the equality of action and reaction seems to be an universal law of nature; but your theory implies a contradiction to this experience. These instances, with many more which it were easy to collect (particularly the supposition of a mind or system of thought that is eternal or, in other words, an animal ingenerable and immortal)—these instances, I say, may teach all of us sobriety in condemning each other, and let us see that as no system of this kind ought ever to be received from a slight analogy, so neither ought any to be rejected on account of a small incongruity. For that is an inconvenience from which we can justly pronounce no one to be exempted.

All religious systems, it is confessed, are subject to great and insuperable difficulties. Each disputant triumphs in his turn, while he carries on an offensive war, and exposes the absurdities, barbarities, and pernicious tenets of his antagonist. But all of them, on the whole, prepare a complete triumph for the *sceptic,* who tells them that no system ought ever to be embraced with regard to such subjects: for this plain reason that no absurdity ought ever to be assented to with regard to any subject. A total suspense of judgment is here our only reasonable resource. And if every attack, as is commonly observed, and no defence among theologians is successful, how complete must be *his* victory who remains always, with all mankind, on the offensive, and has himself no fixed station or abiding city which he is ever, on any occasion, obliged to defend?

PART IX

But if so many difficulties attend the argument a posteriori, said Demea, had we not better adhere to that simple and sublime argument a priori which, by offering to us infallible demonstration, cuts off at once all doubt and difficulty? By this argument, too, we may prove the *infinity* of the Divine attributes, which, I am afraid, can never be ascertained with certainty from any other topic. For how can an effect which either is finite or, for aught we know, may be so—how can such an effect, I say, prove an infinite cause? The unity, too, of the Divine Nature it is very difficult, if not absolutely impossible, to deduce merely from contemplating the works of nature; nor will the uniformity alone of the plan, even were it allowed, give us any assurance of that attribute. Whereas the argument a priori. . . .

You seem to reason, Demea, interposed Cleanthes, as if those advantages and conveniences in the abstract argument were full proofs of its solidity. But it is first proper, in my opinion, to determine what argument of this nature you choose to insist on; and we shall afterwards, from itself, better than from its *useful* consequences, endeavour to determine what value we ought to put upon it.

The argument, replied Demea, which I would insist on is the common one. Whatever exists must have a cause or reason of its existence, it being absolutely impossible for anything to produce itself or be the cause of its own existence. In mounting up, therefore, from effects to causes, we must either go on in tracing an infinite succession, without any ultimate cause at all, or must at last have recourse to some ultimate cause that is *necessarily* existent. Now that the first supposition is absurd may be thus proved. In the infinite chain or succession of causes and effects, each single effect is determined to exist by the power and efficacy of that cause which immediately preceded; but the whole eternal chain or succession, taken together, is not determined or caused by anything, and yet it is evident that it requires a cause or reason, as much as any particular object which begins to exist in time. The question is still reasonable why this particular succession of causes existed from eternity, and not any other succession or no succession at all. If there be no necessarily existent being, any supposition which can be formed is equally possible; nor is there any more absurdity in *nothing's* having existed from eternity than there is in that succession of causes which constitutes the universe. What was it, then, which determined *something* to exist rather than *nothing,* and bestowed being on a particular possibility, exclusive of the rest? *External causes,* there are supposed to be none.

Chance is a word without a meaning. Was it *nothing?* But that can never produce anything. We must, therefore, have recourse to a necessarily existent Being who carries the *reason* of his existence in himself, and who cannot be supposed not to exist, without an express contradiction. There is, consequently, such a Being—that is, there is a Deity.

I shall not leave it to Philo, said Cleanthes, though I know that the starting objections is his chief delight, to point out the weakness of this metaphysical reasoning. It seems to me so obviously ill-grounded, and at the same time of so little consequence to the cause of true piety and religion, that I shall myself venture to show the fallacy of it.

I shall begin with observing that there is an evident absurdity in pretending to demonstrate a matter of fact, or to prove it by arguments a priori. Nothing is demonstrable unless the contrary implies a contradiction. Nothing that is distinctly conceivable implies a contradiction. Whatever we conceive as existent, we can also conceive as nonexistent. There is no being, therefore, whose nonexistence implies a contradiction. Consequently there is no being whose existence is demonstrable. I propose this argument as entirely decisive, and am willing to rest the whole controversy upon it.

It is pretended that the Deity is a necessarily existent being; and this necessity of his existence is attempted to be explained by asserting that, if we knew his whole essence or nature, we should perceive it to be as impossible for him not to exist, as for twice two not to be four. But it is evident that this can never happen, while our faculties remain the same as at present. It will still be possible for us, at any time, to conceive the nonexistence of what we formerly conceived to exist; nor can the mind ever lie under a necessity of supposing any object to remain always in being; in the same manner as we lie under a necessity of always conceiving twice two to be four. The words, therefore, *necessary existence* have no meaning or, which is the same thing, none that is consistent.

But further, why may not the material universe be the necessarily existent Being, according to this pretended explication of necessity? We dare not affirm that we know all the qualities of matter; and, for aught we can determine, it may contain some quali-

ties which, were they known, would make its nonexistence appear as great a contradiction as that twice two is five. I find only one argument employed to prove that the material world is not the necessarily existent Being; and this argument is derived from the contingency both of the matter and the form of the world. "Any particle of matter," it is said, "may be *conceived* to be annihilated, and any form may be *conceived* to be altered. Such an annihilation or alteration, therefore, is not impossible." But it seems a great partiality not to perceive that the same argument extends equally to the Deity, so far as we have any conception of him, and that the mind can at least imagine him to be nonexistent or his attributes to be altered. It must be some unknown, inconceivable qualities which can make his non-existence appear impossible or his attributes unalterable; and no reason can be assigned why these qualities may not belong to matter. As they are altogether unknown and inconceivable, they can never be proved incompatible with it.

Add to this that in tracing an eternal succession of objects it seems absurd to inquire for a general cause or first author. How can anything that exists from eternity have a cause, since that relation implies a priority in time and a beginning of existence?

In such a chain, too, or succession of objects, each part is caused by that which preceded it, and causes that which succeeds it. Where then is the difficulty? But the *whole,* you say, wants a cause. I answer that the uniting of these parts into a whole, like the uniting of several distinct countries into one kingdom, or several distinct members into one body is performed merely by an arbitrary act of the mind, and has no influence on the nature of things. Did I show you the particular causes of each individual in a collection of twenty particles of matter, I should think it very unreasonable should you afterwards ask me what was the cause of the whole twenty. This is sufficiently explained in explaining the cause of the parts.

Though the reasonings which you have urged, Cleanthes, may well excuse me, said Philo, from starting any further difficulties, yet I cannot forbear insisting still upon another topic. It is observed by arithmeticians that the products of 9 compose always either 9 or some lesser product of 9 if you add together all the characters of which any of the former products is composed. Thus, of 18, 27, 36, which are products of 9, you make 9 by adding 1 to 8, 2 to 7, 3 to 6. Thus 369 is a product also of 9; and if you add 3, 6, and 9, you make 18, a lesser product of 9. To a superficial observer so wonderful a regularity may be admired as the effect either of chance or design; but a skillful algebraist immediately concludes it to be the work of necessity, and demonstrates that it must for ever result from the nature of these numbers. Is it not probable, I ask, that the whole economy of the universe is conducted by a like necessity, though no human algebra can furnish a key which solves the difficulty? And instead of admiring the order of natural beings, may it not happen that, could we penetrate into the intimate nature of bodies, we should clearly see why it was absolutely impossible they could ever admit of any other disposition? So dangerous is it to introduce this idea of necessity into the present question! and so naturally does it afford an inference directly opposite to the religious hypothesis!

But dropping all these abstractions, continued Philo, and confining ourselves to more familiar topics, I shall venture to add an observation that the argument a priori has seldom been found very convincing, except to people of a metaphysical head who have accustomed themselves to abstract reasoning, and who, finding from mathematics that the understanding frequently leads to truth through obscurity, and contrary to first appearances, have transferred the same habit of thinking to subjects where it ought not to have place. Other people, even of good sense and the best inclined to religion, feel always some deficiency in such arguments, though they are not perhaps able to explain distinctly where it lies—a certain proof that men ever did and ever will derive their religion from other sources than from this species of reasoning.

PART X

It is my opinion, I own, replied Demea, that each man feels, in a manner, the truth of religion within his own breast, and, from a consciousness of his imbecility and misery rather than from any reasoning, is led to seek protection from that Being on whom he and all nature is dependent. So anxious or so tedious are even the best scenes of life that futurity is still the object of all our hopes and fears. We incessantly look forward and endeavour, by prayers, adoration, and sacrifice, to appease those unknown powers whom we find, by experience, so able to afflict and oppress us. Wretched creatures that we are! What resource for us amidst the innumerable ills of life did not religion suggest some methods of atonement, and appease those terrors with which we are incessantly agitated and tormented?

I am indeed persuaded, said Philo, that the best and indeed the only method of bringing everyone to a due sense of religion is by just representations of the misery and wickedness of men. And for that purpose a talent of eloquence and strong imagery is more requisite than that of reasoning and argument. For is it necessary to prove what everyone feels within himself? It is only necessary to make us feel it, if possible, more intimately and sensibly.

The people, indeed, replied Demea, are sufficiently convinced of this great and melancholy truth. The miseries of life, the unhappiness of man, the general corruptions of our nature, the unsatisfactory enjoyment of pleasures, riches, honours—these phrases have become almost proverbial in all languages. And who can doubt of what all men declare from their own immediate feeling and experience?

In this point, said Philo, the learned are perfectly agreed with the vulgar; and in all letters, *sacred* and *profane,* the topic of human misery has been insisted on with the most pathetic eloquence that sorrow and melancholy could inspire. The poets, who speak from sentiment, without a system, and whose testimony has therefore the more authority, abound in images of this nature. From Homer down to Dr. Young, the whole inspired tribe have ever been sensible that no other representation of things would suit the feeling and observation of each individual.

As to authorities, replied Demea, you need not seek them. Look round this library of Cleanthes. I shall venture to affirm that, except authors of particular sciences, such as chemistry or botany, who have no occasion to treat of human life, there is scarce one of those innumerable writers from whom the sense of human misery has not, in some passage or other, extorted a complaint and confession of it. At least, the chance is entirely on that side; and no one author has ever, so far as I can recollect, been so extravagant as to deny it.

There you must excuse me, said Philo: Leibniz has denied it, and is perhaps the first who ventured upon so bold and paradoxical an opinion; at least, the first who made it essential to his philosophical system.

And by being the first, replied Demea, might he not have been sensible of his error? For is this a subject in which philosophers can propose to make discoveries especially in so late an age? And can any man hope by a simple denial (for the subject scarcely admits of reasoning) to bear down the united testimony of mankind, founded on sense and consciousness?

And why should man, added he, pretend to an exemption from the lot of all other animals? The whole earth, believe me, Philo, is cursed and polluted. A perpetual war is kindled amongst all living creatures. Necessity, hunger, want stimulate the strong and courageous; fear, anxiety, terror agitate the weak and infirm. The first entrance into life gives anguish to the new-born infant and to its wretched parent; weakness, impotence, distress attend each stage of that life, and it is, at last finished in agony and horror.

Observe, too, says Philo, the curious artifices of nature in order to embitter the life of every living being. The stronger prey upon the weaker and keep them in perpetual terror and anxiety. The weaker, too, in their turn, often prey upon the stronger, and vex and molest them without relaxation. Consider that innumerable race of insects, which either are bred on the body of each animal or, flying about, infix their stings in him. These insects have others still less than themselves which torment them. And thus on each hand, before and behind, above and below, every animal is surrounded with enemies which incessantly seek his misery and destruction.

Man alone, said Demea, seems to be, in part, an exception to this rule. For by combination in society he can easily master lions, tigers, and bears, whose greater strength and agility naturally enable them to prey upon him.

On the contrary, it is here chiefly, cried Philo, that the uniform and equal maxims of nature are most apparent. Man, it is true, can, by combination, surmount all his *real* enemies and become master of the whole animal creation; but does he not immediately raise up to himself *imaginary* enemies, the demons of his fancy, who haunt him with superstitious terrors and blast every enjoyment of life? His pleasure, as he imagines, becomes in their eyes a crime; his food and repose give them umbrage and offence; his very sleep and dreams furnish new materials to anxious fear; and even death, his refuge from every other ill, presents only the dread of endless and innumerable woes. Nor does the wolf molest more the timid flock than superstition does the anxious breast of wretched mortals.

Besides, consider, Demea: This very society by which we surmount those wild beasts, our natural enemies, what new enemies does it not raise to us? What woe and misery does it not occasion? Man is the greatest enemy of man. Oppression, injustice, contempt, contumely, violence, sedition, war, calumny, treachery, fraud—by these they mutually torment each other, and they would soon dissolve that society which they had formed were it not for the dread of still greater ills which must attend their separation.

But though these external insults, said Demea, from animals, from men, from all the elements, which assault us from a frightful catalogue of woes, they are nothing in comparison of those which arise within ourselves, from the distempered condition of our mind and body. How many lie under the lingering torment of diseases? Hear the pathetic enumeration of the great poet.

> Intestine stone and ulcer, colic-pangs,
> Demoniac frenzy, moping melancholy,
> And moon-struck madness, pining atrophy
> Marasmus, and wide-wasting pestilence.
> Dire was the tossing, deep the groans: Despair
> Tended the sick, busiest from couch to couch
> And over them triumphant Death his dart
> Shook: but delay'd to strike, though oft invok'd
> With vows, as their chief good and final hope.

The disorders of the mind, continued Demea, though more secret, are not perhaps less dismal and vexatious. Remorse, shame, anguish, rage, disappointment, anxiety, fear, dejection, despair—who has ever passed through life without cruel inroads from these tormentors? How many have scarcely ever felt any better sensations? Labour and poverty, so abhorred by everyone, are the certain lot of the far greater number; and those few privileged persons who enjoy ease and opulence never reach contentment or true felicity. All the goods of life united would not make a very happy man, but all the ills united would make a wretch indeed; and any one of them almost (and who can be free from every one?), nay, often the absence of one good (and who can possess all?) is sufficient to render life ineligible.

Were a stranger to drop on a sudden into this world, I would show him, as a specimen of its ills, an hospital full of diseases, a prison crowded with malefactors and debtors, a field of battle strewed with carcases, a fleet floundering in the ocean, a nation languishing under tyranny, famine, or pestilence. To turn the gay side of life to him and give him a notion of its pleasures—whither should I conduct him? To a ball, to an opera, to court? He might justly think that I was only showing him a diversity of distress and sorrow.

There is no evading such striking instances, said Philo, but by apologies which still further aggravate the charge. Why have all men, I ask, in all ages, complained incessantly of the miseries of life? . . . They have no just reason, says one: these complaints proceed only from their discontented, repining, anxious disposition. . . . And can there possibly, I reply, be a more certain foundation of misery than such a wretched temper?

But if they were really as unhappy as they pretend, says my antagonist, why do they remain in life? . . .

Not satisfied with life, afraid of death—

This is the secret chain, say I, that holds us. We are terrified, not bribed to the continuance of our existence.

It is only a false delicacy, he may insist, which a few refined spirits indulge, and which has spread these complaints among the whole race of mankind. . . . And what is this delicacy, I ask, which you blame? Is it anything but a greater sensibility to all the pleasures and pains of life? And if the man of a delicate, refined temper, by being so much more alive

than the rest of the world, is only so much more unhappy, what judgment must we form in general of human life?

Let men remain at rest, says our adversary, and they will be easy. They are willing artificers of their own misery. . . . No! reply I: an anxious languor follows their repose; disappointment, vexation, trouble, their activity and ambition.

I can observe something like what you mention in some others, replied Cleanthes, but I confess I feel little or nothing of it in myself, and hope that it is not so common as you represent it.

If you feel not human misery yourself, cried Demea, I congratulate you on so happy a singularity. Others, seemingly the most prosperous, have not been ashamed to vent their complaints in the most melancholy strains. Let us attend to the great, the fortunate emperor, Charles V, when tired with human grandeur, he resigned all his extensive dominions into the hands of his son. In the last harangue which he made on that memorable occasion, he publicly avowed *that the greatest prosperities which he had ever enjoyed had been mixed with so many adversities that he might truly say he had never enjoyed any satisfaction or contentment.* But did the retired life in which he sought for shelter afford him any greater happiness? If we may credit his son's account, his repentance commenced the very day of his resignation.

Cicero's fortune, from small beginnings, rose to the greatest lustre and renown; yet what pathetic complaints of the ills of life do his familiar letters, as well as philosophical discourses, contain? And suitably to his own experience, he introduces Cato, the great, the fortunate Cato protesting in his old age that had he a new life in his offer he would reject the present.

Ask yourself, ask any of your acquaintance, whether they would live over again the last ten or twenty years of their life. No! but the next twenty, they say, will be better:

And from the dregs of life, hope to receive
What the first sprightly running could not give.

Thus, at last, they find (such is the greatness of human misery, it reconciles even contradictions) that they complain at once of the shortness of life and of its vanity and sorrow.

And is it possible, Cleanthes, said Philo, that after all these reflections, and infinitely more which might be suggested, you can still persevere in your anthropomorphism, and assert the moral attributes of the Deity, his justice, benevolence, mercy, and rectitude, to be of the same nature with these virtues in human creatures? His power, we allow, is infinite; whatever he wills is executed; but neither man nor any other animal is happy; therefore, he does not will their happiness. His wisdom is infinite; he is never mistaken in choosing the means to any end; but the course of nature tends not to human or animal felicity; therefore, it is not established for that purpose. Through the whole compass of human knowledge there are no inferences more certain and infallible than these. In what respect, then, do his benevolence and mercy resemble the benevolence and mercy of men?

Epicurus' old questions are yet unanswered.

Is he willing to prevent evil, but not able? then is he impotent. Is he able, but not willing? then is he malevolent. Is he both able and willing? whence then is evil?

You ascribe, Cleanthes (and I believe justly), a purpose and intention to nature. But what, I beseech you, is the object of that curious artifice and machinery which she has displayed in all animals—the preservation alone of individuals, and propagation of the species? It seems enough for her purpose, if such a rank be barely upheld in the universe, without any care or concern for the happiness of the members that compose it. No resource for this purpose: no machinery in order merely to give pleasure or ease; no fund of pure joy and contentment; no indulgence without some want or necessity accompanying it. At least, the few phenomena of this nature are over-balanced by opposite phenomena of still greater importance.

Our sense of music, harmony, and indeed beauty of all kinds, gives satisfaction, without being absolutely necessary to the preservation and propagation of the species. But what racking pains, on the other hand, arise from gouts, gravels, megrims, toothaches, rheumatisms, where the injury to the animal machinery is either small or incurable? Mirth, laughter, play, frolic seem gratuitous satisfactions which have no fur-

ther tendency; spleen, melancholy, discontent, superstition are pains of the same nature. How then does the Divine benevolence display itself, in the sense of you anthropomorphites? None but we mystics, as you were pleased to call us, can account for this strange mixture of phenomena, by deriving it from attributes infinitely perfect but incomprehensible.

And have you, at last, said Cleanthes smiling, betrayed your intentions, Philo? Your long agreement with Demea did indeed a little surprise me, but I find you were all the while erecting a concealed battery against me. And I must confess that you have now fallen upon a subject worthy of your noble spirit of opposition and controversy. If you can make out the present point, and prove mankind to be unhappy or corrupted, there is an end at once of all religion. For to what purpose establish the natural attributes of the Deity, while the moral are still doubtful and uncertain?

You take umbrage very easily, replied Demea, at opinions the most innocent and the most generally received, even amongst the religious and devout themselves; and nothing can be more surprising than to find a topic like this—concerning the wickedness and misery of man—charged with no less than atheism and profaneness. Have not all pious divines and preachers who have indulged their rhetoric on so fertile a subject, have they not easily, I say, given a solution of any difficulties which may attend it? This world is but a point in comparison of the universe; this life but a moment in comparison of eternity. The present evil phenomena, therefore, are rectified in other regions, and in some future period of existence. And the eyes of men, being then opened to larger views of things, see the whole connection of general laws, and trace, with adoration, the benevolence and rectitude of the Deity through all the mazes and intricacies of his providence.

No! replied Cleanthes, no! These arbitrary suppositions can never be admitted, contrary to matter of fact, visible and uncontroverted. Whence can any cause be known but from its known effects? Whence can any hypothesis be proved but from the apparent phenomena? To establish one hypothesis upon another is building entirely in the air; and the utmost we ever attain by these conjectures and fictions is to ascertain the bare possibility of our opinion, but never can we, upon such terms, establish its reality.

The only method of supporting Divine benevolence—and it is what I willingly embrace—is to deny absolutely the misery and wickedness of man. Your representations are exaggerated; your melancholy views mostly fictitious; your inferences contrary to fact and experience. Health is more common than sickness; pleasure than pain; happiness than misery. And for one vexation which we meet with, we attain, upon computation, a hundred enjoyments.

Admitting your position, replied Philo, which yet is extremely doubtful, you must at the same time allow that, if pain be less frequent than pleasure, it is infinitely more violent and durable. One hour of it is often able to outweigh a day, a week, a month of our common insipid enjoyments; and how many days, weeks, and months are passed by several in the most acute torments? Pleasure, scarcely in one instance, is ever able to reach ecstasy and rapture; and in no one instance can it continue for any time at its highest pitch and altitude. The spirits evaporate, the nerves relax, the fabric is disordered, and the enjoyment quickly degenerates into fatigue and uneasiness. But pain often, good God, how often! rises to torture and agony; and the longer it continues, it becomes still more genuine agony and torture. Patience is exhausted, courage languishes, melancholy seizes us, and nothing terminates our misery but the removal of its cause or another event which is the sole cure of all evil, but which, from our natural folly, we regard with still greater horror and consternation.

But not to insist upon these topics, continued Philo, though most obvious, certain, and important, I must use the freedom to admonish you, Cleanthes, that you have put the controversy upon a most dangerous issue, and are unawares introducing a total scepticism into the most essential articles of natural and revealed theology. What! no method of fixing a just foundation for religion unless we allow the happiness of human life, and maintain a continued existence even in this world, with all our present pains, infirmities, vexations, and follies, to be eligible and desirable! But this is contrary to everyone's feeling and experience; it is contrary to an authority so established as nothing can subvert. No decisive proofs can ever be produced against this authority; nor is it possible for you to compute, estimate, and compare all the pains and all the pleasures in the lives of all men and of all animals; and thus, by your resting the whole system of religion on a point which, from its very nature, must for ever be uncertain, you tacitly confess that that system is equally uncertain.

But allowing you what never will be believed, at least, what you never possibly can prove, that animal or, at least, human happiness in this life exceeds its misery, you have yet done nothing; for this is not, by any means, what we expect from infinite power, infinite wisdom, and infinite goodness. Why is there any misery at all in the world? Not by chance, surely. From some cause then. Is it from the intention of the Deity? But he is perfectly benevolent. Is it contrary to his intention? But he is almighty. Nothing can shake the solidity of this reasoning, so short, so clear, so decisive, except we assert that these subjects exceed all human capacity, and that our common measures of truth and falsehood are not applicable to them—a topic which I have all along insisted on, but which you have, from the beginning, rejected with scorn and indignation.

But I will be contented to retire still from this intrenchment, for I deny that you can ever force me in it. I will allow that pain or misery in man is *compatible* with infinite power and goodness in the Deity, even in your sense of these attributes: what are you advanced by all these concessions? A mere possible compatibility is not sufficient. You must *prove* these pure, unmixt, and uncontrollable attributes from the present mixt and confused phenomena, and from these alone. A hopeful undertaking! Were the phenomena ever so pure and unmixt, yet, being finite, they would be insufficient for that purpose. How much more, where they are also so jarring and discordant!

Here, Cleanthes, I find myself at ease in my argument. Here I triumph. Formerly, when we argued concerning the natural attributes of intelligence and design, I needed all my sceptical and metaphysical subtilty to elude your grasp. In many views of the universe and of its parts, particularly the latter, the beauty and fitness of final causes strike us with such irresistible force that all objections appear (what I believe they really are) mere cavils and sophisms; nor can we then imagine how it was ever possible for us to repose any weight on them. But there is no view of human life or of the condition of mankind from which, without the greatest violence, we can infer the moral attributes or learn that infinite benevolence, conjoined with infinite power and infinite wisdom, which we must discover by the eyes of faith alone. It is your turn now to tug the labouring oar, and to support your philosophical subtilties against the dictates of plain reason and experience.

PART XI

I scruple not to allow, said Cleanthes, that I have been apt to suspect the frequent repetition of the word *infinite,* which we meet with in all theological writers, to savour more of panegyric than of philosophy, and that any purposes of reasoning, and even of religion, would be better served were we to rest contented with more accurate and more moderate expressions. The terms *admirable, excellent, superlatively great, wise,* and *holy*—these sufficiently fill the imaginations of men, and anything beyond, besides that it leads into absurdities, has no influence on the affections or sentiments. Thus, in thy present subject, if we abandon all human analogy, as seems your intention, Demea, I am afraid we abandon all religion and retain no conception of the great object of our adoration. If we preserve human analogy, we must forever find it impossible to reconcile any mixture of evil in the universe with infinite attributes; much less can we ever prove the latter from the former. But supposing the Author of nature to be finitely perfect, though far exceeding mankind, a satisfactory account may then be given of natural and moral evil, and every untoward phenomenon be explained and adjusted. A less evil may then be chosen in order to avoid a greater; inconveniences be submitted to in order to reach a desirable end; and, in a word, benevolence, regulated by wisdom and limited by necessity, may produce just such a world as the present. You, Philo, who are so prompt at starting views and reflections and analogies, I would gladly hear, at length, without interruption, your opinion of this new theory; and if it deserve our attention, we may afterwards, at more leisure, reduce it into form.

My sentiments, replied Philo, are not worth being made a mystery of; and, therefore, without any ceremony, I shall deliver what occurs to me with regard to the present subject. It must, I think, be allowed that, if a very limited intelligence whom we shall suppose utterly unacquainted with the universe were assured that it were the production of a very good, wise, and powerful Being, however finite, he would, from his conjectures, form *beforehand* a different notion of it from what we find it to be by experience; nor would he ever imagine, merely from these attributes of the cause of which he is informed, that the effect could be so full of vice and misery and disorder, as it appears in this life. Supposing now that this person were brought into the world, still assured that it was the workmanship of such a sublime and benevolent Being, he might, perhaps, be surprised at the disappointment, but would never retract his former belief if founded on any very solid argument, since such a limited intelligence must be sensible of his own blindness and ignorance, and must allow that there may be many solutions of those phenomena which will for ever escape his comprehension. But supposing, which is the real case with regard to man, that this creature is not antecedently convinced of a supreme intelligence, benevolent, and powerful, but is left to gather such a belief from the appearances of things—this entirely alters the case, nor will he ever find any reason for such a conclusion. He may be fully convinced of the narrow limits of his understanding, but this will not help him in forming an inference concerning the goodness of superior powers, since he must form that inference from what he knows, not from what he is ignorant of. The more you exaggerate his weakness and ignorance, the more diffident you render him, and give him the greater suspicion that such subjects are beyond the reach of his faculties. You are obliged, therefore, to reason with him merely from the known phenomena, and to drop every arbitrary supposition or conjecture.

Did I show you a house or palace where there was not one apartment convenient or agreeable, where the windows, doors, fires, passages, stairs, and the whole economy of the building were the source of noise, confusion, fatigue, darkness, and the extremes of heat and cold, you would certainly blame the contrivance, without any further examination. The architect would in vain display his subtilty, and prove to you that, if this door or that window were altered, greater ills would ensue. What he says may be strictly true: the alteration of one particular, while the other parts of the building remain, may only augment the inconveniences. But still you would assert in general that, if the architect had had skill and good intentions, he might have formed such a plan of the whole, and might have adjusted the parts in such a manner as would have remedied all or most of these inconveniences. His ignorance, or even your own ignorance of such a plan, will never convince you of the impossibility of it. If you find any inconveniences and deformities in the building, you will always, without entering into any detail, condemn the architect.

In short, I repeat the question: Is the world, considered in general and as it appears to us in this life, different from what a man or such a limited being would, *beforehand,* expect from a very powerful, wise, and benevolent Deity? It must be strange prejudice to assert the contrary. And from thence I conclude that, however consistent the world may be, allowing certain suppositions and conjectures with the idea of such a Deity, it can never afford us an inference concerning his existence. The consistency is not absolutely denied, only the inference. Conjectures, especially where infinity is excluded from the Divine attributes, may perhaps be sufficient to prove a consistency, but can never be foundations for any inference.

There seem to be *four* circumstances on which depend all or the greatest part of the ills that molest sensible creatures; and it is not impossible but all these circumstances may be necessary and unavoidable. We know so little beyond common life, or even of common life, that, with regard to the economy of a universe, there is no conjecture, however wild, which may not be just, nor any one, however plausible, which may not be erroneous. All that belongs to human understanding, in this deep ignorance and obscurity, is to be sceptical or at least cautious, and not to admit of any hypothesis whatever, much less of any which is supported by no appearance of probability. Now this I assert to be the case with regard to all the causes of evil and the circumstances on which

it depends. None of them appear to human reason in the least degree necessary or unavoidable, nor can we suppose them such, without the utmost license of imagination.

The *first* circumstance which introduces evil is that contrivance or economy of the animal creation by which pains, as well as pleasures, are employed to excite all creatures to action, and make them vigilant in the great work of self-preservation. Now pleasure alone, in its various degrees, seems to human understanding sufficient for this purpose. All animals might be constantly in a state of enjoyment; but when urged by any of the necessities of nature, such as thirst, hunger, weariness, instead of pain, they might feel a diminution of pleasure by which they might be prompted to seek that object which is necessary to their subsistence. Men pursue pleasure as eagerly as they avoid pain; at least, they might have been so constituted. It seems, therefore, plainly possible to carry on the business of life without any pain. Why then is any animal ever rendered susceptible of such a sensation? If animals can be free from it an hour, they might enjoy a perpetual exemption from it, and it required as particular a contrivance of their organs to produce that feeling as to endow them with sight, hearing, or any of the senses. Shall we conjecture that such a contrivance was necessary, without any appearance of reason, and shall we build on that conjecture as on the most certain truth?

But a capacity of pain would not alone produce pain were it not for the *second* circumstance, viz., the conducting of the world by general laws; and this seems nowise necessary to a very perfect Being. It is true, if everything were conducted by particular volitions, the course of nature would be perpetually broken, and no man could employ his reason in the conduct of life. But might not other particular volitions remedy this inconvenience? In short, might not the Deity exterminate all ill, wherever it were to be found, and produce all good, without any preparation or long progress of causes and effects?

Besides, we must consider that, according to the present economy of the world, the course of nature, though supposed exactly regular, yet to us appears not so, and many events are uncertain, and many disappoint our expectations. Health and sickness, calm and tempest, with an infinite number of other accidents whose causes are unknown and variable, have a great influence both on the fortunes of particular persons and on the prosperity of public societies; and indeed all human life, in a manner, depends on such accidents. A being, therefore, who knows the secret springs of the universe might easily, by particular volitions, turn all these accidents to the good of mankind and render the whole world happy, without discovering himself in any operation. A fleet whose purposes were salutary to society might always meet with a fair wind. Good princes enjoy sound health and long life. Persons born to power and authority be framed with good tempers and virtuous dispositions. A few such events as these, regularly and wisely conducted, would change the face of the world, and yet would no more seem to disturb the course of nature or confound human conduct than the present economy of things where the causes are secret and variable and compounded. Some small touches given to Caligula's brain in his infancy might have converted him into a Trajan. One wave, a little higher than the rest, by burying Caesar and his fortune in the bottom of the ocean, might have restored liberty to a considerable part of mankind. There may, for aught we know, be good reasons why Providence interposes not in this manner, but they are unknown to us; and, though the mere supposition that such reasons exist may be sufficient to *save* the conclusion concerning the Divine attributes, yet surely it can never be sufficient to *establish* that conclusion.

If everything in the universe be conducted by general laws, and if animals be rendered susceptible of pain, it scarcely seems possible but some ill must arise in the various shocks of matter and the various concurrence and opposition of general laws; but this ill would be very rare were it not for the *third* circumstance which I proposed to mention, viz., the great frugality with which all powers and faculties are distributed to every particular being. So well adjusted are the organs and capacities of all animals, and so well fitted to their preservation, that, as far as history or tradition reaches, there appears not to be any single species which has yet been extinguished in the universe. Every animal has the requisite endowments, but these endowments are bestowed with so

scrupulous an economy that any considerable diminution must entirely destroy the creature. Wherever one power is increased, there is a proportional abatement in the others. Animals which excel in swiftness are commonly defective in force. Those which possess both are either imperfect in some of their senses or are oppressed with the most craving wants. The human species, whose chief excellence is reason and sagacity, is of all others the most necessitous, and the most deficient in bodily advantages, without clothes, without arms, without food, without lodging, without any convenience of life, except what they owe to their own skill and industry. In short, nature seems to have formed an exact calculation of the necessities of her creatures, and, like a *rigid master,* has afforded them little more powers or endowments than what are strictly sufficient to supply those necessities. An *indulgent parent* would have bestowed a large stock in order to guard against accidents, and secure the happiness and welfare of the creature in the most unfortunate concurrence of circumstances. Every course of life would not have been so surrounded with precipices that the least departure from the true path, by mistake or necessity, must involve us in misery and ruin. Some reserve, some fund, would have been provided to ensure happiness, nor would the powers and the necessities have been adjusted with so rigid an economy. The Author of nature is inconceivably powerful; his force is supposed great, if not altogether inexhaustible, nor is there any reason, as far as we can judge, to make him observe this strict frugality in his dealings with his creatures. It would have been better, were his power extremely limited, to have created fewer animals, and to have endowed these with more faculties for their happiness and preservation. A builder is never esteemed prudent who undertakes a plan beyond what his stock will enable him to finish.

In order to cure most of the ills of human life, I require not that man should have the wings of the eagle, the swiftness of the stag, the force of the ox, the arms of the lion, the scales of the crocodile or rhinoceros; much less do I demand the sagacity of an angel or cherubim. I am contented to take an increase in one single power or faculty of his soul. Let him be endowed with a greater propensity to industry and labour, a more vigorous spring and activity of mind, a more constant bent to business and application. Let the whole species possess naturally an equal diligence with that which many individuals are able to attain by habit and reflection, and the most beneficial consequences, without any allay of ill, is the immediate and necessary result of this endowment. Almost all the moral as well as natural evils of human life arise from idleness; and were our species, by the original constitution of their frame, exempt from this vice or infirmity, the perfect cultivation of land, the improvement of arts and manufactures, the exact execution of every office and duty, immediately follow; and men at once may fully reach that state of society which is so imperfectly attained by the best regulated government. But as industry is a power, and the most valuable of any, nature seems determined, suitably to her usual maxims, to bestow it on man with a very sparing hand, and rather to punish him severely for his deficiency in it than to reward him for his attainments. She has so contrived his frame that nothing but the most violent necessity can oblige him to labour; and she employs all his other wants to overcome, at least in part, the want of diligence, and to endow him with some share of a faculty of which she has thought fit naturally to bereave him. Here our demands may be allowed very humble, and therefore the more reasonable. If we required the endowments of superior penetration and judgment, of a more delicate taste of beauty, of a nicer sensibility to benevolence and friendship, we might be told that we impiously pretend to break the order of nature, that we want to exalt ourselves into a higher rank of being, that the presents which we require, not being suitable to our state and condition, would only be pernicious to us. But it is hard, I dare to repeat it, it is hard that, being placed in a world so full of wants and necessities, where almost every being and element is either our foe or refuses its assistance . . . we should also have our own temper to struggle with, and should be deprived of that faculty which can alone fence against these multiplied evils.

The *fourth* circumstance whence arises the misery and ill of the universe is the inaccurate workmanship of all the springs and principles of the great machine of nature. It must be acknowledged that there are few parts of the universe which seem not to serve some purpose, and whose removal would not produce a visible defect and disorder in the whole. The parts hang all together, nor can one be touched without affecting the rest, in a greater or less degree. But at the same time, it must be observed that none of these parts or principles, however useful, are so accurately adjusted as to keep precisely within those bounds in which their utility consists; but they are, all of them, apt, on every occasion, to run into the one extreme or the other. One would imagine that this grand production had not received the last hand of the maker—so little finished is every part, and so coarse are the strokes with which it is executed. Thus the winds are requisite to convey the vapours along the surface of the globe, and to assist men in navigation; but how often, rising up to tempests and hurricanes, do they become pernicious? Rains are necessary to nourish all the plants and animals of the earth; but how often are they defective? how often excessive? Heat is requisite to all life and vegetation, but is not always found in the due proportion. On the mixture and secretion of the humours and juices of the body depend the health and prosperity of the animal; but the parts perform not regularly their proper function. What more useful than all the passions of the mind, ambition, vanity, love, anger? But how often do they break their bounds and cause the greatest convulsions in society? There is nothing so advantageous in the universe but what frequently becomes pernicious, by its excess or defect; nor has nature guarded, with the requisite accuracy, against all disorder or confusion. The irregularity is never perhaps so great as to destroy any species, but is often sufficient to involve the individuals in ruin and misery.

On the concurrence, then, of these *four* circumstances does all or the greatest part of natural evil depend. Were all living creatures incapable of pain, or were the world administered by particular volitions, evil never could have found access into the universe; and were animals endowed with a large stock of powers and faculties, beyond what strict necessity requires, or were the several springs and principles of the universe so accurately framed as to preserve always the just temperament and medium, there must have been very little ill in comparison of what we feel at present. What then shall we pronounce on this occasion? Shall we say that these circumstances are not necessary, and that they might easily have been altered in the contrivance of the universe? This decision seems too presumptuous for creatures so blind and ignorant. Let us be more modest in our conclusions. Let us allow that, if the goodness of the Deity (I mean a goodness like the human) could be established on any tolerable reasons a priori, these phenomena, however untoward, would not be sufficient to subvert that principle, but might easily, in some unknown manner, be reconcilable to it. But let us still assert that, as this goodness is not antecedently established but must be inferred from the phenomena, there can be no grounds for such an inference while there are so many ills in the universe, and while these ills might so easily have been remedied, as far as human understanding can be allowed to judge on such a subject. I am sceptic enough to allow that the bad appearances, notwithstanding all my reasonings, may be compatible with such attributes as you suppose, but surely they can never prove these attributes. Such a conclusion cannot result from scepticism, but must arise from the phenomena, and from our confidence in the reasonings which we deduce from these phenomena.

Look round this universe. What an immense profusion of beings, animated and organized, sensible and active! You admire this prodigious variety and fecundity. But inspect a little more narrowly these living existences, the only beings worth regarding. How hostile and destructive to each other! How insufficient all of them for their own happiness! How contemptible or odious to the spectator! The whole presents nothing but the idea of a blind nature, impregnated by a great vivifying principle, and pouring forth from her lap, without discernment or parental care, her maimed and abortive children!

Here the Manichaean system occurs as a proper hypothesis to solve the difficulty; and, no doubt, in some respects it is very specious and has more probability than the common hypothesis, by giving a plausible account of the strange mixture of good and ill which appears in life. But if we consider, on the other hand, the perfect uniformity and agreement of the parts of the universe, we shall not discover in it any marks of the combat of a malevolent with a benevolent being. There is indeed an opposition of pains and pleasures in the feelings of sensible creatures; but are not all the operations of nature carried on by an opposition of principles, of hot and cold, moist and dry, light and heavy? The true conclusion is that the original Source of all things is entirely indifferent to all these principles, and has no more regard to good above ill than to heat above cold, or to drought above moisture, or to light above heavy.

There may *four* hypotheses be framed concerning the first causes of the universe: that they are endowed with perfect goodness; that they have perfect malice; that they are opposite and have both goodness and malice; that they have neither goodness nor malice. Mixed phenomena can never prove the two former unmixed principles; and the uniformity and steadiness of general laws seem to oppose the third. The fourth, therefore, seems by far the most probable.

What I have said concerning natural evil will apply to moral with little or no variation; and we have no more reason to infer that the rectitude of the Supreme Being resembles human rectitude than that his benevolence resembles the human. Nay, it will be thought that we have still greater cause to exclude from him moral sentiments, such as we feel them, since moral evil, in the opinion of many, is much more predominant above moral good than natural evil above natural good.

But even though this should not be allowed, and though the virtue which is in mankind should be acknowledged much superior to the vice, yet, so long as there is any vice at all in the universe, it will very much puzzle you anthropomorphites how to account for it. You must assign a cause for it, without having recourse to the first cause. But as every effect must have a cause, and that cause another, you must either carry on the progression *in infinitum* or rest on that original principle, who is the ultimate cause of all things. . . .

Hold! hold! cried Demea: Whither does your imagination hurry you? I joined in alliance with you in order to prove the incomprehensible nature of the Divine Being, and refute the principles of Cleanthes, who would measure everything by human rule and standard. But I now find you running into all the topics of the greatest libertines and infidels, and betraying that holy cause which you seemingly espoused. Are you secretly, then, a more dangerous enemy than Cleanthes himself?

And are you so late in perceiving it? replied Cleanthes. Believe me, Demea, your friend Philo, from the beginning, has been amusing himself at both our expense; and it must be confessed that the injudicious reasoning of our vulgar theology has given him but too just a handle of ridicule. The total infirmity of human reason, the absolute incomprehensibility of the Divine Nature, the great and universal misery, and still greater wickedness of men— these are strange topics, surely, to be so fondly cherished by orthodox divines and doctors. In ages of stupidity and ignorance, indeed, these principles may safely be espoused; and perhaps no views of things are more proper to promote superstition than such as encourage the blind amazement, the diffidence, and melancholy of mankind. But at present. . . .

Blame not so much, interposed Philo, the ignorance of these reverend gentlemen. They know how to change their style with the times. Formerly, it was a most popular theological topic to maintain that human life was vanity and misery, and to exaggerate all the ills and pains which are incident to men. But of late years, divines, we find, begin to retract this position and maintain, though still with some hesitation, that there are more goods than evils, more pleasures than pains, even in this life. When religion stood entirely upon temper and education, it was thought proper to encourage melancholy, as, indeed, mankind never have recourse to superior powers so readily as in that disposition. But as men have now learned to form principles and to draw consequences, it is necessary to change the batteries, and to make use of such arguments as will endure at least some scrutiny and examination. This variation is the same (and from the same causes) with that which I formerly remarked with regard to scepticism.

Thus Philo continued to the last his spirit of opposition, and his censure of established opinions. But I could observe that Demea did not at all relish the latter part of the discourse; and he took occasion soon after, on some pretence or other, to leave the company.

Why God Allows Evil

~

RICHARD SWINBURNE

Richard Swinburne is the Nolloth Professor of the Philosophy of the Christian Religion at the University of Oxford. He has written extensively in support of theism and other tenets of Christianity. His numerous volumes include the trilogy, *The Existence of God, The Coherence of Theism,* and *Faith and Reason.*

The world . . . contains much evil. An omnipotent God could have prevented this evil, and surely a perfectly good and omnipotent God would have done so. So why is there this evil? Is not its existence strong evidence against the existence of God? It would be unless we can construct what is known as a theodicy, an explanation of why God would allow such evil to occur. I believe that that can be done, and I shall outline a theodicy. . . . I emphasize that . . . in writing that God would do this or that, I am not taking for granted the existence of God, but merely claiming that, if there is a God, it is to be expected that he would do certain things, including allowing the occurrence of certain evils; and so, I am claiming, their occurrence is not evidence against his existence.

It is inevitable that any attempt by myself or anyone else to construct a theodicy will sound callous, indeed totally insensitive to human suffering. Many theists, as well as atheists, have felt that any attempt to construct a theodicy evinces an immoral approach to suffering. I can only ask the reader to believe that I am not totally insensitive to human suffering, and that I do mind about the agony of poisoning, child abuse, bereavement, solitary imprisonment, and marital infidelity as much as anyone else. True, I would not in most cases recommend that a pastor give this chapter to victims of sudden distress at their worst moment to read for consolation. But this is not because its arguments are unsound; it is simply that most people in deep distress need comfort, not argument. Yet there is a problem about why God allows evil, and, if the theist does not have (in a cool moment) a satisfactory answer to it, then his belief in God is less than rational, and there is no reason why the atheist should share it. To appreciate the argument of this chapter, each of us needs to stand back a bit from the particular situation of his or her own life and that of close relatives and friends (which can so easily seem the only important thing in the world), and ask very generally what good things would a generous and everlasting God give to human beings in the course of a short earthly life. Of course thrills of pleasure and periods of contentment are good things, and—other things being equal—God would certainly seek to provide plenty of those. But a generous God will seek to give deeper good things than these. He will seek to give us great responsibility for ourselves, each other, and the world, and thus a share in his own creative activity of determining what sort of world it is to be. And he will seek to make our lives valuable, of great use to ourselves and each other. The problem is that God cannot give us these goods in full measure without allowing much evil on the way. . . .

[T]here are plenty of evils, positive bad states, which God could if he chose remove. I divide these into moral evils and natural evils. I understand by "natural evil" all evil which is not deliberately produced by human beings and which is not allowed by human beings to occur as a result of their negligence. Natural evil includes both physical suffering and mental suffering, of animals as well as humans; all the trial of suffering which disease, natural disasters, and accidents unpredictable by humans bring in their train. "Moral evil" I understand as including all evil caused deliberately by humans doing what they ought not to do (or allowed to occur by humans negligently failing to do what they ought to do) *and* also the evil constituted by such deliberate actions or negligent failure. It includes the sensory pain of the blow inflicted by the bad parent on his child, the mental pain of the parent depriving the child of love, the starvation allowed to occur in Africa because of negligence by members of foreign governments who could have prevented it, and also the evil of the parent or politician deliberately bringing about the pain or not trying to prevent the starvation.

MORAL EVIL

The central core of any theodicy must, I believe, be the "free-will defence," which deals—to start with—with moral evil, but can be extended to deal with much natural evil as well. The free-will defence claims that it is a great good that humans have a certain sort of free will which I shall call free and responsible choice, but that, if they do, then necessarily there will be the natural possibility of moral evil. (By the "natural possibility" I mean that it will not be determined in advance whether or not the evil will occur.) A God who gives humans such free will necessarily brings about the possibility, and puts outside his own control whether or not that evil occurs. It is not logically possible—that is, it would be self-contradictory to suppose—that God could give us such free will and yet ensure that we always use it in the right way.

Free and responsible choice is not just free will in the narrow sense of being able to choose between alternative actions, without our choice being causally necessitated by some prior cause. . . . [H]umans could have that kind of free will merely in virtue of being able to choose freely between two equally good and unimportant alternatives. Free and responsible choice is rather free will (of the kind discussed) to make significant choices between good and evil, which make a big difference to the agent, to others, and to the world.

Given that we have free will, we certainly have free and responsible choice. Let us remind ourselves of the difference that humans can make to themselves, others, and the world. Humans have opportunities to give themselves and others pleasurable sensations, and to pursue worthwhile activities—to play tennis or the piano, to acquire knowledge of history and science and philosophy, and to help others to do so, and thereby to build deep personal relations founded upon such sensations and activities. And humans are so made that they can form their characters. Aristotle famously remarked: "we become just by doing just acts, prudent by doing prudent acts, brave by doing brave acts." That is, by doing a just act when it is difficult—when it goes against our natural inclinations (which is what I understand by desires)—we make it easier to do a just act next time. We can gradually change our desires, so that—for example—doing just acts becomes natural. Thereby we can free ourselves from the power of the less good desires to which we are subject. And, by choosing to acquire knowledge and to use it to build machines of various sorts, humans can extend the range of the differences they can make to the world—they can build universities to last for centuries, or save energy for the next generation; and by cooperative effort over many decades they can eliminate poverty. The possibilities for free and responsible choice are enormous.

It is good that the free choices of humans should include *genuine* responsibility for other humans, and that involves the opportunity to benefit *or* harm them. God has the power to benefit or to harm humans. If other agents are to be given a share in his creative work, it is good that they have that power too (although perhaps to a lesser degree). A world in which agents can benefit each other but not do each other harm is one where they have only very limited responsibility for each other. If my responsibility for you is limited to whether or not to give you a camcorder, but I cannot cause you pain, stunt your growth, or limit your education, then I do not have a great deal of responsibility for you. A God who gave

agents only such limited responsibilities for their fellows would not have given much. God would have reserved for himself the all-important choice of the kind of world it was to be, while simply allowing humans the minor choice of filling in the details. He would be like a father asking his elder son to look after the younger son, and adding that he would be watching the elder son's every move and would intervene the moment the elder son did a thing wrong. The elder son might justly retort that, while he would be happy to share his father's work, he could really do so only if he were left to make his own judgements as to what to do within a significant range of the options available to the father. A good God, like a good father, will delegate responsibility. In order to allow creatures a share in creation, he will allow them the choice of hurting and maiming, of frustrating the divine plan. Our world is one where creatures have just such deep responsibility for each other. I cannot only benefit my children, but harm them. One way in which I can harm them is that I can inflict physical pain on them. But there are much more damaging things which I can do to them. Above all I can stop them growing into creatures with significant knowledge, power, and freedom; I can determine whether they come to have the kind of free and responsible choice which I have. The possibility of humans bringing about significant evil is a logical consequence of their having this free and responsible choice. Not even God could give us this choice without the possibility of resulting evil.

Now . . . an action would not be intentional unless it was done for a reason—that is, seen as in some way a good thing (either in itself or because of its consequences). And, if reasons alone influence actions, that regarded by the subject as most important will determine what is done; an agent under the influence of reason alone will inevitably do the action which he regards as overall the best. If an agent does not do the action which he regards as overall the best, he must have allowed factors other than reason to exert an influence on him. In other words, he must have allowed desires for what he regards as good only in a certain respect, but not overall, to influence his conduct. So, in order to have a choice between good and evil, agents need already a certain depravity, in the sense of a system of desires for what they correctly believe to be evil. I need to *want* to overeat, get more than my fair share of money or power, indulge my sexual appetites even by deceiving my spouse or partner, want to see you hurt, if I am to have choice between good and evil. This depravity is itself an evil which is a necessary condition of a greater good. It makes possible a choice made seriously and deliberately, because made in the face of a genuine alternative. I stress that, according to the free-will defence, it is the natural possibility of moral evil which is the necessary condition of the great good, not the actual evil itself. Whether that occurs is (through God's choice) outside God's control and up to us.

Note further and crucially that, if I suffer in consequence of your freely chosen bad action, that is not by any means pure loss for me. In a certain respect it is a good for *me*. My suffering would be pure loss for me if the only good thing in life was sensory pleasure, and the only bad thing sensory pain; and it is because the modern world tends to think in those terms that the problem of evil seems so acute. If these were the only good and bad things, the occurrence of suffering would indeed be a conclusive objection to the existence of God. But we have already noted the great good of freely choosing and influencing our future, that of our fellows, and that of the world. And now note another great good—the good of our life serving a purpose, of being of use to ourselves and others. Recall the words of Christ, "it is more blessed to give than to receive" (as quoted by St. Paul (Acts 20: 35)). We tend to think, when the beggar appears on our doorstep and we feel obliged to give and do give, that that was lucky for him but not for us who happened to be at home. That is not what Christ's words say. They say that *we* are the lucky ones, not just because we have a lot, out of which we can give a little, but because we are privileged to contribute to the beggar's happiness—and that privilege is worth a lot more than money. And, just as it is a great good freely to choose to do good, so it is also a good to be used by someone else for a worthy purpose (so long, that is, that he or she has the right, the authority, to use us in this way). Being allowed to suffer to make possible a great good is a privilege, even if the privilege is forced upon you. Those who are allowed to

die for their country and thereby save their country from foreign oppression are privileged. Cultures less obsessed than our own by the evil of purely physical pain have always recognized that. And they have recognized that it is still a blessing, even if the one who died had been conscripted to fight.

And even twentieth-century man can begin to see that—sometimes—when he seeks to help prisoners, not by giving them more comfortable quarters, but by letting them help the handicapped; or when he pities rather than envies the "poor little rich girl" who has everything and does nothing for anyone else. And one phenomenon prevalent in end-of-century Britain draws this especially to our attention—the evil of unemployment. Because of our system of Social Security, the unemployed on the whole have enough money to live without too much discomfort; certainly they are a lot better off than are many employed in Africa or Asia or Victorian Britain. What is evil about unemployment is not so much any resulting poverty but the uselessness of the unemployed. They often report feeling unvalued by society, of no use, "on the scrap heap." They rightly think it would be a good for them to contribute; but they cannot. Many of them would welcome a system where they were obliged to do useful work in preference to one where society has no use for them.

It follows from that fact that being of use is a benefit for him who is of use, and that those who suffer at the hands of others, and thereby make possible the good of those others who have free and responsible choice, are themselves benefited in this respect. I am fortunate if the natural possibility of my suffering if you choose to hurt me is the vehicle which makes your choice really matter. My vulnerability, my openness to suffering (which necessarily involves my actually suffering if you make the wrong choice), means that you are not just like a pilot in a simulator, where it does not matter if mistakes are made. That our choices matter tremendously, that we can make great differences to things for good or ill, is one of the greatest gifts a creator can give us. And if my suffering is the means by which he can give you that choice, I too am in this respect fortunate. Though of course suffering is in itself a bad thing, my good fortune is that the suffering is not random, pointless suffering. It is suffering which is a consequence of my vulnerability which makes me of such use.

Someone may object that the only good thing is not *being* of use (dying for one's country or being vulnerable to suffering at your hands), but *believing* that one is of use—believing that one is dying for one's country and that this is of use; the "feel-good" experience. But that cannot be correct. Having comforting beliefs is only a good thing if they are true beliefs. It is not a good thing to believe that things are going well when they are not, or that your life is of use when it is not. Getting pleasure out of a comforting falsehood is a cheat. But if I get pleasure out of a true belief, it must be that I regard the state of things which I believe to hold to be a good thing. If I get pleasure out of the true belief that my daughter is doing well at school, it must be that I regard it as a good thing that my daughter does well at school (whether or not I believe that she is doing well). If I did not think the latter, I would not get any pleasure out of believing that she is doing well. Likewise, the belief that I am vulnerable to suffering at your hands, and that that is a good thing, can only be a good thing if being vulnerable to suffering at your hands is itself a good thing (independently of whether I believe it or not). Certainly, when my life is of use and that is a good for me, it is even better if I believe it and get comfort therefrom; but it can only be even better if it is already a good for me whether I believe it or not.

But though suffering may in these ways serve good purposes, does God have the right to allow me to suffer for your benefit, without asking my permission? For surely, an objector will say, no one has the right to allow one person A to suffer for the benefit of another one B without A's consent. We judge that doctors who use patients as involuntary objects of experimentation in medical experiments which they hope will produce results which can be used to benefit others are doing something wrong. After all, if my arguments about the utility of suffering are sound, ought we not all to be causing suffering to others in order that those others may have the opportunity to react in the right way?

There are, however, crucial differences between God and the doctors. The first is that God as the author of our being has certain rights, a certain authority over us, which we do not have over our fellow humans. He is the cause of our existence at each moment of our existence and sustains the laws of nature which give us everything we are and have. To allow someone to suffer for his own good or that of others, one has to stand in some kind of parental relationship towards him. I do not have the right to let some stranger suffer for the sake of some good, when I could easily prevent this, but I do have *some* right of this kind in respect of my own children. I may let the younger son suffer *somewhat* for his own good or that of his brother. I have this right because in small part I am responsible for the younger son's existence, his beginning and continuance. If I have begotten him, nourished, and educated him, I have some limited rights over him in return; to a *very limited* extent I can use him for some worthy purpose. If this is correct, then a God who is so much more the author of our being than are our parents has so much more right in this respect. Doctors do have over us even the rights of parents.

But secondly and all-importantly, the doctors *could* have asked the patients for permission; and the patients, being free agents of some power and knowledge, could have made an informed choice of whether or not to allow themselves to be used. By contrast, God's choice is not about how to use already existing agents, but about the sort of agents to make and the sort of world into which to put them. In God's situation there are no agents to be asked. I am arguing that it is good that one agent A should have deep responsibility for another B (who in turn could have deep responsibility for another C). It is not logically possible for God to have asked B if he wanted things thus, for, if A is to be responsible for B's growth in freedom, knowledge, and power, there will not be a B with enough freedom and knowledge to make any choice, before God has to choose whether or not to give A responsibility for him. One cannot ask a baby into which sort of world he or she wishes to be born. The creator has to make the choice independently of his creatures. He will seek on balance to benefit them—all of them. And, in giving them the gift of life—whatever suffering goes with it—that is a substantial benefit. But when one suffers at the hands of another, often perhaps it is not enough of a benefit to outweigh the suffering. Here is the point to recall that it is an additional benefit to the sufferer that his suffering is the means whereby the one who hurt him had the opportunity to make a significant choice between good and evil which otherwise he would not have had.

Although for these reasons, as I have been urging, God has the right to allow humans to cause each other to suffer, there must be a limit to the amount of suffering which he has the right to allow a human being to suffer for the sake of a great good. A parent may allow an elder child to have the power to do some harm to a younger child for the sake of the responsibility given to the elder child; but there are limits. And there are limits even to the moral right of God, our creator and sustainer, to use free sentient beings as pawns in a greater game. Yet, if these limits were too narrow, God would be unable to give humans much real responsibility; he would be able to allow them only to play a toy game. Still, limits there must be to God's rights to allow humans to hurt each other; and limits there are in the world to the extent to which they can hurt each other, provided above all by the short finite life enjoyed by humans and other creatures—one human can hurt another for no more than eighty years or so. And there are a number of other safety-devices in-built into our physiology and psychology, limiting the amount of pain we can suffer. But the primary safety limit is that provided by the shortness of our finite life. Unending, unchosen suffering would indeed to my mind provide a very strong argument against the existence of God. But that is not the human situation.

So then God, without asking humans, has to choose for them between the kinds of world in which they can live—basically either a world in which there is very little opportunity for humans to benefit or harm each other, or a world in which there is considerable opportunity. How shall he choose? There are clearly reasons for both choices. But it seems to me (just, on balance) that his choosing to create the world in which we have considerable opportunity to benefit or harm each other is to bring about a good at least as great as the evil which he thereby allows to occur. *Of course* the suffering he allows is a bad thing; and, other things being equal, to be avoided.

But having the natural possibility of causing suffering makes possible a greater good. God, in creating humans who (of logical necessity) cannot choose for themselves the kind of world into which they are to come, plausibly exhibits his goodness in making for them the heroic choice that they come into a risky world where they may have to suffer for the good of others.

NATURAL EVIL

Natural evil is not to be accounted for along the same lines as moral evil. Its main role rather, I suggest, is to make it possible for humans to have the kind of choice which the free-will defence extols, and to make available to humans specially worthwhile kinds of choice.

There are two ways in which natural evil operates to give humans those choices. First, the operation of natural laws producing evils gives humans knowledge (if they choose to seek it) of how to bring about such evils themselves. Observing you catch some disease by the operation of natural processes gives me the power either to use those processes to give that disease to other people, or through negligence to allow others to catch it, or to take measures to prevent others from catching the disease. Study of the mechanisms of nature producing various evils (and goods) opens up for humans a wide range of choice. This is the way in which in fact we learn how to bring about (good and) evil. But could not God give us the requisite knowledge (of how to bring about good or evil) which we need in order to have free and responsible choice by a less costly means? Could he not just whisper in our ears from time to time what are the different consequences of different actions of ours? Yes. But anyone who believed that an action of his would have some effect because he believed that God had told him so would see all his actions as done under the all-watchful eye of God. He would not merely believe strongly that there was a God, but would know it with real certainty. That knowledge would greatly inhibit his freedom of choice, would make it very difficult for him to choose to do evil. This is because we all have a natural inclination to wish to be thought well of by everyone, and above all by an all-good God; that we have such an inclination is a very good feature of humans, without which we would be less than human. Also, if we were directly informed of the consequences of our actions, we would be deprived of the choice whether to seek to discover what the consequences were through experiment and hard cooperative work. Knowledge would be available on tap. Natural processes alone give humans knowledge of the effects of their actions without inhibiting their freedom, and if evil is to be a possibility for them they must know how to allow it to occur.

The other way in which natural evil operates to give humans their freedom is that it makes possible certain kinds of action towards it between which agents can choose. It increases the range of significant choice. A particular natural evil, such as physical pain, gives to the sufferer a choice—whether to endure it with patience, or to bemoan his lot. His friend can choose whether to show compassion towards the sufferer, or to be callous. The pain makes possible these choices, which would not otherwise exist. There is no guarantee that our actions in response to the pain will be good ones, but the pain gives us the opportunity to perform good actions. The good or bad actions which we perform in the face of natural evil themselves provide opportunities for further choice—of good or evil stances towards the former actions. If I am patient with my suffering, you can choose whether to encourage or laugh at my patience; if I bemoan my lot, you can teach me by word and example what a good thing patience is. If you are sympathetic, I have then the opportunity to show gratitude for the sympathy; or to be so self-involved that I ignore it. If you are callous, I can choose whether to ignore this or to resent it for life. And so on. I do not think that there can be much doubt that natural evil, such as physical pain, makes available these sorts of choice. The actions which natural evil makes possible are ones which allow us to perform at our best and interact with our fellows at the deepest level.

It may, however, be suggested that adequate opportunity for these great good actions would be provided by the occurrence of moral evil without any need for suffering to be caused by natural processes.

You can show courage when threatened by a gunman, as well as when threatened by cancer; and show sympathy to those likely to be killed by gunmen as well as to those likely to die of cancer. But just imagine all the suffering of mind and body caused by disease, earthquake, and accident unpreventable by humans removed at a stroke from our society. No sickness, no bereavement in consequence of the untimely death of the young. Many of us would then have such an easy life that we simply would not have much opportunity to show courage or, indeed, manifest much in the way of great goodness at all. We need those insidious processes of decay and dissolution which money and strength cannot ward off for long to give us the opportunities, so easy otherwise to avoid, to become heroes.

God has the right to allow natural evils to occur (for the same reason as he has the right to allow moral evils to occur)—up to a limit. It would, of course, be crazy for God to multiply evils more and more in order to give endless opportunity for heroism, but to have *some* significant opportunity for real heroism and consequent character formation is a benefit for the person to whom it is given. Natural evils give to us the knowledge to make a range of choices between good and evil, and the opportunity to perform actions of especially valuable kinds.

There is, however, no reason to suppose that animals have free will. So what about their suffering? Animals had been suffering for a long time before humans appeared on this planet—just how long depends on which animals are conscious beings. The first thing to take into account here is that, while the higher animals, at any rate the vertebrates, suffer, it is most unlikely that they suffer nearly as much as humans do. Given that suffering depends directly on brain events (in turn caused by events in other parts of the body), then, since the lower animals do not suffer at all and humans suffer a lot, animals of intermediate complexity (it is reasonable to suppose) suffer only a moderate amount. So, while one does need a theodicy to account for why God allows animals to suffer, one does not need as powerful a theodicy as one does in respect of humans. One only needs reasons adequate to account for God allowing an amount of suffering much less than that of humans.

That said, there is, I believe, available for animals parts of the theodicy which I have outlined above for humans.

The good of animals, like that of humans, does not consist solely in thrills of pleasure. For animals, too, there are more worthwhile things, and in particular intentional actions, and among them serious significant intentional actions. The life of animals involves many serious significant intentional actions. Animals look for a mate, despite being tired and failing to find one. They take great trouble to build nests and feed their young, to decoy predators and explore. But all this inevitably involves pain (going on despite being tired) and danger. An animal cannot intentionally avoid forest fires, or take trouble to rescue its off-spring from forest fires, unless there exists a serious danger of getting caught in a forest fire. The action of rescuing despite danger simply cannot be done unless the danger exists—and the danger will not exist unless there is a significant natural probability of being caught in the fire. Animals do not choose freely to do such actions, but the actions are nevertheless worthwhile. It is great that animals feed their young, not just themselves; that animals explore when they know it to be dangerous; that animals save each other from predators, and so on. These are the things that give the lives of animals their value. But they do often involve some suffering to some creature.

To return to the central case of humans—the reader will agree with me to the extent to which he or she values responsibility, free choice, and being of use very much more than thrills of pleasure or absence of pain. There is no other way to get the evils of this world into the right perspective, except to reflect at length on innumerable very detailed thought experiments (in addition to actual experiences of life) in which we postulate very different sorts of worlds from our own, and then ask ourselves whether the perfect goodness of God would require him to create one of these (or no world at all) rather than our own. But I conclude with a very small thought experiment, which may help to begin this process. Suppose that you exist in another world before your birth in this one, and are given a choice as to the sort of life you are to have in this one. You are told that you are to have only a short life, maybe

of only a few minutes, although it will be an adult life in the sense that you will have the richness of sensation and belief characteristic of adults. You have a choice as to the sort of life you will have. You can have either a few minutes of very considerable pleasure, of the kind produced by some drug such as heroin, which you will experience by yourself and which will have no effects at all in the world (for example, no one else will know about it); or you can have a few minutes of considerable pain, such as the pain of childbirth, which will have (unknown to you at the time of pain) considerable good effects on others over a few years. You are told that, if you do not make the second choice, those others will never exist—and so you are under no moral obligation to make the second choice. But you seek to make the choice which will make *your* own life the best life for *you* to have led. How will you choose? The choice is, I hope, obvious. You should choose the second alternative.

For someone who remains unconvinced by my claims about the relative strengths of the good and evils involved—holding that, great though the goods are, they do not justify the evils which they involve—there is a fallback position. My arguments may have convinced you of the greatness of the goods involved sufficiently for you to allow that a perfectly good God would be justified in bringing about the evils for the sake of the good which they make possible, if and only if God also provided compensation in the form of happiness after death to the victims whose sufferings make possible the goods. . . . While believing that God does provide at any rate for many humans such life after death, I have expounded a theodicy without relying on this assumption. But I can understand someone thinking that the assumption is needed, especially when we are considering the worst evils. (This compensatory afterlife need not necessarily be the everlasting life of Heaven.)

It remains the case, however, that evil is evil, and there is a substantial price to pay for the goods of our world which it makes possible. God would not be less than perfectly good if he created instead a world without pain and suffering, and so without the particular goods which those evils make possible. Christian, Islamic, and much Jewish tradition claims that

God has created worlds of both kinds—our world, and the Heaven of the blessed. The latter is a marvellous world with a vast range of possible deep goods, but it lacks a few goods which our world contains, including the good of being able to reject the good. A generous God might well choose to give some of us the choice of rejecting the good in a world like ours before giving to those who embrace it a wonderful world in which the former possibility no longer exists.

The Moriarty Hypothesis

~

STEVEN M. CAHN

Steven M. Cahn, editor of this book, is professor of philosophy at the City University of New York Graduate Center. Among his numerous books are *Fate, Logic, and Time, Saints and Scamps: Ethics in Academia,* and *Puzzles & Perplexities: Collected Essays.*

Why does an all-powerful, all-knowing, all-good God allow evil? Theists who seek to answer this question may take comfort in firmly embracing a justification that accommodates all past, present, and future evils, however horrific. But this approach leads to a philosophical pitfall.

To see why, consider the fictional example of Sherlock Holmes and his archfiend, Professor Moriarty. Holmes believed that Moriarty was the "great malignant brain" behind crime in London, the "deep organizing power" that unified "every deviltry" into "one connected whole," the "foul spider which lurks in the centre," "never caught—never so much as suspected."[1] Now suppose Moriarty's power extended throughout the universe, so that all events (perhaps excluding acts of human freedom) were the work of one omnipotent, omniscient, omnimalevolent demon. Let us call this theory "the Moriarty hypothesis."

Does the presence of various goods refute the Moriarty hypothesis? No, for just as theism can be shown to be logically consistent with the world's most horrendous evils, so the Moriarty hypothesis can be shown to be logically consistent with the world's most wonderful goods. While evils can be viewed as logically necessary for the greater good, goods can be viewed as logically necessary for the greater evil.[2]

Assuming, then, that the Moriarty hypothesis is not obviously false and leaving aside speculation about whether a next life may bring greater goods or greater evils, do theists have any different expectations about the events of this life than do those who accept the Moriarty hypothesis?

Consider the following two assessments of the human condition:

1. "[I]s not all life pathetic and futile? . . . We reach. We grasp. And what is left in our hands at the end? A shadow. Or worse than a shadow—misery."
2. "The first entrance into life gives anguish to the new-born infant and to its wretched parent; weakness, impotence, distress attend each stage of that life, and it is at last finished in agony and horror."

Which is the viewpoint of a theist and which that of a believer in the Moriarty hypothesis? As it happens, 1 is uttered by Sherlock Holmes,[3] and 2 by the orthodox believer Demea in Part X of Hume's *Dialogues Concerning Natural Religion.* The positions appear interchangeable.

Both the theist and the believer in the Moriarty hypothesis recognize that life contains happiness as well as misery. No matter how terrible the misery, the theist may regard it as unsurprising; after all, aren't all evils, in principle, explicable? To believers in the Moriarty hypothesis, happiness may be regarded as unsurprising; after all, aren't all goods, in principle, explicable? Supporters of both positions are apt to view events that appear to conflict with their fundamental principles merely as tests of fortitude, opportunities to display strength of commitment.

If defenders of either view modified their beliefs in the light of changing circumstances, then their expectations would differ. But believers are loath to admit doubt. They admire those who stand fast in their faith, regardless of appearances.

Any seemingly contrary evidence can be considered ambiguous. St. Paul says, "we see in a mirror, dimly,"[4] and Sherlock Holmes speaks of seeking the truth "through the veil which shrouded it."[5] If events are so difficult to interpret, they provide little reason for believers to abandon deep-seated tenets. Those who vacillate are typically viewed by other members of their communities as weakhearted and faithless.

One other attempt to differentiate the expectations of the theist and the believer in the Moriarty hypothesis is to suppose that theists have reason to be more optimistic than their counterparts But this presumption is unwarranted. Recall the words from the Book of Ecclesiastes: "I accounted those who died long since more fortunate than those who are still living; and happier than either are those who have not yet come into being and have never witnessed the miseries that go on under the sun."[6] A more pessimistic view is hard to imagine.

We may be living, as the theist supposes, in the best of all possible worlds, but, if so, the best of all possible worlds contains immense torments. On the other hand, we may be living, as the believer in the Moriarty hypothesis supposes, in the worst of all possible worlds, but, if so, the worst of all possible worlds contains enormous delights. Both scenarios offer us reason to be cheerful and reason to be gloomy. Our outlook depends on our personalities, not our theology or demonology.

So, as we seek to understand life's vicissitudes, does it make any difference whether we believe in God or in the Moriarty hypothesis? Not if we hold either of these beliefs unshakeably. For the more tenaciously we cling to one of them, the less it matters which one.

NOTES

1. *The Complete Sherlock Holmes* (Garden City, NY: Doubleday & Company, n.d.), pp. 471, 496, 769. The works cited are "The Final Problem," "The Adventure of the Norwood Builder," and "The Valley of Fear."

2. See my "Cacodaemony," *Analysis* 37 (1977), pp. 69–73.

3. See "The Adventure of the Retired Colourman," p. 1113.

4. I Corinthians 13:12.

5. See "The Final Problem," p. 471.

6. Ecclesiastes 4:2,3. The translation is from *Tanakh: The Holy Scriptures* (Philadelphia: Jewish Publication Society, 1988).

The Will to Believe

WILLIAM JAMES

William James (1842–1910), who taught psychology and philosophy at Harvard University, was a founder of the philosophical view that has come to be known as "pragmatism." His most important works were his *Principles of Psychology* and *The Varieties of Religious Experience.*

I

Let us give the name of hypothesis to anything that may be proposed to our belief; and just as the electricians speak of live and dead wires, let us speak of any hypothesis as either *live* or *dead*. A live hypothesis is one which appeals as a real possibility to him to whom it is proposed. If I ask you to believe in the Mahdi, the notion makes no electric connection with your nature—it refuses to scintillate with any credibility at all. As an hypothesis it is completely dead. To an Arab, however (even if he be not one of the Mahdi's followers), the hypothesis is among the mind's possibilities: It is alive. This shows that deadness and liveness in an hypothesis are not intrinsic properties, but relations to the individual thinker. They are measured by his willingness to act. The maximum of liveness in an hypothesis means willingness to act irrevocably. Practically, that means belief; but there is some believing tendency wherever there is willingness to act at all.

Next, let us call the decision between two hypotheses an *option*. Options may be of several kinds. They may be first, *living* or *dead;* secondly, *forced* or *avoidable;* thirdly, *momentous* or *trivial;* and for our purposes we may call an option a *genuine* option when it is of the forced, living, and momentous kind.

1. A living option is one in which both hypotheses are live ones. If I say to you: "Be a theosophist or be a Mohammedan," it is probably a dead option, because for you neither hypothesis is likely to be alive. But if I say: "Be an agnostic or be a Christian," it is otherwise: trained as you are, each hypothesis makes some appeal, however small, to your belief.

2. Next, if I say to you: "Choose between going out with your umbrella or without it," I do not offer you a genuine option, for it is not forced. You can easily avoid it by not going out at all. Similarly, if I say, "Either love me or hate me," "Either call my theory true or call it false," your option is avoidable. You may remain indifferent to me, neither loving nor hating, and you may decline to offer any judgment as to my theory. But if I say, "Either accept this truth or go without it," I put on you a forced option, for there is no standing place outside of the alternative. Every dilemma based on a complete logical disjunction, with no possibility of not choosing, is an option of this forced kind.

3. Finally, if I were Dr. Nansen and proposed to you to join my North Pole expedition, your option would be momentous; for this would probably be your only similar opportunity, and your choice now would either exclude you from the North Pole sort of immortality altogether or put at least the chance of it into your hands. He who refuses to embrace a unique

William James, *The Will to Believe* (1896).

opportunity loses the prize as surely as if he tried and failed. Per contra, the option is trivial when the opportunity is not unique, when the stake is insignificant, or when the decision is reversible if it later prove unwise. Such trivial options abound in the scientific life. A chemist finds an hypothesis live enough to spend a year in its verification: he believes in it to that extent. But if his experiments prove inconclusive either way, he is quit for his loss of time, no vital harm being done.

It will facilitate our discussion if we keep all these distinctions well in mind.

II

The next matter to consider is the actual psychology of human opinion. When we look at certain facts, it seems as if our passional and volitional nature lay at the root of all our convictions. When we look at others, it seems as if they could do nothing when the intellect had once said its say. Let us take the latter facts up first.

Does it not seem preposterous on the very face of it to talk of our opinions being modifiable at will? Can our will either help or hinder our intellect in its perceptions of truth? Can we, by just willing it, believe that Abraham Lincoln's existence is a myth, and that the portraits of him in *McClure's Magazine* are all of some one else? Can we, by any effort of our will, or by any strength of wish that it were true, believe ourselves well and about when we are roaring with rheumatism in bed, or feel certain that the sum of the two one-dollar bills in our pocket must be a hundred dollars? We can *say* any of these things, but we are absolutely impotent to believe them; and of just such things is the whole fabric of the truths that we do believe in made up—matters of fact, immediate or remote, as Hume said, and relations between ideas, which are either there or not there for us if we see them so, and which if not there cannot be put there by any action of our own.

In Pascal's *Thoughts* there is a celebrated passage known in literature as Pascal's wager. In it he tries to force us into Christianity by reasoning as if our concern with truth resembled our concern with the stakes in a game of chance. Translated freely his words are these: You must either believe or not believe that God is—which will you do? Your human reason cannot say. A game is going on between you and the nature of things which at the day of judgment will bring out either heads or tails. Weigh what your gains and your losses would be if you should stake all you have on heads, or God's existence: if you win in such case, you gain eternal beatitude; if you lose, you lose nothing at all. If there were an infinity of chances, and only one for God in this wager, still you ought to stake your all on God; for though you surely risk a finite loss by this procedure, any finite loss is reasonable, even a certain one is reasonable, if there is but the possibility of infinite gain. Go, then, and take holy water, and have masses said; belief will come and stupefy your scruples. . . . Why should you not? At bottom, what have you to lose?

You probably feel that when religious faith expresses itself thus, in the language of the gaming-table, it is put to its last trumps. Surely Pascal's own personal belief in masses and holy water had far other springs; and this celebrated page of his is but an argument for others, a last desperate snatch at a weapon against the hardness of the unbelieving heart. We feel that a faith in masses and holy water adopted wilfully after such a mechanical calculation would lack the inner soul of faith's reality; and if we were ourselves in the place of the Deity, we should probably take particular pleasure in cutting off believers of this pattern from their infinite reward. It is evident that unless there be some preexisting tendency to believe in masses and holy water, the option offered to the will by Pascal is not a living option. Certainly no Turk ever took to masses and holy water on its account; and even to us Protestants these means of salvation seem such foregone impossibilities that Pascal's logic, invoked for them specifically, leaves us unmoved. As well might the Mahdi write to us, saying, "I am the Expected One whom God has created in his effulgence. You shall be infinitely happy if you confess me; otherwise you shall be cut off from the light of the sun. Weigh, then, your infinite gain if I am genuine against your finite sacrifice if I am not!" His logic would be that of Pascal; but he would vainly use it on us, for the hypothesis he offers us is dead. No tendency to act on it exists in us to any degree.

The talk of believing by our volition seems, then, from one point of view, simply silly. From another point of view it is worse than silly, it is vile. When one turns to the magnificent edifice of the physical sciences, and sees how it was reared; what thousands of disinterested moral lives of men lie buried in its mere foundations; what patience and postponement, what choking down of preference, what submission to the icy laws of outer fact are wrought into its very stones and mortar; how absolutely impersonal it stands in its vast augustness—then how besotted and contemptible seems every little sentimentalist who comes blowing his voluntary smoke-wreaths, and pretending to decide things from out of his private dream! Can we wonder if those bred in the rugged and manly school of science should feel like spewing such subjectivism out of their mouths? The whole system of loyalties which grow up in the schools of science go dead against its toleration; so that it is only natural that those who have caught the scientific fever should pass over to the opposite extreme, and write sometimes as if the incorruptibly truthful intellect ought positively to prefer bitterness and unacceptableness to the heart in its cup.

> It fortifies my soul to know
> That though I perish, Truth is so

sings Clough, while Huxley exclaims: "My only consolation lies in the reflection that, however bad our posterity may become, so far as they hold by the plain rule of not pretending to believe what they have no reason to believe, because it may be to their advantage so to pretend [the word 'pretend' is surely here redundant], they will not have reached the lowest depth of immorality." And that delicious enfant terrible Clifford writes: "Belief is desecrated when given to unproved and unquestioned statements for the solace and private pleasure of the believer. . . . Whoso would deserve well of his fellows in this matter will guard the purity of his belief with a very fanaticism of jealous care, lest at any time it should rest on an unworthy object, and catch a stain which can never be wiped away. . . . If [a] belief has been accepted on insufficient evidence [even though the belief be true, as Clifford on the same page explains] the pleasure is

a stolen one. . . . It is sinful because it is stolen in defiance of our duty to mankind. That duty is to guard ourselves from such beliefs as from a pestilence which may shortly master our own body and then spread to the rest of the town. . . . It is wrong always, everywhere, and for every one, to believe anything upon insufficient evidence."

III

All this strikes one as healthy, even when expressed, as by Clifford, with somewhat too much of robustious pathos in the voice. Free will and simple wishing do seem, in the matter of our credences, to be only fifth wheels to the coach. Yet if any one should thereupon assume that intellectual insight is what remains after wish and will and sentimental preference have taken wing, or that pure reason is what then settles our opinions, he would fly quite as directly in the teeth of the facts.

It is only our already dead hypotheses that our willing nature is unable to bring to life again. But what has made them dead for us is for the most part a previous action of our willing nature of an antagonistic kind. When I say "willing nature," I do not mean only such deliberate volitions as may have set up habits of belief that we cannot now escape from— I mean all such factors of belief as fear and hope, prejudice and passion, imitation and partisanship, the circumpressure of our caste and set. As a matter of fact we find ourselves believing, we hardly know how or why. Mr. Balfour gives the name of "authority" to all those influences, born of the intellectual climate, that make hypotheses possible or impossible for us, alive or dead. Here in this room, we all of us believe in molecules and the conservation of energy, in democracy and necessary progress, in Protestant Christianity and the duty of fighting for "the doctrine of the immortal Monroe," all for no reasons worthy of the name. We see into these matters with no more inner clearness, and probably with much less, than any disbeliever in them might possess. His unconventionality would probably have some grounds to show for its conclusions; but for us, not insight, but the *prestige* of the opinions, is what makes the spark shoot from them and light up our sleeping magazines of faith. Our reason is quite satisfied, in nine hundred and ninety-nine cases out of every thousand of us, if it can find a few arguments that will do to recite in case our credulity is criticized by some one else. Our faith is faith in some one else's faith, and in the greatest matters this is the most the case. . . .

Evidently, then, our non-intellectual nature does influence our convictions. There are passional tendencies and volitions which run before and others which come after belief, and it is only the latter that are too late for the fair; and they are not too late when the previous passional work has been already in their own direction. Pascal's argument, instead of being powerless, then seems a regular clincher, and is the last stroke needed to make our faith in masses and holy water complete. The state of things is evidently far from simple; and pure insight and logic, whatever they might do ideally, are not the only things that really do produce our creeds.

IV

Our next duty, having recognized this mixed-up state of affairs, is to ask whether it be simply reprehensible and pathological, or whether, on the contrary, we must treat it as a normal element in making up our minds. The thesis I defend is, briefly stated, this: *Our passional nature not only lawfully may, but must, decide an option between propositions, whenever it is a genuine option that cannot by its nature be decided on intellectual grounds; for to say, under such circumstances, "Do not decide, but leave the question open," is itself a passional decision—just like deciding yes or no—and is attended with the same risk of losing the truth. . . .*

VII

One more point, small but important, and our preliminaries are done. There are two ways of looking at our duty in the matter of opinion—ways entirely different, and yet ways about whose difference the theory of knowledge seems hitherto to have shown very little concern. *We must know the truth;* and *we must avoid error*—these are our first and great commandments as would-be knowers; but they are not two ways of stating an identical commandment, they are two separable laws. Although it may indeed happen that when we believe the truth A, we escape as an incidental consequence from believing the falsehood B, it hardly ever happens that by merely disbelieving B we necessarily believe A. We may in escaping B fall into believing other falsehoods, C or D, just as bad as B; or we may escape B by not believing anything at all, not even A.

Believe truth! Shun error!—these, we see, are two materially different laws; and by choosing between them we may end by coloring differently our whole intellectual life. We may regard the chase for truth as paramount, and the avoidance of error as secondary; or we may, on the other hand, treat the avoidance of error as more imperative, and let truth take its chance. Clifford, in the instructive passage which I have quoted, exhorts us to the latter course. Believe nothing, he tells us, keep your mind in suspense forever, rather than by closing it on insufficient evidence incur the awful risk of believing lies. You, on the other hand, may think that the risk of being in error is a very small matter when compared with the blessings of real knowledge, and be ready to be duped many times in your investigation rather than postpone indefinitely the chance of guessing true. I myself find it impossible to go with Clifford. We must remember that these feelings of our duty about either truth or error are in any case only expressions of our passional life. Biologically considered, our minds are as ready to grind out falsehood as veracity, and he who says, "Better go without belief forever than believe a lie!" merely shows his own preponderant private horror of becoming a dupe. He may be critical of many of his desires and fears, but this fear he slavishly obeys. He cannot imagine any one questioning its binding force. For my own part, I have also a horror of being duped; but I can believe that worse things than being duped may happen to a man in this world: so Clifford's exhortation has to my ears a thoroughly fantastic sound. It is like a general informing his soldiers that it is better to keep out of battle forever than to risk a single wound. Not so are victories either over enemies or over nature gained. Our errors are surely not such awfully solemn things. In a world where we are so certain to incur them in spite of all our caution, a certain lightness of heart seems healthier than this excessive nervousness on their behalf. At any rate, it seems the fittest thing for the empiricist philosopher.

VIII

And now, after all this introduction, let us go straight at our question. I have said, and now repeat it, that not only as a matter of fact do we find our passional nature influencing us in our opinions, but that there are some options between opinions in which this influence must be regarded both as an inevitable and as a lawful determinant of our choice.

I fear here that some of you my hearers will begin to scent danger, and lend an inhospitable ear. Two first steps of passion you have indeed had to admit as necessary—we must think so as to avoid dupery, and we must think so as to gain truth; but the surest path to those ideal consummations, you will probably consider, is from now onwards to take no further passional step.

Well, of course, I agree as far as the facts will allow. Wherever the option between losing truth and gaining it is not momentous, we can throw the chance of *gaining truth* away, and at any rate save ourselves from any chance of *believing falsehood,* by not making up our minds at all till objective evidence has come. In scientific questions, this is almost always the case; and even in human affairs in general, the need of acting is seldom so urgent that a false belief to act on is better than no belief at all. Law courts, indeed, have to decide on the best evidence attainable for the moment, because a judge's duty is to make law as well as to ascertain it, and (as a learned judge once said to me) few cases are worth spending much time over: the great thing is to have them decided on *any* acceptable principle, and got out of the way. But in our dealings with objective nature we obviously are recorders, not makers, of the truth; and decisions for the mere sake of deciding promptly and getting on to the next business would be wholly out of place. Throughout the breadth of physical nature facts are what they are quite independently of us, and seldom is there any such hurry about them that the risks of

being duped by believing a premature theory need be faced. The questions here are always trivial options, the hypotheses are hardly living (at any rate not living for us spectators), the choice between believing truth or falsehood is seldom forced. The attitude of sceptical balance is therefore the absolutely wise one if we would escape mistakes. What difference, indeed, does it make to most of us whether we have or have not a theory of the Röntgen rays, whether we believe or not in mind-stuff, or have a conviction about the causality of conscious states? It makes no difference. Such options are not forced on us. On every account it is better not to make them, but still keep weighing reasons *pro et contra* with an indifferent hand.

I speak, of course, here of the purely judging mind. For purposes of discovery such indifference is to be less highly recommended, and science would be far less advanced than she is if the passionate desires of individuals to get their own faiths confirmed had been kept out of the game. See for example the sagacity which Spencer and Weismann now display. On the other hand, if you want an absolute duffer in an investigation, you must, after all, take the man who has no interest whatever in its results: he is the warranted incapable, the positive fool. The most useful investigator, because the most sensitive observer, is always he whose eager interest in one side of the question is balanced by an equally keen nervousness lest he become deceived.[1] Science has organized this nervousness into a regular *technique,* her so-called method of verification; and she has fallen so deeply in love with the method that one may even say she has ceased to care for truth by itself at all. It is only truth as technically verified that interests her. The truth of truths might come in merely affirmative form, and she would decline to touch it. Such truth as that, she might repeat with Clifford, would be stolen in defiance of her duty to mankind. Human passions, however, are stronger than technical rules. *"Le coeur a ses raisons,"* as Pascal says, *"que la raison ne connait pas"*[2]; and however indifferent to all but the bare rules of the game the umpire, the abstract intellect, may be, the concrete players who furnish him the materials to judge of are usually, each one of them, in love with some pet "live hypothesis" of his own. Let us agree, however, that wherever there is no forced option, the dispassionately judicial intellect with no pet hypothesis, saving us, as it does, from dupery at any rate, ought to be our ideal.

The question next arises: Are there not somewhere forced options in our speculative questions, and can we (as men who may be interested at least as much in positively gaining truth as in merely escaping dupery) always wait with impunity till the coercive evidence shall have arrived? It seems *a priori* improbable that the truth should be so nicely adjusted to our needs and powers as that. In the great boardinghouse of nature, the cakes and the butter and the syrup seldom come out so even and leave the plates so clean. Indeed, we should view them with scientific suspicion if they did.

IX

Moral questions immediately present themselves as questions whose solution cannot wait for sensible proof. A moral question is a question not of what sensibly exists, but of what is good, or would be good if it did exist. Science can tell us what exists; but to compare the *worths,* both of what exists and of what does not exist, we must consult not science, but what Pascal calls our heart. . . .

Turn now from these wide questions of good to a certain class of questions of fact, questions concerning personal relations, states of mind between one man and another. *Do you like me or not?*—for example. Whether you do or not depends, in countless instances, on whether I meet you halfway, am willing to assume that you must like me, and show you trust and expectation. The previous faith on my part in your liking's existence is in such cases what makes your liking come. But if I stand aloof, and refuse to budge an inch until I have objective evidence, until you shall have done something apt, as the absolutists say, *ad extorquendum assensum meum,* ten to one your liking never comes. How many women's hearts are vanquished by the mere sanguine insistence of some man that they *must* love him! He will not consent to the hypothesis that they cannot. The desire for a certain kind of truth here brings about that special truth's existence; and so it is in innumerable cases of

other sorts. . . . *And where faith in a fact can help create the fact,* that would be an insane logic which should say that faith running ahead of scientific evidence is the "lowest kind of immorality" into which a thinking being can fall. Yet such is the logic by which our scientific absolutists pretend to regulate our lives!

X

In truths dependent on our personal action, then, faith based on desire is certainly a lawful and possibly an indispensable thing.

But now, it will be said, these are all childish human cases, and have nothing to do with great cosmical matters, like the question of religious faith. Let us then pass on to that. Religions differ so much in their accidents that in discussing the religious question we must make it very generic and broad. What then do we now mean by the religious hypothesis? Science says things are; morality says some things are better than other things; and religion says essentially two things.

First, she says that the best things are the more eternal things, the overlapping things, the things in the universe that throw the last stone, so to speak, and say the final word. "Perfection is eternal"—this phrase of Charles Secrétan seems a good way of putting this first affirmation of religion, an affirmation which obviously cannot yet be verified scientifically at all.

The second affirmation of religion is that we are better off even now if we believe her first affirmation to be true.

Now, let us consider what the logical elements of this situation are *in case the religious hypothesis in both its branches be really true.* (Of course, we must admit that possibility at the outset. If we are to discuss the question at all, it must involve a living option. If for any of you religion be a hypothesis that cannot, by any living possibility, be true, then you need go no farther. I speak to the "saving remnant" along.) So proceeding, we see, first, that religion offers itself as a *momentous* option. We are supposed to gain, even now, by our belief, and to lose by our non-belief, a certain vital good. Secondly, religion is a *forced* option, so far as that good goes. We cannot escape the issue by remaining sceptical and waiting for more light, because, although we do avoid error in that way *if religion be untrue,* we lose the good, *if it be true,* just as certainly as if we positively chose to disbelieve. It is as if a man should hesitate indefinitely to ask a certain woman to marry him because he was not perfectly sure that she would prove an angel after he brought her home. Would he not cut himself off from that particular angel-possibility as decisively as if he went and married some one else? Scepticism, then, is not avoidance of option; it is option of a certain particular kind of risk. *Better risk loss of truth than chance of error*—that is your faith-vetoer's exact position. He is actively playing his stake as much as the believer is; he is backing the field against the religious hypothesis, just as the believer is backing the religious hypothesis against the field. To preach scepticism to us as a duty until "sufficient evidence" for religion be found, is tantamount therefore to telling us, when in presence of the religious hypothesis, that to yield to our fear of its being error is wiser and better than to yield to our hope that it may be true. It is not intellect against all passions, then; it is only intellect with one passion laying down its law. And by what, forsooth, is the supreme wisdom of this passion warranted? Dupery for dupery, what proof is there that dupery through hope is so much worse than dupery through fear? I, for one, can see no proof; and I simply refuse obedience to the scientist's command to imitate his kind of option, in a case where my own stake is important enough to give me the right to choose my own form of risk. If religion be true and the evidence for it be still insufficient, I do not wish, by putting your extinguisher upon my nature (which feels to me as if it had after all some business in this matter), to forfeit my sole chance in life of getting upon the winning side—that chance depending, of course, on my willingness to run the risk of acting as if my passional need of taking the world religiously might be prophetic and right.

All this is on the supposition that it really may be prophetic and right, and that, even to us who are discussing the matter, religion is a live hypothesis which may be true. Now, to most of us religion comes in a still further way that makes a veto on our active faith even more illogical. The more perfect and more eternal aspect of the universe is represented in our religions as having personal form. The universe is no longer a mere *It* to us, but a *Thou,* if we are religious; and any relation that may be possible from person to person might be possible here. For instance, although in one sense we are passive portions of the universe, in another we show a curious autonomy, as if we were small active centers on our own account. We feel, too, as if the appeal of religion to us were made to our own active goodwill, as if evidence might be forever withheld from us unless we met the hypothesis halfway to take a trivial illustration: just as a man who in a company of gentlemen made no advances, asked a warrant for every concession, and believed no one's word without proof, would cut himself off by such churlishness from all the social rewards that a more trusting spirit would earn—so here, one who should shut himself up in snarling logicality and try to make the gods extort his recognition willy-nilly, or not get it at all, might cut himself off forever from his only opportunity of making the gods' acquaintance. This feeling, forced on us we know not whence that by obstinately believing that there are gods (although not to do so would be so easy both for our logic and our life) we are doing the universe the deepest service we can, seems part of the living essence of the religious hypothesis. If the hypothesis *were* true in all its parts, including this one, then pure intellectualism, with its veto on our making willing advances, would be an absurdity; and some participation of our sympathetic nature would be logically required. I therefore, for one, cannot see my way to accepting the agnostic rules for truth-seeking, or wilfully agree to keep my willing nature out of the game. I cannot do so for this plain reason, that *a rule of thinking which would absolutely prevent me from acknowledging certain kinds of truth if those kinds of truth were really there, would be an irrational rule.* That for me is the long and short of the formal logic of the situation, no matter what the kinds of truth might materially be.

I confess I do not see how this logic can be escaped. But sad experience makes me fear that some of you may still shrink from radically saying with me, *in abstracto,* that we have the right to believe at our own risk any hypothesis that is live enough to tempt our will. I suspect, however, that if this is so, it is because you have got away from the abstract logical point of view altogether, and are thinking (perhaps without realizing it) of some particular religious hypothesis which for you is dead. The freedom to "believe what we will" you apply to the case of some patent superstition; and the faith you think of is the faith defined by the schoolboy when he said, "Faith is when you believe something that you know ain't true." I can only repeat that this is misapprehension. *In concreto,* the freedom to believe can only cover living options which the intellect of the individual cannot by itself resolve; and living options never seem absurdities to him who has them to consider. When I look at the religious question as it really puts itself to concrete men, and when I think of all the possibilities which both practically and theoretically it involves, then this command that we shall put a stopper on our heart, instincts, and courage, and *wait*—acting of course meanwhile more or less as if religion were *not* true[3]—till doomsday, or till such time as our intellect and senses working together may have raked in evidence enough—this command, I say, seems to me the queerest idol ever manufactured in the philosophic cave. Were we scholastic absolutists, there might be more excuse. If we had an infallible intellect with its objective certitudes, we might feel ourselves disloyal to such a perfect organ of knowledge in not trusting to it exclusively, in not waiting for its releasing word. But if we are empiricists, if we believe that no bell in us

tolls to let us know for certain when truth is in our grasp, then it seems a piece of idle fantasticality to preach so solemnly our duty of waiting for the bell. Indeed we *may* wait if we will—I hope you do not think that I am denying that—but if we do so, we do so at our peril as much as if we believed. In either case we *act,* taking our life in our hands.

NOTES

1. Compare Wilfrid Ward's Essay "The Wish to Believe," in his *Witnesses to the Unseen* (Macmillan & Co., 1893).

2. "The heart has its reasons which reason does not know."

3. Since belief is measured by action, he who forbids us to believe religion to be true, necessarily also forbids us to act as we should if we did believe it to be true. The whole defence of religious faith hinges upon action. If the action required or inspired by the religious hypothesis is in no way different from that dictated by the naturalistic hypothesis, then religious faith is a pure superfluity, better pruned away, and controversy about its legitimacy is a piece of idle trifling, unworthy of serious minds. I myself believe, of course, that the religious hypothesis gives to the world an expression which specifically determines our reactions, and makes them in a large part unlike what they might be on a purely naturalistic scheme of belief.

William James and the Will to Believe

MICHAEL MARTIN

Michael Martin is professor of philosophy at Boston University.

One important thing to notice about James's argument is his subjective and relativistic definition of a live option. For James a live option to person P is simply one that appeals to P as a real possibility. But what appeals to a person as a real possibility may have nothing to do with what the evidence indicates and may be completely irrational. Indeed, certain options that appeal to a person as real possibilities may in fact be impossible, while ones that do not appeal as real possibilities may in the light of the evidence be at least as plausible as, or even more plausible than, the ones the person considers to be real possibilities. For example, granted that Buddhism would not appeal to an average American as a real possibility while Christianity would, it is hard to see why this is a reason for excluding Buddhism from serious consideration when this person is choosing a religion. Perhaps objective investigation would show that Christianity rests on historically dubious evidence and an incoherent ontology and that Buddhism does not suffer from these problems.

I suggest that James should have said that a live option is one that is not improbable in the light of the available evidence. Let us understand "live option" in this new sense, and let us assume with James that in matters of religion, options are live, forced, momentous, and not capable of intellectual resolution. On these assumptions there may be many more genuine options than James ever imagined. For example, Buddhism, Christianity, Islam, Judaism, and Hinduism would become genuine options for every person living in this country. Not only would there be the genuine options of the various living world religions but there would also be the genuine options of various concepts of gods or God within those religions. How is one to choose between them? By hypothesis epistemic arguments cannot help, and it is unclear how beneficial reasons can give a clear answer. How can one tell if one would be better off in this life believing that Christianity or Buddhism is true? And if one makes a choice, which form of Christianity or Buddhism is justified on beneficial grounds?

The second thing to notice is that although James uses rather specific examples (Christianity vs. agnosticism) to illustrate what a live option in the choice of religious hypothesis is, his actual statement of the religious hypothesis is extremely vague and unclear. Recall that the first part of James's religious hypothesis says that "the best things are the more eternal things, the overlapping things, the things in the universe that throw the last stone, so to speak, and say the final word," and the second part says that "we are better off even now if we believe" the first part of the hypothesis. This statement has prompted one commentator on James's work to remark:

"Best" is vague, and "more eternal" comes close to being nonsense: either something is eternal or it is not. To add that the best things are "the overlapping things" and "throw the last stone, so to speak" only adds further mystification. Is James referring to God but embarrassed to say so?

In any case, taken at their face value both parts of the religious hypothesis are normative statements. They seem to have no obvious metaphysical implication. The first part says, in effect, for any X and for any Y, if X is eternal and Y is not, X is better than Y. Let us call this statement B. The second part has the form, it is better to believe B than not to. But unless more is said, there is surely little warrant for either judgment. Mathematical entities such as numbers, at least on a Platonic view of such entities, are eternal. They are timeless and unchanging. But why are numbers better than all noneternal things? One would have thought it at least prima facie debatable that the set of all primes was better than a millennium of world peace and love.

If we give James's religious hypothesis a more specific religious meaning, the first part can perhaps be stated as follows: For any X and for any Y, if X is a perfect and eternal being and Y is neither, X is better than Y. The second part of the hypothesis is that it is better to believe this than not to. On one interpretation the first part of the hypothesis is true by definition. A perfect being is surely better—that is, more perfect—than a less than perfect being. But on other interpretations the religious hypothesis is not true. The expression "is better" is usually used contextually. Something is better for some purposes but not for others. For example, a hammer is better than a pencil for driving a nail, but not for signing one's name. Surely, in this contextual sense, a perfect and eternal being is not always better than some noneternal and less than perfect being. For example, a hammer is better than God if one wants to drive a nail.

But let us concentrate on the sense of "better" that would make the first part of the religious hypothesis true by definition. Given this understanding of the first part of the religious hypothesis, atheists could accept the second part. Atheists could well admit that it is better to believe that an eternal and perfect being is more perfect than a noneternal and nonperfect being, since such a statement is trivially true and it is better to believe that trivially true statements are true than to believe that they are false. It does not follow from this admission that this being actually exists.

However, let us give the religious hypothesis a more metaphysical interpretation. Despite what his words suggest, let us understand James to mean that the religious hypothesis asserts two things:

(1) There exists a perfect and eternal being: God.
(2) It is better in this life to believe that (1) than not to.

One could approach the justification of (2) in a spirit similar to that of Pascal's wager. One might argue that if God exists, then believing in God will result in a better life in this world than not believing. If God does not exist, then believing in God will still bring about a better life in this world than not believing. So in any case it is better to believe in God. Why would one be better off in this life by believing in God than by not believing in God if God exists? Two reasons come to mind. First, if God exists and one believes in Him, He may tend to make one's life better than if one does not believe. On this intervention interpretation, God intervenes in the natural course of events and rewards the faithful. Second, it may just be true, given human nature and the way society is structured, that theists tend to live happier, healthier, and more rewarding lives than nontheists. Let us call this the natural law interpretation. On either the intervention interpretation or the natural law interpretation, belief in God, if God exists, would be preferable. Let us assume further that if God did not exist, given human nature and the way society is structured, theists would tend to live happier, healthier, and more rewarding lives than nontheists. The situation, then, would look like:

	God exists	God does not exist
Believe in God	X_1	X_2
Do not believe in God	Y_1	Y_2

where X_1, X_2, Y_1, and Y_2 are finite values found in this life, such that $X_1 > Y_1$ and $X_2 > Y_2$.

The trouble with James's argument, interpreted in this way, is that there is little empirical reason to suppose that theists are happier and healthier, lead more rewarding lives, and so on than nontheists. It certainly seems to be true that nontheists are capable of living lives with as great an amount of happiness, self-fulfillment, and the like as theists. Nor does it seem to be true that if one is a theist it is more likely that one will achieve happiness and so on in this life than if one is a nontheist. Indeed, an argument could be given for just the opposite conclusion. For example, suppose one picked two children at random, one from a nontheistic family and one from a theistic family in the United States. Which one is more likely to live a healthy and productive life while growing up? From what we know of religious belief and its relation to education, health care, social class, economic level, and the like, the best guess is that the child from the theistic family is more likely to be ill, to have less education, and to end up in some unsatisfying job than the child from a family of nonbelievers. Insofar as health and happiness and a satisfying job are correlated (which seems likely), the child from the nonreligious family is likely to be happier than the child from the religious family as an adult. Further, if we consider two children picked at random from the world at large and not just from the United States, one from a religious family and one from a nonreligious family, the chances surely would improve that the child from a religious family will be worse off than the child from a nonreligious family. The reason is simple. Poverty, ignorance, and sickness are more prevalent in the world at large than in the United States, and we know that religious belief is associated with poverty and lack of education, as well as that poverty and ignorance are associated with disease. Thus one might say that if one had a choice and was interested in staying healthy, getting an education, and getting a challenging job, one should choose not to be born into a religious family.

It still might be maintained that, although theists are less likely to live productive and healthy lives than nontheists, theists are capable of a higher quality of happiness. For example, theists are capable of achieving a state of spiritual tranquility and serenity while nontheists are not and this state is qualitatively better than any state of happiness that a nontheist can reach. In reply, the following points can be made. First, it is not clear that tranquility and serenity are better than, say, the satisfaction of a challenging job. Why should we consider tranquility and serenity a higher sort of happiness? Recall that tranquility and serenity of a sort can be achieved by means of drugs and frontal lobotomies, yet such a state is not particularly desirable. What makes the tranquility and serenity that are achieved by religious means so valuable? Second, even if tranquility and serenity achieved through spiritual insights are so valuable, it is not clear that nontheists cannot achieve them. Surely, this state of mind is not uniquely associated with belief in God. Certain sects of Buddhism, on most interpretations a nontheistic religion, aim to achieve this state of mind, and transcendental meditation claims great success in achieving tranquility and serenity although it makes no assumption about God in the theistic sense.

Let us admit for the sake of argument that theists are capable of achieving a higher degree of happiness, self-fulfillment, and the like than nontheists. It is still not clear that theism would be the best choice. For despite James's neglect of probabilities, they must be taken into account. Although a theist may be able to achieve a higher degree of happiness, and so on, in this life than a nontheist can, the probability of his or her doing so may be lower than that of a nontheist's achieving a more modest degree of happiness. If we compute the expected value, nontheists may be better off. For example, suppose the probability p_1 of achieving the sort of life that theists are capable of is 0.4 while the probability of achieving the sort of life nontheists are capable of is 0.7. Suppose further that the value of happiness that a theist can achieve is 500 while the value of happiness a nontheist can achieve is 300. Then the expected value EV of theistic belief is $0.4 \times 500 = 200$ while the EV of nontheistic belief is $0.7 \times 300 = 210$. Thus with these values and probabilities, nontheism would still be preferable to theism despite the assumption that a higher level of happiness is associated with theism. However, we have seen no reason to suppose that this assumption is true.

Further, as I argued above against Pascal's wager, there are certain values associated with nonbelief that have nothing to do with happiness and the like. Once we bring these values into the computation of EV, we seem to tip the scales toward nonbelief even if belief is associated with more happiness. The possibility of

less happiness and the like may be offset by these other values. As pointed out above, nonbelief puts responsibility for humanity's problems on humans. There is a certain value in self-reliance that may go far in outweighing the value of any happiness and the like that belief in God may produce. Thus it is by no means clear that we are better off even now in believing that God exists. Indeed, nonbelief seems preferable when all the relevant values are taken into account.

Moreover, as we have seen, even on a generous interpretation of James, he seems to suppose that believing that the religious hypothesis is true involves accepting some undifferentiated theism. But as many religious scholars have noted, one does not have religious belief in the abstract; it is always relative to a certain religious tradition. For example, one does not believe in God per se but rather in the God of the Catholic Church or of Islam. Belief in these different Gods leads to very different ways of life, since different ritual, ethical codes, and religious practices are associated with different concepts of God in different religions. Oddly enough, when James discusses live and dead religious options he seems to be aware of the nature of religious belief, but he forgets this when he specifies the content of the religious hypothesis. Furthermore, there are religions in which belief in God, as we understand it, has no important role.

What would be the effect of bringing specific religious beliefs into James's scheme? For one thing, it would complicate the question of whether it would be better to believe the religious hypothesis even now. For there would not be a single religious hypothesis. The question would become whether it would be better even now to embrace religion R_1 or R_2 or R_3 and so on or to embrace none. There would be no a priori reason to suppose that in terms of conduciveness to happiness, health, or whatever, the preferred religion would be theistic or that, on the basis of such values, would be preferred to no religion at all.

So far we have not considered James's claim that there is an epistemological advantage in religious belief. Recall that James can be interpreted as saying at one point that the verification of God's existence in one's experience is facilitated by belief in God. Does this provide a beneficial reason to believe in God?

To see that it is not obvious that it does, recall first that this would be simply one advantage that would have to be weighed against possible disadvantages. Second, on a more plausible conception of live option, any option is live if it is not improbable in the light of the evidence. Therefore, there are surely live religious options where religious belief would not have this epistemological advantage and, indeed, where it would have a disadvantage. Consider a god who reveals himself to his believers less often than to people who are skeptical. After all, he might reason, his followers do not need convincing, whereas skeptics do. Belief in such a god would have a decided epistemological disadvantage. Further, there does not seem to be any more epistemic reason to believe in this god than in the sort of god that James has in mind. Indeed, James's God seems vindictive and ungenerous to withhold evidence from skeptics who may simply be more cautious than believers are. Why should going beyond what the evidence indicates be rewarded even when the reward is new evidence that vindicates the incautious attitude?

In addition to these problems, religious experience varies from one religious tradition to another, and it is often in conflict. If belief in the god of religion R_1 results in the confirmation of R_1, then would belief in the god of religion R_2 result in the confirmation of R_2? If so, since R_1 and R_2 may be incompatible with one another, beliefs in different gods may result in the confirmation of incompatible hypotheses.

Finally, James talks as if believing in God and seeing whether the hypothesis that God exists is confirmed in one's experience is like an experiment. But his procedure lacks an essential element of standard experimental procedure: he does not seem to allow for the *disconfirmation* of the hypothesis by the results of the experiment. Suppose one believes in some god and yet no evidence of his existence is revealed in one's experience. James does not entertain the possibility that this failure would count against the hypothesis that this god exists.

The Hiddenness of God

ROBERT McKIM

Robert McKim is associate professor in the Department of Philosophy and the Program for the Study of Religion at the University of Illinois at Urbana-Champaign.

THE HIDDEN EMPEROR

Once upon a time, in a faraway and geographically isolated land, there was a small community that had lived without contact with other communities for so long that the very memory that there were other peoples had been lost almost entirely. Only a few of the elders could recall from their childhood the stories that used to be told of visitors from afar, of distant peoples and communities, of powerful princes and lords, and of their vast empires. Some of the very oldest people with the best memories could recall that back in the old days there were some who said (or was it that they remembered hearing reports about its having been said?—it was so long ago and so hard to tell) that their territory was actually itself part of one of those great empires, and one that was ruled over by a great and good emperor. But these stories had not been told for so long that even the old people had difficulty remembering them, and the young were downright skeptical.

And then one day there arrived an outsider who claimed to be an emissary and who bore astonishing news. He declared that some of the old stories were true. He said that the small, isolated community was indeed part of a great empire, an empire that stretched farther than anyone could have imagined. And—more astonishing still—the ruler of all this, the emissary said, pointing to the familiar hillsides and fields, to the rude dwellings and away to the horizon in all directions, is a great and wise emperor who deserves loyalty and obedience from all his subjects. And that includes you, said the visitor. And—could it be yet more astonishing?—the emperor is generally known to his subjects throughout the rest of the empire as the "Hidden Emperor," for he never lets himself be seen clearly by any of his subjects. Not even his closest, most loyal, and most devoted servants are sure exactly what he looks like. But it is widely believed that he travels incognito throughout the empire, for he has various remarkable powers that make this possible, including the power to make himself invisible, the power to travel from place to place with great speed, and even the power to understand what people are thinking. Indeed, *so* great are his powers in these respects, said the visitor, that it is hardly an exaggeration to say that he is always present throughout the entire empire.

Never had anything quite like this been heard. Mouths were agape, eyes were wide in astonishment. What are we to do, what does the emperor want from us and what are we to expect from him? people asked. "He wants your loyalty, trust, and obedience, and he offers protection and help in time of trouble," replied the emissary.

At this point a man in the crowd, a tallish bearded man with a puzzled expression, and of the sort that is inclined to twiddle with his beard in an irritating way, replied as follows. "But why," he asked—and the emissary knew what was coming, for he had been through this many times and knew that in every community there is a trouble-maker or two and that beard twiddling and a puzzled expression are among the best indicators that trouble is brewing—"why does the emperor have to be hidden? Why can't we see the emperor for ourselves? I know that it is not my place to ask"—a familiar line to the seasoned emissary, who has heard it all before and can recognize false modesty at a glance—"but why couldn't the emperor's existence and presence be as clear as *your* presence and existence? And"—now for the coup de grâce, thought the emissary, the sign that we are contending here with a *serious* thinker—"if it is important for the emperor to be hidden, why are you here informing us about him?"

After the tall bearded man had spoken, there was silence for a few minutes. The fact was that no one quite knew what would happen next, or what it was proper to say to the emissary. Had the bearded man gone too far? Had he spoken improperly? Would he be reprimanded or punished? Would they all be reprimanded or punished? Should he be silenced?

Then an old woman, known for her wisdom and insight, and of that generation among whom belief in the great emperor had not entirely been lost, spoke up. "I, for one, think that things are much better this way. As long as the emperor, and may he and his blessed relatives live for ever," she added, with a glance at the emissary, "as long as the emperor is hidden, we have a type of freedom that would otherwise be unavailable to us. We are free to decide whether or not to believe that there is an emperor. If the facts of the matter were clear to us, and it were just plain obvious that the emperor exists, belief would be forced on us. As long as the facts are unclear, we are in a position to exercise control over what we think. And even though our esteemed visitor has come to explain the situation to us, we are still in a position to decide whether or not to believe what he says."

At this the bearded man became downright exasperated, saying, "Listen here. What is so great about being able to make up your mind in conditions in which the facts are unclear? Surely if the facts are unclear, we ought simply to believe that the facts are unclear. It's absurd to suggest that there is something especially admirable or good about deciding that the emperor exists under circumstances in which it is unclear whether the emperor exists. Do you think that it would also be good for us to be able to choose whether or not to believe, say, that two plus two equals four in circumstances in which *that* is not clear, or for us to be able to choose what to believe about who our parents are in circumstances in which *that* is not clear?"

"This may seem absurd to you," interjected the woman, "since you are the sort of man who likes to strut around as if you had all the answers to life's questions even though nobody else has quite noticed, but what you have to understand is that this arrangement has the great advantage of permitting our willingness to acknowledge our status as subservient underlings in the emperor's realm to play a role in determining whether or not we believe that the emperor exists."

"And I will tell you," said the woman, warming to her theme and enjoying the attention of the crowd, and what she took to be the approving look of the visiting emissary, "I will tell you about another benefit of our current situation. The fact that we do not know what the emperor looks like permits him to come among us, looking like one of us. Long ago, when I was a little girl, it used to be said that when you entertain a stranger, you should remember that you might be entertaining the emperor. In fact people used to say, 'Every poor stranger is the emperor.' I don't suppose that they really meant it, but you can see what they had in mind. And there was another saying, too, now that I remember it. We used to say, when we wished to show respect for someone, that 'You are He.' Of course, if you knew that a visitor in your house really was the emperor, you would be quite dazed and overwhelmed, and even ashamed by how little you had to offer such a guest."

"Damn it all," said the man with the puzzled look, "this is all nonsense. If the emperor wanted us to believe in him, he would make his existence apparent to us. Don't listen to that old bag. It's as simple as this. If the emperor existed, he would want us to know him and to know about him. If so, he would make his presence apparent to us. He does not do so even though he could do so. The only sensible conclusion is that *there is no emperor. There is no emperor! There is no emperor!*"

After this intemperate outburst yet another voice was heard from the crowd, the voice of one who prides himself on taking a sober, comprehensive, and balanced view of things, and in the process takes himself much too seriously. "Maybe we *are* part of the empire," said this new interlocutor. "Certainly we have some evidence that this is so, not least of which is the fact that our honored visitor, who appears to me to have an open and trustworthy countenance, has come to tell us that this is so. The recollections of some of our senior members are also relevant here. Surely they give us some reason to believe there to be an emperor. But if there is an emperor—and I certainly do not rule out this possibility—it is hard to believe that it matters to him whether we believe that he exists. If it mattered very much to the emperor that we believe that he exists, then surely it would be clearer than it now is that there is an emperor. After all, where has the emperor been all this time? Furthermore, the beliefs that we hold about the emperor under current conditions, if we hold any, ought to reflect the fact that they are held under conditions of uncertainty. Any beliefs we hold in this area ought in fact to be held with tentativeness, and with an awareness that we may be wrong."

In the fullness of time, and after the emissary had gone his way, it came to pass that three schools of thought developed, each of which embraced one of the views that were expressed on that day. There were those who agreed with the old woman, and who were known by their opponents as the "Imperialists." Then there were the Skeptics. All of their bearded members had a strong inclination toward beard-twiddling. And there were the Tentative Believers. They were known to their detractors as "the half-baked believers." So who was right? . . .

THE DISADVANTAGES OF GOD'S HIDDENNESS

If God exists but is hidden, this is a perplexing state of affairs. One reason that it is perplexing is internal to theism and arises from the fact that the theistic traditions place such importance on belief. Typically each theistic tradition asserts that to fail to hold theistic beliefs, and especially to fail to hold its theistic beliefs, or at least what it considers to be the most important among them, is to go wrong in a very serious way whereas to adopt theistic beliefs, and especially the set of theistic beliefs associated with it, is a worthwhile and important thing to do. These traditions say, too, that one ought to regret or even feel guilty about a failure to believe. Yet if God is hidden, belief is more difficult than it would be if God were not hidden. If God exists, and if the facts about God's existence and nature were clear, belief would be ever so much easier for us. The theistic traditions are inclined to hold human beings responsible and even to blame them if they are nonbelievers or if their belief is weak. But does this make any sense?

God's hiddenness creates uncertainty and contributes to profound disagreement about the existence and nature of God. Indeed, I would suggest that it contributes *more* to the occurrence of nonbelief than does the presence of evil in the world (or of *other* evil in the world, if the hiddenness of God is understood as a type of evil). This is not to deny that there are people who are nontheists because of evils that they either encounter or are familiar with; but it seems that the explanation in most cases of how it has come about that people do not believe that God exists (whether they are atheists or agnostics or members of nontheistic religions) is not that they consider God's existence to be incompatible with various evils. Rather, it is that they have nothing that they understand as an awareness of God. They do not understand themselves to be familiar with God. Consequently, they do not even reach a point where evil is perceived as a problem. . . .

Another reason that the hiddenness of God is perplexing has to do with the sort of personal relationship with God that some theists advocate. This is also a reason that is internal to theism, or at least to theism of a certain sort, especially evangelical and fundamentalist Christianity. The personal relationship in question is understood to involve trust, respect, and, above all, ongoing intimate communication. Is it not reasonable to suppose that if God were less hidden, this sort of relationship would be more widespread?

The hiddenness of God, therefore, seems to be a particularly acute problem for strands of theism that emphasize the importance of fellowship and communication with God. But it is also a problem for the other major strands of theism because they all emphasize the importance and value of belief. And

they declare that God cares about us; if God exists and if God cares about us, why does God leave human beings to such an extent in the dark about various religiously important facts? If God does not care about us, there is less to explain. Theism typically requires, too, that we put our trust and confidence in God: But why, then, are the facts about God not more clear? If God exists and the facts about God's existence and nature were more clear, people would be more likely to see that they ought to put their trust and confidence in God and would be more willing and more able to do so.

Another important, and related, disadvantage associated with divine hiddenness is this. If God exists, God is worthy of adoration and worship: given the good, wise, just (etc.) nature of God, and the relation between God and God's creatures, a worshipful response from human beings would be appropriate. For if God exists, God is our Creator and we owe all we have to God. But if many of us are in the dark about the existence and nature of God, then this appropriate human response is made more difficult than it otherwise would be. So part of the cost of divine hiddenness is its contribution to the large-scale failure of human beings to respond to God in ways that seem appropriate in the case of a good, just, and wise creator.

And there are further costs. The profound disagreements about God, and more broadly the profound disagreements that there are about numerous matters of religious importance, often play a role in promoting and exacerbating social conflict. If God exists and if the facts about God were as clear as they could be, there might not be as much room for disagreement, and hence such disagreements would not contribute to social conflict. The mystery surrounding God also provides opportunities for charlatans and frauds to pose as experts on the nature and activities of God, and for religious authorities in numerous traditions to acquire and exercise, and sometimes abuse, power and control over others.

To each of these apparent disadvantages, or costs, of God's hiddenness there corresponds an advantage or benefit that, it appears, would accrue if God were not hidden. Thus if God were not hidden, and the facts about God were clear for all to see, it appears that belief would be easier for us, a personal relationship with God would be facilitated, more people would worship God, religious disagreement would be less likely to exacerbate social tensions, and there would be fewer opportunities for people to pose as experts and to acquire power and influence over others. . . .

There is, then, some reason to think that, if God exists, it must not matter greatly to God whether we believe. This applies to belief that God exists, to various standard theistic beliefs about God, such as beliefs about the activities and character of God, and to belief in God. At least that we should hold such beliefs . . . here and now and under our current circumstances probably does not matter greatly. There is also considerable reason to believe that it is not important that everyone should accept any particular form of theism, such as Judaism or Islam. If it were very important that we should accept theism or any particular form of theism, our circumstances probably would be more conducive to it.

PART 2

~

Epistemology

Introduction

DAVID SOSA

Epistemology (from the Greek *episteme,* knowledge) is the theory of knowledge. Some people *know* what they're talking about. That makes them valuable and interesting. We can learn things from them, and we want to know what they have to say. Other people don't know what they're talking about. But this difference between *knowing* and *not knowing* turns out to be philosophically problematic. Maybe none of us knows a thing! What is knowledge, anyway? And *how* do we know things, if we do?

Consider the old saw, "how do you know you're not dreaming?" René Descartes takes that concern seriously and carefully considers its effects. He entertains *skepticism,* a position in which you *doubt* or refrain from belief. But he finds a way out of this doubt in his second meditation with the *cogito.* Not even the most powerful demon could be fooling you if you think that you're thinking. If you *think* that you're *thinking,* you are. This, for Descartes, staunches the skeptical hemorrhage.

John Locke and George Berkeley can now be seen as concerned with the following question: how must the world be in order that we might have knowledge of it? Locke represents the modern "materialist" point of view of his day, according to which there is a material world, independent of our thoughts about it, with its own material properties and features. Locke found, however, that some of those features are systematically misleading. Dividing qualities into categories, Locke claims that "secondary" qualities are actually mere "powers," and though they may present themselves as akin to primary qualities, in fact they are metaphysically quite different. Berkeley takes skepticism to represent the ultimate absurdity: any position that leads to it must, for that very reason, be mistaken. And impressed with Locke's argument that secondary qualities misrepresent themselves, Berkeley extends the argument so that it affects *any* feature of a material world. If we accept a materialist point of view, Berkeley argues, we will be reduced to skepticism. Instead, we should accept "idealism," which holds that so-called material bodies are constituted precisely by ideas, by psychological items. In a striking passage, Berkeley turns this view into an argument for the existence of God.

G. E. Moore turns the tables on skepticism. He thinks he can refute skepticism and *prove* that the external world exists. "Here is one hand," he urges, holding up his two hands, "and here is another"; in so doing, Moore suggests, he has proved the existence of things outside himself. It's easy to think, however, that Moore's argument is a kind of trick: Ludwig Wittgenstein thought so. He begins his series of reflections by challenging Moore's right to the premise, "here is one hand." But Wittgenstein admits ultimately that "justification comes to an end."

Reading Moore and then Wittgenstein, we may begin to worry that there's something very *deeply* problematic about epistemology. We're trying to understand knowledge. We're worried that maybe we know nothing. To check whether we know anything, it seems that we have to make some assumptions—that we can trust our senses, for example, or that our reasoning is reliable. But that assumption reproduces our problem: do we *know* that we can trust our senses? Is reasoning reliable? Roderick M. Chisholm neatly poses the general problem. Nevertheless he, like Moore, thinks there may be a way out. Moore and Chisholm are *foundationalist internalists*. They think we can use certain internal presentations, about which our knowledge can be basic, as a foundation for much of the rest of our knowledge.

This may be a good time to define our terms. What, exactly, do we mean by "knowledge"? A traditional analysis holds that knowledge requires each of three things, and that all three together are sufficient for knowledge: (1) truth, (2) belief, and (3) justification. So there's no knowing something false; to know something requires that it be true. Second, if you are to know something, you must believe it. If you don't commit yourself to a claim, if you do not accept it as one of your beliefs, then you cannot be said to know it. And, finally, knowledge requires justification: if you believe something illegitimately—you don't have any reason for it, say, and really you shouldn't believe it, but you believe it anyway—and by luck your belief turns out to be true, then we would not say you had *knowledge*. People who know what they're talking about are not just people who get it right. Edmund Gettier considers whether this definition is really adequate. He doesn't show that any of the conditions given so far is unnecessary, but he argues that together they're still not sufficient for knowledge.

Gettier's paper led people like Alvin I. Goldman and Robert Nozick to try to spell out in more detail what else may be required for knowledge. An important development in epistemology is the sort of *externalism* we find in their work. According to Goldman and Nozick, the foundationalist internalism of Moore and Chisholm is unsatisfactory. The sort of warrant required for knowledge is rather a matter of standing in the right relation to your environment. Ultimately, how you are *internally*—what your internal presentations are like—is only part of the story; those presentations have to be reliably rigged up to the external world around you. Even perfect internal duplicates could vary with respect to what they know. Nozick goes on to try to use his definition of knowledge to reject skepticism.

Ernest Sosa (disclosure: he's my father!) investigates the *shape* of the structure of our knowledge. Should we think of our knowledge as *founded,* grounding out in a foundation, like a pyramid or a house? Or are we rather adrift on an ocean of epistemic possibility, required to build and rebuild a raft of knowledge from what we can, sometimes casting off parts of what we've built to make way for new additions? Sosa considers important objections to each of these lines of thought; makes several fine distinctions, and discusses what may be said in reply.

David Lewis, in "Elusive Knowledge," tries to offer an alternative to the foundationalist/coherentist divide. He takes up what we may call a "contextualist" theory of knowledge.

According to contextualism, knowledge is a *relative* phenomenon, in some ways like being tall. Whether you know something is a matter of satisfying standards, but *which* standards need to be satisfied can vary from one context to another.

Finally, W. V. O. Quine and Jaegwon Kim give us a debate about *naturalism.* Exactly what naturalism in epistemology amounts to is itself an important issue. But in Quine, it has to do with thinking of epistemology as a chapter of *psychology,* as a matter of investigating the relationship between the scientific theories we accept and the evidence on which we accept them. The question of when we *should* believe something, the question of *justification,* is at least transformed, maybe eliminated, in favor of the *descriptive* question: how, as a matter of psychological fact, does knowledge happen? Kim, whose Section III offers among other things a valuable summary and interpretation of Quine's paper, points out that the substitute for, or successor to, epistemology offered by Quine cannot avoid the "normative" issue of justification. According to Kim, "for epistemology to go out of the business of justification is for it to go out of business."

Meditations on First Philosophy

~

RENÉ DESCARTES

René Descartes (1596–1650) marks the beginning of modern philosophy. His work ranged widely, including not only the *Discourse on Method* and *Principles of Philosophy,* but also *The World* (defending a heliocentric astronomy, published posthumously), *Geometry* (the Cartesian coordinate system is named for Descartes), *Meteorology, Optics,* and *The Passions of the Soul.* The *Meditations on First Philosophy* is his masterpiece.

MEDITATION I

Of the things which may be brought within the sphere of the doubtful

It is now some years since I detected how many were the false beliefs that I had from my earliest youth admitted as true, and how doubtful was everything I had since constructed on this basis; and from that time I was convinced that I must once for all seriously undertake to rid myself of all the opinions which I had formerly accepted, and commence to build anew from the foundation, if I wanted to establish any firm and permanent structure in the sciences. But as this enterprise appeared to be a very great one, I waited until I had attained an age so mature that I could not hope that at any later date I should be better fitted to execute my design. This reason caused me to delay so long that I should feel that I was doing wrong were I to occupy in deliberation the time that yet remains to me for action. To-day, then, since very opportunely for the plan I have in view I have delivered my mind from every care [and am happily agitated by no passions] and since I have procured for myself an assured leisure in a peaceable retirement, I shall at last seriously and freely address myself to the general upheaval of all my former opinions.

Now for this object it is not necessary that I should show that all of these are false—I shall perhaps never arrive at this end. But inasmuch as reason already persuades me that I ought no less carefully to withhold my assent from matters which are not entirely certain and indubitable than from those which appear to me manifestly to be false, if I am able to find in each one some reason to doubt, this will suffice to justify my rejecting the whole. And for that end it will not be requisite that I should examine each in particular, which would be an endless undertaking; for owing to the fact that the destruction of the foundations of necessity brings with it the downfall of the rest of the edifice, I shall only in the first place attack those principles upon which all my former opinions rested.

All that up to the present time I have accepted as most true and certain I have learned either from the senses or through the senses; but it is sometimes proved to me that these senses are deceptive, and it is wiser not to trust entirely to any thing by which we have once been deceived.

But it may be that although the senses sometimes deceive us concerning things which are hardly perceptible, or very far away, there are yet many others to be met with as to which we cannot reasonably have any doubt, although we recognize them by their means. For example, there is the fact that I am here, seated by the fire, attired in a dressing gown, having this paper in my hands and other similar matters. And how could I deny that these hands and this body are mine, were it not perhaps that I compare myself to certain persons, devoid of sense, whose cerebella are so troubled and clouded by the violent vapours of black bile, that they constantly assure us that they think they are kings when they are really quite poor, or that they are clothed in purple when they are really without covering, or who imagine that they have an earthenware head or are nothing but pumpkins or are made of glass. But they are mad, and I should not be any the less insane were I to follow examples so extravagant.

At the same time I must remember that I am a man, and that consequently I am in the habit of sleeping, and in my dreams representing to myself the same things or sometimes even less probable things, than do those who are insane in their waking moments. How often has it happened to me that in the night I dreamt that I found myself in this particular place, that I was dressed and seated near the fire, whilst in reality I was lying undressed in bed! At this moment it does indeed seem to me that it is with eyes awake that I am looking at this paper; that this head which I move is not asleep, that it is deliberately and of set purpose that I extend my hand and perceive it; what happens in sleep does not appear so clear nor so distinct as does all this. But in thinking over this I remind myself that on many occasions I have in sleep been deceived by similar illusions, and in dwelling carefully on this reflection I see so manifestly that there are no certain indications by which we may clearly distinguish wakefulness from sleep that I am lost in astonishment. And my astonishment is such that it is almost capable of persuading me that I now dream.

Now let us assume that we are asleep and that all these particulars, e.g. that we open our eyes, shake our head, extend our hands, and so on, are but false delusions; and let us reflect that possibly neither our hands nor our whole body are such as they appear to us to be. At the same time we must at least confess that the things which are represented to us in sleep are like painted representations which can only have been formed as the counterparts of something real and true, and that in this way those general things at least, i.e. eyes, a head, hands, and a whole body, are not imaginary things, but things really existent. For, as a matter of fact, painters, even when they study with the greatest skill to represent sirens and satyrs by forms the most strange and extraordinary, cannot give them natures which are entirely new, but merely make a certain medley of the members of different animals; or if their imagination is extravagant enough to invent something so novel that nothing similar has ever before been seen, and that then their work represents a thing purely fictitious and absolutely false, it is certain all the same that the colours of which this is composed are necessarily real. And for the same reason, although these general things, to wit, [a body], eyes, a head, hands, and such like, may be imaginary, we are bound at the same time to confess that there are at least some other objects yet more simple and more universal, which are real and true; and of these just in the same way as with certain real colours, all these images of things which dwell in our thoughts, whether true and real or false and fantastic, are formed.

To such a class of things pertains corporeal nature in general, and its extension, the figure of extended things, their quantity or magnitude and number, as also the place in which they are, the time which measures their duration, and so on.

That is possibly why our reasoning is not unjust when we conclude from this that Physics, Astronomy, Medicine and all other sciences which have as their end the consideration of composite things, are very dubious and uncertain; but that Arithmetic, Geometry and other sciences of that kind which only treat of things that are very simple and very general, without taking great trouble to ascertain whether they are actually existent or not, contain some measure of certainty and an element of the indubitable. For whether I am awake or asleep, two and three together always form five, and the square can never have more than four sides, and it does not seem possible that truths so clear and apparent can be suspected of any falsity [or uncertainty].

Nevertheless I have long had fixed in my mind the belief that an all-powerful God existed by whom I have been created such as I am. But how do I know that He has not brought it to pass that there is no earth, no heaven, no extended body, no magnitude, no place, and that nevertheless [I possess the perceptions of all these things and that] they seem to me to exist just exactly as I now see them? And, besides, as I sometimes imagine that others deceive themselves in the things which they think they know best, how do I know that I am not deceived every time that I add two and three, or count the sides of a square, or judge of things yet simpler, if anything simpler can be imagined? But possibly God has not desired that I should be thus deceived, for He is said to be supremely good. If, however, it is contrary to His goodness to have made me such that I constantly deceive myself, it would also appear to be contrary to His goodness to

permit me to be sometimes deceived, and nevertheless I cannot doubt that He does permit this.

There may indeed be those who would prefer to deny the existence of a God so powerful, rather than believe that all other things are uncertain. But let us not oppose them for the present, and grant that all that is here said of a God is a fable; nevertheless in whatever way they suppose that I have arrived at the state of being that I have reached—whether they attribute it to fate or to accident, or make out that it is by a continual succession of antecedents, or by some other method—since to err and deceive oneself is a defect, it is clear that the greater will be the probability of my being so imperfect as to deceive myself ever, as is the Author to whom they assign my origin the less powerful. To these reasons I have certainly nothing to reply, but at the end I feel constrained to confess that there is nothing in all that I formerly believed to be true, of which I cannot in some measure doubt, and that not merely through want of thought or through levity, but for reasons which are very powerful and maturely considered; so that henceforth I ought not the less carefully refrain from giving credence to these opinions than to that which is manifestly false, if I desire to arrive at any certainty [in the sciences].

But it is not sufficient to have made these remarks, we must also be careful to keep them in mind. For these ancient and commonly held opinions still revert frequently to my mind, long and familiar custom having given them the right to occupy my mind against my inclination and rendered them almost masters of my belief; nor will I ever lose the habit of deferring to them or of placing my confidence in them, so long as I consider them as they really are, i.e. opinions in some measure, doubtful, as I have just shown, and at the same time highly probable, so that there is much more reason to believe in than to deny them. That is why I consider that I shall not be acting amiss, if, taking of set purpose a contrary belief, I allow myself to be deceived, and for a certain time pretend that all these opinions are entirely false and imaginary, until at last, having thus balanced my former prejudices with my latter [so that they cannot divert my opinions more to one side than to the other], my judgment will no longer be dominated by bad usage or turned away from the right knowledge of the truth. For I am assured that there can be neither peril nor error in this course, and that I cannot at present yield too much to distrust, since I am not considering the question of action, but only of knowledge.

I shall then suppose, not that God who is supremely good and the fountain of truth, but some evil genius not less powerful than deceitful, has employed his whole energies in deceiving me; I shall consider that the heavens, the earth, colours, figures, sound, and all other external things are nought but the illusions and dreams of which this genius has availed himself in order to lay traps for my credulity; I shall consider myself as having no hands, no eyes, no flesh, no blood, nor any senses, yet falsely believing myself to possess all these things; I shall remain obstinately attached to this idea, and if by this means it is not in my power to arrive at the knowledge of any truth, I may at least do what is in my power [i.e. suspend my judgment], and with firm purpose avoid giving credence to any false thing, or being imposed upon by this arch deceiver, however powerful and deceptive he may be. But this task is a laborious one, and insensibly a certain lassitude leads me into the course of my ordinary life. And just as a captive who in sleep enjoys an imaginary liberty, when he begins to suspect that his liberty is but a dream, fears to awaken, and conspires with these agreeable illusions that the deception may be prolonged, so insensibly of my own accord I fall back into my former opinions, and I dread awakening from this slumber, lest the laborious wakefulness which would follow the tranquility of this repose should have to be spent not in daylight, but in the excessive darkness of the difficulties which have just been discussed.

MEDITATION II

Of the Nature of the Human Mind; and that it is more easily known than the Body

The Meditation of yesterday filled my mind with so many doubts that it is no longer in my power to forget them. And yet I do not see in what manner I can resolve them; and, just as if I had all of a sudden fallen into very deep water, I am so disconcerted that I can neither make certain of setting my feet on the bottom, nor can I swim and so support myself on the surface. I shall nevertheless make an effort and follow anew the same path as that on which I yesterday entered, i.e. I shall proceed by setting aside all that in which the least doubt could be supposed to exist, just as if I had discovered that it was absolutely false; and I shall ever follow in this road until I have met with something which is certain, or at least, if I can do nothing else, until I have learned for certain that there is nothing in the world that is certain. Archimedes, in order that he might draw the terrestrial globe out of its place, and transport it elsewhere, demanded only that one point should be fixed and immovable; in the same way I shall have the right to conceive high hopes if I am happy enough to discover one thing only which is certain and indubitable.

I suppose, then, that all the things that I see are false; I persuade myself that nothing has ever existed of all that my fallacious memory represents to me. I consider that I possess no senses; I imagine that body, figure, extension, movement and place are but the fictions of my mind. What, then, can be esteemed as true? Perhaps nothing at all, unless that there is nothing in the world that is certain.

But how can I know there is not something different from those things that I have just considered, of which one cannot have the slightest doubt? Is there not some God, or some other being by whatever name we call it, who puts these reflections into my mind? That is not necessary, for is it not possible that I am capable of producing them myself? I myself, am I not at least something? But I have already denied that I had senses and body. Yet I hesitate, for what follows from that? Am I so dependent on body and senses that I cannot exist without these? But I was persuaded that there was nothing in all the world, that there was no heaven, no earth, that there were no minds, nor any bodies: was I not then likewise persuaded that I did not exist? Not at all; of a surety I myself did exist since I persuaded myself of something [or merely because I thought of something]. But there is some deceiver or other, very powerful and very cunning, who ever employs his ingenuity in deceiving me. Then without doubt I exist also if he deceives me, and let him deceive me as much as he will, he can never cause me to be nothing so long as I think that I am something. So that after having reflected well and carefully examined all things, we must come to the definite conclusion that this proposition: I am, I exist, is necessarily true each time that I pronounce it, or that I mentally conceive it.

But I do not yet know clearly enough what I am, I who am certain that I am; and hence I must be careful to see that I do not imprudently take some other object in place of myself, and thus that I do not go astray in respect of this knowledge that I hold to be the most certain and most evident of all that I have formerly learned. That is why I shall now consider anew what I believed myself to be before I embarked upon these last reflections; and of my former opinions I shall withdraw all that might even in a small degree be invalidated by the reasons which I have just brought forward, in order that there may be nothing at all left beyond what is absolutely certain and indubitable.

What then did I formerly believe myself to be? Undoubtedly I believed myself to be a man. But what is a man? Shall I say a reasonable animal? Certainly not; for then I should have to inquire what an animal is, and what is reasonable; and thus from a single question I should insensibly fall into an infinitude of others more difficult; and I should not wish to waste the little time and leisure remaining to me in trying to unravel subtleties like these. But I shall rather stop here to consider the thoughts which of themselves spring up in my mind, and which were not inspired by anything beyond my own nature alone when I applied myself to the consideration of my being. In the first place, then, I considered myself as having a face, hands, arms, and all that system of members composed of bones and flesh as seen in a corpse which I designated by the name of body. In addition to this I considered that I was nourished, that I walked, that I felt, and that I thought, and I referred all these actions to the soul: but I did not stop to consider what the soul was, or if I did stop, I imagined that it was something extremely rare and subtle like a wind, a flame, or an ether, which was spread throughout my grosser parts. As to body I had no manner of doubt about its nature, but thought I had a very clear knowledge of it; and if I had desired to explain it according to the notions that I had then formed of it, I should have described it thus: By the body I understand all that which can be defined by a certain figure: something which can be confined in a certain place, and which can fill a given space in such a way that every other body will be excluded from it; which can be perceived either by touch, or by sight, or by hearing, or by taste, or by smell: which can be moved in many ways not, in truth, by itself, but by something which is foreign to it, by which it is touched [and from which it receives impressions]: for to have the power of self-movement, as also of feeling or of thinking, I did not consider to appertain to the nature of body: on the contrary, I was rather astonished to find that faculties similar to them existed in some bodies.

But what am I, now that I suppose that there is a certain genius which is extremely powerful, and, if I may say so, malicious, who employs all his powers in deceiving me? Can I affirm that I possess the least of all those things which I have just said pertain to the nature of body? I pause to consider, I revolve all these things in my mind, and I find none of which I can say that it pertains to me. It would be tedious to stop to enumerate them. Let us pass to the attributes of soul and see if there is any one which is in me? What of nutrition or walking [the first mentioned]? But if it is so that I have no body it is also true that I can neither walk nor take nourishment. Another attribute is sensation. But one cannot feel without body, and besides I have thought I perceived many things during sleep that I recognised in my waking moments as not having been experienced at all. What of thinking? I find here that thought is an attribute that belongs to me; it alone cannot be separated from me. I am, I exist, that is certain. But how often? Just when I think; for it might possibly be the case if I ceased entirely to think, that I should likewise cease altogether to exist. I do not now admit anything which is not necessarily true: to speak accurately I am not more than a thing which thinks, that is to say a mind or a soul, or an understanding, or a reason, which are terms whose significance was formerly unknown to me. I am, however, a real thing and really exist; but what thing? I have answered: a thing which thinks.

And what more? I shall exercise my imagination [in order to see if I am not something more]. I am not a collection of members which we call the human body: I am not a subtle air distributed through these members, I am not a wind, a fire, a vapour, a breath, nor anything at all which I can imagine or conceive; because I have assumed that all these were nothing. Without changing that supposition I find that I only leave myself certain of the fact that I am somewhat. But perhaps it is true that these same things which I supposed were non-existent because they are unknown to me, are really not different from the self which I know. I am not sure about this, I shall not dispute about it now; I can only give judgment on things that are known to me. I know that I exist, and I inquire what I am, I whom I know to exist. But it is very certain that the knowledge of my existence taken in its precise significance does not depend on things whose existence is not yet known to me; consequently it does not depend on those which I can feign in imagination. And indeed the very term *feign* in imagination proves to me my error, for I really do this if I image myself a something, since to imagine is nothing else than to contemplate the figure or image of a corporeal thing. But I already know for certain that I am, and that it may be that all these images, and, speaking generally, all things that relate to the nature of body are nothing but dreams [and chimeras]. For this reason I see clearly that I have as little reason to say, "I shall stimulate my imagination in order to know more distinctly what I am," than if I were to say, "I am now awake, and I perceive somewhat that is real and true: but because I do not yet perceive it distinctly enough, I shall go to sleep of express purpose, so that my dreams may represent the perception with greatest truth and evidence." And, thus, I know for certain that nothing of all that I can understand by means of my imagination belongs to this knowledge which I have of myself, and that it is necessary to recall the mind from this mode of thought with the utmost diligence in order that it may be able to know its own nature with perfect distinctness.

But what then am I? A thing which thinks. What is a thing which thinks? It is a thing which doubts, understands, [conceives], affirms, denies, wills, refuses, which also imagines and feels.

Certainly it is no small matter if all these things pertain to my nature. But why should they not so pertain? Am I not that being who now doubts nearly everything, who nevertheless understands certain things, who affirms that one only is true, who denies all the others, who desires to know more, is averse from being deceived, who imagines many things, sometimes indeed despite his will, and who perceives many likewise, as by the intervention of the bodily organs? Is there nothing in all this which is as true as it is certain that I exist, even though I should always sleep and though he who has given me being employed all his ingenuity in deceiving me? Is there likewise any one of these attributes which can be distinguished from my thought, or which might be said to be separated from myself? For it is so evident of itself that it is I who doubts, who understands, and who desires, that there is no reason here to add anything to explain it. And I have certainly the power of imagining likewise; for although it may happen (as I formerly supposed) that none of the things which I imagine are true, nevertheless this power of imagining does not cease to be really in use, and it forms part of my thought. Finally, I am the same who feels, that is to say, who perceives certain things, as by the organs of sense, since in truth I see light, I hear noise, I feel heat. But it will be said that these phenomena are false and that I am dreaming. Let it be so; still it is at least quite certain that it seems to me that I see light, that I hear noise and that I feel heat. That cannot be false; properly speaking it is what is in me called feeling; and used in this precise sense that is no other thing than thinking.

From this time I begin to know what I am with a little more clearness and distinction than before; but nevertheless it still seems to me, and I cannot prevent myself from thinking, that corporeal things, whose images are framed by thought, which are tested by the senses, are much more distinctly known than that obscure part of me which does not come under the imagination. Although really it is very strange to say that I know and understand more distinctly these things whose existence seems to me dubious, which are unknown to me, and which do not belong to me, than others of the truth of which I am convinced, which are known to me and which pertain to my real nature, in a word, than myself. But I see clearly how the case stands: my mind loves to wander, and cannot yet suffer itself to be retained within the just limits of truth. Very good, let us once more give it the freest rein, so that, when afterwards we seize the proper occasion for pulling up, it may the more easily be regulated and controlled.

Let us begin by considering the commonest matters, those which we believe to be the most distinctly comprehended, to wit, the bodies which we touch and see; not indeed bodies in general, for these general ideas are usually a little more confused, but let us consider one body in particular. Let us take, for example, this piece of wax: it has been taken quite freshly from the hive, and it has not yet lost the sweetness of the honey which it contains; it still retains somewhat of the odour of the flowers from which it has been culled; its colour, its figure, its size are apparent; it is hard, cold, easily handled, and if you strike it with the finger, it will emit a sound. Finally all the things which are requisite to cause us distinctly to recognise a body, are met with in it. But notice that while I speak and approach the fire what remained of the taste is exhaled, the smell evaporates, the colour alters, the figure is destroyed, the size increases, it becomes liquid, it heats, scarcely can one handle it, and when one strikes it, no sound is emitted. Does the same wax remain after this change? We must confess that it remains; none would judge otherwise. What then did I know so distinctly in this piece of wax? It could certainly be nothing of all that the senses brought to my notice, since all these things which fall under taste, smell, sight, touch, and hearing, are found to be changed, and yet the same wax remains.

Perhaps it was what I now think, viz, that this wax was not that sweetness of honey, not that agreeable scent of flowers, nor that particular whiteness, nor that figure, nor that sound, but simply a body which a little while before appeared to me as perceptible under these forms, and which is now perceptible under others. But what, precisely, is it that I imagine when I form such conceptions? Let us attentively consider this, and, abstracting from all that does not belong to the wax, let us see what remains. Certainly nothing remains excepting a certain extended thing which is flexible and movable. But what is the meaning of flexible and movable? Is it not that I imagine

that this piece of wax being round is capable of becoming square and of passing from a square to a triangular figure? No, certainly it is not that, since I imagine it admits of an infinitude of similar changes, and I nevertheless do not know how to compass the infinitude by my imagination, and consequently this conception which I have of the wax is not brought about by the faculty of imagination. What now is this extension? Is it not also unknown? For it becomes greater when the wax is melted, greater when it is boiled, and greater still when the heat increases; and I should not conceive [clearly] according to truth what wax is, if I did not think that even this piece that we are considering is capable of receiving more variations in extension than I have ever imagined. We must then grant that I could not even understand through the imagination what this piece of wax is, and that it is my mind alone which perceives it. I say this piece of wax in particular, for as to wax in general it is yet clearer. But what is this piece of wax which cannot be understood excepting by the [understanding or] mind? It is certainly the same that I see, touch, imagine, and finally it is the same which I have always believed it to be from the beginning. But what must particularly be observed is that its perception is neither an act of vision, nor of touch, nor of imagination, and has never been such although it may have appeared formerly to be so, but only an intuition of the mind, which may be imperfect and confused as it was formerly, or clear and distinct as it is at present, according as my attention is more or less directed to the elements which are found in it, and of which it is composed.

Yet in the meantime I am greatly astonished when I consider [the great feebleness of mind] and its proneness to fall [insensibly] into error; for although without giving expression to my thoughts I consider all this in my own mind, words often impede me and I am almost deceived by the terms of ordinary language. For we say that we see the same wax, if it is present, and not that we simply judge that it is the same from its having the same colour and figure. From this I should conclude that I knew the wax by means of vision and not simply by the intuition of the mind; unless by chance I remember that, when looking from a window and saying I see men who pass in the street, I really do not see them, but infer that what I see is men, just as I say that I see wax. And yet what do I see from the window but hats and coats which may cover automatic machines? Yet I judge these to be men. And similarly solely by the faculty of judgment which rests in my mind, I comprehend that which I believed I saw with my eyes.

A man who makes it his aim to raise his knowledge above the common should be ashamed to derive the occasion for doubting from the forms of speech invented by the vulgar; I prefer to pass on and consider whether I had a more evident and perfect conception of what the wax was when I first perceived it, and when I believed I knew it by means of the external senses or at least by the common sense as it is called, that is to say by the imaginative faculty, or whether my present conception is clearer now that I have most carefully examined what it is, and in what way it can be known. It would certainly be absurd to doubt as to this. For what was there in this first perception which was distinct? What was there which might not as well have been perceived by any of the animals? But when I distinguish the wax from its external forms, and when, just as if I had taken from it its vestments, I consider it quite naked, it is certain that although some error may still be found in my judgment, I can nevertheless not perceive it thus without a human mind.

But finally what shall I say of this mind, that is, of myself, for up to this point I do not admit in myself anything but mind? What then, I who seem to perceive this piece of wax so distinctly, do I not know myself, not only with much more truth and certainty, but also with much more distinctness and clearness? For if I judge that the wax is or exists from the fact that I see it, it certainly follows much more clearly that I am or that I exist myself from the fact that I see it. For it may be that what I see is not really wax, it may also be that I do not possess eyes with which to see anything; but it cannot be that when I see, or (for I no longer take account of the distinction) when I think I see, that I myself who think am nought. So if I judge that the wax exists from the fact that I touch it, the same thing will follow, to wit, that I am; and if I judge that my imagination, or some other cause, whatever it is, persuades me that wax exists, I shall

still conclude the same. And what I have here remarked of wax may be applied to all other things which are external to me [and which are met with outside of me]. And further, if the [notion or] perception of wax has seemed to me clearer and more distinct, not only after the sight or the touch, but also after many other causes have rendered it quite manifest to me, with how much more [evidence] and distinctness must it be said that I now know myself, since all the reasons which contribute to the knowledge of wax, or any other body whatever, are yet better proofs of the nature of my mind! And there are so many other things in the mind itself which may contribute to the elucidation of its nature, that those which depend on body such as these just mentioned, hardly merit being taken into account.

But finally here I am, having insensibly reverted to the point I desired, for, since it is now manifest to me that even bodies are not properly speaking known by the senses or by the faculty of imagination, but by the understanding only, and since they are not known from the fact that they are seen or touched, but only because they are understood, I see clearly that there is nothing which is easier for me to know than my mind. But because it is difficult to rid oneself so promptly of an opinion to which one was accustomed for so long, it will be well that I should halt a little at this point, so that by the length of my meditation I may more deeply imprint on my memory this new knowledge.

MEDITATION III

Of God: that He exists

I shall now close my eyes, I shall stop my ears, I shall call away all my senses, I shall efface even from my thoughts all the images of corporeal things, or at least (for that is hardly possible) I shall esteem them as vain and false; and thus holding converse only with myself and considering my own nature, I shall try little by little to reach a better knowledge of and a more familiar acquaintanceship with myself. I am a thing that thinks, that is to say, that doubts, affirms, denies, that knows a few things, that is ignorant of many [that loves, that hates], that wills, that desires, that also imagines and perceives; for as I remarked before, although the things which I perceive and imagine are perhaps nothing at all apart from me and in themselves, I am nevertheless assured that these modes of thought that I call perceptions and imaginations, inasmuch only as they are modes of thought, certainly reside [and are met with] in me.

And in the little that I have just said, I think I have summed up all that I really know, or at least all that hitherto I was aware that I knew. In order to try to extend my knowledge further, I shall now look around more carefully and see whether I cannot still discover in myself some other things which I have not hitherto perceived. I am certain that I am a thing which thinks; but do I not then likewise know what is requisite to render me certain of a truth? Certainly in this first knowledge there is nothing that assures me of its truth, excepting the clear and distinct perception of that which I state, which would not indeed suffice to assure me that what I say is true, if it could ever happen that a thing which I conceived so clearly and distinctly could be false; and accordingly it seems to me that already I can establish as a general rule that all things which I perceive very clearly and very distinctly are true.

At the same time I have before received and admitted many things to be very certain and manifest, which yet I afterwards recognised as being dubious. What then were these things? They were the earth, sky, stars and all other objects which I apprehended by means of the senses. But what did I clearly [and distinctly] perceive in them? Nothing more than that the ideas or thoughts of these things were presented to my mind. And not even now do I deny that these ideas are met with in me. But there was yet another thing which I affirmed, and which, owing to the habit which I had formed of believing it, I thought I perceived very clearly, although in truth I did not perceive it at all, to wit, that there were objects outside of me from which these ideas proceeded, and to which they were entirely similar. And it was in this that I erred, or, if perchance my judgment was correct, this was not due to any knowledge arising from my perception.

But when I took anything very simple and easy in the sphere of arithmetic or geometry into consideration, e.g. that two and three together made five, and other things of the sort, were not these present to my mind so clearly as to enable me to affirm that they were true? Certainly if I judged that since such matters could be doubted, this would not have been so for any other reason than that it came into my mind that perhaps a God might have endowed me with such a nature that I may have been deceived even concerning things which seemed to me most manifest. But every time that this preconceived opinion of the sovereign power of a God presents itself to my thought, I am constrained to confess that it is easy to Him, if He wishes it, to cause me to err, even in matters in which I believe myself to have the best evidence. And, on the other hand, always when I direct my attention to things which I believe myself to perceive very clearly, I am so persuaded of their truth that I let myself break out into words such as these: Let who will deceive me, He can never cause me to be nothing while I think that I am, or some day cause it to be true to say that I have never been, it being true now to say that I am, or that two and three make more or less than five, or any such thing in which I see a manifest contradiction. And, certainly, since I have no reason to believe that there is a God who is a deceiver, and as I have not yet satisfied myself that there is a God at all, the reason for doubt which depends on this opinion alone is very slight, and so to speak metaphysical. But in order to be able altogether to remove it, I must inquire whether there is a God as soon as the occasion presents itself; and if I find that there is a God, I must also inquire whether He may be a deceiver; for without a knowledge of these two truths I do not see that I can ever be certain of anything.

An Essay Concerning Human Understanding

~

JOHN LOCKE

John Locke (1632–1704) was a physician and scientist and an Oxford don for much of his life. After an unhappy move from England to Holland, he published his philosophical work, including *An Essay Concerning Human Understanding,* three *Letters Concerning Toleration,* and *Two Treatises of Government,* and, published posthumously, *An Examination of Malebranche's Opinion of Seeing All Things in God.*

CHAPTER VIII

Some Further Considerations Concerning Our Simple Ideas

1. Concerning the simple *ideas* of sensation, it is to be considered that whatsoever is so constituted in nature as to be able, by affecting our senses, to cause any perception in the mind, doth thereby produce in the understanding a simple *idea;* which, whatever be the external cause of it, when it comes to be taken notice of by our discerning faculty, it is by the mind looked on and considered there to be a real *positive idea* in the understanding, as much as any other whatsoever, though perhaps the cause of it be but a privation of the subject.

2. Thus the *ideas* of heat and cold, light and darkness, white and black, motion and rest, are equally clear and *positive ideas* in the mind, though perhaps some of *the causes* which produce them are barely *privations* in those subjects from whence our senses derive those *ideas.* These the understanding, in its view of them, considers all as distinct positive *ideas,* without taking notice of the causes that produce them: which is an inquiry not belonging to the *idea,* as it is in the understanding, but to the nature of the things existing without us. These are two very different things, and carefully to be distinguished: it being

one thing to perceive and know the *idea* of white or black, and quite another to examine what kind of particles they must be and how ranged in the superficies, to make any object appear white or black.

3. A painter or dyer who never inquired into their causes hath the *ideas* of white and black, and other colours, as clearly, perfectly, and distinctly in his understanding, and perhaps more distinctly, than the philosopher who hath busied himself in considering their natures and thinks he knows how far either of them is, in its cause, positive or privative; and the *idea of black* is no less *positive* in his mind than that of white, *however the cause* of that colour in the external object may *be only a privation.*

4. If it were the design of my present undertaking to inquire into the natural causes and manner of perception, I should offer this as a reason *why a privative cause might,* in some cases at least, *produce a positive idea,* viz. that all sensation being produced in us only by different degrees and modes of motion in our animal spirits, variously agitated by external objects, the abatement of any former motion must as necessarily produce a new sensation as the variation or increase of it, and so introduce a new *idea,* which depends only on a different motion of the animal spirits in that organ.

5. But whether this be so or no, I will not here determine but appeal to everyone's own experience

John Locke, *An Essay Concerning Human Understanding.*

whether the shadow of a man, though it consists of nothing but the absence of light (and the more the absence of light is, the more discernible is the shadow) does not, when a man looks on it, cause as clear and positive an *idea* in his mind as a man himself, though covered over with clear sunshine? And the picture of a shadow is a positive thing. Indeed, we have *negative names* which stand not directly for positive *ideas* but for their absence, such as *insipid, silence, nihil,* etc., which words denote positive *ideas,* v.g., *taste, sound, being* with a signification of their absence.

6. And thus one may truly be said to see darkness. For supposing a hole perfectly dark, from whence no light is reflected, it is certain one may see the figure of it, or it may be painted; or, whether the ink I write with makes any other *idea* is a question. The privative causes I have here assigned of positive *ideas* are according to the common opinion; but in truth it will be hard to determine whether there be really any *ideas* from a privative cause, till it be determined *whether rest be any more a privation than motion.*

7. To discover the nature of our *ideas* the better, and to discourse of them intelligibly, it will be convenient to distinguish them as they are *ideas* or perceptions in our minds, and as they are modifications of matter in the bodies that cause such perceptions in us: that so we *may not* think (as perhaps usually is done) that they are exactly the images and *resemblances* of something inherent in the subject: most of those of sensation being in the mind no more the likeness of something existing without us, than the names that stand for them are the likeness of our *ideas,* which yet upon hearing they are apt to excite in us.

8. Whatsoever the mind perceives in itself, or is the immediate object of perception, thought, or understanding, that I call *idea;* and the power to produce any *idea* in our mind, I call *quality* of the subject wherein that power is. Thus a snowball having the power to produce in us the *ideas* of *white, cold,* and *round,* the power to produce those *ideas* in us as they are in the snowball I call *qualities;* and as they are sensations or perceptions in our understandings, I call them *ideas;* which *ideas,* if I speak of sometimes as in the things themselves, I would be understood to mean those qualities in the objects which produce them in us.

9. Qualities thus considered in bodies are:

First, such as are utterly inseparable from the body, in what state soever it be; such as in all the alterations and changes it suffers, all the force can be used upon it, it constantly keeps; and such as sense constantly finds in every particle of matter which has bulk enough to be perceived; and the mind finds inseparable from every particle of matter, though less than to make itself singly be perceived by our senses. V.g., take a grain of wheat, divide it into two parts, each part has still *solidity, extension, figure,* and *mobility;* divide it again, and it retains still the same qualities; and so divide it on, till the parts become insensible: they must retain still each of them all those qualities. For division (which is all that a mill or pestle or any other body does upon another in reducing it to insensible parts) can never take away either solidity, extension, figure, or mobility from any body, but only makes two or more distinct separate masses of matter, of that which was but one before; all which distinct masses, reckoned as so many distinct bodies, after division make a certain number. These I call *original* or *primary qualities* of body; which I think we may observe to produce simple *ideas* in us, viz. solidity, extension, figure, motion or rest, and number.

10. Secondly, such *qualities* which in truth are nothing in the objects themselves but powers to produce various sensations in us by their *primary qualities,* i.e. by the bulk, figure, texture, and motion of their insensible parts, as colours, sounds, tastes, etc. These I call *secondary qualities.* To these might be added a third sort, which are allowed to be barely powers, though they are as much real qualities in the subject as those which I, to comply with the common way of speaking, call *qualities,* but for distinction, *secondary qualities.* For the power in fire to produce a new colour, or consistency in wax or clay, by its primary qualities, is as much a quality in fire as the power it has to produce in me a new *idea* or sensation of warmth or burning, which I felt not before, by the same primary qualities, viz. the bulk, texture, and motion of its insensible parts.

11. The next thing to be considered is how *bodies* produce *ideas* in us; and that is manifestly *by*

impulse, the only way which we can conceive bodies operate in.

12. If then external objects be not united to our minds when they produce *ideas* in it and yet we perceive *these original qualities* in such of them as singly fall under our senses, it is evident that some motion must be thence continued by our nerves or animal spirits, by some parts of our bodies, to the brains or the seat of sensation, there to *produce in our minds the particular* ideas *we have of them.* And since the extension, figure, number, and motion of bodies of an observable bigness may be perceived at a distance *by* the sight, it is evident some singly imperceptible bodies must come from them to the eyes, and thereby convey to the brain some *motion,* which produces these *ideas* which we have of them in us.

13. After the same manner that the *ideas* of these original qualities are produced in us, we may conceive that the *ideas of secondary qualities* are also *produced,* viz. *by the operation of insensible particles on our senses.* For it being manifest that there are bodies and good store of bodies, each whereof are so small that we cannot by any of our senses discover either their bulk, figure, or motion, as is evident in the particles of the air and water and others extremely smaller than those, perhaps as much smaller than the particles of air or water as the particles of air or water are smaller than peas or hail-stones: let us suppose at present that the different motions and figures, bulk and number, of such particles, affecting the several organs of our senses, produce in us those different sensations which we have from the colours and smells of bodies: v.g. that a violet, by the impulse of such insensible particles of matter, of peculiar figures and bulks, and in different degrees and modifications of their motions, causes the *ideas* of the blue colour and sweet scent of that flower to be produced in our minds. It being no more impossible to conceive that God should annex such *ideas* to such motions, with which they have no similitude, than that he should annex the *idea* of pain to the motion of a piece of steel dividing our flesh, with which that *idea* hath no resemblance.

14. What I have said concerning *colours* and *smells* may be understood also of *tastes* and *sounds, and other the like sensible qualities;* which, whatever reality we by mistake attribute to them, are in truth nothing in the objects themselves but powers to produce various sensations in us, and depend *on those primary qualities,* viz. bulk, figure, texture, and motion of parts, as I have said.

15. From whence I think it easy to draw this observation: that the *ideas of primary qualities* of bodies *are resemblances* of them, and their patterns do really exist in the bodies themselves; but the *ideas produced* in us *by* these *secondary qualities have no resemblance* of them at all. There is nothing like our *ideas* existing in the bodies themselves. They are, in the bodies we denominate from them, only a power to produce those sensations in us; and what is sweet, blue, or warm in *idea* is but the certain bulk, figure, and motion of the insensible parts in the bodies themselves, which we call so.

16. *Flame* is denominated *hot* and *light; snow, white* and *cold;* and *manna, white* and *sweet,* from the *ideas* they produce in us. Which qualities are commonly thought to be the same in those bodies that those *ideas* are in us, the one the perfect resemblance of the other, as they are in a mirror, and it would by most men be judged very extravagant if one should say otherwise. And yet he that will consider that *the same fire* that at one distance *produces* in us the sensation of *warmth* does, at a nearer approach, produce in us the far different sensation of *pain,* ought to bethink himself what reason he has to say that his *idea* of *warmth,* which was produced in him by the fire, is actually *in the fire;* and his *idea* of *pain,* which the same fire produced in him the same way, is *not* in the *fire.* Why are whiteness and coldness in snow, and pain not, when it produces the one and the other *idea* in us; and can do neither, but by the bulk, figure, number, and motion of its solid parts?

17. The particular *bulk, number, figure, and motion of the parts of fire or snow are really in them,* whether anyone's senses perceive them or no; and therefore they may be called *real qualities,* because they really exist in those bodies. But *light, heat, whiteness,* or *coldness are no more really in them than sickness or pain is in* manna. Take away the sensation of them; let not the eyes see light or colours, nor the ears hear sounds; let the palate not taste, nor the nose smell; and all colours, tastes, odours, and

sounds, as they are such particular *ideas,* vanish and cease, and are reduced to their causes, i.e. bulk, figure, and motion of parts.

18. A piece of *manna* of a sensible bulk is able to produce in us the *idea* of a round or square figure; and by being removed from one place to another, the *idea* of motion. This *idea* of motion represents it as it really is in the *manna* moving; a circle or square are the same, whether in *idea* or existence, in the mind or in the *manna;* and this, both *motion and figure, are really in the manna,* whether we take notice of them or no: this everybody is ready to agree to. Besides, *manna,* by the bulk, figure, texture, and motion of its parts, has a power to produce the sensations of sickness, and sometimes of acute pains or gripings in us. That these *ideas* of *sickness and pain are not in the* manna, but effects of its operations on us, and are nowhere when we feel them not: this also everyone readily agrees to. And yet men are hardly to be brought to think that *sweetness and whiteness are not really in manna,* which are but the effects of the operations of *manna,* by the motion, size, and figure of its particles, on the eyes and palate, as the pain and sickness caused by *manna* are confessedly nothing but the effects of its operations on the stomach and guts, by the size, motion, and figure of its insensible parts (for by nothing else can a body operate, as has been proved): as if it could not operate on the eyes and palate and thereby produce in the mind particular distinct *ideas* which in itself it has not, as well as we allow it can operate on the guts and stomach and thereby produce distinct *ideas* which in itself it has not. These *ideas* being all effects of the operations of *manna* on several parts of our bodies by the size, figure, number, and motion of its parts, why those produced by the eyes and palate should rather be thought to be really in the *manna* than those produced by the stomach and guts; or why the pain and sickness, *ideas* that are the effects of *manna,* should be thought to be nowhere, when they are not felt: and yet the sweetness and whiteness, effects of the same *manna* on other parts of the body by ways equally as unknown, should be thought to exist in the *manna,* when they are not seen nor tasted, would need some reason to explain.

19. Let us consider the red and white colours in *porphyry.* Hinder light but from striking on it, and its colours vanish: it no longer produces any such *ideas* in us; upon the return of light it produces these appearances on us again. Can anyone think any real alterations are made in the *porphyry* by the presence or absence of light; and that those *ideas* of whiteness and redness are really in *porphyry* in the light, when it is plain *it has no colour in the dark?* It has, indeed, such a configuration of particles, both night and day, as are apt, by the rays of light rebounding from some parts of that hard stone, to produce in us the *idea* of redness, and from others the *idea* of whiteness; but whiteness or redness are not in it at any time, but such a texture that hath the power to produce such a sensation in us.

20. Pound an almond, and the clear white *colour* will be altered into a dirty one, and the sweet *taste* into an oily one. What real alteration can the beating of the pestle make in any body, but an alteration of the *texture* of it?

21. *Ideas* being thus distinguished and understood, we may be able to give an account how the same water, at the same time, may produce the *idea* of cold by one hand and of heat by the other, whereas it is impossible that the same water, if those *ideas* were really in it, should at the same time be both hot and cold. For if we imagine *warmth* as it is *in our hands* to be *nothing but a certain sort and degree of motion in the minute particles of our nerves, or animal spirits,* we may understand how it is possible that the same water may at the same time produce the sensation of heat in one hand and cold in the other; which yet figure never does, that never producing the *idea* of a square by one hand which has produced the *idea* of a globe by another. But if the sensation of heat and cold be nothing but the increase or diminution of the motion of the minute parts of our bodies, caused by the corpuscles of any other body, it is easy to be understood that, if that motion be greater in one hand than in the other, if a body be applied to the two hands, which has in its minute particles a greater motion than in those of one of the hands, and a less than in those of the other, it will increase the motion of the one hand and lessen it in the other, and so cause the different sensations of heat and cold that depend thereon.

22. I have in what just goes before been engaged in physical inquiries a little further than perhaps I

intended. But, it being necessary to make the nature of sensation a little understood; and to make the *difference between the qualities in bodies, and the* ideas *produced by them in the mind,* to be distinctly conceived, without which it were impossible to discourse intelligibly of them: I hope I shall be pardoned this little excursion into natural philosophy, it being necessary in our present inquiry to distinguish the *primary* and *real qualities* of bodies, which are always in them (viz. solidity, extension, figure, number, and motion or rest; and are sometimes perceived by us, viz. when the bodies they are in are big enough singly to be discerned), from those *secondary* and *imputed qualities,* which are but the powers of several combinations of those primary ones, when they operate without being distinctly discerned; whereby we also may come to know what *ideas* are, and what are not, resemblances of something really existing in the bodies we denominate from them.

23. The *qualities,* then, that are in *bodies,* rightly considered, are of *three sorts:*

First, The *bulk, figure, number, situation,* and *motion or rest* of their solid parts. Those are in them, whether we perceive them or no; and when they are of that size that we can discover them, we have by these an *idea* of the thing as it is in itself, as is plain in artificial things. These I call *primary qualities.*

Secondly, The *power* that is in any body, by reason of *its* insensible *primary qualities,* to operate after a peculiar manner on any of our senses, and thereby *produce in us* the *different ideas* of several colours, sounds, smells, tastes, etc. These are usually called sensible qualities.

Thirdly, The *power* that is in any body, *by* reason of the particular constitution of *its primary qualities, to* make such a *change* in the *bulk, figure, texture, and motion of another body,* as to make it operate on our senses differently from what it did before. Thus the sun has a power to make wax white, and fire to make lead fluid. These *are* usually called powers.

The first of these, as has been said, I think may be properly called *real, original,* or *primary qualities,* because they are in the things themselves, whether they are perceived or no; and upon their different modifications it is that the secondary qualities depend.

The other two are only powers to act differently upon other things, which powers result from the different modifications of those primary qualities.

24. But though *these two latter sorts of qualities are powers barely,* and nothing but powers relating to several other bodies and resulting from the different modifications of the original qualities, yet they are generally otherwise thought of. For *the second sort,* viz. the powers to produce several *ideas* in us by our senses, *are looked upon as real qualities in the things* thus affecting us; but *the third sort are called and esteemed barely powers,* v.g. the *idea* of heat or light which we receive by our eyes or touch from the sun are commonly thought *real qualities* existing in the sun and something more than mere powers in it. But when we consider the sun in reference to wax, which it melts or blanches, we look upon the whiteness and softness produced in the wax not as qualities in the sun but effects produced by *powers* in it: whereas, if rightly considered, these qualities of light and warmth, which are perceptions in me when I am warmed or enlightened by the sun, are no otherwise in the sun than the changes, made in the wax when it is blanched or melted, are in the sun. They are all of them equally powers in the sun, depending on its primary qualities; whereby it is able in the one case so to alter the bulk, figure, texture, or motion of some of the insensible parts of my eyes or hands as thereby to produce in me the *idea* of light or heat; and in the other, it is able so to alter the bulk, figure, texture, or motion of the insensible parts of the wax, as to make them fit to produce in me the distinct *ideas* of white and fluid.

25. The reason *why the one are ordinarily taken for real qualities and the other only for bare powers* seems to be because the *ideas* we have of distinct colours, sounds, etc., containing nothing at all in them of bulk, figure, or motion, we are apt to think them the effects of these primary qualities which appear not to our senses to operate in their production, and with which they have not any apparent congruity or conceivable connexion. Hence it is that we are so forward to imagine that those *ideas* are the resemblances of something really existing in the objects themselves, since sensation discovers nothing of bulk, figure, or motion of parts in their pro-

duction, nor can reason show how bodies by their bulk, figure, and motion should produce in the mind the *ideas* of blue or yellow, etc. But in the other case, in the operations of bodies changing the qualities one of another, we plainly discover that the quality produced hath commonly no resemblance with anything in the thing producing it; wherefore we look on it as a bare effect of power. For, though receiving the *idea* of heat or light from the sun, we are apt to think it is a perception and resemblance of such a quality in the sun: yet when we see wax or a fair face receive change of colour from the sun, we cannot imagine that to be the reception or resemblance of anything in the sun, because we find not those different colours in the sun itself. For, our senses being able to observe a likeness or unlikeness of sensible qualities in two different external objects, we forwardly enough conclude the production of any sensible quality in any subject to be an effect of bare power, and not the communication of any quality which was really in the efficient, when we find no such sensible quality in the thing that produced it. But our senses not being able to discover any unlikeness between the *idea* produced in us and the quality of the object producing it, we are apt to imagine that our *ideas* are resemblances of something in the objects, and not the effects of certain powers placed in the modification of their primary qualities, with which primary qualities the *ideas* produced in us have no resemblance.

26. To conclude, beside those before-mentioned *primary qualities* in bodies, viz. bulk, figure, extension, number, and motion of their solid parts: all the rest, whereby we take notice of bodies and distinguish them one from another, are nothing else but several powers in them, depending on those primary qualities; whereby they are fitted, either by immediately operating on our bodies to produce several different *ideas* in us, or else, by operating on other bodies, so to change their primary qualities as to render them capable of producing *ideas* in us different from what before they did. The former of these, I think, may be called *secondary qualities immediately perceivable,* the latter *secondary qualities, mediately perceivable.*

Three Dialogues Between Hylas and Philonous

GEORGE BERKELEY

George Berkeley (1685–1753) published *Three Dialogues Between Hylas and Philonous* when he was just 28 years old. These dialogues followed his unpopular *A Treatise Concerning the Principles of Human Knowledge.* Berkeley, later bishop of Cloyne, is associated with the philosophy known as "idealism" and with its characteristic slogan: *esse est percipi* (to be is to be perceived). His many writings also include *De Motu; Alciphron; The Analyst;* and, not the least, *Siris: A Chain of Philosophical Reflections and Inquiries Concerning the Virtues of Tar-water, and Divers Other Subjects.*

THE FIRST DIALOGUE

Philonous. Good morrow, Hylas. I did not expect to find you abroad so early.

Hylas. It is indeed something unusual; but my thoughts were so taken up with a subject I was discoursing of last night that, finding I could not sleep, I resolved to rise and take a turn in the garden.

George Berkeley, *Three Dialogues Between Hylas and Philonous.*

Phil. It happened well, to let you see what inno- cent and agreeable pleasures you lose every morning. Can there be a pleasanter time of the day or a more delightful season of the year? That purple sky, these wild but sweet notes of birds, the fragrant bloom upon the trees and flowers, the gentle influence of the rising sun—these and a thousand nameless beauties of nature inspire the soul with secret transports; its faculties, too, being at this time fresh and lively, are fit for those meditations which the solitude of a gar- den and tranquility of the morning naturally dispose us to. But I am afraid I interrupt your thoughts, for you seemed very intent on something.

Hyl. It is true, I was, and shall be obliged to you if you will permit me to go on in the same vein; not that I would by any means deprive myself of your company, for my thoughts always flow more easily in conversation with a friend than when I am alone; but my request is that you would suffer me to impart my reflections to you.

Phil. With all my heart, it is what I should have requested myself if you had not prevented me.

Hyl. I was considering the odd fate of those men who have in all ages, through an affectation of being distinguished from the vulgar, or some unaccount- able turn of thought, pretended either to believe noth- ing at all or to believe the most extravagant things in the world. This, however, might be borne if their paradoxes and skepticism did not draw after them some consequences of general disadvantage to mankind. But the mischief lies here: that when men of less leisure see them who are supposed to have spent their whole time in the pursuits of knowledge professing an entire ignorance of all things or advancing such notions as are repugnant to plain and commonly received principles, they will be tempted to entertain suspicions concerning the most impor- tant truths, which they had hitherto held sacred and unquestionable.

Phil. I entirely agree with you as to the ill ten- dency of the affected doubts of some philosophers and fantastical conceits of others. I am even so far gone of late in this way of thinking that I have quit- ted several of the sublime notions I had got in their schools for vulgar opinions. And I give it you on my word, since this revolt from metaphysical notions to the plain dictates of nature and common sense, I find my understanding strangely enlightened, so that I can now easily comprehend a great many things which before were all mystery and riddle.

Hyl. I am glad to find there was nothing in the accounts I heard of you.

Phil. Pray, what were those?

Hyl. You were represented in last night's conver- sation as one who maintained the most extravagant opinion that ever entered into the mind of man, to wit, that there is no such thing as "material substance" in the world.

Phil. That there is no such thing as what philoso- phers call "material substance," I am seriously per- suaded; but if I were made to see anything absurd or skeptical in this, I should then have the same reason to renounce this that I imagine I have now to reject the contrary opinion.

Hyl. What! Can anything be more fantastical, more repugnant to common sense or a more manifest piece of skepticism than to believe there is no such thing as matter?

Phil. Softly, good Hylas. What if it should prove that you, who hold there is, are, by virtue of that opin- ion, a greater skeptic and maintain more paradoxes and repugnances to common sense than I who believe no such thing?

Hyl. You may as soon persuade me the part is greater than the whole, as that, in order to avoid absurdity and skepticism, I should ever be obliged to give up my opinion in this point.

Phil. Well then, are you content to admit that opinion for true which, upon examination, shall appear most agreeable to common sense and remote from skepticism?

Hyl. With all my heart. Since you are for raising disputes about the plainest things in nature, I am con- tent for once to hear what you have to say.

Phil. Pray, Hylas, what do you mean by a "skep- tic?"

Hyl. I mean what all men mean, one that doubts of everything.

Phil. He then who entertains no doubt concerning some particular point, with regard to that point can- not be thought a skeptic.

Hyl. I agree with you.

Phil. Whether does doubting consist in embracing the affirmative or negative side of a question?

Hyl. In neither; for whoever understands English cannot but know that *doubting* signifies a suspense between both.

Phil. He then that denies any point can no more be said to doubt of it than he who affirms it with the same degree of assurance.

Hyl. True.

Phil. And, consequently, for such his denial is no more to be esteemed a skeptic than the other.

Hyl. I acknowledge it.

Phil. How comes it to pass then, Hylas, that you pronounce me a skeptic because I deny what you affirm, to wit, the existence of matter? Since, for aught you can tell, I am as peremptory in my denial as you in your affirmation.

Hyl. Hold, Philonous, I have been a little out in my definition; but every false step a man makes in discourse is not to be insisted on. I said indeed that a "skeptic" was one who doubted of everything; but I should have added: or who denies the reality and truth of things.

Phil. What things? Do you mean the principles and theorems of sciences? But these you know are universal intellectual notions, and consequently independent of matter; the denial therefore of this does not imply the denying them.

Hyl. I grant it. But are there no other things? What think you of distrusting the senses, of denying the real existence of sensible things, or pretending to know nothing of them. Is not this sufficient to denominate a man a skeptic?

Phil. Shall we therefore examine which of us it is that denies the reality of sensible things or professes the greatest ignorance of them, since, if I take you rightly, he is to be esteemed the greatest skeptic?

Hyl. That is what I desire.

Phil. What mean you by "sensible things?"

Hyl. Those things which are perceived by the senses. Can you imagine that I mean anything else?

Phil. Pardon me, Hylas, if I am desirous clearly to apprehend your notions, since this may much shorten our inquiry. Suffer me then to ask you this further question. Are those things only perceived by the senses which are perceived immediately? Or may those things properly be said to be "sensible" which are perceived mediately, or not without the intervention of others?

Hyl. I do not sufficiently understand you.

Phil. In reading a book, what I immediately perceive are the letters, but mediately, or by means of these, are suggested to my mind the notions of God, virtue, truth, etc. Now, that the letters are truly sensible things, or perceived by sense, there is no doubt; but I would know whether you take the things suggested by them to be so too.

Hyl. No, certainly; it were absurd to think God or virtue sensible things, though they may be signified and suggested to the mind by sensible marks with which they have an arbitrary connection.

Phil. It seems, then, that by "sensible things" you mean those only which can be perceived immediately by sense.

Hyl. Right.

Phil. Does it not follow from this that, though I see one part of the sky red, and another blue, and that my reason does thence evidently conclude there must be some cause of that diversity of colors, yet that cause cannot be said to be a sensible thing or perceived by the sense of seeing?

Hyl. It does.

Phil. In like manner, though I hear variety of sounds, yet I cannot be said to hear the causes of those sounds.

Hyl. You cannot.

Phil. And when by my touch I perceive a thing to be hot and heavy, I cannot say, with any truth or propriety, that I feel the cause of its heat or weight.

Hyl. To prevent any more questions of this kind, I tell you once for all that by "sensible things" I mean those only which are perceived by sense, and that in truth the senses perceive nothing which they do not perceive immediately, for they make no inferences. The deducing therefore of causes or occasions from effects and appearances, which alone are perceived by sense, entirely relates to reason.

Phil. This point then is agreed between us—that *sensible things are those only which are immediately perceived by sense.* You will further inform me whether we immediately perceive by sight anything besides light and colors and figures; or by hearing, anything but sounds; by the palate, anything beside tastes; by the smell, besides odors; or by the touch, more than tangible qualities.

Hyl. We do not.

Phil. It seems, therefore, that if you take away all sensible qualities, there remains nothing sensible?

Hyl. I grant it.

Phil. Sensible things therefore are nothing else but so many sensible qualities or combinations of sensible qualities?

Hyl. Nothing else.

Phil. Heat is then a sensible thing?

Hyl. Certainly.

Phil. Does the reality of sensible things consist in being perceived, or is it something distinct from their being perceived, and that bears no relation to the mind?

Hyl. To *exist* is one thing, and to be *perceived* is another.

Phil. I speak with regard to sensible things only; and of these I ask, whether by their real existence you mean a subsistence exterior to the mind and distinct from their being perceived?

Hyl. I mean a real absolute being, distinct from and without any relation to their being perceived.

Phil. Heat therefore, if it be allowed a real being, must exist without the mind?

Hyl. It must.

Phil. Tell me, Hylas, is this real existence equally compatible to all degrees of heat, which we perceive, or is there any reason why we should attribute it to some and deny it to others? And if there be, pray let me know that reason.

Hyl. Whatever degree of heat we perceive by sense, we may be sure the same exists in the object that occasions it.

Phil. What! the greatest as well as the least?

Hyl. I tell you, the reason is plainly the same in respect of both: they are both perceived by sense; nay, the greater degree of heat is more sensibly perceived; and consequently, if there is any difference, we are more certain of its real existence than we can be of the reality of a lesser degree.

Phil. But is not the most vehement and intense degree of heat a very great pain?

Hyl. No one can deny it.

Phil. And is any unperceiving thing capable of pain or pleasure?

Hyl. No, certainly.

Phil. Is your material substance a senseless being or a being endowed with sense and perception?

Hyl. It is senseless, without doubt.

Phil. It cannot, therefore, be the subject of pain?

Hyl. By no means.

Phil. Nor, consequently, of the greatest heat perceived by sense, since you acknowledge this to be no small pain?

Hyl. I grant it.

Phil. What shall we say then of your external object: is it a material substance, or no?

Hyl. It is a material substance with the sensible qualities inhering in it.

Phil. How then can a great heat exist in it, since you own it cannot in a material substance? I desire you would clear this point.

Hyl. Hold, Philonous, I fear I was out in yielding intense heat to be a pain. It should seem rather that pain is something distinct from heat, and the consequence or effect of it.

Phil. Upon putting your hand near the fire, do you perceive one simple uniform sensation or two distinct sensations?

Hyl. But one simple sensation.

Phil. Is not the heat immediately perceived?

Hyl. It is.

Phil. And the pain?

Hyl. True.

Phil. Seeing therefore they are both immediately perceived at the same time, and the fire affects you only with one simple or uncompounded idea, it follows that this same simple idea is both the intense heat immediately perceived and the pain; and, consequently, that the intense heat immediately perceived is nothing distinct from a particular sort of pain.

Hyl. It seems so.

Phil. Again, try in your thoughts, Hylas, if you can conceive a vehement sensation to be without pain or pleasure.

Hyl. I cannot.

Phil. Or can you frame to yourself an idea of sensible pain or pleasure, in general, abstracted from every particular idea of heat, cold, tastes, smells, etc.?

Hyl. I do not find that I can.

Phil. Does it not therefore follow that sensible pain is nothing distinct from those sensations or ideas—in an intense degree?

Hyl. It is undeniable; and, to speak the truth, I begin to suspect a very great heat cannot exist but in a mind perceiving it.

Phil. What! are you then in that *skeptical* state of suspense, between affirming and denying?

Hyl. I think I may be positive in the point. A very violent and painful heat cannot exist without the mind.

Phil. It has not therefore, according to you, any real being?

Hyl. I own it.

Phil. Is it therefore certain that there is no body in nature really hot?

Hyl. I have not denied there is any real heat in bodies. I only say there is no such thing as an intense real heat.

Phil. But did you not say before that all degrees of heat were equally real, or, if there was any difference, that the greater were more undoubtedly real than the lesser?

Hyl. True; but it was because I did not then consider the ground there is for distinguishing between them, which I now plainly see. And it is this: because intense heat is nothing else but a particular kind of painful sensation, and pain cannot exist but in a perceiving being, it follows that no intense heat can really exist in an unperceiving corporeal substance. But this is no reason why we should deny heat in an inferior degree to exist in such a substance.

Phil. But how shall we be able to discern those degrees of heat which exist only in the mind from those which exist without it?

Hyl. That is no difficult matter. You know the least pain cannot exist unperceived; whatever, therefore, degree of heat is a pain exists only in the mind. But as for all other degrees of heat nothing obliges us to think the same of them.

Phil. I think you granted before that no unperceiving being was capable of pleasure any more than of pain.

Hyl. I did.

Phil. And is not warmth, or a more gentle degree of heat than what causes uneasiness, a pleasure?

Hyl. What then?

Phil. Consequently, it cannot exist without the mind in an unperceiving substance, or body.

Hyl. So it seems.

Phil. Since, therefore, as well those degrees of heat that are not painful, as those that are, can exist only in a thinking substance, may we not conclude that external bodies are absolutely incapable of any degree of heat whatsoever?

Hyl. On second thoughts, I do not think it is so evident that warmth is a pleasure as that a great degree of heat is a pain.

Phil. I do not pretend that warmth is as great a pleasure as heat is a pain. But if you grant it to be even a small pleasure, it serves to make good my conclusion.

Hyl. I could rather call it an "indolence." It seems to be nothing more than a privation of both pain and pleasure. And that such a quality or state as this may agree to an unthinking substance, I hope you will not deny.

Phil. If you are resolved to maintain that warmth, or a gentle degree of heat, is no pleasure, I know not how to convince you otherwise than by appealing to your own sense. But what think you of cold?

Hyl. The same that I do of heat. An intense degree of cold is a pain; for to feel a very great cold is to perceive a great uneasiness; it cannot therefore exist without the mind; but a lesser degree of cold may, as well as a lesser degree of heat.

Phil. Those bodies, therefore, upon whose application to our own we perceive a moderate degree of heat must be concluded to have a moderate degree of heat or warmth in them; and those upon whose application we feel a like degree of cold must be thought to have cold in them.

Hyl. They must.

Phil. Can any doctrine be true that necessarily leads a man into an absurdity?

Hyl. Without doubt it cannot.

Phil. Is it not an absurdity to think that the same thing should be at the same time both cold and warm?

Hyl. It is.

Phil. Suppose now one of your hands hot, and the other cold, and that they are both at once put into the same vessel of water, in an intermediate state, will not the water seem cold to one hand, and warm to the other?

Hyl. It will.

Phil. Ought we not therefore, by your principles, to conclude it is really both cold and warm at the same time, that is, according to your own concession, to believe an absurdity?

Hyl. I confess it seems so.

Phil. Consequently, the principles themselves are false, since you have granted that no true principle leads to an absurdity.

Hyl. But, after all, can anything be more absurd than to say, *there is no heat in the fire?*

Phil. To make the point still clearer; tell me whether, in two cases exactly alike, we ought not to make the same judgment?

Hyl. We ought.

Phil. When a pin pricks your finger, does it not rend and divide the fibres of your flesh?

Hyl. It does.

Phil. And when a coal burns your finger, does it any more?

Hyl. It does not.

Phil. Since, therefore, you neither judge the sensation itself occasioned by the pin, nor anything like it to be in the pin, you should not, conformably to what you have now granted, judge the sensation occasioned by the fire, or anything like it, to be in the fire.

Hyl. Well, since it must be so, I am content to yield this point and acknowledge that heat and cold are only sensations existing in our minds. But there still remain qualities enough to secure the reality of external things.

Phil. But what will you say, Hylas, if it shall appear that the case is the same with regard to all other sensible qualities, and that they can no more be supposed to exist without the mind than heat and cold?

Hyl. Then, indeed, you will have done something to the purpose; but that is what I despair of seeing proved.

Phil. Let us examine them in order. What think you of tastes—do they exist without the mind, or no?

Hyl. Can any man in his senses doubt whether sugar is sweet, or wormwood bitter?

Phil. Inform me, Hylas. Is a sweet taste a particular kind of pleasure or pleasant sensation, or is it not?

Hyl. It is.

Phil. And is not bitterness some kind of uneasiness or pain?

Hyl. I grant it.

Phil. If, therefore, sugar and wormwood are unthinking corporeal substances existing without the mind, how can sweetness and bitterness, that is, pleasure and pain, agree to them?

Hyl. Hold, Philonous. I now see what it was [that] deluded me all this time. You asked whether heat and cold, sweetness and bitterness, were not particular sorts of pleasure and pain; to which I answered simply that they were. Whereas I should have thus distinguished: those qualities as perceived by us are pleasures or pains, but not as existing in the external objects. We must not therefore conclude absolutely that there is no heat in the fire or sweetness in the sugar, but only that heat or sweetness, as perceived by us, are not in the fire or sugar. What say you to this?

Phil. I say it is nothing to the purpose. Our discourse proceeded altogether concerning sensible things, which you defined to be "the things we immediately perceive by our senses." Whatever other qualities, therefore, you speak of, as distinct from these, I know nothing of them, neither do they at all belong to the point in dispute. You may, indeed, pretend to have discovered certain qualities which you do not perceive and assert those insensible qualities exist in fire and sugar. But what use can be made of this to your present purpose, I am at a loss to conceive. Tell me then once more, do you acknowledge that heat and cold, sweetness and bitterness (meaning those qualities which are perceived by the senses), do not exist without the mind?

Hyl. I see it is to no purpose to hold out, so I give up the cause as to those mentioned qualities, though I profess it sounds oddly to say that sugar is not sweet.

Phil. But, for your further satisfaction, take this along with you: that which at other times seems sweet shall, to a distempered palate, appear bitter. And nothing can be plainer than that divers persons perceive different tastes in the same food, since that which one man delights in, another abhors. And how could this be if the taste was something really inherent in the food?

Hyl. I acknowledge I know not how.

Phil. In the next place, odors are to be considered. And with regard to these I would fain know whether what has been said of tastes does not exactly agree to them? Are they not so many pleasing or displeasing sensations?

Hyl. They are.

Phil. Can you then conceive it possible that they should exist in an unperceiving thing?

Hyl. I cannot.

Phil. Or can you imagine that filth and ordure affect those brute animals that feed on them out of choice with the same smells which we perceive in them?

Hyl. By no means.

Phil. May we not therefore conclude of smells, as of the other forementioned qualities, that they cannot exist in any but a perceiving substance or mind?

Hyl. I think so.

Phil. Then as to sounds, what must we think of them, are they accidents really inherent in external bodies or not?

Hyl. That they inhere not in the sonorous bodies is plain from hence; because a bell struck in the exhausted receiver of an air-pump sends forth no sound. The air, therefore, must be thought the subject of sound.

Phil. What reason is there for that, Hylas?

Hyl. Because, when any motion is raised in the air, we perceive a sound greater or lesser, in proportion to the air's motion; but without some motion in the air we never hear any sound at all.

Phil. And granting that we never hear a sound but when some motion is produced in the air, yet I do not see how you can infer from thence that the sound itself is in the air.

Hyl. It is this very motion in the external air that produces in the mind the sensation of sound. For, striking on the drum of the ear, it causes a vibration which by the auditory nerves being communicated to the brain, the soul is thereupon affected with the sensation called "sound."

Phil. What! is sound then a sensation?

Hyl. I tell you, as perceived by us it is a particular sensation in the mind.

Phil. And can any sensation exist without the mind?

Hyl. No, certainly.

Phil. How then can sound, being a sensation, exist in the air if by the "air" you mean a senseless substance existing without the mind?

Hyl. You must distinguish, Philonous, between sound as it is perceived by us, and as it is in itself; or (which is the same thing) between the sound we immediately perceive and that which exists without us. The former, indeed, is a particular kind of sensation, but the latter is merely a vibrative or undulatory motion in the air.

Phil. I thought I had already obviated that distinction by the answer I gave when you were applying it in a like case before. But, to say no more of that, are you sure then that sound is really nothing but motion?

Hyl. I am.

Phil. Whatever, therefore, agrees to real sound may with truth be attributed to motion?

Hyl. It may.

Phil. It is then good sense to speak of "motion" as of a thing that is *loud, sweet, acute,* or *grave.*

Hyl. I see you are resolved not to understand me. Is it not evident those accidents or modes belong only to sensible sound, or sound in the common acceptation of the word, but not to sound in the real and philosophic sense, which, as I just now told you, is nothing but a certain motion of the air?

Phil. It seems then there are two sorts of sound—the one vulgar, or that which is heard, the other philosophical and real?

Hyl. Even so.

Phil. And the latter consists in motion?

Hyl. I told you so before.

Phil. Tell me, Hylas, to which of the senses, think you, the idea of motion belongs? To the hearing?

Hyl. No, certainly; but to the sight and touch.

Phil. It should follow then that, according to you, real sounds may possibly be *seen* or *felt,* but never *heard.*

Hyl. Look you, Philonous, you may, if you please, make a jest of my opinion, but that will not alter the truth of things. I own, indeed, the inferences you draw me into sound something oddly, but common language, you know, is framed by, and for the use of, the vulgar. We must not therefore wonder if expressions adapted to exact philosophic notions seem uncouth and out of the way.

Phil. Is it come to that? I assure you I imagine myself to have gained no small point since you make so light of departing from common phrases and opinions, it being a main part of our inquiry to examine whose notions are widest of the common road and most repugnant to the general sense of the world. But can you think it no more than a philosophical paradox to say that "real sounds are never heard," and that the idea of them is obtained by some other sense? And is there nothing in this contrary to nature and the truth of things?

Hyl. To deal ingenuously, I do not like it. And, after the concessions already made, I had as well grant that sounds, too, have no real being without the mind.

Phil. And I hope you will make no difficulty to acknowledge the same of colors.

Hyl. Pardon me; the case of colors is very different. Can anything be plainer than that we see them on the objects?

Phil. The objects you speak of are, I suppose, corporeal substances existing without the mind?

Hyl. They are.

Phil. And have true and real colors inhering in them?

Hyl. Each visible object has that color which we see in it.

Phil. How! is there anything visible but what we perceive by sight?

Hyl. There is not.

Phil. And do we perceive anything by sense which we do not perceive immediately?

Hyl. How often must I be obliged to repeat the same thing? I tell you, we do not.

Phil. Have patience, good Hylas, and tell me once more whether there is anything immediately perceived by the senses except sensible qualities. I know you asserted there was not; but I would now be informed whether you still persist in the same opinion.

Hyl. I do.

Phil. Pray, is your corporeal substance either a sensible quality or made up of sensible qualities?

Hyl. What a question that is! Who ever thought it was?

Phil. My reason for asking was, because in saying "each visible object has that color which we see in it," you make visible objects to be corporeal substances, which implies either that corporeal substances are sensible qualities or else that there is something besides sensible qualities perceived by sight; but as this point was formerly agreed between us, and is still maintained by you, it is a clear consequence that your corporeal substance is nothing distinct from sensible qualities.

Hyl. You may draw as many absurd consequences as you please and endeavor to perplex the plainest things, but you shall never persuade me out of my senses. I clearly understand my own meaning.

Phil. I wish you would make me understand it, too. But, since you are unwilling to have your notion of corporeal substance examined, I shall urge that point no further. Only be pleased to let me know whether the same colors which we see exist in external bodies or some other.

Hyl. The very same.

Phil. What! are then the beautiful red and purple we see on yonder clouds really in them? Or do you imagine they have in themselves any other form than that of a dark mist or vapor?

Hyl. I must own, Philonous, those colors are not really in the clouds as they seem to be at this distance. They are only apparent colors.

Phil. "Apparent" call you them? How shall we distinguish these apparent colors from real?

Hyl. Very easily. Those are to be thought apparent which, appearing only at a distance, vanish upon a nearer approach.

Phil. And those, I suppose, are to be thought real which are discovered by the most near and exact survey.

Hyl. Right.

Phil. Is the nearest and exactest survey made by the help of a microscope or by the naked eye?

Hyl. By a microscope, doubtless.

Phil. But a microscope often discovers colors in

an object different from those perceived by the unassisted sight. And, in case we had microscopes magnifying to any assigned degree, it is certain that no object whatsoever, viewed through them, would appear in the same color which it exhibits to the naked eye.

Hyl. And what will you conclude from all this? You cannot argue that there are really and naturally no colors on objects because by artificial managements they may be altered or made to vanish.

Phil. I think it may evidently be concluded from your own concessions that all the colors we see with our naked eyes are only apparent as those on the clouds, since they vanish upon a more close and accurate inspection which is afforded us by a microscope. Then, as to what you say by way of prevention: I ask you whether the real and natural state of an object is better discovered by a very sharp and piercing sight or by one which is less sharp?

Hyl. By the former without doubt.

Phil. Is it not plain from dioptrics that microscopes make the sight more penetrating and represent objects as they would appear to the eye in case it were naturally endowed with a most exquisite sharpness?

Hyl. It is.

Phil. Consequently, the microscopical representation is to be thought that which best sets forth the real nature of the thing, or what it is in itself. The colors, therefore, by it perceived are more genuine and real than those perceived otherwise.

Hyl. I confess there is something in what you say.

Phil. Besides, it is not only possible but manifest that there actually are animals whose eyes are by nature framed to perceive those things which by reason of their minuteness escape our sight. What think you of those inconceivably small animals perceived by glasses? Must we suppose they are all stark blind? Or, in case they see, can it be imagined their sight has not the same use in preserving their bodies from injuries which appears in that of all other animals? And if it has, is it not evident they must see particles less than their own bodies, which will present them with a far different view in each object from that which strikes our senses? Even our own eyes do not always represent objects to us after the same manner. In the jaundice everyone knows that all things seem

yellow. Is it not therefore highly probable those animals in whose eyes we discern a very different texture from that of ours, and whose bodies abound with different humors, do not see the same colors in every object that we do? From all which should it not seem to follow that all colors are equally apparent, and that none of those which we perceive are really inherent in any outward object?

Hyl. It should.

Phil. The point will be past all doubt if you consider that, in case colors were real properties or affections inherent in external bodies, they could admit of no alteration without some change wrought in the very bodies themselves; but is it not evident from what has been said that, upon the use of microscopes, upon a change happening in the humors of the eye, or a variation of distance, without any manner of real alteration in the thing itself, the colors of any object are either changed or totally disappear? Nay, all other circumstances remaining the same, change but the situation of some objects and they shall present different colors to the eye. The same thing happens upon viewing an object in various degrees of light. And what is more known than that the same bodies appear differently colored by candlelight from what they do in the open day? Add to these the experiment of a prism which, separating the heterogeneous rays of light, alters the color of any object and will cause the whitest to appear of a deep blue or red to the naked eye. And now tell me whether you are still of opinion that every body has its true real color inhering in it; and if you think it has, I would fain know further from you what certain distance and position of the object, what peculiar texture and formation of the eye, what degree or kind of light is necessary for ascertaining that true color and distinguishing it from apparent ones.

Hyl. I own myself entirely satisfied that they are all equally apparent and that there is no such thing as color really inhering in external bodies, but that it is altogether in the light. And what confirms me in this opinion is that in proportion to the light colors are still more or less vivid; and if there be no light, then are there no colors perceived. Besides, allowing there are colors on external objects, yet, how is it possible for us to perceive them? For no external body affects the mind unless it acts first on our organs of sense. But the only action of bodies is motion, and motion cannot be communicated otherwise than by impulse. A distant object, therefore, cannot act on the eye, nor consequently make itself or its properties perceivable to the soul. Whence it plainly follows that it is immediately some contiguous substance which, operating on the eye, occasions a perception of colors; and such is light.

Phil. How! is light then a substance?

Hyl. I tell you, Philonous, external light is nothing but a thin fluid substance whose minute particles, being agitated with a brisk motion and in various manners reflected from the different surfaces of outward objects to the eyes, communicate different motions to the optic nerves; which, being propagated to the brain, cause therein various impressions, and these are attended with the sensations of red, blue, yellow, etc.

Phil. It seems, then, the light does no more than shake the optic nerves.

Hyl. Nothing else.

Phil. And, consequent to each particular motion of the nerves, the mind is affected with a sensation which is some particular color.

Hyl. Right.

Phil. And these sensations have no existence without the mind.

Hyl. They have not.

Phil. How then do you affirm that colors are in the light, since by "light" you understand a corporeal substance external to the mind?

Hyl. Light and colors, as immediately perceived by us, I grant cannot exist without the mind. But in themselves they are only the motions and configurations of certain insensible particles of matter.

Phil. Colors, then, in the vulgar sense, or taken for the immediate objects of sight, cannot agree to any but a perceiving substance.

Hyl. That is what I say.

Phil. Well then, since you give up the point as to those sensible qualities which are alone thought colors by all mankind besides, you may hold what you please with regard to those invisible ones of the philosophers. It is not my business to dispute about them; only I would advise you to bethink yourself whether, considering the inquiry we are upon, it be

prudent for you to affirm—*the red and blue which we see are not real colors, but certain unknown motions and figures which no man ever did or can see are truly so.* Are not these shocking notions, and are not they subject to as many ridiculous inferences as those you were obliged to renounce before in the case of sounds?

Hyl. I frankly own, Philonous, that it is in vain to stand out any longer. Colors, sounds, tastes, in a word, all those termed "secondary qualities," have certainly no existence without the mind. But by this acknowledgment I must not be supposed to derogate anything from the reality of matter or external objects; seeing it is no more than several philosophers maintain, who nevertheless are the farthest imaginable from denying matter. For the clearer understanding of this you must know sensible qualities are by philosophers divided into "primary" and "secondary." The former are extension, figure, solidity, gravity, motion, and rest. And these they hold exist really in bodies. The latter are those above enumerated, or, briefly, all sensible qualities besides the primary, which they assert are only so many sensations or ideas existing nowhere but in the mind. But all this, I doubt not, you are already apprised of. For my part I have been a long time sensible there was such an opinion current among philosophers, but was never thoroughly convinced of its truth till now.

Phil. You are still then of opinion that *extension* and *figures* are inherent in external unthinking substances?

Hyl. I am.

Phil. But what if the same arguments which are brought against secondary qualities will hold good against these also?

Hyl. Why then I shall be obliged to think they too exist only in the mind.

Phil. Is it your opinion the very figure and extension which you perceive by sense exist in the outward object or material substance?

Hyl. It is.

Phil. Have all other animals as good grounds to think the same of the figure and extension which they see and feel?

Hyl. Without doubt, if they have any thought at all.

Phil. Answer me, Hylas. Think you the senses were bestowed upon all animals for their preservation and well-being in life? Or were they given to men alone for this end?

Hyl. I make no question but they have the same use in all other animals.

Phil. If so, is it not necessary they should be enabled by them to perceive their own limbs and those bodies which are capable of harming them?

Hyl. Certainly.

Phil. A mite therefore must be supposed to see his own foot, and things equal or even less than it, as bodies of some considerable dimension, though at the same time they appear to you scarce discernible or at best as so many visible points?

Hyl. I cannot deny it.

Phil. And to creatures less than the mite they will seem yet larger?

Hyl. They will.

Phil. Insomuch that what you can hardly discern will to another extremely minute animal appear as some huge mountain?

Hyl. All this I grant.

Phil. Can one and the same thing be at the same time in itself of different dimensions?

Hyl. That were absurd to imagine.

Phil. But from what you have laid down it follows that both the extension by you perceived and that perceived by the mite itself, as likewise all those perceived by lesser animals, are each of them the true extension of the mite's foot; that is to say, by your own principles you are led into an absurdity.

Hyl. There seems to be some difficulty in the point.

Phil. Again, have you not acknowledged that no real inherent property of any object can be changed without some change in the thing itself?

Hyl. I have.

Phil. But, as we approach to or recede from an object, the visible extension varies, being at one distance ten or a hundred times greater than at another. Does it not therefore follow from hence likewise that it is not really inherent in the object?

Hyl. I own I am at a loss what to think.

Phil. Your judgment will soon be determined if you will venture to think as freely concerning this quality as you have done concerning the rest. Was it not admitted as a good argument that neither heat nor cold was in the water because it seemed warm to one hand and cold to the other?

Hyl. It was.

Phil. Is it not the very same reasoning to conclude there is no extension or figure in an object because to one eye it shall seem little, smooth, and round, when at the same time it appears to the other great, uneven, and angular?

Hyl. The very same. But does this latter fact ever happen?

Phil. You may at any time make the experiment by looking with one eye bare, and with the other through a microscope.

Hyl. I know not how to maintain it, and yet I am loath to give up *extension;* I see so many odd consequences following upon such a concession.

Phil. Odd, say you? After the concessions already made, I hope you will stick at nothing for its oddness. But, on the other hand, should it not seem very odd if the general reasoning which includes all other sensible qualities did not also include extension? If it be allowed that no idea nor anything like an idea can exist in an unperceiving substance, then surely it follows that no figure or mode of extension, which we can either perceive or imagine, or have any idea of, can be really inherent in matter, not to mention the peculiar difficulty there must be in conceiving a material substance, prior to and distinct from extension, to be the *substratum* of extension. Be the sensible quality what it will—figure or sound or color—it seems alike impossible it should subsist in that which does not perceive it.

Hyl. I give up the point for the present, reserving still a right to retract my opinion in case I shall hereafter discover any false step in my progress to it.

Phil. That is a right you cannot be denied. Figures and extension being dispatched, we proceed next to *motion.* Can a real motion in any external body be at the same time both very swift and very slow?

Hyl. It cannot.

Phil. Is not the motion of a body swift in a reciprocal proportion to the time it takes up in describing any given space? Thus a body that describes a mile in an hour moves three times faster than it would in case it described only a mile in three hours.

Hyl. I agree with you.

Phil. And is not time measured by the succession of ideas in our minds?

Hyl. It is.

Phil. And is it not possible ideas should succeed one another twice as fast in your mind as they do in mine, or in that of some spirit of another kind?

Hyl. I own it.

Phil. Consequently, the same body may to another seem to perform its motion over any space in half the time that it does to you. And the same reasoning will hold as to any other proportion; that is to say, according to your principles (since the motions perceived are both really in the object) it is possible one and the same body shall be really moved the same way at once, both very swift and very slow. How is this consistent either with common sense or with what you just now granted?

Hyl. I have nothing to say to it.

Phil. Then as for *solidity;* either you do not mean any sensible quality by that word, and so it is beside our inquiry; or if you do, it must be either hardness or resistance. But both the one and the other are plainly relative to our senses: it being evident that what seems hard to one animal may appear soft to another who has greater force and firmness of limbs. Nor is it less plain that the resistance I feel is not in the body.

Hyl. I own the very sensation of resistance, which is all you immediately perceive, is not in the *body,* but the cause of that sensation is.

Phil. But the causes of our sensations are not things immediately perceived, and therefore not sensible. This point I thought had been already determined.

Hyl. I own it was; but you will pardon me if I seem a little embarrassed; I know not how to quit my old notions.

Phil. To help you out, do but consider that if *extension* be once acknowledged to have no existence without the mind, the same must necessarily be granted of motion, solidity, and gravity, since they all evidently suppose extension. It is therefore superfluous to inquire particularly concerning each of them. In denying extension, you have denied them all to have any real existence.

Hyl. I wonder, Philonous, if what you say be true, why those philosophers who deny the secondary qualities any real existence should yet attribute it to the primary. If there is no difference between them, how can this be accounted for?

Phil. It is not my business to account for every opinion of the philosophers. But, among other reasons which may be assigned for this, it seems probable that pleasure and pain being rather annexed to the former than the latter may be one. Heat and cold, tastes and smells have something more vividly pleasing or disagreeable than the ideas of extension, figure, and motion affect us with. And, it being too visibly absurd to hold that pain or pleasure can be in an unperceiving substance, men are more easily weaned from believing the external existence of the secondary than the primary qualities. You will be satisfied there is something in this if you recollect the difference you made between an intense and more moderate degree of heat, allowing the one a real existence while you denied it to the other. But, after all, there is no rational ground for that distinction, for surely an indifferent sensation is as truly a *sensation* as one more pleasing or painful, and consequently should not any more than they be supposed to exist in an unthinking subject.

Hyl. It is just come into my head, Philonous, that I have somewhere heard of a distinction between *absolute* and *sensible* extension. Now though it be acknowledged that *great* and *small,* consisting merely in the relation which other extended beings have to the parts of our own bodies, do not really inhere in the substances themselves, yet nothing obliges us to hold the same with regard to *absolute* extension, which is something abstracted from *great* and *small,* from this or that particular magnitude or figure. So likewise as to motion: *swift* and *slow* are altogether relative to the succession of ideas in our own minds. But it does not follow, because those modifications of motion exist not without the mind, that therefore absolute motion abstracted from them does not.

Phil. Pray what is it that distinguishes one motion, or one part of extension, from another? Is it not something sensible, as some degree of swiftness or slowness, some certain magnitude or figure peculiar to each?

Hyl. I think so.

Phil. These qualities, therefore, stripped of all sensible properties, are without all specific and numerical differences, as the schools call them.

Hyl. They are.

Phil. That is to say, they are extension in general, and motion in general.

Hyl. Let it be so.

Phil. But it is a universally received maxim that *everything which exists is particular.* How then can motion in general, or extension in general, exist in any corporeal substance?

Hyl. I will take time to solve your difficulty.

Phil. But I think the point may be speedily decided. Without doubt you can tell whether you are able to frame this or that idea. Now I am content to put our dispute on this issue. If you can frame in your thoughts a distinct abstract idea of motion or extension divested of all those sensible modes as swift and slow, great and small, round and square, and the like, which are acknowledged to exist only in the mind, I will then yield the point you contend for. But if you cannot, it will be unreasonable on your side to insist any longer upon what you have no notion of.

Hyl. To confess ingenuously, I cannot.

Phil. Can you even separate the ideas of extension and motion from the ideas of all those qualities which they who make the distinction term "secondary?"

Hyl. What! is it not an easy matter to consider extension and motion by themselves, abstracted from all other sensible qualities? Pray how do the mathematicians treat of them?

Phil. I acknowledge, Hylas, it is not difficult to form general propositions and reasonings about those qualities without mentioning any other, and, in this sense, to consider or treat of them abstractedly. But how does it follow that, because I can pronounce the word "motion" by itself, I can form the idea of it in my mind exclusive of body? Or because theorems may be made of extension and figures, without any mention of *great* or *small,* or any other sensible mode or quality, that therefore it is possible such an abstract

idea of extension, without any particular size or figure or sensible quality, should be distinctly formed and apprehended by the mind? Mathematicians treat of quantity without regarding what other sensible qualities it is attended with, as being altogether indifferent to their demonstrations. But when, laying aside the words, they contemplate the bare ideas, I believe you will find they are not the pure abstracted ideas of extension.

Hyl. But what say you to *pure intellect?* May not abstracted ideas be framed by that faculty?

Phil. Since I cannot frame abstract ideas at all, it is plain I cannot frame them by the help of pure intellect, whatsoever faculty you understand by those words. Besides, not to inquire into the nature of pure intellect and its spiritual objects, as *virtue, reason, God,* or the like, thus much seems manifest that sensible things are only to be perceived by sense or represented by the imagination. Figures, therefore, and extension, being originally perceived by sense, do not belong to pure intellect; but, for your further satisfaction, try if you can frame the idea of any figure abstracted from all particularities of size or even from other sensible qualities.

Hyl. Let me think a little—I do not find that I can.

Phil. And can you think it possible that should really exist in nature which implies a repugnancy in its conception?

Hyl. By no means.

Phil. Since therefore it is impossible even for the mind to disunite the ideas of extension and motion from all other sensible qualities, does it not follow that where the one exist there necessarily the other exist likewise?

Hyl. It should seem so.

Phil. Consequently, the very same arguments which you admitted as conclusive against the secondary qualities are, without any further application of force, against the primary, too. Besides, if you will trust your senses, is it not plain all sensible qualities coexist, or to them appear as being in the same place? Do they ever represent a motion or figure as being divested of all other visible and tangible qualities?

Hyl. You need say no more on this head. I am free to own, if there be no secret error or oversight in our proceedings hitherto, that all sensible qualities are alike to be denied existence without the mind. But my fear is that I have been too liberal in my former concessions, or overlooked some fallacy or other. In short, I did not take time to think.

Phil. For that matter, Hylas, you may take what time you please in reviewing the progress of our inquiry. You are at liberty to recover any slips you might have made, or offer whatever you have omitted which makes for your first opinion.

Hyl. One great oversight I take to be this—that I did not sufficiently distinguish the *object* from the *sensation.* Now, though this latter may not exist without the mind, yet it will not thence follow that the former cannot.

Phil. What object do you mean? The object of the senses?

Hyl. The same.

Phil. It is then immediately perceived?

Hyl. Right.

Phil. Make me to understand the difference between what is immediately perceived and a sensation.

Hyl. The sensation I take to be an act of the mind perceiving; besides which there is something perceived, and this I call the "object." For example, there is red and yellow on that tulip. But then the act of perceiving those colors is in me only, and not in the tulip.

Phil. What tulip do you speak of? Is it that which you see?

Hyl. The same.

Phil. And what do you see besides color, figure, and extension?

Hyl. Nothing.

Phil. What you would say then is that the red and yellow are coexistent with the extension; is it not?

Hyl. That is not all; I would say they have a real existence without the mind, in some unthinking substance.

Phil. That the colors are really in the tulip which I see is manifest. Neither can it be denied that this tulip may exist independent of your mind or mine; but that any immediate object of the senses—that is, any idea, or combination of ideas—should exist in an unthinking substance, or exterior to all minds, is in itself an evident contradiction. Nor can I imagine how this fol-

lows from what you said just now, to wit, that the red and yellow were on the tulip *you saw,* since you do not pretend to *see* that unthinking substance.

Hyl. You have an artful way, Philonous, of diverting our inquiry from the subject.

Phil. I see you have no mind to be pressed that way. To return then to your distinction between *sensation* and *object;* if I take you right, you distinguish in every perception two things, the one an action of the mind, the other not.

Hyl. True.

Phil. And this action cannot exist in, or belong to, any unthinking thing, but whatever besides is implied in a perception may?

Hyl. That is my meaning.

Phil. So that if there was a perception without any act of the mind, it were possible such a perception should exist in an unthinking substance?

Hyl. I grant it. But it is impossible there should be such a perception.

Phil. When is the mind said to be active?

Hyl. When it produces, puts an end to, or changes anything.

Phil. Can the mind produce, discontinue, or change anything but by an act of the will?

Hyl. It cannot.

Phil. The mind therefore is to be accounted *active* in its perceptions so far forth as *volition* is included in them?

Hyl. It is.

Phil. In plucking this flower I am active, because I do it by the motion of my hand, which was consequent upon my volition; so likewise in applying it to my nose. But is either of these smelling?

Hyl. No.

Phil. I act, too, in drawing the air through my nose, because my breathing so rather than otherwise is the effect of my volition. But neither can this be called "smelling," for if it were I should smell every time I breathed in that manner?

Hyl. True.

Phil. Smelling then is somewhat consequent to all this?

Hyl. It is.

Phil. But I do not find my will concerned any further. Whatever more there is—as that I perceive such a particular smell, or any smell at all—this is independent of my will, and therein I am altogether passive. Do you find it otherwise with you, Hylas?

Hyl. No, the very same.

Phil. Then, as to seeing, is it not in your power to open your eyes or keep them shut, to turn them this or that way?

Hyl. Without doubt.

Phil. But does it in like manner depend on your will that in looking on this flower you perceive *white* rather than any other color? Or, directing your open eyes toward yonder part of the heaven, can you avoid seeing the sun? Or is light or darkness the effect of your volition?

Hyl. No, certainly.

Phil. You are then in these respects altogether passive?

Hyl. I am.

Phil. Tell me now whether *seeing* consists in perceiving light and colors or in opening and turning the eyes?

Hyl. Without doubt, in the former.

Phil. Since, therefore, you are in the very perception of light and colors altogether passive, what is become of that action you were speaking of as an ingredient in every sensation? And does it not follow from your own concessions that the perception of light and colors, including no action in it, may exist in an unperceiving substance? And is not this a plain contradiction?

Hyl. I know not what to think of it.

Phil. Besides, since you distinguish the *active* and *passive* in every perception, you must do it in that of pain. But how is it possible that pain, be it as little active as you please, should exist in an unperceiving substance? In short, do but consider the point and then confess ingenuously whether light and colors, tastes, sounds, etc. are not all equally passions or sensations in the soul. You may indeed call them "external objects" and give them in words what subsistence you please. But examine your own thoughts and then tell me whether it be not as I say?

Hyl. I acknowledge, Philonous, that, upon a fair observation of what passes in my mind, I can discover nothing else but that I am a thinking being affected with variety of sensations, neither is it possi-

ble to conceive how a sensation should exist in an unperceiving substance. But then, on the other hand, when I look on sensible things in a different view, considering them as so many modes and qualities, I find it necessary to suppose a material *substratum,* without which they cannot be conceived to exist.

Phil. "Material substratum" call you it? Pray, by which of your senses came you acquainted with that being?

Hyl. It is not itself sensible; its modes and qualities only being perceived by the senses.

Phil. I presume then it was by reflection and reason you obtained the idea of it?

Hyl. I do not pretend to any proper positive idea of it. However, I conclude it exists because qualities cannot be conceived to exist without a support.

Phil. It seems then you have only a relative notion of it, or that you conceive it not otherwise than by conceiving the relation it bears to sensible qualities?

Hyl. Right.

Phil. Be pleased, therefore, to let me know wherein that relation consists.

Hyl. Is it not sufficiently expressed in the term "substratum" or "substance?"

Phil. If so, the word "substratum" should import that it is spread under the sensible qualities or accidents?

Hyl. True.

Phil. And consequently under extension?

Hyl. I own it.

Phil. It is therefore somewhat in its own nature entirely distinct from extension?

Hyl. I tell you extension is only a mode, and matter is something that supports modes. And is it not evident the thing supported is different from the thing supporting?

Phil. So that something distinct from, and exclusive of, extension is supposed to be the *substratum* of extension?

Hyl. Just so.

Phil. Answer me, Hylas, can a thing be spread without extension, or is not the idea of extension necessarily included in *spreading?*

Hyl. It is.

Phil. Whatsoever therefore you suppose spread under anything must have in itself an extension distinct from the extension of that thing under which it is spread?

Hyl. It must.

Phil. Consequently, every corporeal substance being the *substratum* of extension must have in itself another extension by which it is qualified to be a *substratum,* and so on to infinity? And I ask whether this be not absurd in itself and repugnant to what you granted just now, to wit, that the *substratum* was something distinct from and exclusive of extension?

Hyl. Aye, but, Philonous, you take me wrong. I do not mean that matter is *spread* in a gross literal sense under extension. The word "substratum" is used only to express in general the same thing with "substance."

Phil. Well then, let us examine the relation implied in the term "substance." Is it not that it stands under accidents?

Hyl. The very same.

Phil. But that one thing may stand under or support another, must it not be extended?

Hyl. It must.

Phil. Is not therefore this supposition liable to the same absurdity with the former?

Hyl. You still take things in a strict literal sense; that is not fair, Philonous.

Phil. I am not for imposing any sense on your words; you are at liberty to explain them as you please. Only, I beseech you, make me understand something by them. You tell me matter supports or stands under accidents. How! is it as your legs support your body?

Hyl. No; that is the literal sense.

Phil. Pray let me know any sense, literal or not literal, that you understand it in.—How long must I wait for an answer, Hylas?

Hyl. I declare I know not what to say. I once thought I understood well enough what was meant by matter's supporting accidents. But now, the more I think on it, the less can I comprehend it; in short, I find that I know nothing of it.

Phil. It seems then you have no idea at all, neither relative nor positive, of matter; you know neither what it is in itself nor what relation it bears to accidents?

Hyl. I acknowledge it.

Phil. And yet you asserted that you could not conceive how qualities or accidents should really exist without conceiving at the same time a material support of them?

Hyl. I did.

Phil. That is to say, when you conceive the real existence of qualities, you do withal conceive something which you cannot conceive?

Hyl. It was wrong I own. But still I fear there is some fallacy or other. Pray, what think you of this? It is just come into my head that the ground of all our mistake lies in your treating of each quality by itself. Now I grant that each quality cannot singly subsist without the mind. Color cannot without extension, neither can figure without some other sensible quality. But, as the several qualities united or blended together form entire sensible things, nothing hinders why such things may not be supposed to exist without the mind.

Phil. Either, Hylas, you are jesting or have a very bad memory. Though, indeed, we went through all the qualities by name one after another, yet my arguments, or rather your concessions, nowhere tended to prove that the secondary qualities did not subsist each alone by itself, but that they were not *at all* without the mind. Indeed, in treating of figure and motion we concluded they could not exist without the mind, because it was impossible even in thought to separate them from all secondary qualities, so as to conceive them existing by themselves. But then this was not the only argument made use of upon that occasion. But (to pass by all that has been hitherto said and reckon it for nothing, if you will have it so) I am content to put the whole upon this issue. If you can conceive it possible for any mixture or combination of qualities, or any sensible object whatever, to exist without the mind, then I will grant it actually to be so.

Hyl. If it comes to that the point will soon be decided. What more easy than to conceive a tree or house existing by itself, independent of, and unperceived by, any mind whatsoever? I do at this present time conceive them existing after that manner.

Phil. How say you, Hylas, can you see a thing which is at the same time unseen?

Hyl. No, that were a contradiction.

Phil. Is it not as great a contradiction to talk of *conceiving* a thing which is *unconceived?*

Hyl. It is.

Phil. The tree or house, therefore, which you think of is conceived by you?

Hyl. How should it be otherwise?

Phil. And what is conceived is surely in the mind?

Hyl. Without question, that which is conceived is in the mind.

Phil. How then came you to say you conceived a house or tree existing independent and out of all minds whatsoever?

Hyl. That was I own an oversight, but stay, let me consider what led me into it.—It is a pleasant mistake enough. As I was thinking of a tree in a solitary place where no one was present to see it, methought that was to conceive a tree as existing unperceived or unthought of, not considering that I myself conceived it all the while. But now I plainly see that all I can do is to frame ideas in my own mind. I may indeed conceive in my own thoughts the idea of a tree, or a house, or a mountain, but that is all. And this is far from proving that I can conceive them *existing out of the minds of all spirits.*

Phil. You acknowledge then that you cannot possibly conceive how any one corporeal sensible thing should exist otherwise than in a mind?

Hyl. I do.

Phil. And yet you will earnestly contend for the truth of that which you cannot so much as conceive?

Hyl. I profess I know not what to think; but still there are some scruples remain with me. Is it not certain I see things at a distance? Do we not perceive the stars and moon, for example, to be a great way off? Is not this, I say, manifest to the senses?

Phil. Do you not in a dream, too, perceive those or the like objects?

Hyl. I do.

Phil. And have they not then the same appearance of being distant?

Hyl. They have.

Phil. But you do not thence conclude the apparitions in a dream to be without the mind?

Hyl. By no means.

Phil. You ought not therefore to conclude that sensible objects are without the mind, from their appearance or manner wherein they are perceived.

Hyl. I acknowledge it. But does not my sense deceive me in those cases?

Phil. By no means. The idea or thing which you immediately perceive, neither sense nor reason informs you that it actually exists without the mind. By sense you only know that you are affected with such certain sensations of light and colors, etc. And these you will not say are without the mind.

Hyl. True, but, besides all that, do you not think the sight suggests something of *outness* or *distance?*

Phil. Upon approaching a distant object, do the visible size and figure change perpetually or do they appear the same at all distances?

Hyl. They are in a continual change.

Phil. Sight, therefore, does not suggest or any way inform you that the visible object you immediately perceive exists at a distance, or will be perceived when you advance farther onward, there being a continued series of visible objects succeeding each other during the whole time of your approach.

Hyl. It does not; but still I know, upon seeing an object, what object I shall perceive after having passed over a certain distance; no matter whether it be exactly the same or no, there is still something of distance suggested in the case.

Phil. Good Hylas, do but reflect a little on the point, and then tell me whether there be any more in it than this. From the ideas you actually perceive by sight, you have by experience learned to collect what other ideas you will (according to the standing order of nature) be affected with, after such a certain succession of time and motion.

Hyl. Upon the whole, I take it to be nothing else.

Phil. Now is it not plain that if we suppose a man born blind was on a sudden made to see, he could at first have no experience of what may be suggested by sight?

Hyl. It is.

Phil. He would not then, according to you, have any notion of distance annexed to the things he saw, but would take them for a new set of sensations existing only in his mind?

Hyl. It is undeniable.

Phil. But to make it still more plain: is not *distance* a line turned endwise to the eye?

Hyl. It is.

Phil. And can a line so situated be perceived by sight?

Hyl. It cannot.

Phil. Does it not therefore follow that distance is not properly and immediately perceived by sight?

Hyl. It should seem so.

Phil. Again, it is your opinion that colors are at a distance?

Hyl. It must be acknowledged they are only in the mind.

Phil. But do not colors appear to the eye as coexisting in the same place with extension and figures?

Hyl. They do.

Phil. How can you then conclude from sight that figures exist without, when you acknowledge colors do not; the sensible appearance being the very same with regard to both?

Hyl. I know not what to answer.

Phil. But allowing that distance was truly and immediately perceived by the mind, yet it would not thence follow it existed out of the mind. For whatever is immediately perceived is an idea; and can any *idea* exist out of the mind?

Hyl. To suppose that were absurd; but, inform me, Philonous, can we perceive or know nothing besides our ideas?

Phil. As for the rational deducing of causes from effects, that is beside our inquiry. And by the senses you can best tell whether you perceive anything which is not immediately perceived. And I ask you whether the things immediately perceived are other than your own sensations or ideas? You have indeed more than once, in the course of this conversation, declared yourself on those points, but you seem, by this last question, to have departed from what you then thought.

Hyl. To speak the truth, Philonous, I think there are two kinds of objects: the one perceived immediately, which are likewise called "ideas"; the other are real things or external objects, perceived by the mediation of ideas which are their images and representations. Now I own ideas do not exist without the mind, but the latter sort of objects do. I am sorry I did not think of this distinction sooner; it would probably have cut short your discourse.

Phil. Are those external objects perceived by sense or by some other faculty?

Hyl. They are perceived by sense.

Phil. How! is there anything perceived by sense which is not immediately perceived?

Hyl. Yes, Philonous, in some sort there is. For example, when I look on a picture or statue of Julius Caesar, I may be said, after a manner, to perceive him (though not immediately) by my senses.

Phil. It seems then you will have our ideas, which alone are immediately perceived, to be pictures of external things: and that these also are perceived by sense inasmuch as they have a conformity or resemblance to our ideas?

Hyl. That is my meaning.

Phil. And in the same way that Julius Caesar, in himself invisible, is nevertheless perceived by sight, real things, in themselves imperceptible, are perceived by sense.

Hyl. In the very same.

Phil. Tell me, Hylas, when you behold the picture of Julius Caesar, do you see with your eyes any more than some colors and figures, with a certain symmetry and composition of the whole?

Hyl. Nothing else.

Phil. And would not a man who had never known anything of Julius Caesar see as much?

Hyl. He would.

Phil. Consequently, he has his sight and the use of it in as perfect a degree as you?

Hyl. I agree with you.

Phil. Whence comes it then that your thoughts are directed to the Roman emperor, and his are not? This cannot proceed from the sensations or ideas of sense by you then perceived, since you acknowledge you have no advantage over him in that respect. It should seem therefore to proceed from reason and memory, should it not?

Hyl. It should.

Phil. Consequently, it will not follow from that instance that anything is perceived by sense which is not immediately perceived. Though I grant we may, in one acceptation, be said to perceive sensible things mediately by sense—that is, when, from a frequently perceived connection, the immediate perception of ideas by one sense suggest to the mind others, perhaps belonging to another sense, which are wont to be connected with them. For instance, when I hear a coach drive along the streets, immediately I perceive only the sound; but from the experience I have had that such a sound is connected with a coach, I am said to hear the coach. It is nevertheless evident that, in truth and strictness, nothing can be *heard* but *sound;* and the coach is not then properly perceived by sense, but suggested from experience. So likewise when we are said to see a red-hot bar of iron; the solidity and heat of the iron are not the objects of sight, but suggested to the imagination by the color and figure which are properly perceived by that sense. In short, those things alone are actually and strictly perceived by any sense which would have been perceived in case that same sense had then been first conferred on us. As for other things, it is plain they are only suggested to the mind by experience grounded on former perceptions. But, to return to your comparison of Caesar's picture, it is plain, if you keep to that, you must hold the real things or archetypes of our ideas are not perceived by sense, but by some internal faculty of the soul, as reason or memory. I would, therefore, fain know what arguments you can draw from reason for the existence of what you call "real things" or "material objects," or whether you remember to have seen them formerly as they are in themselves, or if you have heard or read of anyone that did.

Hyl. I see, Philonous, you are disposed to raillery; but that will never convince me.

Phil. My aim is only to learn from you the way to come at the knowledge of "material beings." Whatever we perceive is perceived either immediately or mediately—by sense, or by reason and reflection. But, as you have excluded sense, pray show me what reason you have to believe their existence, or what *medium* you can possibly make use of to prove it, either to mine or your own understanding.

Hyl. To deal ingenuously, Philonous, now [that] I consider the point, I do not find I can give you any good reason for it. But this much seems pretty plain, that it is at least possible such things may really exist. And as long as there is no absurdity in supposing them, I am resolved to believe as I did, till you bring good reasons to the contrary.

Phil. What! is it come to this, that you only believe the existence of material objects, and that your belief is founded barely on the possibility of its being true? Then you will have me bring reasons against it, though another would think it reasonable the proof should lie on him who holds the affirmative. And, after all, this very point which you are now resolved to maintain, without any reason, is in effect what you have more than once during this discourse seen good reason to give up. But to pass over all this—if I understand you rightly, you say our ideas do not exist without the mind, but that they are copies, images, or representations of certain originals that do?

Hyl. You take me right.

Phil. They are then like external things?

Hyl. They are.

Phil. Have those things a stable and permanent nature, independent of our senses, or are they in a perpetual change, upon our producing any motions in our bodies, suspending, exerting, or altering our faculties or organs of sense?

Hyl. Real things, it is plain, have a fixed and real nature, which remains the same notwithstanding any change in our senses or in the posture and motion of our bodies; which indeed may affect the ideas in our minds, but it were absurd to think they had the same effect on things existing without the mind.

Phil. How then is it possible that things perpetually fleeting and variable as our ideas should be copies or images of anything fixed and constant? Or, in other words, since all sensible qualities, as size, figure, color, etc., that is, our ideas, are continually changing upon every alteration in the distance, medium, or instruments of sensation—how can any determinate material objects be properly represented or painted forth by several distinct things each of which is so different from and unlike the rest? Or, if you say it resembles some one only of our ideas, how shall we be able to distinguish the true copy from all the false ones?

Hyl. I profess, Philonous, I am at a loss. I know not what to say to this.

Phil. But neither is this all. Which are material objects in themselves—perceptible or imperceptible?

Hyl. Properly and immediately nothing can be perceived but ideas. All material things, therefore, are in themselves insensible and to be perceived only by their ideas.

Phil. Ideas then are sensible, and their archetypes or originals insensible?

Hyl. Right.

Phil. But how can that which is sensible be like that which is insensible? Can a real thing, in itself *invisible,* be like a *color,* or a real thing which is not *audible* be like a *sound?* In a word, can anything be like a sensation or idea, but another sensation or idea?

Hyl. I must own, I think not.

Phil. Is it possible there should be any doubt on the point? Do you not perfectly know your own ideas?

Hyl. I know them perfectly, since what I do not perceive or know can be no part of my idea.

Phil. Consider, therefore, and examine them, and then tell me if there be anything in them which can exist without the mind, or if you can conceive anything like them existing without the mind?

Hyl. Upon inquiry I find it is impossible for me to conceive or understand how anything but an idea can be like an idea. And it is most evident that *no idea can exist without the mind.*

Phil. You are, therefore, by your principles forced to deny the reality of sensible things, since you made it to consist in an absolute existence exterior to the mind. That is to say, you are a downright skeptic. So I have gained my point, which was to show your principles led to skepticism.

Hyl. For the present I am, if not entirely convinced, at least silenced.

Phil. I would fain know what more you would require in order to a perfect conviction. Have you not had the liberty of explaining yourself all manner of ways? Were any little slips in discourse laid hold and insisted on? Or were you not allowed to retract or reinforce anything you had offered, as best served your purpose? Has not everything you could say been heard and examined with all the fairness imaginable? In a word, have you not in every point been convinced out of your own mouth? And, if you can at present discover any flaw in any of your former concessions, or think of any remaining subterfuge, any new distinction, color, or comment whatsoever, why do you not produce it?

Hyl. A little patience, Philonous. I am at present so amazed to see myself ensnared, and as it were imprisoned in the labyrinths you have drawn me into, that on the sudden it cannot be expected I should find my way out. You must give me time to look about me and recollect myself.

Phil. Hark; is not this the college bell?

Hyl. It rings for prayers.

Phil. We will go in then, if you please, and meet here again tomorrow morning. In the meantime, you may employ your thoughts on this morning's discourse and try if you can find any fallacy in it, or invent any new means to extricate yourself.

Hyl. Agreed.

THE SECOND DIALOGUE

Hylas. I beg your pardon, Philonous, for not meeting you sooner. All this morning my head was so filled with our late conversation that I had not leisure to think of the time of the day, or indeed of anything else.

Philonous. I am glad you were so intent upon it, in hopes if there were any mistakes in your concessions, or fallacies in my reasonings from them, you will now discover them to me.

Hyl. I assure you I have done nothing ever since I saw you but search after mistakes and fallacies, and, with that [in] view, have minutely examined the whole series of yesterday's discourse; but all in vain, for the notions it led me into, upon review, appear still more clear and evident; and the more I consider them, the more irresistibly do they force my assent.

Phil. And is not this, think you, a sign that they are genuine, that they proceed from nature and are conformable to right reason? Truth and beauty are in this alike, that the strictest survey sets them both off to advantage, while the false luster of error and disguise cannot endure being reviewed or too nearly inspected.

Hyl. I own there is a great deal in what you say. Nor can anyone be more entirely satisfied of the truth of those odd consequences so long as I have in view the reasonings that lead to them. But when these are out of my thoughts, there seems, on the other hand, something so satisfactory, so natural and intelligible in the modern way of explaining things that I profess I know not how to reject it.

Phil. I know not what way you mean.

Hyl. I mean the way of accounting for our sensations or ideas.

Phil. How is that?

Hyl. It is supposed the soul makes her residence in some part of the brain, from which the nerves take their rise, and are thence extended to all parts of the body; and that outward objects, by the different impressions they make on the organs of sense, communicate certain vibrative motions to the nerves, and these, being filled with spirits, propagate them to the brain or seat of the soul, which, according to the various impressions or traces thereby made in the brain, is variously affected with ideas.

Phil. And call you this an explication of the manner whereby we are affected with ideas?

Hyl. Why not, Philonous; have you anything to object against it?

Phil. I would first know whether I rightly understand your hypothesis. You make certain traces in the brain to be the causes or occasions of our ideas. Pray tell me whether by the "brain" you mean any sensible thing.

Hyl. What else think you I could mean?

Phil. Sensible things are all immediately perceivable; and those things which are immediately perceivable are ideas, and these exist only in the mind. This much you have, if I mistake not, long since agreed to.

Hyl. I do not deny it.

Phil. The brain therefore you speak of, being a sensible thing, exists only in the mind. Now I would fain know whether you think it reasonable to suppose that one idea or thing existing in the mind occasions all other ideas. And if you think so, pray how do you account for the origin of that primary idea or brain itself?

Hyl. I do not explain the origin of our ideas by that brain which is perceivable to sense, this being itself only a combination of sensible ideas, but by another which I imagine.

Phil. But are not things imagined as truly *in the mind* as things perceived?

Hyl. I must confess they are.

Phil. It comes, therefore, to the same thing; and you have been all this while accounting for ideas by certain motions or impressions of the brain, that is, by some alterations in an idea, whether sensible or imaginable it matters not.

Hyl. I begin to suspect my hypothesis.

Phil. Besides spirits, all that we know or conceive are our own ideas. When, therefore, you say all ideas are occasioned by impressions in the brain, do you conceive this brain or no? If you do, then you talk of ideas imprinted in an idea causing that same idea, which is absurd. If you do not conceive it, you talk unintelligibly, instead of forming a reasonable hypothesis.

Hyl. I now clearly see it was a mere dream. There is nothing in it.

Phil. You need not be much concerned at it, for, after all, this way of explaining things, as you called it, could never have satisfied any reasonable man. What connection is there between a motion in the nerves and the sensations of sound or color in the mind? Or how is it possible these should be the effect of that?

Hyl. But I could never think it had so little in it as now it seems to have.

Phil. Well then, are you at length satisfied that no sensible things have a real existence, and that you are in truth an arrant *skeptic?*

Hyl. It is too plain to be denied.

Phil. Look! are not the fields covered with a delightful verdure? Is there not something in the woods and groves, in the rivers and clear springs, that soothes, that delights, that transports the soul? At the prospect of the wide and deep ocean, or some huge mountain whose top is lost in the clouds, or of an old gloomy forest, are not our minds filled with a pleasing horror? Even in rocks and deserts is there not an agreeable wildness? How sincere a pleasure is it to behold the natural beauties of the earth! To preserve and renew our relish for them, is not the veil of night alternately drawn over her face, and does she not change her dress with the seasons? How aptly are the elements disposed! What variety and use in the meanest productions of nature! What delicacy, what beauty, what contrivance in animal and vegetable bodies! How exquisitely are all things suited, as well to their particular ends as to constitute apposite parts of the whole! And while they mutually aid and support, do they not also set off and illustrate each other? Raise now your thoughts from this ball of earth to all those glorious luminaries that adorn the high arch of heaven. The motion and situation of the planets, are they not admirable for use and order? Were those (miscalled "erratic") globes ever known to stray in their repeated journeys through the pathless void? Do they not measure areas round the sun ever proportioned to the times? So fixed, so immutable are the laws by which the unseen Author of nature actuates the universe. How vivid and radiant is the luster of the fixed stars! How magnificent and rich that negligent profusion with which they appear to be scattered throughout the whole azure vault! Yet, if you take the telescope, it brings into your sight a new host of stars that escape the naked eye. Here they seem contiguous and minute, but to a nearer view, immense orbs of light at various distances, far sunk in the abyss of space. Now you must call imagination to your aid. The feeble narrow sense cannot descry innumerable worlds revolving round the central fires, and in those worlds the energy of an all-perfect Mind displayed in endless forms. But neither sense nor imagination are big enough to comprehend the boundless extent with all its glittering furniture. Though the laboring mind exert and strain each power to its utmost reach, there still stands out ungrasped a surplusage immeasurable. Yet all the vast bodies that compose this mighty frame, how distant and remote soever, are by some secret mechanism, some divine art and force linked in a mutual dependence and intercourse with each other, even with this earth, which was almost slipt from my thoughts and lost in the crowd of worlds. Is not the whole system immense, beautiful, glorious beyond expression and beyond thought! What treatment, then, do those philosophers deserve who would deprive these noble and delightful scenes of all reality? How should those principles be entertained that lead us to think all the visible beauty of the creation a false imaginary glare? To be plain, can you expect this skepticism of yours will not be thought extravagantly absurd by all men of sense?

Hyl. Other men may think as they please, but for your part you have nothing to reproach me with. My comfort is you are as much a skeptic as I am.

Phil. There, Hylas, I must beg leave to differ from you.

Hyl. What! have you all along agreed to the premises, and do you now deny the conclusion and leave me to maintain those paradoxes by myself which you led me into? This surely is not fair.

Phil. I deny that I agreed with you in those notions that led to skepticism. You indeed said the *reality* of sensible things consisted in an *absolute existence* out of the minds of spirits, or distinct from their being perceived. And, pursuant to this notion of reality, you are obliged to deny sensible things any real existence; that is, according to your own definition, you profess yourself a skeptic. But I neither said nor thought the reality of sensible things was to be defined after that manner. To me it is evident, for the reasons you allow of, that sensible things cannot exist otherwise than in a mind or spirit. Whence I conclude, not that they have no real existence, but that, seeing they depend not on my thought and have an existence distinct from being perceived by me, *there must be some other mind wherein they exist.* As sure, therefore, as the sensible world really exists, so sure is there an infinite omnipresent Spirit, who contains and supports it.

Hyl. What! this is no more than I and all Christians hold; nay, and all others, too, who believe there is a God and that He knows and comprehends all things.

Phil. Aye, but here lies the difference. Men commonly believe that all things are known or perceived by God, because they believe the being of a God; whereas I, on the other side, immediately and necessarily conclude the being of a God, because all sensible things must be perceived by him.

Hyl. But so long as we all believe the same thing, what matter is it how we come by that belief?

Phil. But neither do we agree in the same opinion. For philosophers, though they acknowledge all corporeal beings to be perceived by God, yet they attribute to them an absolute subsistence distinct from their being perceived by any mind whatever, which I do not. Besides, is there no difference between saying, *there is a God, therefore He perceives all things,* and saying, *sensible things do really exist; and if they really exist, they are necessarily perceived by an infinite mind: therefore there is an infinite mind, or God?* This furnishes you with a direct and immediate demonstration, from a most evident principle, of the *being of a God*. Divines and philosophers had proved beyond all controversy, from the beauty and usefulness of the several parts of the creation, that it was the workmanship of God. But that—setting aside all help of astronomy and natural philosophy, all contemplation of the contrivance, order and adjustment of things—an infinite mind should be necessarily inferred from the bare *existence* of the sensible world is an advantage peculiar to them only who have made this easy reflection, that the sensible world is that which we perceive by our several senses; and that nothing is perceived by the senses besides ideas; and that no idea or archetype of an idea can exist otherwise than in a mind.

Proof of an External World

~

G. E. MOORE

George Edward Moore (1873–1958) led, with Bertrand Russell, an important revolt against the Hegelian idealism popular in England at the turn of the century. Beside *Philosophical Papers,* Moore published three books: *Principia Ethica, Ethics,* and *Some Main Problems of Philosophy.* A defender of common sense, Moore was an important influence on the Bloomsbury Group of artists and intellectuals.

It seems to me that, so far from its being true, as Kant declares to be his opinion, that there is only one possible proof of the existence of things outside of us, namely the one which he has given, I can now give a large number of different proofs, each of which is a perfectly rigorous proof; and that at many other times I have been in a position to give many others. I can prove now, for instance, that two human hands exist. How? By holding up my two hands, and saying, as I make a certain gesture with the right hand, "Here is one hand," and adding, as I make a certain gesture with the left, "and here is another." And if, by doing this, I have proved *ipso facto* the existence of external things, you will all see that I can also do it now in numbers of other ways: there is no need to multiply examples.

But did I prove just now that two human hands were then in existence? I do want to insist that I did; that the proof which I gave was a perfectly rigorous one; and that it is perhaps impossible to give a better or more rigorous proof of anything whatever. Of course, it would not have been a proof unless three conditions were satisfied; namely (1) unless the premiss which I adduced as proof of the conclusion was different from the conclusion I adduced it to prove; (2) unless the premiss which I adduced was something which I *knew* to be the case, and not merely something which I believed but which was by no means certain, or something which, though in fact true, I did not know to be so; and (3) unless the conclusion did really follow from the premiss. But all these three conditions were in fact satisfied by my proof. (1) The premiss which I adduced in proof was quite certainly different from the conclusion, for the conclusion was merely "Two human hands exist at this moment"; but the premiss was something far more specific than this—something which I expressed by showing you my hands, making certain gestures, and saying the words "Here is one hand, and here is another." It is quite obvious that the two were different, because it is quite obvious that the conclusion might have been true, even if the premiss had been false. In asserting the pre-

Reprinted from G. E. Moore, *Philosophical Papers* (London: George Allen & Unwin, 1959), by permission of the publisher.

miss I was asserting much more than I was asserting in asserting the conclusion. (2) I certainly did at the moment *know* that which I expressed by the combination of certain gestures with saying the words "There is one hand and here is another." I *knew* that there was one hand in the place indicated by combining a certain gesture with my first utterance of "here" and that there was another in the different place indicated by combining a certain gesture with my second utterance of "here." How absurd it would be to suggest that I did not know it, but only believed it, and that perhaps it was not the case! You might as well suggest that I do not know that I am now standing up and talking—that perhaps after all I'm not, and that it's not quite certain that I am! And finally (3) it is quite certain that the conclusion did follow from the premiss. This is as certain as it is that if there is one hand here and another here *now,* then it follows that there are two hands in existence *now.*

My proof, then, of the existence of things outside of us did satisfy three of the conditions necessary for a rigorous proof. Are there any other conditions necessary for a rigorous proof, such that perhaps it did not satisfy one of them? Perhaps there may be; I do not know; but I do want to emphasize that, so far as I can see, we all of us do constantly take proofs of this sort as absolutely conclusive proofs of certain conclusions—as finally settling certain questions, as to which we were previously in doubt. Suppose, for instance, it were a question whether there were as many as three misprints on a certain page in a certain book. A says there are, B is inclined to doubt it. How could A prove that he is right? Surely he *could* prove it by taking the book, turning to the page, and pointing to three separate places on it, saying "There's one misprint here, another here, and another here"; surely that is a method by which it *might* be proved! Of course, A would not have proved, by doing this, that there were at least three misprints on the page in question, unless it was certain that there was a misprint in each of the places to which he pointed. But to say that he *might* prove it in this way, is to say that it *might* be certain that there was. And if such a thing as that could ever be certain, then assuredly it was certain just now that there was one hand in one of the two places I indicated and another in the other.

I did, then, just now, give a proof that there were *then* external objects; and obviously, if I did, I could *then* have given many other proofs of the same sort that there were external objects *then,* and could now give many proofs of the same sort that there are external objects *now.*

But, if what I am asked to do is to prove that external objects have existed *in the past,* then I can give many different proofs of this also, but proofs which are in important respects of a different *sort* from those just given. And I want to emphasize that, when Kant says it is a scandal not to be able to give a proof of the existence of external objects, a proof of their existence in the past would certainly *help* to remove the scandal of which he is speaking. He says that, if it occurs to anyone to question their existence, we ought to be able to confront him with a satisfactory proof. But by a person who questions their existence, he certainly means not merely a person who questions whether any exist at the moment of speaking, but a person who questions whether any have *ever* existed; and a proof that some have existed in the past would certainly therefore be relevant to *part* of what such a person is questioning. How then can I prove that there have been external objects in the past? Here is one proof. I can say: "I held up two hands above this desk not very long ago; therefore two hands existed not very long ago; therefore at least two external objects have existed at some time in the past, Q.E.D." This is a perfectly good proof, provided I *know* what is asserted in the premiss. But I *do* know that I held up two hands above this desk not very long ago. As a matter of fact, in this case you all know it too. There's no doubt whatever that I did. Therefore I have given a perfectly conclusive proof that external objects have existed in the past; and you will all see at once that, if this is a conclusive proof, I could have given many others of the same sort, and could now give many others. But it is also quite obvious that this sort of proof differs in important respects from the sort of proof I gave just now that there were two hands existing *then.*

I have, then, given two conclusive proofs of the existence of external objects. The first was a proof that two human hands existed at the time when I gave the proof; the second was a proof that two human hands had existed at a time previous to that at which I gave the proof. These proofs were of a different sort in important respects. And I pointed out that I could have given, then, many other conclusive proofs of both sorts. It is also obvious that I could give many others of both sorts now. So that, if these are the sort of proof that is wanted, nothing is easier than to prove the existence of external objects.

But now I am perfectly well aware that, in spite of all that I have said, many philosophers will still feel that I have not given any satisfactory proof of the point in question. And I want briefly, in conclusion, to say something as to why this dissatisfaction with my proofs should be felt.

One reason why, is, I think, this. Some people understand "proof of an external world" as including a proof of things which I haven't attempted to prove and haven't proved. It is not quite easy to say *what* it is that they want proved—*what* it is that is such that unless they got a proof of it, they would not say that they had a proof of the existence of external things; but I can make an approach to explaining what they want by saying that if I had proved the propositions which I used as *premises* in my two proofs, then they would perhaps admit that I had proved the existence of external things, but, in the absence of such a proof (which, of course, I have neither given nor attempted to give), they will say that I have not given what they mean by a proof of the existence of external things. In other words, they want a proof of what I assert *now* when I hold up my hands and say "Here's one hand and here's another"; and, in the other case, they want a proof of what I assert *now* when I say "I did hold up two hands above this desk just now." Of course, what they really want is not merely a proof of these two propositions, but something like a general statement as to how *any* propositions of this sort may be proved. This, of course, I haven't given; and I do not believe it can be given: if this is what is meant by proof of the existence of external things, I do not believe that any proof of the existence of external things is possible. Of course, in some cases what might be called a proof of propositions which seem like these can be got. If one of you suspected that one of my hands was artificial he might be said to get a proof of my proposition "Here's one hand, and here's another," by coming up

and examining the suspected hand close up, perhaps touching and pressing it, and so establishing that it really was a human hand. But I do not believe that any proof is possible in nearly all cases. How am I to prove now that "Here's one hand, and here's another"? I do not believe I can do it. In order to do it, I should need to prove for one thing, as Descartes pointed out, that I am not now dreaming. But how can I prove that I am not? I have, no doubt, conclusive reasons for asserting that I am not now dreaming; I have conclusive evidence that I am awake: but that is a very different thing from being able to prove it. I could not tell you what all my evidence is; and I should require to do this at least, in order to give you a proof.

But another reason why some people would feel dissatisfied with my proofs is, I think, not merely that they want a proof of something which I haven't proved, but that they think that, if I cannot give such extra proofs, then the proofs that I have given are not conclusive proofs at all. And this, I think, is a definite mistake. They would say: "If you cannot prove your premiss that here is one hand and here is another, then you do not know it. But you yourself have admitted that, if you did not know it, then your proof was not conclusive. Therefore your proof was not, as you say it was, a conclusive proof." This view that, if I cannot prove such things as these, I do not know them, is, I think, the view that Kant was expressing in the sentence which I quoted at the beginning of this lecture, when he implies that so long as we have no proof of the existence of external things, their existence must be accepted merely on *faith*. He means to say, I think, that if I cannot prove that there is a hand here, I must accept it merely as a matter of faith—I cannot know it. Such a view, though it has been very common among philosophers, can, I think, be shown to be wrong—though shown only by the use of premisses which are not known to be true, unless we do know of the existence of external things. I can know things, which I cannot prove; and among things which I certainly did know, even if (as I think) I could not prove them, were the premisses of my two proofs. I should say, therefore, that those, if any, who are dissatisfied with these proofs merely on the ground that I did not know their premisses, have no good reason for their dissatisfaction.

On Certainty

~

LUDWIG WITTGENSTEIN

Ludwig Wittgenstein (1889–1951) is a seminal and polarizing figure in 20th-century philosophy. His early *Tractatus Logico-Philosophicus* and late *Philosophical Investigations* represent pioneering but bifurcating philosophical paths. The author of works too numerous to cite here, on topics including color, mathematics, and psychology, Wittgenstein worked on *On Certainty* during the last 18 months of his life and up to his last days.

1. If you do know that *here is one hand*, we'll grant you all the rest.

When one says that such and such a proposition can't be proved, of course that does not mean that it can't be derived from other propositions; any proposition can be derived from other ones. But they may be no more certain than it is itself. (On this a curious remark by H. Newman.)

2. From its *seeming* to me—or to everyone—to be so, it doesn't follow that it *is* so.

What we can ask is whether it can make sense to doubt it.

3. If e.g. someone says "I don't know if there's a hand here" he might be told "Look closer".—This possibility of satisfying oneself is part of the language-game. Is one of its essential features.

4. "I know that I am a human being." In order to see how unclear the sense of this proposition is, consider its negation. At most it might be taken to mean "I know I have the organs of a human". (E.g. a brain which, after all, no one has ever yet seen.) But what about such a proposition as "I know I have a brain"? Can I doubt it? Grounds for *doubt* are lacking! Everything speaks in its favour, nothing against it. Nevertheless it is imaginable that my skull should turn out empty when it was operated on.

5. Whether a proposition can turn out false after all depends on what I make count as determinants for that proposition.

6. Now, can one enumerate what one knows (like Moore)? Straight off like that, I believe not.—For otherwise the expression "I know" gets misused. And through this misuse a queer and extremely important mental state seems to be revealed.

7. My life shews that I know or am certain that there is a chair over there, or a door, and so on.—I tell a friend e.g. "Take that chair over there", "Shut the door", etc. etc.

8. The difference between the concept of 'knowing' and the concept of 'being certain' isn't of any great importance at all, except where "I know" is meant to mean: I *can't* be wrong. In a law-court, for example, "I am certain" could replace "I know" in every piece of testimony. We might even imagine its being forbidden to say "I know" there. [A passage in *Wilhelm Meister*, where "You know" or "You knew" is used in the sense "You were certain," the facts being different from what he knew.]

9. Now do I, in the course of my life, make sure I know that here is a hand—my own hand, that is?

10. I know that a sick man is lying here? Nonsense! I am sitting at his bedside, I am looking atten-

Reprinted from Ludwig Wittgenstein, *On Certainty* (Oxford: Basil Blackwell, 1969), by permission of Basil Blackwell.

tively into his face.—So I don't know, then, that there is a sick man lying here? Neither the question nor the assertion makes sense. Any more than the assertion "I am here", which I might yet use at any moment, if suitable occasion presented itself.—Then is "2 × 2 = 4" nonsense in the same way, and not a proposition of arithmetic, apart from particular occasions? "2 × 2 = 4" is a true proposition of arithmetic—not "on particular occasions" nor "always"—but the spoken or written sentence "2 × 2 = 4" in Chinese might have a different meaning or be out and out nonsense, and from this is seen that it is only in use that the proposition has its sense. And "I know that there's a sick man lying here", used in an *unsuitable* situation, seems not to be nonsense but rather seems matter-of-course, only because one can fairly easily imagine a situation to fit it, and one thinks that the words "I know that . . ." are always in place where there is no doubt, and hence even where the expression of doubt would be unintelligible.

11. We just do not see how very specialized the use of "I know" is.

12.—For "I know" seems to describe a state of affairs which guarantees what is known, guarantees it as a fact. One always forgets the expression "I thought I knew".

13. For it is not as though the proposition "It is so" could be inferred from someone else's utterance: "I know it is so". Nor from the utterance together with its not being a lie.—But can't I infer "It is so" from my own utterance "I know etc."? Yes; and also "There is a hand there" follows from the proposition "He knows that there's a hand there". But from his utterance "I know . . ." it does not follow that he does know it.

14. That he does know takes some shewing.

15. It needs to be *shewn* that no mistake was possible. Giving the assurance "I know" doesn't suffice. For it is after all only an assurance that I can't be making a mistake, and it needs to be *objectively* established that I am not making a mistake about *that*.

16. "If I know something, then I also know that I know it, etc." amounts to: "I know that" means "I am incapable of being wrong about that". But whether I am so needs to be established objectively.

17. Suppose now I say "I'm incapable of being wrong about this: that is a book" while I point to an object. What would a mistake here be like? And have I any *clear* idea of it?

18. "I know" often means: I have the proper grounds for my statement. So if the other person is acquainted with the language-game, he would admit that I know. The other, if he is acquainted with the language-game, must be able to imagine *how* one may know something of the kind.

19. The statement "I know that here is a hand" may then be continued: "for it's *my* hand that I'm looking at". Then a reasonable man will not doubt that I know.—Nor will the idealist; rather he will say that he was not dealing with the practical doubt which is being dismissed, but there is a further doubt *behind* that one.—That this is an *illusion* has to be shewn in a different way.

20. "Doubting the existence of the external world" does not mean for example doubting the existence of a planet, which later observations proved to exist.— Or does Moore want to say that knowing that here is his hand is different in kind from knowing the existence of the planet Saturn? Otherwise it would be possible to point out the discovery of the planet Saturn to the doubters and say that its existence has been proved, and hence the existence of the external world as well.

21. Moore's view really comes down to this: the concept 'know' is analogous to the concepts 'believe', 'surmise', 'doubt', 'be convinced' in that the statement "I know . . ." can't be a mistake. And if that *is* so, then there can be an inference from such an utterance to the truth of an assertion. And here the form "I thought I knew" is being overlooked.—But if this latter is inadmissible, then a mistake in the *assertion* must be logically impossible too. And anyone who is acquainted with the language-game must realize this—an assurance from a reliable man that he *knows* cannot contribute anything.

22. It would surely be remarkable if we had to believe the reliable person who says "I can't be wrong"; or who says "I am not wrong".

23. If I don't know whether someone has two hands (say, whether they have been amputated or not) I shall believe his assurance that he has two hands, if

he is trustworthy. And if he says he *knows* it, that can only signify to me that he has been able to make sure, and hence that his arms are e.g. not still concealed by coverings and bandages, etc. etc. My believing the trustworthy man stems from my admitting that it is possible for him to make sure. But someone who says that perhaps there are no physical objects makes no such admission.

24. The idealist's question would be something like: "What right have I not to doubt the existence of my hands?" (And to that the answer can't be: I *know* that they exist.) But someone who asks such a question is overlooking the fact that a doubt about existence only works in a language-game. Hence, that we should first have to ask: what would such a doubt be like?, and don't understand this straight off.

25. One may be wrong even about "there being a hand here". Only in particular circumstances is it impossible.—"Even in a calculation one can be wrong—only in certain circumstances one can't."

26. But can it be seen from a *rule* what circumstances logically exclude a mistake in the employment of rules of calculation?

What use is a rule to us here? Mightn't we (in turn) go wrong in applying it?

27. If, however, one wanted to give something like a rule here, then it would contain the expression "in normal circumstances". And we recognize normal circumstances but cannot precisely describe them. At most, we can describe a range of abnormal ones.

28. What is 'learning a rule'?— *This.*

What is 'making a mistake in applying it'?— *This.* And what is pointed to here is something indeterminate.

29. Practice in the use of the rule also shews what is a mistake in its employment.

30. When someone has made sure of something, he says: "Yes, the calculation is right", but he did not infer that from his condition of certainty. One does not infer how things are from one's own certainty.

Certainty is *as it were* a tone of voice in which one declares how things are, but one does not infer from the tone of voice that one is justified.

31. The propositions which one comes back to again and again as if bewitched—these I should like to expunge from philosophical language.

32. It's not a matter of *Moore's* knowing that

there's a hand there, but rather we should not understand him if he were to say "Of course I may be wrong about this". We should ask "What is it like to make such a mistake as that?"—e.g. what's it like to discover that it was a mistake?

33. Thus we expunge the sentences that don't get us any further.

34. If someone is taught to calculate, is he also taught that he can rely on a calculation of his teacher's? But these explanations must after all sometime come to an end. Will he also be taught that he can trust his senses—since he is indeed told in many cases that in such and such a special case you *cannot* trust them?—

Rule and exception.

35. But can't it be imagined that there should be no physical objects? I don't know. And yet "There are physical objects" is nonsense. Is it supposed to be an empirical proposition?—

And is *this* an empirical proposition: "There seem to be physical objects"?

36. "A is a physical object" is a piece of instruction which we give only to someone who doesn't yet understand either what "A" means, or what "physical object" means. Thus it is instruction about the use of words, and "physical object" is a logical concept. (Like colour, quantity, . . .) And that is why no such proposition as: "There are physical objects" can be formulated.

Yet we encounter such unsuccessful shots at every turn.

37. But is it an adequate answer to the scepticism of the idealist, or the assurances of the realist, to say that "There are physical objects" is nonsense? For them after all it is not nonsense. It would, however, be an answer to say: this assertion, or its opposite is a misfiring attempt to express what can't be expressed like that. And that it does misfire can be shewn; but that isn't the end of the matter. We need to realize that what presents itself to us as the first expression of a difficulty, or of its solution, may as yet not be correctly expressed at all. Just as one who has a just censure of a picture to make will often at first offer the censure where it does not belong, and an *investigation* is needed in order to find the right point of attack for the critic.

38. Knowledge in mathematics: Here one has to

keep on reminding oneself of the unimportance of the 'inner process' or 'state' and ask "Why should it be important? What does it matter to me?" What is interesting is how we *use* mathematical propositions.

39. *This* is how calculation is done, in such circumstances a calculation is *treated* as absolutely reliable, as certainly correct.

40. Upon "I know that here is my hand" there may follow the question "How do you know?" and the answer to that presupposes that *this* can be known in *that* way. So, instead of "I know that here is my hand", one might say "Here is my hand", and then add *how* one knows.

41. "I know where I am feeling pain", "I know that I feel it *here*" is as wrong as "I know that I am in pain". But "I know where you touched my arm" is right.

42. One can say "He believes it, but it isn't so", but not "He knows it, but it isn't so". Does this stem from the difference between the mental states of belief and of knowledge? No.—One may for example call "mental state" what is expressed by tone of voice in speaking, by gestures etc. It would thus be *possible* to speak of a mental state of conviction, and that may be the same whether it is knowledge or false belief. To think that different states must correspond to the words "believe" and "know" would be as if one believed that different people had to correspond to the word "I" and the name "Ludwig", because the concepts are different.

43. What sort of proposition is this: "We *cannot* have miscalculated in $12 \times 12 = 144$"? It must surely be a proposition of logic.—But now, is it not the same, or doesn't it come to the same, as the statement $12 \times 12 = 144$?

44. If you demand a rule from which it follows that there can't have been a miscalculation here, the answer is that we did not learn this through a rule, but by learning to calculate.

45. We got to know the *nature* of calculating by learning to calculate.

46. But then can't it be described how we satisfy ourselves of the reliability of a calculation? O yes! Yet no rule emerges when we do so.—But the most important thing is: The rule is not needed. Nothing is lacking. We do calculate according to a rule, and that is enough.

47. *This* is how one calculates. Calculating is *this*. What we learn at school, for example. Forget this transcendent certainty, which is connected with your concept of spirit.

48. However, out of a host of calculations certain ones might be designated as reliable once for all, others as not yet fixed. And now, is this a *logical* distinction?

49. But remember: even when the calculation is something fixed for me, this is only a decision for a practical purpose.

50. When does one say, I know that $\ldots \times \ldots = \ldots$? When one has checked the calculation.

51. What sort of proposition is: "What could a mistake here be like!"? It would have to be a logical proposition. But it is a logic that is not used, because what it tells us is not learned through propositions.— It is a logical proposition; for it does describe the conceptual (linguistic) situation.

52. This situation is thus not the same for a proposition like "At this distance from the sun there is a planet" and "Here is a hand" (namely my own hand). The second can't be called a hypothesis. But there isn't a sharp boundary line between them.

53. So one might grant that Moore was right, if he is interpreted like this: a proposition saying that here is a physical object may have the same logical status as one saying that here is a red patch.

54. For it is not true that a mistake merely gets more and more improbable as we pass from the planet to my own hand. No: at some point it has ceased to be conceivable.

This is already suggested by the following: if it were not so, it would also be conceivable that we should be wrong in *every* statement about physical objects; that any we ever make are mistaken.

55. So is the *hypothesis* possible, that all the things around us don't exist? Would that not be like the hypothesis of our having miscalculated in all our calculations?

56. When one says: "Perhaps this planet doesn't exist and the light-phenomenon arises in some other way", then after all one needs an example of an object which does exist. This doesn't exist,—as *for example* does. . . .

Or are we to say that *certainly* is merely a constructed point to which some things approximate more, some less closely? No. Doubt gradually loses its sense. This language-game just *is* like that.

And everything descriptive of a language-game is part of logic.

57. Now might not "I *know,* I am not just surmising, that here is my hand" be conceived as a proposition of grammar? Hence *not* temporally.—

But in that case isn't it like *this* one: "I know, I am not just surmising, that I am seeing red"?

And isn't the consequence "So there are physical objects" like: "So there are colours"?

58. If "I know etc." is conceived as a grammatical proposition, of course the "I" cannot be important. And it properly means "There is no such thing as a doubt in this case" or "The expression 'I do not know' makes no sense in this case". And of course it follows from this that "I *know*" makes no sense either.

59. "I know" is here a *logical* insight. Only realism can't be proved by means of it.

60. It is wrong to say that the 'hypothesis' that *this* is a bit of paper would be confirmed or disconfirmed by later experience, and that, in "I know that this is a bit of paper," the "I know" either relates to such an hypothesis or to a logical determination.

61. . . . A meaning of a word is a kind of employment of it.

For it is what we learn when the word is incorporated into our language.

62. That is why there exists a correspondence between the concepts 'rule' and 'meaning'.

63. If we imagine the facts otherwise than as they are, certain language-games lose some of their importance, while others become important. And in this way there is an alteration—a gradual one—in the use of the vocabulary of a language.

64. Compare the meaning of a word with the 'function' of an official. And 'different meanings' with 'different functions'.

65. When language-games change, then there is a change in concepts, and with the concepts the meanings of words change.

66. I make assertions about reality, assertions which have different degrees of assurance. How does the degree of assurance come out? What consequences has it?

We may be dealing, for example, with the certainty of memory, or again of perception. I may be sure of something, but still know what test might convince me of error. I am e.g. quite sure of the date of a battle, but if I should find a different date in a recognized work of history, I should alter my opinion, and this would not mean I lost all faith in judging.

67. Could we imagine a man who keeps on making mistakes where we regard a mistake as ruled out, and in fact never encounter one?

E.g. he says he lives in such and such a place, is so and so old, comes from such and such a city, and he speaks with the same certainty (giving all the tokens of it) as I do, but he is wrong.

But what is his relation to this error? What am I to suppose?

68. The question is: what is the logician to say here?

69. I should like to say: "If I am wrong about *this,* I have no guarantee that anything I say is true." But others won't say that about me, nor will I say it about other people.

70. For months I have lived at address A, I have read the name of the street and the number of the house countless times, have received countless letters here and given countless people the address. If I am wrong about it, the mistake is hardly less than if I were (wrongly) to believe I was writing Chinese and not German.

71. If my friend were to imagine one day that he had been living for a long time past in such and such a place, etc. etc., I should not call this a *mistake,* but rather a mental disturbance, perhaps a transient one.

72. Not every false belief of this sort is a mistake.

73. But what is the difference between mistake and mental disturbance? Or what is the difference between my treating it as a mistake and my treating it as mental disturbance?

74. Can we say: a *mistake* doesn't only have a cause, it also has a ground? I.e., roughly: when someone makes a mistake, this can be fitted into what he knows aright.

75. Would this be correct: If I merely believed wrongly that there is a table here in front of me, this might still be a mistake; but if I believe wrongly that I have seen this table, or one like it, every day for sev-

eral months past, and have regularly used it, that isn't a mistake?

76. Naturally, my aim must be to say what the statements one would like to make here, but cannot make significantly.

77. Perhaps I shall do a multiplication twice to make sure, or perhaps get someone else to work it over. But shall I work it over again twenty times, or get twenty people to go over it? And is that some sort of negligence? Would the certainty really be greater for being checked twenty times?

78. And can I give a *reason* why it isn't?

79. That I am a man and not a woman can be verified, but if I were to say I was a woman, and then tried to explain the error by saying I hadn't checked the statement, the explanation would not be accepted.

80. The *truth* of my statements is the test of my *understanding* of these statements.

81. That is to say: if I make certain false statements, it becomes uncertain whether I understand them.

82. What counts as an adequate test of a statement belongs to logic. It belongs to the description of the language-game.

83. The *truth* of certain empirical propositions belongs to our frame of reference.

84. Moore says he *knows* that the earth existed long before his birth. And put like that it seems to be a personal statement about him, even if it is in addition a statement about the physical world. Now it is philosophically uninteresting whether Moore knows this or that, but it is interesting that, and how, it can be known. If Moore had informed us that he knew the distance separating certain stars, we might conclude from that that he had made some special investigations, and we shall want to know what these were. But Moore chooses precisely a case in which we all seem to know the same as he, and without being able to say how. I believe e.g. that I know as much about this matter (the existence of the earth) as Moore does, and if he knows that it is as he says, then *I* know it too. For it isn't, either, as if he had arrived at his proposition by pursuing some line of thought which, while it is open to me, I have not in fact pursued.

85. And what goes into someone's knowing this? Knowledge of history, say? He must know what it means to say: the earth has already existed for such and such a length of time. For not *any* intelligent adult must know that. We see men building and demolishing houses, and are led to ask: "How long has this house been here?" But how does one come on the idea of asking this about a mountain, for example? And have all men the notion of the earth as a *body*, which may come into being and pass away? Why shouldn't I think of the earth as flat, but extending without end in every direction (including depth)? But in that case one might still say "I know that this mountain existed long before my birth."—But suppose I met a man who didn't believe that?

86. Suppose I replaced Moore's "I know" by "I am of the unshakeable conviction"?

87. Can't an assertoric sentence, which was capable of functioning as an hypothesis, also be used as a foundation for research and action? I.e., can't it simply be isolated from doubt, though not according to any explicit rule? It simply gets assumed as a truism, never called in question, perhaps not even everformulated.

88. It may be for example that *all enquiry on our part* is set so as to exempt certain propositions from doubt, if they are everformulated. They lie apart from the route travelled by enquiry.

89. One would like to say: "Everything speaks for, and nothing against the earth's having existed long before. . . ."

Yet might I not believe the contrary after all? But the question is: What would the practical effects of this belief be?—Perhaps someone says: "That's not the point. A belief is what it is whether it has any practical effects or not." One thinks: It is the same adjustment of the human mind anyway.

90. "I know" has a primitive meaning similar to and related to "I see" ("wissen", "videre"). And "I knew he was in the room, but he wasn't in the room" is like "I saw him in the room, but he wasn't there". "I know" is supposed to express a relation, not between me and the sense of a proposition (like "I believe") but between me and a fact. So that the *fact* is taken into my consciousness. (Here is the reason why one wants to say that nothing that goes on in the outer world is really known, but only what happens in the domain of what are called sense-data.) This

would give us a picture of knowing as the perception of an outer event through visual rays which project it as it is into the eye and the consciousness. Only then the question at once arises whether one can be *certain* of this projection. And this picture does indeed show how our *imagination* presents knowledge, but not what lies at the bottom of this presentation.

91. If Moore says he knows the earth existed etc., most of us will grant him that it has existed all that time, and also believe him when he says he is convinced of it. But has he also got the right *ground* for his conviction? For if not, then after all he doesn't *know* (Russell).

92. However, we can ask: May someone have telling grounds for believing that the earth has only existed for a short time, say since his own birth?— Suppose he had always been told that,—would he have any good reason to doubt it? Men have believed that they could make rain; why should not a king be brought up in the belief that the world began with him? And if Moore and this king were to meet and discuss, could Moore really prove his belief to be the right one? I do not say that Moore could not convert the king to his view, but it would be a conversion of a special kind; the king would be brought to look at the world in a different way.

Remember that one is sometimes convinced of the *correctness* of a view by its *simplicity* or *symmetry,* i.e., these are what induce one to go over to this point of view. One then simply says something like: "*That's* how it must be."

93. The propositions presenting what Moore '*knows*' are all of such a kind that it is difficult to imagine *why* anyone should believe the contrary. E.g. the proposition that Moore has spent his whole life in close proximity to the earth.—Once more I can speak of myself here instead of speaking of Moore. What could induce me to believe the opposite? Either a memory, or having been told.—Everything that I have seen or heard gives me the conviction that no man has ever been far from the earth. Nothing in my picture of the world speaks in favour of the opposite.

94. But I did not get my picture of the world by satisfying myself of its correctness; nor do I have it because I am satisfied of its correctness. No: it is the inherited background against which I distinguish between true and false.

95. The propositions describing this world-picture might be part of a kind of mythology. And their role is like that of rules of a game; and the game can be learned purely practically, without learning any explicit rules.

96. It might be imagined that some propositions, of the form of empirical propositions, were hardened and functioned as channels for such empirical propositions as were not hardened but fluid; and that this relation altered with time, in that fluid propositions hardened, and hard ones became fluid.

97. The mythology may change back into a state of flux, the river-bed of thoughts may shift. But I distinguish between the movement of the waters on the river-bed and the shift of the bed itself; though there is not a sharp division of the one from the other.

98. But if someone were to say "So logic too is an empirical science" he would be wrong. Yet this is right: the same proposition may get treated at one time as something to test by experience, at another as a rule of testing.

99. And the bank of that river consists partly of hard rock, subject to no alteration or only to an imperceptible one, partly of sand, which now in one place now in another gets washed away, or deposited.

100. The truths which Moore says he knows, are such as, roughly speaking, all of us know, if he knows them.

101. Such a proposition might be e.g. "My body has never disappeared and reappeared again after an interval."

102. Might I not believe that once, without knowing it, perhaps in a state of unconsciousness, I was taken far away from the earth—that other people even know this, but do not mention it to me? But this would not fit into the rest of my convictions at all. Not that I could describe the system of these convictions. Yet my convictions do form a system, a structure.

103. And now if I were to say "It is my unshakeable conviction that etc.", this means in the present case too that I have not consciously arrived at the conviction by following a particular line of thought, but that it is anchored in all my *questions and answers,* so anchored that I cannot touch it.

104. I am for example also convinced that the sun is not a hole in the vault of heaven.

105. All testing, all confirmation and disconfirmation of a hypothesis takes place already within a system. And this system is not a more or less arbitrary and doubtful point of departure for all our arguments: no, it belongs to the essence of what we call an argument. The system is not so much the point of departure, as the element in which arguments have their life.

106. Suppose some adult had told a child that he had been on the moon. The child tells me the story, and I say it was only a joke, the man hadn't been on the moon; no one has ever been on the moon; the moon is a long way off and it is impossible to climb up there or fly there.—If now the child insists, saying perhaps there is a way of getting there which I don't know, etc. what reply could I make to him? What reply could I make to the adults of a tribe who believe that people sometimes go to the moon (perhaps that is how they interpret their dreams), and who indeed grant that there are no ordinary means of climbing up to it or flying there?—But a child will not ordinarily stick to such a belief and will soon be convinced by what we tell him seriously.

107. Isn't this altogether like the way one can instruct a child to believe in a God, or that none exists, and it will accordingly be able to produce apparently telling grounds for the one or the other?

108. "But is there then no objective truth? Isn't it true, or false, that someone has been on the moon?" If we are thinking within our system, then it is certain that no one has ever been on the moon. Not merely is nothing of the sort ever seriously reported to us by reasonable people, but our whole system of physics forbids us to believe it. For this demands answers to the questions "How did he overcome the force of gravity?" "How could he live without an atmosphere?" and a thousand others which could not be answered. But suppose that instead of all these answers we met the reply: "We don't know *how* one gets to the moon, but those who get there know at once that they are there; and even you can't explain everything." We should feel ourselves intellectually very distant from someone who said this.

109. "An empirical proposition can be *tested*" (we say). But how? and through what?

110. What *counts* as its test?—"But is this an adequate test? And, if so, must it not be recognizable as such in logic?"—As if giving grounds did not come to an end sometime. But the end is not an ungrounded presupposition: it is an ungrounded way of acting.

111. "I *know* that I have never been on the moon." That sounds quite different in the circumstances which actually hold, to the way it would sound if a good many men had been on the moon, and some perhaps without knowing it. In *this* case one could give grounds for this knowledge. Is there not a relationship here similar to that between the general rule of multiplying and particular multiplications that have been carried out?

I want to say: my not having been on the moon is as sure a thing for me as any grounds I could give for it.

112. And isn't that what Moore wants to say, when he says he *knows* all these things?—But is his knowing it really what is in question, and not rather that some of these propositions must be solid for us?

113. When someone is trying to teach us mathematics, he will not begin by assuring us that he *knows* that a + b = b + a.

114. If you are not certain of any fact, you cannot be certain of the meaning of your words either.

115. If you tried to doubt everything you would not get as far as doubting anything. The game of doubting itself presupposes certainty.

116. Instead of "I know . . .", couldn't Moore have said: "It stands fast for me that . . ."? And further: "It stands fast for me and many others. . . ."

117. Why is it not possible for me to doubt that I have never been on the moon? And how could I try to doubt it?

First and foremost, the supposition that perhaps I have been there would strike me as *idle*. Nothing would follow from it, nothing be explained by it. It would not tie in with anything in my life.

When I say "Nothing speaks for, everything against it," this presupposes a principle of speaking for and against. That is, I must be able to say what *would* speak for it.

118. Now would it be correct to say: So far no one has opened my skull in order to see whether there is a brain inside; but everything speaks for, and nothing against, its being what they would find there?

119. But can it also be said: Everything speaks for, and nothing against the table's still being there when no one sees it? For what does speak for it?

120. But if anyone were to doubt it, how would his doubt come out in practice? And couldn't we peacefully leave him to doubt it, since it makes no difference at all?

121. Can one say: "Where there is no doubt there is no knowledge either"?

122. Doesn't one need grounds for doubt?

123. Wherever I look, I find no ground for doubting that. . . .

124. I want to say: We use judgments as principles of judgment.

125. If a blind man were to ask me "Have you got two hands?" I should not make sure by looking. If I were to have any doubt of it, then I don't know why I should trust my eyes. For why shouldn't I test my *eyes* by looking to find out whether I see my two hands? *What* is to be tested by *what*? (Who decides *what* stands fast?)

And what does it mean to say that such and such stands fast?

126. I am not more certain of the meaning of my words than I am of certain judgments. Can I doubt that this colour is called "blue"?

(My) doubts form a system.

127. For how do I know that someone is in doubt? How do I know that he uses the words "I doubt it" as I do?

128. From a child up I learnt to judge like this. *This is* judging.

129. This is how I learned to judge; *this* I got to know *as* judgment.

130. But isn't it experience that teaches us to judge like *this,* that is to say, that it is correct to judge like this? But how does experience *teach* us, then? *We* may derive it from experience, but experience does not direct us to derive anything from experience. If it is the *ground* of our judging like this, and not just the cause, still we do not have a ground for seeing this in turn as a ground.

131. No, experience is not the ground for our game of judging. Nor is its outstanding success.

132. Men have judged that a king can make rain; *we* say this contradicts all experience. Today they judge that aeroplanes and the radio etc. are means for the closer contact of peoples and the spread of culture.

133. Under ordinary circumstances I do not satisfy myself that I have two hands by seeing how it looks. *Why* not? Has experience shown it to be unnecessary? Or (again): Have we in some way learnt a universal law of induction, and do we trust it here too?—But why should we have learnt one *universal* law first, and not the special one straight away?

134. After putting a book in a drawer, I assume it is there, unless. . . . "Experience always proves me right. There is no well attested case of a book's (simply) disappearing." It has *often* happened that a book has never turned up again, although we thought we knew for certain where it was.—But experience does really teach that a book, say, does not vanish away. (E.g. gradually evaporate.) But is it this experience with books etc. that leads us to assume that such a book has not vanished away? Well, suppose we were to find that under particular novel circumstances books did vanish away.—Shouldn't we alter our assumption? Can one give the lie to the effect of experience on our system of assumption?

135. But do we not simply follow the principle that what has always happened will happen again (or something like it)? What does it mean to follow this principle? Do we really introduce it into our reasoning? Or is it merely the *natural law* which our inferring apparently follows? This latter it may be. It is not an item in our considerations.

136. When Moore says he *knows* such and such, he is really enumerating a lot of empirical propositions which we affirm without special testing; propositions, that is, which have a peculiar logical role in the system of our empirical propositions.

137. Even if the most trustworthy of men assures me that he *knows* things are thus and so, this by itself cannot satisfy me that he does know. Only that he believes he knows. That is why Moore's assurance that he knows . . . does not interest us. The propositions, however, which Moore retails as examples of such known truths are indeed interesting. Not because anyone knows their truth, or believes he knows them, but because they all have a *similar* role in the system of our empirical judgments.

138. We don't, for example, arrive at any of them as a result of investigation.

There are e.g. historical investigations and investigations into the shape and also the age of the earth, but not into whether the earth has existed during the last hundred years. Of course many of us have information about this period from our parents and grandparents; but mayn't they be wrong?—"Nonsense!" one will say. "How should all these people be wrong?"—But is that an argument? Is it not simply the rejection of an idea? And perhaps the determination of a concept? For if I speak of a possible mistake here, this changes the role of "mistake" and "truth" in our lives.

139. Not only rules, but also examples are needed for establishing a practice. Our rules leave loop-holes open, and the practice has to speak for itself.

140. We do not learn the practice of making empirical judgments by learning rules: we are taught *judgments* and their connexion with other judgments. A *totality* of judgments is made plausible to us.

141. When we first begin to *believe* anything, what we believe is not a single proposition, it is a whole system of propositions. (Light dawns gradually over the whole.)

142. It is not single axioms that strike me as obvious, it is a system in which consequences and premises give one another *mutual* support.

143. I am told, for example, that someone climbed this mountain many years ago. Do I always enquire into the reliability of the teller of this story, and whether the mountain did exist years ago? A child learns there are reliable and unreliable informants much later than it learns facts which are told it. It doesn't learn *at all* that that mountain has existed for a long time: that is, the question whether it is so doesn't arise at all. It swallows this consequence down, so to speak, together with *what* it learns.

144. The child learns to believe a host of things. I.e. it learns to act according to these beliefs. Bit by bit there forms a system of what is believed, and in that system some things stand unshakeably fast and some are more or less liable to shift. What stands fast does so, not because it is intrinsically obvious or convincing; it is rather held fast by what lies around it.

145. One wants to say "*All* my experiences shew that it is so". But how do they do that? For that proposition to which they point itself belongs to a particular interpretation of them.

"That I regard this proposition as certainly true also characterizes my interpretation of experience."

146. We form *the picture* of the earth as a ball floating free in space and not altering essentially in a hundred years. I said "We form the *picture* etc." and this picture now helps us in the judgment of various situations.

I may indeed calculate the dimensions of a bridge, sometimes calculate that here things are more in favor of a bridge than a ferry, etc. etc.,—but somewhere I must begin with an assumption or a decision.

147. The picture of the earth as a ball is a *good* picture, it proves itself everywhere, it is also a simple picture—in short, we work with it without doubting it.

148. Why do I not satisfy myself that I have two feet when I want to get up from a chair? There is no why. I simply don't. This is how I act.

149. My judgments themselves characterize the way I judge, characterize the nature of judgment.

150. How does someone judge which is his right and which his left hand? How do I know that my judgment will agree with someone else's? How do I know that this colour is blue ? If I don't trust *myself* here, why should I trust anyone else's judgment? Is there a why? Must I not begin to trust somewhere? That is to say: somewhere I must begin with not-doubting; and that is not, so to speak, hasty but excusable: it is part of judging.

151. I should like to say: Moore does not *know* what he asserts he knows, but it stands fast for him, as also for me; regarding it as absolutely solid is part of our *method* of doubt and enquiry.

152. I do not explicitly learn the propositions that stand fast for me. I can *discover* them subsequently like the axis around which a body rotates. This axis is not fixed in the sense that anything holds it fast, but the movement around it determines its immobility.

153. No one ever taught me that my hands don't disappear when I am not paying attention to them. Nor can I be said to presuppose the truth of this proposition in my assertions etc., (as if they rested on it) while it only gets sense from the rest of our procedure of asserting.

154. There are cases such that, if someone gives signs of doubt where we do not doubt, we cannot confidently understand his signs as signs of doubt.

I.e.: if we are to understand his signs of doubt as such, he may give them only in particular cases and may not give them in others.

155. In certain circumstances a man cannot make a *mistake*. ("Can" is here used logically, and the proposition does not mean that a man cannot say anything false in those circumstances.) If Moore were to pronounce the opposite of those propositions which he declares certain, we should not just not share his opinion: we should regard him as demented.

156. In order to make a mistake, a man must already judge in conformity with mankind.

157. Suppose a man could not remember whether he had always had five fingers or two hands? Should we understand him? Could we be sure of understanding him?

158. Can I be making a mistake, for example, in thinking that the words of which this sentence is composed are English words whose, meaning I know?

159. As children we learn facts; e.g., that every human being has a brain, and we take them on trust. I believe that there is an island, Australia, of such-and-such a shape, and so on and so on; I believe that I had great-grandparents, that the people who gave themselves out as my parents really were my parents, etc. This belief may never have been expressed; even the thought that it was so, never thought.

160. The child learns by believing the adult. Doubt comes *after* belief.

161. I learned an enormous amount and accepted it on human authority, and then I found some things confirmed or disconfirmed by my own experience.

162. In general I take as true what is found in text-books, of geography for example. Why? I say: All these facts have been confirmed a hundred times over. But how do I know that? What is my evidence for it? I have a world-picture. Is it true or false? Above all it is the substratum of all my enquiring and asserting. The propositions describing it are not all equally subject to testing.

163. Does anyone ever test whether this table remains in existence when no one is paying attention to it?

We check the story of Napoleon, but not whether all the reports about him are based on sense-deception, forgery and the like. For whenever we test

anything, we are already presupposing something that is not tested. Now am I to say that the experiment which perhaps I make in order to test the truth of a proposition presupposes the truth of the proposition that the apparatus I believe I see is really there (and the like)?

164. Doesn't testing come to an end?

165. One child might say to another: "I know that the earth is already hundreds of years old" and that would mean: I have learnt it.

166. The difficulty is to realize the groundlessness of our believing.

167. It is clear that our empirical propositions do not all have the same status, since one can lay down such a proposition and turn it from an empirical proposition into a norm of description.

Think of chemical investigations. Lavoisier makes experiments with substances in his laboratory and now he concludes that this and that takes place when there is burning. He does not say that it might happen otherwise another time. He has got hold of a definite world-picture—not of course one that he invented: he learned it as a child. I say world-picture and not hypothesis, because it is the matter-of-course foundation for his research and as such also goes unmentioned.

168. But now, what part is played by the presupposition that a substance A always reacts to a substance B in the same way, given the same circumstances? Or is that part of the definition of a substance?

169. One might think that there were propositions declaring that chemistry is *possible*. And these would be propositions of a natural science. For what should they be supported by, if not by experience?

170. I believe what people transmit to me in a certain manner. In this way I believe geographical, chemical, historical facts etc. That is how I *learn* the sciences. Of course learning is based on believing.

If you have learnt that Mont Blanc is 4000 metres high, if you have looked it up on the map, you say you *know* it.

And can it now be said: we accord credence in this way because it has proved to pay?

171. A principal ground for Moore to assume that he never was on the moon is that no one ever was on

the moon or *could* come there; and this we believe on grounds of what we learn.

172. Perhaps someone says "There must be some basic principle on which we accord credence", but what can such a principle accomplish? Is it more than a natural law of 'taking for true'?

173. Is it maybe in my power what I believe? or what I unshakeably believe?

I believe that there is a chair over there. Can't I be wrong? But, can I believe that I am wrong? Or can I so much as bring it under consideration?—And mightn't I also hold fast to my belief whatever I learned later on?! But is my belief then *grounded*?

174. I act with *complete* certainty. But this certainty is my own.

175. "I know it" I say to someone else; and here there is a justification. But there is none for my belief.

176. Instead of "I know it" one may say in some cases "That's how it is—rely upon it." In some cases, however "I learned it years and years ago"; and sometimes: "I am sure it is so."

177. What I know, I believe.

178. The wrong use made by Moore of the proposition "I know . . ." lies in his regarding it as an utterance as little subject to doubt as "I am in pain". And since from "I know it is so" there follows "It is so", then the latter can't be doubted either.

179. It would be correct to say: "I believe . . ." has subjective truth; but "I know . . ." not.

180. Or again "I believe . . ." is an 'expression', but not "I know . . .".

181. Suppose Moore had said "I swear . . ." instead of "I know . . .".

182. The more primitive idea is that the earth *never* had a beginning. No child has reason to ask himself how long the earth has existed, because all change takes place *on* it. If what is called the earth really came into existence at some time—which is

hard enough to picture—then one naturally assumes the beginning as having been an inconceivably long time ago.

183. "It is certain that after the battle of Austerlitz Napoleon. . . . Well, in that case it's surely also certain that the earth existed then."

184. "It is certain that we didn't arrive on this planet from another one a hundred years ago." Well, it's as certain as such things *are*.

185. It would strike me as ridiculous to want to doubt the existence of Napoleon; but if someone doubted the existence of the earth 150 years ago, perhaps I should be more willing to listen, for now he is doubting our whole system of evidence. It does not strike me as if this system were more certain than a certainty within it.

186. "I might suppose that Napoleon never existed and is a fable, but not that the *earth* did not exist 150 years ago."

187. "Do you *know* that the earth existed then?"—"Of course I know that. I have it from someone who certainly knows all about it."

188. It strikes me as if someone who doubts the existence of the earth at that time is impugning the nature of all historical evidence. And I cannot say of this latter that it is definitely *correct.*

189. At some point one has to pass from explanation to mere description.

190. What we call historical evidence points to the existence of the earth a long time before my birth;—the opposite hypothesis has *nothing* on its side.

191. Well, if everything speaks for an hypothesis and nothing against it—is it then certainly true? One may designate it as such.—But does it certainly agree with reality, with the facts?—With this question you are already going round in a circle.

192. To be sure there is justification; but justification comes to an end.

The Problem of the Criterion

~

RODERICK M. CHISHOLM

Roderick M. Chisholm (1916–1999), for many years Romeo Elton Professor at Brown University, is best known for his major contributions in epistemology and metaphysics. But he is also important for bringing—through his work as translator and editor and as director of the Brentano Foundation—Anglo-American philosophy back into contact with a rich Austrian philosophical tradition.

1

"The problem of the criterion" seems to me to be one of the most important and one of the most difficult of all the problems of philosophy. I am tempted to say that one has not begun to philosophize until one has faced this problem and has recognized how unappealing, in the end, each of the possible solutions is. I have chosen this problem as my topic for the Aquinas Lecture because what first set me to thinking about it (and I remain obsessed by it) were two treatises of twentieth century scholastic philosophy. I refer first to P. Coffey's two-volume work, *Epistemology or the Theory of Knowledge,* published in 1917.[1] This led me in turn to the treatises of Coffey's great teacher, Cardinal D. J. Mercier: *Critériologie générale ou théorie générale de la certitude.*[2]

Mercier and, following him, Coffey set the problem correctly, I think, and have seen what is necessary for its solution. But I shall not discuss their views in detail. I shall formulate the problem; then note what, according to Mercier, is necessary if we are to solve the problem; then sketch my own solution; and, finally, note the limitations of my approach to the problem.

2

What is the problem, then? It is the ancient problem of "the diallelus"—the problem of "the wheel" or "the vicious circle." It was put very neatly by Montaigne in his *Essays.* So let us begin by para-paraphrasing his formulation of the puzzle. To know whether things really are as they seem to be, we must have a *procedure* for distinguishing appearances that are true from appearances that are false. But to know whether our procedure is a good procedure, we have to know whether it really *succeeds* in distinguishing appearances that are true from appearances that are false. And we cannot know whether it does really succeed unless we already know which appearances are *true* and which ones are *false.* And so we are caught in a circle.[3]

Let us try to see how one gets into a situation of this sort.

The puzzles begin to form when you ask yourself, "What can I really know about the world?" We all are acquainted with people who think they know a lot more than in fact they do know. I'm thinking of fanatics, bigots, mystics, various types of dogmatists. And we have all heard of people who claim at least to know

Reprinted from Roderick M. Chisholm, *The Foundations of Knowing* (Minneapolis: University of Minnesota Press, 1982), by permission of Marquette University Press.

a lot less than what in fact they do know. I'm thinking of those people who call themselves "skeptics" and who like to say that people cannot know what the world is really like. People tend to become skeptics, temporarily, after reading books on popular science: the authors tell us we cannot know what things are like really (but they make use of a vast amount of knowledge, or a vast amount of what is claimed to be knowledge, to support this skeptical conclusion). And as we know, people tend to become dogmatists, temporarily, as a result of the effects of alcohol, or drugs, or religious and emotional experiences. Then they claim to have an inside view of the world and they think they have a deep kind of knowledge giving them a key to the entire workings of the universe.

If you have a healthy common sense, you will feel that something is wrong with both of these extremes and that the truth is somewhere in the middle: we can know far more than the skeptic says we can know and far less than the dogmatist or the mystic says that he can know. But how are we to decide these things?

3

How do we decide, in any particular case, whether we have a genuine item of knowledge? Most of us are ready to confess that our beliefs far transcend what we really know. There are things we believe that we don't in fact know. And we can say of many of these things that we know that we don't know them. I believe that Mrs. Jones is honest, say, but I don't know it, and I know that I don't know it. There are other things that we don't know, but they are such that we don't know that we don't know them. Last week, say, I thought I knew that Mr. Smith was honest, but he turned out to be a thief. I didn't know that he was a thief, and, moreover, I didn't know that I didn't know that he was a thief; I thought I knew that he was honest. And so the problem is: How are we to distinguish the real cases of knowledge from what only seem to be cases of knowledge? Or, as I put it before, how are we to decide in any particular case whether we have genuine items of knowledge?

What would be a satisfactory solution to our problem? Let me quote in detail what Cardinal Mercier says:

If there is any knowledge which bears the mark of truth, if the intellect does have a way of distinguishing the true and the false, in short, *if there is* a criterion of truth, then this criterion should satisfy three conditions: it should be *internal, objective,* and *immediate.*

It should be *internal.* No reason or rule of truth that is provided by an *external authority* can serve as an ultimate criterion. For the reflective doubts that are essential to criteriology can and should be applied to this authority itself. The mind cannot attain to certainty until it has found *within itself* a sufficient reason for adhering to the testimony of such an authority.

The criterion should be *objective.* The ultimate reason for believing cannot be a merely *subjective* state of the thinking subject. A man is aware that he can reflect upon his psychological states in order to control them. Knowing that he has this ability, he does not, so long as he has not made use of it, have the right to be sure. The ultimate ground of certitude cannot consist in a subjective feeling. It can be found only in that which, objectively, produces this feeling and is adequate to reason.

Finally, the criterion must be *immediate.* To be sure, a certain conviction may rest upon many different reasons some of which are subordinate to others. But if we are to avoid an infinite regress, then we must find a ground of assent that presupposes no other. We must find an *immediate* criterion of certitude.

Is there a criterion of truth that satisfies these three conditions? If so, what is it?[4]

4

To see how perplexing our problem is, let us consider a figure that Descartes had suggested and that Coffey takes up in his dealings with the problem of the criterion.[5] Descartes' figure comes to this.

Let us suppose that you have a pile of apples and you want to sort out the good ones from the bad ones. You want to put the good ones in a pile by themselves and throw the bad ones away. This is a useful thing to do, obviously, because the bad apples tend to infect the good ones and then the good ones become bad, too. Descartes thought our beliefs were like this. The bad ones tend to infect the good ones, so we should look them over very carefully, throw out the bad ones if we can, and then—or so Descartes hoped—we would be left with just a stock of good beliefs on which we could rely completely. But how are we to do the sorting? If we are to sort out the good ones from the bad ones, then, of course, we must have a way of recognizing the good ones. Or at least we must have a way of recognizing the bad ones. And—again, of course—you and I do have a way of recognizing good apples and also of recognizing bad ones. The good ones have their own special feel, look, and taste, and so do the bad ones.

But when we turn from apples to beliefs, the matter is quite different. In the case of the apples, we have a method—a criterion—for distinguishing the good ones from the bad ones. But in the case of the beliefs, we do not have a method or a criterion for distinguishing the good ones from the bad ones. Or, at least, we don't have one yet. The question we started with was: How *are* we to tell the good ones from the bad ones? In other words, we were asking: What is the proper method for deciding which are the good beliefs and which are the bad ones—which beliefs are genuine cases of knowledge and which beliefs are not?

And now, you see, we are on the wheel. First, we want to find out which are the good beliefs and which are the bad ones. To find this out we have to have some way—some method—of deciding which are the good ones and which are the bad ones. But there are good and bad methods—good and bad ways—of sorting out the good beliefs from the bad ones. And so we now have a new problem: How are we to decide which are the good methods and which are the bad ones?

If we could fix on a good method for distinguishing between good and bad methods, we might be all set. But this, of course, just moves the problem to a different level. How are we to distinguish between a good method for choosing good methods? If we continue in this way, of course, we are led to an infinite regress and we will never have the answer to our original question.

What do we do in fact? We do know that there are fairly reliable ways of sorting out good beliefs from bad ones. Most people will tell you, for example, that

if you follow the procedures of science and common sense—if you tend carefully to your observations and if you make use of the canons of logic, induction, and the theory of probability—you will be following the best possible procedure for making sure that you will have more good beliefs than bad ones. This is doubtless true. But how do we know that it is? How do we know that the procedures of science, reason, and common sense are the best methods that we have?

If we do know this, it is because we know that these procedures work. It is because we know that these procedures do in fact enable us to distinguish the good beliefs from the bad ones. We say: "See—these methods turn out good beliefs." But *how* do we know that they do? It can only be that we already know how to tell the difference between the good beliefs and the bad ones.

And now you can see where the skeptic comes in. He'll say this: "You said you wanted to sort out the good beliefs from the bad ones. Then to do this, you apply the canons of science, common sense, and reason. And now, in answer to the question, 'How do you know that that's the right way to do it?,' you say 'Why, I can see that the ones it picks out are the good ones and the ones it leaves behind are the bad ones.' But if you can *see* which ones are the good ones and which ones are the bad ones, why do you think you need a general method for sorting them out?"

5

We can formulate some of the philosophical issues that are involved here by distinguishing two pairs of questions. These are:

A) "*What* do we know? What is the *extent* of our knowledge?"
B) "How are we to decide *whether* we know? What are the *criteria* of knowledge?"

If you happen to know the answers to the first of these pairs of questions, you may have some hope of being able to answer the second. Thus, if you happen to know which are the good apples and which are the bad ones, then maybe you could explain to some other person how he could go about deciding whether or not he has a good apple or a bad one. But if you don't know the answer to the first of these pairs of questions—if you don't know what things you know or how far your knowledge extends—it is difficult to see how you could possibly figure out an answer to the second.

On the other hand, *if,* somehow, you already know the answers to the second of these pairs of questions, then you may have some hope of being able to answer the first. Thus, if you happen to have a good set of directions for telling whether apples are good or bad, then maybe you can go about finding a good one—assuming, of course, that there are some good apples to be found. But if you don't know the answer to the second of these pairs of questions—if you don't know how to go about deciding whether or not you know, if you don't know what the criteria of knowing are—it is difficult to see how you could possibly figure out an answer to the first.

And so we can formulate the position of *the skeptic* on these matters. He will say: "You cannot answer question A until you have answered question B. And you cannot answer question B until you have answered question A. Therefore you cannot answer either question. You cannot know what, if anything, you know, and there is no possible way for you to decide in any particular case." Is there any reply to this?

6

Broadly speaking, there are at least two other possible views. So we may choose among three possibilities.

There are people—philosophers—who think that they do have an answer to B and that, given their answer to B, they can then figure out their answer to A. And there are other people—other philosophers—who have it the other way around: they think that they have an answer to A and that, given their answer to A, they can then figure out the answer to B.

There don't seem to be any generally accepted names for these two different philosophical positions. (Perhaps this is just as well. There are more than enough names, as it is, for possible philosophi-

cal views.) I suggest, for the moment, we use the expressions "methodists" and "particularists." By "methodists," I mean, not the followers of John Wesley's version of Christianity, but those who think they have an answer to B, and who then, in terms of it, work out their answer to A. By "particularists" I mean those who have it the other way around.

7

Thus John Locke was a methodist—in our present, rather special sense of the term. He was able to arrive—somehow—at an answer to B. He said, in effect: "The way you decide whether or not a belief is a good belief—that is to say, the way you decide whether a belief is likely to be a genuine case of knowledge—is to see whether it is derived from sense experience, to see, for example, whether it bears certain relations to your sensations." Just what these relations to our sensations might be is a matter we may leave open, for present purposes. The point is: Locke felt that if a belief is to be credible, it must bear certain relations to the believer's sensations—but he never told us *how* he happened to arrive at this conclusion. This, of course, is the view that has come to be known as "empiricism." David Hume followed Locke in this empiricism and said that empiricism gives us an effective criterion for distinguishing the good apples from the bad ones. You can take this criterion to the library, he said. Suppose you find a book in which the author makes assertions that do not conform to the empirical criterion. Hume said: Commit it to the flames: for it can contain nothing but sophistry and illusion."

8

Empiricism, then, was a form of what I have called "methodism." The empiricist—like other types of methodist—begins with a criterion and then he uses it to throw out the bad apples. There are two objections, I would say, to empiricism. The first—which applies to every form of methodism (in our present sense of the word)—is that the criterion is very broad and far-reaching and at the same time completely arbitrary. How can one *begin* with a broad general-ization? It seems especially odd that the empiricist—who wants to proceed cautiously, step by step, from experience—begins with such a generalization. He leaves us completely in the dark so far as concerns what *reasons* he may have for adopting this particular criterion rather than some other. The second objection applies to empiricism in particular. When we apply the empirical criterion—at least, as it was developed by Hume, as well as by many of those in the nineteenth and twentieth centuries who have called themselves "empiricists"—we seem to throw out, not only the bad apples but the good ones as well, and we are left, in effect, with just a few parings or skins with no meat behind them. Thus Hume virtu-ally conceded that, if you are going to be empiricist, the only matters of fact that you can really know about pertain to the existence of sensations. "'Tis vain," he said, "To ask whether there be body." He meant you cannot know whether any physical things exist—whether there are trees, or houses, or bodies, much less whether there are atoms or other such microscopic particles. All you can know is that there are and have been certain sensations. You cannot know whether there is any you who experiences those sensations—much less whether any other peo-ple exist who experience sensations. And I think, if he had been consistent in his empiricism, he would also have said you cannot really be sure whether there have been any sensations in the past; you can know only that certain sensations exist here and now.

9

The great Scottish philosopher, Thomas Reid, reflected on all this in the eighteenth century. He was serious about philosophy and man's place in the world. He finds Hume saying things implying that we can know only of the existence of certain sensations here and now. One can imagine him saying: "Good Lord! What kind of nonsense is this?" What he did say, among other things, was this: "A traveller of good judgment may mistake his way, and be unawares led into a wrong track; and while the road is fair before him, he may go on without suspicion and be followed by others but, when it ends in a coal pit, it requires no

great judgment to know that he hath gone wrong, nor perhaps to find out what misled him."[6]

Thus Reid, as I interpret him, was not an empiri-cist; nor was he, more generally, what I have called a "methodist." He was a "particularist." That is to say, he thought that he had an answer to question A, and in terms of the answer to question A, he then worked out kind of an answer to question B.[7] An even better example of a "particularist" is the great twentieth century English philosopher, G. E. Moore.

Suppose, for a moment, you were tempted to go along with Hume and say "The only thing about the world I can really know is that there are now sensa-tions of a certain sort. There's a sensation of a man, there's the sound of a voice, and there's a feeling of bewilderment or boredom. But that's all I can really know about." What would Reid say? I can imagine him saying something like this: "Well, you can talk that way if you want to. But you know very well that it isn't true. You know that you are there, that you have a body of such and such a sort and that other people are here, too. And you know about this building and where you were this morning and all kinds of other things as well." G. E. Moore would raise his hand at this point and say: "I know very well this is a hand, and so do you. If you come across some philosophi-cal theory that implies that you and I cannot know that this is a hand, then so much the worse for the theory." I think that Reid and Moore are right, myself, and I'm inclined to think that the "methodists" are wrong.

Going back to our questions A and B, we may summarize the three possible views as follows: there is skepticism (you cannot answer either question without presupposing an answer to the other, and therefore the questions cannot be answered at all); there is "methodism" (you begin with an answer to B); and there is "particularism" (you begin with an answer to A). I suggest that the third possibility is the most reasonable.

10

I would say—and many reputable philosophers would disagree with me—that, to find out whether you know such a thing as that this is a hand, you don't have to apply any test or criterion. Spinoza has it right. "In order to know," he said, "there is no need to know that we know, much less to know that we know that we know."[8]

This is part of the answer, it seems to me, to the puzzle about the diallelus. There are many things that quite obviously, we do know to be true. If I report to you the things I now see and hear and feel—or, if you prefer, the things I now think I see and hear and feel—the chances are that my report will be correct; I will be telling you something I know. And so, too, if you report the things that you think you now see and hear and feel. To be sure, there are hallucinations and illusions. People often think they see or hear or feel things that in fact they do not see or hear or feel. But from this fact—that our senses do sometimes deceive us—it hardly follows that your senses and mine are deceiving you and me right now. One may say similar things about what we remember.

Having these good apples before us, we can look them over and formulate certain criteria of goodness. Consider the senses, for example. One important criterion—one epistemological principle—was formulated by St. Augustine. It is more reasonable, he said, to trust the senses than to distrust them. Even though there have been illusions and hallucinations, the wise thing, when everything seems all right, is to accept the testimony of the senses. I say "when everything seems all right." If on a particular occasion something about *that* particular occasion makes you suspect that particular report of the senses, if, say, you seem to remember having been drugged or hypnotized, or brainwashed, then perhaps you should have some doubts about what you think you see, or hear, or feel, or smell. But if nothing about this particular occasion leads you to suspect what the senses report on this particular occasion, then the wise thing is to take such a report at its face value. In short the senses should be regarded as innocent until there is some positive reason, on some particular occasion, for thinking that they are guilty on that particular occasion.

One might say the same thing of memory. If, on any occasion, you think you remember that such-and-such an event occurred, then the wise thing is to assume that that particular event did occur—unless something special about this particular occasion leads you to suspect your memory.

We have then a kind of answer to the puzzle about the diallelus. We start with particular cases of knowledge and then from those we generalize and formulate criteria of goodness—criteria telling us what it is for a belief to be epistemologically respectable. Let us now try to sketch somewhat more precisely this approach to the problem of the criterion.

[margin note: why is this a good way?]

11

The theory of evidence, like ethics and the theory of value, presupposes an objective right and wrong. To explicate the requisite senses of "right" and "wrong," we need the concept of *right preference*—or, more exactly, the concept of one state of mind being *preferable,* epistemically, to another. One state of mind may be *better,* epistemically, than another. This concept of epistemic preferability is what Cardinal Mercier called an *objective* concept. It is one thing to say, objectively, that one state of mind is *to be preferred* to another. It is quite another thing to say, subjectively, that one state of mind is in fact preferred to another—that someone or other happens to prefer the one state of mind to the other. If a state of mind A is to be preferred to a state of mind B, if it is, as I would like to say, intrinsically preferable to B, then anyone who prefers B to A is *mistaken* in his preference.

Given this concept of epistemic preferability, we can readily explicate the basic concepts of the theory of evidence. We could say, for for example, that a proposition p is *beyond reasonable doubt* provided only that believing *p* is then epistemically preferable for S to withholding *p*—where by "withholding *p*" we mean the state of neither accepting *p* nor its negation. It is evident to me, for example, that many people are here. This means it is epistemically preferable for me to believe that many people are here than for me neither to believe nor to disbelieve that many are people here.

A proposition is *evident* for a person if it is beyond reasonable doubt for that person and is such that his including it among the propositions upon which he bases his decisions is preferable to his not so including it. A proposition is *acceptable* if withholding it is *not* preferable to believing it. And a proposition is *unacceptable* if withholding it *is* preferable to believing it.

Again, some propositions are not beyond reasonable doubt but they may be said to have *some presumption in their favor.* I suppose that the proposition that each of us will be alive an hour from now is one that has some presumption in its favor. We could say that a proposition is of this sort provided only that believing the proposition is epistemically preferable to believing its negation.

Moving in the other direction in the epistemic hierarchy, we could say that a proposition is *certain,* absolutely certain, for a given subject at a given time, if that proposition is then evident to that subject and if there is no other proposition that is such that believing that other proposition is then epistemically preferable for him to believing the given proposition. It is certain for me, I would say, that there seem to be many people here and that 7 and 5 are 12. If this is so, then each of the two propositions is evident to me and there are no other propositions that are such that it would be even better, epistemically, if I were to believe those other propositions.

This concept of epistemic preferability can be axiomatized and made the basis of a system of epistemic logic exhibiting the relations among these and other concepts of the theory of evidence.[9] For present purposes, let us simply note how they may be applied in our approach to the problem of the criterion.

12

Let us begin with the most difficult of the concepts to which we have just referred—that of a proposition being *certain* for a man at a given time. Can we formulate *criteria* of such certainty? I think we can.

Leibniz had said that there are two kinds of immediately evident proposition—the "first truths of fact" and the "first truths of reason." Let us consider each of these in turn.

Among the "first truths of fact," for any man at any given time, I would say, are various propositions about his own state of mind at that time—his thinking certain thoughts, his entertaining certain beliefs, his being in a certain sensory or emotional state. These propositions all pertain to certain states of the man that may be said to manifest or present themselves to him at that time. We could use Meinong's term and say that certain states are "self-presenting," where this concept might be marked off in the following way.

A man's being in a certain state is *self-presenting* to him at a given time provided only that (i) he is in that state at that time and (ii) it is necessarily true that if he is in that state at that time then it is evident to him that he is in that state at that time.

The states of mind just referred to are of this character. Wishing, say, that one were on the moon is a state that is such that a man cannot be in that state without it being evident to him that he is in that state. And so, too, for thinking certain thoughts and having certain sensory or emotional experiences. These states present themselves and are, so to speak, marks of their own evidence. They cannot occur unless it is evident that they occur. I think they are properly called the "first truths of fact." Thus St. Thomas could say that "the intellect knows that it possesses the truth by reflecting on itself."[10]

Perceiving external things and remembering are not states that present themselves. But thinking that one perceives (or seeming to perceive) and thinking that one remembers (or seeming to remember) *are* states of mind that present themselves. And in presenting themselves they may, at least under certain favorable conditions, present something else as well.

Coffey quotes Hobbes as saying that "the inn of evidence has no sign-board."[11] I would prefer saying that these self-presenting states are sign-boards—of the inn of indirect evidence. But these sign-boards need no further sign-boards in order to be presented, for they present themselves.

13

What of the first truths of reason? These are the propositions that some philosophers have called "a priori" and that Leibniz, following Locke, referred to as "maxims" or "axioms." These propositions are all necessary and have a further characteristic that Leibniz described in this way: "You will find in a hundred places that the Scholastics have said that these propositions are evident, *ex terminis,* as soon as the terms are understood, so that they were persuaded that the force of conviction was grounded in the nature of the terms, i.e., in the connection of their ideas."[1] Thus St. Thomas referred to propositions that are "manifest through themselves."[13]

An axiom, one might say, is a necessary proposition such that one cannot understand it without thereby knowing that it is true. Since one cannot know a proposition unless it is evident and one believes it, and since one cannot believe a proposition unless one understands it, we might characterize these first truths of reason in the following way:

A proposition is *axiomatic* for a given subject at a given time provided only that (i) the proposition is one that is necessarily true and (ii) it is also necessarily true that if the person then believes that proposition, the proposition is then evident to him.

We might now characterize the *a priori* somewhat more broadly by saying that a proposition is a priori for a given subject at a given time provided that one or the other of these two things is true: either (i) the proposition is one that is axiomatic for that subject at that time, or else (ii) the proposition is one such that it is evident to the man at that time that the proposition is entailed by a set of propositions that are axiomatic for him at that time.

In characterizing the "first truths of fact" and the "first truths of reason," I have used the expression "evident." But I think it is clear that such truths are not only evident but also certain. And they may be said to be *directly,* or *immediately,* evident.

What, then, of the indirectly evident?

14

I have suggested in rather general terms above what we might say about memory and the senses. These ostensible sources of knowledge are to be treated as innocent until there is positive ground for thinking them guilty. I will not attempt to develop a theory of the indirectly evident at this point. But I will note at least the *kind* of principle to which we might appeal in developing such a theory.

We could *begin* by considering the following two principles, M and P; M referring to memory, and P referring to perception or the senses.

M) For any subject S, if it is evident to S that she seems to remember that *a* was F, then it is beyond reasonable doubt for S that *a* was F.

P) For any subject S, if it is evident to S that she thinks she perceives that *a* is F, then it is evident to S that *a* is F.

"She seems to remember" and "she thinks she perceives" here refer to certain self-presenting states that, in the figure I used above, could be said to serve as sign-boards for the inn of indirect evidence.

But principles M and P, as they stand, are much too latitudinarian. We will find that it is necessary to make qualifications and add more and more conditions. Some of these will refer to the subject's sensory state; some will refer to certain of her other beliefs; and some will refer to the relations of confirmation and mutual support. To set them forth in adequate detail would require a complete epistemology.[14]

So far as our problem of the criterion is concerned, the essential thing to note is this. In formulating such principles we will simply proceed as Aristotle did when he formulated his rules for the syllogism. As "particularists" in our approach to the problem of the criterion, we will fit our rules to the cases—to the apples we know to be good and to the apples we know to be bad. Knowing what we do about ourselves and the world, we have at our disposal certain instances that our rules or principles should countenance, and certain other instances that our rules or principles should rule out or forbid. And, as rational beings, we assume that by investigating these instances we can formulate criteria that any instance must satisfy if it is to be countenanced and we can formulate other criteria that any instance must satisfy if it is to be ruled out or forbidden.

If we proceed in this way we will have satisfied Cardinal Mercier's criteria for a theory of evidence or, as he called it, a theory of certitude. He said that any criterion, or any adequate set of criteria, should be internal, objective, and immediate. The type of criteria I have referred to are certainly *internal,* in his sense of the term. We have not appealed to any external authority as constituting the ultimate test of evidence. (Thus we haven't appealed to "science" or to "the scientists of our culture circle" as constituting the touchstone of what we know.) I would say that our criteria are *objective*. We have formulated them in terms of the concept of epistemic preferability—where the locution "*p* is epistemically preferable to *q* for S" is taken to refer to an objective relation that obtains independently of the actual preferences of any particular subject. The criteria that we formulate, if they are adequate, will be principles that are necessarily true. And they are also *immediate*. Each of them is such that, if it is applicable at any particular time, then the fact that it is then applicable is capable of being directly evident to that particular subject at that particular time.

15

But in all of this I have presupposed the approach I have called "particularism." The "methodist" and the "skeptic" will tell us that we have started in the wrong place. If now we try to reason with them, then, I am afraid, we will be back on the wheel.

What few philosophers have had the courage to recognize is this: we can deal with the problem only by begging the question. It seems to me that, if we do recognize this fact, as we should, then it is unseemly for us to try to pretend that it isn't so.

One may object: "Doesn't this mean, then, that the skeptic is right after all?" I would answer: "Not at all. His view is only one of the three possibilities and in itself has no more to recommend it than the others do. And in favor of our approach there is the fact that we *do* know many things, after all."

NOTES

1. Published in London in 1917 by Longmans, Green and Co.

2. The eighth edition of this work was published in 1923 in Louvain by the Institut Supérieur de Philosophie, and in Paris by Félix Alcan. The first edition was published in 1884. It has been translated into Spanish, Polish, Portuguese and perhaps still other languages, but unfortunately not yet into English.

3. The quotation is a paraphrase. What Montaigne wrote was: "Pour juger des apparences que nous recevons des subjects, il nous faudroit un instrument judicatoire; pour verifier cet instrument, il nous y faut de la demonstration; pour verifier la demonstration, un instrument; nous voyià au rouet. Puisque les sens ne peuvent arrester notre dispute, éstans pleins eux-mesmes d'incertitude, il faut que se soit la raison: sucune raison s'establira sans une sutre raison: nous voyià à reculons jusques à l'infiny." The passage appears in Book 2, Chapter 12 ("An Apologie of Raymond Sebond"); it may be found on page 544 of the Modern Library edition of *The Essays of Montaigne.*

4. *Critériologie,* Op. cit., eighth edition, p. 234.

5. See the reply to the VIIth set of Objections and Coffey, vol. 1, p. 127.

6. Thomas Reid, *Inquiry into the Human Mind,* chap. 1, sec. 8.

7. Unfortunately Cardinal Mercier takes Reid to be what I have called a "methodist." He assumes, incorrectly I think, that Reid defends certain principles (principles that Reid calls principles of "common sense") on the ground that these principles happen to be the deliverance of a faculty called "common sense." See Mercier, pp. 179–81.

8. *On Improvement of the Understanding,* in *Chief Works of Benedict de Spinoza,* vol. 2, trans. R. H. M. Elwes, rev. ed. (London: George Bell and Sons, 1898), p. 13.

9. The logic of these concepts, though with a somewhat different vocabulary, is set forth in Roderick M. Chisholm and Robert Keim, "A System of Epistemic Logic," *Ratio,* 15 (1973).

10. *The Disputed Questions on Truth,* Question One, Article 9; trans. Robert W. Mulligan (Chicago: Henry Regnery Company, 1952).

11. Coffey, vol. 1, p. 146. I have been unable to find this quotation in Hobbes.

12. *New Essays concerning Human Understanding,* book 4, chap. 7, n. 1.

13. *Exposition of the Posterior Analytics of Aristotle,* Lectio 4, No. 10; trans Pierre Conway (Quebec: M. Doyon, 1956).

14. I have attempted to do this to some extent in *Theory of Knowledge* (Englewood Cliffs, NJ: Prentice-Hall, Inc., 1966). Revisions and corrections may be found in my essay "On the Nature of Empirical Evidence" in Roderick M. Chisholm and Robert J. Swartz, eds., *Empirical Knowledge* (Englewood Cliffs, NJ: Prentice-Hall, Inc., 1973).

Is Justified True Belief Knowledge?

~

EDMUND GETTIER

Edmund Gettier is Professor Emeritus at the University of Massachusetts, Amherst. This short piece, published in 1963, seemed to many decisively to refute an otherwise attractive analysis of knowledge. It stimulated a renewed effort, still ongoing, to clarify exactly what knowledge comprises.

Various attempts have been made in recent years to state necessary and sufficient conditions for someone's knowing a given proposition. The attempts have often been such that they can be stated in a form similar to the following:[1]

(a) S knows that P   *IFF*
  (i) P is true,
  (ii) S believes that P, and
  (iii) S is justified in believing that P.

For example, Chisholm has held that the following gives the necessary and sufficient conditions for knowledge:[2]

(b) S knows that P   *IFF*
  (i) S accepts P,
  (ii) S has adequate evidence for P, and
  (iii) P is true.

Ayer has stated the necessary and sufficient conditions for knowledge as follows:[3]

(c) S knows that P   *IFF*
  (i) P is true,
  (ii) S is sure that P is true, and
  (iii) S has the right to be sure that P is true.

I shall argue that (a) is false in that the conditions stated therein do not constitute a *sufficient* condition for the truth of the proposition that S knows that P. The same argument will show that (b) and (c) fail if "has adequate evidence for" or "has the right to be sure that" is substituted for "is justified in believing that" throughout.

I shall begin by noting two points. First, in that sense of "justified" in which S's being justified in believing P is a necessary condition of S's knowing that P, it is possible for a person to be justified in believing a proposition that is in fact false. Secondly, for any proposition P, if S is justified in believing P, and P entails Q, and S deduces Q from P and accepts Q as a result of this deduction, then S is justified in believing Q. Keeping these two points in mind, I shall now present two cases in which the conditions stated in (a) are true for some proposition, though it is at the same time false that the person in question knows that proposition.

CASE I

Suppose that Smith and Jones have applied for a certain job. And suppose that Smith has strong evidence for the following conjunctive proposition:

(d) Jones is the man who will get the job, and Jones has ten coins in his pocket.

Smith's evidence for (d) might be that the president of the company assured him that Jones would in the end be selected, and that he, Smith, had counted the coins in Jones's pocket ten minutes ago. Proposition (d) entails:

   (e) The man who will get the job has ten coins in his pocket.

Let us suppose that Smith sees the entailment from (d) to (e), and accepts (e) on the grounds of (d), for which he has strong evidence. In this case, Smith is clearly justified in believing that (e) is true.

   But imagine, further, that unknown to Smith, he himself, not Jones, will get the job. And, also, unknown to Smith, he himself has ten coins in his pocket. Proposition (e) is then true, though proposition (d), from which Smith inferred (e), is false. In our example, then, all of the following are true: (*i*) (e) is true, (*ii*) Smith believes that (e) is true, and (*iii*) Smith is justified in believing that (e) is true. But it is equally clear that Smith does not *know* that (e) is true; for (e) is true in virtue of the number of coins in Smith's pocket, while Smith does not know how many coins are in Smith's pocket, and bases his belief in (e) on a count of the coins in Jones's pocket, whom he falsely believes to be the man who will get the job.

CASE II

Let us suppose that Smith has strong evidence for the following proposition:

   (f) Jones owns a Ford.

Smith's evidence might be that Jones has at all times in the past within Smith's memory owned a car, and always a Ford, and that Jones has just offered Smith a ride while driving a Ford. Let us imagine, now, that Smith has another friend, Brown, of whose whereabouts he is totally ignorant. Smith selects three place names quite at random and constructs the following three propositions:

   (g) Either Jones owns a Ford, or Brown is in Boston.

   (h) Either Jones owns a Ford, or Brown is in Barcelona.

   (i) Either Jones owns a Ford, or Brown is in Brest-Litovsk.

Each of these propositions is entailed by (f). Imagine that Smith realizes the entailment of each of these propositions he has constructed by (f), and proceeds to accept (g), (h), and (i) on the basis of (f). Smith has correctly inferred (g), (h), and (i) from a proposition for which he has strong evidence. Smith is therefore completely justified in believing each of these three propositions. Smith, of course, has no idea where Brown is.

   But imagine now that two further conditions hold. First, Jones does *not* own a Ford, but is at present driving a rented car. And secondly, by the sheerest coincidence, and entirely unknown to Smith, the place mentioned in proposition (h) happens really to be the place where Brown is. If these two conditions hold, then Smith does *not* know that (h) is true, even though (*i*) (h) is true, (*ii*) Smith does believe that (h) is true, and (*iii*) Smith is justified in believing that (h) is true.

   These two examples show that definition (a) does not state a *sufficient* condition for someone's knowing a given proposition. The same cases, with appropriate changes, will suffice to show that neither definition (b) nor definition (c) do so either.

NOTES

1. Plato seems to be considering some such definition at *Theaetetus* 201, and perhaps accepting one at *Meno* 98.

2. Roderick M. Chisholm, *Perceiving: A Philosophical Study.* (Ithaca, N.Y., 1957), 16.

3. A. J. Ayer. *The Problem of Knowledge* (London, 1956).

Discrimination and Perceptual Knowledge

~

ALVIN I. GOLDMAN

Alvin Goldman is professor of philosophy at Rutgers University. The author of *A Theory of Human Action* and of *Liaisons: Philosophy Meets the Cognitive and Social Sciences* and *Philosophical Applications of Cognitive Science,* in addition to his important work in the theory of knowledge, his name is associated with a position known as "reliabilism" and with the celebrated example of papier-mâché barns given here. His recent interests have focused on the social dimensions of knowledge.

This paper presents a partial analysis of perceptual knowledge, an analysis that will, I hope, lay a foundation for a general theory of knowing. Like an earlier theory I proposed,[1] the envisaged theory would seek to explicate the concept of knowledge by reference to the causal processes that produce (or sustain) belief. Unlike the earlier theory, however, it would abandon the requirement that a knower's belief that *p* be causally connected with the fact, or state of affairs, that *p*.

What kinds of causal processes or mechanisms must be responsible for a belief if that belief is to count as knowledge? They must be mechanisms that are, in an appropriate sense, "reliable." Roughly, a cognitive mechanism or process is reliable if it not only produces true beliefs in actual situations, but would produce true beliefs, or at least inhibit false beliefs, in relevant counterfactual situations. The theory of knowledge I envisage, then, would contain an important counterfactual component.

To be reliable, a cognitive mechanism must enable a person to *discriminate* or *differentiate* between incompatible states of affairs. It must operate in such a way that incompatible states of the world would generate different cognitive responses. Perceptual mechanisms illustrate this clearly. A perceptual mechanism is reliable to the extent that contrary features of the environment (e.g., an object's being red, versus its being yellow) would produce contrary perceptual states of the organism, which would, in turn, produce suitably different beliefs about the environment. Another belief-governing mechanism is a reasoning mechanism, which, given a set of antecedent beliefs, generates or inhibits various new beliefs. A reasoning mechanism is reliable to the extent that its functional procedures would generate new true beliefs from antecedent true beliefs.

My emphasis on discrimination accords with a sense of the verb "know" that has been neglected by philosophers. The O.E.D. lists one (early) sense of "know" as "*to distinguish* (one thing) *from* (another)," as in "I know a hawk from a handsaw" (*Hamlet*) and "We'll teach him to know Turtles from Jayes" (*Merry Wives of Windsor*). Although it no longer has great currency, this sense still survives in such expressions as "I don't know him from Adam," "He doesn't know right from left," and other phrases that readily come to mind. I suspect that this construction is historically important and can be used to shed light on constructions in which "know" takes propositional objects. I suggest that a person is said to know that *p* just in case he *distinguishes* or *discriminates* the truth of *p* from relevant alternatives.

A knowledge attribution imputes to someone the

From *The Journal of Philosophy,* vol. 73 (1976), reprinted by permission of the Journal of Philosophy.

discrimination of a given state of affairs from possible alternatives, but not necessarily all logically possible alternatives. In forming beliefs about the world, we do not normally consider all logical possibilities. And in deciding whether someone knows that p (its truth being assumed), we do not ordinarily require him to discriminate p from all logically possible alternatives. Which alternatives are, or ought to be considered, is a question I shall not fully resolve in this paper, but some new perspectives will be examined. I take up this topic in section I.

I

Consider the following example. Henry is driving in the countryside with his son. For the boy's edification Henry identifies various objects on the landscape as they come into view. "That's a cow," says Henry, "That's a tractor," "That's a silo," "That's a barn," etc. Henry has no doubt about the identity of these objects; in particular, he has no doubt that the last-mentioned object is a barn, which indeed it is. Each of the identified objects has features characteristic of its type. Moreover, each object is fully in view, Henry has excellent eyesight, and he has enough time to look at them reasonably carefully, since there is little traffic to distract him.

Given this information, would we say that Henry *knows* that the object is a barn? Most of us would have little hesitation in saying this, so long as we were not in a certain philosophical frame of mind. Contrast our inclination here with the inclination we would have if we were given some additional information. Suppose we are told that, unknown to Henry, the district he has just entered is full of papier-mâché facsimiles of barns. These facsimiles look from the road exactly like barns, but are really just façades, without back walls or interiors, quite incapable of being used as barns. They are so cleverly constructed that travelers invariably mistake them for barns. Having just entered the district, Henry has not encountered any facsimiles; the object he sees is a genuine barn. But if the object on that site were a facsimile, Henry would mistake it for a barn. Given this new information, we would be strongly inclined to withdraw the claim that Henry *knows* the object is a

barn. How is this change in our assessment to be explained?

Note first that the traditional justified-true-belief account of knowledge is of no help in explaining this change. In both cases Henry truly believes (indeed, is certain) that the object is a barn. Moreover, Henry's "justification" or "evidence" for the proposition that the object is a barn is the same in both cases. Thus, Henry should either know in both cases or not know in both cases. The presence of facsimiles in the district should make no difference to whether or not he knows.

My old causal analysis cannot handle the problem either. Henry's belief that the object is a barn is caused by the presence of the barn; indeed, the causal process is a perceptual one. Nonetheless, we are not prepared to say, in the second version, that Henry knows.

One analysis of propositional knowledge that might handle the problem is Peter Unger's non-accidentality analysis.[2] According to this theory, S knows that p if and only if it is not at all accidental that S is right about its being the case that p. In the initial description of the example, this requirement appears to be satisfied; so we say that Henry knows. When informed about the facsimiles, however, we see that it is accidental that Henry is right about its being a barn. So we withdraw our knowledge attribution. The "non-accidentality" analysis is not very satisfying, however, for the notion of "non-accidentality" itself needs explication. Pending explication, it isn't clear whether it correctly handles all cases.

Another approach to knowledge that might handle our problem is the "indefeasibility" approach.[3] On this view, S knows that p only if S's true belief is justified *and* this justification is not defeated. In an unrestricted form, an indefeasibility theory would say that S's justification j for believing that p is defeated if and only if there is some true proposition q such that the conjunction of q and j does not justify S in believing that p. In slightly different terms, S's justification j is defeated just in case p would no longer be evident for S if q were evident for S. This would handle the barn example, presumably, because the true proposition that there are barn facsimiles in the district is such that, if it were evident for Henry, then it would no longer be evident for him that the object he sees is a barn.

The trouble with the indefeasibility approach is that it is too strong, at least in its unrestricted form. On the foregoing account of "defeat," as Gilbert Harman shows,[4] it will (almost) always be possible to find a true proposition that defeats S's justification. Hence, S will never (or seldom) know. What is needed is an appropriate restriction on the notion of "defeat," but I am not aware of an appropriate restriction that has been formulated thus far.

The approach to the problem I shall recommend is slightly different. Admittedly, this approach will raise problems analogous to those of the indefeasibility theory, problems which will not be fully resolved here. Nevertheless, I believe this approach is fundamentally on the right track.

What, then, is my proposed treatment of the barn example? A person knows that p, I suggest, only if the actual state of affairs in which p is true is *distinguishable* or *discriminable* by him from a relevant possible state of affairs in which p is false. If there is a relevant possible state of affairs in which p is false and which is indistinguishable by him from the actual state of affairs, then he fails to know that p. In the original description of the barn case there is no hint of any relevant possible state of affairs in which the object in question is not a barn but is indistinguishable (by Henry) from the actual state of affairs. Hence, we are initially inclined to say that Henry knows. The information about the facsimiles, however, introduces such a relevant state of affairs. Given that the district Henry has entered is full of barn facsimiles, there is a relevant alternative hypothesis about the object, viz., that it is a facsimile. Since, by assumption, a state of affairs in which such a hypothesis holds is indistinguishable by Henry from the actual state of affairs (from his vantage point on the road), this hypothesis is not "ruled out" or "precluded" by the factors that prompt Henry's belief. So, once apprised of the facsimiles in the district, we are inclined to deny that Henry knows.

Let us be clear about the bearing of the facsimiles on the case. The presence of the facsimiles does not "create" the possibility that the object Henry sees is a facsimile. Even if there were no facsimiles in the dis-

trict, it would be possible that the object on that site is a facsimile. What the presence of the facsimiles does is make this possibility *relevant;* or it makes us *consider* it relevant.

The qualifier "relevant" plays an important role in my view. If knowledge required the elimination of all logically possible alternatives, there would be no knowledge (at least of contingent truths). If only *relevant* alternatives need to be precluded, however, the scope of knowledge could be substantial. This depends, of course, on which alternatives are relevant.

The issue at hand is directly pertinent to the dispute—at least one dispute—between skeptics and their opponents. In challenging a claim to knowledge (or certainty), a typical move of the skeptic is to adduce an unusual alternative hypothesis that the putative knower is unable to preclude: an alternative compatible with his "data." In the skeptical stage of his argument, Descartes says that he is unable to preclude the hypothesis that, instead of being seated by the fire, he is asleep in his bed and dreaming, or the hypothesis that an evil and powerful demon is making it appear to him as if he is seated by the fire. Similarly, Bertrand Russell points out that, given any claim about the past, we can adduce the "skeptical hypothesis" that the world sprang into being five minutes ago, exactly as it then was, with a population that "remembered" a wholly unreal past.[5]

One reply open to the skeptic's opponent is that these skeptical hypotheses are just "idle" hypotheses, and that a person can know a proposition even if there are "idle" alternatives he cannot preclude. The problem, of course, is to specify when an alternative is "idle" and when it is "serious" ("relevant"). Consider Henry once again. Should we say that the possibility of a facsimile before him is a serious or relevant possibility if there are no facsimiles in Henry's district, but only in Sweden? Or if a single such facsimile once existed in Sweden, but none exist now?

There are two views one might take on this general problem. The first view is that there is a "correct" answer, in any given situation, as to which alternatives are relevant. Given a complete specification of Henry's situation, a unique set of relevant alternatives is determined: either a set to which the facsimile alternative belongs or one to which it doesn't belong. According to this view, the semantic content of "know" contains (implicit) rules that map any putative knower's circumstances into a set of relevant alternatives. An analysis of "know" is incomplete unless it specifies these rules. The correct specification will favor either the skeptic or the skeptic's opponent.

The second view denies that a putative knower's circumstances uniquely determine a set of relevant alternatives. At any rate, it denies that the semantic content of "know" contains rules that map a set of circumstances into a single set of relevant alternatives. According to this second view, the verb "know" is simply not so semantically determinate.

The second view need not deny that there are *regularities* governing the alternative hypotheses a speaker (i.e., an attributer or denier of knowledge) thinks of, and deems relevant. But these regularities are not part of the semantic content of "know." The putative knower's circumstances do not *mandate* a unique selection of alternatives; but psychological regularities govern which set of alternatives are in fact selected. In terms of these regularities (together with the semantic content of "know"), we can explain the observed use of the term.

It is clear that some of these regularities pertain to the (description of the) putative knower's circumstances. One regularity might be that the more *likely* it is, given the circumstances, that a particular alternative would obtain (rather than the actual state of affairs), the more probable it is that a speaker will regard this alternative as relevant. Or, the more *similar* the situation in which the alternative obtains to the actual situation, the more probable it is that a speaker will regard this alternative as relevant. It is not only the circumstances of the putative knower's situation, however, that influence the choice of alternatives. The speaker's own linguistic and psychological context are also important. If the speaker is in a class where Descartes's evil demon has just been discussed, or Russell's five-minute-old-world hypothesis, he may think of alternatives he would not otherwise think of and will perhaps treat them seriously. This sort of regularity is entirely ignored by the first view.

What I am calling the "second" view might have two variants. The first variant can be imbedded in Robert Stalnaker's framework for pragmatics.[6] In this framework, a proposition is a function from possible words into truth values; the determinants of a proposition are a sentence and a (linguistic) context. An important contextual element is what the utterer of a sentence presupposes, or takes for granted. According to the first variant of the second view, a sentence of the form "*S* knows that *p*" does not determine a unique proposition. Rather, a proposition is determined by such a sentence together with the speaker's presuppositions concerning the relevant alternatives.[7] Skeptics and nonskeptics might make different presuppositions (both presuppositions being "legitimate"), and, if so, they are simply asserting or denying different propositions.

One trouble with this variant is its apparent implication that, if a speaker utters a knowledge sentence without presupposing a fully determinate set of alternatives, he does not assert or deny any proposition. That seems too strong. A second variant of the second view, then, is that sentences of the form "*S* knows that *p*" express vague or indeterminate propositions (if they express "propositions" at all), which can, but need not, be made more determinate by full specification of the alternatives. A person who *assents* to a knowledge sentence says that *S* discriminates the truth of *p* from relevant alternatives; but he may not have a distinct set of alternatives in mind. (Similarly, according to Paul Ziff, a person who says something is "good" says that it answers to *certain* interests;[8] but he may not have a distinct set of interests in mind.) Someone who *denies* a knowledge sentence more commonly has one or more alternatives in mind as relevant, because his denial may stem from a particular alternative *S* cannot rule out. But even the denier of a knowledge sentence need not have a full set of relevant alternatives in mind.

I am attracted by the second view under discussion, especially its second variant. In the remainder of the paper, however, I shall be officially neutral. In other words, I shall not try to settle the question of whether the semantic content of 'know' contains rules that map the putative knower's situation into a unique set of relevant alternatives. I leave open the question of whether there is a "correct" set of relevant alternatives, and if so, what it is. To this extent, I also leave open the question of whether skeptics or their opponents are "right." In defending my analysis of "perceptually knows," however, I shall have to discuss particular examples. In treating these examples I shall assume some (psychological) regularities concerning the selection of alternatives. Among these regularities is the fact that speakers do not *ordinarily* think of "radical" alternatives, but are caused to think of such alternatives, and take them seriously, if the putative knower's circumstances call attention to them. Since I assume that radical or unusual alternatives are not *ordinarily* entertained or taken seriously, I may appear to side with the opponents of skepticism. My official analysis, however, is neutral on the issue of skepticism.

II

I turn now to the analysis of "perceptually knows." Suppose that Sam spots Judy on the street and correctly identifies her as Judy, i.e., believes she is Judy. Suppose further that Judy has an identical twin, Trudy, and the possibility of the person's being Trudy (rather than Judy) is a relevant alternative. Under what circumstances would we say that Sam *knows* it is Judy?

If Sam regularly identifies Judy as Judy and Trudy as Trudy, he apparently has some (visual) way of discriminating between them (though he may not know how he does it, i.e., what cues he uses). If he does have a way of discriminating between them, which he uses on the occasion in question, we would say that he *knows* it is Judy. But if Sam frequently mistakes Judy for Trudy, and Trudy for Judy, he presumably does not have a way of discriminating between them. For example, he may not have sufficiently distinct (visual) memory "schemata" of Judy and Trudy. So that, on a particular occasion, sensory stimulation from either Judy *or* Trudy would elicit a Judy-identification from him. If he happens to be right that it is Judy, this is just accidental. He doesn't *know* it is Judy.

The crucial question in assessing a knowledge attribution, then, appears to be the truth value of a counterfactual (or set of counterfactuals). Where

Sam correctly identifies Judy as Judy, the crucial counterfactual is: "If the person before Sam were Trudy (rather than Judy), Sam would believe her to be Judy." If this counterfactual is true, Sam doesn't know it is Judy. If this counterfactual is false (and all other counterfactuals involving relevant alternatives are also false), then Sam may know it is Judy.

This suggests the following analysis of (noninferential) perceptual knowledge.

S (noninferentially) *perceptually knows that p* if and only if

(1) *S* (noninferentially) perceptually believes that *p,*
(2) *p* is true, and
(3) there is no relevant contrary *q* of *p* such that, if *q* were true (rather than *p*), then *S* would (still) believe that *p.*

Restricting attention to relevant possibilities, these conditions assert in effect that the only situation in which *S* would believe that *p* is a situation in which *p* is true. In other words, *S*'s believing that *p* is sufficient for the truth of *p.* This is essentially the analysis of noninferential knowledge proposed by D. M. Armstrong in *A Materialist Theory of the Mind* (though without any restriction to "relevant" alternatives), and refined and expanded in *Belief, Truth, and Knowledge.*[9]

This analysis is too restrictive. Suppose Oscar is standing in an open field containing Dack the dachshund. Oscar sees Dack and (noninferentially) forms a belief in (P):

(P) The object over there is a dog.

Now suppose that (Q):

(Q) The object over there is a wolf.

is a relevant alternative to (P) (because wolves are frequenters of this field). Further suppose that Oscar has a tendency to mistake wolves for dogs (he confuses them with malamutes, or German shepherds). Then if the object Oscar saw were Wiley the wolf, rather than Dack the dachshund, Oscar would (still) believe (P). This means that Oscar fails to satisfy the proposed analysis with respect to (P), since (3) is violated. But surely it is wrong to deny—for the indicated reasons—that Oscar *knows* (P) to be true. The mere fact that he would erroneously take a wolf to be a dog hardly shows that he doesn't know a *dachshund* to be a dog! Similarly, if someone looks at a huge redwood and correctly believes it to be a tree, he is not disqualified from knowing it to be a tree merely because there is a very small plant he would wrongly believe to be a tree, i.e., a bonsai tree.

The moral can be formulated as follows. If Oscar believes that a dog is present because of a certain way he is "appeared to," then this true belief fails to be knowledge if there is an alternative situation in which a non-dog produces the same belief by means of the same, or a very similar, appearance. But the wolf situation is not such an alternative: although it would produce in him the same belief, it would not be by means of the same (or a similar) appearance. An alternative that disqualifies a true perceptual belief from being perceptual knowledge must be a "perceptual equivalent" of the actual state of affairs.[10] A *perceptual equivalent* of an actual state of affairs is a possible state of affairs that would produce the same, or a sufficiently similar, perceptual experience.

The relation of perceptual equivalence must obviously be relativized to *persons* (or organisms). The presence of Judy and the presence of Trudy might be perceptual equivalents for Sam, but not for the twins' own mother (to whom the twins look quite different). Similarly, perceptual equivalence must be relativized to *times,* since perceptual discriminative capacities can be refined or enhanced with training or experience, and can deteriorate with age or disease.

How shall we specify alternative states of affairs that are candidates for being perceptual equivalents? First, we should specify the *object* involved. (I assume for simplicity that only one object is in question.) As the Judy-Trudy case shows, the object in the alternative state of affairs need not be identical with the actual object. Sometimes, indeed, we may wish to allow non-actual possible objects. Otherwise our framework will be unable in principle to accommodate some of the skeptic's favorite alternatives, e.g., those involving demons. If the reader's ontological

sensibility is offended by talk of possible objects, I invite him to replace such talk with any preferred substitute.

Some alternative states of affairs involve the same object but different properties. Where the actual state of affairs involves a certain ball painted blue, an alternative might be chosen involving the same ball painted green. Thus, specification of an alternative requires not only an object, but properties of the object (at the time in question). These should include not only the property in the belief under scrutiny, or one of its contraries, but other properties as well, since the property in the belief (or one of its contraries) might not be sufficiently determinate to indicate what the resultant percept would be like. For full generality, let us choose a *maximal set of* (nonrelational) *properties.* This is a set that would exhaustively characterize an object (at a single time) in some possible world.[11]

An object plus a maximal set of (nonrelational) properties still does not fully specify a perceptual alternative. Also needed are relations between the object and the perceiver, plus conditions of the environment. One relation that can affect the resultant percept is *distance.* Another relational factor is *relative orientation,* both of object vis-à-vis perceiver and perceiver vis-à-vis object. The nature of the percept depends, for example, on which side of the object faces the perceiver, and on how the perceiver's bodily organs are oriented, or situated, vis-à-vis the object. Thirdly, the percept is affected by the current state of the *environment,* e.g., the illumination, the presence or absence of intervening objects, and the direction and velocity of the wind.

To cover all such elements, I introduce the notion of a *distance-orientation-environment* relation, for short, a *DOE relation.* Each such relation is a conjunction of relations or properties concerning distance, orientation, and environmental conditions. One DOE relation is expressed by the predicate "*x* is 20 feet from *y,* the front side of *y* is facing *x,* the eyes of *x* are open and focused in *y*'s direction, no opaque object is interposed between *x* and *y,* and *y* is in moonlight."

Since the health of sensory organs can affect percepts, it might be argued that this should be included in these relations, thereby opening the condition of these organs to counterfactualization. For simplicity I neglect this complication. This does not mean that I don't regard the condition of sensory organs as open to counter-factualization. I merely omit explicit incorporation of this factor into our exposition.

We can now give more precision to our treatment of perceptual equivalents. Perceptual states of affairs will be specified by ordered triples, each consisting of (1) an object, (2) a maximal set of nonrelational properties, and (3) a DOE relation. If S perceives object b at t and if b has all the properties in a maximal set J and bears DOE relation R to S at t, then the actual state of affairs pertaining to this perceptual episode is represented by the ordered triple $\langle b, J, R \rangle$. An alternative state of affairs is represented by an ordered triple $\langle c, K, R^* \rangle$, which may (but need not) differ from $\langle b, J, R \rangle$ with respect to one or more of its elements.

Under what conditions is an alternative $\langle c, K, R^* \rangle$ a perceptual equivalent of $\langle b, J, R \rangle$ for person S at time t? I said that a perceptual equivalent is a state of affairs that would produce "the same, or a very similar" perceptual experience. That is not very committal. Must a perceptual equivalent produce exactly the same percept? Given our intended use of perceptual equivalence in the analysis of perceptual knowledge, the answer is clearly No. Suppose that a Trudy-produced percept would be qualitatively distinct from Sam's Judy-produced percept, but similar enough for Sam to mistake Trudy for Judy. This is sufficient grounds for saying that Sam fails to have knowledge. Qualitative identity of percepts, then, is too strong a requirement for perceptual equivalence.

How should the requirement be weakened? We must not weaken it too much, for the wolf alternative might then be a perceptual equivalent of the dachshund state of affairs. This would have the unwanted consequence that Oscar doesn't know Dack to be a dog.

The solution I propose is this. If the percept produced by the alternative state of affairs would not differ from the actual percept in any respect that is causally relevant to S's belief, this alternative situation is a perceptual equivalent for S of the actual situation. Suppose that a Trudy-produced percept would

differ from Sam's Judy-produced percept to the extent of having a different eyebrow configuration. (A difference in shape between Judy's and Trudy's eyebrows does not ensure that Sam's percepts would "register" this difference. I assume, however, that the eyebrow difference would be registered in Sam's percepts.) But suppose that Sam's visual "concept" of Judy does not include a feature that reflects this contrast. His Judy-concept includes an "eyebrow feature" only in the sense that the absence of eyebrows would inhibit a Judy-classification. It does not include a more determinate eyebrow feature, though: Sam hasn't learned to associate Judy with distinctively shaped eyebrows. Hence, the distinctive "eyebrow shape" of his actual (Judy-produced) percept is not one of the percept-features that is causally responsible for his believing Judy to be present. Assuming that a Trudy-produced percept would not differ from his actual percept in any *other* causally relevant way, the hypothetical Trudy-situation is a perceptual equivalent of the actual Judy-situation.

Consider now the dachshund-wolf case. The hypothetical percept produced by a wolf would differ from Oscar's actual percept of the dachshund in respects that *are* causally relevant to Oscar's judgment that a dog is present. Let me elaborate. There are various kinds of objects, rather different in shape, size, color, and texture, that would be classified by Oscar as a dog. He has a number of visual "schemata," we might say, each with a distinctive set of features, such that any percept that "matches" or "fits" one of these schemata would elicit a "dog" classification. (I think of a schema not as a "template," but as a set of more-or-less abstract—though iconic—features.[12]) Now, although a dachshund and a wolf would each produce a dog-belief in Oscar, the percepts produced by these respective stimuli would differ in respects that are causally relevant to Oscar's forming a dog-belief. Since Oscar's dachshund-schema includes such features as having an elongated, sausagelike shape, a smallish size, and droopy ears, these features of the percept are all causally relevant, when a dachshund is present, to Oscar's believing that a dog is present. Since a hypothetical wolf-produced percept would differ in these respects from Oscar's dachshund-produced percept, the hypothetical wolf state of affairs is not a perceptual equivalent of the dachshund state of affairs for Oscar.

The foregoing approach requires us to relativize perceptual equivalence once again, this time to the belief in question, or the property believed to be exemplified. The Trudy-situation is a perceptual equivalent for Sam of the Judy-situation *relative to the property of being* (identical with) *Judy*. The wolf-situation is not a perceptual equivalent for Oscar of the dachshund-situation *relative to the property of being a dog*.

I now propose the following definition of perceptual equivalence:

If object *b* has the maximal set of properties *J* and is in DOE relation *R* to *S* at *t*, if *S* has some percept *P* at *t* that is perceptually caused by *b*'s having *J* and being in *R* to *S* at *t*, and if *P* noninferentially causes *S* to believe (or sustains *S* in believing) of object *b* that it has property *F*, then
⟨*c,K,R**⟩ *is a perceptual equivalent of* ⟨*b,J,R*⟩ *for S at t relative to property F* if and only if
(1) if at *t* object *c* had *K* and were in *R** to *S*, then this would perceptually cause *S* to have some percept *P** at *t*,
(2) *P** would cause *S* noninferentially to believe (or sustain *S* in believing) of object *c* that it has *F*, and
(3) *P** would not differ from *P* in any respect that is causally relevant to *S*'s *F*-belief.

Since I shall analyze the *de re, relational,* or *transparent* sense of "perceptually knows," I shall want to employ, in my analysis, the *de re* sense of "believe." This is why such phrases as "believe . . . *of* object *b*" occur in the definition of perceptual equivalence. For present purposes, I take for granted the notion of (perceptual) *de re* belief. I assume, however, that the object *of which* a person perceptually believes a property to hold is the object he perceives, i.e., the object that "perceptually causes" the percept that elicits the belief. The notion of *perceptual causation* is another notion I take for granted. A person's percept is obviously caused by many objects (or events), not all of which the person is said to perceive. One problem for

the theory of perception is to explicate the notion of perceptual causation, that is, to explain which of the causes of a percept a person is said to perceive. I set this problem aside here.[13] A third notion I take for granted is the notion of a (noninferential) *perceptual belief,* or perceptual "taking." Not all beliefs that are noninferentially caused by a percept can be considered perceptual "takings"; "indirectly" caused beliefs would not be so considered. But I make no attempt to delineate the requisite causal relation.

Several other comments on the definition of perceptual equivalence are in order. Notice that the definition is silent on whether *J* or *K* contains property *F*, i.e., whether *F* is exemplified in either the actual or the alternative states of affairs. The relativization to *F* (in the definiendum) implies that an *F-belief* is produced in both situations, not that *F* is exemplified (in either or both situations). In applying the definition to cases of putative knowledge, we shall focus on cases where *F* belongs to *J* (so *S*'s belief is true in the actual situation) but does not belong to *K* (so *S*'s belief is false in the counterfactual situation). But the definition of perceptual equivalence is silent on these matters.

Though the definition does not say so, I assume it is possible for object *c* to have all properties in *K*, and possible for *c* to be in *R** to *S* while having all properties in *K*. I do not want condition 1 to be vacuously true, simply by having an impossible antecedent.

It might seem as if the antecedent of (1) should include a further conjunct, expressing the supposition that object *b* is absent. This might seem necessary to handle cases in which, if *c* were in *R** to *S*, but *b* remained in its actual relation *R* to *S*, then *b* would "block" *S*'s access to *c*. (For example, *b* might be an orange balloon floating over the horizon, and *c* might be the moon.) This can be handled by the definition as it stands, by construing *R**, where necessary, as including the absence of object *b* from the perceptual scene. (One cannot *in general* hypothesize that *b* is absent, for we want to allow object *c* to be identical with *b*.)

The definition implies that there is no temporal gap between each object's having its indicated properties and DOE relation and the occurrence of the corresponding percept. This simplification is introduced because no general requirement can be laid down about how long it takes for the stimulus energy to reach the perceiver. The intervals in the actual and alternative states may differ because the stimuli might be at different distances from the perceiver.

III

It is time to turn to the analysis of perceptual knowledge, for which the definition of perceptual equivalence paves the way. I restrict my attention to perceptual knowledge of the possession, by physical objects, of nonrelational properties. I also restrict the analysis to *noninferential* perceptual knowledge. This frees me from the complex issues introduced by inference, which require separate treatment.

It may be contended that all perceptual judgment is based on inference and, hence, that the proposed restriction reduces the scope of the analysis to nil. Two replies are in order. First, although cognitive psychology establishes that percepts are affected by cognitive factors, such as "expectancies," it is by no means evident that these causal processes should be construed as inferences. Second, even if we were to grant that there is in fact no noninferential perceptual belief, it would still be of epistemological importance to determine whether noninferential perceptual knowledge of the physical world is conceptually possible. This could be explored by considering merely possible cases of noninferential perceptual belief, and seeing whether, under suitable conditions, such belief would count as knowledge.

With these points in mind, we may propose the following (tentative) analysis:

At t S noninferentially perceptually knows of object b that it has property F if and only if

(1) for some maximal set of nonrelational properties J and some DOE relation R, object b has (all the members of) J at t and is in R to S at t,

(2) F belongs to J,

(3) (A) b's having J and being in R to S at t perceptually causes S at t to have some percept P,[14]

    (B) P noninferentially causes S at t to believe (or sustains S in believing) of object b that it has property F, and

(C) there is no alternative state of affairs $\langle c, K, R^* \rangle$ such that

    (i) $\langle c, K, R^* \rangle$ is a relevant perceptual equivalent of $\langle b, J, R \rangle$ for S at t relative to property F, and

    (ii) F does not belong to K.

Conditions 1 and 2 jointly entail the truth condition for knowledge: S knows b to have F (at t) only if b does have F (at t). Condition 3B contains the belief condition for knowledge, restricted, of course, to (noninferential) perceptual belief. The main work of the conditions is done by 3C. It requires that there be no relevant alternative that is (i) a perceptual equivalent to the actual state of affairs relative to property F, and (ii) a state of affairs in which the appropriate object lacks F (and hence S's F-belief is false).

How does this analysis relate to my theme of a "reliable discriminative mechanism"? A perceptual cognizer may be thought of as a two-part mechanism. The first part constructs percepts (a special class of internal states) from receptor stimulation. The second part operates on percepts to produce beliefs. Now, in order for the conditions of the analysans to be satisfied, each part of the mechanism must be sufficiently discriminating, or "finely tuned." If the first part is not sufficiently discriminating, patterns of receptor stimulation from quite different sources would result in the same (or very similar) percepts, percepts that would generate the same beliefs. If the second part is not sufficiently discriminating, then even if different percepts are constructed by the first part, the same beliefs will be generated by the second part. To be sure, even an undiscriminating bipartite mechanism may produce a belief that, luckily, is true; but there will be other, counterfactual, situations in which such a belief would be false. In this sense, such a mechanism is unreliable. What our analysis says is that S has perceptual knowledge if and only if not only does his perceptual mechanism produce true belief, but there are no relevant counterfactual situations in which the same belief would be produced via an equivalent percept and in which the belief would be false.

Let me now illustrate how the analysis is to be applied to the barn example, where there are facsimiles in Henry's district. Let S = Henry, b = the barn Henry actually sees, and F = the property of being a barn. Conditions 1 through 3B are met by letting J take as its value the set of all nonrelational properties actually possessed by the barn at t, R take as its value the actual DOE relation the barn bears to Henry at t, and P take as its value the actual (visual) percept caused by the barn. Condition 3C is violated, however. There *is* a relevant triple that meets subclauses (i) and (ii), i.e., the triple where c = a suitable barn facsimile, K = a suitable set of properties (excluding, of course, the property of being a barn), and R^* = approximately the same DOE relation as the actual one. Thus, Henry does not (noninferentially) perceptually *know* of the barn that it has the property of being a barn.

In the dachshund-wolf case, S = Oscar, b = Dack the dachshund, and F = being a dog. The first several conditions are again met. Is 3C met as well? There is a relevant alternative state of affairs in which Wiley the wolf is believed by Oscar to be a dog, but lacks that property. This state of affairs doesn't violate 3C, however, since it isn't a *perceptual equivalent* of the actual situation relative to being a dog. So this alternative doesn't disqualify Oscar from knowing Dack to be a dog.

Is there another alternative that *is* a perceptual equivalent of the actual situation (relative to being a dog)? We can imagine a DOE relation in which fancy devices between Wiley and Oscar distort the light coming from Wiley and produce in Oscar a Dack-like visual percept. The question here, however, is whether this perceptual equivalent is *relevant*. Relevance is determined not only by the hypothetical object and its properties, but also by the DOE relation. Since the indicated DOE relation is highly unusual, this will count (at least for a nonskeptic) against the alternative's being relevant and against its disqualifying Oscar from knowing.[15]

The following "Gettierized" example, suggested by Marshall Swain, might appear to present difficulties. In a dark room there is a candle several yards ahead of S which S sees and believes to be ahead of him. But he sees the candle only indirectly, via a system of mirrors (of which he is unaware) that make it appear as if he were seeing it directly.[16] We would surely deny that S knows the candle to be ahead of him. (This case does not really fit our intended analysandum, since the believed property F is relational. This detail can be ignored, however.) Why? If we say, with Harman, that all perceptual belief is based on inference, we can maintain that S infers that the candle is ahead of him from the premise that he sees whatever he sees *directly*. This premise being false, S's knowing is disqualified on familiar grounds.

My theory suggests another explanation, which makes no unnecessary appeal to inference. We deny that S knows, I suggest, because the system of mirrors draws our attention to a perceptual equivalent in which the candle is *not* ahead of S, i.e., a state of affairs where the candle is behind S but reflected in a system of mirrors so that it appears to be ahead of him. Since the actual state of affairs involves a system of reflecting mirrors, we are impelled to count this alternative as relevant, and hence to deny that S knows.

Even in ordinary cases, of course, where S sees a candle directly, the possibility of reflecting mirrors constitutes a perceptual equivalent. In the ordinary case, however, we would not count this as relevant; we would not regard it as a "serious" possibility. The Gettierized case impels us to take it seriously because there the actual state of affairs involves a devious system of reflecting mirrors. So we have an explanation of why people are credited with knowing in ordinary perceptual cases but not in the Gettierized case.

The following is a more serious difficulty for our analysis. S truly believes something to be a tree, but there is a relevant alternative in which an electrode stimulating S's optic nerve would produce an equivalent percept, which would elicit the same belief. Since this is assumed to be a relevant alternative, it ought to disqualify S from knowing. But it doesn't satisfy our definition of a perceptual equivalent, first because the electrode would not be a perceptual cause of the percept (we would not say that S *perceives* the electrode), and second because S would not believe *of the electrode* (nor *of* anything else) that it is a tree. A similar problem arises where the alternative state of affairs would involve S's having a hallucination.

To deal with these cases, we could revise our analysis of perceptual knowledge as follows. (A similar revision in the definition of perceptual equivalence would do the job equally well.) We could reformulate 3C to say that there must neither be a relevant perceptual equivalent of the indicated sort (using our present definition of perceptual equivalence) *nor* a relevant alternative situation in which an equivalent percept occurs and prompts a *de dicto* belief that something has *F*, but where there is nothing that *perceptually* causes this percept and nothing *of which F* is believed to hold. In other words, knowledge can be disqualified by relevant alternative situations where *S* doesn't perceive anything and doesn't have any *de re* (*F*-) belief at all. I am inclined to adopt this solution, but will not actually make this addition to the analysis.

Another difficulty for the analysis is this. Suppose Sam's "schemata" of Judy and Trudy have hitherto been indistinct, so Judy-caused percepts sometimes elicit Judy-beliefs and sometimes Trudy-beliefs, and similarly for Trudy-caused percepts. Today Sam falls down and hits his head. As a consequence a new feature is "added" to his Judy-schema, a mole-associated feature. From now on he will believe someone to be Judy only if he has the sort of percept that would be caused by a Judy-like person with a mole over the left eye. Sam is unaware that this change has taken place and will remain unaware of it, since he isn't conscious of the cues he uses. Until today, neither Judy nor Trudy has had a left-eyebrow mole; but today Judy happens to develop such a mole. Thus, from now on Sam can discriminate Judy from Trudy. Does this mean that he will *know* Judy to be Judy when he correctly identifies her? I am doubtful.

A possible explanation of Sam's not knowing (on future occasions) is that Trudy-with-a-mole is a relevant perceptual equivalent of Judy. This is not Trudy's actual condition, of course, but it might be deemed a relevant possibility. I believe, however, that the mole case calls for a further restriction, one concerning the *genesis* of a person's propensity to form a certain belief as a result of a certain percept. A merely fortuitous or accidental genesis is not enough to support knowledge. I do not know exactly what requirement to impose on the genesis of such a propensity. The mole case intimates that the genesis should involve certain "experience" with objects, but this may be too narrow. I content myself with a very vague addition to our previous conditions, which completes the analysis:

(4) *S*'s propensity to form an *F*-belief as a result of percept *P* has an appropriate genesis.

Of course this leaves the problem unresolved. But the best I can do here is identify the problem.

IV

A few words are in order about the intended significance of my analysis. One of its purposes is to provide an alternative to the traditional "Cartesian" perspective in epistemology. The Cartesian view combines a theory of knowledge with a theory of justification. Its theory of knowledge asserts that *S* knows that *p* at *t* only if *S* is (fully, adequately, etc.) justified at *t* in believing that *p*. Its theory of justification says that *S* is justified at *t* in believing that *p* only if either (A) *p* is self-warranting for *S* at *t,* or (B) *p* is (strongly, adequately, etc.) supported or confirmed by propositions each of which is self-warranting for *S* at *t*. Now propositions about the state of the external world at *t* are not self-warranting. Hence, if *S* knows any such proposition *p* at *t,* there must be some other propositions which strongly support *p* and which are self-warranting for *S* at *t*. These must be propositions about *S*'s mental state at *t* and perhaps some obvious necessary truths. A major task of Cartesian epistemology is to show that there is some such set of self-warranting propositions, propositions that support external-world propositions with sufficient strength.

It is impossible to canvass all attempts to fulfill this project; but none have succeeded, and I do not think that any will. One can conclude either that we have no knowledge of the external world or that Cartesian requirements are too demanding. I presuppose the latter conclusion in offering my theory of perceptual knowledge. My theory requires no justification for external-world propositions that derives entirely from self-warranting propositions. It requires only, in effect, that beliefs in the external world be suitably caused, where "suitably" comprehends a process or mechanism that not only produces true belief in the actual situation, but would not produce false belief in relevant counterfactual situations. If one wishes, one can so employ the term "justification" that belief causation of *this* kind counts as justification. In this sense, of course, my theory does require justification. But this is entirely different from the sort of justification demanded by Cartesianism.

My theory protects the possibility of knowledge by making Cartesian-style justification unnecessary. But it leaves a door open to skepticism by its stance on relevant alternatives. This is not a failure of the theory, in my opinion. An adequate account of the term "know" should make the temptations of skepticism comprehensible, which my theory does. But it should also put skepticism in a proper perspective, which Cartesianism fails to do.

In any event, I put forward my account of perceptual knowledge not primarily as an antidote to skepticism, but as a more accurate rendering of what the term "know" actually means. In this respect it is instructive to test my theory and its rivals against certain metaphorical or analogical uses of "know." A correct definition should be able to explain extended and figurative uses as well as literal uses, for it should explain how speakers arrive at the extended uses from the central ones. With this in mind, consider how tempting it is to say of an electric-eye door that it "knows" you are coming (at least that *something* is coming), or "sees" you coming. The attractiveness of the metaphor is easily explained on my theory: the door has a reliable mechanism for discriminating between something being before it and nothing being there. It has a "way of telling" whether or not something is there: this "way of telling" consists in a mechanism by which objects in certain DOE relations to it have differential effects on its internal state. By contrast, note how artificial it would be to apply more traditional analyses of "know" to the electric-eye door, or to other mechanical detecting devices. How odd it would be to say that the door has "good reasons," "adequate evidence," or "complete justification" for thinking something is there; or that it has "the right to be sure" something is there. The oddity

of these locutions indicates how far from the mark are the analyses of 'know' from which they derive.

The trouble with many philosophical treatments of knowledge is that they are inspired by Cartesian-like conceptions of justification or vindication. There is a consequent tendency to overintellectualize or overrationalize the notion of knowledge. In the spirit of naturalistic epistemology,[17] I am trying to fashion an account of knowing that focuses on more primitive and pervasive aspects of cognitive life, in connection with which, I believe, the term "know" gets its application. A fundamental facet of animate life, both human and infra-human, is telling things apart, distinguishing predator from prey, for example, or a protective habitat from a threatening one. The concept of knowledge has its roots in this kind of cognitive activity.

NOTES

An early version of this paper was read at the 1972 Chapel Hill Colloquium. Later versions were read at the 1973 University of Cincinnati Colloquium, and at a number of other philosophy departments. For comments and criticism, I am especially indebted to Holly Goldman, Bruce Aune, Jaegwon Kim, Louis Loeb, and Kendall Walton.

1. "A Causal Theory of Knowing," this journal LXIV, 12 (June 22, 1967): 357–372; reprinted in M. Roth and L. Galis, eds., *Knowing* (New York: Random House, 1970).

2. "An Analysis of Factual Knowledge," this journal LXV, 6 (Mar. 21, 1968): 157–170; reprinted in Roth and Galis, *op. cit.*

3. See, for example, Keith Lehrer and Thomas Paxson, Jr., "Knowledge: Undefeated Justified True Belief," this journal, LXVI, 8 (Apr. 24, 1969): 225–237, and Peter D. Klein, "A Proposed Definition of Propositional Knowledge," *ibid.*, LXVIII, 16 (Aug. 19, 1971): 471–482.

4. *Thought* (Princeton, N.J.: University Press, 1973), p. 152.

5. *The Analysis of Mind* (London: Allen & Unwin, 1921), pp. 159–160.

6. "Pragmatics," in Donald Davidson and Harman, eds., *Semantics of Natural Language* (Boston: Reidel, 1972).

7. Something like this is suggested by Fred Dretske, in "Epistemic Operators," this journal, LXVII, 24 (Dec. 24, 1970): 1007–1023, p. 1022.

8. That 'good' means *answers to certain interests* is claimed by Ziff in *Semantic Analysis* (Ithaca, N.Y.: Cornell, 1960), ch. VI.

9. *A Materialist Theory of the Mind* (New York: Humanities, 1968), pp. 189 ff., and *Belief, Truth and Knowledge* (New York: Cambridge, 1973), chs. 12 and 13.

10. My notion of a perceptual equivalent corresponds to Jaakko Hintikka's notion of a "perceptual alternative." See "On the Logic of Perception," in N. S. Care and R. H. Grimm, eds., *Perception and Personal Identity* (Cleveland, Ohio: Case Western Reserve, 1969).

11. I have in mind here purely qualitative properties. Properties like *being identical with Judy* would be given by the selected object. If the set of qualitative properties (at a given time) implied which object it was that had these properties, then specification of the object would be redundant, and we could represent states of affairs by ordered pairs of maximal sets of (qualitative) properties and DOE relations. Since this is problematic, however, I include specification of the object as well as the set of (qualitative) properties.

12. For a discussion of iconic schemata, see Michael I. Posner, *Cognition: An Introduction* (Glenview, Ill.: Scott, Foresman, 1973), ch. 3.

13. I take this problem up in "Perceptual Objects," forthcoming in *Synthese.*

14. Should (3A) be construed as implying that *every* property in *J* is a (perceptual) cause of *P?* No. Many of *b*'s properties are exemplified in its interior or at its backside. These are not causally relevant, at least in visual perception. (3A) must therefore be construed as saying that *P* is (perceptually) caused by *b*'s having (jointly) *all* the members of *J,* and leaving open which, among these members, are individually causally relevant. It follows, however, that (3A) does not require that *b's-having-F,* in particular, is a (perceptual) cause of *P,* and this omission might be regarded as objectionable. "Surely," it will be argued, "*S* perceptually knows *b* to have *F* only if *b's-having-F* (perceptually) causes the percept." The reason I omit this requirement is the following. Suppose *F* is the property of being a dog. Can we say that *b's-being-a-dog* is a cause of certain light waves' being reflected? This is very dubious. It is the molecular properties of the surface of the animal that are causally responsible for this transmission of light, and hence for the percept.

One might say that, even if the percept needn't be (perceptually) caused by *b*'s-having-*F,* it must at least be caused by microstructural properties of *b* that *ensure b's-having-F.* As the dog example again illustrates, however, this is too strong. The surface properties of the dog that reflect the light waves do not *ensure* that the object is a dog, either logically or nomologically. Something could have that surface (on one side) and still have a non-dog interior and backside. The problem should be solved, I think, by reliance on whether there are relevant perceptual equivalents. If there are no relevant perceptual equivalents in which *K* excludes being a dog, then the properties of the actual object that are causally responsible for the percept suffice to yield knowledge. We need not require either that the percept be (perceptually) caused by *b*'s-having-*F,* nor by any subset of *J* that "ensures" *b*'s-having-*F.*

15. It is the "unusualness" of the DOE relation that inclines us not to count the alternative as relevant; it is not the mere fact that the DOE relation differs from the actual one. In general, our analysis allows knowledge to be defeated or disqualified by alternative situations in which the DOE relation differs from the DOE relation in the actual state of affairs. Our analysis differs in this respect from Fred Dretske's analysis in "Conclusive Reasons," *Australasian Journal of Philosophy,* IL, 1 (May 1971): 1–22. Dretske's analysis, which ours resembles on a number of points, considers only those counterfactual situations in which everything that is "logically and causally independent of the state of affairs expressed by *P*" (7/8) is the same as in the actual situation. (*P* is the content of *S*'s belief.) This implies that the actual DOE relation cannot be counterfactualized, but must be held fixed. (It may also imply—depending what *P* is—that one cannot counterfactualize the perceived object nor the full set of properties *J.*) This unduly narrows the class of admissible alternatives. Many *relevant* alternatives, that do disqualify knowledge, involve DOE relations that differ from the actual DOE relation.

16. Harman has a similar case, in *Thought,* pp. 22–23. In that case, however, *S* does not see the candle; it is not a cause of his percept. Given our causal requirement for perceptual knowledge, that case is easily handled.

17. Cf. W. V. Quine, "Epistemology Naturalized," in *Ontological Relativity, and Other Essays* (New York: Columbia, 1969).

Knowledge and Scepticism

~

ROBERT NOZICK

Robert Nozick (1938–2002) was Pellegrino University Professor at Harvard University. His early book in political theory, *Anarchy, State, and Utopia,* was very influential, and he followed it with *Philosophical Explanations, The Examined Life, The Nature of Rationality, Socratic Puzzles,* and *Invariances: The Structure of the Objective World.*

You think you are seeing these words, but could you not be hallucinating or dreaming or having your brain stimulated to give you the experience of seeing these marks on paper although no such thing is before you? More extremely, could you not be floating in a tank while super-psychologists stimulate your brain electrochemically to produce exactly the same experiences as you are now having, or even to produce the whole sequence of experiences you have had in your lifetime thus far? If one of these other things was happening, your experience would be exactly the same as it now is. So how can you know none of them is happening? Yet if you do not know these possibilities don't hold, how can you know you are reading this book now? If you do not know you haven't always been floating in the tank at the mercy of the psychologists, how can you know anything—what your name is, who your parents were, where you come from?

The sceptic argues that we do not know what we think we do. Even when he leaves us unconverted, he leaves us confused. Granting that we do know, how *can* we? Given these other possibilities he poses, how is knowledge possible? In answering this question, we do not seek to convince the sceptic, but rather to formulate hypotheses about knowledge and our connection to facts that show how knowledge can exist even given the sceptic's possibilities. These hypotheses must reconcile our belief that we know things with our belief that the sceptical possibilities are logical possibilities.

The sceptical possibilities, and the threats they pose to our knowledge, depend upon our knowing things (if we do) mediately, through or by way of something else. Our thinking or believing that some fact *p* holds is connected somehow to the fact that *p*, but is not itself identical with that fact. Intermediate links establish the connection. This leaves room for the possibility of these intermediate stages holding and producing our belief that *p*, without the fact that *p* being at the other end. The intermediate stages arise in a completely different manner, one not involving the fact that *p* although giving rise to the appearance that *p* holds true.

Are the sceptic's possibilities indeed logically possible? Imagine reading a science fiction story in which someone is raised from birth floating in a tank with psychologists stimulating his brain. The story could go on to tell of the person's reactions when he is brought out of the tank, of how the psychologists convince him of what had been happening to him, or how they fail to do so. This story is coherent, there is nothing self-contradictory or otherwise impossible about it. Nor is there anything incoherent in imagining that you are now in this situation, at a time before being taken out of the tank. To ease the transition out,

Reprinted from Robert Nozick, *Philosophical Explanations* (Cambridge, Mass.: Harvard University Press, 1981), by permission of the publisher.

to prepare the way, perhaps the psychologists will give the person in the tank thoughts of whether floating in the tank is possible, or the experience of reading a book that discusses this possibility, even one that discusses their easing his transition. (Free will presents no insuperable problem for this possibility. Perhaps the psychologists caused all your experiences of choice, including the feeling of freely choosing; or perhaps you do freely choose to act while they, cutting the effector circuit, continue the scenario from there.)

Some philosophers have attempted to demonstrate there is no such coherent possibility of this sort.[1] However, for any reasoning that purports to show this sceptical possibility cannot occur, we can imagine the psychologists of our science fiction story feeding *it* to their tank-subject, along with the (inaccurate) feeling that the reasoning is cogent. So how much trust can be placed in the apparent cogency of an argument to show the sceptical possibility isn't coherent?

The sceptic's possibility is a logically coherent one, in tension with the existence of (almost all) knowledge; so we seek a hypothesis to explain how, even given the sceptic's possibilities, knowledge is possible. We may worry that such explanatory hypotheses are ad hoc, but this worry will lessen if they yield other facts as well, fit in with other things we believe, and so forth. Indeed, the theory of knowledge that follows was not developed in order to explain how knowledge is possible. Rather, the motivation was external to epistemology; only after the account of knowledge was developed for another purpose did I notice its consequences for scepticism, for understanding how knowledge is possible. So whatever other defects the explanation might have, it can hardly be called ad hoc.

I. KNOWLEDGE

[Conditions for Knowledge]

Our task is to formulate further conditions to go alongside

(1) p is true
(2) S believes that p.

We would like each condition to be necessary for knowledge, so any case that fails to satisfy it will not be an instance of knowledge. Furthermore, we would like the conditions to be jointly sufficient for knowledge, so any case that satisfies all of them will be an instance of knowledge. We first shall formulate conditions that seem to handle ordinary cases correctly, classifying as knowledge cases which are knowledge, and as non-knowledge cases which are not; then we shall check to see how these conditions handle some difficult cases discussed in the literature.

One plausible suggestion is causal, something like: the fact that p (partially) causes S to believe that p, that is, (2) because (1). But this provides an inhospitable environment for mathematical and ethical knowledge; also there are well-known difficulties in specifying the type of causal connection. If someone floating in a tank oblivious to everything around him is given (by direct electrical and chemical stimulation of the brain) the belief that he is floating in a tank with his brain being stimulated, then even though that fact is part of the cause of his belief, still he does not know that it is true.

Let us consider a different third condition:

(3) If p were not true, S would not believe that p.

Throughout this work, let us write the subjunctive "if-then" by an arrow, and the negation of a sentence by prefacing "not-" to it. The above condition thus is rewritten as:

(3) not-p → not-(S believes that p).

This subjunctive condition is not unrelated to the causal condition. Often when the fact that p (partially) causes someone to believe that p, the fact also will be causally necessary for his having the belief—without the cause, the effect would not occur. In that case, the subjunctive condition (3) also will be satisfied. Yet this condition is not equivalent to the causal condition. For the causal condition will be satisfied in cases of causal overdetermination, where either two sufficient causes of the effect actually operate, or a back-up cause (of the same effect) would operate if the first one didn't; whereas the subjunctive condition need not hold for these cases.[2] When the two conditions do agree, causality indicates knowledge because it acts in a manner that makes the subjunctive (3) true.

The subjunctive condition (3) serves to exclude cases of the sort first described by Edward Gettier, such as the following. Two other people are in my office and I am justified on the basis of much evidence in believing the first owns a Ford car; though he (now) does not, the second person (a stranger to me) owns one. I believe truly and justifiably that someone (or other) in my office owns a Ford car, but I do not know someone does. Concluded Gettier, knowledge is not simply justified true belief.

The following subjunctive, which specifies condition (3) for this Gettier case, is not satisfied: if no one in my office owned a Ford car, I wouldn't believe that someone did. The situation that would obtain if no one in my office owned a Ford is one where the stranger does not (or where he is not in the office); and in that situation I still would believe, as before, that someone in my office does own a Ford, namely, the first person. So the subjunctive condition (3) excludes this Gettier case as a case of knowledge.

The subjunctive condition is powerful and intuitive, not so easy to satisfy, yet not so powerful as to rule out everything as an instance of knowledge. A subjunctive conditional "if p were true, q would be true," $p \rightarrow q$, does not say that p entails q or that it is logically impossible that p yet not-q. It says that in the situation that would obtain if p were true, q also would be true. This point is brought out especially clearly in recent "possible-worlds" accounts of subjunctives: the subjunctive is true when (roughly) in all those worlds in which p holds true that are closest to the actual world, q also is true. (Examine those worlds in which p holds true closest to the actual world, and see if q holds true in all these.) Whether or not q is true in p worlds that are still farther away from the actual world is irrelevant to the truth of the subjunctive. I do not mean to endorse any particular possible-worlds account of subjunctives, nor am I committed to this type of account.[3] I sometimes shall use it, though, when it illustrates points in an especially clear way.

The subjunctive condition (3) also handles nicely cases that cause difficulties for the view that you know that p when you can rule out the relevant alternatives to p in the context. For, as Gail Stine writes, "what makes an alternative relevant in one context and not another? . . . if on the basis of visual appearances obtained under optimum conditions while driving through the countryside Henry identifies an object as a barn, normally we say that Henry knows that it is a barn. Let us suppose, however, that unknown to Henry, the region is full of expertly made papier-mâché facsimiles of barns. In that case, we would not say that Henry knows that the object is a barn, unless he has evidence against it being a papier-mâché facsimile, which is now a relevant alternative. So much is clear, but what if no such facsimiles exist in Henry's surroundings, although they once did? Are either of these circumstances sufficient to make the hypothesis (that it's a papier-mâché object) relevant? Probably not, but the situation is not so clear."[4] Let p be the statement that the object in the field is a (real) barn, and q the one that the object in the field is a papier-mâché barn. When papier-mâché barns are scattered through the area, if p were false, q would be true or might be. Since in this case (we are supposing) the person still would believe p, the subjunctive

(3) not-$p \rightarrow$ not-(S believes that p)

is not satisfied, and so he doesn't know that p. However, when papier-mâché barns are or were scattered around another country, even if p were false q wouldn't be true, and so (for all we have been told) the person may well know that p. A hypothesis q contrary to p clearly is relevant when if p weren't true, q would be true; when not-$p \rightarrow q$. It clearly is irrelevant when if p weren't true, q also would not be true; when not-$p \rightarrow$ not-q. The remaining possibility is that neither of these opposed subjunctives holds; q might (or might not) be true if p weren't true. In this case, q also will be relevant, according to an account of knowledge incorporating condition (3) and treating subjunctives along the lines sketched above. Thus, condition (3) handles cases that befuddle the "relevant alternatives" account; though that account can adopt the above subjunctive criterion for when an alternative is relevant, it then becomes merely an alternate and longer way of stating condition (3).

Despite the power and intuitive force of the condition that if p weren't true the person would not believe it, this condition does not (in conjunction with the first two conditions) rule out every problem case. There remains, for example, the case of the person in the tank who is brought to believe, by direct electrical and chemical stimulation of his brain, that he is in the tank and is being brought to believe things in this way; he does not know this is true. However, the subjunctive condition is satisfied: if he weren't floating in the tank, he wouldn't believe he was.

The person in the tank does not know he is there, because his belief is not sensitive to the truth. Although it is caused by the fact that is its content, it is not sensitive to that fact. The operators of the tank could have produced any belief, including the false belief that he wasn't in the tank; if they had, he would have believed that. Perfect sensitivity would involve beliefs and facts varying together. We already have one portion of that variation, subjunctively at least: if p were false he wouldn't believe it. This sensitivity as specified by a subjunctive does not have the belief vary with the truth or falsity of p in all possible situations, merely in the ones that would or might obtain if p were false.

The subjunctive condition

(3) not-p → not-(S believes that p)

tells us only half the story about how his belief is sensitive to the truth-value of p. It tells us how his belief state is sensitive to p's falsity, but not how it is sensitive to p's truth; it tells us what his belief state would be if p were false, but not what it would be if p were true.

To be sure, conditions (1) and (2) tell us that p is true and he does believe it, but it does not follow that his believing p is sensitive to p's being true. This additional sensitivity is given to us by a further subjunctive: if p were true, he would believe it.

(4) p → S believes that p.

Not only is p true and S believes it, but if it were true he would believe it. Compare: not only was the photon emitted and did it go to the left, but (it was then

true that): if it were emitted it would go to the left. The truth of antecedent and consequent is not alone sufficient for the truth of a subjunctive; (4) says more than (1) and (2). Thus, we presuppose some (or another) suitable account of subjunctives. According to the suggestion tentatively made above, (4) holds true if not only does he actually truly believe p, but in the 'close' worlds where p is true, he also believes it. He believes that p for some distance out in the p neighbourhood of the actual world; similarly, condition (3) speaks not of the whole not-p neighbourhood of the actual world, but only of the first portion of it. (If, as is likely, these explanations do not help, please use your own intuitive understanding of the subjunctives (3) and (4).)

The person in the tank does not satisfy the subjunctive condition (4). Imagine as actual a world in which he is in the tank and is stimulated to believe he is, and consider what subjunctives are true in that world. It is not true of him there that if he were in the tank he would believe it; for in the close world (or situation) to his own where he is in the tank but they don't give him the belief that he is (much less instil the belief that he isn't) he doesn't believe he is in the tank. Of the person actually in the tank and believing it, it is not true to make the further statement that if he were in the tank he would believe it—so he does not know he is in the tank.

The subjunctive condition (4) also handles a case presented by Gilbert Harman.[5] The dictator of a country is killed; in their first edition, newspapers print the story, but later all the country's newspapers and other media deny the story, falsely. Everyone who encounters the denial believes it (or does not know what to believe and so suspends judgement). Only one person in the country fails to hear any denial and he continues to believe the truth. He satisfies conditions (1)–(3) (and the causal condition about belief) yet we are reluctant to say he knows the truth. The reason is that if he had heard the denials, he too would have believed them, just like everyone else. His belief is not sensitively tuned to the truth, he doesn't satisfy the condition that if it were true he would believe it. Condition (4) is not satisfied.

There is a pleasing symmetry about how this account of knowledge relates conditions (3) and (4), and connects them to the first two conditions. The account has the following form.

(1)
(2)
(3) not-1 → not-2
(4) 1 → 2

I am not inclined, however, to make too much of this symmetry, for I found also that with other conditions experimented with as a possible fourth condition there was some way to construe the resulting third and fourth conditions as symmetrical answers to some symmetrical looking questions, so that they appeared to arise in parallel fashion from similar questions about the components of true belief.

Symmetry, it seems, is a feature of a mode of presentation, not of the contents presented. A uniform transformation of symmetrical statements can leave the results non-symmetrical. But if symmetry attaches to mode of presentation, how can it possibly be a deep feature of, for instance, laws of nature that they exhibit symmetry? (One of my favourite examples of symmetry is due to Groucho Marx. On his radio programme he spoofed a commercial, and ended, "And if you are not completely satisfied, return the unused portion of our product and we will return the unused portion of your money.") Still, to present our subject symmetrically makes the connection of knowledge to true belief especially perspicuous. It seems to me that a symmetrical formulation is a sign of our understanding, rather than a mark of truth. If we cannot understand an asymmetry as arising from an underlying symmetry through the operation of a particular factor, we will not understand why that asymmetry exists in that direction. (But do we also need to understand why the underlying asymmetrical factor holds instead of its opposite?)

A person knows that p when he not only does truly believe it, but also would truly believe it and wouldn't falsely believe it. He not only actually has a true belief, he subjunctively has one. It is true that p and he believes it; if it weren't true he wouldn't believe it, and if it were true he would believe it. To know that p is to be someone who would believe it if it were true, and who wouldn't believe it if it were false.

It will be useful to have a term for this situation when a person's belief is thus subjunctively connected to the fact. Let us say of a person who believes that p, which is true, that when (3) and (4) hold, his belief *tracks* the truth that p. To know is to have a belief that tracks the truth. Knowledge is a particular way of being connected to the world, having a specific real factual connection to the world: tracking it.

II. SCEPTICISM

The sceptic about knowledge argues that we know very little or nothing of what we think we know, or at any rate that this position is no less reasonable than the belief in knowledge. The history of philosophy exhibits a number of different attempts to refute the sceptic: to prove him wrong or show that in arguing against knowledge he presupposes there is some and so refutes himself. Others attempt to show that accepting scepticism is unreasonable, since it is more likely that the sceptic's extreme conclusion is false than that all of his premises are true, or simply because reasonableness of belief just means proceeding in an anti-sceptical way. Even when these counter-arguments satisfy their inventors, they fail to satisfy others, as is shown by the persistent attempts against scepticism. The continuing felt need to refute scepticism, and the difficulty in doing so, attests to the power of the sceptic's position, the depth of his worries.

An account of knowledge should illuminate sceptical arguments and show wherein lies their force. If the account leads us to reject these arguments, this had better not happen too easily or too glibly. To think the sceptic overlooks something obvious, to attribute to him a simple mistake or confusion or fallacy, is to refuse to acknowledge the power of his position and the grip it can have upon us. We thereby cheat ourselves of the opportunity to reap his insights and to gain self-knowledge in understanding why his arguments lure us so. Moreover, in fact, we cannot lay the spectre of scepticism to rest without first hearing what it shall unfold.

Our goal is not, however, to refute scepticism, to prove it is wrong or even to argue that it is wrong. We have elsewhere distinguished between philosophy that attempts to prove, and philosophy that attempts to explain how something is possible. Our task here is to explain how knowledge is possible, given what the sceptic says that we do accept (for example, that it is logically possible that we are dreaming or are floating in the tank). In doing this, we need not convince the sceptic, and we may introduce explanatory hypotheses that he would reject. What is important for our task of explanation and understanding is that *we* find those hypotheses acceptable or plausible, and that they show us how the existence of knowledge fits together with the logical possibilities the sceptic points to, so that these are reconciled within our own belief system. These hypotheses are to explain to ourselves how knowledge is possible, not to prove to someone else that knowledge *is* possible.[6]

Sceptical Possibilities

The sceptic often refers to possibilities in which a person would believe something even though it was false: really, the person is cleverly deceived by others, perhaps by an evil demon, or the person is dreaming, or he is floating in a tank near Alpha Centauri with his brain being stimulated. In each case, the *p* he believes is false, and he believes it even though it is false.

How do these possibilities adduced by the sceptic show that someone does not know that *p?* Suppose that someone is you; how do these possibilities count against your knowing that *p?* One way might be the following. (I shall consider other ways later.) If there is a possible situation where *p* is false yet you believe that *p*, then in that situation you believe that *p* even though it is false. So it appears you do not satisfy condition (3) for knowledge.

(3) If *p* were false, *S* wouldn't believe that *p*.

For a situation has been described in which you do believe that *p* even though *p* is false. How then can it also be true that if *p* were false, you wouldn't believe it? If the sceptic's possible situation shows that (3) is false, and if (3) is a necessary condition for knowledge, then the sceptic's possible situation shows that there isn't knowledge.

So construed, the sceptic's argument plays on condition (3); it aims to show that condition (3) is not satisfied. The sceptic may seem to be putting forth

R: Even if *p* were false, *S* still would believe *p*.

This conditional, with the same antecedent as (3) and the contradictory consequent, is incompatible with the truth of (3). If (3) is true, then R is not. However, R is stronger than the sceptic needs in order to show (3) is false. For (3) is false when if *p* were false, *S* might believe that *p*. This last conditional is weaker than R, and is merely (3)'s denial:

T: not-[not-*p* → not-(*S* believes that *p*)].

Whereas R does not simply deny (3), it asserts an opposing subjunctive of its own. Perhaps the possibility the sceptic adduces is not enough to show that R is true, but it appears at least to establish the weaker T; since this T denies (3), the sceptic's possibility appears to show that (3) is false.

However, the truth of (3) is not incompatible with the existence of a possible situation where the person believes *p* though it is false. The subjunctive

(3) not-*p* → not-(*S* believes *p*)

does not talk of all possible situations in which *p* is false (in which not-*p* is true). It does not say that in all possible situations where not-*p* holds, *S* doesn't believe *p*. To say there is no possible situation in which not-*p* yet *S* believes *p*, would be to say that not-*p* entails not-(*S* believes *p*), or logically implies it. But subjunctive conditionals differ from entailments; the subjunctive (3) is not a statement of entailment. So the existence of a possible situation in which *p* is false yet *S* believes *p* does not show that (3) is false; (3) can be true even though there is a possible situation where not-*p* and *S* believes that *p*.

What the subjunctive (3) speaks of is the situation that would hold if *p* were false. Not every possible situation in which *p* is false is the situation that would hold if *p* were false. To fall into possible worlds talk, the subjunctive (3) speaks of the not-*p* world that is closest to the actual world, or of those not-*p* worlds that are closest to the actual world. And it is of this or these not-p worlds that it says (in them) S does not believe that p. What happens in yet other more distant not-p worlds is no concern of the subjunctive (3).

The sceptic's possibilities (let us refer to them as SK), of the person's being deceived by a demon or dreaming or floating in a tank, count against the subjunctive

(3) if p were false then S wouldn't believe that p

only if (one of) these possibilities would or might obtain if p were false. Condition (3) says: if p were false, S still would not believe p. And this can hold even though there is some situation SK described by the sceptic in which p is false and S believes p. If p were false S still would not believe p, even though there is a situation SK in which p is false and S does believe p, provided that this situation SK wouldn't obtain if p were false. If the sceptic describes a situation SK which would not hold even if p were false then this situation SK doesn't show that (3) is false and so does not (in this way at least) undercut knowledge. Condition C acts to rule out sceptical hypotheses.

C: not-$p \rightarrow$ SK does not obtain.

Any sceptical situation SK which satisfies condition C is ruled out. For a sceptical situation SK to show that we don't know that p, it must fail to satisfy C which excludes it; instead it must be a situation that might obtain if p did not, and so satisfy C's denial:

not-(not-$p \rightarrow$ SK doesn't obtain).

Although the sceptic's imagined situations appear to show that (3) is false, they do not; they satisfy condition C and so are excluded.

The sceptic might go on to ask whether we know that his imagined situations SK are excluded by condition C, whether we know that if p were false SK would not obtain. However, typically he asks something stronger: do we know that his imagined situation SK does not actually obtain? Do we know that we are not being deceived by a demon, dreaming, or

floating in a tank? And if we do not know this, how can we know that p? Thus we are led to the second way his imagined situations might show that we do not know that p.

Sceptical Results

According to our account of knowledge, S knows that the sceptic's situation SK doesn't hold if and only if

(1) SK doesn't hold
(2) S believes that SK doesn't hold
(3) If SK were to hold, S would not believe that SK doesn't hold
(4) If SK were not to hold, S would believe it does not.

Let us focus on the third of these conditions. The sceptic has carefully chosen his situations SK so that if they held we (still) would believe they did not. We would believe we weren't dreaming, weren't being deceived, and so on, even if we were. He has chosen situations SK such that if SK were to hold, S would (still) believe that SK doesn't hold—and this is incompatible with the truth of (3).

Since condition (3) is a necessary condition for knowledge, it follows that we do not know that SK doesn't hold. If it were true that an evil demon was deceiving us, if we were having a particular dream, if we were floating in a tank with our brains stimulated in a specified way, we would still believe we were not. So, we do not know we're not being deceived by an evil demon, we do not know we're not in that tank, and we do not know we're not having that dream. So says the sceptic, and so says our account. And also so we say—don't we? For how could we know we are not being deceived that way, dreaming that dream? If those things *were* happening to us, everything would seem the same to us. There is no way we can know it is not happening for there is no way we could tell if it were happening; and if it were happening we would believe exactly what we do now—in particular, we still would believe that it was not. For this reason, we feel, and correctly, that we don't know—how could we?—that it is not happening to us. It is a virtue of our account that it yields, and explains, this result.

The sceptic asserts we do not know his possibilities don't obtain, and he is right. Attempts to avoid scepticism by claiming we do know these things are bound to fail. The sceptic's possibilities make us uneasy because, as we deeply realize, we do not know they don't obtain; it is not surprising that attempts to show we do know these things leave us suspicious, strike us even as bad faith. Nor has the sceptic merely pointed out something obvious and trivial. It comes as a surprise to realize that we do not know his possibilities don't obtain. It is startling, shocking. For we would have thought, before the sceptic got us to focus on it, that we did know those things, that we did know we were not being deceived by a demon, or dreaming that dream, or stimulated that way in that tank. The sceptic has pointed out that we do not know things we would have confidently said we knew. And if we don't know these things, what can we know? So much for the supposed obviousness of what the sceptic tells us.

Let us say that a situation (or world) is doxically identical for *S* to the actual situation when if *S* were in that situation, he would have exactly the beliefs (*doxa*) he actually does have. More generally, two situations are doxically identical for *S* if and only if he would have exactly the same beliefs in them. It might be merely a curiosity to be told there are non-actual situations doxically identical to the actual one. The sceptic, however, describes worlds doxically identical to the actual world in which almost everything believed is false.[7]

Such worlds are possible because we know mediately, not directly. This leaves room for a divergence between our beliefs and the truth. It is as though we possessed only two-dimensional plane projections of three-dimensional objects. Different three-dimensional objects, oriented appropriately, have the same two-dimensional plane projection. Similarly, different situations or worlds will lead to our having the very same beliefs. What is surprising is how very different the doxically identical world can be—different enough for almost everything believed in it to be false. Whether or not the mere fact that knowledge is mediated always makes room for such a very different doxically identical world, it does so in our case, as the sceptic's possibilities

show. To be shown this is non-trivial, especially when we recall that we do not know the sceptic's possibility doesn't obtain: we do not know that we are not living in a doxically identical world wherein almost everything we believe is false.

What more could the sceptic ask for or hope to show? Even readers who sympathized with my desire not to dismiss the sceptic too quickly may feel this has gone too far, that we have not merely acknowledged the force of the sceptic's position but have succumbed to it.

The sceptic maintains that we know almost none of what we think we know. He has shown, much to our initial surprise, that we do not know his (non-trivial) possibility SK doesn't obtain. Thus, he has shown of one thing we thought we knew, that we didn't and don't. To the conclusion that we know almost nothing, it appears but a short step. For if we do not know we are not dreaming or being deceived by a demon or floating in a tank, then how can I know, for example, that I am sitting before a page writing with a pen, and how can you know that you are reading a page of a book?

However, although our account of knowledge agrees with the sceptic in saying that we do not know that not-SK, it places no formidable barriers before my knowing that I am writing on a page with a pen. It is true that I am, I believe I am, if I weren't I wouldn't believe I was, and if I were, I would believe it. Also, it is true that you are reading a page (please, don't stop now!), you believe you are, if you weren't reading a page you wouldn't believe you were, and if you were reading a page you would believe you were. So according to the account, I do know that I am writing on a page with a pen, and you do know that you are reading a page. The account does not lead to any general scepticism.

Yet we must grant that it appears that if the sceptic is right that we don't know we are not dreaming or being deceived or floating in the tank, then it cannot be that I know I am writing with a pen or that you know you are reading a page. So we must scrutinize with special care the sceptic's "short step" to the conclusion that we don't know these things, for either this step cannot be taken or our account of knowledge is incoherent.

Nonclosure

In taking the "short step," the sceptic assumes that if
S knows that *p* and he knows that "*p* entails *q*" then
he also knows that *q*. In the terminology of the logicians, the sceptic assumes that knowledge is closed
under known logical implication; that the operation
of moving from something known to something else
known to be entailed by it does not take us outside of
the (closed) area of knowledge. He intends, of
course, to work things backwards, arguing that since
the person does not know that *q*, assuming (at least
for the purposes of argument) that he does know that
p entails *q*, it follows that he does not know that *p*.
For if he did know that *p*, he would also know that *q*,
which he doesn't.

The details of different sceptical arguments vary
in their structure, but each one will assume some
variant of the principle that knowledge is closed
under known logical implication. If we abbreviate
"knowledge that *p*" by "*Kp*" and abbreviate "entails"
by the fishhook sign "-3," we can write this principle of closure as the subjunctive principle

P: $K(p -3 q) \& Kp \rightarrow Kq$.

If a person were to know that *p* entails *q* and he were
to know that *p* then he would know that *q*. The statement that *q* follows by *modus ponens* from the other
two stated as known in the antecedent of the subjunctive principle P; this principle counts on the person to draw the inference to *q*.

You know that your being in a tank on Alpha Centauri entails your not being in place *X* where you are.
(I assume here a limited readership.) And you know
also the contrapositive, that your being at place *X*
entails that you are not then in a tank on Alpha Centauri. If you knew you were at *X* you would know
you're not in a tank (of a specified sort) at Alpha Centauri. But you do not know this last fact (the sceptic
has argued and we have agreed) and so (he argues)
you don't know the first. Another intuitive way of
putting the sceptic's argument is as follows. If you
know that two statements are incompatible and you
know the first is true then you know the denial of the
second. You know that your being at *X* and your

being in a tank on Alpha Centauri are incompatible;
so if you knew you were at *X* you would know you
were not in the (specified) tank on Alpha Centauri.
Since you do not know the second, you don't know
the first.

No doubt, it is possible to argue over the details of
principle P, to point out it is incorrect as it stands. Perhaps, though *Kp*, the person does not know that he
knows that *p* (that is, not-*KKp*) and so does not draw
the inference to *q*. Or perhaps he doesn't draw the
inference because not-$KK(p -3 q)$. Other similar
principles face their own difficulties: for example, the
principle that $K(p \rightarrow q) \rightarrow (Kp \rightarrow Kq)$ fails if *Kp* stops
$p \rightarrow q$ from being true, that is, if $Kp \rightarrow$ not-$(p \rightarrow q)$;
the principle that $K(p -3 q) \rightarrow K(Kp \rightarrow Kq)$ faces difficulties if *Kp* makes the person forget that $(p -3 q)$
and so he fails to draw the inference to *q*. We seem
forced to pile *K* upon *K* until we reach something like
$KK(p -3 q) \& KKp \rightarrow Kq$; this involves strengthening considerably the antecedent of P and so is not useful for the sceptic's argument that *p* is not known.
(From a principle altered thus, it would follow at best
that it is not known that *p* is known.)

We would be ill-advised, however, to quibble over
the details of P. Although these details are difficult to
get straight, it will continue to appear that something
like P is correct. If *S* knows that "*p* entails *q*," and he
knows that *p* and knows that "(*p* and *p* entails *q*)
entails *q*" and he does draw the inference to *q* from
all this and believes *q* via the process of drawing this
inference, then will he not know that *q*? And what is
wrong with simplifying this mass of detail by writing
merely principle P, provided we apply it only to cases
where the mass of detail holds, as it surely does in the
sceptical cases under consideration? For example, I
do realize that my being in the Van Leer Foundation
Building in Jerusalem entails that I am not in a tank
on Alpha Centauri; I am capable of drawing inferences now; I do believe I am not in a tank on Alpha
Centauri (though not solely via this inference,
surely); and so forth. Won't this satisfy the correctly
detailed principle, and shouldn't it follow that I know
I am not (in that tank) on Alpha Centauri? The sceptic agrees it should follow; so he concludes from the
fact that I don't know I am not floating in the tank on
Alpha Centauri that I don't know I am in Jerusalem.

Uncovering difficulties in the details of particular formulations of P will not weaken the principle's intuitive appeal; such quibbling will seem at best like a wasp attacking a steamroller, at worst like an effort in bad faith to avoid being pulled along by the sceptic's argument.

Principle P is wrong, however, and not merely in detail. Knowledge is not closed under known logical implication. S knows that p when S has a true belief that p, and S wouldn't have a false belief that p (condition (3)) and S would have a true belief that p (condition (4)). Neither of these latter two conditions is closed under known logical implication.

Let us begin with condition

(3) if p were false, S wouldn't believe that p.

When S knows that p, his belief that p is contingent on the truth of p, contingent in the way the subjunctive condition (3) describes. Now it might be that p entails q (and S knows this), that S's belief that p is subjunctively contingent on the truth of p, that S believes q, yet his belief that q is not subjunctively dependent on the truth of q, in that it (or he) does not satisfy:

(3') if q were false, S wouldn't believe that q.

For (3') talks of what S would believe if q were false, and this may be a very different situation from the one that would hold if p were false, even though p entails q. That you were born in a certain city entails that you were born on earth.[8] Yet contemplating what (actually) would be the situation if you were not born in that city is very different from contemplating what situation would hold if you weren't born on earth. Just as those possibilities are very different, so what is believed in them may be very different. When p entails q (and not the other way around) p will be a stronger statement than q, and so not-q (which is the antecedent of (3')) will be a stronger statement than not-p (which is the antecedent of (3)). There is no reason to assume you will have the same beliefs in these two cases, under these suppositions of differing strengths.

There is no reason to assume the (closest) not-p world and the (closest) not-q world are doxically identical for you, and no reason to assume, even though p entails q, that your beliefs in one of these worlds would be a (proper) subset of your beliefs in the other.

Consider now the two statements:

p = I am awake and sitting on a chair in Jerusalem;
q = I am not floating in a tank on Alpha Centauri being stimulated by electrochemical means to believe that p.

The first one entails the second: p entails q. Also, I know that p entails q; and I know that p. If p were false, I would be standing or lying down in the same city, or perhaps sleeping there, or perhaps in a neighbouring city or town. If q were false, I would be floating in a tank on Alpha Centauri. Clearly these are very different situations, leading to great differences in what I then would believe. If p were false, if I weren't awake and sitting on a chair in Jerusalem, I would not believe that p. Yet if q were false, if I was floating in a tank on Alpha Centauri, I would believe that q, that I was not in the tank, and indeed, in that case, I would still believe that p. According to our account of knowledge, I know that p yet I do not know that q, even though (I know) p entails q.

This failure of knowledge to be closed under known logical implication stems from the fact that condition (3) is not closed under known logical implication; condition (3) can hold of one statement believed while not of another known to be entailed by the first. It is clear that any account that includes as a necessary condition for knowledge the subjunctive condition (3), not-$p \rightarrow$ not-(S believes that p), will have the consequence that knowledge is not closed under known logical implication.

When p entails q and you believe each of them, if you do not have a false belief that p (since p is true) then you do not have a false belief that q. However, if you are to know something not only don't you have a false belief about it, but also you wouldn't have a false belief about it. Yet, we have seen how it may be that p entails q and you believe each and you wouldn't have a false belief that p yet you might have a false belief that q (that is, it is not the case that you wouldn't have one). Knowledge is not closed under the known logical implication because 'wouldn't have a false belief that' is not closed under known logical implication.

If knowledge were the same as (simply) true belief then it would be closed under known logical implication (provided the implied statements were believed). Knowledge is not simply true belief, however; additional conditions are needed. These further conditions will make knowledge open under known logical implication, even when the entailed statement is believed, when at least one of the further conditions itself is open. Knowledge stays closed (only) if all of the additional conditions are closed. I lack a general non-trivial characterization of those conditions that are closed under known logical implication; possessing such an illuminating characterization, one might attempt to prove that no additional conditions of that sort could provide an adequate analysis of knowledge.

Still, we can say the following. A belief that p is knowledge that p only if it somehow varies with the truth of p. The causal condition for knowledge specified that the belief was "produced by" the fact, but that condition did not provide the right sort of varying with the fact. The subjunctive conditions (3) and (4) are our attempt to specify that varying. But however an account spells this out, it will hold that whether a belief that p is knowledge partly depends on what goes on with the belief in some situations when p is false. An account that says nothing about what is believed in any situation when p is false cannot give us any mode of varying with the fact.

Because what is preserved under logical implication is truth, any condition that is preserved under known logical implication is most likely to speak only of what happens when p, and q, are true, without speaking at all of what happens when either one is false. Such a condition is incapable of providing "varies with"; so adding only such conditions to true belief cannot yield an adequate account of knowledge.

A belief's somehow varying with the truth of what is believed is not closed under known logical implication. Since knowledge that p involves such variation, knowledge also is not closed under known logical implication. The sceptic cannot easily deny that

knowledge involves such variation, for his argument that we don't know that we're not floating in that tank, for example, uses the fact that knowledge does involve variation. ("If you were floating in the tank you would still think you weren't, so you don't know that you're not.") Yet, though one part of his argument uses that fact that knowledge involves such variation, another part of his argument presupposes that knowledge does not involve any such variation. This latter is the part that depends upon knowledge being closed under known logical implication, as when the sceptic argues that since you don't know that not-SK, you don't know you are not floating in the tank, then you also don't know, for example, that you are now reading a book. That closure can hold only if the variation does not. The sceptic cannot be right both times. According to our view he is right when he holds that knowledge involves such variation and so concludes that we don't know, for example, that we are not floating in that tank; but he is wrong when he assumes knowledge is closed under known logical implication and concludes that we know hardly anything.[9]

Knowledge is a real factual relation, subjunctively specifiable, whose structure admits our standing in this relation, tracking, to p without standing in it to some q which we know p to entail. Any relation embodying some variation of belief with the fact, with the truth (value), will exhibit this structural feature. The sceptic is right that we don't track some particular truths—the ones stating that his sceptical possibilities SK don't hold—but wrong that we don't stand in the real knowledge-relation of tracking to many other truths, including ones that entail these first mentioned truths we believe but don't know.

The literature on scepticism contains writers who endorse these sceptical arguments (or similar narrower ones), but confess their inability to maintain their sceptical beliefs at times when they are not focusing explicitly on the reasoning that led them to sceptical conclusions. The most notable example of this is Hume:

> I am ready to reject all belief and reasoning, and can look upon no opinion even as more probable or likely than another . . . Most fortunately it happens

that since reason is incapable of dispelling these clouds, nature herself suffices to that purpose, and cures me of this philosophical melancholy and delirium, either by relaxing this bent of mind, or by some avocation, and lively impression of my senses, which obliterate all these chimeras. I dine, I play a game of backgammon, I converse, and am merry with my friends; and when after three or four hours' amusement, I would return to these speculations, they appear so cold, and strained, and ridiculous, that I cannot find in my heart to enter into them any farther. (*A Treatise of Human Nature,* Book I, Part IV, section VII.)

The great subverter of Pyrrhonism or the excessive principles of skepticism is action, and employment, and the occupations of common life. These principles may flourish and triumph in the schools; where it is, indeed, difficult, if not impossible, to refute them. But as soon as they leave the shade, and by the presence of the real objects, which actuate our passions and sentiments, are put in opposition to the more powerful principles of our nature, they vanish like smoke, and leave the most determined skeptic in the same condition as other mortals . . . And though a Pyrrhonian may throw himself or others into a momentary amazement and confusion by his profound reasonings; the first and most trivial event in life will put to flight all his doubts and scruples, and leave him the same, in every point of action and speculation, with the philosophers of every other sect, or with those who never concerned themselves in any philosophical researches. When he awakes from his dream, he will be the first to join in the laugh against himself, and to confess that all his objections are mere amusement. (*An Enquiry Concerning Human Understanding,* Section XII, Part II.)

The theory of knowledge we have presented explains why sceptics of various sorts have had such difficulties in sticking to their far-reaching sceptical conclusions "outside the study," or even inside it when they are not thinking specifically about sceptical arguments and possibilities SK.

The sceptic's arguments do show (but show only) that we don't know the sceptic's possibilities SK do not hold; and he is right that we don't track the fact that SK does not hold. (If it were to hold, we would still think it didn't.) However, the sceptic's arguments don't show we do not know other facts (including

facts that entail not-SK) for we do track these other facts (and knowledge is not closed under known logical entailment). Since we do track these other facts—you, for example, the fact that you are reading a book; I, the fact that I am writing on a page—and the sceptic tracks such facts too, it is not surprising that when he focuses on them, on his relationship to such facts, the sceptic finds it hard to remember or maintain his view that he does not know those facts. Only by shifting his attention back to his relationship to the (different) fact that not-SK, which relationship is not tracking, can he revive his sceptical belief and make it salient. However, this sceptical triumph is evanescent, it vanishes when his attention turns to other facts. Only by fixating on the sceptical possibilities SK can he maintain his sceptical virtue; otherwise, unsurprisingly, he is forced to confess to sins of credulity.

NOTES

1. See Hilary Putnam, *Reason, Truth and History* (Cambridge, 1981), ch. 1.

2. I should note here that I assume bivalence throughout this chapter, and consider only statements that are true if and only if their negations are false.

3. See Robert Stalnaker, "A Theory of Conditionals," in N. Rescher, ed., *Studies in Logical Theory* (Oxford 1968); David Lewis, *Counterfactuals* (Cambridge 1973); and Jonathan Bennett's critical review of Lewis, "Counterfactuals and Possible Worlds," *Canadian Journal of Philosophy,* 4/2 (Dec. 1974), 381–402. Our purposes require, for the most part, no more than an intuitive understanding of subjunctives.

4. G. C. Stine, "Skepticism, Relevant Alternatives and Deductive Closure," *Philosophical Studies,* 29 (1976), 252, who attributes the example to Carl Ginet.

5. Gilbert Harman, *Thought* (Princeton; 1973), ch. 9, 142–54.

6. From the perspective of explanation rather than proof, the extensive philosophical discussion, deriving from Charles S. Peirce, of whether the sceptic's doubts are real is beside the point. The problem of explaining how knowledge is possible would remain the same, even if no one ever claimed to doubt that there was knowledge.

7. I say almost everything, because there still could be some true beliefs such as "I exist." More limited sceptical possibilities present worlds doxically identical to the actual

world in which almost every belief of a certain sort is false, for example, about the past, or about other people's mental states.

8. Here again I assume a limited readership, and ignore possibilities such as those described in James Blish, *Cities in Flight* (New York, 1982).

9. Reading an earlier draft of this chapter, friends pointed out to me that Fred Dretske already had defended the view that knowledge (as one among many epistemic concepts) is not closed under known logical implication. (See his "Epistemic Operators," *Journal of Philosophy,* 67, (1970), 1007–23.) Furthermore, Dretske presented a subjunctive condition for knowledge (in his "Conclusive Reasons," *Australasian Journal of Philosophy,* 49, (1971), 1–22), holding that *S* knows that *p* on the basis of reasons *R* only if: *R* would not be the case unless *p* were the case. Here Dretske ties the evidence subjunctively to the fact, and the belief based on the evidence subjunctively to the fact through the evidence. The independent statement and

delineation of the position here I hope will make clear its many merits.

After Goldman's paper on a causal theory of knowledge, in *Journal of Philosophy,* 64, (1967), an idea then already "in the air," it required no great leap to consider subjunctive conditions. Some 2 months after the first version of this chapter was written, Goldman himself published a paper on knowledge utilizing counterfactuals ("Discrimination and Perceptual Knowledge," Essay II in this collection), also talking of relevant possibilities (without using the counterfactuals to identify which possibilities are relevant); and R. Shope has called my attention to a paper of L. S. Carrier ("An Analysis of Empirical Knowledge," *Southern Journal of Philosophy,* 9, (1971), 3–11) that also used subjunctive conditions including our condition (3). Armstrong's reliability view of knowledge (*Belief, Truth and Knowledge,* Cambridge, 1973, pp. 166, 169) involved a lawlike connection between the belief that *p* and the state of affairs that makes it true. Clearly, the idea is one whose time has come.

The Raft and the Pyramid: Coherence Versus Foundations in the Theory of Knowledge

~

ERNEST SOSA

Ernest Sosa, Romeo Elton Professor at Brown University and professor of philosophy at Rutgers University, is recognized for contributions in epistemology, metaphysics, and philosophy of mind. He is the author of *Knowledge in Perspective,* developing his "virtue perspectivism," which gives due credit to both foundationalist and coherentist currents.

Contemporary epistemology must choose between the solid security of the ancient foundationalist pyramid and the risky adventure of the new coherentist raft. Our main objective will be to understand, as deeply as we can, the nature of the controversy and the reasons for and against each of the two options. But first of all we take note of two underlying assumptions.

1. TWO ASSUMPTIONS

(A1) Not everything believed is known, but nothing can be known without being at least believed (or accepted, presumed, taken for granted, or the like) in some broad sense. What additional requirements must a belief fill in order to be knowledge? There are

Reprinted from Ernest Sosa, *Knowledge in Perspective: Selected Essays in Epistemology* (Cambridge, England: Cambridge University Press, 1991), by permission of the publisher.

surely at least the following two: (a) it must be true, and (b) it must be justified (or warranted, reasonable, correct, or the like).

(A2) Let us assume, moreover, with respect to the second condition A1(b): first, that it involves a normative or evaluative property; and, second, that the relevant sort of justification is that which pertains to knowledge: epistemic (or theoretical) justification. Someone seriously ill may have two sorts of justification for believing he will recover: the practical justification that derives from the contribution such belief will make to his recovery and the theoretical justification provided by the lab results, the doctor's diagnosis and prognosis, and so on. Only the latter is relevant to the question whether he knows.

2. KNOWLEDGE AND CRITERIA (OR CANONS, METHODS, OR THE LIKE)

a. There are two key questions of the theory of knowledge:

  (i) What do we know?
  (ii) How do we know?

The answer to the first would be a list of bits of knowledge or at least of types of knowledge: of the self, of the external world, of other minds, and so on. An answer to the second would give us criteria (or canons, methods, principles, or the like) that would explain how we know whatever it is that we do know.

b. In developing a theory of knowledge, we can begin either with a(i) or with a(ii). Particularism would have us begin with an answer to a(i) and only then take up a(ii) on the basis of that answer. Quite to the contrary, methodism would reverse that order. The particularist thus tends to be antiskeptical on principle. But the methodist is as such equally receptive to skepticism and to the contrary. Hume, for example, was no less a methodist than Descartes. Each accepted, in effect, that only the obvious and what is proved deductively on its basis can possibly be known.

c. What, then, is the obvious? For Descartes it is what we know by intuition, what is clear and distinct, what is indubitable and credible with no fear of error. Thus for Descartes basic knowledge is always an infallible belief in an indubitable truth. All other knowledge must stand on that basis through deductive proof. Starting from such criteria (canons, methods, etc.), Descartes concluded that knowledge extended about as far as his contemporaries believed.[1] Starting from similar criteria, however, Hume concluded that both science and common sense made claims far beyond their rightful limits.

d. Philosophical posterity has rejected Descartes's theory for one main reason: that it admits too easily as obvious what is nothing of the sort. Descartes's reasoning is beautifully simple: God exists; no omnipotent perfectly good being would descend to deceit; but if our common sense beliefs were radically false, that would represent deceit on His part. Therefore, our common sense beliefs must be true or at least cannot be radically false. But in order to buttress this line of reasoning and fill in details, Descartes appeals to various principles that appear something less than indubitable.

e. For his part, Hume rejects all but a miniscule portion of our supposed common sense knowledge. He establishes first that there is no way to prove such supposed knowledge on the basis of what is obvious at any given moment through reason or experience. And he concludes, in keeping with this methodism, that in point of fact there really is no such knowledge.

3. TWO METAPHORS: THE RAFT AND THE PYRAMID

Both metaphors concern the body or system of knowledge in a given mind. But the mind is of course a more complex marvel than is sometimes supposed. Here I do not allude to the depths plumbed by Freud, nor even to Chomsky's. Nor need we recall the labyrinths inhabited by statesman and diplomats, nor the rich patterns of some novels or theories. We need look no further than the most common, everyday beliefs. Take, for instance, the belief that driving tonight will be dangerous. Brief reflection should reveal that any of us with that belief will join to it several other closely related beliefs on which the given belief depends for its existence or (at least) its justification. Among such beliefs we could presumably find some or all of the following: that the road will be icy or snowy; that driving on ice or snow is dangerous; that it will rain or snow tonight; that the temperature will be below freezing; appropriate beliefs about the forecast and its reliability; and so on.

How must such beliefs be interrelated in order to help justify my belief about the danger of driving tonight? Here foundationalism and coherentism disagree, each offering its own metaphor. Let us have a closer look at this dispute, starting with foundationalism.

Both Descartes and Hume attribute to human knowledge an architectonic structure. There is a nonsymmetric relation of physical support such that any two floors of a building are tied by that relation: one of the two supports (or at least helps support) the other. And there is, moreover, a part with a special status: the foundation, which is supported by none of the floors while supporting them all.

With respect to a body of knowledge K (in someone's possession), foundationalism implies that K can be divided into parts $K_1, K_2, \ldots$, such that there is some nonsymmetric relation R (analogous to the relation of physical support) which orders those parts in such a way that there is one—call it F—that bears R to every other part while none of them bears R in turn to F.

According to foundationalism, each piece of knowledge lies on a pyramid like that in Figure 1. The nodes of such a pyramid (for a proposition P relative to a subject S and a time t) must obey the following requirements:

a. The set of all nodes that succeed (directly) any given node must serve jointly as a base that properly supports that node (for S at t).
b. Each node must be a proposition that S is justified in believing at t.
c. If a node is not self-evident (for S at t), it must have successors (that serve jointly as a base that properly supports that node).
d. Each branch of an epistemic pyramid must terminate.

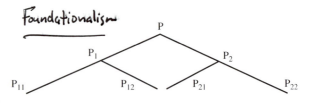

Figure 1

For the foundationalist Descartes, for instance, each terminating node must be an indubitable proposition that S believes at t with no possibility of error. As for the nonterminal nodes, each of them represents inferential knowledge, derived by deduction from more basic beliefs.

Such radical foundationalism suffers from a fatal weakness that is twofold:

(a) there are not so many perfectly obvious truths as Descartes thought; and
(b) once we restrict ourselves to what is truly obvious in any given context, very little of one's supposed common sense knowledge can be proved on that basis.

If we adhere to such radical foundationalism, therefore, we are just wrong in thinking we know so much.

Note that in citing such a "fatal weakness" of radical foundationalism, we favor particularism as against the methodism of Descartes and Hume. For we reject the methods or criteria of Descartes and Hume when we realize that they plunge us in a deep skepticism. If such criteria are incompatible with our enjoyment of the rich body of knowledge that we commonly take for granted, then as good particularists we hold on to the knowledge and reject the criteria.

If we reject radical foundationalism, however, what are we to put in its place? Here epistemology faces a dilemma that different epistemologists resolve differently. Some reject radical foundationalism but retain some more moderate form of foundationalism. Others react more vigorously, however, by rejecting all forms of foundationalism in favor of a radically different coherentism. Coherentism is associated with idealism—of both the German and the British variety—and has recently acquired new vigor and interest.

The coherentists reject the metaphor of the pyramid in favor of one that they owe to the positivist Neurath, according to whom our body of knowledge is a raft that floats free of any anchor or tie. Repairs must be made afloat, and though no part is untouchable, we must stand on some in order to replace or repair others. Not every part can go at once.

According to the new metaphor, what justifies a belief is not that it can be an infallible belief with an indubitable object, nor that it have been proved deductively on such a basis, but that it cohere with a comprehensive system of beliefs.

4.   A COHERENTIST CRITIQUE OF FOUNDATIONALISM

What reasons do coherentists offer for their total rejection of foundationalism? The argument that follows below summarizes much of what is alleged against foundationalism. But first we must distinguish between subjective states that incorporate a propositional attitude and those that do not. A propositional attitude is a mental state of someone with a proposition for its object: beliefs, hopes, and fears provide examples. By way of contrast, a headache does not incorporate any such attitude. One can of course be conscious of a headache, but the headache itself does not constitute or incorporate any attitude with a proposition for its object. With this distinction in the background, here is the antifoundationalist argument, which has two lemmas—a(iv) and b(iii)—and a principal conclusion.

a.   (i) If a mental state incorporates a propositional attitude, then it does not give us direct contact with reality, e.g., with pure experience, unfiltered by concepts or beliefs.

(ii) If a mental state does not give us direct contact with reality, then it provides no guarantee against error.

(iii) If a mental state provides no guarantee against error, then it cannot serve as a foundation for knowledge.

(iv) Therefore, if a mental state incorporates a propositional attitude, then it cannot serve as a foundation for knowledge.

b.   (i) If a mental state does not incorporate a propositional attitude, then it is an enigma how such a state can provide support for any hypothesis, raising its credibility selectively by contrast with its alternatives. (If the mental state has no conceptual or propositional content, then what logical relation can it possibly bear to any hypothesis? Belief in a hypothesis would be a propositional attitude with the hypothesis itself as object. How can one depend logically for such a belief on an experience with no propositional content?)

(ii) If a mental state has no propositional content and cannot provide logical support for any hypothesis, then it cannot serve as a foundation for knowledge.

(iii) Therefore, if a mental state does not incorporate a propositional attitude, then it cannot serve as a foundation for knowledge.

c.   Every mental state either does or does not incorporate a propositional attitude.

d.   Therefore, no mental state can serve as a foundation for knowledge. (From a(iv), b(iii), and c.)

According to the coherentist critic, foundationalism is run through by this dilemma. Let us take a closer look.[2]

In the first place, what reason is there to think, in accordance with premise b(i), that only propositional attitudes can give support to their own kind? Consider practices—e.g., broad policies or customs. Could not some person or group be justified in a practice because of its consequences: that is, could not the consequences of a practice make it a good practice? But among the consequences of a practice may surely be found, for example, a more just distribution of goods and less suffering than there would be under its alternatives. And neither the more just distribution nor the lower degree of suffering is a propositional attitude. This provides an example in which propositional attitudes (the intentions that sustain the practice) are justified by consequences that are not propositional attitudes. That being so, is it not conceivable that the justification of belief that matters for knowledge be analogous to the objective justification by consequences that we find in ethics?

Is it not possible, for instance, that a belief that there is something red before one be justified in part because it has its origin in one's visual experience of red when one looks at an apple in daylight? If we accept such examples, they show us a source of justification that serves as such without incorporating a propositional attitude.

As for premise a(iii), it is already under suspicion from our earlier exploration of premise b(i). A mental state M can be nonpropositional and hence not a candidate for so much as truth, much less infallibility, while it serves, in spite of that, as a foundation of knowledge. Leaving that aside, let us suppose that the relevant mental state is indeed propositional. Must it then be infallible in order to serve as a foundation of justification and knowledge? That is so far from being obvious that it seems more likely false when compared with an analogue in ethics. With respect to beliefs, we may distinguish between their being true and their being justified. Analogously, with respect to actions, we may distinguish between their being optimal (best of all alternatives, all things considered) and their being (subjectively) justified. In practical deliberation on alternatives for action, is it inconceivable that the most *eligible* alternative *not* be objectively the best, all things considered? Can there not be another alternative—perhaps a most repugnant one worth little if any consideration—that in point of fact would have a much better total set of consequences and would thus be better, all things considered? Take the physician attending to Frau Hitler at the birth of little Adolf. Is it not possible that if he had acted less morally, that would have proved better in the fullness of time? And if that is so in ethics, may not its likeness hold good in epistemology? Might there not be justified (reasonable, warranted) beliefs that are not even true, much less infallible? That seems to me not just a conceivable possibility, but indeed a familiar fact of everyday life, where observational beliefs too often prove illusory but no less reasonable for being false.

If the foregoing is on the right track, then the antifoundationalist is far astray. What has led him there?

As a diagnosis of the antifoundationalist argument before us, and more particularly of its second lemma, I would suggest that it rests on an Intellectualist Model of Justification.

According to such a model, the justification of belief (and psychological states generally) is parasitical on certain logical relations among propositions. For example, my belief (i) that the streets are wet is justified by my pair of beliefs (ii) that it is raining, and (iii) that if it is raining, the streets are wet. Thus we have a structure such as this:

B(Q) is justified by the fact that B(Q) is grounded on (B(P), B(P $\supset$ Q)).

And according to an Intellectualist Model, this is parasitical on the fact that

P and (P $\supset$ Q) together logically imply Q.

Concerning this attack on foundationalism I will argue (a) that it is useless to the coherentist, since if the antifoundationalist dilemma impales the foundationalist, a form of it can be turned against the coherentist to the same effect; (b) that the dilemma would be lethal not only to foundationalism and coherentism but also to the very possibility of substantive epistemology; and (c) that a form of it would have the same effect on normative ethics.

(a) According to coherentism, what justifies a belief is its membership in a coherent and comprehensive set of beliefs. But whereas being grounded on B(P) and (B(P $\supset$ Q) is a property of a belief B(Q) that yields immediately the logical implication of Q by [P and (P $\supset$ Q)] as the logical source of that property's justificatory power, the property of being a member of a coherent set is not one that immediately yields any such implication.

It may be argued, nevertheless, (i) that the property of being a member of a coherent set would supervene in any actual instance on the property of being a member of a particular set α that is in fact coherent, and (ii) that this would enable us to preserve our Intellectualist Model, since (iii) the justification of the member belief B(Q) by its membership in α would then be parasitical on the logical relations among the beliefs in α which constitute the coherence of that set of beliefs, and (iv) the justification of B(Q) by the fact that it is part of a coherent set would then be *indirectly* parasitical on logical relations among propositions after all.

But if such an indirect form of parasitism is allowed, then the experience of pain may perhaps be said to justify belief in its existence parasitically on the fact that P logically implies P! The Intellectualist Model seems either so trivial as to be dull, or else sharp enough to cut equally against both foundationalism and coherentism.

(b) If (i) only propositional attitudes can justify such propositional attitudes as belief, and if (ii) to do so they must in turn be justified by yet other propositional attitudes, it seems clear that (iii) there is no hope of constructing a complete epistemology, one which would give us, in theory, an account of what the justification of any justified belief would supervene on. For (i) and (ii) would rule out the possibility of a finite regress of justification.

(c) If only propositional attitudes can justify propositional attitudes, and if to do so they must in turn be justified by yet other propositional attitudes, it seems clear that there is no hope of constructing a complete normative ethics, one which would give us, in theory, an account of what the justification of any possible justified action would supervene upon. For the justification of an action presumably depends on the intentions it embeds and the justification of these, and here we are already within the net of propositional attitudes from which, for the Intellectualist, there is no escape.

It seems fair to conclude that our coherentist takes his antifoundationalist zeal too far. His antifoundationalist argument helps expose some valuable insights but falls short of its malicious intent. The foundationalist emerges showing no serious damage. Indeed, he now demands equal time for a positive brief in defense of his position.

5.   THE REGRESS ARGUMENT

a. The regress argument in epistemology concludes that we must countenance beliefs that are justified in the absence of justification by other beliefs. But it reaches that conclusion only by rejecting the possibility in principle of an infinite regress of justification. It thus opts for foundational beliefs justified in some noninferential way by ruling out a chain or pyramid of justification that has justifiers, and justifiers of justifiers, and so on *without end*. One may well find this too short a route to foundationalism, however, and demand more compelling reasons for thus rejecting an infinite regress as vicious. We shall find indeed that it is not easy to meet this demand.

b. We have seen how even the most ordinary of everyday beliefs is the tip of an iceberg. A closer look below the surface reveals a complex structure that ramifies with no end in sight. Take again my belief that driving will be dangerous tonight, at the tip of an iceberg, (I), that looks like Figure 2. The immediate cause of my belief that driving will be hazardous tonight is the sound of raindrops on the windowpane. All but one or two members of the underlying iceberg are as far as they can be from my thoughts at the time. In what sense, then, do they form an iceberg whose tip breaks the calm surface of my consciousness?

Here I will assume that the members of (I) are beliefs of the subject, even if unconscious or subconscious, that causally buttress and thus justify his prediction about the driving conditions.

Can the iceberg extend without end? It may appear obvious that it cannot do so, and one may jump to the conclusion that any piece of knowledge must be ultimately founded on beliefs that are *not* (inferentially) justified or warranted by other beliefs. This is a doctrine of *epistemic foundationalism*.

Let us focus not so much on the *giving* of justification as on the *having* of it. *Can* there be a belief that is justified in part by other beliefs, some of which are in turn justified by yet other beliefs, and so on without end? Can there be an endless regress of justification?

(I)

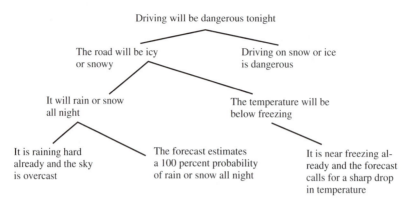

Figure 2

c. There are several familiar objections to such a regress:

(i) *Objection:* "It is incompatible with human limitations. No human subject could harbor the required infinity of beliefs."

Reply: It is mere presumption to fathom with such assurance the depths of the mind, and especially its unconscious and dispositional depths. Besides, our object here is the nature of epistemic justification in itself and not only that of such justification as is accessible to humans. Our question is not whether humans could harbor an infinite iceberg of justification. Our question is rather whether *any* mind, no matter how deep, could do so. Or is it ruled out *in principle* by the very nature of justification?

(ii) *Objection:* "An infinite regress is indeed ruled out in principle, for if justification were thus infinite how could it possibly end?"

Reply: (i) If the end mentioned is *temporal,* then why must there be such an end? In the first place, the subject may be eternal. Even if he is not eternal, moreover, why must belief acquisition and justification occur seriatim? What precludes an infinite body of beliefs acquired at a single stroke? Human limitations may rule this out for humans, but we have yet to be shown that it is precluded in

principle, by the very nature of justification. (ii) If the end mentioned is justificatory, on the other hand, then to ask how justification could possibly end is just to beg the question.

(iii) *Objection:* "Let us make two assumptions: first, that S's belief of q justifies his belief of p only if it works together with a justified belief on his part that q provides good evidence for p; and, second, that if S is to be justified in believing p on the basis of his belief of q and is to be justified in believing q on the basis of his belief of r, then S must be justified in believing that r provides good evidence for p via q. These assumptions imply that an actual regress of justification requires belief in an infinite proposition. Since no one (or at least no human) can believe an infinite proposition, no one (no human) can be a subject of such an actual regress."[3]

Reply: Neither of the two assumptions is beyond question, but even granting them both, it may still be doubted that the conclusion follows. It is true that each finitely complex belief of the form "r provides good evidence for p via $q_1, \ldots, q_n$" will *omit* how some members of the full infinite regress are epistemically tied to belief of p. But that seems irrelevant given the fact that for each member r of the regress, such that r is tied epistemically to belief of p, there *is* a finite belief of the required sort ("r provides good evidence for p via $q_1, \ldots, q_n$") that ties the two together. Consequently, there is no apparent reason to suppose—even granted the two assumptions—that an infinite regress will require a single belief in an infinite proposition, and not just an infinity of beliefs in increasingly complex finite propositions.

(iv) *Objection:* "But if it is allowed that justification extend infinitely, then it is too easy to justify any belief at all or too many beliefs altogether. Take, for instance, the belief that there are perfect numbers greater than 100. And suppose a mind powerful enough to believe every member of the following sequence:

(σ1) There is at least one perfect number > 100
       There are at least two perfect numbers > 100
             "   three   "   "

If such a believer has no other belief about perfect numbers save the belief that a perfect number is a whole number equal to the sum of its whole factors, then surely he is *not* justified in believing that there are perfect numbers greater than 100. He is quite unjustified in believing any of the members of sequence (σ1), in spite of the fact that a challenge to any can be met easily by appeal to its successor. Thus it cannot be allowed after all that justification extend infinitely, and an infinite regress is ruled out."

Reply: We must distinguish between regresses of justification that are actual and those that are merely potential. The difference is *not* simply that an actual regress is composed of actual beliefs. For even if all members of the regress are actual beliefs, the regress may still be *merely potential* in the following sense: while it is true that *if* any member *were* justified then its predecessors *would* be, still none is in fact justified. Anyone with our series of beliefs about perfect numbers in the absence of any further relevant information on such numbers would presumably be the subject of such a merely potential justificatory regress.

(v) *Objection:* "But defenders of infinite justificatory regresses cannot distinguish thus between actual regresses and those that are merely potential. There is no real distinction to be drawn between the two. For if any regress ever justifies the belief at its head, then every regress must always do so. But obviously not every regress does so (as we have seen by examples), and hence no regress can do so."[4]

Reply: One can in fact distinguish between actual justificatory regresses and merely potential ones, and one can do so both abstractly and by examples.

What an actual regress has that a merely potential regress lacks is the property of containing only justified beliefs as members. What they both share is the property of containing no member without successors that would jointly justify it.

Recall our regress about perfect numbers greater than 100: i.e., there is at least one; there are at least two; there are at least three; and so on. Each member has a successor that would justify it, but no member is justified (in the absence of further information external to the regress). That is therefore a merely potential infinite regress. As for an actual regress, I see no compelling reason why someone (if not a human, then some more powerful mind) could not hold an infinite series of actually justified beliefs as follows:

(σ2) There is at least one even number
       There are at least two even numbers
             "   three   "

It may be that no one could be the subject of such a series of justified beliefs unless he had a proof that there is a denumerable infinity of even numbers. But even if that should be so, it would not take away the fact of the infinite regress of potential justifiers, each of which is actually justified, and hence it would not take away the fact of the actual endless regress of justification.

The objection under discussion is confused, moreover, on the nature of the issue before us. Our question is *not* whether there can be an infinite potential regress, each member of which would be justified by its successors, such that the belief at its head is justified in virtue of its position there, at the head of such a regress. The existence and even the possibility of a single such regress with a belief at its head that was *not* justified in virtue of its position there would of course settle that question in the negative. Our question is, rather, whether there can be an actual infinite regress of justification, and the fact that a belief at the head of a potential regress might still fail to be justified despite its position does *not* settle this question. For even if there can be a merely potential regress with an unjustified belief at its head, that leaves open the possibility of an infinite regress, each member of which is justified by its immediate successors working jointly, where every member of the regress is in addition actually justified.

6.   THE RELATION OF JUSTIFICATION AND FOUNDATIONALIST STRATEGY

The foregoing discussion is predicated on a simple conception of justification such that a set of beliefs ß conditionally justifies (*would* justify) a belief X iff, necessarily, if all members of ß are justified then X is also justified (if it exists). The fact that on such a conception of justification actual endless regresses—such as (σ2)—seem quite possible blocks a straightforward regress argument in favor of foundations. For it shows that an actual infinite regress cannot be dismissed out of hand.

Perhaps the foundationalist could introduce some relation of justification—presumably more complex and yet to be explicated—with respect to which it could be argued more plausibly that an actual endless regress is out of the question.

There is, however, a more straightforward strategy open to the foundationalist. For he *need not* object to the possibility of an endless regress of justification. His essential creed is the more positive belief that every justified belief must be at the head of a termi-

nating regress. Fortunately, to affirm the universal necessity of a terminating regress is *not* to deny the bare possibility of a nonterminating regress. For a single belief can trail at once regresses of both sorts: one terminating and one not. Thus the proof of the denumerably infinite cardinality of the set of evens may provide for a powerful enough intellect a *terminating* regress for each member of the *endless* series of justified beliefs:

(σ2)   There is at least one even number
There are at least two even numbers
"   three   "

At the same time, it is obvious that each member of (σ2) lies at the head of an actual endless regress of justification, on the assumption that each member is conditionally justified by its successor, which is in turn actually justified.

"Thank you so much," the foundationalist may sneer, "but I really do not need that kind of help. Nor do I need to be reminded of my essential creed, which I know as well as anyone. Indeed my rejection of endless regresses of justification is only a means of supporting my view that every justified belief must rest ultimately on foundations, on a terminating regress. You reject that strategy much too casually, in my view, but I will not object here. So we put that strategy aside. And now, my helpful friend, just what do we put in its place?"

Fair enough. How then could one show the need for foundations if an endless regress is not ruled out?

7.   TWO LEVELS OF FOUNDATIONALISM

a. We need to distinguish, first, between two forms of foundationalism: one *formal,* the other *substantive.* A type of *formal foundationalism* with respect to a normative or evaluative property φ is the view that the conditions (actual and possible) within which φ would apply can be specified in general, perhaps recursively. *Substantive foundationalism* is only a particular way of doing so, and coherentism is another.

Simpleminded hedonism is the view that:

(i) every instance of pleasure is good,

(ii) everything that causes something good is itself good, and

(iii) everything that is good is so in virtue of (i) or (ii) above.

Simpleminded hedonism is a type of formal foundationalism with respect to the good.

Classical foundationalism in epistemology is the view that:

(i) every infallible, indubitable belief is justified,

(ii) every belief deductively inferred from justified beliefs is itself justified, and

(iii) every belief that is justified is so in virtue of (i) or (ii) above.

Classical foundationalism is a type of formal foundationalism with respect to epistemic justification.

Both of the foregoing theories—simpleminded hedonism in ethics, and classical foundationalism in epistemology—are of course flawed. But they both remain examples of formal foundationalist theories.

b. One way of arguing in favor of formal foundationalism in epistemology is to formulate a convincing formal foundationalist theory of justification. But classical foundationalism in epistemology no longer has for many the attraction that it had for Descartes, nor has any other form of epistemic foundationalism won general acceptance. Indeed epistemic foundationalism has been generally abandoned and its advocates have been put on the defensive by the writings of Wittgenstein, Quine, Sellars, Rescher, Aune, Harman, Lehrer, and others. It is lamentable that in our headlong rush away from foundationalism we have lost sight of the different types of foundationalism (formal vs. substantive) and of the different grades of each type. Too many of us now see it as a blur to be decried and avoided. Thus our present attempt to bring it all into better focus.

c. If we cannot argue from a generally accepted foundationalist theory, what reason is there to accept formal foundationalism? There is no reason to think that the conditions (actual and possible) within which an object is spherical are generally specifiable in non-geometric terms. Why should we think that the con-

ditions (actual and possible) within which a belief is epistemically justified are generally specifiable in nonepistemic terms?

So far as I can see, the main reason for accepting formal foundationalism in the absence of an actual, convincing formal foundationalist theory is the very plausible idea that epistemic justification is subject to the supervenience that characterizes normative and evaluative properties generally. Thus, if a car is a good car, then any physical replica of that car must be just as good. If it is a good car in virtue of such properties as being economical, little prone to break down, etc., then surely any exact replica would share all such properties and would thus be equally good. Similarly, if a belief is epistemically justified, it is presumably so in virtue of its character and its basis in perception, memory, or inference (if any). Thus any belief exactly like it in its character and its basis must be equally well justified. Epistemic justification is supervenient. The justification of a belief supervenes on such properties of it as its content and its basis (if any) in perception, memory, or inference. Such a doctrine of supervenience may itself be considered, with considerable justice, a grade of foundationalism. For it entails that every instance of justified belief is founded on a number of its nonepistemic properties, such as its having a certain basis in perception, memory, and inference, or the like.

But there are higher grades of foundationalism as well. There is, for instance, the doctrine that the conditions (actual and possible) within which a belief would be epistemically justified *can be specified* in general, perhaps recursively (and by reference to such notions as perception, memory, and inference).

A higher grade yet of formal foundationalism requires not only that the conditions for justified belief be specifiable, in general, but that they be specifiable by a simple, comprehensive theory.

d. Simpleminded hedonism is a formal foundationalist theory of the highest grade. If it is true, then in every possible world goodness supervenes on pleasure and causation in a way that is recursively specifiable by means of a very simple theory.

Classical foundationalism in epistemology is also a formal foundationalist theory of the highest grade. If it is true, then in every possible world epistemic justification supervenes on infallibility-cumindubitability and deductive inference in a way that is recursively specifiable by means of a very simple theory.

Surprisingly enough, coherentism may also turn out to be formal foundationalism of the highest grade, provided only that the concept of coherence is itself both simple enough and free of any normative or evaluative admixture. Given these provisos, coherentism explains how epistemic justification supervenes on the nonepistemic in a theory of remarkable simplicity: a belief is justified iff it has a place within a system of beliefs that is coherent and comprehensive.

It is a goal of ethics to explain how the ethical rightness of an action supervenes on what is not ethically evaluative or normative. Similarly, it is a goal of epistemology to explain how the epistemic justification of a belief supervenes on what is not epistemically evaluative or normative. If coherentism aims at this goal, that imposes restrictions on the notion of coherence, which must now be conceived innocent of epistemically evaluative or normative admixture. Its substance must therefore consist of such concepts as explanation, probability, and logical implication—with these conceived, in turn, innocent of normative or evaluative content.

e. We have found a surprising kinship between coherentism and substantive foundationalism, both of which turn out to be varieties of a deeper foundationalism. This deeper foundationalism is applicable to any normative or evaluative property ϕ, and it comes in three grades. The *first* or lowest is simply the supervenience of ϕ; the idea that whenever something has ϕ its having it is founded on certain others of its properties which fall into certain restricted sorts. The *second* is the explicable supervenience of ϕ: the idea that there are formulable principles that explain in quite general terms the conditions (actual and possible) within which ϕ applies. The *third* and highest is the easily explicable supervenience of ϕ: the idea that there is a *simple* theory that explains the conditions within which ϕ applies. We have found the coherentist and the substantive foundationalist sharing a primary goal: the development of a formal foundationalist theory of the highest grade. For they both want a simple theory that explains precisely how epistemic justification supervenes, in general, on the nonepistemic. This insight gives us an unusual view-

point on some recent attacks against foundationalism. Let us now consider as an example a certain simple form of argument distilled from the recent antifoundationalist literature.[5]

8. DOXASTIC ASCENT ARGUMENTS

Several attacks on foundationalism turn on a sort of "doxastic ascent" argument that calls for closer scrutiny.[6] Here are two examples:

A. A belief B is foundationally justified for S in virtue of having property F only if S is justified in believing (1) that most at least of his beliefs with property F are true, and (2) that B has property F. But this means that belief B is not foundational after all, and indeed that the very notion of (empirical) foundational belief is incoherent.

It is sometimes held, for example, that perceptual or observational beliefs are often justified through their origin in the exercise of one or more of our five senses in standard conditions of perception. The advocate of doxastic ascent would raise a vigorous protest, however, for in his view the mere fact of such sensory prompting is impotent to justify the belief prompted.

Such prompting must be coupled with the further belief that one's senses work well in the circumstances, or the like. For we are dealing here with *knowledge,* which requires not blind faith but *reasoned* trust. But now surely the further belief about the reliability of one's senses itself cannot rest on blind faith but requires its own backing of reasons, and we are off on the regress.

B. A belief B of proposition P is foundationally justified for S only if S is justified in believing that there are no factors present that would cause him to make mistakes on the matter of the proposition P. But, again, this means that belief B is not foundational after all and indeed that the notion of (empirical) foundational belief is incoherent.

From the vantage point of formal foundationalism, neither of these arguments seems conclusive. In the first place, as we have seen, what makes a belief foundational (formally) is its having a property that is nonepistemic (not evaluative in the epistemic or cognitive mode), and does not involve inference from other beliefs, but guarantees, via a necessary principle, that the belief in question is justified. A belief B is made foundational by having some such nonepistemic property that yields its justification. Take my belief that I am in pain in a context where it is caused by my being in pain. The property that my belief then has, of being a self-attribution of pain caused by one's own pain, is, let us suppose, a nonepistemic property that yields the justification of any belief that has it. So my belief that I am in pain is in that context foundationally justified. Along with my belief that I am in pain, however, there come other beliefs that are equally well justified, such as my belief that someone is in pain. Thus I am foundationally justified in believing that I am in pain only if I am justified in believing that someone is in pain. Those who object to foundationalism as in A or B above are hence mistaken in thinking that their premises would refute foundationalism. The fact is that they would not touch it. For a belief is no less foundationally justified for having its justification yoked to that of another closely related belief.

The advocate of arguments like A and B must apparently strengthen his premises. He must apparently claim that the beliefs whose justification is entailed by the foundationally justified status of belief B must in some sense function as a *necessary source* of the justification of B. And this would of course preclude giving B foundationally justified status. For if the *being justified* of those beliefs is an *essential* part of the source of the justification of B, then it is ruled out that there be a wholly *nonepistemic* source of B's justification.

That brings us to a second point about A and B, for it should now be clear that these cannot be selectively aimed at foundationalism. In particular, they seem neither more nor less valid objections to coherentism than to foundationalism, or so I will now argue about each of them in turn.

(A′) A belief X is justified for S in virtue of membership in a coherent set only if S is justified in believing (1) that most at least of his

beliefs with the property of thus cohering are true, and (2) that X has that property.

Any coherentist who accepts A seems bound to accept A′. For what could he possibly appeal to as a relevant difference? But A′ is a quicksand of endless depth. (How is he justified in believing A′(1)? Partly through justified belief that *it* coheres? And what would justify *this*? And so on. . . .)

(B′) A belief X is justified for S only if S is justified in believing that there are no factors present that would cause him to make mistakes on the subject matter of that belief.

Again, any coherentist who accepts B seems bound to accept B′. But this is just another road to the quicksand. (For S is justified in believing that there are no such factors only if . . . and so on.)

Why are such regresses vicious? The key is again, to my mind, the doctrine of supervenience. Such regresses are vicious because they would be logically incompatible with the supervenience of epistemic justification on such nonepistemic facts as the totality of a subject's beliefs, his cognitive and experiential history, and as many other nonepistemic facts as may seem at all relevant. The idea is that there is a set of such nonepistemic facts surrounding a justified belief such that no belief could possibly have been surrounded by those very facts without being justified. Advocates of A or B run afoul of such supervenience, since they are surely committed to the more general views derivable from either of A or B by deleting "foundationally" from its first sentence. In each case the more general view would then preclude the possibility of supervenience, since it would entail that the source of justification *always* includes an *epistemic* component.

9. COHERENTISM AND SUBSTANTIVE FOUNDATIONALISM

a. The notions of coherentism and substantive foundationalism remain unexplicated. We have relied so far on our intuitive grasp of them. In this section we shall consider reasons for the view that substantive foundationalism is superior to coherentism. To assess these reasons, we need some more explicit account of the difference between the two.

By coherentism we shall mean any view according to which the ultimate sources of justification for any belief lie in relations among that belief and other beliefs of the subject: explanatory relations, perhaps, or relations of probability or logic.

According to substantive foundationalism, as it is to be understood here, there are ultimate sources of justification other than relations among beliefs. Traditionally these additional sources have pertained to the special content of the belief or its special relations to the subjective experience of the believer.

b. The view that justification is a matter of relations among beliefs is open to an objection from alternative coherent systems or detachment from reality, depending on one's perspective. From the latter perspective the body of beliefs is held constant and the surrounding world is allowed to vary; from the former it is the surrounding world that is held constant while the body of beliefs is allowed to vary. In either case, according to the coherentist, there could be no effect on the justification for any belief.

Let us sharpen the question before us as follows. Is there reason to think that there is at least one system B′, alternative to our actual system of beliefs B, such that B′ contains a belief X with the following properties:

(i) in our present nonbelief circumstances we would not be justified in having belief X even if we accepted along with that belief (as our total system of beliefs) the entire belief system B′ in which it is embedded (no matter how acceptance of B′ were brought about); and

(ii) that is so despite the fact that belief X coheres within B′ at least as fully as does some actual justified belief of ours within our actual belief system B (where the justification of that actual justified belief is alleged by the coherentist to derive solely from its coherence within our actual body of beliefs B).

The coherentist is vulnerable to counterexamples of this sort right at the surface of his body of beliefs, where we find beliefs with minimal coherence, whose detachment and replacement with contrary beliefs would have little effect on the coherence of the body. Thus take my belief that I have a headache when I do have a splitting headache, and let us suppose that this *does* cohere within my present body of beliefs. (Thus I have no reason to doubt my present introspective beliefs, and so on. And if my belief does *not* cohere, so much the worse for coherentism, since my belief is surely justified.) Here then we have a perfectly justified or warranted belief. And yet such a belief may well have relevant relations of explanation, logic, or probability with at most a small set of other beliefs of mine at the time: say, that I am not free of headache, that I am in pain, that someone is in pain, and the like. If so, then an equally coherent alternative is not far to seek. Let everything remain constant, *including* the splitting headache, except for the following: replace the belief that I have a headache with the belief that I do *not* have a headache, the belief that I am in pain with the belief that I am *not* in pain, the belief that someone is in pain with the belief that someone is *not* in pain, and so on. I contend that my resulting hypothetical system of beliefs would cohere as fully as does my actual system of beliefs, and yet my hypothetical belief that I do *not* have a headache would not therefore be justified. What makes this difference concerning justification between my actual belief that I have a headache and the hypothetical belief that I am free of headache, each as coherent as the other within its own system, if not the actual splitting headache? But the headache is *not* itself a belief nor a relation among beliefs and is thus in no way constitutive of the internal coherence of my body of beliefs.

Some might be tempted to respond by alleging that one's belief about whether or not one has a headache is always *infallible*. But since we could devise similar examples for the various sensory modalities and propositional attitudes, the response given for the case of headache would have to be generalized. In effect, it would have to cover "peripheral" beliefs generally—beliefs at the periphery of one's body of beliefs, minimally coherent with the rest. These peripheral beliefs would all be said to be infallible. That is, again, a possible response, but it leads to a capitulation by the coherentist to the radical foundationalist on a crucial issue that has traditionally divided them: the infallibility of beliefs about one's own subjective states.

What is more, not all peripheral beliefs are about one's own subjective states. The direct realist is probably right that some beliefs about our surroundings are uninferred and yet justified. Consider my present belief that the table before me is oblong. This presumably coheres with such other beliefs of mine as that the table has the same shape as the piece of paper before me, which is oblong, and a different shape than the window frame here, which is square, and so on. So far as I can see, however, there is no insurmountable obstacle to replacing that whole set of coherent beliefs with an equally coherent set as follows: that the table before me is square, that the table has the same shape as the square window frame, and a different shape than the piece of paper, which is oblong, and so on. The important points are (a) that this replacement may be made without changing the rest of one's body of beliefs or any aspect of the world beyond, including one's present visual experience of something oblong, not square, as one looks at the table before one; and (b) that is so, in part, because of the fact (c) that the subject need not have any beliefs about his present sensory experience.

Some might be tempted to respond by alleging that one's present experience is *self-intimating,* i.e., always necessarily taken note of and reflected in one's beliefs. Thus if anyone has visual experience of something oblong, then he believes that he has such experience. But this would involve a further important concession by the coherentist to the radical foundationalist, who would have been granted two of his most cherished doctrines: the infallibility of introspective belief and the self-intimation of experience.

10. THE FOUNDATIONALIST'S DILEMMA

The antifoundationalist zeal of recent years has left several forms of foundationalism standing. These all share the conviction that a belief can be justified not only by its coherence within a comprehensive system but also by an appropriate combination of observational content and origin in the use of the senses in standard conditions. What follows presents a dilemma for any foundationalism based on any such idea.

a. We may surely suppose that beings with observational mechanisms radically unlike ours might also have knowledge of their environment. (That seems possible even if the radical difference in observational mechanisms precludes overlap in substantive concepts and beliefs.)

b. Let us suppose that there is such a being, for whom experience of type ϕ (of which we have no notion) has a role with respect to his beliefs of type ϕ analogous to the role that our visual experience has with respect to our visual beliefs. Thus we might have a schema such as the following:

Human	Extraterrestrial being
Visual experience	ϕ experience
Experience of something red	Experience of something F
Belief that there is something red before one	Belief that there is something F before one

c. It is often recognized that our visual experience intervenes in two ways with respect to our visual beliefs: as cause and as justification. But these are not wholly independent. Presumably, the justification of the belief that something here is red derives at least in part from the fact that it originates in a visual experience of something red that takes place in normal circumstances.

d. Analogously, the extraterrestrial belief that something here has the property of being F might be justified partly by the fact that it originates in a ϕ experience of something F that takes place in normal circumstances.

e. A simple question presents the foundationalist's dilemma: regarding the epistemic principle that underlies our justification for believing that something here is red on the basis of our visual experience of something red, is it proposed as a fundamental principle or as a derived generalization? Let us compare the famous Principle of Utility of value theory, according to which it is best for that to happen which, of all the possible alternatives in the circumstances, would bring with it into the world the greatest balance of pleasure over pain, joy over sorrow, happiness over unhappiness, content over discontent, or the like. Upon this fundamental principle one may then base various generalizations, rules of thumb, and maxims of public health, nutrition, legislation, etiquette, hygiene, and so on. But these are all then derived generalizations which rest for their validity on the fundamental principle. Similarly, one may also ask, with respect to the generalizations advanced by our foundationalist, whether these are proposed as fundamental principles or as derived maxims or the like. This sets him face to face with a dilemma, each of whose alternatives is problematic. If his proposals are meant to have the status of secondary or derived maxims, for instance, then it would be quite unphilosophical to stop there. Let us turn, therefore, to the other alternative.

f. On reflection it seems rather unlikely that epistemic principles for the justification of observational beliefs by their origin in sensory experience could have a status more fundamental than that of derived generalizations. For by granting such principles fundamental status we would open the door to a multitude of equally basic principles with no unifying factor. There would be some for vision, some for hearing, etc., without even mentioning the corresponding extraterrestrial principles.

g. It may appear that there is after all an idea, however, that unifies our multitude of principles. For they all involve sensory experience and sensible characteristics. But what is a sensible characteristic? Aristotle's answer appeals to examples: colors, shapes, sounds, and so on. Such a notion might enable us to unify perceptual epistemic principles under some more fundamental principle such as the following:

If σ is a sensible characteristic, then the belief that there is something with σ before one is (prima facie) justified if it is based on a visual experience of something with σ in conditions that are normal with respect to σ.

h. There are at least two difficulties with such a suggestion, however, and neither one can be brushed aside easily. First, it is not clear that we can have a viable notion of sensible characteristic on the basis of examples so diverse as colors, shapes, tones, odors, and so on. Second, the authority of such a principle apparently derives from contingent circumstances concerning the reliability of beliefs prompted by sensory experiences of certain sorts. According to the foundationalist, our visual beliefs are justified by their origin in our visual experience or the like. Would such beliefs be equally well justified in a world where beliefs with such an origin were nearly always false?

i. In addition, finally, even if we had a viable notion of such characteristics, it is not obvious that fundamental knowledge of reality would have to derive causally or otherwise from sensory experience of such characteristics. How could one impose reasonable limits on extraterrestrial mechanisms for noninferential acquisition of beliefs? Is it not possible that such mechanisms need not always function through sensory experience of any sort? Would such beings necessarily be denied any knowledge of their surroundings and indeed of any contingent spatio-temporal fact? Let us suppose them to possess a complex system of true beliefs concerning their surroundings, the structures below the surface of things, exact details of history and geography, all constituted by concepts none of which corresponds to any of our sensible characteristics. What then? Is it not possible that their basic beliefs should all concern fields of force, waves, mathematical structures, and numerical assignments to variables in several dimensions? This is no doubt an exotic notion, but even so it still seems conceivable. And if it is in fact possible, what then shall we say of the noninferential beliefs of such beings? Would we have to concede the existence of special epistemic principles that can validate their noninferential beliefs? Would it not be preferable to formulate more abstract principles that can cover both human and extraterrestrial foundations? If such more abstract principles are in fact accessible, then the less general principles that define the human foundations and those that define the extraterrestrial foundations are both derived principles whose validity depends on that of the more abstract principles. In this the human and extraterrestrial epistemic principles would resemble rules of good nutrition for an infant and an adult. The infant's rules would of course be quite unlike those valid for the adult. But both would still be based on a more fundamental principle that postulates the ends of well-being and good health. What more fundamental principles might support both human and extraterrestrial knowledge in the way that those concerning good health and well-being support rules of nutrition for both the infant and the adult?

11. RELIABILISM: AN ETHICS OF MORAL VIRTUES AND AN EPISTEMOLOGY OF INTELLECTUAL VIRTUES

In what sense is the doctor attending Frau Hitler justified in performing an action that brings with it far less value than one of its accessible alternatives? According to one promising idea, the key is to be found in the rules that he embodies through stable dispositions. His action is the result of certain stable virtues, and there are no equally virtuous alternate *dispositions* that, given his cognitive limitations, he might have embodied with equal or better total consequences, and that would have led him to infanticide in the circumstances. The important move for our purpose is the stratification of justification. Primary justification attaches to virtues and other dispositions, to stable dispositions to act, through their greater contribution of value when compared with alternatives. Secondary justification attaches to particular acts in virtue of their source in virtues or other such justified dispositions.

The same strategy may also prove fruitful in epistemology. Here primary justification would apply to *intellectual* virtues, to stable dispositions for belief acquisition, through their greater contribution toward getting us to the truth. Secondary justification would then attach to particular beliefs in virtue of their source in intellectual virtues or other such justified dispositions.[7]

That raises parallel questions for ethics and epistemology. We need to consider more carefully the concept of a virtue and the distinction between moral and intellectual virtues. In epistemology, there is reason to think that the most useful and illuminating notion of intellectual virtue will prove broader than our tradition would suggest and must give due weight not only to the subject and his intrinsic nature but also to his environment and to his epistemic community. This is a large topic, however, to which I hope some of us will turn with more space, and insight, than I can now command.

12. SUMMARY

1. *Two assumptions:* (A1) that for a belief to constitute knowledge it must be (a) true and (b) justified; and (A2) that the justification relevant to whether or not one knows is a sort of epistemic or theoretical justification to be distinguished from its practical counterpart.

2. *Knowledge and criteria.* Particularism is distinguished from methodism: the first gives priority to particular examples of knowledge over general methods of criteria, whereas the second reverses that order. The methodism of Descartes leads him to an elaborate dogmatism whereas that of Hume leads him to a very simple skepticism. The particularist is, of course, antiskeptical on principle.

3. *Two metaphors: the raft and the pyramid.* For the foundationalist every piece of knowledge stands at the apex of a pyramid that rests on stable and secure foundations whose stability and security does not derive from the upper stories or sections. For the coherentist a body of knowledge is a free-floating raft every plank of which helps directly or indirectly to

keep all the others in place, and no plank of which would retain its status with no help from the others.

4. *A coherentist critique of foundationalism.* No mental state can provide a foundation for empirical knowledge. For if such a state is propositional, then it is fallible and hence no secure foundation. But if it is *not* propositional, then how can it possibly serve as a foundation for belief? How can one infer or justify anything on the basis of a state that, having no propositional content, must be logically dumb? An analogy with ethics suggests a reason to reject this dilemma. Other reasons are also advanced and discussed.

5. *The regress argument.* In defending his position, the foundationalist often attempts to rule out the very possibility of an infinite regress of justification (which leads him to the necessity for a foundation). Some of his arguments to that end are examined.

6. *The relation of justification and foundationalist strategy.* An alternative foundationalist strategy is exposed, one that does not require ruling out the possibility of an infinite regress of justification.

7. *Two levels of foundationalism.* Substantive foundationalism is distinguished from formal foundationalism, three grades of which are exposed: first, the supervenience of epistemic justification; second, its explicable supervenience; and, third, its supervenience explicable by means of a simple theory. There turns out to be a surprising kinship between coherentism and substantive foundationalism, both of which aim at a formal foundationalism of the highest grade, at a theory of the greatest simplicity that explains how epistemic justification supervenes on nonepistemic factors.

8. *Doxastic ascent arguments.* The distinction between formal and substantive foundationalism provides an unusual viewpoint on some recent attacks against foundationalism. We consider doxastic ascent arguments as an example.

9. *Coherentism and substantive foundationalism.* It is argued that substantive foundationalism is superior since coherentism is unable to account adequately for the epistemic status of beliefs at the "periphery" of a body of beliefs.

10. *The foundationalist's dilemma.* All foundationalism based on sense experience is subject to a fatal dilemma.

11. *Reliabilism.* An alternative to foundationalism of sense experience is sketched.

NOTES

1. But Descartes's methodism was at most partial. James Van Cleve has supplied the materials for a convincing argument that the way out of the Cartesian circle is through a particularism of basic knowledge. (See James Van Cleve, "Foundationalism, Epistemic Principles, and the Cartesian Circle," *Philosophical Review* 88 (1979): 55–91.) But this is, of course, compatible with methodism on inferred knowledge. Whether Descartes subscribed to such methodism is hard (perhaps impossible) to determine, since in the end he makes room for all the kinds of knowledge required by particularism. But his language when he introduces the method of hyperbolic doubt, and the order in which he proceeds, suggest that he did subscribe to such methodism.

2. Cf. Laurence Bonjour, "The Coherence Theory of Truth," *Philosophical Studies* 30 (1976):281–312; and, especially, Michael Williams, *Groundless Belief* (New Haven: Yale University Press, 1977); and L. Bonjour, "Can Empirical Knowledge Have a Foundation?" *American Philosophical Quarterly* 15 (1978): 1–15.

3. Cf. Richard Foley, "Inferential Justification and the Infinite Regress," *American Philosophical Quarterly* 15 (1978): 311–16.

4. Cf. John Post, "Infinite Regresses of Justification and of Explanation," *Philosophical Studies* 38 (1980): 31–52.

5. The argument of this whole section is developed in greater detail in my paper "The Foundations of Foundationalism," *Nous* 14 (1980): 547–65; see Chapter 9 herein.

6. For some examples of the influence of doxastic ascent arguments, see Wilfrid Sellars's writing in epistemology: e.g., "Empiricism and the Philosophy of Mind," in *Science, Perception and Reality* (London: Routledge & Kegan Paul, 1963), ch. 5, especially section VIII, and particularly p. 168. Also I. T. Oakley, "An Argument for Skepticism Concerning Justified Beliefs," *American Philosophical Quarterly* 13 (1976): 221–8; and Bonjour, "Can Empirical Knowledge Have a Foundation?"

7. This puts in a more traditional perspective the contemporary effort to develop a "causal theory of knowing." From our viewpoint, this effort is better understood not as an attempt to *define* propositional knowledge but as an attempt to formulate fundamental principles of justification.

Cf. D. Armstrong, *Belief, Truth and Knowledge* (Cambridge, 1973); and that of F. Dretske, A. Goldman, and M. Swain, whose relevant already published work is included in *Essays on Knowledge and Justification,* ed. G. Pappas and M. Swain (Ithaca and London, 1978). But the theory is still under development by Goldman and Swain, who have reached general conclusions about it similar to those suggested here, though not necessarily—so far as I know—for the same reasons or in the same overall context.

Elusive Knowledge

DAVID LEWIS

David Lewis (1941–2001) was Class of 1943 University Professor of Philosophy at Princeton University. His contributions spanned philosophical logic, philosophy of language, philosophy of mind, philosophy of science, metaphysics, and epistemology. In *On the Plurality of Worlds,* he defended his challenging metaphysical position, "modal realism." He was also the author of the books *Convention, Counterfactuals, Parts of Classes,* and several volumes of collected papers.

We know a lot. I know what food penguins eat. I know that phones used to ring, but nowadays squeal, when someone calls up. I know that Essendon won the 1993 Grand Final. I know that here is a hand, and here is another.

We have all sorts of everyday knowledge, and we have it in abundance. To doubt that would be absurd. At any rate, to doubt it in any serious and lasting way would be absurd; and even philosophical and temporary doubt, under the influence of argument, is more than a little peculiar. It is a Moorean fact that we know a lot. It is one of those things that we know better than we know the premises of any philosophical argument to the contrary.

Besides knowing a lot that is everyday and trite, I myself think that we know a lot that is interesting and esoteric and controversial. We know a lot about things unseen: tiny particles and pervasive fields, not to mention one another's underwear. Sometimes we even know what an author meant by his writings. But on these questions, let us agree to disagree peacefully with the champions of "post-knowledgeism." The most trite and ordinary parts of our knowledge will be problem enough.

For no sooner do we engage in epistemology—the systematic philosophical examination of knowledge—than we meet a compelling argument that we know next to nothing. The sceptical argument is nothing new or fancy. It is just this: it seems as if knowledge must be by definition infallible. If you claim that S knows that P, and yet you grant that S cannot eliminate a certain possibility in which not-P, it certainly seems as if you have granted that S does not after all know that P. To speak of fallible knowledge, of knowledge despite uneliminated possibilities of error, just *sounds* contradictory.

Blind Freddy can see where this will lead. Let your paranoid fantasies rip—CIA plots, hallucinogens in the tap water, conspiracies to deceive, old Nick himself—and soon you find that uneliminated

Reprinted from *Australasian Journal of Philosophy, 74,* (1996), by permission of the *Australasian Journal of Philosophy.*

possibilities of error are everywhere. Those possibilities of error are farfetched, of course, but possibilities all the same. They bite into even our most everyday knowledge. We never have infallible knowledge.

Never—well, hardly ever. Some say we have infallible knowledge of a few simple, axiomatic necessary truths; and of our own present experience. They say that I simply cannot be wrong that a part of a part of something is itself a part of that thing; or that it seems to me now (as I sit here at the keyboard) exactly as if I am hearing clicking noises on top of a steady whirring. Some say so. Others deny it. No matter; let it be granted, at least for the sake of the argument. It is not nearly enough. If we have only that much infallible knowledge, yet knowledge is by definition infallible, then we have very little knowledge indeed—not the abundant everyday knowledge we thought we had. That is still absurd.

So we know a lot; knowledge must be infallible; yet we have fallible knowledge or none (or next to none). We are caught between the rock of fallibilism and the whirlpool of scepticism. Both are mad!

Yet fallibilism is the less intrusive madness. It demands less frequent corrections of what we want to say. So, if forced to choose, I choose fallibilism. (And so say all of us.) We can get used to it, and some of us have done. No joy there—we know that people can get used to the most crazy philosophical sayings imaginable. If you are a contented fallibilist, I implore you to be honest, be naive, hear it afresh. "He knows, yet he has not eliminated all possibilities of error." Even if you've numbed your ears, doesn't this overt, explicit fallibilism *still* sound wrong?

Better fallibilism than scepticism; but it would be better still to dodge the choice. I think we can. We will be alarmingly close to the rock, and also alarmingly close to the whirlpool, but if we steer with care, we can—just barely—escape them both.

Maybe epistemology is the culprit. Maybe this extraordinary pastime robs us of our knowledge. Maybe we do know a lot in daily life; but maybe when we look hard at our knowledge, it goes away. But only when we look at it harder than the sane ever do in daily life; only when we let our paranoid fantasies rip. That is when we are forced to admit that there always are uneliminated possibilities of error, so that we have fallible knowledge or none.

Much that we say is context-dependent, in simple ways or subtle ways. Simple: "it's evening" is truly said when, and only when, it is said in the evening. Subtle: it could well be true, and not just by luck, that Essendon played rottenly, the Easybeats played brilliantly, yet Essendon won. Different contexts evoke different standards of evaluation. Talking about the Easybeats we apply lax standards, else we could scarcely distinguish their better days from their worse ones. In talking about Essendon, no such laxity is required. Essendon won because play that is rotten by demanding standards suffices to beat play that is brilliant by lax standards.

Maybe ascriptions of knowledge are subtly context-dependent, and maybe epistemology is a context that makes them go false. Then epistemology would be an investigation that destroys its own subject matter. If so, the sceptical argument might be flawless, when we engage in epistemology—and only then![1]

If you start from the ancient idea that justification is the mark that distinguishes knowledge from mere opinion (even true opinion), then you well might conclude that ascriptions of knowledge are context-dependent because standards for adequate justification are context-dependent. As follows: opinion, even if true, deserves the name of knowledge only if it is adequately supported by reasons; to deserve that name in the especially demanding context of epistemology, the arguments from supporting reasons must be especially watertight; but the special standards of justification that this special context demands never can be met (well, hardly ever). In the strict context of epistemology we know nothing, yet in laxer contexts we know a lot.

But I myself cannot subscribe to this account of the context-dependence of knowledge, because I question its starting point. I don't agree that the mark of knowledge is justification.[2] First, because justification is not sufficient: your true opinion that you will lose the lottery isn't knowledge, whatever the odds. Suppose you know that it is a fair lottery with one winning ticket and many losing tickets, and you know how many losing tickets there are. The greater the number of losing tickets, the better is your justification for believing you will lose. Yet there is no number great enough to transform your fallible opinion into knowledge—after all, you just might win. No justification is good enough—or none short of a watertight deductive argument, and all but the sceptics will agree that this is too much to demand.[3]

Second, because justification is not always necessary. What (non-circular) argument supports our reliance on perception, on memory, and on testimony?[4] And yet we do gain knowledge by these means. And sometimes, far from having supporting arguments, we don't even know how we know. We once had evidence, drew conclusions, and thereby gained knowledge; now we have forgotten our reasons, yet still we retain our knowledge. Or we know the name that goes with the face, or the sex of the chicken, by relying on subtle visual cues, without knowing what those cues may be.

The link between knowledge and justification must be broken. But if we break that link, then it is not—or not entirely, or not exactly—by raising the standards of justification that epistemology destroys knowledge. I need some different story.

To that end, I propose to take the infallibility of knowledge as my starting point.[5] Must infallibilist epistemology end in scepticism? Not quite. Wait and see. Anyway, here is the definition. Subject S *knows* proposition P iff P holds in every possibility left uneliminated by S's evidence; equivalently, iff S's evidence eliminates every possibility in which not-P.

The definition is short, the commentary upon it is longer. In the first place, there is the proposition, P. What I choose to call "propositions" are individuated coarsely, by necessary equivalence. For instance, there is only one necessary proposition. It holds in every possibility; hence in every possibility left uneliminated by S's evidence, no matter who S may be and no matter what his evidence may be. So the necessary proposition is known always and everywhere. Yet this known proposition may go unrecognised when presented in impenetrable linguistic disguise, say as the proposition that every even number is the sum of two primes. Likewise, the known proposition that I have two hands may go unrecognised when presented as the proposition that the number of my hands is the least number n such that every even number is the sum of n primes. (Or if you doubt the

necessary existence of numbers, switch to an example involving equivalence by logic alone.) These problems of disguise shall not concern us here. Our topic is modal, not hyperintensional, epistemology.[6]

Next, there are the possibilities. We needn't enter here into the question whether these are concreta, abstract constructions, or abstract simples. Further, we needn't decide whether they must always be maximally specific possibilities, or whether they need only be specific enough for the purpose at hand. A possibility will be specific enough if it cannot be split into subcases in such a way that anything we have said about possibilities, or anything we are going to say before we are done, applies to some subcases and not to others. For instance, it should never happen that proposition P holds in some but not all subcases; or that some but not all sub-cases are eliminated by S's evidence.

But we do need to stipulate that they are not just possibilities as to how the whole world is; they also include possibilities as to which part of the world is oneself, and as to when it now is. We need these possibilities *de se et nunc* because the propositions that may be known include propositions *de se et nunc.*[7] Not only do I know that there are hands in this world somewhere and somewhen. I know that *I* have hands, or anyway I have them *now.* Such propositions aren't just made true or made false by the whole world once and for all. They are true for some of us and not for others, or true at some times and not others, or both.

Further, we cannot limit ourselves to "real" possibilities that conform to the actual laws of nature, and maybe also to actual past history. For propositions about laws and history are contingent, and may or may not be known.

Neither can we limit ourselves to "epistemic" possibilities for S—possibilities that S does not know not to obtain. That would drain our definition of content. Assume only that knowledge is closed under strict implication. (We shall consider the merits of this assumption later.) Remember that we are not distinguishing between equivalent propositions. Then knowledge of a conjunction is equivalent to knowledge of every conjunct. P is the conjunction of all propositions not-W, where W is a possibility in which not-P. That suffices to yield an equivalence: S knows that P iff, for every possibility W in which not-P, S knows that not-*W*. Contraposing and cancelling a double negation: iff every possibility which *S* does not know not to obtain is one in which *P*. For short: iff *P* holds throughout *S*'s epistemic possibilities. Yet to get this far, we need no substantive definition of knowledge at all! To turn this into a substantive definition, in fact the very definition we gave before, we need to say one more thing: *S*'s epistemic possibilities are just those possibilities that are uneliminated by *S*'s evidence.

So, next, we need to say what it means for a possibility to be eliminated or not. Here I say that the uneliminated possibilities are those in which the subject's entire perceptual experience and memory are just as they actually are. There is one possibility that actually obtains (for the subject and at the time in question); call it *actuality*. Then a possibility *W* is *uneliminated* iff the subject's perceptual experience and memory in *W* exactly match his perceptual experience and memory in actuality. (If you want to include other alleged forms of basic evidence, such as the evidence of our extrasensory faculties, or an innate disposition to believe in God, be my guest. If they exist, they should be included. If not, no harm done if we have included them conditionally.)

Note well that we do not need the "pure sense-datum language" and the "incorrigible protocol statements" that for so long bedevilled foundationalist epistemology. It matters not at all whether there are words to capture the subject's perceptual and memory evidence, nothing more and nothing less. If there are such words, it matters not at all whether the subject can hit upon them. The given does not consist of basic axioms to serve as premises in subsequent arguments. Rather, it consists of a match between possibilities.

When perceptual experience *E* (or memory) eliminates a possibility *W*, that is not because the propositional content of the experience conflicts with *W*. (Not even if it is the narrow content.) The propositional content of our experience could, after all, be false. Rather, it is the existence of the experience that conflicts with *W*: *W* is a possibility in which the subject is not having experience *E*. Else we would need to tell some fishy story of how the experience has some sort of infallible, ineffable, purely phenomenal propositional content. . . . Who needs that? Let *E*

have propositional content *P*. Suppose even—something I take to be an open question—that *E* is, in some sense, fully characterized by *P*. Then I say that *E* eliminates *W* iff *W* is a possibility in which the subject's experience or memory has content different from *P*. I do *not* say that *E* eliminates *W* iff *W* is a possibility in which *P* is false.

Maybe not every kind of sense perception yields experience; maybe, for instance, the kinaesthetic sense yields not its own distinctive sort of sense-experience but only spontaneous judgements about the position of one's limbs. If this is true, then the thing to say is that kinaesthetic evidence eliminates all possibilities except those that exactly resemble actuality with respect to the subject's spontaneous kinaesthetic judgements. In saying this, we would treat kinaesthetic evidence more on the model of memory than on the model of more typical senses.

Finally, we must attend to the word "every." What does it mean to say that every possibility in which not-*P* is eliminated? An idiom of quantification, like "every," is normally restricted to some limited domain. If I say that every glass is empty, so it's time for another round, doubtless I and my audience are ignoring most of all the glasses there are in the whole wide world throughout all of time. They are outside the domain. They are irrelevant to the truth of what was said.

Likewise, if I say that every uneliminated possibility is one in which *P*, or words to that effect, I am doubtless ignoring some of all the uneliminated alternative possibilities that there are. They are outside the domain, they are irrelevant to the truth of what was said.

But, of course, I am not entitled to ignore just any possibility I please. Else true ascriptions of knowledge, whether to myself or to others, would be cheap indeed. I may properly ignore some uneliminated possibilities; I may not properly ignore others. Our definition of knowledge requires a sotto voce proviso. *S knows* that *P* iff *S*'s evidence eliminates every possibility in which not-*P*—Psst!—except for those possibilities that we are properly ignoring.

Unger suggests an instructive parallel.[8] Just as *P* is known iff there are no uneliminated possibilities of error, so likewise a surface is flat iff there are no bumps on it. We must add the proviso: Psst!— except for those bumps that we are properly ignoring. Else we will conclude, absurdly, that nothing is flat. (Simplify by ignoring departures from flatness that consist of gentle curvature.)

We can restate the definition. Say that we *presuppose* proposition *Q* iff we ignore all possibilities in which not-*Q*. To close the circle: we *ignore* just those possibilities that falsify our presuppositions. *Proper* presupposition corresponds, of course, to proper ignoring. Then *S* knows that *P* iff *S*'s evidence eliminates every possibility in which not-*P*—Psst!— except for those possibilities that conflict with our proper presuppositions.[9]

The rest of (modal) epistemology examines the sotto voce proviso. It asks: what may we properly presuppose in our ascriptions of knowledge? Which of all the uneliminated alternative possibilities may not properly be ignored? Which ones are the "relevant alternatives"?—relevant, that is, to what the subject does and doesn't know?[10] In reply, we can list several rules.[11] We begin with three prohibitions: rules to tell us what possibilities we may not properly ignore.

First, there is the *Rule of Actuality*. The possibility that actually obtains is never properly ignored; actuality is always a relevant alternative; nothing false may properly be presupposed. It follows that only what is true is known, wherefore we did not have to include truth in our definition of knowledge. The rule is "externalist"—the subject himself may not be able to tell what is properly ignored. In judging which of his ignorings are proper, hence what he knows, we judge his success in knowing—not how well he tried.

When the Rule of Actuality tells us that actuality may never be properly ignored, we can ask: *whose* actuality? Ours, when we ascribe knowledge or ignorance to others? Or the subject's? In simple cases, the question is silly. (In fact, it sounds like the sort of pernicious nonsense we would expect from someone who mixes up what is true with what is believed.) There is just one actual world, we the ascribers live in that world, the subject lives there too, so the subject's actuality is the same as ours.

But there are other cases, less simple, in which the question makes perfect sense and needs an answer.

Someone may or may not know who he is; someone may or may not know what time it is. Therefore I insisted that the propositions that may be known must include propositions *de se et nunc;* and likewise that the possibilities that may be eliminated or ignored must include possibilities *de se et nunc.* Now we have a good sense in which the subject's actuality may be different from ours. I ask today what Fred knew yesterday. In particular, did he then know who he was? Did he know what day it was? Fred's actuality is the possibility *de se et nunc* of being Fred on September 19th at such-and-such possible world; whereas my actuality is the possibility *de se et nunc* of being David on September 20th at such-and-such world. So far as the world goes, there is no difference: Fred and I are worldmates, his actual world is the same as mine. But when we build subject and time into the possibilities *de se et nunc,* then his actuality yesterday does indeed differ from mine today.

What is more, we sometimes have occasion to ascribe knowledge to those who are off at other possible worlds. I didn't read the newspaper yesterday. What would I have known if I had read it? More than I do in fact know. (More and less: I do in fact know that I left the newspaper unread, but if I had read it, I would not have known that I had left it unread.) I-who-did-not-read-the-newspaper am here at this world, ascribing knowledge and ignorance. The subject to whom I am ascribing that knowledge and ignorance, namely I-as-I-would-have-been-if-I-had-read-the-newspaper, is at a different world. The worlds differ in respect at least of a reading of the newspaper. Thus the ascriber's actual world is not the same as the subject's. (I myself think that the ascriber and the subject are two different people: the subject is the ascriber's otherworldly counterpart. But even if you think the subject and the ascriber are the same identical person, you must still grant that this person's actuality qua subject differs from his actuality qua ascriber.)

Or suppose we ask modal questions about the subject: what must he have known, what might he have known? Again we are considering the subject as he is not here, but off at other possible worlds. Likewise if we ask questions about knowledge of knowledge: what does he (or what do we) know that he knows?

So the question "whose actuality?" is not a silly question after all. And when the question matters, as it does in the cases just considered, the right answer is that it is the subject's actuality, not the ascriber's, that never can be properly ignored.

Next, there is the *Rule of Belief.* A possibility that the subject believes to obtain is not properly ignored, whether or not he is right to so believe. Neither is one that he ought to believe to obtain—one that evidence and arguments justify him in believing—whether or not he does so believe.

That is rough. Since belief admits of degree, and since some possibilities are more specific than others, we ought to reformulate the rule in terms of degree of belief, compared to a standard set by the unspecificity of the possibility in question. A possibility may not be properly ignored if the subject gives it, or ought to give it, a degree of belief that is sufficiently high, and high not just because the possibility in question is unspecific.

How high is "sufficiently high"? That may depend on how much is at stake. When error would be especially disastrous, few possibilities may be properly ignored. Then even quite a low degree of belief may be "sufficiently high" to bring the Rule of Belief into play. The jurors know that the accused is guilty only if his guilt has been proved beyond reasonable doubt.[12]

Yet even when the stakes are high, some possibilities still may be properly ignored. Disastrous though it would be to convict an innocent man, still the jurors may properly ignore the possibility that it was the dog, marvellously well-trained, that fired the fatal shot. And, unless they are ignoring other alternatives more relevant than that, they may rightly be said to know that the accused is guilty as charged. Yet if there had been reason to give the dog hypothesis a slightly less negligible degree of belief—if the world's greatest dog-trainer had been the victim's mortal enemy—then the alternative would be relevant after all.

This is the only place where belief and justification enter my story. As already noted, I allow justified true belief without knowledge, as in the case of your belief that you will lose the lottery. I allow knowl-edge without justification, in the cases of face recognition and chicken sexing. I even allow knowledge without belief, as in the case of the timid student who knows the answer but has no confidence that he has it right, and so does not believe what he knows.[13] Therefore any proposed converse to the Rule of Belief should be rejected. A possibility that the subject does not believe to a sufficient degree, and ought not to believe to a sufficient degree, may nevertheless be a relevant alternative and not properly ignored.

Next, there is the *Rule of Resemblance.* Suppose one possibility saliently resembles another. Then if one of them may not be properly ignored, neither may the other. (Or rather, we should say that if one of them may not properly be ignored *in virtue of rules other than this rule,* then neither may the other. Else nothing could be properly ignored; because enough little steps of resemblance can take us from anywhere to anywhere.) Or suppose one possibility saliently resembles two or more others, one in one respect and another in another, and suppose that each of these may not properly be ignored (in virtue of rules other than this rule). Then these resemblances may have an additive effect, doing more together than any one of them would separately.

We must apply the Rule of Resemblance with care. Actuality is a possibility uneliminated by the subject's evidence. Any other possibility W that is likewise uneliminated by the subject's evidence thereby resembles actuality in one salient respect: namely, in respect of the subject's evidence. That will be so even if W is in other respects very dissimilar to actuality—even if, for instance, it is a possibility in which the subject is radically deceived by a demon. Plainly, we dare not apply the Rules of Actuality and Resemblance to conclude that any such W is a relevant alternative—that would be capitulation to scepticism. The Rule of Resemblance was never meant to apply to *this* resemblance! We seem to have an ad hoc exception to the Rule, though one that makes good sense in view of the function of attributions of knowledge. What would be better, though, would be to find a way to reformulate the Rule so as to get the needed exception without ad hocery. I do not know how to do this.

It is the Rule of Resemblance that explains why you do not know that you will lose the lottery, no matter what the odds are against you and no matter how sure you should therefore be that you will lose. For every ticket, there is the possibility that it will win. These possibilities are saliently similar to one another: so either every one of them may be properly ignored, or else none may. But one of them may not properly be ignored: the one that actually obtains.

The Rule of Resemblance also is the rule that solves the Gettier problems: other cases of justified true belief that are not knowledge.[14]

(1) I think that Nogot owns a Ford, because I have seen him driving one; but unbeknownst to me he does not own the Ford he drives, or any other Ford. Unbeknownst to me, Havit does own a Ford, though I have no reason to think so because he never drives it, and in fact I have often seen him taking the tram. My justified true belief is that one of the two owns a Ford. But I do not know it; I am right by accident. Diagnosis: I do not know, because I have not eliminated the possibility that Nogot drives a Ford he does not own whereas Havit neither drives nor owns a car. This possibility may not properly be ignored. Because, first, actuality may not properly be ignored; and, second, this possibility saliently resembles actuality. It resembles actuality perfectly so far as Nogot is concerned; and it resembles actuality well so far as Havit is concerned, since it matches actuality both with respect to Havit's carless habits and with respect to the general correlation between carless habits and carlessness. In addition, this possibility saliently resembles a third possibility: one in which Nogot drives a Ford he owns while Havit neither drives nor owns a car. This third possibility may not properly be ignored, because of the degree to which it is believed. This time, the resemblance is perfect so far as Havit is concerned, rather good so far as Nogot is concerned.

(2) The stopped clock is right twice a day. It says 4:39, as it has done for weeks. I look at it at 4:39; by luck I pick up a true belief. I have ignored the uneliminated possibility that I looked at it at 4:22 while it was stopped saying 4:39. That possibility was not properly ignored. It resembles actuality perfectly so far as the stopped clock goes.

(3) Unbeknownst to me, I am travelling in the land of the bogus barns; but my eye falls on one of the few real ones. I don't know that I am seeing a barn, because I may not properly ignore the possibility that I am seeing yet another of the abundant bogus barns. This possibility saliently resembles actuality in respect of the abundance of bogus barns, and the scarcity of real ones, hereabouts.

(4) Donald is in San Francisco, just as I have every reason to think he is. But, bent on deception, he is writing me letters and having them posted to me by his accomplice in Italy. If I had seen the phoney letters, with their Italian stamps and postmarks, I would have concluded that Donald was in Italy. Luckily, I have not yet seen any of them. I ignore the uneliminated possibility that Donald has gone to Italy and is sending me letters from there. But this possibility is not properly ignored, because it resembles actuality both with respect to the fact that the letters are coming to me from Italy and with respect to the fact that those letters come, ultimately, from Donald. So I don't know that Donald is in San Francisco.

Next, there is the *Rule of Reliability*. This time, we have a presumptive rule about what *may* be properly ignored; and it is by means of this rule that we capture what is right about causal or reliabilist theories of knowing. Consider processes whereby information is transmitted to us: perception, memory, and testimony. These processes are fairly reliable.[15] Within limits, we are entitled to take them for granted. We may properly presuppose that they work without a glitch in the case under consideration. Defeasibly—*very* defeasibly!—a possibility in which they fail may properly be ignored.

My visual experience, for instance, depends causally on the scene before my eyes, and what I believe about the scene before my eyes depends in turn on my visual experience. Each dependence covers a wide and varied range of alternatives.[16] Of course, it is possible to hallucinate—even to hallucinate in such a way that all my perceptual experience and memory would be just as they actually are. That possibility never can be eliminated. But it can be ignored. And if it is properly ignored—as it mostly is—then vision gives me knowledge. Sometimes, though, the possibility of hallucination is not properly ignored; for sometimes we really do hallucinate. The Rule of Reliability may be defeated by the Rule of Actuality. Or it may be defeated by the Rules of Actuality and of Resemblance working together, in a Gettier problem: if I am not hallucinating, but unbeknownst to me I live in a world where people mostly do hallucinate and I myself have only narrowly escaped, then the uneliminated possibility of hallucination is too close to actuality to be properly ignored.

We do not, of course, presuppose that nowhere ever is there a failure of, say, vision. The general presupposition that vision is reliable consists, rather, of a standing disposition to presuppose, concerning whatever particular case may be under consideration, that we have no failure in that case.

In similar fashion, we have two permissive *Rules of Method.* We are entitled to presuppose—again, very defeasibly—that a sample is representative; and that the best explanation of our evidence is the true explanation. That is, we are entitled properly to ignore possible failures in these two standard methods of nondeductive inference. Again, the general rule consists of a standing disposition to presuppose reliability in whatever particular case may come before us.

Yet another permissive rule is the *Rule of Conservatism.* Suppose that those around us normally do ignore certain possibilities, and it is common knowledge that they do. (They do, they expect each other to, they expect each other to expect each other to, . . .) Then—again, very defeasibly!—these generally ignored possibilities may properly be ignored. We are permitted, defeasibly, to adopt the usual and mutually expected presuppositions of those around us.

(It is unclear whether we need all four of these permissive rules. Some might be subsumed under others. Perhaps our habits of treating samples as representative, and of inferring to the best explanation, might count as normally reliable processes of transmission of information. Or perhaps we might subsume the Rule of Reliability under the Rule of Conservatism, on the ground that the reliable processes whereby we gain knowledge are familiar, are generally relied upon, and so are generally presupposed to be normally reliable. Then the only extra work done by the

Rule of Reliability would be to cover less familiar—and merely hypothetical?—reliable processes, such as processes that relied on extrasensory faculties. Likewise, *mutatis mutandis,* we might subsume the Rules of Method under the Rule of Conservatism. Or we might instead think to subsume the Rule of Conservatism under the Rule of Reliability, on the ground that what is generally presupposed tends for the most part to be true, and the reliable processes whereby this is so are covered already by the Rule of Reliability. Better redundancy than incompleteness, though. So, leaving the question of redundancy open, I list all four rules.)

Our final rule is the *Rule of Attention.* But it is more a triviality than a rule. When we say that a possibility is properly ignored, we mean exactly that; we do not mean that it *could have been* properly ignored. Accordingly, a possibility not ignored at all is ipso facto not properly ignored. What is and what is not being ignored is a feature of the particular conversational context. No matter how far-fetched a certain possibility may be, no matter how properly we might have ignored it in some other context, if in *this* context we are not in fact ignoring it but attending to it, then for us now it is a relevant alternative. It is in the contextually determined domain. If it is an uneliminated possibility in which not-*P*, then it will do as a counter-example to the claim that *P* holds in every possibility left uneliminated by *S*'s evidence. That is, it will do as a counter-example to the claim that *S* knows that *P.*

Do some epistemology. Let your fantasies rip. Find uneliminated possibilities of error everywhere. Now that you are attending to them, just as I told you to, you are no longer ignoring them, properly or otherwise. So you have landed in a context with an enormously rich domain of potential counter-examples to ascriptions of knowledge. In such an extraordinary context, with such a rich domain, it never can happen (well, hardly ever) that an ascription of knowledge is true. Not an ascription of knowledge to yourself (either to your present self or to your earlier self, untainted by epistemology); and not an ascription of knowledge to others. That is how epistemology destroys knowledge. But it does so only temporarily.

The pastime of epistemology does not plunge us forevermore into its special context. We can still do a lot of proper ignoring, a lot of knowing, and a lot of true ascribing of knowledge to ourselves and others, the rest of the time.

What is epistemology all about? The epistemology we've just been doing, at any rate, soon became an investigation of the ignoring of possibilities. But to investigate the ignoring of them was ipso facto not to ignore them. Unless this investigation of ours was an altogether atypical sample of epistemology, it will be inevitable that epistemology must destroy knowledge. That is how knowledge is elusive. Examine it, and straightway it vanishes.

Is resistance useless? If you bring some hitherto ignored possibility to our attention, then straightway we are not ignoring it at all, so *a fortiori* we are not properly ignoring it. How can this alteration of our conversational state be undone? If you are persistent, perhaps it cannot be undone—at least not so long as you are around. Even if we go off and play backgammon, and afterward start our conversation afresh, you might turn up and call our attention to it all over again.

But maybe you called attention to the hitherto ignored possibility by mistake. You only suggested that we ought to suspect the butler because you mistakenly thought him to have a criminal record. Now that you know he does not—that was the *previous* butler—you wish you had not mentioned him at all. You know as well as we do that continued attention to the possibility you brought up impedes our shared conversational purposes. Indeed, it may be common knowledge between you and us that we would all prefer it if this possibility could be dismissed from our attention. In that case we might quickly strike a tacit agreement to speak just as if we were ignoring it; and after just a little of that, doubtless it really would be ignored.

Sometimes our conversational purposes are not altogether shared, and it is a matter of conflict whether attention to some far-fetched possibility would advance them or impede them. What if some farfetched possibility is called to our attention not by a sceptical philosopher, but by counsel for the defence? We of the jury may wish to ignore it, and wish it had not been mentioned. If we ignored it now, we would bend the rules of cooperative conversation; but we may have good reason to do exactly that. (After all, what matters most to us as jurors is not whether we can truly be said to know; what really matters is what we should believe to what degree, and whether or not we should vote to convict.) We would ignore the far-fetched possibility if we could—but can we? Perhaps at first our attempted ignoring would be make-believe ignoring, or self-deceptive ignoring; later, perhaps, it might ripen into genuine ignoring. But in the meantime, do we know? There may be no definite answer. We are bending the rules, and our practices of context-dependent attributions of knowledge were made for contexts with the rules unbent.

If you are still a contented fallibilist, despite my plea to hear the sceptical argument afresh, you will probably be discontented with the Rule of Attention. You will begrudge the sceptic even his very temporary victory. You will claim the right to resist his argument not only in everyday contexts, but even in those peculiar contexts in which he (or some other epistemologist) busily calls your attention to far-fetched possibilities of error. Further, you will claim the right to resist without having to bend any rules of cooperative conversation. I said that the Rule of Attention was a triviality: that which is not ignored at all is not properly ignored. But the Rule was trivial only because of how I had already chosen to state the *sotto voce* proviso. So you, the contented fallibilist, will think it ought to have been stated differently. Thus, perhaps: "Psst!—except for those possibilities we *could* properly have ignored". And then you will insist that those far-fetched possibilities of error that we attend to at the behest of the sceptic are nevertheless possibilities we could properly have ignored. You will say that no amount of attention can, by itself, turn them into relevant alternatives.

If you say this, we have reached a standoff. I started with a puzzle: how can it be, when his conclusion is so silly, that the sceptic's argument is so irresistible? My Rule of Attention, and the version of the proviso that made that Rule trivial, were built to explain how the sceptic manages to sway us—why his argument seems irresistible, however temporarily. If you continue to find it eminently resistible in all contexts, you have no need of any such explanation. We just disagree about the explanandum phenomenon.

I say S knows that P iff P holds in every possibility left uneliminated by S's evidence—Psst!—except for those possibilities that *we* are properly ignoring. "We" means: the speaker and hearers of a given context; that is, those of us who are discussing S's knowledge together. It is our ignorings, not S's own ignorings, that matter to what we can truly say about S's knowledge. When we are talking about our own knowledge or ignorance, as epistemologists so often do, this is a distinction without a difference. But what if we are talking about someone else?

Suppose we are detectives; the crucial question for our solution of the crime is whether S already *knew*, when he bought the gun, that he was vulnerable to blackmail. We conclude that he did. *We* ignore various far-fetched possibilities, as hard-headed detectives should. But S does not ignore them. S is by profession a sceptical epistemologist. He never ignores much of anything. If it is our own ignorings that matter to the truth of our conclusion, we may well be right that S already knew. But if it is S's ignorings that matter, then we are wrong, because S never knew much of anything. I say we may well be right; so it is our own ignorings that matter, not S's.

But suppose instead that we are epistemologists considering what S knows. If we are well-informed about S (or if we are considering a well-enough specified hypothetical case), then if S attends to a certain possibility, we attend to S's attending to it. But to attend to S's attending to it is ipso facto to attend to it ourselves. In that case, unlike the case of the detectives, the possibilities we are properly ignoring must be among the possibilities that S himself ignores. We may ignore fewer possibilities than S does, but not more.

Even if S himself is neither sceptical nor an epistemologist, he may yet be clever at thinking up far-fetched possibilities that are uneliminated by his evidence. Then again, we well-informed epistemologists who ask what S knows will have to attend to the possibilities that S thinks up. Even if S's idle cleverness does not lead S himself to draw sceptical conclusions, it nevertheless limits the knowledge that we can truly ascribe to him when attentive to his state of mind. More simply: his cleverness limits his knowledge. He would have known more, had he been less imaginative.[17]

Do I claim you can know P just by presupposing it?! Do I claim you can know that a possibility W does not obtain just by ignoring it? Is that not what my analysis implies, provided that the presupposing and the ignoring are proper? Well, yes. And yet I do not claim it. Or rather, I do not claim it for any specified P or W. I have to grant, in general, that knowledge just by presupposing and ignoring *is* knowledge; but it is an *especially* elusive sort of knowledge, and consequently it is an unclaimable sort of knowledge. You do not even have to practise epistemology to make it vanish. Simply *mentioning* any particular case of this knowledge, aloud or even in silent thought, is a way to attend to the hitherto ignored possibility, and thereby render it no longer ignored, and thereby create a context in which it is no longer true to ascribe the knowledge in question to yourself or others. So, just as we should think, presuppositions alone are not a basis on which to *claim* knowledge.

In general, when S knows that P some of the possibilities in which not-P are eliminated by S's evidence and others of them are properly ignored. There are some that can be eliminated, but cannot properly be ignored. For instance, when I look around the study without seeing Possum the cat, I thereby eliminate various possibilities in which Possum is in the study; but had those possibilities not been eliminated, they could not properly have been ignored. And there are other possibilities that never can be eliminated, but can properly be ignored. For instance, the possibility that Possum is on the desk but has been made invisible by a deceiving demon falls normally into this class (though not when I attend to it in the special context of epistemology).

There is a third class: not-P possibilities that might either be eliminated or ignored. Take the far-fetched possibility that Possum has somehow managed to get into a closed drawer of the desk—maybe he jumped in when it was open, then I closed it without noticing him. That possibility could be eliminated by opening the drawer and making a thorough examination. But if uneliminated, it may nevertheless be ignored, and in many contexts that ignoring would be proper. If I look all around the study, but without checking the closed drawers of the desk, I may truly be said to know that Possum is not in the study—or at any rate, there are many contexts in which that may truly be said. But if I did check all the closed drawers, then I would know *better* that Possum is not in the study. My knowledge would be better in the second case because it would rest more on the elimination of not-*P* possibilities, less on the ignoring of them.[18,19]

Better knowledge is more stable knowledge: it stands more chance of surviving a shift of attention in which we begin to attend to some of the possibilities formerly ignored. If, in our new shifted context, we ask what knowledge we may truly ascribe to our earlier selves, we may find that only the better knowledge of our earlier selves still deserves the name. And yet, if our former ignorings were proper at the time, even the worse knowledge of our earlier selves could truly have been called knowledge in the former context.

Never—well, hardly ever—does our knowledge rest entirely on elimination and not at all on ignoring. So hardly ever is it quite as good as we might wish. To that extent, the lesson of scepticism is right—and right permanently, not just in the temporary and special context of epistemology.[20]

What is it all for? Why have a notion of knowledge that works in the way I described? (Not a compulsory question. Enough to observe that short-cuts—like satisficing, like having indeterminate degrees of belief—that we resort to because we are not smart enough to live up to really high, perfectly Bayesian, standards of rationality. You cannot maintain a record of exactly which possibilities you have eliminated so far, much as you might like to. It is easier to keep track of which possibilities you have eliminated if you—Psst!—ignore many of all the possibilities there are. And besides, it is easier to list some of the propositions that are true in *all* the uneliminated, unignored possibilities than it is to find propositions

that are true in *all and only* the uneliminated, unignored possibilities.

If you doubt that the word "know" bears any real load in science or in metaphysics, I partly agree. The serious business of science has to do not with knowledge per se; but rather, with the elimination of possibilities through the evidence of perception, memory, etc., and with the changes that one's belief system would (or might or should) undergo under the impact of such eliminations. Ascriptions of knowledge to yourself or others are a very sloppy way of conveying very incomplete information about the elimination of possibilities. It is as if you had said:

> The possibilities eliminated, whatever else they may also include, at least include all the not-*P* possibilities; or anyway, all of those except for some we are presumably prepared to ignore just at the moment.

The only excuse for giving information about what really matters in such a sloppy way is that at least it is easy and quick! But it *is* easy and quick; whereas giving full and precise information about which possibilities have been eliminated seems to be extremely difficult, as witness the futile search for a "pure observation language." If I am right about how ascriptions of knowledge work, they are a handy but humble approximation. They may yet be indispensable in practice, in the same way that other handy and humble approximations are.

If we analyse knowledge as a modality, as we have done, we cannot escape the conclusion that knowledge is closed under (strict) implication.[21] Dretske has denied that knowledge is closed under implication; further, he has diagnosed closure as the fallacy that drives arguments for scepticism. As follows: the proposition that I have hands implies that I am not a handless being, and a *fortiori* that I am not a handless being deceived by a demon into thinking that I have hands. So, by the closure principle, the proposition that I know I have hands implies that I know that I am not handless and deceived. But I don't know that I am not handless and deceived—for how can I eliminate that possibility? So, by *modus tollens,* I don't know that I have hands. Dretske's advice is to resist scepticism by denying closure. He says that although having hands *does* imply not being handless and deceived, yet knowing that I have hands *does not* imply knowing that I am not handless and deceived. I do know the former, I do not know the latter.[22]

What Dretske says is close to right, but not quite. Knowledge *is* closed under implication. Knowing that I have hands *does* imply knowing that I am not handless and deceived. Implication preserves truth—that is, it preserves truth in any given, fixed context. But if we switch contexts midway, all bets are off. I say (1) pigs fly; (2) what I just said had fewer than three syllables (true); (3) what I just said had fewer than four syllables (false). So "less than three" does not imply "less than four"? No! The context switched midway, the semantic value of the context-dependent phrase "what I just said" switched with it. Likewise in the sceptical argument the context switched midway, and the semantic value of the context-dependent word "know" switched with it. The premise "I know that I have hands" was true in its everyday context, where the possibility of deceiving demons was properly ignored. The mention of that very possibility switched the context midway. The conclusion "I know that I am not handless and deceived" was false in *its* context, because that was a context in which the possibility of deceiving demons was being mentioned, hence was not being ignored, hence was not being properly ignored. Dretske gets the phenomenon right, and I think he gets the diagnosis of scepticism right; it is just that he misclassifies what he sees. He thinks it is a phenomenon of logic, when really it is a phenomenon of pragmatics. Closure, rightly understood, survives the test. If we evaluate the conclusion for truth not with respect to the context in which it was uttered, but instead with respect to the different context in which the premise was uttered, then truth is preserved. And if, *per impossibile,* the conclusion could have been said in the same unchanged context as the premise, truth would have been preserved.

A problem due to Saul Kripke turns upon the closure of knowledge under implication. *P* implies that any evidence against *P* is misleading. So, by closure, whenever you know that *P,* you know that any evi-

dence against *P* is misleading. And if you know that evidence is misleading, you should pay it no heed. Whenever we know—and we know a lot, remember—we should not heed any evidence tending to suggest that we are wrong. But that is absurd. Shall we dodge the conclusion by denying closure? I think not. Again, I diagnose a change of context. At first, it was stipulated that *S* knew, whence it followed that *S* was properly ignoring all possibilities of error. But as the story continues, it turns out that there is evidence on offer that points to some particular possibility of error. Then, by the Rule of Attention, that possibility is no longer properly ignored, either by *S* himself or by we who are telling the story of *S.* The advent of that evidence destroys *S*'s knowledge, and thereby destroys *S*'s licence to ignore the evidence lest he be misled.

There is another reason, different from Dretske's, why we might doubt closure. Suppose two or more premises jointly imply a conclusion. Might not someone who is compartmentalized in his thinking—as we all are—know each of the premises but fail to bring them together in a single compartment? Then might he not fail to know the conclusion? Yes; and I would not like to plead idealization-of-rationality as an excuse for ignoring such cases. But I suggest that we might take not the whole compartmentalized thinker, but rather each of his several overlapping compartments, as our "subjects." That would be the obvious remedy if his compartmentalization amounted to a case of multiple personality disorder; but maybe it is right for milder cases as well.[23]

A compartmentalized thinker who indulges in epistemology can destroy his knowledge, yet retain it as well. Imagine two epistemologists on a bushwalk. As they walk, they talk. They mention all manner of far-fetched possibilities of error. By attending to these normally ignored possibilities they destroy the knowledge they normally possess. Yet all the while they know where they are and where they are going! How so? The compartment in charge of philosophical talk attends to far-fetched possibilities of error. The compartment in charge of navigation does not. One compartment loses its knowledge, the other retains its knowledge. And what does the entire compartmentalized thinker know? Not an altogether felicitous question. But if we need an answer, I suppose the best thing to say is that *S* knows that *P* iff any one of *S*'s compartments knows that *P*. Then we can say what we would offhand want to say: yes, our philosophical bushwalkers still know their whereabouts.

Context-dependence is not limited to the ignoring and non-ignoring of far-fetched possibilities. Here is another case. Pity poor Bill! He squanders all his spare cash on the pokies, the races, and the lottery. He will be a wage slave all his days. We know he will never be rich. But if he wins the lottery (if he wins big), then he will be rich. Contrapositively: his never being rich, plus other things we know, imply that he will lose. So, by closure, if we know that he will never be rich, we know that he will lose. But when we discussed the case before, we concluded that we cannot know that he will lose. All the possibilities in which Bill loses and someone else wins saliently resemble the possibility in which Bill wins and the others lose; one of those possibilities is actual; so by the Rules of Actuality and of Resemblance, we may not properly ignore the possibility that Bill wins. But there is a loophole: the resemblance was required to be salient. Salience, as well as ignoring, may vary between contexts. Before, when I was explaining how the Rule of Resemblance applied to lotteries, I saw to it that the resemblance between the many possibilities associated with the many tickets was sufficiently salient. But this time, when we were busy pitying poor Bill for his habits and not for his luck, the resemblance of the many possibilities was not so salient. At that point, the possibility of Bill's winning was properly ignored; so then it was true to say that we knew he would never be rich. Afterward I switched the context. I mentioned the possibility that Bill might win, wherefore that possibility was no longer properly ignored. (Maybe there were two separate reasons why it was no longer properly ignored, because maybe I also made the resemblance between the many possibilities more salient.) It was true at first that we knew that Bill would never be rich. And at that point it was also true that we knew he would lose—but that was only true so long as it remained unsaid! (And maybe unthought as well.) Later, after the change in context, it was no longer true that we

knew he would lose. At that point, it was also no longer true that we knew he would never be rich.

But wait. Don't you smell a rat? Haven't I, by my own lights, been saying what cannot be said? (Or whistled either.) If the story I told was true, how have I managed to tell it? In trendyspeak, is there not a problem of reflexivity? Does not my story deconstruct itself?

I said: *S* knows that *P* iff *S*'s evidence eliminates every possibility in which not-*P*—Psst!—except for those possibilities that we are properly ignoring. That "psst" marks an attempt to do the impossible—to mention that which remains unmentioned. I am sure you managed to make believe that I had succeeded. But I could not have done.

And I said that when we do epistemology, and we attend to the proper ignoring of possibilities, we make knowledge vanish. First we do know, then we do not. But I had been doing epistemology when I said that. The uneliminated possibilities were *not* being ignored—not just then. So by what right did I say even that we used to know?[24]

In trying to thread a course between the rock of fallibilism and the whirlpool of scepticism, it may well seem as if I have fallen victim to both at once. For do I not say that there are all those uneliminated possibilities of error? Yet do I not claim that we know a lot? Yet do I not claim that knowledge is, by definition, infallible knowledge?

I did claim all three things. But not all at once! Or if I did claim them all at once, that was an expository shortcut, to be taken with a pinch of salt. To get my message across, I bent the rules. If I tried to whistle what cannot be said, what of it? I relied on the cardinal principle of pragmatics, which overrides every one of the rules I mentioned: interpret the message to make it make sense—to make it consistent, and sensible to say.

When you have context-dependence, ineffability can be trite and unmysterious. Hush! [moment of silence] I might have liked to say, just then, "All of us are silent." It was true. But I could not have said it truly, or whistled it either. For by saying it aloud, or by whistling, I would have rendered it false.

I could have said my say fair and square, bending

no rules. It would have been tiresome, but it could have been done. The secret would have been to resort to "semantic ascent." I could have taken great care to distinguish between (1) the language I use when I talk about knowledge, or whatever, and (2) the second language that I use to talk about the semantic and pragmatic workings of the first language. If you want to hear my story told that way, you probably know enough to do the job for yourself. If you can, then my informal presentation has been good enough.

NOTES

1. The suggestion that ascriptions of knowledge go false in the context of epistemology is to be found in Barry Stroud, "Understanding Human Knowledge in General" in Marjorie Clay and Keith Lehrer (eds.), *Knowledge and Skepticism* (Boulder: Westview Press, 1989); and in Stephen Hetherington, "Lacking Knowledge and Justification by Theorising About Them" (lecture at the University of New South Wales, August 1992). Neither of them tells the story just as I do, however it may be that their versions do not conflict with mine.

2. Unless, like some, we simply define "justification" as "whatever it takes to turn true opinion into knowledge" regardless of whether what it takes turns out to involve argument from supporting reasons.

3. The problem of the lottery was introduced in Henry Kyburg, *Probability and the Logic of Rational Belief* (Middletown, CT: Wesleyan University Press, 1961), and in Carl Hempel, "Deductive-Nomological vs. Statistical Explanation" in Herbert Feigl and Grover Maxwell (eds.), *Minnesota Studies in the Philosophy of Science*, Vol. II (Minneapolis: University of Minnesota Press, 1962). It has been much discussed since, as a problem both about knowledge and about our everyday, non-quantitative concept of belief.

4. The case of testimony is less discussed than the others; but see C. A. J. Coady, *Testimony: A Philosophical Study* (Oxford: Clarendon Press, 1992) pp. 79–129.

5. I follow Peter Unger, *Ignorance: A Case for Scepticism* (New York: Oxford University Press, 1975). But I shall not let him lead me into scepticism.

6. See Robert Stalnaker, *Inquiry* (Cambridge, MA: MIT Press, 1984) pp. 59–99.

7. See my 'Attitudes *De Dicto* and *De Se*', *The Philosophical Review* 88 (1979) pp. 513–543; and R. M. Chisholm, "The Indirect Reflexive" in C. Diamond and J. Teichman (eds.), *Intention and Intentionality: Essays in Honour of G. E. M. Anscombe* (Brighton: Harvester, 1979).

8. Peter Unger, *Ignorance*, chapter II. I discuss the case, and briefly foreshadow the present paper, in my "Scorekeeping in a Language Game," *Journal of Philosophical Logic* 8 (1979) pp. 339–359, esp. pp. 353–355.

9. See Robert Stalnaker, "Presuppositions," *Journal of Philosophical Logic* 2 (1973) pp. 447–457; and "Pragmatic Presuppositions" in Milton Munitz and Peter Unger (eds.), *Semantics and Philosophy* (New York: New York University Press, 1974). See also my "Scorekeeping in a Language Game."

The definition restated in terms of presupposition resembles the treatment of knowledge in Kenneth S. Ferguson, *Philosophical Scepticism* (Cornell University doctoral dissertation, 1980).

10. See Fred Dretske, "Epistemic Operators," *The Journal of Philosophy* 67 (1970) pp. 1007–1022, and "The Pragmatic Dimension of Knowledge," *Philosophical Studies* 40 (1981) pp. 363–378; Alvin Goldman, "Discrimination and Perceptual Knowledge," *The Journal of Philosophy* 73 (1976) pp. 771–791; G. C. Stine, "Skepticism, Relevant Alternatives, and Deductive Closure," *Philosophical Studies* 29 (1976) pp. 249–261; and Stewart Cohen, "How to be A Fallibilist," *Philosophical Perspectives* 2 (1988) pp. 91–123.

11. Some of them, but only some, taken from the authors just cited.

12. Instead of complicating the Rule of Belief as I have just done, I might equivalently have introduced a separate Rule of High Stakes saying that when error would be especially disastrous, few possibilities are properly ignored.

13. A. D. Woozley, "Knowing and Not Knowing," *Proceedings of the Aristotelian Society* 53 (1953) pp. 151–172; Colin Radford, "Knowledge—by Examples," *Analysis* 27 (1966) pp. 1–11.

14. See Edmund Gettier, "Is Justified True Belief Knowledge?," *Analysis* 23 (1963) pp. 121–123. Diagnoses have varied widely. The four examples below come from: (1) Keith Lehrer and Thomas Paxson Jr., "Knowledge: Undefeated True Belief," *The Journal of Philosophy* 66 (1969) pp. 225–237; (2) Bertrand Russell, *Human Knowledge: Its Scope and Limits* (London: Allen and Unwin, 1948) p. 154; (3) Alvin Goldman, "Discrimination and Perceptual Knowledge," op. cit.; (4) Gilbert Harman, *Thought* (Princeton, NJ: Princeton University Press, 1973) p. 143.

Though the lottery problem is another case of justified true belief without knowledge, it is not normally counted among the Gettier problems. It is interesting to find that it yields to the same remedy.

15. See Alvin Goldman, "A Causal Theory of Knowing," *The Journal of Philosophy* 64 (1967) pp. 357–372; D.

M. Armstrong, *Belief, Truth and Knowledge* (Cambridge: Cambridge University Press, 1973).

16. See my "Veridical Hallucination and Prosthetic Vision," *Australasian Journal of Philosophy* 58 (1980) pp. 239–249. John Bigelow has proposed to model knowledge-delivering processes generally on those found in vision.

17. See Catherine Elgin, "The Epistemic Efficacy of Stupidity," *Synthese* 74 (1988) pp. 297–311. The "efficacy" takes many forms; some to do with knowledge (under various rival analyses), some to do with justified belief. See also Michael Williams, *Unnatural Doubts: Epistemological Realism and the Basis of Scepticism* (Oxford: Blackwell, 1991) pp. 352–355, on the instability of knowledge under reflection.

18. Mixed cases are possible: Fred properly ignores the possibility W_1 which Ted eliminates; however, Ted properly ignores the possibility W_2 which Fred eliminates. Ted has looked in all the desk drawers but not the file drawers, whereas Fred has checked the file drawers but not the desk. Fred's knowledge that Possum is not in the study is better in one way, Ted's is better in another.

19. To say truly that X is known, I must be properly ignoring any uneliminated possibilities in which not-X; whereas to say truly that Y is better known than X, I must be attending to some such possibilities. So I cannot say both in a single context. If I say "X is known, but Y is better known," the context changes in mid-sentence: some previously ignored possibilities must stop being ignored. That can happen easily. Saying it the other way around— "Y is better known than X, but even X is known"—is harder, because we must suddenly start to ignore previously unignored possibilities. That cannot be done, really; but we could bend the rules and make believe we had done it, and

no doubt we would be understood well enough. Saying "X is flat, but Y is flatter" (that is, "X has no bumps at all, but Y has even fewer or smaller bumps") is a parallel case. And again, "Y is flatter, but even X is flat" sounds clearly worse—but not altogether hopeless.

20. Thanks here to Stephen Hetherington. While his own views about better and worse knowledge are situated within an analysis of knowledge quite unlike mine, they withstand transplantation.

21. A proof-theoretic version of this closure principle is common to all "normal" modal logics: if the logic validates an inference from zero or more premises to a conclusion, then also it validates the inference obtained by prefixing the necessity operator to each premise and to the conclusion. Further, this rule is all we need to take us from classical sentential logic to the least normal modal logic. See Brian Chellas, *Modal Logic: An Introduction* (Cambridge: Cambridge University Press, 1980) p. 114.

22. Dretske, "Epistemic Operators." My reply follows the lead of Stine, "Skepticism, Relevant Alternatives, and Deductive Closure," op. cit.; and (more closely) Cohen, "How to be a Fallibilist," op. cit.

23. See Stalnaker, *Inquiry*, pp. 79–99.

24. Worse still: by what right can I even say that we used to be in a position to say truly that we knew? Then, we were in a context where we properly ignored certain uneliminated possibilities of error. Now, we are in a context where we no longer ignore them. If *now* I comment retrospectively upon the truth of what was said *then,* which context governs: the context now or the context then? I doubt there is any general answer, apart from the usual principle that we should interpret what is said so as to make the message make sense.

Epistemology Naturalized

~

W. V. O. QUINE

W. V. O. Quine (1908–2000) was one of the most distinguished philosophers of the 20th century. For many years Edgar Pierce Professor of Philosophy at Harvard University, Quine is renowned for emphasizing *naturalism,* as he does here. Among his most significant works are "Two Dogmas of Empiricism," "On What There Is," and the book *Word and Object.*

Epistemology is concerned with the foundations of science. Conceived thus broadly, epistemology includes the study of the foundations of mathematics as one of its departments. Specialists at the turn of the century thought that their efforts in this particular department were achieving notable success: mathematics seemed to reduce altogether to logic. In a more recent perspective this reduction is seen to be better describable as a reduction to logic and set theory. This correction is a disappointment epistemologically, since the firmness and obviousness that we associate with logic cannot be claimed for set theory. But still the success achieved in the foundations of mathematics remains exemplary by comparative standards, and we can illuminate the rest of epistemology somewhat by drawing parallels to this department.

Studies in the foundations of mathematics divide symmetrically into two sorts, conceptual and doctrinal. The conceptual studies are concerned with meaning, the doctrinal with truth. The conceptual studies are concerned with clarifying concepts by defining them, some in terms of others. The doctrinal studies are concerned with establishing laws by proving them, some on the basis of others. Ideally the obscurer concepts would be defined in terms of the clearer ones so as to maximize clarity, and the less

obvious laws would be proved from the more obvious ones so as to maximize certainty. Ideally the definitions would generate all the concepts from clear and distinct ideas, and the proofs would generate all the theorems from self-evident truths.

The two ideals are linked. For, if you define all the concepts by use of some favored subset of them, you thereby show how to translate all theorems into these favored terms. The clearer these terms are, the likelier it is that the truths couched in them will be obviously true, or derivable from obvious truths. If in particular the concepts of mathematics were all reducible to the clear terms of logic, then all the truths of mathematics would go over into truths of logic; and surely the truths of logic are all obvious or at least potentially obvious, i.e., derivable from obvious truths by individually obvious steps.

This particular outcome is in fact denied us, however, since mathematics reduces only to set theory and not to logic proper. Such reduction still enhances clarity, but only because of the interrelations that emerge and not because the end terms of the analysis are clearer than others. As for the end truths, the axioms of set theory, these have less obviousness and certainty to recommend them than do most of the mathematical theorems that we would derive from them. Moreover, we know from Gödel's work that no

Reprinted from W. V. O. Quine, *Ontological Relativity and Other Essays* (New York: Columbia University Press, 1969), by permission of the publisher.

consistent axiom system can cover mathematics even when we renounce self-evidence. Reduction in the foundations of mathematics remains mathematically and philosophically fascinating, but it does not do what the epistemologist would like of it: it does not reveal the ground of mathematical knowledge, it does not show how mathematical certainty is possible.

Still there remains a helpful thought, regarding epistemology generally, in that duality of structure which was especially conspicuous in the foundations of mathematics. I refer to the bifurcation into a theory of concepts, or meaning, and a theory of doctrine, or truth; for this applies to the epistemology of natural knowledge no less than to the foundations of mathematics. The parallel is as follows. Just as mathematics is to be reduced to logic, or logic and set theory, so natural knowledge is to be based somehow on sense experience. This means explaining the notion of body in sensory terms; here is the conceptual side. And it means justifying our knowledge of truths of nature in sensory terms; here is the doctrinal side of the bifurcation.

Hume pondered the epistemology of natural knowledge on both sides of the bifurcation, the conceptual and the doctrinal. His handling of the conceptual side of the problem, the explanation of body in sensory terms, was bold and simple: he identified bodies outright with the sense impressions. If common sense distinguishes between the material apple and our sense impressions of it on the ground that the apple is one and enduring while the impressions are many and fleeting, then, Hume held, so much the worse for common sense; the notion of its being the same apple on one occasion and another is a vulgar confusion.

Nearly a century after Hume's *Treatise*, the same view of bodies was espoused by the early American philosopher Alexander Bryan Johnson.[1] "The word iron names an associated sight and feel," Johnson wrote.

What then of the doctrinal side, the justification of our knowledge of truths about nature? Here, Hume despaired. By his identification of bodies with impressions he did succeed in construing some singular statements about bodies as indubitable truths, yes; as truths about impressions, directly known. But general statements, also singular statements about the future, gained no increment of certainty by being construed as about impressions.

On the doctrinal side, I do not see that we are farther along today than where Hume left us. The Humean predicament is the human predicament. But on the conceptual side there has been progress. There the crucial step forward was made already before Alexander Bryan Johnson's day, although Johnson did not emulate it. It was made by Bentham in his theory of fictions. Bentham's step was the recognition of contextual definition, or what he called paraphrasis. He recognized that to explain a term we do not need to specify an object for it to refer to, nor even specify a synonymous word or phrase; we need only show, by whatever means, how to translate all the whole sentences in which the term is to be used. Hume's and Johnson's desperate measure of identifying bodies with impressions ceased to be the only conceivable way of making sense of talk of bodies, even granted that impressions were the only reality. One could undertake to explain talk of bodies in terms of talk of impressions by translating one's whole sentences about bodies into whole sentences about impressions, without equating the bodies themselves to anything at all.

This idea of contextual definition, or recognition of the sentence as the primary vehicle of meaning, was indispensable to the ensuing developments in the foundations of mathematics. It was explicit in Frege, and it attained its full flower in Russell's doctrine of singular descriptions as incomplete symbols.

Contextual definition was one of two resorts that could be expected to have a liberating effect upon the conceptual side of the epistemology of natural knowledge. The other is resort to the resources of set theory as auxiliary concepts. The epistemologist who is willing to eke out his austere ontology of sense impressions with these set-theoretic auxiliaries is suddenly rich: he has not just his impressions to play with, but sets of them, and sets of sets, and so on up. Constructions in the foundations of mathematics have shown that such set-theoretic aids are a powerful addition; after all, the entire glossary of concepts of classical mathematics is constructible from them. Thus equipped, our epistemologist may not need either to identify bodies with impressions or to settle for contextual definition; he may hope to find in some subtle construction of sets upon sets of sense impressions a category of objects enjoying just the formula properties that he wants for bodies.

The two resorts are very unequal in epistemological status. Contextual definition is unassailable. Sentences that have been given meaning as wholes are undeniably meaningful, and the use they make of their component terms is therefore meaningful, regardless of whether any translations are offered for those terms in isolation. Surely Hume and A. B. Johnson would have used contextual definition with pleasure if they had thought of it. Recourse to sets, on the other hand, is a drastic ontological move, a retreat from the austere ontology of impressions. There are philosophers who would rather settle for bodies outright than accept all these sets, which amount, after all, to the whole abstract ontology of mathematics.

This issue has not always been clear, however, owing to deceptive hints of continuity between elementary logic and set theory. This is why mathematics was once believed to reduce to logic, that is, to an innocent and unquestionable logic, and to inherit these qualities. And this is probably why Russell was content to resort to sets as well as to contextual definition when in *Our Knowledge of the External World* and elsewhere he addressed himself to the epistemology of natural knowledge, on its conceptual side.

To account for the external world as a logical construct of sense data—such, in Russell's terms, was the program. It was Carnap, in his *Der logische Aufbau der Welt* of 1928, who came nearest to executing it.

This was the conceptual side of epistemology; what of the doctrinal? There the Humean predicament remained unaltered. Carnap's constructions, if carried successfully to completion, would have enabled us to translate all sentences about the world into terms of sense data, or observation, plus logic and set theory. But the mere fact that a sentence is *couched* in terms of observation, logic, and set theory does not mean that it can be *proved* from observation sentences by logic and set theory. The most modest of generalizations about observable traits will cover more cases than its utterer can have had occasion

actually to observe. The hopelessness of grounding natural science upon immediate experience in a firmly logical way was acknowledged. The Cartesian quest for certainty had been the remote motivation of epistemology, both on its conceptual and its doctrinal side; but that quest was seen as a lost cause. To endow the truths of nature with the full authority of immediate experience was as forlorn a hope as hoping to endow the truths of mathematics with the potential obviousness of elementary logic.

What then could have motivated Carnap's heroic efforts on the conceptual side of epistemology, when hope of certainty on the doctrinal side was abandoned? There were two good reasons still. One was that such constructions could be expected to elicit and clarify the sensory evidence for science, even if the inferential steps between sensory evidence and scientific doctrine must fall short of certainty. The other reason was that such constructions would deepen our understanding of our discourse about the world, even apart from questions of evidence; it would make all cognitive discourse as clear as observation terms and logic and, I must regretfully add, set theory.

It was sad for epistemologists, Hume and others, to have to acquiesce in the impossibility of strictly deriving the science of the external world from sensory evidence. Two cardinal tenets of empiricism remained unassailable, however, and so remain to this day. One is that whatever evidence there *is* for science *is* sensory evidence. The other, to which I shall recur, is that all inculcation of meanings of words must rest ultimately on sensory evidence. Hence the continuing attractiveness of the idea of a *logischer Aufbau* in which the sensory content of discourse would stand forth explicitly.

If Carnap had successfully carried such a construction through, how could he have told whether it was the right one? The question would have had no point. He was seeking what he called a *rational reconstruction*. Any construction of physicalistic discourse in terms of sense experience, logic, and set theory would have been seen as satisfactory if it made the physicalistic discourse come out right. If there is one way there are many, but any would be a great achievement.

But why all this creative reconstruction, all this make-believe? The stimulation of his sensory receptors is all the evidence anybody has had to go on, ultimately, in arriving at his picture of the world. Why not just see how this construction really proceeds? Why not settle for psychology? Such a surrender of the epistemological burden to psychology is a move that was disallowed in earlier times as circular reasoning. If the epistemologist's goal is validation of the grounds of empirical science, he defeats his purpose by using psychology or other empirical science in the validation. However, such scruples against circularity have little point once we have stopped dreaming of deducing science from observations. If we are out simply to understand the link between observation and science, we are well advised to use any available information, including that provided by the very science whose link with observation we are seeking to understand.

But there remains a different reason, unconnected with fears of circularity, for still favoring creative reconstruction. We should like to be able to *translate* science into logic and observation terms and set theory. This would be a great epistemological achievement, for it would show all the rest of the concepts of science to be theoretically superfluous. It would legitimize them—to whatever degree the concepts of set theory, logic, and observation are themselves legitimate—by showing that everything done with the one apparatus could in principle be done with the other. If psychology itself could deliver a truly translational reduction of this kind, we should welcome it; but certainly it cannot, for certainly we did not grow up learning definitions of physicalistic language in terms of a prior language of set theory, logic, and observation. Here, then, would be good reason for persisting in a rational reconstruction: we want to establish the essential innocence of physical concepts, by showing them to be theoretically dispensable.

The fact is, though, that the construction which Carnap outlined in *Der logische Aufbau der Welt* does not give translational reduction either. It would not even if the outline were filled in. The crucial point comes where Carnap is explaining how to assign sense qualities to positions in physical space and time. These assignments are to be made in such a way

as to fulfill, as well as possible, certain desiderata which he states, and with growth of experience the assignments are to be revised to suit. This plan, however illuminating, does not offer any key to *translating* the sentences of science into terms of observation, logic, and set theory.

We must despair of any such reduction. Carnap had despaired of it by 1936, when, in "Testability and meaning,"[2] he introduced so-called *reduction forms* of a type weaker than definition. Definitions had shown always how to translate sentences into equivalent sentences. Contextual definition of a term showed how to translate sentences containing the term into equivalent sentences lacking the term. Reduction forms of Carnap's liberalized kind, on the other hand, do not in general give equivalences; they give implications. They explain a new term, if only partially, by specifying some sentences which are implied by sentences containing the term, and other sentences which imply sentences containing the term.

It is tempting to suppose that the countenancing of reduction forms in this liberal sense is just one further step of liberalization comparable to the earlier one, taken by Bentham, of countenancing contextual definition. The former and sterner kind of rational reconstruction might have been represented as a fictitious history in which we imagined our ancestors introducing the terms of physicalistic discourse on a phenomenalistic and set-theoretic basis by a succession of contextual definitions. The new and more liberal kind of rational reconstruction is a fictitious history in which we imagine our ancestors introducing those terms by a succession rather of reduction forms of the weaker sort.

This, however, is a wrong comparison. The fact is rather that the former and sterner kind of rational reconstruction, where definition reigned, embodied no fictitious history at all. It was nothing more nor less than a set of directions—or would have been, if successful—for accomplishing everything in terms of phenomena and set theory that we now accomplish in terms of bodies. It would have been a true reduction by translation, a legitimation by elimination. *Definire est eliminare.* Rational reconstruction by Carnap's later and looser reduction forms does none of this.

To relax the demand for definition, and settle for a kind of reduction that does not eliminate, is to renounce the last remaining advantage that we supposed rational reconstruction to have over straight psychology; namely, the advantage of translational reduction. If all we hope for is a reconstruction that links science to experience in explicit ways short of translation, then it would seem more sensible to settle for psychology. Better to discover how science is in fact developed and learned than to fabricate a fictitious structure to a similar effect.

The empiricist made one major concession when he despaired of deducing the truths of nature from sensory evidence. In despairing now even of translating those truths into terms of observation and logico-mathematical auxiliaries, he makes another major concession. For suppose we hold, with the old empiricist Peirce, that the very meaning of a statement consists in the difference its truth would make to possible experience. Might we not formulate, in a chapter-length sentence in observational language, all the difference that the truth of a given statement might make to experience, and might we not then take all this as the translation? Even if the difference that the truth of the statement would make to experience ramifies indefinitely, we might still hope to embrace it all in the logical implications of our chapter-length formulation, just as we can axiomatize an infinity of theorems. In giving up hope of such translation, then, the empiricist is conceding that the empirical meanings of typical statements about the external world are inaccessible and ineffable.

How is this inaccessibility to be explained? Simply on the ground that the experiential implications of a typical statement about bodies are too complex for finite axiomatization, however lengthy? No; I have a different explanation. It is that the typical statement about bodies has no fund of experiential implications it can call its own. A substantial mass of theory, taken together, will commonly have experiential implications; this is how we make verifiable predictions. We may not be able to explain why we arrive at theories which make successful predictions, but we do arrive at such theories.

Sometimes also an experience implied by a theory fails to come off; and then, ideally, we declare the theory false. But the failure falsifies only a block of theory as a whole, a conjunction of many statements. The failure shows that one or more of those statements is false, but it does not show which. The predicted experiences, true and false, are not implied by any one of the component statements of the theory rather than another. The component statements simply do not have empirical meanings, by Peirce's standard; but a sufficiently inclusive portion of theory does. If we can aspire to a sort of *logischer Aufbau der Welt* at all, it must be to one in which the texts slated for translation into observational and logico-mathematical terms are mostly broad theories taken as wholes, rather than just terms or short sentences. The translation of a theory would be a ponderous axiomatization of all the experiential difference that the truth of the theory would make. It would be a queer translation, for it would translate the whole but none of the parts. We might better speak in such a case not of translation but simply of observational evidence for theories; and we may, following Peirce, still fairly call this the empirical meaning of the theories.

These considerations raise a philosophical question even about ordinary unphilosophical translation, such as from English into Arunta or Chinese. For, if the English sentences of a theory have their meaning only together as a body, then we can justify their translation into Arunta only together as a body. There will be no justification for pairing off the component English sentences with component Arunta sentences, except as these correlations make the translation of the theory as a whole come out right. Any translations of the English sentences into Arunta sentences will be as correct as any other, so long as the net empirical implications of the theory as a whole are preserved in translation. But it is to be expected that many different ways of translating the component sentences, essentially different individually, would deliver the same empirical implications for the theory as a whole; deviations in the translation of one component sentence could be compensated for in the translation of another component sentence. Insofar, there can be no ground for saying which of two glaringly unlike translations of individual sentences is right.

For an uncritical mentalist, no such indeterminacy threatens. Every term and every sentence is a label attached to an idea, simple or complex, which is stored in the mind. When on the other hand we take a verification theory of meaning seriously, the indeterminacy would appear to be inescapable. The Vienna Circle espoused a verification theory of meaning but did not take it seriously enough. If we recognize with Peirce that the meaning of a sentence turns purely on what would count as evidence for its truth, and if we recognize with Duhem that theoretical sentences have their evidence not as single sentences but only as larger blocks of theory, then the indeterminacy of translation of theoretical sentences is the natural conclusion. And most sentences, apart from observation sentences, are theoretical. This conclusion, conversely, once it is embraced, seals the fate of any general notion of propositional meaning or, for that matter, state of affairs.

Should the unwelcomeness of the conclusion persuade us to abandon the verification theory of meaning? Certainly not. The sort of meaning that is basic to translation, and to the learning of one's own language, is necessarily empirical meaning and nothing more. A child learns his first words and sentences by hearing and using them in the presence of appropriate stimuli. These must be external stimuli, for they must act both on the child and on the speaker from whom he is learning. Language is socially inculcated and controlled; the inculcation and control turn strictly on the keying of sentences to shared stimulation. Internal factors may vary *ad libitum* without prejudice to communication as long as the keying of language to external stimuli is undisturbed. Surely one has no choice but to be an empiricist so far as one's theory of linguistic meaning is concerned.

What I have said of infant learning applies equally to the linguist's learning of a new language in the field. If the linguist does not lean on related languages for which there are previously accepted translation practices, then obviously he has no data but the concomitances of native utterance and observable stimulus situation. No wonder there is indeterminacy of translation—for of course only a small fraction of our utterances report concurrent external stimulation. Granted, the linguist will end up with unequivocal

translations of everything; but only by making many arbitrary choices—arbitrary even though unconscious—along the way. Arbitrary? By this I mean that different choices could still have made everything come out right that is susceptible in principle to any kind of check.

Let me link up, in a different order, some of the points I have made. The crucial consideration behind my argument for the indeterminacy of translation was that a statement about the world does not always or usually have a separable fund of empirical consequences that it can call its own. That consideration served also to account for the impossibility of an epistemological reduction of the sort where every sentence is equated to a sentence in observational and logico-mathematical terms. And the impossibility of that sort of epistemological reduction dissipated the last advantage that rational reconstruction seemed to have over psychology.

Philosophers have rightly despaired of translating everything into observational and logico-mathematical terms. They have despaired of this even when they have not recognized, as the reason for this irreducibility, that the statements largely do not have their private bundles of empirical consequences. And some philosophers have seen in this irreducibility the bankruptcy of epistemology. Carnap and the other logical positivists of the Vienna Circle had already pressed the term "metaphysics" into pejorative use, as connoting meaninglessness; and the term "epistemology" was next. Wittgenstein and his followers, mainly at Oxford, found a residual philosophical vocation in therapy: in curing philosophers of the delusion that there were epistemological problems.

But I think that at this point it may be more useful to say rather that epistemology still goes on, though in a new setting and a clarified status. Epistemology, or something like it, simply falls into place as a chapter of psychology and hence of natural science. It studies a natural phenomenon, viz., a physical human subject. This human subject is accorded a certain experimentally controlled input—certain patterns of irradiation in assorted frequencies, for instance—and in the fullness of time the subject delivers as output a description of the three-dimensional external world and its history. The relation between the meager input and the torrential output is a relation that we are prompted to study for somewhat the same reasons that always prompted epistemology; namely, in order to see how evidence relates to theory, and in what ways one's theory of nature transcends any available evidence.

Such a study could still include, even, something like the old rational reconstruction, to whatever degree such reconstruction is practicable; for imaginative constructions can afford hints of actual psychological processes, in much the way that mechanical simulations can. But a conspicuous difference between old epistemology and the epistemological enterprise in this new psychological setting is that we can now make free use of empirical psychology.

The old epistemology aspired to contain, in a sense, natural science; it would construct it somehow from sense data. Epistemology in its new setting, conversely, is contained in natural science, as a chapter of psychology. But the old containment remains valid too, in its way. We are studying how the human subject of our study posits bodies and projects his physics from his data, and we appreciate that our position in the world is just like his. Our very epistemological enterprise, therefore, and the psychology wherein it is a component chapter, and the whole of natural science wherein psychology is a component book—all this is our own construction or projection from stimulations like those we were meting out to our epistemological subject. There is thus reciprocal containment, though containment in different senses: epistemology in natural science and natural science in epistemology.

This interplay is reminiscent again of the old threat of circularity, but it is all right now that we have stopped dreaming of deducing science from sense data. We are after an understanding of science as an institution or process in the world, and we do not intend that understanding to be any better than the science which is its object. This attitude is indeed one that Neurath was already urging in Vienna Circle days, with his parable of the mariner who has to rebuild his boat while staying afloat in it.

One effect of seeing epistemology in a psychological setting is that it resolves a stubborn old enigma of epistemological priority. Our retinas are irradi-

ated in two dimensions, yet we see things as three-dimensional without conscious inference. Which is to count as observation—the unconscious two-dimensional reception or the conscious three-dimensional apprehension? In the old epistemological context the conscious form had priority, for we were out to justify our knowledge of the external world by rational reconstruction, and that demands awareness. Awareness ceased to be demanded when we gave up trying to justify our knowledge of the external world by rational reconstruction. What to count as observation now can be settled in terms of the stimulation of sensory receptors, let consciousness fall where it may.

The Gestalt psychologists' challenge to sensory atomism, which seemed so relevant to epistemology forty years ago, is likewise deactivated. Regardless of whether sensory atoms or Gestalten are what favor the forefront of our consciousness, it is simply the stimulations of our sensory receptors that are best looked upon as the input to our cognitive mechanism. Old paradoxes about unconscious data and inference, old problems about chains of inference that would have to be completed too quickly—these no longer matter.

In the old anti-psychologistic days the question of epistemological priority was moot. What is epistemologically prior to what? Are Gestalten prior to sensory atoms because they are noticed, or should we favor sensory atoms on some more subtle ground? Now that we are permitted to appeal to physical stimulation, the problem dissolves; A is epistemologically prior to B if A is causally nearer than B to the sensory receptors. Or, what is in some ways better, just talk explicitly in terms of causal proximity to sensory receptors and drop the talk of epistemological priority.

Around 1932 there was debate in the Vienna Circle over what to count as observation sentences, or *Protokollsätze*.[3] One position was that they had the form of reports of sense impressions. Another was that they were statements of an elementary sort about the external world, e.g., "A red cube is standing on the table." Another, Neurath's, was that they had the form of reports of relations between percipients and external things: "Otto now sees a red cube on the table." The worst of it was that there seemed to be no objective way of settling the matter: no way of making real sense of the question.

Let us now try to view the matter unreservedly in the context of the external world. Vaguely speaking, what we want of observation sentences is that they be the ones in closest causal proximity to the sensory receptors. But how is such proximity to be gauged? The idea may be rephrased this way: observation sentences are sentences which, as we learn language, are most strongly conditioned to concurrent sensory stimulation rather than to stored collateral information. Thus let us imagine a sentence queried for our verdict as to whether it is true or false; queried for our assent or dissent. Then the sentence is an observation sentence if our verdict depends only on the sensory stimulation present at the time.

But a verdict cannot depend on present stimulation to the exclusion of stored information. The very fact of our having learned the language evinces much storing of information, and of information without which we should be in no position to give verdicts on sentences however observational. Evidently then we must relax our definition of observation sentence to read thus: a sentence is an observation sentence if all verdicts on it depend on present sensory stimulation and on no stored information beyond what goes into understanding the sentence.

This formulation raises another problem: how are we to distinguish between information that goes into understanding a sentence and information that goes beyond? This is the problem of distinguishing between analytic truth, which issues from the mere meanings of words, and synthetic truth, which depends on more than meanings. Now I have long maintained that this distinction is illusory. There is one step toward such a distinction, however, which does make sense: a sentence that is true by mere meanings of words should be expected, at least if it is simple, to be subscribed to by all fluent speakers in the community. Perhaps the controversial notion of analyticity can be dispensed with, in our definition of observation sentence, in favor of this straightforward attribute of community-wide acceptance.

This attribute is of course no explication of analyticity. The community would agree that there have been black dogs, yet none who talk of analyticity would call this analytic. My rejection of the analyticity notion just means drawing no line between what goes into the mere understanding of the sentences of a language and what else the community sees eye-to-eye on. I doubt that an objective distinction can be made between meaning and such collateral information as is community-wide.

Turning back then to our task of defining observation sentences, we get this: an observation sentence is one on which all speakers of the language give the same verdict when given the same concurrent stimulation. To put the point negatively, an observation sentence is one that is not sensitive to differences in past experience within the speech community.

This formulation accords perfectly with the traditional role of the observation sentence as the court of appeal of scientific theories. For by our definition the observation sentences are the sentences on which all members of the community will agree under uniform stimulation. And what is the criterion of membership in the same community? Simply general fluency of dialogue. This criterion admits of degrees, and indeed we may usefully take the community more narrowly for some studies than for others. What count as observation sentences for a community of specialists would not always so count for a larger community.

There is generally no subjectivity in the phrasing of observation sentences, as we are now conceiving them; they will usually be about bodies. Since the distinguishing trait of an observation sentence is intersubjective agreement under agreeing stimulation, a corporeal subject matter is likelier than not.

The old tendency to associate observation sentences with a subjective sensory subject matter is rather an irony when we reflect that observation sentences are also meant to be the intersubjective tribunal of scientific hypotheses. The old tendency was due to the drive to base science on something firmer and prior in the subject's experience; but we dropped that project.

The dislodging of epistemology from its old status of first philosophy loosed a wave, we saw, of epistemological nihilism. This mood is reflected somewhat in the tendency of Polányi, Kuhn, and the late Russell Hanson to belittle the role of evidence and to accentuate cultural relativism. Hanson ventured even to discredit the idea of observation, arguing that so-called observations vary from observer to observer with the amount of knowledge that the observers bring with them. The veteran physicist looks at some apparatus and sees an x-ray tube. The neophyte, looking at the same place, observes rather "a glass and metal instrument replete with wires, reflectors, screws, lamps, and pushbuttons."[4] One man's observation is another man's closed book or flight of fancy. The notion of observation as the impartial and objective source of evidence for science is bankrupt. Now my answer to the x-ray example was already hinted a little while back: what counts as an observation sentence varies with the width of community considered. But we can also always get an absolute standard by taking in all speakers of the language, or most.[5] It is ironical that philosophers, finding the old epistemology untenable as a whole, should react by repudiating a part which has only now moved into clear focus.

Clarification of the notion of observation sentence is a good thing, for the notion is fundamental in two connections. These two correspond to the duality that I remarked upon early in this lecture: the duality between concept and doctrine, between knowing what a sentence means and knowing whether it is true. The observation sentence is basic to both enterprises. Its relation to doctrine, to our knowledge of what is true, is very much the traditional one: observation sentences are the repository of evidence for scientific hypotheses. Its relation to meaning is fundamental too, since observation sentences are the ones we are in a position to learn to understand first, both as children and as field linguists. For observation sentences are precisely the ones that we can correlate with observable circumstances of the occasion of utterance or assent, independently of variations in the past histories of individual informants. They afford the only entry to a language.

The observation sentence is the cornerstone of semantics. For it is, as we just saw, fundamental to the learning of meaning. Also, it is where meaning is firmest. Sentences higher up in theories have no empirical consequences they can call their own; they confront the tribunal of sensory evidence only in more or less inclusive aggregates. The observation sentence, situated at the sensory periphery of the body scientific, is the minimal verifiable aggregate; it has an empirical content all its own and wears it on its sleeve.

The predicament of the indeterminacy of translation has little bearing on observation sentences. The equating of an observation sentence of our language to an observation sentence of another language is mostly a matter of empirical generalization; it is a matter of identity between the range of stimulations that would prompt assent to the one sentence and the range of stimulations that would prompt assent to the other.[6]

It is no shock to the preconceptions of old Vienna to say that epistemology now becomes semantics. For epistemology remains centered as always on evidence, and meaning remains centered as always on verification; and evidence is verification. What is likelier to shock preconceptions is that meaning, once we get beyond observation sentences, ceases in general to have any clear applicability to single sentences; also that epistemology merges with psychology, as well as with linguistics.

This rubbing out of boundaries could contribute to progress, it seems to me, in philosophically interesting inquiries of a scientific nature. One possible area is perceptual norms. Consider, to begin with, the linguistic phenomenon of phonemes. We form the habit, in hearing the myriad variations of spoken sounds, of treating each as an approximation to one or another of a limited number of norms—around thirty altogether—constituting so to speak a spoken alphabet. All speech in our language can be treated in practice as sequences of just those thirty elements, thus rectifying small deviations. Now outside the realm of language also there is probably only a rather limited alphabet of perceptual norms altogether, toward which we tend unconsciously to rectify all perceptions. These, if experimentally identified, could be taken as epistemological building blocks, the working elements of experience. They might prove in part to be culturally variable, as phonemes are, and in part universal.

Again there is the area that the psychologist Donald T. Campbell calls evolutionary epistemology.[7] In this area there is work by Hüseyin Yilmaz, who shows how some structural traits of color perception could have been predicted from survival value.[8] And a more emphatically epistemological topic that evolution helps to clarify is induction, now that we are allowing epistemology the resources of natural science.

NOTES

1. A. B. Johnson, A *Treatise on Language* (New York, 1836; Berkeley, 1947).

2. *Philosophy of Science* 3 (1936), 419–471; 4 (1937), 1–40.

3. Carnap and Neurath in *Erkenntnis* 3 (1932), 204–228.

4. N. R. Hanson, "Observation and interpretation," in S. Morgenbesser, ed., *Philosophy of Science Today* (New York: Basic Books, 1966).

5. This qualification allows for occasional deviants such as the insane or the blind. Alternatively, such cases might be excluded by adjusting the level of fluency of dialogue whereby we define sameness of language. (For prompting this note and influencing the development of this paper also in more substantial ways I am indebted to Burton Dreben.)

6. Cf. Quine, *Word and Object,* pp. 31–46, 68.

7. D. T. Campbell, "Methodological suggestions from a comparative psychology of knowledge processes," *Inquiry* 2 (1959), 152–182.

8. Hüseyin Yilmaz, "On color vision and a new approach to general perception," in E. E. Bernard and M. R. Kare, eds., *Biological Prototypes and Synthetic Systems* (New York: Plenum, 1962); "Perceptual invariance and the psychophysical law," *Perception and Psychophysics* 2 (1967), 533–538.

What Is "Naturalized Epistemology"?

JAEGWON KIM

Jaegwon Kim is William Herbert Perry Faunce Professor of Philosophy at Brown University. After pioneering early work on events and on the valuable philosophical concept known as "supervenience," in addition to work in the theory of knowledge, Kim has been especially interested in philosophy of mind. His books include *Supervenience and Mind* and *Mind in a Physical World.*

1. EPISTEMOLOGY AS A NORMATIVE INQUIRY

Descartes' epistemological inquiry in the *Meditations* begins with this question: What propositions are worthy of belief? In the *First Meditation* Descartes canvasses beliefs of various kinds he had formerly held as true and finds himself forced to conclude that he ought to reject them, that he ought not to accept them as true. We can view Cartesian epistemology as consisting of the following two projects: to identify the criteria by which we ought to regulate acceptance and rejection of beliefs, and to determine what we may be said to know according to those criteria. Descartes' epistemological agenda has been the agenda of Western epistemology to this day. The twin problems of identifying criteria of justified belief and coming to terms with the skeptical challenge to the possibility of knowledge have defined the central tasks of theory of knowledge since Descartes. This was as true of the

Reprinted from J. Tomberlin, ed., *Philosophical Perspectives, Vol. 2: Epistemology* (Atascadero, Calif.: Ridgeview Publishing Co., 1988), by permission of the publisher.

empiricists, of Locke and Hume and Mill, as of those who more closely followed Descartes in the rationalist path.[1]

It is no wonder then that modern epistemology has been dominated by a single concept, that of *justification,* and two fundamental questions involving it: What conditions must a belief meet if we are justified in accepting it as true? and What beliefs are we in fact justified in accepting? Note that the first question does not ask for an "analysis" or "meaning" of the term "justified belief." And it is generally assumed, even if not always explicitly stated, that not just any statement of a necessary and sufficient condition for a belief to be justified will do. The implicit requirement has been that the stated conditions must constitute "criteria" of justified belief, and for this it is necessary that the conditions be stated *without the use of epistemic terms.* Thus, formulating conditions of justified belief in such terms as "adequate evidence," "sufficient ground," "good reason," "beyond a reasonable doubt," and so on, would be merely to issue a promissory note redeemable only when these epistemic terms are themselves explained in a way that accords with the requirement.[2]

This requirement, while it points in the right direction, does not go far enough. What is crucial is this: *the criteria of justified belief must be formulated on the basis of descriptive or naturalistic terms alone, without the use of any evaluative or normative ones, whether epistemic or of another kind.*[3] Thus, an analysis of justified belief that makes use of such terms as "intellectual requirement"[4] and "having a right to be sure"[5] would not satisfy this generalized condition; although such an analysis can be informative and enlightening about the inter-relationships of these normative concepts, it will not, on the present conception, count as a statement of *criteria* of justified belief, unless of course these terms are themselves provided with nonnormative criteria. What is problematic, therefore, about the use of epistemic terms in stating criteria of justified belief is not its possible circularity in the usual sense; rather it is the fact that these epistemic terms are themselves essentially normative. We shall later discuss the rationale of this strengthened requirement.

As many philosophers have observed,[6] the two questions we have set forth, one about the criteria of justified belief and the other about what we can be said to know according to those criteria, constrain each other. Although some philosophers have been willing to swallow skepticism just because what we regard as correct criteria of justified belief are seen to lead inexorably to the conclusion that none, or very few, of our beliefs are justified, the usual presumption is that our answer to the first question should leave our epistemic situation largely unchanged. That is to say, it is expected to turn out that according to the criteria of justified belief we come to accept, we know, or are justified in believing, pretty much what we reflectively think we know or are entitled to believe.

Whatever the exact history, it is evident that the concept of justification has come to take center stage in our reflections on the nature of knowledge. And apart from history, there is a simple reason for our preoccupation with justification: it is the only specifically epistemic component in the classic tripartite conception of knowledge. Neither belief nor truth is a specifically epistemic notion: belief is a psychological concept and truth a semantical-metaphysical one. These concepts may have an implicit epistemological dimension, but if they do, it is likely to be through their involvement with essentially normative epistemic notions like justification, evidence, and rationality. Moreover, justification is what makes knowledge itself a normative concept. On surface at least, neither truth nor belief is normative or evaluative (I shall argue below, though, that belief does have an essential normative dimension). But justification manifestly is normative. If a belief is justified for us, then it is *permissible* and *reasonable,* from the epistemic point of view, for us to hold it, and it would be *epistemically irresponsible* to hold beliefs that contradict it. If we consider believing or accepting a proposition to be an "action" in an appropriate sense, belief justification would then be a special case of justification of action, which in its broadest terms is the central concern of normative ethics. Just as it is the business of normative ethics to delineate the conditions under which acts and decisions are justified from the moral point of view, so it is the business of epistemology to identify and analyze the conditions under which beliefs, and perhaps other propositional attitudes, are justified from the epistemological point of view. It probably is only an historical accident that we standardly speak of "normative ethics" but not of "normative epistemology." Epistemology is a normative discipline as much as, and in the same sense as, normative ethics.

We can summarize our discussion thus far in the following points: that justification is a central concept of our epistemological tradition, that justification, as it is understood in this tradition, is a normative concept, and in consequence that epistemology itself is a normative inquiry whose principal aim is a systematic study of the conditions of justified belief. I take it that these points are uncontroversial, although of course there could be disagreement about the details—for example, about what it means to say a concept or theory is "normative" or "evaluative."

2. THE FOUNDATIONALIST STRATEGY

In order to identify the target of the naturalistic critique—in particular, Quine's—it will be useful to take a brief look at the classic response to the epistemological program set forth by Descartes. Descartes' approach to the problem of justification is a familiar story, at least as the textbook tells it: it takes the form of what is now commonly called "foundationalism". The foundationalist strategy is to divide the task of explaining justification into two stages: first, to identify a set of beliefs that are "directly" justified in that they are justified without deriving their justified status from that of any other belief, and then to explain how other beliefs may be "indirectly" or "inferentially" justified by standing in an appropriate relation to those already justified. Directly justified beliefs, or "basic beliefs," are to constitute the foundation upon which the superstructure of "nonbasic" or "derived" beliefs is to rest. What beliefs then are directly justified, according to Descartes? Subtleties aside, he claimed that beliefs about our own present conscious states are among them. In what does their justifica-

tion consist? What is it about these beliefs that make them directly justified? Somewhat simplistically again, Descartes' answer is that they are justified because they are *indubitable,* that the attentive and reflective mind *cannot but assent* to them. How are nonbasic beliefs justified? By "deduction"—that is, by a series of inferential steps, or "intuitions", each of which is indubitable. If, therefore, we take Cartesian indubitability as a psychological notion, Descartes' epistemological theory can be said to meet the desideratum of providing nonepistemic, naturalistic criteria of justified belief.

Descartes' foundationalist program was inherited, in its essential outlines, by the empiricists. In particular, his "mentalism," that beliefs about one's own current mental state are epistemologically basic, went essentially unchallenged by the empiricists and positivists, until this century. Epistemologists have differed from one another chiefly in regard to two questions: first, what else belonged in our corpus of basic beliefs, and second, how the derivation of the nonbasic part of our knowledge was to proceed. Even the Logical Positivists were, by and large, foundationalists, although some of them came to renounce Cartesian mentalism in favor of a "physicalistic basis."[7] In fact, the Positivists were foundationalists twice over: for them "observation," whether phenomenological or physical, served not only as the foundation of knowledge but as the foundation of all "cognitive meaning"—that is, as both an epistemological and a semantic foundation.

3. QUINE'S ARGUMENTS

It has become customary for epistemologists who profess allegiance to a "naturalistic" conception of knowledge to pay homage to Quine as the chief contemporary provenance of their inspiration—especially to his influential paper "Epistemology Naturalized."[8] Quine's principal argument in this paper against traditional epistemology is based on the claim that the Cartesian foundationalist program has failed—that the Cartesian "quest for certainty" is "a lost cause." While this claim about the hopelessness of the Cartesian "quest for certainty" is nothing new, using it to discredit the very conception of normative epistemology is new, something that any serious student of epistemology must contend with.

Quine divides the classic epistemological program into two parts: *conceptual reduction* whereby physical terms, including those of theoretical science, are reduced, via definition, to terms referring to phenomenal features of sensory experience, and *doctrinal reduction* whereby truths about the physical world are appropriately obtained from truths about sensory experience. The "appropriateness" just alluded to refers to the requirement that the favored epistemic status ("certainty" for classic epistemologists, according to Quine) of our basic beliefs be transferred, essentially undiminished, to derived beliefs, a necessary requirement if the derivational process is to yield knowledge from knowledge. What derivational methods have this property of preserving epistemic status? Perhaps there are none, given our proneness to err in framing derivations as in anything else, not to mention the possibility of lapses of attention and memory in following lengthy proofs. But logical deduction comes as close to being one as any; it can at least be relied on to transmit truth, if not epistemic status. It could perhaps be argued that no method can preserve certainty unless it preserves (or is known to preserve) truth; and if this is so, logical deduction is the only method worth considering. I do not know whether this was the attitude of most classic epistemologists; but Quine assumes that if deduction doesn't fill their bill, nothing will.

Quine sees the project of conceptual reduction as culminating in Carnap's *Der Logische Aufbau der Welt.* As Quine sees it, Carnap "came nearest to executing" the conceptual half of the classic epistemological project. But coming close is not good enough. Because of the holistic manner in which empirical meaning is generated by experience, no reduction of the sort Carnap and others so eagerly sought could in principle be completed. For definitional reduction requires point-to-point meaning relations[9] between physical terms and phenomenal terms, something that Quine's holism tells us cannot be had. The second half of the program, doctrinal reduction, is in no better shape; in fact, it was the one to stumble first, for, according to Quine, its impossibility was decisively

demonstrated long before the *Aufbau,* by Hume in his celebrated discussion of induction. The "Humean predicament" shows that theory cannot be logically deduced from observation; there simply is no way of deriving theory from observation that will transmit the latter's epistemic status intact to the former.

I don't think anyone wants to disagree with Quine in these claims. It is not possible to "validate" science on the basis of sensory experience, if "validation" means justification through logical deduction. Quine of course does not deny that our theories depend on observation for evidential support; he has said that sensory evidence is the only evidence there is. To be sure, Quine's argument against the possibility of conceptual reduction has a new twist: the application of his "holism". But his conclusion is no surprise; "translational phenomenalism" has been moribund for many years.[10] And, as Quine himself notes, his argument against the doctrinal reduction, the "quest for certainty", is only a restatement of Hume's "skeptical" conclusions concerning induction: induction after all is not deduction. Most of us are inclined, I think, to view the situation Quine describes with no great alarm, and I rather doubt that these conclusions of Quine's came as news to most epistemologists when "Epistemology Naturalized" was first published. We are tempted to respond: of course we can't define physical concepts in terms of sense-data; of course observation "underdetermines" theory. That is why observation is observation and not theory.

So it is agreed on all hands that the classical epistemological project, conceived as one of deductively validating physical knowledge from indubitable sensory data, cannot succeed. But what is the moral of this failure? What should be its philosophical lesson to us? Having noted the failure of the Cartesian program, Quine goes on:[11]

The stimulation of his sensory receptors is all the evidence anybody has had to go on, ultimately, in arriving at his picture of the world. Why not just see how this construction really proceeds? Why not settle for psychology? Such a surrender of the epistemological burden to psychology is a move that was disallowed in earlier times as circular reasoning. If the epistemologist's goal is validation of the grounds of empirical science, he defeats his purpose by using psychology or other empirical science in the validation. However, such scruples against circularity have little point once we have stopped dreaming of deducing science from observation. If we are out simply to understand the link between observation and science, we are well advised to use any available information, including that provided by the very science whose link with observation we are seeking to understand.

And Quine has the following to say about the failure of Carnap's reductive program in the *Aufbau:*[12]

> To relax the demand for definition, and settle for a kind of reduction that does not eliminate, is to renounce the last remaining advantage that we supposed rational reconstruction to have over straight psychology; namely, the advantage of translational reduction. If all we hope for is a reconstruction that links science to experience in explicit ways short of translation, then it would seem more sensible to settle for psychology. Better to discover how science is in fact developed and learned than to fabricate a fictitious structure to a similar effect.

If a task is entirely hopeless, if we know it cannot be executed, no doubt it is rational to abandon it; we would be better off doing something else that has some hope of success. We can agree with Quine that the "validation"—that is, logical deduction—of science on the basis of observation cannot be had; so it is rational to abandon this particular epistemological program, if indeed it ever was a program that anyone seriously undertook. But Quine's recommendations go further. In particular, there are two aspects of Quine's proposals that are of special interest to us: first, he is not only advising us to quit the program of "validating science," but urging us to take up another specific project, an empirical psychological study of our cognitive processes; second, he is also claiming that this new program replaces the old, that both programs are part of something appropriately called "epistemology." Naturalized epistemology is to be a kind of epistemology after all, a "successor subject"[13] to classical epistemology.

How should we react to Quine's urgings? What should be our response? The Cartesian project of validating science starting from the indubitable foundation of first-person psychological reports (perhaps with the help of certain indubitable first principles) is not the whole of classical epistemology—or so it would seem at first blush. In our characterization of classical epistemology, the Cartesian program was seen as one possible response to the problem of epistemic justification, the two-part project of identifying the criteria of epistemic justification and determining what beliefs are in fact justified according to those criteria. In urging "naturalized epistemology" on us, Quine is not suggesting that we give up the Cartesian foundationalist solution and explore others within the same framework[14]—perhaps, to adopt some sort of "coherentist" strategy, or to require of our basic beliefs only some degree of "initial credibility" rather than Cartesian certainty, or to permit some sort of probabilistic derivation in addition to deductive derivation of nonbasic knowledge, or to consider the use of special rules of evidence, like Chisholm's "principles of evidence,"[15] or to give up the search for a derivational process that transmits undiminished certainty in favor of one that can transmit diminished but still useful degrees of justification. Quine's proposal is more radical than that. He is asking us to set aside the entire framework of justification-centered epistemology. That is what is new in Quine's proposals. Quine is asking us to put in its place a purely descriptive, causal-nomological science of human cognition.[16]

How should we characterize in general terms the difference between traditional epistemological programs, such as foundationalism and coherence theory, on the one hand and Quine's program of naturalized epistemology on the other? Quine's stress is on the *factual* and *descriptive* character of his program; he says, "Why not see how [the construction of theory from observation] *actually proceeds?* Why not settle for psychology?";[17] again, "Better to *discover how science is in fact developed and learned than....* [18] We are given to understand that in contrast traditional epistemology is not a descriptive, factual inquiry. Rather, it is an attempt at a "validation" or "rational reconstruction" of science. Validation, according to Quine, proceeds via deduction, and rational reconstruction via definition. However, their *point* is justificatory—that is, to rationalize our sundry knowledge claims. So Quine is asking us to set aside what is "rational" in rational reconstruction.

Thus, it is normativity that Quine is asking us to repudiate. Although Quine does not explicitly characterize traditional epistemology as "normative" or "prescriptive," his meaning is unmistakable. Epistemology is to be "a chapter of psychology," a law-based predictive-explanatory theory, like any other theory within empirical science; its principal job is to see how human cognizers develop theories (their "picture of the world") from observation ("the stimulation of their sensory receptors"). Epistemology is to go out of the business of justification. We earlier characterized traditional epistemology as essentially normative; we see why Quine wants us to reject it. Quine is urging us to replace a normative theory of cognition with a descriptive science.

4.   LOSING KNOWLEDGE FROM EPISTEMOLOGY

If justification drops out of epistemology, knowledge itself drops out of epistemology. For our concept of knowledge is inseparably tied to that of justification. As earlier noted, knowledge itself is a normative notion. Quine's nonnormative, naturalized epistemology has no room for our concept of knowledge. It is not surprising that, in describing naturalized epistemology, Quine seldom talks about knowledge; instead, he talks about "science" and "theories" and "representations." Quine would have us investigate how sensory stimulation "leads" to "theories" and "representation" of the world. I take it that within the traditional scheme these "theories" and "representations" correspond to beliefs, or systems of beliefs; thus, what Quine would have us do is to investigate how sensory stimulation leads to the formation of beliefs about the world.

But in what sense of "lead"? I take it that Quine has in mind a causal or nomological sense. He is urging us to develop a theory, an empirical theory, that uncovers lawful regularities governing the processes through which organisms come to develop beliefs about their environment as a causal result of having their sensory receptors stimulated in certain ways. Quine says:[19]

[Naturalized epistemology] studies a natural phenomenon, viz., a physical human subject. This human subject is accorded experimentally controlled input—certain patterns of irradiation in assorted frequencies, for instance—and in the fullness of time the subject delivers as output a description of the three-dimensional external world and its history. *The relation between the meager input and torrential output* is a relation that we are prompted to study for somewhat the same reasons that always prompted epistemology; namely, in order to see *how evidence relates to theory,* and in what ways one's theory of nature transcends any available evidence.

The relation Quine speaks of between "meager input" and "torrential output" is a causal relation; at least it is qua causal relation that the naturalized epistemologist investigates it. It is none of the naturalized epistemologist's business to assess whether, and to what degree, the input "justifies" the output, how a given irradiation of the subject's retinas makes it "reasonable" or "rational" for the subject to emit certain representational output. His interest is strictly causal and nomological: he wants us to look for patterns of lawlike dependencies characterizing the input-output relations for this particular organism and others of a like physical structure.

If this is right, it makes Quine's attempt to relate his naturalized epistemology to traditional epistemology look at best lame. For in what sense is the study of causal relationships between physical stimulation of sensory receptors and the resulting cognitive output a way of "seeing how evidence relates to theory" in an epistemologically relevant sense? The causal relation between sensory input and cognitive output is a relation between "evidence" and "theory"; however, it is not an *evidential relation*. This can be seen from the following consideration: the nomological patterns that Quine urges us to look for are certain to vary from species to species, depending on the particular way each biological (and possibly nonbiological) species processes information, but the evidential relation in its proper normative sense must abstract from such factors and concern itself only with the degree to which evidence supports hypothesis.

In any event, the concept of evidence is inseparable from that of justification. When we talk of "evidence" in an epistemological sense we are talking about justification: one thing is "evidence" for another just in case the first tends to enhance the reasonableness or justification of the second. And such evidential relations hold in part because of the "contents" of the items involved, not merely because of the causal or nomological connections between them. A strictly nonnormative concept of evidence is not our concept of evidence; it is something that we do not understand.[20]

None of us, I think, would want to quarrel with Quine about the interest or importance of the psychological study of how our sensory input causes our epistemic output. This is only to say that the study of human (or other kinds of) cognition is of interest. That isn't our difficulty; our difficulty is whether, and in what sense, pursuing Quine's "epistemology" is a way of doing epistemology—that is, a way of studying "how evidence relates to theory." Perhaps, Quine's recommendation that we discard justification-centered epistemology is worth pondering; and his exhortation to take up the study of psychology perhaps deserves to be heeded also. What is mysterious is why this recommendation has to be coupled with the rejection of normative epistemology (if normative epistemology is not a possible inquiry, why shouldn't the would-be epistemologist turn to, say, hydrodynamics or ornithology rather than psychology?). But of course Quine is saying more; he is saying that an understandable, if misguided, motivation (that is, seeing "how evidence relates to theory") does underlie our proclivities for indulgence in normative epistemology, but that we would be better served by a scientific study of human cognition than normative epistemology.

But it is difficult to see how an "epistemology" that has been purged of normativity, one that lacks an appropriate normative concept of justification or evidence, can have anything to do with the concerns of traditional epistemology. And unless naturalized epistemology and classical epistemology share some of their central concerns, it's difficult to see how one could *replace* the other, or be a way (a better way) of doing the other.[21] To be sure, they both investigate "how evidence relates to theory." But putting the matter this way can be misleading, and has perhaps

misled Quine: the two disciplines do not investigate the same relation. As lately noted, normative epistemology is concerned with the evidential relation properly so-called—that is, the relation of justification—and Quine's naturalized epistemology is meant to study the causal-nomological relation. For epistemology to go out of the business of justification is for it to go out of business.[22] . . .

Two important themes underlie these convictions: first, values, though perhaps not reducible to facts, must be "consistent" with them in that objects that are indiscernible in regard to fact must be indiscernible in regard to value; second, there must be nonvaluational "reasons" or "grounds" for the attribution of values, and these "reasons" or "grounds" must be *generalizable*—that is, they are covered by *rules* or *norms*. These two ideas correspond to "weak supervenience" and "strong supervenience" that I have discussed elsewhere.[23] Belief in the supervenience of value upon fact, arguably, is fundamental to the very concepts of value and valuation.[24] Any valuational concept, to be significant, must be governed by a set of criteria, and these criteria must ultimately rest on factual characteristics and relationships of objects and events being evaluated. There is something deeply incoherent about the idea of an infinitely descending series of valuational concepts, each depending on the one below it as its criterion of application.[25]

It seems to me, therefore, that epistemological supervenience is what underlies our belief in the possibility of normative epistemology, and that we do not need new inspirations from the sciences to acknowledge the existence of naturalistic criteria for epistemic and other valuational concepts. The case of normative ethics is entirely parallel: belief in the possibility of normative ethics is rooted in the belief that moral properties and relations are supervenient upon nonmoral ones. Unless we are prepared to disown normative ethics as a viable philosophical inquiry, we had better recognize normative epistemology as one, too.[26] We should note, too, that epistemology is likely to parallel normative ethics in regard to the degree to which scientific results are relevant or useful to its development.[27] Saying this of course leaves large room for disagreement concerning how relevant and useful, if at all, empirical psychology of human motivation and action can be to the development and confirmation of normative ethical theories.[28] In any event, once the normativity of epistemology is clearly taken note of, it is no surprise that epistemology and normative ethics share the same metaphilosophical fate. Naturalized epistemology makes no more, and no less, sense than naturalized normative ethics.[29]

NOTES

1. In making these remarks I am only repeating the familiar textbook history of philosophy; however, what *our* textbooks say about the history of a philosophical concept has much to do with *our* understanding of that concept.

2. Alvin Goldman explicitly states this requirement as a desideratum of his own analysis of justified belief in "What is Justified Belief?," in George S. Pappas (ed.), *Justification and Knowledge* (Dordrecht: Reidel, 1979), p. 1. Roderick M. Chisholm's definition of "being evident" in his *Theory of Knowledge,* 2nd ed. (Englewood Cliffs, N.J.: Prentice-Hall, 1977) does not satisfy this requirement as it rests ultimately on an unanalyzed epistemic concept of one belief being *more reasonable than* another. What does the real "criteriological" work for Chisholm is his "principles of evidence." See especially (A) on p. 73 of *Theory of Knowledge,* which can usefully be regarded as an attempt to provide nonnormative, descriptive conditions for certain types of justified beliefs.

3. The basic idea of this stronger requirement seems implicit in Roderick Firth's notion of "warrant-increasing property" in his "Coherence, Certainty, and Epistemic Priority," *Journal of Philosophy* 61 (1964): 545–57. It seems that William P. Alston has something similar in mind when he says, " . . . like any evaluative property, epistemic justification is a supervenient property, the application of which is based on more fundamental properties" (at this point Alston refers to Firth's paper cited above), in "Two Types of Foundationalism," *Journal of Philosophy* 73 (1976): 165–85 (the quoted remark occurs on p. 170). Although Alston doesn't further explain what he means by "more fundamental properties," the context makes it plausible to suppose that he has in mind nonnormative, descriptive properties. . . .

4. See Chisholm, ibid., p. 14. Here Chisholm refers to a "person's responsibility or duty *qua* intellectual being."

5. This term was used by A. J. Ayer to characterize the difference between lucky guessing and knowing; see *The Problem of Knowledge* (New York & London: Penguin Books, 1956), p. 33.

6. Notably by Chisholm in *Theory of Knowledge,* 1st ed., ch. 4.

7. See Rudolf Carnap, "Testability and Meaning," *Philosophy of Science* 3 (1936), and 4 (1937). We should also note the presence of a strong coherentist streak among some positivists; see, e.g., Carl G. Hempel, "On the Logical Positivists' Theory of Truth," *Analysis* 2 (1935): 49–59, and "Some Remarks on 'Facts' and Propositions," *Analysis* 2 (1935): 93–96.

8. In W.V. Quine, *Ontological Relativity and Other Essays* (New York: Columbia University Press, 1969). Also see his *Word and Object* (Cambridge: MIT Press, 1960); *The Roots of Reference* (La Salle, Ill.: Open Court, 1973); (with Joseph Ullian) *The Web of Belief* (New York: Random House, 1970); and especially "The Nature of Natural Knowledge" in Samuel Guttenplan (ed.), *Mind and Language* (Oxford: Clarendon Press, 1975). See Frederick F. Schmitt's excellent bibliography on naturalistic epistemology in Hilary Kornblith (ed.), *Naturalizing Epistemology* (Cambridge: MIT/Bradford, 1985).

9. Or confirmational relations, given the Positivists' verificationist theory of meaning.

10. I know of no serious defense of it since Ayer's *The Foundations of Empirical Knowledge* (London: Macmillan, 1940).

11. "Epistemology Naturalized," pp. 75–76.

12. Ibid., p. 78.

13. To use an expression of Richard Rorty's in *Philosophy and the Mirror of Nature* (Princeton: Princeton University Press, 1979), p. 11.

14. Elliott Sober makes a similar point: "And on the question of whether the failure of a foundationalist programme shows that questions of justification cannot be answered, it is worth noting that Quine's advice 'Since Carnap's foundationalism failed, why not settle for psychology' carries weight only to the degree that Carnapian epistemology exhausts the possibilities of epistemology", in "Psychologism," *Journal of Theory of Social Behaviour* 8 (1978): 165–191.

15. See Chisholm, *Theory of Knowledge,* 2nd ed., ch. 4.

16. "If we are seeking only the causal mechanism of our knowledge of the external world, and not a justification of that knowledge in terms prior to science . . . ," Quine, "Grades of Theoreticity," in L. Foster and J.W. Swanson (eds.), *Experience and Theory* (Amherst: University of Massachusetts Press, 1970), p. 2.

17. Ibid., p. 75. Emphasis added.

18. Ibid., p. 78. Emphasis added.

19. Ibid., p. 83. Emphasis added.

20. But aren't there those who advocate a "causal theory" of evidence or justification? I want to make two brief

points about this. First, the nomological or causal input/output relations are not in themselves evidential relations, whether these latter are understood causally or otherwise. Second, a causal theory of evidence attempts to state *criteria* for "e is evidence for h" in causal terms; even if this is successful, it does not necessarily give us a causal "definition" or "reduction" of the concept of evidence. . . .

21. I am not saying that Quine is under any illusion on this point. My remarks are directed rather at those who endorse Quine without, it seems, a clear appreciation of what is involved.

22. Here I am drawing chiefly on Donald Davidson's writings on radical interpretation. See Essays 9, 10, and 11 in his *Inquiries into Truth and Interpretation* (Oxford: Clarendon Press, 1984). See also David Lewis, "Radical Interpretation," *Synthese* 27 (1974): 331–44.

23. See "Concepts of Supervenience," *Philosophy and Phenomenological Research* 65 (1984): 153–76.

24. Ernest Sosa, too, considers epistemological supervenience as a special case of the supervenience of valuational properties on naturalistic conditions, in "The Foundation of Foundationalism," *Nous* 14 (1980): 547–64; especially p. 551. See also James Van Cleve's instructive discussion in his "Epistemic Supervenience and the Circle of Belief," The *Monist* 68 (1985): 90–104; especially, pp. 97–99.

25. Perhaps one could avoid this kind of criteriological regress by embracing directly apprehended valuational properties (as in ethical intuitionism) on the basis of which criteria for other valuational properties could be formulated. The denial of the supervenience of valuational concepts on factual characteristics, however, would sever the essential connection between value and fact on which, it seems, the whole point of our valuational activities depends. In the absence of such supervenience, the very notion of valuation would lose its significance and relevance. The elaboration of these points, however, would have to wait for another occasion; but see Van Cleve's paper cited in the preceding note for more details.

26. Quine will not disagree with this: he will "naturalize" them both. For his views on values see "The Nature of Moral Values" in Alvin I. Goldman and Jaegwon Kim (eds.), *Values and Morals* (Dordrecht: Reidel, 1978). For a discussion of the relationship between epistemic and ethical concepts see Roderick Firth, "Are Epistemic Concepts Reducible to Ethical Concepts?" in the same volume.

27. For discussions of this and related issues see Alvin I. Goldman, *Epistemology and Cognition* (Cambridge: Harvard University Press, 1986).

28. For a detailed development of a normative ethical theory that exemplifies the view that it is crucially relevant,

see Richard B. Brandt, *A Theory of the Good and the Right* (Oxford: The Clarendon Press, 1979).

29. An early version of this paper was read at a meeting of the Korean Society for Analytic Philosophy in 1984 in Seoul. An expanded version was presented at a symposium at the Western Division meetings of the American Philosophical Association in April, 1985, and at the epistemology conference at Brown University in honor of Roderick Chisholm in 1986. I am grateful to Richard Foley and Robert Audi who presented helpful comments at the APA session and the Chisholm Conference respectively. I am also indebted to Terence Horgan and Robert Meyers for helpful comments and suggestions.

REFERENCES

Alston, William P., "Two Types of Foundationalism" *Journal of Philosophy* 73 (1976): 165–85.

Armstrong, David M., *Truth, Belief and Knowledge* (London: Cambridge University Press, 1973).

Ayer, A.J., *The Foundations of Empirical Knowledge* (London: Macmillan, 1940).

Ayer, A.J., *The Problem of Knowledge* (New York & London: Penguin Books, 1956).

Brandt, Richard B., *A Theory of the Good and the Right* (Oxford: The Clarendon Press, 1979).

Carnap, Rudolf, "Testability and Meaning," *Philosophy of Science* 3 (1936), and 4 (1937).

Chisholm, Roderick M., *Theory of Knowledge,* 2nd ed. (Englewood Cliffs, N.J.: Prentice-Hall, 1977).

Davidson, Donald, *Inquiries into Truth and Interpretation* (Oxford: Clarendon Press, 1984).

Firth, Roderick, "Coherence, Certainty, and Epistemic Priority," *Journal of Philosophy* 61 (1964): 545–57.

Firth, Roderick, "Are Epistemic Concepts Reducible to Ethical Concepts?" in Goldman, Alvin I. and Jaegwon Kim (eds.), *Values and Morals* (Dordrecht: Reidel, 1978).

Goldman, Alvin I., "What is Justified Belief?," in George S. Pappas (ed.), *Justification and Knowledge* (Dordrecht: Reidel, 1979).

Goldman, Alvin I., *Epistemology and Cognition* (Cambridge: Harvard University Press, 1986).

Hare, R.M., *The Language of Morals* (London: Oxford University Press, 1952).

Hempel, Carl G., "On the Logical Positivists' Theory of Truth," *Analysis* 2 (1935): 49–59.

Hempel, Carl G., "Some Remarks on 'Facts' and Propositions," *Analysis* 2 (1935): 93–96.

Kim, Jaegwon, "Concepts of Supervenience," *Philosophy and Phenomenological Research* 65 (1984): 153–176.

Kim, Jaegwon, "Psychophysical Laws," in Ernest LePore and Brian McLaughlin (eds.), *Actions and Events: Perspectives on the Philosophy of Donald Davidson* (Oxford: Blackwell, 1985).

Kitcher, Phillip, *The Nature of Mathematical Knowledge* (New York: Oxford University Press, 1983).

Kornblith, Hilary, "The Psychological Turn," *Australasian Journal of Philosophy* 60 (1982): 238–253.

Kornblith, Hilary, (ed.), *Naturalizing Epistemology* (Cambridge: MIT/Bradford, 1985).

Kornblith, Hilary, "What is Naturalistic Epistemology?," in Kornblith (ed.), *Naturalizing Epistemology.*

Lewis, David, "Radical Interpretation," *Synthese* 27 (1974): 331–44.

Moore, G.E., "A Reply to My Critics", in P.A. Schilpp (ed.), *The Philosophy of G. E. Moore* (Chicago & Evanston: Open Court, 1942).

Quine, W.V., *Word and Object* (Cambridge: MIT Press, 1960).

Quine, W.V., *Ontological Relativity and Other Essays* (New York: Columbia University Press, 1969).

Quine, W.V., (with Joseph Ullian), *The Web of Belief* (New York: Random House, 1970).

Quine, W.V., "Grades of Theoreticity," in L. Foster and J. W. Swanson (eds.), *Experience and Theory* (Amherst: University of Massachusetts Press, 1970).

Quine, W. V., *The Roots of Reference* (La Salle, IL,: Open Court, 1973); Quine, W.V., "The Nature of Natural Knowledge" in Samuel Guttenplan (ed.), *Mind and Language* (Oxford: Clarendon Press, 1975).

Quine, W.V., "The Nature of Moral Values" in Alvin I. Goldman and Jaegwon Kim (eds.), *Values and Morals* (Dordrecht: Reidel, 1978).

Rorty, Richard, *Philosophy and the Mirror of Nature* (Princeton: Princeton University Press, 1979).

Sober, Elliott, "Psychologism," *Journal of Theory of Social Behavior* 8 (1978): 165–191.

Sosa, Ernest, "The Foundation of Foundationalism," *Nous* 14 (1980): 547–64.

Van Cleve, James, "Epistemic Supervenience and the Circle of Belief," *The Monist* 68 (1985): 90–104.

PART 3

~

Philosophy of Science

Introduction

L. A. PAUL

Scientists construct scientific theories about the physical world that enable us to manipulate objects and predict and understand the occurrence of events. Philosophers of science, on the other hand, analyze the nature of scientific inferences, methods, explanations, and theories to determine science's contribution to our knowledge of the world. Philosophers of science do so by investigating, among other things, how well we can justify claims made by scientific theories, whether the theorems of scientific theories are true or even approximately true, what laws of nature may be, and how science discovers them.

One of the most important issues philosophers of science address involves the nature of the inferences that we use to construct general claims and predict what will happen in certain circumstances. In science, as in everyday life, it seems that we rely on *induction* to make predictions about what to expect in the future. Induction is a process whereby we use our experience about the past and the present to make generalizations that we expect will hold in the future, or at least in the next instance. For example, on every morning of my past experience, the sun has come up in the east, and it has come up in the east on this morning as well. On the basis of my experience, I can use induction to construct the generalization that *the sun comes up every morning in the east.* Using this inductive generalization, I predict that tomorrow morning the sun will come up in the east.

David Hume calls into question the justifiability of the reasoning that scientists (and everyday people) use to make claims about unobserved matters of fact. When scientists want to predict something will happen or make claims about parts of the universe they have not observed, they rely on inductive generalizations. Hume asks: on what grounds are we rationally justified in relying on such generalizations? If our justification is that in the past the future has resembled the past, this won't do, for in order to infer that the future will resemble the past from the fact that in the past the future has resembled the past, we have to assume that the future will resemble the past. But to assume here that the future will resemble the past is circular, and hence rationally unjustified, which seems to imply that scientific reasoning based on inductive generalization is also rationally unjustified.

Brian Skyrms discusses Hume's argument in terms of the problem of providing a rational justification of inductive reasoning or inductive logic. Skyrms shows how Hume's arguments place us in a dilemma: we cannot use deductively valid arguments to rationally justify the use of induction, and if we try to use inductively strong arguments to rationally justify induction, we beg the question.

Perhaps the only way out of the dilemma is to deny that it exists: in an effort to sidestep Hume's skeptical paradox, Gilbert Harman argues that warranted scientific reasoning and prediction about unobserved matters of fact rely on inference to the best explanation (IBE). IBE is the principle that the best explanation of the facts is also the true explanation; hence, it licenses the inference from an explanation being the best explanation of a fact to the explanation's being a true explanation of that fact. If Harman is correct, and if IBE can be rationally justified, then science can escape Hume's paradox.

To understand how we use IBE to identify patterns and discover uniformities of nature, also called "laws of nature," we must understand the role of empirical methods in collecting data and constructing scientific theories. Rudolf Carnap discusses how we use the experimental method to discover empirical facts and make inferences about laws of nature.

Once we discover the laws of nature, how do we use our knowledge of these laws to understand the world? Carl G. Hempel explores how we determine that lawlike statements describe laws and presents a theory of scientific explanation. Hempel calls his account of explanation the deductive-nomological or D-N model of explanation. The D-N model (a species of what is called a "covering-law model") is designed to show how descriptions of matters of empirical fact taken together with statements of laws of nature can deductively imply a description of the phenomenon to be explained. Hempel holds that when we describe a law of nature, we describe a matter of objective fact and that only true lawlike statements describe laws. Laws of nature, since they apply universally, are "covering laws." Hempel's account provides us with a picture of scientific theorizing as a procedure whereby we describe and explain the world by fitting together empirical facts with covering laws.

Nancy Cartwright challenges the idea that describing nature and explaining nature fit together in the way that Hempel and others have assumed. Covering-law models hold that we have scientific explanations in virtue of the fact that the phenomena explained are subsumed by universally true laws of nature. But as Cartwright shows, many scientific phenomena for which we have perfectly good scientific explanations are explained by regularities that hold only under special circumstances (ceteris paribus regularities) rather than covering laws. Cartwright's article shows that theories of scientific explanation need significant revision in order to account for the role of ceteris paribus regularities.

Nelson Goodman raises a new problem (the "new riddle of induction") for scientific realists who hold that results of predictions can be used to confirm the truth of scientific theories. His worry is formulated in terms of projectibility: when can we be sure that a lawlike claim that is part of a scientific theory is projectible, that is, that it describes the sort of regularity that is eligible to be a law of nature? Goodman argues that the problem of distinguishing projectible generalizations from nonprojectible generalizations is a serious problem. If, when making predictions, scientists cannot be sure they are relying upon projectible generalizations, they cannot use the results of their predictions to confirm the objective truth of their theories.

A further objection to the scientific realist challenges the realist's picture of science as a cumulative process of the discovery and refinement of objective knowledge. Thomas Kuhn argues that the role of scientific revolutions in scientific development is to facilitate radical theoretical changes in which old theories are discarded and entirely new theories are adopted in their place. Hence, science does not give us a cumulative increase of knowledge of the world; rather, it gives us a succession of wholly different conceptions of the world.

Richard Boyd defends the realist conception of science that scientific theories are (at least approximately) true against the problems raised by Kuhn, Goodman and others. He argues that the scientific method gives us a successful guide to facts about the empirical world and that scientific realism gives us an adequate explanation for the success of the scientific method. Those who challenge realism by raising concerns about projectibility and the like have no adequate explanation for the success of science; hence, we should prefer the realist conception of science to the opposing "antirealist" or "instrumentalist" conception of science.

The selections included in this section represent only a sampling of the philosophical analyses of science advanced by past and current philosophers of science. Debate on almost every topic addressed continues to flourish in contemporary philosophical circles. Although there is no definitive agreement among the contributors as to what constitutes science's contribution to our knowledge of the world, a careful reading of the text should help the thoughtful reader to develop a broader, deeper, and more sophisticated philosophical conception of science and scientific knowledge.

An Enquiry Concerning Human Understanding

~

DAVID HUME

David Hume (1711–1776) was a Scottish philosopher and leading exponent of British empiricism. His books include the *Treatise of Human Nature, An Enquiry Concerning the Principles of Morals,* and *Dialogues Concerning Natural Religion.*

When it is asked, *What is the nature of all our reasonings concerning matter of fact?* the proper answer seems to be, that they are founded on the relation of cause and effect. When again it is asked, *What is the foundation of all our reasonings and conclusions concerning that relation?* it may be replied in one word, Experience. But if we still carry on our sifting humour, and ask, *What is the foundation of all conclusions from experience?* this implies a new question, which may be of more difficult solution and explication. Philosophers, that give themselves airs of superior

wisdom and sufficiency, have a hard task when they encounter persons of inquisitive dispositions, who push them from every corner to which they retreat, and who are sure at last to bring them to some dangerous dilemma. The best expedient to prevent this confusion, is to be modest in our pretensions; and even to discover the difficulty ourselves before it is objected to us. By this means, we may make a kind of merit of our very ignorance.

I shall content myself, in this section, with an easy task, and shall pretend only to give a negative answer to the question here proposed.

David Hume, *An Essay Concerning Human Understanding.*

I say then, that, even after we have experience of the operations of cause and effect, our conclusions from that experience are *not* founded on reasoning, or any process of the understanding. This answer we must endeavour both to explain and to defend.

It must certainly be allowed, that nature has kept us at a great distance from all her secrets, and has afforded us only the knowledge of a few superficial qualities of objects; while she conceals from us those powers and principles on which the influence of these objects entirely depends. Our senses inform us of the colour, weight, and consistence of bread; but neither sense nor reason can ever inform us of those qualities which fit it for the nourishment and support of a human body. Sight or feeling conveys an idea of the actual motion of bodies; but as to that wonderful force or power, which would carry on a moving body for ever in a continued change of place, and which bodies never lose but by communicating it to others; of this we cannot form the most distant conception. But notwithstanding this ignorance of natural powers[1] and principles, we always presume, when we see like sensible qualities, that they have like secret powers, and expect that effects, similar to those which we have experienced, will follow from them. If a body of like colour and consistence with that bread, which we have formerly eat, be presented to us, we make no scruple of repeating the experiment, and foresee, with certainty, like nourishment and support. Now this is a process of the mind or thought, of which I would willingly know the foundation. It is allowed on all hands that there is no known connexion between the sensible qualities and the secret powers; and consequently, that the mind is not led to form such a conclusion concerning their constant and regular conjunction, by anything which it knows of their nature. As to past *Experience,* it can be allowed to give *direct* and *certain* information of those precise objects only, and that precise period of time, which fell under its cognizance: but why this experience should be extended to future times, and to other objects, which for aught we know, may be only in appearance similar; this is the main question on which I would insist. The bread, which I formerly eat, nourished me; that is, a body of such sensible qualities was, at that time, endued with such secret powers: but does it follow, that other bread must also nourish me at another time, and that like sensible qualities must always be attended with like secret powers? The consequence seems nowise necessary. At least, it must be acknowledged that there is here a consequence drawn by the mind; that there is a certain step taken; a process of thought, and an inference, which wants to be explained. These two propositions are far from being the same, *I have found that such an object has always been attended with such an effect,* and *I foresee, that other objects, which are, in appearance, similar, will be attended with similar effects.* I shall allow, if you please, that the one proposition may justly be inferred from the other: I know, in fact, that it always is inferred. But if you insist that the inference is made by a chain of reasoning, I desire you to produce that reasoning. The connexion between these propositions is not intuitive. There is required a medium, which may enable the mind to draw such an inference, if indeed it be drawn by reasoning and argument. What that medium is, I must confess, passes my comprehension; and it is incumbent on those to produce it, who assert that it really exists, and is the origin of all our conclusions concerning matter of fact.

This negative argument must certainly, in process of time, become altogether convincing, if many penetrating and able philosophers shall turn their enquiries this way and no one be ever able to discover any connecting proposition or intermediate step, which supports the understanding in this conclusion. But as the question is yet new, every reader may not trust so far to his own penetration, as to conclude, because an argument escapes his enquiry, that therefore it does not really exist. For this reason it may be requisite to venture upon a more difficult task;

30

and enumerating all the branches of human knowledge, endeavour to show that none of them can afford such an argument.

All reasonings may be divided into two kinds, namely, demonstrative reasoning, or that concerning relations of ideas, and moral reasoning, or that concerning matter of fact and existence. That there are no demonstrative arguments in the case seems evident; since it implies no contradiction that the course of nature may change, and that an object, seemingly like those which we have experienced, may be attended with different or contrary effects. May I not clearly and distinctly conceive that a body, falling from the clouds, and which, in all other respects, resembles snow, has yet the taste of salt or feeling of fire? Is there any more intelligible proposition than to affirm, that all the trees will flourish in December and January, and decay in May and June? Now whatever is intelligible, and can be distinctly conceived, implies no contradiction, and can never be proved false by any demonstrative argument or abstract reasoning *à priori*.

If we be, therefore, engaged by arguments to put trust in past experience, and make it the standard of our future judgement, these arguments must be probable only, or such as regard matter of fact and real existence, according to the division above mentioned. But that there is no argument of this kind, must appear, if our explication of that species of reasoning be admitted as solid and satisfactory. We have said that all arguments concerning existence are founded on the relation of cause and effect; that our knowledge of that relation is derived entirely from experience; and that all our experimental conclusions proceed upon the supposition that the future will be conformable to the past. To endeavour, therefore, the proof of this last supposition by probable arguments, or arguments regarding existence, must be evidently going in a circle, and taking that for granted, which is the very point in question.

31 In reality, all arguments from experience are founded on the similarity which we discover among natural objects, and by which we are induced to expect effects similar to those which we have found to follow from such objects. And though none but a fool or madman will ever pretend to dispute the authority of experience, or to reject that great guide of human life, it may surely be allowed a philosopher to have so much curiosity at least as to examine the principle of human nature, which gives this mighty authority to experience, and makes us draw advantage from that similarity which nature has placed among different objects. From causes which appear *similar* we expect similar effects. This is the sum of all our experimental conclusions. Now it seems evident that, if this conclusion were formed by reason, it would be as perfect at first, and upon one instance, as after ever so long a course of experience. But the case is far otherwise. Nothing so like as eggs; yet no one, on account of this appearing similarity, expects the same taste and relish in all of them. It is only after a long course of uniform experiments in any kind, that we attain a firm reliance and security with regard to a particular event. Now where is that process of reasoning which, from one instance, draws a conclusion, so different from that which it infers from a hundred instances that are nowise different from that single one? This question I propose as much for the sake of information, as with an intention of raising difficulties. I cannot find, I cannot imagine any such reasoning. But I keep my mind still open to instruction, if any one will vouchsafe to bestow it on me.

Should it be said that, from a number of uniform experiments, we *infer* a connexion between the sensible qualities and the secret powers; this, I must confess, seems the same difficulty, couched in different terms. The question still recurs, on what process of argument this *inference* is founded? Where is the medium, the interposing ideas, which join propositions so very wide of each other? It is confessed that the colour, consistence, and other sensible qualities of bread appear not, of

32

themselves, to have any connexion with the secret powers of nourishment and support. For otherwise we could infer these secret powers from the first appearance of these sensible qualities, without the aid of experience; contrary to the sentiment of all philosophers, and contrary to plain matter of fact. Here, then, is our natural state of ignorance with regard to the powers and influence of all objects. How is this remedied by experience? It only shows us a number of uniform effects, resulting from certain objects, and teaches us that those particular objects, at that particular time, were endowed with such powers and forces. When a new object, endowed with similar sensible qualities, is produced, we expect similar powers and forces, and look for a like effect. From a body of like colour and consistence with bread we expect like nourishment and support. But this surely is a step or progress of the mind, which wants to be explained. When a man says, *I have found, in all past instances, such sensible qualities conjoined with such secret powers:* And when he says, *Similar sensible qualities will always be conjoined with similar secret powers,* he is not guilty of a tautology, nor are these propositions in any respect the same. You say that the one proposition is an inference from the other. But you must confess that the inference is not intuitive; neither is it demonstrative: Of what nature is it, then? To say it is experimental, is begging the question. For all inferences from experience suppose, as their foundation, that the future will resemble the past, and that similar powers will be conjoined with similar sensible qualities. If there be any suspicion that the course of nature may change, and that the past may be no rule for the future, all experience becomes useless, and can give rise to no inference or conclusion. It is impossible, therefore, that any arguments from experience can prove this resemblance of the past to the future; since all these arguments are founded on the supposition of that resemblance. Let the course of things be allowed hitherto ever so regular; that alone, without

some new argument or inference, proves not that, for the future, it will continue so. In vain do you pretend to have learned the nature of bodies from your past experience. Their secret nature, and consequently all their effects and influence, may change, without any change in their sensible qualities. This happens sometimes, and with regard to some objects: Why may it not happen always, and with regard to all objects? What logic, what process of argument secures you against this supposition? My practice, you say, refutes my doubts. But you mistake the purport of my question. As an agent, I am quite satisfied in the point; but as a philosopher, who has some share of curiosity, I will not say scepticism, I want to learn the foundation of this inference. No reading, no enquiry has yet been able to remove my difficulty, or give me satisfaction in a matter of such importance. Can I do better than propose the difficulty to the public, even though, perhaps, I have small hopes of obtaining a solution? We shall at least, by this means, be sensible of our ignorance, if we do not augment our knowledge.

I must confess that a man is guilty of unpardonable arrogance who concludes, because an argument has escaped his own investigation, that therefore it does not really exist. I must also confess that, though all the learned, for several ages, should have employed themselves in fruitless search upon any subject, it may still, perhaps, be rash to conclude positively that the subject must, therefore, pass all human comprehension. Even though we examine all the sources of our knowledge, and conclude them unfit for such a subject, there may still remain a suspicion, that the enumeration is not complete, or the examination not accurate. But with regard to the present subject, there are some considerations which seem to remove all this accusation of arrogance or suspicion of mistake.

It is certain that the most ignorant and stupid peasants—nay infants, nay even brute beasts—improve by experience, and learn the qualities of natural objects, by observing the effects which result from them. When a child has felt the sensation of pain from touching the flame of a candle, he will be careful not to put his hand near any candle; but will expect a similar effect from a cause which is similar in its sensible qualities and appearance. If you assert, therefore, that the understanding of the child is led into this conclusion by any process of argument or ratiocination, I may justly require you to produce that argument; nor have you any pretence to refuse so equitable a demand. You cannot say that the argument is abstruse, and may possibly escape your enquiry; since you confess that it is obvious to the capacity of a mere infant. If you hesitate, therefore, a moment, or if, after reflection, you produce any intricate or profound argument, you, in a manner, give up the question, and confess that it is not reasoning which engages us to suppose the past resembling the future, and to expect similar effects from causes which are, to appearance, similar. This is the proposition which I intended to enforce in the present section. If I be right, I pretend not to have made any mighty discovery. And if I be wrong, I must acknowledge myself to be indeed a very backward scholar; since I cannot now discover an argument which, it seems, was perfectly familiar to me long before I was out of my cradle.

NOTE

1. The word, Power, is here used in a loose and popular sense. The more accurate explication of it would give additional evidence to this argument.

The Traditional Problem of Induction

～

BRIAN SKYRMS

Brian Skryms is professor of logic and philosophy of science at the University of California at Irvine. He has made important contributions to theories of inductive logic, game theory, and decision theory. His books include *Choice and Chance, Causal Necessity,* and *The Dynamics of Rational Deliberation.*

INTRODUCTION

[I]nductive logic is used to shape our expectations of that which is as yet unknown on the basis of those facts that are already known; for instance, to shape our expectations of the future on the basis of our knowledge of the past and present. Our problem is the rational justification of the use of a system of scientific inductive logic, rather than some other system of inductive logic, for this task.

The Scottish philosopher David Hume first raised this problem, which we shall call the *traditional problem of induction,* in full force.[1] Hume gave the problem a cutting edge, for he advanced arguments designed to show that no such rational justification of inductive logic is possible, no matter what the details of a system of scientific inductive logic turn out to be. The history of philosophical discussion of inductive logic since Hume has been in large measure occupied with attempts to circumvent the difficulties he raised. . . .

Reprinted from *Choice and Chance* (Belmont, Calif.: Wadsworth, 1986), by permission of the publishers.

Hume's Argument

Before we can meaningfully discuss arguments which purport to show that it is impossible to rationally justify scientific induction, we must be clear on what would be required to rationally justify a system of inductive logic. Presumably we could rationally justify such a system if we could show that it is well suited for the uses to which it is put. One of the most important uses of inductive logic is in setting up our predictions of the future.[2] Inductive logic figures in these predictions by way of *epistemic probabilities*. If a claim about the future has high epistemic probability, we predict that it will prove true. And, more generally, we expect something more or less strongly as its epistemic probability is higher or lower. The epistemic probability of a statement is just the inductive probability of the argument which embodies all available information in its premises. Thus the epistemic probability of a statement depends on two things: (i) the stock of knowledge and (ii) the inductive logic used to grade the strength of the argument from that stock of knowledge to the conclusion.

Now obviously what we want is for our predictions to be correct. If we could get by with deductively valid arguments we could be assured of true predictions all the time. Deductively valid arguments lead from true premises always to true conclusions and the statements comprising our stock of knowledge are known to be true. But deductively valid arguments are too conservative to leap from the past and present to the future. For this sort of daring behavior we will have to rely on inductively strong arguments—and we will have to give up the comfortable assurance that we will be right all the time.

How about most of the time? Let us call the sort of argument used to set up an epistemic probability an e-argument. That is, an *e-argument* is an argument which has, as its premises, some stock of knowledge. We might hope, then, that inductively strong e-arguments will give us *true conclusions most of the time.* Remember that there are *degrees* of inductive strength and that, on the basis of our present knowledge, we do not always simply predict or not-predict that an event will occur, but anticipate it with various *degrees of confidence.* We might hope further that inductively *stronger* e-arguments have true conclusions *more*

often than inductively *weaker* ones. Finally, since we think that it is useful to gather evidence to enlarge our stock of knowledge, we might hope that inductively strong e-arguments give us true conclusions more often when the stock of knowledge embodied in the premises is great than when it is small.

The last consideration really has to do with justifying epistemic probabilities as tools for prediction. The epistemic probability is the inductive probability of an argument embodying *all* our stock of knowledge in its premises. The requirement that it embody *all* our knowledge, and not just some part of it, is known as the Total Evidence Condition.[3] If we could show that basing our predictions on more knowledge gives us better success ratios, we would have justified the total evidence condition.

The other considerations have to do with justifying the other determinant of epistemic probability—the inductive logic which assigns inductive probabilities to arguments.

We are now ready to suggest what is required to rationally justify a system of inductive logic:

Rational Justification

A system of inductive logic is rationally justified if and only if it is shown that the arguments to which it assigns high inductive probability yield true conclusions from true premises most of the time, and the e-arguments to which it assigns higher inductive probability yield true conclusions from true premises more often than the arguments to which it assigns lower inductive probability.

It is this sense of rational justification, or something quite close to it, that Hume has in mind when he advances his arguments to prove that a rational justification of scientific induction is impossible.

If scientific induction is to be rationally justified in . . . [this] sense, we must establish that the arguments to which it assigns high inductive probability yield true conclusions from true premises most of the time. By what sort of reasoning, asks Hume, could we establish such a conclusion? If the argument that we must use is to have any force whatsoever, it must be either deductively valid or inductively strong. Hume proceeds to show that neither sort of argument could do the job.

Suppose we try to rationally justify scientific inductive logic by means of a deductively valid argument. The only premises we are entitled to use in this argument are those that state things we know. Since we do not know what the future will be like (if we did, we would have no need of an inductive logic on which to base our predictions), the premises can contain knowledge of only the past and present. But if the argument is deductively valid, then the conclusion can make no factual claims that are not already made by the premises. Thus the conclusion of the argument can only refer to the past and present, not to the future, for the premises made no factual claims about the future. Such a conclusion cannot, however, be adequate to rationally justify scientific induction.

To rationally justify scientific induction we must show that e-arguments to which it assigns high inductive probability yield true conclusions from true premises most of the time. And "most of the time" does not mean most of the time in only the past and present; it means most of the time, *past, present, and future.* It is conceivable that a certain type of argument might have given us true conclusions from true premises in the past and might cease to do so in the future. Since our conclusion cannot tell us how successful arguments will be in the future, it cannot establish that the e-arguments to which scientific induction assigns high probability will give us true conclusions from true premises *most of the time.* Thus we cannot use a deductively valid argument to rationally justify induction.

Suppose we try to rationally justify scientific induction by means of an inductively strong argument. We construct our argument, whatever it may be, and present it as an inductively strong argument. "Why do you think that this is an inductively strong argument?" Hume might ask. "Because it has a high inductive probability," we would reply. "And what system of inductive logic assigns it a high probability?" "Scientific induction, of course." What Hume has pointed out is that if we attempt to rationally justify scientific induction by use of an inductively strong argument, we are in the position of having to *assume* that scientific induction is reliable in order to prove that scientific induction is reliable; we are

reduced to begging the question. Thus we cannot use an inductively strong argument to rationally justify scientific induction.

A common argument is that scientific induction is justified because it has been quite successful in the past. On reflection, however, we see that this argument is really an attempt to justify induction by means of an inductively strong argument, and thus begs the question. More explicitly, the argument reads something like this:

> Arguments that are judged by scientific inductive logic to have high inductive probability have given us true conclusions from true premises most of the time in the past.

> Such arguments will give us true conclusions from true premises most of the time, past, present, and future.

It should be obvious that this argument is not deductively valid. At best it is assigned high inductive probability by a system of scientific inductive logic. But the point at issue is whether we should put our faith in such a system.

We can view the traditional problem of induction from a different perspective by discussing it in terms of the *principle of the uniformity of nature.* Although we do not have the details of a system of scientific induction in hand, we do know that it must accord well with common sense and scientific practice, and we are reasonably familiar with both. A few examples will illustrate a general principle which appears to underlie both scientific and common-sense judgments of inductive strength.

If you were to order filet mignon in a restaurant, and a friend were to object that filet mignon would corrode your vitals and lead to quick and violent death, it would seem quite sufficient to respond that you had often eaten filet mignon without any of the dire consequences he predicted. That is, you would intuitively judge the following argument to be inductively strong:

> I have eaten filet mignon many times and it has never corroded my vitals.

> Filet mignon will not now corrode my vitals.

Suppose a scientist is asked whether a rocket would work in reaches of space beyond the range of our telescopes. He replies that it would, and to back up his answer appeals to certain principles of theoretical physics. When asked what evidence he has for these principles, he can refer to a great mass of observed phenomena that corroborate them. The scientist is then judging the following argument to be inductively strong:

Principles A, B, and C correctly describe the behavior of material bodies in all of the many situations we have observed.

Principles A, B, and C correctly describe the behavior of material bodies in those reaches of space that we have not as yet observed.

There appears to be a common assumption underlying the judgments that these arguments are inductively strong. As a steak eater you assume that the future will be like the past, that types of food that proved healthful in the past will continue to prove so in the future. The scientist assumes that the distant reaches of space are like the nearer ones, that material bodies obey the same general laws in all areas of space. Thus it seems that underlying our judgments of inductive strength in both common sense and science is the presupposition that nature is uniform or, as it is sometimes put, that like causes produce like effects throughout all regions of space and time. Thus we can say that a system of scientific induction will base its judgments of inductive strength on the presupposition that *nature is uniform* (and in particular that the future will resemble the past).

We ought to realize at this point that we have only a vague, intuitive understanding of the principle of the uniformity of nature, gleaned from examples rather than specified by precise definitions. This rough understanding is sufficient for the purposes at hand. But we should bear in mind that the task of giving an *exact* definition of the principle, a definition of the sort that would be presupposed by a system of scientific inductive logic, is as difficult as the construction of such a system itself. One of the problems is that nature is simply not uniform in all respects, the future does not resemble the past in all respects. Bertrand Russell once speculated that the chicken on

slaughter-day might reason that whenever the humans came it had been fed, so when the humans would come today it would also be fed. The chicken thought that the future would resemble the past, but it was dead wrong.

The future may resemble the past, but it does not do so in all respects. And we do not know beforehand what those respects are nor to what degree the future resembles the past. Our ignorance of what these respects are is a deep reason behind the total evidence condition. Looking at more and more evidence helps us reject spurious patterns which we might otherwise project into the future. Trying to say exactly *what* about nature we believe is uniform thus turns out to be a surprisingly delicate task.

But suppose that a subtle and sophisticated version of the principle of the uniformity of nature can be formulated which adequately explains the judgments of inductive strength rendered by scientific inductive logic. Then if nature is indeed uniform in the required sense (past, present, and future), e-arguments judged strong by scientific induction will indeed give us true conclusions most of the time. Therefore the problem of rationally justifying scientific induction could be reduced to the problem of establishing that nature is uniform.

But by what reasoning could we establish such a conclusion? If an argument is to have any force whatsoever it must be either deductively valid or inductively strong. A deductively valid argument could not be adequate, for if the information in the premises consists solely of our knowledge of the past and present, then the conclusion cannot tell us that nature will be uniform in the future. The conclusion of a deductively valid argument can make no factual claims that are not already made by the premises, and factual claims about the future are not factual claims about the past and present. But if we claim to have established the principle of the uniformity of nature by an argument that is rated inductively strong by scientific inductive logic, we are open to a challenge as to why we should place our faith in such arguments. But we cannot reply "Because nature is uniform," for that is precisely what we are trying to establish.

Let us summarize the traditional problem of induction. It appears that to rationally justify a system of scientific inductive logic we would have to establish that the e-arguments it judges to be inductively strong give us true conclusions most of the time. If we try to prove that this is the case by means of a deductively valid argument whose premises state things we already know, then the conclusion must fall short of the desired goal. But to try to rationally justify scientific induction by means of an argument that scientific induction judges to be inductively strong is to beg the question. The same difficulties arise if we attempt to justify scientific inductive logic by establishing that nature is uniform.

NOTES

1. I have taken some liberties with Hume and have given the traditional problem of induction a new twist for reasons that will become apparent.

2. Its other uses do not differ in ways essential to the argument.

3. Sometimes the Total Evidence Condition is stated as the requirement that an e-argument embody only all our *relevant* knowledge. This comes to the same thing, however, since by definition, the remainder of our stock of knowledge is irrelevant just in case its addition or deletion from the premises makes no difference to the probability.

The Inference to the Best Explanation

GILBERT HARMAN

Gilbert Harman is professor of philosophy at Princeton University. He has made important contributions in many areas, including ethics, epistemology, philosophy of mind, and the philosophy of language. His books include *Thought, The Nature of Morality,* and *Explaining Value.*

I wish to argue that enumerative induction should not be considered a warranted form of nondeductive inference in its own right.[1] I claim that, in cases where it appears that a warranted inference is an instance of enumerative induction, the inference should be described as a special case of another sort of inference, which I shall call "the inference to the best explanation."

The form of my argument in the first part of this paper is as follows: I argue that even if one accepts enumerative induction as one form of nondeductive inference, one will have to allow for the existence of "the inference to the best explanation." Then I argue that all warranted inferences which may be described as instances of enumerative induction must also be described as instances of the inference to the best explanation.

So, on my view, either (a) enumerative induction is not always warranted or (b) enumerative induction is always warranted but is an uninteresting special case of the more general inference to the best explanation. Whether my view should be expressed as (a) or (b) will depend upon a particular interpretation of "enumerative induction."

In the second part of this paper, I attempt to show how taking the inference to the best explanation (rather than enumerative induction) to be the basic form of nondeductive inference enables one to account for an interesting feature of our use of the word "know." This provides an additional reason for

Reprinted from the *Philosophical Review,* 74 (1965).

describing our inferences as instances of the inference to the best explanation rather than as instances of enumerative induction.

I

"The inference to the best explanation" corresponds approximately to what others have called "abduction," "the method of hypothesis," "hypothetic inference," "the method of elimination," "eliminative induction," and "theoretical inference." I prefer my own terminology because I believe that it avoids most of the misleading suggestions of the alternative terminologies.

In making this inference one infers, from the fact that a certain hypothesis would explain the evidence, to the truth of that hypothesis. In general, there will be several hypotheses which might explain the evidence, so one must be able to reject all such alternative hypotheses before one is warranted in making the inference. Thus one infers, from the premise that a given hypothesis would provide a "better" explanation for the evidence than would any other hypothesis, to the conclusion that the given hypothesis is true.

There is, of course, a problem about how one is to judge that one hypothesis is sufficiently better than another hypothesis. Presumably such a judgment will be based on considerations such as which hypothesis is simpler, which is more plausible, which explains more, which is less *ad hoc,* and so forth. I do not wish to deny that there is a problem about explaining the exact nature of these considerations; I will not, however, say anything more about this problem.

Uses of the inference to the best explanation are manifold. When a detective puts the evidence together and decides that it *must* have been the butler, he is reasoning that no other explanation which accounts for all the facts is plausible enough or simple enough to be accepted. When a scientist infers the existence of atoms and subatomic particles, he is inferring the truth of an explanation for various data which he wishes to account for. These seem the obvious cases; but there are many others. When we infer that a witness is telling the truth, our inference goes as follows: (i) we infer that he says what he does because he believes it; (ii) we infer that he believes

what he does because he actually did witness the situation which he describes. That is, our confidence in his testimony is based on our conclusion about the most plausible explanation for that testimony. Our confidence fails if we come to think there is some other possible explanation for his testimony (if, for example, he stands to gain a great deal from our believing him). Or, to take a different sort of example, when we infer from a person's behavior to some fact about his mental experience, we are inferring that the latter fact explains better than some other explanation what he does.

It seems to me that these examples of inference (and, of course, many other similar examples) are easily described as instances of the inference to the best explanation. I do not see, however, how such examples may be described as instances of enumerative induction. It may seem plausible (at least prima facie) that the inference from scattered evidence to the proposition that the butler did it may be described as a complicated use of enumerative induction; but it is difficult to see just how one would go about filling in the details of such an inference. Similar remarks hold for the inference from testimony to the truth of that testimony. But whatever one thinks about these two cases, the inference from experimental data to the theory of subatomic particles certainly does not seem to be describable as an instance of enumerative induction. The same seems to be true for most inferences about other people's mental experiences.

I do not pretend to have a conclusive proof that such inferences cannot be made out to be complicated uses of enumerative induction. But I do think that the burden of proof here shifts to the shoulders of those who would defend induction in this matter, and I am confident that any attempt to account for these inferences as inductions will fail. Therefore, I assert that even if one permits himself the use of enumerative induction, he will still need to avail himself of at least one other form of nondeductive inference.

As I shall now try to show, however, the opposite does not hold. If one permits himself the use of the inference to the best explanation, one will not still need to use enumerative induction (as a separate form of inference). Enumerative induction, as a separate form of nondeductive inference, is superfluous.

All cases in which one appears to be using it may also be seen as cases in which one is making an inference to the best explanation.

Enumerative induction is supposed to be a kind of inference that exemplifies the following form. From the fact that all observed A's are B's we may infer that all A's are B's (or we may infer that at least the next A will probably be a B). Now, in practice we always know more about a situation than that all observed A's are B's, and before we make the inference, it is good inductive practice for us to consider the total evidence. Sometimes, in the light of the total evidence, we are warranted in making our induction, at other times not. So we must ask ourselves the following question: under what conditions is one permitted to make an inductive inference?

I think it is fair to say that, if we turn to inductive logic and its logicians for an answer to this question, we shall be disappointed. If, however, we think of the inference as an inference to the best explanation, we can explain when a person is and when he is not warranted in making the inference from "All observed A's are B's" to "All A's are B's." The answer is that one is warranted in making this inference whenever the hypothesis that all A's are B's is (in the light of all the evidence) a better, simpler, more plausible (and so forth) hypothesis than is the hypothesis, say, that someone is biasing the observed sample in order to make us think that all A's are B's. On the other hand, as soon as the total evidence makes some other, competing hypothesis plausible, one may not infer from the past correlation in the observed sample to a complete correlation in the total population.

The inference from "All observed A's are B's" to "The next observed A will be B" may be handled in the same way. Here, one must compare the hypothesis that the next A will be different from the preceding A's with the hypothesis that the next A will be similar to preceding A's. As long as the hypothesis that the next A will be similar is a better hypothesis in the light of all the evidence, the supposed induction is warranted. But if there is no reason to rule out a change, then the induction is unwarranted.

I conclude that inferences which appear to be applications of enumerative induction are better described as instances of the inference to the best

explanation. My argument has been (1) that there are many inferences which cannot be made out to be applications of enumerative induction but (2) that we can account for when it is proper to make inferences which appear to be applications of enumerative induction, if we describe these inferences as instances of the inference to the best explanation.

II

I now wish to give a further reason for describing our inferences as instances of the inference to the best explanation rather than enumerative induction.[2] Describing our inference as enumerative induction disguises the fact that our inference makes use of certain lemmas, whereas, as I show below, describing the inference as one to the best explanation exposes these lemmas. These intermediate lemmas play a part in the analysis of knowledge based on inference. Therefore, if we are to understand such knowledge, we must describe our inference as inference to the best explanation.

Let me begin by mentioning a fact about the analysis of "know" which is often overlooked.[3] It is now generally acknowledged by epistemologists that, if a person is to know, his belief must be both true and warranted. We shall assume that we are now speaking of a belief which is based on a (warranted) inference.[4] In this case, it is not sufficient for knowledge that the person's final belief be true. If these intermediate propositions are warranted but false, then the person cannot be correctly described as *knowing* the conclusion. I will refer to this necessary condition of knowledge as "the condition that the lemmas be true."

To illustrate this condition, suppose I read on the philosophy department bulletin board that Stuart Hampshire is to read a paper at Princeton tonight. Suppose further that this warrants my believing that Hampshire will read a paper at Princeton tonight. From this belief, we may suppose I infer that Hampshire will read a paper (somewhere) tonight. This belief is also warranted. Now suppose that, unknown to me, tonight's meeting was called off several weeks ago, although no one has thought to remove the announcement from the bulletin board. My belief that Hampshire will read a paper at Princeton tonight is false. It follows that I do not know whether or not Hampshire will read a paper (somewhere) tonight, even if I am right in believing that he will. Even if I am accidentally right (because Hampshire has accepted an invitation to read a paper at N.Y.U.), I do not know that Hampshire will read a paper tonight. The condition that the lemmas be true has not been met in this case.

I will now make use of the condition that the lemmas be true in order to give a new reason for describing the inferences on which belief is based as instances of the inference to the best explanation rather than of enumerative induction. I will take two different sorts of knowledge (knowledge from authority and knowledge of mental experiences of other people) and show how our ordinary judgment of when there is and when there is not knowledge is to be accounted for in terms of our belief that the inference involved must make use of certain lemmas. Then I will argue that the use of these lemmas can be understood only if the inference is in each case described as the inference to the best explanation.

First, consider what lemmas are used in obtaining knowledge from an authority. Let us imagine that the authority in question either is a person who is an expert in his field or is an authoritative reference book. It is obvious that much of our knowledge is based on authority in this sense. When an expert tells us something about a certain subject, or when we read about the subject, we are often warranted in believing that what we are told or what we read is correct. Now one condition that must be satisfied if our belief is to count as knowledge is that our belief must be true. A second condition is this: what we are told or what we read cannot be there by mistake. That is, the speaker must not have made a slip of the tongue which affects the sense. Our belief must not be based on reading a misprint. Even if the slip of the tongue or the misprint has changed a falsehood into truth, by accident, we still cannot get knowledge from it. This indicates that the inference which we make from testimony to truth must contain as a lemma the proposition that the utterance is there because it is believed and not because of a slip of the tongue or typewriter. Thus our account of this inference must show the role played by such a lemma.

My other example involves knowledge of mental experience gained from observing behavior. Suppose we come to know that another person's hand hurts by seeing how he jerks it away from a hot stove which he has accidentally touched. It is easy to see that our inference here (from behavior to pain) involves as lemma the proposition that the pain is responsible for the sudden withdrawal of the hand. (We do not know the hand hurts, even if we are right about the pain being there, if in fact there is some alternative explanation for the withdrawal.) Therefore, in accounting for the inference here, we will want to explain the role of this lemma in the inference.

My claim is this: if we describe the inferences in the examples as instances of the inference to the best explanation, then we easily see how lemmas such as those described above are an essential part of the inference. On the other hand, if we describe the inferences as instances of enumerative induction,[5] then we obscure the role of such lemmas. When the inferences are described as basically inductive, we are led to think that the lemmas are, in principle, eliminable. They are not so eliminable. If we are to account properly for our use of the word "know," we must remember that these inferences are instances of the inference to the best explanation.

In both examples, the role of the lemmas in our inference is explained only if we remember that we must infer an explanation of the data. In the first example we infer that the best explanation for our reading or hearing what we do is given by the hypothesis that the testimony is the result of expert belief expressed without slip of tongue or typewriter. From this intermediate lemma we infer the truth of the testimony. Again, in making the inference from behavior to pain, we infer the intermediate lemma that the best explanation for the observed behavior is given by the hypothesis that this behavior results from the agent's suddenly being in pain.

If in the first example we think of ourselves as using enumerative induction, then it seems in principle possible to state all the relevant evidence in statements about the correlation between (on the one hand) testimony of a certain type of person about a certain subject matter, where this testimony is given in a certain manner, and (on the other hand) the truth of that testimony. Our inference appears to be completely described by saying that we infer from the correlation between testimony and truth in the past to the correlation in the present case. But, as we have seen, this is not a satisfactory account of the inference which actually does back up our knowledge, since this account cannot explain the essential relevance of whether or not there is a slip of the tongue or a misprint. Similarly, if the inference used in going from behavior to pain is thought of as enumerative induction, it would again seem that getting evidence is in principle just a matter of finding correlations between behavior and pain. But this description leaves out the essential part played by the lemma whereby the inferred mental experience must figure in the explanation for the observed behavior.

If we think of the inferences which back up our knowledge as inferences to the best explanation, then we shall easily understand the role of lemmas in these inferences. If we think of our knowledge as based on enumerative induction (and we forget that induction is a special case of the inference to the best explanation), then we will think that inference is solely a matter of finding correlations which we may project into the future, and we will be at a loss to explain the relevance of the intermediate lemmas. If we are adequately to describe the inferences on which our knowledge rests, we must think of them as instances of the inference to the best explanation.

I have argued that enumerative induction should not be considered a warranted form of inference in its own right. I have used two arguments: (a) we can best account for when it is proper to make inferences which appear to be applications of enumerative induction by describing these inferences as instances of the inference to the best explanation; and (b) we can best account for certain necessary conditions of one's having knowledge (for example, which is knowledge from authority or which is knowledge of another's mental experience gained through observing his behavior) if we explain these conditions in terms of the condition that the lemmas be true and if we think of the inference on which knowledge is based as the inference to the best explanation rather than as enumerative induction.

NOTES

1. Enumerative induction infers from observed regularity to universal regularity or at least to regularity in the next instance.

2. In what follows, when I speak of "describing an inference as an instance of enumerative induction," I understand this phrase to rule out thought of the inference as an instance of the inference to the best explanation. I have no objection to talking of enumerative induction where one recognizes the inference as a special case of the inference to the best explanation.

3. But see Edmund L. Gettier, "Is Justified True Belief Knowledge?," *Analysis,* 23 (1963), 121–123 and Clark, "Knowledge and Grounds: A Comment on Mr. Gettier's Paper," *Analysis,* 24 (1963), 46–48.

4. Cf. "How Belief Is Based on Inference," *The Journal of Philosophy,* LXI (1964), 353–360.

5. See note 2.

The Experimental Method

~

RUDOLF CARNAP

Rudolf Carnap (1891–1970) was a logical positivist who made important contributions to philosophy of science, logic, and philosophy of language. His books include *Der logische Aufbau der Welt* (tr. *The Logical Structure of the World*), *Logische Syntax der Sprache* (tr. *The Logical Syntax of Language*), and *Meaning and Necessity.*

One of the great distinguishing features of modern science, as compared to the science of earlier periods, is its emphasis on what is called the "experimental method." As we have seen, all empirical knowledge rests finally on observations, but these observations can be obtained in two essentially different ways. In the non-experimental way, we play a passive role. We simply look at the stars or at some flowers, note similarities and differences, and try to discover regularities that can be expressed as laws. In the experimental way, we take an active role. Instead of being onlookers, we *do* something that will produce better observational results than those we find by merely looking at nature. Instead of waiting until nature provides situations for us to observe, we try to create such situations. In brief, we make experiments.

The experimental method has been enormously fruitful. The great progress physics has made in the last two hundred years, especially in the last few decades, would have been impossible without the experimental method. If this is so, one might ask, why is the experimental method not used in all fields of science? In some fields it is not as easy to use as it is in physics. In astronomy, for example, we cannot give a planet a push in some other direction to see what would happen to it. Astronomical objects are out of reach; we can only observe and describe them. Sometimes astronomers can create conditions in the laboratory similar to those, say, on the surface of the sun or moon and then observe what happens in the laboratory under those conditions. But this is not really an astronomical experiment. It is a physical experiment that has some relevance for astronomical knowledge. . . .

The experimental method is especially fruitful in fields in which there are quantitative concepts that can be accurately measured. How does the scientist plan an experiment? It is hard to describe the general nature of experiments, because there are so many different kinds, but a few general features can be pointed out.

First of all, we try to determine the relevant factors involved in the phenomenon we wish to investigate. Some factors—but not too many—must be left aside as irrelevant. In an experiment in mechanics, for example, involving wheels, levers, and so on, we may decide to disregard friction. We know that friction is involved, but we think its influence is too small to justify complicating the experiment by considering it. Similarly, in an experiment with slow-moving bodies, we may choose to neglect air resistance. If we are working with very high velocities, such as a missile moving at a supersonic speed, we can no longer neglect air resistance. In short, the scientist leaves out only those factors whose influence on his experiment will, he thinks, be insignificant. Sometimes, in order to keep an experiment from being too complicated,

Reprinted from *An Introduction to the Philosophy of Science* (New York: Dover Books, 1995), by permission of the publisher.

he may even have to neglect factors he thinks may have important effects.

After having decided on the relevant factors, we devise an experiment in which some of those factors are kept constant while others are permitted to vary. Suppose we are dealing with a gas in a vessel, and we wish to keep the temperature of the gas as constant as we can. We immerse the vessel in a water-bath of much larger volume. (The specific heat of the gas is so small in relation to the specific heat of the water that, even if the temperature of the gas is varied momentarily, as by compression or expansion, it will quickly go back to its old temperature.) Or we may wish to keep a certain electrical current at a constant rate of flow. Perhaps this is done by having an ammeter so that, if we observe an increase or decrease in the current, we can alter the resistance and keep the current constant. In such ways as these we are able to keep certain magnitudes constant while we observe what happens when other magnitudes are varied.

Our final aim is to find laws that connect *all* the relevant magnitudes; but, if a great many factors are involved, this may be a complicated task. At the beginning, therefore, we restrict our aim to lower-level laws that connect *some* of the factors. The simplest first step, if there are k magnitudes involved, is to arrange the experiment so that k-2 magnitudes are kept constant. This leaves two magnitudes, M_1 and M_2, that we are free to vary. We change one of them and observe how the other behaves. Maybe M_2 goes down whenever M_1 is increased. Or perhaps, as M_1 is increased, M_2 goes first up and then down. The value of M_2 is a function of the value of M_1. We can plot this function as a curve on a sheet of graph paper and perhaps determine the equation that expresses the function. We will then have a restricted law: If magnitudes M_3, M_4, M_5 . . . are kept constant, and M_1 is increased, M_2 varies in a way expressed by a certain equation. But this is only the beginning. We continue our experiment, controlling other sets of k-2 factors, so that we can see how other pairs of magnitudes are functionally related. Later, we experiment in the same way with triples, keeping everything constant except three magnitudes. In some cases, we may be able to guess, from our laws relating to pairs, some or all of the laws concerning the triples. Then we aim

for still more general laws involving four magnitudes, and finally for the most general, sometimes quite complicated, laws that cover all the relevant factors.

As a simple example, consider the following experiment with a gas. We have made the rough observation that the temperature, volume, and pressure of a gas often vary simultaneously. We wish to know exactly how these three magnitudes are related to one another. A fourth relevant factor is what gas we are using. We may experiment with other gases later, but at first we decide to keep this factor constant by using only pure hydrogen. We put the hydrogen in a cylindrical vessel (see Figure 1) with a movable piston on which a weight can be placed. We can easily measure the volume of the gas, and we can vary the pressure by changing the weight on the piston. The temperature is regulated and measured by other means.

Before we proceed with experiments to determine how the three factors—temperature, volume, and pressure—are related, we need to make some preliminary experiments to make sure that there are no other relevant factors. Some factors we might suspect of being relevant turn out not to be. For example, is the shape of the vessel containing the gas relevant? We know that in some experiments (for example, the distribution of an electrical charge and its surface potential) the shape of the object involved is important. Here it is not difficult to determine that the shape of the vessel is irrelevant; only the volume is important. We can draw on our knowledge of nature to rule out many other factors. An astrologer may come into the laboratory and ask: "Have you checked on where the planets are today? Their positions may have some influence on your experiment." We consider this an irrelevant factor because we believe the planets are too far away to have an influence.

Our assumption of the irrelevance of the planets is correct, but it would be a mistake to think that we can automatically exclude various factors simply because we believe they have no influence. There is no way to be really sure until experimental tests have been made. Imagine that you live before the invention of radio. Someone places a box on your table and tells you that if someone sings at a certain spot, one

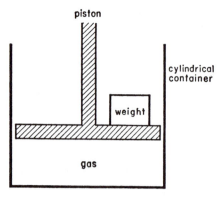

Figure 1

thousand miles away, you will hear the apparatus in this box sing exactly the same song, in the same pitch and rhythm. Would you believe it? You would probably reply: "Impossible! There are no electric wires attached to this box. I know from my experience that nothing happening one thousand miles away could have any effect on what is happening in this room."

That is exactly the same reasoning by which we decided that the positions of the planets could not affect our experiments with hydrogen! It is obvious that we must be very cautious. Sometimes there are influences we cannot know about until they are discovered. For this reason, the very first step in our experiment—determining the relevant factors—is sometimes a difficult one. Moreover, it is a step that is often not explicitly mentioned in the reports of investigations. A scientist describes only the apparatus he used, the experiment he performed, what he discovered about the relations between certain magnitudes. He does not add, "and in addition I found out that such and such factors have no influence on the results". In most cases, when enough is known about the field in which the investigation is made, the scientist will take for granted that other factors are irrelevant. He may be quite right. But in new fields, one must be extremely cautious. Of course, nobody would think that a laboratory experiment could be influenced by whether we look at the apparatus from a distance of ten inches or ten feet or whether we are in a kind or angry disposition when we look at it. These factors are probably irrelevant, but absolutely sure we cannot be. If anyone suspects that these are relevant factors, an experiment must be made to rule them out.

Practical considerations prevent us, of course, from testing every factor that might be relevant. Thousands of remote possibilities can be tested, and there simply is not time to examine all of them. We must proceed according to common sense and correct our assumptions only if something unexpected happens that forces us to consider relevant a factor we had previously neglected. Will the color of leaves on trees outside a laboratory influence the wave length of light used in an experiment? Will a piece of apparatus function differently depending on whether its legal owner is in New York or Chicago or on how he feels about the experiment? We obviously do not have time to test such factors. We assume that the mental attitude of the equipment's owner has no physical influence on the experiment, but members of certain tribes may differ. They may believe that the gods will assist the experiment only if the owner of the apparatus wants the experiment made and not if the pretended owner wishes it. Cultural beliefs thus sometimes influence what is considered relevant. In most cases, a scientist thinks about the problem, makes a common-sense guess about what factors are worth considering, and perhaps performs a few preliminary experiments to rule out factors about which he is doubtful.

Assume that we have decided that the factors relevant to our experiment with hydrogen are temperature, pressure, and volume. In our vessel the nature and total amount of the gas remain the same because we keep it in a closed vessel. We are free, therefore, to test relationships among the three factors. If we maintain a constant temperature but increase the pressure, we discover that the volume varies inversely with the pressure. That is, if we double the pressure, the volume decreases to half its former amount. If we triple the pressure, the volume decreases to one third. This is the famous experiment performed in the seventeenth century by the Irish physicist Robert Boyle. The law he discovered, known as Boyle's law, states that if the temperature of a confined gas remains the same, the product of the volume and pressure is constant.

Next we keep the pressure constant (by leaving the same weight on the piston) but vary the temperature. We then discover that the volume increases when the gas is heated and decreases when it is cooled; and, by measuring volume and temperature, we find that volume is proportional to temperature. (This is sometimes called Charles's law, after the French scientist Jacques Charles.) We must be careful not to use either the Fahrenheit or the centigrade scale, but a scale in which zero is "absolute zero" or −273 degrees on the centigrade scale. This is the "absolute scale", or "Kelvin scale", introduced by Lord Kelvin, a nineteenth-century Scottish physicist. It is now an easy step to an experimental verification of a general law covering all three factors. Such a law is, in fact, suggested by the two laws we have already obtained, but the general law has more empirical con-

tent than the two laws taken together. This general law states that if the amount of a confined gas remains constant, the product of the pressure and volume equals the product of the temperature and R ($P \cdot V = T \cdot R$). In this equation, R is a constant that varies with the amount of gas under consideration. This general law gives the relationships among all three magnitudes and is therefore of significantly greater efficiency in making predictions than the other two laws combined. If we know the value of any two of the three variable magnitudes, we can easily predict the third.

Aspects of Scientific Explanation

～

CARL G. HEMPEL

Carl G. Hempel (1905–1997) made central contributions to logical positivist accounts of scientific confirmation, explanation, and laws. He published several important articles and books, including the widely influential "Studies in the Logic of Explanation" and *Aspects of Scientific Explanation*.

1. INTRODUCTION

Among the many factors that have prompted and sustained inquiry in the diverse fields of empirical science, two enduring human concerns have provided the principal stimulus for man's scientific efforts.

One of them is of a practical nature. Man wants not only to survive in the world, but also to improve his strategic position in it. This makes it important for him to find reliable ways of foreseeing changes in his environment and, if possible, controlling them to his advantage. The formulation of laws and theories that permit the prediction of future occurrences are among the proudest achievements of empirical science; and the extent to which they answer man's quest for foresight and control is indicated by the vast scope of their practical applications, which range

from astronomic predictions to meteorological, demographic, and economic forecasts, and from physico-chemical and biological technology to psychological and social control.

The second basic motive for man's scientific quest is independent of such practical concerns; it lies in his sheer intellectual curiosity, in his deep and persistent desire to know and to understand himself and his world. So strong, indeed, is this urge that in the absence of more reliable knowledge, myths are often invoked to fill the gap. But in time, many such myths give way to scientific conceptions of the what and the why of empirical phenomena.

What is the nature of the explanations empirical science can provide? What understanding of empirical phenomena do they convey? This essay attempts to shed light on these questions by examining in

Reprinted from *Aspects of Scientific Explanation* (New York: Free Press, 1965), by permission of the publisher.

some detail the form and the function of some of the major types of explanatory account that have been advanced in different areas of empirical science.

The terms "empirical science" and "scientific explanation" will here be understood to refer to the entire field of empirical inquiry, including the natural and the social sciences as well as historical research. This broad use of the two terms is not intended to pre-judge the question of the logical and methodological similarities and differences between different areas of empirical inquiry, except for indicating that the procedures used in those different areas will be taken to conform to certain basic standards of objectivity. According to these standards, hypotheses and theo-ries—including those invoked for explanatory pur-poses—must be capable of test by reference to pub-licly ascertainable evidence, and their acceptance is always subject to the proviso that they may have to be abandoned if adverse evidence or more adequate hypotheses or theories should be found.

A scientific explanation may be regarded as an answer to a why-question, such as: "Why do the plan-ets move in elliptical orbits with the sun at one focus?," "Why does the moon look much larger when it is near the horizon than when it is high in the sky?," "Why did the television apparatus on Ranger VI fail?," "Why are children of blue-eyed parents always blue-eyed?," "Why did Hitler go to war against Rus-sia?." There are other modes of formulating what we will call *explanation-seeking questions:* we might ask what caused the failure of the television apparatus on Ranger VI, or what led Hitler to his fateful decision. But a why-question always provides an adequate, if perhaps sometimes awkward, standard phrasing.

Sometimes the subject matter of an explanation, or the *explanandum,* is indicated by a noun, as when we ask for an explanation of the aurora borealis. It is important to realize that this kind of phrasing has a clear meaning only in so far as it can be restated in terms of why-questions. Thus, in the context of an explanation, the aurora borealis must be taken to be characterized by certain distinctive general features, each of them describable by a that-clause, for exam-ple: that it is normally found only in fairly high north-ern latitudes; that it occurs intermittently; that sunspot maxima, with their eleven-year cycle, are regularly accompanied by maxima in the frequency and brightness of aurora borealis displays; that an aurora shows characteristic spectral lines of rare atmospheric gases, and so on. And to ask for an explanation of the aurora borealis is to request an explanation of *why* auroral displays occur in the fash-ion indicated and *why* they have physical characteris-tics such as those just mentioned. Indeed, requests for an explanation of the aurora borealis, of the tides, of solar eclipses in general or of some individual solar eclipse in particular, or of a given influenza epidemic, and the like have a clear meaning only if it is under-stood what aspects of the phenomenon in question are to be explained; and in that case the explanatory problem can again be expressed in the form "Why is it the case that *p?*," where the place of "*p*" is occu-pied by an empirical statement specifying the explanandum. Questions of this type will be called *explanation-seeking why-questions.*

Not all why-questions call for explanations, how-ever. Some of them solicit reasons in support of an assertion. Thus, statements such as "Hurricane Delila will veer out into the Atlantic," "He must have died of a heart attack," "Plato would have disliked Stravin-sky's music" might be met with the question "Why should this be so?," which seeks to elicit, not an explanation, but evidence or grounds or reasons in support of the given assertion. Questions of this kind will be called *reason-seeking* or *epistemic.* To put them into the form "Why should it be the case that *p?*" is misleading; their intent is more adequately conveyed by a phrasing such as "Why should it be believed that *p?*" or "What reasons are there for believing that *p?*."

An explanation-seeking why-question normally presupposes that the statement occupying the place of '*p*' is true, and asks for an explanation of the pre-sumptive fact, event, or state of affairs described by it; an epistemic why-question does not presuppose the truth of the corresponding statement, but on the contrary, solicits reasons for believing it true. An appropriate answer to the former will therefore offer an explanation of a presumptive empirical phenome-non; whereas an appropriate answer to the latter will offer validating or justifying grounds in support of a statement. . . .

2. DEDUCTIVE-NOMOLOGICAL EXPLANATION

2.1 Fundamentals

D-N Explanation and the concept of Law

In his book, *How We Think,* John Dewey describes a phenomenon he observed one day while washing dishes. Having removed some glass tumblers from the hot suds and placed them upside down on a plate, he noticed that soap bubbles emerged from under the tumbler's rims, grew for a while, came to a standstill and finally receded into the tumblers. Why did this happen? Dewey outlines an explanation to this effect: Transferring the tumblers to the plate, he had trapped cool air in them; that air was gradually warmed by the glass, which initially had the temperature of the hot suds. This led to an increase in the volume of the trapped air, and thus to an expansion of the soap film that had formed between the plate and the tumblers' rims. But gradually, the glass cooled off, and so did the air inside, and as a result, the soap bubbles receded.

The explanation here outlined may be regarded as an argument to the effect that the phenomenon to be explained, *the explanandum phenomenon,* was to be expected in virtue of certain explanatory facts. These fall into two groups: (i) particular facts and (ii) uniformities expressible by means of general laws. The first group includes facts such as these: the tumblers had been immersed in soap suds of a temperature considerably higher than that of the surrounding air; they were put, upside down, on a plate on which a puddle of soapy water had formed that provided a connecting soap film, and so on. The second group of explanatory facts would be expressed by the gas laws and by various other laws concerning the exchange of heat between bodies of different temperature, the elastic behavior of soap bubbles, and so on. While some of these laws are only hinted at by such phrasings as 'the warming of the trapped air led to an increase in its pressure', and others are not referred to even in this oblique fashion, they are clearly presupposed in the claim that certain stages in the process yielded others as their results. If we imagine the various explicit or tacit explanatory assumptions to be

fully stated, then the explanation may be conceived as a deductive argument of the form

$$\text{(D-N)} \quad \left.\begin{array}{l} C_1, C_2, \ldots, C_k \\[1mm] L_1, L_2, \ldots, L_r \end{array}\right\} \text{Explanans } S$$
$$\overline{\qquad E \qquad} \quad \text{Explanandum-sentence}$$

Here, $C_1, C_2, \ldots, C_k$ are sentences describing the particular facts invoked; $L_1, L_2, \ldots, L_r$ are the general laws on which the explanation rests. Jointly these sentences will be said to form the *explanans S,* where S may be thought of alternatively as the set of the explanatory sentences or as their conjunction. The conclusion E of the argument is a sentence describing the explanandum-phenomenon; I will call E the explanandum-sentence or explanandum-statement; the word "explanandum" alone will be used to refer either to the explanandum-phenomenon or to the explanandum-sentence: the context will show which is meant.

The kind of explanation whose logical structure is suggested by the schema (D-N) will be called *deductive-nomological explanation* or D-N *explanation* for short; for it effects a deductive subsumption of the explanandum under principles that have the character of general laws. Thus a D-N explanation answers the question "*Why* did the explanandum-phenomenon occur?" by showing that the phenomenon resulted from certain particular circumstances, specified in $C_1, C_2, \ldots, C_k$, in accordance with the laws $L_1, L_2, \ldots, L_r$. By pointing this out, the argument shows that, given the particular circumstances and the laws in question, the occurrence of the phenomenon *was to be expected;* and it is in this sense that the explanation enables us to *understand why* the phenomenon occurred.

In a D-N explanation, then, the explanandum is a logical consequence of the explanans. Furthermore, reliance on general laws is essential to a D-N explanation; it is in virtue of such laws that the particular facts cited in the explanans possess explanatory relevance to the explanandum phenomenon. Thus, in the case of Dewey's soap bubbles, the gradual warming of the cool air trapped under the hot tumblers would constitute a mere accidental antecedent rather than an explanatory factor for the growth of the bubbles, if it were not for the gas laws, which connect the two events. But what if the explanandum sentence E in an argument of the form (D-N) is a logical consequence of the sentences $C_1, C_2, \ldots, C_k$ alone? Then, surely, no empirical laws are *required* to deduce E from the explanans; and any laws included in the latter are gratuitous, dispensable premises. Quite so; but in this case, the argument would not count as an explanation. For example, the argument:

The soap bubbles first expanded and then receded

The soap bubbles first expanded

though deductively valid, clearly cannot qualify as an explanation of why the bubbles first expanded. The same remark applies to all other cases of this kind. A D-N explanation will have to contain, in its explanans, some general laws that are *required* for the deduction of the explanandum, i.e. whose deletion would make the argument invalid.

If the explanans of a given D-N explanation is true, i.e. if the conjunction of its constituent sentences is true, we will call the *explanation true;* a true explanation, of course, has a true explanandum as well. Next, let us call a *D-N explanation more or less strongly supported or confirmed* by a given body of evidence according as its explanans is more or less strongly confirmed by the given evidence. (One factor to be considered in appraising the empirical soundness of a given explanation will be the extent to which its explanans is supported by the total relevant evidence available.) Finally, by a *potential D-N explanation,* let us understand any argument that has the character of a D-N explanation except that the sentences constituting its explanans need not be true. In a potential D-N explanation, therefore, $L_1, L_2, \ldots, L_r$ will be what Goodman has called *lawlike sentences,* i.e. sentences that are like laws except for possibly being false. Sentences of this kind will also be referred to as *nomic* or *nomological.* We use the notion of a potential explanation, for example, when we ask whether a novel and as yet untested law or theory would provide an explanation for some empir-

ical phenomenon; or when we say that the phlogiston theory, though now discarded, afforded an explanation for certain aspects of combustion. Strictly speaking, only true lawlike statements can count as laws—one would hardly want to speak of false laws of nature. But for convenience I will occasionally use the term "law" without implying that the sentence in question is true, as in fact, I have done already in the preceding sentence.

The characterization of laws as true lawlike sentences raises the important and intriguing problem of giving a clear characterization of lawlike sentences without, in turn, using the concept of law. This problem has proved to be highly recalcitrant, and I will make here only a few observations on certain aspects of it that are relevant also to the analysis of scientific explanation.

Lawlike sentences can have many different logical forms. Some paradigms of nomic sentences, such as "All gases expand when heated under constant pressure" may be construed as having the simple universal conditional form "$(x) (Fx \supset Gx)$", others involve universal as well as existential generalization, as does the sentence "For every chemical compound there exists a range of temperatures and pressures at which the compound is liquid"; many of the lawlike sentences and theoretical principles of the physical sciences assert more or less complex mathematical relationships between different quantitative variables.

But lawlike sentences cannot be characterized in terms of their form alone. For example, not all sentences of the simple universal conditional form just mentioned are lawlike; hence, even if true, they are not laws. The sentences "All members of the Greenbury School Board for 1964 are bald" and "All pears in this basket are sweet" illustrate this point. Goodman has pointed out a characteristic that distinguishes laws from such nonlaws: The former can, whereas the latter cannot, sustain counterfactual and subjunctive conditional statements. Thus the law about the expansion of gases can serve to support statements such as "If the oxygen in this cylinder had been heated (were heated) under constant pressure then it would have expanded (would expand)"; whereas the statement about the School Board lends no support at all to the subjunctive conditional "If

Robert Crocker were a member of the Greenbury School Board for 1964 then he would be bald."

We might add that the two kinds of sentence differ analogously in explanatory power. The gas law, in combination with suitable particular data, such as that the oxygen in the cylinder was heated under constant pressure, can serve to explain why the volume of the gas increased; but the statement about the School Board, analogously combined with a statement such as "Harry Smith is a member of the Greenbury School Board for 1964" cannot explain why Harry Smith is bald.

But though these observations shed light on the concept of lawlikeness they afford no satisfactory explication of it; for one of them presupposes an understanding of counterfactual and of subjunctive conditional statements, which present notorious philosophical difficulties; the other makes use of the idea of explanation to clarify the concept of a lawlike statement; and we are here trying conversely to characterize a certain type of explanation with the help of concepts which include that of lawlike statement.

Now, our examples of non-lawlike sentences share a characteristic that might seem to afford a criterion for the distinction we seek to draw; namely, each of them applies to only a finite number of individual cases or instances. Must not a general law be conceived as admitting of indefinitely many instances?

Surely a lawlike sentence must not be *logically* limited to a finite number of instances: it must not be logically equivalent to a finite conjunction of singular sentences, or, briefly, it must be of *essentially generalized form*. Thus, the sentence "Every element of the class consisting of the objects *a, b,* and *c* has the property *P*" is not lawlike; for it is logically equivalent to the conjunction "*Pa · Pb · Pc,*" and clearly a sentence of this kind cannot support counterfactual conditionals or provide explanations.

But our two earlier nonlawlike generalizations are not ruled out by this condition: they are not logically equivalent to corresponding finite conjunctions since they do not state specifically who are the members of the School Board, or what particular pears are in the basket. Should we, then, deny lawlike status also to any general sentence which—by empirical accident, so to speak—has only a finite number of instances?

This would surely be ill-advised. Suppose, for example, that from the basic laws of celestial mechanics a general statement is derived concerning the relative motion of the components of a double star in the special case where those components are of exactly equal mass. Is this statement to be termed a law only if it has been established that there exist at least two (or perhaps more) instances of this special kind of double star? Or consider the general statement, derivable from Newton's laws of gravitation and of motion, which deals, in a manner similar to Galileo's law, with the free fall of physical bodies near the surface of a spherical mass having the same density as the Earth, but twice its radius. Should this statement not be called a law unless it had been shown to have several instances—even though it is a logical consequence of a set of laws with many instances?

Besides, there appears to be only an inessential "difference in degree" between a general statement that happens to have just one instance and another which happens to have two or some other finite number. But, then, how many instances would a law be required to have? To insist on some particular finite number would be arbitrary; and the requirement of an infinite number of actual instances would raise obvious difficulties. Clearly, the concept of scientific law cannot reasonably be subjected to any condition concerning the number of instances, except for the requirement barring logical equivalence with singular statements.

Besides, we should note that the concept, presupposed in the preceding discussion, of a "case" or an "instance" of a general statement is by no means as clear as it might seem. Consider, for example, general statements of the form, "All objects with the property *F* also have the property *G*," or briefly "All *F* are *G*." It seems natural to accept the criterion that a particular object *i* is an instance of such a statement if and only if *i* has the property *F* and the property *G,* or briefly, if *i* is both *F* and *G*. This would imply that if there are no objects with the property *F* at all, the general statement has no instances. Yet, the statement is logically equivalent with "All non-*G* are non-*F,*" which, under the contemplated criterion, may well have instances even if there are no *F*. Thus, the general statement, "All unicorns feed on clover" would have no instance, but its equivalent "Anything that does not feed on clover is not a unicorn" would have many—perhaps infinitely many—instances. An analogous remark might well be true of the law mentioned earlier concerning double stars whose components have equal mass. Hence, the contemplated criterion of instantiation, which seems quite obvious at first, has the consequence that of two logically equivalent general statements, one may have no instances, the other, infinitely many. But this makes the criterion unacceptable since such equivalent sentences express the same law and thus should be instantiated by the same objects.

For laws of the simple kind just considered, the following alternative definition of instantiation will suffice to assign the same instances to equivalent statements: an object i is an instance of the statement "All F are G" if and only if it is not the case that i is F but not G. However, for laws of more complex logical form, the concept of instance raises further problems. But these need not be pursued here, for I am not proposing that a law must satisfy certain minimum conditions concerning the number of its instances.

There is yet another common trait of our non-lawlike generalizations that seems to hold promise as a criterion for the distinction here under discussion: they contain terms, such as "this basket" and "the Greenbury School Board for 1964," which directly or indirectly refer to particular objects, persons, or places; whereas the terms occurring in Newton's laws or in the gas laws involve no such reference. In an earlier article on the subject, Oppenheim and I suggested, therefore, that the constituent predicates of what we called fundamental lawlike sentences must all be such that the specification of their meaning requires no reference to any one particular object or location. We noted, however, that this characterization still is not satisfactory for purposes of explication because the idea of "the meaning" of a given term is itself far from being clear.

Besides, reference to particular individuals does not always deprive a general statement of explanatory power, as is illustrated by Galileo's law for free fall, whose full formulation makes reference to the earth. Now it is true that, with qualifications soon to be stated, Galileo's law may be regarded as derivable

from the laws of Newtonian theory, which have the character of fundamental lawlike sentences, so that an explanation based on Galileo's law can also be effected by means of fundamental laws. But it certainly cannot be taken for granted that all other laws mentioning particular individuals can similarly be derived from fundamental laws. . . .

Though the preceding discussion has not led to a fully satisfactory general characterization of lawlike sentences and thus of laws, it will, I hope, have clarified to some extent the sense in which those concepts will be understood in the present study.

The examples we have considered so far illustrate the deductive explanation of particular occurrences by means of empirical laws. But empirical science raises the question "Why?" also in regard to the uniformities expressed by such laws and often answers it, again, by means of a deductive-nomological explanation, in which the uniformity in question is subsumed under more inclusive laws or under theoretical principles. For example, the questions of why freely falling bodies move in accordance with Galileo's law and why the motion of the planets exhibit the uniformities expressed by Kepler's laws are answered by showing that these laws are but special consequences of the Newtonian laws of gravitation and of motion. Similarly, the uniformities expressed by the laws of geometrical optics, such as those of the rectilinear propagation of light and of reflection and refraction, are accounted for by subsumption under the principles of wave optics. For brevity, an explanation of a uniformity expressed by a law will sometimes be elliptically referred to as an explanation of the law in question.

It should be noted, however, that in the illustrations just mentioned, the theory invoked does not, strictly speaking, imply the presumptive general laws to be explained; rather, it implies that those laws hold only within a limited range, and even there, only approximately. Thus, Newton's law of gravitation implies that the acceleration of a freely falling body is not constant, as Galileo's law asserts, but undergoes a very slight but steady increase as the body approaches the ground. But while, strictly speaking, Newton's law contradicts Galileo's, it shows that the latter is almost exactly satisfied in free fall over short distances. In slightly greater detail, we might say that the Newtonian theory of gravitation and of motion implies its own laws concerning free fall under various circumstances. According to one of these, the acceleration of a small object falling freely toward a homogeneous spherical body varies inversely as the square of its distance from the center of the sphere, and thus increases in the course of the fall; and the uniformity expressed by this law is explained in a strictly deductive sense by the Newtonian theory. But when conjoined with the assumption that the earth is a homogeneous sphere of specified mass and radius, the law in question implies that for free fall over short distances near the surface of the earth, Galileo's law holds to a high degree of approximation; in this sense, the theory might be said to provide an *approximative D-N explanation* of Galileo's law.

Again, in the case of planetary motion, the Newtonian theory implies that since a planet is subject to gravitational attraction not only from the Sun, but also from the other planets, its orbit will not be exactly elliptical, but will show certain perturbations. Hence, as Duhem noted, Newton's law of gravitation, far from being an inductive generalization based on Kepler's laws, is, strictly speaking, incompatible with them. One of its important credentials is precisely the fact that it enables the astronomer to compute the deviations of the planets from the elliptic orbits Kepler had assigned to them.

A similar relation obtains between the principles of wave optics and the laws of geometrical optics. For example, the former calls for a diffractive "bending" of light around obstacles—a phenomenon ruled out by the conception of light as composed of rays traveling in straight lines. But in analogy to the preceding illustration, the wave-theoretical account implies that the laws of rectilinear propagation, of reflection, and of refraction as formulated in geometrical optics are satisfied to a very high degree of approximation within a limited range of cases, including those which provided experimental support for the laws in their original formulation.

In general, an explanation based on theoretical principles will both broaden and deepen our understanding of the empirical phenomena concerned. It will achieve an increase in breadth because the the-

ory will usually cover a wider range of occurrences than do the empirical laws previously established. For example, Newton's theory of gravitation and of motion governs free fall not only on the earth, but also on other celestial bodies; and not only planetary motions, but also the relative motion of double stars, the orbits of comets and of artificial satellites, the movements of pendulums, certain aspects of the tides, and many other phenomena. And a theoretical explanation deepens our understanding for at least two reasons. First, it reveals the different regularities exhibited by a variety of phenomena, such as those just mentioned in reference to Newton's theory, as manifestations of a few basic laws. Secondly, as we noted, the generalizations previously accepted as correct statements of empirical regularities will usually appear as approximations only of certain lawlike statements implied by the explanatory theory, and to be very nearly satisfied only within a certain limited range. And in so far as tests of the laws in their earlier formulation were confined to cases in that range, the theoretical account also indicates why those laws, though not generally true, should have been found confirmed.

When a scientific theory is superseded by another in the sense in which classical mechanics and electrodynamics were superseded by the special theory of relativity, then the succeeding theory will generally have a wider explanatory range, including phenomena the earlier theory could not account for; and it will as a rule provide approximative explanations for the empirical laws implied by its predecessor. Thus, special relativity theory implies that the laws of the classical theory are very nearly satisfied in cases involving motion only at velocities which are small compared to that of light.

The general conception of explanation by deductive subsumption under general laws or theoretical principles, as it has been outlined in this section, will be called the *deductive nomological-model,* or the *D-N model of explanation;* the laws invoked in such an explanation will also be referred to, in William Dray's suggestive phrase, as *covering laws.* Unlike Dray, however, I will not refer to the D-N model as the covering-law model, for I will subsequently introduce a second basic model of scientific explanation which also relies on covering laws, but which is not of deductive-nomological form. The term 'covering-law model' will then serve to refer to both of those models.

As the schema (D-N) plainly indicates, a deductive-nomological explanation is not conceived as invoking only one covering law; and our illustrations show how indeed many different laws may be invoked in explaining one phenomenon. A purely logical point should be noted here, however. If an explanation is of the form (D-N), then the laws $L_1, L_2, \ldots, L_r$ invoked in its explanans logically imply a law L^* which by itself would suffice to explain the explanandum event by reference to the particular conditions noted in the sentences $C_1, C_2, \ldots, C_k$. This law L^* is to the effect that whenever conditions of the kind described in the sentences $C_1, C_2, \ldots, C_k$ are realized then an event of the kind described by the explanandum-sentence occurs. Consider an example: A chunk of ice floats in a large beaker of water at room temperature. Since the ice extends above the surface, one might expect the water level to rise as the ice melts; actually, it remains unchanged. Briefly, this can be explained as follows: According to Archimedes' principle, a solid body floating in a liquid displaces a volume of liquid that has the same weight as the body itself. Hence, the chunk of ice has the same weight as the water displaced by its submerged portion. Since melting does not change the weight, the ice turns into a mass of water of the same weight, and hence also of the same volume, as the water initially displaced by its submerged portion; consequently, the water level remains unchanged. The laws on which this account is based include Archimedes' principle, a law concerning the melting of ice at room temperature; the principle of the conservation of mass; and so on. None of these laws mentions the particular glass of water or the particular piece of ice with which the explanation is concerned. Hence the laws imply not only that as this particular piece of ice melts in this particular glass, the water level remains unchanged, but rather the general statement L^* that under the same *kind* of circumstance, i.e., when any piece of ice floats in water in any glass at room temperature, the same *kind* of phenomenon will occur, i.e., the water level will remain unchanged. The law L^* will usually be "weaker" than the laws $L_1, L_2, \ldots, L_r$; i.e., while being logically implied by the conjunction of those laws, it will not, in general, imply that conjunction. Thus, in our illustration one of the original explanatory laws applies also to the floating of a piece of marble on mercury or of a boat on water, whereas L^* deals only with the case of ice floating on water. But clearly, L^* in conjunction with $C_1, C_2, \ldots, C_k$ logically implies E and could indeed be used to explain, in this context, the event described by E. We might therefore refer to L^* as a *minimal covering law* implicit in a given D-N explanation. But while such laws might be used for explanatory purposes, the D-N model by no means restricts deductive-nomological explanations to the use of minimal laws. Indeed such a restriction would fail to do justice to one important objective of scientific inquiry, namely, that of establishing laws and theories of broad scope, under which narrower generalizations may then be subsumed as special cases or as close approximations of such.

The Truth Doesn't Explain Much

⌒

NANCY CARTWRIGHT

Nancy Cartwright is professor of philosophy and chair of the Centre for Philosophy of Natural and Social Science at the London School of Economics and Political Science. She is a major contributor to contemporary philosophy of science and philosophy of social science. Her books include *Nature's Capacities and Their Measurement* and *The Dappled World: A Study of the Boundaries of Science*.

INTRODUCTION

Scientific theories must tell us both what is true in nature, and how we are to explain it. I shall argue that these are entirely different functions and should be kept distinct. Usually the two are conflated. The second is commonly seen as a by-product of the first. Scientific theories are thought to explain by dint of the descriptions they give of reality. Once the job of describing is done, science can shut down. That is all there is to do. To describe nature—to tell its laws, the values of its fundamental constants, its mass distributions—is ipso facto to lay down how we are to explain it.

This is a mistake, I shall argue; a mistake that is fostered by the covering-law model of explanation. The covering-law model supposes that all we need to know are the laws of nature—and a little logic, perhaps a little probability theory—and then we know which factors can explain which others. For example, in the simplest deductive-nomological version, the covering-law model says that one factor explains another just in case the occurrence of the second can be deduced from the occurrence of the first given the laws of nature. . . .

A good deal of criticism has been aimed at Hempel's original covering-law models. Much of the criticism objects that these models let in too much. On Hempel's account it seems we can explain Henry's failure to get pregnant by his taking birth control pills, and we can explain the storm by the falling barometer. My objection is quite the opposite. Covering-law models let in too little. With a covering-law model we can explain hardly anything, even the things of which we are most proud—like the role of DNA in the inheritance of genetic characteristics, or the formation of rainbows when sunlight is refracted through raindrops. We cannot explain these phenomena with a covering-law model, I shall argue, because we do not have laws that cover them. Covering laws are scarce.

Many phenomena which have perfectly good scientific explanations are not covered by any laws. No true laws, that is. They are at best covered by ceteris paribus generalizations—generalizations that hold only under special conditions, usually ideal conditions. The literal translation is "other things being equal"; but it would be more apt to read "ceteris paribus" as "other things being *right*."

Sometimes we act as if this does not matter. We have in the back of our minds an "understudy" picture of ceteris paribus laws: ceteris paribus laws are real laws; they can stand in when the laws we would like to see are not available and they can perform all the same functions, only not quite so well. But this will not do. Ceteris paribus generalizations, read literally without the "ceteris paribus" modifier, are

Reprinted from *How the Laws of Physics Lie* (Oxford: Oxford University Press, 1983).

false. They are not only false, but held by us to be false; and there is no ground in the covering-law picture for false laws to explain anything. On the other hand, with the modifier the ceteris paribus generalizations may be true, but they cover only those few cases where the conditions are right. For most cases, either we have a law that purports to cover, but cannot explain because it is acknowledged to be false, or we have a law that does not cover. Either way, it is bad for the covering-law picture.

1.   CETERIS PARIBUS LAWS

When I first started talking about the scarcity of covering laws, I tried to summarize my view by saying "There are no exceptionless generalizations." Then a friend asked, "How about 'All men are mortal'?" She was right. I had been focusing too much on the equations of physics. A more plausible claim would have been that there are no exceptionless quantitative laws in physics. Indeed not only are there no exceptionless laws, but in fact our best candidates are known to fail. This is something like the Popperian thesis that *every theory is born refuted*. Every theory we have proposed in physics, even at the time when it was most firmly entrenched, was known to be deficient in specific and detailed ways. I think this is also true for every precise quantitative law within a physics theory.

But this is not the point I had wanted to make. Some laws are treated, at least for the time being, as if they were exceptionless, whereas others are not, even though they remain "on the books." Snell's law (about the angle of incidence and the angle of refraction for a ray of light) is a good example of this latter kind. In the optics text I use for reference (Miles V. Klein, *Optics*),[1] it first appears on page 21, and without qualification:

Snell's Law: At an interface between dielectric media, there is (also) a *refracted ray* in the second medium, lying in the plane of incidence, making an angle θ_t with the normal, and obeying Snell's law:

$$\sin \theta / \sin \theta_t = n_2/n_1$$

where v_1 and v_2 are the velocities of propagation in the two media, and $n_1 = (c/v_1)$, $n_2 = (c/v_2)$ are the indices of refraction.

It is only some 500 pages later, when the law is derived from the "full electromagnetic theory of light," that we learn that Snell's law as stated on page 21 is true only for media whose optical properties are *isotropic*. (In anisotropic media, "there will generally be *two* transmitted waves.") So what is deemed true is not really Snell's law as stated on page 21, but rather a refinement of Snell's law:

Refined Snell's Law: For any two media which are optically isotropic, at an interface between dielectrics there is a refracted ray in the second medium, lying in the plane of incidence, making an angle θ_t with the normal, such that:

$$\sin \theta / \sin \theta_t = n_2/n_1.$$

The Snell's law of page 21 in Klein's book is an example of a ceteris paribus law, a law that holds only in special circumstances—in this case when the media are both isotropic. Klein's statement on page 21 is clearly not to be taken literally. Charitably, we are inclined to put the modifier 'ceteris paribus' in front to hedge it. But what does this ceteris paribus modifier do? With an eye to statistical versions of the covering law model . . . we may suppose that the unrefined Snell's law is not intended to be a universal law, as literally stated, but rather some kind of statistical law. The obvious candidate is a crude statistical law: *for the most part,* at an interface between dielectric media there is *a* refracted ray . . . But this will not do. For *most* media are optically anisotropic, and in an anisotropic medium there are *two* rays. I think there are no more satisfactory alternatives. If ceteris paribus laws are to be true laws, there are no statistical laws with which they can generally be identified.

2.   WHEN LAWS ARE SCARCE

Why do we keep Snell's law on the books when we both know it to be false and have a more accurate refinement available? There are obvious pedagogic reasons. But are there serious scientific ones? I think there are, and these reasons have to do with the task of explaining. Specifying which factors are explanatorily relevant to which others is a job done by science over and above the job of laying out the laws of nature. Once the laws of nature are known, we still have to decide what kinds of factors can be cited in explanation.

One thing that ceteris paribus laws do is to express our explanatory commitments. They tell what kinds of explanations are permitted. We know from the refined Snell's law that in any isotropic medium, the angle of refraction can be explained by the angle of incidence, according to the equation $\sin \theta / \sin \theta_t = n_2/n_1$. To leave the unrefined Snell's law on the books is to signal that the same kind of explanation can be given even for some anisotropic media. The pattern of explanation derived from the ideal situation is employed even where the conditions are less than ideal; and we assume that we can understand what happens in *nearly* isotropic media by rehearsing how light rays behave in pure isotropic cases.

This assumption is a delicate one . . . For the moment I intend only to point out that it *is* an assumption, and an assumption which (prior to the "full electromagnetic theory") goes well beyond our knowledge of the facts of nature. We *know* that in isotropic media, the angle of refraction is due to the angle of incidence under the equation $\sin \theta / \sin \theta_t = n_2/n_1$. We *decide* to explain the angles for the two refracted rays in anisotropic media in the same manner. We may have good reasons for the decision; in this case if the media are nearly isotropic, the two rays will be very close together, and close to the angle predicted by Snell's law; or we believe in continuity of physical processes. But still this decision is not forced by our knowledge of the laws of nature.

Obviously this decision could not be taken if we also had on the books a second refinement of Snell's law, implying that in any anisotropic media the angles are quite different from those given by Snell's law. But laws are scarce, and often we have no law at all about what happens in conditions that are less than ideal.

Covering-law theorists will tell a different story about the use of ceteris paribus laws in explanation. From their point of view, ceteris paribus explanations are elliptical for genuine covering law explanations from true laws which we do not yet know. When we use a ceteris paribus "law" which we know to be false, the covering-law theorist supposes us to be making a bet about what form the true law takes. For example, to retain Snell's unqualified law would be to bet that the (at the time unknown) law for anisotropic media will entail values "close enough" to those derived from the original Snell law.

I have two difficulties with this story. The first arises from an extreme metaphysical possibility, in which I in fact believe. Covering-law theorists tend to think that nature is well-regulated; in the extreme, that there is a law to cover every case. I do not. I imagine that natural objects are much like people in societies. Their behaviour is constrained by some specific laws and by a handful of general principles, but it is not determined in detail, even statistically. What happens on most occasions is dictated by no law at all. This is not a metaphysical picture that I urge. My claim is that this picture is as plausible as the alternative. God may have written just a few laws and grown tired. We do not know whether we are in a tidy universe or an untidy one. Whichever universe we are in, the ordinary commonplace activity of giving explanations ought to make sense.

The second difficulty for the ellipsis version of the covering-law account is more pedestrian. Elliptical explanations are not explanations: they are at best assurances that explanations are to be had. The law that is supposed to appear in the complete, correct D-N explanation is not a law we have in our theory, not a law that we can state, let alone test. There may be covering-law explanations in these cases. But those explanations are not our explanations; and those unknown laws cannot be our grounds for saying of a nearly isotropic medium, "$\sin \theta_t \approx k(n_2/n_1)$ *because* $\sin \theta = k$."

What then are our grounds? I assert only what they are not: they are not the laws of nature. The laws of nature that we know at any time are not enough to tell us what kinds of explanations can be given at that time. That requires a decision; and it is just this decision that covering-law theorists make when they wager about the existence of unknown laws. We may believe in these unknown laws, but we do so on no ordinary grounds: they have not been tested, nor are they derived from a higher level theory. Our grounds for believing in them are only as good as our reasons for adopting the corresponding explanatory strategy, and no better.

3. WHEN LAWS CONFLICT

I have been maintaining that there are not enough covering laws to go around. Why? The view depends on the picture of science that I mentioned earlier. Science is broken into various distinct domains: hydrodynamics, genetics, laser theory, . . . We have many detailed and sophisticated theories about what happens within the various domains. But we have little theory about what happens in the intersection of domains. . . .

For example, (ceteris paribus) adding salt to water decreases the cooking time of potatoes; taking the water to higher altitudes increases it. Refining, if we speak more carefully we might say instead, 'Adding salt to water while keeping the altitude constant decreases the cooking time; whereas increasing the altitude while keeping the saline content fixed increases it' . . .

But neither of these tells what happens when we both add salt to the water and move to higher altitudes.

Here we think that probably there is a precise answer about what would happen, even though it is not part of our common folk wisdom. But this is not always the case. I discuss this in detail in the next essay. Most real life cases involve some combination of causes; and general laws that describe what happens in these complex cases are not always available. Although both quantum theory and relativity are highly developed, detailed, and sophisticated, there is no satisfactory theory of relativistic quantum mechanics. A more detailed example from transport theory is given in the next essay. The general lesson is this: where theories intersect, laws are usually hard to come by.

4. WHEN EXPLANATIONS CAN BE GIVEN ANYWAY

So far, I have only argued half the case. I have argued that covering laws are scarce, and that ceteris paribus laws are no true laws. It remains to argue that, nevertheless, ceteris paribus laws have a fundamental explanatory role. But this is easy, for most of our explanations are explanations from ceteris paribus laws.

Let me illustrate with a humdrum example. Last year I planted camellias in my garden. I know that camellias like rich soil, so I planted them in composted manure. On the other hand, the manure was still warm, and I also know that camellia roots cannot take high temperatures. So I did not know what to expect. But when many of my camellias died, despite otherwise perfect care, I knew what went wrong. The camellias died because they were planted in hot soil.

This is surely the right explanation to give. Of course, I cannot be absolutely certain that this explanation is the correct one. Some other factor may have been responsible, nitrogen deficiency or some genetic defect in the plants, a factor that I did not notice, or may not even have known to be relevant. But this uncertainty is not peculiar to cases of explanation. It is just the uncertainty that besets all of our judgements about matters of fact. We must allow for oversight; still, since I made a reasonable effort to eliminate other menaces to my camellias, we may have some confidence that this is the right explanation.

So we have an explanation for the death of my camellias. But it is not an explanation from any true covering law. There is no law that says that camellias just like mine, planted in soil which is both hot and rich, die. To the contrary, they do not all die. Some thrive; and probably those that do, do so *because* of the richness of the soil they are planted in. We may insist that there must be some differentiating factor which brings the case under a covering law: in soil which is rich and hot, camellias of one kind die; those of another thrive. I will not deny that there may be such a covering law. I merely repeat that our ability to give this humdrum explanation precedes our knowledge of that law. On the Day of Judgment, when all laws are known, these may suffice to explain all phenomena. But in the meantime we do give explanations; and it is the job of science to tell us what kinds of explanations are admissible.

In fact I want to urge a stronger thesis. If, as is possible, the world is not a tidy deterministic system, this job of telling how we are to explain will be a job which is still left when the descriptive task of science is complete. Imagine for example (what I suppose actually to be the case) that the facts about camellias are irreducibly statistical. Then it is possible to know all the general nomological facts about camellias which there are to know—for example, that 62 percent of all camellias in just the circumstances of my camellias die, and 38 per cent survive. But one would not thereby know how to explain what happened in my garden. You would still have to look to the *Sunset Garden Book* to learn that the *heat* of the soil explains the perishing, and the *richness* explains the plants that thrive.

5.   CONCLUSION

Most scientific explanations use ceteris paribus laws. These laws, read literally as descriptive statements,

are false, not only false but deemed false even in the context of use. This is no surprise: we want laws that unify; but what happens may well be varied and diverse. We are lucky that we can organize phenomena at all. There is no reason to think that the principles that best organize will be true, nor that the principles that are true will organize much.

NOTE

1. Miles V. Klein, *Optics* (New York: John Wiley and Sons, 1970), p. 21, italics added. θ is the angle of incidence.

The New Riddle of Induction

NELSON GOODMAN

Nelson Goodman (1906–1998) made important contributions to aesthetics, epistemology, metaphysics, logic, and the philosophy of science. His books include *The Structure of Appearance, Languages of Art,* and *Ways of Worldmaking.*

Confirmation of a hypothesis by an instance depends rather heavily upon features of the hypothesis other than its syntactical form. That a given piece of copper conducts electricity increases the credibility of statements asserting that other pieces of copper conduct electricity, and thus confirms the hypothesis that all copper conducts electricity. But the fact that a given man now in this room is a third son does not increase the credibility of statements asserting that other men now in this room are third sons, and so does not confirm the hypothesis that all men now in this room are third sons. Yet in both cases our hypothesis is a generalization of the evidence statement. The difference is that in the former case the hypothesis is

a *lawlike* statement; while in the latter case, the hypothesis is a merely contingent or accidental generality. Only a statement that is *lawlike*—regardless of its truth or falsity or its scientific importance—is capable of receiving confirmation from an instance of it; accidental statements are not. Plainly, then, we must look for a way of distinguishing lawlike from accidental statements.

So long as what seems to be needed is merely a way of excluding a few odd and unwanted cases that are inadvertently admitted by our definition of confirmation, the problem may not seem very hard or very pressing. We fully expect that minor defects will be found in our definition and that the necessary refinements will have to be worked out patiently one after another. But some further examples will show that our present difficulty is of a much graver kind.

Suppose that all emeralds examined before a certain time *t* are green. At time *t,* then, our observations support the hypothesis that all emeralds are green; and this is in accord with our definition of confirmation. Our evidence statements assert that emerald *a* is green, that emerald *b* is green, and so on; and each confirms the general hypothesis that all emeralds are green. So far, so good.

Now let me introduce another predicate less familiar than "green." It is the predicate "grue" and it applies to all things examined before *t* just in case they are green but to other things just in case they are blue. Then at time *t* we have, for each evidence statement asserting that a given emerald is green, a parallel evidence statement asserting that that emerald is grue. And the statements that emerald *a* is grue, that emerald *b* is grue, and so on, will each confirm the general hypothesis that all emeralds are grue. Thus according to our definition, the prediction that all emeralds subsequently examined will be green and the prediction that all will be grue are alike confirmed by evidence statements describing the same observations. But if an emerald subsequently examined is grue, it is blue and hence not green. Thus although we are well aware which of the two incompatible predictions is genuinely confirmed, they are equally well confirmed according to our present definition. Moreover, it is clear that if we simply choose an appropriate predicate, then on the basis of these same observations we shall have equal confirmation, by our definition, for any prediction whatever about other emeralds—or indeed about anything else.[1] As in our earlier example, only the predictions subsumed under lawlike hypothesis are genuinely confirmed; but we have no criterion as yet for determining lawlikeness. And now we see that without some such criterion, our definition not merely includes a few unwanted cases, but is so completely ineffectual that it virtually excludes nothing. We are left once again with the intolerable result that anything confirms anything. This difficulty cannot be set aside as an annoying detail to be taken care of in due course. It has to be met before our definition will work at all.

Nevertheless, the difficulty is often slighted because on the surface there seem to be easy ways of dealing with it. Sometimes, for example, the problem is thought to be . . . [that we are], making tacit and illegitimate use of information outside the stated evidence: the information, for example, that different samples of one material are usually alike in conductivity, and the information that different men in a lecture audience are usually not alike in the number of their older brothers. But while it is true that such information is being smuggled in, this does not by itself settle the matter as it settles the matter of the ravens. There the point was that when the smuggled information is forthrightly declared, its effect upon the confirmation of the hypothesis in question is immediately and properly registered by the definition we are using. On the other hand, if to our initial evidence we add statements concerning the conductivity of pieces of other materials or concerning the number of older brothers of members of other lecture audiences, this will not in the least affect the confirmation, according to our definition, of the hypothesis concerning copper or of that concerning this lecture audience. Since our definition is insensitive to the bearing upon hypotheses of evidence so related to them, even when the evidence is fully declared, the difficulty about accidental hypotheses cannot be explained away on the ground that such evidence is being surreptitiously taken into account.

A more promising suggestion is to explain the matter in terms of the effect of this other evidence not directly upon the hypothesis in question but *indi*rectly through other hypotheses that *are* confirmed, according to our definition, by such evidence. Our information about other materials does by our definition confirm such hypotheses as that all pieces of iron conduct electricity, that no pieces of rubber do, and so on; and these hypotheses, the explanation runs, impart to the hypothesis that all pieces of copper conduct electricity (and also to the hypothesis that none do) the character of lawlikeness—that is, amenability to confirmation by direct positive instances when found. On the other hand, our information about other lecture audiences *dis*confirms many hypotheses to the effect that all the men in one audience are third sons, or that none are; and this strips any character of lawlikeness from the hypothesis that all (or the hypothesis that none) of the men in *this* audience are third sons. But clearly if this course is to be followed, the circumstances under which hypotheses are thus related to one another will have to be precisely articulated.

The problem, then, is to define the relevant way in which such hypotheses must be alike. Evidence for the hypothesis that all iron conducts electricity enhances the lawlikeness of the hypothesis that all zirconium conducts electricity, but does not similarly affect the hypothesis that all the objects on my desk conduct electricity. Wherein lies the difference? The first two hypotheses fall under the broader hypothesis—call it "*H*"—that every class of things of the same material is uniform in conductivity; the first and third fall only under some such hypothesis as—call it "*K*"—that every class of things that are either all of the same material or all on a desk is uniform in conductivity. Clearly the important difference here is that evidence for a statement affirming that one of the classes covered by *H* has the property in question increases the credibility of any statement affirming that another such class has this property; while nothing of the sort holds true with respect to *K*. But this is only to say that *H* is lawlike and *K* is not. We are faced anew with the very problem we are trying to solve: the problem of distinguishing between lawlike and accidental hypotheses.

The most popular way of attacking the problem takes its cue from the fact that accidental hypotheses seem typically to involve some spatial or temporal restriction, or reference to some particular individual. They seem to concern the people in some particular room, or the objects on some particular person's desk; while lawlike hypotheses characteristically concern all ravens or all pieces of copper whatsoever. Complete generality is thus very often supposed to be a sufficient condition of lawlikeness; but to define this complete generality is by no means easy. Merely to require that the hypothesis contain no term naming, describing, or indicating a particular thing or location will obviously not be enough. The troublesome hypothesis that all emeralds are grue contains no such term; and where such a term does occur, as in hypotheses about men in *this room*, it can be sup-

pressed in favor of some predicate (short or long, new or old) that contains no such term but applies only to exactly the same things. One might think, then, of excluding not only hypotheses that actually contain terms for specific individuals but also all hypotheses that are equivalent to others that do contain such terms. But, as we have just seen, to exclude only hypotheses of which *all* equivalents contain such terms is to exclude nothing. On the other hand, to exclude all hypotheses that have *some* equivalent containing such a term is to exclude everything; for even the hypotheses

All grass is green

has as an equivalent

All grass in London or elsewhere is green.

The next step, therefore, has been to consider ruling out predicates of certain kinds. A syntactically universal hypothesis is lawlike, the proposal runs, if its predicates are "purely qualitative" or "non-positional". This will obviously accomplish nothing if a purely qualitative predicate is then conceived either as one that is equivalent to some expression free of terms for specific individuals, or as one that is equivalent to no expression that contains such a term; for this only raises again the difficulties just pointed out. The claim appears to be rather that at least in the case of a simple enough predicate we can readily determine by direct inspection of its meaning whether or not it is purely qualitative. But even aside from obscurities in the notion of 'the meaning' of a predicate, this claim seems to me wrong. I simply do not know how to tell whether a predicate is qualitative or positional, except perhaps by completely begging the question at issue and asking whether the predicate is "well-behaved"—that is, whether simple syntactically universal hypotheses applying it are lawlike.

This statement will not go unprotested. "Consider," it will be argued, "the predicates 'blue' and 'green' and the predicate 'grue' introduced earlier, and also the predicate 'bleen' that applies to emeralds examined before time *t* just in case they are blue and to other emeralds just in case they are green. Surely it is clear," the argument runs, "that the first two are purely qualitative and the second two are not; for the meaning of each of the latter two plainly involves reference to a specific temporal position." To this I reply that indeed I do recognize the first two as well-behaved predicates admissible in lawlike hypotheses, and the second two as ill-behaved predicates. But the argument that the former but not the latter are purely qualitative seems to me quite unsound. True enough, if we start with "blue" and "green", then "grue" and "bleen" will be explained in terms of "blue" and "green" and a temporal term. But equally truly, if we start with "grue" and "bleen", then "blue" and "green" will be explained in terms of "grue" and "bleen" and a temporal term; "green", for example, applies to emeralds examined before time *t* just in case they are grue, and to other emeralds just in case they are bleen. Thus qualitativeness is an entirely relative matter and does not by itself establish any dichotomy of predicates. This relativity seems to be completely overlooked by those who contend that the qualitative character of a predicate is a criterion for its good behavior.

Of course, one may ask why we need worry about such unfamiliar predicates as "grue" or about accidental hypotheses in general, since we are unlikely to use them in making predictions. If our definition works for such hypotheses as are normally employed, isn't that all we need? In a sense, yes; but only in the sense that we need no definition, no theory of induction, and no philosophy of knowledge at all. We get along well enough without them in daily life and in scientific research. But if we seek a theory at all, we cannot excuse gross anomalies resulting from a proposed theory by pleading that we can avoid them in practice. The odd cases we have been considering are clinically pure cases that, though seldom encountered in practice, nevertheless display to best advantage the symptoms of a widespread and destructive malady.

We have so far neither any answer nor any promising clue to an answer to the question what distinguishes lawlike or confirmable hypotheses from accidental or non-confirmable ones; and what may at first have seemed a minor technical difficulty has taken on the stature of a major obstacle to the development of a satisfactory theory of confirmation. It is this problem that I call the new riddle of induction.

THE PERVASIVE PROBLEM OF PROJECTION

At the beginning of this lecture, I expressed the opinion that the problem of induction is still unsolved, but that the difficulties that face us today are not the old ones; and I have tried to outline the changes that have taken place. The problem of justifying induction has been displaced by the problem of defining confirmation, and our work upon this has left us with the residual problem of distinguishing between confirmable and non-confirmable hypotheses. One might say roughly that the first question was "Why does a positive instance of a hypothesis give any grounds for predicting further instances?"; that the newer question was "What is a positive instance of a hypothesis?"; and that the crucial remaining question is "What hypotheses are confirmed by their positive instances?"

The vast amount of effort expended on the problem of induction in modern times has thus altered our afflictions but hardly relieved them. The original difficulty about induction arose from the recognition that anything may follow upon anything. Then, in attempting to define confirmation in terms of the converse of the consequence relation, we found ourselves with the distressingly similar difficulty that our definition would make any statement confirm any other. And now, after modifying our definition drastically, we still get the old devastating result that any statement will confirm any statement. Until we find a way of exercising some control over the hypotheses to be admitted, our definition makes no distinction whatsoever between valid and invalid inductive inferences.

The real inadequacy of Hume's account lay not in his descriptive approach but in the imprecision of his description. Regularities in experience, according to him, give rise to habits of expectation; and thus it is predictions conforming to past regularities that are normal or valid. But Hume overlooks the fact that some regularities do and some do not establish such habits; that predictions based on some regularities are valid while predictions based on other regularities are not. Every word you have heard me say has occurred prior to the final sentence of this lecture; but that does not, I hope, create any expectation that every word you will hear me say will be prior to that sentence. Again, consider our case of emeralds. All those examined before time *t* are green; and this leads us to expect, and confirms the prediction, that the next one will be green. But also, all those examined are grue; and this does not lead us to expect, and does not confirm the prediction, that the next one will be grue. Regularity in greenness confirms the prediction of further cases; regularity in grueness does not. To say that valid predictions are those based on past regularities, without being able to say *which* regularities, is thus quite pointless. Regularities are where you find them, and you can find them anywhere. As we have seen, Hume's failure to recognize and deal with this problem has been shared even by his most recent successors.

As a result, what we have in current confirmation theory is a definition that is adequate for certain cases that so far can be described only as those for which it is adequate. The theory works where it works. A hypothesis is confirmed by statements related to it in the prescribed way provided it is so confirmed. This is a good deal like having a theory that tells us that the area of a plane figure is one-half the base times the altitude, without telling us for what figures this holds. We must somehow find a way of distinguishing law-like hypotheses, to which our definition of confirmation applies, from accidental hypotheses, to which it does not.

Today I have been speaking solely of the problem of induction, but what has been said applies equally to the more general problem of projection. As pointed out earlier, the problem of prediction from past to future cases is but a narrower version of the problem of projecting from any set of cases to others. We saw that a whole cluster of troublesome problems concerning dispositions and possibility can be reduced to this problem of projection. That is why the new riddle of induction, which is more broadly the problem of distinguishing between projectible and non-projectible hypotheses, is as important as it is exasperating.

NOTE

1. For instance, we shall have equal confirmation, by our present definition, for the prediction that roses subsequently examined will be blue. Let "emerose" apply just to emeralds examined before time *t,* and to roses examined later. Then all emeroses so far examined are grue, and this confirms the hypothesis that all emeroses are grue and hence the prediction that roses subsequently examined will be blue. The problem raised by such antecedents has been little noticed, but is no easier to meet than that raised by similarly perverse consequents.

The Structure of Scientific Revolutions

~

THOMAS S. KUHN

Thomas S. Kuhn (1922–1996) was an historian and philosopher of science. His book *The Structure of Scientific Revolutions* is a seminal work on the nature and importance of scientific development and scientific revolutions that revolutionized the field of philosophy of science.

What are scientific revolutions and what is their function in scientific development? . . . [S]cientific revolutions are here taken to be those noncumulative developmental episodes in which an older paradigm is replaced in whole or in part by an incompatible new one. There is more to be said, however, and an essential part of it can be introduced by asking one further question. Why should a change of paradigm be called a revolution? In the face of the vast and essential differences between political and scientific development, what parallelism can justify the metaphor that finds revolutions in both?

One aspect of the parallelism must already be apparent. Political revolutions are inaugurated by a growing sense, often restricted to a segment of the political community, that existing institutions have ceased adequately to meet the problems posed by an environment that they have in part created. In much the same way, scientific revolutions are inaugurated by a growing sense, again often restricted to a narrow subdivision of the scientific community, that an existing paradigm has ceased to function adequately in the exploration of an aspect of nature to which that paradigm itself had previously led the way. In both political and scientific development the sense of malfunction that can lead to crisis is prerequisite to revolution. Furthermore, though it admittedly strains the metaphor, that parallelism holds not only for the major paradigm changes, like those attributable to Copernicus and Lavoisier, but also for the far smaller ones associated with the assimilation of a new sort of phenomenon, like oxygen or X-rays. Scientific revolutions . . . need seem revolutionary only to those whose paradigms are affected by them. To outsiders they may, like the Balkan revolutions of the early twentieth century, seem normal parts of the developmental process. Astronomers, for example, could accept X-rays as a mere addition to knowledge, for their paradigms were unaffected by the existence of the new radiation. But for men like Kelvin, Crookes, and Roentgen, whose research dealt with radiation theory or with cathode ray tubes, the emergence of X-rays necessarily violated one paradigm as it created another. That is why these rays could be discovered only through something's first going wrong with normal research.

This genetic aspect of the parallel between political and scientific development should no longer be open to doubt. The parallel has, however, a second and more profound aspect upon which the significance of the first depends. Political revolutions aim to change political institutions in ways that those institutions themselves prohibit. Their success therefore necessitates the partial relinquishment of one set of institutions in favor of another, and in the interim, society is not fully governed by institutions at all. Initially it is

Reprinted from *The Structure of Scientific Revolutions* (Chicago: University of Chicago Press, 1962), by permission of the publisher.

crisis alone that attenuates the role of political institutions as we have already seen it attenuate the role of paradigms. In increasing numbers individuals become increasingly estranged from political life and behave more and more eccentrically within it. Then, as the crisis deepens, many of these individuals commit themselves to some concrete proposal for the reconstruction of society in a new institutional framework. At that point the society is divided into competing camps or parties, one seeking to defend the old institutional constellation, the others seeking to institute some new one. And, once that polarization has occurred, *political recourse fails.* Because they differ about the institutional matrix within which political change is to be achieved and evaluated, because they acknowledge no supra-institutional framework for the adjudication of revolutionary difference, the parties to a revolutionary conflict must finally resort to the techniques of mass persuasion, often including force. Though revolutions have had a vital role in the evolution of political institutions, that role depends upon their being partially extrapolitical or extrainstitutional events.

The remainder of this essay aims to demonstrate that the historical study of paradigm change reveals very similar characteristics in the evolution of the sciences. Like the choice between competing political institutions, that between competing paradigms proves to be a choice between incompatible modes of community life. Because it has that character, the choice is not and cannot be determined merely by the evaluative procedures characteristic of normal science, for these depend in part upon a particular paradigm, and that paradigm is at issue. When paradigms enter, as they must, into a debate about paradigm choice, their role is necessarily circular. Each group uses its own paradigm to argue in that paradigm's defense.

The resulting circularity does not, of course, make the arguments wrong or even ineffectual. The man who premises a paradigm when arguing in its defense can nonetheless provide a clear exhibit of what scientific practice will be like for those who adopt the new view of nature. That exhibit can be immensely persuasive, often compellingly so. Yet, whatever its force, the status of the circular argument is only that

of persuasion. It cannot be made logically or even probabilistically compelling for those who refuse to step into the circle. The premises and values shared by the two parties to a debate over paradigms are not sufficiently extensive for that. As in political revolutions, so in paradigm choice—there is no standard higher than the assent of the relevant community. To discover how scientific revolutions are effected, we shall therefore have to examine not only the impact of nature and of logic, but also the techniques of persuasive argumentation effective within the quite special groups that constitute the community of scientists.

To discover why this issue of paradigm choice can never be unequivocally settled by logic and experiment alone, we must shortly examine the nature of the differences that separate the proponents of a traditional paradigm from their revolutionary successors. That examination is the principal object of this section and the next. We have, however, already noted numerous examples of such differences, and no one will doubt that history can supply many others. What is more likely to be doubted than their existence—and what must therefore be considered first—is that such examples provide essential information about the nature of science. Granting that paradigm rejection has been a historic fact, does it illuminate more than human credulity and confusion? Are there intrinsic reasons why the assimilation of either a new sort of phenomenon or a new scientific theory must demand the rejection of an older paradigm?

First notice that if there are such reasons, they do not derive from the logical structure of scientific knowledge. In principle, a new phenomenon might emerge without reflecting destructively upon any part of past scientific practice. Though discovering life on the moon would today be destructive of existing paradigms (these tell us things about the moon that seem incompatible with life's existence there), discovering life in some less well-known part of the galaxy would not. By the same token, a new theory does not have to conflict with any of its predecessors. It might deal exclusively with phenomena not previously known, as the quantum theory deals (but, significantly, not exclusively) with subatomic phenomena unknown before the twentieth century. Or again, the new theory might be simply a higher level theory than those known before, one that linked together a whole group of lower level theories without substantially changing any. Today, the theory of energy conservation provides just such links between dynamics, chemistry, electricity, optics, thermal theory, and so on. Still other compatible relationships between old and new theories can be conceived. Any and all of them might be exemplified by the historical process through which science has developed. If they were, scientific development would be genuinely cumulative. New sorts of phenomena would simply disclose order in an aspect of nature where none had been seen before. In the evolution of science new knowledge would replace ignorance rather than replace knowledge of another and incompatible sort.

Of course, science (or some other enterprise, perhaps less effective) might have developed in that fully cumulative manner. Many people have believed that it did so, and most still seem to suppose that cumulation is at least the ideal that historical development would display if only it had not so often been distorted by human idiosyncrasy. There are important reasons for that belief. . . . Nevertheless, despite the immense plausibility of that ideal image, there is increasing reason to wonder whether it can possibly be an image of *science.* After the pre-paradigm period the assimilation of all new theories and of almost all new sorts of phenomena has in fact demanded the destruction of a prior paradigm and a consequent conflict between competing schools of scientific thought. Cumulative acquisition of unanticipated novelties proves to be an almost non-existent exception to the rule of scientific development. The man who takes historic fact seriously must suspect that science does not tend toward the ideal that our image of its cumulativeness has suggested. Perhaps it is another sort of enterprise.

If, however, resistant facts can carry us that far, then a second look at the ground we have already covered may suggest that cumulative acquisition of novelty is not only rare in fact but improbable in principle. Normal research, which *is* cumulative, owes its success to the ability of scientists regularly to select problems that can be solved with conceptual and instrumental techniques close to those already in existence. (That is why an excessive concern with useful problems, regardless of their relation to existing knowledge and technique, can so easily inhibit scientific development.) The man who is striving to solve a problem defined by existing knowledge and technique is not, however, just looking around. He knows what he wants to achieve, and he designs his instruments and directs his thoughts accordingly. Unanticipated novelty, the new discovery, can emerge only to the extent that his anticipations about nature and his instruments prove wrong. Often the importance of the resulting discovery will itself be proportional to the extent and stubbornness of the anomaly that foreshadowed it. Obviously, then, there must be a conflict between the paradigm that discloses anomaly and the one that later renders the anomaly law-like. The examples of discovery through paradigm destruction . . . did not confront us with mere historical accident. There is no other effective way in which discoveries might be generated.

The same argument applies even more clearly to the invention of new theories. There are, in principle, only three types of phenomena about which a new theory might be developed. The first consists of phenomena already well explained by existing paradigms, and these seldom provide either motive or point of departure for theory construction. When they do . . . the theories that result are seldom accepted, because nature provides no ground for discrimination. A second class of phenomena consists of those whose nature is indicated by existing paradigms but whose details can be understood only through further theory articulation. These are the phenomena to which scientists direct their research much of the time, but that research aims at the articulation of existing paradigms rather than at the invention of new ones. Only when these attempts at articulation fail do scientists encounter the third type of phenomena, the recognized anomalies whose characteristic feature is their stubborn refusal to be assimilated to existing paradigms. This type alone gives rise to new theories. Paradigms provide all phenomena except anomalies with a theory-determined place in the scientist's field of vision.

But if new theories are called forth to resolve anomalies in the relation of an existing theory to nature, then the successful new theory must somewhere permit predictions that are different from those derived from its predecessor. That difference could not occur if the two were logically compatible. In the process of being assimilated, the second must displace the first. Even a theory like energy conservation, which today seems a logical superstructure that relates to nature only through independently established theories, did not develop historically without paradigm destruction. Instead, it emerged from a crisis in which an essential ingredient was the incompatibility between Newtonian dynamics and some recently formulated consequences of the caloric theory of heat. Only after the caloric theory had been rejected could energy conservation become part of science.[1] And only after it had been part of science for some time could it come to seem a theory of a logically higher type, one not in conflict with its predecessors. It is hard to see how new theories could arise without these destructive changes in beliefs about nature. Though logical inclusiveness remains a permissible view of the relation between successive scientific theories, it is a historical implausibility.

A century ago it would, I think, have been possible to let the case for the necessity of revolutions rest at this point. But today, unfortunately, that cannot be done because the view of the subject developed above cannot be maintained if the most prevalent contemporary interpretation of the nature and function of scientific theory is accepted. That interpretation, closely associated with early logical positivism and not categorically rejected by its successors, would restrict the range and meaning of an accepted theory so that it could not possibly conflict with any later theory that made predictions about some of the same natural phenomena. The best-known and the strongest case for this restricted conception of a scientific theory emerges in discussions of the relation between contemporary Einsteinian dynamics and the older dynamical equations that descend from Newton's *Principia*. From the viewpoint of this essay these two theories are fundamentally incompatible in the sense illustrated by the relation of Copernican to Ptolemaic astronomy: Einstein's theory can be accepted only with the recognition that Newton's was wrong. Today this remains a minority view.[2] We must therefore examine the most prevalent objections to it.

The gist of these objections can be developed as follows. Relativistic dynamics cannot have shown Newtonian dynamics to be wrong, for Newtonian dynamics is still used with great success by most engineers and, in selected applications, by many physicists. Furthermore, the propriety of this use of the older theory can be proved from the very theory that has, in other applications, replaced it. Einstein's theory can be used to show that predictions from Newton's equations will be as good as our measuring instruments in all applications that satisfy a small number of restrictive conditions. For example, if Newtonian theory is to provide a good approximate solution, the relative velocities of the bodies considered must be small compared with the velocity of light. Subject to this condition and a few others, Newtonian theory seems to be derivable from Einsteinian, of which it is therefore a special case.

But, the objection continues, no theory can possibly conflict with one of its special cases. If Einsteinian science seems to make Newtonian dynamics wrong, that is only because some Newtonians were so incautious as to claim that Newtonian theory yielded entirely precise results or that it was valid at very high relative velocities. Since they could not have had any evidence for such claims, they betrayed the standards of science when they made them. In so far as Newtonian theory was ever a truly scientific theory supported by valid evidence, it still is. Only extravagant claims for the theory—claims that were never properly parts of science—can have been shown by Einstein to be wrong. Purged of these merely human extravagances, Newtonian theory has never been challenged and cannot be.

Some variant of this argument is quite sufficient to make any theory ever used by a significant group of competent scientists immune to attack. The much-maligned phlogiston theory, for example, gave order to a large number of physical and chemical phenomena. It explained why bodies burned—they were rich in phlogiston—and why metals had so many more properties in common than did their ores. The metals were all compounded from different elementary earths combined with phlogiston, and the latter, common to all metals, produced common properties. In addition, the phlogiston theory accounted for a number of reactions in which acids were formed by the combustion of substances like carbon and sulphur. Also, it explained the decrease of volume when combustion occurs in a confined volume of air—the phlogiston released by combustion "spoils" the elasticity of the air that absorbed it, just as fire "spoils" the elasticity of a steel spring.[3] If these were the only phenomena that the phlogiston theorists had claimed for their theory, that theory could never have been challenged. A similar argument will suffice for any theory that has ever been successfully applied to any range of phenomena at all.

But to save theories in this way, their range of application must be restricted to those phenomena and to that precision of observation with which the experimental evidence in hand already deals.[4] Carried just a step further (and the step can scarcely be avoided once the first is taken), such a limitation prohibits the scientist from claiming to speak "scientifically" about any phenomenon not already observed. Even in its present form the restriction forbids the scientist to rely upon a theory in his own research whenever that research enters an area or seeks a degree of precision for which past practice with the theory offers no precedent. These prohibitions are logically unexceptionable. But the result of accepting them would be the end of the research through which science may develop further.

By now that point too is virtually a tautology. Without commitment to a paradigm there could be no normal science. Furthermore, that commitment must extend to areas and to degrees of precision for which there is no full precedent. If it did not, the paradigm could provide no puzzles that had not already been solved. Besides, it is not only normal science that depends upon commitment to a paradigm. If existing theory binds the scientist only with respect to existing applications, then there can be no surprises, anomalies, or crises. But these are just the signposts that point the way to extraordinary science. If positivistic restrictions on the range of a theory's legitimate applicability are taken literally, the mechanism that tells the scientific community what problems may lead to fundamental change must cease to function. And when that occurs, the community will inevitably return to something much like its pre-paradigm state, a condition in which all members practice science but

in which their gross product scarcely resembles science at all. Is it really any wonder that the price of significant scientific advance is a commitment that runs the risk of being wrong?

More important, there is a revealing logical lacuna in the positivist's argument, one that will reintroduce us immediately to the nature of revolutionary change. Can Newtonian dynamics really be *derived* from relativistic dynamics? What would such a derivation look like? Imagine a set of statements, $E_1, E_2, \ldots, E_n$, which together embody the laws of relativity theory. These statements contain variables and parameters representing spatial position, time, rest mass, etc. From them, together with the apparatus of logic and mathematics, is deducible a whole set of further statements including some that can be checked by observation. To prove the adequacy of Newtonian dynamics as a special case, we must add to the E_i's additional statements, like $(v/c)^2 \ll 1$, restricting the range of the parameters and variables. This enlarged set of statements is then manipulated to yield a new set, $N_1, N_2, \ldots, N_m$, which is identical in form with Newton's laws of motion, the law of gravity, and so on. Apparently Newtonian dynamics has been derived from Einsteinian, subject to a few limiting conditions.

Yet the derivation is spurious, at least to this point. Though the N_i's are a special case of the laws of relativistic mechanics, they are not Newton's Laws. Or at least they are not unless those laws are reinterpreted in a way that would have been impossible until after Einstein's work. The variables and parameters that in the Einsteinian E_i's represented spatial position, time, mass, etc., still occur in the N_i's; and they there still represent Einsteinian space, time, and mass. But the physical referents of these Einsteinian concepts are by no means identical with those of the Newtonian concepts that bear the same name. (Newtonian mass is conserved; Einsteinian is convertible with energy. Only at low relative velocities may the two be measured in the same way, and even then they must not be conceived to be the same.) Unless we change the definitions of the variables in the N_i's, the statements we have derived are not Newtonian. If we do change them, we cannot properly be said to have *derived* Newton's Laws, at least not in any sense of "derive" now generally recognized. Our argument has, of course, explained why Newton's Laws ever seemed to work. In doing so it has justified, say, an automobile driver in acting as though he lived in a Newtonian universe. An argument of the same type is used to justify teaching earth-centered astronomy to surveyors. But the argument has still not done what it purported to do. It has not, that is, shown Newton's Laws to be a limiting case of Einstein's. For in the passage to the limit it is not only the forms of the laws that have changed. Simultaneously we have had to alter the fundamental structural elements of which the universe to which they apply is composed.

This need to change the meaning of established and familiar concepts is central to the revolutionary impact of Einstein's theory. Though subtler than the changes from geocentrism to heliocentrism, from phlogiston to oxygen, or from corpuscles to waves, the resulting conceptual transformation is no less decisively destructive of a previously established paradigm. We may even come to see it as a prototype for revolutionary reorientations in the sciences. Just because it did not involve the introduction of addi-

tional objects or concepts, the transition from Newtonian to Einsteinian mechanics illustrates with particular clarity the scientific revolution as a displacement of the conceptual network through which scientists view the world.

NOTES

1. Silvanus P. Thompson, *Life of William Thomson Baron Kelvin of Largs* (London, 1910), I, 266–81.

2. See, for example, the remarks by P. P. Wiener in *Philosophy of Science*, XXV (1958), 298.

3. James B. Conant, *Overthrow of the Phlogiston Theory* (Cambridge, 1950), pp. 13–16; and J. R. Partington, *A Short History of Chemistry* (2d ed.; London, 1951), pp. 85–88. The fullest and most sympathetic account of the phlogiston theory's achievements is by H. Metzger, *Newton, Stahl, Boerhaave et la doctrine chimique* (Paris, 1930), Part II.

4. Compare the conclusions reached through a very different sort of analysis by R. B. Braithwaite, *Scientific Explanation* (Cambridge, 1953), pp. 50–87, esp. p. 76.

Realism and the Theory-Dependence of Experimental Design

~

RICHARD N. BOYD

Richard N. Boyd is professor of philosophy at Cornell University. He is a leading exponent of scientific realism, and his articles include "On the Current Status of Scientific Realism," "Scientific Realism and Naturalistic Epistemology," and "Determinism, Laws and Predictability in Principle."

I. REALISM AND THE THEORY-DEPENDENCE OF EXPERIMENTAL DESIGN

In several papers . . . I have argued that scientific realism provides the only scientifically reasonable explanation for the reliability of certain important features of scientific methodology which are crucial in experimental design and in the assessment of experimental evidence. Roughly speaking, these are the features of scientific methodology relevant to the assessment of the "degree of confirmation" of a pro-

Reprinted from *Images of Science,* eds. Paul M. Churchland and Clifford A. Hooker (Chicago: University of Chicago Press, 1985), by permission of the publisher.

posed theory, given a body of observational evidence (if we choose to employ the standard empiricist terminology). In the present section, I want to expand upon this claim and to offer arguments for it in somewhat greater detail.

To begin with, it is important to understand what sort of reliability of methodology is to be explained. If scientific realism is true, then the methodological practices of science provide a reliable guide to approximate truth about theoretical matters and, no doubt, only scientific realism could provide a satisfactory explanation for this fact. But it would be question-begging to suggest that this provides any good reason to accept scientific realism; after all, only realists believe that the methodology of science is reliable in this sense, anyway. What I propose to do is to take advantage of the fact that antirealists in the philosophy of science are typically selective in their skepticism and to define the reliability of the methods of science in such a way that no questions are begged against the position of the typical antirealist. Call a theory instrumentally reliable if it makes approximately true predictions about observable phenomena. Call a methodology instrumentally reliable if it is a reliable guide to the acceptance of theories which are themselves instrumentally reliable. For the antirealist against whom my arguments are directed, it is uncontroversial that the actual methods of science are instrumentally reliable in this sense, although it may of course be a matter for philosophical dispute just which features of actual scientific practice explain this reliability. The arguments I am discussing here are directed against only the selectively skeptical antirealist; I have nothing to say to "the Skeptic."

Let us suppose that some scientific theory T has been proposed and that a body E of experimental results has been obtained which is consonant with the predictions of T. Imagine that T is an ordinary medium-sized theory of the sort which scientists routinely confirm or disconfirm in the course of what Kuhn calls "normal science." (Scientific realism must have something to say about the acceptance of large-scale paradigm-fixing theories as well, but it is a matter of controversy whether there is a reliable methodology for such cases, and so I want here to examine the more commonplace instances of theory

testing. . . .) Questions regarding the extent to which T is confirmed by the evidence E may be fruitfully divided into three categories:

1. *The question of "projectability."* One of the things which Goodman has taught us is that something important about inductive inference can be learned by examining the *unrefuted* inductive generalizations which no one ought to accept. Goodman formulates the issue in terms of the projectability of predicates in simple inductive generalizations, but it is clear that the issue he raises is more general. We can think of any sufficiently general theory as representing the proposal to consider as projectable certain possible patterns in observable data, *viz.,* those patterns which the theory predicts. In general, the methodological acceptability of such a proposal will not depend soley upon the projectability of the individual predicates contained in the theory in question considered in isolation, but also on the structure of the theory itself. . . . T will receive significant evidential support from E only if T represents a projectable pattern in possible observational data.

2. *The question of experimental controls and experimental artifacts.* Suppose that T represents a projectable pattern in possible observational data, and suppose further that the data in E represent apparently confirming evidence for T, whatever this latter constraint might come to. It will still be methodologically inappropriate to accept T as well confirmed unless there is reason to believe that the experiments involved in the production of these data were well designed. There must have been experimental controls for the influence of factors irrelevant to the assessment of T; in particular, the data which appear to confirm T must not be artifacts of the design of the experiments in question rather than genuine tests of the empirical adequacy of T. The analogous constraint applies, of course, to the case in which T is apparently disconfirmed by E.

3. *The question of "sampling."* Suppose that T represents a projectable pattern and that the experiments whose results are reflected in E are individually well designed. If we now ask how well, or to what extent, T is confirmed by E, we face head on the methodological analogue of the pure epistemologist's problem of induction. T will typically have infi-

nitely many different observational consequences, and the problem of assessing the extent to which E confirms T comes down to the question of which (typically relatively small) finite subsets of those consequences are such that their confirmation bestows significant confirmation on all the rest. (For the realist, of course, the problem is broader; one needs to know which such subsets bestow significant confirmation on the theory taken literally as a description of [partly] unobservable reality. Here, as in the case of the definition of reliability of methodology, I frame the issue in a way which does not beg the question against the antirealist.)

We may, I think, frame this question in a revealing way. The question is whether the consequences of T which have been tested are—in an epistemically appropriate sense—*a representative sample* of all the observational consequences of T. We cannot have checked out all of the (epistemically) possible ways in which T could "go wrong" with respect to observational prediction; there are, after all, infinitely many such ways. What we want to know is whether the experimental studies in question involve a representative sample of those ways, so that, if T hasn't gone wrong where we've tested it, then we can be justified in believing that it isn't going to go (very far) wrong at all. (Actually, this description is somewhat idealized; in the actual history of science, well-established theories have often turned out to be very wrong indeed in some of their empirical predictions. What is important is that we—rightly—expect experimental confirmation of a theory to warrant our belief that it will prove instrumentally reliable in a wide range of applications whose limits we cannot set in advance. The problem of identifying a relevantly representative sample of the observational predictions of a proposed theory is hardly rendered easier by this complication.)

The Theory-Dependence of the Answers to These Questions

The ways in which scientists answer these fundamental questions regarding the assessment of experimental evidence are quite profoundly dependent upon their prior theoretical commitments. That this is

generally true of scientific methodology is now uncontroversial; Kuhn, Quine, both H. Putnams, Goodman, Glymour, and van Fraassen have all emphasized this point without, of course, all drawing realist conclusions. It will be important for our purposes to examine in some detail the ways in which theoretical considerations are involved in answering the three questions about experimental evidence which we have just identified.

1. *Projectability.* Kuhn correctly insists that in mature sciences the basic form of solutions to particular research problems is tightly circumscribed by the theoretical and research tradition (the "paradigm"), and van Fraassen agrees that the acceptance of particular theories involves the scientist "in a certain sort of research programme." The proposed theory T whose degree of confirmation by E is to be estimated will not be a serious candidate for confirmation at all unless it arises as a proposed solution to some problem: the extension of an existing theory to some new area of application, perhaps, or the explanation of some particular phenomena or observations. The theoretical tradition very sharply constrains such proposals; a proposed solution is unacceptable unless it is *theoretically* plausible in the light of existing theories, unless it is one of the solutions suggested by the existing "paradigm." Only those patterns in observable data are considered projectable which correspond to theoretically plausible theoretical proposals. Two facts about the theory-dependence of such projectability judgments are important for our concerns.

In the first place, such judgments sharply limit the generalizations *about observables* which we take to be confirmable. Suppose, as is typically the case, that T is put forward to account for some particular (finite) set of observational data. Of course, there will be infinitely many possible theories which would accommodate those data. Even if we take two such theories to be equivalent if they are empirically equivalent (or, better, if their respective integrations into the existing theoretical tradition would be empirically equivalent), there will remain infinitely many equivalence classes, each representing one possible observational generalization from the initial data. The effect of our theory-dependent judgments of projectability is to restrict our attention to a quite small finite number of these possible generalizations. Only the generalizations in this small set are potentially confirmable by observations, given the prevailing standards for the assessment of scientific evidence.

Secondly, the projectability judgments in question are genuinely *theory*-dependent. The judgments of theoretical plausibility which these projectability judgments reflect depend upon the *theoretical* structure both of the proposed solutions and of the received theoretical tradition. Proposed problem solutions are plausible, for instance, when the unobservable mechanisms they postulate are relevantly similar to the mechanisms postulated in the received theoretical tradition, where the relevant respects of similarity are likewise dependent on the theoretical structures postulated in the tradition. If the received body of theories were replaced by some quite different but empirically equivalent body of theories, then judgments of theoretical plausibility would pick out quite different problem solutions as acceptable and thus typically identify quite different patterns as projectable. As Kuhn insists, the ontology of the received "paradigm" is crucial in determining the range of acceptable problem solutions (and thus the range of projectable patterns in data).

2. Experimental artifacts. Suppose that *T* is theoretically plausible and thus represents a projectable pattern in observable data, and suppose that the experimental results in *E* appear to support (or refute) *T*. If these results are really to be evidentially relevant, then there must be reason to think that the results favorable (or unfavorable) to *T* were not the result of features of the experimental situation which are irrelevant to the assessment of *T*. Of course, it is impossible to control for all epistemically possible experimental artifacts (of which there is an infinite number). Instead, we rely upon established theory to indicate the conditions under which the presence of experimental artifacts is to be suspected and the sorts of experimental controls which will permit us to avoid or discount for their effects. This is, I think, uncontroversial. It is also uncontroversial—although it is not much stressed in the literature—that our theory-dependent judgments in this area cut down the number of epistemically possible artifactual effects we actually control for from infinitely many to rather few.

What may be more controversial is whether or not these judgments are theory-dependent in the broader sense that they depend on the *theoretical* structure of the relevant background theories rather than just on their observational consequences. It might seem that they do not. Consider, for example, the commonplace that one must, in experiments involving electrical phenomena, control for the 60Hz hum induced by the alternating current in ordinary electrical wiring. Of course, the background theories which draw our attention to this sort of possible artifact have a complex theoretical structure, postulating electrons and electrical and magnetic fields and so forth. But, in order to know that we must shield various pieces of apparatus, all we need to know is that unless we do there will appear a certain sort of signal in our recording equipment superimposed on whatever signal comes from the preparation we are studying. If this sort of situation always obtains in cases of controlling for experimental artifacts, then it would appear that the methodological judgments which govern such controls do not depend on the theoretical structure of the relevant background theories.

Even if this were the case, there would, of course, be a significant way in which the identification of necessary experimental controls depends on the *theoretical* structure of the theories in the relevant theoretical tradition: the judgments of "projectability" which governed the acceptance of the generalizations about observables reflected in the currently accepted theories would have themselves depended on the *theoretical* structure of the earlier stages in the theoretical tradition. More importantly, it is by no means the case that the identification of relevant possible experimental artifacts depends solely on the observational consequences of the relevant background theories. This is so for two related reasons. In the first place, sound methodology often requires that we control for possible experimental artifacts whose effects are not by any means *predicted* by the received body of the theories but whose interference with the intended function of the experimental apparatus is *suggested* by those theories. Whatever may be the ultimate "rational reconstruction" of our practice, it is true that, in the typical case, the way in which the possible artifactual effects are suggested is that there are (typically unobservable) mechanisms postulated by the received theories about which it is *theoretically* plausible that either these mechanisms or mechanisms similar to them will produce the artifactual effects in question. Thus, we identify relevant possible experimental artifacts by something like "inductive" inference from theoretical premises, and the sorts of possible artifacts which we thereby identify depend dramatically on the theoretical structure of the theories which are the premises of these inferences.

We may see the same sort of theoretical-structure-dependent inferences in another methodologically important strategy for the identification of relevant possible experimental artifacts. Good methodology often requires that we control in one experimental situation E for some possible artifact A because we have already encountered similar artifacts A' in similar experimental situations E'. In the typical case, the possible artifact will be described in partly theoretical language, and the relevant respects of similarity (between E and E' and between A and A') will be determined by theoretical considerations—by considerations about the structure and effects of the unobservable mechanisms which the received theories postulate as operating in the relevant natural systems. In this case, too, whatever the ultimate reconstruction might be, the theoretical structure of the accepted theories, and not just their observational consequences, plays a crucial role in the identification of the relevant possible artifacts.

Two important points of similarity thus emerge about the way in which sound scientific methodology controls for the possibility of experimental artifacts and the way in which the problem of projectability is solved. In the first place, while there are infinitely many epistemically possible experimental artifacts which might affect any given experiment, scientific attention is paid to only a small finite number. In this regard, the identification of relevant possible experimental artifacts resembles the assessment of projectability: from an infinity of epistemic possibilities, the scientific method identifies a small finite number as methodologically relevant. The identification of relevant possible experimental artifacts resembles the solution to the problem of projectability in another crucial way: in each case the relevant methodology

depends on the theoretical structure of the currently accepted scientific theories; were those theories replaced by others which are empirically equivalent but theoretically divergent, quite different methodological practices would be identified as appropriate. In both cases, scientists behave as though their methodology were determined by inductive inferences from the theoretical principles embodied in the received theoretical tradition.

3. *Sampling.* The pattern discernible in our examination of the ways in which scientific methodology handles the issues of projectability and experimental artifacts is even more striking in the case of the solution to the problem of "sampling." It is a fair statement of the most basic methodological principle governing the assessment of experimental evidence that a proposed theory T should be tested under conditions representative of those in which it is most reasonable to think that the theory will fail, if it's going to fail at all. The identification of these conditions rests upon *theoretical* criticism of that theory. The proposed theory T will, typically, postulate various mechanisms, entities, processes, etc., as factors in the phenomena to which it applies. Theoretical criticism involves the identification of alternative conceptions of the mechanisms, processes, etc., involved which are theoretically plausible—that is, which are suggested by the sorts of mechanisms, entities, etc., which are postulated by the received body of theories. These theoretically plausible alternatives to T will suggest circumstances in which the observational predictions of T might be expected to be wrong. It is under (representative instances of) these circumstances that T must be tested if it is to be well confirmed. This is the central methodological principle of experimental design.

Plainly, the methodological solution to the problem of sampling is theory-dependent. Moreover, whatever the "rational reconstruction" of this methodology might be, scientists do not in practice distinguish sharply between unobservable mechanisms, processes, entities, etc., and observable ones in identifying ways in which a proposed theory might reasonably be expected to fail. Indeed, inferences which look for all the world like inductive inferences from accepted premises about unobservables to conclusions about unobservables play an absolutely crucial role in the sort of theoretical criticism we are discussing. Thus, in the present case, as in the case of the methodological solutions to the problems of projectability and of experimental artifacts, the ways in which scientific methodology is theory-dependent are such that, if the existing body of theories were replaced by an empirically equivalent but theoretically divergent body of theories, our methodological judgments *regarding the "degree of confirmation" of generalizations about observables* would be profoundly different.

Projectability and Induction About Unobservables

The ways in which the features of scientific methodology just discussed depend on the theoretical structure of the received body of background theories may be seen more clearly if we consider a standard way in which philosophers in the tradition of logical positivism have treated the feature of theory testing which I have presented under the heading "Sampling." It has been widely recognized that at any given time in the history of science, and for any given problem or issue, there are typically only a very few theories "in the field" and contending for acceptance. The practice of testing a proposed theory against its most plausible rivals might, in this context, be seen as simply an application of the same pragmatic principle which dictates that, if there are only a very few brands of band saw available, one should evaluate each before making a purchase. This sort of description gives the appearance of reducing the methodological principle we have been discussing to a *merely* pragmatic level, denying it any special epistemic relevance.

Of course, such an interpretation *would not* deprive the practices we have been discussing either of their theory-dependence or of their epistemic importance. So long as the relevant rival theories are identified in the theory-dependent way described in the section on projectability, then the practice would be as theory-dependent as one could wish. Moreover, if testing proposed theories against instrumental rivals in the way suggested represented *the* methodological solution to the problem of "sampling," then it has epistemic importance however much it may also

have a purely pragmatic justification. What is most interesting in this context, however, is that the actual methodological practice of scientists departs in a revealing way from that suggested by the pragmatic account. In order for the pragmatic picture to have any plausibility, we must think of a proposed theory as competing against other possible predictive instruments roughly as powerful as itself. The rival "theories" against which it must be tested must be theories in the sense of fairly well developed systems with some significant predictive power. One does, after all, test band saws against other band saws.

While it is true that sound scientific methodology does require that a proposed theory should be tested against similarly well articulated rivals which are approximately equally theoretically plausible (roughly, that's what being a rival *theory* means, beyond having been invented in the first place), what is striking about the methodological practices which constitute the solution to the problem of sampling is that they may also require that a proposed theory be tested against a mere hunch, which has no deductive predictive consequences whatsoever. Suppose that a proposed theory T postulates a particular sort of unobservable mechanism as operating in the systems to which T applies, and imagine that T is sufficiently well worked out that (using well-established auxiliary hypotheses) it is possible to obtain experimentally testable predictions from T. Suppose, also, that theoretical criticism of T identifies alternative possible mechanisms, plausible in the light of received theories. Under these circumstances, it becomes necessary to try to pit T's conception of the matter against the alternative in some sort of experimental situation *even if* the alternative account is not nearly so thoroughly worked out as T and even if, for that reason, it yields (together with relevant auxiliary hypotheses) *no* definite predictions about observables at all. Under these circumstances, what sound methodology dictates is the identification of experimental circumstances under which the sorts of observations which it is *theoretically plausible* to expect given the alternative conception are different from those which one would expect given T's account of the relevant mechanisms.

By way of example, suppose that T provides an account of the reaction mechanisms for some biochemical process and that T is worked out in sufficient detail that it has (together with well-confirmed auxiliary hypotheses) significant deductive observational consequences. Suppose that a rival conception of the relevant reaction mechanisms is suggested by theoretically plausible considerations but that this rival conception is insufficiently well developed to have specific testable deductive consequences. It might nevertheless be possible to test T against the rival conception. Suppose that, in the case of better-studied systems, those systems to which mechanisms like those proposed by T and ascribed by the received theories are much more sensitive to some particular class of chemical agent than those to which mechanisms like those proposed in the alternative are ascribed (note here that the relevant respects of likeness will be determined by the content of theoretical descriptions of the systems in question, and the theoretical content of the relevant background theories, *and* that the class of chemical agents in question may similarly be theoretically defined). Under such circumstances, sound methodology will dictate subjecting the biochemical systems to which T applies to chemical agents in the relevant class; data indicating considerable sensitivity to such agents will be especially important for the confirmation of T precisely because they will constitute a test of T against the theoretically plausible rival conception of the relevant reaction mechanisms. Note that in the present case the rival conception need not have any *deductive* observational consequences regarding the experimental situations in question. Instead, reasoning by analogy *at the theoretical level* makes it *theoretically plausible* to expect low sensitivity if the rival conception is true. T is tested against a theoretically plausible hunch about how it might go wrong.

Indeed, the role of considerations of theoretical plausibility in theory testing can go even deeper; a proposed theory may be pitted against a theoretically plausible rival in a particular experimental setting even though neither the rival *nor* the proposed theory have (when taken together with appropriate well-confirmed auxiliary hypotheses) any deductive observational predictions about the results of the experiments in question! In the example we have been considering, the appropriateness of the experimental test in question does not depend on the theory T's having any observational deductive predictions

about the results of the experiment. All that is required is that it be *theoretically* plausible that a test of the sensitivity of the relevant biochemical systems to the specific chemical agent will provide an indication of which of the two accounts of reaction mechanisms (if either) is right. We may test T by pitting a hunch about the outcome of experimentation which is theoretically plausible given T (and the body of received theories) against an experimental hunch which is theoretically plausible on the assumption of the rival conception of reaction mechanisms. Even though we have assumed that T makes a significant number of deductive observational predictions, we need not assume that it makes any *deductive* predictions about the outcome of this crucial experimental test! In sciences which deal with complex systems, instances of theory testing which fit the model just presented are by no means uncommon. Indeed, it may be a good idea to ask whether in describing the instrumental application of theories (rather than their confirmation)—when defining empirical adequacy, for example—the idealization that it is the *deductive* observational consequences of a theory (together with auxiliary hypotheses) rather than its *inductive* consequences that are relevant may not be fundamentally misleading; but that is a topic for another paper.

In any event, what we may learn from these examples is that, in practice, inductive inferences in science extend to inferences with theoretical premises and theoretical conclusions. Just as there are theory-dependent judgments about which possible patterns in observables are projectable, so there are judgments about which patterns in the properties or behavior of "theoretical entities" are projectable. Just as there are theory-dependent judgments of the "degree of confirmation" of instrumental claims by empirical data, so there are theory-dependent judgments of the plausibility of various theoretical claims in the light of other considerations both empirical and theoretical. Indeed, whatever the correct philosophical analysis of this matter, scientific methodology does not dictate any significant distinction between inductive inferences about observables and what certainly look like inductive inferences about unobservables. Finally, and most strikingly, the very methodological principles which govern scientific induction about observables are, in practice, parasitic upon "inductive" inferences about unobservables.

An Argument for Scientific Realism

It will be evident how one may argue for scientific realism on the basis of the theory-dependence of experimental methodology. Consider the question, why are the methodological practices of science instrumentally reliable? Both scientific realists and (almost all) empiricists agree that these practices are instrumentally reliable, but they differ sharply in their capacity to explain this reliability. So theory-dependent are the most basic principles for the assessment of experimental evidence that it must be concluded that these are principles for applying the knowledge which is reflected in currently accepted theories as a guide to the proper methods for the evidential assessment of new theoretical proposals; any other conclusion makes the instrumental success of the scientific method a miracle.

According to the empiricist, the knowledge reflected in the existing body of accepted theories at any time in the history of science is entirely instrumental knowledge: the most we know on the basis of experimental evidence is that the existing body of theories is empirically adequate. Thus, the replacement of existing theories by an empirically equivalent set of theories would leave the knowledge they embody unchanged. Thus, the empiricist can explain the epistemic adequacy of only those theory-dependent features of scientific methodology whose dictates are preserved under the substitution, for the actual body of accepted theories, of any other empirically equivalent one. But, as we have just seen, *none* of the central methodological principles which govern the evaluation of scientific evidence have this property! The consistent empiricist cannot explain the instrumental reliability of the methodology which scientists actually employ.

The scientific realist, on the other hand, has no difficulty in providing the required explanation. According to the realist, existing theories provide approximate knowledge not only of relations between observables, but also of the unobservable structures which underlie observable phenomena. In applying theory-dependent evidential standards, scientists use existing theoretical (and observational) knowledge as a guide to the articulation and experimental assessment of new theories. The judgments of projectability, identification of experimental artifacts, and theoretical criticisms of proposed theories which look ever so much like inductive inferences *are* inductive inferences from acquired theoretical knowledge to new theoretical conclusions. When a theoretical proposal is theoretically plausible in the light of the existing theoretical tradition, what that means is that it is supported by an inductive inference at the theoretical level from previously acquired theoretical knowledge.

Judgments of "projectability" are thus just what they look like "preanalytically": they represent the identification of theoretical proposals for which there are good inductive reasons to believe that they are (approximately) true and thus for which there is good reason to believe that they will eventually be articulated into empirically adequate theories. The role of experimentation is to choose between the various theoretical proposals which pass this preliminary test for probable (approximate) truth.

Similarly, the judgments of theoretical plausibility by which possible experimental artifacts are identified turn out to be inductive inferences from theoretical knowledge which result in reliable assessments of the evidential likelihood that various unobservable factors will influence the outcome of experiments. Finally, the methodological solution to the problem of sampling really does consist in identifying—by reliable inductive inference from theoretical knowledge—the most plausible rivals to a proposed theory and the experimental conditions under which they can be effectively pitted against it. The reliability of scientific methodology in guiding induction about observables turns out to be largely parasitic upon the reliability of the methodology in applying existing theoretical knowledge to guide the establishment of new theoretical knowledge. . . . Only this explanation, the realist maintains, can account both for the reliability of the scientific method and for the fact that seemingly inductive reasoning about theoretical matters is so central to it.

PART 4

~

Metaphysics

Introduction

DELIA GRAFF

What is there? What could there be? What are things like? How do they interact with each other? The aim of metaphysics is to refine and provide answers to such questions. Of course, it is not only metaphysicians who do so. The zoologist investigating whether there are as yet undiscovered mammalian species wants to answer the question *what is there?* A worried mother may want to know how things (her children) interact with each other. Metaphysics is the *philosophical* approach to *philosophical* formulations of such questions. What distinguishes the philosophical approaches or formulations from the nonphilosophical? This is itself a philosophical question, not easy to answer in a completely satisfying way.

Still, there is much truth in saying that the questions of metaphysics are about the nature of reality at a very abstract and general level, and are typically addressed through reason rather than empirical investigation. The readings collected here cover a variety of topics within metaphysics. Some questions in metaphysics are *ontological:* they are concerned with what kinds of things there are. One ontological question is whether every existent is located in space, or whether there are abstract existents as well. A second question is: if someone says, "my pen is red," the truth of what they say requires there to be a pen in the world, but does it also require that there be a property, *redness,* for the pen to have, and also a relation of *belonging to* holding between the pen and the speaker that makes the use of the possessive pronoun "my" correct? A further question, for one who admits in addition to particulars also properties and relations, is whether the property of *redness* that one red pen has is the very same property of *redness* had by some other red pen. To answer this question affirmatively is to admit the existence of *universals.* The question is an ancient one. In the history of philosophy, there have been those who admit particulars but not universals, and those who admit universals but not particulars. In the selections by Bertrand Russell and David Armstrong, we find arguments that both particulars and universals must be admitted as "fundamental constituents of reality."

The next set of readings address questions about the *material constitution* of particulars. We commonly think of material objects, such as human bodies, as having parts, such as fingers and toes. Do material objects also have *arbitrary* parts? Is there, for example, such a thing as the northern half of the Eiffel Tower or an undetached part of my right arm shaped exactly like a bust of Mozart? One may defend an affirmative answer to this question by arguing that it is merely a reflection of human interests and not of an underlying metaphysical reality that we have names for some types of parts of objects but not others. Yet if there were arbitrary parts of material objects, then it seems we would have to accept that if an object, such as a statue, could survive the destruction of some of its parts, such as its limbs, then it could become identical to something, namely its torso, to which it had not always been identical. We find such an argument elaborated and defended in Peter van Inwagen's essay "The Doctrine of Arbitrary Undetached Parts." In "Many, But Almost One," David Lewis addresses problems that arise when we realize that the everyday objects around us have *vague boundaries* and that many precise objects—some containing, others lacking, a certain molecule as part—are equally good candidates for being *identical* to the cloud above you, or to the cat on your mat.

The excerpt from John Locke's *Essay Concerning Human Understanding* includes his views on material constitution. Locke holds that, unlike plants and animals, inanimate objects such as a lump of clay cannot survive the destruction of any of their parts. Also, unlike van Inwagen and Lewis, Locke holds that it is possible for distinct objects (such as a horse and its body) to exist in the same location for the entire duration of their existence as long as they are not of the same kind.

In the excerpt Locke also presents his famous "memory criterion" of identity for persons, which allows for the metaphysical possibility of bodily transfer. Sydney Shoemaker argues that memory criteria and bodily criteria are both important for questions about the identity of a person over time. Derek Parfit contends that relations other than identity over time are what matter to us in questions of survival.

It is natural to think that identity over time is a prerequisite for *motion:* that in order for an object to *move,* the very same object must be at one time in a certain location and at a later time in a different location. Aristotle presents and responds to Zeno of Elea's paradoxes of time and motion in the excerpt from Book VI of his *Physics.* The conclusion of one of Zeno's paradoxes is that it is impossible for Achilles, however fast he runs, to catch up with the moving tortoise, however slow and however small its lead. Max Black argues that philosophers have been wrong to think that modern mathematics, in particular its understanding of convergent infinite series, helps in solving Zeno's paradoxes. He contends instead that Achilles can catch the tortoise only if doing so does not require him to cover infinitely many nonoverlapping distances.

The remaining selections deal with the topics of *causation, fatalism, determinism,* and *freedom of the will.* David Hume argues that our concept of *causation* cannot involve the idea of any "necessary connexion" between objects or events because we have no experience of necessary connections but only of "constant conjunctions" of events of one kind being followed by those of another. David Lewis proposes that causation should be analyzed by appeal to *counterfactual* conditionals—such as "if this event had not happened, then that event would not have happened." Lewis contends that his analysis has advantages over "regularity" analyses of causation he regards as descending from Hume.

Aristotle's antifatalism comes out in the excerpt from his *De Interpretatione.* Aristotle believes that the future is open, that, for example, it is not now necessary that there will be a sea battle tomorrow, nor is it now necessary that there will not be one. On one interpretation, we find Aristotle arguing in the passage that if the openness of the future is to be preserved, we must give up the principle of bivalence—the principle that every statement is either true or false. Since Aristotle does accept the Law of Excluded Middle, he proposes that we must allow that such disjunctions "either there will be a sea battle tomorrow or there will not be" can be true without either of their disjuncts being true. Richard Taylor defends this interpretation of Aristotle's "sea battle argument," providing important clarification of the sense of *necessity* at issue in the question whether "everything that happens happens of necessity" and addressing a variety of objections to Aristotle's argument, including one involving the possibility of omniscience.

The final metaphysical debate we encounter relates causation and determinism to human freedom. It is agreed that humans can be morally praiseworthy or blameworthy only if they have free will. A. J. Ayer argues that free will is compatible with determinism, the thesis that the laws of nature, together with the past state of the world, leave open only one possible future. Roderick Chisholm contends that free will is not compatible with determinism. The debate between compatibilists and incompatibilists plays out further in the articles by Harry Frankfurt and Peter van Inwagen. Frankfurt strengthens the case for compatibilism by arguing against "the principle of alternate possibilities," according to which agents are morally responsible for their actions only if they could have done otherwise. The crux of Frankfurt's argument is that an agent may be morally responsible for an action when he performs it *because* he chose to, despite the presence of an intervening threat or force that would have either compelled him to choose as he did or caused him to act as he did even if he had not so chosen. Van Inwagen strengthens the case for the incompatibilism of free will and determinism by setting out an explicit argument for it. Van Inwagen's argument places a burden on compatibilists to say either which of van Inwagen's premises they reject or where they find fault with his conception of freedom or determinism.

Philosophers disagree about whether in doing metaphysics we are discovering truths about reality as it is "in itself," or whether we are rather discovering truths about the structure of our conceptualization of reality. In any case, from the very abstract (Are there universals?) to the practical (Is punishment ever appropriate?), grappling with the questions of metaphysics requires us to subject our most commonly held convictions to rational scrutiny. It is hoped that the reader discovers the enjoyment and fulfillment of exercising this distinctively human ability.

On the Relations of Universals and Particulars

~

BERTRAND RUSSELL

Bertrand Russell (1872–1970) is considered to be one of the founders of analytic philosophy. His impact on the fields of logic, philosophy of language, philosophy of mathematics, metaphysics, and epistemology has been enormous. *Principia Mathematica,* written with A. N. Whitehead, is among his most important works. Russell is also known as a social critic and political activist. He received the Order of Merit in 1949 and the Nobel Prize for literature in 1950.

The purpose of the following paper is to consider whether there is a fundamental division of the objects with which metaphysics is concerned into two classes, universals and particulars, or whether there is any method of overcoming this dualism. My own opinion is that the dualism is ultimate; on the other hand, many men with whom, in the main, I am in close agreement, hold that it is not ultimate. I do not feel the grounds in favour of its ultimate nature to be very conclusive, and in what follows I should lay stress rather on the distinctions and considerations introduced during the argument than on the conclusion at which the argument arrives.

It is impossible to begin our discussion with sharp definitions of universals and particulars, though we may hope to reach such definitions in the end. At the beginning, we can only roughly indicate the kind of facts that we wish to analyse and the kind of distinctions that we wish to examine. There are several cognate distinctions which produce confusion by intermingling, and which it is important to disentangle before advancing into the heart of our problem.

The first distinction that concerns us is the distinction between percepts and concepts, i.e., between objects of acts of perception and objects of acts of conception. If there is a distinction between particulars and universals, percepts will be among particulars, while concepts will be among universals. Opponents of universals, such as Berkeley and Hume, will maintain that concepts are derivable from percepts, as faint copies, or in some other way. Opponents of particulars will maintain that the apparent particularity of percepts is illusory, and that, though the act of perception may differ from the act of conception, yet its objects differ only by their greater complexity, and are really composed of constituents which are, or might be, concepts.

But the distinction of percepts and concepts is too psychological for an ultimate metaphysical distinction. Percepts and concepts are respectively the relata of two different relations, perception and conception, and there is nothing in their definitions to show whether, or how, they differ. Moreover, the distinction of percepts and concepts, in itself, is incapable of being extended to entities which are not objects of cognitive acts. Hence we require some other distinction expressing the intrinsic difference which we seem to feel between percepts and concepts.

A cognate distinction, which effects part at least of what we want, is the distinction between things which exist in time and things which do not. In order to avoid any question as to whether time is relative or absolute, we may say that an entity x "exists in time" provided x is not itself a moment or part of time, and

From *Proceedings of the Aristotelian Society, 12.*

some such proposition as "*x* is before *y* or simultaneous with *y* or after *y*" is true of *x*. (It is not to be assumed that *before, simultaneous,* and *after* are mutually exclusive: if *x* has duration, they will not be so.) Prima facie, a percept exists in time, in the above sense, while a concept does not. The object of perception is simultaneous with the act of perception, while the object of conception seems indifferent to the time of conceiving and to all time. Thus, prima facie, we have here the non-psychological distinction of which we were in search. But the same controversies will break out as in the case of percepts and concepts. The man who reduces concepts to percepts will say that nothing is really out of time, and that the appearance of this in the case of concepts is illusory. The man who reduces percepts to concepts may either, like most idealists, deny that anything is in time, or, like some realists, maintain that concepts can and do exist in time.

In addition to the above distinction as regards time, there is a distinction as regards space which, as we shall find, is very important in connexion with our present question. Put as vaguely as possible, this is a distinction which divides entities into three classes: (*a*) those which are not in any place, (*b*) those which are in one place at one time, but never in more than one, (*c*) those which are in many places at once. To make this threefold division precise, we should have to discuss what we mean by a place, what we mean by "in," and how the different kinds of space—visual, tactile, physical—produce different forms of this threefold division. For the present I will merely illustrate what I mean by examples. Relations, obviously, do not exist anywhere in space. Our bodies, we think, exist in one place at a time, but not in more than one. General qualities, such as whiteness, on the contrary, may be said to be in many places at once: we may say, in a sense, that whiteness is in every place where there is a white thing. This division of entities will be discussed later; for the present I merely wish to indicate that it requires examination.

In addition to the above psychological and metaphysical distinctions, there are two logical distinctions which are relevant in the present enquiry. In the first place, there is the distinction between relations and entities which are not relations. It has been cus-tomary for philosophers to ignore or reject relations, and speak as if all entities were either subjects or predicates. But this custom is on the decline, and I shall assume without further argument that there are such entities as relations. Philosophy has, so far as I know, no common name for all entities which are not relations. Among such entities are included not only all the things that would naturally be called particulars, but also all the universals that philosophers are in the habit of considering when they discuss the relation of particulars to universals, for universals are generally conceived as common properties of particulars, in fact, as predicates. For our purpose it is hardly worth while to invent a technical term *ad hoc;* I shall therefore speak of entities which are not relations simply as *non-relations.*

The second logical distinction which we require is one which may or may not be identical in extension with that between relations and non-relations, but is certainly not identical in intention. It may be expressed as the distinction between verbs and substantives, or, more correctly, between the objects denoted by verbs and the objects denoted by substantives. (Since this more correct expression is long and cumbrous, I shall generally use the shorter phrase to mean the same thing. Thus, when I speak of verbs, I mean the objects denoted by verbs, and similarly for substantives.) The nature of this distinction emerges from the analysis of complexes. In most complexes, if not in all, a certain number of different entities are combined into a single entity by means of a relation. "*A*'s hatred for *B*," for example, is a complex in which *hatred* combines *A* and *B* into one whole; "*C*'s belief that *A* hates *B*" is a complex in which *belief* combines *A* and *B* and *C* and hatred into one whole, and so on. A relation is distinguished as dual, triple, quadruple, etc., or dyadic, triadic, tetradic, etc., according to the number of terms which it unites in the simplest complexes in which it occurs. Thus in the above examples, hatred is a dual relation and belief is a quadruple relation. The capacity for combining terms into a single complex is the defining characteristic of what I call *verbs.* The question now arises: Are there complexes which consist of a single term and a verb? "*A* exists" might serve as an example of what is possibly such a complex. It is the possibility that there may be complexes of this kind which makes it impossible to decide off-hand that verbs are the same as relations. There may be verbs which are philosophically as well as grammatically intransitive. Such verbs, if they exist, may be called *predicates,* and the propositions in which they are attributed may be called subject-predicate propositions.

If there are no such verbs as those whose possibility we have been considering, i.e., if all verbs are relations, it will follow that subject-predicate propositions, if there are any, will express a *relation* of subject to predicate. Such propositions will then be definable as those that involve a certain relation called *predication.* Even if there are subject-predicate propositions in which the predicate is the verb, there will still be equivalent propositions in which the predicate is related to the subject; thus '*A* exists', for example, will be equivalent to "*A* has existence." Hence the question whether predicates are verbs or not becomes unimportant. The more important question is whether there is a specific relation of predication, or whether what are grammatically subject-predicate propositions are really of many different kinds, no one of which has the characteristics one naturally associates with subject-predicate propositions. This question is one to which we shall return at a later stage.

The above logical distinctions are relevant to our enquiry because it is natural to regard particulars as entities which can only be subjects or terms of relations, and cannot be predicates or relations. A particular is naturally conceived as a *this* or something intrinsically analogous to a *this;* and such an entity seems incapable of being a predicate or a relation. A universal, on this view, will be anything that is a predicate or a relation. But if there is no specific relation of predication, so that there is no class of entities which can properly be called predicates, then the above method of distinguishing particulars and universals fails. The question whether philosophy must recognize two ultimately distinct kinds of entities, particulars and universals, turns, as we shall see more fully later on, on the question whether non-relations are of two kinds, subjects and predicates, or rather terms which can only be subjects and terms which may be either subjects or predicates. And this question turns on whether there is an ultimate simple asymmetrical relation which may be called predica-

tion, or whether all apparent subject-predicate propositions are to be analysed into propositions of other forms, which do not require a radical difference of nature between the apparent subject and the apparent predicate.

The decision of the question whether there is a simple relation of predication ought perhaps to be possible by inspection, but for my part I am unable to come to any decision in this way. I think, however, that it can be decided in favour of predication by the analysis of *things* and by considerations as to spatio-temporal diversity. This analysis and these considerations will also show the way in which our purely logical question is bound up with the other questions as to particulars and universals which I raised at the beginning of this paper.

The common-sense notion of things and their qualities is, I suppose, the source of the conception of subject and predicate, and the reason why language is so largely based on this conception. But the thing, like other common-sense notions, is a piece of half-hearted metaphysics, which neither gives crude data nor gives a tenable hypothesis as to a reality behind the data. A thing, of the everyday sort, is constituted by a bundle of sensible qualities belonging to various senses, but supposed all to coexist in one continuous portion of space. But the common space which should contain both visual and tactile qualities is not the space of either visual or tactile perception: it is a constructed "real" space, belief in which has, I suppose, been generated by association. And in crude fact, the visual and tactile qualities of which I am sensible are not in a common space, but each in its own space. Hence if the thing is to be impartial as between sight and touch, it must cease to have the actual qualities of which we are sensible, and become their common cause or origin or whatever vaguer word can be found. Thus the road is opened to the metaphysical theories of science and to the metaphysical theories of philosophy: the thing may be a number of electric charges in rapid motion, or an idea in the mind of God, but it is certainly not what the senses perceive.

The argument against things is trite, and I need not labour it. I introduce it here only in order to illustrate a consequence which is sometimes overlooked. Realists who reject particulars are apt to regard a thing as reducible to a number of qualities coexisting in one place. But, apart from other objections to this view, it is doubtful whether the different qualities in question ever do coexist in one place. If the qualities are sensible, the place must be in a sensible space; but this makes it necessary that the qualities should belong to only one sense, and it is not clear that genuinely different qualities belonging to one sense ever coexist in a single place in a perceptual space. If, on the other hand, we consider what may be called "real" space, i.e. the inferred space containing the "real" objects which we suppose to be the causes of our perceptions, then we no longer know what is the nature of the qualities, if any, which exist in this 'real' space, and it is natural to replace the bundle of qualities by a collection of pieces of matter having whatever characteristics the science of the moment may prescribe. Thus in any case the bundle of coexisting qualities in the same place is not an admissible substitute for the thing.

For our purposes, the "real" object by which science or philosophy replaces the thing is not important. We have rather to consider the relations of sensible objects in a single sensible space, say that of sight.

The theory of sensible qualities which dispenses with particulars will say, if the same shade of colour is found in two different places, that what exists is the shade of colour itself, and that what exists in the one place is identical with what exists in the other. The theory which admits particulars will say, on the contrary, that two numerically different *instances* of the shade of colour exist in the two places: in this view, the shade of colour itself is a universal and a predicate of both the instances, but the universal does not exist in space and time. Of the above two views, the first, which does not introduce particulars, dispenses altogether with predication as a fundamental relation: according to this view, when we say "this thing is white," the fundamental fact is that whiteness exists here. According to the other view, which admits particulars, what exists here is something of which whiteness is a predicate—not, as for common sense, the thing with many other qualities, but an instance of whiteness, a particular of which whiteness is the only predicate except shape and brightness and whatever else is necessarily connected with whiteness.

Of the above two theories, one admits only what would naturally be called universals, while the other admits both universals and particulars. Before examining them, it may be as well to examine and dismiss the theory which admits only particulars, and dispenses altogether with universals. This is the theory advocated by Berkeley and Hume in their polemic against "abstract ideas." Without tying ourselves down to their statements, let us see what can be made of this theory. The general name "white," in this view, is defined for a given person at a given moment by a particular patch of white which he sees or imagines; another patch is called white if it has exact likeness in colour to the standard patch. In order to avoid making the colour a universal, we have to suppose that "exact likeness" is a simple relation, not analysable into community of predicates; moreover, it is not the general relation of likeness that we require, but a more special relation, that of colour-likeness, since two patches might be exactly alike in shape or size but different in colour. Thus, in order to make the theory of Berkeley and Hume workable, we must assume an ultimate relation of colour-likeness, which holds between two patches which would commonly be said to have the same colour. Now, prima facie, this relation of colour-likeness will itself be a universal or an "abstract idea," and thus we shall still have failed to avoid universals. But we may apply the same analysis to colour-likeness. We may take a standard particular case of colour-likeness, and say that anything else is to be called a colour-likeness if it is exactly like our standard case. It is obvious, however, that such a process leads to an endless regress: we explain the likeness of two terms as consisting in the likeness which their likeness bears to the likeness of two other terms, and such a regress is plainly vicious. Likeness at least, therefore, must be admitted as a universal, and, having admitted one universal, we have no longer any reason to reject others. Thus the whole complicated theory, which had no motive except to avoid universals, falls to the ground. Whether or not there are particulars, there must be relations which are universals in the sense that (*a*) they are concepts, not percepts; (*b*) they do not exist in time; (*c*) they are verbs, not substantives.

It is true that the above argument does not prove that there are universal qualities as opposed to universal relations. On the contrary, it shows that universal qualities *can,* so far as logic can show, be replaced by exact likenesses of various kinds between particulars.

This view has, so far as I know, nothing to recommend it beyond its logical possibility. But from the point of view of the problem whether there are particulars, it has no bearing on the argument. It is a view which is only possible if there are particulars, and it demands only an easy re-statement of subject-predicate propositions: instead of saying that an entity has such and such a predicate, we shall have to say that there are entities to which it has such and such a specific likeness. I shall therefore in future ignore this view, which in any case assumes our main thesis, namely, the existence of particulars. To the grounds in favour of this thesis we must now return.

When we endeavoured to state the two theories as to sensible qualities, we had occasion to consider two white patches. On the view which denies particulars, whiteness itself exists in both patches: a numerically single entity, whiteness, exists in all places that are white. Nevertheless, we speak of *two* white patches, and it is obvious that, in some sense, the patches are two, not one. It is this spatial plurality which makes the difficulty of the theory that denies particulars.

Without attempting, as yet, to introduce all the necessary explanations and distinctions, we may state the argument for particulars roughly as follows. It is logically possible for two exactly similar patches of white, of the same size and shape, to exist simultaneously in different places. Now, whatever may be the exact meaning of "existing in different places," it is self-evident that, in such a case, there are two different patches of white. Their diversity might, if we adopted the theory of absolute position, be regarded as belonging, not to the white itself which exists in the two places, but to the complexes "whiteness in this place" and "whiteness in that place." This would derive their diversity from the diversity of this place and that place; and since places cannot be supposed to differ as to qualities, this would require that the places should be particulars. But if we reject absolute position, it will become impossible to distinguish the two patches as two, unless each, instead of being the universal whiteness, is an *instance* of whiteness. It might be thought that the two might be distinguished by means of other qualities in the same place as the one but not in the same place as the other. This, however, presupposes that the two patches are already

distinguished as numerically diverse, since otherwise what is in the same place as the one must be in the same place as the other. Thus the fact that it is logically possible for precisely similar things to coexist in two different places, but that things in different places at the same time cannot be numerically identical, forces us to admit that it is particulars, i.e., *instances* of universals, that exist in places, and not universals themselves.

The above is the outline of our argument. But various points in it have to be examined and expanded before it can be considered conclusive. In the first place, it is not necessary to assert that there ever are two exactly similar existents. It is only necessary to perceive that our judgment that this and that are two different existents is not necessarily based on any difference of qualities, but may be based on difference of spatial position alone; and that difference of qualities, whether or not it always in fact accompanies numerical difference, is not logically necessary in order to insure numerical difference where there is difference of spatial position.

Again, it is not easy to state exactly what sort of spatial distribution in perceived space warrants us in asserting plurality. Before we can use space as an argument for particulars, we must be clear on this point. We are accustomed to concede that a thing cannot be in two places at once, but this common-sense maxim, unless very carefully stated, will lead us into inextricable difficulties. Our first business, therefore, it to find out how to state this maxim in an unobjectionable form.

In rational dynamics, where we are concerned with matter and "real" space, the maxim that nothing can be in two places at once is taken rigidly, and any matter occupying more than a point of space is regarded as at least theoretically divisible. Only what occupies a bare point is simple and single. This view is straight-forward, and raises no difficulties as applied to "real" space.

But as applied to perceived space, such a view is quite inadmissible. The immediate object of (say) visual perception is always of finite extent. If we suppose it to be, like the matter corresponding to it in "real" space, composed of a collection of entities, one for each point which is not empty, we shall have to suppose two things, both of which seem incredible, namely: (1) that every immediate object of visual (or tactile) perception is infinitely complex; (2) that every such object is always composed of parts which are by their very nature imperceptible. It seems quite impossible that the immediate object of perception should have these properties. Hence we must suppose that an indivisible object of visual perception may occupy a finite extent of visual space. In short, we must, in dividing any complex object of visual perception, reach, after a finite number of steps, a *minimum sensible,* which contains no plurality although it is of finite extent. Visual space may, in a sense, be infinitely *divisible,* for, by attention alone, or by the microscope, the immediate object of perception can be changed in a way which introduces complexity where formerly there was simplicity; and to this process no clear limit can be set. But this is a process which substitutes a new immediate object in place of the old one, and the new object, though more subdivided than the old one, will still consist of only a finite number of parts. We must therefore admit that the space of perception is not infinitely divided, and does not consist of points, but is composed of a finite though constantly varying number of surfaces or volumes, continually breaking up or joining together according to the fluctuations of attention. If there is a "real" geometrical space corresponding to the space of perception, an infinite number of points in the geometrical space will have to correspond to a single simple entity in the perceived space.

It follows from this that, if we are to apply to the immediate objects of perception the maxim that a thing cannot be in two places at once, a "place" must not be taken to be a point, but must be taken to be the extent occupied by a single object of perception. A white sheet of paper, for example, may be seen as a single undivided object, or as an object consisting of two parts, an upper and a lower or a right hand and a left hand part, or again as an object consisting of four parts, and so on. If we on this account consider that, even when the sheet appeared as an undivided object, its upper and lower halves were in different places, then we shall have to say that the undivided object was in both these places at once. But it is better to say that, when the sheet appeared as an undivided object,

this object occupied only one "place," though the place corresponded to what were afterwards two places. Thus a "place" may be defined as the space occupied by one undivided object of perception.

With this definition, the maxim that a thing cannot be in two places at once might seem to reduce to a tautology. But this maxim, though it may need rewording, will still have a substantial significance, to be derived from the consideration of spatial relations. It is obvious that perceived spatial relations cannot hold between points, but must hold between the parts of a single complex object of perception. When the sheet of paper is perceived as consisting of two halves, an upper and a lower, these two halves are combined into a complex whole by means of a spatial relation which holds directly between the two halves, not between supposed smaller subdivisions which in fact do not exist in the immediate object of perception. Perceived spatial relations, therefore, must have a certain roughness, not the neat smooth properties of geometrical relations between points. What, for example, shall we say of distance? The distance between two simultaneously perceived objects will have to be defined by the perceived objects between them; in the case of two objects which touch, like the two halves of the sheet of paper, there is no distance between them. What remains definite is a certain order; by means of right and left, up and down, and so on, the parts of a complex object of perception acquire a spatial order, which is definite, though not subject to quite the same laws as geometrical order. The maxim that a thing cannot be in two places at once will then become the maxim that every spatial relation implies diversity of its terms, i.e., that nothing is to the right of itself, or above itself, and so on. In that case, given two white patches, one of which is to the right of the other, it will follow that there is not a single thing, whiteness, which is to the right of itself, but that there are two different things, instances of whiteness, of which one is to the right of the other. In this way our maxim will support the conclusion that there must be particulars as well as universals. But the above outline of an argument needs some amplification before it can be considered conclusive. Let us therefore examine, one by one, the steps of the argument.

Let us suppose, for the sake of definiteness, that within one field of vision we perceive two separated patches of white on a ground of black. It may then be taken as quite certain that the two patches are two and not one. The question is: Can we maintain that there are two if what exists in each is the universal whiteness?

If absolute space is admitted, we can of course say that it is the difference of place that makes the patches two; there is whiteness in this place, and whiteness in that place. From the point of view of our main problem, which is as to the existence of particulars, such a view would prove our thesis, since this place and that place would be or imply particulars constituting absolute space. But from the point of view of our immediate problem, which is concerned with plurality in perceived space, we may reject the above view on the ground that, whatever may be the case with "real" space, perceived space is certainly not absolute, i.e., absolute positions are not among objects of perception. Thus the whiteness here and the whiteness there cannot be distinguished as complexes of which this place and that place are respectively constituents.

Of course the whitenesses may be of different shapes, say one round and one square, and then they could be distinguished by their shapes. It will be observed that, with the view adopted above as to the nature of perceived space, it is perfectly possible for a simple object of perception to have a shape: the shape will be a quality like another. Since a simple object of perception may be of finite extent, there is no reason to suppose that a shape must imply spatial divisibility in the object of perception. Hence our two patches may be respectively round and square, and yet not be spatially divisible. It is obvious, however, that this method of distinguishing the two patches is altogether inadequate. The two patches are just as easily distinguished if both are square or both are round. So long as we can see both at once, no degree of likeness between them causes the slightest difficulty in perceiving that there are two of them. Thus difference of shape, whether it exists or not, is not what makes the patches two entities instead of one.

It may be said that the two patches are distinguished by the difference in their relations to other things. For example, it may happen that a patch of red

is to the right of one and to the left of the other. But this does not imply that the patches are two unless we know that one thing cannot be both to the right and to the left of another. This, it might be said, is obviously false. Suppose a surface of black with a small white space in the middle. Then the whole of the black may form only one simple object of perception, and would seem to be both to the right and to the left of the white space which it entirely surrounds. I think it would be more true to say, in this case, that the black is neither to the right nor to the left of the white. But right and left are complicated relations involving the body of the percipient. Let us take some other simpler relation, say that of surrounding, which the black surface has to the white patch in our example. Suppose we have another white patch, of exactly the same size and shape, entirely surrounded by red. Then, it may be said, the two patches of white are distinguished by difference of relation, since one is surrounded by black and the other by red. But if this ground of distinction is to be valid, we must know that it is impossible for one entity to be both wholly and immediately surrounded by black and wholly and immediately surrounded by red. I do not mean to deny that we do know this. But two things deserve notice—first, that it is not an analytic proposition; second, that it presupposes the numerical diversity of our two patches of white.

We are so accustomed to regarding such relations as "inside" and "outside" as incompatible that it is easy to suppose a *logical* incompatibility, although in fact the incompatibility is a characteristic of space, not a result of logic. I do not know what are the unanalysable spatial relations of objects of perception, whether visual or tactile, but whatever they are they must have the kind of characteristics which are required in order to generate an order. They, or some of them, must be asymmetrical, i.e., such that they are incompatible with their converses: for example, supposing "inside" to be one of them, a thing which is inside another must not also be outside it. They, or some of them, must also be transitive, i.e., such that, for example, if x is inside y and y is inside z, then x is inside z—supposing, for the sake of illustration, "inside" to be among fundamental spatial relations. Probably some further properties will be required, but these at least are essential, in view of the fact that there is such a thing as spatial order. It follows that some at least of the fundamental spatial relations must be such as no entity can have to itself. It is indeed self-evident that spatial relations fulfil these conditions. But these conditions are not demonstrable by purely logical considerations: they are synthetic properties of perceived spatial relations.

It is in virtue of these self-evident properties that the numerical diversity of the two patches of white is self-evident. They have the relation of being outside each other, and this requires that they should be two, not one. They may or may not have intrinsic differences—of shape, or size, or brightness, or any other quality—but whether they have or not they are two, and it is obviously logically possible that they should have no intrinsic differences whatever. It follows from this that the terms of spatial relations cannot be universals or collections of universals, but must be particulars capable of being exactly alike and yet numerically diverse.

It is very desirable, in such discussions as that on which we are at present engaged, to be able to talk of "places" and of things or qualities "occupying" places, without implying absolute position. It must be understood that, on the view which adopts relative position, a "place" is not a precise notion. But its usefulness arises as follows: Suppose a set of objects, such as the walls and furniture of a room, to retain their spatial relations unchanged for a certain length of time, while a succession of other objects, say people who successively sit in a certain chair, have successively a given set of spatial relations to the relatively fixed objects. Then the people have, one after the other, a given set of properties, consisting in spatial relations to the walls and furniture. Whatever has this given set of properties at a given moment is said to "occupy" a certain place, the "place" itself being merely a fixed set of spatial relations to certain objects whose spatial relations to each other do not change appreciably during the time considered. Thus when we say that one thing can only be in one place at one time, we mean that it can only have one set of spatial relations to a given set of objects at one time.

It might be argued that, since we have admitted that a simple object of perception may be of finite extent, we have admitted that it may be in many places at once, and therefore may be outside itself. This, how-

ever, would be a misunderstanding. In perceived space, the finite extent occupied by a simple object of perception is not divided into many places. It is a single place occupied by a single thing. There are two different ways in which this place may "correspond" to many places. First, if there is such a thing as "real" space with geometrical properties, the one place in perceived space will correspond to an infinite number of points in "real" space, and the single entity which is the object of perception will correspond to many physical entities in "real" space. Secondly, there is a more or less partial correspondence between perceived space at one time and perceived space at another. Suppose that we attend closely to our white patch, and meanwhile no other noticeable changes occur in the field of vision. Our white patch may, and often does, change as the result of attention—we may perceive differences of shade or other differentiations, or, without differences of quality, we may merely observe parts in it which make it complex and introduce diversity and spatial relations within it. We consider, naturally, that we are still looking at the same thing as before, and that what we see now was there all along. Thus we conclude that our apparently simple white patch was not really simple. But, in fact, the object of perception is not the same as it was before; what may be the same is the physical object supposed to correspond to the object of perception. This physical object is, of course, complex. And the perception which results from attention will be in one sense more correct than that which perceived a simple object, because, if attention reveals previously unnoticed differences, it may be assumed that there are corresponding differences in the 'real' object which corresponds to the object of perception. Hence the perception resulting from attention gives more information about the 'real' object than the other perception did: but the object of perception itself is no more and no less real in the one case than in the other—that is to say, in both cases it is an object which exists when perceived, but which there is no reason to believe existent except when it is perceived.

In perceived space, the spatial unit is not a point, but a simple object of perception or an ultimate constituent in a complex object of perception. This is the reason why, although two patches of white which are visibly separated from each other must be two, a continuous area of white may not be two. A continuous area, if not too large, may be a single object of perception not consisting of parts, which is impossible for two visibly separated areas. The spatial unit is variable, constantly changing its size, and subject to every fluctuation of attention, but it must occupy a continuous portion of perceived space, since otherwise it would be perceived as plural.

The argument as to numerical diversity which we have derived from perceived space may be reinforced by a similar argument as regards the contents of different minds. If two people are both believing that two and two are four, it is at least theoretically possible that the meanings they attach to the words *two* and *and* and *are* and *four* are the same, and that therefore, so far as the objects of their beliefs are concerned, there is nothing to distinguish the one from the other. Nevertheless, it seems plain that there are two entities, one the belief of the one man and the other the belief of the other. A particular belief is a complex of which something which we may call a subject is a constituent; in our case, it is the diversity of the subjects that produces the diversity of the beliefs. But these subjects cannot be mere bundles of general qualities. Suppose one of our men is characterized by benevolence, stupidity, and love of puns. It would not be correct to say: "Benevolence, stupidity, and love of puns believe that two and two are four." Nor would this become correct by the addition of a larger number of general qualities. Moreover, however many qualities we add, it remains possible that the other subject may also have them; hence qualities cannot be what constitutes the diversity of the subjects. The only respect in which two different subjects *must* differ is in their relations to particulars: for example, each will have to the other relations which he does not have to himself. But it is not logically impossible that everything concerning one of the subjects and otherwise only concerning universals might be true of the other subject. Hence, even when differences in regard to such propositions occur, it is not these differences that constitute the diversity of the two subjects. The subjects, therefore, must be regarded as particulars, and as radically different from any collection of those general qualities which may be predicated of them.

It will be observed that, according to the general principles which must govern any correspondence of real things with objects of perception, any principle which introduces diversity among objects of perception must introduce a corresponding diversity among real things. I am not now concerned to argue as to what grounds exist for assuming a correspondence, but, if there is such a correspondence, it must be supposed that diversity in the effects—i.e., the perceived objects—implies diversity in the causes—i.e., the real objects. Hence if I perceive two objects in the field of vision, we must suppose that at least two real objects are concerned in causing my perception.

The essential characteristic of particulars, as they appear in perceived space, is that they cannot be in two places at once. But this is an unsatisfactory way of stating the matter, owing to the doubt as to what a "place" is. The more correct statement is that certain perceptible spatial relations imply diversity of their terms; for example, if x is above y, x and y must be different entities. So long, however, as it is understood that this is what is meant, no harm is done by the statement that a thing cannot be in two places at once.

We may now return to the question of particulars and universals with a better hope of being able to state precisely the nature of the opposition between them. It will be remembered that we began with three different oppositions: (1) that of percept and concept, (2) that of entities existing in time and entities not existing in time, (3) that of substantives and verbs. But in the course of our discussion a different opposition developed itself, namely, (4) that between entities which can be in one place, but not in more than one, at a given time, and entities which either cannot be anywhere or can be in several places at one time. What makes a particular patch of white particular, whereas whiteness is universal, is the fact that the particular patch cannot be in two places simultaneously, whereas the whiteness, if it exists at all, exists wherever there are white things. This opposition, as stated, might be held not to apply to thoughts. We might reply that a man's thoughts are in his head; but without going into this question, we may observe that there certainly is some relation between a man's thoughts and his head (or some part of it) which there is not between his thoughts and other things in space.

We may extend our definition of particulars so as to cover this relation. We may say that a man's thought "belongs to" the place where his head is. We may then define a particular in our fourth sense as an entity which cannot be in or belong to more than one place at one time, and a universal as an entity which either cannot be in or belong to any place, or can be in or belong to many places at once. This opposition has certain affinities with the three earlier oppositions, which must be examined.

(1) Owing to the admission of particulars in our fourth sense, we can make an absolute division between percepts and concepts. The universal whiteness is a concept, whereas a particular white patch is a percept. If we had not admitted particulars in our fourth sense, percepts would have been identical with certain concepts.

(2) For the same reason, we are able to say that such general qualities as whiteness never exist in time, whereas the things that do exist in time are all particulars in our fourth sense. The converse, that all particulars in our fourth sense exist in time, holds in virtue of their definition. Hence the second and fourth senses of the opposition of particulars and universals are co-extensive.

(3) The third opposition, that of substantives and verbs, presents more difficulties, owing to the doubt whether predicates are verbs or not. In order to evade this doubt, we may substitute another opposition, which will be co-extensive with substantives and verbs if predicates are verbs, but not otherwise. This other opposition puts predicates and relations on one side, and everything else on the other. What is not a predicate or relation is, according to one traditional definition, a substance. It is true that, when substance was in vogue, it was supposed that a substance must be indestructible, and this quality will not belong to our substances. For example, what a man sees when he sees a flash of lightning is a substance in our sense. But the importance of indestructibility was metaphysical, not logical. As far as logical properties are concerned, our substances will be fairly analogous to traditional substances. Thus we have the opposition of substances on the one hand and predicates and relations on the other hand. The theory which rejects particulars allows entities commonly classed as predicates—e.g. white—to exist; thus the distinction between substances and predicates is obliterated by this theory. Our theory, on the contrary, preserves the distinction. In the world we know, substances are identical with particulars in our fourth sense, and predicates and relations with universals.

It will be seen that, according to the theory which assumes particulars, there is a specific relation of subject to predicate, unless we adopt the view—considered above in connexion with Berkeley and Hume—that common sensible qualities are really derivative from specific kinds of likeness. Assuming this view to be false, ordinary sensible qualities will be predicates of the particulars which are instances of them. The sensible qualities themselves do not exist in time in the same sense in which the instances do. Predication is a relation involving a fundamental logical difference between its two terms. Predicates may themselves have predicates, but the predicates of predicates will be radically different from the predicates of substances. The predicate, on this view, is never part of the subject, and thus no true subject-predicate proposition is analytic. Propositions of the form "All *A* is *B*" are not really subject-predicate propositions, but express relations of predicates; such propositions may be analytic, but the traditional confusion of them with true subject-predicate propositions has been a disgrace to formal logic.

The theory which rejects particulars, and assumes that, e.g., whiteness itself exists wherever (as common sense would say) there are white things, dispenses altogether with predication as a fundamental relation. 'This is white', which, on the other view, expresses a relation between a particular and whiteness, will, when particulars are rejected, really state that whiteness is one of the qualities in this place, or has certain spatial relations to certain other qualities. Thus the question whether predication is an ultimate simple relation may be taken as distinguishing the two theories; it is ultimate if there are particulars, but not otherwise. And if predication is an ultimate relation, the best definition of particulars is that they are entities which can only be subjects of predicates or terms of relations, i.e., that they are (in the logical sense) substances. This definition is preferable to one introducing space or time, because space and time are accidental characteristics of the world with which we happen to be acquainted, and therefore are destitute of the necessary universality belonging to purely logical categories.

We have thus a division of all entities into two classes: (1) particulars, which enter into complexes only as the subjects of predicates or the terms of relations, and, if they belong to the world of which we have experience, exist in time, and cannot occupy more than one place at one time in the space to which they belong; (2) universals, which can occur as predicates or relations in complexes, do not exist in time, and have no relation to one place which they may not simultaneously have to another. The ground for regarding such a division as unavoidable is the self-evident fact that certain spatial relations imply diversity of their terms, together with the self-evident fact that it is logically possible for entities having such spatial relations to be wholly indistinguishable as to predicates.

Properties

~

D. M. ARMSTRONG

David Malet Armstrong, an Australian metaphysician and philosopher of mind, is Emeritus Professor of Philosophy at the University of Sydney. His books include *A Materialist Theory of the Mind, Universals: An Opinionated Introduction, A Combinatorial Theory of Possibility,* and *A World of States of Affairs.* He is a foundation fellow of the Australian Academy of the Humanities and was made an officer of the Order of Australia in 1993.

In the present climate of metaphysics nothing is more important, I think, than the recognition of properties and relations as fundamental constituents of reality. Once properties and relations are admitted, further questions can be raised. Should we, as our languages seem to urge us, admit alongside properties and relations, things, particulars, which have the properties and between which relations hold? Or should we instead try to construct particulars out of properties and relations, or even out of properties alone, or relations alone? Again, should we take properties and relations as universals, that is, should we take it that different particulars can have the very same property, in the full strict sense of the word "same," and that different pairs, triples . . . *n*-tuples . . . can be related by the very same relation? Or should we instead hold that properties and relations are particulars (abstract particulars, tropes, moments) so that each particular has its own properties that no other particular can have, and pairs, etc. of particulars each their own relations? A third issue: should we allow that properties and relations themselves can be propertied and stand in relations? Or should we instead with Brian Skyrms allow nothing but a first level of properties and relations?[1]

These issues, and others, about properties and relations are of the greatest interest. And because an answer to one of the questions does not in any obvious way pre-empt the answer to any of the others, we have here a sort of metaphysician's paradise in which philosophers can wander, arguing. But before these issues can be joined there must be established the

Reprinted from *Language, Truth and Ontology,* edited by K. Mulligan (Dordrecht: Kluwer, 1992), by permission of Kluwer Academic Publishers and the author.

fundamental point: that there are in reality properties and relations. In this paper, I will largely confine myself to properties.

1. WHY WE SHOULD ADMIT PROPERTIES

The great deniers of properties and relations are of two sorts: those who put their faith in *predicates* and those who appeal to *sets* (classes). Some seem to take their comfort from both at once. The resort to predicates was, I suppose, given encouragement by the great Linguistic Turn, with its hope of solving philosophical problems by semantic ascent. This turn gained us some important insights at the cost of a fundamental misdirection of philosophical energy. The appeal to sets was one effect of the immense development of set theory in this century. This raised the hope of resolving all sorts of philosophical problems by a series of set-theoretical technical fixes.

To appreciate the utter implausibility of the attempt to evade properties by means of predicates it is perhaps sufficient to consider a case where a thing's property changes. A cold thing becomes hot. For one who puts his or her faith in predicates this is a matter first of the predicate "cold," or its semantic equivalent, *applying to* or *being true of* the object, and, second, the predicate "hot" becoming applicable after "cold" loses applicability. Properties in the object are but metaphysical shadows cast on that object by the predicates.

But what have predicates to do with the temperature of the object? The change in the object could have occurred even if the predicates had never existed. Furthermore, the change is something intrinsic to the object, and has nothing to do with the way the object stands to language.

I think that one has to be pretty far gone in what might be called Linguistic Idealism to find predicates much of a substitute for properties. But sets are a somewhat more serious matter. After all, to substitute classes for genuine properties is at least to remain a realist, even if a reductivist realist, about properties. Even so, an account of properties in terms of classes is still full of difficulties.

First, there is what might be called the "Promiscuity problem"—a fairly close relative of the grue prob-

lem. Sets abound, and only a very few of them are of the slightest interest. Most of the uninteresting ones are uninteresting because they are utterly heterogeneous, that is, the members of the set have nothing in common. In particular, for most sets there is no common property, *F,* such that the set is the set of *all the F*s. The result is that mere sets are insufficient to give an account of properties: at best having a property is a matter of membership of a set *of a certain sort.*

Indeed, not only are most sets too poor to support properties, others, it seems are too prosperous, and support more than one property. This is the problem for a class account of properties that all philosophers are conversant with. It is the coextension problem, the problem of the renates and the cordates, the creatures with kidneys and the creatures with hearts.

Returning to the Promiscuity problem, which I judge to be a much more serious fundamental problem, there are various ways that an account of properties in terms of class might move under pressure. One solution, pioneered by Anthony Quinton, is to introduce a new, fundamental, and so not further analyzable, notion of a *natural* class.[2] Some classes are natural, most are not. The natural ones admit of degrees of naturalness, but no analysis of naturalness is possible.

Of the difficulties that such an account faces, I shall here call attention to but one. (A problem concerning relations will be mentioned when the resemblance theory is discussed.) It is similar to the difficulty urged a moment ago against an account of properties in terms of predicates. It was said that when a thing changes temperature, it is the thing itself that changes. The change in the applicability of certain predicates is, fairly obviously, subsequent and secondary. In the same way, consider the natural class consisting of all and only the objects having temperature *T.* Let *a* be a member of this class. What have the *other* members of the class, or at any rate the other members that are wholly distinct from *a,* to do with *a*'s temperature? After all there would appear to be a possible world in which these other members do not exist, or where they exist but lack temperature *T.*

Somewhat more attractive than a Natural Class theory is a Resemblance account. According to one version of this view, talk about properties of a particular has as its ontological ground a suitable relation of resemblance holding between the particular in question and suitable paradigms. It might seem that such a view falls victim to the argument just advanced against Predicate and Class accounts. What have the paradigms to do with the *being* of the properties of things that suitably resemble the paradigms? I used to think that this was a good argument against a Resemblance analysis as well as Predicate and Class accounts. But I have recently come to think that the consideration that resemblance is an *internal* relation, based upon the nature of its terms, will block the argument in the case of a Resemblance theory.[3] Details must be left aside here.

But it is worth noticing that the Resemblance theory, like a Class theory (and a Natural Class theory), is unable to distinguish between different but coextensive properties. In a paradigm version, for instance, it would not be possible to set up different paradigms for the different properties. In any case, the detail required to work out a Resemblance theory is considerable, and trouble may lurk in the elaborate constructions required. There is also trouble concerning relations. The problem is that when a has R to b, and c has "the same" R to d, the resemblance has to hold between the way a stands to b, on the one hand, and the way c stands to d, on the other. This formulation already involves the notion of relation in the phrase "stands to." How to eliminate this? It seems that the Resemblance theory will have to use the same device that a Class theory uses, and identify the terms that resemble with the ordered sets $\langle a,b \rangle$ and $\langle c,d \rangle$. This still involves the relational notion of *order*, and if that is to be eliminated the device of Wiener or Kuratowski will have to be employed and each ordered pair identified with unordered classes of classes. This has a consequence that is also a consequence for a class theory: different classes of classes will each serve as a's having R to b, and, much worse, the same class of classes can be used for different relations between a and b. Such arbitrariness strongly suggests that the classes in question do no more than represent, map, the state of affairs of a's having R to b. The classes are not *identical* with the state of affairs, which is what is needed for metaphysical analysis.

A final criticism that I will make of the Resemblance theory leads us directly to the postulation of

properties. I begin by noticing that a traditional argument against the Resemblance analysis is that the resemblance relation is not a two-termed but a three-termed affair. If a resembles b, in general, they resemble in certain *respects*, and fail to resemble in other *respects*. But respects are uncomfortably close to properties, which the Resemblance theory proposes to do without.

I do not think that this traditional objection is at all conclusive as it stands. The Resemblance theorist can argue that the metaphysically fundamental relation of resemblance is two-termed (though admitting of degrees like the relations of *being distant from* or *more massive than*). It can then be argued that respects and resemblance in respects supervene upon the network of two-term resemblances which are fundamental. But the Resemblance theorist remains in some embarrassment when he comes to explain the formal properties of his fundamental relation. He has to say that the two-termed relation is non-transitive. There is an exception: the limiting case of exact resemblance. But in general: if a resembles b to degree D and b resembles c to the same degree, the degree to which a resembles c can take any value. Why is this? The Resemblance theory, it seems, must take it as a primitive, not to be further analysed, fact. A Property theory, however, can *derive* this non-transitivity. It is a matter of a res'embling b in respect of a certain set of properties, b resembling c in respect of a *different* set of properties. This can naturally be expected to produce a different degree of resemblance between the pairs $\langle a,b \rangle$ and $\langle a,c \rangle$. The transitivity of exact resemblance is also explained, since in such a case the properties of $a,b,$ and c are the same. Explanatory power is a virtue, and lack of explanation a defect, in metaphysics as much as science.

The above argument led us from resemblance to properties. But I believe that the explanatory power of a theory which gives real existence to properties (and relations) is seen most clearly in connection with *causation* and *natural law*. Suppose that the water in the kettle is heated by the fire. We surely want to deny that it is the whole fire, qua token, that causes the heating of the water. The fire, first of all, must be in the right *relations* to the kettle, say underneath, and the kettle must in turn *contain* the water.

Still more importantly, the fire must be *hot*. Consider how this is explained by an account in terms of predicates. The predicate "underneath" applies to the pair of the fire and the kettle, the predicate "hot" to the fire and, eventually, to the water. But when we have said that these predicates apply, we have surely not said enough. The situation cries out for explanation. It is surely something definite *about* these three things that allows the predicates to apply. Must there not be something quite specific about the things which allows, indeed ensures, that these predicates apply? The predicates require *ontological correlates*. The predicate theory does have correlates indeed, but they are no more than the objects themselves, and so are far too coarse.

It is little better to appeal to classes, even natural classes. What has this fire's heating this water in this kettle, here and now, to do with the fire's membership of the class of hot things? A satisfactory correlate must be found "within" the fire. A sophisticated Resemblance theory can, I think, appeal to the *natures* of the resembling things, natures from which the resemblances flow. The natures are suitably internal, but are as coarse as the things themselves (indeed, should perhaps be identified with the things themselves).

As with causes, so with laws. I am not speaking of law-*statements* but of the ontological correlates of true law-statements, that in the world which makes true law-statements true. Suppose it be a truth that gravitational force between bodies is equal to the product of their masses divided by the square of their distance. This appears to be a certain connection between the properties of massive things. One can try to translate the corresponding law-statements into statements of universal quantification where the subject-terms are nothing but first-order particulars. But although statements about first-order particulars may follow from law-statements, the latter as is well known, say something more, a more that is plausibly a link between properties. And even if one denies this, perhaps because one thinks that properties are not universals but particulars, it still seems that the ontological correlates of true law-statements must involve properties. How else can one pick out the uniformities which the law-statements entail?

Why has there been such hostility to properties (and relations) among so many contemporary leaders of analytic philosophy? Is it just the Ockhamist spirit? Do without properties and relations if you can! Or is it the influence of Quine, with his doctrine that the predicate of a true statement carries no ontological implications? (Together with his nasty remarks about "McX," the upholder of universals.)[4] All these things, maybe, and others. But I think that upholders of properties and relations also have something to answer for. As so often happens, in philosophy and elsewhere, an excellent case has been ignored because its advocates overdid things and made exaggerated claims. Simply put, they found far too many properties.

What has happened is that for each distinct predicate, upholders of properties have been inclined to postulate, corresponding to it, a distinct property. Synonymous predicates, "father" and "male parent," were generally thought to apply in virtue of just one property. But for non-synonymous predicates, each its own property. To self-contradictory predicates, perhaps, no property corresponds. But for each of the rest, a property of its own.

As a very beginning one might eliminate from this monstrous regiment of properties all those where the corresponding predicate fails to apply, is not true of, anything. After all, the argument for properties that I advanced was for something in particulars which would allow the application of predicates. No application, no property. There is a tendency, whose rationale I do not really understand, to think of properties as necessary beings. A necessary being, if it is possible, exists, and so, if properties are necessary beings, all non-self-contradictory properties exist. But if, as I think we should, we take properties to be contingent beings, then it seems reasonable to deny that there are uninstantiated properties.

This is not to deny that it may be convenient from time to time to talk about, to make ostensible reference to, uninstantiated properties. No body is perfectly elastic, so there is no property of *being perfectly elastic*. But it may be useful to compare more or less elastic bodies in the degree to which they approach the unreachable perfect elasticity. A useful fiction, however, is still a fiction.

If predicates actually apply to, are actually true of, things, then, of course, it is perfectly legitimate to introduce *a sense* in which the things automatically have a property corresponding to just that predicate. Indeed, this is a very useful sense, a point that I have in the past tended to overlook. To make use of Carnap's phrases, the *material mode* is much less fatiguing to the imagination and the intellect than is the *formal mode.* Such properties, however, cut no ontological ice. The properties that are of ontological interest and which we are concerned with here, are those constituents of objects, of particulars, which serve as the ground in the objects for the application of predicates. And concerning these properties, the true properties I am inclined to say, there is no reason to think that to each distinct predicate that has application corresponds its own distinct property in the object. Indeed, there is much reason to think the opposite.

Instead of approaching the matter of such properties directly, it may be helpful to think in the first place in terms of "good" or "bad" predicates, where good and bad are to be assessed in terms of our purely theoretical interests: the sort of predicates that the spectator of all time and eternity might find attractive. And here, I think, we are led on to Plato's marvellous image of carving the beast (the great beast of reality) at the joints. The carving may be more or less precise. But as the carving is the more and more precise, so we reach predicates that are of greater and greater theoretical value, predicates more and more fit to appear in the formulations of an exact science. At the limit, monadic predicates apply in virtue of strict properties. An upholder of universals will conceive of these properties as strictly identical in their different instances. A believer in particularized properties, in tropes, will deny identity but allow the symmetrical and transitive relation of exact similarity. It is properties thus conceived that serve as the ontological foundation for the application of predicates, most predicates at any rate, to first-order particulars.

How do we determine what these ontological properties are? The answer, in part, is the same as the answer to the question "How do kangaroos make love?". With difficulty. In the epistemic state of nature, the only predicates to which we can give much trust are those suggested by ordinary experience and ordinary life. We cannot but take it that these predicates carve out properties that approximate to some of the joints to some extent. In that state of nature, we cannot but think that blue is better than grue. But in the present age we take ourselves to have advanced beyond the epistemic state of nature, and to have sciences that we speak of as "mature." There we will find the predicates that constitute our most educated guess about what are the true properties and relations. Property-realism, whether the properties be taken as universals or particulars, should be an *a posteriori,* a scientific, realism.

If we combine an *a posteriori* or scientific realism about properties (and relations) with the speculative but attractive thesis of physicalism, then we shall look to physics, the most mature science of all, for *our best predicates so far.* Physics (perhaps it will have to be a cosmological physics as well as the physics of the very small) shows promise of giving an explanatory account of the workings of the whole space-time realm, and thus, perhaps, the whole of being. And it shows promise of doing this in terms of a quite restricted range of fundamental properties and relations. These properties and relations are for the most part quantitative in nature, and the laws that govern them are functional in nature. I will just note that quantities and functions seem to me to involve rather deep problems for the property-realist. (Happily, though, the problems for the alternative positions, such as Predicate and Class Nominalism, seem to be far worse.)

Keith Campbell has suggested, in his new book *Abstract Particulars,* which puts forward a trope metaphysics, that a metaphysics of this physicalist sort is not particularly economical with properties.[5] For suppose that some fundamental quantity such as length is really continuous. We will then be faced with the necessity to postulate continuum-many length-properties corresponding to each different length taken as a type. Some lengths may not be instantiated, but that will not bring the number down.

Continuum-many properties is a lot of properties, to be sure. But let us remember a remark that Mr Reagan made when he was Governor of California. Speaking of the Sequoia tree, he said "seen one, seen them all." If you have seen one length, then given only some mathematics, which is topic-neutral, you can grasp the notion of lengths of any length. The class of length-types is a unitary thing, and in taking lengths to be fundamental properties, if you do so, you are making a quite economical postulation. And it may be that a relatively small number of quantities such as length are the only fundamental quantities that physics requires us to postulate.

2.   UNIVERSALS VS. TROPES

So much in defense of properties, although much more could be said. In the second part of my paper I will take up an issue *within* the theory of properties, an issue that has enjoyed quite a lot of recent discussion. It is the question whether we should take properties to be universals or particulars. There are those who admit both universal and particular properties into their ontology. Perhaps Aristotle and even Plato were among them. But I think that this position sins against economy. If you have universals, you can do without the particularized properties, and vice-versa. So for me, and I think for most contemporary metaphysicians, the question is which should we choose.

I was brought up by my teacher, John Anderson, to reject the Particularist position. (He used to criticize G. F. Stout's view.) I still favor the Universalist view, but recently I come to think that tropes have more to be said for them than I have allowed previously. In particular, I now see more clearly how tropes can serve as substitutes for universals in many respects.

A Trope theory is best combined with a resemblance theory, and developed as a sophisticated Resemblance Nominalism. Of particular importance here is the notion of *exact resemblance.* If we work with ordinary particulars, then, with the possible exception of such things as fundamental particles, exact resemblance is a theoretical ideal. We all remember Leibniz's unfortunate courtiers searching vainly for identical leaves in the garden. But if we move to the much thinner *tropes,* then exact resemblances may be achievable. Two tropes that are constituents of different things might resemble exactly in mass, in length, in charge, and so on. The plausible

examples are again found at fundamental levels. Thus, it is at present believed that the charge on each electron is exactly the same. 'Exactly the same' appears to assume *identity* of charge in different electrons. But it can be rendered in the language of tropes by saying instead that the different charge-tropes associated with the different electrons are all exactly similar. The interesting thing about exact similarity is that it is symmetrical *and transitive.* (Less than exact similarly is not transitive, even for tropes.) As a result, the relation of exact similarity is an equivalence relation, partitioning the field of tropes into equivalence classes. Tropes will then do much the same work as universals. Suppose that a believer in universals and a believer in tropes have co-ordinated their views in the following way. For each universal property postulated, the trope theorist postulates a class of exactly similar tropes, with universals and tropes properties of the very same class of things. For each class of exactly similar tropes postulated, the Realist postulates a class of thing which all have the same property, with tropes and universals properties of the very same class of things. What inferiority is there in the Trope theory?

I used to think that the Universals theory had an important advantage here. Where we have what the trope theorist thinks of as exact similarity of tropes, we do not scruple to speak of *sameness* of property. Even a trope theorist will allow that by the lights of our present physics electrons have *exactly the same* charge. But "same" means identical does it not? Yet the trope theory denies identity.

However, I have become convinced that in our ordinary usage "same" does not always mean identical. There is what Bishop Butler so brilliantly characterized as a "loose and popular" sense of the word "same."[6] Butler was thinking about the replacement over time of particles in an object such as a human body. We say the *same* body but we don't really mean it. It is only a loose and popular identity. By itself, even if we accept it, Butler's point is rather frustrating. What rules are we going by when we use "same" in the loose and popular way? Here I am indebted to a Sydney student, Peter Anstey. He suggested that we are prepared to use "same" in this relaxed way only if the things said to be the same are both members of a relevant equivalence class. Though different, the things said to be the same must both be members of the same class, where "same class" is, of course, taken in the *strict* sense.

If one takes *portions of the lives of organisms* as a field, then it seems that they fall into equivalence classes, where the members of any one class constitute the totality of the life of a single organism (fission, fusion, and so on being neglected). It is of course difficult to spell out just what the equivalence relation is: "identity over time" is a puzzling subject. But, if Anstey is right, it must be in virtue of this equivalence relation that we assert "identity," and assert it even though we believe that *strict* identity is not involved. (A further suggestion by Anstey. Is this relevant to the topic of 'relevant identity'? When *a* and *b* are "the same *F*" but not "the same *G*," is this because the identity is loose and popular, and two different equivalence relations are involved?)

This is, alas, good news for the tropes. When we say that two electrons have the very same charge, then according to the Trope theory *strictly* the tropes involved are not identical. But the two tropes are both members of a relevant equivalence class, where the equivalence relation is exact similarity, and so can be said to be "the same" in a loose and popular sense.

Unfortunately, this is not all the good news for the Trope theory. A very important topic in the theory of properties (and relations) is that of their *resemblance*. Particulars resemble: that is clear enough. But so do properties. The colors all resemble each other, so do the shapes, the masses, the lengths. One property can resemble another more than it does a third. Redness is more like orange than it is like yellow. A kilo is more like a pound than it is like an ounce.

We may think of the whole field of properties as arranged in a multidimensional order. This order appears to be largely objective, and is to be interpreted as a resemblance-order. For properties to stand near to each other in the order is for them to resemble each other quite closely.

If these properties are universals, then it will be natural to construe these resemblances between properties in accordance with the old slogan "all resemblance is partial identity." That is how I construe it myself. Resembling universals have common constituents, with either one of the properties con-

taining all the constituents of the other universals and more besides, or else a mere overlap in constituents. I say "constituents" rather than "part" because I think that this partial identity is not the simple sort of partial identity envisaged by the mereological calculus, the calculus of whole and part. (A point that confused me for many years.) I cannot go further into the matter here. To do so would involve getting into a huge new topic: the theory of facts or states of affairs.[7]

But however all this may be, an upholder of tropes can deal with the resemblance of properties in a way that parallels the treatment of the topic by an upholder of universals. We have seen the potential to set up a one–one correlation between properties taken as universals, on the one side, and equivalence classes of exactly similar tropes, on the other. To make the matter vivid, select just one trope from each of these equivalence classes and range each of these tropes opposite to its corresponding universal. This structure of tropes will exactly reflect the multidimensional resemblance structure of the universals.

How resemblance is interpreted will presumably differ in the two structures. The Trope theory is not under pressure to interpret resemblance between tropes as partial identity, a move that is indeed against the spirit of trope theory, although that option would be open. (Similarly, it is an option for the Universals theory to treat resemblance between *universals* as primitive and unanalyzable, although that goes against the spirit of a Universals theory.) A Trope theory, with exact resemblance already treated as a primitive, will presumably embrace the view that, in fundamental cases at least, lesser degrees of resemblance between tropes are also primitive and unanalyzable. But the point I want principally to make here is that the Trope theory is in as good a position as the Universals theory to deal with the difficult topic of resemblance of properties. The friends of the tropes can say to the friends of the universals: "Anything you can do, I can do better, or at least equally well."

But I finish now by saying I do not believe in the tropes. First, there is the question, already touched upon, of the Axioms of Resemblance. The trope theorist requires such axioms. *First,* there is symmetry. If *a* resembles *b* to degree *D*, then *b* resembles *a* to degree *D. Second,* there is failure of transitivity. If *a* resembles *b* to degree *D*, and *b* resembles *c* to degree

D, then it is not normally the case that *a* resembles *c* to degree *D*. This holds for tropes as much as for ordinary particulars. However, *third,* transitivity is restored for a special case. If *a* exactly resembles *b,* and *b* exactly resembles *c,* then *a* exactly resembles *c.* This transitivity is a particular case of a more general principle: if *a* resembles *b* to degree *D* and *b* exactly resembles *c,* then *a* resembles *c* to degree *D.* Resemblance to degree *D* is preserved under the substitution of exact resemblers.

For the trope theorist these necessities are *brute* necessities, fundamental necessities that cannot be explained further. The Universals theory need carry no such ontological baggage. The symmetry of resemblance is simply the symmetry of identity. The transitivity of exact resemblance is the transitivity of identity. The non-transitivity of ordinary resemblance is the non-transitivity of partial identity. The Axioms of Resemblance are but particular cases of the axioms that govern identity.

Explanation is a virtue in metaphysics, as elsewhere. I submit that this startlingly easy deduction of the properties of resemblance from the entirely uncontroversial properties of identity is a major advantage of the Universals theory. It enables one to see the intuitive force behind the old, inconclusive, criticism brought against Resemblance Nominalisms that resemblance is resemblance *in identical respects.*

My second reason for rejecting the Trope theory is more controversial, depending as it does on views that would be contested by many. It is that I think that universals are required to get a satisfactory account of laws of nature.

I note again that by laws of nature I mean not true law statements, but that entity, state of affairs, in the world that makes true law statements true. I believe that the contemporary orthodoxy on laws of nature— that basically they are mere regularities in the four-dimensional scenery—is in a similar position to that enjoyed by the regimes in power in Eastern Europe until a few months ago, if "enjoyed" is the right word. No doubt the end to Regularity theories of law will not come so suddenly, though, because inside their own subject philosophers are great conservatives.

Regularity theories of laws face the grue problem. That, I think, can only be got over by introducing properties, sparse properties, into one's ontology.

However, the properties could, I think, be tropes as well as being universals, so there is no advantage to universals here. More to the present point, even with properties given, Regularity theories make laws into *molecular* states of affairs. These tokens of a certain phenomenon behave in a certain way, so do these, so do all instances of the phenomenon. There is here no *inner connection* between, say, cause and effect in the individual tokens that fall under the causal law. This conclusion can, I think, be enforced by noting with Reichenbach and others that only some cosmic regularities are manifestations of law; by the difficulty in seeing how such a molecular state of affairs could "sustain counterfactuals"; and by the incredible shifts that are necessary to accommodate probabilistic laws within a regularity approach.

Only a higher-order fact about the universals involved in the individual positive instances falling under the law can, as far as I can see, provide the atomic state of affairs that will solve these difficulties. If *being an F* ensures or makes probable to some degree that the *F,* or something related to it, is a *G,* with *F* and *G* universals, then I think that an internal connection is provided. More controversially, I think it can also be seen that such a connection automatically, analytically, and yet non-trivially provides for a regularity or statistical distribution to flow from the connection. Indeed, I think that, although postulating such a connection does not cure wooden legs or halt tooth decay, it does go a great way to help us with the problem of induction.[8]

So: my idea is that a Universals theory can provide us with a satisfactory account of laws of nature, while a Trope theory cannot. It is a controversial and complex argument, which cannot be assessed in any hurry. But even without this, the Trope theory still needs its Axioms of Resemblance, and that is a clear-cut disadvantage. I know of no such compensating disadvantage for the view that properties are universals.

NOTES

1. Brian Skyrms, "Tractarian Nominalism," *Philosophical Studies,* 40(1981), 199–206.

2. Anthony Quinton, "Properties and Classes," *Proceedings of the Aristotelian Society,* 58 (1957–8), 33–58;

The Nature of Things (London: Routledge & Kegan Paul, 1973).

3. See my *Universals: An Opinionated Introduction* (Boulder, Colorado: Westview Press, 1989), chapter 3, §11.

4. See Willard Van Orman Quine, "On What There Is," in *From a Logical Point of View* (Cambridge, MA: Harvard University Press, 1953).

5. Keith Campbell, *Abstract Particulars* (Oxford: Blackwell, 1990), p. 13.

6. Joseph Butler (1736), "Of Personal Identity" in *Personal Identity,* edited by John Perry (Berkeley: University of California Press, 1975), 99–105.

7. See my *Universals: An Opinionated Introduction.*

8. For all this see my *What Is a Law of Nature?* (Cambridge: Cambridge University Press, 1983).

The Doctrine of Arbitrary Undetached Parts

PETER VAN INWAGEN

Peter van Inwagen is John Cardinal O'Hara Professor of Philosophy at the University of Notre Dame. His writings are centered in metaphysics and philosophical theology. His books include *Material Beings, The Possibility of Resurrection and Other Essays in Christian Apologetics,* and *God, Knowledge and Mystery.*

1. Many philosophers accept what I shall call the Doctrine of Arbitrary Undetached Parts (DAUP). Adherents of this doctrine believe in such objects as the northern half of the Eiffel Tower, the middle two-thirds of the cigar Uncle Henry is smoking, and the thousands (at least) of overlapping perfect duplicates of Michelangelo's *David* that were hidden inside the block of marble from which (as they see it) Michelangelo liberated the *David.* Moreover, they do not believe in only *some* "undetached parts"; they believe, so to speak, in *all* of them. The following statement of DAUP, though it is imperfect in some respects, at least captures the *generality* of the doctrine I mean to denote by that name:

For every material object[1] M, if R is the region of space occupied[2] by M at time *t,* and if sub-R is *any* occupiable[3] sub-region of R *whatever,* there exists a material object that occupies the region sub-R at *t.*

(It should be obvious that DAUP, so defined, entails the existence of the northern half of the Eiffel Tower[4] and the other items in the above list.) This definition or statement or whatever it is of DAUP has, as I have said, certain imperfections as a statement of the doctrine I wish to describe certain philosophers as holding. One was mentioned in note 4. Another is this: there are philosophers who hold what is recognizable as a version of DAUP who would not be willing to admit regions of space into their ontologies.[5] Here is a third: this statement entails that material objects have boundaries so sharp that they occupy regions that are sets of points; and no adherent of DAUP that I know of would accept such a thesis about material objects. But these defects are irrelevant to the points that will be raised in the sequel and I shall not attempt to formulate a statement of DAUP that remedies them. For our purposes, therefore, DAUP may be identified with my imperfect statement of it.

Pacific Philosophical Quarterly, 62. Copyright © 1981 by Blackwell Publishers. Reprinted by permission of Blackwell Publishers.

What I want to say about DAUP involves only two components of that doctrine: (i) the arbitrariness of the parts—a *part* of an object is of course an object that occupies a sub-region of the region occupied by that object—whose existence it asserts ("... *any* occupiable sub-region of R *whatever* ...") and (ii) the concreteness and materiality of these parts. The second of these features calls for a brief comment. A philosopher might hold that, e.g., the northern half of the Eiffel Tower exists, but identify this item in his ontology with some *abstract* object, such as the pair whose first term is the Eiffel Tower and whose second term is the northern half of the region of space occupied by the Eiffel Tower. (If this idea were to be applied to moving, flexible objects or to objects that grow or shrink, it would have to be radically elaborated; I mean only to provide a vague, general picture of how one might identify parts with abstract objects.) This paper is not addressed to that philosopher's doctrine. It is addressed to DAUP, which holds that, e.g., the northern half of the Eiffel Tower is a concrete material particular in the same sense as that in which the Eiffel Tower itself is a concrete material particular.

2. The Doctrine of Arbitrary Undetached Parts is false. It is also mischievous: it has caused a great deal of confusion in our thinking about material objects. But I shall not attempt to show that it is mischievous. I shall be content to show that it is false.

As a first step towards showing this, I shall show that DAUP entails a thesis very close to *mereological essentialism:* it entails the thesis that it is impossible for an object to lose any of its parts; that is, it entails the thesis that if a part is removed from an object, and no new part is added to the "remainder," then that object must therewith cease to exist. This is a weaker thesis than mereological essentialism proper, which entails that if a part is removed from an object, then that object must therewith cease to exist *whether or not* any part is added to the remainder.[6] We may call this weaker doctrine *Mereological Near-Essentialism* (MNE). I shall not raise the question whether DAUP entails mereological essentialism proper; it will do for my purposes to show that it entails MNE. (A parenthetical note. We are speaking at a very high level of abstraction. I have not said what it would be for an

object to "lose" a part. An adherent of DAUP may very well believe in the existence of "scattered objects," that is, objects that are not "in one piece."[7] Whether he does or not will depend on which regions he takes to be occupiable in the sense of note 3. Someone who accepts the existence of scattered objects might very well accept the following account of cutting a cake. If I cut a cake and separate the newly cut piece from the remainder, I have not caused anything to "lose a piece"; I have merely changed a certain cake from a non-scattered to a scattered object. Thus, in this context and at this level of generality, it is not clear just what "losing a part" may come down to. Still, the *annihilation* of a part would seem to be sufficient for the losing of it. In any case, the loss of parts is possible or it isn't. If it is, then MNE refers to just those possible cases that count as losses of parts, whether by separation or annihilation. If it isn't, MNE is a vacuously necessary truth and is thus entailed by DAUP.)

I shall now show that DAUP entails MNE. Assume that DAUP is true and MNE false. It follows from the falsity of MNE that there is a time (which for simplicity's sake I shall assume to be the present) such there could be objects O and P such that P is a part of O at that time and such that O could survive the subsequent loss of P. Suppose such objects exist. By DAUP there is an object that occupies just that region of space that is the set-theoretic difference between the region occupied by O and the region occupied by P.[8] Call this object O-minus. O-minus is numerically diverse from O, since they occupy different regions of space and have different parts. Now suppose O were to lose P; for good measure let us suppose P to be annihilated, all other parts of O remaining unchanged, except for such changes in them as may be logically necessitated by the annihilation of P. It would seem that O-minus would still exist. Admittedly, this is not a formally demonstrable consequence of DAUP. Nevertheless, the proposition that a thing cannot cease to exist *simply* because something that was *not* a part of it is "detached" from it seems to be a sufficiently obvious conceptual truth that we may in good conscience use it as a premise. We have seen that O could (logically) have survived the annihilation of P. Let us suppose it has. What is the relation (now) between O and O-minus? Only one answer would seem to be possible: identity. "Each" is a material object, after all, and "they" now have the same boundaries, and, in fact, share all their "momentary" physical properties. Someone *might* say that O and O-minus are two material objects that now have the same size, shape, position, weight, orientation in space, linear velocity, angular velocity, and so on, these two objects being numerically distinct simply in virtue of their having different histories. But this *I* cannot conceive of; if the meaning of 'material object' is such as to allow the conceptual possibility of this, then I do not understand 'material object' and therefore do not understand DAUP. We have reached the conclusion that O is now O-minus. But O and O-minus were once diverse (when P was a part of O) and thus we have arrived at a violation of the principle of the transitivity of identity. Hence we must reject our assumption that MNE is false, and we have shown that DAUP entails MNE.[9]

I should be the last to deny that there are disputable steps in this argument. In the next section we shall apply this general argument to a particular case, and I shall try to leave no disputable contention undefended. What I shall say may, I hope, be applied to the general case.

Let us agree for the nonce that I have shown that DAUP entails MNE. So what? Why shouldn't the proponent of DAUP simply accept MNE? No reason, I suppose. Unless there is some object that is known to be capable of surviving the loss of a part.

3. There is. We ourselves, we men and women, are such objects. Or at least we are if we *have* parts; whether or not we have parts is a question the correct answer to which depends on the correct answer to the general, theoretical questions raised in this paper. But, at any rate, we all too frequently undergo, and often survive, episodes of the sort that it is correct to describe in ordinary speech as "losing a finger" or "losing a leg." I wish to examine in detail one such episode—a fictional one involving a real person—on the assumption that DAUP is true. (We shall reach an absurd result—that identity is not transitive—and we shall therefore have to conclude that DAUP is false.) We have already seen, in the preceding section, in abstract outline, what our examination of this episode will reveal.

Consider Descartes and his left leg.[10] (The adherent of DAUP is going to have a certain amount of trouble with Descartes's left leg: there are, according to DAUP, an enormous number of objects that are equally good candidates for the office of "Descartes's left leg." I shall not address this problem. I shall assume in the sequel that some one of these candidates has been chosen, by fair means or foul, to fill this office.) If DAUP is true, then at any moment during Descartes's life, there was a thing (problems of multiplicity aside) that was his left leg at that moment. Let us pick some moment, call it t_0, during Descartes's life, and let "L" designate the thing that was his leg at the moment. There *also* existed at that moment, according to DAUP, a thing we shall call *D-minus*, the thing that occupied at t_0 the region of space that was the set-theoretic difference between the region occupied by Descartes and the region occupied by L. Obviously, Descartes and D-minus were not the same thing (at t_0), since, at t_0, they were differently shaped. Now suppose that at t (shortly after t_0), L and D-minus became separated from each other; for good measure, let us suppose that L was then annihilated.

It would seem that after this episode—which I assume could be correctly described in the idiom of everyday life like this: Descartes's left leg was cut off and then destroyed—D-minus still existed. The survival by D-minus of its separation from L is not a formal consequence of DAUP. Still, how can we avoid this conclusion? It seems simply *true,* an inescapable consequence of the requirement of DAUP that the undetached parts of material objects be themselves, in the same sense, material objects. What "material objects" are may not be altogether clear. But if you can cause a thing to cease to exist by detaching from it (or even by destroying) something that was *not* one of its parts but simply part of its *environment,* while leaving the arrangement of all *its* parts wholly unchanged, if you can do *that,* then, I maintain, you have not got anything that can properly be called a material object.

It would seem that after this episode, Descartes still existed. One can, after all, survive the loss of a leg.

But if both Descartes and D-minus survived the severance of L from D-minus at *t,* what was the relation between them immediately after *t?* Only one answer is possible: they were then identical. If they were not, then we should have to admit that there was a time at which there were two material objects having the *same* size, shape, position, orientation, attitude, mass, velocity (both linear and angular), and color. Someone *might* say this, I suppose, but I should not understand him and I suspect that no one else would either.

We may also reach the conclusion that Descartes and D-minus were identical after *t* by a slightly different route. Before *t,* D-minus was *ex hypothesi* a part of Descartes. At *t,* Descartes lost L and lost no other parts (save parts of him that overlapped L). Therefore, after *t* Decartes had D-minus as a part. But, clearly, after *t,* no part of Descartes was "larger" than D-minus—that is, no part of Descartes had D-minus as a *proper* part. Therefore, Descartes (after t) had D-minus as an improper part. Therefore, after *t,* Descartes and D-minus were identical.

Our argument has led us to this conclusion: that there was a time at which Descartes and D-minus were identical. And, as we have noted, there was an earlier time at which they were *not* identical. But if this is correct, then there was once an object that had earlier been two objects, which is a plain violation of the principle of the transitivity of identity. I mean it is a violation of the principle of the transitivity of identity *simpliciter,* by the way, and not of a principle that claims transitivity for some "specialized" version of identity like "identity through time." So far as I can see, there is no relation called "identity through time," unless those words are simply another name for identity *simpliciter.* We may represent explicitly the violation of the transitivity of identity I contend we have arrived at as follows. If our argument is correct then all four of the following propositions are true:

> The thing that was D-minus before *t* =
> the thing that was D-minus after *t*
> The thing that was D-minus after *t* =
> the thing that was Descartes after *t*
> The thing that was Descartes after *t* =
> the thing that was Descartes before *t*
> The thing that was D-minus before *t* ≠
> the thing that was Descartes before *t.*[11]

Thus our reductio has been accomplished, and we must conclude that there was never any such thing as D-minus. Therefore, DAUP is false, for DAUP entails that there was such a thing as D-minus.

We can, in fact, easily reach an even more striking conclusion: L does not exist either: there was never any such thing as Descartes's left leg. We need only one premise to reach this conclusion, namely that if L existed, D-minus did too. And this premise seems quite reasonable, for it would seem wholly arbitrary to accept the existence of L and to deny the existence of D-minus. In more senses than one, L and D-minus stand or fall together. If these things existed, they would be things of the same sort. Each would be an *arbitrary* undetached part of a certain man.[12] This fact may be disguised by our having (problems of multiplicity and vagueness aside) what is a customary and idiomatic name for L if it is a name for anything: "Descartes's left leg." But this is a linguistic accident that reflects our interests. (We may imagine a race of rational beings who raise human beings as meat animals. Suppose these beings, for religious reasons, never eat left legs. They might very well have in their language some customary and idiomatic phrase that stands to D-minus in the same relation as that in which the English phrase "Descartes's left leg" stands to L.)

If our argument against DAUP also leads to the conclusion that there never was any such thing as Descartes's left leg (which I am willing to grant), this may lead some people to think that there *must* be something wrong with the argument. Here is a leg (one is tempted to say) and here is another leg, and therefore van Inwagen is wrong. I am not entirely out of sympathy with this reaction. If a philosophical argument leads us to deny something that every human being in history has believed, then it is a pretty good bet that something is wrong with the argument. But I doubt that in saying that there never was any such thing as Descartes's left leg[13] I am denying anything that has been believed, as the Church says, *ubique et ab omnibus.*[14] The proposition I mean to express by the words "There never was any such thing as Descartes's left leg" does not, as I see it, entail the falsity of, e.g., the proposition that Descartes scratched his left leg on the morning of his eleventh birthday. I think I could show this. To make good this claim, I should at least have to provide some reason for thinking that sentences that apparently involve reference to or quantification over the limbs of animals can be translated into sentences that don't even apparently involve such reference or quantification. I believe I could do this, but this is not the place for it. My purpose in the present paragraph is to explain what sort of position my position on the nonexistence of Descartes's left leg is, and not to defend that position. (My position is comparable to that of many other philosophers who have denied the existence of various objects in order to escape the paradoxical consequences that they thought, rightly or wrongly, would follow from the existence of such objects. Philosophers who have denied the existence of the material substrate have not, in general, denied the existence of tables and chairs; philosophers who have denied the existence of sense-data have not, in general, denied the existence of perception or even the existence of a distinction between appearance and reality; philosophers who have denied the existence of pains have not, in general, denied the existence of pain.)

Nonetheless, an argument that leads to the conclusion that there never was any such thing as Descartes's left leg is at least prima facie objectionable. But all the objections to this argument I know of involve principles or lead to conclusions that, in my view at least, are more objectionable than the proposition that Descartes's left leg did not exist. In the remainder of this section and in the two sections that follow I shall examine these objections.

There are four objections, or types of objection, that I shall simply dismiss.

I shall simply dismiss any objection that involves a denial of the principle of the transitivity of identity. People who take this line are, as Professor Geach would say, "not to be heard." Anyone who rejects the principle of the transitivity of identity simply does not understand the difference between the number one and the number two.

I shall simply dismiss any objection that involves the contention that it would have been logically impossible for Descartes to survive the loss of a leg.[15] I do not know if anyone would say this, but if anyone would, he too is not to be heard.

I shall simply dismiss any objection that involves the contention that it would have been impossible for D-minus to survive being separated from L.

I shall simply dismiss any objection that involves the contention that it was possible for Descartes and D-minus to have been numerically distinct material objects having the same momentary physical properties. (I would not go so far as to say that such objections are not to be heard. I dismiss them because I cannot understand them and therefore have nothing to say about them.)

I know of two objections to my argument that are worthy of extended consideration. I shall call them the *Chisholm Objection* and the *Lewis Objection*. I will discuss them in the two sections that follow.

4. *The Chisholm Objection.* It will not have escaped the reader's attention that my argument assumes that Descartes was a flesh-and-blood object that, when unmutilated, was shaped like a statute of Descartes. Many philosophers, including Descartes, would reject this assumption. Though I am myself convinced of its truth beyond all doubt and beyond all possibility of conversion by philosophical argument, I admit that it is highly controversial. To be sure, few philosophers would deny either that there was once a flesh-and-blood object shaped like a statute of Descartes or that that object was somehow intimately related to Descartes. But many philosophers would deny what seems evident to me: that he (that thing that thought) *was* that object. These philosophers would say that that object was not Descartes but rather his *body*. The philosopher who thus distinguishes between Descartes and his body and who wishes to accept the existence of D-minus may reply to the argument of Section 3 as follows:

> I can accept the existence of D-minus, and I can accept the proposition that Descartes was capable of surviving the loss of a leg, and I can accept the principle of the transitivity of identity, and your arguments do not show that my acceptance of these things forces upon me the desperate expedient of admitting that it is conceptually possible for there to be two conterminous material objects. I need only say—and I *do* say it—that D-minus was not a part of Descartes but only a part of Descartes's *body*.

And this response is perfectly proper. But this is not the end of the matter, for certain consequences follow upon it.

First, though my imaginary philosopher has escaped the consequences of the assumption that D-minus was a part of Descartes, he must nonetheless face the consequences of conceding that D-minus was a part of Descartes's body. Here is one: that Descartes's body (that is, the thing that at any given moment was the body Descartes had *then*) could not have survived the loss of a part. This could be easily shown by a trivial modification of the argument of Section 3. Moreover, since, as a matter of empirical fact, human bodies are (to speak with the vulgar) constantly exchanging matter with their surroundings, he must concede that Descartes is continually "changing bodies"; and not just every now and then, but hundreds of times every second. Well, perhaps he will be willing to say this. We have shown independently of any considerations involving persons and their bodies that DAUP entails MNE, and the continual changing of one's body is a consequence of the proposition that at any given time one has some body or other, together with MNE and certain empirical facts about the human organism.

There is, however, a much more serious and far-reaching consequence of our imaginary philosopher's objection to the argument of Section 3. Of those philosophers I know of who have thought about these matters, only Roderick Chisholm has seen the inevitability of this consequence.[16] I therefore call the above objection to the argument of Section 3 the *Chisholm Objection,* provided that it is understood to include the consequence I shall set forth in the following paragraphs.

If DAUP is true, then a human being, if he lasts from one moment to the next, cannot during that interval lose any parts. This is simply a consequence of the fact that DAUP entails MNE. Now there may be some "everyday" material objects that endure for appreciable periods of time according to the strict standards of endurance entailed by MNE. The Hope Diamond, say, or a fly in amber. But none of these observable, enduring material things is you or I. Therefore, if DAUP is true, and if you and I last from one moment to the next, we cannot be everyday

material objects. I concede that there are observable material things other than the statue-shaped flesh-and-blood objects that *I* think you and I are that, according to reputable philosophers, are what you and I are. For example, some reputable philosophers think that you and I are living human brains. But such views are no more consistent with DAUP than is my own, for no such view is consistent with MNE and, therefore, no such view is consistent with DAUP. (Suppose for example that I am a brain. Surely I can survive the loss of some part of myself; a single cell, say. Let P be a part of me I can survive the loss of. Let B-minus be the object that occupies the region that is the set-theoretic difference between the region occupied by my brain—that is, by me—and the region occupied by P . . .)

It would seem, therefore, that (given our persistence through time, the transitivity of identity, and so on) it follows from DAUP that we are not observable material things, or, at any rate, that we are not material things of any sort that *has* so far been observed. Therefore, anyone who accepts DAUP must either accept the thesis that we are not material things or else accept the thesis that we are material things of a kind very different from any kind that has ever been observed.

The difficulties with the thesis that we are, contrary to all appearances, immaterial things, are well known.

Let us examine the thesis that we are material things of a sort that has never been observed. Anyone who accepts this may reasonably be expected to answer the question, *Why* have we so far gone unobserved? It cannot be for want of people's poking and prying inside human bodies. There are, I think, three possible answers.

(i) We have gone unobserved because we are very small; perhaps as small as or smaller than a single cell. Presumably an object that small, or even a bit larger, might be located inside our bodies—inside our brains if anywhere, I should think—and have escaped the attention of the most assiduous physiologists.

(ii) We have gone unobserved because we are made of some sort of subtle matter (the "nameless and unknown" soul-stuff of Epicurus and Lucretius) that can affect gross, everyday matter—or else we should not have charge of our bodies—but which affects it to such a small degree that physicists have not yet taken note of its effects.

(iii) We have gone unobserved because we are far from our bodies, with which we interact at a distance.

We may note that (i), (ii) and (iii) are not exclusive alternatives: perhaps we are at once tiny, subtle, and far away.

Let us call an object a *Chisholm Object* if it is a concrete particular that thinks and wills and is the cause of the voluntary movements of a human body and is in practice unobservable, either because it is immaterial (a Cartesian ego) or, if material, tiny or made of subtle matter or remote from the human body it controls.

We may now state the Chisholm Objection more adequately:

> Your argument has a false premise: that D-minus was a part of Descartes. Moreover, there is no true proposition that you could use in place of the proposition that D-minus was a part of Descartes in some reconstructed argument against DAUP, for Descartes was a Chisholm Object; if he ever lost a part, he lost it in 1650 (the year of his death) or later. Moreover, in the strict, philosophical sense (to borrow Bishop Butler's fine phrase) of *same* it is very unlikely that there was any appreciable interval throughout which Descartes had the same body.

I think that this is the only possible objection to my argument that is not demonstrably wrong. I have nothing to say against it except that I do not believe a word of it. But that is a psychological report, not an argument. Doubtless there are philosophers who find equally incredible my contention that, in the strict, philosophical senses of *was* and *thing,* there never was any such thing as Descartes's left leg.

I think that the arguments of this section and the preceding section show that anyone who accepts DAUP should also accept the proposition that every person is a Chisholm Object. For my part, I say so

much the worse for DAUP. At any rate, I am fairly sure that few philosophers would find acceptance of the propositions the Chisholm Objection commits its adherents to an acceptable price to pay for DAUP.

5. *The Lewis Objection.* One philosopher who balks at paying this price and who is nevertheless attracted to DAUP is David Lewis.[17] Lewis argues, à la Gaunilon, that my reasoning must be faulty since parallel reasoning leads to an obviously false conclusion.[18]

Consider the Austro-Hungarian Empire in, say, 1900. In 1900, Austria existed and Hungary existed and these two countries composed the Empire. That is, they did not overlap and the portion of the earth's surface occupied by one or the other was just exactly the portion of the earth's surface occupied by the Empire. Thus in a very obvious sense, these two countries stood to the Empire as L and D-minus (if such there were) stood to Descartes. Now (the Lewis Objection runs) consider the following argument:

> Suppose that the Martians had totally destroyed Hungary and had left the territory occupied by Austria untouched. We can only suppose that Austria would have survived this destruction of Hungary. We can only suppose that the Austro-Hungarian Empire (whose capital at Vienna of course escaped destruction) would also have survived the destruction of Hungary. (True, "the Austro-Hungarian Empire" might not have been a very good *name* for it thereafter; but the example of the Holy Roman Empire shows that the name of an empire need not be a *good* name.) Empires and other states can increase and decrease in extent and can gain and lose parts without losing their identities (consider, for example, the fact that the United States survived the admission into the Union of Alaska and Hawaii). The act we have supposed the Martians to have performed would have caused the Empire to lose a part without causing it to cease to exist. Now what would have been the relation between Austria and the Empire after the destruction of Hungary? We can only suppose that it would have been identity, for what distinction would there have been between them? Moreover, Austria would have been the largest part of the Empire, and, according to any accept-

able mereology, the largest part of a thing is its sole improper part, itself. But this is to suppose that the Empire might have been Austria at one time and not at another, which would be a violation of the principle of the transitivity of identity. Since the principle of the transitivity of identity is a necessary truth, only one conclusion is possible: Austria did not exist in 1900. Moreover, since Hungary existed in 1900 if and only if Austria did, Hungary did not exist in 1900 either.

Since the conclusion of this argument is absurd, there must be something wrong with the argument. But the argument is sound if and only if our earlier reductio arguments are sound. Therefore they are not sound.

I reject the Lewis Objection. I believe it contains a false premise: that after the destruction of Hungary, Austria and the Empire would have been identical. I say they would merely have occupied the same territory. They would have differed in many of their properties. Two examples would be historical properties (the Empire would have had the property *having had Hungary as a part;* Austria would not have had it) and modal properties (the Empire would have had the property *possibly having Bavaria as a part;* Austria would not have had it).

As to the "largest part" argument, though one politico-geographical entity may correctly be said to be "part" of another, "part" in this sense does not obey the laws of any mereology I know of.[19] Call this relation the *PG-part relation.* It would seem that it should be defined as follows: A is a PG-part of B if the territory occupied by A is a part (in the standard, spatial sense) of the territory occupied by B. If this definition is accepted—and what are the alternatives?—then there would seem to be only one natural definition of "A is a larger PG-part of B than C is" and only one natural definition of "A is a proper PG-part of B", in fact, these definitions are so natural it would be pedantic to state them. But it follows from these natural definitions that there need be no such thing as the largest PG-part of a politico-geographical entity, and, moreover, that a politico-geographical entity may have improper PG-parts other than itself. Take, for example, the City of Washington and the District of Columbia. Each of these is an improper PG-part of the other, and yet, by the principle of the

non-identity of discernibles, they are numerically diverse. For example, the District of Columbia has the properties *having been the same size throughout its existence, not being a city,* and *having had Georgetown as a PG-part in 1850;* Washington has none of them. If matters had gone as we imagined with Austria and the Austro-Hungarian Empire, then this would have been just their situation: each would have been an improper PG part of the other.

Therefore, the Lewis Objection fails, since the "parallel" argument Lewis produces, though it indeed has an absurd conclusion, is not really parallel to the *reductio* arguments of sections 2 and 3. In a nutshell, the reason is this: "parts" of material objects and "parts" of politico-geographical entities do not work the same way. If an "improper part" of a material object is a material object that occupies the same region of space as that object, then every material object has exactly one improper part: itself. If an "improper part" of a politico-geographical entity that occupies the same territory as that entity, then every politico-geographical entity has *at least* one improper part: itself; but some have more.

6. The Chisholm Objection I cannot accept. The Lewis Objection fails. I therefore find no reason to doubt the soundness of our reductio arguments, and I conclude that, though (I have no doubt) there are undetached parts, there are not "just any" undetached parts. That is, I conclude that DAUP is false. In this, the final section, I will show how what has been said in the earlier sections may be applied to another sort of "part."

Some philosophers would call "parts" of the sort we have been talking about, 'spatial parts'. They would oppose them to *temporal* parts. I fully accept the arguments of Chisholm and Geach for the conclusion that the idea of a temporal part is incoherent.[20] I simply do not understand what these things are supposed to be, and I do not think this is my fault. I think that no one understands what they are supposed to be, though of course plenty of philosophers think they do. (If anyone who thinks he does understand temporal parts feels inclined to charge me with conceptual arrogance, I invite him to consider the following list: the Absolute Idea; impossible objects; Cartesian egos; bare particulars; things-in-themselves; pure acts of will; simple, non-natural properties; logically perfect languages; sense-data. I think it very likely that he will find that there is at least one item on this list that he has no glimmering of an understanding of. Yet each of them has been believed in by great philosophers. Anyone, therefore, who fails to understand some item on this list is no less conceptually arrogant than I.) But if I do not understand temporal parts, I at any rate understand what parameters are supposed by most philosophers who say they believe in them to individuate them: to each persisting object and each occupiable interval of time such that that object exists at every moment in that interval, there corresponds a *concrete* particular that is a temporal part of that object.[21] (Of course if some philosopher wishes to call an object-interval pair a "temporal part" of its first term, I have no objection.) So far as I know, no philosopher who believes there are *any* temporal parts thinks that there could be some occupiable sub-interval of the interval during which a given object exists that is *not* occupied by a temporal part of that object. That is to say, all philosophers who accept the existence of (proper) temporal parts, would accept what might be called the Doctrine of Arbitrary Temporal Parts (DATP)[22]:

> For every persisting object P, if I is the interval of time occupied by P and if sub-I is *any* occupiable sub-interval of I *whatever,* there exists a persisting object that occupies the interval sub-I and which, for every moment *t* that falls within sub-I, has at *t* exactly the same momentary properties[23] that P has.

This doctrine is formally very similar to DAUP. (The differences in structure can, I think, be traced to the fact that there are three spatial dimensions and only one temporal dimension.)

There is at least one philosopher, the author of this paper, who thinks that while there *are* undetached spatial parts, comparatively few of the occupiable regions that fall wholly within a given material object are occupied. (See note 9.) *I* think this because I think that the cells living things are made of are, in a sense I cannot here explore, *unitary* things, things having an entelechy; in this respect they are like the men, women, and dogs (Thurber's list) of which they are

parts. It is very hard to see how anyone could take a similar attitude toward temporal parts. I reject the Doctrine of Undetached Arbitrary (Spatial) Parts. But if there were temporal parts, then they would *all* be "arbitrary": there are no temporal analogues of cells.

Or perhaps this is wrong. Perhaps there is one sort of temporal part such that one could affirm the existence of parts of this sort and, without appearing to be placing wholly arbitrary restrictions on one's ontology, deny the existence of all other (proper) temporal parts. I am thinking of *instantaneous* temporal parts, those that occupy a mathematical instant of time, an interval of measure 0. In what follows, I am going to adopt the arguments that were employed earlier in this paper against DAUP to the task of showing that DATP is false. I think that anyone who, perhaps impressed by my argument, rejects DATP and who wants to believe in *some* temporal parts has only one possibility open to him: he must believe in the improper temporal part of an object (i.e., the object itself) and he must believe in all the instantaneous parts of the object and in no other parts. He must, for example, believe in Descartes and he must believe in the part of Descartes that occupied *t,* where *t* is any *instant* of time at which Descartes existed, and he must *not* believe in the part of Descartes that occupied the year 1625. I shall offer no arguments against *this* doctrine of temporal parts.

I said in the preceding paragraph that I should argue that DATP was false. I spoke loosely. DATP is not false. It is meaningless because the notion of a temporal part is meaningless. Or, at any rate, *I* don't understand it. But I *can* give an argument that *would* be an argument for the falsity of DATP if that doctrine made any sense. I can do this because, as I said above, though I do not understand the notion of a temporal part, I know what parameters are supposed to individuate temporal parts. Moreover, I can justifiably assume that discourse about temporal parts must satisfy certain formal constraints that I am familiar with from my understanding of parts *simpliciter.* But this self-justification is too abstract to convey much. Let us turn to the argument.

Our argument against DAUP depended on its being possible for a thing to lose its parts, or, more accurately, for its parts to become separated or to be annihilated. Nothing like this can figure in an argument about temporal parts: no one would suppose that two "adjoining" temporal parts of a thing might become separated or that a temporal part of a thing might cease to exist. (I *think*. I'm feeling my way about in the dark, you understand. The chair I'm sitting on is supposed to be a temporal part of itself and *it* could cease to exist.) At any rate, I won't assume this is possible. But one can assume, I think, that adjoining temporal parts of a thing might not have been in "contact"; not, perhaps, that there might have been an interval between them, but, at any rate, that one of them might not have existed. Take Descartes, for example. Let L be the temporal part of Descartes that occupied the last year of Descartes's existence.[24] Let D-minus be the temporal part of Descartes that occupied the interval from Descartes's birth (or conception or whenever it was he began to exist) to the moment exactly one year before Descartes ceased to exist. Though L and D-minus were in fact "joined" to each other, there would not seem to have been any necessity to this: there are surely possible worlds in which D-minus exists and L does not, either because *no* temporal part of Descartes adjoins D-minus or because some part other than L does.

Now if this is so, then it is easy to adapt our earlier methods to the task of deducing an absurdity from the proposition that there was such a thing as D-minus. If there was such a thing as D-minus, then there was such a thing as L, and the relations that held between D-minus, L, and Descartes are those that were described in the preceding paragraph. In that case, obviously, D-minus and Descartes were not identical. But suppose, as seems possible, that Descartes had ceased to exist exactly one year earlier than he in fact did; or, if you like, suppose, as seems possible, that D-minus had not been "attached to L" or "continuous with L" (or however one should put it). What then would have been the relationship that held between D-minus and Descartes? What could it have been but identity? To suppose otherwise is to suppose that a thing might have had two improper temporal parts. But if D-minus and Descartes could have been identical, then there are two things that could have been one thing. This is not only a violation of an obvious *modal* principle about identity ("*x*

$\neq y \supset \Box x \neq y$"), it is a violation of the principle of the transitivity of identity *simpliciter*. This may be seen from inspection of the following four propositions (in which "*t*" denotes the moment exactly one year before the moment at which Descartes ceased to exist):

> D-minus = the thing that would have been D-minus if Descartes had ceased to exist at *t*
> The thing that would have been D-minus if Descartes had ceased to exist at *t* = the thing that would have been Descartes if Descartes had ceased to exist at *t*
> The thing that would have been Descartes if Descartes had ceased to exist at *t* = Descartes D-minus ≠ Descartes.[25]

I have not presented any explicit argument for the conclusion that all four of these propositions can be derived from the assumption that D-minus exists (and would have existed if Descartes had ceased to exist at *t*). I should do so if this paper consisted solely of an attack on DATP. But I have devoted a good deal of space to an argument showing that DAUP entails a violation of the principle of the transitivity of identity, and I believe the reader will find it an easy task to construct the arguments I *would* give (if pressed) for the conclusion that DATP entails a violation of that principle.

I conclude that DATP fails for much the same reason that DAUP fails. More exactly, I conclude that if anyone ever does provide some explanation of the notion of a temporal part (thus bringing DATP into existence: at present there is no such doctrine), then DATP *will* fail for much the same reason that DAUP fails.

NOTES

1. I shall not define *material object*.
2. I shall assume that the space we inhabit is a three-dimensional continuum of *points*. A *region* is any set of points. Suppose we agree that we know what it means to say that a given point in space *lies within* a given material object at a given moment. Then an object *occupies* a certain region at a certain moment if that region is the set contain-

ing all and only those points that lie within that object at that moment.

3. A region of space is *occupiable* if it is possible (in what Plantinga calls "the broadly logical sense") for it to be occupied by a material object. Presumably not all regions of space are occupiable. Consider a spherical region S; consider that sub-region of S that consists of just the points within S that are at distances from the center of S that have irrational measures: it is certainly hard to see how this sub-region could be occupied by a material object. I shall not discuss occupiability further, however, since its exact nature is not relevant to the issues that we shall be taking up. For an interesting proposal about occupiable regions, see Richard Cartwright's fine paper. "Scattered Objects" in *Analysis and Metaphysics* ed. by Keith Lehrer (Dordrecht: D. Reidel, 1975). If we accept Cartwright's account of what it is for a region to be occupiable (to be what he calls a "receptacle"), then DAUP is an immediate consequence of (though it does not entail) what he calls the *Covering Principle*.

4. More precisely: DAUP entails that, for any time *t*, if the Eiffel Tower exists at *t*, and if the northern half of the space it occupies at *t* is then occupiable—and I think no one would want to deny *that*—then there exists an object at *t* that occupies that space, an object it would certainly be natural to call "the northern half of the Eiffel Tower." There is a thesis that DAUP intuitively "ought" to entail that my statement of it does *not* entail. Consider two times *t* and *t'*. Suppose that the Eiffel Tower exists and has the same location and orientation in space at both these times. Suppose that at both these times it consists of the same girders, struts, and rivets, arranged in the same way. The thesis: the thing that is the northern half of the Eiffel Tower at *t* is identical with the thing that is the northern half of the Eiffel Tower at *t'*. I regard the failure of my statement of DAUP to entail this thesis as a defect in that statement. (I *think* this entailment fails to hold. It certainly cannot be shown formally to hold. For all I know, however, there may be some feature of the concept of a material object in virtue of which it *does* hold.)

5. Argle for example. See "Holes" by David and Stephanie Lewis, *The Australasian Journal of Philosophy,* 48 (1970).

6. Mereological essentialism proper also entails that a thing could not have "started out with" different parts, which is not a consequence of the weaker thesis. For general discussions of mereological essentialism, see Roderick M. Chisholm, "Parts as Essential to Their Wholes," *The Review of Metaphysics* XXVI (1973) and *Person and Object: A Metaphysical Study* (La Salle: Open Court, 1976), Appendix B.

7. "Scattered objects" is Cartwright's term. See his article of that title (cited in note 3, above) for a precise definition of 'scattered object'.

8. Here I assume the following principle: if A is a material object and B is (a material object that is) a part of A and if R_A is the region occupied by A and R_B is the region occupied by B, then R_A minus R_B is occupiable. If there is any doubt about this principle, it could be proved as follows. Imagine that B was annihilated and that all else remained the same. Then R_A *would be* occupied by a material object (even if it hadn't been before the annihilation of B). This principle is, strictly speaking, false if certain views about occupiability are correct, since it assumes that both "closed" and "open" regions are occupiable. (This is an implicit assumption of our little proof.) Those who care about such things will see that this assumption could be removed at the cost of a little elaboration that would not materially affect the use made of the principle in the body of the paper. Those who wish to deny the existence of "scattered objects" may wish to append the clause 'if topologically connected' to the principle.

9. A very similar argument can be found in Cartwright, *op. cit.,* pp. 164–166. Someone might argue that if the above argument is sound, then it can be extended in the following way to prove not simply that MNE follows from DAUP but that MNE is true *simpliciter:* Either there are undetached parts or there aren't; if there aren't, then MNE is vacuously true; if there are, then our argument can be used to show that MNE is true. This reaction conflates DAUP with the thesis that there are undetached parts. Any argument like the one I have presented in the text would have to employ some principle that allowed the arguer pass from the existence of the object O and the part P to the existence of the object O-minus. This is just what DAUP allows one to do. (Of course there are weaker principles that would legitimize this inference.) Therefore, if one rejects DAUP (and if one accepts no other principle that would legitimize the inference of the existence of O-minus from the existence of O and P), one can consistently believe in the existence of undetached parts that are not essential to their wholes. I, for example, believe that there exists a cell in my right hand that is an undetached part of me and such that I could survive the loss of it. I can consistently believe this because I do not think that there is any such object as "I-minus-that-cell"; that is, if R is the region of space I occupy and r is the region of space that cell occupies, I do not think that there exists any object that occupies the region R-r.

10. The following reflections on Descartes and his left leg supersede those contained in my paper "Philosophers and the Words 'Human Body,'" in *Time and Cause: Essays Presented to Richard Taylor,* (Dordrecht: D. Reidel, 1980).

11. The first and third of these four propositions I take to be trivial logical truths. Or, at least, to follow trivially from the propositions that D-minus existed before and after *t* and that Descartes existed before and after *t*.

12. Perhaps I am wrong about this. If I am, if a leg is like a cell (say), and unlike the left half of cell, in being a non-arbitrary part of a human being, then I am wrong about something that is of no great import, since I am not saying that there are *no* undetached parts (cf. *n*. 9). But whether or not there was such a thing as L, there was certainly no such thing as D-minus. And the non-existence of D-minus is sufficient to refute DAUP. Nevertheless, I think I am right and that L did not exist. I will assert this rather than suspend judgment because I think that if my thesis about parts entails that L did not exist, then my thesis has an extremely counter-intuitive consequence and I do not wish to make my thesis look more plausible than it is by glossing over its more implausible consequences.

13. There's the bit where you say it.

14. There's the bit where you take it back.

15. Some philosophers distinguish between survival and identity. I have no idea what they mean by this. When I say that a certain person survived a certain adventure, what I say entails that a person who existed before the adventure and a person who existed after the adventure were the same person.

16. My knowledge of Chisholm's views on this question comes entirely from a paper I heard him read in 1978. He has recently told me, however, that I have not misrepresented him.

17. Lewis holds that "persons and their bodies are identical." See his "Counterparts of Persons and Their Bodies," *The Journal of Philosophy* LXVIII (1971).

18. This argument was communicated to me in a letter. The wording of the argument in the text is mine. It is my fault and not Lewis's that the political details of the example are inaccurate. I should like to apologize to anyone who cares about the constitution of the Dual Monarchy.

19. By a 'politico-geographical entity', I mean an entity that (i) is a political entity—is brought into existence by human beings' entering into political relations with one another—and (ii) extends over part of the Earth's surface. (Strictly speaking, this is a definition of a *terrestrial* politico-geographical entity). Thus the Caspian Sea is not a politico-geographical entity because it fails to satisfy condition (i). The Congress of the United States fails to satisfy condition (ii). The United States, the British Commonwealth, Paris, Nova Scotia, and the territorial waters of Peru are politico-geographical entities.

20. See Geach's British Academy Lecture "Some Problems about Time," reprinted in *Logic Matters* (Oxford: Blackwell, 1972) and Appendix A to Chisholm's *Person and Object*.

21. An object *occupies* a set of moments of time if it exists at every moment in that set and at no other moments. A set of moments of time is an *occupiable interval* if it is possible in the broadly logical sense for there to be some object that occupies it. Presumably not all sets of moments of time are occupiable intervals. Cf. *n*. 3.

22. I do not say "*undetached* temporal parts." A detached temporal part of a thing, presumably, would be something that *used to be* a temporal part of that thing. None of the friends of temporal parts, so far as I know, has found any use for such a notion.

23. It is well known that grave difficulties attend the notion of a "momentary" property. But I do not see how to state DATP without using it. I shall not exploit these difficulties in what follows, however, and thus *I* am under no obligation to explain momentary properties.

24. Some people believe that Descartes has never ceased to exist. The argument I shall present does not really require that we assume that Descartes has ceased to exist but only that we assume that it is *possible* for him to cease to exist.

25. The first and third of these four propositions I take to be trivial logical truths. Or, at least, to follow trivially from the propositions that D-minus existed and would have existed if Descartes had ceased to exist at t and that Descartes existed and would have existed if he had ceased to exist at *t*. Cf. *n*. 11.

Many, but Almost One

~

DAVID LEWIS

David Lewis (1941–2001), a leading metaphysician of our time, has produced significant and groundbreaking work in nearly every area of philosophy. His books include
Convention, Counterfactuals, On the Plurality of Worlds, and five collections of essays.
Lewis taught at Princeton University for three decades and became Class of 1943 University Professor of Philosophy. He was also an honorary fellow of the Australian Academy of the Humanities.

THE PROBLEM OF THE MANY

Think of a cloud—just one cloud, and around it clear
blue sky. Seen from the ground, the cloud may seem
to have a sharp boundary. Not so. The cloud is a
swarm of water droplets. At the outskirts of the cloud
the density of the droplets falls off. Eventually they
are so few and far between that we may hesitate to
say that the outlying droplets are still part of the
cloud at all; perhaps we might better say only that
they are near the cloud. But the transition is gradual.
Many surfaces are equally good candidates to be the
boundary of the cloud. Therefore many aggregates of
droplets, some more inclusive and some less inclusive (and some inclusive in different ways then others), are equally good candidates to be the cloud.
Since they have equal claim, how can we say that the
cloud is one of these aggregates rather than another?
But if all of them count as clouds, then we have many
clouds rather than one. And if none of them count,
each one being ruled out because of the competition
from the others, then we have no cloud. How is it,
then, that we have just one cloud? And yet we do.

This is Unger's (1980) "problem of the many."
Once noticed, we can see that it is everywhere, for
all things are swarms of particles. There are always

outlying particles, questionably parts of the thing, not
definitely included and not definitely not included.
So there are always many aggregates, differing by a
little bit here and a little bit there, with equal claim to
be the thing. We have many things or we have none,
but anyway not the one thing we thought we had.
That is absurd.

Think of a rusty nail, and the gradual transition
from steel, to steel with bits of rust scattered through,
to rust adhering to the nail, to rust merely resting on
the nail. Or think of a cathode, and its departing electrons. Or think of anything that undergoes evapora-
tion or erosion or abrasion. Or think of yourself, or
any organism, with parts that gradually come loose in
metabolism or excretion or perspiration or shedding
of dead skin. In each case, a thing has questionable
parts, and therefore is subject to the problem of the
many.

If, as I think, things perdure through time by having temporal parts, then questionable temporal parts
add to the problem of the many. If a person comes
into existence gradually (whether over weeks or over
years or over nanoseconds doesn't matter for our
present purpose) then there are questionable temporal parts at the beginning of every human life. Likewise at the end, even in the most sudden death imag-

Reprinted from *Ontology, Causality, and Mind,* eds. J. Bacon, K. Campbell, and L. Reinhardt (Cambridge, England: Cambridge
University Press, 1993), by permission of the publisher.

inable. Do you think you are one person?—No, there are many aggregates of temporal parts, differing just a little at the ends, with equal claim to count as persons, and equal claim to count as you. Are all those equally good claims good enough? If so, you are many. If not, you are none. Either way we get the wrong answer. For undeniably you are one.

If, as some think but I do not,[1] ordinary things extend through other possible worlds, then the problem of the many takes on still another dimension. Here in this world we have a ship, the *Enigma;* there in another world is a ship built at about the same time, to plans that are nearly the same but not quite, using many of the same planks and some that are not the same. It is questionable whether the ship in that other world is *Enigma* herself, or just a substitute. If *Enigma* is a thing that extends through worlds, then the question is whether *Enigma* includes as a part what's in that other world. We have two versions of *Enigma,* one that includes this questionable otherworldly part and one that excludes it. They have equal claim to count as ships, and equal claim to count as *Enigma.* We have two ships, coinciding in this world but differing in their full extent. Or else we have none; but anyway not the one ship we thought we had.

THE PARADOX OF 1001 CATS

Cat Tibbles is alone on the mat. Tibbles has hairs h_1, $h_2, \ldots, h_{1000}$. Let c be Tibbles including all these hairs; let c_1 be all of Tibbles except for h_1; and similarly for $c_2, \ldots, c_{1000}$. Each of these c's is a cat. So instead of one cat on the mat, Tibbles, we have at least 1001 cats—which is absurd. This is P. T. Geach's (1980, pp. 215–16) paradox of 1001 cats.

Why should we think that each c_n is a cat? Because, says Geach, "c_n would clearly be a cat were the hair h_n plucked out, and we cannot reasonably suppose that plucking out a hair *generates* a cat, so c_n must already have been a cat" (p. 215). This need not convince us. We can reply that plucking out h_n turns c_n from a mere proper part of cat Tibbles into the whole of a cat. No new cat is generated, since the cat that c_n becomes the whole of is none other than Tibbles. Nor do c_n and Tibbles ever become identical *simpliciter*—of course not, since what's true about

c_n's past still differs from what's true about Tibbles's past. Rather, c_n becomes the whole of cat Tibbles in the sense that c_n's post-plucking temporal part is identical with Tibbles's post-plucking temporal part. So far, so good; except for those, like Geach, who reject the idea of temporal parts. The rest of us have no paradox yet.

But suppose it is spring, and Tibbles is shedding. When a cat sheds, the hairs do not come popping off; they become gradually looser, until finally they are held in place only by the hairs around them. By the end of this gradual process, the loose hairs are no longer parts of the cat. Sometime before the end, they are questionable parts: not definitely still parts of the cat, not definitely not. Suppose each of $h_1, h_2, \ldots, h_{1000}$ is at this questionable stage. Now indeed all of $c_1, c_2, \ldots, c_{1000}$, and also c which includes all the questionable hairs, have equal claim to be a cat, and equal claim to be Tibbles. So now we have 1001 cats. (Indeed, we have many more than that. For instance there is the cat that includes all but the four hairs h_6, h_{408}, h_{882}, and h_{907}.) The paradox of 1001 cats, insofar as it is a real paradox, is another instance of Unger's problem of the many.

To deny that there are many cats on the mat, we must either deny that the many are cats, or else deny that the cats are many. We may solve the paradox by finding a way to disqualify candidates for cathood: there are the many, sure enough, but the many are not all cats. At most one of them is. Perhaps the true cat is one of the many; or perhaps it is something else altogether, and none of the many are cats. Or else, if we grant that all the candidates are truly cats, we must find a way to say that these cats are not truly different from one another. I think both alternatives lead to successful solutions, but we shall see some unsuccessful solutions as well.

TWO SOLUTIONS BY DISQUALIFICATION: NONE OF THE MANY ARE CATS

We could try saying that not one of the c's is a cat; they are many, sure enough, but not many cats. Tibbles, the only genuine cat on the mat, is something else, different from all of them.

One way to disqualify the many is to invoke the alleged distinction between things and the parcels of matter that constitute them. We could try saying that the c's are not cats. Rather, they are cat-constituting parcels of matter. Tibbles is the cat that each of them constitutes.[2]

This dualism of things and their constituters is unparsimonious and unnecessary. It was invented to solve a certain problem, but a better solution to that problem lies elsewhere, as follows. We know that the matter of a thing may exist before and after the thing does; and we know that a thing may gain and lose matter while it still exists, as a cat does, or a wave or a flame. The dualists conclude that the matter is not the thing; constitution is not identity; there are things, there are the parcels of matter that temporarily constitute those things; these are items of two different categories, related by the special relation of constitution. We must agree, at least, that the temporally extended thing is not the temporally extended parcel of matter that temporarily constitutes that thing. But constitution may be identity, all the same, if it is identity between temporal parts. If some matter constitutes a cat for one minute, then a minute-long temporal segment of the cat is identical to a minute-long temporal segment of the matter. The cat consists entirely of the matter that constitutes it, in this sense: The whole of the cat, throughout the time it lives, consists entirely of temporal segments of various parcels of matter. At any moment, if we disregard everything not located at that moment, the cat and the matter that then constitutes it are identical.[3]

So only those who reject the notion of temporal parts have any need for the dualism of things and constituters. But suppose we accept it all the same. At best, this just transforms the paradox of 1001 cats into the paradox of 1001 cat-constituters. Is that an improvement? We all thought there was only one cat on the mat. After distinguishing Tibbles from her constituter, would we not still want to think there was only one cat-constituter on the mat?

Further, even granted that Tibbles has many constituters, I still question whether Tibbles is the only cat present. The constituters are cat-like in size, shape, weight, inner structure, and motion. They vibrate and set the air in motion—in short, they purr (especially when you pat them). Any way a cat can be at a moment, cat-constituters also can be; anything a cat can do at a moment, cat-constituters also can do. They are all too cat-like not to be cats. Indeed, they may have unfeline pasts and futures, but that doesn't show that they are never cats; it only shows that they do not remain cats for very long. Now we have the paradox of 1002 cats: Tibbles the constituted cat, and also the 1001 all-too-feline cat-constituters. Nothing has been gained.

I conclude that invoking the dualism of cats and cat-constituters to solve the paradox of 1001 cats does not succeed.

A different way to disqualify the many appeals to a doctrine of vagueness in nature. We could try saying that cat Tibbles is a vague object, and that the c's are not cats but rather alternative precisifications of a cat.

In one way, at least, this solution works better than the one before. This time, I cannot complain that at best we only transform the paradox of 1001 cats into the paradox of 1001 cat-precisifications, because that is no paradox. If indeed there are vague objects and precisifications, it is only to be expected that one vague object will have many precisifications.

If the proposal is meant to solve our paradox, it must be meant as serious metaphysics. It cannot just be a way of saying 'in the material mode' that the words "Tibbles" and "cat" are vague, and that this vagueness makes it indefinite just which hairs are part of the cat Tibbles. Rather, the idea must be that material objects come in two varieties, vague and precise; cats are vague, the c's are precise, and that is why none of the c's is a cat.

This new dualism of vague objects and their precisifications is, again, unparsimonious and unnecessary. The problem it was made to solve might better be solved another way. It is absurd to think that we have decided to apply the name "Tibbles" to a certain precisely delimited object; or that we have decided to apply the term "cat" to each of certain precisely delimited objects. But we needn't conclude that these words must rather apply to certain *im*precisely delimited, vague objects. Instead we should conclude that we never quite made up our minds just what these words apply to. We have made up our minds that "Tibbles" is to name one or another Tibbles-precisification, but we never decided just which one; we decided that "cat" was to apply to some and only some cat-precisifications, but again we never decided just which ones. (Nor did we ever decide just which things our new-found terms "Tibbles-precisification" and "cat-precisification" were to apply to.) It was very sensible of us not to decide. We probably couldn't have done it if we'd tried; and even if we could have, doing it would have been useless folly. Semantic indecision will suffice to explain the phenomenon of vagueness.[4] We need no vague objects.

Further, I doubt that I have any correct conception of a vague object. How, for instance, shall I think of an object that is vague in its spatial extent? The closest I can come is to superimpose three pictures. There is the *multiplicity* picture, in which the vague object gives way to its many precisifications, and the vagueness of the object gives way to differences between precisifications. There is the *ignorance* picture, in which the object has some definite but secret extent. And there is the *fadeaway* picture, in which the presence of the object admits of degree, in much the way that the presence of a spot of illumination admits of degree, and the degree diminishes as a function of the distance from the region where the object is most intensely present. None of the three pictures is right. Each one in its own way replaces the alleged vagueness of the object by precision. But if I cannot think of a vague object except by juggling these mistaken pictures, I have no correct conception.[5]

I can complain as before that we end up with a paradox of 1002 cats: Tibbles the vague cat, and also the 1001 precise cats. Once again, the cat-precisifications are all too cat-like. More so than the cat-constituters, in fact: The precisifications are cat-like not just in what they can do and how they can be at a moment, but also over time. They would make good pets—especially since 1001 of them will not eat you out of house and home!

Don't say that the precisifications cannot be cats because cats cannot be precise objects. Surely there could be cats in a world where nature is so much less gradual that the problem of the many goes away. It could happen that cats have no questionable parts at all, neither spatial nor temporal. (In this world, when

cats shed in the spring, the hairs *do* come popping off.) So it is at least possible that cat-like precise objects are genuine cats. If so, how can the presence of one vague cat spoil their cathood?

I conclude that invoking the dualism of vague objects and their precisifications to solve the paradox of 1001 cats does not succeed.

A BETTER SOLUTION BY DISQUALIFICATION: ONE OF THE MANY IS A CAT

Since all of the many are so cat-like, there is only one credible way to deny that all of them are cats. When is something very cat-like, yet not a cat?—When it is just a little less than a whole cat, almost all of a cat with just one little bit left out. Or when it is just a little more than a cat, a cat plus a little something extra. Or when it is both a little more and a little less.

Suppose we say that one of our many is exactly a cat, no more and no less; and that each of the rest is disqualified because it is a little less than a cat, or a little more, or both more and less. This invokes no unparsimonious and unnecessary dualisms; it disqualifies all but one of the many without denying that they are very cat-like; it leaves us with just one cat. All very satisfactory.

The trouble, so it seems, is that there is no saying which one is a cat. That is left altogether arbitrary. Settling it takes a semantic decision, and that is the decision we never made (and shouldn't have made, and maybe couldn't have made). No secret fact could answer the question, for we never decided how the answer would depend on secret facts. Which one deserves the name "cat" is up to us. If we decline to settle the question, nothing else will settle it for us.[6]

We cannot deny the arbitrariness. What we can deny, though, is that it is trouble. What shall we do, if semantic indecision is inescapable, and yet we wish to carry on talking? The answer, surely, is to exploit the fact that very often our unmade semantic decisions don't matter. Often, what you want to say will be true under all different ways of making the unmade decision. Then if you say it, even if by choice or by necessity you leave the decision forever unmade, you still speak truthfully. It makes no difference just what you meant, what you say is true regardless. And if it makes no difference just what you meant, likewise it makes no difference that you never made up your mind just what to mean. You say that a famous architect designed Fred's house; it never crossed your mind to think whether by "house" you meant something that did or that didn't include the attached garage; neither does some established convention or secret fact decide the issue; no matter, you knew that what you said was true either way.

This plan for coping with semantic indecision is van Fraassen's (1966) method of *supervaluations.* Call a sentence *super-true* if and only if it is true under all ways of making the unmade semantic decisions; *super-false* if and only if it is false under all ways of making those decisions; and if it is true under some ways and false under others, then it suffers a super-truth-value gap. Super-truth, with respect to a language interpreted in an imperfectly decisive way, replaces truth *simpliciter* as the goal of a cooperative speaker attempting to impart information. We can put it another way: Whatever it is that we do to determine the "intended" interpretation of our language determines not one interpretation but a range of interpretations. (The range depends on context, and is itself somewhat indeterminate.) What we try for, in imparting-information, is truth of what we say under all the intended interpretations.

Each intended interpretation of our language puts one of the cat candidates on the mat into the extension of the word "cat," and excludes all the rest. Likewise each intended interpretation picks out one cat candidate, the same one, as the referent of "Tibbles." Therefore it is super-true that there is just one cat, Tibbles, on the mat. Because it is super-true, you are entitled to affirm it. And so you may say what you want to say: there is one cat. That is how the method of supervaluations solves the paradox of 1001 cats.

Objection. Just one of the candidates is a cat, no more and no less. But don't try to say which one it is. Nothing you might say would be super-true. For it is exactly this semantic decision that remains unmade; it is exactly in this respect that the intended interpretations differ. Although it is super-true that something is a cat on the mat, there is nothing such that it is super-true of it that *it* is a cat on the mat. (It's like

the old puzzle: I owe you a horse, but there's no horse such that I owe you that horse.) This is peculiar.

Reply. So it is. But once you know the reason why, you can learn to accept it.

Objection.[7] Supervaluationism works too well: it stops us from ever stating the problem in the first place. The problem supposedly was that all the many candidates had equal claim to cathood. But under the supervaluationist rule, that may not be said. For under any one way of making the unmade decision, one candidate is picked as a cat. So under any one way of making the decision, the candidates do *not* have equal claim. What's true under all ways of making the decision is super-true. So what's super-true, and what we should have said, is that the candidates do *not* have equal claim. Then what's the problem? And yet the problem was stated. So supervaluationism is mistaken.

Reply. What's mistaken is a fanatical supervaluationism, which automatically applies the supervaluationist rule to any statement whatever, never mind that the statement makes no sense that way. The rule should instead be taken as a defeasible presumption. What defeats it, sometimes, is the cardinal principle of pragmatics: The right way to take what is said, if at all possible, is the way that makes sense of the message. Since the supervaluationist rule would have made hash of our statement of the problem, straightway the rule was suspended. We are good at making these accommodations; we don't even notice when we do it. Under the supervaluationist rule, it's right to say that there's only one cat, and so the candidates have unequal claim. Suspending the rule, it's right to say that the candidates have equal claim, and that all of them alike are not definitely not cats. Suspending the rule, it's even right to say that they are all cats! Is this capitulation to the paradox?—No; it's no harm to admit that in *some* sense there are many cats. What's intolerable is to be without any good and natural sense in which there is only one cat.

Objection.[8] The supervaluationist's notion of indeterminate reference is conceptually derivative from the prior notion of reference *simpliciter.* But if the problem of the many is everywhere, and semantic indecision is inescapable, then reference *simpliciter* never happens. To the extent that we gain concepts by "fixing the reference" on actual examples, we are in no position to have the concept of reference. Then neither are we in a position to have the derivative concept of indeterminate reference due to semantic indecision.

Reply. We don't need actual examples to have the concept. We have plenty of imaginary examples of reference *simpliciter,* uncomplicated by semantic indecision. These examples are set in sharper worlds than ours: worlds where clouds have no outlying droplets, where cats shed their hairs instantaneously, and so on. When we picked up the concept of reference, in childhood, we probably took for granted that our own world was sharp in just that way. (When not puzzling over the problem of the many, maybe we half-believe it still.) We fixed the reference of "reference" on these imaginary examples in the sharp world we thought we lived in—and if any theory of reference says that cannot be done, so much the worse for it.

I conclude that the supervaluationist solution to the paradox of 1001 cats, and to the problem of the many generally, is successful. But is it the only successful solution?—I think not. I turn now to the other sort of solution: the kind which concedes that the many are cats, but seeks to deny that the cats are really many.

RELATIVE IDENTITY: THE MANY ARE NOT DIFFERENT CATS

Geach himself favours one such solution. The paradox of 1001 cats serves as a showcase for his doctrine of relative identity.

> Everything falls into place if we realize that the number of cats on the mat is the number of *different* cats on the mat; and c_{13}, c_{279}, and c are not three different cats, they are one and the same cat. Though none of these 1001 lumps of feline tissue is the same lump of feline tissue as another, each is the same cat as any other: each of them, then, is a cat, but there is only one cat on the mat, and our original story

> stands. . . . The price to pay is that we must regard '——is the same cat as——' as expressing only a certain equivalence relation, not an absolute identity restricted to cats; but this price, I have elsewhere argued, must be paid anyhow, for there is no such absolute identity as logicians have assumed. (1980, p. 216)

"Same cat" is a relation of partial indiscernibility, restricted to respects of comparison somehow associated with the term "cat," and discernibility by just a few hairs doesn't count. "Same lump of feline tissue" is a different relation of partial indiscernibility, and a more discerning one.

I agree that sometimes we say "same," and mean by it not "absolute identity" but just some relation of partial indiscernibility. I also agree that sometimes we count by relations of partial indiscernibility. As I once wrote:

> If an infirm man wishes to know how many roads he must cross to reach his destination, I will count by identity-along-his-path rather than by identity. By crossing the Chester A. Arthur Parkway and Route 137 at the brief stretch where they have merged, he can cross both by crossing only one road. (1976, p. 27)

I'll happily add that for that brief stretch, the two roads are the same. But though I don't object to this positive part of Geach's view, it doesn't ring true to apply it as he does to the case of the cats.

If you ask me to say whether c_{13}, c_{279}, and c are the same or different, I may indeed be of two minds about how to answer. I might say they're different—after all, I know how they differ! Or I might say they're the same, because the difference is negligible, so I duly ignore it. (Not easy to do while attending to the example as I now am; if I attend to my ignoring of something, ipso facto I no longer ignore it.) But if you add the noun phrase, either "same cat" or "same lump of feline tissue," it seems to me that I am no less hesitant than before. Just as I was of two minds about "same," so I am still of two minds about "same cat" and "same lump of feline tissue."

Other cases are different. If you ask me "same or different?" when you hold Monday's *Melbourne Age* in one hand and Tuesday's *Age* in the other, or when you hold one Monday *Age* in each hand, again I won't know how to answer. But if you ask me "same or different newspaper?" or "same or different issue?" or "same or different copy?" then I'll know just what to say. We can dispute his explanation of what happens, but at least the phenomenon happens exactly as Geach says it does. Not so, I think, for the case of "same cat" versus "same lump."

Something else is lacking in Geach's solution. In other cases where it comes natural to count by a relation other than identity, it seems that identity itself—"absolute identity"—is not far away. Local identity, as between the Arthur Parkway and Route 137 for the stretch where they have merged, is identity *simpliciter* of spatial parts. Likewise temporary identity, as between a thing and the matter that temporarily constitutes it, is identity *simpliciter* of temporal parts. Qualitative identity is identity *simpliciter* of qualitative character. The newspaper that Monday's *Age* is an issue of and the newspaper that Tuesday's *Age* is an issue of are identical *simpliciter;* likewise my copy and your copy of Monday's *Age* are copies of the identical issue. But Geach never tells us what the "same cat" relation has to do with identity *simpliciter.*

He wouldn't, of course, because he thinks "there is no such absolute identity as logicians have assumed." (Nor would he accept all my examples above; certainly not the one about temporary identity and identity of temporal parts.) But Geach's case against absolute identity is unconvincing. It seems to come down to a challenge: If Geach is determined to construe all that I say in terms of relations of partial indiscernibility, is there any way I can stop him? Can I *force* him to understand? (What's more, can I do it with one hand tied behind my back? Can I do it, for instance, without ever using the second-order quantification that Geach (1967) also challenges?) I suppose not. But I don't see why that should make me doubt that I know the difference between identity and indiscernibility.

We have the concept of identity, *pace* Geach; and if we are to justify denying that the cats are many, we need to show that they are interrelated by a relation closely akin to identity itself. Geach has not shown this, and wouldn't wish to show it. Nevertheless it

can be shown, as we shall soon see. But at that point we shall have a solution that bypasses Geach's doctrine of relative identity altogether.

PARTIAL IDENTITY: THE MANY ARE ALMOST ONE

What is the opposite of identity? *Non*-identity, we'd offhand say. Anything is identical to itself; otherwise we have two "different" things, two "distinct" things; that is, two non-identical things. Of course it's true that things are either identical or non-identical, and never both. But the real opposite of identity is distinctness: not distinctness in the sense of non-identity, but rather distinctness in the sense of non-overlap (what is called "disjointness" in the jargon of those who reserve "distinct" to mean "non-identical"). We have a spectrum of cases. At one end we find the complete identity of a thing with itself: it and itself are entirely identical, not at all distinct. At the opposite end we find the case of two things that are entirely distinct: They have no part in common. In between we find all the cases of partial overlap: things with parts in common and other parts not in common. (Sometimes one of the overlappers is part of the other, sometimes not.) The things are not entirely identical, not entirely distinct, but some of each. They are partially identical, partially distinct. There may be more overlap or less. Some cases are close to the distinctness end of the spectrum: Siamese twins who share only a finger are almost completely distinct, but not quite. Other cases are close to the identity end. For instance, any two of our cat-candidates overlap almost completely. They differ by only a few hairs. They are not quite completely identical, but they are almost completely identical and very far from completely distinct.

It's strange how philosophers have fixed their attention on one end of the spectrum and forgotten how we ordinarily think of identity and distinctness. You'd think the philosophers of common sense and ordinary language would have set us right long ago, but in fact it was Armstrong (1978, Vol. 2, pp. 37–8) who did the job. Overshadowed though it is by Armstrong's still more noteworthy accomplishments, this service still deserves our attention and gratitude.

Assume our cat-candidates are genuine cats. (Set aside, for now, the supervaluationist solution.) Then, strictly speaking, the cats are many. No two of them are completely identical. But any two of them are almost completely identical; their differences are negligible, as I said before. We have many cats, each one almost identical to all the rest.

Remember how we translate statements of number into the language of identity and quantification. "There is one cat on the mat" becomes "For some x, x is a cat on the mat, and every cat on the mat is identical to x." That's false, if we take "identical" to express the complete and strict identity that lies at the end of the spectrum. But the very extensive overlap of the cats does approximate to complete identity. So what's true is that for some x, x is a cat on the mat, and every cat on the mat is almost identical to x. In this way, the statement that there is one cat on the mat is almost true. The cats are many, but almost one. By a blameless approximation, we may say simply that there is one cat on the mat. Is that true?—Sometimes we'll insist on stricter standards, sometimes we'll be ambivalent, but for most contexts it's true enough. Thus the idea of partial and approximate identity affords another solution to the paradox of 1001 cats.

The added noun phrase has nothing to do with it. Because of their extensive overlap, the many are almost the same cat; they are almost the same lump of feline tissue; and so on for any other noun phrase that applies to them all. Further, the relation of almost-identity, closely akin to the complete identity that we call identity *simpliciter*, is not a relation of partial indiscernibility. Of course we can expect almost-identical things to be very similar in a great many ways: size, shape, location, weight, purring, behaviour, not to mention relational properties like location and ownership. But it is hard to think of any very salient respect in which almost-identical things are guaranteed to be entirely indiscernible. Finally, the relation of almost-identity, in other words extensive overlap, is not in general an equivalence relation. Many steps of almost-identity can take us from one thing to another thing that is entirely distinct from the first. We may hope that almost-identity, when restricted to the many cats as they actually are, will be an equivalence relation; but even that is not entirely

guaranteed. It depends on the extent to which the cats differ, and on the threshold for almost-identity (and both of these are matters that we will, very sensibly, leave undecided). What this solution has in common with Geach's is just that we count the cats by a relation other than strict, 'absolute' identity. Beyond that, the theories differ greatly.[9]

ONE SOLUTION TOO MANY?

We find ourselves with two solutions, and that is one more than we needed. Shall we now choose between the way of supervaluation and the way of partial identity? I think not. We might better combine them. We shall see how each can assist the other.

Here is how to combine them. In the first place, there are two kinds of intended interpretations of our language. Given many almost-identical cat-candidates, some will put every (good enough) candidate into the extension of "cat"; others will put exactly one. Context will favour one sort of interpretation or the other, though not every context will settle the matter. Sometimes, especially in our offhand and unphilosophical moments, context will favour the second, one-cat sort of interpretation; and then the supervaluation rule, with nothing to defeat it, will entitle us to say that there is only one cat. But sometimes, for instance when we have been explicitly attending to the many candidates and noting that they are equally catlike, context will favour the first, many-cat sort of interpretation. (If we start with one-cat interpretations, and we say things that the supervaluation rule would make hash of, not only is the rule suspended but also the many-cat interpretations come into play.) But even then, we still want some good sense in which there is just one cat (though we may want a way to say the opposite as well). That is what almost-identity offers.

This is one way that almost-identity helps a combined solution. It is still there even when we discuss the paradox of 1001 cats, and we explicitly choose to say that the many are all cats, and we thereby make the supervaluation solution go away.

Perhaps it helps in another way too. The supervaluation rule is more natural in some applications than in others. For instance it seems artificial to apply it to a case of unrelated homonyms. "You said you were going to the bank. Is that true? No worries, you bank at the ANZ, it's right down by the river, so what you said was true either way!"—I don't think such a response is utterly forbidden, but it's peculiar in a way that other applications of the supervaluation rule are not. The two interpretations of "bank" are so different that presumably you did make up your mind which one you meant. So the means for coping with semantic indecision are out of place. The supervaluation rule comes natural only when the alternative interpretations don't differ too much. If they are one-cat interpretations that differ only by picking almost-identical cats, that's one way for them not to differ much.

How, on the other hand, do supervaluations help the combined solution? Why not let almost-identity do the whole job?

For one thing, not every case of the problem of the many is like the paradox of 1001 cats. The almost-identity solution won't always work well.[10] We've touched on one atypical case already: if not a problem of the many, at least a problem of two. Fred's house taken as including the garage, and taken as not including the garage, have equal claim to be his house. The claim had better be good enough, else he has no house. So Fred has two houses. No! We've already seen how to solve this problem by the method of supervaluations. (If that seemed good to you, it shows that the difference between the interpretations was not yet enough to make the supervaluation rule artificial.) But although the two house-candidates overlap very substantially, having all but the garage in common, they do not overlap nearly as extensively as the cats do. Though they are closer to the identity end of the spectrum than the distinctness end, we cannot really say they're almost identical. So likewise we cannot say that the two houses are almost one.

For another thing, take a statement different from the statements of identity and number that have concerned us so far. Introduce a definite description: "The cat on the mat includes hair h_{17}." The obvious response to this statement, I suppose, is that it is gappy. It has no definite truth-value, or no definite super-truth-value, as the case may be. But how can we get that answer if we decide that all the cat-

candidates are cats, forsake supervaluations, and ask almost-identity to do the whole job? We might subject the definite description to Russellian translation:

(R1) There is something that is identical to all and only cats on the mat, and that includes h_{17}.

Or equivalently:

(R2) Something is identical to all and only cats on the mat, and every cat on the mat includes h_{17}.

Both these translations come out false, because nothing is strictly identical to all and only cats on the mat. That's not the answer we wanted. So we might relax "identical" to "almost identical." When we do, the translations are no longer equivalent: (R1)-relaxed is true, (R2)-relaxed is false. Maybe we're in a state of semantic indecision between (R1)-relaxed and (R2)-relaxed; if so, we could apply the supervaluation rule to get the desired gappiness. Or we might apply the supervaluation rule more directly. Different one-cat interpretations pick out different things as the cat, some that include h_{17} and some that don't. Under any particular one-cat interpretation the Russellian translations are again equivalent, and different one-cat interpretations give them different truth values; so the translations, and likewise the original sentence, suffer super-truth-value gaps. Or more simply, different one-cat interpretations differ in the referent of "the cat", some of these referents satisfy "includes h_{17}" and some don't, so again we get a super-truth-value gap. Whichever way we go, supervaluations give us the gappiness we want. It's hard to see how else to get it.

NOTES

1. See Lewis (1986a, pp. 210–20).

2. This is the solution advanced in Lowe (1982).

3. The dualism of things and their constituters is also meant to solve a modal problem: Even at one moment, the thing might have been made of different matter, so what might have been true of it differs from what might have

been true of its matter, so constitution cannot be identity. This problem too has a better solution. We should allow that what is true of a given thing at a given world is a vague and inconstant matter. Conflicting answers, equally correct, may be evoked by different ways of referring to the same thing, e.g., as cat or as cat-constituter. My counterpart theory affords this desirable inconstancy; many rival theories do also. See Lewis (1986a, pp. 248–63).

4. Provided that there exist the many precisifications for us to be undecided between. If you deny this, you will indeed have need of vague objects. See van Inwagen (1990, pp. 213–83).

5. I grant that the hypothesis of vague objects, for all its faults, can at least be made consistent. If there are vague objects, no doubt they sometimes stand in relations of "vague identity" to one another. We might think that when *a* and *b* are vaguely identical vague objects, the identity statement *a* = *b* suffers a truth-value gap; but in fact this conception of vague identity belongs to the theory of vagueness as semantic indecision. As Gareth Evans showed, it doesn't mix with the idea that vague identity is due to vagueness in nature. For if *a* and *b* are vaguely identical, they differ in respect of vague identity to *a*; but nothing, however peculiar it may be, differs in any way from itself; so the identity *a* = *b* is definitely false. See Evans (1978). (Evans' too-concise paper invites misunderstanding, but his own testimony confirms my interpretation. See Lewis 1988.) To get a consistent theory of vague objects, different from the bastard theory that is Evans's target, we must disconnect 'vague identity' from truth-value gaps in identity statements. Even if *a* = *b* is definitely false, *a* and *b* can still be 'vaguely identical' in the sense of sharing some but not all of their precisifications.

6. I do not think reference is entirely up to our choice. Some things are by their nature more eligible than others to be referents or objects of thought, and when we do nothing to settle the contest in favour of the less eligible, then the more eligible wins by default; see Lewis (1984). That's no help here: nature is gradual, no handy joint in nature picks out one of the *c*'s from all the rest.

7. Here I'm indebted to remarks of Saul Kripke many years ago. At his request, I note that what I have written here may not correspond exactly to the whole of what he said on that occasion.

8. Here I'm indebted to Andrew Strauss (personal communication, 1989).

9. There is another way we sometimes count by a rela-tion other than strict identity. You draw two diagonals in a square; you ask me how many triangles; I say there are four; you deride me for ignoring the four large triangles and counting only the small ones. But the joke is on you. For I was within my rights as a speaker of ordinary language, and you couldn't see it because you insisted on counting by strict identity. I meant that, for some *w, x, y, z,* (1) *w, x, y,* and *z* are triangles; (2) *w* and *x* are distinct, and . . . and so are *y* and *z* (six clauses); and (3) for any triangle *t,* either *t* and *w* are not distinct, or . . . or *t* and *z* are not distinct (four clauses). And by 'distinct' I meant non-overlap rather than non-identity, so what I said was true.

10. Here I'm indebted to Phillip Bricker (personal communication, 1990).

REFERENCES

Armstrong, D. M. 1978. *Universals and Scientific Realism,* 2 vols. (Cambridge University Press).

Evans, Gareth. 1978. "Can There be Vague Objects?," *Analysis* 38: 208. Reprinted in *Collected Papers* (Oxford University Press, 1985).

Geach, P. T. 1967. "Identity," *Review of Metaphysics* 21: 3–12. Reprinted in *Logic Matters* (Oxford: Blackwell, 1972), pp. 238–47.

——— 1980. *Reference and Generality,* 3rd ed. (Ithaca, NY: Cornell University Press).

Lewis, David. 1976. "Survival and Identity." In *The Identities of Persons,* ed. Amélie Rorty (Berkeley: University of California Press), pp. 17–40. Reprinted in Lewis, *Philosophical Papers,* vol. 1 (Oxford University Press, 1983), pp. 55–72.

——— 1984. "Putnam's Paradox," *Australasian Journal of Philosophy* 62: 221–36.

——— 1986a. *On the Plurality of Worlds* (Oxford: Blackwell).

——— 1988. "Vague Identity: Evans Misunderstood," *Analysis* 48: 128–30.

Lowe, E. J. 1982. "The Paradox of the 1,001 Cats," *Analysis* 42: 27–30.

Unger, Peter. 1980. "The Problem of the Many," *Midwest Studies in Philosophy* 5: 411–67.

van Fraassen, Bas C. 1966. "Singular Terms, Truth-Value Gaps, and Free Logic," *Journal of Philosophy* 63: 481–95.

van Inwagen, Peter. 1990. *Material Beings* (Ithaca, NY: Cornell University Press).

Of Identity and Diversity

~

JOHN LOCKE

John Locke (1632–1704) was a British philosopher known for his empiricism in epistemology and metaphysics and his social contract theory in political philosophy. In addition to his most important work, *An Essay Concerning Human Understanding,* his writings include *A Letter Concerning Toleration* and *Two Treatises of Government.*

CHAPTER XXVII • OF IDENTITY AND DIVERSITY

1. *Wherein Identity consists.* Another occasion the mind often takes of comparing is the very being of things, when, considering anything as existing at any determined time and place, we compare it with itself existing at another time, and thereon form the ideas of *identity* and *diversity.* When we see anything to be in any place in any instant of time, we are sure (be it what it will) that it is that very thing, and not another which at that same time exists in another place, how like and undistinguishable soever it may be in all other respects; and in this consists *identity,* when the ideas it is attributed to vary not at all from what they were that moment wherein we consider their former existence, and to which we compare the present. For we never finding, nor conceiving it possible, that two things of the same kind should exist in the same place at the same time, we rightly conclude that whatever exists anywhere at any time excludes all of the same kind, and is there itself alone. When therefore we demand whether anything be the same or no, it refers always to something that existed such a time in such a place, which it was certain, at that instant, was the same with itself, and no other. From whence it follows that one thing cannot have two beginnings of existence, nor two things one beginning; it being impossible for two things of the same kind to be or

exist in the same instant, in the very same place; or one and the same thing in different places. That, therefore, that had one beginning, is the same thing; and that which had a different beginning in time and place from that, is not the same, but diverse. That which has made the difficulty about this relation has been the little care and attention used in having precise notions of the things to which it is attributed.

2. *Identity of Substances.* We have the ideas but of three sorts of substances: (1) God. (2) Finite intelligences. (3) Bodies. First, God is without beginning, eternal, unalterable, and everywhere, and therefore concerning his identity there can be no doubt. Secondly, finite spirits having had each its determinate time and place of beginning to exist, the relation to that time and place will always determine to each of them its identity, as long as it exists. Thirdly, the same will hold of every particle of matter, to which no addition or subtraction of matter being made, it is the same. For, though these three sorts of substances, as we term them, do not exclude one another out of the same place, yet we cannot conceive but that they must necessarily each of them exclude any of the same kind out of the same place; or else the notions and names of identity and diversity would be in vain, and there could be no such distinctions of substances, or anything else one from another. *Identity of Modes.* All other things being but modes or relations ultimately terminated in substances, the identity and

From John Locke, *An Essay Concerning Human Understanding.*

diversity of each particular existence of them too will be by the same way determined; only as to things whose existence is in succession, such as are the actions of finite beings, v.g. *motion* and *thought,* both which consist in a continued train of succession, concerning their diversity there can be no question; because, each perishing the moment it begins, they cannot exist in different times, or in different places, as permanent beings can at different times exist in distant places; and therefore no motion or thought, considered as at different times, can be the same, each part thereof having a different beginning of existence.

3. *Principium Individuationis.* From what has been said, it is easy to discover what is so much inquired after, the *principium individuationis;* and that, it is plain, is existence itself; which determines a being of any sort to a particular time and place, incommunicable to two beings of the same kind. This, though it seems easier to conceive in simple substances or modes, yet, when reflected on, is not more difficult in compounded ones, if care be taken to what it is applied: v.g. let us suppose an atom, i.e. a continued body under one immutable superficies, existing in a determined time and place; it is evident that, considered in any instant of its existence, it is in that instant the same with itself. For, being at that instant what it is, and nothing else, it is the same, and so must continue as long as its existence is continued; for so long it will be the same, and no other. In like manner, if two or more atoms be joined together into the same mass, every one of those atoms will be the same, by the foregoing rule; and whilst they exist united together, the mass, consisting of the same atoms, must be the same mass, or the same body, let the parts be never so differently jumbled. But if one of these atoms be taken away, or one new one added, it is no longer the same mass or the same body. In the state of living creatures, their identity depends not on a mass of the same particles, but on something else. For in them the variation of great parcels of matter alters not the identity: an oak growing from a plant to a great tree, and then lopped, is still the same oak; and a colt grown up to a horse, sometimes fat, sometimes lean, is all the while the same horse: though, in both these cases, there may be a manifest change of the

parts, so that truly they are not either of them the same masses of matter, though they be truly one of them the same oak, and the other the same horse. The reason whereof is that in these two cases—a mass of matter and a living body—identity is not applied to the same thing.

4. *Identity of Vegetables.* We must therefore consider wherein an oak differs from a mass of matter, and that seems to me to be in this, that the one is only the cohesion of particles of matter any how united, the other such a disposition of them as constitutes the parts of an oak, and such an organization of those parts as is fit to receive and distribute nourishment, so as to continue and frame the wood, bark, and leaves, &c., of an oak, in which consists the vegetable life. That being then one plant which has such an organization of parts in one coherent body, partaking of one common life, it continues to be the same plant as long as it partakes of the same life, though that life be communicated to new particles of matter vitally united to the living plant, in a like continued organization conformable to that sort of plants. For this organization, being at any one instant in any one collection of matter, is in that particular concrete distinguished from all other, and is that individual life; which existing constantly from that moment both forwards and backwards, in the same continuity of insensibly succeeding parts united to the living body of the plant, it has that identity which makes the same plant, and all the parts of it, parts of the same plant, during all the time that they exist united in that continued organization, which is fit to convey that common life to all the parts so united.

5. *Identity of Animals.* The case is not so much different in *brutes* but that anyone may hence see what makes an animal and continues it the same. Something we have like this in machines, and may serve to illustrate it. For example, what is a watch? It is plain it is nothing but a fit organization or construction of parts to a certain end, which, when a sufficient force is added to it, it is capable to attain. If we would suppose this machine one continued body, all whose organized parts were repaired, increased, or diminished by a constant addition or separation of insensible parts, with one common life, we should have something very much like the body of an animal;

with this difference, that in an animal the fitness of the organization, and the motion wherein life consists, begin together, the motion coming from within; but in machines the force, coming sensibly from without, is often away when the organ is in order, and well fitted to receive it.

6. *Identity of Man.* This also shows wherein the identity of the same *man* consists: viz. in nothing but a participation of the same continued life, by constantly fleeting particles of matter, in succession vitally united to the same organized body. He that shall place the identity of man in anything else, but, like that of other animals, in one fitly organized body, taken in any one instant, and from thence continued, under one organization of life, in several successively fleeting particles of matter united to it, will find it hard to make an embryo, one of years, mad and sober, the same man, by any supposition, that will not make it possible for Seth, Ismael, Socrates, Pilate, St. Austin, and Cæsar Borgia to be the same man. For if the identity of *soul alone* makes the same *man,* and there be nothing in the nature of matter why the same individual spirit may not be united to different bodies, it will be possible that those men, living in distant ages, and of different tempers, may have been the same man; which way of speaking must be from a very strange use of the word *man,* applied to an idea out of which body and shape are excluded. And that way of speaking would agree yet worse with the notions of those philosophers who allow of transmigration, and are of opinion that the souls of men may, for their miscarriages, be detruded into the bodies of beasts, as fit habitations, with organs suited to the satisfaction of their brutal inclinations. But yet I think nobody, could he be sure that the soul of Heliogabalus were in one of his hogs, would yet say that hog were a *man* or *Heliogabalus.*

7. *Identity suited to the Idea.* It is not therefore unity of substance that comprehends all sorts of identity, or will determine it in every case; but to conceive and judge of it aright, we must consider what idea the word it is applied to stands for; it being one thing to be the same *substance,* another the same *man,* and a third the same *person,* if *person, man,* and *substance* are three names standing for three different ideas; for such as is the idea belonging to that name, such must

be the identity; which, if it had been a little more carefully attended to, would possibly have prevented a great deal of that confusion which often occurs about this matter, with no small seeming difficulties, especially concerning *personal* identity, which therefore we shall in the next place a little consider.

8. *Same man.* An animal is a living organized body; and consequently the same animal, as we have observed, is the same continued *life* communicated to different particles of matter, as they happen successively to be united to that organized living body. And whatever is talked of other definitions, ingenuous observation puts it past doubt that the idea in our minds, of which the sound 'man' in our mouths is the sign, is nothing else but of an animal of such a certain form. Since I think I may be confident that, whoever should see a creature of his own shape or make, though it had no more reason all its life than a cat or a parrot, would call him still a man; or whoever should hear a cat or a parrot discourse, reason, and philosophize, would call or think it nothing but a cat or a parrot; and say the one was a dull irrational man, and the other a very intelligent rational parrot. For I presume it is not the idea of a thinking or rational being alone that makes the idea of a man in most people's sense, but of a body, so and so shaped, joined to it; and if that be the idea of a man, the same successive body not shifted all at once must, as well as the same immaterial spirit, go to the making of the same man.

9. *Personal Identity.* This being premised, to find wherein personal identity consists, we must consider what *person* stands for; which, I think, is a thinking intelligent being, that has reason and reflection, and can consider itself as itself, the same thinking thing, in different times and places; which it does only by that consciousness which is inseparable from thinking, and, as it seems to me, essential to it; it being impossible for anyone to perceive without perceiving that he does perceive. When we see, hear, smell, taste, feel, meditate, or will anything, we know that we do so. Thus it is always as to our present sensations and perceptions; and by this everyone is to himself that which he calls *self;* it not being considered, in this case, whether the same self be continued in the same or divers substances. For, since consciousness always accompanies thinking, and it is that that

makes everyone to be what he calls self, and thereby distinguishes himself from all other thinking things, in this alone consists personal identity, i.e. the sameness of a rational being; and as far as this consciousness can be extended backwards to any past action or thought, so far reaches the identity of that person; it is the same self now it was then; and it is by the same self with this present one that now reflects on it, that that action was done.

10. *Consciousness makes personal Identity.* But it is further inquired whether it be the same identical substance. This few would think they had reason to doubt of, if these perceptions, with their consciousness, always remained present in the mind, whereby the same thinking thing would be always consciously present, and, as would be thought, evidently the same to itself. But that which seems to make the difficulty is this, that this consciousness being interrupted always by forgetfulness, there being no moment of our lives wherein we have the whole train of all our past actions before our eyes in one view, but even the best memories losing the sight of one part whilst they are viewing another; and we sometimes, and that the greatest part of our lives, not reflecting on our past selves, being intent on our present thoughts, and in sound sleep having no thoughts at all, or at least none with that consciousness which remarks our waking thoughts; I say, in all these cases, our consciousness being interrupted, and we losing the sight of our past selves, doubts are raised whether we are the same thinking thing, i.e. the same substance or no. Which, however reasonable or unreasonable, concerns not *personal* identity at all. The question being what makes the same person; and not whether it be the same identical substance, which always thinks in the same person, which, in this case, matters not at all; different substances, by the same consciousness (where they do partake in it) being united into one person, as well as different bodies by the same life are united into one animal, whose identity is preserved in that change of substances by the unity of one continued life. For, it being the same consciousness that makes a man be himself to himself, personal identity depends on that only, whether it be annexed only to one individual substance, or can be continued in a succession of several substances. For as far as

any intelligent being *can* repeat the idea of any past action with the same consciousness it had of it at first, and with the same consciousness it has of any present action, so far it is the same personal self. For it is by the consciousness it has of its present thoughts and actions, that it is *self to itself* now, and so will be the same self, as far as the same consciousness can extend to actions past or to come; and would be by distance of time, or change of substance, no more two persons, than a man be two men by wearing other clothes today than he did yesterday, with a long or a short sleep between; the same consciousness uniting those distant actions into the same person, whatever substances contributed to their production.

11. *Personal Identity in Change of Substances.* That this is so, we have some kind of evidence in our very bodies, all whose particles, whilst vitally united to this same thinking conscious self, so that *we feel* when they are touched, and are affected by, and conscious of good or harm that happens to them, are a part of ourselves, i.e. of our thinking conscious self. Thus, the limbs of his body are to everyone a part of himself; he sympathizes and is concerned for them. Cut off a hand, and thereby separate it from that consciousness he had of its heat, cold, and other affections, and it is then no longer a part of that which is himself, any more than the remotest part of matter. Thus, we see the substance whereof personal self consisted at one time may be varied at another, without the change of personal identity; there being no question about the same person, though the limbs which but now were a part of it be cut off.

12. *Whether in the Change of thinking Substances.* But the question is whether, if the same substance which thinks be changed, it can be the same person; or, remaining the same, it can be different persons?

And to this I answer: first, this can be no question at all to those who place thought in a purely material animal constitution, void of an immaterial substance. For, whether their supposition be true or no, it is plain they conceive personal identity preserved in something else than identity of substance, as animal identity is preserved in identity of life, and not of substance. And therefore those who place thinking in an immaterial substance only, before they can come to deal with these men, must show why personal identity cannot be preserved in the change of immaterial substances, or variety of particular immaterial substances, as well as animal identity is preserved in the change of material substances, or variety of particular bodies; unless they will say, it is one immaterial spirit that makes the same life in brutes, as it is one immaterial spirit that makes the same person in men; which the Cartesians at least will not admit, for fear of making brutes thinking things too.

13. But next, as to the first part of the question, whether, if the same thinking substance (supposing immaterial substances only to think) be changed, it can be the same person, I answer, that cannot be resolved but by those who know what kind of substances they are that do think; and whether the consciousness of past actions can be transferred from one thinking substance to another. I grant, were the same consciousness the same individual action, it could not; but, it being a present representation of a past action, why it may not be possible that that may be represented to the mind to have been which really never was, will remain to be shown. And therefore how far the consciousness of past actions is annexed to any individual agent, so that another cannot possibly have it, will be hard for us to determine, till we know what kind of action it is that cannot be done without a reflex act of perception accompanying it, and how performed by thinking substances, who cannot think without being conscious of it. But that which we call the same consciousness, not being the same individual act, why one intellectual substance may not have represented to it, as done by itself, what *it* never did, and was perhaps done by some other agent—why, I say, such a representation may not possibly be without reality of matter of fact, as well as several representations in dreams are, which yet whilst dreaming we take for true, will be difficult to conclude from the nature of things.

14. As to the second part of the question, whether, the same immaterial substance remaining, there may be two distinct persons; which question seems to me to be built on this, whether the same immaterial being, being conscious of the actions of its past duration, may be wholly stripped of all the consciousness of its past existence, and lose it beyond the power of ever retrieving again, and so as it were beginning a

new account from a new period, have a consciousness that cannot reach beyond this new state. All those who hold pre-existence are evidently of this mind, since they allow the soul to have no remaining consciousness of what it did in that pre-existent state, either wholly separate from body, or informing any other body; and, if they should not, it is plain experience would be against them. So that personal identity, reaching no further than consciousness reaches, a pre-existent spirit, not having continued so many ages in a state of silence, must needs make different persons. Let anyone reflect upon himself, and conclude that he has in himself an immaterial spirit, which is that which thinks in him, and, in the constant change of his body keeps him the same: and is that which he calls himself; let him also suppose it to be the same soul that was in Nestor or Thersites at the siege of Troy (for souls being, as far as we know anything of them, in their nature indifferent to any parcel of matter, the supposition has no apparent absurdity in it), which it may have been, as well as it is now the soul of any other man; but he now having no consciousness of any of the actions either of Nestor or Thersites, does or can he conceive himself the same person with either of them? Can he be concerned in either of their actions? attribute them to himself, or think them his own, more than the actions of any other man that ever existed? So that this consciousness, not reaching to any of the actions of either of those men, he is no more one *self* with either of them than if the soul or immaterial spirit that now informs him had been created, and began to exist, when it began to inform his present body; though it were never so true that the same *spirit* that informed Nestor's or Thersites's body were numerically the same that now informs his. But let him once find himself conscious of any of the actions of Nestor, he then finds himself the same person with Nestor.

15. And thus may we be able, without any difficulty, to conceive the same person at the resurrection, though in a body not exactly in make or parts the same which he had here, the same consciousness going along with the soul that inhabits it. But yet the soul alone, in the change of bodies, would scarce to anyone but to him that makes the soul the man, be enough to make the same man. For should the soul of

a prince, carrying with it the consciousness of the prince's past life, enter and inform the body of a cobbler, as soon as deserted by his own soul, everyone sees he would be the same *person* with the prince, accountable only for the prince's actions; but who would say it was the same *man?* The body too goes to the making the man, and would, I guess, to everybody determine the man in this case, wherein the soul, with all its princely thoughts about it, would not make another man; but he would be the same cobbler to everyone besides himself. I know that, in the ordinary way of speaking, 'the same person' and 'the same man' stand for one and the same thing. And indeed everyone will always have a liberty to speak as he pleases, and to apply what articulate sounds to what ideas he thinks fit, and change them as often as he pleases. But yet, when we will inquire what makes the same *spirit, man,* or *person,* we must fix the ideas of spirit, man, or person in our minds; and having resolved with ourselves what we mean by them, it will not be hard to determine, in either of them, or the like, when it is the same, and when not.

18. *Object of Reward and Punishment.* In this personal identity is founded all the right and justice of reward and punishment; happiness and misery being that for which everyone is concerned for *himself,* and not mattering what becomes of any substance, not joined to, or affected with that consciousness.

19. To punish Socrates waking for what sleeping Socrates thought, and waking Socrates was never conscious of, would be no more of right than to punish one twin for what his brother-twin did, whereof he knew nothing, because their outsides were so like, that they could not be distinguished; for such twins have been seen.

20. But yet possibly it will still be objected, suppose I wholly lose the memory of some parts of my life, beyond a possibility of retrieving them, so that perhaps I shall never be conscious of them again; yet am I not the same person that did those actions, had those thoughts that I once was conscious of, though I have now forgot them? To which I answer that we must here take notice what the word *I* is applied to; which, in this case, is the man only. And the same man being presumed to be the same person, *I* is easily here supposed to stand also for the same person.

But if it be possible for the same man to have distinct incommunicable consciousness at different times, it is past doubt the same man would at different times make different persons; which, we see, is the sense of mankind in the solemnest declaration of their opinions, human laws not punishing the mad man for the sober man's actions, nor the sober man for what the mad man did; thereby making them two persons, which is somewhat explained by our way of speaking in English when we say such an one is *not himself,* or is *beside himself;* in which phrases it is insinuated, as if those who now, or at least first used them, thought that self was changed; the self-same person was no longer in that man.

22. But is not a man drunk and sober the same person? Why else is he punished for the fact he commits when drunk, though he be never afterwards conscious of it? Just as much the same person as a man that walks, and does other things in his sleep, is the same person, and is answerable for any mischief he shall do in it. Human laws punish both, with a justice suitable to their way of knowledge, because, in these cases, they cannot distinguish certainly what is real, what counterfeit; and so the ignorance in drunkenness or sleep is not admitted as a plea. For, though punishment be annexed to personality, and personality to consciousness, and the drunkard perhaps be not conscious of what he did, yet human judicatures justly punish him, because the fact is proved against him, but want of consciousness cannot be proved for him. But in the Great Day, wherein the secrets of all hearts shall be laid open, it may be reasonable to think, no one shall be made to answer for what he knows nothing of, but shall receive his doom, his conscience accusing or excusing him.

23. *Consciousness alone makes Self.* Nothing but consciousness can unite remote existences into the same person; the identity of substance will not do it, for whatever substance there is, however framed, without consciousness there is no person; and a carcass may be a person, as well as any sort of substance be so, without consciousness.

Could we suppose two distinct incommunicable consciousnesses acting the same body, the one constantly by day, the other by night; and, on the other side, the same consciousness acting by intervals two distinct bodies: I ask, in the first case, whether the day- and the night-man would not be two as distinct persons as Socrates and Plato? And whether, in the second case, there would not be one person in two distinct bodies, as much as one man is the same in two distinct clothings? Nor is it at all material to say that this same, and this distinct, consciousness, in the cases above mentioned, is owing to the same and distinct immaterial substances, bringing it with them to those bodies; which, whether true or no, alters not the case, since it is evident the personal identity would equally be determined by the consciousness, whether that consciousness were annexed to some individual immaterial substance or no. For, granting that the thinking substance in man must be necessarily supposed immaterial, it is evident that immaterial thinking thing may sometimes part with its past consciousness, and be restored to it again, as appears in the forgetfulness men often have of their past actions; and the mind many times recovers the memory of a past consciousness, which it had lost for twenty years together. Make these intervals of memory and forgetfulness to take their turns regularly by day and night, and you have two persons with the same immaterial spirit, as much as in the former instance two persons with the same body. So that self is not determined by identity or diversity of substance, which it cannot be sure of, but only by identity of consciousness.

25. I agree, the more probable opinion is that this consciousness is annexed to, and the affection of, one individual immaterial substance.

But let men, according to their diverse hypotheses, resolve of that as they please. This every intelligent being, sensible of happiness or misery, must grant: that there is something that is *himself,* that he is concerned for, and would have happy; that this self has existed in a continued duration more than one instant, and therefore it is possible may exist, as it has done, months and years to come, without any certain bounds to be set to its duration; and may be the same self, by the same consciousness continued on for the future. And thus, by this consciousness he finds himself to be the same self which did such or such an action some years since, by which he comes to be happy or miserable now. In all which account of self, the same numerical *substance* is not considered as

making the same self; but the same continued *consciousness,* in which several substances may have been united, and again separated from it, which, whilst they continued in a vital union with that wherein this consciousness then resided, made a part of that same self. Thus any part of our bodies, vitally united to that which is conscious in us, makes a part of ourselves; but upon separation from the vital union by which that consciousness is communicated, that which a moment since was part of ourselves is now no more so than a part of another man's self is a part of me; and it is not impossible but in a little time may become a real part of another person. And so we have the same numerical substance become a part of two different persons, and the same person preserved under the change of various substances. Could we suppose any spirit wholly stripped of all its memory or consciousness of past actions, as we find our minds always are of a great part of ours, and sometimes of them all, the union or separation of such a spiritual substance would make no variation of personal identity, any more than that of any particle of matter does. Any substance vitally united to the present thinking being is a part of that very same self which now is; anything united to it by a consciousness of former actions makes also a part of the same self, which is the same both then and now.

26. *Person a Forensic Term. Person,* as I take it, is the name for this self. Wherever a man finds what he calls himself, there, I think, another may say is the same person. It is a forensic term, appropriating actions and their merit, and so belongs only to intelligent agents, capable of a law, and happiness, and misery. This personality extends itself beyond present existence to what is past, only by consciousness, whereby it becomes concerned and accountable, owns and imputes to itself past actions, just upon the same ground and for the same reason as it does the present. All which is founded in a concern for happiness, the unavoidable concomitant of consciousness; that which is conscious of pleasure and pain desiring that that self that is conscious should be happy. And therefore whatever past actions it cannot reconcile or appropriate to that present self by consciousness, it can be no more concerned in than if they had never been done; and to receive pleasure or pain, i.e. reward

or punishment, on the account of any such action, is all one as to be made happy or miserable in its first being, without any demerit at all. For, supposing a man punished now for what he had done in another life, whereof he could be made to have no consciousness at all, what difference is there between that punishment and being created miserable? And therefore, conformable to this, the apostle tells us that, at the great day, when everyone shall *receive according to his doings, the secrets of all hearts shall be laid open.* The sentence shall be justified by the consciousness all persons shall have that *they themselves,* in what bodies soever they appear, or what substances soever that consciousness adheres to, are the *same* that committed those actions, and deserve that punishment for them.

Personal Identity and Memory

~

SYDNEY SHOEMAKER

Sydney Shoemaker is Susan Linn Sage Professor of Philosophy at Cornell University. He has written on various topics in metaphysics, epistemology, and philosophy of mind. His books include *Self-Knowledge and Self-Identity, Identity, Cause and Mind: Philosophical Essays,* and *The First-Person Perspective, and Other Essays.*

PERSONAL IDENTITY AND MEMORY

Persons, unlike other things, make statements about their own pasts, and can be said to know these statements to be true. This fact would be of little importance, as far as the problem of personal identity is concerned, if these statements were always grounded in the ways in which people's statements about the past histories of things other than themselves are grounded. But while our statements about our own pasts are sometimes based on diaries, photographs, fingerprints, and the like, normally they are not. Normally they are based on our own memories, and the way in which one's memory provides one with knowledge concerning one's own past is quite unlike the way in which it provides one with knowledge concerning the past history of another person or thing. It is largely for this reason, I believe, that in addition to whatever problems there are about the notion of identity in general there has always been felt to be a special problem about *personal* identity. It is, for example, the way in which one knows one's own past that has led some philosophers to hold that personal identity is the only *real* identity that we have any knowledge of, the identity we ascribe to ships and stones being only, as Thomas Reid expressed it, "something which, for convenience of speech, we call identity."[1] What I wish to do in this paper is to consider how the concept of memory and the concept of personal identity are related. In particular, I want to consider the view that memory provides a criterion of personal identity, or, as H. P. Grice expressed it some years ago, that "the self is a logical construction and is to be defined in terms of memory."[2]

1. Clearly the concepts of memory and personal identity are not logically independent. As has often been pointed out, it is a logical truth that, if a person remembers[3] a past event, then he, the very person who remembers, must have been a witness to that event. It is partly this logical truth that has led some

Reprinted from *The Journal of Philosophy* (1959) by permission of the publisher and the author.

philosophers to hold that personal identity can be wholly or partially defined in terms of memory. And this view may seem to be supported by the fact that we sometimes use, as grounds for saying that a person was present when an event occurred, the fact that he apparently remembers the event, i.e., is able to give a correct and detailed account of it and does not appear to have anything other than his own memory on the basis of which he could know of it.

But it does not seem, off-hand, that these considerations force us to accept this view. For it might be held that while there is a logical relationship between the concepts of memory and personal identity, this is because the former is definable or analyzable in terms of the latter, and not *vice versa*. The assertion that a person A remembers an event X can plausibly be analyzed as meaning (1) that A now has knowledge of X, (2) that A's knowledge is not grounded inductively or based on the testimony of other persons, and (3) that A witnessed X when it occurred. To know with certainty that A remembers X, it might be held, we would have to know all three of these conditions were satisfied, and we could know that (3) is satisfied only if we had a criterion of personal identity by which we could judge that A, the person who now has knowledge of X, is identical with one of the persons who witnessed X. Obviously our criterion of identity here could not be the fact that A remembers X, for we could know this fact only if we had already established that such an identity holds.

The view just described, I think, must be the view of any philosopher who thinks that the identity of a human body is the sole criterion of personal identity. And this view seems compatible with the fact that sometimes, when we do not have independent grounds for saying that a person witnessed an event, we accept his being able to describe the event as evidence that he was a witness to it. For it might be held that in such cases we are reasoning inductively. We have, it might be said, found out empirically (using bodily identity as our criterion of personal identity) that when someone claims to remember a past event it is generally the case that such an event did occur and that he was a witness to it. On this view it is an inductively established correlation, and not any logical relationship between memory and personal iden-

tity, that justifies us in using the memory claims of persons as evidence for identity judgments about them.

2. On the view just described the criteria of personal identity are simply the criteria of bodily identity (i.e., I suppose, spatiotemporal continuity). But it is often argued that bodily identity is not even a necessary condition of personal identity, let alone a sufficient condition, and the same arguments have been alleged to show that memory is a criterion of personal identity. We must now consider some of these arguments.

Considerable attention has been paid, in discussions of personal identity, to so-called "puzzle cases," ostensible cases of what I will call "bodily transfer." It has been argued that if certain imaginable events were to occur we would be obliged to say, or at least would have good grounds for saying, that someone had changed bodies, i.e., had come to have a body that is numerically different from the body that had been his in the past. Locke, it may be recalled, thought it conceivable that the soul of a prince might "enter and inform" the body of a cobbler, "carrying with it the consciousness of the prince's past life," and said that if this happened the cobbler would become "the same person with the prince, accountable only for the prince's actions."[4] And it is certainly imaginable that a cobbler, living somewhere in the Bronx, might awake some morning and show great surprise at the appearance of his body, that he might claim to find his surroundings, and the persons who claim to know him, totally unfamiliar, that he might exhibit a detailed knowledge of the past life of Prince Philip, reporting the Prince's actions as his own, and that he might, in his subsequent behavior, exhibit all of the mannerisms, interests, and personality and character traits that Prince Philip had displayed in the past. Let us imagine this happening immediately after the death of the man now known as Prince Philip.

What we say about such cases is clearly relevant to the question whether memory is a criterion of personal identity. If the above case inclines us to say that bodily transfer is possible, this is largely because the cobbler is imagined to be able to describe in detail, thereby giving evidence of being able to remember, the past life of Prince Philip. That this so much inclines us to admit the possibility of bodily transfer, whether or not we do admit it, seems to be grounds for saying that bodily identity is not our sole criterion of personal identity, and that memory, and perhaps also sameness of personality, has a place among our criteria.

Many philosophers have held that personal identity and bodily identity are logically quite distinct. This view is implied by the Cartesian conception of the mind (or soul) as a substance distinct from the body, and it also seems to be implied by the view of Locke, that it is "same consciousness" that "makes" the same person, and by the views of those philosophers, such as Hume and (at one time) Russell, who have held that the persistence of a person through time consists simply in the occurrence of a series of mental events ("perceptions," "experiences") that are bound together by a non-physical relationship of "co-personality" (perhaps the relation "being the memory of"). In short, it is implied by any view according to which the identity of a person is essentially the identity of a mind, and according to which a mind (whether regarded as a Cartesian "spiritual substance" or a Humeian "bundle" of mental events) is something logically distinct from a human body. To hold such a view is to admit the possibility of bodily transfer, and it is partly the prevalence of such views that accounts for the attention that philosophers have paid to "puzzle cases" such as the one I have described. But it is hardly plausible to suppose that those who have held such views have come to hold them because they have been persuaded by such cases that bodily transfer is possible. For even if it is admitted that such cases would be cases of bodily transfer, it by no means follows that personal identity and bodily identity are logically independent. It does not follow that bodily transfer could become the rule rather than the exception, and it certainly does not follow that a person could exist without having a body at all. Indeed, the view that bodily transfer is possible is quite compatible with a completely behavioristic view concerning the nature of mind and a completely materialistic conception of the nature of a person. After all, in the case I have imagined it is bodily and behavioral facts (the behavior of the cobbler and the past behavior of Prince Philip) that incline one to say that a bodily transfer has occurred.

So while such cases provide some grounds for thinking that memory is among the criteria of personal identity, we must look further if we wish to account for the plausibility of the view that the criteria of personal identity are "mental" or "psychological," one version of which being the view that memory is, to the exclusion of bodily identity, the sole criterion of personal identity. But we need not look much further; all that we have to do, in fact, is to describe such cases in the first person rather than in the third person. For it is when one considers the way in which one knows, or seems to know, one's *own* identity that it becomes plausible to regard personal identity as something logically independent of bodily identity. One does not have to observe, or (it seems) know anything about, the present state of one's body in order to make past tense statements about oneself on the basis of memory. But such statements imply the persistence of a person through time, and it is natural to regard them as expressing knowledge of one's own identity, knowledge that a "present self" (that to which the word "I" refers) is identical with a "past self" (the person who did such and such in the past). One is inclined to suppose that the real criteria of personal identity must be criteria that one uses in making statements about one's own identity. And since it appears that one can make such statements, and know them to be true, without first knowing the facts that would justify an assertion about the identity of one's body, the conclusion would seem to be that bodily identity cannot be a criterion of personal identity. The real criteria of personal identity, it seems, cannot be bodily or behavioral criteria of any sort, but must be criteria that one can know to be satisfied in one's own case without knowing anything about one's body. For similar reasons one is inclined to reject the view that the notion of memory is definable or analyzable in terms of the notion of personal identity. For when one says that one remembers a past event it is surely not the case that one has first established that one is the same as someone who witnessed the event, and then concluded, on the basis of this fact and others, that one remembers the event. That one remembers an event seems, from one's own point of view, a brute, unanalyzable fact. But if there is a logical relationship between the concepts of memory and personal identity, and if the former is not definable or analyzable in terms of the latter, what seems to follow is that the latter is somehow definable in terms of the former, and that memory provides the criterion of personal identity.

3. Whether or not memory is *a* criterion of personal identity, it is not *the* criterion. As I will argue later, it cannot be the sole criterion that we use in making identity statements about other persons. And while it is true that one does not use bodily identity as a criterion of personal identity when one says on the basis of memory that one did something in the past, this is not because one uses something else as a criterion, but is rather because one uses no criterion at all.

Suppose that I make the statement "I broke the front window yesterday." If this statement is based on a criterion of personal identity it must be the case that I know that someone broke the front window yesterday, and that I have found out, by use of my criterion, that that person was myself. And my statement must be based, at least in part, on what I know about that person as he was at the time at which he broke the window. Let us suppose that my own memory is my only source of knowledge concerning the past event in question, for that is the sort of case that we are interested in. Then my statement must be a conclusion from what I remember about the person who broke the window yesterday, and perhaps from other facts as well (facts about my "present self"), and my criterion of identity must be what justifies me in drawing this conclusion from these facts. Presumably, if I had remembered different facts about that person I would have drawn a different conclusion, namely that he was not myself. It should be noted that, if all of this were so, then, strictly speaking, it would be incorrect for me to say "*I remember* that I broke the front window yesterday." For if my statement "I broke the front window yesterday" expresses a conclusion *from* what I remember it is not itself a memory statement, i.e., is not simply a description or report of what I actually remember. We must distinguish statements that are "based" on memory simply in the sense of being memory statements from those that are "based" on memory in the sense of being

conclusions drawn from remembered facts.[5] If one thinks that one cannot make a first person past tense statement except on the basis of a criterion of identity, one must accept the consequence that no such statement can be a memory statement. In the case at hand, if my statement is grounded on a criterion of identity then what I actually remember cannot be that *I* broke the window yesterday, but must be that someone of such and such a description broke the window, the assertion that it was myself being a conclusion from what I remember about the person.

Now it is a logical truth, as I have already said, that if a person remembers a past event then he, that same person, must have been a witness to the event, i.e., must have been present when it occurred and in a position to know of its occurrence. So if I remember someone breaking the front window yesterday it follows that I was present at the time. And since, if I remember this, I am entitled to say "I remember someone breaking the front window yesterday," I am also entitled to say "I was present yesterday when the front window was broken." But this last statement is a first person past tense statement, so let us see whether it can be grounded on any criterion of personal identity. Clearly it cannot be. It is not, as it would have to be if based on a criterion of identity, a conclusion from what I know about someone who existed in the past. What I know about the past, in the case we are considering, is what I remember, but this statement is not a conclusion from *what* I remember at all; it is a conclusion from the fact *that I remember something*, not from any of the facts that I remember.

But if I can know that I was present when an action was done without using a criterion of identity, why can't I know in this way that I did the action? Is it that I must employ a criterion in order to know *which* of the persons present was myself? In that case, presumably, I would not need to employ my criterion if I remembered that only one person was present, for that person would obviously have to be myself. But the trouble is that he would have to be myself *no matter what* I remembered about him. i.e., even if the remembered facts were such that I would have to conclude, in accordance with my criterion, that he was *not* myself. If I had a criterion of identity that I could use in such cases, it seems to me, it would be possible for me to remember someone doing a certain action, discover by the use of my criterion that he was not myself, and then find, by consulting my memory of the event, that he was the only person present when the action was done. And clearly this is not possible.

It is sometimes suggested that one is able to identify a remembered "past self" as one's own self by the fact that one is able to remember the private thoughts, feelings, sensations, etc., of that self. There does seem to be a sense in which my own thoughts and feelings are the only ones that I can remember. Certainly they are the only ones that I can remember *having*. But it is a mistake to conclude from this that memory is used as a first person criterion of personal identity. The sentence "I remember having a headache yesterday" does not differ in meaning from the sentence "I remember my having a headache yesterday." But if what I remember when I remember a past headache is *my having* a headache, or that *I* had a headache, my statement "I had a headache" is a memory statement, not a conclusion from what I remember, and cannot be grounded on any criterion of identity. If, however, what I remember is that someone had a headache, or that a headache occurred, it is clear that the remembered facts provide no grounds for the conclusion that *I* had a headache. Nor can we say, as some have said, that the relation "being the memory of" is the relation of "co-personality" between mental events, and that I know that a past sensation was mine because I have established that one of my present mental states is a memory of it and therefore co-personal with it. For, contrary to what Hume and others seem to have supposed, in the sort of case we are considering it makes no sense to speak of comparing one's present memory with a past sensation and finding that the one is the memory of (on Hume's theory, that it resembles) the other. One could make such a comparison only if one knew of the past sensation on some grounds other than one's memory of it, and our concern here is with cases in which one's memory is one's only source of knowledge concerning the past events in question. In such a case, comparing a past sensation with one's memory of it could only be comparing one's memory with itself—and comparing something with itself (if that means anything) is certainly not a way of discovering whether two events are related in a certain way. One

can raise the question whether two events are related in a particular way (in *any* given way) only if one knows of the occurrence of both events. And if one knows of one of the events on the basis of memory, one must, in inquiring whether it is related in some way to the other event, be relying on one's memory of it, and clearly cannot be raising any question as to whether one does remember it (or whether one of one's present mental states is a memory of it). Indeed, if one's knowledge of a past sensation is memory knowledge it is misleading to say that one knows that one remembers a particular past sensation. It makes sense to speak of knowing that one remembers a particular event (knowing of an event that one remembers it) only where it would also make sense to speak of knowing of that event that one does not remember it (as is the case if one's knowledge of an event is based on something other than, or in addition to, one's memory). When I say that I have a headache I am not mentioning some particular headache and reporting, as a fact that I know about it, that it is experienced by me; likewise, when I say that I remember a headache I am not, in most cases, saying of some particular headache that I remember it. Normally I can identify a past sensation only as one that I remember (or, as I should prefer to say, one that I remember having). And when this is so there cannot arise any question concerning the ownership of the sensation, and there is no room for the employment of criteria of ownership or criteria of personal identity.

4. If, as I have argued, one does not use criteria of identity in making statements about one's own past on the basis of memory, the criteria of personal identity must be third person criteria. And if memory were the sole criterion of personal identity it would have to be the sole criterion that we use in making identity statements about persons other than ourselves. It is easily shown, however, that if we did not have some criterion other than memory that we could use in making statements of personal identity we could not use what others remember, or claim to remember, as evidence of any sort (criteriological or otherwise) for identity statements about them.

To begin with, if the word "remember" is to have any meaning it must be possible to establish whether someone is using it correctly. If some of the utterances that persons make are to count as memory claims, and therefore as evidence of what they remember or seem to remember, it must be possible to establish what a person means by the words he utters. But establishing what a person means by a term, or whether he is using it correctly, involves observing his use of it in various circumstances and over a period of time. This, of course, involves being able to know that it was one and the same person who uttered a given word on two different occasions, and to be able to know this one must have a criterion of identity. What could this criterion be if not bodily identity? It could not be any "psychological" criterion (such as memory or sameness of personality), for the use of such criteria (if criteria they are) involves accepting what a person says as indicating what his psychological state is (e.g., that he seems to remember doing a certain thing), and one could not do this if one were trying to establish what he means by, or whether he understands, the expressions he is using. In *some* circumstances, at least, bodily identity must be a criterion of personal identity.

Moreover, memory claims can be mistaken, and there must, accordingly, be such a thing as checking on the truth of a memory claim, i.e., establishing whether a person remembers something without taking his word for it that he does. And this, if he claims to have done a certain thing in the past, would involve establishing whether he, the person who claims this, is the same as someone who did do such an action in the past. In establishing this we could not use memory as our criterion of personal identity, and it is difficult to see what we could use if not bodily identity. And if, in such cases, we could not use bodily identity (or something other than memory) as a criterion of identity, it would not be possible to establish whether someone understands the use of the term "remember," and that term could not so much as have a meaning. It is, I believe, a logical or conceptual truth, not a contingent truth, that memory beliefs, and therefore honest memory claims, are generally true.[6] If someone frequently prefaced past tense statements with the words "I remember that," and these statements generally turned out to be false, this would be grounds for saying that he did not understand the use

of these words. We would not think that we had succeeded in teaching a child the use of the word "remember" if he commonly said "I remember doing such and such" when he had not done the thing in question. Again, suppose that we had discovered a new people whose language we did not know, and that someone had proposed a way of translating their language that involved regarding a certain class of statements (or utterances) as memory statements. Clearly, if all or most of those statements turned out to be false if translated as proposed, there could be no reason for accepting that way of translating them as correct, and there would be every reason for rejecting it as mistaken. But if it is a conceptual truth that memory claims are generally true, establishing that someone understands the use of the term "remember" must surely involve establishing whether his memory claims (or what appear to be his memory claims) are true or false. And to be able to do this we must have something other than memory that we can use as a criterion of personal identity.

5. The arguments of the last section may seem to give support to the view that bodily identity is, to the exclusion of memory, the sole criterion of personal identity. But this view seems to me to be mistaken. Bodily identity is certainly *a* criterion of personal identity, and if it were not, I have argued, nothing else could be so much as evidence of personal identity. But I do not think that it can be the sole criterion, and I think that there is an important sense in which memory, though certainly not the sole criterion, is one of the criteria.

Let us consider one consequence of the view that bodily identity is the sole criterion of personal identity. As I said in section 1, if this view were correct it would have to be the case that we are reasoning inductively when we use the fact that someone claims to remember something as grounds for a statement about his past. It would be a contingent fact, one that we have discovered empirically, that most memory claims are true, or that people generally remember what they claim to remember. This would, indeed, be nothing other than the fact that the memory claims that issue from the mouth of a certain body generally correspond to events in the past history of that same body. But I have argued that it is a logical fact, not a contingent fact, that memory claims are generally true. If this is so, inferences of the form "He claims to remember doing X, so he probably did X" are not simply inductive inferences, for they are warranted by a generalization that is logically rather than empirically true.[7]

Now let us return briefly to the case of the cobbler and the prince. If one is inclined to use the memory claims of the cobbler as grounds that he is (has become) the prince, the inference one is inclined to make is not of the form "He claims to remember doing X, so he probably did do X," but is of a more complex sort. Roughly, it is of the form "He claims to remember doing X, Y, and Z under such and such circumstances and at such and such times and places, and X, Y, and Z were done by someone under precisely those circumstances and at those times and places, so there is reason to believe that he is the person who did those actions." But it seems to me that if inferences of the first sort are not inductive, neither are inferences of the second sort. And I think that to say that inferences of the second sort are legitimate (as they certainly are, at least under certain circumstances), and that they are noninductive, is tantamount to saying that memory is a criterion of personal identity.

It should be noted that if such inferences were merely inductive, and if bodily identity were the sole criterion of personal identity, it would be patently absurd to make such an inference in a case in which the body of the person making a memory claim is known not to be identical with the body of the person who did the action that he claims to remember. The absurdity would be that of asserting something to be true, or probably true, on the basis of indirect evidence, when one has direct and conclusive evidence that it is false. But in the imaginary case I have described, the claim that the cobbler is (has become) the prince does not, I think, strike us as having *this* sort of absurdity. I have not attempted to say whether, if the events I have described were to occur, it would be correct to say that the cobbler had become the prince, and I do not know how this question could be settled. But this in itself seems to me significant. The fact that such cases so much as incline us to admit the

possibility of bodily transfer, or leave us in doubt as to what to say, seems to me prima facie evidence that memory is a criterion of personal identity. It is not as if our doubts were due to ignorance of empirical facts that, if known, would settle the issue. Doubts of that sort are easily removed, for we need only add further details to the description of the case. But if, knowing all of the relevant facts, we are in doubt as to how we should answer a question of identity, this is surely an indication that the case is such that the question is not unambiguously decidable by our criterion of identity. This, in turn, suggests that there is a conflict of criteria. In the case at hand, our doubts are evidence that one criterion of personal identity, namely bodily identity, is in conflict with another, namely memory.

But now I must try to meet an objection. It might be argued that while the inference "He claims to remember doing X, so he probably did X" is not inductive, we are nevertheless reasoning inductively when we take what a person says as evidence for a statement about his past history. For what justifies us in taking the sounds that a person utters as expressing a memory claim? As was argued earlier, if a question arises as to whether a person understands the use of the word "remember," or is using it to mean what we mean by it, the question can be settled only by establishing, independently of what he says, whether the things that he claims (or apparently claims) to remember are things he actually did, endured, or witnessed in the past. If in a number of cases it turns out that the actions that he apparently claims to remember having done are actions that he actually did, this is evidence that he does understand the use of such words as "remember," and that his apparent memory claims are really memory claims and can generally be relied upon. Must it not be much the same sort of considerations, i.e., our having observed certain correlations between the sounds that people utter and what they have done in the past, that justifies our general reliance on people's memory claims, or rather our acceptance of people's utterances as memory claims? If so, it would seem that our use of people's memory claims as evidence for statements about their own pasts, including identity statements about them, is, in the end, inductively based. Though it is a logical fact that memory claims are generally true, what does this come to except the fact that if there did not exist correlations of the sort mentioned none of the utterances of persons would be memory claims? But the existence of such correlations is a contingent fact, and it is on this contingent fact, it might be argued, that inferences of the sort "He claims to remember doing X, so he probably did X" are ultimately based. As for the case of the cobbler and the prince, it might be argued that if what I said in section 4 is correct then the facts that I have imagined would be evidence, not that the cobbler had become the prince, but rather that his utterances were not memory claims at all, and that he did not understand the use of the term "remember."

To take the last point first, suppose that we were in doubt as to whether the cobbler really understood the words that he was using. Could we not satisfy ourselves that he did by observing his subsequent behavior, and by establishing (using bodily identity as our criterion of personal identity) that when he claims to have done an action that occurred *after* the alleged bodily transfer it is generally the case that he did do that action? When we are trying to establish whether a person understands the words he utters we must, I have argued, use bodily identity as a criterion of identity, but it does not follow from this that there cannot, in exceptional cases, be personal identity in the absence of bodily identity.

As for the rest of the objection, it is certainly true that unless there existed certain correlations between the sounds people utter and events in the past histories of those who utter them it would be impossible to have knowledge of the past that is based on the memory claims of other persons. These correlations are those that must exist if any of the utterances that people make are to be memory claims. But it cannot be the case, I believe, that we regard certain of the utterances of other persons as memory claims *because* we have established, inductively, that such correlations hold. To be sure, from the fact that a person utters the sounds that I would utter if making a certain memory claim it does not necessarily follow that he speaks the language that I speak and means by those sounds what I would mean by them. Under exceptional circumstances I might raise a question as to whether what sounds to me like a memory claim is really one,

and such a question could be settled empirically, by observing the behavior of the person who made the claim. But except when we have definite grounds for supposing the contrary, we must, I believe, regard other persons as speaking a language, our own if the words sound familiar, without having any general empirical justification for doing so. Let us consider whether it would be possible for me to question whether there is anyone at all (other than myself) who speaks the language that I speak, and then to discover empirically, by observing correlations between the sounds people utter and their present and past behavior, that those around me do speak the language that I speak and that certain of their utterances are memory claims and can generally be relied upon. In carrying on such an investigation I would, of course, have to rely on my own memory. But ones's memory can be mistaken. It is essential to the very notion of memory that there be a distinction between remembering something and merely seeming to remember something. And for there to be such a distinction there must be such a thing as checking up on one's own memory and finding that one does, or does not, remember what one seems to remember. As Wittgenstein pointed out,[8] there are and must be circumstances in which we would accept other sorts of evidence concerning the past as more authoritative than our own memories. But an important—I think essential—check on one's own memory is the testimony of other persons. And this sort of check would not be available to me if I could not even regard the utterances of other persons as testimony until I had completed my investigation and established the required set of correlations. Unless there were some persons whose utterances I would be willing to accept as memory claims without having conducted such an investigation I would in effect be admitting no distinction between remembering and merely seeming to remember, and I could therefore make no distinction between finding the correlations and merely seeming to have found them.

It is, I should like to say, part of the concept of a person that persons are capable of making memory statements about their own pasts. Since it is a conceptual truth that memory statements are generally true, it is a conceptual truth that persons are capable of knowing their own pasts in a special way, a way that does not involve the use of criteria of personal identity, and it is a conceptual truth (or a logical fact) that the memory claims that a person makes can be used by others as grounds for statements about the past history of that person. This, I think, is the kernel of truth that is embodied in the view that personal identity can be defined in terms of memory.

NOTES

1. Thomas Reid, *Essays on the Intellectual Powers of Man,* ed. by A. D. Woozley (London: Macmillan, 1941), p. 206.

2. H. P. Grice, "Personal Identity," *Mind,* Vol. L (October, 1941), p. 340.

3. I use "remember" in its most common sense, in which "I remember that P" entails "P," and "I remember X occurring" entails "X occurred."

4. John Locke, *An Essay Concerning Human Understanding,* Vol. I, ed. by Fraser (Oxford: The Clarendon Press, 1894), p. 457.

5. Roughly speaking, a statement is a memory statement if (supposing it to be an honest assertion) it cannot be false unless the speaker has misremembered. A conclusion from what is remembered, on the other hand, can be false without there being a mistaken memory. E.g., I mistakenly identify the man I saw as John when in fact it was his identical twin.

6. The word "generally" is vague, but I doubt if this can be made much more precise. This statement should perhaps be qualified so as to apply only to memory beliefs concerning the *recent* past.

7. We can, of course, have inductive grounds for believing that one person's memory claims are exceptionally reliable and that another's are exceptionally unreliable.

8. Ludwig Wittgenstein, *Philosophical Investigations* (Oxford: Basil Blackwell, 1953), Pt. I, paras. 56 and 265.

Personal Identity

DEREK PARFIT

Derek Parfit, on the philosophy faculty of New York University, is a senior research fellow of All Souls College, Oxford, and a fellow of the British Academy and the American Academy of Arts and Sciences. He specializes in ethics, metaphysics, and the philosophy of mind. He is the author of *Reasons and Persons.*

We can, I think, describe cases in which, though we know the answer to every other question, we have no idea how to answer a question about personal identity. These cases are not covered by the criteria of personal identity that we actually use.

Do they present a problem?

It might be thought that they do not, because they could never occur. I suspect that some of them could. (Some, for instance, might become scientifically possible.) But I shall claim that even if they did they would present no problem.

My targets are two beliefs: one about the nature of personal identity, the other about its importance.

The first is that in these cases the question about identity must have an answer.

No one thinks this about, say, nations or machines. Our criteria for the identity of these do not cover certain cases. No one thinks that in these cases the questions "Is it the same nation?" or "Is it the same machine?" must have answers.

Some people believe that in this respect they are different. They agree that our criteria of personal

Reprinted from *The Philosophical Review, 80* (1971).

identity do not cover certain cases, but they believe that the nature of their own identity through time is, somehow, such as to guarantee that in these cases questions about their identity must have answers. This belief might be expressed as follows: "Whatever happens between now and any future time, either I shall still exist, or I shall not. Any future experience will either be *my* experience, or it will not."

This first belief—in the special nature of personal identity—has, I think, certain effects. It makes people assume that the principle of self-interest is more rationally compelling than any moral principle. And it makes them more depressed by the thought of aging and of death.

I cannot see how to disprove this first belief. I shall describe a problem case. But this can only make it seem implausible.

Another approach might be this. We might suggest that one cause of the belief is the projection of our emotions. When we imagine ourselves in a problem case, we do feel that the question "Would it be me?" must have an answer. But what we take to be a bafflement about a further fact may be only the bafflement of our concern.

I shall not pursue this suggestion here. But one cause of our concern is the belief which is my second target. This is that unless the question about identity has an answer, we cannot answer certain important questions (questions about such matters as survival, memory, and responsibility).

Against this second belief my claim will be this. Certain important questions do presuppose a question about personal identity. But they can be freed of this presupposition. And when they are, the question about identity has no importance.

I

We can start by considering the much-discussed case of the man who, like an amoeba, divides.[1]

Wiggins has recently dramatized this case.[2] He first referred to the operation imagined by Shoemaker.[3] We suppose that my brain is transplanted into someone else's (brainless) body, and that the resulting person has my character and apparent memories of my life. Most of us would agree, after thought, that the resulting person is me. I shall here assume such agreement.[4]

Wiggins then imagined his own operation. My brain is divided, and each half is housed in a new body. Both resulting people have my character and apparent memories of my life.

What happens to me? There seem only three possibilities: (1) I do not survive; (2) I survive as one of the two people; (3) I survive as both.

The trouble with (1) is this. We agreed that I could survive if my brain were successfully transplanted. And people have in fact survived with half their brains destroyed. It seems to follow that I could survive if half my brain were successfully transplanted and the other half were destroyed. But if this is so, how could I *not* survive if the other half were also successfully transplanted? How could a double success be a failure?

We can move to the second description. Perhaps one success is the maximum score. Perhaps I shall be one of the resulting people.

The trouble here is that in Wiggins' case each half of my brain is exactly similar, and so, to start with, is each resulting person. So how can I survive as only one of the two people? What can make me one of them rather than the other?

It seems clear that both of these descriptions—that I do not survive, and that I survive as one of the people—are highly implausible. Those who have accepted them must have assumed that they were the only possible descriptions.

What about our third description: that I survive as both people?

It might be said, "If 'survive' implies identity, this description makes no sense—you cannot be two people. If it does not, the description is irrelevant to a problem about identity."

I shall later deny the second of these remarks. But there are ways of denying the first. We might say, "What we have called 'the two resulting people' are not two people. They are one person. I do survive Wiggins' operation. Its effect is to give me two bodies and a divided mind."

It would shorten my argument if this were absurd. But I do not think it is. It is worth showing why.

We can, I suggest, imagine a divided mind. We can imagine a man having two simultaneous experiences, in having each of which he is unaware of having the other.

We may not even need to imagine this. Certain actual cases, to which Wiggins referred, seem to be best described in these terms. These involve the cutting of the bridge between the hemispheres of the brain. The aim was to cure epilepsy. But the result appears to be, in the surgeon's words, the creation of "two separate spheres of consciousness,"[5] each of which controls one half of the patient's body. What is experienced in each is, presumably, experienced by the patient.

There are certain complications in these actual cases. So let us imagine a simpler case.

Suppose that the bridge between my hemispheres is brought under my voluntary control. This would enable me to disconnect my hemispheres as easily as if I were blinking. By doing this I would divide my mind. And we can suppose that when my mind is divided I can, in each half, bring about reunion.

This ability would have obvious uses. To give an example: I am near the end of a maths exam, and see two ways of tackling the last problem. I decide to divide my mind, to work, with each half, at one of two calculations, and then to reunite my mind and write a fair copy of the best result.

What shall I experience?

When I disconnect my hemispheres, my consciousness divides into two streams. But this division is not something that I experience. Each of my two streams of consciousness seems to have been straightforwardly continuous with my one stream of consciousness up to the moment of division. The only changes in each stream are the disappearance of half my visual field and the loss of sensation in, and control over, half my body.

Consider my experiences in what we can call my "right-handed" stream. I remember that I assigned my right hand to the longer calculation. This I now begin. In working at this calculation I can see, from the movements of my left hand, that I am also working at the other. But I am not aware of working at the other. So I might, in my right-handed stream, wonder how, in my left-handed stream, I am getting on.

My work is now over. I am about to reunite my mind. What should I, in each stream, expect? Simply that I shall suddenly seem to remember just having thought out two calculations, in thinking out each of which I was not aware of thinking out the other. This,

I submit, we can imagine. And if my mind was divided, these memories are correct.

In describing this episode, I assumed that there were two series of thoughts, and that they were both mine. If my two hands visibly wrote out two calculations, and if I claimed to remember two corresponding series of thoughts, this is surely what we should want to say.

If it is, then a person's mental history need not be like a canal, with only one channel. It could be like a river, with islands, and with separate streams.

To apply this to Wiggins' operation: we mentioned the view that it gives me two bodies and a divided mind. We cannot now call this absurd. But it is, I think, unsatisfactory.

There were two features of the case of the exam that made us want to say that only one person was involved. The mind was soon reunited, and there was only one body. If a mind was permanently divided and its halves developed in different ways, the point of speaking of one person would start to disappear. Wiggins' case, where there are also two bodies, seems to be over the borderline. After I have had his operation, the two "products" each have all the attributes of a person. They could live at opposite ends of the earth. (If they later met, they might even fail to recognize each other.) It would become intolerable to deny that they were different people.

Suppose we admit that they are different people. Could we still claim that I survived as both, using "survive" to imply identity?

We could. For we might suggest that two people could compose a third. We might say, "I do survive Wiggins' operation as two people. They can be different people, and yet be me, in just the way in which the Pope's three crowns are one crown."[6]

This is a possible way of giving sense to the claim that I survive as two different people, using "survive" to imply identity. But it keeps the language of identity only by changing the concept of a person. And there are obvious objections to this change.[7]

The alternative, for which I shall argue, is to give up the language of identity. We can suggest that I survive as two different people without implying that I am these people.

When I first mentioned this alternative, I mentioned this objection: "If your new way of talking does not imply identity, it cannot solve our problem. For that is about identity. The problem is that all the possible answers to the question about identity are highly implausible."

We can now answer this objection.

We can start by reminding ourselves that this is an objection only if we have one or both of the beliefs which I mentioned at the start of this paper.

The first was the belief that to any question about personal identity, in any describable case, there must be a true answer. For those with this belief, Wiggins' case is doubly perplexing. If all the possible answers are implausible, it is hard to decide which of them is true, and hard even to keep the belief that one of them must be true. If we give up this belief, as I think we should, these problems disappear. We shall then regard the case as like many others in which, for quite unpuzzling reasons, there *is* no answer to a question about identity. (Consider "Was England the same nation after 1066?")

Wiggins' case makes the first belief implausible. It also makes it trivial. For it undermines the second belief. This was the belief that important questions turn upon the question about identity. (It is worth pointing out that those who have only this second belief do not think that there must *be* an answer to this question, but rather that we must decide upon an answer.)

Against this second belief my claim is this. Certain questions do presuppose a question about personal identity. And because these questions *are* important, Wiggins' case does present a problem. But we cannot solve this problem by answering the question about identity. We can solve this problem only by taking these important questions and prizing them apart from the question about identity. After we have done this, the question about identity (though we might for the sake of neatness decide it) has no further interest.

Because there are several questions which presuppose identity, this claim will take some time to fill out.

We can first return to the question of survival. This is a special case, for survival does not so much presuppose the retaining of identity as seem equivalent to it. It is thus the general relation which we need to prize apart from identity. We can then consider particular relations, such as those involved in memory and intention.

"Will I survive?" seems, I said, equivalent to "Will there be some person alive who is the same person as me?"

If we treat these questions as equivalent, then the least unsatisfactory description of Wiggins' case is, I think, that I survive with two bodies and a divided mind.

Several writers have chosen to say that I am neither of the resulting people. Given our equivalence, this implies that I do not survive, and hence, presumably, that even if Wiggins' operation is not literally death, I ought, since I will not survive it, to regard it *as* death. But this seemed absurd.

It is worth repeating why. An emotion or attitude can be criticized for resting on a false belief, or for being inconsistent. A man who regarded Wiggins' operation as death must, I suggest, be open to one of these criticisms.

He might believe that his relation to each of the resulting people fails to contain some element which is contained in survival. But how can this be true? We agreed that he *would* survive if he stood in this very same relation to only *one* of the resulting people. So it cannot be the nature of this relation which makes it fail, in Wiggins' case, to be survival. It can only be its duplication.

Suppose that our man accepts this, but still regards division as death. His reaction would now seem wildly inconsistent. He would be like a man who, when told of a drug that could double his years of life, regarded the taking of this drug as death. The only difference in the case of division is that the extra years are to run concurrently. This is an interesting difference. But it cannot mean that there are *no* years to run.

I have argued this for those who think that there must, in Wiggins' case, be a true answer to the question about identity. For them, we might add, "Perhaps the original person does lose his identity. But there may be other ways to do this than to die. One other way might be to multiply. To regard these as the same is to confuse nought with two."

For those who think that the question of identity is up for decision, it would be clearly absurd to regard

Wiggins' operation as death. These people would have to think, "We could have chosen to say that I should be one of the resulting people. If we had, I should not have regarded it as death. But since we have chosen to say that I am neither person, I *do*." This is hard even to understand.[8]

My first conclusion, then, is this. The relation of the original person to each of the resulting people contains all that interests us—all that matters—in any ordinary case of survival. This is why we need a sense in which one person can survive as two.[9]

One of my aims in the rest of this paper will be to suggest such a sense. But we can first make some general remarks.

II

Identity is a one-one relation. Wiggins' case serves to show that what matters in survival need not be one-one.

Wiggins' case is of course unlikely to occur. The relations which matter are, in fact, one-one. It is because they are that we can imply the holding of these relations by using the language of identity.

This use of language is convenient. But it can lead us astray. We may assume that what matters *is* identity and, hence, has the properties of identity.

In the case of the property of being one-one, this mistake is not serious. For what matters is in fact one-one. But in the case of another property, the mistake *is* serious. Identity is all-or-nothing. Most of the relations which matter in survival are, in fact, relations of degree. If we ignore this, we shall be led into quite ill-grounded attitudes and beliefs.

The claim that I have just made—that most of what matters are relations of degree—I have yet to support. Wiggins' case shows only that these relations need not be one-one. The merit of the case is not that it shows this in particular, but that it makes the first break between what matters and identity. The belief that identity *is* what matters is hard to overcome. This is shown in most discussions of the problem cases which actually occur: cases, say, of amnesia or of brain damage. Once Wiggins' case has made one breach in this belief, the rest should be easier to remove.[10]

To turn to a recent debate: most of the relations which matter can be provisionally referred to under the heading "psychological continuity" (which includes causal continuity). My claim is thus that we use the language of personal identity in order to imply such continuity. This is close to the view that psychological continuity provides a criterion of identity.

Williams has attacked this view with the following argument. Identity is a one-one relation. So any criterion of identity must appeal to a relation which is logically one-one. Psychological continuity is not logically one-one. So it cannot provide a criterion.[11]

Some writers have replied that it is enough if the relation appealed to is always in fact one-one.[12]

I suggest a slightly different reply. Psychological continuity is a ground for speaking of identity when it is one-one.

If psychological continuity took a one-many or branching form, we should need, I have argued, to abandon the language of identity. So this possibility would not count against this view.

We can make a stronger claim. This possibility would count in its favor.

The view might be defended as follows. Judgments of personal identity have great importance. What gives them their importance is the fact that they imply psychological continuity. This is why, whenever there is such continuity, we ought, if we can, to imply it by making a judgment of identity.

If psychological continuity took a branching form, no coherent set of judgments of identity could correspond to, and thus be used to imply, the branching form of this relation. But what we ought to do, in such a case, is take the importance which would attach to a judgment of identity and attach this importance directly to each limb of the branching relation. So this case helps to show that judgments of personal identity do derive their importance from the fact that they imply psychological continuity. It helps to show that when we can, usefully, speak of identity, this relation is our ground.

This argument appeals to a principle which Williams put forward.[13] The principle is that an important judgment should be asserted and denied only on importantly different grounds.

Williams applied this principle to a case in which one man is psychologically continuous with the dead Guy Fawkes, and a case in which two men are. His argument was this. If we treat psychological continuity as a sufficient ground for speaking of identity, we shall say that the one man is Guy Fawkes. But we could not say that the two men are, although we should have the same ground. This disobeys the principle. The remedy is to deny that the one man is Guy Fawkes, to insist that sameness of the body is necessary for identity.

Williams' principle can yield a different answer. Suppose we regard psychological continuity as more important than sameness of the body.[14] And suppose that the one man really is psychologically (and causally) continuous with Guy Fawkes. If he is, it would disobey the principle to deny that he is Guy Fawkes, for we have the same important ground as in a normal case of identity. In the case of the two men, we again have the same important ground. So we ought to take the importance from the judgment of identity and attach it directly to this ground. We ought to say, as in Wiggins' case, that each limb of the branching relation is as good as survival. This obeys the principle.

To sum up these remarks: even if psychological continuity is neither logically, nor always in fact, one-one, it can provide a criterion of identity. For this can appeal to the relation of *non-branching* psychological continuity, which is logically one-one.[15]

The criterion might be sketched as follows. "*X* and *Y* are the same person if they are psychologically continuous and there is no person who is contemporary with either and psychologically continuous with the other." We should need to explain what we mean by "psychologically continuous" and say how much continuity the criterion requires. We should then, I think, have described a sufficient condition for speaking of identity.[16]

We need to say something more. If we admit that psychological continuity might not be one-one, we need to say what we ought to do if it were not one-one. Otherwise our account would be open to the objections that it is incomplete and arbitrary.[17]

I have suggested that if psychological continuity took a branching form, we ought to speak in a new way, regarding what we describe as having the same

significance as identity. This answers these objections.[18]

We can now return to our discussion. We have three remaining aims. One is to suggest a sense of "survive" which does not imply identity. Another is to show that most of what matters in survival are relations of degree. A third is to show that none of these relations needs to be described in a way that presupposes identity.

We can take these aims in the reverse order.

III

The most important particular relation is that involved in memory. This is because it is so easy to believe that its description must refer to identity.[19] This belief about memory is an important cause of the view that personal identity has a special nature. But it has been well discussed by Shoemaker[20] and by Wiggins.[21] So we can be brief.

It may be a logical truth that we can only remember our own experiences. But we can frame a new concept for which this is not a logical truth. Let us call this "*q*-memory."

To sketch a definition[22] I am *q*-remembering an experience if (1) I have a belief about a past experience which seems in itself like a memory belief, (2) someone did have such an experience, and (3) my belief is dependent upon this experience in the same way (whatever that is) in which a memory of an experience is dependent upon it.

According to (1) *q*-memories seem like memories. So I *q*-remember *having* experiences.

This may seem to make *q*-memory presuppose identity. One might say, "My apparent memory of *having* an experience is an apparent memory of *my* having an experience. So how could I *q*-remember my having other people's experiences?"

This objection rests on a mistake. When I seem to remember an experience, I do indeed seem to remember *having* it.[23] But it cannot be a part of what I seem to remember about this experience that I, the person who now seems to remember it, am the person who had this experience.[24] That I am is something that I automatically assume. (My apparent memories sometimes come to me simply as the belief that *I* had a certain experience.) But it is something that I am justified in assuming only because I do not in fact have q-memories of other people's experiences.

Suppose that I did start to have such q-memories. If I did, I should cease to assume that my apparent memories must be about my own experiences. I should come to assess an apparent memory by asking two questions: (1) Does it tell me about a past experience? (2) If so, whose?

Moreover (and this is a crucial point) my apparent memories would now come to me *as* q-memories. Consider those of my apparent memories which do come to me simply as beliefs about my past: for example, "I did that." If I knew that I could q-remember other people's experiences, these beliefs would come to me in a more guarded form: for example, "Someone—probably I—did that." I might have to work out who it was.

I have suggested that the concept of q-memory is coherent. Wiggins' case provides an illustration. The resulting people, in his case, both have apparent memories of living the life of the original person. If they agree that they are not this person, they will have to regard these as only q-memories. And when they are asked a question like "Have you heard this music before?" they might have to answer "I am sure that I q-remember hearing it. But I am not sure whether I remember hearing it. I am not sure whether it was I who heard it, or the original person."

We can next point out that on our definition every memory is also a q-memory. Memories are, simply, q-memories of one's own experiences. Since this is so, we could afford now to drop the concept of memory and use in its place the wider concept q-memory. If we did, we should describe the relation between an experience and what we now call a "memory" of this experience in a way which does not presuppose that they are had by the same person.[25]

This way of describing this relation has certain merits. It vindicates the "memory criterion" of personal identity against the charge of circularity.[26] And it might, I think, help with the problem of other minds.

But we must move on. We can next take the relation between an intention and a later action. It may be a logical truth that we can intend to perform only our own actions. But intentions can be redescribed as q-intentions. And one person could q-intend to perform another person's actions.

Wiggins' case again provides the illustration. We are supposing that neither of the resulting people is the original person. If so, we shall have to agree that the original person can, before the operation, q-intend to perform their actions. He might, for example, q-intend, as one of them, to continue his present career, and, as the other, to try something new.[27] (I say "q-intend *as* one of them" because the phrase "q-intend *that* one of them" would not convey the directness of the relation which is involved. If I intend that someone else should do something, I cannot get him to do it simply by forming this intention. But if I am the original person, and he is one of the resulting people, I can.)

The phrase "q-intend *as* one of them" reminds us that we need a sense in which one person can survive as two. But we can first point out that the concepts of q-memory and q-intention give us our model for the others that we need: thus, a man who can q-remember could q-recognize, and be a q-witness of, what he has never seen; and a man who can q-intend could have q-ambitions, make q-promises, and be q-responsible for.

To put this claim in general terms: many different relations are included within, or are a consequence of, psychological continuity. We describe these relations in ways which presuppose the continued existence of one person. But we could describe them in new ways which do not.

This suggests a bolder claim. It might be possible to think of experiences in a wholly "impersonal" way. I shall not develop this claim here. What I shall try to describe is a way of thinking of our own identity through time which is more flexible, and less misleading, than the way in which we now think.

This way of thinking will allow for a sense in which one person can survive as two. A more important feature is that it treats survival as a matter of degree.

IV

We must first show the need for this second feature. I shall use two imaginary examples.

The first is the converse of Wiggins' case: fusion. Just as division serves to show that what matters in survival need not be one-one, so fusion serves to show that it can be a question of degree.

Physically, fusion is easy to describe. Two people come together. While they are unconscious, their two bodies grow into one. One person then wakes up.

The psychology of fusion is more complex. One detail we have already dealt with in the case of the exam. When my mind was reunited, I remembered just having thought out two calculations. The one person who results from a fusion can, similarly, q-remember living the lives of the two original people. None of their q-memories need be lost.

But some things must be lost. For any two people who fuse together will have different characteristics, different desires, and different intentions. How can these be combined?

We might suggest the following. Some of these will be compatible. These can coexist in the one resulting person. Some will be incompatible. These, if of equal strength, can cancel out, and if of different strengths, the stronger can be made weaker. And all these effects might be predictable.

To give examples—first, of compatibility: I like Palladio and intend to visit Venice. I am about to fuse with a person who likes Giotto and intends to visit Padua. I can know that the one person we shall become will have both tastes and both intentions. Second, of incompatibility: I hate red hair, and always vote Labour. The other person loves red hair, and always votes Conservative. I can know that the one person we shall become will be indifferent to red hair, and a floating voter.

If we were about to undergo a fusion of this kind, would we regard it as death?

Some of us might. This is less absurd than regarding division as death. For after my division the two resulting people will be in every way like me, while after my fusion the one resulting person will not be wholly similar. This makes it easier to say, when faced with fusion, "I shall not survive," thus continuing to regard survival as a matter of all-or-nothing.

This reaction is less absurd. But here are two analogies which tell against it.

First, fusion would involve the changing of some of our characteristics and some of our desires. But only the very self-satisfied would think of this as

death. Many people welcome treatments with these effects.

Second, someone who is about to fuse can have, beforehand, just as much "intentional control" over the actions of the resulting individual as someone who is about to marry can have, beforehand, over the actions of the resulting couple. And the choice of a partner for fusion can be just as well considered as the choice of a marriage partner. The two original people can make sure (perhaps by "trial fusion") that they do have compatible characters, desires, and intentions.

I have suggested that fusion, while not clearly survival, is not clearly failure to survive, and hence that what matters in survival can have degrees.

To reinforce this claim we can now turn to a second example. This is provided by certain imaginary beings. These beings are just like ourselves except that they reproduce by a process of natural division.

We can illustrate the histories of these imagined beings with the aid of a diagram. The lines on the diagram represent the spatiotemporal paths which would be traced out by the bodies of these beings. We can call each single line (like the double line) a "branch"; and we can call the whole structure a "tree." And let us suppose that each "branch" corresponds to what is thought of as the life of one individual. These individuals are referred to as "A," "B + 1," and so forth.

Now, each single division is an instance of Wiggins' case. So A's relation to both B + 1 and B + 2 is just as good as survival. But what of A's relation to B + 30?

I said earlier that what matters in survival could be provisionally referred to as "psychological continuity." I must now distinguish this relation from another, which I shall call "psychological connectedness."

Let us say that the relation between a q-memory and the experience q-remembered is a "direct" relation. Another "direct" relation is that which holds between a q-intention and the q-intended action. A third is that which holds between different expressions of some lasting q-characteristic.

"Psychological connectedness," as I define it, requires the holding of these direct psychological relations. "Connectedness" is not transitive, since

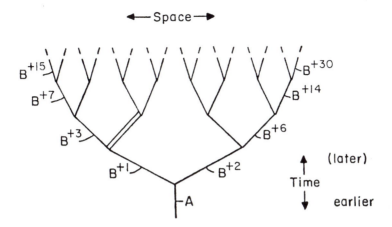

these relations are not transitive. Thus, if X q-remembers most of Y's life, and Y q-remembers most of Z's life, it does not follow that X q-remembers most of Z's life. And if X carries out the q-intentions of Y, and Y carries out the q-intentions of Z, it does not follow that X carries out the q-intentions of Z.

"Psychological continuity," in contrast, only requires overlapping chains of direct psychological relations. So "continuity" *is* transitive.

To return to our diagram. A *is* psychologically continuous with $B + 30$. There are between the two continuous chains of overlapping relations. Thus, A has q-intentional control over $B + 2$, $B + 2$ has q-intentional control over $B + 6$, and so on up to $B + 30$. Or $B + 30$ can q-remember the life of $B + 14$, $B + 14$ can q-remember the life of $B + 6$, and so on back to A.[28]

A, however, need *not* be psychologically connected to $B + 30$. Connectedness requires direct relations. And if these beings are like us, A cannot stand in such relations to every individual in his indefinitely long "tree." Q-memories will weaken with the passage of time, and then fade away. Q-ambitions, once fulfilled, will be replaced by others. Q-characteristics will gradually change. In general, A stands in fewer and fewer direct psychological relations to an individual in his "tree" the more remote that individual is. And if the individual is (like $B + 30$) sufficiently remote, there may be between the two *no* direct psychological relations.

Now that we have distinguished the general relations of psychological continuity and psychological connectedness, I suggest that connectedness is a more important element in survival. As a claim about our own survival, this would need more arguments than I have space to give. But it seems clearly true for my imagined beings. A is as close psychologically to $B + 1$ as I today am to myself tomorrow. A is as distant from $B + 30$ as I am from my great-great-grandson.

Even if connectedness is not more important than continuity, the fact that one of these is a relation of degree is enough to show that what matters in survival can have degrees. And in any case the two relations are quite different. So our imagined beings would need a way of thinking in which this difference is recognized.

V

What I propose is this.

First, A can think of any individual, anywhere in his "tree," as "a descendant self." This phrase implies psychological continuity. Similarly, any later individual can think of any earlier individual on the single path[29] which connects him to A as "an ancestral self."

Since psychological continuity is transitive, "being an ancestral self of" and "being a descendant self of" are also transitive.

To imply psychological connectedness I suggest the phrases "one of my future selves" and "one of my past selves."

These are the phrases with which we can describe Wiggins' case. For having past and future selves is, what we needed, a way of continuing to exist which does not imply identity through time. The original person does, in this sense, survive Wiggins' operation: the two resulting people are his later selves. And they can each refer to him as "my past self." (They can share a past self without being the same self as each other.)

Since psychological connectedness is not transitive, and is a matter of degree, the relations "being a past self of" and "being a future self of" should themselves be treated as relations of degree. We allow for this series of descriptions: "my most recent self," "one of my earlier selves," "one of my distant selves," "hardly one of *my* past selves (I can only *q*-remember a few of his experiences)," and, finally, "not in any way one of *my* past selves—just an ancestral self."

This way of thinking would clearly suit our first imagined beings. But let us now turn to a second kind of being. These reproduce by fusion as well as by division.[30] And let us suppose that they fuse every autumn and divide every spring. This yields the following diagram:

If *A* is the individual whose life is represented by the three-lined "branch," the two-lined "tree" represents those lives which are psychologically continuous with *A*'s life. (It can be seen that each individual has his own "tree," which overlaps with many others.)

For the imagined beings in this second world, the phrases "an ancestral self" and "a descendant self" would cover too much to be of much use. (There may well be pairs of dates such that every individual who ever lived before the first date was an ancestral self of every individual who ever will live after the second date.) Conversely, since the lives of each individual last for only half a year, the word "I" would cover too little to do all of the work which it does for us. So part of this work would have to be done, for these second beings, by talk about past and future selves.

We can now point out a theoretical flaw in our proposed way of thinking. The phrase "a past self of" implies psychological connectedness. Being a past self of is treated as a relation of degree, so that this phrase can be used to imply the varying degrees of psychological connectedness. But this phrase can imply only the degrees of connectedness between different lives. It cannot be used within a single life. And our way of delimiting successive lives does not refer to the degrees of psychological connectedness. Hence there is no guarantee that this phrase, "a past self of," could be used whenever it was needed. There is no guarantee that psychological connectedness will not vary in degree within a single life.

This flaw would not concern our imagined beings. For they divide and unite so frequently, and their lives are in consequence so short, that within a single life psychological connectedness would always stand at a maximum.

But let us look, finally, at a third kind of being.

In this world there is neither division nor union. There are a number of everlasting bodies, which gradually change in appearance. And direct psychological relations, as before, hold only over limited periods of time. This can be illustrated with a third diagram (given on the next page). In this diagram the two shadings represent the degrees of psychological connectedness to their two central points.

These beings could not use the way of thinking that we have proposed. Since there is no branching of psychological continuity, they would have to regard themselves as immortal. It might be said that this is what they are. But there is, I suggest, a better description.

Our beings would have one reason for thinking of themselves as immortal. The parts of each "line" are all psychologically continuous. But the parts of each

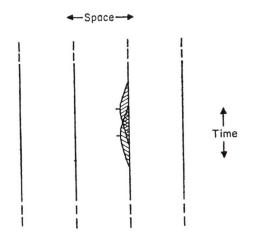

"line" are not all psychologically connected. Direct psychological relations hold only between those parts which are close to each other in time. This gives our beings a reason for *not* thinking of each "line" as corresponding to one single life. For if they did, they would have no way of implying these direct relations. When a speaker says, for example, "I spent a period doing such and such," his hearers would not be entitled to assume that the speaker has any memories of this period, that his character then and now are in any way similar, that he is now carrying out any of the plans or intentions which he then had, and so forth. Because the word "I" would carry none of these implications, it would not have for these "immortal" beings the usefulness which it has for us.[31]

To gain a better way of thinking, we must revise the way of thinking that we proposed above. The revision is this. The distinction between successive selves can be made by reference, not to the branching of psychological continuity, but to the degrees of psychological connectedness. Since this connectedness is a matter of degree, the drawing of these distinctions can be left to the choice of the speaker and be allowed to vary from context to context.

On this way of thinking, the word "I" can be used to imply the greatest degree of psychological connectedness. When the connections are reduced, when there has been any marked change of character or style of life, or any marked loss of memory, our imagined beings would say, "It was not I who did that, but an earlier self." They could then describe in what ways, and to what degree, they are related to this earlier self.

This revised way of thinking would suit not only our "immortal" beings. It is also the way in which we ourselves could think about our lives. And it is, I suggest, surprisingly natural.

One of its features, the distinction between successive selves, has already been used by several writers. To give an example, from Proust: "we are incapable, while we are in love, of acting as fit predecessors of the next persons who, when we are in love no longer, we shall presently have become. . . ."[32]

Although Proust distinguished between successive selves, he still thought of one person as being these different selves. This we would not do on the way of thinking that I propose. If I say, "It will not be me, but one of my future selves," I do not imply that I will be that future self. He is one of my later selves, and I am one of his earlier selves. There is no underlying person who we both are.

To point out another feature of this way of thinking. When I say, "There is no person who we both are," I am only giving my decision. Another person could say, "It will be you," thus deciding differently. There is no question of either of these decisions being a mistake. Whether to say "I," or "one of my future selves," or "a descendant self" is entirely a matter of choice. The matter of fact, which must be agreed, is only whether the disjunction applies. (The question "Are X and Y the same person?" thus becomes "Is X *at least* an ancestral [or descendant] self of Y?")

VI

I have tried to show that what matters in the continued existence of a person are, for the most part, relations of degree. And I have proposed a way of thinking in which this would be recognized.

I shall end by suggesting two consequences and asking one question.

It is sometimes thought to be especially rational to act in our own best interests. But I suggest that the principle of self-interest has no force. There are only two genuine competitors in this particular field. One is the principle of biased rationality: do what will best achieve what you actually want. The other is the principle of impartiality: do what is in the best interests of everyone concerned.

The apparent force of the principle of self-interest derives, I think, from these two other principles.

The principle of self-interest is normally supported by the principle of biased rationality. This is because most people care about their own future interests.

Suppose that this prop is lacking. Suppose that a man does not care what happens to him in, say, the more distant future. To such a man, the principle of self-interest can only be propped up by an appeal to the principle of impartiality. We must say, "Even if you don't care, you ought to take what happens to you then equally into account." But for this, as a special claim, there seem to me no good arguments. It can only be supported as part of the general claim, "You ought to take what happens to everyone equally into account."[33]

The special claim tells a man to grant an *equal* weight to all the parts of his future. The argument for this can only be that all the parts of his future are *equally* parts of *his* future. This is true. But it is a truth too superficial to bear the weight of the argument. (To give an analogy: The unity of a nation is, in its nature, a matter of degree. It is therefore only a superficial truth that all of a man's compatriots are *equally* his compatriots. This truth cannot support a good argument for nationalism.)[34]

I have suggested that the principle of self-interest has no strength of its own. If this is so, there is no special problem in the fact that what we ought to do can be against our interests. There is only the general problem that it may not be what we want to do.

The second consequence which I shall mention is implied in the first. Egoism, the fear not of near but of distant death, the regret that so much of one's *only* life should have gone by—these are not, I think, wholly natural or instinctive. They are all strengthened by the beliefs about personal identity which I have been attacking. If we give up these beliefs, they should be weakened.

My final question is this. These emotions are bad, and if we weaken them we gain. But can we achieve this gain without, say, also weakening loyalty to, or love of, other particular selves? As Hume warned, the "refined reflections which philosophy suggests . . . cannot diminish . . . our vicious passions . . . without diminishing . . . such as are virtuous. They are . . . applicable to all our affections. In vain do we hope to direct their influence only to one side."[35]

That hope *is* vain. But Hume had another: that more of what is bad depends upon false belief. This is also my hope.

NOTES

1. Implicit in John Locke, *Essay Concerning Human Understanding,* ed. by John W. Yolton (London, 1961), Vol. II, Ch. XXVII, sec. 18, and discussed by (among others) A. N. Prior in "Opposite Number," *Review of Metaphysics,* II (1957–1958), and "Time, Existence and Identity," *Proceedings of the Aristotelian Society,* LVII (1965–1966); J. Bennett in "The Simplicity of the Soul," *Journal of Philosophy,* LXIV (1967); and R. Chisholm and S. Shoemaker in "The Loose and Popular and the Strict and the Philosophical Senses of Identity," in *Perception and Personal Identity: Proceedings of the 1967 Oberlin Colloquium in Philosophy,* ed. by Norman Care and Robert H. Grimm (Cleveland, 1967).

2. In David Wiggins, *Identity and Spatio-Temporal Continuity* (Oxford, 1967), p. 50.

3. In *Self-Knowledge and Self-Identity* (Ithaca, N. Y., 1963), p. 22.

4. Those who would disagree are not making a mistake. For them my argument would need a different case. There must be some multiple transplant, faced with which these people would both find it hard to believe that there must be an answer to the question about personal identity, and be able to be shown that nothing of importance turns upon this question.

5. R. W. Sperry, in *Brain and Conscious Experience,* ed. by J. C. Eccles (New York, 1966), p. 299.

6. Cf. David Wiggins, op. cit, p. 40.

7. Suppose the resulting people fight a duel. Are there three people fighting, one on each side, and one on both? And suppose one of the bullets kills. Are there two acts, one murder and one suicide? How many people are left alive? One? Two? (We could hardly say, "One and a half.") We could talk in this way. But instead of saying that the resulting people *are* the original person—so that the pair is a trio—it would be far simpler to treat them as a pair, and

describe their relation to the original person in some new way. (I owe this suggested way of talking, and the objections to it, to Michael Woods.)

8. Cf. Sydney Shoemaker, in *Perception and Personal Identity: Proceedings of the 1967 Oberlin Colloquim in Philosophy,* loc. cit.

9. Cf. David Wiggins, op. cit., p. 54.

10. Bernard Williams' "The Self and the Future," *Philosophical Review,* LXXIX (1970), 161–180, is relevant here. He asks the question "Shall I survive?" in a range of problem cases, and he shows how natural it is to believe (1) that this question must have an answer, (2) that the answer must be all-or-nothing, and (3) that there is a "risk" of our reaching the *wrong* answer. Because these beliefs are so natural, we should need in undermining them to discuss their causes. These, I think, can be found in the ways in which we misinterpret what it is to remember (cf. Sec. III) and to anticipate (cf. Williams' "Imagination and the Self," *Proceedings of the British Academy,* LII [1966], 105–124); and also in the way in which certain features of our egoistic concern—e.g., that it is simple, and applies to all imaginable cases—are "projected" onto its object. (For another relevant discussion, see Terence Penelhum's *Survival and Disembodied Existence* [London, 1970], final chapters.)

11. "Personal Identity and Individuation," *Proceedings of the Aristotelian Society,* LVII (1956–1957), 229–253; also *Analysis,* 21 (1960–1961), 43–48.

12. J. M. Shorter, "More about Bodily Continuity and Personal Identity," *Analysis,* 22 (1961–1962), 79–85; and Mrs. J. M. R. Jack (unpublished), who requires that this truth be embedded in a causal theory.

13. *Analysis,* 21 (1960–1961), 44.

14. For the reasons given by A. M. Quinton in "The Soul," *Journal of Philosophy,* LIX (1962), 393–409.

15. Cf. S. Shoemaker, "Persons and Their Pasts," *American Philosophical Quarterly,* 7 (1970), 269–285, and "Wiggins on Identity," *Philosophical Review,* LXXIX (1970), 542.

16. But not a necessary condition, for in the absence of psychological continuity bodily identity might be sufficient.

17. Cf. Bernard Williams, "Personal Identity and Individuation," *Proceedings of the Aristotelian Society,* LVII (1956–1957), 240–241, and *Analysis,* 21 (1960–1961), 44; and also Wiggins, op. cit., p. 38: "if coincidence under [the concept] *f* is to be *genuinely* sufficient we must not withhold identity . . . simply because transitivity is threatened."

18. Williams produced another objection to the "psychological criterion," that it makes it hard to explain the difference between the concepts of identity and exact sim-

ilarity (*Analysis,* 21 [1960–1961], 48). But if we include the requirement of causal continuity we avoid this objection (and one of those produced by Wiggins in his note 47).

19. Those philosophers who have held this belief, from Butler onward, are too numerous to cite.

20. Op. cit.

21. In a paper on Butler's objection to Locke (not yet published).

22. I here follow Shoemaker's "quasi-memory." Cf. also Penelhum's "retrocognition," in his article on "Personal Identity," in the *Encyclopedia of Philosophy,* ed. by Paul Edwards.

23. As Shoemaker put it, I seem to remember the experience "from the inside" (op. cit.).

24. This is what so many writers have overlooked. Cf. Thomas Reid: "My memory testifies not only that this was done, but that it was done by me who now remember it" ("Of Identity," in *Essays on the Intellectual Powers of Man,* ed. by A. D. Woozley [London, 1941], p. 203). This mistake is discussed by A. B. Palma in "Memory and Personal Identity," *Australasian Journal of Philosophy,* 42 (1964), 57.

25. It is not logically necessary that we only *q*-remember our own experiences. But it might be necessary on other grounds. This possibility is intriguingly explored by Shoemaker in his "Persons and Their Pasts" (op. cit.). He shows that *q*-memories can provide a knowledge of the world only if the observations which are *q*-remembered trace out fairly continuous spatiotemporal paths. If the observations which are *q*-remembered traced out a network of frequently interlocking paths, they could not, I think, be usefully ascribed to persisting observers, but would have to be referred to in some more complex way. But in fact the observations which are *q*-remembered trace out single and separate paths; so we can ascribe them to ourselves. In other words, it is epistemologically necessary that the observations which are *q*-remembered should satisfy a certain general condition, one particular form of which allows them to be usefully self-ascribed.

26. Cf. Wiggins' paper on Butler's objection to Locke.

27. There are complications here. He could form *divergent q*-intentions only if he could distinguish, in advance, between the resulting people (e.g., as "the left-hander" and "the right-hander"). And he could be confident that such divergent *q*-intentions would be carried out only if he had reason to believe that neither of the resulting people would change their (inherited) mind. Suppose he was torn between duty and desire. He could not solve this dilemma by *q*-intending, as one of the resulting people, to do his duty, and, as the other, to do what he desires. For the one he *q*-intended to do his duty would face the same dilemma.

28. The chain of continuity must run in one direction of time. *B* + 2 is not, in the sense I intend, psychologically continuous with *B* + 1.

29. Cf. David Wiggins, op. cit.

30. Cf. Sydney Shoemaker in "Persons and Their Pasts," op. cit.

31. Cf. Austin Duncan Jones, "Man's Mortality," *Analysis,* 28 (1967–1968), 65–70.

32. *Within a Budding Grove* (London, 1949), I, 226 (my own translation).

33. Cf. Thomas Nagel's *The Possibility of Altruism* (Oxford, 1970), in which the special claim is in effect defended as part of the general claim.

34. The unity of a nation we seldom take for more than what it is. This is partly because we often think of nations, not as units, but in a more complex way. If we thought of ourselves in the way that I proposed, we might be less likely to take our own identity for more than what it is. We are, for example, sometimes told, "It is irrational to act against your own interests. After all, it will be *you* who will regret it." To this we could reply, "No, not me. Not even one of my future selves. Just a descendant self."

35. "The Sceptic," in "Essays Moral, Political and Literary," *Hume's Moral and Political Philosophy* (New York, 1959), p. 349.

Of Motion

~

ARISTOTLE

Aristotle (384–322 B.C.) was born in Stagira in northern Greece. He was a student of Plato and a tutor of Alexander the Great. His works range from logic and metaphysics to ethics and politics as well as biology, physics, and meteorology.

BOOK V

8. Since everything to which motion or rest is natural is in motion or at rest in the natural time, place, and manner, that which is coming to a stand, when it is coming to a stand, must be in motion; for if it is not in motion it must be at rest; but that which is at rest cannot be coming to rest. From this it evidently follows that coming to a stand must occupy a period of time; for the motion of that which is in motion occupies a period of time, and that which is coming to a stand has been shown to be in motion: consequently coming to a stand must occupy a period of time.

Again, since the terms "quicker" and "slower" are used only of that which occupies a period of time, and the process of coming to a stand may be quicker or slower, the same conclusion follows.

And that which is coming to a stand must be coming to a stand in any part of the primary time in which it is coming to a stand. For if it is coming to a stand in neither of two parts into which the time may be divided, it cannot be coming to a stand in the whole time, with the result that that which is coming to a stand will not be coming to a stand. If on the other hand it is coming to a stand in only one of the two parts, the whole cannot be the primary time in which it is coming to a stand; for it is coming to a stand in this derivatively, as we said before in the case of things in motion.

And just as there is no primary time in which that which is in motion is in motion, so too there is no primary time in which that which is coming to a stand is coming to a stand, there being no primary stage either of being in motion or of coming to a stand. For

Reprinted from *Physics,* translated by W. D. Ross (Oxford: Oxford University Press, 1950), by permission of the publisher.

let AB be the primary time in which a thing is coming to a stand. Now AB cannot be without parts; for there cannot be motion in that which is without parts, because a moving thing would have moved for a part of it, and that which is coming to a stand has been shown to be in motion. But since AB is divisible, the thing is coming to a stand in every one of its parts; for we have shown above that it is coming to a stand in every one of the parts in which it is primarily coming to a stand. Since, then, that in which primarily a thing is coming to a stand must be a period of time and not something indivisible, and since all time is infinitely divisible, there cannot be anything in which primarily it is coming to a stand.

Nor again can there be a primary time at which a thing at rest was resting; for it cannot have been resting in that which has no parts, because there cannot be motion in that which is indivisible, and that in which rest takes place is the same as that in which motion takes place (for we said that rest occurs if a thing which naturally moves is not moving when and at a time in which motion would be natural to it). Again, we say that a thing rests when it is now in the same state as it was in earlier, judging rest not by any one point but by at least two: consequently that in which a thing is at rest cannot be without parts. Since, then, it is divisible, it must be a period of time, and the thing must be at rest in every one of its parts, as may be shown by the same method as that used above.

So there can be no primary time; and the reason is that rest and motion are always in time, and there is no primary time—nor magnitude nor in fact anything continuous; for everything continuous is divisible into an infinite number of parts.

And since everything that is in motion is in motion in time and changes from something to something, in the time in which in its own right (i.e. not merely in a part of the time) something moves, it is impossible that that which is in motion should be over against some particular thing primarily. For if a thing—itself and each of its parts—occupies the same space for a definite period of time, it is at rest; for it is in just these circumstances that we use the term "being at rest"—when at one now after another it can be said with truth that a thing, itself and its parts, occupies the same space. So if this is being at rest it is impos-

sible for that which is changing to be as a whole, at the time when it is primarily changing, over against any particular thing (for the whole period of time is divisible), so that in one part of it after another it will be true to say that the thing, itself and its parts, occupies the same space. If this is not so and the aforesaid proposition is true only at a single now, then the thing will be over against a particular thing not for any period of time but only at a moment that limits the time. It is true that at any now it is always over against something; but it is not at rest; for at a now it is not possible for anything to be either in motion or at rest. So while it is true to say that that which is in motion is at a now not in motion and is opposite some particular thing, it cannot in a period of time be at rest over against anything; for that would involve the conclusion that that which is in locomotion is at rest.

9. Zeno's reasoning, however, is fallacious, when he says that if everything when it occupies an equal space is at rest, and if that which is in locomotion is always in a now, the flying arrow is therefore motionless. This is false; for time is not composed of indivisible nows any more than any other magnitude is composed of indivisibles.

Zeno's arguments about motion, which cause so much trouble to those who try to answer them, are four in number. The first asserts the non-existence of motion on the ground that that which is in locomotion must arrive at the half-way stage before it arrives at the goal. This we have discussed above.

The second is the so-called Achilles, and it amounts to this, that in a race the quickest runner can never overtake the slowest, since the pursuer must first reach the point whence the pursued started, so that the slower must always hold a lead. This argument is the same in principle as that which depends on bisection, though it differs from it in that the spaces with which we have successively to deal are not divided into halves. The result of the argument is that the slower is not overtaken; but it proceeds along the same lines as the bisection-argument (for in both a division of the space in a certain way leads to the result that the goal is not reached, though the Achilles goes further in that it affirms that even the runner most famed for his speed must fail in his pursuit of the slowest), so that the solution too must be the same. And the claim that that which holds a lead is never overtaken is false: it is not overtaken while it holds a lead; but it is overtaken nevertheless if it is granted that it traverses the finite distance. These then are two of his arguments.

The third is that already given above, to the effect that the flying arrow is at rest, which result follows from the assumption that time is composed of moments: if this assumption is not granted, the conclusion will not follow.

The fourth argument is that concerning equal bodies which move alongside equal bodies in the stadium from opposite directions—the ones from the end of the stadium, the others from the middle—at equal speeds, in which he thinks it follows that half the time is equal to its double. The fallacy consists in requiring that a body travelling at an equal speed travels for an equal time past a moving body and a body of the same size at rest. That is false. E.g. let the stationary equal bodies be AA; let BB be those starting from the middle of the A's (equal in number and in magnitude to them); and let CC be those starting from the end (equal in number and magnitude to them, and equal in speed to the B's). Now it follows that the first B and the first C are at the end at the same time, as they are moving past one another. And it follows that the C has passed all the A's and the B half; so that the time is half, for each of the two is alongside each for an equal time. And at the same time it follows that the first B has passed all the C's. For at the same time the first B and the first C will be at opposite ends, being an equal time alongside each of the B's as alongside each of the A's, as he says, because both are an equal time alongside the A's. That is the argument, and it rests on the stated falsity.

Nor in reference to contradictory change shall we find anything impossible—e.g. if it is argued that if a thing is changing from not-white to white, and is in neither condition, then it will be neither white nor not-white; for the fact that it is not *wholly* in either condition will not preclude us from calling it white or not-white. We call a thing white or not-white not because it is wholly either one or the other, but because most of its parts or the most essential parts of it are so: not being in a certain condition is different from not being wholly in that condition. So, too, in

the case of being and not-being and all other conditions which stand in a contradictory relation: while the changing thing must of necessity be in one of the two opposites, it is never wholly in either.

Again, in the case of circles and spheres and everything that moves within its own dimensions, it is argued that they will be at rest, on the ground that such things, themselves and their parts, will occupy the same position for a period of time, and that therefore they will be at once at rest and in motion. For, first, the parts do not occupy the same place for any period of time; and secondly, the whole also is always changing to a different position; for the circumference from A is not the same as that from B or C or any other point except accidentally, as a musical man is the same as a man. Thus one is always changing into another, and the thing will never be at rest. And it is the same with the sphere and everything else which moves within its own dimensions.

10. That having been demonstrated, we next assert that that which is without parts cannot be in motion except accidentally, i.e. in so far as the body or the magnitude to which it belongs is in motion, just as that which is in a boat may be in motion in consequence of the locomotion of the boat, or a part may be in motion in virtue of the motion of the whole. (By "that which is without parts" I mean that which is quantitatively indivisible.) For parts have different motions—those in virtue of themselves, and those in virtue of the motion of the whole. The distinction may be seen most clearly in the case of a sphere, in which the velocities of the parts near the centre and of those on the surface are different from one another and from that of the whole; this implies that there is not one motion. As we have said, then, that which is without parts can be in motion in the sense in which a man sitting in a boat is in motion when the boat is travelling, but it cannot be in motion of itself. For suppose that it is changing from AB to BC—either from one magnitude to another, or from one form to another, or from some state to its contradictory—and let D be the primary time in which it undergoes the change. Then in the time in which it is changing it must be either in AB or in BC or partly in one and partly in the other; for this, as we saw, is true of everything that is changing. Now it cannot be partly

in each of the two; for then it would be divisible into parts. Nor again can it be in BC; for then it will have changed, whereas the assumption is that it is changing. It remains, then, that in the time in which it is changing, it is in AB. That being so, it will be at rest; for, as we saw, to be in the same condition for a period of time is to be at rest. So it is not possible for that which has no parts to be in motion or to change in any way; for only one condition could have made it possible for it to have motion, viz. that time should be composed of nows, in which case at any now it would have moved or changed, so that it would never be in motion, but would always have been moving. But this we have already shown to be impossible: time is not composed of nows, just as a line is not composed of points, and motion is not composed of movings; for this theory simply makes motion consist of indivisibles in exactly the same way as time is made to consist of nows or a length of points.

Again, it may be shown in the following way that there can be no motion of a point or of any other indivisible. That which is in motion can never traverse a space greater than itself without first traversing a space equal to or less than itself. That being so, it is evident that the point also must first traverse a space equal to or less than itself. But since it is indivisible, it is impossible for it to traverse a lesser space first: so it will have to traverse a distance equal to itself. Thus the line will be composed of points; for the point, as it continually traverses a distance equal to itself, will be a measure of the whole line. But since this is impossible, it is likewise impossible for the indivisible to be in motion.

Again, since motion is always in time and never in a now, and all time is divisible, for everything that is in motion there must be a time less than that in which it traverses a distance as great as itself. For that in which it is in motion will be a time, because all motion is in time; and all time has been shown above to be divisible. Therefore, if a point is in motion, there must be a time less than that in which it has itself traversed its own length. But this is impossible; for in less time it must traverse less distance, and thus the indivisible will be divisible into something less, just as the time is so divisible; for that which is without parts and indivisible could be in motion only if it were possible to move in an indivisible now; for in the two questions— that of motion in a now and that of motion of something indivisible—the same principle is involved.

No change is infinite; for every change, whether between contradictories or between contraries, is a change from something to something. Thus in contradictory changes the positive or the negative is the limit, e.g. being is the limit of coming to be and not-being is the limit of ceasing to be; and in contrary changes the particular contraries are the limits, since these are the extreme points of the change, and consequently of every alteration; for alteration is always dependent upon some contraries. Similarly for increase and decrease: the limit of increase is to be found in the complete magnitude proper to the peculiar nature of the thing, while the limit of decrease is the loss of such magnitude. Locomotion, it is true, we cannot show to be finite in this way, since it is not always between contraries. But since that which cannot be cut (in the sense that it is not possible that it should be cut, the term 'cannot' being used in several ways)—since it is not possible that that which in this sense cannot be cut should be being cut, and generally that that which cannot come to be should be coming to be, it follows that it is not possible that that which cannot have changed should be changing to that to which it cannot have changed. If, then, that which is in locomotion is to be changing to something, it must be capable of having changed. Consequently its motion is not infinite, and it will not be in locomotion over an infinite distance; for it cannot have traversed such a distance.

It is evident, then, that a change cannot be infinite in the sense that it is not defined by limits. But it remains to be considered whether it is possible in the sense that one and the same change may be infinite in respect of the time which it occupies. If it is not one change, it would seem that there is nothing to prevent its being infinite; e.g. if a locomotion be succeeded by an alteration and that by an increase and that again by a coming to be: in this way there may be motion for ever so far as the time is concerned; but it will not be one motion, because all these motions do not compose one. If it is to be one, no motion can be infinite in respect of the time that it occupies, with the single exception of rotatory locomotion.

Achilles and the Tortoise

~

MAX BLACK

Max Black (1909–1988) was professor of philosophy at Cornell University. He was influential in philosophy of language, philosophy of art, philosophy of science, and philosophy of mathematics. His books include *The Nature of Mathematics, Language and Philosophy* and *Models and Metaphors: Studies in Language and Philosophy.*

1. Suppose Achilles runs ten times as fast as the tortoise and gives him a hundred yards start. In order to win the race. Achilles must first make up for his initial handicap by running a hundred yards; but when he has done this and has reached the point where the tortoise started, the animal has had time to advance ten yards. While Achilles runs these ten yards, the tortoise gets one yard ahead; when Achilles has run this yard, the tortoise is a tenth of a yard ahead; and so on, without end. Achilles never catches the tortoise, because the tortoise always holds a lead, however small.

This is approximately the form in which the so-called "Achilles" paradox has come down to us. Aristotle, who is our primary source for this and the other paradoxes attributed to Zeno, summarises the argument as follows: "In a race the quickest runner can never overtake the slowest, since the pursuer must first reach the point whence the pursued started, so that the slower must always hold a lead" (Physics, 239^b).[1]

2. It would be a waste of time to prove, by independent argument, that Achilles will pass the tortoise. Everybody knows this already, and the puzzle arises because the conclusion of Zeno's argument is known to be absurd. We must try to find out, if we can, exactly what mistake is committed in this argument.[2]

3. A plausible answer that has been repeatedly offered[3] takes the line that "this paradox of Zeno is based upon a mathematical fallacy" (A. N. Whitehead, *Process and Reality* (1929), 107).

Consider the lengths that Achilles has to cover, according to our version of the paradox. They are, successively, a hundred yards, ten yards, one yard, a tenth of a yard, and so on. So the total number of yards he must travel in order to catch the tortoise is

$$100 + 10 + 1 + 1/10 + \ldots$$

This is a convergent geometrical series whose sum can be expressed in decimal notion as $111.\dot{1}$, that is to say exactly $111^1/_9$. When Achilles has run this number of yards, he will be dead level with his competitor; and at any time thereafter he will be actually ahead.

A similar argument applies to the time needed for Achilles to catch the tortoise. If we suppose that Achilles can run a hundred yards in ten seconds, the number of seconds he needs in order to catch up is

$$10 + 1 + 1/10 + 1/100 + \ldots$$

This, too, is a convergent geometrical series, whose sum is expressed in decimal notation $11.\dot{1}$, that is to say exactly $11^1/_9$. This, as we should expect, is one tenth of the number we previously obtained.

We can check the calculation without using infinite series at all. The relative velocity with which Achilles overtakes the tortoise is nine yards per sec-

Reprinted from *Analysis, 11* (1951).

ond. Now the number of seconds needed to cancel the initial gap of a hundred yards at a relative velocity of pursuit of nine yards per second is 100 divided by 9 or $11\frac{1}{9}$. This is exactly the number we previously obtained by summing the geometrical series representing the times needed by Achilles. During this time, moreover, since Achilles is actually travelling at ten yards per second, the actual distance he travels is $10 \times 11\frac{1}{9}$, or $111\frac{1}{9}$, as before. Thus we have confirmed our first calculation by an argument not involving the summation of infinite series.

4. According to this type of solution, the fallacy in Zeno's argument is due to the use of the words "never" and "always." Given the premise that "the pursuer must first reach the point whence the pursued started," it does *not* follow, as alleged, that the quickest runner "never" overtakes the slower: Achilles does catch the tortoise at some time—that is to say at a time exactly $11\frac{1}{9}$ seconds from the start. It is wrong to say that the tortoise is "always" in front: there is a place—a place exactly $111\frac{1}{9}$ yards from Achilles' starting point—where the two are dead level. Our calculations have showed this, and Zeno failed to see that only a finite time and finite space are needed for the infinite series of steps that Achilles is called upon to make.

5. This kind of mathematical solution has behind it the authority of Descartes and Peirce and Whitehead[4]—to mention no lesser names—yet I cannot see that it goes to the heart of the matter. It tells us, correctly, when and where Achilles and the tortoise will meet, *if* they meet; but it fails to show that Zeno was wrong in claiming they *could not* meet.

Let us be clear about what is meant by the assertion that the sum of the infinite series.

$$100 + 10 + 1 + 1/10 + 1/100 + \ldots$$

is $111\frac{1}{9}$. It does not mean, as the naive might suppose, that mathematicians have succeeded in adding together an infinite number of terms. As Frege pointed out in a similar connection,[5] this remarkable feat would require an infinite supply of paper, an infinite quantity of ink, and an infinite amount of time. If we had to add all the terms together, we could never prove that the series had a finite sum. To say that the

sum of the series is $111\frac{1}{9}$ is to say that if enough terms of the series are taken, the difference between the sum of that *finite number* of terms and the number $111\frac{1}{9}$ becomes, and stays, as small as we please. (Or to put it another way: Let n be any number less than $111\frac{1}{9}$. We can always find a finite number of terms of the series whose sum will be less than $111\frac{1}{9}$ but greater than n).

Since this is all that is meant by saying that the infinite series has a sum, it follows that the "summation" of all the terms of an infinite series is not the same thing as the summation of a finite set of numbers. In one case we can get the answers by working out a finite number of additions; in the other case we *must* "perform a limit operation," that is to say, prove that there is a number whose difference from the sum of the initial members of the series can be made to remain as small as we please.

6. Now let us apply this to the race. The series of distances traversed by Achilles is convergent. This means that if Achilles takes enough steps whose sizes are given by the series 100 yards, 10 yards, 1 yard, 1/10 yard, etc. the distance *still to go* to the meeting point eventually becomes, and stays, as small as we please. After the first step he still has $11\frac{1}{9}$ yards to go; after the second, only $1\frac{1}{9}$ yard; after the third, no more than $\frac{1}{9}$ yard; and so on. The distance still to go is reduced by ten at each move.

But the distance, however much reduced, still remains to be covered; and after each step there are infinitely many steps still to be taken. The logical difficulty is that Achilles seems called upon to perform *an infinite series of tasks;* and it does not help to be told that the tasks become easier and easier, or need progressively less and less time in the doing. Achilles may get nearer to the place and time of his rendezvous, but his task remains just as hard, for he still has to perform what seems to be logically impossible. It is just as hard to draw a very small square circle as it is to draw an enormous one: we might say both tasks are infinitely hard. The logical difficulty is not in the extent of the distance Achilles has to cover but in the apparent impossibility of his travelling any distance whatsoever. I think Zeno had enough mathematical knowledge to understand that if Achilles could run $111\frac{1}{9}$ yards—that is to say, keep going for

$11^1/_9$ seconds—he would indeed have caught the tortoise. The difficulty is to understand how Achilles could arrive anywhere at all without first having performed an infinite series of acts.

7. The nature of the difficulty is made plainer by a second argument of Zeno, known as the "Dichotomy" which, according to Aristotle, is "the same in principle" (*Physics,* 239^b). In order to get from one point to another, Achilles must first reach a third point midway between the two; similarly, in order to reach this third point he must first reach a fourth point; to reach this point he must first reach another point; and so on, without end. To reach *any* point, he must first reach a nearer one. So, in order to get moving, Achilles must already have performed an infinite series of acts—must, as it were, have travelled along the series of points from the infinitely distant and *open* "end."[6] This is an even more astounding feat than the one he accomplishes in winning the race against the tortoise.

The two arguments are complementary: the "Achilles" shows that the runner cannot reach any place, even if he gets started; while the "Dichotomy" shows that he cannot get started, *i.e.* cannot leave any place he has reached.

8. Mathematicians have sometimes said that the difficulty of conceiving the performance of an infinite series of tasks is factitious. All it shows, they say, is the weakness of human imagination and the folly of the attempt to make a mental image of mathematical relationships. The line really does have infinitely many points, and there is no logical impediment to Achilles' making an infinite number of steps in a finite time. I will try to show that this way of thinking about the race is untenable.

9. I am going to argue that the expression, "infinite series of acts," is self-contradictory, and that failure to see this arises from confusing a series of acts with a series of numbers generated by some mathematical law. (By an "act" I mean something marked off from its surroundings by having a definite beginning and end.)

In order to establish this by means of an illustration I shall try to make plain some of the absurd consequences of talking about "counting an infinite number of marbles." And in order to do this I shall find it convenient to talk about counting an infinite

number of marbles as if I supposed it was sensible to talk in this way. But I want it to be understood all the time that I do not think it sensible to talk in this way, and that my aim in so talking is to show how absurd this way of talking is. Counting may seem a very special kind of "act" to choose, but I hope to be able to show that the same considerations will apply to an infinite series of any kinds of acts.

10. Suppose we want to find out the number of things in a given collection, presumably identified by some description. Unless the things are mathematical or logical entities it will be impossible to deduce the size of the collection from the description alone; and somebody will have to do the work of taking a census. Of course he can do this without having any idea of how large the collection will turn out to be: his instructions may simply take the form, "Start counting and keep on until there is nothing left in the collection to count." This implies that there will be a point at which there will be "nothing left to count," so that the census-taker will then know his task to have been completed.

Now suppose we can know that the collection is infinite. If, knowing this, we were to say "Start counting and continue until there is nothing left to count" we should be practicing a deception. For our census-taker would be led to suppose that sooner or later there would be nothing left to count, while all the time we would know this supposition to be false. An old recipe for catching guinea pigs is to put salt on their tails. Since they have no tails, this is no recipe at all. To avoid deception we should have said, in the case of the infinite collection, "Start counting and *never* stop." This should be enough to tell an intelligent census-taker that the collection is infinite, so that there is no sense in trying to count it.

If somebody says to me "Count all the blades of grass in Hyde Park" I might retort "It's too difficult; I haven't enough time." But if some cosmic bully were to say "Here is an infinite collection; go ahead and count it," only logical confusion could lead me to mutter "Too difficult; not enough time." The trouble is that, no matter what I do, the result of all my work will not and cannot count as compliance with the instructions. If somebody commands me to obey a certain "instruction," and is then obliging enough to add that nothing that I can do will count as compliance with that instruction, only confusion could lead me to suppose that any task had been set.

11. Some writers, however, have said that the difficulty of counting an infinite collection is just a matter of *lack of time*. If only we could count faster and faster, the whole job could be done in a finite time; there would still never be a time at which we were ending, but there would be a time at which we already would have ended the count. It is not necessary to finish counting; it is sufficient that the counting shall have been finished.

Very well. Since the task is too much for human capacity, let us imagine a machine that can do it. Let us suppose that upon our left a narrow tray stretches into the distance as far as the most powerful telescope can follow; and that this tray or slot is full of marbles. Here, at the middle, where the line of marbles begins, there stands a kind of mechanical scoop; and to the right, a second, but empty tray, stretching away into the distance beyond the farthest reach of vision. Now the machine is started. During the first minute of its operation, it seizes a marble and transfers it to the empty tray; then it rests a minute. In the next half-minute the machine seizes a second marble on the left, transfers it, and rests half-a-minute. The third marble is moved in a quarter of a minute, with a corresponding pause; the next in one eighth of a minute; and so until the movements are so fast that all we can see is a grey blur. But at the end of exactly four minutes the machine comes to a halt, and we now see that the left-hand tray that was full seems to be empty, while the right-hand tray that was empty seems full of marbles.

Let us call this an *infinity machine.* And since it is the first of several to be described let us give it the name "Alpha."

12. I hope nobody will object that the wear and tear on such a machine would be too severe; or that it would be too hard to construct! We are dealing with the logical coherence of ideas, not with the practicability of mechanical devices. If we can conceive of such a machine without contradiction, that will be enough; and believers in the "actual infinite" will have been vindicated.

13. An obvious difficulty in conceiving of an infinity machine is this. How are we supposed to know that there are infinitely many marbles in the left-hand tray at the outset? Or, for that matter, that there are infinitely many on the right when the machine has stopped? Everything we can observe of Alpha's operations (and no matter how much we slow it down!) is consistent with there having been involved only a very large, though still finite, number of marbles.

14. Now there is a simple and instructive way of making certain that the machine shall have infinitely many marbles to count. Let there be only *one* marble in the left-hand tray to begin with, and let some device always return *that same marble* while the machine is resting. Let us give the name "Beta" to a machine that works in this way. From the standpoint of the machine, as it were, the task has not changed. The difficulty of performance remains exactly the same whether the task, as in Alpha's case, is to transfer an infinite series of qualitatively similar but different marbles; or whether the task, as in Beta's case, is constantly to transfer the *same* marble that is immediately returned to its original position. Imagine Alpha and Beta both at work side by side on their respective tasks: every time the one moves, so does the other; if one succeeds in its task, so must the other; and if it is impossible for either to succeed, it is impossible for *each.*

15. The introduction of our second machine, Beta, shows clearly that the infinite count really is impossible. For the single marble is always returned, and each move of the machine accomplished nothing. A man given the task of filling three holes by means of two pegs can always fill the third hole by transferring one of the pegs; but this automatically creates another empty place, and it won't help in the least to run through this futile series of operations faster and faster. (We don't get any nearer to the end of the rainbow by running faster). Now our machine, Beta, is in just this predicament: the very act of transferring the marble from left to right immediately causes it to be returned again; the operation is self-defeating and it is logically impossible for its end to be achieved. Now if this is true for Beta, it must be true also for Alpha, as we have already seen.

16. When Hercules tried to cut off the heads of Hydra, two heads immediately grew where one had been removed. It is rumoured that the affair has been incorrectly reported: Zeus, the all powerful, took pity on Hercules and eased his labor. It was decreed that only *one* head should replace the head that had been

cut off and that Hercules should have the magical power to slash faster and faster in geometrical progression. If this is what really happened, had Hercules any cause to be grateful? Not a bit. Since the head that was sliced off immediately grew back again, Hercules was getting nowhere, and might just as well have kept his sword in its scabbard.

17. Somebody may still be inclined to say that nevertheless when the machine Beta finally comes to rest (at the end of the four minutes of its operation) the single marble might after all be found in the right-hand tray, and this, if it happened, would *prove* that the machine's task had been accomplished. However, it is easy to show that this suggestion will not work.

I said, before, that "some device" always restored the marble to its original position in the left-hand tray. Now the most natural device to use for this purpose is another machine—Gamma, say—working like Beta but *from right to left*. Let it be arranged that no sooner does Beta move the marble from left to right than Gamma moves it back again. The successive working periods and pauses of Gamma are then equal in length to those of Beta, except that Gamma is working while Beta is resting, and vice versa. The task of Gamma, moreover, is exactly parallel to that of Beta, that is, to transfer the marble an infinite number of times from one side to the other. If the result of the whole four minutes' operation by the first machine is to transfer the marble from left to right, the result of the whole four minutes' operation by the second machine must be to transfer the marble from right to left. But there is only one marble and it must end somewhere! Hence neither machine can accomplish its task, and our description of the infinity machines involves a contradiction.

18. These consideration show, if I am not mistaken, that the outcome of the infinite machine's work is independent of what the machine is supposed to have done antecedently. The marble might end up on the right, on the left, or nowhere. When Hercules ended his slashing, Zeus had to decide whether the head should still be in position or whether, after all, Hercules' strenuous efforts to do the impossible should be rewarded.

Hercules might have argued that every time a head appeared, he had cut it off, so no head ought to

remain; but the Hydra could have retorted, with equal force, that after a head had been removed another had always appeared in its place, so a head ought to remain in position. The two contentions cancel one another and neither would provide a ground for Zeus' decision.

Even Zeus, however, could not abrogate the continuity of space and motion; and this, if I am not mistaken, is the source of the contradiction in our description of the machine Beta. The motion of the marble is represented, graphically, by a curve with an infinite number of oscillations, the rapidity of the oscillations increasing constantly as approach is made to the time at which the machine comes to rest. Now to say that motion is continuous is to deny that any real motion can be represented by a curve of this character. Yet every machine that performed an infinite series of acts in a finite time would have to include a part that oscillated "infinitely fast", as it were, in this impossible fashion. For the beginning of every spatio-temporal act is marked by a change in the velocity or in some other magnitude characterizing the agent.

19. It might be thought that the waiting-intervals in the operations of the three infinity machines so far described have been essential to the argument. And it might be objected that the steps Achilles takes are performed consecutively and without intervening pauses. I will now show that the pauses are not essential.

Consider for this purpose two machines, Delta and Epsilon, say, that begin to work with a single marble each, but in opposite directions. Let Delta start with the marble *a* and Epsilon with the marble *b*. Now suppose the following sequence of operations: while Delta transfers marble *a* from left to right in one minute, Epsilon transfers marble *b* from right to left; then Delta moves *b* from left to right in half a minute while Epsilon returns *a* from right to left during the same time; and so on, indefinitely, with each operation taking half the time of its predecessor. During the time that either machine is transporting a marble, its partner is placing the other marble in position for the next move.[7] Once again, the total tasks of Delta and Epilson are exactly parallel: if the first is to succeed, both marbles must end on the right, but if the second is to succeed, both must end on the left. Hence neither can succeed, and there is a contradiction in our description of the machines.

20. Nor will it help to have a machine—Phi, say—, transferring marbles that become progressively smaller in geometrical progression.[8] For, by an argument already used, we can suppose that while Phi is performing its operations, one of the machines already described is going through its paces at the same rates and at the same times. If Phi could complete its task, Alpha, Beta, Gamma, Delta and Epsilon would have to be able to complete their respective tasks. And we have already seen that this is not possible. The size of the successive tasks has nothing to do with the logical impossibility of performing an infinite series of operations. Indeed it should be clear by this time that the logical possibility of the existence of any one of the machines depends upon the logical possibility of the existence of all of them or, indeed, of any machine that could count an infinite number of objects. If the idea of the existence of any one of them is self-contradictory, the same must be true for each of them. The various descriptions of these different hypothetical devices simply make it easier for us to see that one and all are logically impossible. And though a good deal more needs to be said about this, I hope I have said enough to show why I think this notion of counting an infinite collection is self-contradictory.

21. If we now reconsider for a moment the arguments that have been used in connection with our six infinity machines, we can easily see that no use was made of the respects in which counting differs from any other series of acts. Counting differs from other series of acts by the conventional assignment of numerals to each stage of the count, and it differs in other respects, too. But every series of acts is like counting in requiring the successive doing of things, each having a beginning and end in space or time. And this is all that was used or needed in our arguments. Since our arguments in no way depended upon the specific peculiarities of counting they would apply, as I said at the outset, to any infinite series of acts.

22. And now let us return to Achilles. If it really were necessary for him to perform an infinite number

of *acts* or, as Aristotle says "to pass over or severally to come in contact with infinite things" (*Physics,* 233ᵃ), it would indeed be logically impossible for him to pass the tortoise. But all the things he really does are finite in number; a finite number of steps, heart beats, deep breaths, cries of defiance, and so on. The track on which he runs has a finite number of pebbles, grains of earth, and blades of grass,[9] each of which in turn has a finite, though enormous number of atoms. For all of these are things that have a beginning and end in space or time. But if anybody says we must imagine that the atoms themselves occupy space and so are divisible "in thought", he is no longer talking about spatiotemporal things. To divide a thing "in thought" is merely to halve the numerical interval which we have assigned to it. Or else it is to suppose what is in fact physically impossible beyond a certain point, the actual separation of the physical thing into discrete parts. We can of course choose to say that we shall represent a distance by a numerical interval, and that every part of that numerical interval shall also count as representing a distance; then it will be true a priori that there are infinitely many "distances." But the class of what will then be called "distances" will be a series of pairs of numbers, not an infinite series of spatio-temporal things. The infinity of this series is then a feature of one way in which we find it useful to *describe* the physical reality; to suppose that therefore Achilles has to *do* an infinite number of things would be as absurd as to suppose that because I can attach two numbers to an egg I must make some special effort to hold its halves together.

23. To summarise: I have tried to show that the popular mathematical refutation of Zeno's paradoxes will not do, because it simply assumes that Achilles can perform an infinite series of acts. By using the illustration of what would be involved in counting an infinite number of marbles, I have tried to show that the notion of an infinite series of acts is self-contradictory. For any material thing, whether machine or person, that set out to do an infinite number of acts would be committed to performing a motion that was discontinuous and therefore impossible. But Achilles is not called upon to do the logically impossible; the illusion that he must do so is created by our

failure to hold separate the finite number of real things that the runner has to accomplish and the infinite series of numbers by which we describe what he actually does. We create the illusion of the infinite tasks by the kind of mathematics that we use to describe space, time, and motion.

NOTES

1. Aristotle's solution seems to be based upon a distinction between two meanings of 'infinite'—(i) as meaning "infinite in extent," (ii) as meaning "infinitely divisible." "For there are two senses in which length and time and generally anything continuous are called "infinite": they are called so either in respect of divisibility or in respect of their extremities. So while a thing in a finite time cannot come in contact with things quantitatively infinite, it can come in contact with things infinite in respect of divisibility; for in this sense the time itself is also infinite . . ." (*Physics,* 233ª). This type of answer has been popular (cf. e.g. J. S. Mill, *System of Logic,* 5th ed., 389–390). Several writers object that infinite divisibility of the line implies its actually having an infinite number of elements—and so leaves the puzzle unresolved. But see H. R. King, "Aristotle and the paradoxes of Zeno," *Journal of Philosophy* 46 (1949), 657–670.

For references to the vast literature on this and the other arguments of Zeno, see F. Cajori, "The history of Zeno's arguments on motion," *American Mathematical Monthly* 22 (1915), 1–6, 39–47, 77–82, 109–115, 143–149, 179–186, 253–258, 292–297.

2. It has sometimes been held e.g. by Paul Tannery in *Revue Philosophique* 20 (1885) that Zeno's arguments were sound. "Tannery's explanation of the four arguments, particularly of the 'Arrow' and 'Stade' raises these paradoxes from childish arguments to arguments with conclusions which follow with compelling force . . . it exhibits Zeno as a logician of the first rank" (Cajori, op. cit., 6).

Cf. Russell's remark that the arguments of Zeno "are not, however, on any view, mere foolish quibbles: they are serious arguments, raising difficulties which it has taken two thousand years to answer, and which even now are fatal to the teachings of most philosophers" (*Our Knowledge of the External World* (1926), 175).

3. In addition to the reference to Whitehead, see for instance Descartes (letter to Clerselier, Adam and Tannery, ed. of *Works* 4, 445–447), and Peirce (Collected Papers, 6.177–6.182). Peirce says " . . . this silly little catch presents no difficulty at all to a mind adequately trained in mathematics and in logic . . ." (6.177).

4. See note.

5. *Grundgesetze der Arithmetik* 2 (1903); §124. Or see my translation in *Philosophical Review* 59 (1950), 332.

6. This, at any rate, is the usual interpretation, though I cannot see that Aristotle was thinking of anything more than an argument resembling the "Achilles" in all respects except that of the ratio in which the distance is divided. For the contrary view see, for instance, Sir Thomas Heath, *Mathematics in Aristotle* (1949), 135–6.

7. An alternative arrangement would be to have three similar machines constantly circulating three marbles.

8. Somebody might say that if the marble moved by Beta eventually shrunk to nothing there would be no problem about its final location!.

9. Cf. Peirce: "I do not think that if each pebble were broken into a million pieces the difficulty of getting over the road would necessarily have been increased; and I don't see why it should if one of these millions—or all of them— had been multiplied into an infinity" (Op. cit., 6.182).

Of the Idea of Necessary Connection

~

DAVID HUME

David Hume (1711–1776), born in Scotland, was a leading empiricist philosopher. His most important work, *A Treatise of Human Nature,* is a seminal contribution to metaphysics, epistemology, moral philosophy, and philosophy of science.

SECTION VII • OF THE IDEA OF NECESSARY CONNECTION

Part I

The great advantage of the mathematical sciences above the moral consists in this, that the ideas of the former, being sensible, are always clear and determinate, the smallest distinction between them is immediately perceptible, and the same terms are still expressive of the same ideas without ambiguity or variation. An oval is never mistaken for a circle, nor a hyperbola for an ellipsis. The isosceles and scalenum are distinguished by boundaries more exact than vice and virtue, right and wrong. If any term be defined in geometry, the mind readily, of itself substitutes on all occasions the definition for the term defined, or, even when no definition is employed, the object itself may be presented to the senses and by that means be steadily and clearly apprehended. But the finer sentiments of the mind, the operations of the understanding, the various agitations of the passions, though really in themselves distinct, easily escape us when surveyed by reflection, nor is it in our power to recall the original object as often as we have occasion to contemplate it. Ambiguity, by this means, is gradually introduced into our reasonings: similar objects are readily taken to be the same, and the conclusion becomes at last very wide of the premises.

One may safely, however, affirm that if we consider these sciences in a proper light, their advantages and disadvantages nearly compensate each other and reduce both of them to a state of equality. If the mind, with greater facility, retains the ideas of geometry clear and determinate, it must carry on a much longer and more intricate chain of reasoning and compare ideas much wider of each other in order to reach the abstruser truths of that science. And if moral ideas are apt, without extreme care, to fall into obscurity and confusion, the inferences are always much shorter in these disquisitions, and the intermediate steps which lead to the conclusion much fewer than in the sciences which treat of quantity and number. In reality, there is scarcely a proposition in Euclid so simple as not to consist of more parts than are to be found in any moral reasoning which runs not into chimera and conceit. Where we trace the principles of the human mind through a few steps, we may be very well satisfied with our progress, considering how soon nature throws a bar to all our inquiries concerning causes and reduces us to an acknowledgment of our ignorance. The chief obstacle, therefore, to our improvements in the moral or metaphysical sciences is the obscurity of the ideas and ambiguity of the terms. The principal difficulty in the mathematics is the length of inferences and compass of thought requisite to the forming of any conclusion. And, perhaps, our

From David Hume, *An Enquiry Concerning Human Understanding.*

progress in natural philosophy is chiefly retarded by the want of proper experiments and phenomena, which are often discovered by chance and cannot always be found when requisite, even by the most diligent and prudent inquiry. As moral philosophy seems hitherto to have received less improvement than either geometry or physics, we may conclude that if there be any difference in this respect among these sciences, the difficulties which obstruct the progress of the former require superior care and capacity to be surmounted.

There are no ideas which occur in metaphysics more obscure and uncertain than those of "power," "force," "energy," or "necessary connection," of which it is every moment necessary for us to treat in all our disquisitions. We shall, therefore, endeavor in this Section to fix, if possible, the precise meaning of these terms and thereby remove some part of that obscurity which is so much complained of in this species of philosophy.

It seems a proposition which will not admit of much dispute that all our ideas are nothing but copies of our impressions, or, in other words, that it is impossible for us to *think* of anything which we have not antecedently *felt,* either by our external or internal senses. I have endeavored to explain and prove this proposition, and have expressed my hopes that by a proper application of it men may reach a greater clearness and precision in philosophical reasonings than what they have hitherto been able to attain. Complex ideas may, perhaps, be well known by definition, which is nothing but an enumeration of those parts or simple ideas that compose them. But when we have pushed up definitions to the most simple ideas and find still some ambiguity and obscurity, what resources are we then possessed of? By what invention can we throw light upon these ideas and render them altogether precise and determinate to our intellectual view? Produce the impressions or original sentiments from which the ideas are copied. These impressions are all strong and sensible. They admit not of ambiguity. They are not only placed in a full light themselves, but may throw light on their correspondent ideas, which lie in obscurity. And by this means we may perhaps attain a new microscope or species of optics by which, in the moral sciences,

the most minute and most simple ideas may be so enlarged as to fall readily under our apprehension and be equally known with the grossest and most sensible ideas that can be the object of our inquiry.

To be fully acquainted, therefore, with the idea of power or necessary connection, let us examine its impression and, in order to find the impression with greater certainty, let us search for it in all the sources from which it may possibly be derived.

When we look about us towards external objects and consider the operation of causes, we are never able, in a single instance, to discover any power or necessary connection, any quality which binds the effect to the cause and renders the one an infallible consequence of the other. We only find that the one does actually in fact follow the other. The impulse of one billiard ball is attended with motion in the second. This is the whole that appears to the *outward* senses. The mind feels no sentiment or *inward* impression from this succession of objects: consequently, there is not, in any single particular instance of cause and effect, anything which can suggest the idea of power or necessary connection.

From the first appearance of an object we never can conjecture what effect will result from it. But were the power or energy of any cause discoverable by the mind, we could foresee the effect, even without experience, and might, at first, pronounce with certainty concerning it by mere dint of thought and reasoning.

In reality, there is no part of matter that does ever, by its sensible qualities, discover any power or energy, or give us ground to imagine that it could produce anything, or be followed by any other object, which we could denominate its effect. Solidity, extension, motion—these qualities are all complete in themselves and never point out any other event which may result from them. The scenes of the universe are continually shifting, and one object follows another in an uninterrupted succession; but the power or force which actuates the whole machine is entirely concealed from us and never discovers itself in any of the sensible qualities of body. We know that, in fact, heat is a constant attendant of flame; but what is the connection between them we have no room so much as to conjecture or imagine. It is impossible, therefore, that the idea of power can be derived from the contemplation of bodies in single instances of their operation, because no bodies ever discover any power which can be the original of this idea.[1]

Since, therefore, external objects as they appear to the senses give us no idea of power or necessary connection by their operation in particular instances, let us see whether this idea be derived from reflection on the operations of our own minds and be copied from any internal impression. It may be said that we are every moment conscious of internal power while we feel that, by the simple command of our will, we can move the organs of our body or direct the faculties of our mind. An act of volition produces motion in our limbs or raises a new idea in our imagination. This influence of the will we know by consciousness. Hence we acquire the idea of power or energy, and are certain that we ourselves and all other intelligent beings are possessed of power. This idea, then, is an idea of reflection since it arises from reflecting on the operations of our own mind and on the command which is exercised by will both over the organs of the body and faculties of the soul.

We shall proceed to examine this pretension and, first, with regard to the influence of volition over the organs of the body. This influence, we may observe, is a fact which, like all other natural events, can be known only by experience, and can never be foreseen from any apparent energy or power in the cause which connects it with the effect and renders the one an infallible consequence of the other. The motion of our body follows upon the command of our will. Of this we are every moment conscious. But the means by which this is effected, the energy by which the will performs so extraordinary an operation—of this we are so far from being immediately conscious that it must forever escape our most diligent inquiry.

For, *first,* is there any principle in all nature more mysterious than the union of soul with body, by which a supposed spiritual substance acquires such an influence over a material one that the most refined thought is able to actuate the grossest matter? Were we empowered by a secret wish to remove mountains or control the planets in their orbit, this extensive authority would not be more extraordinary, nor more beyond our comprehension. But if, by consciousness,

we perceived any power or energy in the will, we must know this power; we must know its connection with the effect; we must know the secret union of soul and body, and the nature of both these substances by which the one is able to operate in so many instances upon the other.

Secondly, we are not able to move all the organs of the body with a like authority, though we cannot assign any reason, besides experience, for so remarkable a difference between one and the other. Why has the will an influence over the tongue and fingers, not over the heart and liver? This question would never embarrass us were we conscious of a power in the former case, not in the latter. We should then perceive, independent of experience, why the authority of the will over organs of the body is circumscribed within such particular limits. Being in that case fully acquainted with the power or force by which it operates, we should also know why its influence reaches precisely to such boundaries, and no further.

A man suddenly struck with a palsy in the leg or arm, or who had newly lost those members, frequently endeavors, at first, to move them and employ them in their usual offices. Here he is as much conscious of power to command such limbs as a man in perfect health is conscious of power to actuate any member which remains in its natural state and condition. But consciousness never deceives. Consequently, neither in the one case nor in the other are we ever conscious of any power. We learn the influence of our will from experience alone. And experience only teaches us how one event constantly follows another, without instructing us in the secret connection which binds them together and renders them inseparable.

Thirdly, we learn from anatomy that the immediate object of power in voluntary motion is not the member itself which is moved, but certain muscles and nerves and animal spirits, and, perhaps, something still more minute and more unknown, through which the motion is successfully propagated ere it reach the member itself whose motion is the immediate object of volition. Can there be a more certain proof that the power by which this whole operation is performed, so far from being directly and fully known by an inward sentiment or consciousness, is to the last degree mysterious and unintelligible? Here the mind wills a certain event; immediately another event, unknown to ourselves and totally different from the one intended, is produced. This event produces another, equally unknown, till, at last, through a long succession the desired event is produced. But if the original power were felt, it must be known; were it known, its effect must also be known, since all power is relative to its effect. And, *vice versa,* if the effect be not known, the power cannot be known nor felt. How indeed can we be conscious of a power to move our limbs when we have no such power, but only that to move certain animal spirits which, though they produce at last the motion of our limbs, yet operate in such a manner as is wholly beyond our comprehension?

We may therefore conclude from the whole, I hope, without any temerity, though with assurance, that our idea of power is not copied from any sentiment or consciousness of power within ourselves when we give rise to animal motion or apply our limbs to their proper use and office. That their motion follows the command of the will is a matter of common experience, like other natural events; but the power or energy by which this is effected, like that in other natural events, is unknown and inconceivable.[2]

Shall we then assert that we are conscious of a power or energy in our own minds when, by an act or command of our will, we raise up a new idea, fix the mind to the contemplation of it, turn it on all sides, and at last dismiss it for some other idea when we think that we have surveyed it with sufficient accuracy? I believe the same arguments will prove that even this command of the will gives us no real idea of force or energy.

First, it must be allowed that when we know a power, we know that very circumstance in the cause by which it is enabled to produce the effect, for these are supposed to be synonymous. We must, therefore, know both the cause and effect and the relation between them. But do we pretend to be acquainted with the nature of the human soul and the nature of an idea, or the aptitude of the one to produce the other? This is a real creation, a production of something out of nothing, which implies a power so great that it may seem, at first sight, beyond the reach of any being less than infinite. At least it must be owned that such a power is not felt, nor known, nor even conceivable by the mind. We only feel the event, namely, the existence of an idea consequent to a command of the will; but the manner in which this operation is performed, the power by which it is produced, is entirely beyond our comprehension.

Secondly, the command of the mind over itself is limited, as well as its command over the body; and these limits are not known by reason or any acquaintance with the nature of cause and effect, but only by experience and observation, as in all other natural events and in the operation of external objects. Our authority over our sentiments and passions is much weaker than that over our ideas; and even the latter authority is circumscribed within very narrow boundaries. Will any one pretend to assign the ultimate reason of these boundaries, or show why the power is deficient in one case, not in another.

Thirdly, this self-command is very different at different times. A man in health possesses more of it than one languishing with sickness. We are more master of our thoughts in the morning than in the evening; fasting, than after a full meal. Can we give any reason for these variations except experience? Where then is the power of which we pretend to be conscious? Is there not here, either in a spiritual or material substance, or both, some secret mechanism or structure of parts upon which the effect depends, and which, being entirely unknown to us, renders the power or energy of the will equally unknown and incomprehensible?

Volition is surely an act of the mind with which we are sufficiently acquainted. Reflect upon it. Consider it on all sides. Do you find anything in it like this creative power by which it raises from nothing a new idea and, with a kind of *fiat,* imitates the omnipotence of its Maker, if I may be allowed so to speak, who called forth into existence all the various scenes of nature? So far from being conscious of this energy in the will, it requires as certain experience as that of which we are possessed to convince us that such extraordinary effects do ever result from a simple act of volition.

The generality of mankind never find any difficulty in accounting for the more common and familiar operations of nature, such as the descent of heavy bodies, the growth of plants, the generation of animals, or the nourishment of bodies by food; but suppose that in all these cases they perceive the very force or energy of the cause by which it is connected with its effect, and is forever infallible in its operation. They acquire, by long habit, such a turn of mind that upon the appearance of the cause they immediately expect, with assurance, its usual attendant, and hardly conceive it possible that any other event could result from it. It is only on the discovery of extraordinary phenomena, such as earthquakes, pestilence, and prodigies of any kind, that they find themselves at a loss to assign a proper cause and to explain the manner in which the effect is produced by it. It is usual for men, in such difficulties, to have recourse to some invisible intelligent principle as the immediate cause of that event which surprises them, and which they think cannot be accounted for from the common powers of nature. But philosophers, who carry their scrutiny a little further, immediately perceive that, even in the most familiar events, the energy of the cause is as unintelligible as in the most unusual, and that we only learn by experience the frequent conjunction of objects, without being ever able to comprehend anything like connection between them. Here, then, many philosophers think themselves obliged by reason to have recourse, on all occasions, to the same principle which the vulgar never appeal to but in cases that appear miraculous and supernatural. They acknowledge mind and intelligence to be, not only the ultimate and original cause of all things, but the immediate and sole cause of every event which appears in nature. They pretend that those objects which are commonly denominated "causes" are in reality nothing but "occasions," and that the true and direct principle of every effect is not any power or force in nature, but a volition of the Supreme Being, who wills that such particular objects should forever be conjoined with each other. Instead of saying that one billiard ball moves another by a force which it has derived from the author of nature, it is the Deity himself, they say, who, by a particular volition, moves the second ball, being determined to this operation by the impulse of the first ball, in consequence of those general laws which he has laid down to himself in the government of the universe. But philosophers, advancing still in their inquiries, discover that as we are totally ignorant of the power on which depends the mutual operation of bodies, we are no less ignorant of

that power on which depends the operation of mind on body, or of body on mind; nor are we able, either from our senses or consciousness, to assign the ultimate principle in the one case more than in the other. The same ignorance, therefore, reduces them to the same conclusion. They assert that the Deity is the immediate cause of the union between soul and body, and that they are not the organs of sense which, being agitated by external objects, produce sensations in the mind; but that it is a particular volition of our omnipotent Maker which excites such a sensation in consequence of such a motion in the organ. In like manner, it is not any energy in the will that produces local motion in our members: It is God himself, who is pleased to second our will, in itself impotent, and to command that motion which we erroneously attribute to our own power and efficacy. Nor do philosophers stop at this conclusion. They sometimes extend the same inference to the mind itself in its internal operations. Our mental vision or conception of ideas is nothing but a revelation made to us by our Maker. When we voluntarily turn our thoughts to any object and raise up its image in the fancy, it is not the will which creates that idea, it is the universal Creator who discovers it to the mind and renders it present to us.

Thus, according to these philosophers, everything is full of God. Not content with the principle that nothing exists but by his will, that nothing possesses any power but by his concession, they rob nature and all created beings of every power in order to render their dependence on the Deity still more sensible and immediate. They consider not that by this theory they diminish, instead of magnifying, the grandeur of those attributes which they affect so much to celebrate. It argues, surely, more power in the Deity to delegate a certain degree of power to inferior creatures than to produce everything by his own immediate volition. It argues more wisdom to contrive at first the fabric of the world with such perfect foresight that of itself, and by its proper operation, it may serve all the purposes of Providence than if the great Creator were obliged every moment to adjust its parts and animate by his breath all the wheels of that stupendous machine.

But if we would have a more philosophical confutation of this theory, perhaps the two following reflections may suffice:

First, it seems to me that this theory of the universal energy and operation of the Supreme Being is too bold ever to carry conviction with it to a man sufficiently apprised of the weakness of human reason and the narrow limits to which it is confined in all its operations. Though the chain of arguments which conduct to it were ever so logical, there must arise a strong suspicion, if not an absolute assurance, that it has carried us quite beyond the reach of our faculties when it leads to conclusions so extraordinary and so remote from common life and experience. We are got into fairyland long ere we have reached the last steps of our theory; and *there* we have no reason to trust our common methods of arguments or to think that our usual analogies and probabilities have any authority. Our line is too short to fathom such immense abysses. And however we may flatter ourselves that we are guided, in every step which we take, by a kind of verisimilitude and experience, we may be assured that this fancied experience has no authority when we thus apply it to subjects that lie entirely out of the sphere of experience. But on this we shall have occasion to touch afterwards.

Secondly, I cannot perceive any force in the arguments on which this theory is founded. We are ignorant, it is true, of the manner in which bodies operate on each other. Their force or energy is entirely incomprehensible. But are we not equally ignorant of the manner or force by which a mind, even the Supreme Mind, operates, either on itself or on body? Whence, I beseech you, do we acquire any idea of it? We have no sentiment or consciousness of this power in ourselves. We have no idea of the Supreme Being but what we learn from reflection on our own faculties. Were our ignorance, therefore, a good reason for rejecting anything, we should be led into that principle of denying all energy in the Supreme Being, as much as in the grossest matter. We surely comprehend as little the operations of the one as of the other. Is it more difficult to conceive that motion may arise from impulse than that it may arise from volition? All we know is our profound ignorance in both cases.[3]

Part II

But to hasten to a conclusion of this argument, which is already drawn out to too great a length: We have

sought in vain for an idea of power or necessary connection in all the sources from which we could suppose it to be derived. It appears that in single instances of the operation of bodies we never can, by our utmost scrutiny, discover anything but one event following another, without being able to comprehend any force or power by which the cause operates or any connection between it and its supposed effect. The same difficulty occurs in contemplating the operations of mind on body, where we observe the motion of the latter to follow upon the volition of the former, but are not able to observe or conceive the tie which binds together the motion and volition, or the energy, by which the mind produces this effect. The authority of the will over its own faculties and ideas is not a whit more comprehensible, so that, upon the whole, there appears not, throughout all nature, any one instance of connection which is conceivable by us. All events seem entirely loose and separate. One event follows another, but we never can observe any tie between them. They seem *conjoined,* but never *connected.* And as we can have no idea of anything which never appeared to our outward sense or inward sentiment, the necessary conclusion *seems* to be that we have no idea of connection or power at all, and that these words are absolutely without any meaning when employed either in philosophical reasonings or common life.

But there still remains one method of avoiding this conclusion, and one source which we have not yet examined. When any natural object or event is presented, it is impossible for us, by any sagacity or penetration, to discover, or even conjecture, without experience, what event will result from it, or to carry our foresight beyond that object which is immediately present to the memory and senses. Even after one instance or experiment where we have observed a particular event to follow upon another, we are not entitled to form a general rule or foretell what will happen in like cases, it being justly esteemed an unpardonable temerity to judge the whole course of nature from one single experiment, however accurate or certain. But when one particular species of events has always, in all instances, been conjoined with another, we make no longer any scruple of foretelling one upon the appearance of the other, and of employing that reasoning which can alone assure us of any matter of fact or existence. We then call the one object "cause," the other "effect." We suppose that there is some connection between them, some power in the one by which it infallibly produces the other and operates with the greatest certainty and strongest necessity.

It appears, then, that this idea of a necessary connection among events arises from a number of similar instances which occur, of the constant conjunction of these events; nor can that idea ever be suggested by any one of these instances surveyed in all possible lights and positions. But there is nothing in a number of instances, different from every single instance, which is supposed to be exactly similar, except only that after a repetition of similar instances the mind is carried by habit, upon the appearance of one event, to expect its usual attendant and to believe that it will exist. This connection, therefore, which we *feel* in the mind, this customary transition of the imagination from one object to its usual attendant, is the sentiment or impression from which we form the idea of power or necessary connection. Nothing further is in the case. Contemplate the subject on all sides, you will never find any other origin of that idea. This is the sole difference between one instance, from which we can never receive the idea of connection, and a number of similar instances by which it is suggested. The first time a man saw the communication of motion by impulse, as by the shock of two billiard balls, he could not pronounce that the one event was *connected,* but only that it was *conjoined* with the other. After he has observed several instances of this nature, he then pronounces them to be *connected.* What alteration has happened to give rise to this new idea of *connection?* Nothing but that he now *feels* these events to be *connected* in his imagination, and can readily foretell the existence of one from the appearance of the other. When we say, therefore, that one object is connected with another, we mean only that they have acquired a connection in our thought and give rise to this inference by which they become proofs of each other's existence—a conclusion which is somewhat extraordinary, but which seems founded on sufficient evidence. Nor will its evidence be weakened by any general diffidence of the understanding or skeptical suspicion concerning every conclusion which is new and extraordinary. No conclusions can be more agreeable to skepticism than

such as make discoveries concerning the weakness and narrow limits of human reason and capacity.

And what stronger instance can be produced of the surprising ignorance and weakness of the understanding than the present? For surely, if there be any relation among objects which it imports us to know perfectly, it is that of cause and effect. On this are founded all our reasonings concerning matter of fact or existence. By means of it alone we attain any assurance concerning objects which are removed from the present testimony of our memory and senses. The only immediate utility of all sciences is to teach us how to control and regulate future events by their causes. Our thoughts and inquiries are, therefore, every moment employed about this relation; yet so imperfect are the ideas which we form concerning it that it is impossible to give any just definition of cause, except what is drawn from something extraneous and foreign to it. Similar objects are always conjoined with similar. Of this we have experience. Suitably to this experience, therefore, we may define a cause to be *an object followed by another, and where all the objects, similar to the first, are followed by objects similar to the second.* Or, in other words, *where, if the first object had not been, the second never had existed.* The appearance of a cause always conveys the mind, by a customary transition, to the idea of the effect. Of this also we have experience. We may, therefore suitably to this experience, form another definition of cause and call it *an object followed by another, and whose appearance always conveys the thought to that other.* But though both these definitions be drawn from circumstances foreign to the cause, we cannot remedy this inconvenience or attain any more perfect definition which may point out that circumstance in the cause which gives it a connection with its effect. We have no idea of this connection, nor even any distinct notion what it is we desire to know when we endeavor at a conception of it. We say, for instance, that the vibration of this string is the cause of this particular sound. But what do we mean by that affirmation? We either mean *that this vibration is followed by this sound, and that all similar vibrations have been followed by similar sounds; or, that this vibration is followed by this sound, and that, upon the appearance of one, the mind anticipates the senses and forms immediately an idea of the other.* We may consider the relation of cause and effect in either of these two lights; but beyond these we have no idea of it.[4]

To recapitulate, therefore, the reasonings of this Section: Every idea is copied from some preceding impression or sentiment; and where we cannot find any impression, we may be certain that there is no idea. In all single instances of the operation of bodies or minds there is nothing that produces any impression, nor consequently can suggest any idea, of power or necessary connection. But when many uniform instances appear, and the same object is always followed by the same event, we then begin to entertain the notion of cause and connection. We then *feel* a new sentiment or impression, to wit, a customary connection in the thought or imagination between one object and its usual attendant; and this sentiment is the original of that idea which we seek for. For as this idea arises from a number of similar instances, and not from any single instance, it must arise from that circumstance in which the number of instances differ from every individual instance. But this customary connection or transition of the imagination is the only circumstance in which they differ. In every other particular they are alike. The first instance which we saw of motion, communicated by the shock of two billiard balls (to return to this obvious illustration), is exactly similar to any instance that may at present occur to us, except only that we could not at first *infer* one event from the other, which we are enabled to do at present, after so long a course of uniform experience. I know not whether the reader will readily apprehend this reasoning. I am afraid that, should I multiply words about it or throw it into a greater variety of lights, it would only become more obscure and intricate. In all abstract reasonings there is one point of view which, if we can happily hit, we shall go further towards illustrating the subject than by all the eloquence in the world. This point of view we should endeavor to reach, and reserve the flowers of rhetoric for subjects which are more adapted to them.

NOTES

1. Mr. Locke, in his chapter of Power, says that, finding from experience that there are several new productions in matter, and concluding that there must somewhere be a power capable of producing them, we arrive at last by this reasoning at the idea of power. But no reasoning can ever give us a new, original simple idea, as this philosopher himself confesses. This, therefore, can never be the origin of that idea.

2. It may be pretended, that the resistance which we meet with in bodies, obliging us frequently to exert our force and call up all our power, this gives us the idea of force and power. It is this *nisus* or strong endeavor of which we are conscious, that is the original impression from which this idea is copied. But, *first*, we attribute power to a vast number of objects where we never can suppose this resistance or exertion of force to take place: to the Supreme Being, who never meets with any resistance; to the mind in its command over its ideas and limbs, in common thinking and motion, where the effect follows immediately upon the will, without any exertion or summoning up of force; to inanimate matter, which is not capable of this sentiment. *Secondly,* this sentiment of an endeavor to overcome resistance has no known connection with any event: What follows it we know by experience, but could not know it *a priori.* It must, however, be confessed that the animal *nisus* which we experience, though it can afford no accurate precise idea of power, enters very much into that vulgar, inaccurate idea which is formed of it.

3. I need not examine at length the *vis inertiae* which is so much talked of in the new philosophy, and which is ascribed to matter. We find by experience that a body at rest or in motion continues forever in its present state, till put from it by some new cause; and that a body impelled takes as much motion from the impelling body as it acquires itself. These are facts. When we call this a *vis inertiae,* we only mark these facts, without pretending to have any idea of the inert power, in the same manner as, when we talk of gravity, we mean certain effects without comprehending that active power. It was never the meaning of Sir Isaac Newton to rob second causes of all force or energy, though some of his followers have endeavored to establish that theory upon his authority. On the contrary, that great philosopher had recourse to an ethereal active fluid to explain his universal attraction, though he was so cautious and modest as to allow that it was a mere hypothesis not to be insisted on without more experiments. I must confess that there is something in the fate of opinions a little extraordinary. Descartes insinuated that doctrine of the universal and sole efficacy of the Deity, without insisting on it. Malebranche and other Cartesians made it the foundation of all their philosophy. It had, however, no authority in England. Locke, Clarke, and Cudworth never so much as take notice of it, but suppose all along that matter has a real, though subor-

dinate and derived, power. By what means has it become so prevalent among our modern metaphysicians?

4. According to these explications and definitions, the idea of *power* is relative as much as that of *cause;* and both have a reference to an effect, or some other event constantly conjoined with the former. When we consider the *unknown* circumstance of an object by which the degree or quantity of its effect is fixed and determined, we call that its power. And accordingly, it is allowed by all philosophers that the effect is the measure of the power. But if they had any idea of power as it is in itself, why could they not measure it in itself? The dispute, whether the force of a body in motion be as its velocity, or the square of its velocity; this dispute, I say, needed not be decided by comparing its effects in equal or unequal times, but by direct mensuration and comparison.

As to the frequent use of the words "force," "power," "energy," etc., which everywhere occur in common conversation as well as in philosophy, that is no proof that we are acquainted, in any instance, with the connecting principle between cause and effect, or can account ultimately for the production of one thing by another. These words, as commonly used, have very loose meanings annexed to them, and their ideas are very uncertain and confused. No animal can put external bodies in motion without the sentiment of a *nisus* or endeavor; and every animal has a sentiment or feeling from the stroke or blow of an external object that is in motion. These sensations, which are merely animal, and from which we can *a priori* draw no inference, we are apt to transfer to inanimate objects, and to suppose that they have some such feelings whenever they transfer or receive motion. With regard to energies, which are exerted without our annexing to them any idea of communicated motion, we consider only the constant experienced conjunction of the events; and as we *feel* a customary connection between the ideas, we transfer that feeling to the objects, as nothing is more usual than to apply to external bodies every internal sensation which they occasion.

Causation

DAVID LEWIS

David Lewis (1941–2001) was professor of philosophy at Princeton University.

Hume defined causation twice over. He wrote "we may define a cause to be *an object followed by another, and where all the objects, similar to the first, are followed by objects similar to the second.* Or, in other words, *where, if the first object had not been, the second never had existed.*"[1]

Descendants of Hume's first definition still dominate the philosophy of causation: a causal succession is supposed to be a succession that instantiates a regularity. To be sure, there have been improvements. Nowadays we try to distinguish the regularities that count—the "causal laws"—from mere accidental regularities of succession. We subsume causes and effects under regularities by means of descriptions they satisfy, not by over-all similarity. And we allow a cause to be only one indispensable part, not the whole, of the total situation that is followed by the effect in accordance with a law. In present-day regularity analyses, a cause is defined (roughly) as any member of any minimal set of actual conditions that are jointly sufficient, given the laws, for the existence of the effect.

More precisely, let C be the proposition that c exists (or occurs) and let E be the proposition that e exists. Then c causes e, according to a typical regularity analysis,[2] iff (1) C and E are true; and (2) for some nonempty set $\mathscr{L}$ of true law-propositions and some set $\mathscr{F}$ of true propositions of particular fact, $\mathscr{L}$

Reprinted from *The Journal of Philosophy, 70* (1973), by permission of the author.

and $\mathscr{F}$ jointly imply $C \supset E$, although $\mathscr{L}$ and $\mathscr{F}$ jointly do not imply E and $\mathscr{F}$ alone does not imply $C \supset E$.[3]

Much needs doing, and much has been done, to turn definitions like this one into defensible analyses. Many problems have been overcome. Others remain: in particular, regularity analyses tend to confuse causation itself with various other causal relations. If c belongs to a minimal set of conditions jointly sufficient for e, given the laws, then c may well be a genuine cause of e. But c might rather be an effect of e: one which could not, given the laws and some of the actual circumstances, have occurred otherwise than by being caused by e. Or c might be an epiphenomenon of the causal history of e: a more or less inefficacious effect of some genuine cause of e. Or c might be a preempted potential cause of e: something that did not cause e, but that would have done so in the absence of whatever really did cause e.

It remains to be seen whether any regularity analysis can succeed in distinguishing genuine causes from effects, epiphenomena, and preempted potential causes—and whether it can succeed without falling victim to worse problems, without piling on the epicycles, and without departing from the fundamental idea that causation is instantiation of regularities. I have no proof that regularity analyses are beyond repair, nor any space to review the repairs that have been tried. Suffice it to say that the prospects look dark. I think it is time to give up and try something else.

A promising alternative is not far to seek. Hume's "other words"—that if the cause had not been, the effect never had existed—are no mere restatement of his first definition. They propose something altogether different: a counterfactual analysis of causation.

The proposal has not been well received. True, we do know that causation has something or other to do with counterfactuals. We think of a cause as something that makes a difference, and the difference it makes must be a difference from what would have happened without it. Had it been absent, its effects—some of them, at least, and usually all—would have been absent as well. Yet it is one thing to mention these platitudes now and again, and another thing to rest an analysis on them. That has not seemed worth

while.[4] We have learned all too well that counterfactuals are ill understood, wherefore it did not seem that much understanding could be gained by using them to analyze causation or anything else. Pending a better understanding of counterfactuals, moreover, we had no way to fight seeming counterexamples to a counterfactual analysis.

But counterfactuals need not remain ill understood, I claim, unless we cling to false preconceptions about what it would be like to understand them. Must an adequate understanding make no reference to unactualized possibilities? Must it assign sharply determinate truth conditions? Must it connect counterfactuals rigidly to covering laws? Then none will be forthcoming. So much the worse for those standards of adequacy. Why not take counterfactuals at face value: as statements about possible alternatives to the actual situation, somewhat vaguely specified, in which the actual laws may or may not remain intact? There are now several such treatments of counterfactuals, differing only in details.[5] If they are right, then sound foundations have been laid for analyses that use counterfactuals.

In this paper, I shall state a counterfactual analysis, not very different from Hume's second definition, of some sorts of causation. Then I shall try to show how this analysis works to distinguish genuine causes from effects, epiphenomena, and preempted potential causes.

My discussion will be incomplete in at least four ways. Explicit preliminary settings-aside may prevent confusion.

1. I shall confine myself to causation among *events,* in the everyday sense of the word: flashes, battles, conversations, impacts, strolls, deaths, touchdowns, falls, kisses, and the like. Not that events are the only things that can cause or be caused; but I have no full list of the others, and no good umbrella-term to cover them all.

2. My analysis is meant to apply to causation in particular cases. It is not an analysis of causal generalizations. Presumably those are quantified statements involving causation among particular events (or non-events), but it turns out not to be easy to match up the causal generalizations of natural language with the available quantified forms. A sentence

of the form "c-events cause E-events," for instance, can mean any of

(a) For some c in C and some e in E, c causes e.
(b) For every e in E, there is some c in C such that c causes e.
(c) For every c in C, there is some e in E such that c causes e. not to mention further ambiguities. Worse still, "Only c-events cause E-events" ought to mean
(d) For every c, if there is some e in E such that c causes e, then c is in C.

if "only" has its usual meaning. But no; it unambiguously means (b) instead! These problems are not about causation, but about our idioms of quantification.

3. We sometimes single out one among all the causes of some event and call it "the" cause, as if there were no others. Or we single out a few as the "causes," calling the rest mere "causal factors" or "causal conditions." Or we speak of the "decisive" or "real" or "principal" cause. We may select the abnormal or extraordinary causes, or those under human control, or those we deem good or bad, or just those we want to talk about. I have nothing to say about these principles of invidious discrimination.[6] I am concerned with the prior question of what it is to be one of the causes (unselectively speaking). My analysis is meant to capture a broad and nondiscriminatory concept of causation.

4. I shall be content, for now, if I can give an analysis of causation that works properly under determinism. By determinism I do not mean any thesis of universal causation, or universal predictability-in-principle, but rather this: the prevailing laws of nature are such that there do not exist any two possible worlds which are exactly alike up to some time, which differ thereafter, and in which those laws are never violated. Perhaps by ignoring indeterminism I squander the most striking advantage of a counterfactual analysis over a regularity analysis: that it allows undetermined events to be caused.[7] I fear, however, that my present analysis cannot yet cope with all varieties of causation under indeterminism. The needed repair would take us too far into disputed questions about the foundations of probability.

COMPARATIVE SIMILARITY

To begin, I take as primitive a relation of *comparative over-all* similarity among possible worlds. We may say that one world is *closer to actuality* than another if the first resembles our actual world more than the second does, taking account of all the respects of similarity and difference and balancing them off one against another.

(More generally, an arbitrary world w can play the role of our actual world. In speaking of our actual world without knowing just which world is ours, I am in effect generalizing over all worlds. We really need a three-place relation: world w_1 is closer to world w than world w_2 is. I shall henceforth leave this generality tacit.)

I have not said just how to balance the respects of comparison against each other, so I have not said just what our relation of comparative similarity is to be. Not for nothing did I call it primitive. But I have said what *sort* of relation it is, and we are familiar with relations of that sort. We do make judgments of comparative overall similarity—of people, for instance— by balancing off many respects of similarity and difference. Often our mutual expectations about the weighting factors are definite and accurate enough to permit communication. I shall have more to say later about the way the balance must go in particular cases to make my analysis work. But the vagueness of over-all similarity will not be entirely resolved. Nor should it be. The vagueness of similarity does infect causation, and no correct analysis can deny it.

The respects of similarity and difference that enter into the overall similarity of worlds are many and varied. In particular, similarities in matters of particular fact trade off against similarities of law. The prevailing laws of nature are important to the character of a world; so similarities of law are weighty. Weighty, but not sacred. We should not take it for granted that a world that conforms perfectly to our actual laws is ipso facto closer to actuality than any world where those laws are violated in any way at all. It depends on the nature and extent of the violation, on the place of the violated laws in the total system of laws of nature, and on the countervailing similarities and differences in other respects. Likewise, similarities or differences of particular fact may be more or less weighty, depending on their nature and extent. Comprehensive and exact similarities of particular fact throughout large spatiotemporal regions seem to have special weight. It may be worth a small miracle to prolong or expand a region of perfect match.

Our relation of comparative similarity should meet two formal constraints. (1) It should be a weak ordering of the worlds: an ordering in which ties are permitted, but any two worlds are comparable. (2) Our actual world should be closest to actuality, resembling itself more than any other world resembles it. We do *not* impose the further constraint that for any set A of worlds there is a unique closest A-world, or even a set of A-worlds tied for closest. Why not an infinite sequence of closer and closer A-worlds, but no closest?

COUNTERFACTUALS AND COUNTERFACTUAL DEPENDENCE

Given any two propositions A and C, we have their *counterfactual* $A \square \rightarrow C$: the proposition that if A were true, then C would also be true. The operation $\square \rightarrow$ is defined by a rule of truth, as follows. $A \square \rightarrow C$ is true (at a world w) iff either (1) there are no possible A-worlds (in which case $A \square \rightarrow C$ is *vacuous*), or (2) some A-world where C holds is closer (to w) than is any A-world where C does not hold. In other words, a counterfactual is nonvacuously true iff it takes less of a departure from actuality to make the consequent true along with the antecedent than it does to make the antecedent true without the consequent.

We did not assume that there must always be one or more closest A-worlds. But if there are, we can simplify: $A \square \rightarrow C$ is nonvacuously true iff C holds at all the closest A-worlds.

We have not presupposed that A is false. If A is true, then our actual world is the closest A-world, so $A \square \rightarrow C$ is true iff C is. Hence $A \square \rightarrow C$ implies the material conditional $A \supset C$; and A and C jointly imply $A \square \rightarrow C$.

Let $A_1, A_2, \ldots$ be a family of possible propositions, no two of which are compossible; let $C_1, C_2, \ldots$ be another such family (of equal size). Then if all the counterfactuals $A_1 \square \rightarrow C_1, A_2 \square \rightarrow C_2, \ldots$

between corresponding propositions in the two families are true, we shall say that the C's *depend counterfactually* on the A's. We can say it like this in ordinary language: whether C_1 or C_2 or . . . depends (counterfactually) on whether A_1 or A_2 or. . . .

Counterfactual dependence between large families of alternatives is characteristic of processes of measurement, perception, or control. Let $R_1, R_2, \ldots$ be propositions specifying the alternative readings of a certain barometer at a certain time. Let $P_1, P_2, \ldots$ specify the corresponding pressures of the surrounding air. Then, if the barometer is working properly to measure the pressure, the R's must depend counterfactually on the P's. As we say it: the reading depends on the pressure. Likewise, if I am seeing at a certain time, then my visual impressions must depend counterfactually, over a wide range of alternative possibilities, on the scene before my eyes. And if I am in control over what happens in some respect, then there must be a double counterfactual dependence, again over some fairly wide range of alternatives. The outcome depends on what I do, and that in turn depends on which outcome I want.[8]

CAUSAL DEPENDENCE AMONG EVENTS

If a family $C_1, C_2, \ldots$ depends counterfactually on a family $A_1, A_2, \ldots$ in the sense just explained, we will ordinarily be willing to speak also of causal dependence. We say, for instance, that the barometer reading depends causally on the pressure, that my visual impressions depend causally on the scene before my eyes, or that the outcome of something under my control depends causally on what I do. But there are exceptions. Let $G_1, G_2 \ldots$ be alternative possible laws of gravitation, differing in the value of some numerical constant. Let $M_1, M_2, \ldots$ be suitable alternative laws of planetary motion. Then the M's may depend counterfactually on the G's, but we would not call this dependence causal. Such exceptions as this, however, do not involve any sort of dependence among distinct particular events. The hope remains that causal dependence among events, at least, may be analyzed simply as counterfactual dependence.

We have spoken thus far of counterfactual dependence among propositions, not among events.

Whatever particular events may be, presumably they are not propositions. But that is no problem, since they can at least be paired with propositions. To any possible event e, there corresponds the proposition $O(e)$ that holds at all and only those worlds where e occurs. This $O(e)$ is the proposition that e occurs.[9] (If no two events occur at exactly the same worlds—if, that is, there are no absolutely necessary connections between distinct events—we may add that this correspondence of events and propositions is one to one.) Counterfactual dependence among events is simply counterfactual dependence among the corresponding propositions.

Let c_1, c_2, ... and e_1, e_2, ... be distinct possible events such that no two of the c's and no two of the e's are compossible. Then I say that the family e_1, e_2, ... of events *depends causally* on the family c_1, c_2, ... iff the family $O(e_1)$, $O(e_2)$, ... of propositions depends counterfactually on the family $O(c_1)$, $O(c_2)$, ... As we say it: whether e_1 or e_2 or ... occurs depends on whether c_1 or c_2 or ... occurs.

We can also define a relation of dependence among single events rather than families. Let c and e be two distinct possible particular events. Then e *depends causally* on c iff the family $O(e)$, $\sim O(e)$ depends counterfactually on the family $O(c)$, $\sim O(c)$. As we say it: whether e occurs or not depends on whether c occurs or not. The dependence consists in the truth of two counterfactuals: $O(c) \square \rightarrow O(e)$ and $\sim O(c) \square \rightarrow \sim O(e)$. There are two cases. If c and e do not actually occur, then the second counterfactual is automatically true because its antecedent and consequent are true: so e depends causally on c iff the first counterfactual holds. That is, iff e would have occurred if c had occurred. But if c and e are actual events, then it is the first counterfactual that is automatically true. Then e depends causally on c iff, if c had not been, e never had existed. I take Hume's second definition as my definition not of causation itself, but of causal dependence among actual events.

CAUSATION

Causal dependence among actual events implies causation. If c and e are two actual events such that e would not have occurred without c, then c is a cause of e. But I reject the converse. Causation must always

be transitive; causal dependence may not be; so there can be causation without causal dependence. Let c, d, and e be three actual events such that d would not have occurred without c and e would not have occurred without d. Then c is a cause of e even if e would still have occurred (otherwise caused) without c.

We extend causal dependence to a transitive relation in the usual way. Let c, d, e, ... be a finite sequence of actual particular events such that d depends causally on c, e on d, and so on throughout. Then this sequence is a *causal chain*. Finally, one event is a *cause* of another iff there exists a causal chain leading from the first to the second. This completes my counterfactual analysis of causation.

COUNTERFACTUAL VERSUS NOMIC DEPENDENCE

It is essential to distinguish counterfactual and causal dependence from what I shall call *nomic dependence*. The family C_1, C_2, ... of propositions depends nomically on the family A_1, A_2, ... iff there are a nonempty set $\mathcal{L}$ of true law-propositions and a set $\mathcal{F}$ of true propositions of particular fact such that $\mathcal{L}$ and $\mathcal{F}$ jointly imply (but $\mathcal{F}$ alone does not imply) all the material conditionals $A_1 \supset C_1$, $A_2 \supset C_2$, ... between the corresponding propositions in the two families. (Recall that these same material conditionals are implied by the counterfactuals that would comprise a counterfactual dependence.) We shall say also that the nomic dependence holds *in virtue of* the premise sets $\mathcal{L}$ and $\mathcal{F}$.

Nomic and counterfactual dependence are related as follows. Say that a proposition B is *counterfactually independent* of the family A_1, A_2, ... of alternatives iff B would hold no matter which of the A's were true—that is, iff the counterfactuals $A_1 \square \rightarrow B$, $A_2 \square \rightarrow B$, ... all hold. If the C's depend nomically on the A's in virtue of the premise sets $\mathcal{L}$ and $\mathcal{F}$, and if in addition (all members of) $\mathcal{L}$ and $\mathcal{F}$ are counterfactually independent of the A's, then it follows that the C's depend counterfactually on the A's. In that case, we may regard the nomic dependence in virtue of $\mathcal{L}$ and $\mathcal{F}$ as explaining the counterfactual dependence. Often, perhaps always, counterfactual dependences may be thus explained. But the requirement of counterfactual independence is indispensable. Unless $\mathcal{L}$

and $\mathscr{F}$ meet that requirement, nomic dependence in virtue of $\mathscr{L}$ and $\mathscr{F}$ does not imply counterfactual dependence, and, if there is counterfactual dependence anyway, does not explain it.

Nomic dependence is reversible, in the following sense. If the family $C_1, C_2, \ldots$ depends nomically on the family $A_1, A_2, \ldots$ in virtue of $\mathscr{L}$ and $\mathscr{F}$, then also $A_1, A_2, \ldots$ depends nomically on the family AC_1, $AC_2, \ldots$, in virtue of $\mathscr{L}$ and $\mathscr{F}$, where A is the disjunction $A_1 \vee A_2 \vee \ldots$. Is counterfactual dependence likewise reversible? That does not follow. For, even if $\mathscr{L}$ and $\mathscr{F}$ are independent of $A_1, A_2, \ldots$ and hence establish the counterfactual dependence of the C's on the A's, still they may fail to be independent of AC_1, $AC_2, \ldots$, and hence may fail to establish the reverse counterfactual dependence of the A's on the AC's. Irreversible counterfactual dependence is shown below: @ is our actual world, the dots are the other worlds, and distance on the page represents similarity "distance."

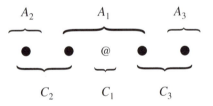

The counterfactuals $A_1 \; \Box \!\!\rightarrow C_1$, $A_2 \; \Box \!\!\rightarrow C_2$, and $A_3 \; \Box \!\!\rightarrow C_3$ hold at the actual world; wherefore the C's depend on the A's. But we do not have the reverse dependence of the A's on the AC's, since instead of the needed $AC_2 \; \Box \!\!\rightarrow A_2$ and $AC_3 \; \Box \!\!\rightarrow A_3$ we have $AC_2 \; \Box \!\!\rightarrow A_1$ and $AC_3 \; \Box \!\!\rightarrow A_1$.

Just such irreversibility is commonplace. The barometer reading depends counterfactually on the pressure—that is as clear-cut as counterfactuals ever get—but does the pressure depend counterfactually on the reading? If the reading had been higher, would the pressure have been higher? Or would the barometer have been malfunctioning? The second sounds better: a higher reading would have been an incorrect reading. To be sure, there are actual laws and circumstances that imply and explain the actual accuracy of the barometer, but these are no more sacred than the actual laws and circumstances that imply and explain the actual pressure. Less sacred, in fact.

When something must give way to permit a higher reading, we find it less of a departure from actuality to hold the pressure fixed and sacrifice the accuracy, rather than vice versa. It is not hard to see why. The barometer, being more localized and more delicate than the weather, is more vulnerable to slight departures from actuality.[10]

We can now explain why regularity analyses of causation (among events, under determinism) work as well as they do. Suppose that event c causes event e according to the sample regularity analysis that I gave at the beginning of this paper, in virtue of premise sets $\mathscr{L}$ and $\mathscr{F}$. It follows that $\mathscr{L}$, $\mathscr{F}$, and $\sim O(c)$ jointly do not imply $O(e)$. Strengthen this: suppose further that they do imply $\sim O(e)$. If so, the family $O(e), \sim O(e)$, depends nomically on the family $O(c), \sim O(c)$ in virtue of $\mathscr{L}$ and $\mathscr{F}$. Add one more supposition: that $\mathscr{L}$ and $\mathscr{F}$ are counterfactually independent of $O(c)$, $\sim O(c)$. Then it follows according to my counterfactual analysis that e depends counterfactually and causally on c, and hence that c causes e. If I am right, the regularity analysis gives conditions that are almost but not quite sufficient for explicable causal dependence. That is not quite the same thing as causation; but causation without causal dependence is scarce, and if there is inexplicable causal dependence we are (understandably!) unaware of it.[11]

EFFECTS AND EPIPHENOMENA

I return now to the problems I raised against regularity analyses, hoping to show that my counterfactual analysis can overcome them.

The *problem of effects,* as it confronts a counterfactual analysis, is as follows. Suppose that c causes a subsequent event e, and that e does not also cause c. (I do not rule out closed causal loops a priori, but this case is not to be one.) Suppose further that, given the laws and some of the actual circumstances, c could not have failed to cause e. It seems to follow that if the effect e had not occurred, then its cause c would not have occurred. We have a spurious reverse causal dependence of c on e, contradicting our supposition that e did not cause c.

The *problem of epiphenomena,* for a counterfactual analysis, is similar. Suppose that e is an epiphenomenal effect of a genuine cause c of an effect f.

That is, c causes first e and then f, but e does not cause f. Suppose further that, given the laws and some of the actual circumstances, c could not have failed to cause e; and that, given the laws and others of the circumstances, f could not have been caused otherwise than by c. It seems to follow that if the epiphenomenon e had not occurred, then its cause c would not have occurred and the further effect f of that same cause would not have occurred either. We have a spurious causal dependence of f on e, contradicting our supposition that e did not cause f.

One might be tempted to solve the problem of effects by brute force: insert into the analysis a stipulation that a cause must always precede its effect (and perhaps a parallel stipulation for causal dependence). I reject this solution. (1) It is worthless against the closely related problem of epiphenomena, since the epiphenomenon e does precede its spurious effect f. (2) It rejects a priori certain legitimate physical hypotheses that posit backward or simultaneous causation. (3) It trivializes any theory that seeks to define the forward direction of time as the predominant direction of causation.

The proper solution to both problems, I think, is flatly to deny the counterfactuals that cause the trouble. If e had been absent, it is not that c would have been absent (and with it f, in the second case). Rather, c would have occurred just as it did but would have failed to cause e. It is less of a departure from actuality to get rid of e by holding c fixed and giving up some or other of the laws and circumstances in virtue of which c could not have failed to cause e, rather than to hold those laws and circumstances fixed and get rid of e by going back and abolishing its cause c. (In the second case, it would of course be pointless not to hold f fixed along with c.) The causal dependence of e on c is the same sort of irreversible counterfactual dependence that we have considered already.

To get rid of an actual event e with the least overall departure from actuality, it will normally be best not to diverge at all from the actual course of events until just before the time of e. The longer we wait, the more we prolong the spatiotemporal region of perfect match between our actual world and the selected alternative. Why diverge sooner rather than later? Not to avoid violations of laws of nature. Under determinism *any* divergence, soon or late, requires some violation of the actual laws. If the laws were held sacred, there would be no way to get rid of e without changing all of the past; and nothing guarantees that the change could be kept negligible except in the recent past. That would mean that if the present were ever so slightly different, then all of the past would have been different—which is absurd. So the laws are not sacred. Violation of laws is a matter of degree. Until we get up to the time immediately before e is to occur, there is no general reason why a later divergence to avert e should need a more severe violation than an earlier one. Perhaps there are special reasons in special cases—but then these may be cases of backward causal dependence.

PREEMPTION

Suppose that c_1 occurs and causes e; and that c_2 also occurs and does not cause e, but would have caused e if c_1 had been absent. Thus c_2 is a potential alternate cause of e, but is preempted by the actual cause c_1. We may say that c_1 and c_2 overdetermine e, but they do so asymmetrically.[12] In virtue of what difference does c_1 but not c_2 cause e?

As far as causal dependence goes, there is no difference: e depends neither on c_1 nor on c_2. If either one had not occurred, the other would have sufficed to cause e. So the difference must be that, thanks to c_1, there is no causal chain from c_2 to e; whereas there is a causal chain of two or more steps from c_1 to e. Assume for simplicity that two steps are enough. Then e depends causally on some intermediate event d, and d in turn depends on c_1. Causal dependence is here intransitive: c_1 causes e via d even though e would still have occurred without c_1.

So far, so good. It remains only to deal with the objection that e does *not* depend causally on d, because if d had been absent then c_1 would have been absent and c_2, no longer preempted, would have caused e. We may reply by denying the claim that if d had been absent then c_1 would have been absent. That is the very same sort of spurious reverse dependence of cause on effect that we have just rejected in simpler cases. I rather claim that if d had been absent, c_1 would somehow have failed to cause d. But c_1 would still have been there to interfere with c_2, so e would not have occurred.

NOTES

1. *An Enquiry concerning Human Understanding,* Section VII.

2. Not one that has been proposed by any actual author in just this form, so far as I know.

3. I identify a *proposition,* as is becoming usual, with the set of possible worlds where it is true. It is not a linguistic entity. Truth-functional operations on propositions are the appropriate Boolean operations on sets of worlds; logical relations among propositions are relations of inclusion, overlap, etc. among sets. A sentence of a language *expresses* a proposition iff the sentence and the proposition are true at exactly the same worlds. No ordinary language will provide sentences to express all propositions; there will not be enough sentences to go around.

4. One exception: Aardon Lyon, "Causality," *British Journal for Philosophy of Science,* XVIII, 1 (May 1967): 1–20.

5. See, for instance, Robert Stalnaker, "A Theory of Conditionals," in Nicholas Rescher, ed., *Studies in Logical Theory* (Oxford: Blackwell, 1968); and my *Counterfactuals* (Oxford: Blackwell, 1973).

6. Except that Morton G. White's discussion of causal selection, in *Foundations of Historical Knowledge* (New York: Harper & Row, 1965), pp. 105–181, would meet my needs, despite the fact that it is based on a regularity analysis.

7. That this ought to be allowed is argued in G. E. M. Anscombe, *Causality and Determination: An Inaugural Lecture* (Cambridge: University Press, 1971); and in Fred Dretske and Aaron Snyder, "Causal Irregularity," *Philosophy of Science,* XXXIX, 1 (March 1972): 69–71.

8. Analyses in terms of counterfactual dependence are found in two papers of Alvin I. Goldman: "Toward a Theory of Social Power," *Philosophical Studies,* XXIII (1972): 221–268; and "Discrimination and Perceptual Knowledge," presented at the 1972 Chapel Hill Colloquium.

9. Beware: if we refer to a particular event *e* by means of some description that *e* satisfies, then we must take care not to confuse $O(e)$, the proposition that *e* itself occurs, with the different proposition that some event or other occurs which satisfies the description. It is a contingent matter, in general, what events satisfy what descriptions. Let *e* be the death of Socrates—the death he actually died, to be distinguished from all the different deaths he might have died instead. Suppose that Socrates had fled, only to be eaten by a lion. Then *e* would not have occurred, and $O(e)$ would have been false; but a different event would have satisfied the description 'the death of Socrates' that I used to refer to *e.* Or suppose that Socrates had lived and died just as he actually did, and afterwards was resurrected and killed again and resurrected again, and finally became immortal. Then no event would have satisfied the description. (Even if the temporary deaths are real deaths, neither of the two can be *the* death.) But *e* would have occurred, and $O(e)$ would have been true. Call a description of an event *e* rigid iff (1) nothing but *e* could possibly satisfy it, and (2) *e* could not possibly occur without satisfy it. I have claimed that even such common-place descriptions as 'the death of Socrates' are nonrigid, and in fact I think that rigid descriptions of events are hard to find. That would be a problem for anyone who needed to associate with every possible event *e* a sentence $\phi(e)$ true at all and only those worlds where *e* occurs. But we need no such sentences—only propositions, which may or may not have expressions in our language.

10. Granted, there are contexts or changes of wording that would incline us the other way. For some reason, "If the reading had been higher, that would have been because the pressure was higher" invites my assent more than "If the reading had been higher, the pressure would have been higher." The counterfactuals from readings to pressures are much less clear-cut than those from pressures to readings. But it is enough that some legitimate resolutions of vagueness give an irreversible dependence of readings on pressures. Those are the resolutions we want at present, even if they are not favored in all contexts.

11. I am not here proposing a repaired regularity analysis. The repaired analysis would gratuitously rule out inexplicable causal dependence, which seems bad. Nor would it be squarely in the tradition of regularity analyses any more. Too much else would have been added.

12. I shall not discuss symmetrical cases of overdetermination, in which two over-determining factors have equal claim to count as causes. For me these are useless as test cases because I lack firm naive opinions about them.

The Sea-Battle Tomorrow

ARISTOTLE

Aristotle (384–322 B.C.), the famed Greek thinker, made important contributions to virtually every area of philosophical inquiry.

CHAPTER 9

With regard to what is and what has been it is necessary for the affirmation or the negation to be true or false. And with universals taken universally it is always necessary for one to be true and the other false, and with particulars too, as we have said; but with universals not spoken of universally it is not necessary. But with particulars that are going to be it is different.

For if every affirmation or negation is true or false it is necessary for everything either to be the case or not to be the case. For if one person says that something will be and another denies this same thing, it is clearly necessary for one of them to be saying what is true—if every affirmation is true or false; for both will not be the case together under such circumstances. For if it is true to say that it is white or is not white, it is necessary for it to be white or not white; and if it is white or is not white, then it was true to say or deny this. If it is not the case it is false, if it is false it is not the case. So it is necessary for the affirmation or the negation to be true. It follows that nothing either is or is happening, or will be or will not be, by chance or as chance has it, but everything of necessity and not as chance has it (since either he who says or he who denies is saying what is true). For otherwise it might equally well happen or not happen, since what is as chance has it is no more thus than not thus, nor will it be.

Again, if it is white now it was true to say earlier that it would be white; so that it was always true to say of anything that has happened that it would be so. But if it was always true to say that it was so, or would be so, it could not not be so, or not be going to be so. But if something cannot not happen it is impossible for it not to happen; and if it is impossible for something not to happen it is necessary for it to happen. Everything that will be, therefore, happens necessarily. So nothing will come about as chance has it or by chance; for if by chance, not of necessity.

Nor, however, can we say that neither is true—that it neither will be nor will not be so. For, firstly, though the affirmation is false the negation is not true, and though the negation is false the affirmation, on this view, is not true. Moreover, if it is true to say that something is white and large, both have to hold of it, and if true that they will hold tomorrow, they will have to hold tomorrow; and if it neither will be nor will not be the case tomorrow, then there is no "as chance has it." Take a sea-battle: it would *have* neither to happen nor not to happen.

These and others like them are the absurdities that follow if it is necessary, for every affirmation and negation either about universals spoken of universally or about particulars, that one of the opposites be true and the other false, and that nothing of what happens is as chance has it, but everything is and happens of necessity. So there would be no need to deliberate or to take trouble (thinking that if we do this,

Reprinted from *Aristotle's Categories and De Interpretatione,* translated by J. L. Ackrill (Oxford: Oxford University Press, 1963), by permission of the publisher.

this will happen, but if we do not, it will not). For there is nothing to prevent someone's having said ten thousand years beforehand that this would be the case, and another's having denied it; so that whichever of the two was true to say then, will be the case of necessity. Nor, of course, does it make any difference whether any people made the contradictory statements or not. For clearly this is how the actual things are even if someone did not affirm it and another deny it. For it is not because of the affirming or denying that it will be or will not be the case, nor is it a question of ten thousand years beforehand rather than any other time. Hence, if in the whole of time the state of things was such that one or the other was true, it was necessary for this to happen, and for the state of things always to be such that everything that happens happens of necessity. For what anyone has truly said would be the case cannot not happen; and of what happens it was always true to say that it would be the case.

But what if this is impossible? For we see that what will be has an origin both in deliberation and in action, and that, in general, in things that are not always actual there is the possibility of being and of not being; here both possibilities are open, both being and not being, and, consequently, both coming to be and not coming to be. Many things are obviously like this. For example, it is possible for this cloak to be cut up, and yet it will not be cut up but will wear out first. But equally, its not being cut up is also possible, for it would not be the case that it wore out first unless its not being cut up were possible. So it is the same with all other events that are spoken of in terms of this kind of possibility. Clearly, therefore, not everything

is or happens of necessity: some things happen as chance has it, and of the affirmation and the negation neither is true rather than the other; with other things it is one rather than the other and as a rule, but still it is possible for the other to happen instead.

What is, necessarily is, when it is; and what is not, necessarily is not, when it is not. But not everything that is, necessarily is; and not everything that is not, necessarily is not. For to say that everything that is, is of necessity, when it is, is not the same as saying unconditionally that it is of necessity. Similarly with what is not. And the same account holds for contradictories: everything necessarily is or is not, and will be or will not be; but one cannot divide and say that one or the other is necessary. I mean, for example: it is necessary for there to be or not to be a sea-battle tomorrow; but it is not necessary for a sea-battle to take place tomorrow, nor for one not to take place — though it is necessary for one to take place or not to take place. So, since statements are true according to how the actual things are, it is clear that wherever these are such as to allow of contraries as chance has it, the same necessarily holds for the contradictories also. This happens with things that are not always so or are not always not so. With these it is necessary for one or the other of the contradictories to be true or false—not, however, this one or that one, but as chance has it; or for one to be true *rather* than the other, yet not *already* true or false.

Clearly, then, it is not necessary that of every affirmation and opposite negation one should be true and the other false. For what holds for things that are does not hold for things that are not but may possibly be or not be; with these it is as we have said.

The Problem of Future Contingencies

⌒

RICHARD TAYLOR

Richard Taylor is Professor Emeritus of philosophy at the University of Rochester. Previously, he taught at Brown University and Columbia University. He is the author of numerous books, including *Metaphysics, Action and Purpose,* and *Good and Evil.* In addition, he is renowned internationally for his knowledge of apiculture, the keeping of bees.

Aristotle believed that any statement which asserts or denies, concerning a contingent event, that it is going to occur, is neither true nor false, the world being as yet indeterminate with regard to the existence or nonexistence of such things.[1]

Few doctrines from antiquity have engendered more controversy than this one, as indicated by the rash of polemic that has broken out over it again in the last few years.[2] Medieval philosophers, following Boethius, found in it a thorny problem of reconciling liberty with divine omniscience; Lukasiewicz, more recently, revived Aristotle's arguments to provide an interpretation for his three-valued logic, while other writers still find it necessary to take account of essentially the same arguments in dealing with metaphysical problems of time. Nearly all the Scholastics discarded Aristotle's arguments as inconsistent with Christian presuppositions, while modern logicians have tended to dismiss them as paralogisms. C. A. Baylis rejected all of them, as reinterpreted by Lukasiewicz, as fallacious,[3] and W. V. Quine has disdained one of the conclusions as "Aristotle's fantasy."[4] Applying them to metaphysical puzzles, Gilbert Ryle treats such arguments as confusions of categories,[5] while Donald Williams has pronounced Aristotle's reasoning "so swaggeringly invalid that the student can hardly believe he meant it," and his conclusion "as nearly incredible as any proposition could be."[6]

The prevailing opinion, then, is, and always has been, that Aristotle was muddled in these arguments and that his conclusion was false. I want to show, on the contrary, that he was exceptionally profound and that at least one important part of his doctrine is true. And if, as I believe, Aristotle was right, some far-reaching consequences follow. The conclusion yields, for instance, (1) in metaphysics, the view, much fought over lately, that time has not only an intrinsic order, as does space, but also an intrinsic sense or asymmetry, as space has not; (2) in logic, an area of applicability of a three-valued system, and (3) in theology, a revision of the traditional notion of divine omniscience.

I shall proceed as follows: In the first section, to set forth Aristotle's thesis and three of the arguments for it which I regard as valid; in the second, to clarify these arguments and elicit their presuppositions; and finally, to defend Aristotle's opinion against all the important objections I know of. The reader can thus probably find in this last section his own objection, if he has one, and satisfy himself whether it has been answered.

Reprinted from *The Philosophical Review, 66* (1957).

I. ARISTOTLE'S OPINION

The Thesis

Aristotle, as I understand him, maintains that all propositions are either true or are false, with the sole exception of a limited class of propositions about the future, viz., those that assert the occurrence, or nonoccurrence, of some future contingency. Concerning these (only) he held (a) that they are, antecedently, not true and yet not false, but (b) that any disjunction of such a proposition with its denial is necessarily true.[7]

And by a "future contingency" is meant any event which belongs not to the present or past, but which in the nature of things, and not merely in relation to our knowledge or ignorance of things, might or might not occur in the future.

The Arguments

There seem to be three distinct arguments for this, somewhat mixed together and admixed with other considerations. They are predicated on two assumptions, so I shall state first the assumptions and then, paraphrastically, the arguments.

The first assumption is a correspondence theory of truth, the minimum requirement of which is that in the case of any true proposition asserting some predicate of a particular individual, there is (tenselessly) a fact consisting of that individual having that predicate. This raises problems of its own, but we can ignore them. The second assumption is that there are genuine ambiguities in the future, i.e., that sometimes various mutually incompatible events are each of them future possibilities. We shall see what this means shortly.

(1) The first argument is this: Suppose all propositions, including those about future contingencies, are now either true or are false. Then if one man says today that a particular event—e.g., a sea fight—will occur tomorrow, and another denies this, what one of them says must correspond to a fact forthcoming, positive or negative, and what the other says must fail to correspond. But in that case it must already be true that a sea fight definitely will take place, such that

there is now no possibility that it might not, or else that it definitely will not take place, such that there is now no possibility that it nevertheless might. This, however, is false; for on such a view "nothing is or takes place fortuitously [ἀπὸ τύχης], either in the present or in the future, and there are no real alternatives; everything takes place of necessity and is fixed . . . for the meaning of the word 'fortuitous' in regard to present or future events is that reality is so constituted that it may issue in either of two opposite directions."[8]

Two qualifications are added to this and the following arguments. First, that it does not matter how far in advance a prediction is made: "A man may predict an event ten thousand years beforehand, and another may predict the reverse; that which was truly predicted at the moment in the past will of necessity take place in the fullness of time."[9] Second, that it is irrelevant whether such propositions about the future ever *are* actually stated or entertained, for "it is manifest that the circumstances are not influenced by the fact of an affirmation or denial on the part of anyone."[10]

(2) The second argument concerns propositions about past contingencies considered in relation to the time when the event in question was as yet future, and unlike the first it is stated categorically rather than disjunctively. It is this: Consider an object which is now white, e.g., a table. Now on the supposition that every proposition is true, or if not true then false, it must have been true before the table became white, or even existed, that it would become white; indeed, it must have been true from all eternity. But if it was always true that it would become white, then it was never really possible that it might not, "and when a thing cannot not come to be, it is impossible that it should not come to be, and when it is impossible that it should not come to be, it must come to be." So again, "it results from this that nothing is uncertain or fortuitous,"[11] that "there are no real alternatives, but that all that is or takes place is the outcome of necessity."[12] This, however, is false, for

in those things which are not continuously actual there is a potentiality in either direction [τὸ δυνατὸν εἶναι καὶ μή]. Such things may either be or not be;

events also therefore may either take place or not take place. . . . So it is therefore with all other events which possess this kind of potentiality. It is therefore plain that it is not of necessity that everything is or takes place; but in some instances there are real alternatives, in which case the affirmation is no more true and no more false than the denial.[13]

(3) The third argument is exceedingly succint and straight-forward, being but a combination of the two aforementioned assumptions and a conclusion therefrom. It is simply this: "Since propositions correspond with facts, it is evident that when in future events there is a real alternative, and a potentiality in contrary directions [τὰ ἐναντία ἐνδέχεσθαι], the corresponding affirmation and denial have the same character."[14] We could express this otherwise, but no better, by saying that if the world is such that something which has not happened nevertheless might occur or might fail to occur in the future, and if this contingency or "potentiality in contrary directions" belongs to the nature of things and is not merely relative to our knowledge or ignorance of things, then it expresses the *whole* truth about such an event to say that it might happen, or it might not.

It will be noticed that the arguments I have summarized bear only on part (a) of Aristotle's thesis, viz., that future contingency statements neither are true nor are false, and do nothing to prove part (b), viz., that any disjunction of one such proposition and its denial is nevertheless necessarily true; and it is, in fact, only the former that I shall consider. It may be that the truth of (a) would require a revision of (b), as I believe it would, but we shall have enough on our hands if we say what needs to be said concerning (a).

II.   COMMENT

These arguments are valid, though terribly susceptible of misinterpretation. In this section I shall (a) formulate a more careful statement of the doctrine of real contingencies, upon which Aristotle's and my own forthcoming arguments rest, and (b) indicate the senses in which the modal terms involved should be taken.

The Doctrine of Real Contingencies

Most critics have tended to treat Aristotle's arguments simply as articles of logic, interpreting such key words as "necessary" as logical modalities, predicable of propositions, such that the question then becomes that of whether these arguments constitute logically valid inferences—as they plainly do not, unless further assumptions are introduced. From the mere fact that a statement is true, it hardly follows that it is logically necessary—unless one is prepared to abandon any distinction between contingent and necessary truths.[15] I should maintain, then, that Aristotle's arguments are derived from a metaphysical assumption: the assumption, namely, that there are real ambiguities in nature, i.e., from a doctrine of real contingencies.

This doctrine is best understood in terms of what it *denies,* namely, universal causal determinism, which is to the effect that (as it has just recently been well put) "without exception . . . the present (including the present character and behavior of human beings) is the only present that could exist, given the past that did exist, and the future will be the only future that could exist, given the particular present that now is."[16] Belief in determinism, that is, involves the belief that, for any event that ever happens, there are conditions given which nothing else could happen. And since the causal conditions of events, or the occurrences of such conditions, are themselves events, this proposition does entail that the past and present states of the world, in their totality, are compatible with only one future, that the future is unambiguous, save in reference to our powers of prediction.

The denial of this is simply that *some* events are not such as described. This view has sometimes—I think by Aristotle—been thought plausible only as applied to the choices or decisions of men. But however narrowly construed, if this view is true then determinism, as formulated above, is absolutely false, the past and the present states of the world *are* compatible with any of several alternative futures, and "future possibilities" are real ones, not just logical or relative possibilities.

I shall give no argument for this view of real contingencies; indeed, I think it can be neither proved nor disproved, though I happen to believe it. For the purpose of the present discussion, it may be regarded as an hypothesis only, such that our problem can be formulated as the following hypothetical one: If the doctrine of real contingencies is true, was Aristotle right in believing that some propositions—viz., those asserting or denying the existence in the future of contingent things—are neither true nor false?

That Aristotle believed in real contingencies is, I think, beyond doubt, but I shall not prove it here, it being an historical question. Two articles of his philosophy do, however, deserve to be mentioned, as clarifying somewhat the doctrine in question.

The first is his rarely formulated theory of the fortuitous. According to this, as I understand it, any causally connected series of events is such that each member is caused by its predecessor, if it has a predecessor, and in this sense comes about "of necessity." The beginning of such a series, however—e.g., the ultimate cause of the choice or decision of a living being, or perhaps of a man—"no longer points to something further," and thus, Aristotle says, is "the starting-point for the fortuitous, and will have nothing else as cause of its coming to be."[17] Such a conception involves an unusual conception of causation, according to which some things—e.g., men and other active things, in the strict sense of "active"—can be "originative sources of motion," but Aristotle evidently did believe this (as I do), and whether it is unusual or not is in any case irrelevant.

The other doctrine, closely connected with the first, and alluded to in the arguments I have paraphrased, is that of rational and nonrational capacities (δυνάμες μετὰ λόγου and δυνάμες ἄλογοι).[18] A nonrational capacity is the disposition of something toward a unique state under given conditions—which is, of course, what philosophers normally have in mind in speaking of capacities or dispositions. Sugar placed in warm water, for instance, can only dissolve; it cannot sometimes dissolve, sometimes ignite, and sometimes do nothing. Water, heated to a certain point, can only boil, it cannot solidify; the sun can only warm us, under given conditions, not sometimes warm and sometimes chill us. Rational capacities, on the other hand, are "capacities for opposites [δυνάμεις τῶν ἐναντίων]," and characterize (to-

gether with nonrational ones) only living things, perhaps only rational beings.[19] These are dispositions to do any of two or more incompatible things under a given set of conditions, that is, dispositions that are really ambiguous. Such capacities are not utterly ambiguous—indeed, the states or acts to which a thing having such a capacity may tend, in given circumstances, may be as few as two—but the important thing is that such a disposition is not toward some unique state. Moreover, such capacities are not manifest "necessarily," i.e., from ordinary causal processes; if they were, then, being capacities for opposites, they would result in incompatible states at the same time, which is impossible. Something further is needed, then, to "decide," and this is what Aristotle calls "desire or will [ὄρεξις ἢ προαίρεσις]."[20] And this, again, is something which is not simply the actualization of another capacity, rational or nonrational, but is instead simply the act of an active being—i.e., of a being which acts and is not merely acted upon—considered as an "originative source of movement," not itself entirely determined to one thing rather than another by any fixed causal connections.

Now either of these doctrines—which really amount to much the same thing—would yield a theory of real contingencies. And both, I submit, are plausible in the light of what we take ourselves, as active beings, to be, but I shall not prove them.

Modal Predicates

Nothing is so apt to mislead as Aristotle's use of such concepts as "necessary" and "possible," so I shall now clarify these.

Given a meaning for any one of the four modal terms—"necessary," "possible," "impossible," and "contingent"—the others can forthwith be defined in terms of it. Given, for instance, a meaning for "necessary," the remaining three predicates can be explicated as follows:

x is possible $\equiv \sim(\sim x$ is necessary)
x is impossible $\equiv \sim x$ is necessary
x is contingent $\equiv \sim(x$ is necessary). $\sim(\sim x$ is necessary),

substituting for "*x*" a statement, an event, or whatever the sense of the modal term requires, and letting "~*x*" designate, not simply the absence of *x*, but something not compossible with *x*, in the sense of the modality in question.

These definitions, which are of course empty until a meaning is given to the basic modal term, exhibit one important point that is easily overlooked, viz., that the possible and the contingent are *not* the same. Whatever is contingent is possible, but not vice versa; for if anything is necessary, then it is also possible, but not therefore contingent.[21]

In the light of these definitions four more or less familiar senses of necessity and hence also, derivatively, of contingency, can be distinguished in roughly the following way:

(1) *Logical necessity* is predicable of a *statement* or *proposition* and corresponds to analyticity. Thus

necessarily $p \equiv$ "p" is analytic,

and a logically contingent statement is thus one which is neither analytic nor self-contradictory.[22]

(2) *Epistemic necessity* is predicable of events and states, though only in a derivative way, and corresponds to what is known to be. Thus

necessarily $e \equiv e$ is known to exist,

and an epistemically contingent event is one concerning which it is not known whether it exists (has existed, will exist) or not—one which, "for all we know," might exist, or might not. This is indeed a strange kind of contingency and is in fact no real contingency at all, being only a reflection of someone's knowledge or ignorance of things, but it is nevertheless the commonest sense of contingency embodied in ordinary speech. If, for instance, someone says before opening a drawer that it might or might not contain his necktie, he only means that he does not yet know; if some one says it might rain a week hence, he ordinarily means only that he does not know that it will not. On the other hand, one who knows, say, that Mr. Jones is in New York cannot really consider it possible that he is not.[23]

(3) *Nomical necessity,* also called "causal" and "etiological," is necessitation by causation and is predicable of an event. Thus

necessarily $e \equiv$ there is (was, will be) a cause for e,

and a nomically contingent event is therefore one neither the occurrence nor nonoccurrence of which has a cause.[24] Derivatively, an event causally dependent, remotely or proximately, upon a contingent event would itself be contingent, prior to the occurrence of any member of the causal series of which it was itself a member. Of course it is customary to deny that causation does involve necessitation, and this is correct if such necessity be considered logical (and thus predicable only of statements or propositions), but on the other hand there is a fairly clear sense in which, for instance, water *cannot but* boil under certain conditions, or a man who is decapitated *must* die, and so forth, and it is simply the modality expressed by such words as "cannot but" or "must" in such uses which is here called "nomical." Also, some would deny that there *are* any contingent events, in this sense, but I have only made it an hypothesis that there are, and I am in any case not trying to prove they exist by defining them.

(4) *Temporal necessity,* which might less misleadingly be called "irrevocability" or "unalterability,"[25] applies to any event that has happened, and is thus relative to a date. Thus

necessarily $e \equiv e$ has already occurred,

and a temporally contingent event is thus simply one which has not yet occurred, an event temporally incompatible with it having likewise not yet occurred. This is perhaps the strangest kind of contingency yet, but no questions are begged by introducing it. What this notion calls attention to is just this obvious, and in other contexts trivial, fact: that nothing that may be in the past is in any way revocable or alterable by what might happen now, whereas this is plainly not the case with such things as may be yet to come. The lapse of time by itself thus imposes a kind of necessity on things; things once capable of being otherwise, or of not existing at all, are no longer so. Until an event has happened, it is sometimes possible that it might not, but once it has happened, it is no longer possible that it did not—and this, despite the fact that it is still possible that it did not happen in any or all of the three foregoing senses of "possible." All this is surely a truism of sorts, but it does indicate an indubitable sense in which past things, but not future things, are by now "of necessity."

It must be added that none of the above distinctions purports to be an enlightening *analysis* of any modal concept. Indeed, I am sure that some senses of necessity cannot be analyzed at all without circularity; it is very doubtful, for instance, whether "cause" can be so analyzed, especially if causal statements be regarded as warranting counterfactual inferences. My only object, then, has been to distinguish these several senses sufficiently to prevent confusion in what follows.

Real and Relative Contingencies

To speak of an event as contingent is to say, loosely, that it might or might not happen, that its occurrence is neither necessitated nor ruled out; but this, in the light of the foregoing distinctions, can mean any of several things.

It might mean (a) that a statement asserting its occurrence is logically contingent. But this is not remotely what Aristotle was thinking. In saying that the assumption of truth for a prediction requires necessarily the occurrence of what is predicted, he emphatically does not mean that such an assumption entails that the prediction is necessary or its denial self-contradictory—it is events, not statements, which are spoken of as necessary or contingent.[26] Moreover, this interpretation would abolish any distinction between logically necessary and contingent statements, or between false and self-contradictory ones, which would be an absurdity, especially if ascribed to Aristotle.

Again, to speak of an event as contingent might mean (b) that it is uncertain, i.e., not known, whether the event has occurred, is occurring, or will occur.[27] I have called this kind of contingency "epistemic"; it can also be called "relative," being always relative to someone's knowledge of things. If, for instance, an

Athenian had said in 400 B.C. that Socrates might or might not die of poisoning, he would have meant in part at least that it was not known whether this would happen. Now being a very ordinary sense of contingency, it is exceedingly easy to force it upon Aristotle's arguments; indeed, many philosophers have insisted that this is the only kind of "contingency," other than logical, that is intelligible.[28] But it would be absurdly incorrect to so interpret Aristotle: from the mere fact that this or that person may not *know* whether something is going to happen, it hardly follows that it is neither true nor false that it *is* going to happen,[29] and Aristotle cannot be considered so dull as to have imagined that anything of this sort *does* follow.

Or again, one might mean by contingency (c) that natural causal processes are themselves ambiguous with respect to some outcome or other, that it is really undetermined by anything past or present whether an event of a given description is going to happen. This sort of contingency, which I have called "nomical," might also be called "real" contingency, being not relative to this or that man's powers of prediction but rather belonging to the very nature of things. And it is what our aforementioned Athenian could further have meant in saying that Socrates might or might not die of poisoning; that is, he might have meant, especially if he were philosophical, not only that *he* was uncertain about the outcome of things but that it was "uncertain," i.e., as yet undetermined, by nature; that the state of the world was then causally compatible with either of at least two futures, the one containing that event and the other not. And it is in *this* sense that I would understand Aristotle, since (i) I believe that some things are contingent in this sense, (ii) we have good reasons to think that Aristotle thought so too, and (iii) this interpretation is absolutely required in order that Aristotle's thesis can be rendered even plausible.

Finally, reference to an event as contingent might mean (d) that the outcome, i.e., its occurrence or nonoccurrence, has not already been decided one way or the other by the mere lapse of time—which is what I have called "temporal" contingency. One might, in short, simply be making the point that an event of a given description has not happened *yet*.

Now one naturally wants to think that this is all Aristotle had in mind—else why should he have regarded contingencies as belonging to the future only, never to the past? But this, too, would be wrong. Aristotle did not hold that *all* statements having reference to the future are neither true nor false, though he can hardly have doubted that such statements do indeed have reference to things that have not happened yet.

Aristotle's doctrine should, therefore, be construed as one concerning not merely contingent events, in the sense of real or nomical contingency—as this belongs to past events no less than to future ones—and not merely events of the future, or temporally contingents things—as some of these may be already determined—but as one concerning the *combination* of these. And it is this combination of modal notions which makes his arguments so enormously liable to confusion and at the same time so profound. His claim is, therefore, that (a) if an event of a given description is really contingent in the sense given, i.e., not yet nomically determined, and (b) if the outcome of things, i.e., the occurrence or nonoccurrence of the event in question, has not already been decided merely by the lapse of time, such that it irrevocably has happened or has failed to happen—in short, if the thing in question is a future contingency—then (c) any statement asserting or denying that it will happen is not (yet) true, but also not (yet) false.

Summary.—We can now summarize the argument in this fashion. Using the general notion "incapable of being otherwise" and "necessary" interchangeably, we may say:

If the statement "*e* has happened" is *true,* given a descriptive interpretation for "*e*," then the event *e* is no longer capable of being otherwise; i.e., it is unalterable, with respect to its occurring, failing to occur, or occurring otherwise than as described, by anything that happens between the time of *e* and the present, (however nomically contingent *e* may be). Or, calling this statement "*p*,"

(1) ("*p*" is true) ⊃ (necessarily, *e*).

Note that this is *not* saying either (a) that since one proposition necessarily entails another, then it entails that that other is necessary, nor (b) that "*e* has hap-pened" is logically necessary, nor (c) that a proposition can entail an event, nor (d) that the truth of "*p*" entails that *e* is nomically determined, nor (e) that *p* is the cause of *e*.

By identical reasoning, if the statement "*e* will happen" is *true,* given a descriptive interpretation for "*e*," then the event *e* is henceforth incapable of being otherwise; i.e., it is unalterable, with respect to its occurring, failing to occur, or occurring otherwise than as described, by anything that happens between the time of *e* and the present (however nomically contingent *e* may be). Calling this statement "*q*,"

(2) ("*q*" is true) ⊃ (necessarily, *e*).

And note here, too, that this is not to be given an interpretation similar to *any* of the five just rejected.

Now one feels no inclination to deny the consequent of (1). That is, once an event has happened, it *is* incapable of being otherwise, i.e., it is *now* impossible that it should not have happened, however nomically contingent it may have been. Hence, one feels no inclination to deny the antecedent, viz., that the statement may be true.

But we *do* deny the consequent of (2), i.e., we deny that *e* is incapable of being otherwise—for instance, that it is incapable of not occurring at all—so long as it is as yet future, *unless* something else already exists nomically sufficient for its occurrence, i.e., unless *e,* though future, is already causally necessitated by what exists already, and hence is not a real contingency. Denying the consequent (with this important qualification), then, we deny also the antecedent, viz., that the statement "*q*" is true. By similar inference, we deny also that "*q*" is false.

III.   ANSWERS TO OBJECTIONS

First Objection.—The truth values of propositions are no function of time. More precisely, a correspondence theory of truth, such as Aristotle assumes, does not at all require the *present* existence of facts for propositions to agree or conflict with, but only the existence of such facts at some time or other.

C. A. Baylis directed this criticism at Lukasiewicz' arguments,[30] which are essentially those of Aristotle, and Donald Williams has on the same and other grounds rejected *all* theories which deny truth about the future.[31] Baylis suggests that it is no better to argue that a proposition referring to the future cannot be true or false, on the ground that there is *not yet* any definite fact with which it can agree or conflict, than to argue that one referring to the past cannot be true or false, on the ground that there is *no longer* any fact to make it such; and both Aristotle and Lukasiewicz, like everyone else, admit that statements about the past are either true or are false. And Donald Williams, making the same point, says that "all these arguments are strangely selective . . . in making much of supposed difficulties about the future which are quietly ignored as they equally affect the past and present."[32]

Reply.—This criticism quite misses the point, for Aristotle's argument is not to the effect that because some facts do not yet exist, propositions about them are neither true nor false. It was not just their temporal distance that bothered him, but their contingency, or rather, the contingency of some of them. There is thus in Aristotle's philosophy no general denial of truth about the future. The motions of the heavenly bodies and the alterations of the seasons, for instance, are entirely "according to necessity," he thought. Hence, being uniform and determined, nothing stands in the way of there being truths about them in advance of their occurring.[33] We can thus see how little force there is in Williams' remark that "even Aristotle, when he said 'All men are mortal,' did not mean merely that all men living at the moment were mortal,"[34] or his further comment that reference to an eclipse tomorrow, rather than to a sea fight, "would not find us half so receptive of the suggestion of its unreality."[35] Neither man's mortality nor celestial motions are among those "things that can be otherwise."

Second Objection.—All temporal references in statements are in principle eliminable, if replaced by explicit references to dates; that is, variations of tense, and hence explicit or implicit references to *nows* and *thens,* can be eliminated from statements altogether without changing their meanings and hence without changing their truth values. The advantage in doing so is that there is removed any temptation to think of the truth values of tensed statements as changing with the lapse of time; any propo-

sition, when so expressed with date or time, appears as an eternal truth, if a truth at all. Instead, for instance, of saying, "Socrates was executed," and thereby having on our hands a tensed statement which it might be tempting to think could not have been true during Socrates' lifetime, but which became true immediately thereafter, one can just say, tenselessly, "Socrates *is* executed in 399 B.C.," which amounts to the same thing. And this is fatal to Aristotle's thesis, for if the statements, e.g., "There will be a sea fight tomorrow" and "There was a sea fight yesterday," uttered on separate days with a day intervening and both referring to the same event, are equivalent to "There is a sea fight on—," the date replacing the blank, then it is obviously impossible to say that some of these are true, or are false, while one of them is neither.

St. Thomas thought that what is essentially this view holds for all propositions, necessary or contingent, known to God, since "His knowledge is measured by eternity,"[36] and logicians have tended to take the same view in order to facilitate logical analysis.[37] Bertrand Russell,[38] A. J. Ayer,[39] Nelson Goodman,[40] and J. N. Findlay[41] have all advocated the elimination of tense for certain purposes to achieve clarity and precision, the last declaring that "if we avoided the adverbs 'here' and 'there,' if we purged our language of tenses, and talked exclusively in terms of dates and tenseless participles, we should never be involved in difficulties." Indeed, it has been persuasively argued that it was only by historical accident that variations ever came to be made on verbs to indicate temporal rather than spatial direction in the first place, and that such variations can, in any case, be eliminated, just as we avoid "spatial tenses" by explicit reference, when necessary, to locations.[42] It is in terms of this view that Donald Williams is able to speak of "the totality of being, of facts, or of events as spread out eternally in the dimension of time as well as the dimensions of space"[43] and to say that "there 'exists' an eternal world total in which past and future events are as determinately located, characterized, and truly describable as are southern events and western events."[44]

Reply.—First, this argument begs the question by simply *assuming* that future contingency statements are already either true or false—precisely the thing at issue—and then offering those very statements, irrelevantly adorned with dates, as an argument.[45]

Secondly, the objection is mistaken anyway, for in fact one *cannot* convey the same information and avoid the systematic ambiguity of "now" and "then" just by substituting dates for tenses. This can be done *only* if an additional statement is supplied in order to complete the information so easily completed by the use of tense, and this additional statement must contain a temporal reference relative to *now*.[46] That is, it must be a statement to the effect that the date mentioned is earlier than, contemporaneous with, or future to *now*—precisely the thing that the use of dates was intended to avoid. Upon being told, for instance, that "Socrates is executed in 399 B.C.," I by no means get the idea that he has already *been* executed, unless I am *also* told, or happen somehow to know, that 399 B.C. is *before now,* that it is *now past.* Of course nearly everyone does know this, but only because we happen to have been taught how past and future times can be designated by numbers and what numbers designate, at various times, what is designated by "now." An ignorant man might not know this at all; but he would have to be more than ignorant to have no sense of the difference between things past and things yet to come.

Third objection.—From the truth of a statement that an event of a given description has happened, there is no temptation to infer that it *had* to happen, or that its occurrence was in any way necessitated by this posterior truth. Indeed, it might be quite *certain* that it happened, or even that it happened contingently—from which it plainly follows, not that it was not contingent after all, but that it was. But similarly, from the truth of a statement that an event of a given description *will* happen, it does not at all follow that it *must* happen, or that its occurrence is somehow necessitated by this anterior truth, but only that it will in fact occur. Indeed, it might be quite *certain* that it will occur, or even that it will occur contingently—from which it plainly follows, not that it will not be contingent after all, but that it will. Aristotle's confusion thus results from the feeling that if it is antecedently true that an event of a certain kind will happen, then that event is by that truth *obliged* to hap-

pen and that hence there is nothing anyone can do to prevent it—whereas all that follows is that nothing will in fact be done to prevent it, that no condition nomically sufficient to prevent it will arise.[47]

More precisely, let *e* be some event, such as my coughing tomorrow, which, let us assume, is going to happen, and *f* another event, such as my taking cough medicine meanwhile, which is not going to happen but which would be such that, if it did happen, it would prevent *e*. Consider, then, these four statements:

(1)   *e* will occur.
(2)   If *f* were to occur, then *e* would not occur.
(3)   *f* will not occur.
(4)   *f* might occur.

Now it is evident (a) that the first two of these statements entail the third, and (b) all four may be true. Hence, (c) no combination of them can entail that the last is false. Therefore, the truth of (1) cannot entail that *e must* happen, or that it cannot be prevented, because (4), which we can assume is also true, entails the opposite, viz., that something might happen which would prevent it.

Reply.—This argument also begs the question, for it just *assumes* that our thesis is mistaken and conceals that assumption by applying it, not to the event *e,* to which our attention is mainly directed, but to *another* event, *f,* concerning which the very same difficulties that were initially raised concerning *e* now arise all over again.

For if, in the first place, *f* is a real and not a relative future contingency—that is, if nothing has yet occurred which is nomically sufficient either for the occurrence of *f* or for its nonoccurrence—then it is not already true that it will occur, on the basis of the arguments heretofore given. By the same token, it is not yet true that it will not. Therefore, if it is assumed that statement (4) is true, and "might" is given the sense of real contingency, then it cannot be simply assumed that (3) is true also without begging the question. If (4) is true, then (3), according to Aristotle's and my arguments, is neither true nor false.

But if, on the other hand, *f* is not a real future contingency, then something already exists which is nomically sufficient either for its occurrence or for its nonoccurrence; i.e., either *f* or *not-f* is already nomically determined. But in that case, though (3) may indeed be true, (4) is no longer true, if "might" is given the sense of real contingency; for *f* is now by hypothesis not a contingency, whereas statement (4) asserts that it is.

So in either case, premise (b) of the argument, that all four statements may be true, must be rejected; or at any rate, it clearly cannot be used to *refute* our thesis but can be accepted only *after* our thesis has been refuted without using it.

Fourth objection.—One cannot find any general difference between past and forthcoming events, other than the difference in time, and Aristotle does not rest his thesis upon the mere futurity of future contingencies, this being something they have in common with future necessities. For when the various senses of "contingent" are examined, it is found that past and future events are contingent in the same ways and that the only difference left between them *is* a merely temporal one.

The same logical possibilities apply to both predictions and retrodictions, for instance, the only logical impossibility being, in either case, that an event of a given description both does and does not occur.[48] Again, the same epistemic possibilities apply in both cases, there being ever so many things of the past concerning which we know nothing and can only say that, for all we know, they might have existed, or might not. Indeterminacy, again, belongs to past events no less than to future ones, if it belongs to anything at all, a causally undetermined event being no less so by the mere accident of being now past. So we are left with no way of distinguishing future contingencies from past ones other than by their temporal direction from us, which is by hypothesis irrelevant.

If, accordingly, statements about future contingencies are neither true nor false, then we should accept the same conclusion as applied to past ones, or else say, as Aristotle did not, that the mere futurity of an event, unlike pastness, renders statements about it neither true nor false. Or else, conversely—and this is what most philosophers believe—if there are truths about past events, including contingent ones, there is no reason for doubting that there are truths about future ones too.[49]

Reply.—It is not the futurity of future contingencies, nor the nomical contingency of them, upon which our thesis rests, but the combination of the two. When something has *happened,* then however contingent it may have been, its occurring excludes the possibility of something incompatible with it happening at the same time, whereas in the case of some (not all) ostensibly future things, nothing *has* happened to exclude the possibility of something else happening then instead. In Aristotelian concepts, this is to say that when a potentiality in opposite directions has become actualized in one of these directions, there ceases to be any potentiality for the opposite, the antecedent alternative possibilities having been forever foreclosed by the one that has now become actual.[50] Nothing, however, now excludes any real contingency for the future and nothing will, *until* it is excluded by the realization of its opposite or of something nomically sufficient for the realization of its opposite; that is, until it has ceased to be a *future* contingency.

Putting this another way, we can say that there is only one possible past but many possible futures. There are, indeed, ordinary interpretations according to which this is absurd, but there is another according to which it is true. It is part of what people mean in saying, as Aristotle said, that the past cannot be "undone," no matter what indeterminism or haphazardness there may be in it.[51] The past consists of everything that has happened, and even if we should suppose that any or all of these things might easily have been otherwise, the fact that they have happened renders impossible forever after the occurrence of anything else in their place. The future, too, consists of everything that will happen; but here, nothing has happened to preclude the occurrence of *either* of two or more incompatible events. Concerning a future contingency, we can say only *if* it occurs then the occurrence of anything incompatible with it is excluded; but concerning a past contingency, we express the fact by saying *since* it occurred everything incompatible with its occurring is excluded.[52] The future *is* alterable, and not merely in the trivial sense of being alterable by our own forthcoming efforts but by the mere *lapse of time,* which itself reduces to zero what were once many alternative future possibilities.[53] One may indeed say that when tomorrow comes, we shall find its contents as fully determinate and exclusive of things incompatible with those contents as we now find the contents of yesterday, and this is true; but it only means that with the lapse of time, what were once alternative possibilities have dwindled until reduced to zero by those which have become actual.[54]

If, then, in the sense explained, there is no longer any real contingency in things past, we do not express the whole truth in any statement about the past other than by saying of an event of this or that description that it *did happen* or that it *did not.* In the case of future contingencies, however, it expresses the *whole* truth to say of one of them that it *might happen* or it *might not.*[55] It cannot be true now that it will, for this means more than "might," nor can it be true now that it will not, for this means more than "might not." The lapse of time, and not merely the increase of our knowledge and experience, can confute our statement that it will happen as well as our statement that it will not, whereas only the increase of knowledge, and not merely the lapse of time, can confute our beliefs about things past and done.[56]

Fifth Objection.—Aristotle's arguments rest on a common amphiboly, treating as equivalent certain statements which can indeed be expressed in the same way but which are really quite different in what they assert. One is

necessarily, *p* or *not-p,*

understood in the first place as meaning that the whole disjunction is necessary (which is true) but then understood to mean that one or other of the disjuncts by itself is necessary (which hardly follows). Another is

if *p,* then necessarily *p,*

understood first as meaning that the whole hypothetical statement is necessary (which is true) and then to mean that the consequent, by itself, is necessary (which is by no means the same).

Moreover, if every true proposition is in some sense necessary, then every false one must in a simi-

lar sense be impossible; indeed, Aristotle says as much: "That which is must needs be when it is, and that which is not must needs not be when it is not."[57] But if we combine these suppositions with his further claim that a proposition may be contingent, we can, by elementary rules of logical inference, get the absurd result that if a proposition is contingent, then it is false and hence impossible, but also that it is true and hence necessary. Thus, in obvious notation:

(1) $p \supset Np$
(2) $\sim(Np) \supset \sim p$
(3) $Cp \supset \sim p,$

and so on. And:

(4) $\sim p \supset Ip$
(5) $\sim(Ip) \supset p$
(6) $Cp \supset p,$

and so on. And this is absurd.

Reply.—If Aristotle had argued (1) that it is necessary that every proposition or its denial is true, and that therefore every proposition is itself necessarily true, or its denial necessarily true, or (2) that a proposition necessarily entails itself, and therefore necessarily entails that it is itself a necessary proposition, then his arguments would be as "swaggeringly invalid" as Donald Williams, who ascribes them to Aristotle, has claimed.[58] But in fact he says nothing like this. Someone might be tempted to adopt Aristotle's thesis on the basis of such amphibolies, but Aristotle did not,[59] and neither do I.

The reductio ad absurdum of the second part of this criticism is question begging, for it simply *assumes* that if a proposition is not true, then it is false, and if not false, then true—precisely the point at issue. Thus, the transposition of step 2 is sufficient for asserting "$\sim p$" only if this is read *not-p.* This cannot be equated with "*p* is false" without begging the question. Again, step 5 is not even correctly symbolized; the consequent must read "$\sim(\sim p)$," meaning "it is not the case that *not-p*"—which does not mean that *p* is true. Moreover, step 3 is accomplished only by substituting "contingent" for "not necessary," and step 6 by substituting the same for "not impossible."

But "contingent" means "not necessary *and* not impossible"; it does not mean "not necessary *or* not impossible." A thing which is impossible is indeed not necessary—but not therefore contingent; similarly, a thing which is necessary is indeed not impossible—but again, not therefore contingent. These distinctions are simply obliterated by this kind of criticism.

Sixth objection.—Whether or not there is any omniscient being, the conception of one involves no evident absurdity. But an omniscient being would by definition know everything, and hence everything that is going to happen, and a being less than omniscient can know something of the future. And if any man or god might know which of various alternative contingent things are going to happen, then it must already be true, though not therefore necessary, that those things will happen, and that things incompatible with them, while not impossible, will not happen.[60]

Reply.—An omniscient being would not be one who knows everything, simply, but one who knows everything that is knowable.[61] If there is anything that cannot be known—and of course there are infinitely many such things, for example, all false propositions—then even an omniscient being cannot be expected to know it. This kind of qualification was presupposed by the Scholastics when God's *omnipotence* was considered, the view of St. Thomas being, for example, that God can do only whatever is metaphysically capable of being done; if anything is inherently impossible, then it is idle to expect that God should do it.[62]

With this qualification, the question becomes whether things that are future and contingent are knowable. Now of course they are not knowable by inductive inference, but that is *not* the question. The question is whether *any* degree of prescient or sapient power would enable one to know which of several alternative contingencies will in time come about, assuming there are real contingencies.

It seems evident that it would not. For in the first place, knowledge can be only knowledge of what is true, and it has been our main point to prove that statements about future contingencies are neither true nor false. To argue, then, that such statements must be true, since they are known to God, if there is a God, is plainly circular.

Secondly, if the future is partially undetermined and in its very nature ambiguous, an omniscient being would have to comprehend it just that way. This alone would be knowledge of the future; to see it as otherwise, to comprehend it as already determinate and to judge exactly what is going to happen, is not knowledge but only the obscurity of guesswork and error.[63] Of course on this view an omniscient being would know more at one time than at another, but this need not be inconsistent with the idea of omniscience; at any time such a being would know all there is to know, and this ought surely to suffice.[64]

I think the only rejoinder that can be made to this is that, as Boethius and many others after him put it, "foreknowledge is not the cause of any necessity in things to come."[65] This point is iterated often, as if it left nothing more to be settled. Gilbert Ryle, for instance, observing that neither an "anterior truth" nor the knowledge of it could *cause* any event to happen, adds the similar point that propositions can never *entail* events but only other propositions.[66] Now all this true, but it is irrelevant to what is here being asserted. I am not saying, nor did Aristotle, that foreknowledge would *cause* this thing or that to happen,[67] or that propositions, known or unknown, *entail* events, all of which is surely nonsense, but rather that the supposition of foreknowledge *is* inconsistent with the claim that any of several alternative futures might become real, using "might" in the sense of real and not relative contingency. For the assumption that any one of these futures, no matter which, is already known, and hence will in fact come into being, is incompatible with the theory of real contingency, viz., that some other future is no less likely to come into being than that one.

Seventh objection.—Suppose someone, "*A*," indulged in prophecy, asserting, "Henry will sneeze tomorrow," and another person, "*B*," following Aristotle's principles, replied, "No, he might, or he might not; it cannot yet be true either that he will or that he will not, this being in the realm of contingencies." Tomorrow comes, and Henry sneezes. *A*, it would seem, can now say, "I said he would sneeze, and he did, so what I said was true, while you, in denying that what I said was true, are now shown to have been wrong." This comment by *A* seems reasonable, for it certainly seems that yesterday *A* had something that *B* did not have—namely, a true opinion. Of course, *B* did not say Henry would not sneeze, but still, his opinion was not as good as *A*'s—for *A*'s opinion, we now discover, was true, while *B*'s was just noncommittal.

Reply.—The most this argument can be claimed to prove is that *either* A's prophecy was true *or* that it *became* true, just as it became fulfilled,[68] through the lapse of time and the reduction to zero of alternative possibilities. There is nothing in it to show that it *was* antecedently true, any more than that it was antecedently fulfilled. Or, to put it otherwise, all the argument shows is the trivial fact that when "tomorrow" had ceased to be tomorrow and had become today, it contained just those events which then happened; it does not show that, on the day before, it was *going* to contain those rather than alternative ones.[69] No advantage, in the way of true opinion, can be claimed by *A* as having obtained when he first made his prediction, for all he can claim is that it was *fulfilled*—which suffices for any wagers that were made. The apparent advantage of his opinion over *B*'s is only an ex post facto sort of one—much like the advantage one might have who, by taking one path rather than another, stumbles upon a fortune. *B*, on the other hand, has had from the beginning a real advantage, for he claimed the future to be ambiguous and unsettled—as in fact it then was. His opinion, unlike *A*'s, did not have to wait to become true but was true from the start. It only *became* an inadequate opinion, but not disconfirmed, when *A*'s prediction came true, that is, when the event in question ceased to be a future contingency and to admit of any possibility of being otherwise.

It might be said that if we allow *B*'s opinion to have been true in advance, then nothing prevents *A*'s opinion from having been true as well. But this overlooks the fact that *A*'s statement concerns a future contingency, whereas there is nothing of contingency in *B*'s proposition that Henry might sneeze or he might not. We need not wait upon anything to see whether this is so.

Again, it might be said that *A*'s statement can be reformulated to say, "The belief that Henry will sneeze, while perhaps not true now, will become true" and that this assertion is about a future contingency no less than the first. But this complication introduces nothing new into the original argument; for *B* could reply that it might become true or it might not, the rest of the argument then proceeding exactly as before, only with more words.

NOTES

1. *De Int.*, ch. ix.

2. See C. A. Baylis, "Are Some Propositions neither True nor False?" *Philosophy of Science,* III (1936), 156–166; Donald Williams, "The Sea Fight Tomorrow," in *Structure, Method and Meaning,* ed. by P. Henle, H. M. Kallen, and S. K. Langer (New York, 1951), pp. 280–306; A. N. Prior, "Three-valued Logic and Future Contingents," *Philosophical Quarterly,* III (1953), 317–326; Leonard Linsky, "Professor Donald Williams on Aristotle," *Philosophical Review,* LXIII (1954), 250–252; Donald Williams, "Professor Linsky on Aristotle," *ibid.,* 253–255; Gilbert Ryle, "It Was to Be," in *Dilemmas* (Cambridge, 1954), pp. 15–35; R. J. Butler, "Aristotle's Sea Fight and Three-valued Logic," *Philosophical Review,* LXIV (1955), 264–274; G. E. M. Anscombe, "Aristotle and the Sea Battle,"*Mind,* n.s., LXV (1956), 1–15.

3. Op. cit.

4. "On a So-called Paradox," *Mind,* n.s., LXII (1953), 65.

5. Op. cit. Cf. the introductory lecture of this collection.

6. "The Sea Fight Tomorrow," pp. 284, 291.

7. Aristotle believed that "$p \lor \sim p$" is true for any interpretation of "*p*," including statements of future contingencies, if understood in the *sensus compositionis.* Neither "true" nor "false" can be predicated of the constituents of an interpretation of that law, however, if "*p*" is a statement about a future contingency. Aristotle could accordingly accept the first but not the other two of the following formulations as applying to any statements whatever, including future contingency statements: (1) "If a statement is true, its denial is false, and if false, its denial is true"; (2) "Each statement is ture, or, if not true, then false"; (3) "If two propositions contradict each other, one must be true."

8. *De. Int.* 18^b 5–9. All quotations are from the Oxford translation of E. M. Edghill, ed. by W. D. Ross.

9. Ibid., 18^b 33–36.

10. Ibid., 18^b 36–38. Cf. Ryle, op. cit., pp. 16–17.

11. *De Int.* 18^b 13–16.

12. Ibid., 18^b 30–31.

13. Ibid., 19^a 9–20.

14. Ibid., 19^a 32–35.

15. Linsky, op. cit., p. 252, interprets Aristotle as abolishing this distinction, comparing his philosophy to that of Leibniz in this respect. Cf. Butler, op. cit., pp. 267–268.

16. H. Van Rensselaer Wilson, "Causal Discontinuity in Fatalism and Indeterminism," *Journal of Philosophy,* LII (1955), 70.

17. *Met.,* bk. VI, ch. iii. Cf. *De Gen. et Corr.,* 337^a 34 ff.; also, W. D. Ross, *Aristotle,* (London, 1949), p. 164.

18. See *Met.* 1046^a 38–1046^b 25; *Phys.* 251^a 28.

19. *Met.* 1047^b 1–1048^a 16. See also H. H. Joachim, *The Nicomachean Ethics* (Oxford, 1951), pp. 108–110. This distinction is not consistently maintained, for Aristotle sometimes connects contingency with *matter* as such. See also *Met.* 1050^b 6–14: "Every potency is at one and the same time a potency of the opposite."

20. *Met.* 1047^b 35–1048^a 11. Cf. Joachim, op. cit., p. 109.

21. See *De. Int.,* ch. xiii; also Yehoshua Bar-Hillel, "Mr. Weiss on the Paradox of Necessary Truth," *Philosophical Studies,* VI (1955), 92–93.

22. Cf. W. V. Quine, "Notes on Existence and Necessity," *Journal of Philosophy,* XL (1943), 121.

23. Cf. Nelson Goodman, "On Likeness of Meaning," in *Semantics and the Philosophy of Language,* ed. by Leonard Linsky (Urbana, Ill., 1952), p. 68.

24. "Nomic necessity" has been used by R. B. Braithwaite and W. E. Johnson. "Etiological necessity" has been used by C. J. Ducasse.

25. Cf. Butler, op. cit., p. 269.

26. Prior, op. cit., p. 324, has shown that Aristotle was not thinking of logical necessity in these arguments.

27. Cf. Anscombe, op. cit., p. 12.

28. Hobbes is an excellent example: "All propositions concerning future things, contingent or not contingent . . . are either necessarily true, or necessarily false; but we call them contingent because we do not yet know whether they be true or false; whereas their verity depends not upon our knowledge, but upon the foregoing of their causes" (*The Metaphysical System of Hobbes,* Open Court edition, ed. by M. W. Calkins, pp. 78–79). Cf. C. J. Ducasse, "Truth, Verifiability, and Propositions about the Future," *Philosophy of Science,* VIII (1941), 331–333.

29. Cf. Baylis, op. cit., p. 163.

30. Ibid., p. 162.

31. "The Sea Fight Tomorrow," pp. 294 ff.

32. Ibid., pp. 294–295.

33. *De Gen. et. Corr.,* 337^b 35; *Met.,* 1015^b 14; *E. N.* 1139^b 24. Cf. Anscombe, op. cit., pp. 6–7.

34. "The Sea Fight Tomorrow," p. 286.

35. Ibid., p. 290.

36. *Summa Theologica,* pt. I, q. 14, art. 13. Donald Williams expresses the same idea ("The Sea Fight Tomorrow," p. 283): "The most accidental and ephemeral proposition—that the dog's tail twitches at just such and such a moment, for example—is likewise an eternal truth, if it is true at all. It was true when the sun was formed; it will be true when the sun explodes or is extinguished."

37. Cf. W. V. Quine, *Elementary Logic* (Boston, 1941), p. 6, (quoted by Williams, "The Sea Fight Tomorrow," p. 286).

38. *Inquiry into Meaning and Truth* (London, 1940), p. 113.

39. *Philosophical Essays* (London, 1954), p. 186.

40. *The Structure of Appearance* (Cambridge, Mass., 1951), p. 297.

41. "Time: A Treatment of Some Puzzles," in *Essays on Logic and Language,* ed. by Antony Flew (New York, 1951), p. 53.

42. Williams, "The Sea Fight Tomorrow," pp. 287 ff. Cf. his "The Myth of Passage," *Journal of Philosophy,* XLVIII (1951), 459–460.

43. "The Sea Fight Tomorrow," p. 282.

44. Ibid., pp. 305–306.

45. Cf. Paul Weiss, *Nature and Man* (New York, 1947), p. 12.

46. Cf. Butler, op. cit., p. 273.

47. This argument is familiar from Leibniz, who the in *Discourse on Metaphysics* (Art. 13) argued that whatever is going to happen is already "assured" or "certain," but not therefore any more "necessary" than what has already happened. The same point was well made by Thomas Reid (*Essays on the Intellectual and Active Powers of Man* (1790), vol. I, Essay III, ch. ii), and more recently by Ryle, who asks, "Why does the slogan 'Whatever is, always was to be' seem to imply that nothing can be helped, where the obverse slogan 'Whatever is, will always have been' does not seem to imply this?" (op. cit., p. 21).

48. Cf. Baylis, op. cit., pp. 161–162.

49. Cf. Reid, op. cit., vol. III, Essay IV, ch. x.

50. See G. Grote, *Aristotle* (London, 1880), pp. 115–116. Cf. Paul Weiss, "The Past: Its Nature and Reality," *Review of Metaphysics,* V (1952), 508–509.

51. *E. N.* 1139^b: "No one deliberates about the past, but about what is future and capable of being otherwise, while what is past is not capable of not having taken place; hence Agathos is right in saying 'For this alone is lacking even to God, to make undone things that have once been done.'" Cf. St. Thomas, *S.T.* pt. I, Q. 25, art. 4, and Weiss, "The Past: Its Nature and Reality," p. 511.

52. Cf. Anscombe, op. cit., p. 11.

53. Donald Williams writes that "as for the irrevocability of past time, it seems to be no more than the trivial fact that the particular events of 1902, let us say, can not also be the events of 1952" ("The Myth of Passage," p. 465). But so also, the events of 2002 cannot also be the events of 1952; yet the future is alterable.

54. This point is taken from Charles Hartshorne, *Man's Vision of God* (Chicago, 1941), p. 101.

55. Cf. Mary and Arthur Prior, "Erotetic Logic," *Philosophical Review,* LXIV (1955), 57–58.

56. Donald Williams remarks that "there is a wholly unacceptable suggestion in these passages that an event may be contingent before it happens and necessary afterward; that indeed all present and past events . . . are necessary. But in so far as he is persuaded of the truth of his first proposition, it must be by deduction from his own metaphysics of potentiality and tendency, rather than by logic or observation" ("The Sea Fight Tomorrow," pp. 290–291). I think this interpretation is right but the evaluation wrong.

57. *De Int.* 19ᵃ 23–24. But notice that this is a temporal, and not an ordinary hypothetical statement.

58. "The Sea Fight Tomorrow," pp. 291–292.

59. As Linsky, op. cit., p. 251 and Butler, op. cit., pp. 267–268, have both pointed out.

60. Cf. St. Thomas, *S.T.* pt. I, Q. 22, art. 4. For a brief history of Scholastic opinion on this point, see Philotheus Boehner's edition and study of Ockham's *Tractatus de praedestinatione et de praescientia Dei et de futuris contingentibus,* Franciscan Institute Publications (St. Bonaventure, N.Y., 1945), pp. 75 ff.

61. Cf. Weiss, *Nature and Man,* p. 13.

62. *S.T* pt. I, Q. 25, art. 3.

63. Hartshorne, op. cit., p. 98. Cf. Boethius, *The Consolation of Philosophy* (Loeb Classical Library), p. 387.

64. Hartshorne (op. cit., pp. 104, 139) calls this conception of omniscience "the Principle of Gersonides," after Levy ben Gerson (fourteenth century) who may have been its originator.

65. Op. cit., p. 385. Cf. E. Gilson, *The Philosophy of St. Thomas Aquinas* (St. Louis, 1941), p. 119.

66. Op. cit., pp. 21–23.

67. Aristotle explicitly denied it (*De. Int.* 19ᵇ 36).

68. Essentially this point is made by Ryle, op. cit., pp. 19–20: "A prophecy is not fulfilled until the event forecast has happened. . . . The establishment of incorrectness certainly cancels 'true' but not, as a rule, so fiercely as to incline us to say 'false.'"

69. Cf. Hartshorne, op. cit., p. 103.

Freedom and Necessity

A. J. AYER

Alfred Jules Ayer (1910–1989) taught at Oxford University and the University of London. He was Wykeham Professor of Logic at Oxford from 1959 to 1978. His book *Language, Truth and Logic* is a classic source in English for verificationism and logical positivism. He is also the author of *The Problem of Knowledge.* He was knighted in 1970.

WHEN I am said to have done something of my own free will it is implied that I could have acted otherwise; and it is only when it is believed that I could have acted otherwise that I am held to be morally responsible for what I have done. For a man is not thought to be morally responsible for an action that it was not in his power to avoid. But if human behaviour is entirely governed by causal laws, it is not clear how any action that is done could ever have been avoided. It may be said of the agent that he would

Reprinted from *Philosophical Essays* (London: Macmillan; New York: St. Martin's Press, 1954), by permission of Macmillan, London and Basingstoke.

have acted otherwise if the causes of his action had been different, but they being what they were, it seems to follow that he was bound to act as he did. Now it is commonly assumed both that men are capable of acting freely, in the sense that is required to make them morally responsible, and that human behaviour is entirely governed by causal laws: and it is the apparent conflict between these two assumptions that gives rise to the philosophical problem of the freedom of the will.

Confronted with this problem, many people will be inclined to agree with Dr. Johnson: "Sir, we *know* our will is free, and *there's* an end on't." But, while this does very well for those who accept Dr. Johnson's premiss, it would hardly convince anyone who denied the freedom of the will. Certainly, if we do know that our wills are free, it follows that they are so. But the logical reply to this might be that since our wills are not free, it follows that no one can know that they are: so that if anyone claims, like Dr. Johnson, to know that they are, he must be mistaken. What is evident, indeed, is that people often believe themselves to be acting freely; and it is to this "feeling" of freedom that some philosophers appeal when they wish, in the supposed interests of morality, to prove that not all human action is causally determined. But if these philosophers are right in their assumption that a man cannot be acting freely if his action is causally determined, then the fact that someone feels free to do, or not to do, a certain action does not prove that he really is so. It may prove that the agent does not himself know what it is that makes him act in one way rather than another: but from the fact that a man is unaware of the causes of his action, it does not follow that no such causes exist.

So much may be allowed to the determinist; but his belief that all human actions are subservient to causal laws still remains to be justified. If, indeed, it is necessary that every event should have a cause, then the rule must apply to human behaviour as much as to anything else. But why should it be supposed that every event must have a cause? The contrary is not unthinkable. Nor is the law of universal causation a necessary presupposition of scientific thought. The scientist may try to discover causal laws, and in many cases he succeeds; but sometimes he has to be con-

tent with statistical laws, and sometimes he comes upon events which, in the present state of his knowledge, he is not able to subsume under any law at all. In the case of these events he assumes that if he knew more he would be able to discover some law, whether causal or statistical, which would enable him to account for them. And this assumption cannot be disproved. For however far he may have carried his investigation, it is always open to him to carry it further; and it is always conceivable that if he carried it further he would discover the connection which had hitherto escaped him. Nevertheless, it is also conceivable that the events with which he is concerned are not systematically connected with any others: so that the reason why he does not discover the sort of laws that he requires is simply that they do not obtain.

Now in the case of human conduct the search for explanations has not in fact been altogether fruitless. Certain scientific laws have been established; and with the help of these laws we do make a number of successful predictions about the ways in which different people will behave. But these predictions do not always cover every detail. We may be able to predict that in certain circumstances a particular man will be angry, without being able to prescribe the precise form that the expression of his anger will take. We may be reasonably sure that he will shout, but not sure how loud his shout will be, or exactly what words he will use. And it is only a small proportion of human actions that we are able to forecast even so precisely as this. But that, it may be said, is because we have not carried our investigations very far. The science of psychology is still in its infancy and, as it is developed, not only will more human actions be explained, but the explanations will go into greater detail. The ideal of complete explanation may never in fact be attained: but it is theoretically attainable. Well, this may be so: and certainly it is impossible to show a priori that it is not so: but equally it cannot be shown that it is. This will not, however, discourage the scientist who, in the field of human behaviour, as elsewhere, will continue to formulate theories and test them by the facts. And in this he is justified. For since he has no reason a priori to admit that there is a limit to what he can discover, the fact that he also cannot be sure that there is no limit does not make it unreasonable for him to devise theories, nor, having devised them, to try constantly to improve them.

But now suppose it to be claimed that, so far as men's actions are concerned, there is a limit: and that this limit is set by the fact of human freedom. An obvious objection is that in many cases in which a person feels himself to be free to do, or not to do, a certain action, we are even now able to explain, in causal terms, why it is that he acts as he does. But it might be argued that even if men are sometimes mistaken in believing that they act freely, it does not follow that they are always so mistaken. For it is not always the case that when a man believes that he has acted freely we are in fact able to account for his action in causal terms. A determinist would say that we should be able to account for it if we had more knowledge of the circumstances, and had been able to discover the appropriate natural laws. But until those discoveries have been made, this remains only a pious hope. And may it not be true that, in some cases at least, the reason why we can give no causal explanation is that no causal explanation is available; and that this is because the agent's choice was literally free, as he himself felt it to be?

The answer is that this may indeed be true, inasmuch as it is open to anyone to hold that no explanation is possible until some explanation is actually found. But even so it does not give the moralist what he wants. For he is anxious to show that men are capable of acting freely in order to infer that they can be morally responsible for what they do. But if it is a matter of pure chance that a man should act in one way rather than another, he may be free but can hardly be responsible. And indeed when a man's actions seem to us quite unpredictable, when, as we say, there is no knowing what he will do, we do not look upon him as a moral agent. We look upon him as a lunatic.

To this it may be objected that we are not dealing fairly with the moralist. For when he makes it a condition of my being morally responsible that I should act freely, he does not wish to imply that it is purely a matter of chance that I act as I do. What he wishes to imply is that my actions are the result of my own free choice: and it is because they are the result of my own free choice that I am held to be morally responsible for them.

Responsibility

But now we must ask how it is that I come to make my choice. Either it is an accident that I choose to act as I do or it is not. If it is a accident, then it is merely a matter of chance that I did not choose otherwise; and if it is merely a matter of chance that I did not choose otherwise, it is surely irrational to hold me morally responsible for choosing as I did. But if it is not an accident that I choose to do one thing rather than another, then presumably there is some causal explanation of my choice: and in that case we are led back to determinism.

Again, the objection may be raised that we are not doing justice to the moralist's case. His view is not that it is a matter of chance that I choose to act as I do, but rather that my choice depends upon my character. Nevertheless he holds that I can still be free in the sense that he requires; for it is I who am responsible for my character. But in what way am I responsible for my character? Only, surely, in the sense that there is a causal connection between what I do now and what I have done in the past. It is only this that justifies the statement that I have made myself what I am: and even so this is an over-simplification, since it takes no account of the external influences to which I have been subjected. But, ignoring the external influences, let us assume that it is in fact the case that I have made myself what I am. Then it is still legitimate to ask how it is that I have come to make myself one sort of person rather than another. And if it be answered that it is a matter of my strength of will, we can put the same question in another form by asking how it is that my will has the strength that it has and not some other degree of strength. Once more, either it is an accident or it is not. If it is an accident, then by the same argument as before, I am not morally responsible, and if it is not an accident we are led back to determinism.

Furthermore, to say that my actions proceed from my character or, more colloquially, that I act in character, is to say that my behaviour is consistent and to that extent predictable: and since it is, above all, for the actions that I perform in character that I am held to be morally responsible, it looks as if the admission of moral responsibility, so far from being incompatible with determinism, tends rather to presuppose it. But how can this be so if it is a necessary condition of moral responsibility that the person who is held responsible should have acted freely? It seems that if we are to retain this idea of moral responsibility, we must either show that men can be held responsible for actions which they do not do freely, or else find some way of reconciling determinism with the freedom of the will.

It is no doubt with the object of effecting this reconciliation that some philosophers have defined freedom as the consciousness of necessity. And by so doing they are able to say not only that a man can be acting freely when his action is causally determined, but even that his action must be causally determined for it to be possible for him to be acting freely. Nevertheless this definition has the serious disadvantage that it gives to the word "freedom" a meaning quite different from any that it ordinarily bears. It is indeed obvious that if we are allowed to give the word "freedom" any meaning that we please, we can find a meaning that will reconcile it with determinism: but this is no more a solution of our present problem than the fact that the word "horse" could be arbitrarily used to mean what is ordinarily meant by "sparrow" is a proof that horses have wings. For suppose that I am compelled by another person to do something "against my will." In that case, as the word "freedom" is ordinarily used, I should not be said to be acting freely: and the fact that I am fully aware of the constraint to which I am subjected makes no difference to the matter. I do not become free by becoming conscious that I am not. It may, indeed, be possible to show that my being aware that my action is causally determined is not incompatible with my acting freely: but it by no means follows that it is in this that my freedom consists. Moreover, I suspect that one of the reasons why people are inclined to define freedom as the consciousness of necessity is that they think that if one is conscious of necessity one may somehow be able to master it. But this is a fallacy. It is like someone's saying that he wishes he could see into the future, because if he did he would know what calamities lay in wait for him and so would be able to avoid them. But if he avoids the calamities then they don't lie in the future and it is not true that he foresees them. And similarly if I am able to master necessity, in the sense of escaping the operation of a nec-

essary law, then the law in question is not necessary. And if the law is not necessary, then neither my freedom nor anything else can consist in my knowing that it is.

Let it be granted, then, when we speak of reconciling freedom with determination we are using the word "freedom" in an ordinary sense. It still remains for us to make this usage clear: and perhaps the best way to make it clear is to show what it is that freedom, in this sense, is contrasted with. Now we began with the assumption that freedom is contrasted with causality: so that a man cannot be said to be acting freely if his action is causally determined. But this assumption has led us into difficulties and I now wish to suggest that it is mistaken. For it is not, I think, causality that freedom is to be contrasted with, but constraint. And while it is true that being constrained to do an action entails being caused to do it, I shall try to show that the converse does not hold. I shall try to show that from the fact that my action is causally determined it does not necessarily follow that I am constrained to do it: and this is equivalent to saying that it does not necessarily follow that I am not free.

If I am constrained, I do not act freely. But in what circumstances can I legitimately be said to be constrained? An obvious instance is the case in which I am compelled by another person to do what he wants. In a case of this sort the compulsion need not be such as to deprive one of the power of choice. It is not required that the other person should have hypnotized me, or that he should make it physically impossible for me to go against his will. It is enough that he should induce me to do what he wants by making it clear to me that, if I do not, he will bring about some situation that I regard as even more undesirable than the consequences of the action that he wishes me to do. Thus, if the man points a pistol at my head I may still choose to disobey him: but this does not prevent its being true that if I do fall in with his wishes he can legitimately be said to have compelled me. And if the circumstances are such that no reasonable person would be expected to choose the other alternative, then the action that I am made to do is not one for which I am held to be morally responsible.

A similar, but still somewhat different, case is that in which another person has obtained an habitual ascendancy over me. Where this is so, there may be no question of my being induced to act as the other person wishes by being confronted with a still more disagreeable alternative: for if I am sufficiently under his influence this special stimulus will not be necessary. Nevertheless I do not act freely, for the reason that I have been deprived of the power of choice. And this means that I have acquired so strong a habit of obedience that I no longer go through any process of deciding whether or not to do what the other person wants. About other matters I may still deliberate; but as regards the fulfilment of this other person's wishes, my own deliberations have ceased to be a causal factor in my behaviour. And it is in this sense that I may be said to be constrained. It is not, however, necessary that such constraint should take the form of subservience to another person. A kleptomaniac is not a free agent, in respect of his stealing, because he does not go through any process of deciding whether or not to steal. Or rather, if he does go through such a process, it is irrelevant to his behaviour. Whatever he resolved to do, he would steal all the same. And it is this that distinguishes him from the ordinary thief.

But now it may be asked whether there is any essential difference between these cases and those in which the agent is commonly thought to be free. No doubt the ordinary thief does go through a process of deciding whether or not to steal, and no doubt it does affect his behaviour. If he resolved to refrain from stealing, he could carry his resolution out. But if it be allowed that his making or not making this resolution is causally determined, then how can he be any more free than the kleptomaniac? It may be true that unlike the kleptomaniac he could refrain from stealing if he chose: but if there is a cause, or set of causes, which necessitate his choosing as he does, how can he be said to have the power of choice? Again, it may be true that no one now compels me to get up and walk across the room: but if my doing so can be causally explained in terms of my history or my environment, or whatever it may be, then how am I any more free than if some other person had compelled me? I do not have the feeling of constraint that I have when a pistol is manifestly pointed at my head; but the chains of causation by which I am bound are no less effective for being invisible.

The answer to this is that the cases I have mentioned as examples of constraint do differ from the others: and they differ just in the ways that I have tried to bring out. If I suffered from a compulsion neurosis, so that I got up and walked across the room, whether I wanted to or not, or if I did so because somebody else compelled me, then I should not be acting freely. But if I do it now, I shall be acting freely, just because these conditions do not obtain; and the fact that my action may nevertheless have a cause is, from this point of view, irrelevant. For it is not when my action has any cause at all, but only when it has a special sort of cause, that it is reckoned not to be free.

But here it may be objected that, even if this distinction corresponds to ordinary usage, it is still very irrational. For why should we distinguish, with regard to a person's freedom, between the operations of one sort of cause and those of another? Do not all causes equally necessitate? And is it not therefore arbitrary to say that a person is free when he is necessitated in one fashion but not when he is necessitated in another? *Question*

That all causes equally necessitate is indeed a tautology, if the word "necessitate" is taken merely as equivalent to "cause": but if, as the objection requires, it is taken as equivalent to "constrain" or "compel," then I do not think that this proposition is true. For all that is needed for one event to be the cause of another is that, in the given circumstances, the event which is said to be the effect would not have occurred if it had not been for the occurrence of the event which is said to be the cause, or vice versa, according as causes are interpreted as necessary, or sufficient, conditions: and this fact is usually deducible from some causal law which states that whenever an event of the one kind occurs then, given suitable conditions, an event of the other kind will occur in a certain temporal or spatio-temporal relationship to it. In short, there is an invariable concomitance between the two classes of events; but there is no compulsion, in any but a metaphorical sense. Suppose, for example, that a psycho-analyst is able to account for some aspect of my behaviour by referring it to some lesion that I suffered in my childhood. In that case, it may be said that my childhood experience, together with certain other events, necessitates my behaving as I do. But all that this involves is that it is found to be true in general that when people have had certain experiences as children, they subsequently behave in certain specifiable ways; and my case is just another instance of this general law. It is in this way indeed that my behaviour is explained. But from the fact that my behaviour is capable of being explained, in the sense that it can be subsumed under some natural law, it does not follow that I am acting under constraint.

If this is correct, to say that I could have acted otherwise is to say, first, that I should have acted otherwise if I had so chosen; secondly, that my action was voluntary in the sense in which the actions, say, of the kleptomaniac are not; and thirdly, that nobody compelled me to choose as I did: and these three conditions may very well be fulfilled. When they are fulfilled, I may be said to have acted freely. But this is not to say that it was a matter of chance that I acted as I did, or, in other words, that my action could not be explained. And that my actions should be capable of being explained is all that is required by the postulate of determinism.

If more than this seems to be required it is, I think, because the use of the very word "determinism" is in some degree misleading. For it tends to suggest that one event is somehow in the power of another, whereas the truth is merely that they are factually correlated. And the same applies to the use, in this context, of the word "necessity" and even of the word "cause" itself. Moreover, there are various reasons for this. One is the tendency to confuse causal with logical necessitation, and so to infer mistakenly that the effect is contained in the cause. Another is the uncritical use of a concept of force which is derived from primitive experiences of pushing and striking. A third is the survival of an animistic conception of causality, in which all causal relationships are modelled on the example of one person's exercising

authority over another. As a result we tend to form an imaginative picture of an unhappy effect trying vainly to escape from the clutches of an overmastering cause. But, I repeat, the fact is simply that when an event of one type occurs, an event of another type occurs also, in a certain temporal or spatio-temporal relation to the first. The rest is only metaphor. And it is because of the metaphor, and not because of the fact, that we come to think that there is an antithesis between causality and freedom.

Nevertheless, it may be said, if the postulate of determinism is valid, then the future can be explained in terms of the past: and this means that if one knew enough about the past one would be able to predict the future. But in that case what will happen in the future is already decided. And how then can I be said to be free? What is going to happen is going to happen and nothing that I do can prevent it. If the determinist is right, I am the helpless prisoner of fate.

But what is meant by saying that the future course of events is already decided? If the implication is that some person has arranged it, then the proposition is false. But if all that is meant is that it is possible, in principle, to deduce it from a set of particular facts about the past, together with the appropriate general laws, then, even if this is true, it does not in the least entail that I am the helpless prisoner of fate. It does not even entail that my actions make no difference to the future: for they are causes as well as effects; so that if they were different their consequences would be different also. What it does entail is that my behaviour can be predicted: but to say that my behaviour can be predicted is not to say that I am acting under constraint. It is indeed true that I cannot escape my destiny if this is taken to mean no more than that I shall do what I shall do. But this is a tautology, just as it is a tautology that what is going to happen is going to happen. And such tautologies as these prove nothing whatsoever about the freedom of the will.

 Acting freely

Human Freedom and the Self

◠

RODERICK M. CHISHOLM

Roderick Chisholm (1916–1999) was a philosopher at Brown University. He is known for his adverbial theory of perception, foundationalism in the theory of knowledge, and incompatibilsm about freedom and determinism. His books include *Perceiving: A Philosophical Study, Person and Object: A Metaphysical Study,* and *A Realistic Theory of Categories: An Essay on Ontology.*

"A staff moves a stone, and is moved by a hand, which is moved by a man."

—*Aristotle, Physics, 256a.*

1. The metaphysical problem of human freedom might be summarized in the following way: Human beings are responsible agents; but this fact appears to conflict with a deterministic view of human action (the view that every event that is involved in an act is caused by some other event); and it *also* appears to conflict with an indeterministic view of human action (the view that the act, or some event that is essential to the act, is not caused at all.) To solve the problem, I believe, we must make somewhat far-reaching assumptions about the self or the agent—about the man who performs the act.

Perhaps it is needless to remark that, in all likelihood, it is impossible to say anything significant about this ancient problem that has not been said before.[1]

2. Let us consider some deed, or misdeed, that may be attributed to a responsible agent: one man, say, shot another. If the man *was* responsible for what he did, then, I would urge, what was to happen at the time of the shooting was something that was entirely up to the man himself. There was a moment at which it was true, both that he could have fired the shot and also that he could have refrained from firing it. And if this is so, then, even though he did fire it, he could have done something else instead. (He didn't find himself firing the shot "against his will," as we say.) I think we can say, more generally, then, that if a man is responsible for a certain event or a certain state of affairs (in our example, the shooting of another man), then that event or state of affairs was brought about by some act of his, and the act was something that was in his power either to perform or not to perform.

But now if the act which he *did* perform was an act that was also in his power *not* to perform, then it could not have been caused or determined by any event that was not itself within his power either to bring about or not to bring about. For example, if what we say he did was really something that was brought about by a second man, one who forced his hand upon the trigger, say, or who, by means of hypnosis, compelled him to perform the act, then since the act was caused by the *second* man it was nothing that was within the power of the *first* man to prevent. And precisely the same thing is true, I think, if instead of referring to a second man who compelled the first one, we speak instead of the *desires* and *beliefs* which the first man happens to have had. For if what we say he did was really something that was brought about by his own beliefs and desires, if these

The Lindley Lecture, 1964. Copyright © 1964 by the Department of Philosophy, University of Kansas. Reprinted by permission of the Department of Philosophy and of the University of Kansas.

beliefs and desires in the particular situation in which he happened to have found himself caused him to do just what it was that we say he did do, then, since *they* caused it, *he* was unable to do anything other than just what it was that he did do. It makes no difference whether the cause of the deed was internal or external; if the cause was some state or event for which the man himself was not responsible, then he was not responsible for what we have been mistakenly calling his act. If a flood caused the poorly constructed dam to break, then, given the flood and the constitution of the dam, the break, we may say, *had* to occur and nothing could have happened in its place. And if the flood of desire caused the weak-willed man to give in, then he, too, had to do just what it was that he did do and he was no more responsible than was the dam for the results that followed. (It is true, of course, that if the man is responsible for the beliefs and desires that he happens to have, then he may also be responsible for the things they lead him to do. But the question now becomes: *is* he responsible for the beliefs and desires he happens to have? If he is, then there was a time when they were within his power either to acquire or not to acquire, and we are left, therefore, with our general point.)

One may object: But surely if there were such a thing as a man who is really *good,* then he would be responsible for things that he would do; yet, he would be unable to do anything other than just what it is that he does do, since, being good, he will always choose to do what is best. The answer, I think, is suggested by a comment that Thomas Reid makes upon an ancient author. The author had said of Cato, "He was good because he could not be otherwise," and Reid observes: "This saying, if understood literally and strictly, is not the praise of Cato, but of his constitution, which was no more the work of Cato than his existence."[2] If Cato was himself responsible for the good things that he did, then Cato, as Reid suggests, was such that, although he had the power to do what was not good, he exercised his power only for that which was good.

All of this, if it is true, may give a certain amount of comfort to those who are tender-minded. But we should remind them that it also conflicts with a familiar view about the nature of God—with the view that

St. Thomas Aquinas expresses by saying that "every movement both of the will and of nature proceeds from God as the Prime Mover."[3] If the act of the sinner *did* proceed from God as the Prime Mover, then God was in the position of the second agent we just discussed—the man who forced the trigger finger, or the hypnotist—and the sinner, so-called, was *not* responsible for what he did. (This may be a bold assertion, in view of the history of western theology, but I must say that I have never encountered a single good reason for denying it.)

There is one standard objection to all of this and we should consider it briefly.

3. The objection takes the form of a stratagem—one designed to show that determinism (and divine providence) is consistent with human responsibility. The stratagem is one that was used by Jonathan Edwards and by many philosophers in the present century, most notably, G. E. Moore.[4]

One proceeds as follows: The expression

(a) He could have done otherwise,

it is argued, means no more nor less than

(b) If he had chosen to do otherwise, then he would have done otherwise.

(In place of "chosen," one might say "tried," "set out," "decided," "undertaken," or "willed.") The truth of statement (b), it is then pointed out, is consistent with determinism (and with divine providence); for even if all of the man's actions were causally determined, the man could still be such that, *if* he had chosen otherwise, then he would have done otherwise. What the murderers saw, let us suppose, along with his beliefs and desires, *caused* him to fire the shot; yet he was such that *if,* just then, he had chosen or decided *not* to fire the shot, then he would not have fired it. All of this is certainly possible. Similarly, we could say, of the dam, that the flood caused it to break and also that the dam was such that, *if* there had been no flood or any similar pressure, then the dam would have remained intact. And therefore, the argument proceeds, if (b) is consistent with determinism, and if (a) and (b) say the same thing, then (a) is also consistent with determinism; hence we can say that the agent *could* have done otherwise even though he was caused to do what he did do; and therefore determinism and moral responsibility are compatible.

Is the argument sound? The conclusion follows from the premises, but the catch, I think, lies in the first premiss—the one saying that statement (a) tells us no more nor less than what statement (b) tells us. For (b), it would seem, could be true while (a) is false. That is to say, our man might be such that, if he had chosen to do otherwise, then he would have done otherwise, and yet *also* such that he could not have done otherwise. Suppose, after all, that our murderer could not have *chosen,* or could not have *decided,* to do otherwise. Then the fact that he happens also to be a man such that, if he had chosen not to shoot he would not have shot, would make no difference. For if he could *not* have chosen *not* to shoot, then he could not have done anything other than just what it was that he did do. In a word: from our statement (b) above ("If he had chosen to do otherwise, then he would have done otherwise"), we cannot make an inference to (a) above ("He could have done otherwise") unless we can *also* assert:

(c) He could have chosen to do otherwise.

And therefore, if we must reject this third statement (c), then, even though we may be justified in asserting (b), we are not justified in asserting (a). If the man could not have chosen to do otherwise, then he would not have done otherwise—*even if* he was such that, if he *had* chosen to do otherwise, then he would have done otherwise.

The stratagem in question, then, seems to me not to work, and I would say, therefore, that the ascription of responsibility conflicts with a deterministic view of action.

4. Perhaps there is less need to argue that the ascription of responsibility also conflicts with an indeterministic view of action—with the view that the act, or some event that is essential to the act, is not caused at all. If the act—the firing of the shot—was not caused at all, if it was fortuitous or capricious, happening so to speak out of the blue, then, presumably, no one—and nothing—was responsible for the act. Our conception of action, therefore, should be neither deterministic nor indeterministic. Is there any other possibility?

5. We must not say that every event involved in the act is caused by some other event; and we must not say that the act is something that is not caused at all. The possibility that remains, therefore, is this: We should say that at least one of the events that are involved in the act is caused, not by any other events, but by something else instead. And this something else can only be the agent—the man. If there is an event that is caused, not by other events, but by the man, then there are some events involved in the act that are not caused by other events. But if the event in question is caused by the man then it *is* caused and we are not committed to saying that there is something involved in the act that is not caused at all.

But this, of course, is a large consequence, implying something of considerable importance about the nature of the agent or the man.

6. If we consider only inanimate natural objects, we may say that causation, if it occurs, is a relation between *events* or *states of affairs.* The dam's breaking was an event that was caused by a set of other events—the dam being weak, the flood being strong, and so on. But if a man is responsible for a particular deed, then, if what I have said is true, there is some event, or set of events, that is caused, *not* by other events or states of affairs, but by the agent, whatever he may be.

I shall borrow a pair of medieval terms, using them, perhaps, in a way that is slightly different from that for which they were originally intended. I shall say that when one event or state of affairs (or set of events or states of affairs) causes some other event or state of affairs, then we have an instance of *transeunt* causation. And I shall say that when an *agent,* as distinguished from an event, causes an event or state of affairs, then we have an instance of *immanent* causation.

The nature of what is intended by the expression "immanent causation" may be illustrated by this sentence from Aristotle's *Physics:* "Thus, a staff moves a stone, and is moved by a hand, which is moved by a man." (VII, 5, 256a, 6–8) If the man was responsible, then we have in this illustration a number of instances of causation—most of them transeunt but at least one of them immanent. What the staff did to the stone was an instance of transeunt causation, and thus we may describe it as a relation between events: "the motion of the staff caused the motion of the stone." And similarly for what the hand did to the staff: "the motion of the hand caused the motion of the staff." And, as we know from physiology, there are still other events which caused the motion of the hand. Hence we need not introduce the agent at this particular point, as Aristotle does—we *need* not, though we *may*. We *may* say that the hand was moved by the man, but we may *also* say that the motion of the hand was caused by the motion of certain muscles; and we may say that the motion of the muscles was caused by certain events that took place within the brain. But some event, and presumably one of those that took place within the brain, was caused by the agent and not by any other events.

There are, of course, objections to this way of putting the matter; I shall consider the two that seem to me to be most important.

7. One may object, firstly: "If the *man* does anything, then, as Aristotle's remark suggests, what he does is to move the *hand*. But he certainly does not *do* anything to his brain—he may not even know that he *has* a brain. And if he doesn't do anything to the brain, and if the motion of the hand was caused by something that happened within the brain, then there is no point in appealing to 'immanent causation' as being something incompatible with 'transeunt causation'—for the whole thing, after all, is a matter of causal relations among events or states of affairs."

The answer to this objection, I think, is this: It is true that the agent does not *do* anything with his brain, or to his brain, in the sense in which he *does* something with his hand and does something to the staff. But from this it does not follow that the agent was not the immanent cause of something that happened within his brain.

We should note a useful distinction that has been proposed by Professor A. I. Melden—namely, the distinction between 'making something A happen' and "doing A."[5] If I reach for the staff and pick it up, then one of the things that I *do* is just that—reach for the staff and pick it up. And if it is something that I do,

then there is a very clear sense in which it may be said to be something that I know that I do. If you ask me, "Are you doing something, or trying to do something, with the staff?" I will have no difficulty in finding an answer. But in doing something with the staff, I also make various things happen which are not in this same sense things that I do: I will make various air-particles move; I will free a number of blades of grass from the pressure that had been upon them; and I may cause a shadow to move from one place to another. If these are merely things that I make happen, as distinguished from things that I do, then I may know nothing whatever about them; I may not have the slightest idea that, in moving the staff, I am bringing about any such thing as the motion of air-particles, shadows, and blades of grass.

We may say, in answer to the first objection, therefore, that it is true that our agent does nothing to his brain or with his brain; but from this it does not follow that the agent is not the immanent cause of some event within his brain; for the brain event may be something which, like the motion of the air-particles, he made happen in picking up the staff. The only difference between the two cases is this: in each case, he made something happen when he picked up the staff; but in the one case—the motion of the air-particles or of the shadows—it was the motion of the staff that caused the event to happen; and in the other case—the event that took place in the brain—it was this event that caused the motion of the staff.

The point is, in a word, that whenever a man does something A, then (by "immanent causation") he makes a certain cerebral event happen, and this cerebral event (by 'transeunt causation') makes A happen.

8. The second objection is more difficult and concerns the very concept of "immanent causation," or causation by an agent, as this concept is to be interpreted here. The concept is subject to a difficulty which has long been associated with that of the prime mover unmoved. We have said that there must be some event A, presumably some cerebral event, which is caused not by any other event, but by the agent. Since A was not caused by any other event, then the agent himself cannot be said to have undergone any change or produced any other event (such as "an act of will" or the like) which brought A about.

But if, when the agent made A happen, there was no event involved other than A itself, no event which could be described as *making* A happen, what did the agent's causation consist of? What, for example, is the difference between A's just happening, and the agents' *causing* A to happen? We cannot attribute the difference to any event that took place within the agent. And so far as the event A itself is concerned, there would seem to be no discernible difference. Thus Aristotle said that the activity of the prime mover is nothing in addition to the motion that it produces, and Suarez said that "the action is in reality nothing but the effect as it flows from the agent."[6] Must we conclude, then, that there is no more to the man's action in causing event A than there is to the event A's happening by itself? Here we would seem to have a distinction without a difference—in which case we have failed to find a *via media* between a deterministic and an indeterministic view of action.

The only answer, I think, can be this: that the difference between the man's causing A, on the one hand, and the event A just happening, on the other, lies in the fact that, in the first case but not the second, the event A *was* caused and was caused by the man. There was a brain event A; the agent did, in fact, cause the brain event; but there was nothing that he did to cause it.

This answer may not entirely satisfy and it will be likely to provoke the following question: "But what are you really *adding* to the assertion that A happened when you utter the words 'The agent *caused* A to happen'"? As soon as we have put the question this way, we see, I think, that whatever difficulty we may have encountered is one that may be traced to the concept of causation generally—whether "immanent" or "transeunt." The problem, in other words, is not a problem that is peculiar to our conception of human action. It is a problem that must be faced by anyone who makes use of the concept of causation at all; and therefore, I would say, it is a problem for everyone but the complete indeterminist.

For the problem, as we put it, referring just to "immanent causation," or causation by an agent, was this: "What is the difference between saying, of an event A, that A just happened and saying that someone caused A to happen?" The analogous problem,

which holds for "transeunt causation," or causation by an event, is this: "What is the difference between saying, of two events A and B, that B happened and then A happened, and saying that B's happening was the *cause* of A's happening?" And the only answer that one can give is this—that in the one case the agent was the cause of A's happening and in the other case event B was the cause of A's happening. The nature of transeunt causation is no more clear than is that of immanent causation.

9. But we may plausibly say—and there is a respectable philosophical tradition to which we may appeal—that the notion of immanent causation, or causation by an agent, is in fact more clear than that of transeunt causation, or causation by an event, and that it is only by understanding our own causal efficacy, as agents, that we can grasp the concept of *cause* at all. Hume may be said to have shown that we do not derive the concept of *cause* from what we perceive of external things. How, then, do we derive it? The most plausible suggestion, it seems to me, is that of Reid, once again: namely that "the conception of an efficient cause may very probably be derived from the experience we have had . . . of our own power to produce certain effects."[7] If we did not understand the concept of immanent causation, we would not understand that of transeunt causation.

10. It may have been noted that I have avoided the term "free will" in all of this. For even if there is such a faculty as "the will," which somehow sets our acts agoing, the question of freedom, as John Locke said, is not the question "*whether the will be free*"; it is the question "*whether a man be free.*"[8] For if there is a "will," as a moving faculty, the question is whether the man is free to will to do these things that he does will to do—and also whether he is free *not* to will any of those things that he does will to do, and, again, whether he is free to will any of those things that he does not will to do. Jonathan Edwards tried to restrict himself to the question—"Is the man free to do what it is that he wills?"—but the answer to this question will not tell us whether the man is responsible for what it is that he *does* will to do. Using still another pair of medieval terms, we may say that the metaphysical problem of freedom does not concern the *actus imperatus;* it does not concern the question

whether we are free to accomplish whatever it is that we will or set out to do; it concerns the *actus elicitus,* the question whether we are free to will or to set out to do those things that we do will or set out to do.

11. If we are responsible, and if what I have been trying to say is true, then we have a prerogative which some would attribute only to God: each of us, when we act, is a prime mover unmoved. In doing what we do, we cause certain events to happen, and nothing—or no one—causes us to cause those events to happen.

12. If we are thus prime movers unmoved and if our actions, or those for which we are responsible, are not causally determined, then they are not causally determined by our *desires.* And this means that the relation between what we want or what we desire, on the one hand, and what it is that we do, on the other, is not as simple as most philosophers would have it.

We may distinguish between what we might call the "Hobbist approach" and what we might call the "Kantian approach" to this question. The Hobbist approach is the one that is generally accepted at the present time, but the Kantian approach, I believe, is the one that is true. According to Hobbism, if we *know,* of some man, what his beliefs and desires happen to be and how strong they are, if we know what he feels certain of, what he desires more than anything else, and if we know the state of his body and what stimuli he is being subjected to, then we may *deduce,* logically, just what it is that he will do—or, more accurately, just what it is that he will try, set out, or undertake to do. Thus Professor Melden has said that "the connection between wanting and doing is logical."[9] But according to the Kantian approach to our problem, and this is the one that I would take, there is no such logical connection between wanting and doing, nor need there even be a causal connection. No set of statements about a man's desires, beliefs, and stimulus situation at any time implies any statement telling us what the man will try, set out, or undertake to do at that time. As Reid put it, though we may "reason from men's motives to their actions and, in many cases, with great probability," we can never do so "with absolute certainty."[10]

Interesting point This means that, in one very strict sense of the terms, there can be no science of man. If we think of science as a matter of finding out what laws happen

to hold, and if the statement of a law tells us what kinds of events are caused by what other kinds of events, then there will be human actions which we cannot explain by subsuming them under any laws. We cannot say, "It is causally necessary that, given such and such desires and beliefs, and being subject to such and such stimuli, the agent will do so and so." For at times the agent, if he chooses, may rise above his desires and do something else instead.

But all of this is consistent with saying that, perhaps more often than not, our desires do exist under conditions such that those conditions necessitate us to act. And we may also say, with Leibniz, that at other times our desires may "incline without necessitating."

13. Leibniz's phrase presents us with our final philosophical problem. What does it mean to say that a desire, or a motive, might "incline without necessitating"? There is a temptation, certainly, to say that "to incline" means to cause and that "not to necessitate" means not to cause, but obviously we cannot have it both ways.

Nor will Leibniz's own solution do. In his letter to Coste, he puts the problem as follows: "When a choice is proposed, for example to go out or not to go out, it is a question whether, with all the circumstances, internal and external, motives, perceptions, dispositions, impressions, passions, inclinations taken together, I am still in a contingent state, or whether I am necessitated to make the choice, for example, to go out; that is to say, whether this proposition true and determined in fact, *In all these circumstances taken together I shall choose to go out,* is contingent or necessary."[11] Leibniz's answer might be put as follows: in one sense of the terms "necessary" and "contingent," the proposition "In all these circumstances taken together I shall choose to go out," may be said to be contingent and not necessary, and in another sense of these terms, it may be said to be necessary and not contingent. But the sense in which the proposition may be said to be contingent, according to Leibniz, is only this: there is no logical contradiction involved in denying the proposition. And the sense in which it may be said to be necessary is this: since "nothing ever occurs without cause or determining reason," the proposition is causally necessary. "Whenever all the circumstances taken together are such that the balance of deliberation is heavier on one side than on the other, it is certain and infallible that that is the side that is going to win out." But if what we have been saying is true, the proposition "In all these circumstances taken together I shall choose to go out," may be causally as well as logically contingent. Hence we must find another interpretation for Leibniz's statement that our motives and desires may incline us, or influence us, to choose without thereby necessitating us to choose.

Let us consider a public official who has some moral scruples but who also, as one says, could be had. Because of the scruples that he does have, he would never take any positive steps to receive a bribe—he would not actively solicit one. But his morality has its limits and he is also such that, if we were to confront him with a fait accompli or to let him see what is about to happen ($10,000 in cash is being deposited behind the garage), then he would succumb and be unable to resist. The general situation is a familiar one and this is one reason that people pray to be delivered from temptation. (It also justifies Kant's remark: "And how many there are who may have led a long blameless life, who are only *fortunate* in having escaped so many temptations."[12] Our relation to the misdeed that we contemplate may not be a matter simply of being able to bring it about or not to bring it about. As St. Anselm noted, there are at least four possibilities. We may illustrate them by reference to our public official and the event which is his receiving the bribe, in the following way: (i) he may be able to bring the event about himself (*facere esse*), in which case he would actively cause himself to receive the bribe; (ii) he may be able to refrain from bringing it about himself (*non facere esse*), in which case he would not himself do anything to insure that he receive the bribe; (iii) he may be able to do something to prevent the event from occurring (*facere non esse*), in which case he would make sure that the $10,000 was *not* left behind the garage; or (iv) he may be unable to do anything to prevent the event from occurring (*non facere non esse*), in which case, though he may not solicit the bribe, he would allow himself to keep it.[13] We have envisaged our official as a man who can resist the temptation to (i) but cannot resist the temptation to (iv): he can refrain

from bringing the event about himself, but he cannot bring himself to do anything to prevent it.

Let us think of "inclination without necessitation," then, in such terms as these. First we may contrast the two propositions:

(1) He can resist the temptation to do something in order to make A happen;
(2) He can resist the temptation to allow A to happen (i.e. to do nothing to prevent A from happening).

We may suppose that the man has some desire to have A happen and thus has a motive for making A happen. His motive for making A happen, I suggest, is one that *necessitates* provided that, because of the motive, (1) is false; he cannot resist the temptation to do something in order to make A happen. His motive for making A happen is one that *inclines* provided that, because of the motive, (2) is false; like our public official, he cannot bring himself to do anything to prevent A from happening. And therefore we can say that this motive for making A happen is one that *inclines but does not necessitate* provided that, because of the motive, (1) is true and (2) is false; he can resist the temptation to make it happen but he cannot resist the temptation to allow it to happen.

NOTES

1. The general position to be presented here is suggested in the following writings, among others: Aristotle, *Eudemian Ethics,* bk. ii ch. 6; *Nicomachean Ethics,* bk. iii, ch. 1–5; Thomas Reid, *Essays on the Active Powers of Man;* C. A. Campbell, "Is 'Free Will' a Pseudo-Problem?" *Mind,* 1951, 441–65; Roderick M. Chisholm, "Responsibility and Avoidability," and Richard Taylor, "Determination and the Theory of Agency," in *Determinism and Freedom in the Age of Modern Science* ed. Sidney Hook (New York, 1958).

2. Thomas Reid, *Essays on the Active Powers of Man,* essay iv, ch. 4 (*Works,* 600).

3. *Summa Theologica,* First Part of the Second Part, qu. vi ("On the Voluntary and Involuntary").

4. Jonathan Edwards, *Freedom of the Will* (New Haven, 1957); G. E. Moore, *Ethics* (Home University Library, 1912), ch. 6.

5. A. I. Melden, *Free Action* (London, 1961), espe-

cially ch. 3. Mr. Meldern's own views, however, are quite the contrary of those that are proposed here.

6. Aristotle, *Physics,* bk. iii, ch. 3; Suarez, *Disputationes Metaphysicae,* Disputation 18, s. 10.

7. Reid, *Works.* 524.

8. *Essay concerning Human Understanding,* bk. ii, ch. 21.

9. Melden, 166.

10. Reid, *Works,* 608, 612.

11. "Lettre à Mr. Coste de la Nécessité et de la Contingence" (1707) in *Opera Philosophica,* ed. Erdmann, 447–9.

12. In the Preface to the *Metaphysical Elements of Ethics,* in *Kant's Critique of Practical Reason and Other Works on the Theory of Ethics,* ed. T. K. Abbott (London, 1959), 303.

13. Cf. D. P. Henry, "Saint Anselm's *De 'Grammatico',*" *Philosophical Quarterly,* x (1960), 115–26. St. Anselm noted that (i) and (iii), respectively, may be thought of as forming the upper left and the upper right corners of a square of opposition, and (ii) and (iv) the lower left and the lower right.

Alternative Possibilities and Moral Responsibility

HARRY G. FRANKFURT

Harry G. Frankfurt is professor of philosophy at Princeton University. His major areas of interest include moral philosophy, philosophy of mind and action, and 17th-century rationalism. He is the author of *Demons, Dreamers, and Madmen: The Defense of Reason in Descartes' Meditations. The Importance of What We Care About* and *Necessity, Volition, and Love* are published collections of his essays.

A dominant role in nearly all recent inquiries into the free-will problem has been played by a principle which I shall call "the principle of alternate possibilities." This principle states that a person is morally responsible for what he has done only if he could have done otherwise. Its exact meaning is a subject of controversy, particularly concerning whether someone who accepts it is thereby committed to believing that moral responsibility and determinism are incompatible. Practically no one, however, seems inclined to deny or even to question that the principle of alternate possibilities (construed in some way or other) is true. It has generally seemed so overwhelmingly plausible that some philosophers have even characterized it as an a priori truth. People whose accounts of free will or of moral responsibility are radically at odds evidently find in it a firm and convenient common ground upon which they can profitably take their opposing stands.

But the principle of alternate possibilities is false. A person may well be morally responsible for what he has done even though he could not have done otherwise. The principle's plausibility is an illusion, which can be made to vanish by bringing the relevant moral phenomena into sharper focus.

I

In seeking illustrations of the principle of alternate possibilities, it is most natural to think of situations in which the same circumstances both bring it about that a person does something and make it impossible for him to avoid doing it. These include, for example, situations in which a person is coerced into doing

Reprinted from *The Journal of Philosophy, 66* (1969), by permission of the publisher.

something, or in which he is impelled to act by a hypnotic suggestion, or in which some inner compulsion drives him to do what he does. In situations of these kinds there are circumstances that make it impossible for the person to do otherwise, and these very circumstances also serve to bring it about that he does whatever it is that he does.

However, there may be circumstances that constitute sufficient conditions for a certain action to be performed by someone and that therefore make it impossible for the person to do otherwise, but that do not actually impel the person to act or in any way produce his action. A person may do something in circumstances that leave him no alternative to doing it, without these circumstances actually moving him or leading him to do it—without them playing any role, indeed, in bringing it about that he does what he does.

An examination of situations characterized by circumstances of this sort casts doubt, I believe, on the relevance to questions of moral responsibility of the fact that a person who has done something could not have done otherwise. I propose to develop some examples of this kind in the context of a discussion of coercion and to suggest that our moral intuitions concerning these examples tend to disconfirm the principle of alternate possibilities. Then I will discuss the principle in more general terms, explain what I think is wrong with it, and describe briefly and without argument how it might appropriately be revised.

II

It is generally agreed that a person who has been coerced to do something did not do it freely and is not morally responsible for having done it. Now the doctrine that coercion and moral responsibility are mutually exclusive may appear to be no more than a somewhat particularized version of the principle of alternate possibilities. It is natural enough to say of a person who has been coerced to do something that he could not have done otherwise. And it may easily seem that being coerced deprives a person of freedom and of moral responsibility simply because it is a special case of being unable to do otherwise. The principle of alternate possibilities may in this way derive some credibility from its association with the

very plausible proposition that moral responsibility is excluded by coercion.

It is not right, however, that it should do so. The fact that a person was coerced to act as he did may entail both that he could not have done otherwise and that he bears no moral responsibility for his action. But his lack of moral responsibility is not entailed by his having been unable to do otherwise. The doctrine that coercion excludes moral responsibility is not correctly understood, in other words, as a particularized version of the principle of alternate possibilities.

Let us suppose that someone is threatened convincingly with a penalty he finds unacceptable and that he then does what is required of him by the issuer of the threat. We can imagine details that would make it reasonable for us to think that the person was coerced to perform the action in question, that he could not have done otherwise, and that he bears no moral responsibility for having done what he did. But just what is it about situations of this kind that warrants the judgment that the threatened person is not morally responsible for his act?

This question may be approached by considering situations of the following kind. Jones decides for reasons of his own to do something, then someone threatens him with a very harsh penalty (so harsh that any reasonable person would submit to the threat) unless he does precisely that, and Jones does it. Will we hold Jones morally responsible for what he has done? I think this will depend on the roles we think were played, in leading him to act, by his original decision and by the threat.

One possibility is that $Jones_1$ is not a reasonable man: he is, rather, a man who does what he has once decided to do no matter what happens next and no matter what the cost. In that case, the threat actually exerted no effective force upon him. He acted without any regard to it, very much as if he were not aware that it had been made. If this is indeed the way it was, the situation did not involve coercion at all. The threat did not lead $Jones_1$ to do what he did. Nor was it in fact sufficient to have prevented him from doing otherwise: if his earlier decision had been to do something else, the threat would not have deterred him in the slightest. It seems evident that in these circumstances the fact that $Jones_1$ was threatened in no way reduces the moral responsibility he would otherwise bear for his act. This example, however, is not a counterexample either to the doctrine that coercion excuses or to the principle of alternate possibilities. For we have supposed that Jones$_1$ is a man upon whom the threat had no coercive effect and, hence, that it did not actually deprive him of alternatives to doing what he did.

Another possibility is that Jones$_2$ was stampeded by the threat. Given that threat, he would have performed that action regardless of what decision he had already made. The threat upset him so profoundly, moreover, that he completely forgot his own earlier decision and did what was demanded of him entirely because he was terrified of the penalty with which he was threatened. In this case, it is not relevant to his having performed the action that he had already decided on his own to perform it. When the chips were down he thought of nothing but the threat, and fear alone led him to act. The fact that at an earlier time Jones$_2$ had decided for his own reasons to act in just that way may be relevant to an evaluation of his character; he may bear full moral responsibility for having made *that* decision. But he can hardly be said to be morally responsible for his action. For he performed the action simply as a result of the coercion to which he was subjected. His earlier decision played no role in bringing it about that he did what he did, and it would therefore be gratuitous to assign it a role in the moral evaluation of his action.

Now consider a third possibility. Jones$_3$ was neither stampeded by the threat nor indifferent to it. The threat impressed him, as it would impress any reasonable man, and he would have submitted to it wholeheartedly if he had not already made a decision that coincided with the one demanded of him. In fact, however, he performed the action in question on the basis of the decision he had made before the threat was issued. When he acted, he was not actually motivated by the threat but solely by the considerations that had originally commended the action to him. It was not the threat that led him to act, though it would have done so if he had not already provided himself with a sufficient motive for performing the action in question.

No doubt it will be very difficult for anyone to know, in a case like this one, exactly what happened.

Did Jones$_3$ perform the action because of the threat, or were his reasons for acting simply those which had already persuaded him to do so? Or did he act on the basis of two motives, each of which was sufficient for his action? It is not impossible, however, that the situation should be clearer than situations of this kind usually are. And suppose it is apparent to us that Jones$_3$ acted on the basis of his own decision and not because of the threat. Then I think we would be justified in regarding his moral responsibility for what he did as unaffected by the threat even though, since he would in any case have submitted to the threat, he could not have avoided doing what he did. It would be entirely reasonable for us to make the same judgment concerning his moral responsibility that we would have made if we had not known of the threat. For the threat did not in fact influence his performance of the action. He did what he did just as if the threat had not been made at all.

III

The case of Jones$_3$ may appear at first glance to combine coercion and moral responsibility, and thus to provide a counterexample to the doctrine that coercion excuses. It is not really so certain that it does so, however, because it is unclear whether the example constitutes a genuine instance of coercion. Can we say of Jones$_3$ that he was coerced to do something, when he had already decided on his own to do it and when he did it entirely on the basis of that decision? Or would it be more correct to say that Jones$_3$ was not coerced to do what he did, even though he himself recognized that there was an irresistible force at work in virtue of which he had to do it? My own linguistic intuitions lead me toward the second alternative, but they are somewhat equivocal. Perhaps we can say either of these things, or perhaps we must add a qualifying explanation to whichever of them we say.

This murkiness, however, does not interfere with our drawing an important moral from an examination of the example. Suppose we decide to say that Jones$_3$ was *not* coerced. Our basis for saying this will clearly be that it is incorrect to regard a man as being coerced to do something unless he does it *because* of the coercive force exerted against him. The fact that an irresistible threat is made will not, then, entail that the person who receives it is coerced to do what he does. It will also be necessary that the threat is what actually accounts for his doing it. On the other hand, suppose we decide to say that Jones$_3$ *was* coerced. Then we will be bound to admit that being coerced does not exclude being morally responsible. And we will also surely be led to the view that coercion affects the judgment of a person's moral responsibility only when the person acts as he does because he is coerced to do so—i.e., when the fact that he is coerced is what accounts for his action.

Whichever we decide to say, then, we will recognize that the doctrine that coercion excludes moral responsibility is not a particularized version of the principle of alternate possibilities. Situations in which a person who does something cannot do otherwise because he is subject to coercive power are either not instances of coercion at all, or they are situations in which the person may still be morally responsible for what he does if it is not because of the coercion that he does it. When we excuse a person who has been coerced, we do not excuse him because he was unable to do otherwise. Even though a person is subject to a coercive force that precludes his performing any action but one, he may nonetheless bear full moral responsibility for performing that action.

IV

To the extent that the principle of alternate possibilities derives its plausibility from association with the doctrine that coercion excludes moral responsibility, a clear understanding of the latter diminishes the appeal of the former. Indeed the case of Jones$_3$ may appear to do more than illuminate the relationship between the two doctrines. It may well seem to provide a decisive counterexample to the principle of alternate possibilities and thus to show that this principle is false. For the irresistibility of the threat to which Jones$_3$ is subjected might well be taken to mean that he cannot but perform the action he performs. And yet the threat, since Jones$_3$ performs the action without regard to it, does not reduce his moral responsibility for what he does.

The following objection will doubtless be raised against the suggestion that the case of Jones$_3$ is a counterexample to the principle of alternate possibilities. There is perhaps a sense in which Jones$_3$ cannot do otherwise than perform the action he performs, since he is a reasonable man and the threat he encounters is sufficient to move any reasonable man. But it is not this sense that is germane to the principle of alternate possibilities. His knowledge that he stands to suffer an intolerably harsh penalty does not mean that Jones$_3$, strictly speaking, *cannot* perform any action but the one he does perform. After all it is still open to him, and this is crucial, to defy the threat if he wishes to do so and to accept the penalty his action would bring down upon him. In the sense in which the principle of alternate possibilities employs the concept of "could have done otherwise," Jones$_3$'s inability to resist the threat does not mean that he cannot do otherwise than perform the action he performs. Hence the case of Jones$_3$ does not constitute an instance contrary to the principle.

I do not propose to consider in what sense the concept of "could have done otherwise" figures in the principle of alternate possibilities, nor will I attempt to measure the force of the objection I have just described.[1] For I believe that whatever force this objection may be thought to have can be deflected by altering the example in the following way.[2] Suppose someone—Black, let us say—wants Jones$_4$ to perform a certain action. Black is prepared to go to considerable lengths to get his way, but he prefers to avoid showing his hand unnecessarily. So he waits until Jones$_4$ is about to make up his mind what to do, and he does nothing unless it is clear to him (Black is an excellent judge of such things) that Jones$_4$ is going to decide to do something *other* than what he wants him to do. If it does become clear that Jones$_4$ is going to decide to do something else, Black takes effective steps to ensure that Jones$_4$ decides to do, and that he does do, what he wants him to do.[3] Whatever Jones$_4$'s initial preferences and inclinations, then, Black will have his way.

What steps will Black take, if he believes he must take steps, in order to ensure that Jones$_4$ decides and acts as he wishes? Anyone with a theory concerning what "could have done otherwise" means may answer this question for himself by describing whatever measures he would regard as sufficient to guarantee that, in the relevant sense, Jones$_4$ cannot do otherwise. Let Black pronounce a terrible threat, and in this way both force Jones$_4$ to perform the desired action and prevent him from performing a forbidden one. Let Black give Jones$_4$ a potion, or put him under hypnosis, and in some such way as these generate in Jones$_4$ an irresistible inner compulsion to perform the act Black wants performed and to avoid others. Or let Black manipulate the minute processes of Jones$_4$'s brain and nervous system in some more direct way, so that causal forces running in and out of his synapses and along the poor man's nerves determine that he chooses to act and that he does act in the one way and not in any other. Given any conditions under which it will be maintained that Jones$_4$ cannot do otherwise, in other words, let Black bring it about that those conditions prevail. The structure of the example is flexible enough, I think, to find a way around any charge of irrelevance by accommodating the doctrine on which the charge is based.[4]

Now suppose that Black never has to show his hand because Jones$_4$, for reasons of his own, decides to perform and does perform the very action Black wants him to perform. In that case, it seems clear, Jones$_4$ will bear precisely the same moral responsibility for what he does as he would have borne if Black had not been ready to take steps to ensure that he do it. It would be quite unreasonable to excuse Jones$_4$ for his action, or to withhold the praise to which it would normally entitle him, on the basis of the fact that he could not have done otherwise. This fact played no role at all in leading him to act as he did. He would have acted the same even if it had not been a fact. Indeed, everything happened just as it would have happened without Black's presence in the situation and without his readiness to intrude into it.

In this example there are sufficient conditions for Jones$_4$'s performing the action in question. What action he performs is not up to him. Of course it is in a way up to him whether he acts on his own or as a result of Black's intervention. That depends upon what action he himself is inclined to perform. But whether he finally acts on his own or as a result of Black's intervention, he performs the same action. He has no alternative but to do what Black wants him

to do. If he does it on his own, however, his moral responsibility for doing it is not affected by the fact that Black was lurking in the background with sinister intent, since this intent never comes into play.

V

The fact that a person could not have avoided doing something is a sufficient condition of his having done it. But, as some of my examples show, this fact may play no role whatever in the explanation of why he did it. It may not figure at all among the circumstances that actually brought it about that he did what he did, so that his action is to be accounted for on another basis entirely. Even though the person was unable to do otherwise, that is to say, it may not be the case that he acted as he did *because* he could not have done otherwise. Now if someone had no alternative to performing a certain action but did not perform it because he was unable to do otherwise, then he would have performed exactly the same action even if he *could* have done otherwise. The circumstances that made it impossible for him to do otherwise could have been subtracted from the situation without affecting what happened or why it happened in any way. Whatever it was that actually led the person to do what he did, or that made him do it, would have led him to do it or made him do it even if it had been possible for him to do something else instead.

Thus it would have made no difference, so far as concerns his action or how he came to perform it, if the circumstances that made it impossible for him to avoid performing it had not prevailed. The fact that he could not have done otherwise clearly provides no basis for supposing that he *might* have done otherwise if he had been able to do so. When a fact is in this way irrelevant to the problem of accounting for a person's action it seems quite gratuitous to assign it any weight in the assessment of his moral responsibility. Why should the fact be considered in reaching a moral judgment concerning the person when it does not help in any way to understand either what made him act as he did or what, in other circumstances, he might have done?

This, then, is why the principle of alternate possibilities is mistaken. It asserts that a person bears no moral responsibility—that is, he is to be excused—for having performed an action if there were circumstances that made it impossible for him to avoid performing it. But there may be circumstances that make it impossible for a person to avoid performing some action without those circumstances in any way bringing it about that he performs that action. It would surely be no good for the person to refer to circumstances of this sort in an effort to absolve himself of moral responsibility for performing the action in question. For those circumstances, by hypothesis, actually had nothing to do with his having done what he did. He would have done precisely the same thing, and he would have been led or made in precisely the same way to do it, even if they had not prevailed.

We often do, to be sure, excuse people for what they have done when they tell us (and we believe them) that they could not have done otherwise. But this is because we assume that what they tell us serves to explain why they did what they did. We take it for granted that they are not being disingenuous, as a person would be who cited as an excuse the fact that he could not have avoided doing what he did but who knew full well that it was not at all because of this that he did it.

What I have said may suggest that the principle of alternate possibilities should be revised so as to assert that a person is not morally responsible for what he has done if he did it because he could not have done otherwise. It may be noted that this revision of the principle does not seriously affect the arguments of those who have relied on the original principle in their efforts to maintain that moral responsibility and determinism are incompatible. For if it was causally determined that a person perform a certain action, then it will be true that the person performed it because of those causal determinants. And if the fact that it was causally determined that a person perform a certain action means that the person could not have done otherwise, as philosophers who argue for the incompatibility thesis characteristically suppose, then the fact that it was causally determined that a person perform a certain action will mean that the person performed it because he could not have done otherwise. The revised principle of alternate possibilities will entail, on this assumption concerning the meaning of "could have done otherwise," that a person is not morally responsible for what he has done if it was causally determined that he do it. I do not believe, however, that this revision of the principle is acceptable.

Suppose a person tells us that he did what he did because he was unable to do otherwise; or suppose he makes the similar statement that he did what he did because he had to do it. We do often accept statements like these (if we believe them) as valid excuses, and such statements may well seem at first glance to invoke the revised principle of alternate possibilities. But I think that when we accept such statements as valid excuses it is because we assume that we are being told more than the statements strictly and literally convey. We understand the person who offers the excuse to mean that he did what he did *only because* he was unable to do otherwise, or *only because* he had to do it. And we understand him to mean, more particularly, that when he did what he did it was not because that was what he really wanted to do. The principle of alternate possibilities should thus be replaced, in my opinion, by the following principle: a person is not morally responsible for what he has done if he did it only because he could not have done otherwise. This principle does not appear to conflict with the view that moral responsibility is compatible with determinism.

The following may all be true: there were circumstances that made it impossible for a person to avoid doing something; these circumstances actually played a role in bringing it about that he did it, so that it is correct to say that he did it because he could not have done otherwise; the person really wanted to do what he did; he did it because it was what he really wanted to do, so that it is not correct to say that he did what he did only because he could not have done otherwise. Under these conditions, the person may well be morally responsible for what he has done. On the other hand, he will not be morally responsible for what he has done if he did it only because he could not have done otherwise, even if what he did was something he really wanted to do.

NOTES

1. The two main concepts employed in the principle of alternate possibilities are "morally responsible" and "could have done otherwise." To discuss the principle without ana-

lyzing either of these concepts may well seem like an attempt at piracy. The reader should take notice that my Jolly Roger is now unfurled.

2. After thinking up the example that I am about to develop I learned that Robert Nozick, in lectures given several years ago, had formulated an example of the same general type and had proposed it as a counterexample to the principle of alternate possibilities.

3. The assumption that Black can predict what $Jones_4$ will decide to do does not beg the question of determinism. We can imagine that $Jones_4$ has often confronted the alternatives—A and B—that he now confronts, and that his face has invariably twitched when he was about to decide to do A and never when he was about to decide to do B. Knowing this, and observing the twitch, Black would have a basis for prediction. This does, to be sure, suppose that there is some

sort of causal relation between $Jones_4$'s state at the time of the twitch and his subsequent states. But any plausible view of decision or of action will allow that reaching a decision and performing an action both involve earlier and later phases, with causal relations between them, and such that the earlier phases are not themselves part of the decision or of the action. The example does not require that these earlier phases be deterministically related to still earlier events.

4. The example is also flexible enough to allow for the elimination of Black altogether. Anyone who thinks that the effectiveness of the example is undermined by its reliance on a human manipulator, who imposes his will on $Jones_4$, can substitute for Black a machine programmed to do what Black does. If this is still not good enough, forget both Black and the machine and suppose that their role is played by natural forces involving no will or design at all.

The Incompatibility of Free Will and Determinism

PETER VAN INWAGEN

Peter van Inwagen is John Cardinal O'Hara Professor of Philosophy at the University of Notre Dame.

In this paper I shall define a thesis I shall call "determinism," and argue that it is incompatible with the thesis that we are able to act otherwise than we do (i.e. is incompatible with "free will"). Other theses, some of them very different from what *I* shall call "determinism," have at least an equal right to this name, and, therefore, I do not claim to show that *every* thesis that could be called "determinism" without historical impropriety is incompatible with free will. I shall, however, assume without argument that what I call 'determinism' is legitimately so called.

In Part I, I shall explain what I mean by "determinism." In Part II, I shall make some remarks about "can." In Part III, I shall argue that free will and deter-

minism are incompatible. In Part IV, I shall examine some possible objections to the argument of Part III. I shall not attempt to establish the truth or falsity of determinism, or the existence or non-existence of free will.

I

In defining "determinism." I shall take for granted the notion of a proposition (that is, of a non-linguistic bearer of truth-value), together with certain allied notions such as denial, conjunction, and entailment. Nothing in this paper will depend on the special features of any particular account of propositions. The reader may think of them as functions from possible worlds to truth-values or in any other way he likes, provided they have their usual features (e.g. they are either true or false; the conjunction of a true and a false proposition is a false proposition; they obey the law of contraposition with respect to entailment).

Our definition of "determinism" will also involve the notion of "the state of the entire physical world" (hereinafter, "the state of the world") at an instant. I shall leave this notion largely unexplained, since the argument of this paper is very nearly independent of its content. Provided the following two conditions are met, the reader may flesh out "the state of the world" in any way he likes:

(i) Our concept of "state" must be such that, given that the world is in a certain state at a certain time, nothing follows *logically* about its states at other times. For example, we must not choose a concept of "state" that would allow as part of a description of the momentary state of the world, the clause, " . . . and, at *t*, the world is such that Jones's left hand will be raised 10 seconds later than *t*."

(ii) If there is some observable change in the way things are (e.g. if a white cloth becomes blue, a warm liquid cold, or if a man raises his hand), this change must entail some change in the state of the world. That is, our concept of "state" must not be so theoretical, so divorced from what is observably true, that it be possible for the world to be in the *same* state at t_1 and t_2, although (for example) Jones's hand is raised at t_1 and not at t_2.

We may now define "determinism." We shall apply this term to the conjunction of these two theses:

(a) For every instant of time, there is a proposition that expresses the state of the world at that instant.

(b) If *A* and *B* are any propositions that express the state of the world at some instants, then the conjunction of *A* with the laws of physics entails *B*.

By a proposition that expresses the state of the world at time *t*, I mean a true proposition that asserts of some state that, at *t*, the world is in that state. The reason for our first restriction on the content of "state"

should now be evident: if it were not for this restriction, "the state of the world" could be defined in such a way that determinism was trivially true. We could, without this restriction, build sufficient information about the past and future into each proposition that expresses the state of the world at an instant, that, for every pair of such propositions, each *by itself* entails the other. And in that case, determinism would be a mere tautology, a thesis applicable to every conceivable state of affairs.

This amounts to saying that the "laws of physics" clause on our definition does some work: whether determinism is true depends in the character of the laws of physics. For example, if all physical laws were vague propositions like "In every nuclear reaction, momentum is *pretty nearly* conserved," or "Force is *approximately* equal to mass times acceleration," then determinism would be false.

This raises the question, What is a law of physics? First, a terminological point. I do not mean the application of this term to be restricted to those laws that belong to physics in the narrowest sense of the world. I am using "law of physics" in the way some philosophers use "law of nature." Thus, a law about chemical valences is a law of physics in my sense, even if chemistry is not ultimately "reducible" to physics. I will not use the term "law of nature," because, conceivably, *psychological* laws, including laws (if such there be) about the voluntary behaviour of rational agents, might be included under this term.[1] Rational agents are, after all, in some sense part of "Nature." Since I do not think that everything I shall say about laws of physics is true of such "voluntaristic laws," I should not want to use, instead of "laws of physics," some term like "laws of nature" that might legitimately be applied to voluntaristic laws. Thus, for all that is said in this paper, it may be that some version of determinism based on voluntaristic laws is compatible with free will.[2] Let us, then, understand by "law of physics" a law of nature that is not about the voluntary behaviour of rational agents.

But this does not tell us what "laws of nature" are. There would probably be fairly general agreement that a proposition cannot be a law of nature unless it is true and contingent, and that no proposition is a law of nature if it entails the existence of some concrete individual, such as Caesar or the earth. But the proposition that there is no solid gold sphere 20 feet in diameter (probably) satisfies these conditions, though it is certainly not a law of nature.

It is also claimed sometimes that a law of nature must "support its counter-factuals." There is no doubt something to this. Consider, however, the proposition, "Dogs die if exposed to virus V." The claim that this proposition supports its counter-factuals is, I think, equivalent to the claim that "Every dog is such that if it were exposed to virus V, it would die" is *true*. Let us suppose that this latter proposition *is* true, the quantification being understood as being over all dogs, past, present, and future. Its truth, it seems to me, is quite consistent with its being the case that dog-breeders *could* (but will not) institute a programme of selective breeding that *would* produce a sort of dog that is immune to virus V. But if dog-breeders *could* do this, then clearly "Dogs die if exposed to virus V" is not a law of nature, since in that case the truth of the corresponding universally quantified counter-factual depends upon an accidental circumstance: if dog-breeders were to institute a certain programme of selective breeding they are quite capable of instituting, then "Every dog is such that if it were exposed to virus V, it would die" would be false. Thus a proposition may "support its counter-factuals" and yet not be a law of nature.

I do not think that any philosopher has succeeded in giving a (non-trivial) set of individually necessary and jointly sufficient conditions for a proposition's being a law of nature or of physics. *I* certainly do not know of any such set. Fortunately, for the purposes of this paper we need not know how to analyse the concept "law of physics." I shall, in Part III, argue that certain statements containing "law of physics" are analytic. But this can be done in the absence of a satisfactory analysis of "law of physics." In fact, it would hardly be possible for one to *provide* an analysis of some concept if one had no pre-analytic convictions about what statements involving that concept are analytic.

For example, we do not have to have a satisfactory analysis of memory to know that "No one can remember future events" is analytic. And if someone devised an analysis of memory according to which it was possible to remember future events, then, however attractive the analysis was in other respects, it would have to be rejected. The analyticity of "No one can remember future events" is one of the *data* that anyone who investigates the concept of memory must take account of. Similarly, the claims I shall make on behalf of the concept of physical law seem to me to be basic and evident enough to be data that an analysis of this concept must take account of: any analysis on which these claims did not 'come out true' would be for that very reason defective.

II

It seems to be generally agreed that the concept of free will should be understood in terms of the *power* or *ability* of agents to act otherwise than they in fact do. To deny that men have free will is to assert that what a man *does* do and what he *can* do coincide. And almost all philosophers[3] agree that a necessary condition for holding an agent responsible for an act is believing that that agent *could have* refrained from performing that act.[4]

There is, however, considerably less agreement as to how "can" (in the relevant sense) should be analysed. This is one of the most difficult questions in philosophy. It is certainly a question to which I do not know any non-trivial answer. But, as I said I should do in the case of "law of physics," I shall make certain conceptual claims about "can" (in the "power" or "ability" sense) in the absence of any analysis. Any suggested analysis of "can" that does not support these claims will either be neutral with respect to them, in which case it will be incomplete, since it will not settle *all* conceptual questions about "can," or it will be inconsistent with them, in which case the arguments I shall present in support of these claims will, in effect, be arguments that the analysis fails. In Part IV, I shall expand on this point as it applies to one particular analysis of "can," the well-known "conditional" analysis.

I shall say no more than this about the meaning of "can." I shall, however, introduce an idiom that will be useful in talking about ability and inability in complicated cases. Without this idiom, the statement of our argument would be rather unwieldy. We shall sometimes make claims about an agent's abilities by using sentences of the form:

S can render [could have rendered] . . . false.

where " . . ." may be replaced by names of propositions.[5] Our ordinary claims about ability can easily be translated into this idiom. For example, we translate:

He could have reached Chicago by midnight.

as

He could have rendered the proposition that he did not reach Chicago by midnight false.

and, of course, the translation from the special idiom to the ordinary idiom is easy enough in such simple cases. If we were interested only in everyday ascriptions of ability, the new idiom would be useless. Using it, however, we may make ascriptions of ability that it would be very difficult to make in the ordinary idiom. Consider, for example, the last true proposition asserted by Plato. (Let us assume that this description is, as logicians say, "proper.") One claim that we might make about Aristotle is that he could have rendered this proposition false. Now, presumably, we have no way of discovering *what* proposition the last true proposition asserted by Plato was. Still, the claim about Aristotle would seem to be either true or false. To discover its truth-value, we should have to discover under what conditions the last true proposition asserted by Plato (i.e. that proposition having as one of its accidental properties, the property of being the last true proposition asserted by Plato) would be false, and then discover whether it was within Aristotle's power to produce these conditions. For example, suppose that if Aristotle had lived in Athens from the time of Plato's death till the time of his own death, then the last true proposition asserted by Plato (whatever it was) would be false. Then, if Aristotle could have lived (i.e. if he had it within his power to live) in Athens throughout this period, he could have rendered the last true proposition asserted by Plato false. On the other hand, if the last true proposition asserted by Plato is the proposi-

tion that the planets do not move in perfect circles, then Aristotle could not have rendered the last true proposition asserted by Plato false, since it was not within his power to produce any set of conditions sufficient for the falsity of this proposition.[6]

It is obvious that the proposition expressed by "Aristotle could have rendered the last true proposition asserted by Plato false," is a proposition that we should be hard put to express without using the idiom of rendering propositions false, or at least, without using some very similar idiom. We shall find this new idiom very useful in discussing the relation between free will (a thesis about abilities) and determinism (a thesis about certain propositions).

III

I shall now imagine a case in which a certain man, after due deliberation, refrained from performing a certain contemplated act. I shall then argue that, if determinism is true, then that man *could not have* performed that act. Because this argument will not depend on any features peculiar to our imagined case, the incompatibility of free will and determinism *in general* will be established, since, as will be evident, a parallel argument could easily be constructed for the case of any agent and any unperformed act.

Here is the case. Let us suppose there was once a judge who had only to raise his right hand at a certain time, *T*, to prevent the execution of a sentence of death upon a certain criminal, such a hand-raising being the sign, according to the conventions of the judge's country, of a granting of special clemency. Let us further suppose that the judge—call him "*J*"—refrained from raising his hand at that time, and that this inaction resulted in the criminal's being put to death. We may also suppose that the judge was unbound, uninjured, and free from paralysis; that he decided not to raise his hand at *T* only after a period of calm, rational, and relevant deliberation; that he had not been subjected to any "pressure" to decide one way or the other about the criminal's death; that he was not under the influence of drugs, hypnosis, or anything of that sort; and finally, that there was no element in his deliberations that would have been of any special interest to a student of abnormal psychology.

Now the argument. In this argument, which I shall refer to as the "main argument," I shall use "T_0" to denote some instant of time earlier than J's birth, "P_0" to denote the proposition that expresses the state of the world at T_0, "P" to denote the proposition that expresses the state of the world at T, and "L" to denote the conjunction into a single proposition of all laws of physics. (I shall regard L itself as a law of physics, on the reasonable assumption that if A and B are laws of physics, then the conjunction of A and B is a law of physics.) The argument consists of seven statements, the seventh of which follows from the first six:

(1) If determinism is true, then the conjunction of P_0 and L entails P.
(2) If J had raised his hand at T, then P would be false.
(3) If (2) is true, then if J could have raised his hand at T, J could have rendered P false.[7]
(4) If J could have rendered P false, and if the conjunction of P_0 and L entails P, then J could have rendered the conjunction of P_0 and L false.
(5) If J could have rendered the conjunction of P_0 and L false, then J could have rendered L false.
(6) J could not have rendered L false.
∴(7) If determinism is true, J could not have raised his hand at T.

That (7) follows from (1) through (6) can easily be established by truthfunctional logic. Note that all conditionals in the argument except for (2) are truth-functional. For purposes of establishing the *validity* of this argument, (2) may be regarded as a simple sentence. Let us examine the premises individually.

(1) This premiss follows from the definition of determinism.

(2) If J had raised his hand at T, then the world would have been in a different state at T from the state it was in fact in. (See our second condition on the content of "the state of the world.") And, therefore, if J had raised his hand at T, some contrary of P would express the state of the world at T. It should be emphasized that "P" does not *mean* "the proposition

that expresses the state of the world at T." Rather, "P" *denotes* the proposition that expresses the state of the world at T. In Kripke's terminology, "P" is being used as a *rigid designator,* while "the proposition that expresses the state of the world at T" is perforce non-rigid.[8]

(3) Since J's hand being raised at T would have been sufficient for the falsity of P, there is, if J could have raised his hand, at least one condition sufficient for the falsity of P and J could have produced.

(4) This premiss may be defended as an instance of the following general principle:

> If S can render R false, and if Q entails R, then S can render Q false.

This principle seems to be analytic. For if Q entails R, then the denial of R entails the denial of Q. Thus, any condition sufficient for the falsity of R is also sufficient for the falsity of Q. Therefore, if there is some condition that S can produce that is sufficient for the falsity of R, there is some condition (that same condition) that S can produce that is sufficient for the falsity of Q.

(5) This premiss may be defended as an instance of the following general principle, which I take to be analytic:

> If Q is a true proposition that concerns only states of affairs that obtained before S's birth, and if S can render the conjunction of Q and R false, then S can render R false.

Consider, for example, the propositions expressed by

> The Spanish Armada was defeated in 1588.

and

> Peter van Inwagen never visits Alaska.

The conjunction of these two propositions is quite possibly true. At any rate, let us assume it is true. Given that it is true, it seems quite clear that I can render it false if and only if I can visit Alaska. If, for some reason, it is not within my power ever to visit

Alaska, then I *cannot* render it false. This is a quite trivial assertion, and the general principle (above) of which it is an instance is hardly less trivial. And it seems incontestable that premiss (5) is also an instance of this principle.

(6) I shall argue that if anyone *can* (i.e. has it within his power to) render some proposition false, then that proposition is not a law of physics. This I regard as a conceptual truth, one of the data that must be taken account of by anyone who wishes to give an analysis of "can" or "law." It is this connection between these two concepts, I think, that is at the root of the incompatibility of free will and determinism.

In order to see this connection, let us suppose that both of the following are true:

(A) Nothing ever travels faster than light.
(B) Jones, a physicist, can construct a particle accelerator that would cause protons to travel at twice the speed of light.

It follows from (A) that Jones will never exercise the power that (B) ascribes to him. But whatever the reason for Jones's failure to act on his ability to render (A) false, it is clear that (A) and (B) are consistent, and that (B) entails that (A) is not a law of physics. For given that (B) is true, then Jones is able to conduct an experiment that would falsify (A); and surely it is a feature of any proposition that is a physical law that no one *can* conduct an experiment that would show it to be false.

Of course, most propositions that look initially as if they might be physical laws, but which are later decided to be non-laws, are rejected because of experiments that are actually performed. But this is not essential. In order to see this, let us elaborate the example we have been considering. Let us suppose that Jones's ability to render (A) false derives from the fact that he has discovered a mathematically rigorous proof that under certain conditions *C,* realizable in the laboratory, protons would travel faster than light. And let us suppose that this proof proceeds from premises so obviously true that all competent physicists accept his conclusion without reservation. But suppose that conditions *C* never obtain in nature, and that actually to produce them in the laboratory

would require such an expenditure of resources that Jones and his colleagues decide not to carry out the experiment. And suppose that, as a result, conditions *C* are never realized and nothing ever travels faster than light. It is evident that if all this were true, we should have to say that (A), while *true,* is not a law of physics. (Though, of course, "Nothing ever travels faster than light except under conditions *C*" might be a law.)

The laboratories and resources that figure in this example are not essential to its point. If Jones *could* render some proposition false by performing *any* act he does not in fact perform, even such a simple act as raising his hand at a certain time, this would be sufficient to show that that proposition is not a law of physics.

This completes my defence of the premisses of the main argument. In the final part of this paper, I shall examine objections to this argument suggested by the attempts of various philosophers to establish the compatibility of free will and determinism.

IV

The most useful thing a philosopher who thinks that the main argument does not prove its point could do would be to try to show that some premiss of the argument is false or incoherent, or that the argument begs some important question, or contains a term that is used equivocally, or something of that sort. In short, he should get down to cases. Some philosophers, however, might continue to hold that free will and determinism, in the sense of Part I, are compatible, but decline to try to point out a mistake in the argument. For (such a philosopher might argue) we have, in everyday life, *criteria* for determining whether an agent could have acted otherwise than he did, and these criteria determine the *meaning* of "could have acted otherwise"; to know the meaning of this phrase is simply to know how to apply these criteria. And since these criteria make no mention of determinism, anyone who thinks that free will and determinism are incompatible is simply confused.[9]

As regards the argument of Part III (this philosopher might continue), this argument is very complex, and this complexity must simply serve to hide some error, since its conclusion is absurd. We must treat this argument like the infamous "proof" that zero equals one: It may be amusing and even instructive to find the hidden error (if one has nothing better to do), but it would be a waste of time to take seriously any suggestion that it is sound.

Now I suppose we do have "criteria," in some sense of this over-used word, for the application of "could have done otherwise," and I will grant that knowing the criteria for the application of a term can plausibly be identified with knowing its meaning. Whether the criteria for applying 'could have done otherwise' can (as at least one philosopher has supposed[10]) be taught by simple ostension is another question. However this may be, the "criteria" argument is simply invalid. To see this, let us examine a simpler argument that makes the same mistake.

Consider the doctrine of "predestinarianism." Predestinarians hold (i) that if an act is foreseen it is not free, and (ii) that all acts are foreseen by God. (I do not claim that anyone has ever held this doctrine in precisely this form.) Now suppose we were to argue that predestinarianism must be compatible with free will, since our criteria for applying "could have done otherwise" make no reference to predestinarianism. Obviously this argument would be invalid, since predestinarianism is incompatible with free will. And the only difference I can see between this argument and the "criteria" argument for the compatibility of free will and determinism is that predestinarianism, unlike determinism, is *obviously* incompatible with free will. But, of course, theses may be incompatible with one another even if this incompatibility is not obvious. Even if determinism cannot, like predestinarianism, be seen to be incompatible with free will on the basis of a simple formal inference, there is, nonetheless, a conceptual connection between the two theses (as we showed in our defence of premiss (6)). The argument of Part III is intended to draw out the implications of this connection. There may well be a mistake in the argument, but I do not see why anyone should think that the very idea of such an argument is misconceived.

It has also been argued that free will *entails* determinism, and, being itself a consistent thesis, is *a fortiori* compatible with determinism. The argument, put briefly, is this. To say of some person on some particular occasion that he acted freely is obviously to say at least that *he* acted on that occasion. Suppose, however, that we see someone's arm rise and it later turns out that there was *no cause whatsoever* for his arm's rising. Surely we should have to say that *he* did not really raise his arm at all. Rather, his arm's rising was a mere chance happening, that, like a muscular twitch, had nothing to do with *him,* beyond the fact that it happened to involve a part of his body. A necessary condition for this person's really having raised his hand is that *he* caused his hand to rise. And surely "*he* caused" means "*his* character, desires, and beliefs caused."[11]

I think that there is a great deal of confusion in this argument, but to expose this confusion would require a lengthy discussion of many fine points in the theory of agency. I shall only point out that if this argument is supposed to refute the conclusion of Part III, it is an *ignoratio elenchi.* For I did not conclude that free will is incompatible with the thesis that every event has a cause, but rather with determinism as defined in Part I. And the denial of this thesis does not entail that there are uncaused events.

Of course, one might try to construct a similar but relevant argument for the falsity of the conclusion of Part III. But, so far as I can see, the plausibility of such an argument would depend on the plausibility of supposing that if the present movements of one's body are not completely determined by physical law and the state of the world before one's birth, then these present movements are not one's own doing, but, rather, mere random happenings. And I do not see the least shred of plausibility in this supposition.

I shall finally consider the popular "conditional analysis" argument for the compatibility of free will and determinism. According to the advocates of this argument—let us call them 'conditionalists'—what statements of the form:

(8) *S* could have done *X*

mean is:

(9) If *S* had chosen to do *X, S* would have done *X*.[12]

For example, "Smith could have saved the drowning child" means, "If Smith had chosen to save the drowning child, Smith would have saved the drowning child." Thus, even if determinism is true (the conditionalists argue), it is possible that Smith did not save but *could have* saved the drowning child, since the conjunction of determinism with "Smith did not save the child" does not entail the falsity of "If Smith had chosen to save the child, Smith would have saved the child."

Most of the controversy about this argument centres around the question whether (9) is a correct analysis of (8). I shall not enter into the debate about whether this analysis is correct. I shall instead question the relevance of this debate to the argument of Part III. For it is not clear that the main argument would be unsound if the conditional analysis *were* correct. Clearly the argument is *valid* whether or not (8) and (9) mean the same. But suppose the premises of the main argument were rewritten so that every clause they contain that is of form (8) is replaced by the corresponding clause of form (9)—should we then see that any of these premises is false? Let us try this with premiss (6), which seems, prima facie, to be the crucial premiss of the argument. We have:

(6a) It is not the case that if *J* had chosen to render *L* false, *J* would have rendered *L* false.

Now (6a) certainly seems true: If someone chooses to render false some proposition *R*, and if *R* is a law of physics, then surely he will fail. This little argument for (6a) *seems* obviously sound. But we cannot overlook the possibility that someone might discover a mistake in it and, perhaps, even construct a convincing argument that (6a) is false. Let us, therefore, assume for the sake of argument that (6a) is demonstrably false. What would this show? I submit that it would show that (6a) does not mean the same as (6), since (6) is, as I have argued, *true*.

The same dilemma confronts the conditionalist if he attempts to show, on the basis of the conditional analysis, that any of the other premises of the argument is false. Consider the argument got by replacing every clause of form (8) in the main argument with the corresponding clause of form (9). If all the prem-

isses of this new argument are true, the main argument is, according to the conditionalist's own theory, sound. If, on the other hand, any of the premises of the new argument is false, then (*I* would maintain) this premiss is a counter-example to the conditional analysis. I should not be begging the question against the conditionalist in maintaining this, since I have given arguments for the truth of each of the premises of the main argument, and nowhere in these arguments do I assume that the conditional analysis is wrong.

Of course, any or all of my arguments in defence of the premises of the main argument may contain some mistake. But unless the conditionalist could point to some such mistake, he would not accomplish much by showing that some statement he *claimed* was equivalent to one of its premises was false.[13]

NOTES

1. For example, "If a human being is not made to feel ashamed of lying before his twelfth birthday, then he will lie whenever he believes it to be to his advantage."

2. In "The Compatibility of Free Will and Determinism," *Philosophical Review,* 1962, J. V. Canfield argues convincingly for a position that we might represent in this terminology as the thesis that a determinism based on voluntaristic laws could be compatible with free will.

3. See, however, Harry Frankfurt, "Alternate Possibilities and Moral Responsibility," *Journal of Philosophy,* 1969.

4. Actually, the matter is rather more complicated than this, since we may hold a man responsible for an act we believe he could not have refrained from, provided we are prepared to hold him responsible for his being unable to refrain.

5. In all the cases we shall consider, ". . ." will be replaced by names of *true* propositions. For the sake of logical completeness, we may stipulate that any sentence formed by replacing ". . ." with the name of a *false* proposition is trivially true. Thus, "Kant could have rendered the proposition that $7 + 5 = 13$ false" is trivially true.

6. Steven M. Cahn and Richard Taylor have argued (most explicitly in "Time, Truth and Ability" by "Diodorus Cronus," *Analysis,* 1965 that every true proposition is such that, necessarily, no one is able to render it false. On my view, this thesis is mistaken, and their arguments for it can be shown to be unsound. I shall not, however, argue for this

here. I shall argue in Part III that we are unable to render *certain sorts of* true proposition false, but my arguments will depend on special features of these sorts of proposition. I shall, for example, argue that no one can render false a law of physics; but I shall not argue that this is the case because laws of physics are *true,* but because of other features that they possess.

7. "*J* could have raised his hand at *T*" is ambiguous. It might mean either (roughly) "*J* possessed, at *T* the ability to raise his hand," on "*J* possessed the ability to bring it about that his hand rose at *T.*" If *J* was unparalysed at *T* but paralysed at all earlier instants, then the latter of these would be false, though the former might be true. I mean "*J* could have raised his hand at *T*" in the latter sense.

8. See Saul Kripke, "Identity and Necessity," in *Identity and Individuation,* ed. Milton K. Munitz (New York, 1971).

9. Cf. Antony Flew, "Divine Omniscience and Human Freedom," *New Essays in Philosophical Theology,* ed. Antony Flew and Alasdair MacIntyre (London: SCM Press, 1955), 149–51 in particular.

10. Flew, loc cit.

11. Cf. R. E. Hobart, "Free Will as Involving Determination and Inconceivable Without It," *Mind,* 1934; A. J. Ayer, "Freedom and Necessity," in his collected *Philosophical Essays* (New York, 1954) P. H. Nowell-Smith, "Freewill and Moral Responsibility," *Mind,* 1948, J. J. C. Smart, "Free Will, Praise, and Blame," *Mind,* 1961.

12. Many other verbs besides "choose" figure in various philosophers' conditional analyses of ability: e.g. "wish," "want," "will," "try," "set oneself." Much of the important contemporary work on this analysis, by G. E. Moore, P. H. Nowell-Smith, J. L. Austin, Keith Lehrer, Roderick Chisholm, and others, is collected in *The Nature of Human Action,* ed. Myles Brand (Glenview Ill., 1970). See also "Fatalism and Determinism," by Wilfrid Sellars, in *Freedom and Determinism,* ed. Keith Lehrer (New York, 1966), 141–74.

13. For an argument in some respects similar to what I have called the "main argument," see Carl Ginet's admirable article, "Might We Have No Choice?" in Lehrer, 87–104. Another argument similar to the main argument, which is (formally) much simpler than the main argument, but which is stated in language very different from that of traditional statements of the free-will problem, can be found in my "A Formal Approach to the Problem of Free Will and Determinism," *Theoria,* 1974.

PART 5

~

Philosophy of Mind

Introduction

JESSE J. PRINZ

How do mental states relate to physical states of the brain? This question, called the *mind-body problem,* has challenged philosophers for ages. It has also captured the attention of practitioners in more recent fields, such as psychology, neuroscience, and computer science. This section illustrates important insights from all these areas.

Perplexity about the mind-body relation stems from the fact that mental states have two distinctive properties that are difficult to fit into prevailing views about the nature of the physical world. First, mental states feel like something. It feels like something to have a pain, to see a sunset, or to experience joy. The property of feeling like something is termed *phenomenology.* The units of a phenomenological experience—shooting pains, patches of color, tingles of joy—are called *qualia.*

The second distinctive property of mental states is that they represent things. If you believe it is raining, your belief is about rain. Philosophers call the property of representing or being about something *intentionality.* Many mental states, including beliefs, desires, fears, and perceptions, exhibit intentionality.

Phenomenology and intentionality seem quite different from ordinary physical properties. Consider the property of being a liquid. We can explain liquidity by appealing to chemical microstructure. The molecules of a liquid are loosely packed. But phenomenology and intentionality resist explanation by appeal to microstructure. It is far from obvious how electrical impulses in neurons could feel like something or represent something.

The first five readings offer different solutions to the mind-body problem. René Descartes defends *substance dualism,* the view that mind and body are different kinds of substances. We can clearly imagine the mind existing without the body, and thus, Descartes concludes, the two must be distinct. Substance dualism faces a serious objection. If mental states are nonphysical, it is mysterious how they ever influence physical behavior. Every physical event has an identifiable physical cause. If mental states are nonphysical, the can have no causal impact on the physical world. This apparent consequence of dualism, called *epiphenomenalism,* is sometimes regarded as a fatal flaw.

Eager to reconnect mind and behavior, psychologist B. F. Skinner offers a philosophical defense of *behaviorism,* a view that takes several forms. *Methodological behaviorists* claim that science can explain behavior by appeal to external conditions without reference to inner mental states; we drink because we are deprived of water. But methodological behaviorism is compatible with the claim that inner mental states exist and with the claim that they are nonphysical. Skinner prefers *radical behaviorism,* the view that inner mental states are mere fictions. This odd thesis seems to fly in the face of introspection: we seem to experience thoughts, perceptions, and feelings. Skinner responds by arguing that these are not inner mental states at all but, rather, behaviors that are too subtle to observe. The feeling of thirst is really covert drinking behavior. Skinner also embraces *logical behaviorism,* the view that some mental terms can be translated into terms describing behavior, behavioral dispositions, or external conditions that promote behavior. "I am thirsty" may mean "I am pursuing drinks," "I will drink," or "I have not had a drink recently."

Radical behaviorism is a form of *physicalism* (also called *materialism*), the view that mental states are physical. J. J. C. Smart defends another form of physicalism, called the *identity theory.* Rather than deny their existence, he argues that inner mental states are identical with brain states. Smart believes that people are drawn to dualism because mental and physical terms have different meanings. But terms with different meanings often turn out to refer to the same thing, as with the terms "lightening" and "electrical discharge from atmospheric vapor."

Fodor rejects both behaviorism and the identity theory. Mental states cannot be behavioral dispositions because the same mental state can cause different behaviors. Thirst will only lead to water consumption if one has certain mental states, such as the belief that water will quench thirst and the desire for satiation. Mental states cannot be brain states because mental states can exist in creatures that lack brains (*multiple realizability*). A Martian can believe that it is raining even if Martian nervous systems are made out of green goo rather than neurons.

In place of behaviorism and the identity theory, Fodor defends *functionalism.* Functionalists assert that something counts as being a particular mental state by virtue of the causal role it plays within an organism. To take a simplified example, thirst may be characterized as the state that is caused by water deprivation, and causes water consumption when one desires satiation and believes that water will satiate. Two things should be noticed here. First, whereas behaviorists would try to explain thirst by appeal to external conditions and behavior alone, this characterization of thirst makes reference to other mental states, namely, beliefs and desires. These other mental states can be defined by appeal to their own causal roles, which may involve still other mental states, and so on. Second, functionalism allows for multiple realizability because different kinds of stuff can play the same causal role. Neurons may play the thirst role in us, while green goo plays the thirst role in Martians. In theory, the thirst role could even be realized by a nonphysical substance, so functionalism is compatible with dualism. But most functionalists believe that only physical things can play causal roles, and, thus, most functionalists are physicalists.

Fodor urges functionalists to regard the mind as a computer. Computers work by manipulating inner symbols in accordance with rules. Inner symbols are characterized by functional roles. For example, the multiplication symbol used by a math program running in a standard desktop computer has a different physical realization than a multiplication symbol in a pocket calculator or computer made from vacuum tubes. They all count as multiplication symbols, because of the role they play in the programs. Fodor speculates that intentionality may be explained in the same way. Mental states are inner symbols that represent what they do in virtue of the roles they play in our minds.

If minds are computers, perhaps we could build a computer that has a mind. Perhaps artificial intelligence is possible. That is the topic of the next three readings. Allan Turing devises a test for artificial intelligence: if a computer cannot be distinguished from a human being in conversation, it can be said to think. John Searle disagrees. He imagines a system that could pass the *Turing test* (as it is now known) but lacks intelligence. Searle uses the same argument to try to show that artificial intelligence is impossible and to refute the claim that the mind is a computer. Intentionality depends on biological properties of the brain, not symbol manipulation. A functionalist response is presented by Zenon Pylyshyn. He says symbol manipulation can explain intentionality, and the biochemistry of the brain cannot.

Functionalists are less sure about how to explain phenomenology. This is the topic of the next four readings. It seems that two phenomenological different states could play exactly the same functional role. The state that causes me to say "red" when I see a strawberry may feel totally different from the state that plays the same role in you. If so, qualia cannot be determined by causal roles. Terrance Horgan responds to this *inverted spectrum* objection to functionalism by defending a hybrid theory. He says functionalism must join forces with the identity theory to explain phenomenology.

Frank Jackson thinks that neither functionalism nor the identity theory can explain phenomenology. In his *knowledge argument,* he argues against all forms of physicalism by showing that one can have exhaustive knowledge of the physical world and still lack knowledge of phenomenology. In opposing physicalism, Jackson is forced to admit that qualia may be epiphenomenal. He says epiphenomenalism is less objectionable than it seems. Paul Churchland argues that Jackson's knowledge argument commits a fallacy of equivocation: it uses the same word in two different ways. Daniel Dennett contends that epiphenomenalism is unacceptable. If qualia have no causal impact on the world, we have no reason to think they exist. Despite these replies, neither author gives a clear picture of how brain states could have phenomenal character. Why does one pattern of neuron activation feel like red, rather than green, or nothing at all? Until such questions are answered, the debate about the mind-body problem will wage on.

Meditations on First Philosophy

〜

RENÉ DESCARTES

René Descartes (1596–1650) was a French philosopher, mathematician, and scientist. He was a leading defender of rationalism and is often regarded as the first modern philosopher. His works include *Discourse on Method* and *Passions of the Soul.*

SIXTH MEDITATION

The existence of material things, and the real distinction between mind and body

It remains for me to examine whether material things exist. And at least I now know they are capable of existing, in so far as they are the subject-matter of pure mathematics, since I perceive them clearly and distinctly. For there is no doubt that God is capable of creating everything that I am capable of perceiving in this manner; and I have never judged that something could not be made by him except on the grounds that there would be a contradiction in my perceiving it distinctly. The conclusion that material things exist is also suggested by the faculty of imagination, which I am aware of using when I turn my mind to material things. For when I give more attentive consideration to what imagination is, it seems to be nothing else but an application of the cognitive faculty to a body which is intimately present to it, and which therefore exists.

To make this clear, I will first examine the difference between imagination and pure understanding. When I imagine a triangle, for example, I do not merely understand that it is a figure bounded by three lines, but at the same time I also see the three lines with my mind's eye as if they were present before me; and this is what I call imagining. But if I want to think of a chiliagon, although I understand that it is a figure consisting of a thousand sides just as well as I understand the triangle to be a three-sided figure, I do not in the same way imagine the thousand sides or see them as if they were present before me. It is true that since I am in the habit of imagining something whenever I think of a corporeal thing, I may construct in my mind a confused representation of some figure; but it is clear that this is not a chiliagon. For it differs in no way from the representation I should form if I were thinking of a myriagon, or any figure with very many sides. Moreover, such a representation is useless for recognizing the properties which distinguish a chiliagon from other polygons. But suppose I am dealing with a pentagon: I can of course understand the figure of a pentagon, just as I can the figure of a chiliagon, without the help of the imagination; but I can also imagine a pentagon, by applying my mind's eye to its five sides and the area contained within them. And in doing this I notice quite clearly that imagination requires a peculiar effort of mind which is not required for understanding; this additional effort of mind clearly shows the difference between imagination and pure understanding.

Besides this, I consider that this power of imagining which is in me, differing as it does from the power of understanding, is not a necessary constituent of my own essence, that is, of the essence of my mind. For if I lacked it, I should undoubtedly remain the same individual as I now am; from which it seems to follow that it depends on something distinct from myself. And I can easily understand that, if there does exist some body to which the mind is so joined that it can apply itself to contemplate it, as it were, whenever it pleases, then it may possibly be this very body that enables me to imagine corporeal things. So the difference between this mode of thinking and pure understanding may simply be this: when the mind understands, it in some way turns towards itself and inspects one of the ideas which are within it; but when it imagines, it turns towards the body and looks at something in the body which conforms to an idea understood by the mind or perceived by the senses. I can, as I say, easily understand that this is how imagination comes about, if the body exists; and since there is no other equally suitable way of explaining imagination that comes to mind, I can make a probable conjecture that the body exists. But this is only a probability; and despite a careful and comprehensive investigation, I do not yet see how the distinct idea of corporeal nature which I find in my imagination can provide any basis for a necessary inference that some body exists.

But besides that corporeal nature which is the subject-matter of pure mathematics, there is much else that I habitually imagine, such as colours, sounds, tastes, pain and so on—though not so distinctly. Now I perceive these things much better by means of the senses, which is how, with the assistance of memory, they appear to have reached the imagination. So in order to deal with them more fully, I must pay equal attention to the senses, and see whether the things which are perceived by means of that mode of thinking which I call "sensory perception" provide me with any sure argument for the existence of corporeal things.

To begin with, I will go back over all the things which I previously took to be perceived by the senses, and reckoned to be true; and I will go over my reasons for thinking this. Next, I will set out my reasons for subsequently calling these things into doubt. And finally I will consider what I should now believe about them.

First of all then, I perceived by my senses that I had a head, hands, feet and other limbs making up the body which I regarded as part of myself, or perhaps even as my whole self. I also perceived by my senses that this body was situated among many other bodies which could affect it in various favourable or unfavourable ways; and I gauged the favourable effects by a sensation of pleasure, and the unfavourable ones by a sensation of pain. In addition to pain and pleasure, I also had sensations within me of hunger, thirst, and other such appetites, and also of physical propensities towards cheerfulness, sadness, anger and similar emotions. And outside me, besides the extension, shapes and movements of bodies, I also had sensations of their hardness and heat, and of the other tactile qualities. In addition, I had sensations of light, colours, smells, tastes and sounds, the variety of which enabled me to distinguish the sky, the earth, the seas, and all other bodies, one from another. Considering the ideas of all these qualities which presented themselves to my thought, although the ideas were, strictly speaking, the only immediate objects of my sensory awareness, it was not unreasonable for me to think that the items which I was perceiving through the senses were things quite distinct from my thought, namely bodies which produced the ideas. For my experience was that these ideas came to me quite without my consent, so that I could not have sensory awareness of any object, even if I wanted to, unless it was present to my sense organs; and I could not avoid having sensory awareness of it when it was present. And since the ideas perceived by the senses were much more lively and vivid and even, in their own way, more distinct than any of those which I deliberately formed through meditating or which I found impressed on my memory, it seemed impossible that they should have come from within me; so the only alternative was that they came from other things. Since the sole source of my knowledge of these things was the ideas themselves, the supposition that the things resembled the ideas was bound to occur to me. In addition, I remembered that the use of my senses had come first, while the use of my reason came only later; and I saw that the ideas which I formed myself were less vivid than those which I perceived with the senses and were, for the most part, made up of elements of sensory ideas. In this way I easily convinced myself that I had nothing at all in the intellect which I had not previously had in sensation. As for the body which by some special right I called 'mine', my belief that this body, more than any other, belonged to me had some justification. For I could never be separated from it, as I could from other bodies; and I felt all my appetites and emotions in, and on account of, this body; and finally, I was aware of pain and pleasurable ticklings in parts of this body, but not in other bodies external to it. But why should that curious sensation of pain give rise to a particular distress of mind; or why should a certain kind of delight follow on a tickling sensation? Again, why should that curious tugging in the stomach which I call hunger tell me that I should eat, or a dryness of the throat tell me to drink, and so on? I was not able to give any explanation of all this, except that nature taught me so. For there is absolutely no connection (at least that I can understand) between the tugging sensation and the decision to take food, or between the sensation of something causing pain and the mental apprehension of distress that arises from that sensation. These and other judgements that I made concerning sensory objects, I was apparently taught to make by nature; for I had already made up my mind that this was how things were, before working out any arguments to prove it.

Later on, however, I had many experiences which gradually undermined all the faith I had had in the senses. Sometimes towers which had looked round from a distance appeared square from close up; and enormous statues standing on their pediments did not seem large when observed from the ground. In these and countless other such cases, I found that the judgements of the external senses were mistaken. And this applied not just to the external senses but to the internal senses as well. For what can be more internal than pain? And yet I had heard that those who had had a leg or an arm amputated sometimes still seemed to feel pain intermittently in the missing part of the body. So even in my own case it was apparently not quite certain that a particular limb was hurting, even if I felt pain in it. To these reasons for doubting, I recently added two very general ones. The first was that every sensory experience I have ever thought I was having while awake I can also think of myself as sometimes having while asleep;

and since I do not believe that what I seem to perceive in sleep comes from things located outside me, I did not see why I should be any more inclined to believe this of what I think I perceive while awake. The second reason for doubt was that since I did not know the author of my being (or at least was pretending not to), I saw nothing to rule out the possibility that my natural constitution made me prone to error even in matters which seemed to me most true. As for the reasons for my previous confident belief in the truth of the things perceived by the senses, I had no trouble in refuting them. For since I apparently had natural impulses towards many things which reason told me to avoid, I reckoned that a great deal of confidence should not be placed in what I was taught by nature. And despite the fact that the perceptions of the senses were not dependent on my will, I did not think that I should on that account infer that they proceeded from things distinct from myself, since I might perhaps have a faculty not yet known to me which produced them.

But now, when I am beginning to achieve a better knowledge of myself and the author of my being, although I do not think I should heedlessly accept everything I seem to have acquired from the senses, neither do I think that everything should be called into doubt.

First, I know that everything which I clearly and distinctly understand is capable of being created by God so as to correspond exactly with my understanding of it. Hence the fact that I can clearly and distinctly understand one thing apart from another is enough to make me certain that the two things are distinct, since they are capable of being separated, at least by God. The question of what kind of power is required to bring about such a separation does not affect the judgement that the two things are distinct. Thus, simply by knowing that I exist and seeing at the same time that absolutely nothing else belongs to my nature or essence except that I am a thinking thing, I can infer correctly that my essence consists solely in the fact that I am a thinking thing. It is true that I may have (or, to anticipate, that I certainly have) a body that is very closely joined to me. But nevertheless, on the one hand I have a clear and distinct idea of myself, in so far as I am simply a thinking, non-extended thing; and on the other hand I have a distinct idea of body, in so far as this is simply an extended, non-thinking thing. And accordingly, it is certain that I am really distinct from my body, and can exist without it.

Besides this, I find in myself faculties for certain special modes of thinking, namely imagination and sensory perception. Now I can clearly and distinctly understand myself as a whole without these faculties; but I cannot, conversely, understand these faculties without me, that is, without an intellectual substance to inhere in. This is because there is an intellectual act included in their essential definition; and hence I perceive that the distinction between them and myself corresponds to the distinction between the modes of a thing and the thing itself. Of course I also recognize that there are other faculties (like those of changing position, of taking on various shapes, and so on) which, like sensory perception and imagination, cannot be understood apart from some substance for them to inhere in, and hence cannot exist without it. But it is clear that these other faculties, if they exist, must be in a corporeal or extended substance and not an intellectual one; for the clear and distinct conception of them includes extension, but does not include any intellectual act whatsoever. Now there is in me a passive faculty of sensory perception, that is, a faculty for receiving and recognizing the ideas of sensible objects; but I could not make use of it unless there was also an active faculty, either in me or in something else, which produced or brought about these ideas. But this faculty cannot be in me, since clearly it presupposes no intellectual act on my part, and the ideas in question are produced without my cooperation and often even against my will. So the only alternative is that it is in another substance distinct from me—a substance which contains either formally or eminently all the reality which exists objectively in the ideas produced by this faculty (as I have just noted). This substance is either a body, that is, a corporeal nature, in which case it will contain formally ⟨and in fact⟩ everything which is to be found objectively ⟨or representatively⟩ in the ideas; or else it is God, or some creature more noble than a body, in which case it will contain eminently whatever is to be found in the ideas. But since God is not a deceiver, it is quite clear that he does not transmit the ideas to me either directly from himself, or indirectly, via some creature which contains the objective reality of the ideas not formally but only eminently. For God has given me no faculty at all for recognizing any such source for these ideas; on the contrary, he has given me a great propensity to believe that they are produced by corporeal things. So I do not see how God could be understood to be anything but a deceiver if the ideas were transmitted from a source other than corporeal things. It follows that corporeal things exist. They may not all exist in a way that exactly corresponds with my sensory grasp of them, for in many cases the grasp of the senses is very obscure and confused. But at least they possess all the properties which I clearly and distinctly understand. . . .

There is nothing that my own nature teaches me more vividly than that I have a body, and that when I feel pain there is something wrong with the body, and that when I am hungry or thirsty the body needs food and drink, and so on. So I should not doubt that there is some truth in this.

Nature also teaches me, by these sensations of pain, hunger, thirst and so on, that I am not merely present in my body as a sailor is present in a ship, but that I am very closely joined and, as it were, intermingled with it, so that I and the body form a unit. If this were not so, I, who am nothing but a thinking thing, would not feel pain when the body was hurt, but would perceive the damage purely by the intellect, just as a sailor perceives by sight if anything in his ship is broken. Similarly, when the body needed food or drink, I should have an explicit understanding of the fact, instead of having confused sensations of hunger and thirst. For these sensations of hunger, thirst, pain and so on are nothing but confused modes of thinking which arise from the union and, as it were, intermingling of the mind with the body.

I am also taught by nature that various other bodies exist in the vicinity of my body, and that some of these are to be sought out and others avoided. And from the fact that I perceive by my senses a great variety of colours, sounds, smells and tastes, as well as differences in heat, hardness and the like, I am correct in inferring that the bodies which are the source of these various sensory perceptions possess differences corresponding to them, though perhaps not resembling them. Also, the fact that some of the perceptions are agreeable to me while others are disagreeable makes it quite certain that my body, or rather my whole self, in so far as I am a combination of body and mind, can be affected by the various beneficial or harmful bodies which surround it. . . .

And yet it is not unusual for us to go wrong even in cases where nature does urge us towards something. Those who are ill, for example, may desire food or drink that will shortly afterwards turn out to be bad for them. Perhaps it may be said that they go wrong because their nature is disordered, but this does not remove the difficulty. A sick man is no less one of God's creatures than a healthy one, and it seems no less a contradiction to suppose that he has received from God a nature which deceives him. Yet a clock constructed with wheels and weights observes all the laws of its nature just as closely when it is badly made and tells the wrong time as when it completely fulfils the wishes of the clockmaker. In the same way, I might consider the body of a man as a kind of machine equipped with and made up of bones, nerves, muscles, veins, blood and skin in such a way that, even if there were no mind in it, it would still perform all the same movements as it now does in those cases where movement is not under the control of the will or, consequently, of the mind. I can easily see that if such a body suffers from dropsy, for example, and is affected by the dryness of the throat which normally produces in the mind the sensation of thirst, the resulting condition of the nerves and other parts will dispose the body to take a drink, with the result that the disease will be aggravated. Yet this is just as natural as the body's being stimulated by a similar dryness of the throat to take a drink when there is no such illness and the drink is beneficial. Admittedly, when I consider the purpose of the clock, I may say that it is departing from its nature when it does not tell the right time; and similarly when I consider the mechanism of the human body, I may think that, in relation to the movements which normally occur in it, it too is deviating from its nature if the throat is dry at a time when drinking is not beneficial to its continued health. But I am well aware that "nature" as I have just used it has a very different sig-

nificance from "nature" in the other sense. As I have just used it, "nature" is simply a label which depends on my thought; it is quite extraneous to the things to which it is applied, and depends simply on my comparison between the idea of a sick man and a badly-made clock, and the idea of a healthy man and a well-made clock. But by 'nature' in the other sense I understand something which is really to be found in the things themselves; in this sense, therefore, the term contains something of the truth.

When we say, then, with respect to the body suffering from dropsy, that it has a disordered nature because it has a dry throat and yet does not need drink, the term "nature" is here used merely as an extraneous label. However, with respect to the composite, that is, the mind united with this body, what is involved is not a mere label, but a true error of nature, namely that it is thirsty at a time when drink is going to cause it harm. It thus remains to inquire how it is that the goodness of God does not prevent nature, in this sense, from deceiving us.

The first observation I make at this point is that there is a great difference between the mind and the body, inasmuch as the body is by its very nature always divisible, while the mind is utterly indivisible. For when I consider the mind, or myself in so far as I am merely a thinking thing, I am unable to distinguish any parts within myself; I understand myself to be something quite single and complete. Although the whole mind seems to be united to the whole body, I recognize that if a foot or arm or any other part of the body is cut off, nothing has thereby been taken away from the mind. As for the faculties of willing, of understanding, of sensory perception and so on, these cannot be termed parts of the mind, since it is one and the same mind that wills, and understands and has sensory perceptions. By contrast, there is no corporeal or extended thing that I can think of which in my thought I cannot easily divide into parts; and this very fact makes me understand that it is divisible. This one argument would be enough to show me that the mind is completely different from the body, even if I did not already know as much from other considerations.

My next observation is that the mind is not immediately affected by all parts of the body, but only by the brain, or perhaps just by one small part of the brain, namely the part which is said to contain the "common" sense. Every time this part of the brain is in a given state, it presents the same signals to the mind, even though the other parts of the body may be in a different condition at the time. This is established by countless observations, which there is no need to review here.

I observe, in addition, that the nature of the body is such that whenever any part of it is moved by another part which is some distance away, it can always be moved in the same fashion by any of the parts which lie in between, even if the more distant part does nothing. For example, in a cord ABCD, if one end D is pulled so that the other end A moves, the exact same movement could have been brought about if one of the intermediate points B or C had been pulled, and D had not moved at all. In similar fashion, when I feel a pain in my foot, physiology tells me that this happens by means of nerves distributed throughout the foot, and that these nerves are like cords which go from the foot right up to the brain. When the nerves are pulled in the foot, they in turn pull on inner parts of the brain to which they are attached, and produce a certain motion in them; and nature has laid it down that this motion should produce in the mind a sensation of pain, as occurring in the foot. But since these nerves, in passing from the foot to the brain, must pass through the calf, the thigh, the lumbar region, the back and the neck, it can happen that, even if it is not the part in the foot but one of the intermediate parts which is being pulled, the same motion will occur in the brain as occurs when the foot is hurt, and so it will necessarily come about that the mind feels the same sensation of pain. And we must suppose the same thing happens with regard to any other sensation.

My final observation is that any given movement occurring in the part of the brain that immediately affects the mind produces just one corresponding sensation; and hence the best system that could be devised is that it should produce the one sensation which, of all possible sensations, is most especially and most frequently conducive to the preservation of the healthy man. And experience shows that the sensations which nature has given us are all of this kind; and so there is absolutely nothing to be found in them

that does not bear witness to the power and goodness of God. For example, when the nerves in the foot are set in motion in a violent and unusual manner, this motion, by way of the spinal cord, reaches the inner parts of the brain, and there gives the mind its signal for having a certain sensation, namely the sensation of a pain as occurring in the foot. This stimulates the mind to do its best to get rid of the cause of the pain, which it takes to be harmful to the foot. It is true that God could have made the nature of man such that this particular motion in the brain indicated something else to the mind; it might, for example, have made the mind aware of the actual motion occurring in the brain, or in the foot, or in any of the intermediate regions; or it might have indicated something else entirely. But there is nothing else which would have been so conducive to the continued well-being of the body. In the same way, when we need drink, there arises a certain dryness in the throat; this sets in motion the nerves of the throat, which in turn move the inner parts of the brain. This motion produces in the mind a sensation of thirst, because the most useful thing for us to know about the whole business is that we need drink in order to stay healthy. And so it is in the other cases.

It is quite clear from all this that, notwithstanding the immense goodness of God, the nature of man as a combination of mind and body is such that it is bound to mislead him from time to time. For there may be some occurrence, not in the foot but in one of the other areas through which the nerves travel in their route from the foot to the brain, or even in the brain itself; and if this cause produces the same motion which is generally produced by injury to the foot, then pain will be felt as if it were in the foot. This deception of the senses is natural, because a given motion in the brain must always produce the same sensation in the mind; and the origin of the motion in question is much more often going to be something which is hurting the foot, rather than something existing elsewhere. So it is reasonable that this motion should always indicate to the mind a pain in the foot rather than in any other part of the body. Again, dryness of the throat may sometimes arise not, as it normally does, from the fact that a drink is necessary to the health of the body, but from some quite opposite cause, as happens in the case of the man with dropsy. Yet it is much better that it should mislead on this occasion than that it should always mislead when the body is in good health. And the same goes for the other cases.

This consideration is the greatest help to me, not only for noticing all the errors to which my nature is liable, but also for enabling me to correct or avoid them without difficulty. For I know that in matters regarding the well-being of the body, all my senses report the truth much more frequently than not. Also, I can almost always make use of more than one sense to investigate the same thing; and in addition, I can use both my memory, which connects present experiences with preceding ones, and my intellect, which has by now examined all the causes of error. Accordingly, I should not have any further fears about the falsity of what my senses tell me every day; on the contrary, the exaggerated doubts of the last few days should be dismissed as laughable. This applies especially to the principal reason for doubt, namely my inability to distinguish between being asleep and being awake. For I now notice that there is a vast difference between the two, in that dreams are never linked by memory with all the other actions of life as waking experiences are. If, while I am awake, anyone were suddenly to appear to me and then disappear immediately, as happens in sleep, so that I could not see where he had come from or where he had gone to, it would not be unreasonable for me to judge that he was a ghost, or a vision created in my brain, rather than a real man. But when I distinctly see where things come from and where and when they come to me, and when I can connect my perceptions of them with the whole of the rest of my life without a break, then I am quite certain that when I encounter these things I am not asleep but awake. And I ought not to have even the slightest doubt of their reality if, after calling upon all the senses as well as my memory and my intellect in order to check them, I receive no conflicting reports from any of these sources. For from the fact that God is not a deceiver it follows that in cases like these I am completely free from error. But since the pressure of things to be done does not always allow us to stop and make such a meticulous check, it must be admitted that in this human life we are often liable to make mistakes about particular things, and we must acknowledge the weakness of our nature.

The Causes of Behavior

~

B. F. SKINNER

B. F. Skinner (1904–1990) was an American psychologist who spent his career at Harvard University. He was a leading proponent of behaviorism, which had a significant influence on philosophy. Skinner's books include *Science and Human Behavior, Walden Two,* and *Beyond Freedom and Dignity.*

Why do people behave as they do? It was probably first a practical question: How could a person anticipate and hence prepare for what another person would do? Later it would become practical in another sense: How could another person be induced to behave in a given way? Eventually it became a matter of understanding and explaining behavior. It could always be reduced to a question about causes.

Reprinted from *About Behaviorism* (New York: Alfred A. Knopf, 1974), by permission of the publisher.

We tend to say, often rashly, that if one thing follows another, it was probably caused by it—following the ancient principle of *post hoc, ergo propter hoc* (after this, therefore because of this). Of many examples to be found in the explanation of human behavior, one is especially important here. The person with whom we are most familiar is ourself; many of the things we observe just before we behave occur within our body, and it is easy to take them as the causes of our behavior. If we are asked why we have spoken sharply to a friend, we may reply, "Because I felt angry." It is true that we felt angry before, or as, we spoke, and so we take our anger to be the cause of our remark. Asked why we are not eating our dinner, we may say, "Because I do not feel hungry." We often feel hungry when we eat and hence conclude that we eat because we feel hungry. Asked why we are going swimming, we may reply, "Because I feel like swimming." We seem to be saying, "When I have felt like this before, I have behaved in such and such a way." Feelings occur at just the right time to serve as causes of behavior, and they have been cited as such for centuries. We assume that other people feel as we feel when they behave as we behave.

But where are these feelings and states of mind? Of what stuff are they made? The traditional answer is that they are located in a world of nonphysical dimensions called the mind and that they are mental. But another question then arises: How can a mental event cause or be caused by a physical one? If we want to predict what a person will do, how can we discover the mental causes of his behavior, and how can we produce the feelings and states of mind which will induce him to behave in a given way? Suppose, for example, that we want to get a child to eat a nutritious but not very palatable food. We simply make sure that no other food is available, and eventually he eats. It appears that in depriving him of food (a physical event) we have made him feel hungry (a mental event), and that because he has felt hungry, he has eaten the nutritious food (a physical event). But how did the physical act of deprivation lead to the feeling of hunger, and how did the feeling move the muscles involved in ingestion? There are many other puzzling questions of this sort. What is to be done about them? . . .

METHODOLOGICAL BEHAVIORISM

The mentalistic problem can be avoided by going directly to the prior physical causes while bypassing intermediate feelings or states of mind. The quickest way to do this is to confine oneself to what an early behaviorist, Max Meyer, called the "psychology of the other one": consider only those facts which can be objectively observed in the behavior of one person in its relation to his prior environmental history. If all linkages are lawful, nothing is lost by neglecting a supposed nonphysical link. Thus, if we know that a child has not eaten for a long time, and if we know that he therefore feels hungry and that because he feels hungry he then eats, then we know that if he has not eaten for a long time, he will eat. And if by making other food inaccessible, we make him feel hungry, and if because he feels hungry he then eats a special food, then it must follow that by making other food inaccessible, we induce him to eat the special food. . . .

With respect to its own goals, methodological behaviorism was successful. It disposed of many of the problems raised by mentalism and freed itself to work on its own projects without philosophical digressions. By directing attention to genetic and environmental antecedents, it offset an unwarranted concentration on an inner life. It freed us to study the behavior of lower species, where introspection (then regarded as exclusively human) was not feasible, and to explore similarities and differences between man and other species. Some concepts previously associated with private events were formulated in other ways.

But problems remained. Most methodological behaviorists granted the existence of mental events while ruling them out of consideration. Did they really mean to say that they did not matter, that the middle stage in that three-stage sequence of physical-mental-physical contributed nothing—in other words, that feelings and states of mind were merely epiphenomena? It was not the first time that anyone had said so. The view that a purely physical world could be self-sufficient had been suggested centuries before, in the doctrine of psychophysical parallelism, which held that there were two worlds—one of mind and one of matter—and that neither had any effect on the other. Freud's demonstration of the unconscious, in which an awareness of feelings or states of mind seemed unnecessary, pointed in the same direction.

But what about other evidence? Is the traditional *post hoc, ergo propter hoc* argument entirely wrong? Are the feelings we experience just before we behave wholly unrelated to our behavior? What about the power of mind over matter in psychosomatic medicine? What about psychophysics and the mathematical relation between the magnitudes of stimuli and sensations? What about the stream of consciousness? What about the intrapsychic processes of psychiatry, in which feelings produce or suppress other feelings and memories evoke or mask other memories? What about the cognitive processes said to explain perception, thinking, the construction of sentences, and artistic creation? Must all this be ignored because it cannot be studied objectively?

RADICAL BEHAVIORISM

The statement that behaviorists deny the existence of feelings, sensations, ideas, and other features of mental life needs a good deal of clarification. Methodological behaviorism and some versions of logical positivism ruled private events out of bounds because there could be no public agreement about their validity. Introspection could not be accepted as a scientific practice, and the psychology of people like Wilhelm Wundt and Edward B. Titchener was attacked accordingly. Radical behaviorism, however, takes a different line. It does not deny the possibility of self-observation or self-knowledge or its possible usefulness, but it questions the nature of what is felt or observed and hence known. It restores introspection but not what philosophers and introspective psychologists had believed they were "specting," and it raises the question of how much of one's body one can actually observe.

Mentalism kept attention away from the external antecedent events which might have explained behavior, by seeming to supply an alternative explanation. Methodological behaviorism did just the reverse: by dealing exclusively with external antecedent events it turned attention away from self-observation and self-knowledge. Radical behaviorism restores some kind of balance. It does not insist upon truth by agreement and can therefore consider events taking place in the private world within the skin. It does not call these events unobservable, and it does not dismiss them as subjective. It simply questions the nature of the object observed and the reliability of the observations.

The position can be stated as follows: what is felt or introspectively observed is not some nonphysical world of consciousness, mind, or mental life but the observer's own body. This does not mean, as I shall show later, that introspection is a kind of physiological research, nor does it mean (and this is the heart of the argument) that what are felt or introspectively observed are the causes of behavior. An organism behaves as it does because of its current structure, but most of this is out of reach of introspection. At the moment we must content ourselves, as the methodological behaviorist insists, with a person's genetic and environmental histories. What are introspectively observed are certain collateral products of those histories. . . .

Our increasing knowledge of the control exerted by the environment makes it possible to examine the effect of the world within the skin and the nature of self-knowledge. It also makes it possible to interpret a wide range of mentalistic expressions. For example, we can look at those features of behavior which have led people to speak of an act of will, of a sense of purpose, of experience as distinct from reality, of innate or acquired ideas, of memories, meanings, and the personal knowledge of the scientist, and of hundreds of other mentalistic things or events. Some can be "translated into behavior," others discarded as unnecessary or meaningless.

In this way we repair the major damage wrought by mentalism. When what a person does is attributed to what is going on inside him, investigation is brought to an end. Why explain the explanation? For twenty-five hundred years people have been preoccupied with feelings and mental life, but only recently has any interest been shown in a more precise analysis of the role of the environment. Ignorance of that role led in the first place to mental fictions, and it has been perpetuated by the explanatory practices to which they gave rise. . . .

Consider the report "I am, was, or will be hungry." "I am hungry" may be equivalent to "I have hunger pangs," and if the verbal community had some means of observing the contractions of the stomach associated with pangs, it could pin the response to these stimuli alone. It may also be equivalent to "I am eating actively." A person who observes that he is eating voraciously may say, "I really am hungry," or, in retrospect, "I was hungrier than I thought," dismissing other evidence as unreliable. "I am hungry" may also be equivalent to "It has been a long time since I have had anything to eat," although the expression is most likely to be used in describing future behavior: "If I miss my dinner, I shall be hungry." "I am hungry" may also be equivalent to "I feel like eating" in the sense of "I have felt this way before when I have started to eat." It may be equivalent to "I am covertly engaging in behavior similar to that involved in getting and consuming food" or "I am fantasying eating" or "I am thinking of things I like to eat" or "I am 'eating to myself.'" To say, "I am hungry," may be to report several or all of these conditions. . . .

PERCEIVING

Perhaps the most difficult problem faced by behaviorism has been the treatment of conscious content. Are we not all familiar with colors, sounds, tastes, and smells which have no counterparts in the physical world? What is their place in a behavioristic account? . . .

In the traditional view a person responds to the world around him in the sense of acting upon it. Etymologically, to experience the world is to test it, and to perceive it is to capture it—to take it in and possess it. For the Greeks, to know was to be intimate with. A person could not, of course, capture and possess the real world, but he could make copies of it, and these were the so-called data—the givens—with which, in lieu of reality, he worked. He could store them in his memory and later retrieve and act upon them more or less as he might have done when they were first given. . . .

The Copy Theory

Those who believe that we see copies of the world may contend that we never see the world itself, but it is at least equally plausible to say that we never see

anything else. The copy theory of perception is most convincing with respect to visual stimuli. They are frequently copied in works of art as well as in optical systems of mirrors and lenses, and hence it is not difficult to imagine some plausible system of storage. It is much less convincing to say that we do not hear the sounds made by an orchestra but rather some inner reproduction. Music has temporal patterns, and only recently have copies been available which might lend themselves to a mental metaphor. The argument is wholly unconvincing in the field of taste and odor, where it is not easy to imagine copies distinguishable from the real thing, and it is seldom if ever made in the case of feeling. When we feel the texture of a sheet of paper, we feel the paper, not some internal representation. Possibly we do not need copies of tastes, odors, and feelings, since we are already physically intimate with them, and for presumably the same reason we are said to feel internal states like hunger or anger rather than copies.

The trouble is that the notion of an inner copy makes no progress whatsoever in explaining either sensory control or the psychology or physiology of perception. The basic difficulty was formulated by Theophrastus more than two thousand years ago:

> . . . with regard to hearing, it is strange of him [Empedocles] to imagine that he has really explained how creatures hear, when he has ascribed the process to internal sounds and assumed that the ear produces a sound within, like a bell. By means of this internal sound we might hear sounds without, but how should we hear this internal sound itself? The old problem would still confront us.

Similarly, as a modern authority has pointed out, it is as difficult to explain how we see a picture in the occipital cortex of the brain as to explain how we see the outside world, which it is said to represent. The *behavior* of seeing is neglected in all such formulations. It can take its proper place only if attention is given to other terms in the contingencies responsible for stimulus control.

Seeing in the Absence of the Thing Seen

When a person recalls something he once saw, or engages in fantasy, or dreams a dream, surely he is not under the control of a current stimulus. Is he not then seeing a copy? Again, we must turn to his environmental history for an answer. After hearing a piece of music several times, a person may hear it when it is not being played, though probably not as richly or as clearly. So far as we know, he is simply doing in the absence of the music some of the things he did in its presence. Similarly, when a person sees a person or place in his imagination, he may simply be doing what he does in the presence of the person or place. Both "reminiscing" and "remembering" once meant "being mindful of again" or "bringing again to mind"—in other words, seeing again as one once saw. . . .

Behaviorism has been accused of "relegating one of the paramount concerns of the earlier psychologists—the study of the image—to a position of not just neglect, but disgrace." I believe, on the contrary, that it offers the only way in which the subject of imaging or imagining can be put in good order.

Seeing in the absence of the thing seen is familiar to almost everyone, but the traditional formulation is a metaphor. We tend to act to produce stimuli which are reinforcing when seen. If we have found the city of Venice reinforcing (we refer to one reinforcing effect when we call it beautiful), we may go to Venice in order to be thus reinforced. If we cannot go, we may buy pictures of Venice—realistic pictures in color of its most beautiful aspects, although a black-and-white sketch may be enough. Or we may see Venice by reading about it if we have acquired the capacity to visualize while reading. . . . With no external support whatsoever, we may simply "see Venice" because we are reinforced when we do so. We say that we daydream about Venice. The mistake is to suppose that because we create physical stimuli which enable us to see Venice more effectively by going to Venice or buying a picture, we must therefore create *mental* stimuli to be seen in memory. All we need to say is that if we are reinforced for seeing Venice, we are likely to engage in that behavior—that is, the behavior of seeing Venice—even when there is very little in the immediate setting which bears a resemblance to the city. According to one dictionary, fantasy is defined as "the act or function of forming images or representations in direct perception or in memory," but we could say as well that it is the act or function of seeing in direct perception or in memory.

We may also see a thing in its absence, not because we are immediately reinforced when we do so, but because we are then able to engage in behavior which is subsequently reinforced. Thus, we may see Venice in order to tell a friend how to find his way to a particular part of the city. If we were together in the city itself, we might take him along a given route, but we can "take ourselves along the route visually" when we are not there and describe it to him. We can do so more effectively by pointing to a map or a sketch of the route, but we do not consult a "cognitive map" when we describe what we see in "calling the city to mind." Knowing a city means possessing the behavior of getting about in it; it does not mean possessing a map to be followed in getting about. One may construct such a map from the actual city or by seeing the city when absent from it, but visualizing a route through a city in order to describe it to a friend is seeing *as* (not *what*) one sees in going through the city. . . .

Seeing in the absence of the thing seen is most dramatically exemplified in dreaming when asleep. Current stimulation is then minimally in control, and a person's history and resulting states of deprivation and emotion get their chance. Freud emphasized the significance of wishes and fears plausibly inferred from dreaming, but unfortunately he was responsible for emphasizing the distinction between seeing and what is seen. The dreamer engaged in dream work; he staged the dream as a theatrical producer stages a play and then took his place in the audience and watched it. But dreaming is perceptual *behavior,* and the difference between behavior when asleep and when awake, either in or out of a relevant setting, is simply a difference in the controlling conditions.

Rapid eye movements during sleep seem to confirm this interpretation. When most actively dreaming, people move their eyes about as if they were observing a visual presentation. (The middle-ear muscles also seem to move during dreams involving auditory perception.) It has been argued that eye movement, as well as ear-muscle movement, show that "physiological input" affects dreaming, but such behavior is quite clearly a physiological *output.* We can scarcely suppose that the iconic representations observed in dreaming are under the eyelids or in the outer ear.

There are many ways of getting a person to see when there is nothing to be seen, and they can all be analyzed as the arrangement of contingencies which strengthen perceptual behavior. Certain practices in behavior therapy, in which the patient is asked to imagine various conditions or events, have been criticized as not genuinely behavioral because they make use of images. But there are no images in the sense of private copies, there is perceptual behavior; and the measures taken by the psychotherapist are designed to strengthen it. A change takes place in the patient's behavior if what he sees (hears, feels, and so on) has the same positively or negatively reinforcing effect as if he were seeing the things themselves. It is seldom if ever enough simply to instruct the patient to "have feelings," to ask him to feel sexually excited or nauseated, but he may be shown pornographic or nauseating material or be asked to "visualize as clearly as possible" a sexual or disgusting episode.

That a person may see things when there is nothing to be seen must have been a strong reason why the world of the mind was invented. It was hard enough to imagine how a copy of the current environment could get into the head where it could be "known," but there was at least a world outside which might account for it. But pure images seem to indicate a pure mind stuff. It is only when we ask how either the world or a copy of the world is seen that we lose interest in copies. Seeing does not require a thing seen.

Sensations and Brain Processes

~

J. J. C. SMART

J. J. C. Smart is emeritus professor of philosophy at Australian National University. He is one of the most influential defenders of the mind-brain identity theory. Some of his many papers are collected in *Essays Metaphysical and Moral.*

This paper takes its departure from arguments to be found in U. T. Place's "Is Consciousness a Brain Process?" I have had the benefit of discussing Place's thesis in a good many universities in the United States and Australia, and I hope that the present paper answers objections to his thesis which Place has not considered and that it presents his thesis in a more nearly unobjectionable form. This paper is meant also to supplement the paper "The 'Mental' and the 'Physical,'" by H. Feigl, which in part argues for a similar thesis to Place's.

Suppose that I report that I have at this moment a roundish, blurry-edged after-image which is yellow-ish towards its edge and is orange towards its center. What is it that I am reporting? One answer to this question might be that I am not reporting anything, that when I say that it looks to me as though there is a roundish yellowy-orange patch of light on the wall I am expressing some sort of *temptation,* the temptation to say that there *is* a roundish yellowy-orange patch on the wall (though I may know that there is not such a patch on the wall). This is perhaps Wittgenstein's view in the *Philosophical Investigations* (see §§ 367, 370). Similarly, when I "report" a pain, I am not really reporting anything (or, if you like, I am reporting in a queer sense of "reporting"), but am

Reprinted from *The Philosophical Review, 68* (1959).

doing a sophisticated sort of wince. (See § 244: "The verbal expression of pain replaces crying and does not describe it." Nor does it describe anything else?) I prefer most of the time to discuss an after-image rather than a pain, because the word "pain" brings in something which is irrelevant to my purpose: the notion of "distress." I think that "he is in pain" entails "he is in distress," that is, that he is in a certain agitation-condition. Similarly, to say "I am in pain" may be to do more than "replace pain behavior": it may be partly to report something, though this something is quite nonmysterious, being an agitation-condition, and so susceptible of behavioristic analysis. The suggestion I wish if possible to avoid is a different one, namely that "I am in pain" is a genuine report, and that what it reports is an irreducibly psychical something. And similarly the suggestion I wish to resist is also that to say "I have a yellowish-orange after-image" is to report something irreducibly psychical.

Why do I wish to resist this suggestion? Mainly because of Occam's razor. It seems to me that science is increasingly giving us a viewpoint whereby organisms are able to be seen as physicochemical mechanisms: it seems that even the behavior of man himself will one day be explicable in mechanistic terms. There does seem to be, so far as science is concerned, nothing in the world but increasingly complex arrangements of physical constituents. All except for one place: in consciousness. That is, for a full description of what is going on in a man you would have to mention not only the physical processes in his tissues, glands, nervous system, and so forth, but also his states of consciousness: his visual, auditory, and tactual sensations, his aches and pains. That these should be *correlated* with brain processes does not help, for to say that they are *correlated* is to say that they are something "over and above." You cannot correlate something with itself. You correlate footprints with burglars, but not Bill Sikes the burglar with Bill Sikes the burglar. So sensations, states of consciousness, do seem to be the one sort of thing left outside the physicalist picture, and for various reasons I just cannot believe that this can be so. That everything should be explicable in terms of physics (together of course with descriptions of the ways in which the parts are put together—roughly, biology is to physics as radio-

engineering is to electromagnetism) except the occurrence of sensations seems to me to be frankly unbelievable. Such sensations would be "nomological danglers," to use Feigl's expression. It is not often realized how odd would be the laws whereby these nomological danglers would dangle. It is sometimes asked, "Why can't there be psychophysical laws which are of a novel sort, just as the laws of electricity and magnetism were novelties from the standpoint of Newtonian mechanics?" Certainly we are pretty sure in the future to come across new ultimate laws of a novel type, but I expect them to relate simple constituents: for example, whatever ultimate particles are then in vogue. I cannot believe that ultimate laws of nature could relate simple constituents to configurations consisting of perhaps billions of neurons (and goodness knows how many billion billions of ultimate particles) all put together for all the world as though their main purpose in life was to be a negative feedback mechanism of a complicated sort. Such ultimate laws would be like nothing so far known in science. They have a queer "smell" to them. I am just unable to believe in the nomological danglers themselves, or in the laws whereby they would dangle. If any philosophical arguments seemed to compel us to believe in such things, I would suspect a catch in the argument. In any case it is the object of this paper to show that there are no philosophical arguments which compel us to be dualists.

The above is largely a confession of faith, but it explains why I find Wittgenstein's position (as I construe it) so congenial. For on this view there are, in a sense, no sensations. A man is a vast arrangement of physical particles, but there are not, over and above this, sensations or states of consciousness. There are just behavioral facts about this vast mechanism, such as that it expresses a temptation (behavior disposition) to say "there is a yellowish-red patch on the wall" or that it goes through a sophisticated sort of wince, that is, says "I am in pain." Admittedly Wittgenstein says that though the sensation "is not a something," it is nevertheless "not a nothing either" (§304), but this need only mean that the word "ache" has a use. An ache is a thing, but only in the innocuous sense in which the plain man, in the first paragraph of Frege's *Foundations of Arithmetic,* answers the question "What is the number one?" by "a thing." It should be noted that when I assert that to say "I have a yellowish-orange after-image" is to express a temptation to assert the physical-object statement "There is a yellowish-orange patch on the wall," I mean that saying "I have a yellowish-orange after-image" is (partly) the exercise of the disposition which is the temptation. It is not to *report* that I have the temptation, any more than is "I love you" normally a report that I love someone. Saying "I love you" is just part of the behavior which is the exercise of the disposition of loving someone.

Though for the reasons given above, I am very receptive to the above "expressive" account of sensation statements, I do not feel that it will quite do the trick. Maybe this is because I have not thought it out sufficiently, but it does seem to me as though, when a person says "I have an after-image," he *is* making a genuine report, and that when he says "I have a pain," he *is* doing more than "replace pain-behavior," and that "this more" is not just to say that he is in distress. I am not so sure, however, that to admit this is to admit that there are nonphysical correlates of brain processes. Why should not sensations just be brain processes of a certain sort? There are, of course, well-known (as well as lesser-known) philosophical objections to the view that reports of sensations are reports of brain-processes, but I shall try to argue that these arguments are by no means as cogent as is commonly thought to be the case.

Let me first try to state more accurately the thesis that sensations are brain-processes. It is not the thesis that, for example, "after-image" or "ache" means the same as "brain process of sort X" (where "X" is replaced by a description of a certain sort of brain process). It is that, in so far as "after-image" or "ache" is a report of a process, it is a report of a process that *happens to be* a brain process. It follows that the thesis does not claim that sensation statements can be *translated* into statements about brain processes. Nor does it claim that the logic of a sensation statement is the same as that of a brain-process statement. All it claims is that in so far as a sensation statement is a report of something, that something is in fact a brain process. Sensations are nothing over and above brain processes. Nations are nothing "over

and above" citizens, but this does not prevent the logic of nation statements being very different from the logic of citizen statements, nor does it insure the translatability of nation statements into citizen statements. (I do not, however, wish to assert that the relation of sensation statements to brain-process statements is very like that of nation statements to citizen statements. Nations do not just *happen to be* nothing over and above citizens, for example. I bring in the "nations" example merely to make a negative point: that the fact that the logic of A-statements is different from that of B-statements does not insure that A's are anything over and above B's.)

REMARKS ON IDENTITY

When I say that a sensation is a brain process or that lightning is an electric discharge, I am using "is" in the sense of strict identity. (Just as in the—in this case necessary—proposition "7 is identical with the smallest prime number greater than 5.") When I say that a sensation is a brain process or that lightning is an electric discharge I do not mean just that the sensation is somehow spatially or temporally continuous with the brain process or that the lightning is just spatially or temporally continuous with the discharge. When on the other hand I say that the successful general is the same person as the small boy who stole the apples I mean only that the successful general I see before me is a time slice of the same four-dimensional object of which the small boy stealing apples is an earlier time slice. However, the four-dimensional object which has the general-I-see-before-me for its late time slice is identical in the strict sense with the four-dimensional object which has the small-boy-stealing-apples for an early time slice. I distinguish these two senses of "is identical with" because I wish to make it clear that the brain-process doctrine asserts identity in the *strict* sense.

I shall now discuss various possible objections to the view that the processes reported in sensation statements are in fact processes in the brain. Most of us have met some of these objections in our first year as philosophy students. All the more reason to take a good look at them. Others of the objections will be more recondite and subtle.

Objection 1. Any illiterate peasant can talk perfectly well about his after-images, or how things look or feel to him, or about his aches and pains, and yet he may know nothing whatever about neurophysiology. A man may, like Aristotle, believe that the brain is an organ for cooling the body without any impairment of his ability to make true statements about his sensations. Hence the things we are talking about when we describe our sensations cannot be processes in the brain.

Reply. You might as well say that a nation of slugabeds, who never saw the Morning Star or knew of its existence, or who had never thought of the expression "the Morning Star," but who used the expression "the Evening Star" perfectly well, could not use this expression to refer to the same entity as we refer to (and describe as) "the Morning Star."

You may object that the Morning Star is in a sense not the very same thing as the Evening Star, but only something spatiotemporally continuous with it. That is, you may say that the Morning Star is not the Evening Star in the strict sense of "identity" that I distinguished earlier.

There is, however, a more plausible example. Consider lightning. Modern physical science tells us that lightning is a certain kind of electrical discharge due to ionization of clouds of water vapor in the atmosphere. This, it is now believed, is what the true nature of lightning is. Note that there are not two things: a flash of lightning and an electrical discharge. There is one thing, a flash of lightning, which is described scientifically as an electrical discharge to the earth from a cloud of ionized water molecules. The case is not at all like that of explaining a footprint by reference to a burglar. We say that what lightning really is, what its true nature as revealed by science is, is an electrical discharge. (It is not the true nature of a footprint to be a burglar.)

To forestall irrelevant objections, I should like to make it clear that by "lightning" I mean the publicly observable physical object, lightning, not a visual sense-datum of lightning. I say that the publicly observable physical object lightning is in fact the electrical discharge, not just a correlate of it. The sense-datum, or rather the having of the sense-datum, the

"look" of lightning, may well in my view be a correlate of the electrical discharge. For in my view it is a brain state *caused* by the lightning. But we should no more confuse sensations of lightning with lightning than we confuse sensations of a table with the table.

In short, the reply to Objection 1 is that there can be contingent statements of the form "A is identical with B," and a person may well know that something is an A without knowing that it is a B. An illiterate peasant might well be able to talk about his sensations without knowing about his brain processes, just as he can talk about lightning though he knows nothing of electricity.

Objection 2. It is only a contingent fact (if it is a fact) that when we have a certain kind of sensation there is a certain kind of process in our brain. Indeed it is possible, though perhaps in the highest degree unlikely, that our present physiological theories will be as out of date as the ancient theory connecting mental processes with goings on in the heart. It follows that when we report a sensation we are not reporting a brain-process.

Reply. The objection certainly proves that when we say "I have an after-image" we cannot *mean* something of the form "I have such and such a brain-process." But this does not show that what we report (having an after-image) is not *in fact* a brain process. "I see lightning" does not *mean* "I see an electrical discharge." Indeed, it is logically possible (though highly unlikely) that the electrical discharge account of lightning might one day be given up. Again, "I see the Evening Star" does not *mean* the same as "I see the Morning Star," and yet "The Evening Star and the Morning Star are one and the same thing" is a contingent proposition. Possibly Objection 2 derives some of its apparent strength from a "Fido"—Fido theory of meaning. If the meaning of an expression were what the expression named, then of course it *would* follow from the fact that "sensation" and "brain-process" have different meanings that they cannot name one and the same thing.

Objection 3. Even if Objections 1 and 2 do not prove that sensations are something over and above brain-processes, they do prove that the qualities of sensations are something over and above the qualities of brain-processes. That is, it may be possible to get out of asserting the existence of irreducibly psychic processes, but not out of asserting the existence of irreducibly psychic *properties.* For suppose we identify the Morning Star with the Evening Star. Then there must be some properties which logically imply that of being the Morning Star, and quite distinct properties which entail that of being the Evening Star. Again, there must be some properties (for example, that of being a yellow flash) which are logically distinct from those in the physicalist story.

Indeed, it might be thought that the objection succeeds at one jump. For consider the property of "being a yellow flash." It might seem that this property lies inevitably outside the physicalist framework within which I am trying to work (either by "yellow" being an objective emergent property of physical objects, or else by being a power to produce yellow sense-data, where "yellow," in this second instantiation of the word, refers to a purely phenomenal or introspectible quality). I must therefore digress for a moment and indicate how I deal with secondary qualities. I shall concentrate on color.

First of all, let me introduce the concept of a normal percipient. One person is more a normal percipient than another if he can make color discriminations that the other cannot. For example, if A can pick a lettuce leaf out of a heap of cabbage leaves, whereas B cannot though he can pick a lettuce leaf out of a heap of beetroot leaves, then A is more normal than B. (I am assuming that A and B are not given time to distinguish the leaves by their slight difference in shape, and so forth.) From the concept of "more normal than" it is easy to see how we can introduce the concept of "normal." Of course, Eskimos may make the finest discriminations at the blue end of the spectrum, Hottentots at the red end. In this case the concept of a normal percipient is a slightly idealized one, rather like that of "the mean sun" in astronomical chronology. There is no need to go into such subtleties now. I say that "This is red" means something roughly like "A normal percipient would not easily pick this out of a clump of geranium petals though he would pick it out of a clump of lettuce leaves." Of course it does not exactly mean this: a person might know the meaning of "red" without knowing anything about geraniums, or even about normal percipients. But the point is that a person can be *trained* to say "This is red" of objects which would not easily be picked out of geranium petals by a normal percipient, and so on. (Note that even a color-blind person can reasonably assert that something is red, though of course he needs to use another human being, not just himself, as his "color meter.") This account of secondary qualities explains their unimportance in physics. For obviously the discriminations and lack of discriminations made by a very complex neurophysiological mechanism are hardly likely to correspond to simple and nonarbitrary distinctions in nature.

I therefore elucidate colors as powers, in Locke's sense, to evoke certain sorts of discriminatory responses in human beings. They are also, of course, powers to cause sensations in human beings (an account still nearer Locke's). But these sensations, I am arguing, are identifiable with brain processes.

Now how do I get over the objection that a sensation can be identified with a brain process only if it has some phenomenal property, not possessed by brain processes, whereby one-half of the identification may be, so to speak, pinned down?

Reply. My suggestion is as follows. When a person says, "I see a yellowish-orange after-image," he is saying something like this: *"There is something going on which is like what is going on when* I have my eyes open, am awake, and there is an orange illuminated in good light in front of me, that is, when I really see an orange." (And there is no reason why a person should not say the same thing when he is having a veridical sense-datum, so long as we construe "like" in the last sentence in such a sense that something can be like itself.) Notice that the italicized words, namely "there is something going on which is like what is going on when," are all quasilogical or topic-neutral words. This explains why the ancient Greek peasant's reports about his sensations can be neutral between dualistic metaphysics or my materialistic metaphysics. It explains how sensations can be brain-processes and yet how a man who reports them need know nothing about brain-processes. For he reports them only very abstractly as "something going on which is like what is going on when. . . ." Similarly, a person may say "someone is in the room," thus reporting truly that the doctor is in the room, even though he has never heard of doctors. (There are not two people in the room: "someone" *and* the doctor.) This account of sensation statements also explains the singular elusiveness of "raw feels"—why no one seems to be able to pin any properties on them. Raw feels, in my view, are colorless for the very same reason that *something* is colorless. This does not mean that sensations do not have plenty of properties, for if they are brain-processes they certainly have lots of neurological properties. It only means that in speaking of them as being like or unlike one another we need not know or mention these properties.

This, then, is how I would reply to Objection 3. The strength of my reply depends on the possibility of our being able to report that one thing is like another without being able to state the respect in which it is like. I do not see why this should not be so. If we think cybernetically about the nervous system we can envisage it as able to respond to certain likenesses of its internal processes without being able to do more. It would be easier to build a machine which would tell us, say on a punched tape, whether or not two objects were similar, than it would be to build a machine which would report wherein the similarities consisted.

Objection 4. The after-image is not in physical space. The brain-process is. So the after-image is not a brain-process.

Reply. This is an *ignoratio elenchi.* I am not arguing that the after-image is a brain-process, but that the experience of having an after-image is a brain-process. It is the *experience* which is reported in the introspective report. Similarly, if it is objected that the after-image is yellowy-orange, my reply is that it is the experience of seeing yellowy-orange that is being described, and this experience is not a yellowy-orange something. So to say that a brain-process cannot be yellowy-orange is not to say that a brain-process cannot in fact be the experience of having a yellowy-orange after-image. There is, in a sense, no

such thing as an after-image or a sense-datum, though there is such a thing as the experience of having an image, and this experience is described indirectly in material object language, not in phenomenal language, for there is no such thing. We describe the experience by saying, in effect, that it is like the experience we have when, for example, we really see a yellowy-orange patch on the wall. Trees and wallpaper can be green, but not the experience of seeing or imagining a tree or wallpaper. (Or if they are described as green or yellow this can only be in a derived sense.)

Objection 5. It would make sense to say of a molecular movement in the brain that it is swift or slow, straight or circular, but it makes no sense to say this of the experience of seeing something yellow.

Reply. So far we have not given sense to talk of experiences as swift or slow, straight or circular. But I am not claiming that "experience" and "brain-process" mean the same or even that they have the same logic. "Somebody" and "the doctor" do not have the same logic, but this does not lead us to suppose that talking about somebody telephoning is talking about someone over and above, say, the doctor. The ordinary man when he reports an experience is reporting that something is going on, but he leaves it open as to what sort of thing is going on, whether in a material solid medium or perhaps in some sort of gaseous medium, or even perhaps in some sort of nonspatial medium (if this makes sense). All that I am saying is that "experience" and "brain-process" may in fact refer to the same thing, and if so we may easily adopt a convention (which is not a change in our present rules for the use of experience words but an addition to them) whereby it would make sense to talk of an experience in terms appropriate to physical processes.

Objection 6. Sensations are private, brain processes are *public.* If I sincerely say, "I see a yellowish-orange after-image," and I am not making a verbal mistake, then I cannot be wrong. But I can be wrong about a brain-process. The scientist looking into my brain might be having an illusion. Moreover, it makes sense to say that two or more people are observing the same brain-process but not that two or more people are reporting the same inner experience.

Reply. This shows that the language of introspective reports has a different logic from the language of material processes. It is obvious that until the brain-process theory is much improved and widely accepted there will be no *criteria* for saying "Smith has an experience of such-and-such a sort" *except* Smith's introspective reports. So we have adopted a rule of language that (normally) what Smith says goes.

Objection 7. I can imagine myself turned to stone and yet having images, aches, pains, and so on.

Reply. I can imagine that the electrical theory of lightning is false, that lightning is some sort of purely optical phenomenon. I can imagine that lightning is not an electrical discharge. I can imagine that the Evening Star is not the Morning Star. But it is. All the objection shows is that "experience" and "brain-process" do not have the same meaning. It does not show that an experience is not in fact a brain process.

This objection is perhaps much the same as one which can be summed up by the slogan: "What can be composed of nothing cannot be composed of anything." The argument goes as follows: on the brain-process thesis the identity between the brain-process and the experience is a contingent one. So it is logically possible that there should be no brain-process, and no process of any other sort either (no heart process, no kidney process, no liver process). There would be the experience but no "corresponding" physiological process with which we might be able to identify it empirically.

I suspect that the objector is thinking of the experience as a ghostly entity. So it is composed of something, not of nothing, after all. On his view it is composed of ghost stuff, and on mine it is composed of brain stuff. Perhaps the counter-reply will be that the experience is simple and uncompounded, and so it is not composed of anything after all. This seems to be a quibble, for, if it were taken seriously, the remark "What can be composed of nothing cannot be composed of anything" could be recast as an a priori argument against Democritus and atomism and for

Descartes and infinite divisibility. And it seems odd that a question of this sort could be settled a priori. We must therefore construe the word "composed" in a very weak sense, which would allow us to say that even an indivisible atom is composed of something (namely, itself). The dualist cannot really say that an experience can be composed of nothing. For he holds that experiences are something over and above material processes, that is, that they are a sort of ghost stuff. (Or perhaps ripples in an underlying ghost stuff.) I say that the dualist's hypothesis is a perfectly intelligible one. But I say that experiences are not to be identified with ghost stuff but with brain stuff. This is another hypothesis, and in my view a very plausible one. The present argument cannot knock it down a priori.

Objection 8. The "beetle in the box" objection (see Wittgenstein, *Philosophical Investigations,* §293). How could descriptions of experiences, if these are genuine reports, get a foothold in language? For any rule of language must have public criteria for its correct application.

Reply. The change from describing how things are to describing how we feel is just a change from uninhibitedly saying "this is so" to saying "this looks so." That is, when the naïve person might be tempted to say, "There is a patch of light on the wall which moves whenever I move my eyes" or "A pin is being stuck into me," we have learned how to resist this temptation and say "It *looks as though* there is a patch of light on the wallpaper" or "It *feels as though* someone were sticking a pin into me." The introspective account tells us about the individual's state of consciousness in the same way as does "I see a patch of light" or "I feel a pin being stuck into me": it differs from the corresponding perception statement in so far as it withdraws any claim about what is actually going on in the external world. From the point of view of the psychologist, the change from talking about the environment to talking about one's perceptual sensations is simply a matter of disinhibiting certain reactions. These are reactions which one normally suppresses because one has learned that in the prevailing circumstances they are unlikely to provide a good indication of the state of the environment. To say that something looks green to me is simply to say that my experience is like the experience I get when I see something that really is green. In my reply to Objection 3, I pointed out the extreme openness or generality of statements which report experiences. This explains why there is no language of private qualities. (Just as "someone," unlike "the doctor," is a colorless word.)

If it is asked what is the difference between those brain processes which, in my view, are experiences and those brain processes which are not, I can only reply that it is at present unknown. I have been tempted to conjecture that the difference may in part be that between perception and reception (in D. M. MacKay's terminology) and that the type of brain process which is an experience might be identifiable with MacKay's active "matching response." This, however, cannot be the whole story, because sometimes I can perceive something unconsciously, as when I take a handkerchief out of a drawer without being aware that I am doing so. But at the very least, we can classify the brain processes which are experiences as those brain processes which are, or might have been, causal conditions of those pieces of verbal behavior which we call reports of immediate experience.

I have now considered a number of objections to the brain-process thesis. I wish now to conclude with some remarks on the logical status of the thesis itself. U. T. Place seems to hold that it is a straight-out scientific hypothesis. If so, he is partly right and partly wrong. If the issue is between (say) a brain-process thesis and a heart thesis, or a liver thesis, or a kidney thesis, then the issue is a purely empirical one, and the verdict is overwhelmingly in favor of the brain. The right sorts of things don't go on in the heart, liver, or kidney, nor do these organs possess the right sort of complexity of structure. On the other hand, if the issue is between a brain-or-liver-or-kidney thesis (that is, some form of materialism) on the one hand and epiphenomenalism on the other hand, then the issue is not an empirical one. For there is no conceivable experiment which could decide between materialism and epiphenomenalism. This latter issue is not like the average straight-out empirical issue in sci-

ence, but like the issue between the nineteenth-century English naturalist Philip Gosse and the orthodox geologists and paleontologists of his day. According to Gosse, the earth was created about 4000 B.C. exactly as described in *Genesis*, with twisted rock strata, "evidence" of erosion, and so forth, and all sorts of fossils, all in their appropriate strata, just as if the usual evolutionist story had been true. Clearly this theory is in a sense irrefutable: no evidence can possibly tell against it. Let us ignore the theological setting in which Philip Gosse's hypothesis had been placed, thus ruling out objections of a theological kind, such as "what a queer God who would go to such elaborate lengths to deceive us." Let us suppose that it is held that the universe just *began* in 4004 B.C. with the initial conditions just everywhere as they were in 4004 B.C., and in particular that our own planet began with sediment in the rivers, eroded cliffs, fossils in the rocks, and so on. No scientist would ever entertain this as a serious hypothesis, consistent though it is with all possible evidence. The hypothesis offends against the principles of parsimony and simplicity. There would be far too many brute and inexplicable facts. Why are pterodactyl bones just as they are? No explanation in terms of the evolution of pterodactyls from earlier forms of life would any longer be possible. We would have millions of facts about the world as it was in 4004 B.C. that just have to be *accepted*.

The issue between the brain-process theory and epiphenomenalism seems to be of the above sort. (Assuming that a behavioristic reduction of introspective reports is not possible.) If it be agreed that there are no cogent philosophical arguments which force us into accepting dualism, and if the brain process theory and dualism are equally consistent with the facts, then the principles of parsimony and simplicity seem to me to decide overwhelmingly in favor of the brain-process theory. As I pointed out earlier, dualism involves a large number of irreducible psychophysical laws (whereby the "nomological danglers" dangle) of a queer sort, that just have to be taken on trust, and are just as difficult to swallow as the irreducible facts about the paleontology of the earth with which we are faced on Philip Gosse's theory.

The Mind-Body Problem

~

JERRY A. FODOR

Jerry A. Fodor is professor of philosophy at Rutgers University. He is renowned for defending the view that we think in an inner language, akin to the symbolic codes used in ordinary computers. Fodor's highly influential works include *The Language of Thought, The Modularity of Mind,* and *Psychosemantics.*

Modern philosophy of science has been devoted largely to the formal and systematic description of the successful practices of working scientists. The philosopher does not try to dictate how scientific inquiry and argument ought to be conducted. Instead he tries to enumerate the principles and practices that have contributed to good science. The philosopher has devoted the most attention to analyzing the methodological peculiarities of the physical sciences. The analysis has helped to clarify the nature of confirmation, the logical structure of scientific theories, the formal properties of statements that express laws and the question of whether theoretical entities actually exist.

It is only rather recently that philosophers have become seriously interested in the methodological tenets of psychology. Psychological explanations of behavior refer liberally to the mind and to states, operations and processes of the mind. The philosophical difficulty comes in stating in unambiguous language what such references imply.

Traditional philosophies of mind can be divided into two broad categories: dualist theories and materialist theories. In the dualist approach the mind is a nonphysical substance. In materialist theories the mental is not distinct from the physical; indeed, all mental states, properties, processes and operations are in principle identical with physical states, proper-

ties, processes and operations. Some materialists, known as behaviorists, maintain that all talk of mental causes can be eliminated from the language of psychology in favor of talk of environmental stimuli and behavioral responses. Other materialists, the identity theorists, contend that there are mental causes and that they are identical with neurophysiological events in the brain.

In the past fifteen years a philosophy of mind called functionalism that is neither dualist nor materialist has emerged from philosophical reflection on developments in artificial intelligence, computational theory, linguistics, cybernetics and psychology. All these fields, which are collectively known as the cognitive sciences, have in common a certain level of abstraction and a concern with systems that process information. Functionalism, which seeks to provide a philosophical account of this level of abstraction, recognizes the possibility that systems as diverse as human beings, calculating machines and disembodied spirits could all have mental states. In the functionalist view the psychology of a system depends not on the stuff it is made of (living cells, metal or spiritual energy) but on how the stuff is put together. Functionalism is a difficult concept, and one way of coming to grips with it is to review the deficiencies of the dualist and materialist philosophies of mind it aims to displace.

The chief drawback of dualism is its failure to account adequately for mental causation. If the mind is nonphysical, it has no position in physical space. How, then, can a mental cause give rise to a behavioral effect that has a position in space? To put it another way, how can the nonphysical give rise to the physical without violating the laws of the conservation of mass, of energy and of momentum?

The dualist might respond that the problem of how an immaterial substance can cause physical events is not much obscurer than the problem of how one physical event can cause another. Yet there is an important difference: there are many clear cases of physical causation but not one clear case of nonphysical causation. Physical interaction is something philosophers, like all other people, have to live with. Nonphysical interaction, however, may be no more than an artifact of the immaterialist construal of the mental. Most philosophers now agree that no argument has successfully demonstrated why mind-body causation should not be regarded as a species of physical causation.

Dualism is also incompatible with the practices of working psychologists. The psychologist frequently applies the experimental methods of the physical sciences to the study of the mind. If mental processes were different in kind from physical processes, there would be no reason to expect these methods to work in the realm of the mental. In order to justify their experimental methods many psychologists urgently sought an alternative to dualism.

In the 1920s John B. Watson of Johns Hopkins University made the radical suggestion that behavior does not have mental causes. He regarded the behavior of an organism as its observable responses to stimuli, which he took to be the causes of its behavior. Over the next thirty years psychologists such as B. F. Skinner of Harvard University developed Watson's ideas into an elaborate world view in which the role of psychology was to catalogue the laws that determine causal relations between stimuli and responses. In this "radical behaviorist" view the problem of explaining the nature of the mind-body interaction vanishes; there is no such interaction.

Radical behaviorism has always worn an air of paradox. For better or worse, the idea of mental cau-

sation is deeply ingrained in our everyday language and in our ways of understanding our fellow men and ourselves. For example, people commonly attribute behavior to beliefs, to knowledge and to expectations. Brown puts gas in his tank because he believes the car will not run without it. Jones writes not "acheive" but "achieve" because he knows the rule about putting *i* before *e*. Even when a behavioral response is closely tied to an environmental stimulus, mental processes often intervene. Smith carries an umbrella because the sky is cloudy, but the weather is only part of the story. There are apparently also mental links in the causal chain: observation and expectation. The clouds affect Smith's behavior only because he observes them and because they induce in him an expectation of rain.

The radical behaviorist is unmoved by appeals to such cases. He is prepared to dismiss references to mental causes, however plausible they may seem, as the residue of outworn creeds. The radical behaviorist predicts that as psychologists come to understand more about the relations between stimuli and responses they will find it increasingly possible to explain behavior without postulating mental causes.

The strongest argument against behaviorism is that psychology has not turned out this way; the opposite has happened. As psychology has matured, the framework of mental states and processes that is apparently needed to account for experimental observations has grown all the more elaborate. Particularly in the case of human behavior psychological theories satisfying the methodological tenets of radical behaviorism have proved largely sterile, as would be expected if the postulated mental processes are real and causally effective.

Nevertheless, many philosophers were initially drawn to radical behaviorism because, paradoxes and all, it seemed better than dualism. Since a psychology committed to immaterial substances was unacceptable, philosophers turned to radical behaviorism because it seemed to be the only alternative materialist philosophy of mind. The choice, as they saw it, was between radical behaviorism and ghosts.

By the early 1960s philosophers began to have doubts that dualism and radical behaviorism exhausted the possible approaches to the philosophy of mind. Since the two theories seemed unattractive, the right strategy might be to develop a materialist philosophy of mind that nonetheless allowed for mental causes. Two such philosophies emerged, one called logical behaviorism and the other called the central-state identity theory.

Logical behaviorism is a semantic theory about what mental terms mean. The basic idea is that attributing a mental state (say thirst) to an organism is the same as saying that the organism is disposed to behave in a particular way (for example to drink if there is water available). On this view every mental ascription is equivalent in meaning to an if-then statement (called a behavioral hypothetical) that expresses a behavioral disposition. For example, "Smith is thirsty" might be taken to be equivalent to the dispositional statement "If there were water available, then Smith would drink some." By definition a behavioral hypothetical includes no mental terms. The if-clause of the hypothetical speaks only of stimuli and the then-clause speaks only of behavioral responses. Since stimuli and responses are physical events, logical behaviorism is a species of materialism.

The strength of logical behaviorism is that by translating mental language into the language of stimuli and responses it provides an interpretation of psychological explanations in which behavioral effects are attributed to mental causes. Mental causation is simply the manifestation of a behavioral disposition. More precisely, mental causation is what happens when an organism has a behavioral disposition and the if-clause of the behavioral hypothetical expressing the disposition happens to be true. For example, the causal statement "Smith drank some water because he was thirsty" might be taken to mean "If there were water available, then Smith would drink some, and there was water available."

I have somewhat oversimplified logical behaviorism by assuming that each mental ascription can be translated by a unique behavioral hypothetical. Actually the logical behaviorist often maintains that it takes an open-ended set (perhaps an infinite set) of behavioral hypotheticals to spell out the behavioral disposition expressed by a mental term. The mental ascription "Smith is thirsty" might also be satisfied by the hypothetical "If there were orange juice available, then Smith would drink some" and by a host of other hypotheticals. In any event the logical behaviorist does not usually maintain he can actually enumerate all the hypotheticals that correspond to a behavioral disposition expressing a given mental term. He only insists that in principle the meaning of any mental term can be conveyed by behavioral hypotheticals.

The way the logical behaviorist has interpreted a mental term such as thirsty is modeled after the way many philosophers have interpreted a physical disposition such as fragility. The physical disposition "The glass is fragile" is often taken to mean something like "If the glass were struck, then it would break." By the same token the logical behaviorist's analysis of mental causation is similar to the received analysis of one kind of physical causation. The causal statement "The glass broke because it was fragile" is taken to mean something like "If the glass were struck, then it would break, and the glass was struck."

By equating mental terms with behavioral dispositions the logical behaviorist has put mental terms on a par with the nonbehavioral dispositions of the physical sciences. That is a promising move, because the analysis of nonbehavioral dispositions is on relatively solid philosophical ground. An explanation attributing the breaking of a glass to its fragility is surely something even the staunchest materialist can accept. By arguing that mental terms are synonymous with dispositional terms, the logical behaviorist has provided something the radical behaviorist could not: a materialist account of mental causation.

Nevertheless, the analogy between mental causation as construed by the logical behaviorist and physical causation goes only so far. The logical behaviorist treats the manifestation of a disposition as the sole form of mental causation whereas the physical sciences recognize additional kinds of causation. There is the kind of causation where one physical event causes another, as when the breaking of a glass is attributed to its having been struck. In fact, explanations that involve event-event causation are presumably more basic than dispositional explanations, because the manifestation of a disposition (the breaking of a fragile glass) always involves event-event causation and not vice versa. In the realm of the mental many examples of event-event causation involve one mental state's causing another, and for this kind of causation logical behaviorism provides no analysis. As a result the logical behaviorist is committed to the tacit and implausible assumption that psychology requires a less robust notion of causation than the physical sciences require.

Event-event causation actually seems to be quite common in the realm of the mental. Mental causes typically give rise to behavioral effects by virtue of their interaction with other mental causes. For example, having a headache causes a disposition to take aspirin only if one also has the desire to get rid of the headache, the belief that aspirin exists, the belief that taking aspirin reduces headaches and so on. Since mental states interact in generating behavior, it will be necessary to find a construal of psychological explanations that posits mental processes: causal sequences of mental events. It is this construal that logical behaviorism fails to provide.

Such considerations bring out a fundamental way in which logical behaviorism is quite similar to radical behaviorism. It is true that the logical behaviorist, unlike the radical behaviorist, acknowledges the existence of mental states. Yet since the underlying tenet of logical behaviorism is that references to mental states can be translated out of psychological explanations by employing behavioral hypotheticals, all talk of mental states and processes is in a sense heuristic. The only facts to which the behaviorist is actually committed are facts about relations between stimuli and responses. In this respect logical behaviorism is just radical behaviorism in a semantic form. Although the former theory offers a construal of mental causation, the construal is Pickwickian. What does not really exist cannot cause anything, and the logical behaviorist, like the radical behaviorist, believes deep down that mental causes do not exist.

An alternative materialist theory of the mind to logical behaviorism is the central-state identity theory. According to this theory, mental events, states and processes are identical with neurophysiological events in the brain, and the property of being in a certain mental state (such as having a headache or believing it will rain) is identical with the property of being in a certain neurophysiological state. On this basis it is easy to make sense of the idea that a behavioral effect might sometimes have a chain of mental causes; that will be the case whenever a behavioral effect is contingent on the appropriate sequence of neurophysiological events.

The central-state identity theory acknowledges that it is possible for mental causes to interact causally without ever giving rise to any behavioral effect, as when a person thinks for a while about what he ought to do and then decides to do nothing. If mental processes are neurophysiological, they must have the causal properties of neurophysiological processes. Since neurophysiological processes are presumably physical processes, the central-state identity theory ensures that the concept of mental causation is as rich as the concept of physical causation.

The central-state identity theory provides a satisfactory account of what the mental terms in psychological explanations refer to, and so it is favored by psychologists who are dissatisfied with behaviorism. The behaviorist maintains that mental terms refer to nothing or that they refer to the parameters of stimulus-response relations. Either way the existence of mental entities is only illusory. The identity theorist, on the other hand, argues that mental terms refer to neurophysiological states. Thus he can take seriously the project of explaining behavior by appealing to its mental causes.

The chief advantage of the identity theory is that it takes the explanatory constructs of psychology at face value, which is surely something a philosophy of mind ought to do if it can. The identity theory shows how the mentalistic explanations of psychology could be not mere heuristics but literal accounts of the causal history of behavior. Moreover, since the identity theory is not a semantic thesis, it is immune to many arguments that cast in doubt logical behaviorism. A drawback of logical behaviorism is that the observation "John has a headache" does not seem to mean the same thing as a statement of the form "John is disposed to behave in such and such a way." The identity theorist, however, can live with the fact that "John has a headache" and "John is in such and such a brain state" are not synonymous. The assertion of the identity theorist is not that these sentences mean the same thing but only that they are rendered true (or false) by the same neurophysiological phenomena.

The identity theory can be held either as a doctrine about mental particulars (John's current pain or Bill's fear of animals) or as a doctrine about mental universals, or properties (having a pain or being afraid of animals). The two doctrines, called respectively token physicalism and type physicalism, differ in strength and plausibility. Token physicalism maintains only that all the mental particulars that happen to exist are neurophysiological, whereas type physicalism makes the more sweeping assertion that all the mental particulars there could possibly be are neurophysiological. Token physicalism does not rule out the logical possibility of machines and disembodied spirits having mental properties. Type physicalism dismisses this possibility because neither machines nor disembodied spirits have neurons.

Type physicalism is not a plausible doctrine about mental properties even if token physicalism is right about mental particulars. The problem with type physicalism is that the psychological constitution of a system seems to depend not on its hardware, or physical composition, but on its software, or program. Why should the philosopher dismiss the possibility that silicon-based Martians have pains, assuming that the silicon is properly organized? And why should the philosopher rule out the possibility of machines having beliefs, assuming that the machines are correctly programmed? If it is logically possible that Martians and machines could have mental properties, then mental properties and neurophysiological processes cannot be identical, however much they may prove to be coextensive.

What it all comes down to is that there seems to be a level of abstraction at which the generalizations of psychology are most naturally pitched. This level of abstraction cuts across differences in the physical composition of the systems to which psychological generalizations apply. In the cognitive sciences, at least, the natural domain for psychological theorizing seems to be all systems that process information. The problem with type physicalism is that there are possible information-processing systems with the same psychological constitution as human beings but not the same physical organization. In principle all kinds of physically different things could have human software.

This situation calls for a relational account of mental properties that abstracts them from the physical structure of their bearers. In spite of the objections to logical behaviorism that I presented above, logical behaviorism was at least on the right track in offering a relational interpretation of mental properties: to have a headache is to be disposed to exhibit a certain pattern of relations between the stimuli one encounters and the responses one exhibits. If that is what having a headache is, however, there is no reason in principle why only heads that are physically similar to ours can ache. Indeed, according to logical behaviorism, it is a necessary truth that any system that has our stimulus-response contingencies also has our headaches.

All of this emerged ten or fifteen years ago as a nasty dilemma for the materialist program in the philosophy of mind. On the one hand the identity theorist (and not the logical behaviorist) had got right the causal character of the interactions of mind and body. On the other the logical behaviorist (and not the identity theorist) had got right the relational character of mental properties. Functionalism has apparently been able to resolve the dilemma. By stressing the distinction computer science draws between hardware and software the functionalist can make sense of both the causal and the relational character of the mental.

The intuition underlying functionalism is that what determines the psychological type to which a mental particular belongs is the causal role of the particular in the mental life of the organism. Functional individuation is differentiation with respect to causal role. A headache, for example, is identified with the type of mental state that among other things causes a disposition for taking aspirin in people who believe aspirin relieves a headache, causes a desire to rid oneself of the pain one is feeling, often causes someone who speaks English to say such things as "I have a headache" and is brought on by overwork, eyestrain and tension. This list is presumably not complete. More will be known about the nature of a headache as psychological and physiological research discovers more about its causal role.

Functionalism construes the concept of causal role in such a way that a mental state can be defined by its causal relations to other mental states. In this respect functionalism is completely different from logical behaviorism. Another major difference is that functionalism is not a reductionist thesis. It does not foresee, even in principle, the elimination of mentalistic concepts from the explanatory apparatus of psychological theories.

The difference between functionalism and logical behaviorism is brought out by the fact that functionalism is fully compatible with token physicalism. The functionalist would not be disturbed if brain events turn out to be the only things with the functional properties that define mental states. Indeed, most functionalists fully expect it will turn out that way.

Since functionalism recognizes that mental particulars may be physical, it is compatible with the idea that mental causation is a species of physical causation. In other words, functionalism tolerates the materialist solution to the mind-body problem provided by the central-state identity theory. It is possible for the functionalist to assert both that mental properties are typically defined in terms of their relations and that interactions of mind and body are typically causal in however robust a notion of causality is required by psychological explanations. The logical behaviorist can endorse only the first assertion and the type physicalist only the second. As a result functionalism seems to capture the best features of the materialist alternatives to dualism. It is no wonder that functionalism has become increasingly popular.

Machines provide good examples of two concepts that are central to functionalism: the concept that mental states are interdefined and the concept that they can be realized by many systems. The illustration . . . contrasts a behavioristic Coke machine with a mentalistic one. Both machines dispense a Coke for 10 cents. (The price has not been affected by inflation.) The states of the machines are defined by reference to their causal roles, but only one machine would satisfy the behaviorist. Its single state (SO) is completely specified in terms of stimuli and responses. SO is the state a machine is in if, and only if, given a dime as the input, it dispenses a Coke as the output.

The machine in the illustration has interdefined states ($S1$ and $S2$), which are characteristic of functionalism. $S1$ is the state a machine is in if, and only if, (1) given a nickel, it dispenses nothing and proceeds to $S2$, and (2) given a dime, it dispenses a Coke and stays in $S1$. $S2$ is the state a machine is in if, and

only if, (1) given a nickel, it dispenses a Coke and proceeds to $S1$, and (2) given a dime, it dispenses a Coke and a nickel and proceeds to $S1$. What $S1$ and $S2$ jointly amount to is the machine's dispensing a Coke if it is given a dime, dispensing a Coke and a nickel if it is given a dime and a nickel and waiting to be given a second nickel if it has been given a first one.

Since $S1$ and $S2$ are each defined by hypothetical statements, they can be viewed as dispositions. Nevertheless, they are not behavioral dispositions because the consequences an input has for a machine in $S1$ or $S2$ are not specified solely in terms of the output of the machine. Rather, the consequences also involve the machine's internal states.

Nothing about the way I have described the behavioristic and mentalistic Coke machines puts constraints on what they could be made of. Any system whose states bore the proper relations to inputs, outputs and other states could be one of these machines. No doubt it is reasonable to expect such a system to be constructed out of such things as wheels, levers and diodes (token physicalism for Coke machines). Similarly, it is reasonable to expect that our minds may prove to be neurophysiological (token physicalism for human beings).

Nevertheless, the software description of a Coke machine does not logically require wheels, levers and diodes for its concrete realization. By the same token, the software description of the mind does not logically require neurons. As far as functionalism is concerned a Coke machine with states $S1$ and $S2$ could be made of ectoplasm, if there is such stuff and if its states have the right causal properties. Functionalism allows for the possibility of disembodied Coke machines in exactly the same way and to the same extent that it allows for the possibility of disembodied minds.

To say that $S1$ and $S2$ are interdefined and realizable by different kinds of hardware is not, of course, to say that a Coke machine has a mind. Although interdefinition and functional specification are typical features of mental states, they are clearly not sufficient for mentality. . . .

An obvious objection to functionalism as a theory of the mind is that the functionalist definition is not limited to mental states and processes. Catalysts, Coke machines, valve openers, pencil sharpeners, mousetraps and ministers of finance are all in one way or another concepts that are functionally defined, but none is a mental concept such as pain, belief and desire. What, then, characterizes the mental? And can it be captured in a functionalist framework?

The traditional view in the philosophy of mind has it that mental states are distinguished by their having what are called either qualitative content or intentional content. I shall discuss qualitative content first.

It is not easy to say what qualitative content is; indeed, according to some theories, it is not even possible to say what it is because it can be known not by description but only by direct experience. I shall nonetheless attempt to describe it. Try to imagine looking at a blank wall through a red filter. Now change the filter to a green one and leave everything else exactly the way it was. Something about the character of your experience changes when the filter does, and it is this kind of thing that philosophers call qualitative content. I am not entirely comfortable about introducing qualitative content in this way, but it is a subject with which many philosophers are not comfortable.

The reason qualitative content is a problem for functionalism is straightforward. Functionalism is committed to defining mental states in terms of their causes and effects. It seems, however, as if two mental states could have all the same causal relations and yet could differ in their qualitative content. Let me illustrate this with the classic puzzle of the inverted spectrum.

It seems possible to imagine two observers who are alike in all relevant psychological respects except that experiences having the qualitative content of red for one observer would have the qualitative content of green for the other. Nothing about their behavior need reveal the difference because both of them see ripe tomatoes and flaming sunsets as being similar in color and both of them call that color "red." Moreover, the causal connection between their (qualitatively distinct) experiences and their other mental states could also be identical. Perhaps they both think of Little Red Riding Hood when they see ripe toma-

toes, feel depressed when they see the color green and so on. It seems as if anything that could be packed into the notion of the causal role of their experiences could be shared by them, and yet the qualitative content of the experiences could be as different as you like. If this is possible, then the functionalist account does not work for mental states that have qualitative content. If one person is having a green experience while another person is having a red one, then surely they must be in different mental states.

The example of the inverted spectrum is more than a verbal puzzle. Having qualitative content is supposed to be a chief factor in what makes a mental state conscious. Many psychologists who are inclined to accept the functionalist framework are nonetheless worried about the failure of functionalism to reveal much about the nature of consciousness. Functionalists have made a few ingenious attempts to talk themselves and their colleagues out of this worry, but they have not, in my view, done so with much success. (For example, perhaps one is wrong in thinking one can imagine what an inverted spectrum would be like.) As matters stand, the problem of qualitative content poses a serious threat to the assertion that functionalism can provide a general theory of the mental.

Functionalism has fared much better with the intentional content of mental states. Indeed, it is here that the major achievements of recent cognitive science are found. To say that a mental state has intentional content is to say that it has certain semantic properties. For example, for Enrico to believe Galileo was Italian apparently involves a three-way relation between Enrico, a belief and a proposition that is the content of the belief (namely the proposition that Galileo was Italian). In particular it is an essential property of Enrico's belief that it is about Galileo (and not about, say, Newton) and that it is true if, and only if, Galileo was indeed Italian. Philosophers are divided on how these considerations fit together, but it is widely agreed that beliefs involve semantic properties such as expressing a proposition, being true or false and being about one thing rather than another.

It is important to understand the semantic properties of beliefs because theories in the cognitive sciences are largely about the beliefs organisms have. Theories of learning and perception, for example, are chiefly accounts of how the host of beliefs an organism has are determined by the character of its experiences and its genetic endowment. The functionalist account of mental states does not by itself provide the required insights. Mousetraps are functionally defined, yet mousetraps do not express propositions and they are not true or false.

There is at least one kind of thing other than a mental state that has intentional content: a symbol. Like thoughts, symbols seem to be about things. If someone says "Galileo was Italian," his utterance, like Enrico's belief, expresses a proposition about Galileo that is true or false depending on Galileo's homeland. This parallel between the symbolic and the mental underlies the traditional quest for a unified treatment of language and mind. Cognitive science is now trying to provide such a treatment.

The basic concept is simple but striking. Assume that there are such things as mental symbols (mental representations) and that mental symbols have semantic properties. On this view having a belief involves being related to a mental symbol, and the belief inherits its semantic properties from the mental symbol that figures in the relation. Mental processes (thinking, perceiving, learning and so on) involve causal interactions among relational states such as having a belief. The semantic properties of the words and sentences we utter are in turn inherited from the semantic properties of the mental states that language expresses.

Associating the semantic properties of mental states with those of mental symbols is fully compatible with the computer metaphor, because it is natural to think of the computer as a mechanism that manipulates symbols. A computation is a causal chain of computer states and the links in the chain are operations on semantically interpreted formulas in a machine code. To think of a system (such as the nervous system) as a computer is to raise questions about the nature of the code in which it computes and the semantic properties of the symbols in the code. In fact, the analogy between minds and computers actually implies the postulation of mental symbols. There is no computation without representation.

The representational account of the mind, however, predates considerably the invention of the computing machine. It is a throwback to classical epistemology, which is a tradition that includes philosophers as diverse as John Locke, David Hume, George Berkeley, René Descartes, Immanuel Kant, John Stuart Mill and William James.

Hume, for one, developed a representational theory of the mind that included five points. First, there exist "Ideas," which are a species of mental symbol. Second, having a belief involves entertaining an Idea. Third, mental processes are causal associations of Ideas. Fourth, Ideas are like pictures. And fifth, Ideas have their semantic properties by virtue of what they resemble: the Idea of John is about John because it looks like him.

Contemporary cognitive psychologists do not accept the details of Hume's theory, although they endorse much of its spirit. Theories of computation provide a far richer account of mental processes than the mere association of Ideas. And only a few psychologists still think that imagery is the chief vehicle of mental representation. Nevertheless, the most significant break with Hume's theory lies in the abandoning of resemblance as an explanation of the semantic properties of mental representations.

Many philosophers, starting with Berkeley, have argued that there is something seriously wrong with the suggestion that the semantic relation between a thought and what the thought is about could be one of resemblance. Consider the thought that John is tall. Clearly the thought is true only of the state of affairs consisting of John's being tall. A theory of the semantic properties of a thought should therefore explain how this particular thought is related to this particular state of affairs. According to the resemblance theory, entertaining the thought involves having a mental image that shows John to be tall. To put it another way, the relation between the thought that John is tall and his being tall is like the relation between a tall man and his portrait.

The difficulty with the resemblance theory is that any portrait showing John to be tall must also show him to be many other things: clothed or naked, lying, standing or sitting, having a head or not having one, and so on. A portrait of a tall man who is sitting down resembles a man's being seated as much as it resembles a man's being tall. On the resemblance theory it is not clear what distinguishes thoughts about John's height from thoughts about his posture.

The resemblance theory turns out to encounter paradoxes at every turn. The possibility of construing beliefs as involving relations to semantically interpreted mental representations clearly depends on having an acceptable account of where the semantic properties of the mental representations come from. If resemblance will not provide this account, what will?

The current idea is that the semantic properties of a mental representation are determined by aspects of its functional role. In other words, a sufficient condition for having semantic properties can be specified in causal terms. This is the connection between functionalism and the representational theory of the mind. Modern cognitive psychology rests largely on the hope that these two doctrines can be made to support each other.

No philosopher is now prepared to say exactly how the functional role of a mental representation determines its semantic properties. Nevertheless, the functionalist recognizes three types of causal relation among psychological states involving mental representations, and they might serve to fix the semantic properties of mental representations. The three types are causal relations among mental states and stimuli, mental states and responses and some mental states and other ones.

Consider the belief that John is tall. Presumably the following facts, which correspond respectively to the three types of causal relation, are relevant to determining the semantic properties of the mental representation involved in the belief. First, the belief is a normal effect of certain stimulations, such as seeing John in circumstances that reveal his height. Second, the belief is the normal cause of certain behavioral effects, such as uttering "John is tall." Third, the belief is a normal cause of certain other beliefs and a normal effect of certain other beliefs. For example,

anyone who believes John is tall is very likely also to believe someone is tall. Having the first belief is normally causally sufficient for having the second belief. And anyone who believes everyone in the room is tall and also believes John is in the room will very likely believe John is tall. The third belief is a normal effect of the first two. In short, the functionalist maintains that the proposition expressed by a given mental representation depends on the causal properties of the mental states in which that mental representation figures.

The concept that the semantic properties of mental representations are determined by aspects of their functional role is at the center of current work in the cognitive sciences. Nevertheless, the concept may not be true. Many philosophers who are unsympathetic to the cognitive turn in modern psychology doubt its truth, and many psychologists would probably reject it in the bald and unelaborated way that I have sketched it. Yet even in its skeletal form, there is this much to be said in its favor: It legitimizes the notion of mental representation, which has become increasingly important to theorizing in every branch of the cognitive sciences. Recent advances in formulating and testing hypotheses about the character of mental representations in fields ranging from phonetics to computer vision suggest that the concept of mental representation is fundamental to empirical theories of the mind.

The behaviorist has rejected the appeal to mental representation because it runs counter to his view of the explanatory mechanisms that can figure in psychological theories. Nevertheless, the science of mental representation is now flourishing. The history of science reveals that when a successful theory comes into conflict with a methodological scruple, it is generally the scruple that gives way. Accordingly the functionalist has relaxed the behaviorist constraints on psychological explanations. There is probably no better way to decide what is methodologically permissible in science than by investigating what successful science requires.

Computing Machinery and Intelligence

〜

ALAN TURING

Alan Turing (1912–1954) was a British mathematician and major contributor to the foundations of computer science. His theoretical work contributed to the development of the digital computer, and his reflections on artificial intelligence continue to provoke philosophical debate.

1. THE IMITATION GAME

I propose to consider the question, "Can machines think?" This should begin with definitions of the meaning of the terms "machine" and "think." The definitions might be framed so as to reflect so far as possible the normal use of the words, but this attitude is dangerous. If the meaning of the words "machine" and "think" are to be found by examining how they are commonly used it is difficult to escape the conclusion that the meaning and the answer to the question, "Can machines think?" is to be sought in a statistical survey such as a Gallup poll. But this is absurd. Instead of attempting such a definition I shall replace the question by another, which is closely related to it and is expressed in relatively unambiguous words.

The new form of the problem can be described in terms of a game which we call the "imitation game." It is played with three people, a man (A), a woman (B), and an interrogator (C) who may be of either sex. The interrogator stays in a room apart from the other two. The object of the game for the interrogator is to determine which of the other two is the man and which is the woman. He knows them by labels X and Y, and at the end of the game he says either "X is A and Y is B" or "X is B and Y is A." The interrogator is allowed to put questions to A and B thus:

C: Will X please tell me the length of his or her hair?

Now suppose X is actually A, then A must answer. It is A's object in the game to try and cause C to make the wrong identification. His answer might therefore be

"My hair is shingled, and the longest strands are about nine inches long."

In order that tones of voice may not help the interrogator the answers should be written, or better still, typewritten. The ideal arrangement is to have a teleprinter communicating between the two rooms. Alternatively the question and answers can be repeated by an intermediary. The object of the game for the third player (B) is to help the interrogator. The best strategy for her is probably to give truthful answers. She can add such things as "I am the woman, don't listen to him!" to her answers, but it will avail nothing as the man can make similar remarks.

We now ask the question, "What will happen when a machine takes the part of A in this game?" Will the interrogator decide wrongly as often when the game is played like this as he does when the game is played between a man and a woman? These questions replace our original, "Can machines think?"

Reprinted from *Mind, 59* (1950) by permission of Oxford University Press.

2. CRITIQUE OF THE NEW PROBLEM

As well as asking, "What is the answer to this new form of the question," one may ask, "Is this new question a worthy one to investigate?" This latter question we investigate without further ado, thereby cutting short an infinite regress.

The new problem has the advantage of drawing a fairly sharp line between the physical and the intellectual capacities of a man. No engineer or chemist claims to be able to produce a material which is indistinguishable from the human skin. It is possible that at some time this might be done, but even supposing this invention available we should feel there was little point in trying to make a "thinking machine" more human by dressing it up in such artificial flesh. The form in which we have set the problem reflects this fact in the condition which prevents the interrogator from seeing or touching the other competitors, or hearing their voices. Some other advantages of the proposed criterion may be shown up by specimen questions and answers. Thus:

Q: Please write me a sonnet on the subject of the Forth Bridge.
A: Count me out on this one. I never could write poetry.
Q: Add 34957 to 70764
A: (Pause about 30 seconds and then give as answer) 105621.
Q: Do you play chess?
A: Yes.
Q: I have K at my K1, and no other pieces. You have only K at K6 and R at RI. It is your move. What do you play?
A: (After a pause of 15 seconds) R-R8 mate.

The question and answer method seems to be suitable for introducing almost any one of the fields of human endeavour that we wish to include. We do not wish to penalise the machine for its inability to shine in beauty competitions, nor to penalise a man for losing in a race against an aeroplane. The conditions of our game make these disabilities irrelevant. The "witnesses" can brag, if they consider it advisable, as much as they please about their charms, strength or heroism, but the interrogator cannot demand practical demonstrations.

The game may perhaps be criticised on the ground that the odds are weighted too heavily against the machine. If the man were to try and pretend to be the machine he would clearly make a very poor showing. He would be given away at once by slowness and inaccuracy in arithmetic. May not machines carry out something which ought to be described as thinking but which is very different from what a man does? This objection is a very strong one, but at least we can say that if, nevertheless, a machine can be constructed to play the imitation game satisfactorily, we need not be troubled by this objection.

It might be urged that when playing the "imitation game" the best strategy for the machine may possibly be something other than imitation of the behaviour of a man. This may be, but I think it is unlikely that there is any great effect of this kind. In any case there is no intention to investigate here the theory of the game, and it will be assumed that the best strategy is to try to provide answers that would naturally be given by a man.

3. THE MACHINES CONCERNED IN THE GAME

The question which we put in §1 will not be quite definite until we have specified what we mean by the word "machine." It is natural that we should wish to permit every kind of engineering technique to be used in our machines. We also wish to allow the possibility than an engineer or team of engineers may construct a machine which works, but whose manner of operation cannot be satisfactorily described by its constructors because they have applied a method which is largely experimental. Finally, we wish to exclude from the machines men born in the usual manner. It is difficult to frame the definitions so as to satisfy these three conditions. One might for instance insist that the team of engineers should be all of one sex, but this would not really be satisfactory, for it is probably possible to rear a complete individual from a single cell of the skin (say) of a man. To do so would be a feat of biological technique deserving of the very highest praise, but we would not be inclined to regard it as a case of "constructing a thinking machine." This prompts us to abandon the requirement that every kind of technique should be permitted. We are the more ready to do so in view of the fact that the present interest in "thinking machines" has been aroused by a particular kind of machine, usually called an "electronic computer" or "digital computer." Following this suggestion we only permit digital computers to take part in our game.

This restriction appears at first sight to be a very drastic one. I shall attempt to show that it is not so in reality. To do this necessitates a short account of the nature and properties of these computers.

It may also be said that this identification of machines with digital computers, like our criterion for "thinking," will only be unsatisfactory if (contrary to my belief), it turns out that digital computers are unable to give a good showing in the game.

There are already a number of digital computers in working order, and it may be asked, "Why not try the experiment straight away? It would be easy to satisfy the conditions of the game. A number of interrogators could be used, and statistics compiled to show how often the right identification was given." The short answer is that we are not asking whether all digital computers would do well in the game nor whether the computers at present available would do well, but whether there are imaginable computers which would do well. But this is only the short answer. We shall see this question in a different light later.

4.   DIGITAL COMPUTERS

The idea behind digital computers may be explained by saying that these machines are intended to carry out any operations which could be done by a human computer. The human computer is supposed to be following fixed rules; he has no authority to deviate from them in any detail. We may suppose that these rules are supplied in a book, which is altered whenever he is put on to a new job. He has also an unlimited supply of paper on which he does his calculations. He may also do his multiplications and additions on a "desk machine," but this is not important.

If we use the above explanation as a definition we shall be in danger of circularity of argument. We avoid this by giving an outline of the means by which the desired effect is achieved. A digital computer can usually be regarded as consisting of three parts:

   (i) Store.
  (ii) Executive unit.
 (iii) Control.

The store is a store of information, and corresponds to the human computer's paper, whether this is the paper on which he does his calculations or that on which his book of rules is printed. In so far as the human computer does calculations in his head a part of the store will correspond to his memory.

The executive unit is the part which carries out the various individual operations involved in a calculation. What these individual operations are will vary from machine to machine. Usually fairly lengthy operations can be done such as "Multiply 3540675445 by 7076345687" but in some machines only very simple ones such as "Write down 0" are possible.

We have mentioned that the "book of rules" supplied to the computer is replaced in the machine by a part of the store. It is then called the "table of instructions." It is the duty of the control to see that these instructions are obeyed correctly and in the right order. The control is so constructed that this necessarily happens.

The information in the store is usually broken up into packets of moderately small size. In one machine, for instance, a packet might consist of ten decimal digits. Numbers are assigned to the parts of the store in which the various packets of information are stored, in some systematic manner. A typical instruction might say—

"Add the number stored in position 6809 to that in 4302 and put the result back into the latter storage position."

Needless to say it would not occur in the machine expressed in English. It would more likely be coded in a form such as 6809430217. Here 17 says which of various possible operations is to be performed on the two numbers. In this case the operation is that described above, *viz.* "Add the number. . . ." It will be noticed that the instruction takes up 10 digits and so forms one packet of information, very conveniently. The control will normally take the instructions to be obeyed in the order of the positions in which they are stored, but occasionally an instruction such as

"Now obey the instruction stored in position 5606, and continue from there"

may be encountered, or again

"If position 4505 contains 0 obey next the instruction stored in 6707, otherwise continue straight on."

Instructions of these latter types are very important because they make it possible for a sequence of operations to be repeated over and over again until some condition is fulfilled, but in doing so to obey, not fresh instructions on each repetition, but the same ones over and over again. To take a domestic analogy. Suppose Mother wants Tommy to call at the cobbler's every morning on his way to school to see if her shoes are done, she can ask him afresh every morning. Alternatively she can stick up a notice once and for all in the hall which he will see when he leaves for school and which tells him to call for the shoes, and also to destroy the notice when he comes back if he has the shoes with him.

The reader must accept it as a fact that digital computers can be constructed, and indeed have been constructed, according to the principles we have described, and that they can in fact mimic the actions of a human computer very closely.

The book of rules which we have described our human computer as using is of course a convenient fiction. Actual human computers really remember what they have got to do. If one wants to make a machine mimic the behaviour of the human computer in some complex operation one has to ask him how it is done, and then translate the answer into the form of an instruction table. Constructing instruction tables is usually described as "programming." To "programme a machine to carry out the operation A" means to put the appropriate instruction table into the machine so that it will do A.

An interesting variant on the idea of a digital computer is a "digital computer with a random element." These have instructions involving the throwing of a die or some equivalent electronic process; one such instruction might for instance be, "Throw the die and put the resulting number into store 1000." Sometimes such a machine is described as having free will (though I would not use this phrase myself). It is not normally possible to determine from observing a machine whether it has a random element, for a similar effect can be produced by such devices as making the choices depend on the digits of the decimal for π.

Most actual digital computers have only a finite store. There is no theoretical difficulty in the idea of a computer with an unlimited store. Of course only a finite part can have been used at any one time. Likewise only a finite amount can have been constructed, but we can imagine more and more being added as required. Such computers have special theoretical interest and will be called infinitive capacity computers.

The idea of a digital computer is an old one. Charles Babbage, Lucasian Professor of Mathematics at Cambridge from 1828 to 1839, planned such a machine, called the Analytical Engine, but it was never completed. Although Babbage had all the essential ideas, his machine was not at that time such a very attractive prospect. The speed which would have been available would be definitely faster than a human computer but something like 100 times slower than the Manchester machine, itself one of the slower of the modern machines. The storage was to be purely mechanical, using wheels and cards.

The fact that Babbage's Analytical Engine was to be entirely mechanical will help us to rid ourselves of a superstition. Importance is often attached to the fact that modern digital computers are electrical, and that the nervous system also is electrical. Since Babbage's machine was not electrical, and since all digital computers are in a sense equivalent, we see that this use of electricity cannot be of theoretical importance. Of course electricity usually comes in where fast signalling is concerned, so that it is not surprising that we find it in both these connections. In the nervous system chemical phenomena are at least as important as electrical. In certain computers the storage system is mainly acoustic. The feature of using electricity is thus seen to be only a very superficial similarity. If we wish to find such similarities we should look rather for mathematical analogies of function.

5.   UNIVERSALITY OF DIGITAL COMPUTERS

The digital computers considered in the last section may be classified amongst the "discrete state machines." These are the machines which move by sudden jumps or clicks from one quite definite state to another. These states are sufficiently different for the possibility of confusion between them to be ignored. Strictly speaking there are no such machines. Everything really moves continuously. But there are many kinds of machine which can profitably be *thought of* as being discrete state machines. For instance in considering the switches for a lighting system it is a convenient fiction that each switch must be definitely on or definitely off. There must be intermediate positions, but for most purposes we can forget about them. As an example of a discrete state machine we might consider a wheel which clicks round through 120° once a second, but may be stopped by a lever which can be operated from outside; in addition a lamp is to light in one of the positions of the wheel. This machine could be described abstractly as follows. The internal state of the machine (which is described by the position of the wheel) may be q_1, q_2 or q_3. There is an input signal i_0 or i_1 (position of lever). The internal state at any moment is determined by the last state and input signal according to the table

	Last State		
	q_1	q_2	q_3
Input i_0	q_2	q_3	q_1
i_1	q_1	q_2	q_3

The output signals, the only externally visible indication of the internal state (the light) are described by the table

State	q_1	q_2	q_3
Output	o_0	o_0	o_1

This example is typical of discrete state machines. They can be described by such tables provided they have only a finite number of possible states.

It will seem that given the initial state of the machine and the input signals it is always possible to predict all future states. This is reminiscent of Laplace's view that from the complete state of the universe at one moment of time, as described by the positions and velocities of all particles, it should be possible to predict all future states. The prediction which we are considering is, however, rather nearer to practicability than that considered by Laplace. The system of the "universe as a whole" is such that quite small errors in the initial conditions can have an overwhelming effect at a later time. The displacement of a single electron by a billionth of a centimetre at one moment might make the difference between a man being killed by an avalanche a year later, or escaping. It is an essential property of the mechanical systems which we have called "discrete state machines" that this phenomenon does not occur. Even when we consider the actual physical machines instead of the idealised machines, reasonably accurate knowledge of the state at one moment yields reasonably accurate knowledge any number of steps later.

As we have mentioned, digital computers fall within the class of discrete state machines. But the number of states of which such a machine is capable is usually enormously large. For instance, the number for the machine now working at Manchester it about $2^{165,000}$, *i.e.* about $10^{50,000}$. Compare this with our example of the clicking wheel described above, which had three states. It is not difficult to see why the number of states should be so immense. The computer includes a store corresponding to the paper used by a human computer. It must be possible to write into the store any one of the combinations of symbols which might have been written on the paper. For simplicity suppose that only digits from 0 to 9 are used as symbols. Variations in handwriting are ignored. Suppose the computer is allowed 100 sheets of paper each containing 50 lines each with room for 30 digits. Then the number of states is $10^{100 \times 50 \times 30}$, *i.e.*

$10^{150,000}$. This is about the number of states of three Manchester machines put together. The logarithm to the base two of the number of states is usually called the "storage capacity" of the machine. Thus the Manchester machine has a storage capacity of about 165,000 and the wheel machine of our example about 1·6. If two machines are put together their capacities must be added to obtain the capacity of the resultant machine. This leads to the possibility of statements such as "The Manchester machine contains 64 magnetic tracks each with a capacity of 2560, eight electronic tubes with a capacity of 1280. Miscellaneous storage amounts to about 300 making a total of 174,380."

Given the table corresponding to a discrete state machine it is possible to predict what it will do. There is no reason why this calculation should not be carried out by means of a digital computer. Provided it could be carried out sufficiently quickly the digital computer could mimic the behaviour of any discrete state machine. The imitation game could then be played with the machine in question (as B) and the mimicking digital computer (as A) and the interrogator would be unable to distinguish them. Of course the digital computer must have an adequate storage capacity as well as working sufficiently fast. Moreover, it must be programmed afresh for each new machine which it is desired to mimic.

This special property of digital computers, that they can mimic any discrete state machine, is described by saying that they are *universal* machines. The existence of machines with this property has the important consequence that, considerations of speed apart, it is unnecessary to design various new machines to do various computing processes. They can all be done with one digital computer, suitably programmed for each case. It will be seen that as a consequence of this all digital computers are in a sense equivalent.

We may now consider again the point raised at the end of §3. It was suggested tentatively that the question, "Can machines think?" should be replaced by "Are there imaginable digital computers which would do well in the imitation game?" If we wish we can make this superficially more general and ask "Are there discrete state machines which would do

well?" But in view of the universality property we see that either of these questions is equivalent to this, "Let us fix our attention on one particular digital computer C. Is it true that by modifying this computer to have an adequate storage, suitably increasing its speed of action, and providing it with an appropriate programme, C can be made to play satisfactorily the part of A in the imitation game, the part of B being taken by a man?"

6. CONTRARY VIEWS ON THE MAIN QUESTION

We may now consider the ground to have been cleared and we are ready to proceed to the debate on our question, "Can machines think?" and the variant of it quoted at the end of the last section. We cannot altogether abandon the original form of the problem, for opinions will differ as to the appropriateness of the substitution and we must at least listen to what has to be said in this connexion.

It will simplify matters for the reader if I explain first my own beliefs in the matter. Consider first the more accurate form of the question. I believe that in about fifty years' time it will be possible to programme computers, with a storage capacity of about 10^9, to make them play the imitation game so well that an average interrogator will not have more than 70 per cent. chance of making the right identification after five minutes of questioning. The original question, "Can machines think?" I believe to be too meaningless to deserve discussion. Nevertheless I believe that at the end of the century the use of words and general educated opinion will have altered so much that one will be able to speak of machines thinking without expecting to be contradicted. I believe further that no useful purpose is served by concealing these beliefs. The popular view that scientists proceed inexorably from well-established fact to well-established fact, never being influenced by any unproved conjecture, is quite mistaken. Provided it is made clear which are proved facts and which are conjecture, no harm can result. Conjectures are of great importance since they suggest useful lines of research.

I now proceed to consider opinions opposed to my own.

(1) The Theological Objection

Thinking is a function of man's immortal soul. God has given an immortal soul to every man and woman, but not to any other animal or to machines. Hence no animal or machine can think.

I am unable to accept any part of this, but will attempt to reply in theological terms. I should find the argument more convincing if animals were classed with men, for there is a greater difference, to my mind, between the typical animate and the inanimate than there is between man and the other animals. The arbitrary character of the orthodox view becomes clearer if we consider how it might appear to a member of some other religious community. How do Christians regard the Moslem view that women have no souls? But let us leave this point aside and return to the main argument. It appears to me that the argument quoted above implies a serious restriction of the omnipotence of the Almighty. It is admitted that there are certain things that He cannot do such as making one equal to two, but should we not believe that He has freedom to confer a soul on an elephant if He sees fit? We might expect that He would only exercise this power in conjunction with a mutation which provided the elephant with an appropriately improved brain to minister to the needs of this soul. An argument of exactly similar form may be made for the case of machines. It may seem different because it is more difficult to "swallow." But this really only means that we think it would be less likely that He would consider the circumstances suitable for conferring a soul. The circumstances in question are discussed in the rest of this paper. In attempting to construct such machines we should not be irreverently usurping His power of creating souls, any more than we are in the procreation of children: rather we are, in either case, instruments of His will providing mansions for the souls that He creates.

However, this is mere speculation. I am not very impressed with theological arguments whatever they may be used to support. Such arguments have often been found unsatisfactory in the past. In the time of Galileo it was argued that the texts, "And the sun stood still . . . and hasted not to go down about a whole day" (Joshua x. 13) and "He laid the foundations of the earth, that it should not move at any time" (Psalm cv. 5) were an adequate refutation of the Copernican theory. With our present knowledge such an argument appears futile. When that knowledge was not available it made a quite different impression.

(2) The "Heads in the Sand" Objection

"The consequences of machines thinking would be too dreadful. Let us hope and believe that they cannot do so."

This argument is seldom expressed quite so openly as in the form above. But it affects most of us who think about it at all. We like to believe that Man is in some subtle way superior to the rest of creation. It is best if he can be shown to be *necessarily* superior, for then there is no danger of him losing his commanding position. The popularity of the theological argument is clearly connected with this feeling. It is likely to be quite strong in intellectual people, since they value the power of thinking more highly than others, and are more inclined to base their belief in the superiority of Man on this power.

I do not think that this argument is sufficiently substantial to require refutation. Consolation would be more appropriate: perhaps this should be sought in the transmigration of souls.

(3) The Mathematical Objection

There are a number of results of mathematical logic which can be used to show that there are limitations to the powers of discrete-state machines. The best known of these results is known as Gödel's theorem, and shows that in any sufficiently powerful logical system statements can be formulated which can neither be proved nor disproved within the system, unless possibly the system itself is inconsistent. There are other, in some respects similar, results due to Church, Kleene, Rosser, and Turing. The latter result is the most convenient to consider, since it refers directly to machines, whereas the others can only be used in a comparatively indirect argument: for instance if Gödel's theorem is to be used we need in addition to have some means of describing logical systems in terms of machines, and machines in terms of logical systems. The result in question refers to a type of machine which is essentially a digital computer with an infinite capacity. It states that there are certain things that such a machine cannot do. If it is rigged up to give answers to questions as in the imitation game, there will be some questions to which it will either give a wrong answer, or fail to give an answer at all however much time is allowed for a reply. There may, of course, be many such questions, and questions which cannot be answered by one machine may be satisfactorily answered by another. We are of course supposing for the present that the questions are of the kind to which an answer "Yes" or "No" is appropriate, rather than questions such as "What do you think of Picasso?" The questions that we know the machines must fail on are of this type, "Consider the machine specified as follows. . . . Will this machine ever answer 'Yes' to any question?" The dots are to be replaced by a description of some machine in a standard form, which could be something like that used in §5. When the machine described bears a certain comparatively simple relation to the machine which is under interrogation, it can be shown that the answer is either wrong or not forthcoming. This is the mathematical result: it is argued that it proves a disability of machines to which the human intellect is not subject.

The short answer to this argument is that although it is established that there are limitations to the powers of any particular machine, it has only been stated, without any sort of proof, that no such limitations apply to the human intellect. But I do not think this view can be dismissed quite so lightly. Whenever one of these machines is asked the appropriate critical question, and gives a definite answer, we know that this answer must be wrong, and this gives us a certain feeling of superiority. Is this feeling illusory? It is no doubt quite genuine, but I do not think too much importance should be attached to it. We too often give wrong answers to questions ourselves to be justified in being very pleased at such evidence of fallibility on the part of the machines. Further, our superiority can only be felt on such an occasion in relation to the one machine over which we have scored our petty triumph. There would be no question of triumphing simultaneously over *all* machines. In short,

then, there might be men cleverer than any given machine, but then again there might be other machines cleverer again, and so on.

Those who hold to the mathematical argument would, I think, mostly be willing to accept the imitation game as a basis for discussion. Those who believe in the two previous objections would probably not be interested in any criteria.

(4) The Argument from Consciousness

This argument is very well expressed in Professor Jefferson's Lister Oration for 1949, from which I quote. "Not until a machine can write a sonnet or compose a concerto because of thoughts and emotions felt, and not by the chance fall of symbols, could we agree that machine equals brain—that is, not only write it but know that it had written it. No mechanism could feel (and not merely artificially signal, an easy contrivance) pleasure at its successes, grief when its valves fuse, be warmed by flattery, be made miserable by its mistakes, be charmed by sex, be angry or depressed when it cannot get what it wants."

This argument appears to be a denial of the validity of our test. According to the most extreme form of this view the only way by which one could be sure that a machine thinks is to *be* the machine and to feel oneself thinking. One could then describe these feelings to the world, but of course no one would be justified in taking any notice. Likewise according to this view the only way to know that a *man* thinks is to be that particular man. It is in fact the solipsist point of view. It may be the most logical view to hold but it makes communication of ideas difficult. A is liable to believe "A thinks but B does not" whilst B believes "B thinks but A does not." Instead of arguing continually over this point it is usual to have the polite convention that everyone thinks.

I am sure that Professor Jefferson does not wish to adopt the extreme and solipsist point of view. Probably he would be quite willing to accept the imitation game as a test. The game (with the player B omitted) is frequently used in practice under the name of viva voce to discover whether some one really understands something or has "learnt it parrot fashion." Let us listen in to a part of such a viva voce:

Interrogator: In the first line of your sonnet which reads "Shall I compare thee to a summer's day," would not "a spring day" do as well or better?

Witness: It wouldn't scan.

Interrogator: How about "a winter's day"? That would scan all right.

Witness: Yes, but nobody wants to be compared to a winter's day.

Interrogator: Would you say Mr. Pickwick reminded you of Christmas?

Witness: In a way.

Interrogator: Yet Christmas is a winter's day, and I do not think Mr. Pickwick would mind the comparison.

Witness: I don't think you're serious. By a winter's day one means a typical winter's day, rather than a special one like Christmas.

And so on. What would Professor Jefferson say if the sonnet-writing machine was able to answer like this in the viva voce? I do not know whether he would regard the machine as "merely artificially signalling" these answers, but if the answers were as satisfactory and sustained as in the above passage I do not think he would describe it as "an easy contrivance." This phrase is, I think, intended to cover such devices as the inclusion in the machine of a record of someone reading a sonnet, with appropriate switching to turn it on from time to time.

In short then, I think that most of those who support the argument from consciousness could be persuaded to abandon it rather than be forced into the solipsist position. They will then probably be willing to accept our test.

I do not wish to give the impression that I think there is no mystery about consciousness. There is, for instance, something of a paradox connected with any attempt to localise it. But I do not think these mysteries necessarily need to be solved before we can answer the question with which we are concerned in this paper.

(5) Arguments from Various Disabilities

These arguments take the form, "I grant you that you can make machines do all the things you have mentioned but you will never be able to make one to do X." Numerous features X are suggested in this connexion. I offer a selection:

> Be kind, resourceful, beautiful, friendly, have initiative, have a sense of humour, tell right from wrong, make mistakes, fall in love, enjoy strawberries and cream, make some one fall in love with it, learn from experience, use words properly, be the subject of its own thought, have as much diversity of behaviour as a man, do something really new. . . .

No support is usually offered for these statements. I believe they are mostly founded on the principle of scientific induction. A man has seen thousands of machines in his lifetime. From what he sees of them he draws a number of general conclusions. They are ugly, each is designed for a very limited purpose, when required for a minutely different purpose they are useless, the variety of behaviour of any one of them is very small, etc., etc. Naturally he concludes that these are necessary properties of machines in general. Many of these limitations are associated with the very small storage capacity of most machines. (I am assuming that the idea of storage capacity is extended in some way to cover machines other than discrete-state machines. The exact definition does not matter as no mathematical accuracy is claimed in the present discussion.) A few years ago, when very little had been heard of digital computers, it was possible to elicit much incredulity concerning them, if one mentioned their properties without describing their construction. That was presumably due to a similar application of the principle of scientific induction. These applications of the principle are of course largely unconscious. When a burnt child fears the fire and shows that he fears it by avoiding it, I should say that he was applying scientific induction. (I could of course also describe his behaviour in many other ways.) The works and customs of mankind do not seem to be very suitable material to which to apply scientific induction. A very large part of space-time must be investigated, if reliable results are to be obtained. Otherwise we may (as most English children do) decide that everybody speaks English, and that it is silly to learn French.

There are, however, special remarks to be made

about many of the disabilities that have been mentioned. The inability to enjoy strawberries and cream may have struck the reader as frivolous. Possibly a machine might be made to enjoy this delicious dish, but any attempt to make one do so would be idiotic. What is important about this disability is that it contributes to some of the other disabilities, *e.g.* to the difficulty of the same kind of friendliness occurring between man and machine as between white man and white man, or between black man and black man.

The claim that "machines cannot make mistakes" seems a curious one. One is tempted to retort, "Are they any the worse for that?" But let us adopt a more sympathetic attitude, and try to see what is really meant. I think this criticism can be explained in terms of the imitation game. It is claimed that the interrogator could distinguish the machine from the man simply by setting them a number of problems in arithmetic. The machine would be unmasked because of its deadly accuracy. The reply to this is simple. The machine (programmed for playing the game) would not attempt to give the *right* answers to the arithmetic problems. It would deliberately introduce mistakes in a manner calculated to confuse the interrogator. A mechanical fault would probably show itself through an unsuitable decision as to what sort of a mistake to make in the arithmetic. Even this interpretation of the criticism is not sufficiently sympathetic. But we cannot afford the space to go into it much further. It seems to me that this criticism depends on a confusion between two kinds of mistake. We may call them "errors of functioning" and "errors of conclusion." Errors of functioning are due to some mechanical or electrical fault which causes the machine to behave otherwise than it was designed to do. In philosophical discussions one likes to ignore the possibility of such errors; one is therefore discussing "abstract machines." These abstract machines are mathematical fictions rather than physical objects. By definition they are incapable of errors of functioning. In this sense we can truly say that "machines can never make mistakes." Errors of conclusion can only arise when some meaning is attached to the output signals from the machine. The machine might, for instance, type out mathematical equations, or sentences in English. When a false proposition is typed we say that the

machine has committed an error of conclusion. There is clearly no reason at all for saying that a machine cannot make this kind of mistake. It might do nothing but type out repeatedly "0 = 1." To take a less perverse example, it might have some method for drawing conclusions by scientific induction. We must expect such a method to lead occasionally to erroneous results.

The claim that a machine cannot be the subject of its own thought can of course only be answered if it can be shown that the machine has *some* thought with *some* subject matter. Nevertheless, "the subject matter of a machine's operations" does seem to mean something, at least to the people who deal with it. If, for instance, the machine was trying to find a solution of the equation $x^2 - 40x - 11 = 0$ one would be tempted to describe this equation as part of the machine's subject matter at that moment. In this sort of sense a machine undoubtedly can be its own subject matter. It may be used to help in making up its own programmes, or to predict the effect of alterations in its own structure. By observing the results of its own behaviour it can modify its own programmes so as to achieve some purpose more effectively. These are possibilities of the near future, rather than Utopian dreams.

The criticism that a machine cannot have much diversity of behaviour is just a way of saying that it cannot have much storage capacity. Until fairly recently a storage capacity of even a thousand digits was very rare.

The criticisms that we are considering here are often disguised forms of the argument from consciousness. Usually if one maintains that a machine *can* do one of these things, and describes the kind of method that the machine could use, one will not make much of an impression. It is thought that the method (whatever it may be, for it must be mechanical) is really rather base. Compare the parenthesis in Jefferson's statement quoted on p. 21.

(6) Lady Lovelace's Objection

Our most detailed information of Babbage's Analytical Engine comes from a memoir by Lady Lovelace. In it she states, "The Analytical Engine has no pretensions to *originate* anything. It can do *whatever we know how to order it* to perform" (her italics). This statement is quoted by Hartree who adds: "This does not imply that it may not be possible to construct electronic equipment which will 'think for itself,' or in which, in biological terms, one could set up a conditioned reflex, which would serve as a basis for 'learning.' Whether this is possible in principle or not is a stimulating and exciting question, suggested by some of these recent developments. But it did not seem that the machines constructed or projected at the time had this property."

I am in thorough agreement with Hartree over this. It will be noticed that he does not assert that the machines in question had not got the property, but rather that the evidence available to Lady Lovelace did not encourage her to believe that they had it. It is quite possible that the machines in question had in a sense got this property. For suppose that some discrete-state machine has the property. The Analytical Engine was a universal digital computer, so that, if its storage capacity and speed were adequate, it could by suitable programming be made to mimic the machine in question. Probably this argument did not occur to the Countess or to Babbage. In any case there was no obligation on them to claim all that could be claimed.

This whole question will be considered again under the heading of learning machines.

A variant of Lady Lovelace's objection states that a machine can "never do anything really new." This may be parried for a moment with the saw, "There is nothing new under the sun." Who can be certain that "original work" that he has done was not simply the growth of the seed planted in him by teaching, or the effect of following well-known general principles. A better variant of the objection says that a machine can never "take us by surprise." This statement is a more direct challenge and can be met directly. Machines take me by surprise with great frequency. This is largely because I do not do sufficient calculation to decide what to expect them to do, or rather because, although I do a calculation, I do it in a hurried, slipshod fashion, taking risks. Perhaps I say to myself, "I suppose the voltage here ought to be the same as there: anyway let's assume it is." Naturally I am often wrong, and the result is a surprise for me for by the time the experiment is done these assumptions have been forgotten. These admissions lay me open to lectures on the subject of my vicious ways, but do not throw any doubt on my credibility when I testify to the surprises I experience.

I do not expect this reply to silence my critic. He will probably say that such surprises are due to some creative mental act on my part, and reflect no credit on the machine. This leads us back to the argument from consciousness, and far from the idea of surprise. It is a line of argument we must consider closed, but it is perhaps worth remarking that the appreciation of something as surprising requires as much of a "creative mental act" whether the surprising event originates from a man, a book, a machine or anything else.

The view that machines cannot give rise to surprises is due, I believe, to a fallacy to which philosophers and mathematicians are particularly subject. This is the assumption that as soon as a fact is presented to a mind all consequences of that fact spring into the mind simultaneously with it. It is a very useful assumption under many circumstances, but one too easily forgets that it is false. A natural consequence of doing so is that one then assumes that there is no virtue in the mere working out of consequences from data and general principles.

(7) Argument from Continuity in the Nervous System

The nervous system is certainly not a discrete-state machine. A small error in the information about the size of a nervous impulse impinging on a neuron, may make a large difference to the size of the outgoing impulse. It may be argued that, this being so, one cannot expect to be able to mimic the behaviour of the nervous system with a discrete-state system.

It is true that a discrete-state machine must be different from a continuous machine. But if we adhere to the conditions of the imitation game, the interrogator will not be able to take any advantage of this difference. The situation can be made clearer if we consider some other simpler continuous machine. A differential analyser will do very well. (A differential analyser is a certain kind of machine not of the discrete-state type used for some kinds of calculation.) Some of these provide their answers in a typed form, and so are suitable for taking part in the game. It would not be possible for a digital computer to predict exactly what answers the differential analyser would give to a problem, but it would be quite capable of giving the right sort of answer. For instance, if asked to give the value of π (actually about 3.1416) it would be reasonable to choose at random between the values 3.12, 3.13, 3.14, 3.15, 3.16 with the probabilities of 0.05, 0.15, 0.55, 0.19, 0.06 (say). Under these circumstances it would be very difficult for the interrogator to distinguish the differential analyser from the digital computer.

(8) The Argument from Informality of Behaviour

It is not possible to produce a set of rules purporting to describe what a man should do in every conceivable set of circumstances. One might for instance have a rule that one is to stop when one sees a red traffic light, and to go if one sees a green one, but what if by some fault both appear together? One may perhaps decide that it is safest to stop. But some further difficulty may well arise from this decision later. To attempt to provide rules of conduct to cover every eventuality, even those arising from traffic lights, appears to be impossible. With all this I agree.

From this it is argued that we cannot be machines. I shall try to reproduce the argument, but I fear I shall hardly do it justice. It seems to run something like this. "If each man had a definite set of rules of conduct by which he regulated his life he would be no better than a machine. But there are no such rules, so men cannot be machines." The undistributed middle is glaring. I do not think the argument is ever put quite like this, but I believe this is the argument used nevertheless. There may however be a certain confusion between "rules of conduct" and "laws of behaviour" to cloud the issue. By "rules of conduct" I mean precepts such as "Stop if you see red lights," on which one can act, and of which one can be conscious. By "laws of behaviour" I mean laws of nature as applied to a man's body such as "if you pinch him he will squeak." If we substitute "laws of behaviour which regulate his life" for "laws of conduct by

which he regulates his life" in the argument quoted the undistributed middle is no longer insuperable. For we believe that it is not only true that being regulated by laws of behaviour implies being some sort of machine (though not necessarily a discrete-state machine), but that conversely being such a machine implies being regulated by such laws. However, we cannot so easily convince ourselves of the absence of complete laws of behaviour as of complete rules of conduct. The only way we know of for finding such laws is scientific observation, and we certainly know of no circumstances under which we could say, "We have searched enough. There are no such laws."

We can demonstrate more forcibly that any such statement would be unjustified. For suppose we could be sure of finding such laws if they existed. Then given a discrete-state machine it should certainly be possible to discover by observation sufficient about it to predict its future behaviour, and this within a reasonable time, say a thousand years. But this does not seem to be the case. I have set up on the Manchester computer a small programme using only 1000 units of storage, whereby the machine supplied with one sixteen figure number replies with another within two seconds. I would defy anyone to learn from these replies sufficient about the programme to be able to predict any replies to untried values. . . .

7.   LEARNING MACHINES

The reader will have anticipated that I have no very convincing arguments of a positive nature to support my views. If I had I should not have taken such pains to point out the fallacies in contrary views. Such evidence as I have I shall now give.

Let us return for a moment to Lady Lovelace's objection, which stated that the machine can only do what we tell it to do. One could say that a man can "inject" an idea into the machine, and that it will respond to a certain extent and then drop into quiescence, like a piano string struck by a hammer. Another simile would be an atomic pile of less than critical size: an injected idea is to correspond to a neutron entering the pile from without. Each such neutron will cause a certain disturbance which eventually dies away. If, however, the size of the pile is sufficiently increased, the disturbance caused by such an incoming neutron will very likely go on and on increasing until the whole pile is destroyed. Is there a corresponding phenomenon for minds, and is there one for machines? There does seem to be one for the human mind. The majority of them seem to be "sub-critical," i.e. to correspond in this analogy to piles of subcritical size. An idea presented to such a mind will on average give rise to less than one idea in reply. A smallish proportion are super-critical. An idea presented to such a mind may give rise to a whole "theory" consisting of secondary, tertiary and more remote ideas. Animals minds seem to be very definitely sub-critical. Adhering to this analogy we ask, "Can a machine be made to be super-critical?"

The "skin of an onion" analogy is also helpful. In considering the functions of the mind or the brain we find certain operations which we can explain in purely mechanical terms. This we say does not correspond to the real mind: it is a sort of skin which we must strip off if we are to find the real mind. But then in what remains we find a further skin to be stripped off, and so on. Proceeding in this way do we ever come to the "real" mind, or do we eventually come to the skin which has nothing in it? In the latter case the whole mind is mechanical. (It would not be a discrete-state machine however. We have discussed this.)

These last two paragraphs do not claim to be convincing arguments. They should rather be described as "recitations tending to produce belief."

The only really satisfactory support that can be given for the view expressed at the beginning of §6, will be that provided by waiting for the end of the century and then doing the experiment described. But what can we say in the meantime? What steps should be taken now if the experiment is to be successful?

As I have explained, the problem is mainly one of programming. Advances in engineering will have to be made too, but it seems unlikely that these will not be adequate for the requirements. Estimates of the storage capacity of the brain vary from 10^{10} to 10^{15} binary digits. I incline to the lower values and believe that only a very small fraction is used for the higher types of thinking. Most of it is probably used for the retention of visual impressions. I should be surprised if more than 10^9 was required for satisfactory playing

of the imitation game, at any rate against a blind man. (Note—The capacity of the *Encyclopaedia Britannica,* 11th edition, is 2×10^9.) A storage capacity of 10^7 would be a very practicable possibility even by present techniques. It is probably not necessary to increase the speed of operations of the machines at all. Parts of modern machines which can be regarded as analogues of nerve cells work about a thousand times faster than the latter. This should provide a "margin of safety" which could cover losses of speed arising in many ways. Our problem then is to find out how to programme these machines to play the game. At my present rate of working I produce about a thousand digits of programme a day, so that about sixty workers, working steadily through the fifty years might accomplish the job, if nothing went into the waste-paper basket. Some more expeditious method seems desirable.

In the process of trying to imitate an adult human mind we are bound to think a good deal about the process which has brought it to the state that it is in. We may notice three components,

(*a*) The initial state of the mind, say at birth,
(*b*) The education to which it has been subjected,
(*c*) Other experience, not to be described as education, to which it has been subjected.

Instead of trying to produce a programme to simulate the adult mind, why not rather try to produce one which simulates the child's? If this were then subjected to an appropriate course of education one would obtain the adult brain. Presumably the child-brain is something like a note-book as one buys it from the stationers. Rather little mechanism, and lots of blank sheets. (Mechanism and writing are from our point of view almost synonymous.) Our hope is that there is so little mechanism in the child-brain that something like it can be easily programmed. The amount of work in the education we can assume, as a first approximation, to be much the same as for the human child.

We have thus divided our problem into two parts. The child-programme and the education process. These two remain very closely connected. We cannot expect to find a good child-machine at the first attempt. One must experiment with teaching one such machine and see how well it learns. One can then try another and see if it is better or worse. There is an obvious connection between this process and evolution, by the identifications

Structure of the child machine = Hereditary material
Changes „   „   = Mutations
Natural selection   = Judgment of the experimenter

One may hope, however, that this process will be more expeditious than evolution. The survival of the fittest is a slow method for measuring advantages. The experimenter, by the exercise of intelligence, should be able to speed it up. Equally important is the fact that he is not restricted to random mutations. If he can trace a cause for some weakness he can probably think of the kind of mutation which will improve it.

It will not be possible to apply exactly the same teaching process to the machine as to a normal child. It will not, for instance, be provided with legs, so that it could not be asked to go out and fill the coal scuttle. Possibly it might not have eyes. But however well these deficiencies might be overcome by clever engineering, one could not send the creature to school without the other children making excessive fun of it. It must be given some tuition. We need not be too concerned about the legs, eyes, etc. The example of Miss Helen Keller shows that education can take place provided that communication in both directions between teacher and pupil can take place by some means or other.

We normally associate punishments and rewards with the teaching process. Some simple child-machines can be constructed or programmed on this sort of principle. The machine has to be so constructed that events which shortly preceded the occurrence of a punishment-signal are unlikely to be repeated, whereas a reward-signal increased the probability of repetition of the events which led up to it. These definitions do not presuppose any feelings on the part of the machine. I have done some experiments with one such child-machine, and succeeded in teaching it a few things, but the teaching method was too unorthodox for the experiment to be considered really successful.

The use of punishments and rewards can at best be a part of the teaching process. Roughly speaking, if the teacher has no other means of communicating to the pupil, the amount of information which can reach him does not exceed the total number of rewards and punishments applied. By the time a child has learnt to repeat "Casabianca" he would probably feel very sore indeed, if the text could only be discovered by a "Twenty Questions" technique, every "NO" taking the form of a blow. It is necessary therefore to have some other "unemotional" channels of communication. If these are available it is possible to teach a machine by punishments and rewards to obey orders given in some language, e.g. a symbolic language. These orders are to be transmitted through the "unemotional" channels. The use of this language will diminish greatly the number of punishments and rewards required.

Opinions may vary as to the complexity which is suitable in the child machine. One might try to make it as simple as possible consistently with the general principles. Alternatively one might have a complete system of logical inference "built in."[1] In the latter case the store would be largely occupied with definitions and propositions. The propositions would have various kinds of status, e.g. well-established facts, conjectures, mathematically proved theorems, statements given by an authority, expressions having the logical form of proposition but not belief-value. Certain propositions may be described as "imperatives." The machine should be so constructed that as soon as an imperative is classed as "well-established" the appropriate action automatically takes place. To illustrate this, suppose the teacher says to the machine, "Do your homework now." This may cause "Teacher says 'Do your homework now'" to be included amongst the well-established facts. Another such fact might be, "Everything that teacher says is true." Combining these may eventually lead to the imperative, "Do your homework now," being included amongst the well-established facts, and this, by the construction of the machine, will mean that the homework actually gets started, but the effect is very satisfactory. The processes of inference used by the machine need not be such as would satisfy the most exacting logicians. There might for instance be no hierarchy of types. But this need not mean that type fallacies will occur, any more than we are bound to fall over unfenced cliffs. Suitable imperatives (expressed *within* the systems, not forming part of the rules of the system) such as "Do not use a class unless it is a subclass of one which has been mentioned by teacher' can have a similar effect to "Do not go too near the edge."

The imperatives that can be obeyed by a machine that has no limbs are bound to be of a rather intellectual character, as in the example (doing homework) given above. Important amongst such imperatives will be ones which regulate the order in which the rules of the logical system concerned are to be applied. For at each stage when one is using a logical system, there is a very large number of alternative steps, any of which one is permitted to apply, so far as obedience to the rules of the logical system is concerned. These choices make the difference between a brilliant and a footling reasoner, not the difference between a sound and a fallacious one. Propositions leading to imperatives of this kind might be "When Socrates is mentioned, use the syllogism in Barbara" or "If one method has been proved to be quicker than another, do not use the slower method." Some of these may be "given by authority," but others may be produced by the machine itself, e.g. by scientific induction.

The idea of a learning machine may appear paradoxical to some readers. How can the rules of operation of the machine change? They should describe completely how the machine will react whatever its history might be, whatever changes it might undergo. The rules are thus quite time-invariant. This is quite true. The explanation of the paradox is that the rules which get changed in the learning process are of a rather less pretentious kind, claiming only an ephemeral validity. The reader may draw a parallel with the Constitution of the United States.

An important feature of a learning machine is that its teacher will often be very largely ignorant of quite what is going on inside, although he may still be able to some extent to predict his pupil's behaviour. This should apply most strongly to the later education of a machine arising from a child-machine of well-tried design (or programme). This is in clear contrast with

normal procedure when using a machine to do computations: one's object is then to have a clear mental picture of the state of the machine at each moment in the computation. This object can only be achieved with a struggle. The view that "the machine can only do what we know how to order it to do,"[2] appears strange in face of this. Most of the programmes which we can put into the machine will result in its doing something that we cannot make sense of at all, or which we regard as completely random behaviour. Intelligent behaviour presumably consists in a departure from the completely disciplined behaviour involved in computation, but a rather slight one, which does not give rise to random behaviour, or to pointless repetitive loops. Another important result of preparing our machine for its part in the imitation game by a process of teaching and learning is that "human fallibility" is likely to be omitted in a rather natural way, *i.e.* without special "coaching." . . . Processes that are learnt do not produce a hundred per cent. certainty of result; if they did they could not be unlearnt.

It is probably wise to include a random element in a learning machine. Λ random element is rather useful when we are searching for a solution of some problem. Suppose for instance we wanted to find a number between 50 and 200 which was equal to the square of the sum of its digits, we might start at 51 then try 52 and go on until we got a number that worked. Alternatively we might choose numbers at random until we got a a good one. This method has the advantage that it is unnecessary to keep track of the values that have been tried, but the disadvantage that one may try the same one twice, but this is not very important if there are several solutions. The systematic method has the disadvantage that there may be an enormous block without any solutions in the region which has to be investigated first. Now the learning process may be regarded as a search for a form of behaviour which will satisfy the teacher (or some other criterion). Since there is probably a very large number of satisfactory solutions the random method seems to be better than the systematic. It should be noticed that it is used in the analogous process of evolution. But there the systematic method is not possible. How could one keep track of the different genetical combinations that had been tried, so as to avoid trying them again?

We may hope that machines will eventually compete with men in all purely intellectual fields. But which are the best ones to start with? Even this is a difficult decision. Many people think that a very abstract activity, like the playing of chess, would be best. It can also be maintained that it is best to provide the machine with the best sense organs that money can buy, and then teach it to understand and speak English. This process could follow the normal teaching of a child. Things would be pointed out and named, etc. Again I do not know what the right answer is, but I think both approaches should be tried.

We can only see a short distance ahead, but we can see plenty there that needs to be done.

NOTES

1. Or rather "programmed in" for our child-machine will be programmed in a digital computer. But the logical system will not have to be learnt.

2. Compare Lady Lovelace's statement, which does not contain the word "only."

Can Computers Think?

JOHN SEARLE

John R. Searle is professor of philosophy at the University of California at Berkeley. He is well known for his writing on speech acts and his critique of artificial intelligence. His books include *Speech Acts: An Essay in the Philosophy of Language, Intentionality: An Essay in the Philosophy of Mind,* and *The Rediscovery of the Mind.*

Though we do not know in detail how the brain functions, we do know enough to have an idea of the general relationships between brain processes and mental processes. Mental processes are caused by the behaviour of elements of the brain. At the same time, they are realised in the structure that is made up of those elements. I think this answer is consistent with the standard biological approaches to biological phenomena. Indeed, it is a kind of commonsense answer to the question, given what we know about how the world works. However, it is very much a minority point of view. The prevailing view in philosophy, psychology, and artificial intelligence is one which emphasises the analogies between the functioning of the human brain and the functioning of digital computers. According to the most extreme version of this view, the brain is just a digital computer and the mind is just a computer program. One could summarise this view—I call it "strong artificial intelligence," or "strong AI"—by saying that the mind is to the brain, as the program is to the computer hardware.

This view has the consequence that there is nothing essentially biological about the human mind. The brain just happens to be one of an indefinitely large number of different kinds of hardware computers that could sustain the programs which make up human intelligence. On this view, any physical system whatever that had the right program with the right inputs and outputs would have a mind in exactly the same sense that you and I have minds. So, for example, if you made a computer out of old beer cans powered by windmills; if it had the right program, it would have to have a mind. And the point is not that for all we know it might have thoughts and feelings, but rather that it must have thoughts and feelings, because that is all there is to having thoughts and feelings: implementing the right program.

Most people who hold this view think we have not yet designed programs which are minds. But there is pretty much general agreement among them that it's only a matter of time until computer scientists and workers in artificial intelligence design the appropriate hardware and programs which will be the equivalent of human brains and minds. These will be artificial brains and minds which are in every way the equivalent of human brains and minds.

Many people outside of the field of artificial intelligence are quite amazed to discover that anybody could believe such a view as this. So, before criticising it, let me give you a few examples of the things that people in this field have actually said. Herbert Simon of Carnegie-Mellon University says that we already have machines that can literally think. There is no question of waiting for some future machine, because existing digital computers already have thoughts in exactly the same sense that you and I do. Well, fancy that! Philosophers have been worried for centuries about whether or not a machine could think, and now we discover that they already have such machines at Carnegie-Mellon. Simon's colleague Alan Newell claims that we have now discovered (and notice that Newell says "discovered" and not "hypothesised" or "considered the possibility," but we have *discovered*) that intelligence is just a matter of physical symbol manipulation; it has no essential connection with any specific kind of biological or physical wetware or hardware. Rather, any system whatever that is capable of manipulating physical symbols in the right way is capable of intelligence in the same literal sense as human intelligence of human beings. Both Simon and Newell, to their credit, emphasise that there is nothing metaphorical about these claims; they mean them quite literally. Freeman Dyson is quoted as having said that computers have an advantage over the rest of us when it comes to evolution. Since conscious-

ness is just a matter of formal processes, in computers these formal processes can go on in substances that are much better able to survive in a universe that is cooling off than beings like ourselves made of our wet and messy materials. Marvin Minsky of MIT says that the next generation of computers will be so intelligent that we will "be lucky if they are willing to keep us around the house as household pets." My all-time favourite in the literature of exaggerated claims on behalf of the digital computer is from John McCarthy, the inventor of the term "artificial intelligence." McCarthy says even "machines as simple as thermostats can be said to have beliefs." And indeed, according to him, almost any machine capable of problem-solving can be said to have beliefs. I admire McCarthy's courage. I once asked him: "What beliefs does your thermostat have?" And he said: "My thermostat has three beliefs—it's too hot in here, it's too cold in here, and it's just right in here." As a philosopher, I like all these claims for a simple reason. Unlike most philosophical theses, they are reasonably clear, and they admit of a simple and decisive refutation. It is this refutation that I am going to undertake in this chapter.

The nature of the refutation has nothing whatever to do with any particular stage of computer technology. It is important to emphasise this point because the temptation is always to think that the solution to our problems must wait on some as yet uncreated technological wonder. But in fact, the nature of the refutation is completely independent of any state of technology. It has to do with the very definition of a digital computer, with what a digital computer is.

It is essential to our conception of a digital computer that its operations can be specified purely formally; that is, we specify the steps in the operation of the computer in terms of abstract symbols— sequences of zeroes and ones printed on a tape, for example. A typical computer "rule" will determine symbol on its tape, then it will perform a certain operation such as erasing the symbol or printing another symbol and then enter another state such as moving the tape one square to the left. But the symbols have no meaning; they have no semantic content; they are not about anything. They have to be specified purely in terms of their formal or syntactical structure. The zeroes and ones, for example, are just numerals; they don't even stand for numbers. Indeed, it is this feature of digital computers that makes them so powerful. One and the same type of hardware, if it is appropriately designed, can be used to run an indefinite range of different programs. And one and the same program can be run on an indefinite range of different types of hardwares.

But this feature of programs, that they are defined purely formally or syntactically, is fatal to the view that mental processes and program processes are identical. And the reason can be stated quite simply. There is more to having a mind than having formal or syntactical processes. Our internal mental states, by definition, have certain sorts of contents. If I am thinking about Kansas City or wishing that I had a cold beer to drink or wondering if there will be a fall in interest rates, in each case my mental state has a certain mental content in addition to whatever formal features it might have. That is, even if my thoughts occur to me in strings of symbols, there must be more to the thought than the abstract strings, because strings by themselves can't have any meaning. If my thoughts are to be *about* anything, then the strings must have a *meaning* which makes the thoughts about those things. In a word, the mind has more than a syntax, it has a semantics. The reason that no computer program can ever be a mind is simply that a computer program is only syntactical, and minds are more than syntactical. Minds are semantical, in the sense that they have more than a formal structure, they have a content.

To illustrate this point I have designed a certain thought-experiment. Imagine that a bunch of computer programmers have written a program that will enable a computer to simulate the understanding of Chinese. So, for example, if the computer is given a question in Chinese, it will match the question against its memory, or data base, and produce appropriate answers to the questions in Chinese. Suppose for the sake of argument that the computer's answers are as good as those of a native Chinese speaker. Now then, does the computer, on the basis of this, understand Chinese, does it literally understand Chinese, in the way that Chinese speakers understand Chinese? Well, imagine that you are locked in a room,

and in this room are several baskets full of Chinese symbols. Imagine that you (like me) do not understand a word of Chinese, but that you are given a rule book in English for manipulating these Chinese symbols. The rules specify the manipulations of the symbols purely formally, in terms of their syntax, not their semantics. So the rule might say: "Take a squiggle-squiggle sign out of basket number one and put it next to a squoggle-squoggle sign from basket number two." Now suppose that some other Chinese symbols are passed into the room, and that you are given further rules for passing back Chinese symbols out of the room. Suppose that unknown to you the symbols passed into the room are called 'questions' by the people outside the room, and the symbols you pass back out of the room are called "answers to the questions." Suppose, furthermore, that the programmers are so good at designing the programs and that you are so good at manipulating the symbols, that very soon your answers are indistinguishable from those of a native Chinese speaker. There you are locked in your room shuffling your Chinese symbols and passing out Chinese symbols in response to incoming Chinese symbols. On the basis of the situation as I have described it, there is no way you could learn any Chinese simply by manipulating these formal symbols.

Now the point of the story is simply this: by virtue of implementing a formal computer program from the point of view of an outside observer, you behave exactly as if you understood Chinese, but all the same you don't understand a word of Chinese. But if going through the appropriate computer program for understanding Chinese is not enough to give *you* an understanding of Chinese, then it is not enough to give *any other digital computer* an understanding of Chinese. And again, the reason for this can be stated quite simply. If you don't understand Chinese, then no other computer could understand Chinese because no digital computer, just by virtue of running a program, has anything that you don't have. All that the computer has, as you have, is a formal program for manipulating uninterpreted Chinese symbols. To repeat, a computer has a syntax, but no semantics. The whole point of the parable of the Chinese room is to remind us of a fact that we knew all along.

Understanding a language, or indeed, having mental states at all, involves more than just having a bunch of formal symbols. It involves having an interpretation, or a meaning attached to those symbols. And a digital computer, as defined, cannot have more than just formal symbols because the operation of the computer, as I said earlier, is defined in terms of its ability to implement programs. And these programs are purely formally specifiable—that is, they have no semantic content.

We can see the force of this argument if we contrast what it is like to be asked and to answer questions in English, and to be asked and to answer questions in some language where we have no knowledge of any of the meanings of the words. Imagine that in the Chinese room you are also given questions in English about such things as your age or your life history, and that you answer these questions. What is the difference between the Chinese case and the English case? Well again, if like me you understand no Chinese and you do understand English, then the difference is obvious. You understand the questions in English because they are expressed in symbols whose meanings are known to you. Similarly, when you give the answers in English you are producing symbols which are meaningful to you. But in the case of the Chinese, you have none of that. In the case of the Chinese, you simply manipulate formal symbols according to a computer program, and you attach no meaning to any of the elements.

Various replies have been suggested to this argument by workers in artificial intelligence and in psychology, as well as philosophy. They all have something in common; they are all inadequate. And there is an obvious reason why they have to be inadequate, since the argument rests on a very simple logical truth, namely, syntax alone is not sufficient for semantics, and digital computers insofar as they are computers have, by definition, a syntax alone.

I want to make this clear by considering a couple of the arguments that are often presented against me.

Some people attempt to answer the Chinese room example by saying that the whole system understands Chinese. The idea here is that though I, the person in the room manipulating the symbols do not understand Chinese, I am just the central processing unit of the computer system. They argue that it is the whole system, including the room, the baskets full of symbols and the ledgers containing the programs and perhaps other items as well, taken as a totality, that understands Chinese. But this is subject to exactly the same objection I made before. There is no way that the system can get from the syntax to the semantics. I, as the central processing unit have no way of figuring out what any of these symbols means; but then neither does the whole system.

Another common response is to imagine that we put the Chinese understanding program inside a robot. If the robot moved around and interacted causally with the world, wouldn't that be enough to guarantee that it understood Chinese? Once again the inexorability of the semantics-syntax distinction overcomes this manoeuvre. As long as we suppose that the robot has only a computer for a brain then, even though it might behave exactly as if it understood Chinese, it would still have no way of getting from the syntax to the semantics of Chinese. You can see this if you imagine that I am the computer. Inside a room in the robot's skull I shuffle symbols without knowing that some of them come in to me from television cameras attached to the robot's head and others go out to move the robot's arms and legs. As long as all I have is a formal computer program, I have no way of attaching any meaning to any of the symbols. And the fact that the robot is engaged in causal interactions with the outside world won't help me to attach any meaning to the symbols unless I have some way of finding out about that fact. Suppose the robot picks up a hamburger and this triggers the symbol for hamburger to come into the room. As long as all I have is the symbol with no knowledge of its causes or how it got there, I have no way of knowing what it means. The causal interactions between the robot and the rest of the world are irrelevant unless those causal interactions are represented in some mind or other. But there is no way they can be if all that the so-called mind consists of is a set of purely formal, syntactical operations.

It is important to see exactly what is claimed and what is not claimed by my argument. Suppose we ask the question that I mentioned at the beginning: "Could a machine think?" Well, in one sense, of course, we are all machines. We can construe the stuff inside our heads as a meat machine. And of course, we can all think. So, in one sense of "machine," namely that sense in which a machine is just a physical system which is capable of performing certain kinds of operations, in that sense, we are all machines, and we can think. So, trivially, there are machines that can think. But that wasn't the question that bothered us. So let's try a different formulation of it. Could an artefact think? Could a man-made machine think? Well, once again, it depends on the kind of artefact. Suppose we designed a machine that was molecule-for-molecule indistinguishable from a human being. Well then, if you can duplicate the causes, you can presumably duplicate the effects. So once again, the answer to that question is, in principle at least trivially yes. If you could build a machine that had the same structure as a human being, then presumably that machine would be able to think. Indeed, it would be a surrogate human being. Well, let's try again.

The question isn't: "Can a machine think?" or: "Can an artefact think?" The question is: "Can a digital computer think?" But once again we have to be very careful in how we interpret the question. From a mathematical point of view, anything whatever can be described *as if* it were a digital computer. And that's because it can be described as instantiating or implementing a computer program. In an utterly trivial sense, the pen that is on the desk in front of me can be described as a digital computer. It just happens to have a very boring computer program. The program says: "Stay there." Now since in this sense, anything whatever is a digital computer, because anything whatever can be described as implementing a computer program, then once again, our question gets a trivial answer. Of course our brains are digital computers, since they implement any number of computer programs. And of course our brains can think. So once again, there is a trivial answer to the question. But that wasn't really the question we were trying to ask. The question we wanted to ask is this: "Can a digital computer, as defined, think?" That is to say: "Is instantiating or implementing the right computer program with the right inputs and outputs, sufficient for, or constitutive of, thinking?" And to this

question, unlike its predecessors, the answer is clearly "no." And it is "no" for the reason that we have spelled out, namely, the computer program is defined purely syntactically. But thinking is more than just a matter of manipulating meaningless symbols, it involves meaningful semantic contents. These semantic contents are what we mean by "meaning."

It is important to emphasise again that we are not talking about a particular stage of computer technology. The argument has nothing to do with the forthcoming, amazing advances in computer science. It has nothing to do with the distinction between serial and parallel processes, or with the size of programs, or the speed of computer operations, or with computers that can interact causally with their environment or even with the invention of robots. Technological progress is always grossly exaggerated, but even subtracting the exaggeration, the development of computers has been quite remarkable, and we can reasonably expect that even more remarkable progress will be made in the future. No doubt we will be much better able to simulate human behaviour on computers than we can at present, and certainly much better than we have been able to in the past. The point I am making is that if we are talking about having mental states, having a mind, all of these simulations are simply irrelevant. It doesn't matter how good the technology is, or how rapid the calculations made by the computer are. If it really is a computer, its operations have to be defined syntactically, whereas consciousness, thoughts, feelings, emotions, and all the rest of it involve more than a syntax. Those features, by definition, the computer is unable to *duplicate* however powerful may be its ability to *simulate*. The key distinction here is between duplication and simulation. And no simulation by itself ever constitutes duplication.

What I have done so far is give a basis to the sense that those citations I began this talk with are really as preposterous as they seem. There is a puzzling question in this discussion though, and that is: 'Why would anybody ever have thought that computers could think or have feelings and emotions and all the rest of it?' After all, we can do computer simulations of any process whatever that can be given a formal description. So, we can do a computer simulation of the flow of money in the British economy, or the pattern of power distribution in the Labour party. We can do computer simulation of rain storms in the home counties, or warehouse fires in East London. Now, in each of these cases, nobody supposes that the computer simulation is actually the real thing; no one supposes that a computer simulation of a storm will leave us all wet, or a computer simulation of a fire is likely to burn the house down. Why on earth would anyone in his right mind suppose a computer simulation of mental processes actually had mental processes? I don't really know the answer to that, since the idea seems to me, to put it frankly, quite crazy from the start. But I can make a couple of speculations.

First of all, where the mind is concerned, a lot of people are still tempted to some sort of behaviourism. They think if a system behaves as if it understood Chinese, then it really must understand Chinese. But we have already refuted this form of behaviourism with the Chinese room argument. Another assumption made by many people is that the mind is not a part of the biological world, it is not a part of the world of nature. The strong artificial intelligence view relies on that in its conception that the mind is purely formal; that somehow or other, it cannot be treated as a concrete product of biological processes like any other biological product. There is in these discussions, in short, a kind of residual dualism. AI partisans believe that the mind is more than a part of the natural biological world; they believe that the mind is purely formally specifiable. The paradox of this is that the AI literature is filled with fulminations against some view called 'dualism', but in fact, the whole thesis of strong AI rests on a kind of dualism. It rests on a rejection of the idea that the mind is just a natural biological phenomenon in the world like any other.

I want to conclude this chapter by putting together the thesis of the last chapter and the thesis of this one. Both of these theses can be stated very simply. And indeed, I am going to state them with perhaps excessive crudeness. But if we put them together I think we get a quite powerful conception of the relations of minds, brains and computers. And the argument has a very simple logical structure, so you can see whether it is valid or invalid. The first premise is:

1. *Brains cause minds.*

Now, of course, that is really too crude. What we mean by that is that mental processes that we consider to constitute a mind are caused, entirely caused, by processes going on inside the brain. But let's be crude, let's just abbreviate that as three words—brains cause minds. And that is just a fact about how the world works. Now let's write proposition number two:

2. *Syntax is not sufficient for semantics.*

That proposition is a conceptual truth. It just articulates our distinction between the notion of what is purely formal and what has content. Now, to these two propositions—that brains cause minds and that syntax is not sufficient for semantics—let's add a third and a fourth:

3. *Computer programs are entirely defined by their formal, or syntactical, structure.*

That proposition, I take it, is true by definition; it is part of what we mean by the notion of a computer program.

4. *Minds have mental contents; specifically, they have semantic contents.*

And that, I take it, is just an obvious fact about how our minds work. My thoughts, and beliefs, and desires are about something, or they refer to something, or they concern states of affairs in the world; and they do that because their content directs them at these states of affairs in the world. Now, from these four premises, we can draw our first conclusion; and it follows obviously from premises 2, 3, and 4:

CONCLUSION 1. *No computer program by itself is sufficient to give a system a mind. Programs, in short, are not minds, and they are not by themselves sufficient for having minds.*

Now, that is a very powerful conclusion, because it means that the project of trying to create minds solely by designing programs is doomed from the start. And it is important to re-emphasise that this has nothing to do with any particular state of technology or any particular state of the complexity of the program. This is a purely formal, or logical, result from a set of axioms which are agreed to by all (or nearly all) of the disputants concerned. That is, even most of the hardcore enthusiasts for artificial intelligence agree that in fact, as a matter of biology, brain processes cause mental states, and they agree that programs are defined purely formally. But if you put these conclusions together with certain other things that we know, then it follows immediately that the project of strong AI is incapable of fulfilment.

However, once we have got these axioms, let's see what else we can derive. Here is a second conclusion:

CONCLUSION 2. *The way that brain functions cause minds cannot be solely in virtue of running a computer program.*

And this second conclusion follows from conjoining the first premise together with our first conclusion. That is, from the fact that brains cause minds and that programs are not enough to do the job, it follows that the way that brains cause minds can't be solely by running a computer program. Now that also I think is an important result, because it has the consequence that the brain is not, or at least is not just, a digital computer. We saw earlier that anything can trivially be described as if it were a digital computer, and brains are no exception. But the importance of this conclusion is that the computational properties of the brain are simply not enough to explain its functioning to produce mental states. And indeed, that ought to seem a commonsense scientific conclusion to us anyway because all it does is remind us of the fact that brains are biological engines; their biology matters. It is not, as several people in artificial intelligence have claimed, just an irrelevant fact about the mind that it happens to be realised in human brains.

Now, from our first premise, we can also derive a third conclusion:

CONCLUSION 3. *Anything else that caused minds would have to have causal powers at least equivalent to those of the brain.*

And this third conclusion is a trivial consequence of our first premise. It is a bit like saying that if my petrol engine drives my car at seventy-five miles an hour, then any diesel engine that was capable of doing that would have to have a power output at least equivalent to that of my petrol engine. Of course, some other system might cause mental processes using entirely different chemical or biochemical features from those the brain in fact uses. It might turn out that there are beings on other planets, or in other solar systems, that have mental states and use an entirely different biochemistry from ours. Suppose that Martians arrived on earth and we concluded that they had mental states. But suppose that when their heads were opened up, it was discovered that all they had inside was green slime. Well still, the green slime, if it functioned to produce consciousness and all the rest of their mental life, would have to have causal powers equal to those of the human brain. But now, from our first conclusion, that programs are not enough, and our third conclusion, that any other system would have to have causal powers equal to the brain, conclusion four follows immediately:

CONCLUSION 4. *For any artefact that we might build which had mental states equivalent to human mental states, the implementation of a computer program would not by itself be sufficient. Rather the artefact would have to have powers equivalent to the powers of the human brain.*

The upshot of this discussion I believe is to remind us of something that we have known all along: namely, mental states are biological phenomena. Consciousness, intentionality, subjectivity and mental causation are all a part of our biological life history, along with growth, reproduction, the secretion of bile, and digestion.

The "Causal Power" of Machines

⌒

ZENON PYLYSHYN

Zenon Pylyshyn is professor of psychology and director of the Rutgers Center for Cognitive Science at Rutgers University. He has made contributions to research on artificial intelligence, mental imagery, and visual attention. He defends a computational account of human intelligence in *Computation and Cognition: Toward a Foundation for Cognitive Science.*

WHAT KIND OF STUFF CAN REFER?

Searle would have us believe that computers, qua formal symbol manipulators, necessarily lack the quality of intentionality, or the capacity to understand and to refer, because they have different "causal powers" from us. Although just what having different causal powers amounts to (other than not being capable of intentionality) is not spelled out, it appears at least that systems that are functionally identical need not have the same "causal powers." Thus the relation of equivalence with respect to causal powers is a refinement of the relation of equivalence with respect to function. What Searle wants to claim is that only systems that are equivalent to humans in this stronger sense can have intentionality. His thesis thus hangs on the assumption that intentionality is tied very closely to specific material properties—indeed, that it is literally *caused* by them. From that point of view it would be extremely unlikely that any system not made of protoplasm—or something essentially identical to protoplasm—can have intentionality. Thus if more and more of the cells in your brain were to be replaced by integrated circuit chips, programmed in such a way as to keep the input-output *function* of each unit identical to that of the unit being replaced, you would in all likelihood just keep right on speaking exactly as you are doing now except that you

would eventually stop *meaning* anything by it. What we outside observers might take to be words would become for you just certain noises that circuits caused you to make.

Searle presents a variety of seductive metaphors and appeals to intuition in support of this rather astonishing view. For example, he asks: why should we find the view that intentionality is tied to detailed properties of the material composition of the system so surprising, when we so readily accept the parallel claim in the case of lactation? Surely it's obvious that only a system with certain causal powers can produce milk; but then why should the same not be true of the ability to refer? Why this example should strike Searle as even remotely relevant is not clear, however. The product of lactation is a *substance,* milk, whose essential defining properties are, naturally, physical and chemical ones (although nothing prevents the production of synthetic milk using a process that is materially very different from mammalian lactation). Is Searle then proposing that intentionality is a *substance* secreted by the brain, and that a possible test for intentionality might involve, say, titrating the brain tissue that realized some putative mental episodes?

Similarly, Searle says that it's obvious that merely having a program can't possibly be a sufficient condition for intentionality . . . A machine would not have

Reprinted from *The Behavioral and Brain Sciences, 3,* (1980) by permission of Cambridge University Press.

intentionality because such objects "are the wrong kind of stuff to have intentionality in the first place." But what is the right kind of stuff? Is it cell assemblies, individual neurons, protoplasm, protein molecules, atoms of carbon and hydrogen, elementary particles? Let Searle name the level, and it can be simulated perfectly well using "the wrong kind of stuff." Clearly it isn't the *stuff* that has the intentionality. . . . Searle presents no argument for the assumption that what makes the difference between being able to refer and not being able to refer—or to display any other capacity—is a "finer grained" property of the system than can be captured in a *functional* description. Furthermore, it's obvious from Searle's own argument that the nature of the stuff cannot be what is relevant, since the monolingual English speaker who has memorized the formal rules is supposed to be an example of a system made of the *right* stuff and yet it allegedly still lacks the relevant intentionality.

Having said all this, however, one might still want to maintain that in some cases—perhaps in the case of Searle's example—it might be appropriate to say that *nothing* refers, or that the symbols are not being used in a way that refers to something. But if we wanted to deny that these symbols referred, it would be appropriate to ask what licences us *ever* to say that a symbol refers. There are at least three different approaches to answering that question: Searle's view that it is the nature of the embodiment of the symbol (of the brain substance itself), the traditional functionalist view that it is the *functional role* that the symbol plays in the overall behavior of the system, and the view associated with philosophers like Kripke and Putnam, that it is in the nature of the causal connection that the symbol has with certain past events. The latter two are in fact compatible insofar as specifying the functional role of a symbol in the behavior of a system does not preclude specifying its causal interactions with an environment. It is noteworthy that Searle does not even consider the possibility that a purely formal computational model might constitute an essential part of an adequate theory, where the latter also contained an account of the system's transducers and an account of how the symbols came to acquire the role that they have in the functioning of the system.

FUNCTIONALISM AND REFERENCE

The functionalist view is currently the dominant one in both AI and information-processing psychology. In the past, mentalism often assumed that reference was established by relations of similarity; an image referred to a horse if it *looked* sufficiently like a horse. Mediational behaviorism took it to be a simple causal remnant of perception: a brain event referred to a certain object if it shared some of the properties of brain events that occur when that object is perceived. But information-processing psychology has opted for a level of description that deals with the informational, or encoded, aspects of the environment's effects on the organism. On this view it has typically been assumed that what a symbol represents can be seen by examining how the symbol enters into relations with other symbols and with transducers. It is this position that Searle is quite specifically challenging. My own view is that although Searle is right in pointing out that some versions of the functionalist answer are in a certain sense incomplete, he is off the mark both in his diagnosis of where the problem lies and in his prognosis as to just how impoverished a view of mental functioning the cognitivist position will have to settle for. . . .

The sense in which a functionalist answer might be incomplete is if it failed to take the further step of specifying what it was about the system that *warranted* the ascription of one particular semantic content to the functional states (or to the symbolic expressions that express that state) rather than some other logically possible content. A cognitive theory claims that the system behaves in a certain way *because* certain expressions represent certain things (that is, have a certain *semantic* interpretation). It is, furthermore, essential that it do so: otherwise we would not be able to subsume certain classes of regular behaviors in a single generalization of the sort "the system does X because the state S represents such and such" (for example, the person ran out of the building because he believed that *it was on fire*). . . . But the particular interpretation appears to be extrinsic to the theory inasmuch as the system would behave in exactly the same way without the interpretation. Thus Searle concludes that it is only *we,* the theorists, who take the expression to represent, say, that the building is on fire. The system doesn't take it to *represent* anything because it literally doesn't know what the expression refers to: only we theorists do. That being the case, the system can't be said to behave in a certain way *because* of what it represents. This is in contrast with the way in which *our* behavior is determined: we *do* behave in certain ways because of what our thoughts are about. . . .

The last few steps, however, are non sequiturs. The fact that it was we, the theorists, who provided the interpretation of the expressions doesn't by itself mean that such an interpretation is simply a matter of convenience, or that there is a sense in which the interpretation is ours rather than the system's. Of course it's logically possible that the interpretation is only in the mind of the theorist and that the system behaves the way it does for entirely different reasons. But even if that happened to be true, it wouldn't follow simply from the fact that the AI theorist was the one who came up with the interpretation. Much depends on his reasons for coming up with that interpretation. In any case, the question of whether the semantic interpretation resides in the head of the programmer or in the machine is the wrong question to ask. A more relevant question would be: what fixes the semantic interpretation of functional states, or what latitude does the theorist have in assigning a semantic interpretation to the states of the system?

When a computer is viewed as a self-contained device for processing formal symbols, we have a great deal of latitude in assigning semantic interpretations to states. Indeed, we routinely change our interpretation of the computer's functional states, sometimes viewing them as numbers, sometimes as alphabetic characters, sometimes as words or descriptions of a scene, and so on. Even where it is difficult to think of a coherent interpretation that is different from the one the programmer had in mind, such alternatives are always possible in principle. However, if we equip the machine with transducers and allow it to interact freely with both natural and linguistic environments, and if we endow it with the power to make (syntactically specified) inferences, it is anything but obvious what latitude, if any, the theorist (who knows how the transducers operate, and therefore knows what they respond to) would still have in assigning a coherent interpretation to the functional states in such a way as to capture psychologically relevant regularities in behavior.

THE ROLE OF INTUITIONS

Suppose such connections between the system and the world as mentioned above (and possibly other considerations that no one has yet considered) uniquely constrained the possible interpretations that could be placed on representational states. Would this solve the problem of justifying the ascription of particular semantic contents to these states? Here I suspect that one would run into differences of opinion that may well be unresolvable, simply because they are grounded on different intuitions. For example there immediately arises the question of whether we possess a privileged interpretation of our own thoughts that must take precedence over such functional analyses. And if so, then there is the further question of whether being *conscious* is what provides the privileged access; and hence the question of what one is to do about the apparent necessity of positing unconscious mental processes. So far as I can see the *only* thing that recommends that particular view is the intuition that, whatever may be true of other creatures, I at least *know* what *my* thoughts refer to because I have direct experiential access to the referents of my thoughts. Even if we did have strong intuitions about such cases, there is good reason to believe that such intuitions should be considered as no more than secondary sources of constraint, whose validity should be judged by how well theoretical systems based on them perform. We cannot take as sacred anyone's intuitions about such things as whether another creature has intentionality—especially when such intuitions rest (as Searle's do, by his own admission) on knowing what the creature (or machine) is *made of* (for instance, Searle is prepared to admit that other creatures might have intentionality if "we can see that the beasts are made of similar stuff to ourselves"). Clearly, intuitions based on nothing but such anthropocentric chauvinism cannot form the foundation of a science of cognition. . . .

What is frequently neglected in discussions of intentionality is that we cannot state with any degree of precision what it is that entitles us to claim that *people* refer (though there are one or two general ideas, such as those discussed above), and therefore that arguments against the intentionality of computers typically reduce to "argument from ignorance." If we knew what it was that warranted our saying that people refer, we might also be in a position to claim that the ascription of semantic content to formal computational expressions—though it is in fact accomplished in practice by "inference to the best explanation"—was in the end warranted in exactly the same way. Humility, if nothing else, should prompt us to admit that there's a lot we don't know about how we ought to describe the capacities of future robots and other computing machines, even when we do know how their electronic circuits operate.

Functionalism, Qualia, and the Inverted Spectrum

TERRANCE HORGAN

Terence Horgan is professor of philosophy at the University of Memphis. He has written numerous articles in philosophy of mind, language, epistemology, and other areas. He is the author, with John Tienson, of *Connectionism and the Philosophy of Psychology.*

I

Functionalism is the doctrine that every mental state-type may be fully defined by means of its typical causal connections to sensory stimulation, behavior, and other mental state-types similarly defined. Some philosophers, myself included, believe that although functionalism is plausible as regards certain aspects of mentality, nevertheless there is one aspect that is incapable, in principle, of being analyzed functionally: viz., the qualitative, or phenomenal, content of our mental states—i.e., *what it is like* to undergo these states. What we mean by the notion of qualitative content, and why we think that this aspect of mentality cannot be accommodated by functionalism, are nicely summarized by Jerry Fodor:

> Try to imagine looking at a blank wall through a red filter. Now change the filter to a green one and leave everything else exactly the way it was. Something about the character of your experience changes

when the filter does, and it is this kind of thing that philosophers call qualitative content. . . .

The reason qualitative content is a problem for functionalism is straightforward. Functionalism is committed to defining mental states in terms of their causes and effects. It seems, however, as if two mental states could have all the same causal relations and yet could differ in their qualitative content. Let me illustrate this with the classic puzzle of the inverted spectrum.

It seems possible to imagine two observers who are alike in all relevant psychological respects except that experiences having the qualitative content of red for one observer would have the qualitative content of green for the other. Nothing about their behavior need reveal the difference because both of them see ripe tomatoes and flaming sunsets as being similar in color and both of them call that color "red." Moreover, the causal connection between their (qualitatively distinct) experiences and their other mental states could also be identical. Perhaps they both think of Little Red Riding Hood

Reprinted from *Philosophy and Phenomenological Research, 44* (1984), by permission of the International Phenomenological Society.

when they see ripe tomatoes, feel depressed when they see the color green and so on. It seems as if anything that could be packed into the notion of the causal role of their experience could be shared by them, and yet the qualitative content of the experiences could be as different as you like. If this is possible, then the functionalist account does not work for mental states that have qualitative content. If one person is having a green experience while another person is having a red one, then surely they must be in different mental states.

It would seem that if all mental states are fully definable functionally, then the inverted-spectrum thought experiment Fodor describes should be conceptually incoherent. Yet many of us find it remarkably easy to perform such thought experiments, and this makes us very suspicious of claims that they are incoherent. Instead, we find ourselves concluding that functionalism, whatever its virtues in other respects, cannot accommodate qualia. . . .

II

Let us now return to the inverted-spectrum objection to functionalism. To fix our attention on a concrete case, we shall suppose that Jack is a normal color-perceiver, but that Jill has, from the moment of her birth onward, unusual neural "wiring" in the intermediate portions of her visual system—wiring which systematically causes the retinal stimulations induced by light of any given wavelength to generate in her visual cortex the same neural activity that is generated in us by the "spectral inverse" of that wavelength. Thus, if brain state G and brain state R are the state-types induced in John's visual cortex by green objects and red objects respectively, then G is induced in Jill by red objects and R is induced in her by green objects. Nonetheless, since Jill has learned color words in the same ostensive manner John has, she uses those words in the same way he does. Let us further suppose that G plays *completely* the same causal role in Jill that R plays in Jack, and vice versa; thus, if Jack thinks of Little Red Riding Hood when looking at ripe tomatoes then so does Jill, and if Jack becomes depressed when he looks at green objects then so does Jill, and so on.

Thought experiments like this initially seem problematic for functionalism. For when Jack and Jill both look at grass, they surely differ mentally despite being in functionally identical states—a fact that seems to imply that there is more to mentality than what is functionally definable. But now we see how the functionalist can reply to this line of reasoning. He can say that although Jack and Jill are in functionally identical states under one relativization (the one that relativizes Jack's mental states to mankind, and Jill's to her unusual subpopulation), they are in functionally *different* states under another relativization (the one that relativizes both Jack's and Jill's mental states to mankind). Thus, the functionalist can deny that the case of Jack and Jill shows there is more to mentality than is functionally definable. He can say instead that under one relativization, Jack and Jill differ neither functionally nor mentally when they look at grass, whereas under the other relativization they differ *both* functionally and mentally. According to this account, we really commit a subtle form of equivocation if we claim that Jack and Jill differ mentally despite being in functionally identical states: viz., equivocation between two contextually appropriate ways of relativizing mental-state ascriptions.

Should we qualia-lovers concede that this analysis successfully disarms the inverted-spectrum objection to functionalism? I submit that we should not, and for a reason that takes much less time to state then does the analysis itself. For it is just self-evident, I submit, that the qualitative content of Jill's experience when she looks at grass is an absolute, intrinsic feature of her mental life—not a feature that is implicitly population-relative. There is, absolutely and non-relatively, *something it is like* for Jill when she looks at grass. Furthermore, this feature differs from the corresponding intrinsic, non-relative feature of Jack's mental life when he looks at grass: what it is like for Jill when she looks at grass is the same as what it is like for Jack when he looks at grassy red stuff. Hence their mental states when looking at grass are intrinsically, unqualifiedly different. This difference remains present even if we relativize all *functional* state-ascriptions in such a way that Jack and Jill are in functionally-identical states when looking at grass. Thus, the phenomenal content of color experience does indeed go beyond what is functionally definable. Functionalism cannot accommodate qualia.

As I said, I take the intrinsic, non-relative nature of qualia to be a self-evident fact, a fact which unavoidably impresses itself upon most of us who actually experience these states. The point is virtually impossible to *argue* for, however, because it depends upon an individual's first-person perspective toward his own mental life. Functionalists can, and do, resolutely insist that they are aware of no such features in their own mental life; and since the rest of us lack first-person access to their mental states, we cannot refute them. We can only describe cases like that of Jack and Jill, and ask whether it is not absolutely, undeniably *obvious* that there is an intrinsic, non-population-relative difference between Jack's mental state when looking at grass and Jill's.

Dialectically, we seem to have reached an impasse. Initially it appeared that functionalists were required to take the heroic step of denying the intelligibility of inverted-spectrum stories, and hence that the evident intelligibility of such stories constituted evidence against them. But it turns out that functionalists can make sense of inverted spectra by invoking population-relativization. The qualia-lovers reply that this approach leaves out of account the allegedly self-evident fact that the qualitative content of our mental states is an intrinsic, non-population-relative feature of those states. The functionalists respond by denying that this is a fact at all, let alone a self-evident one. Deadlock.

I shall not try to break this deadlock. Instead, I shall simply direct the subsequent discussion at those who consider it obvious, as I do, that the qualitative aspects of mentality are not definable functionally. I shall propose a theory of mind that makes room for qualia as non-functional mental state-types. If you are not among those to whom the remaining portion of the paper is addressed, and you find yourself wondering what it is about our mental life that is allegedly left out by functional definitions, I can only join with Ned Block in replying with the words once used by Louis Armstrong when he was asked what jazz is: "If you got to ask, you ain't never gonna get to know."

III

I propose a two-part theory. Phenomenal state-types (i.e., qualia) are to be identified with neurophysiological state-types; the identities involved are necessary identities, because the qualia-names involved (as well as the neurophysiological state-names) are rigid designators. Non-phenomenal state-types, on the other hand, are to be construed functionally. . . .

Can we expect all the mental state-types we recognize in everyday mentalese to be neatly separable by means of the phenomenal/non-phenomenal distinction? Not necessarily. It may turn out that many garden-variety mental state-types are really hybrid types, involving both a phenomenal component and a non-phenomenal component. A plausible candidate for such hybrid status, I suggest, is the philosopher's favorite mental state: pain. I think there are really two state-types instantiated in any clear-cut instance of pain: (1) *phenomenal* pain, the "raw feel" of pain experiences (and the element not definable functionally); and (2) *functional* pain, the state-type which, by definition, has typical causes such as harmful forces impinging upon the creature's surface, and typical effects such as avoidance-behavior. Hybrid types, on the view I am proposing, are instantiated when both the relevant purely-phenomenal type and the relevant purely-functional type are instantiated—even if these latter are not explicitly countenanced in everyday mentalese.

IV

Let us now consider how this theory, which I shall call *partial functionalism,* fares in comparison to full-fledged functionalism. One important advantage of partial functionalism, of course, is that it explicitly accommodates the deeply-felt intuition that the phenomenal aspects of mentality are not definable functionally: the intuition that functionalism leaves out what it is like to undergo mental states like pain, thirst, seeing red, and seeing green.

Another positive feature of partial functionalism is that it not only accommodates this intuition, but it does so while still preserving a fully naturalistic conception of a human being as physico-chemical system whose behavior is completely explainable, in principle, solely in physicochemical terms. For although I am claiming that the qualitative content of our mental life is not definable functionally, I am not thereby rendering it something occult—something apart from the uninterrupted nexus of physico-chemical causation within the human central nervous system. On the contrary, I am claiming that qualia are nothing other than certain neurophysiological state-types. They are not higher-level state-types whose presence and causal efficacy in human beings are mysterious from the perspective of natural science.

One reason for the current wide appeal of functionalism, I think, is that this doctrine seems to mesh so nicely with a naturalistic conception of human beings. Under functionalism it is no more difficult to understand how humans, regarded naturalistically, can undergo mental states than it is to understand how the physical devices we call computers can undergo "computational" states—i.e., states defined abstractly in terms of the computer's program, its "software." Mentality is to physico-chemical activity in humans as computational activity is to physico-chemical activity in computers.

I am claiming that phenomenal state-types are, in Keith Gunderson's happy phrase, "program resistant." I.e., the capacity to instantiate them does not arise by virtue of a creature's software, the functional organization of its physico-chemical components. But I espouse naturalism nonetheless, for my contention is that phenomenal state-types are *hardware* state-types rather than software state-types. They are program resistant because they are identical, and necessarily identical, to physico-chemical state-types—not because they are occult state-types that no mere physico-chemical system could instantiate.

But although partial functionalism does seem compatible with the granola conception of human beings, nevertheless one might object that it is theoretically less unified than full-fledged functionalism, and that this fact counts seriously against it.

I deny neither the desirability of theoretical simplicity nor the fact that my theory is somewhat more complex than functionalism. But a theory of mind should not be rendered simple at the cost of failing to accommodate seemingly obvious facts about our

mental life—like the fact that in an inverted spectrum situation like that of Jack and Jill, the two persons differ mentally in an absolute, non-population-relative way. Furthermore, since I am not positing qualia as state-types over and above physico-chemical state-types, the greater complexity of my theory concerns only the workings of mental terminology; the ontology of this theory is at least as parsimonious as functionalism's ontology.

Another potential objection to partial functionalism is the charge that it is chauvinistic, in a way that functionalism is not. Surely, the objection goes, a Martian could undergo the same qualia we do even if his neurological hardware were vastly different from our own. Functionalism allows for this possibility, but partial functionalism does not.

Since my theory is partly functionalist, I can grant the plasticity of non-phenomenal mental states, i.e., the realizability of such states in creatures vastly different from ourselves in physico-chemical structure. But is it really plausible to say the same about qualia? I submit that it is not, unless one holds that qualia too are functionally definable. For, if we deny that qualia are functional states, then the most natural way to accommodate them naturalistically is to suppose that they are identical with specific physico-chemical states of the human brain—or at any rate, of brains relevantly similar to human brains. And it then becomes plausible to *deny* the plasticity of qualia, and to contend that a Martian, with his radically different physical makeup, must experience either different qualia than ours or no qualia at all.

The prospect of Martians who are functionally similar to us but who either lack qualia altogether or else have dramatically different qualia, raises with a vengeance the traditional problem of other minds. If partial functionalism is correct, how could we ever tell whether Martians have qualia? Their functional organization would be compatible with both (1) the supposition that their mental lives are qualitatively as rich as our own, and (2) the alternative supposition that they are zombies whose mental lives are qualitatively empty.

Suppose we came to know and like Martians, and to have frequent profound intellectual intercourse with them—including philosophical discussions about mind. At some point, no doubt we would raise the topic of functionalism, the doctrine that all mental state-types are fully definable in terms of typical causal connections to sensory inputs, behavioral outputs, and other similarly-defined mental states. Once we were satisfied that they understood this thesis, we could simply *ask* them whether they find that in their own case, there is more to mentality than what is functionally definable. To make the question more specific, we could describe a Martian version of our earlier inverted-spectrum story, involving a Martian Jack and a Martian Jill, and then ask them whether these two individuals would differ mentally in some absolute, non-population-relative way. If they said yes, we would have grounds for inferring that they have qualia; if no, we would have grounds for inferring that they do not.

Admittedly, the matter might be complicated by the existence of some Martian philosophers who really have qualia but still resolutely deny that there is more to theory mentality than what is functionally definable—just as certain human philosophers do. Still, we could obtain evidence for or against Martian qualia by determining whether the issue was *controversial* among philosophically-inclined Martians. If, by and large, they tended to accede to a Lewis-style analysis of inverted-spectrum cases, we could infer that they probably have no qualia. If, on the other hand, many of them insisted that something crucial is left out by such an analysis, and that "If you got to

ask" what it is "you ain't never gonna get to know," then we could infer that they probably do have qualia—the stubbornness of the Martian functionalists notwithstanding.

But even if it is possible, under partial functionalism, to know whether or not Martians have qualia, it very well might not be possible to know what these qualia are like. After all, "knowing what a mental state is like" involves being in, or remembering being in, that state yourself—or at any rate, being in, or remembering being in, sufficiently similar states. And since Martian qualia would be physico-chemical state-types instantiatable by creatures with a Martian-like physical composition, we humans might simply lack the neural hardware that is necessary to undergo Martian qualia. And if we could not undergo them, we could not "know what they are like."

Does this show that there is something occult and theoretically mysterious about qualia after all? I think not. For I have been claiming that part of what we mean by "knowing what a mental state is like" is "having undergone that state, or a similar one, oneself." Thus, if we can explain scientifically why humans cannot undergo the physical state-types which are identical to Martian qualia, we will thereby explain *why* humans cannot know what Martian qualia are like. Furthermore, it is still perfectly possible to know *what* they are, even if we cannot know what they are like: they are specific physico-chemical state-types.

Epiphenomenal Qualia

~

FRANK JACKSON

Frank Jackson is professor of philosophy at Australian National University. He has made influential contributions to several areas of philosophy and is the author of a widely discussed critique of physicalism. His books include *Perception: A Representative Theory* and *From Metaphysics to Ethics: A Defense of Conceptual Analysis.*

It is undeniable that the physical, chemical and biological sciences have provided a great deal of information about the world we live in and about ourselves. I will use the label "physical information" for this kind of information, and also for information that automatically comes along with it. For example, if a medical scientist tells me enough about the processes that go on in my nervous system, and about how they relate to happenings in the world around me, to what has happened in the past and is likely to happen in the future, to what happens to other similar and dissimilar organisms, and the like, he or she tells me—if I am clever enough to fit it together appropriately—about what is often called the functional role of those states in me (and in organisms in general in similar cases). This information, and its kin, I also label "physical."

I do not mean these sketchy remarks to constitute a definition of "physical information," and of the correlative notions of physical property, process, and so on, but to indicate what I have in mind here. It is well known that there are problems with giving a precise definition of these notions, and so of the thesis of Physicalism that all (correct) information is physical information. But—unlike some—I take the question of definition to cut across the central problems I want to discuss in this paper.

I am what is sometimes known as a "qualia freak." I think that there are certain features of the bodily sensations especially, but also of certain perceptual experiences, which no amount of purely physical information includes. Tell me everything physical there is to tell about what is going on in a living brain, the kind of states, their functional role, their relation to what goes on at other times and in other brains, and so on and so forth, and be I as clever as can be in fitting it all together, you won't have told me about the hurtfulness of pains, the itchiness of itches, pangs of jealousy, or about the characteristic experience of tasting a lemon, smelling a rose, hearing a loud noise or seeing the sky.

There are many qualia freaks, and some of them say that their rejection of Physicalism is an unargued intuition. I think that they are being unfair to themselves. They have the following argument. Nothing you could tell of a physical sort captures the smell of a rose, for instance. Therefore, Physicalism is false. By our lights this is a perfectly good argument. It is obviously not to the point to question its validity, and the premise is intuitively obviously true both to them and to me.

I must, however, admit that it is weak from a polemical point of view. There are, unfortunately for us, many who do not find the premise intuitively obvious. The task then is to present an argument whose premises are obvious to all, or at least to as many as possible. This I try to do in §I with what I will call "the Knowledge argument." . . . In §IV I tackle the ques-

Reprinted from *The Philosophical Quarterly, 32,* by permission of the journal.

tion of the causal role of qualia. The major factor in stopping people from admitting qualia is the belief that they would have to be given a causal role with respect to the physical world and especially the brain; and it is hard to do this without sounding like someone who believes in fairies. I seek in §IV to turn this objection by arguing that the view that qualia are epiphenomenal is a perfectly possible one.

I. THE KNOWLEDGE ARGUMENT FOR QUALIA

People vary considerably in their ability to discriminate colours. Suppose that in an experiment to catalogue this variation Fred is discovered. Fred has better colour vision than anyone else on record; he makes every discrimination that anyone has ever made, and moreover he makes one that we cannot even begin to make. Show him a batch of ripe tomatoes and he sorts them into two roughly equal groups and does so with complete consistency. That is, if you blindfold him, shuffle the tomatoes up, and then remove the blindfold and ask him to sort them out again, he sorts them into exactly the same two groups.

We ask Fred how he does it. He explains that all ripe tomatoes do not look the same colour to him, and in fact that this is true of a great many objects that we classify together as red. He sees two colours where we see one, and he has in consequence developed for his own use two words "red$_1$" and "red$_2$" to mark the difference. Perhaps he tells us that he has often tried to teach the difference between red$_1$ and red$_2$ to his friends but has got nowhere and has concluded that the rest of the world is red$_1$-red$_2$ colour-blind—or perhaps he has had partial success with his children, it doesn't matter. In any case he explains to us that it would be quite wrong to think that because "red" appears in both "red$_1$" and "red$_2$" that the two colours are shades of the one colour. He only uses the common term "red" to fit more easily into our restricted usage. To him red$_1$ and red$_2$ are as different from each other and all the other colours as yellow is from blue. And his discriminatory behaviour bears this out: he sorts red$_1$ from red$_2$ tomatoes with the greatest of ease in a wide variety of viewing circumstances. Moreover, an investigation of the physiological basis of Fred's exceptional ability reveals that Fred's optical system is able to separate out two groups of wavelengths in the red spectrum as sharply as we are able to sort out yellow from blue.

I think that we should admit that Fred can see, really see, at least one more colour than we can; red$_1$ is a different colour from red$_2$. We are to Fred as a totally red-green colour-blind person is to us. H. G. Wells' story "The Country of the Blind" is about a sighted person in a totally blind community. This person never manages to convince them that he can see, that he has an extra sense. They ridicule this sense as quite inconceivable, and treat his capacity to avoid falling into ditches, to win fights and so on as precisely that capacity and nothing more. We would be making their mistake if we refused to allow that Fred can see one more colour than we can.

What kind of experience does Fred have when he sees red$_1$ and red$_2$? What is the new colour or colours like? We would dearly like to know but do not; and it seems that no amount of physical information about Fred's brain and optical system tells us. We find out perhaps that Fred's cones respond differentially to certain light waves in the red section of the spectrum that make no difference to ours (or perhaps he has an extra cone) and that this leads in Fred to a wider range of those brain states responsible for visual discriminatory behaviour. But none of this tells us what we really want to know about his colour experience. There is something about it we don't know. But we know, we may suppose, everything about Fred's body, his behaviour and dispositions to behaviour and about his internal physiology, and everything about his history and relation to others that can be given in physical accounts of persons. We have all the physical information. Therefore, knowing all this is *not* knowing everything about Fred. It follows that Physicalism leaves something out.

To reinforce this conclusion, imagine that as a result of our investigations into the internal workings of Fred we find out how to make everyone's physiology like Fred's in the relevant respects; or perhaps Fred donates his body to science and on his death we are able to transplant his optical system into someone else—again the fine detail doesn't matter. The important point is that such a happening would create enormous interest. People would say, "At last we will know what it is like to see the extra colour, at last we will know how Fred has differed from us in the way he has struggled to tell us about for so long". Then it cannot be that we knew all along all about Fred. But *ex hypothesi* we did know all along everything about Fred that features in the physicalist scheme; hence the physicalist scheme leaves something out.

Put it this way. *After* the operation, we will know *more* about Fred and especially about his colour experiences. But beforehand we had all the physical information we could desire about his body and brain, and indeed everything that has ever featured in physicalist accounts of mind and consciousness. Hence there is more to know than all that. Hence Physicalism is incomplete.

Fred and the new colour(s) are of course essentially rhetorical devices. The same point can be made with normal people and familiar colours. Mary is a brilliant scientist who is, for whatever reason, forced to investigate the world from a black and white room *via* a black and white television monitor. She specialises in the neurophysiology of vision and acquires, let us suppose, all the physical information there is to obtain about what goes on when we see ripe tomatoes, or the sky, and use terms like "red," "blue," and so on. She discovers, for example, just which wave-length combinations from the sky stimulate the retina, and exactly how this produces *via* the central nervous system the contraction of the vocal chords and expulsion of air from the lungs that results in the uttering of the sentence "The sky is blue." (It can hardly be denied that it is in principle possible to obtain all this physical information from black and white television, otherwise the Open University would of *necessity* need to use colour television.)

What will happen when Mary is released from her black and white room or is given a colour television monitor? Will she *learn* anything or not? It seems just obvious that she will learn something about the world and our visual experience of it. But then it is inescapable that her previous knowledge was incomplete. But she had *all* the physical information. Ergo there is more to have than that, and Physicalism is false.

Clearly the same style of Knowledge argument could be deployed for taste, hearing, the bodily sen-

sations and generally speaking for the various mental states which are said to have (as it is variously put) raw feels, phenomenal features or qualia. The conclusion in each case is that the qualia are left out of the physicalist story. And the polemical strength of the Knowledge argument is that it is so hard to deny the central claim that one can have all the physical information without having all the information there is to have. . . .

IV.   THE BOGEY OF EPIPHENOMENALISM

Is there any really *good* reason for refusing to countenance the idea that qualia are causally impotent with respect to the physical world? I will argue for the answer no, but in doing this I will say nothing about two views associated with the classical epiphenomenalist position. The first is that mental *states* are inefficacious with respect to the physical world. All I will be concerned to defend is that it is possible to hold that certain *properties* of certain mental states, namely those I've called qualia, are such that their possession or absence makes no difference to the physical world. The second is that the mental is *totally* causally inefficacious. For all I will say it may be that you have to hold that the instantiation of *qualia* makes a difference to *other mental states* though not to anything physical. Indeed general considerations to do with how you could come to be aware of the instantiation of qualia suggest such a position.

Three reasons are standardly given for holding that a quale like the hurtfulness of a pain must be causally efficacious in the physical world, and so, for instance, that its instantiation must sometimes make a difference to what happens in the brain. None, I will argue, has any real force. (I am much indebted to Alec Hyslop and John Lucas for convincing me of this.)

(i) It is supposed to be just obvious that the hurtfulness of pain is partly responsible for the subject seeking to avoid pain, saying "It hurts" and so on. But, to reverse Hume, anything can fail to cause anything. No matter how often *B* follows *A,* and no matter how initially obvious the causality of the connection seems, the hypothesis that *A* causes *B* can be overturned by an over-arching theory which shows the two as distinct effects of a common underlying causal process.

To the untutored the image on the screen of Lee Marvin's fist moving from left to right immediately followed by the image of John Wayne's head moving in the same general direction looks as causal as anything. And of course throughout countless Westerns images similar to the first are followed by images similar to the second. All this counts for precisely nothing when we know the over-arching theory concerning how the relevant images are both effects of an underlying causal process involving the projector and the film. The epiphenomenalist can say exactly the same about the connection between, for example, hurtfulness and behaviour. It is simply a consequence of the fact that certain happenings in the brain cause both.

(ii) The second objection relates to Darwin's Theory of Evolution. According to natural selection the traits that evolve over time are those conducive to physical survival. We may assume that qualia evolved over time—we have them, the earliest forms of life do not—and so we should expect qualia to be conducive to survival. The objection is that they could hardly help us to survive if they do nothing to the physical world.

The appeal of this argument is undeniable, but there is a good reply to it. Polar bears have particularly thick, warm coats. The Theory of Evolution explains this (we suppose) by pointing out that having a thick, warm coat is conducive to survival in the Arctic. But having a thick coat goes along with having a heavy coat, and having a heavy coat is *not* conducive to survival. It slows the animal down.

Does this mean that we have refuted Darwin because we have found an evolved trait—having a heavy coat—which is not conducive to survival? Clearly not. Having a heavy coat is an unavoidable concomitant of having a warm coat (in the context, modern insulation was not available), and the advantages for survival of having a warm coat outweighed the disadvantages of having a heavy one. The point is that all we can extract from Darwin's theory is that we should expect any evolved characteristic to be *either* conducive to survival *or* a by-product of one that is so conducive. The epiphenomenalist holds that qualia fall into the latter category. They are a by-product of certain brain processes that are highly conducive to survival.

(iii) The third objection is based on a point about how we come to know about other minds. We know about other minds by knowing about other behaviour, at least in part. The nature of the inference is a matter of some controversy, but it is not a matter of controversy that it proceeds from behaviour. That is why we think that stones do not feel and dogs do feel. But, runs the objection, how can a person's behaviour provide any reason for believing he has qualia like mine, or indeed any qualia at all, unless this behaviour can be regarded as the *outcome* of the qualia. Man Friday's footprint was evidence of Man Friday because footprints are causal outcomes of feet attached to people. And an epiphenomenalist cannot regard behaviour, or indeed anything physical, as an outcome of qualia.

But consider my reading in *The Times* that Spurs won. This provides excellent evidence that *The Telegraph* has also reported that Spurs won, despite the fact that (I trust) *The Telegraph* does not get the results from *The Times*. They each send their own reporters to the game. *The Telegraph*'s report is in no sense an outcome of *The Times*', but the latter provides good evidence for the former nevertheless.

The reasoning involved can be reconstructed thus. I read in *The Times* that Spurs won. This gives me reason to think that Spurs won because I know that Spurs' winning is the most likely candidate to be what caused the report in *The Times*. But I also know that Spurs' winning would have had many effects, including almost certainly a report in *The Telegraph*.

I am arguing from one effect back to its cause and out again to another effect. The fact that neither effect causes the other is irrelevant. Now the epiphenomenalist allows that qualia are effects of what goes on in the brain. Qualia cause nothing physical but are caused by something physical. Hence the epiphenomenalist can argue from the behaviour of others to the qualia of others by arguing from the behaviour of others back to its causes in the brains of others and out again to their qualia.

You may well feel for one reason or another that this is a more dubious chain of reasoning than its model in the case of newspaper reports. You are right. The problem of other minds is a major philosophical problem, the problem of other newspaper reports is not. But there is no special problem of Epiphenomenalism as opposed to, say, Interactionism here.

There is a very understandable response to the three replies I have just made. "All right, there is no knockdown refutation of the existence of epiphenomenal qualia. But the fact remains that they are an excrescence. They *do* nothing, they *explain* nothing, they serve merely to soothe the intuitions of dualists, and it is left a total mystery how they fit into the world view of science. In short we do not and cannot understand the how and why of them."

This is perfectly true; but is no objection to qualia, for it rests on an overly optimistic view of the human animal, and its powers. We are the products of Evolution. We understand and sense what we need to understand and sense in order to survive. Epiphenomenal qualia are totally irrelevant to survival. At no stage of our evolution did natural selection favour those who could make sense of how they are caused and the laws governing them, or in fact why they exist at all. And that is why we can't.

It is not sufficiently appreciated that Physicalism is an extremely optimistic view of our powers. If it is true, we have, in very broad outline admittedly, a grasp of our place in the scheme of things. Certain matters of sheer complexity defeat us—there are an awful lot of neurons—but in principle we have it all. But consider the antecedent probability that everything in the Universe be of a kind that is relevant in some way or other to the survival of homo sapiens. It is very low surely. But then one must admit that it is very likely that there is a part of the whole scheme of things, maybe a big part, which no amount of evolution will ever bring us near to knowledge about or understanding. For the simple reason that such knowledge and understanding is irrelevant to survival.

Physicalists typically emphasise that we are a part of nature on their view, which is fair enough. But if we are a part of nature, we are as nature has left us after however many years of evolution it is, and each step in that evolutionary progression has been a matter of chance constrained just by the need to preserve or increase survival value. The wonder is that we understand as much as we do, and there is no wonder that there should be matters which fall quite outside our comprehension. Perhaps exactly how epiphenomenal qualia fit into the scheme of things is one such.

This may seem an unduly pessimistic view of our capacity to articulate a truly comprehensive picture of our world and our place in it. But suppose we discovered living on the bottom of the deepest oceans a sort of sea slug which manifested intelligence. Perhaps survival in the conditions required rational powers. Despite their intelligence, these sea slugs have only a very restricted conception of the world by comparison with ours, the explanation for this being the nature of their immediate environment. Nevertheless they have developed sciences which work surprisingly well in these restricted terms. They also have philosophers, called slugists. Some call themselves tough-minded slugists, others confess to being soft-minded slugists.

The tough-minded slugists hold that the restricted terms (or ones pretty like them which may be introduced as their sciences progress) suffice in principle to describe everything without remainder. These tough-minded slugists admit in moments of weakness to a feeling that their theory leaves something out. They resist this feeling and their opponents, the soft-minded slugists, by pointing out—absolutely correctly—that no slugist has ever succeeded in spelling out how this mysterious residue fits into the highly successful view that their sciences have and are developing of how their world works.

Our sea slugs don't exist, but they might. And there might also exist super beings which stand to us as we stand to the sea slugs. We cannot adopt the perspective of these super beings, because we are not them, but the possibility of such a perspective is, I think, an antidote to excessive optimism.

Jackson's Knowledge Argument

~

PAUL M. CHURCHLAND

Paul M. Churchland is professor of philosophy at the University of California at San Diego. He is a leading defender of the view that we must study the brain in order to understand the mind. His books include *Scientific Realism and the Plasticity of Mind, Matter and Consciousness,* and *The Engine of Reason, The Seat of the Soul: A Philosophical Journey into the Brain.*

Imagine a brilliant neuroscientist named Mary, who has lived her entire life in a room that is rigorously controlled to display only various shades of black, white, and grey. She learns about the outside world by means of a black/white television monitor, and, being brilliant, she manages to transcend these obstacles. She becomes the world's greatest neuroscientist, all from within this room. In particular, she comes to know everything there is to know about the physical structure and activity of the brain and its visual system, of its actual and possible states.

But there would still be something she did *not* know, and could not even imagine, about the actual experiences of all the other people who live outside her black/white room, and about her possible experiences were she finally to leave her room: the nature of the experience of seeing a ripe tomato, what it is like to see red or have a sensation-of-red. Therefore, complete knowledge of the physical facts of visual perception and its related brain activity *still leaves something out.* Therefore, materialism cannot give an adequate reductionist account of all mental phenomena.

To give a conveniently tightened version of this argument:

(1) Mary knows everything there is to know about brain states and their properties.

(2) It is not the case that Mary knows everything there is to know about sensations and their properties.

Therefore, by Leibniz's law,

(3) Sensations and their properties ≠ brain states and their properties.

THE FIRST SHORTCOMING

This defect is simplicity itself. "Knows about" may be transparent in both premises, but it is not *univocal* in both premises. (David Lewis and Laurence Nemirow have both raised this same objection, though their analysis of the ambiguity at issue differs from mine.) Jackson's argument is valid only if 'knows about' is univocal in both premises. But the kind of knowledge addressed in premise 1 seems pretty clearly to be different from the kind of knowledge addressed in (2). Knowledge in (1) seems to be a matter of having mastered a set of sentences or propositions, the kind one finds written in neuroscience texts, whereas knowledge in (2) seems to be a matter of having a representation of redness in some prelinguistic or sublinguistic medium of representation for sensory variables, or to be a matter of being able to *make* certain sensory discriminations, or something along these lines.

Reprinted from *The Journal of Philosophy, 82* (1985), by permission of the publisher and the author.

Lewis and Nemirow plump for the "ability" analysis of the relevant sense of "knows about," but they need not be so narrowly committed, and the complaint of equivocation need not be so narrowly based. As my alternative gloss illustrates, other analyses of "knowledge by acquaintance" are possible, and the charge of equivocation will be sustained so long as the type of knowledge invoked in premise 1 is distinct from the type invoked in premise 2. Importantly, they do seem very different, even in advance of a settled analysis of the latter.

In short, the difference between a person who knows all about the visual cortex but has never enjoyed a sensation of red, and a person who knows no neuroscience but knows well the sensation of red, may reside not in *what* is respectively known by each (brain states by the former, qualia by the latter), but rather in the different *type* of knowledge each has *of exactly the same thing*. The difference is in the manner of the knowing, not in the nature of the thing(s) known. If one replaces the ambiguous occurrences of 'knows about' in Jackson's argument with the two different expansions suggested above, the resulting argument is a clear non sequitur.

(a) Mary has mastered the complete set of true propositions about people's brain states.
(b) Mary does *not* have a representation of redness in her prelinguistic medium of representation for sensory variables.
Therefore, by Leibniz's law,
(c) The redness sensation ≠ any brain state.

Premises a and b are compossible, even on a materialist view. But they do not entail (c).

In sum, there are pretty clearly more ways of "having knowledge" than having mastered a set of sentences. And nothing in materialism precludes this. The materialist can freely admit that one has "knowledge" of one's sensations in a way that is independent of the scientific theories one has learned. This does not mean that sensations are beyond the reach of physical science. *It just means that the brain uses more modes and media of representation than the simple storage of sentences.* And this proposition is pretty obviously true: almost certainly the brain uses

a considerable variety of modes and media of representation, perhaps hundreds of them. Jackson's argument, and Nagel's, exploit this variety illegitimately: both arguments equivocate on "knows about."

This criticism is supported by the observation that, if Jackson's form of argument were sound, it would prove far too much. Suppose that Jackson were arguing, not against materialism, but against dualism: against the view that there exists a nonmaterial substance—call it "ectoplasm"—whose hidden constitution and nomic intricacies ground all mental phenomena. Let our cloistered Mary be an "ectoplasmologist" this time, and let her know$_1$ everything there is to know about the ectoplasmic processes underlying vision. There would still be something she did not know$_2$: what it is like to see red. Dualism is therefore inadequate to account for all mental phenomena!

This argument is as plausible as Jackson's, and for the same reason: it exploits the same equivocation. But the truth is, such arguments show nothing, one way or the other, about how mental phenomena might be accounted for.

THE SECOND SHORTCOMING

There is a further shortcoming with Jackson's argument, one of profound importance for understanding one of the most exciting consequences to be expected from a successful neuroscientific account of mind. I draw your attention to the assumption that even a utopian knowledge of neuroscience *must* leave Mary hopelessly in the dark about the subjective qualitative nature of sensations not-yet-enjoyed. It is true, of course, that no sentence of the form "*x* is a sensation-of-red" will be deducible from premises restricted to the language of neuroscience. But this is no point against the reducibility of phenomenological properties. As we saw in section *I,* direct deducibility is an intolerably strong demand on reduction, and if this is all the objection comes to, then there is no objection worth addressing. What the defender of emergent qualia must have in mind here, I think, is the claim that Mary could not even *imagine* what the relevant experience would be like, despite her exhaustive neuroscientific knowledge, and hence must still be missing certain crucial information.

This claim, however, is simply false. Given the truth of premise 1, premise 2 seems plausible to Jackson . . . only because none of these philosophers has adequately considered how much one might know if, as premise 1 asserts, one knew *everything* there is to know about the physical brain and nervous system. In particular, none of these philosophers has even begun to consider the changes in our introspective apprehension of our internal states that could follow upon a wholesale revision in our conceptual framework for our internal states.

The fact is, we can indeed imagine how neuroscientific information would give Mary detailed information about the qualia of various sensations. Recall our earlier discussion of the transformation of perception through the systematic reconceptualization of the relevant perceptual domain. In particular, suppose that Mary has learned to conceptualize her inner life, even in introspection, in terms of the completed neuroscience we are to imagine. So she does not identify her visual sensations crudely as "a sensation-of-black," "a sensation-of-grey," or "a sensation-of-white"; rather she identifies them more revealingly as various spiking frequencies in the nth layer of the occipital cortex (or whatever). If Mary has the relevant neuroscientific concepts for the sensational states at issue (viz., sensations-of-*red*), but has never yet been *in* those states, she may well be able to imagine being in the relevant cortical state, and imagine it with substantial success, even in advance of receiving external stimuli that would actually produce it.

One test of her ability in this regard would be to give her a stimulus that would (finally) produce in her the relevant state (viz., a spiking frequency of 90 hz in the gamma network: a "sensation-of-red" to us), and see whether she can identify it correctly *on introspective grounds alone,* as "a spiking frequency of 90 hz: the kind a tomato would cause." It does not seem to me to be impossible that she should succeed in this, and do so regularly on similar tests for other states, conceptualized clearly by her, but not previously enjoyed.

This may seem to some an outlandish suggestion, but the following will show that it is not. Musical chords are auditory phenomena that the young and unpracticed ear hears as undivided wholes, discrim-

inable one from another, but without elements or internal structure. A musical education changes this, and one comes to hear chords as groups of discriminable notes. If one is sufficiently practiced to have absolute pitch, one can even name the notes of an apprehended chord. And the reverse is also true: if a set of notes is specified verbally, a trained pianist or guitarist can identify the chord and recall its sound in auditory imagination. Moreover, a really skilled individual can construct, in auditory imagination, the sound of a chord he may never have heard before, and certainly does not remember. Specify for him a relatively unusual one—an F#9th*add* 13th for example—and let him brood for a bit. Then play for him three or four chords, one of which is the target, and see whether he can pick it out as the sound that meets the description. Skilled musicians can do this. Why is a similar skill beyond all possibility for Mary?

"Ah," it is tempting to reply, "musicians can do this only because chords are audibly structured sets of elements. Sensations of color are not."

But neither did chords seem, initially, to be structured sets of elements. They also seemed to be undifferentiated wholes. Why should it be unthinkable that sensations of color possess a comparable internal structure, unnoticed so far, but awaiting our determined and informed inspection? Jackson's argument, to be successful, must rule this possibility out, and it is difficult to see how he can do this *a priori.* Especially since there has recently emerged excellent empirical evidence to suggest that *our sensations of color are indeed structured sets of elements.*

The retinex theory of color vision recently proposed by Edwin Land[1] represents any color apprehendable by the human visual system as being uniquely specified by its joint position along three vertices—its reflectance efficiencies at three critical wavelengths, those wavelengths to which the retina's triune cone system is selectively responsive. Since colors are apprehended by us, it is a good hypothesis that those three parameters are represented in our visual systems and that our sensations of color are in some direct way determined by them. Sensations of color may turn out literally to *be* three-element chords in some neural medium! In the face of all this, I do not see why it is even briefly plausible to insist that it is utterly impossible for a conceptually sophisticated Mary accurately to imagine, and subsequently to pick out, color sensations she has not previously enjoyed. We can already foresee how it might actually be done.

The preceding argument does not collapse the distinction (between knowledge-by-description and knowledge-by-acquaintance) urged earlier in the discussion of equivocation. But it does show that the "taxonomies" that reside in our prelinguistic media of representation can be profoundly shaped by the taxonomies that reside in the linguistic medium, especially if one has had long practice at the observational discrimination of items that answer to those linguistically embodied categories. This is just a further illustration of the plasticity of human perception.

I do not mean to suggest, of course, that there will be no limits to what Mary can imagine. Her brain is finite, and its specific anatomy will have specific limitations. For example, if a bat's brain includes computational machinery that the human brain simply lacks (which seems likely), then the subjective character of *some* of the bat's internal states may well be beyond human imagination. Clearly, however, the

elusiveness of the bat's inner life here stems not from the metaphysical "emergence" of its internal qualia, but only from the finite capacities of our idiosyncratically human brains. Within those sheerly structural limitations, our imaginations may soar far beyond what Jackson, Nagel, and Robinson suspect, if we possess a neuroscientific conceptual framework that is at last adequate to the intricate phenomena at issue.

I suggest then, that those of us who prize the flux and content of our subjective phenomenological experience need not view the advance of materialistic neuroscience with fear and foreboding. Quite the contrary. The genuine arrival of a materialist kinematics and dynamics for psychological states and cognitive processes will constitute not a gloom in which our inner life is suppressed or eclipsed, but rather a dawning, in which its marvelous intricacies are finally *revealed*—most notably, if we apply ourselves, in direct self-conscious introspection.

NOTE

1. "The Retinex Theory of Color Vision," *Scientific American* (December 1977): 108–128.

Consciousness Explained

DANIEL C. DENNETT

Daniel C. Dennett is professor of philosophy at Tufts University. He has been a leading voice in philosophy of mind and has written on such topics as intentionality, consciousness, and free will. His books include *Brainstorms* and *The Intentional Stance*.

I am interested in directly considering the conclusion that Jackson himself draws from his example: visual experiences have qualia that are "epiphenomenal."

The term "epiphenomena" is in common use today by both philosophers and psychologists (and

other cognitive scientists). It is used with the presumption that its meaning is familiar and agreed upon, when in fact, philosophers and cognitive scientists use the term with entirely different meanings— a strange fact made even stranger to me by the fact

Reprinted from *Consciousness Explained* (Boston: Little Brown & Company, 1991), by permission of the publisher.

that although I have pointed this out time and again, no one seems to care. Since "epiphenomenalism" often seems to be the last remaining safe haven for qualia, and since this appearance of safety is due entirely to the confusion between these two meanings, I must become a scold, and put those who use the term on the defensive.

According to the *Shorter Oxford English Dictionary,* the term "epiphenomenon" first appears in 1706 as a term in pathology, "a secondary appearance or symptom." The evolutionary biologist Thomas Huxley (1874) was probably the writer who extended the term to its current use in psychology, where it means a *nonfunctional* property or by-product. Huxley used the term in his discussion of the evolution of consciousness and his claim that epiphenomenal properties (like the "whistle of the steam engine") could not be explained by natural selection.

Here is a clear instance of this use of the word:

> Why do people who are thinking hard bite their lips and tap their feet? Are these actions just epiphenomena that accompany the core processes of feeling and thinking or might they themselves be integral parts of these processes? [Zajonc and Markus, 1984, p. 74]

Notice that the authors mean to assert that these actions, while perfectly detectable, play no enabling role, no designed role, in the processes of feeling and thinking; they are nonfunctional. In the same spirit, the hum of the computer is epiphenomenal, as is your shadow when you make yourself a cup of tea. Epiphenomena are mere by-products, but as such they are products with lots of effects in the world: tapping your feet makes a recordable noise, and your shadow has its effects on photographic film, not to mention the slight cooling of the surfaces it spreads itself over.

The standard philosophical meaning is different: "x is epiphenomenal" means "x is an effect but itself has no effects in the physical world whatever." . . . Are these meanings really so different? Yes, as different as the meanings of *murder* and *death.* The philosophical meaning is stronger: Anything that has no effects whatever in the physical world surely has no effects on the function of anything, but the con-

verse doesn't follow, as the example from Zajonc and Markus makes obvious.

In fact, the philosophical meaning is too strong; it yields a concept of no utility whatsoever. Since x has no physical effects (according to this definition), no instrument can detect the presence of x directly or indirectly; the way the world goes is not modulated in the slightest by the presence or absence of x. How then, could there ever be any empirical reason to assert the presence of x? Suppose, for instance, that Otto insists that he (for one) has epiphenomenal qualia. Why does he say this? Not because they have some effect on him, somehow guiding him or alerting him as he makes his avowals. By the very definition of epiphenomena (in the philosophical sense), Otto's heartfelt avowals that he has epiphenomena *could not* be evidence for himself or anyone else that he does have them, since he would be saying exactly the same thing even if he didn't have them. But perhaps Otto has some "internal" evidence?

Here there's a loophole, but not an attractive one. Epiphenomena, remember, are defined as having no effect in the *physical* world. If Otto wants to embrace out-and-out dualism, he can claim that his epiphenomenal qualia have no effects in the physical world, but do have effects in his (nonphysical) mental world. . . . For instance, they *cause some of his (nonphysical) beliefs,* such as his belief that he has epiphenomenal qualia. But this is just a temporary escape from embarrassment. For now on pain of contradiction, his beliefs, in turn, can have no effect in the physical world. If he suddenly lost his epiphenomenal qualia, he would no longer believe he had them, but he'd still go right on *saying* he did. He just wouldn't believe what he was saying! (Nor could he tell you that he didn't believe what he was saying, or do anything at all that revealed that he no longer believed what he was saying.) So the only way Otto could "justify" his belief in epiphenomena would be by retreating into a solipsistic world where there is only himself, his beliefs and his qualia, cut off from all effects in the world. Far from being a "safe" way of being a materialist and having your qualia too, this is at best a way of endorsing the most radical solipsism, by cutting off your mind—your beliefs and your experiences—from any commerce with the material world.

If qualia are epiphenomenal in the standard philosophical sense, their occurrence can't explain the way things happen (in the material world) since, by definition, things would happen exactly the same without them. There could not be an empirical reason, then, for believing in epiphenomena. Could there be another sort of reason for asserting their existence? What sort of reason? An *a priori* reason, presumably. But what? No one has ever offered one—good, bad, or indifferent—that I have seen. If someone wants to object that I am being a "verificationist" about these epiphenomena, I reply: Isn't everyone a verificationist about *this* sort of assertion? Consider, for instance, the hypothesis that there are fourteen epiphenomenal gremlins in each cylinder of an internal combustion engine. These gremlins have no mass, no energy, no physical properties; they do not make the engine run smoother or rougher, faster or slower. There is *and could be* no empirical evidence of their presence, and no empirical way in principle of distinguishing this hypothesis from its rivals: there are twelve or thirteen or fifteen . . . gremlins. By what principle does one defend one's wholesale dismissal of such nonsense? A verificationist principle, or just plain common sense?

> Ah, but there's a difference! [says Otto.] There is no independent motivation for taking the hypothesis of these gremlins seriously. You just made them up on the spur of the moment. Qualia, in contrast, have been around for a long time, playing a major role in our conceptual scheme!

And what if some benighted people have been thinking for generations that gremlins made their cars go, and by now have been pushed back by the march of science into the forlorn claim that the gremlins are there, all right, but are epiphenomenal? Is it a mistake for us to dismiss their "hypothesis" out of hand? Whatever the principle is that we rely on when we give the back of our hand to such nonsense, it suffices to dismiss the doctrine that qualia are epiphenomenal in this philosophical sense. These are not views that deserve to be discussed with a straight face.

It's hard to believe that the philosophers who have recently described their views as epiphenomenalism can be making such a woebegone mistake. Are they,

perhaps, just asserting that qualia are epiphenomenal in Huxley's sense? Qualia, on this reading, *are* physical effects and *have* physical effects; they just aren't functional. Any materialist should be happy to admit that this hypothesis is true—if we identify qualia with reactive dispositions, for instance. As we noted in the discussion of enjoyment, even though some bulges or biases in our quality spaces are functional—or used to be functional—others are just brute happenstance. Why don't I like broccoli? Probably for no reason at all; my negative reactive disposition is purely epiphenomenal, a by-product of my wiring with no significance. It has no function, but has plenty of effects. In any designed system, some properties are crucial while others are more or less revisable *ad lib*. Everything has to be some way or another, but often the ways don't matter. The gear shift lever on a car may have to be a certain length and a certain strength, but whether it is round or square or oval in cross section is an epiphenomenal property, in Huxley's sense.

If we think of all the properties of our nervous systems that enable us to see, hear, smell, taste, and touch things, we can divide them, roughly, into the properties that play truly crucial roles in mediating the information processing, and the epiphenomal properties that are more or less revisable *ad lib*. . . . When a philosopher surmises that qualia are epiphenomenal properties of brain states, this might mean that qualia could turn out to be local variations in the heat generated by neuronal metabolism. That cannot be what epiphenomenalists have in mind, can it? If it is, then qualia as epiphenomena are no challenge to materialism.

The time has come to put the burden of proof squarely on those who persist in using the term. The philosophical sense of the term is simply ridiculous; Huxley's sense is relatively clear and unproblematic—and irrelevant to the philosophical arguments. No other sense of the term has any currency. So if anyone claims to uphold a variety of epiphenomenalism, try to be polite, but ask: What *are* you talking about?

Notice, by the way, that this equivocation between two senses of "epiphenomenal" also infects the discussion of zombies. A philosopher's zombie, you will recall, is behaviorally indistinguishable from a normal human being, but is not conscious. There is nothing it is like to be a zombie; it just seems that way to observers (including itself, as we saw in the previous chapter). Now this can be given a strong or weak interpretation, depending on how we treat this indistinguishability to observers. If we were to declare that *in principle,* a zombie is indistinguishable from a conscious person, then we would be saying that genuine consciousness is epiphenomenal *in the ridiculous* sense. That is just silly. So we could say instead that consciousness might be epiphenomenal in the Huxley sense: although there was some way of distinguishing zombies from real people (who knows, maybe zombies have green brains), the difference doesn't show up as a functional difference *to observers.* Equivalently, human bodies with green brains don't harbor observers, while other human bodies do. On this hypothesis, we would be able in principle to distinguish the inhabited bodies from the uninhabited bodies by checking for brain color. This is also silly, of course, and dangerously silly, for it echoes the sort of utterly unmotivated prejudices that have denied full personhood to people on the basis of the color of their skin. It is time to recognize the idea of the possibility of zombies for what it is: not a serious philosophical idea but a preposterous and ignoble relic of ancient prejudices. Maybe women aren't really conscious! Maybe Jews! What pernicious nonsense. As Shylock says, drawing our attention, quite properly, to "merely behavioral" criteria:

> Hath not a Jew eyes? Hath not a Jew hands, organs, dimensions, senses, affections, passions; fed with the same food, hurt with the same weapons, subject to the same diseases, heal'd by the same means, warm'd and cool'd by the same winter and summer, as a Christian is? If you prick us, do we not bleed? If you tickle us, do we not laugh? If you poison us, do we not die?

There is another way to address the possibility of zombies, and in some regards I think it is more satisfying. Are zombies possible? They're not just possible, they're actual. We're all zombies. Nobody is conscious—not in the systematically mysterious way that supports such doctrines as epiphenomenalism! I can't prove that no such sort of consciousness exists. I also cannot prove that gremlins don't exist. The best I can do is show that there is no respectable motivation for believing in it.

PART 6

~

Philosophy of Language

Introduction

ROBIN JESHION

What is the relationship between the world, our thought about the world, and language? How can a mere linguistic symbol represent or refer to something in the world? What is the role of the mind in linguistic representation? Who determines what words mean, the speaker or the linguistic community? What makes us so adept at understanding others? These are just some of the fundamental issues that are discussed in philosophy of language.

Philosophers and linguists distinguish three subfields of study: syntax, semantics, and pragmatics. Syntax is the study of the way in which sentences are constructed from their parts. It is a study of pure linguistic forms construed in isolation of their meanings. Although syntax has bearing upon philosophy, research in pure syntax is, by and large, confined to linguistics. Semantics is the study of the meaning, truth, and reference. Semantic theories try to account for how words refer and sentences express facts about the worlds. Pragmatics has two branches. One branch aims to understand the speech acts, things that we *do* with language. The other branch aims to explicate the ways in which we communicate far more than what we explicitly say.

Although meaning, truth, and reference have been discussed throughout the history of philosophy, even in ancient times, philosophy of language is a newcomer on the scene. The first truly systematic study in semantics is Gottlob Frege's remarkable 1892 essay "On Sense and Reference." Frege not only laid out a comprehensive semantic theory, he also framed the most important problems that any semantic theory needs to answer.

Frege opens his discussion with a challenge to any semantic theory that takes the semantic content of a referring term to be exclusively its referent. For example, if the semantic contents of "Mark Twain" and "Samuel Clemens" are just their referents—a certain man—then a problem ensues. For the statement "Mark Twain is Samuel Clemens" is informative. Yet how could it be informative if what is being expressed by it is exactly the same as what is expressed by "Mark Twain is Mark Twain," which is uninformative? To solve this puzzle, Frege concluded that, in addition to a referent, terms like "Mark Twain" have what he called a *sense,* a mode of presentation of the term's referent. A sense can usefully be thought of as a kind of descriptive characterization. The sense of "Mark Twain" might be "the author of *Huckleberry Finn.*" Frege applied his duel notions of sense and reference not only to names and definite descriptions, but to full declarative sentences. What we grasp in understanding a sentence is, for Frege, the sentence's sense—a certain thought. The sentence's truth value is its reference. He also explained how the sense of a full sentence is built up from the senses of its parts, and how the reference of the sentence is a function of the references of its parts. Frege's system links together semantics with mentalistic matters like the content of our thought and epistemic matters like informativeness. Bertrand Russell's brilliant 1905 article "On Denoting" addresses many of the same issues as Frege's "On Sense and Reference," but Russell is guided by a different epistemological concern. Whereas Frege aimed to account for a language's informativeness, Russell was concerned to preserve the idea that we could only have thoughts about things with which we are acquainted. And Russell's views on acquaintance are decidedly offbeat. He thought, for example, that even if you and I someday met in Times Square, we would not be acquainted with each other. To be acquainted with something, we need to grasp that object in its entirety, and there must be no room for mistaken identification. We are each only acquainted with our own sense perceptions (*not* the objects we perceive), universals, and, possibly, ourselves.

How did these views on acquaintance drive Russell's semantic theory? Any propositions we can grasp are composed entirely of constituents with which we can be acquainted. Consequently, for Russell, constituents of sentences must denote only our sense perceptions, universals, or (possibly) our selves. So Russell would treat a sentence like "Mark Twain had a moustache" as "The author of *Huckleberry Finn* had a moustache" and analyze that as "There is one and only individual that authored *Huckleberry Finn* and that individual had a moustache." This move to identify the semantic content of a proper name with a description and offer a quantified analysis of the sentence allows him to preserve his condition on acquaintance. For it is not Mark Twain the man that we "grasp" in understanding the sentence, but rather the property—universal—of being an author of *Huckleberry Finn.* Russell's way of analyzing these statements allowed him to provide an elegant solution to puzzles about sentences that have no referent (such as "The present king of France is bald.") and to explain how we express thoughts about things that do not exist.

Saul Kripke launches a full-scale assault on the Frege-Russell descriptivist theory of the semantics of names. His 1970 lectures were ground-breaking because the arguments were rooted on careful separation of the epistemological distinction between a priori and a posteriori justification and the metaphysical distinction between necessity and possibility, as well as on a theory of possible worlds and metaphysical essentialism. Kripke's fundamental claim is that proper names function as *rigid designators,* terms that refer to the same object in all possible worlds in which they refer to any object at all. Names consequently have a different semantics than ordinary definite descriptions. For example, in the actual world the definite description "the inventor of bifocals" refers to Ben Franklin. But we can imagine that in some other possible world, Ben Franklin got scooped and someone else invented them. In that other possible world, "the inventor of bifocals" refers to that other person. But in that very world in which Ben Franklin got scooped, the name "Ben Franklin" nevertheless refers to Ben Franklin. This point suggests that the descriptivist view that takes names as synonymous with a description, or a cluster of descriptions, stands in need of significant alteration.

In addition to arguing against the Frege-Russell view, Kripke advocated a return to the view of John Stuart Mill that names have reference, but no sense. We use proper names—and do so legitimately—even when we lack identifying information about the referent of the name. How then do we succeed in referring with a name? According to Kripke, we refer to the name's bearer because we use names with the intention to refer to that individual that other speakers in our community refer to when they use the name. A name's reference is determined by following the use of the name through the linguistic community all the way back to the reference-fixing of the name.

In the next selection, we return to Frege for discussion that focuses on the nature of thoughts. One of the highlights is his analysis of the semantics of indexicals such as "I". According to Frege, as a referring term, "I" must have both sense and reference. But, what could be the sense of "I"? After all, when I use "I", I refer to me, and when you use "I" you refer to you. So, since sense determines reference, the sense of "I" in my mouth must differ from the sense of "I" in your mouth. Frege recognized this oddity, yet preserved his core doctrine by regarding "I" as shifting its sense with the speaker. When I refer to myself by using "I", I have a mode of presentation of myself that is known only to me, that is, in principle, entirely ungraspable to others.

In "The Problem of the Essential Indexical," John Perry takes Frege to task. He argues against any Fregean analysis of essential indexicals like "I", "now", and "here" that takes such terms as having a sense that determines reference. Perry's striking idea is that if "I" has a descriptive mode of presentation, "I"-thoughts would not generate their primary function of initiating agency. For example, if I am to be spurred on to clean up the sugar-trail from my broken sugar-sack, I must recognize that I—thought of directly, nondescriptively—am the one making the mess. Thinking of myself as, say, the silliest philosopher in Trader Joe's will not do. For to rouse the requisite action, I must recognize that I am the silliest philosopher in Trader Joe's. Perry shows that the same style of argument applies to "now" and "here".

Our last two selections are on pragmatics. The first is by John Austin, the second by Paul Grice. Until the mid-20th century, most philosophers took declarative sentences as the primary linguistic items that stand in need of analysis. Other uses of language were largely ignored. In *How to Do Things with Words,* Austin changed all that. He did so by explicating a notion of a performative utterance. With a performative utterance with which a speaker performs an act by saying something. Suppose I say to my son "I promise to give you an ice cream cone right after dinner". By making that utterance, I haven't described a state of affairs; I have, rather, executed something. With my words, I have promised. Austin spelled out an enormous range of performative utterances and embarked on an analysis of the conditions for their successful performance.

Paul Grice developed a distinct topic within pragmatics. He explained how it is that what we express or convey with our words outstrips what we say. To put a slight spin on one of Grice's many wonderful examples in "Logic and Conversation," suppose that you are asked to evaluate your professor's teaching. You write "Well, she does know how to read. And she always gets to class on time." Obviously, you're expressing that your professor's performance has been less than stellar. Yet you haven't said that with your words. You have implicated it. How then do we know what you have expressed? Grice characterizes a notion of implicature and advances an ingenious theory explaining how certain rules that govern conversations determine what is expressed by a sentence in a given context.

On Sense and Meaning

~

GOTTLOB FREGE

Gottlob Frege (1848–1925), a German mathematician and philosopher of mathematics, was the founder of modern mathematical logic and a leading figure in the philosophy of language.

Equality[1] gives rise to challenging questions which are not altogether easy to answer. Is it a relation? A relation between objects, or between names or signs of objects? In my *Begriffsschrift* I assumed the latter. The reasons which seem to favour this are the following: $a = a$ and $a = b$ are obviously statements of differing cognitive value; $a = a$ holds a priori and, according to Kant, is to be labelled analytic, while statements of the form $a = b$ often contain very valuable extensions of our knowledge and cannot always be established a priori. The discovery that the rising sun is not new every morning, but always the same, was one of the most fertile astronomical discoveries. Even today the re-identification of a small planet or a comet is not always a | matter of course. Now if we were to regard equality as a relation between that which the names "a" and "b" designate, it would seem that $a = b$ could not differ from $a = a$ (i.e. provided $a = b$ is true). A relation would thereby be expressed of a thing to itself, and indeed one in which each thing stands to itself but to no other thing. What we apparently want to state by $a = b$ is that the signs or names "a" and "b" designate the same thing, so that those signs themselves would be under discussion; a relation between them would be asserted. But this relation would hold between the names or signs only in so far as they named or designated something. It would be mediated by the connection of each of the two signs with the same designated thing. But this is

arbitrary. Nobody can be forbidden to use any arbitrarily producible event or object as a sign for something. In that case the sentence $a = b$ would no longer refer to the subject matter, but only to its mode of designation; we would express no proper knowledge by its means. But in many cases this is just what we want to do. If the sign "a" is distinguished from the sign "b" only as an object (here, by means of its shape), not as a sign (i.e. not by the manner in which it designates something), the cognitive value of $a = a$ becomes essentially equal to that of $a = b$, provided $a = b$ is true. A difference can arise only if the difference between the signs corresponds to a difference in the mode of presentation of the thing designated. Let a, b, c be the lines connecting the vertices of a triangle with the midpoints of the opposite sides. The point of intersection of a and b is then the same as the point of intersection of b and c. So we have different designations for the same point, and these names ("point of intersection of a and b," "point of intersection of b and c") likewise indicate the mode of presentation; and hence the statement contains actual knowledge.

It is natural, now, to think of there being connected with a sign (name, combination of words, written mark), besides that which the sign designates, which may be called the meaning of the sign, also what I should like to call the *sense* of the sign, wherein the mode of presentation is contained. In our example,

Reprinted from the *Translations from the Philosophical Writings of Gottlob Frege*, 3rd ed., ed. P. T. Geach and Max Black (Oxford, Blackwell Publishers, 1980), by permission of the publisher.

accordingly, the | meaning of the expressions "the point of intersection of *a* and *b*" and "the point of intersection of *b* and *c*" would be the same, but not their sense. The meaning of "evening star" would be the same as that of "morning star," but not the sense.

It is clear from the context that by sign and name I have here understood any designation figuring as a proper name, which thus has as its meaning a definite object (this word taken in the widest range), but not a concept or a relation. . . . The designation of a single object can also consist of several words or other signs. For brevity, let every such designation be called a proper name.

The sense of a proper name is grasped by everybody who is sufficiently familiar with the language or totality of designations to which it belongs;[2] but this serves to illuminate only a single aspect of the thing meant, supposing it to have one. Comprehensive knowledge of the thing meant would require us to be able to say immediately whether any given sense attaches to it. To such knowledge we never attain.

The regular connection between a sign, its sense, and what it means is of such a kind that to the sign there corresponds a definite sense and to that in turn a definite thing meant, while to a given thing meant (an object) there does not belong only a single sign. The same sense has different expressions in different languages or even in the same language. To be sure, exceptions to this regular behaviour occur. To every expression belonging to a complete totality of signs, there should certainly correspond a definite sense; but natural languages often do not satisfy this condition, and one must be content if the same word has the same sense in the same context. It may perhaps be granted that every grammatically well-formed expression figuring as a proper name always has a sense. But this is not to say that to the sense there also corresponds a thing meant. The words "the celestial body most distant from the Earth" have a sense, but it is very doubtful if there is also a thing they mean. The expression 'the least rapidly convergent series' has a sense but demonstrably there is nothing it means, since for every given convergent series, another convergent, but less rapidly convergent, series can be found. In grasping a sense, one is not certainly assured of meaning anything.

If words are used in the ordinary way, what one intends to speak of is what they mean. It can also happen, however, that one wishes to talk about the words themselves or their sense. This happens, for instance, when the words of another are quoted. One's own words then first designate words of the other speaker, and only the latter have their usual meaning. We then have signs of signs. In writing, the words are in this case enclosed in quotation marks. Accordingly, a word standing between quotation marks must not be taken as having its ordinary meaning.

In order to speak of the sense of an expression "A" one may simply use the phrase "the sense of the expression 'A.'" In indirect speech one talks about the sense, e.g., of another person's remarks. It is quite clear that in this way of speaking words do not have their customary meaning but designate what is usually their sense. In order to have a short expression, we will say: In indirect speech, words are used *indirectly* or have their *indirect* meaning. We distinguish accordingly the *customary* from the *indirect* meaning of a word; and its *customary* sense from its *indirect* sense. The indirect meaning of a word is accordingly its customary sense. Such exceptions must always be borne in mind if the mode of connection between sign, sense, and meaning in particular cases is to be correctly understood.

The meaning and sense of a sign are to be distinguished from the associated idea. If what a sign means is an object perceivable by the senses, my idea of it is an internal image,[3] arising from memories of sense impressions which I have had and acts, both internal and external, which I have performed. Such an idea is often imbued with feeling; the clarity of its separate parts varies and oscillates. The same sense is not always connected, even in the same man, with the same idea. The idea is subjective: one man's idea is not that of another. There result, as a matter of course, a variety of differences in the ideas associated with the same sense. A painter, a horseman, and a zoologist will probably connect different ideas with the name "Bucephalus." This constitutes an essential distinction between the idea and sign's sense, which may be the common property of many people, and so is not a part or a mode of the individual mind. For one can hardly deny that mankind has a common store of thoughts which is transmitted from one generation to another.[4]

In the light of this, one need have no scruples in speaking simply of *the* sense, whereas in the case of an idea one must, strictly speaking, add whom it belongs to and at what time. It might perhaps be said: Just as one man connects this idea, and another that idea, with the same word, so also one man can associate this sense and another that sense. But there still remains a difference in the mode of connection. They are not prevented from grasping the same sense; but they cannot have the same idea. *Si duo idem faciunt, non est idem.* If two persons picture the same thing, each still has his own idea. It is indeed sometimes possible to establish differences in the ideas, or even in the sensations, of different men; but an exact comparison is not possible, because we cannot have both ideas together in the same consciousness.

The meaning of a proper name is the object itself which we designate by using it; the idea which we have in that case is wholly subjective; in between lies the sense, which is indeed no longer subjective like the idea, but is yet not the object itself. The following analogy will perhaps clarify these relationships. Somebody observes the Moon through a telescope. I compare the Moon itself to the meaning; it is the object of the observation, mediated by the real image projected by the object glass in the interior of the telescope, and by the retinal image of the observer. The former I compare to the sense, the latter is like the idea or experience. The optical image in the telescope is indeed one-sided and dependent upon the standpoint of observation; but it is still objective, inasmuch as it can be used by several observers. At any rate it could be arranged for several to use it simultaneously. But each one would have his own retinal image. On account of the diverse shapes of the observers' eyes, even a geometrical congruence could hardly be achieved, and an actual coincidence would be out of the question. This analogy might be developed still further, by assuming A's retinal image made visible to B; or A might also see his own retinal image in a mirror. In this way we might perhaps show how an idea can itself be taken as an object, but as such is not for the observer what it directly is for the person having the idea. But to pursue this would take us too far afield.

We can now recognize three levels of difference between words, expressions, or whole sentences. The difference may concern at most the ideas, or the sense but not the meaning, or, finally, the meaning as well. With respect to the first level, it is to be noted that, on account of the uncertain connection of ideas with words, a difference may hold for one person, which another does not find. The difference between a translation and the original text should properly not overstep the first level. To the possible difference here belong also the colouring and shading which poetic eloquence seeks to give to the sense. Such colouring and shading are not objective, and must be evoked by each hearer or reader according to the hints of the poet or the speaker. Without some affinity in human ideas art would certainly be impossible; but it can never be exactly determined how far the intentions of the poet are realized.

In what follows there will be no further discussion of ideas and experiences; they have been mentioned here only to ensure that the idea aroused in the hearer by a word shall not be confused with its sense or its meaning.

To make short and exact expressions possible, let the following phraseology be established:

A proper name (word, sign, sign combination, expression) *expresses* its sense, *means* or *designates* its meaning. By employing a sign we express its sense and designate its meaning.

Idealists or sceptics will perhaps long since have objected: "You talk, without further ado, of the Moon as an object; but how do you know that the name 'the Moon' has any meaning? How do you know that anything whatsoever has a meaning?" I reply that when we say "the Moon," we do not intend to speak of our idea of the Moon, nor are we satisfied with the sense alone, but we presuppose a meaning. To assume that in the sentence "The Moon is smaller than the Earth" the idea of the Moon is in question, would be flatly to misunderstand the sense. If this is what the speaker wanted, he would use the phrase "my idea of the Moon." Now we can of course be mistaken in the presupposition, and such mistakes have indeed occurred. But the question whether the presupposition is perhaps always mistaken need | not be answered here; in order to justify mention of that which a sign means it is enough, at first, to point our intention in speaking or thinking. (We must then add the reservation: provided such a meaning exists.)

So far we have considered the sense and meaning only of such expressions, words, or signs as we have called proper names. We now inquire concerning the sense and meaning of an entire assertoric sentence. Such a sentence contains a thought.[5] Is this thought, now, to be regarded as its sense or its meaning? Let us assume for the time being that the sentence does mean something. If we now replace one word of the sentence by another having the same meaning, but a different sense, this can have no effect upon the meaning of the sentence. Yet we can see that in such a case the thought changes; since, e.g., the thought in the sentence "The morning star is a body illuminated by the Sun." differs from that in the sentence "The evening star is a body illuminated by the Sun." Anybody who did not know that the evening star is the morning star might hold the one thought to be true, the other false. The thought, accordingly, cannot be what is meant by the sentence, but must rather be considered as its sense. What is the position now with regard to the meaning? Have we a right even to inquire about it? Is it possible that a sentence as a whole has only a sense, but no meaning? At any rate, one might expect that such sentences occur, just as there are parts of sentences having sense but no meaning. And sentences which contain proper names without meaning will be of this kind. The sentence "Odysseus was set ashore at Ithaca while sound asleep" obviously has a sense. But since it is doubtful whether the name "Odysseus," occurring therein, means anything, it is also doubtful whether the whole sentence does. Yet it is certain, nevertheless, that anyone who seriously took the sentence to be true or false would ascribe to the name "Odysseus" a meaning, not merely a sense; for it is of what the name means that the predicate is affirmed or denied. Whoever does not admit the name has meaning can neither apply nor withhold the predicate. But in that case it would be superfluous to advance to what the name means; one could be satisfied with the sense, if one wanted to go no further than the thought. If it were a question only of the sense of the sentence, the thought, it would be needless to bother with what is meant by a part of the sentence; only the sense, not the

meaning, of the part is relevant to the sense of the whole sentence. The thought remains the same whether "Odysseus" means something or not. The fact that we concern ourselves at all about what is meant by a part of the sentence indicates that we generally recognize and expect a meaning for the sentence itself. The thought loses value for us as soon as we recognize that the meaning of one of its parts is missing. We are therefore justified in not being satisfied with the sense of a sentence, and in inquiring also as to its meaning. But now why do we want every proper name to have not only a sense, but also a meaning? Why is the thought not enough for us? Because, and to the extent that, we are concerned with its truth-value. This is not always the case. In hearing an epic poem, for instance, apart from the euphony of the language we are interested only in the sense of the sentences and the images and feelings thereby aroused. The question of truth would cause us to abandon aesthetic delight for an attitude of scientific investigation. Hence it is a matter of no concern to us whether the name "Odysseus," for instance, has meaning, so long as we accept the poem as a work of art.[6] It is the striving for truth that drives us always to advance from the sense to the thing meant.

We have seen that the meaning of a sentence may always be sought, whenever the meaning of its components is involved; and that this is the case when and only when we are inquiring after the truth-value.

We are therefore driven into accepting the *truth-value* of a sentence as constituting what it means. By the truth-value of a sentence I understand the circumstance that it is true or false. There are no further truth-values. For brevity I call the one the True, the other the False. Every assertoric sentence concerned with what its words mean is therefore to be regarded as a proper name, and its meaning, if it has one, is either the True or the False. These two objects are recognized, if only implicitly, by everybody who judges something to be true—and so even by a sceptic. The designation of the truth-values as objects may appear to be an arbitrary fancy or perhaps a mere play upon words, from which no profound consequences could be drawn. What I am calling an object can be more exactly discussed only in connection with concept and relation. . . . But so much should already be clear, that in every judgement, no matter how trivial, the step from the level of thoughts to the level of meaning (the objective) has already been taken.

One might be tempted to regard the relation of the thought to the True not as that of sense to meaning, but rather as that of subject to predicate. One can, indeed, say: "The thought that 5 is a prime number is true." But closer examination shows that nothing more has been said than in the simple sentence "5 is a prime number." The truth claim arises in each case from the form of the assertoric sentence, and when the latter lacks its usual force, e.g., in the mouth of an actor upon the stage, even the sentence "The thought that 5 is a prime number is true" contains only a thought, and indeed the same thought as the simple "5 is a prime number." It follows that the relation of the thought to the True may not be compared with that of subject to predicate.

Subject and predicate (understood in the logical sense) are just elements of thought; they stand on the same level for knowledge. By combining subject and predicate, one reaches only a thought, never passes from sense to meaning, never from a thought to its truth-value. One moves at the same level but never advances from one level to the next. A truth-value cannot be a part of a thought, any more than, say, the Sun can, for it is not a sense but an object.

If our supposition that the meaning of a sentence is its truth-value is correct, the latter must remain unchanged when a part of the sentence is replaced by an expression with the same meaning. And this is in fact the case. Leibniz gives the definition: "*Eadem sunt, quae sibi mutuo substitui possunt, salva veritate.*" If we are dealing with sentences for which the meaning of their component parts is at all relevant, then what feature except the truth-value can be found that belongs to such sentences quite generally and remains unchanged by substitutions of the kind just mentioned?

If now the truth-value of a sentence is its meaning, then on the one hand all true sentences have the same meaning and so, on the other hand, do all false sentences. From this we see that in the meaning of the sentence all that is specific is obliterated. We can never be concerned only with the meaning of a sentence; but again the mere thought alone yields no knowledge, but only the thought together with its

meaning, i.e. its truth-value. Judgements can be regarded as advances from a thought to a truth-value. Naturally this cannot be a definition. Judgement is something quite peculiar and incomparable. One might also say that judgements are distinctions of parts within truth-values. Such distinction occurs by a return to the thought. To every sense attaching to a truth-value would correspond its own manner of analysis. However, I have here used the word "part" in a special sense. I have in fact transferred the relation between the parts and the whole of the sentence to its meaning, by calling the meaning of a word part of the meaning of the sentence, if the word itself is a part of the sentence. This way of speaking can certainly be attacked, because the total meaning and one part of it do not suffice to determine the remainder, and because the word "part" is already used of bodies in another sense. A special term would need to be invented.

The supposition that the truth value of a sentence is what it means shall now be put to further test. We have found that the truth-value of a sentence remains unchanged when an expression is replaced by another with the same meaning: but we have not yet considered the case in which the expression to be replaced is itself a sentence. Now if our view is correct, the truth-value of a sentence containing another as part must remain unchanged when the part is replaced by another sentence having the same truth-value. Exceptions are to be expected when the whole sentence or its part is direct or indirect quotation; for in such cases as we have seen, the words do not have their customary meaning. In direct quotation, a sentence designates another sentence, and in indirect speech a thought.

We are thus led to consider subordinate sentences or clauses. These occur as parts of a sentence complex, which is, from the logical standpoint, likewise a sentence—a main sentence. . . .

Let us compare, for instance, the two sentences "Copernicus believed that the planetary orbits are circles" and "Copernicus believed that the apparent motion of the Sun is produced by the real motion of the Earth." One subordinate clause can be substituted for the other without harm to the truth. The main clause and the subordinate clause together have as their sense only a single thought, and the truth of the whole includes neither the truth nor the untruth of the subordinate clause. In such cases it is not permissible to replace one expression in the subordinate clause by another having the same customary meaning, but only by one having the same indirect meaning, i.e. the same customary sense. Somebody might conclude: The meaning of a sentence is not its truth-value, for in that case it could always be replaced by another sentence of the same truth-value. But this proves too much; one might just as well claim that the meaning of 'morning star' is not Venus, since one may not always say 'Venus' in place of 'morning star'. One has the right to conclude only that the meaning of a sentence is not *always* its truth-value, and that 'morning star' does not I always mean the planet Venus, viz. when the word has its indirect meaning. An exception of such a kind occurs in the subordinate clause just considered, which has a thought as its meaning. . . .

Let us return to our starting point.

If we found "$a = a$" and "$a = b$" to have different cognitive values, the explanation is that for the purpose of acquiring knowledge, the sense of the sentence, viz., the thought expressed by it, is no less relevant than its meaning, i.e. its truth-value. If now $a = b$, then indeed what is meant by "b" is the same as what is meant by "a", and hence the truth-value of '$a = b$' is the same as that of "$a = a$". In spite of this, the sense of "b" may differ from that of "a", and thereby the thought expressed in '$a = b$' differs from that of "$a = a$". In that case the two sentences do not have the same cognitive value. If we understand by "judgement" the advance from the thought to its truth-value, as in the present paper, we can also say that the judgements are different.

NOTES

1. I use this word in the sense of identity and understand '$a = b$' to have the sense of 'a is the same as b' or 'a and b coincide'.

2. In the case of an actual proper name such as "Aristotle" opinions as to the sense may differ. It might, for instance, be taken to be the following: the pupil of Plato and teacher of Alexander the Great. Anybody who does this will attach another sense to the sentence "Aristotle was born in Stagira" than will a man who takes as the sense of the name: the teacher of Alexander the Great who was born in Stagira. So long as the thing meant remains the same, such variations of sense may be tolerated, although they are to be avoided in the theoretical structure of a demonstrative science and ought not to occur in a perfect language.

3. We may include with ideas direct experiences: here, sense-impressions and acts themselves take the place of the traces which they have left in the mind. The distinction is unimportant for our purpose, especially since memories of sense-impressions and acts always go along with such impressions and acts themselves to complete the perpetual image. One may on the other hand understand direct experience as including any object in so far as it is sensibly perceptible or spatial.

4. Hence it is inadvisable to use the word "idea" to designate something so basically different.

5. By a thought I understand not the subjective performance of thinking but its objective content, which is capable of being the common property of several thinkers.

6. It would be desirable to have a special term for signs intended to have only sense. If we name them say, representations, the words of the actors on the stage would be representations; indeed the actor himself would be a representation.

7. A judgement, for me is not the mere grasping of a thought, but the admission of its truth.

On Denoting

~

BERTRAND RUSSELL

Bertrand Russell (1872–1970) was one of the preeminent philosophers of the 20th century.

By a "denoting phrase" I mean a phrase such as any one of the following: a man, some man, any man, every man, all men, the present King of England, the present King of France, the centre of mass of the solar system at the first instant of the twentieth century, the revolution of the earth round the sun, the revolution of the sun round the earth. Thus a phrase is denoting solely in virtue of its *form*. We may distinguish three cases: (1) A phrase may be denoting, and yet not denote anything; e.g., "the present King of France." (2) A phrase may denote one definite object; e.g., "the present King of England" denotes a certain man. (3) A phrase may denote ambiguously; e.g., "a man" denotes not many men, but an ambiguous man. The interpretation of such phrases is a matter of considerable difficulty; indeed, it is very hard to frame any theory not susceptible of formal refutation. All the difficulties with which I am acquainted are met, so far as I can discover, by the theory which I am about to explain.

The subject of denoting is of very great importance, not only in logic and mathematics, but also in theory of knowledge. For example, we know that the centre of mass of the solar system at a definite instant is some definite point, and we can affirm a number of propositions about it; but we have no immediate *acquaintance* with this point, which is only known to us by description. The distinction between *acquaintance* and *knowledge about* is the distinction between the things we have presentations of, and the things we only reach by means of denoting phrases. It often happens that we know that a certain phrase denotes unambiguously, although we have no acquaintance with what it denotes; this occurs in the above case of the centre of mass. In perception we have acquaintance with the objects of perception, and in thought we have acquaintance with objects of a more abstract logical character; but we do not necessarily have acquaintance with the objects denoted by phrases composed of words with whose meanings we are acquainted. To take a very important instance: there seems no reason to believe that we are ever acquainted with other people's minds, seeing that these are not directly perceived; hence what we know about them is obtained through denoting. All thinking has to start from acquaintance; but it succeeds in thinking *about* many things with which we have no acquaintance.

The course of my argument will be as follows. I shall begin by stating the theory I intend to advocate; I shall then discuss the theories of Frege and Meinong, showing why neither of them satisfies me; then I shall give the grounds in favour of my theory; and finally I shall briefly indicate the philosophical consequences of my theory.

My theory, briefly, is as follows. I take the notion of the *variable* as fundamental; I use "$C(x)$" to mean a proposition[1] in which x is a constituent, where x, the variable, is essentially and wholly undetermined. Then we can consider the two notions "$C(x)$ is always true" and "$C(x)$ is sometimes true."[2] Then *everything* and *nothing* and *something* (which are the most prim-

From *Mind,* 14 (1905).

itive of denoting phrases) are to be interpreted as follows:

C (everything) means "C(x) is always true";
C (nothing) means "'C(x) is false' is always true";
C (something) means "It is false that 'C(x) is false' is always true."[3]

Here the notion "C(x) is always true" is taken as ultimate and indefinable, and the others are defined by means of it. *Everything, nothing,* and *something* are not assumed to have any meaning in isolation, but a meaning is assigned to *every* proposition in which they occur. This is the principle of the theory of denoting I wish to advocate: that denoting phrases never have any meaning in themselves, but that every proposition in whose verbal expression they occur has a meaning. The difficulties concerning denoting are, I believe, all the result of a wrong analysis of propositions whose verbal expressions contain denoting phrases. The proper analysis, if I am not mistaken, may be further set forth as follows.

Suppose now we wish to interpret the proposition, "I met a man." If this is true, I met some definite man; but that is not what I affirm. What I affirm is, according to the theory I advocate:

"'I met x, and x is human' is not always false."

Generally, defining the class of men as the class of objects having the predicate *human,* we say that:

"C (a man)" means "'C(x) and x is human' is not always false." This leaves "a man," by itself, wholly destitute of meaning, but gives a meaning to every proposition in whose verbal expression "a man" occurs.

Consider next the proposition "all men are mortal." This proposition is really hypothetical and states that *if* anything is a man, it is mortal. That is, it states that if x is a man, x is mortal, whatever x may be. Hence, substituting "x is human" for "x is a man," we find:

"All men are mortal" means "'If x is human, x is mortal' is always true."

This is what is expressed in symbolic logic by saying that "all men are mortal" means "'x is human' implies 'x is mortal' for all values of x." More generally, we say:

"C (all men)" means "'If x is human, then C(x) is true' is always true."

Similarly

"C (no men)" means "'If x is human, then C(x) is false' is always true."
"C (some men)" will mean the same as "C (a man),"[4] and
"C (a man)" means "It is false that 'C(x) and x is human' is always false."
"C (every man)" will mean the same as "C (all men)."

It remains to interpret phrases containing *the.* These are by far the most interesting and difficult of denoting phrases. Take as an instance "the father of Charles II was executed." This asserts that there was an x who was the father of Charles II and was executed. Now *the,* when it is strictly used, involves uniqueness; we do, it is true, speak of "*the* son of So-and-so" even when So-and-so has several sons, but it would be more correct to say "*a* son of So-and-so." Thus for our purposes we take *the* as involving uniqueness. Thus when we say "x was *the* father of Charles II" we not only assert that x had a certain relation to Charles II, but also that nothing else had this relation. The relation in question, without the assumption of uniqueness, and without any denoting phrases, is expressed by "x begat Charles II." To get an equivalent of "x was the father of Charles II," we must add, "If y is other than x, y did not beget Charles II," or, what is equivalent, "If y begat Charles II, y is identical with x." Hence "x is the father of Charles II" becomes: "x begat Charles II; and 'if y begat Charles II, y is identical with x' is always true of y."

Thus "the father of Charles II was executed" becomes: "It is not always false of x that x begat Charles II and that x was executed and that 'if y begat Charles II, y is identical with x' is always true of y."

This may seem a somewhat incredible interpretation; but I am not at present giving reasons, I am merely *stating* the theory.

To interpret "*C* (the father of Charles II)," where *C* stands for any statement about him, we have only to substitute *C*(*x*) for "*x* was executed" in the above. Observe that, according to the above interpretation, whatever statement *C* may be, "*C* (the father of Charles II)" implies:

"It is not always false of *x* that 'if *y* begat Charles II, *y* is identical with *x*' is always true of *y*,"

which is what is expressed in common language by "Charles II had one father and no more." Consequently if this condition fails, *every* proposition of the form "*C* (the father of Charles II)" is false. Thus e.g. every proposition of the form "*C* (the present King of France)" is false. This is a great advantage in the present theory. I shall show later that it is not contrary to the law of contradiction, as might be at first supposed.

The above gives a reduction of all propositions in which denoting phrases occur to forms in which no such phrases occur. Why it is imperative to effect such a reduction, the subsequent discussion will endeavour to show.

The evidence for the above theory is derived from the difficulties which seem unavoidable if we regard denoting phrases as standing for genuine constituents of the propositions in whose verbal expressions they occur. Of the possible theories which admit such constituents the simplest is that of Meinong. This theory regards any grammatically correct denoting phrase as standing for an *object*. Thus "the present King of France," "the round square," etc., are supposed to be genuine objects. It is admitted that such objects do not *subsist*, but nevertheless they are supposed to be objects. This is in itself a difficult view; but the chief objection is that such objects, admittedly, are apt to infringe the law of contradiction. It is contended, for example, that the existent present King of France exists, and also does not exist; that the round square is round, and also not round, etc. But this is intolerable; and if any theory can be found to avoid this result, it is surely to be preferred.

The above breach of the law of contradiction is avoided by Frege's theory. He distinguishes, in a denoting phrase, two elements, which we may call the *meaning* and the *denotation*. Thus "the centre of mass of the solar system at the beginning of the twentieth century" is highly complex in *meaning,* but its *denotation* is a certain point, which is simple. The solar system, the twentieth century, etc., are constituents of the *meaning;* but the *denotation* has no constituents at all.[5] One advantage of this distinction is that it shows why it is often worth while to assert identity. If we say "Scott is the author of *Waverley,*" we assert an identity of denotation with a difference of meaning. . . .

One of the first difficulties that confront us, when we adopt the view that denoting phrases *express* a meaning and *denote* a denotation,[6] concerns the cases in which the denotation appears to be absent. If we say "the King of England is bald," that is, it would seem, not a statement about the complex *meaning* "the King of England," but about the actual man denoted by the meaning. But now consider "the King of France is bald." By parity of form, this also ought to be about the denotation of the phrase "the King of France." But this phrase, though it has a *meaning* provided "the King of England" has a meaning, has certainly no denotation, at least in any obvious sense. Hence one would suppose that "the King of France is bald" ought to be nonsense; but it is not nonsense, since it is plainly false. Or again consider such a proposition as the following: "If *u* is a class which has only one member, then that one member is a member of *u*," or, as we may state it, "If *u* is a unit class, *the u* is a *u*." This proposition ought to be *always* true, since the conclusion is true whenever the hypothesis is true. But "the *u*" is a denoting phrase, and it is the denotation, not the meaning, that is said to be a *u*. Now if *u* is *not* a unit class, "the *u*" seems to denote nothing; hence our proposition would seem to become nonsense as soon as *u* is not a unit class.

Now it is plain that such propositions do *not* become nonsense merely because their hypotheses are false. The King in *The Tempest* might say, "If Ferdinand is not drowned, Ferdinand is my only son." Now "my only son" is a denoting phrase, which, on the face of it, has a denotation when, and only when, I have exactly one son. But the above statement would nevertheless have remained true if Ferdinand had been in fact drowned. Thus we must either provide a denotation in cases in which it is at first sight absent, or we must abandon the view that the denotation is what is concerned in propositions which contain denoting phrases. The latter is the course that I advocate. The former course may be taken, as by Meinong, by admitting objects which do not subsist, and denying that they obey the law of contradiction; this, however, is to be avoided if possible. Another way of taking the same course (so far as our present alternative is concerned) is adopted by Frege, who provides by definition some purely conventional denotation for the cases in which otherwise there would be none. Thus "the King of France," is to denote the null-class; "the only son of Mr. So-and-so" (who has a fine family of ten), is to denote the class of all his sons; and so on. But this procedure, though it may not lead to actual logical error, is plainly artificial, and does not give an exact analysis of the matter. Thus if we allow that denoting phrases, in general, have the two sides of meaning and denotation, the cases where there seems to be no denotation cause difficulties both on the assumption that there really is a denotation and on the assumption that there really is none.

A logical theory may be tested by its capacity for dealing with puzzles, and it is a wholesome plan, in thinking about logic, to stock the mind with as many puzzles as possible, since these serve much the same purpose as is served by experiments in physical science. I shall therefore state three puzzles which a theory as to denoting ought to be able to solve; and I shall show later that my theory solves them.

(1) If *a* is identical with *b*, whatever is true of the one is true of the other, and either may be substituted for the other in any proposition without altering the truth or falsehood of that proposition. Now George IV wished to know whether Scott was the author of *Waverley;* and in fact Scott *was* the author of *Waverley.* Hence we may substitute *Scott* for *the author of "Waverley,"* and thereby prove that George IV wished to know whether Scott was Scott. Yet an interest in the law of identity can hardly be attributed to the first gentleman of Europe.

(2) By the law of excluded middle, either "*A* is *B*" or "*A* is not *B*" must be true. Hence either "the present King of France is bald" or "the present King of France is not bald" must be true. Yet if we enumerated the things that are bald, and then the things that are not bald, we should not find the present King of France in either list. Hegelians, who love a synthesis, will probably conclude that he wears a wig.

(3) Consider the proposition "*A* differs from *B*." If this is true, there is a difference between *A* and *B,* which fact may be expressed in the form "the difference between *A* and *B* subsists." But if it is false that *A* differs from *B,* then there is no difference between *A* and *B,* which fact may be expressed in the form "the difference between *A* and *B* does not subsist." But how can a non-entity be the subject of a proposition? "I think, therefore I am" is no more evident than "I am the subject of a proposition, therefore I am," provided "I am" is taken to assert subsistence or being,[7] not existence. Hence, it would appear, it must always be self-contradictory to deny the being of anything; but we have seen, in connexion with Meinong, that to admit being also sometimes leads to contradictions. Thus if *A* and *B* do not differ, to suppose either that there is, or that there is not, such an object as "the difference between *A* and *B,*" seems equally impossible. . . .

It remains to show how all the puzzles we have been considering are solved by the theory explained at the beginning of this article.

According to the view which I advocate, a denoting phrase is essentially *part* of a sentence, and does not, like most single words, have any significance on its own account. If I say "Scott was a man," that is a statement of the form "*x* was a man," and it has "Scott" for its subject. But if I say "the author of *Waverley* was a man," that is not a statement of the form "*x* was a man," and does not have "the author of *Waverley*" for its subject. Abbreviating the statement made at the beginning of this article, we may put, in place of "the author of *Waverley* was a man," the following: "One and only one entity wrote *Waverley,* and that one was a man." (This is not so strictly what is meant as what was said earlier; but it is easier to follow.) And speaking generally, suppose we wish to say that the author of *Waverley* had the property ϕ, what we wish to say is equivalent to "One and only one entity wrote *Waverley,* and that one had the property ϕ."

The explanation of *denotation* is now as follows. Every proposition in which "the author of *Waverley*" occurs being explained as above, the proposition "Scott was the author of *Waverley*" (i.e. "Scott was identical with the author of *Waverley*") becomes "One and only one entity wrote *Waverley*, and Scott was identical with that one"; or, reverting to the wholly explicit form: "It is not always false of *x* that *x* wrote *Waverley*, that it is always true of *y* that if *y* wrote *Waverley y* is identical with *x*, and that Scott is identical with *x*." Thus if "*C*" is a denoting phrase, it may happen that there is one entity *x* (there cannot be more than one) for which the proposition "*x* is identical with *C*" is true, this proposition being interpreted as above. We may then say that the entity *x* is the denotation of the phrase "*C*." Thus Scott is the denotation of "the author of *Waverley*." . . .

The puzzle about George IV's curiosity is now seen to have a very simple solution. The proposition "Scott was the author of *Waverley*," which was written out in its unabbreviated form in the preceding paragraph, does not contain any constituent "the author of *Waverley*" for which we could substitute "Scott." This does not interfere with the truth of inferences resulting from making what is *verbally* the substitution of "Scott" for "the author of *Waverley*," so long as "the author of *Waverley*" has what I call a *primary* occurrence in the proposition considered. The difference of primary and secondary occurrences of denoting phrases is as follows:

When we say: "George IV wished to know whether so-and-so," or when we say "So-and-so is surprising" or "So-and-so is true," etc., the "so-and-so" must be a proposition. Suppose now that "so-and-so" contains a denoting phrase. We may either eliminate this denoting phrase from the subordinate proposition "so-and-so," or from the whole proposition in which "so-and-so" is a mere constituent. Different propositions result according to which we do. I have heard of a touchy owner of a yacht to whom a guest, on first seeing it, remarked, "I thought your yacht was larger than it is"; and the owner replied, "No, my yacht is not larger than it is." What the guest meant was, "The size that I thought your yacht was is greater than the size your yacht is"; the meaning attributed to him is, "I thought the size of your yacht was greater than the size of your yacht." To return to

George IV and *Waverley*, when we say, "George IV wished to know whether Scott was the author of *Waverley*," we normally mean "George IV wished to know whether one and only one man wrote *Waverley* and Scott was that man"; but we *may* also mean: "One and only one man wrote *Waverley*, and George IV wished to know whether Scott was that man." In the latter, "the author of *Waverley*" has a *primary* occurrence; in the former, a *secondary*. The latter might be expressed by "George IV wished to know, concerning the man who in fact wrote *Waverley*, whether he was Scott." This would be true, for example, if George IV had seen Scott at a distance, and had asked "Is that Scott?" A *secondary* occurrence of a denoting phrase may be defined as one in which the phrase occurs in a proposition *p* which is a mere constituent of the proposition we are considering, and the substitution for the denoting phrase is to be effected in *p*, not in the whole proposition concerned. The ambiguity as between primary and secondary occurrences is hard to avoid in language; but it does no harm if we are on our guard against it. In symbolic logic it is of course easily avoided.

The distinction of primary and secondary occurrences also enables us to deal with the question whether the present King of France is bald or not bald, and generally with the logical status of denoting phrases that denote nothing. If "*C*" is a denoting phrase, say "the term having the property *F*," then

> "*C* has the property ϕ" means "one and only one term has the property *F*, and that one has the property ϕ."[8]

If now the property *F* belongs to no terms, or to several, it follows that '*C* has the property ϕ' is false for *all* values of ϕ. Thus "the present King of France is bald" is certainly false; and "the present King of France is not bald" is false if it means

> "There is an entity which is now King of France and is not bald," but is true if it means
> "It is false that there is an entity which is now King of France and is bald."

That is, "the King of France is not bald" is false if the occurrence of "the King of France" is *primary*, and true if it is *secondary*. Thus all propositions in which "the King of France" has a primary occurrence are false; the denials of such propositions are true, but in them "the King of France" has a secondary occurrence. Thus we escape the conclusion that the King of France has a wig.

We can now see also how to deny that there is such an object as the difference between *A* and *B* in the case when *A* and *B* do not differ. If *A* and *B* do differ, there is one and only one entity *x* such that "*x* is the difference between *A* and *B*" is a true proposition; if *A* and *B* do not differ, there is no such entity *x*. Thus according to the meaning of denotation lately explained, "the difference between *A* and *B*" has a denotation when *A* and *B* differ, but not otherwise. This difference applies to true and false propositions generally. If "*a R b*" stands for "*a* has the relation *R* to *b*," then when *a R b* is true, there is such an entity as the relation *R* between *a* and *b*; when *a R b* is false, there is no such entity. Thus out of any proposition we can make a denoting phrase, which denotes an entity if the proposition is true, but does not denote an entity if the proposition is false. E.g., it is true (at least we will suppose so) that the earth revolves round the sun, and false that the sun revolves round the earth; hence "the revolution of the earth round the sun" denotes an entity, while "the revolution of the sun round the earth" does not denote an entity.[9]

The whole realm of non-entities, such as "the round square," "the even prime other than 2," "Apollo," "Hamlet," etc., can now be satisfactorily dealt with. All these are denoting phrases which do not denote anything. A proposition about Apollo means what we get by substituting what the classical dictionary tells us is meant by Apollo, say "the sun-god." All propositions in which Apollo occurs are to be interpreted by the above rules for denoting phrases. If "Apollo" has a primary occurrence, the proposition containing the occurrence is false; if the occurrence is secondary, the proposition may be true. So again "the round square is round" means "there is one and only one entity *x* which is round and square, and that entity is round," which is a false proposition, not, as Meinong maintains, a true one. "The most perfect Being has all perfections; existence is a perfection; therefore the most perfect Being exists" becomes:

"There is one and only one entity *x* which is most perfect; that one has all perfections; existence is a perfection; therefore that one exists." As a proof, this fails for want of a proof of the premiss "there is one and only one entity *x* which is most perfect." . . .[10]

The usefulness of *identity* is explained by the above theory. No one outside a logic-book ever wishes to say "*x* is *x*," and yet assertions of identity are often made in such forms as "Scott was the author of *Waverley*" or "thou art the man." The meaning of such propositions cannot be stated without the notion of identity, although they are not simply statements that Scott is identical with another term, the author of *Waverley*, or that thou art identical with another term, the man. The shortest statement of "Scott is the author of *Waverley*" seems to be "Scott wrote *Waverley*; and it is always true of *y* that if *y* wrote *Waverley*, *y* is identical with Scott." It is in this way that identity enters into "Scott is the author of *Waverley*"; and it is owing to such uses that identity is worth affirming.

One interesting result of the above theory of denoting is this: when there is anything with which we do not have immediate acquaintance, but only definition by denoting phrases, then the propositions in which this thing is introduced by means of a denoting phrase do not really contain this thing as a constituent, but contain instead the constituents expressed by the several words of the denoting phrase. Thus in every proposition that we can apprehend (i.e. not only in those whose truth or falsehood we can judge of, but in all that we can think about), all the constituents are really entities with which we have immediate acquaintance. Now such things as matter (in the sense in which matter occurs in physics) and the minds of other people are known to us only by denoting phrases, i.e. we are not *acquainted* with them, but we know them as what has such and such properties. Hence, although we can form propositional functions $C(x)$ which must hold of such and such a material particle, or of So-and-so's mind, yet we are not acquainted with the propositions which affirm these things that we know must be true, because we cannot apprehend the actual entities concerned. What we know is "So-and-so has a mind which has such and such properties" but we do not know "*A* has such and such properties," where *A* is the mind in question. In such a case, we know the properties of a thing without having acquaintance with the thing itself, and without, consequently, knowing any single proposition of which the thing itself is a constituent.

Of the many other consequences of the view I have been advocating, I will say nothing. I will only beg the reader not to make up his mind against the view—as he might be tempted to do, on account of its apparently excessive complication—until he has attempted to construct a theory of his own on the subject of denotation. This attempt, I believe, will convince him that, whatever the true theory may be, it cannot have such a simplicity as one might have expected beforehand.

NOTES

1. More exactly, a propositional function.

2. The second of these can be defined by means of the first, if we take it to mean, "It is not true that '$C(x)$ is false' is always true."

3. I shall sometimes use, instead of this complicated phrase, the phrase "$C(x)$ is not always false," or "$C(x)$ is sometimes true," supposed *defined* to mean the same as the complicated phrase.

4. Psychologically "C (a man)" has a suggestion of *only one,* and "C (some men)" has a suggestion of *more than one;* but we may neglect these suggestions in a preliminary sketch.

5. Frege distinguishes the two elements of meaning and denotation everywhere, and not only in complex denoting phrases. Thus it is the *meanings* of the constituents of a denoting complex that enter into its *meaning,* not their *denotation.* In the proposition "Mont Blanc is over 1,000 metres high," it is, according to him, the *meaning* of "Mont Blanc," not the actual mountain, that is a constituent of the *meaning* of the proposition.

6. In this theory, we shall say that the denoting phrase *expresses* a meaning; and we shall say both of the phrase and of the meaning that they *denote* a denotation. In the other theory, which I advocate, there is no *meaning,* and only sometimes a *denotation.*

7. I use these as synonyms.

8. This is the abbreviated, not the stricter, interpretation.

9. The propositions from which such entities are derived are not identical either with these entities or with the propositions that these entities have being.

10. The argument can be made to prove validly that all members of the class of most perfect Beings exist; it can also be proved formally that this class cannot have *more* than one member; but, taking the definition of perfection as possession of all positive predicates, it can be proved almost equally formally that the class does not have even one member.

Naming and Necessity

~

SAUL A. KRIPKE

Saul A. Kripke, who taught at Princeton University, is a leading American logician and philosopher of language. The lectures reprinted here were delivered in 1970.

The first topic in the pair of topics is naming. By a name here I will mean a proper name, i.e., the name of a person, a city, a country, etc. It is well known that modern logicians also are very interested in definite descriptions: phrases of the form 'the x such that φx', such as 'the man who corrupted Hadleyburg'. Now, if one and only one man ever corrupted Hadleyburg, then that man is the referent, in the logician's sense, of that description. We will use the term 'name' so that it does *not* include definite descriptions of that sort, but only those things which in ordinary language would be called 'proper names'. If we want a common term to cover names and descriptions, we may use the term 'designator'.

It is a point, made by Donnellan, that under certain circumstances a particular speaker may use a definite description to refer, not to the proper referent, in the sense that I've just defined it, of that description, but to something else which he wants to single out and which he thinks is the proper referent of the description, but which in fact isn't. So you may say, 'The man over there with the champagne in his glass is happy', though he actually only has water in his glass. Now, even though there is no champagne in his glass, and there may be another man in the room who does have champagne in his glass, the speaker *intended* to refer, or maybe, in some sense of 'refer', *did* refer, to the man he thought had the champagne in his glass. Nevertheless, I'm just going to use the term 'referent of the description' to mean the object uniquely satisfying the conditions in the definite description. This is the sense in which it's been used in the logical tradition. So, if you have a description of the form 'the x such that φx', and there is exactly one x such that φx, that is the referent of the description.

Now, what is the relation between names and descriptions? There is a well known doctrine of John Stuart Mill, in his book *A System of Logic,* that names have denotation but not connotation. To use one of his examples, when we use the name 'Dartmouth' to describe a certain locality in England, it may be so called because it lies at the mouth of the Dart. But even, he says, had the Dart (that's a river) changed its course so that Dartmouth no longer lay at the mouth of the Dart, we could still with propriety call this place 'Dartmouth', even though the name may suggest that it lies at the mouth of the Dart. Changing Mill's terminology, perhaps we should say that a name such as 'Dartmouth' *does* have a 'connotation' to some people, namely, it *does* connote (not to me—I never thought of this) that any place called 'Dartmouth' lies at the mouth of the Dart. But then in some way it doesn't have a 'sense'. At least, it is not part of

the *meaning* of the name 'Dartmouth' that the town so named lies at the mouth of the Dart. Someone who said that Dartmouth did not lie at the Dart's mouth would not contradict himself.

It should not be thought that every phrase of the form 'the x such that Fx' is always used in English as a description rather than a name. I guess everyone has heard about The Holy Roman Empire, which was neither holy, Roman nor an empire. Today we have The United Nations. Here it would seem that since these things can be so-called even though they are not Holy Roman United Nations, these phrases should be regarded not as definite descriptions, but as names. In the case of some terms, people might have doubts as to whether they're names or descriptions; like 'God'—does it describe God as the unique divine being or is it a name of God? But such cases needn't necessarily bother us.

Now here I am making a distinction which is certainly made in language. But the classical tradition of modern logic has gone very strongly against Mill's view. Frege and Russell both thought, and seemed to arrive at these conclusions independently of each other, that Mill was wrong in a very strong sense: really a proper name, properly used, simply was a definite description abbreviated or disguised. Frege specifically said that such a description gave the sense of the name.[1]

Now the reasons against Mill's view and in favor of the alternative view adopted by Frege and Russell are really very powerful; and it is hard to see—though one may be suspicious of this view because names don't seem to be disguised descriptions—how the Frege-Russell view, or some suitable variant, can fail to be the case.

Let me give an example of some of the arguments which seem conclusive in favor of the view of Frege and Russell. The basic problem for any view such as Mill's is how we can determine what the referent of a name, as used by a given speaker, is. According to the description view, the answer is clear. If 'Joe Doakes' is just short for 'the man who corrupted Hadleyburg', then whoever corrupted Hadleyburg uniquely is the referent of the name 'Joe Doakes'. However, if there is *not* such a descriptive content to the name, then how do people ever use names to refer to things at all? Well, they may be in a position to point to some things and thus determine the references of certain names ostensively. This was Russell's doctrine of acquaintance, which he thought the so-called genuine or proper names satisfied. But of course ordinary names refer to all sorts of people, like Walter Scott, to whom we can't possibly point. And our reference here seems to be determined by our knowledge of them. Whatever we know about them determines the referent of the name as the unique thing satisfying those properties. For example, if I use the name 'Napoleon', and someone asks, 'To whom are you referring?', I will answer something like, 'Napoleon was emperor of the French in the early part of the nineteenth century; he was eventually defeated at Waterloo', thus giving a uniquely identifying description to determine the referent of the name. Frege and Russell, then, appear to give the natural account of how reference is determined here; Mill appears to give none.

There are subsidiary arguments which, though they are based on more specialized problems, are also motivations for accepting the view. One is that sometimes we may discover that two names have the same referent, and express this by an identity statement. So, for example (I guess this is a hackneyed example), you see a star in the evening and it's called 'Hesperus'. (That's what we call it in the evening, is that right?—I hope it's not the other way around.) We see a star in the morning and call it 'Phosphorus'. Well, then, in fact we find that it's not a star, but is the planet Venus and that Hesperus and Phosphorus are in fact the same. So we express this by 'Hesperus is Phosphorus'. Here we're certainly not just saying of an object that it's identical with itself. This is something that we discovered. A very natural thing to say is that the real content [is that] the star which we saw in the evening is the star which we saw in the morning (or, more accurately, that the thing which we saw in the evening is the thing which we saw in the morning). This, then, gives the real meaning of the identity statement in question; and the analysis in terms of descriptions does this.

Also we may raise the question whether a name has any reference at all when we ask, e.g., whether Aristotle ever existed. It seems natural here to think that what is questioned is not whether this *thing*

(man) existed. Once we've *got* the thing, we know that it existed. What really is queried is whether anything answers to the properties we associate with the name—in the case of Aristotle, whether any one Greek philosopher produced certain works, or at least a suitable number of them.

It would be nice to answer all of these arguments. I am not entirely able to see my way clear through every problem of this sort that can be raised. Furthermore, I'm pretty sure that I won't have time to discuss all these questions in these lectures. Nevertheless, I think it's pretty certain that the view of Frege and Russell is false.

Many people have said that the theory of Frege and Russell is false, but, in my opinion, they have abandoned its letter while retaining its spirit, namely, they have used the notion of a cluster concept. Well, what is this? The obvious problem for Frege and Russell, the one which comes immediately to mind, is already mentioned by Frege himself. He said,

> In the case of genuinely proper names like 'Aristotle' opinions as regards their sense may diverge. As such may, e.g., be suggested: Plato's disciple and the teacher of Alexander the Great. Whoever accepts this sense will interpret the meaning of the statement 'Aristotle was born in Stagira', differently from one who interpreted the sense of 'Aristotle' as the Stagirite teacher of Alexander the Great. As long as the nominatum remains the same, these fluctuations in sense are tolerable. But they should be avoided in the system of a demonstrative science and should not appear in a perfect language.[2]

So, according to Frege, there is some sort of looseness or weakness in our language. Some people may give one sense to the name 'Aristotle', others may give another. But of course it is not only that; even a single speaker when asked 'What description are you willing to substitute for the name?' may be quite at a loss. In fact, he may know many things about him; but any particular thing that he knows he may feel clearly expresses a contingent property of the object. If 'Aristotle' meant *the man who taught Alexander the Great,* then saying 'Aristotle was a teacher of Alexander the Great' would be a mere tautology. But surely it isn't; it expresses the fact that Aristotle taught Alexander the Great, something we could discover to be false. So, *being the teacher of Alexander the Great* cannot be part of [the sense of] the name.

The most common way out of this difficulty is to say 'really it is not a weakness in ordinary language that we can't substitute a *particular* description for the name; that's all right. What we really associate with the name is a *family* of descriptions.' A good example of this is (if I can find it) in *Philosophical Investigations,* where the idea of family resemblances is introduced and with great power.

> Consider this example. If one says 'Moses did not exist', this may mean various things. It may mean: the Israelites did not have a *single* leader when they withdrew from Egypt—or: their leader was not called Moses—or: there cannot have been anyone who accomplished all that the Bible relates of Moses— . . . But when I make a statement about Moses,—am I always ready to substitute some *one* of those descriptions for 'Moses'? I shall perhaps say: by 'Moses' I understand the man who did what the Bible relates of Moses, or at any rate, a good deal of it. But how much? Have I decided how much must be proved false for me to give up my proposition as false? Has the name 'Moses' got a fixed and unequivocal use for me in all possible cases?[3]

According to this view, and a *locus classicus* of it is Searle's article on proper names,[4] the referent of a name is determined not by a single description but by some cluster or family. Whatever in some sense satisfies enough or most of the family is the referent of the name. I shall return to this view later. It may seem, as an analysis of ordinary language, quite a bit more plausible than that of Frege and Russell. It may seem to keep all the virtues and remove the defects of this theory. . . .

Let me return to the question about names which I raised. As I said, there is a popular modern substitute for the theory of Frege and Russell; it is adopted even by such a strong critic of many views of Frege and Russell, especially the latter, as Strawson.[5] The substitute is that, although a name is not a disguised description it either abbreviates, or anyway its reference is determined by, some cluster of descriptions. The question is whether this is true. As I also said,

there are stronger and weaker versions of this. The stronger version would say that the name is simply *defined,* synonymously, as the cluster of descriptions. It will then be necessary, not that Moses had any particular property in this cluster, but that he had the disjunction of them. There couldn't be any counterfactual situation in which he didn't do any of those things. I think it's clear that this is very implausible. People *have* said it—or maybe they haven't been intending to say that, but were using 'necessary' in some other sense. At any rate, for example, in Searle's article on proper names:

> To put the same point differently, suppose we ask, 'why do we have proper names at all?' Obviously to refer to individuals. 'Yes but descriptions could do that for us'. But only at the cost of specifying identity conditions every time reference is made: Suppose we agree to drop 'Aristotle' and use, say, 'the teacher of Alexander', then it is a necessary truth that the man referred to is Alexander's teacher—but it is a contingent fact that Aristotle ever went into pedagogy (though I am suggesting that it is a necessary fact that Aristotle has the logical sum, inclusive disjunction, of properties commonly attributed to him).[6]

Such a suggestion, if 'necessary' is used in the way I have been using it in this lecture, must clearly be false. (Unless he's got some very interesting essential property commonly attributed to Aristotle.) Most of the things commonly attributed to Aristotle are things that Aristotle might not have done at all. In a situation in which he didn't do them, we would describe that as a situation in which *Aristotle* didn't do them. This is not a distinction of scope, as happens sometimes in the case of descriptions, where someone might say that the man who taught Alexander might not have taught Alexander; though it could not have been true that: the man who taught Alexander didn't teach Alexander. This is Russell's distinction of scope. (I won't go into it.) It seems to me clear that this is not the case here. Not only is it true *of* the man Aristotle that he might not have gone into pedagogy; it is also true that we use the term 'Aristotle' in such a way that, in thinking of a counterfactual situation in which Aristotle didn't go into any of the fields and do any of the achievements we commonly attribute to him, still we would say that was a situation in which *Aristotle* did not do these things. Well there are some things like the date, the period he lived in, that might be more imagined as necessary. Maybe those are things we commonly attribute to him. There are exceptions. Maybe it's hard to imagine how he could have lived 500 years later than he in fact did. That certainly raises at least a problem. But take a man who doesn't have any idea of the date. Many people just have some vague cluster of his most famous achievements. Not only each of these singly, but the possession of the entire disjunction of these properties, is just a contingent fact about Aristotle; and the statement that Aristotle had this disjunction of properties is a contingent truth. . . .

What is the true picture of what's going on? Maybe reference doesn't really take place at all! After all, we don't really know that any of the properties we use to identify the man are right. We don't know that they pick out a unique object. So what *does* make my use of 'Cicero' into a name of *him?* The picture which leads to the cluster-of-descriptions theory is something like this: One is isolated in a room; the entire community of other speakers, everything else, could disappear; and one determines the reference for himself by saying—'By "Gödel" I shall mean the man, whoever he is, who proved the incompleteness of arithmetic'. Now you can do this if you want to. There's nothing really preventing it. You can just stick to that determination. If that's what you do, then if Schmidt discovered the incompleteness of arithmetic you *do* refer to him when you say 'Gödel did such and such'.

But that's not what most of us do. Someone, let's say, a baby, is born; his parents call him by a certain name. They talk about him to their friends. Other people meet him. Through various sorts of talk the name is spread from link to link as if by a chain. A speaker who is on the far end of this chain, who has heard about, say Richard Feynman, in the market place or elsewhere, may be referring to Richard Feynman even though he can't remember from whom he first heard of Feynman or from whom he ever heard of Feynman. He knows that Feynman is a famous physicist. A certain passage of communication reaching ultimately to

the man himself does reach the speaker. He then is referring to Feynman even though he can't identify him uniquely. He doesn't know what a Feynman diagram is, he doesn't know what the Feynman theory of pair production and annihilation is. Not only that: he'd have trouble distinguishing between Gell-Mann and Feynman. So he doesn't have to know these things, but, instead, a chain of communication going back to Feynman himself has been established, by virtue of his membership in a community which passed the name on from link to link, not by a ceremony that he makes in private in his study: 'By "Feynman" I shall mean the man who did such and such and such and such'.

How does this view differ from Strawson's suggestion, mentioned before, that one identifying reference may borrow its credentials from another? Certainly Strawson had a good insight in the passage quoted; on the other hand, he certainly shows a difference at least in emphasis from the picture I advocate, since he confines the remark to a footnote. The main text advocates the cluster-of-descriptions theory. Just because Strawson makes his remark in the context of a description theory, his view therefore differs from mine in one important respect. Strawson apparently requires that the speaker must *know* from whom he got his reference, so that he can say: 'By "Gödel" I mean the man *Jones* calls "Gödel"'. If he does not remember how he picked up the reference, he cannot give such a description. The present theory sets no such requirement. As I said, I may well not remember from whom I heard of Gödel, and I may think I remember from which people I heard the name, but wrongly.

These considerations show that the view advocated here can lead to consequences which actually *diverge* from those of Strawson's footnote. Suppose that the speaker has heard the name 'Cicero' from Smith and others, who use the name to refer to a famous Roman orator. He later thinks, however, that he picked up the name from Jones, who (unknown to the speaker) uses 'Cicero' as the name of a notorious German spy and has never heard of any orators of the ancient world. Then, according to Strawson's paradigm, the speaker must determine his reference by the resolution, 'I shall use "Cicero" to refer to the man whom Jones calls by that name', while on the present view, the referent will be the orator in spite of the speaker's false impression about where he picked up the name. The point is that Strawson, trying to fit the chain of communication view into the description theory, relies on what the speaker *thinks* was the source of his reference. If the speaker has forgotten his source, the description Strawson uses is unavailable to him; if he misremembers it, Strawson's paradigm can give the wrong results. On our view, it is not how the speaker thinks he got the reference, but the actual chain of communication, which is relevant.

I think I said the other time that philosophical theories are in danger of being false, and so I wasn't going to present an alternative theory. Have I just done so? Well, in a way; but my characterization has been far less specific than a real set of necessary and sufficient conditions for reference would be. Obviously the name is passed on from link to link. But of course not every sort of causal chain reaching from me to a certain man will do for me to make a reference. There may be a causal chain from our use of the term 'Santa Claus' to a certain historical saint, but still the children, when they use this, by this time probably do not refer to that saint. So other conditions must be satisfied in order to make this into a really rigorous theory of reference. I don't know that I'm going to do this because, first, I'm sort of too lazy at the moment; secondly, rather than giving a set of necessary and sufficient conditions which will work for a term like reference, I want to present just a *better picture* than the picture presented by the received views.

Haven't I been very unfair to the description theory? Here I have stated it very precisely—more precisely, perhaps, than it has been stated by any of its advocates. So then it's easy to refute. Maybe if I tried to state mine with sufficient precision in the form of six or seven or eight theses, it would also turn out that when you examine the theses one by one, they will all be false. That might even be so, but the difference is this. What I think the examples I've given show is not simply that there's some technical error here or some mistake there, but that the whole picture given by this theory of how reference is determined seems to be wrong from the fundamentals. It seems to be wrong

to think that we give ourselves some properties which somehow qualitatively uniquely pick out an object and determine our reference in that manner. What I am trying to present is a better picture—a picture which, if more details were to be filled in, might be refined so as to give more exact conditions for reference to take place.

One might never reach a set of necessary and sufficient conditions. I don't know, I'm always sympathetic to Bishop Butler's 'Everything is what it is and not another thing'—in the nontrivial sense that philosophical analyses of some concept like reference, in completely different terms which make no mention of reference, are very apt to fail. Of course in any particular case when one is given an analysis one has to look at it and see whether it is true or false. One can't just cite this maxim to oneself and then turn the page. But more cautiously, I want to present a better picture without giving a set of necessary and sufficient conditions for reference. Such conditions would be very complicated, but what is true is that it's in virtue of our connection with other speakers in the community, going back to the referent himself, that we refer to a certain man.

There may be some cases where the description picture is true, where some man really gives a name by going into the privacy of his room and saying that the referent is to be the unique thing with certain identifying properties. 'Jack the Ripper' was a possible example which I gave. Another was 'Hesperus'. Yet another case which can be forced into this description is that of meeting someone and being told his name. Except for a belief in the description theory, in its importance in other cases, one probably wouldn't think that that was a case of giving oneself a description, i.e., 'the guy I'm just meeting now'. But one can put it in these terms if one wishes, and if one has never heard the name in any other way. Of course, if you're introduced to a man and told, 'That's Einstein', you've heard of him before, it may be wrong, and so on. But maybe in some cases such a paradigm works—especially for the man who first gives someone or something a name. Or he points to a star and says, 'That is to be Alpha Centauri'. So he can really make himself this ceremony: 'By "Alpha Centauri" I shall mean the star right over there with such and such coordinates'. But in general this picture fails. In general our reference depends not just on what we think ourselves, but on other people in the community, the history of how the name reached one, and things like that. It is by following such a history that one gets to the reference.

More exact conditions are very complicated to give. They seem in a way somehow different in the case of a famous man and one who isn't so famous. For example, a teacher tells his class that Newton was famous for being the first man to think there's a force pulling things to the earth; I think that's what little kids think Newton's greatest achievement was. I won't say what the merits of such an achievement would be, but, anyway, we may suppose that just being told that this was the sole content of Newton's discovery gives the students a false belief *about Newton,* even though they have never heard of him before. If, on the other hand, the teacher uses the name 'George Smith'—a man by that name is actually his next door neighbor—and says that George Smith first squared the circle, does it follow from this that the students have a false belief about the teacher's neighbor? The teacher doesn't tell them that Smith is his neighbor, nor does he believe Smith first squared the circle. He isn't particularly trying to get any belief *about the neighbor* into the students' heads. He tries to inculcate the belief that there was a man who squared the circle, but not a belief about any particular man—he just pulls out the first name that occurs to him—as it happens, he uses his neighbor's name. It doesn't seem clear in that case that the students have a false belief about the neighbor, even though there is a causal chain going back to the neighbor. I am not sure about this. At any rate more refinements need to be added to make this even begin to be a set of necessary and sufficient conditions. In that sense it's not a theory, but is supposed to give a better picture of what is actually going on.

A rough statement of a theory might be the following: An initial 'baptism' takes place. Here the object may be named by ostension, or the reference of the name may be fixed by a description. When the name is 'passed from link to link', the receiver of the name must, I think, intend when he learns it to use it with the same reference as the man from whom he

heard it. If I hear the name 'Napoleon' and decide it would be a nice name for my pet aardvark, I do not satisfy this condition. (Perhaps it is some such failure to keep the reference fixed which accounts for the divergence of present uses of 'Santa Claus' from the alleged original use.)

Notice that the preceding outline hardly *eliminates* the notion of reference; on the contrary, it takes the notion of intending to use the same reference as a given. There is also an appeal to an initial baptism which is explained in terms either of fixing a reference by a description, or ostension (if ostension is not to be subsumed under the other category). (Perhaps there are other possibilities for initial baptisms.) Further, the George Smith case casts some doubt as to the sufficiency of the conditions. Even if the teacher does refer to his neighbor, is it clear that he has passed on his reference to the pupils? Why shouldn't their belief be about any other man named 'George Smith'? If he says that Newton was hit by an apple, somehow his task of transmitting a reference is easier, since he has communicated a common misconception about Newton.

To repeat, I may not have presented a theory, but I do think that I have presented a better picture than that given by description theorists.

NOTES

1. Strictly speaking, of course, Russell says that the names don't abbreviate descriptions and don't have any sense; but then he also says that, just because the things that we call "names" do abbreviate descriptions, they're not really names. So, since "Walter Scott," according to Russell, does abbreviate a description, "Walter Scott" is not a name; and the only names that really exist in ordinary language are, perhaps, demonstratives such as "this" or "that," used on a particular occasion to refer to an object with which the speaker is "acquainted" in Russell's sense. Though we won't put things the way Russell does, we could describe Russell as saying that names, as they are ordinarily called, *do* have sense. They have sense in a strong way, namely, we should be able to give a definite description such that the referent of the name, by definition, is the object satisfying the description. Russell himself, since he eliminates descriptions from his primitive notation, seems to hold in "On Denoting" that the notion of

"sense" is illusory. In reporting Russell's views, we thus deviate from him in two respects. First, we stipulate that 'names' shall be names as ordinarily conceived, not Russell's "logically proper names"; second, we regard descriptions, and their abbreviations, as having sense.

2. Gottlob Frege, "On Sense and Nominatum," translated by Herbert Feigl in *Readings in Philosophical Analysis* (ed. by Herbert Feigl and Wilfrid Sellars), Appleton Century Crofts, 1949, p. 86.

3. Ludwig Wittgenstein, *Philosophical Investigations,* translated by G. E. M. Anscombe, MacMillan, 1953, §79.

4. John R. Searle, "Proper Names," *Mind* 67 (1958), 166–73.

5. P. F. Strawson, *Individuals,* Methuen, London, 1959, Ch. 6.

6. Searle, in Caton, *Philosophy and Ordinary Language,* p. 160.

Thoughts

GOTTLOB FREGE

Gottlob Frege (1848–1925) was a foremost figure in the development of the philosophy of language.

Just as "beautiful" points the ways for aesthetics and "good" for ethics, so do words like "true" for logic. All sciences have truth as their goal; but logic is also concerned with it in a quite different way: logic has much the same relation to truth as physics has to weight or heat. To discover truths is the task of all sciences; it falls to logic to discern the laws of truth. The word "law" is used in two senses. When we speak of moral or civil laws we mean prescriptions, which ought to be obeyed but with which actual occurrences are not always in conformity. Laws of nature are general features of what happens in nature, and occurrences in nature are always in accordance with them. It is rather in this sense that I speak of laws of truth. Here of course it is not a matter of what happens but of what is. From the laws of truth there follow prescriptions about asserting, thinking, judging, inferring. And we may very well speak of laws of thought in this way too. But there is at once a danger here of confusing different things. People may very well interpret the expression "law of thought" by analogy with "law of nature" and then have in mind general features of thinking as a mental occurrence. A law of thought in this sense would be a psychological law. And so they might come to believe that logic deals with the mental process of thinking and with the psychological laws in accordance with which this takes place. That would be misunderstanding the task of logic, for truth has not here been given its proper place. Error and superstition have causes just as much as correct cognition. Whether what you take for true is false or true, your so taking it comes about in accordance with psychological laws. A derivation from these laws, an explanation of a mental process that ends in taking something to be true, can never take the place of proving what is taken to be true. But may not logical laws also have played a part in this mental process? I do not want to dispute this, but if it is a question of truth this possibility is not enough. For it is also possible that something non-logical played a part in the process and made it swerve from the truth. We can decide only after we have come to

Reprinted from *Collected Papers on Mathematics, Logic, and Philosophy,* ed. Brian McGuinness (Oxford: Basil Blackwell, 1984), by permission of the publisher.

know the laws of truth; but then we can probably do without the derivation and explanation of the mental process, if our concern is to decide whether the process terminates in *justifiably* taking something to be true. In order to avoid any misunderstanding and prevent the blurring of the boundary between psychology and logic, I assign to logic the task of discovering the laws of truth, not the laws of taking things to be true or of thinking. The meaning of the word 'true' is spelled out in the laws of truth.

But first I shall attempt to outline roughly how I want to use "true" in this connection, so as to exclude irrelevant uses of the word. "True" is not to be used here in the sense of "genuine" or "veracious"; nor yet in the way it sometimes occurs in discussion of artistic questions, when, for example, people speak of truth in art, when truth is set up as the aim of art, when the truth of a work of art or true feeling is spoken of. Again, the word "true" is prefixed to another word in order to show that the word is to be understood in its proper, unadulterated sense. This use too lies off the path followed here. What I have in mind is that sort of truth which it is the aim of science to discern.

Grammatically, the word "true" looks like a word for a property. So we want to delimit more closely the region within which truth can be predicated, the region in which there is any question of truth. We find truth predicated of pictures, ideas, sentences, and thoughts. It is striking that visible and audible things turn up here along with things which cannot be perceived with the senses. This suggests that shifts of meaning have taken place. So indeed they have! Is a picture considered as a mere visible and tangible thing really true, and a stone or a leaf not true? Obviously we could not call a picture true unless there were an intention involved. A picture is meant to represent something. (Even an idea is not called true in itself, but only with respect to an intention that the idea should correspond to something.) It might be supposed from this that truth consists in a correspondence of a picture to what it depicts. Now a correspondence is a relation. But this goes against the use of the word "true," which is not a relative term and contains no indication of anything else to which something is to correspond. If I do not know that a picture is meant to represent Cologne Cathedral then I do not know what to compare the picture with in order to decide on its truth. A correspondence, moreover, can only be perfect if the corresponding things coincide and so just are not different things. It is supposed to be possible to test the genuineness of a bank-note by comparing it stereoscopically with a genuine one. But it would be ridiculous to try to compare a gold piece stereoscopically with a twenty-mark note. It would only be possible to compare an idea with a thing if the thing were an idea too. And then, if the first did correspond perfectly with the second, they would coincide. But this is not at all what people intend when they define truth as the correspondence of an idea with something real. For in this case it is essential precisely that the reality shall be distinct from the idea. But then there can be no complete correspondence, no complete truth. So nothing at all would be true; for what is only half true is untrue. Truth does not admit of more and less.— But could we not maintain that there is truth when there is correspondence in a certain respect? But which respect? For in that case what ought we to do so as to decide whether something is true? We should have to inquire whether it is *true* that an idea and a reality, say, correspond in the specified respect. And then we should be confronted by a question of the same kind, and the game could begin again. So the attempted explanation of truth as correspondence breaks down. And any other attempt to define truth also breaks down. For in a definition certain characteristics would have to be specified. And in application to any particular case the question would always arise whether it were *true* that the characteristics were present. So we should be going round in a circle. So it seems likely that the content of the word 'true' is *sui generis* and indefinable.

When we ascribe truth to a picture we do not really mean to ascribe a property which would belong to this picture quite independently of other things; we always have in mind some totally different object and we want to say that the picture corresponds in some way to this object. "My idea corresponds to Cologne Cathedral" is a sentence, and now it is a matter of the truth of this sentence. So what is improperly called the truth of pictures and ideas is reduced to the truth of sentences. What is it that we call a sentence? A series of sounds, but only if it has a sense (this is not meant to convey that *any* series of sounds that has a sense is a sentence). And when we call a sentence true we really mean that its sense is true. And hence the only thing that raises the question of truth at all is the sense of sentences. Now is the sense of a sentence an idea? In any case, truth does not consist in correspondence of the sense with something else, for otherwise the question of truth would get reiterated to infinity.

Without offering this as a definition, I mean by "a thought" something for which the question of truth can arise at all. So I count what is false among thoughts no less than what is true.[1] So I can say: thoughts are senses of sentences, without wishing to assert that the sense of every sentence is a thought. The thought, in itself imperceptible by the senses, gets clothed in the perceptible garb of a sentence, and thereby we are enabled to grasp it. We say a sentence *expresses* a thought.

A thought is something imperceptible: anything the senses can perceive is excluded from the realm of things for which the question of truth arises. Truth is not a quality that answers to a particular kind of sense-impressions. So it is sharply distinguished from the qualities we call by the names "red," "bitter," "lilac-smelling." But do we not see that the Sun has risen? and do we not then also see that this is true? That the Sun has risen is not an object emitting rays that reach my eyes; it is not a visible thing like the Sun itself. That the Sun has risen is recognized to be true on the basis of sense-impressions. But being true is not a sensible, perceptible, property. A thing's being magnetic is also recognized on the basis of sense-impressions of the thing, although this property does not answer, any more than truth does, to a particular kind of sense-impressions. So far these properties agree. However, we do need sense-impressions in order to recognize a body as magnetic. On the other hand, when I find it is true that I do not smell anything at this moment, I do not do so on the basis of sense-impressions.

All the same it is something worth thinking about that we cannot recognize a property of a thing without at the same time finding the thought *this thing has this property* to be true. So with every property of a

thing there is tied up a property of a thought, namely truth. It is also worth noticing that the sentence "I smell the scent of violets" has just the same content as the sentence "It is true that I smell the scent of violets." So it seems, then, that nothing is added to the thought by my ascribing to it the property of truth. And yet is it not a great result when the scientist after much hesitation and laborious researches can finally say "My conjecture is true"? The meaning of the word "true" seems to be altogether sui generis. May we not be dealing here with something which cannot be called a property in the ordinary sense at all? In spite of this doubt I will begin by expressing myself in accordance with ordinary usage, as if truth were a property, until some more appropriate way of speaking is found.

In order to bring out more precisely what I mean by "a thought," I shall distinguish various kinds of sentences.[2] We should not wish to deny sense to a command, but this sense is not such that the question of truth could arise for it. Therefore I shall not call the sense of a command a thought. Sentences expressing wishes or requests are ruled out in the same way. Only those sentences in which we communicate or assert something come into the question. But here I do not count exclamations in which one vents one's feelings, groans, sighs, laughs—unless it has been decided by some special convention that they are to communicate something. But how about interrogative sentences? In a word-question we utter an incomplete sentence, which is meant to be given a true sense just by means of the completion for which we are asking. Word-questions are accordingly left out of consideration here. Propositional questions are a different matter. We expect to hear "yes" or "no." The answer "yes" means the same as an assertoric sentence, for in saying "yes" the speaker presents as true the thought that was already completely contained in the interrogative sentence. This is how a propositional question can be formed from any assertoric sentence. And this is why an exclamation cannot be regarded as a communication: no corresponding propositional question can be formed. An interrogative sentence and an assertoric one contain the same thought; but the assertoric sentence contains something else as well, namely assertion. The interrogative sentence contains something more too, namely a request. Therefore two things must be distinguished in an assertoric sentence: the content, which it has in common with the corresponding propositional question; and assertion. The former is the thought or at least contains the thought. So it is possible to express a thought without laying it down as true. The two things are so closely joined in an assertoric sentence that it is easy to overlook their separability. Consequently we distinguish:

(1) the grasp of a thought—thinking,
(2) the acknowledgement of the truth of a thought—the act of judgement,
(3) the manifestation of this judgement—assertion.

We have already performed the first act when we form a propositional question. An advance in science usually takes place in this way: first a thought is grasped, and thus may perhaps be expressed in a propositional question; after appropriate investigations, this thought is finally recognized to be true. We express acknowledgement of truth in the form of an assertoric sentence. We do not need the word "true" for this. And even when we do use it the properly assertoric force does not lie in it, but in the assertoric sentence-form; and where this form loses its assertoric force the word "true" cannot put it back again. This happens when we are not speaking seriously. As stage thunder is only sham thunder and a stage fight only a sham fight, so stage assertion is only sham assertion. It is only acting, only fiction. When playing his part the actor is not asserting anything; nor is he lying, even if he says something of whose falsehood he is convinced. In poetry we have the case of thoughts being expressed without being actually put forward as true, in spite of the assertoric form of the sentence; although the poem may suggest to the hearer that he himself should make an assenting judgement. Therefore the question still arises, even about what is presented in the assertoric sentence-form, whether it really contains an assertion. And this question must be answered in the negative if the requisite seriousness is lacking. It is unimportant whether the word "true" is used here. This explains

why it is that nothing seems to be added to a thought by attributing to it the property of truth.

An assertoric sentence often contains, over and above a thought and assertion, a third component not covered by the assertion. This is often meant to act on the feelings and mood of the hearer, or to arouse his imagination. Words like "regrettably" and "fortunately" belong here. Such constituents of sentences are more strongly prominent in poetry, but are seldom wholly absent from prose. They occur more rarely in mathematical, physical, or chemical expositions than in historical ones. What are called the humanities are closer to poetry, and are therefore less scientific, than the exact sciences, which are drier in proportion to being more exact; for exact science is directed toward truth and truth alone. Therefore all constituents of sentences not covered by the assertoric force do not belong to scientific exposition; but they are sometimes hard to avoid, even for one who sees the danger connected with them. Where the main thing is to approach by way of intimation what cannot be conceptually grasped, these constituents are fully justified. The more rigorously scientific an exposition is, the less the nationality of its author will be discernible and the easier it will be to translate. On the other hand, the constituents of language to which I here want to call attention make the translation of poetry very difficult, indeed make perfect translation almost always impossible, for it is just in what largely makes the poetic value that languages most differ.

It makes no difference to the thought whether I use the word "horse" or "steed" or "nag" or "prad." The assertoric force does not cover the ways in which these words differ. What is called mood, atmosphere, illumination in a poem, what is portrayed by intonation and rhythm, does not belong to the thought.

Much in language serves to aid the hearer's understanding, for instance emphasizing part of a sentence by stress or word-order. Here let us bear in mind words like "still" and "already." Someone using the sentence "Alfred has still not come" actually says "Alfred has not come," and at the same time hints—but only hints—that Alfred's arrival is expected. Nobody can say: Since Alfred's arrival is not expected, the sense of the sentence is false. The way that "but" differs from "and" is that we use it to intimate that what follows it contrasts with what was to be expected from what preceded it. Such conversational suggestions make no difference to the thought. A sentence can be transformed by changing the verb from active to passive and at the same time making the accusative into the subject. In the same way we may change the dative into the nominative and at the same time replace "give" by "receive." Naturally such transformations are not trivial in every respect; but they do not touch the thought, they do not touch what is true or false. If the inadmissibility of such transformations were recognized as a principle, then any profound logical investigation would be hindered. It is just as important to ignore distinctions that do not touch the heart of the matter, as to make distinctions which concern essentials. But what is essential depends on one's purpose. To a mind concerned with the beauties of language, what is trivial to the logician may seem to be just what is important.

Thus the content of a sentence often goes beyond the thought expressed by it. But the opposite often happens too; the mere wording, which can be made permanent by writing or the gramophone, does not suffice for the expression of the thought. The present tense is used in two ways: first, in order to indicate a time; second, in order to eliminate any temporal restriction, where timelessness or eternity is part of the thought—consider for instance the laws of mathematics. Which of the two cases occurs is not expressed but must be divined. If a time-indication is conveyed by the present tense one must know when the sentence was uttered in order to grasp the thought correctly. Therefore the time of utterance is part of the expression of the thought. If someone wants to say today what he expressed yesterday using the word "today," he will replace this word with "yesterday." Although the thought is the same its verbal expression must be different in order that the change of sense which would otherwise be effected by the differing times of utterance may be cancelled out. The case is the same with words like "here" and "there." In all such cases the mere wording, as it can be preserved in writing, is not the complete expression of the thought; the knowledge of certain conditions accompanying the utterance, which are used as means of expressing the thought, is needed for us to grasp the thought correctly. Pointing the finger, hand gestures, glances may belong here too. The same utterance containing the word "I" in the mouths of different men will express different thoughts of which some may be true, others false.

The occurrence of the word "I" in a sentence gives rise to some further questions.

Consider the following case. Dr. Gustav Lauben says, "I was wounded," Leo Peter hears this and remarks some days later, "Dr. Gustav Lauben was wounded." Does this sentence express the same thought as the one Dr. Lauben uttered himself? Suppose that Rudolph Lingens was present when Dr. Lauben spoke and now hears what is related by Leo Peter. If the same thought was uttered by Dr. Lauben and Leo Peter, then Rudolph Lingens, who is fully master of the language and remembers what Dr. Lauben said in his presence, must now know at once from Leo Peter's report that he is speaking of the same thing. But knowledge of the language is a special thing when proper names are involved. It may well be the case that only a few people associate a definite thought with the sentence "Dr. Lauben was wounded." For complete understanding one needs in this case to know the expression "Dr. Gustav Lauben." Now if both Leo Peter and Rudolph Lingens mean by "Dr. Gustav Lauben," the doctor who is the only doctor living in a house known to both of them, then they both understand the sentence "Dr. Gustav Lauben was wounded" in the same way; they associate the same thought with it. But it is also possible that Rudolph Lingens does not know Dr. Lauben personally and does not know that it was Dr. Lauben who recently said "I was wounded." In this case Rudolph Lingens cannot know that the same affair is in question. I say, therefore, in this case: the thought which Leo Peter expresses is not the same as that which Dr. Lauben uttered.

Suppose further that Herbert Garner knows that Dr. Gustav Lauben was born on 13 September, 1875 in N.N. and this is not true of anyone else; suppose, however, that he does not know where Dr. Lauben now lives nor indeed anything else about him. On the other hand, suppose Leo Peter does not know that Dr. Lauben was born on 13 September 1875, in N.N. Then as far as the proper name "Dr. Gustav Lauben" is concerned, Herbert Garner and Leo Peter do not speak the same language, although they do in fact refer to the same man with this name; for they do not know that they are doing so. Therefore Herbert Garner does not associate the same thought with the sentence "Dr. Gustav Lauben was wounded" as Leo Peter wants to express with it. To avoid the awkwardness that Herbert Garner and Leo Peter are not speaking the same language, I shall suppose that Leo Peter uses the proper name "Dr. Lauben" and Herbert Garner uses the proper name "Gustav Lauben." Then it is possible that Herbert Garner takes the sense of the sentence "Dr. Lauben was wounded" to be true but is misled by false information into taking the sense of the sentence "Gustav Lauben was wounded" to be false. So given our assumptions these thoughts are different.

Accordingly, with a proper name, it is a matter of the way that the object so designated is presented. This may happen in different ways, and to every such way there corresponds a special sense of a sentence containing the proper name. The different thoughts thus obtained from the same sentences correspond in truth-value, of course; that is to say, if one is true then all are true, and if one is false than all are false. Nevertheless the difference must be recognized. So we must really stipulate that for every proper name there shall be just one associated manner of presentation of the object so designated. It is often unimportant that this stipulation should be fulfilled, but not always.

Now everyone is presented to himself in a special and primitive way, in which he is presented to no-one else. So, when Dr. Lauben has the thought that he was wounded, he will probably be basing it on this primitive way in which he is presented to himself. And only Dr. Lauben himself can grasp thoughts specified in this way. But now he may want to communicate with others. He cannot communicate a thought he alone can grasp. Therefore, if he now says "I was wounded," he must use "I" in a sense which can be grasped by others, perhaps in the sense of "he who is speaking to you at this moment"; by doing this he makes the conditions accompanying his utterance serve towards the expression of a thought. . . .

I now return to the question: is a thought an idea? If other people can assent to the thought I express in the Pythagorean theorem just as I do, then it does not belong to the content of my consciousness, I am not

its owner; yet I can, nevertheless, acknowledge it as true. However, if what is taken to be the content of the Pythagorean theorem by me and by somebody else is not the same thought at all, we should not really say "*the* Pythagorean theorem," but "*my* Pythagorean theorem," "*his* Pythagorean theorem," and these would be different, for the sense necessarily goes with the sentence. In that case my thought may be the content of my consciousness and his thought the content of his. Could the sense of my Pythagorean theorem be true and the sense of his false? . . .

If every thought requires an owner and belongs to the contents of his consciousness, then the thought has this owner alone; and there is no science common to many on which many could work, but perhaps I have my science, a totality of thoughts whose owner I am, and another person has his. Each of us is concerned with contents of his own consciousness. No contradiction between the two sciences would then be possible, and it would really be idle to dispute about truth; as idle, indeed almost as ludicrous, as for two people to dispute whether a hundred-mark note were genuine, where each meant the one he himself had in his pocket and understood the word 'genuine' in his own particular sense. If someone takes thoughts to be ideas, what he then accepts as true is, on his own view, the content of consciousness, and does not properly concern other people at all. If he heard from me the opinion that a thought is not an idea he could not dispute it, for, indeed, it would not now concern him.

So the result seems to be: thoughts are neither things in the external world nor ideas.

A third realm must be recognized. Anything belonging to this realm has it in common with ideas that it cannot be perceived by the senses, but has it in common with things that it does not need an owner so as to belong to the contents of his consciousness. Thus for example the thought we have expressed in the Pythagorean theorem is timelessly true, true independently of whether anyone takes it to be true. It needs no owner. It is not true only from the time when it is discovered; just as a planet, even before anyone saw it, was in interaction with other planets.[3] . . .

We are not owners of thoughts as we are owners of our ideas. We do not *have* a thought as we have, say, a sense-impression, but we also do not *see* a thought as we see, say, a star. So it is advisable to choose a special expression; the word "grasp" suggests itself for the purpose.[4] To the grasping of thoughts there must then correspond a special mental capacity, the power of thinking. In thinking we do not produce thoughts, we grasp them. For what I have called thoughts stand in the closest connection with truth. What I acknowledge as true, I judge to be true quite apart from my acknowledging its truth or even thinking about it. That someone thinks it has nothing to do with the truth of a thought. . . .

How does a thought act? By being grasped and taken to be true. This is a process in the inner world of a thinker which may have further consequences in this inner world, and which may also encroach on the sphere of the will and make itself noticeable in the outer world as well. If, for example, I grasp the thought we express by the theorem of Pythagoras, the consequence may be that I recognize it to be true, and further that I apply it in making a decision, which brings about the acceleration of masses. This is how our actions are usually led up to by acts of thinking and judging. And so thoughts may indirectly influence the motion of masses. The influence of man on man is brought about for the most part by thoughts. People communicate thoughts. How do they do this? They bring about changes in the common external world, and these are meant to be perceived by someone else, and so give him a chance to grasp a thought and take it to be true. Could the great events of world history have come about without the communication of thoughts? And yet we are inclined to regard thoughts as unactual, because they appear to do nothing in relation to events, whereas thinking, judging, stating, understanding, in general doing things, are affairs that concern men. How very different the actuality of a hammer appears, compared with that of a thought! How different a process handing over a hammer is from communicating a thought! The hammer passes from one control to another, it is gripped, it undergoes pressure, and thus its density, the disposition of its parts, is locally changed. There is nothing of all this with a thought. It does not leave the control of the communicator by being communicated, for after all man has no power over it. When a thought is grasped, it at first only brings about changes in the

inner world of the one who grasps it; yet it remains untouched in the core of its essence, for the changes it undergoes affect only inessential properties. There is lacking here something we observe everywhere in physical process—reciprocal action. Thoughts are not wholly unactual but their actuality is quite different from the actuality of things. And their action is brought about by a performance of the thinker; without this they would be inactive, at least as far as we can see. And yet the thinker does not create them but must take them as they are. They can be true without being grasped by a thinker; and they are not wholly unactual even then, at least if they *could* be grasped and so brought into action.

NOTES

1. So, similarly, people have said "a judgement is something which is either true or false." In fact I use the word "thought" more or less in the sense "judgement" has in the writings of logicians. I hope it will become clear in the sequel why I choose "thought." Such an explanation has been objected to on the ground that it makes a division of judgements into true and false judgements—perhaps the least significant of all possible divisions among judgements. But I cannot see that it is a logical fault that a division is given along with the explanation. As for the division's being significant, we shall perhaps find we must hold it in no small esteem, if, as I have said, it is the word "true" that points the way for logic.

2. I am not using the word "sentence" here in quite the same sense as grammar does, which also includes subordinate clauses. An isolated subordinate clause does not always have a sense about which the question of truth can arise, whereas the complex sentence to which it belongs has such a sense.

3. A person sees a thing, has an idea, grasps or thinks a thought. When he grasps or thinks a thought he does not create it but only comes to stand in a certain relation to what already existed—a different relation from seeing a thing or having an idea.

4. The expression "grasp" is as metaphorical as "content of consciousness." The nature of language does not permit anything else. What I hold in my hand can certainly be regarded as the content of my hand; but all the same it is the content of my hand in quite another and a more extraneous way than are the bones and muscles of which the hand consists or again the tensions these undergo.

The Problem of the Essential Indexical

$\sim$

JOHN PERRY

John Perry, a noted American metaphysician and philosopher of language, is H.W. Stuart Professor of Philosophy at Stanford University.

I once followed a trail of sugar on a supermarket floor, pushing my cart down the aisle on one side of a tall counter and back the aisle on the other, seeking the shopper with the torn sack to tell him he was making a mess. With each trip around the counter, the trail became thicker. But I seemed unable to catch up. Finally it dawned on me. I was the shopper I was trying to catch.

I believed at the outset that the shopper with a torn sack was making a mess. And I was right. But I did not believe that I was making a mess. That seems to be something I came to believe. And when I came to believe that, I stopped following the trail around the counter and rearranged the torn sack in my cart. My change in beliefs seems to explain my change in behavior. My aim in this paper is to make a key point about the characterization of this change, and of beliefs in general.

At first, characterizing the change seems easy. My beliefs changed, didn't they, in that I came to have a new one, namely, *that I am making a mess*. But things are not so simple.

The reason they are not is the importance of the word "I" in my expression of what I came to believe. When we replace it with other designations of me, we no longer have an explanation of my behavior and so, it seems, no longer an attribution of the same belief. It seems to be an *essential* indexical. But without such a replacement, all we have to identify the belief is the sentence "I am making a mess." But that sentence by itself does not seem to identify the crucial belief, for if someone else had said it, they would have expressed a different belief, a false one.

I argue that the essential indexical poses a problem for various otherwise plausible accounts of belief. I first argue that it is a problem for the view that belief is a relation between subjects and propositions conceived as bearers of truth and falsity. The problem is not solved merely by replacing or supplementing this with a notion of *de re* belief. Nor is it solved by moving to a notion of a proposition that, rather than true or false absolutely is only true or false at an index or in a context (at a time, for a speaker, say). Its solution requires us to make a sharp distinction between objects of belief and belief states, and to realize that the connection between them is not so intimate as might have been supposed.

LOCATING BELIEFS

I want to introduce two more examples. In the first, a professor, who desires to attend the department meeting on time and believes correctly that it begins at noon, sits motionless in his office at that time. Suddenly, he begins to move. What explains his action? A change in belief. He believed all along that the department meeting starts at noon; he came to believe, as he would have put it, that it starts *now*.

The author of the book *Hiker's Guide to the Desolation Wilderness* stands in the wilderness beside Gilmore Lake, looking at the Mt. Tallac trail as it leaves the lake and climbs the mountain. He desires

Reprinted from *The Problem of the Essential Indexical* (Oxford: Oxford University Press, 1993), by permission of the publisher.

to leave the wilderness. He believes that the best way out from Gilmore Lake is to follow the Mt. Tallac trail up the mountain to Cathedral Peaks trail, on to the Floating Island trail, emerging at Spring Creek Tract Road. But he does not move. He is lost. He is not sure whether he is standing beside Gilmore Lake, looking at Mt. Tallac, or beside Clyde Lake looking at Jack's Peak, or beside Eagle Lake looking at one of the Maggie peaks. Then he begins to move along the Mt. Tallac trail. If asked, he would have explained the crucial change in his beliefs this way: "I came to believe that *this* is the Mt. Tallac trail and *that* is Gilmore Lake."

In these three cases, the subjects in explaining their actions would use indexicals to characterize certain beliefs they came to have. These indexicals are essential, in that replacement of them by other terms destroys the force of the explanation, or at least requires certain assumptions to be made to preserve it.

Suppose I had said, in the manner of de Gaulle, "I came to believe that John Perry is making a mess." I would no longer have explained why I stopped and looked in my own cart. To explain that, I would have to add, "and I believe that I am John Perry," bringing in the indexical again. After all, suppose I had really given my explanation in the manner of de Gaulle, and said "I came to believe that de Gaulle is making a mess." That would not have explained my stopping at all. But it really would have explained it every bit as much as "I came to believe John Perry is making a mess." For if I added "and I believe that I am de Gaulle," the explanations would be on par. The only reason "I came to believe John Perry is making a mess" seems to explain my action is our natural assumption that I did believe I was John Perry and did not believe I was de Gaulle. So replacing the indexical "I" with another term designating the same person really does, as claimed, destroy the explanation.

Similarly, our professor, as he sets off down the hall, might say "I believe the meeting starts at noon." In accepting the former as an explanation, we would be assuming he believes it is *now* noon. If he believed it was now 5 P.M., he would not have explained his departure by citing his belief that the meeting starts at noon, unless he was a member of a department with very long meetings. After all, he believed that the meeting started at noon all along, so that belief can hardly explain a change in his behavior. Basically similar remarks apply to the lost author.

I shall use the term "locating beliefs" to refer to one's beliefs about where one is, when it is, and who one is. Such beliefs seem essentially indexical. Imagine two lost campers who trust the same guidebook but disagree about where they are. If we were to try to characterize the beliefs of these campers without the use of indexicals, it would seem impossible to bring out this disagreement. If, for example, we characterized their beliefs by the set of "eternal sentences," drawn from the guidebook they would mark "true," there is no reason to suppose that the sets would differ. They could mark all of the same sentences "true," and still disagree in their locating beliefs. It seems that there has to be some indexical element in the characterization of their beliefs to bring out this disagreement. But as we shall see, there is no room for this indexical element in the traditional way of looking at belief, and even when its necessity is recognized, it is not easy to see how to fit it in.

THE DOCTRINE OF PROPOSITIONS

I shall first consider how the problem appears to a traditional way of thinking of belief. The doctrines I describe were held by Frege, but I shall put them in a way that does not incorporate his terminology or the details of his view. This traditional way, which I call the "doctrine of propositions," has three main tenets. The first is that belief is a relation between a subject and an object, the latter being denoted, in a canonical belief report, by a that-clause. So "Carter believes that Atlanta is the capital of Georgia" reports that a certain relation, *believing,* obtains between Carter and a certain object—at least in a suitably wide sense of the object—*that Atlanta is the capital of Georgia.* These objects are called *propositions.*

The second and the third tenets concern such objects. The second is that they have a truth-value in an absolute sense, as opposed to merely being true for a person or at a time. The third has to do with how we individuate them. It is necessary, for *that S* and *that S′* to be the same, that they have the same truth-value. But it is not sufficient, for *that the sea is salty* and *that milk is white* are not the same proposition. It is necessary that they have the same truth condition, in the sense that they attribute to the same objects the same relation. But this also is not sufficient, for *that Atlanta is the capital of Georgia* and *that Atlanta is the capital of the largest state east of the Mississippi* are not the same proposition. Carter, it seems, might believe the first but not the second. Propositions must not only have the same truth-value and concern the same objects and relations, but also involve the same concepts. For Frege, this meant that if *that S = that S′*, *S* and *S′* must have the same sense. Others might eschew senses in favor of properties and relations, others take concepts to be just words, so that sameness of propositions is just sameness of sentences. What these approaches have in common is the insistence that propositions must be individuated in a more "fine-grained" way than is provided by truth-value or the notion of truth conditions employed above.

THE PROBLEM

It is clear that the essential indexical is a problem for the doctrine of propositions. What answer can it give to the question, "What did I come to believe when I straightened up the sugar?" The sentence "I am making a mess" does not identify a proposition. For this sentence is not true or false absolutely, but only as said by one person or another; had another shopper said it when I did, he would have been wrong. So the sentence by which I identify what I came to believe does not identify, by itself, a proposition. There is a *missing conceptual ingredient:* a sense for which I am the reference, or a complex of properties I alone have, or a singular term that refers to no one but me. To identify the proposition I came to believe, the advocate of the doctrine of propositions must identify this missing conceptual ingredient.

An advocate of the doctrine of propositions, his attention drawn to indexicals, might take this attitude towards them: they are communicative shortcuts. Just before I straightened up the sack I must have come to believe some propositions with the structure α *is making a mess,* where α is some concept that I alone "fit" (to pick a phrase neutral among the different notions of a concept). When I say "I believe I am

making a mess," my hearers know that I believe some such proposition of this form; which one in particular is not important for the purposes at hand.

If this is correct, we should be able to identify the proposition I came to believe, even if doing so is not necessary for ordinary communicative purposes. But then the doctrine of propositions is in trouble, for any candidate will fall prey to the problems mentioned above. If *that α is making a mess* is what I came to believe, then "I came to believe that A is making a mess," where A expressed α, should be an even better explanation than the original, where I used "I" as a communicative shortcut. But, as we saw, any such explanation will be defective, working only on the assumption that I believed that I was α.

To this it might be replied that though there may be no replacement for "I" that generally preserves explanatory force, all that needs to be claimed is that there is such a replacement on each occasion. The picture is this. On each occasion that I use "I," there is some concept I have in mind that fits me uniquely, and which is the missing conceptual ingredient in the proposition that remains incompletely identified when I characterize my beliefs. The concept I use to think of myself is not necessarily the same each time I do so, and of course I must use a different one than others do, since it must fit me and not them. Because there is no general way of replacing the "I" with a term that gets at the missing ingredient, the challenge to do so in response to a particular example is temporarily embarrassing. But the doctrine of propositions does not require a general answer.

This strategy does not work for two reasons. First, even if I was thinking of myself as, say, the only bearded philosopher in a Safeway store west of the Mississippi, the fact that I came to believe that the only such philosopher was making a mess explains my action only on the assumption that I believed that I was the only such philosopher, which brings in the indexical again. Second, in order to provide me with an appropriate proposition as the object of belief, the missing conceptual ingredient will have to fit me. Suppose I was thinking of myself in the way described, but that I was not bearded and was not in a Safeway store—I had forgotten that I had shaved and gone to the A&P instead. Then the proposition supplied by this strategy would be false, while what I came to believe, *that I was making a mess,* was true.

This strategy assumes that whenever I have a belief I would characterize by using a sentence with an indexical *d,*

I believe that . . . *d* . . .

that there is some conceptual ingredient *c,* such that it is also true that,

I believe that *d* is *c*

and that, on this second point, I am right. But there is no reason to believe this would always be so. Each time I say "I believe it is *now* time to rake the leaves," I need not have some concept that uniquely fits the time at which I speak.

From the point of view of the doctrine of propositions, belief reports such as "I believe that I am making a mess" are deficient, for there is a missing conceptual ingredient. From the point of view of locating beliefs, there is something lacking in the propositions offered by the doctrine, a missing indexical ingredient.

The problem of the essential indexical reveals that something is badly wrong with the traditional doctrine of propositions. But the traditional doctrine has its competitors anyway, in response to philosophical pressures from other directions. Perhaps attention to these alternative or supplementary models of belief will provide a solution to our problem.

DE RE BELIEF

One development in the philosophy of belief seems quite promising in this respect. It involves qualifying the third tenet of the doctrine of propositions, to allow a sort of proposition individuated by an object or sequence of objects, and a part of a proposition of the earlier sort. The motivation for this qualification or supplementation comes from a type of belief report, which gives rise to the same problem, that of the missing conceptual ingredient, as does the problem of the essential indexical.

The third tenet of the doctrine of propositions is motivated by the failure of substitutivity of coreferen-

tial terms within the that-clause following "believes." But there seems to be a sort of belief report, or a way of understanding some belief reports, that allows such substitution, and such successful substitution becomes a problem for a theory designed to explain its failure. For suppose Patrick believes that, as he would put it, the dean is wise. Patrick does not know Frank, much less know that he lives next to the dean, and yet I might in certain circumstances say "Patrick believes Frank's neighbor is wise." Or I might say "There is someone whom Patrick believes to be wise," and later on identify that someone as "Frank's neighbor." The legitimacy of this cannot be understood on the unqualified doctrine of propositions; I seem to have gone from one proposition, *that the dean of the school is wise,* to another, *that Frank's neighbor is wise;* but the fact that Patrick believes the first seems to be no reason he should believe the second. And the quantification into the belief report seems to make no sense at all on the doctrine of propositions, for the report does not relate Patrick to an individual known variously as "the dean" and "Frank's neighbor," but only with a concept expressed by the first of these terms.

The problem here is just that of a missing conceptual ingredient. It looked in the original report as if Patrick was being said to stand in the relation of a belief to a certain proposition, a part of which was a conceptual ingredient expressed by the words of "the dean." But if I am permitted to exchange those words for others, "Frank's neighbor," which are not conceptually equivalent, then apparently the initial part of the proposition he was credited with belief in was not the conceptual ingredient identified by "the dean" after all. So what proposition was it Patrick was originally credited with belief in? And "There is someone such that Patrick believes that he is wise" seems to credit Patrick with belief in a proposition, without telling us which one. For after the "believes" we have only "he is wise," where the "he" does not give us an appropriate conceptual ingredient, but functions as a variable ranging over individuals.

We do seem in some circumstances to allow such substitutivity, and make ready sense of quantification into belief reports. So the doctrine of propositions must be qualified. We can look upon this sort of belief as involving a relation to a new sort of proposition, consisting of an object or sequence of objects and a conceptual ingredient, a part of a proposition of the original kind, or what we might call an "open proposition." This sort of belief and this kind of proposition we call "*de re,*" the sort of belief and the sort of proposition that fits the original doctrine, "*de dicto.*" Taken this way, we analyze "Patrick believes that the dean of the school is wise," as reporting a relation between Patrick and a proposition consisting of a certain person variously describable as "the dean" and "Frank's neighbor" and something, *that x is wise,* which would yield a proposition with the addition of an appropriate conceptual ingredient. Since the dean himself, and not just a concept expressed by the words "the dean" is involved, substitution holds and quantification makes sense.

Here, as in the case of the essential indexical, we were faced with a missing conceptual ingredient. Perhaps, then, this modification of the third tenet will solve the earlier problem as well. But it will not. Even if we suppose—as I think we should—that when I said "I believe that I am making a mess" I was reporting a *de re* belief, our problem will remain.

One problem emerges when we look at accounts that have been offered of the conditions under which a person has a *de re* belief. The most influential treatments of *de re* belief have tried to explain it in terms of *de dicto* belief or something like it. Some terminological regimentation is helpful here. Let us couch reports of *de re* belief in terms "*X believes of a that he is so and so,*" reserving the simpler "*X believes that a is so and so*" for *de dicto* belief. The simplest account of *de re* belief in terms of *de dicto* belief is this:

X believes of *y* that he is so and so

just in case

there is a concept α such that α fits *y* and *X* believes that α is so and so.

Now it is clear that if this is our analysis of *de re* belief, the problem of the essential indexical is still with us. For we are faced with the same problem we had before. I can believe that I am making a mess, even if there is no concept α such that I alone fit α

and I believe that α is making a mess. Since I do not have any *de dicto* belief of the sort, on this account I do not have a *de re* belief of the right sort either. So, even allowing *de re* belief, we still do not have an account of the belief I acquired.

Now this simple account of *de re* belief has not won many adherents, because it is commonly held that *de re* belief is a more interesting notion than it allows. This proposal trivializes it. Suppose Nixon is the next President. Since I believe that the next President will be the next President, I would on this proposal believe of Nixon that he is the next President, even though I am thoroughly convinced that Nixon will not be the next President.

To get a more interesting or useful notion of *de re* belief, philosophers have suggested that there are limitations on the conceptual ingredient involved in the *de dicto* belief that yields the *de re* belief. Kaplan, for example, requires not only that there be some α such that I believe that α will be the next President and that α denotes Nixon, for me to believe of Nixon that he will be the next President, but also that α be a *vivid name of Nixon for me.* Hintikka requires that α denote the same individual in every possible world compatible with what I believe. Each of these philosophers explains these notions in such a way that in the circumstances imagined, I would not believe of Nixon that he is the next President.

However well these proposals deal with other phenomena connected with *de re* belief, they cannot help with the problem of the essential indexical. They tighten the requirements laid down by the original proposal, but those were apparently already too restrictive. If in order to believe that I am making a mess I need not have any conceptual ingredient α that fits me, a fortiori I am not required to have one that is a vivid name of myself for me, or one that picks out the same individual in every possible world compatible with what I believe.

Perhaps this simply shows that the approach of explaining *de re* belief in terms of *de dicto* belief in incorrect. I think it does show that. But even so, the problem remains. Suppose we do not insist on an account of *de re* belief in terms of *de dicto* belief, but merely suppose that whenever we ascribe a belief, and cannot find a suitable complete proposition to serve as the object because of a missing conceptual ingredient, we are dealing with *de re* belief. Then we will ascribe a *de re* belief to me in the supermarket, I believed *of* John Perry that he was making a mess. But it will not be my having such a *de re* belief that explains my action.

Suppose there were mirrors at either end of the counter so that as I pushed my cart down the aisle in pursuit I saw myself in the mirror. I take what I see to be the reflection of the messy shopper going up the aisle on the other side, not realizing that what I am really seeing is a reflection of a reflection of myself. I point and say, truly, "I believe that he is making a mess." In trying to find a suitable proposition for me to believe, we would be faced with the same sorts of problems we had with my earlier report, in which I used "I" instead of "he." We would not be able to eliminate an indexical element in the term referring to me. So here we have *de re* belief; I believe of John Perry that he is making a mess. But then that I believe of John Perry that he is making a mess does not explain my stopping; in the imagined circumstances I would accelerate, as would the shopper I was trying to catch. But then, even granting that when I say "I believe that I am making a mess" I attribute to myself a certain *de re* belief, the belief of John Perry that he is making a mess, our problem remains.

If we look at it with the notion of a locating belief in mind, the failure of the introduction of *de re* belief to solve our problems is not surprising. *De re* propositions remain nonindexical. Propositions individuated in part by objects remain as insensitive to what is essential in locating beliefs as those individuated wholly by concepts. Saying that I believed of John Perry that he was making a mess leaves out the crucial change, that I came to think of the messy shopper not merely as the shopper with the torn sack, or the man in the mirror, but as *me*.

RELATIVIZED PROPOSITIONS

It seems that to deal with essential indexicality we must somehow incorporate the indexical element into what is believed, the object of belief. If we do so, we come up against the second tenet of the doctrine of propositions, that such objects are true or false absolutely. But the tools for abandoning this tenet have been provided in recent treatments of the semantics of modality, tense, and indexicality. So this seems a promising direction.

In possible-worlds semantics for necessity and possibility we have the notion of truth at a world. In a way this does not involve a new notion of a proposition and in a way it does. When Frege insisted that his "thoughts" were true or false absolutely, he did not mean that they had the same truth-value in all possible worlds. Had he used a possible-worlds framework, he would have had their truth-values vary from world to world, and simply insisted on a determinate truth-value in each world and in particular in the actual world. In a way, then, taking propositions to be functions from possible worlds to truth-values is just a way of looking at the old notion of a proposition.

Still, this way of looking at it invites generalization that takes us away from the old notion. From a technical point of view, the essential idea is that a proposition is, or is represented by, a function from an index to a truth-value; when we get away from modality, this same technical idea may be useful, though something other than possible worlds are taken as indices. To deal with temporal operators, we can use the notion of truth at a time. Here the indices will be times, and our propositions will be functions from times to truth-values. For example, *that Elizabeth is Queen of England* is a proposition true in 1960 but not in 1940. Hence "At some time or other Elizabeth is Queen of England" is true, simpliciter.

Now consider "I am making a mess." Rather than thinking of this as partially identifying an absolutely true proposition, with the "I" showing the place of the missing conceptual ingredient, why not think of it as completely identifying a new-fangled proposition, that is true or false only *at a person?* More precisely, it is one that is true or false at a time and a person, since though true when I said it, it has since occasionally been false.

If we ignore possibility and necessity, it seems that regarding propositions as functions to truth-values from indices that are pairs of persons and times will do the trick, and that so doing will allow us to exploit relations between elements within the indices to formulate rules that bring out differences between indexicals. "I am tired now" is true at the pair consisting of the person a and the time t if and only if a is tired at t, while "You will be tired" is true at the same index if and only if the addressee of *a* at *t* is tired at some time later than *t*.

Does this way of looking at the matter solve the problem of the essential indexical? I say "I believe that I am making a mess." On our amended doctrine of propositions, this ascribes a relation between me and *that I am making a mess,* which is a function from indices to truth-values. The belief report seems to completely specify the relativized proposition involved; there is no missing conceptual ingredient. So the problem must be solved.

But it is not. I believed that certain proposition, *that I am making a mess* was true—true for me. So belief that this proposition was true for me then does not differentiate me from some other shopper, who believes *that I am making a mess* was true for John Perry. So this belief cannot be what explains my stopping and searching my cart for the torn sack. Once we have adopted these new-fangled propositions, which are only true at times for persons, we have to admit also that we believe them as true for persons at times, and not absolutely. And then our problem returns.

Clearly an important distinction must be made. All believing is done by persons at times, or so we may suppose. But the time of belief and the person doing the believing cannot be generally identified with the person and time relative to which the propositions believed is held true. You now believe that *that I am making a mess* was true for me, then, but you certainly do not believe it is true for you now, unless you are reading this in a supermarket. Let us call *you* and *now* the context of belief, and *me* and *then* the context of evaluation. The context of belief may be the same as the context of evaluation, but need not be.

Now the mere fact that I believed that proposition *that I am making a mess* to be true for someone at some time did not explain my stopping the cart. You believe so now, and doubtless have no more desire to mess up supermarkets than I did. But you are not bending over to straighten up a sack of sugar.

The fact that I believed this proposition true for Perry at the time he was in the supermarket does not explain my behavior either. For so did the other shopper. And you also now believe this proposition was true for Perry at the time he was in the supermarket.

The important difference seems to be that for me the context of belief was just the context of evalua-

tion, but for the other shopper it was not and for you it is not. But this does not do the trick either.

Consider our tardy professor. He is doing research on indexicals, and has written on the board "My meeting starts now." He believes that the proposition expressed by this sentence is true at noon for him. He has believed so for hours, and at noon the context of belief comes to be the context of evaluation. These facts give us no reason to expect him to move.

Or suppose I think to myself that the person making the mess should say so. Turning my attention to the proposition, I certainly believe *that I am making a mess* is true for the person who ought to be saying it (or the person in the mirror, or the person at the end of the trail of sugar) at that time. The context of evaluation is just the context of belief. But there is no reason to suppose I would stop my cart.

One supposes that in these cases the problem is that the context of belief is not believed to be the context of evaluation. But formulating the required belief will simply bring up the problem of the essential indexical again. Clearly and correctly we want the tardy professor, when he finally sees he must be off to the meeting, to be ready to say "I believe that the time at which it is true *that the meeting starts now* is now." On the present proposal, we analyze the belief he thereby ascribes to himself as belief in the proposition *that the time at which it is true that the meeting starts now is now.* But he certainly can believe at noon that this whole proposition is true at noon, without being ready to say "It is starting now" and leave. We do not yet have a solution to the problem of the essential indexical.

LIMITED ACCESSIBILITY

One may take all that has been said so far as an argument for the existence of a special class of propositions, propositions of limited accessibility. For what have we really shown? All attempts to find a formula of the form "A is making a mess," with which any of us at any time could express what I believed, have failed. But one might argue that we can hardly suppose that there was not anything that I believed; surely I believed just that proposition which I expressed, on that occasion, with the words "I am making a mess." That we cannot find a sentence that always expresses this proposition when said by anyone does not show that it does not exist. Rather it should lead us to the conclusion that there is a class of propositions that can only be expressed in special circumstances. In particular, only I could express the proposition I expressed when I said "I am making a mess." Others can see, perhaps by analogy with their own case, that there is a proposition that I express, but it is in a sense inaccessible to them.

Similarly, at noon on the day of the meeting, we could all express the proposition the tardy professor expressed with the words "The meeting starts now." But once that time has passed, the proposition becomes inaccessible. We can still identify it as the proposition that was expressed by those words at that time. But we cannot express it with those words any longer, for with each passing moment they express a different proposition. And we can find no other words to express it.

The advocate of such a stock of propositions of limited accessibility may not need to bring in special propositions accessible only at certain places. For it is plausible to suppose that other indexicals can be eliminated in favor of "I" and "now." Perhaps "That is Gilmore Lake" just comes to "What I see now in front of me is Gilmore Lake." But elimination of either "I" or "now" in favor of the other seems impossible.

Such a theory of propositions of limited accessibility seems acceptable, even attractive, to some philosophers. Its acceptability or attractiveness will depend on other parts of one's metaphysics; if one finds plausible reasons elsewhere for believing in a universe that has, in addition to our common world, myriads of private perspectives, the idea of propositions of limited accessibility will fit right in. I have no knockdown argument against such propositions, or the metaphysical schemes that find room for them. But I believe only in a common actual world. And I do not think the phenomenon of essential indexicality forces me to abandon this view.

THE OBVIOUS SOLUTION?

Let us return to the device of the true/false exam. Suppose the lost author had been given such an exam before and after he figured out where he was. Would we expect any differences in his answers? Not so long as the statements contained no indexicals. "Mt. Tallac is higher than either of the Maggie Peaks" would have been marked the same way before and after, the same way he would have marked it at home in Berkeley. His mark on that sentence would tell us nothing about where he thought he was. But if the exam were to contain such sentences as "That is Gilmore Lake in front of me," we would expect a dramatic change, from "False" or "Unsure" to "True."

Imagine such an exam given to various lost campers in different parts of the Wilderness. We could classify the campers by their answers, and such a classification would be valuable for prediction and explanation. Of all the campers who marked "This is Gilmore Lake" with "True," we would say they believed that they were at Gilmore Lake. And we should expect them to act accordingly; if they possessed the standard guidebook and wished to leave the Wilderness, we might expect what is, given one way of looking at it, the same behavior: taking the path up the mountain above the shallow end of the lake before them.

Now consider all the good-hearted people who have ever been in a supermarket, noticed sugar on the floor, and been ready to say "I am making a mess." They all have something important in common, something that leads us to expect their next action to be that of looking into their grocery carts in search of the torn sack. Or consider all the responsible professors who have ever uttered "The department meeting is starting now." They too have something important in common; they are in a state that will lead those just down the hall to go to the meeting, those across campus to curse and feel guilty, those on leave to smile.

What the members within these various groups have in common is not what they believe. There is no *de dicto* proposition that all the campers or shoppers or professors believe. And there is no person whom all the shoppers believe to be making a mess, no lake all the campers believe to be Gilmore Lake, and no time at which all the professors believe their meetings to be starting.

We are clearly classifying the shoppers, campers and professors into groups corresponding to what we have been calling "relativized propositions"—abstract objects corresponding to sentences containing indexicals. But what members of each group have in common, which makes the groups significant, is not belief that a certain relativized proposition is true. Such belief, as we saw, is belief that such a proposition is true at some context of evaluation. Now all of the shoppers believe that *that I am making a mess* is true at some context of evaluation or other, but so does everyone else who has ever given it a moment's thought. And similar remarks apply to the campers and the professors.

If believing the same relativized proposition is not what the members of each of the groups have in common with one another, why is it being used as a principle of classification? I propose we look at things in this way. The shoppers, for example, are all in a certain belief state, a state that, given normal desires and other belief states they can be expected to be in, will lead each of them to examine his cart. But although they are all in the same belief state (not the same *total* belief state, of course), they do not all have the same belief (believe the same thing, have the relation of belief to the same object).

We use sentences with indexicals or relativized propositions to individuate belief states, for the purposes of classifying believers in ways useful for explanation and prediction. That is, belief states individuated in this way enter into our commonsense theory about human behavior and more sophisticated theories emerging from it. We expect all good-hearted people in the state that leads them to say "I am making a mess" to examine their grocery carts, no matter what belief they have in virtue of being in that state. That we individuate belief states in this way doubtless has something to do with the fact that one criterion for being in the states we postulate—at least for articulate, sincere adults—is being disposed to utter the indexical sentence in question. A good philosophy of mind should explain this in detail; my aim is merely to get clear about what it is that needs explaining.

The proposal, then, is that there is not an identity, or even an isomorphic correspondence, but only a systematic relationship between the belief states one is in and what one thereby believes. The opposite assumption, that belief states should be classified by propositions believed, seems to be built right into traditional philosophies of belief. Given this assumption, whenever we have believers in the same belief state, we must expect to find a proposition they all believe, and differences in belief state lead us to expect a difference in proposition believed. The bulk of this paper consisted in following such leads to nowhere (or to propositions of limited accessibility).

Consider a believer whose belief states are characterized by a structure of sentences with indexicals or relativized propositions (those marked "true" in a very comprehensive exam, if we are dealing with an articulate, sincere adult). This structure, together with the context of belief—the time and identity of the speaker—will yield a structure of *de re* propositions. The sequence of objects will consist of the values that the indexicals take in the context. The open propositions will be those yielded by the relativized proposition when shorn of its indexical elements. These are what the person believes, in virtue of being in the states he is in, when and where he is in them.

This latter structure is important, and classifications of believers by *what* they believe are appropriate for many purposes. For example, usually, when a believer moves from context to context, his belief states adjust to preserve beliefs held. As time passes, I go from the state corresponding to "The meeting will begin" to the one corresponding to "The meeting is beginning" and finally to "The meeting has begun." All along I believe of noon that it is when the meeting begins. But I believe it in different ways. And to these different ways of believing the same thing, different actions are appropriate: preparation, movement, apology. Of course, if the change of context is not noted, the adjustment of belief states will not occur, and a wholesale change from believing truly to believing falsely may occur. This is what happened to Rip Van Winkle. He awakes in the same belief states he fell asleep in twenty years earlier, unadjusted to the dramatic change in context, and so with a whole new set of beliefs, such as that he is a young man, mostly false.

We have here a metaphysically benign form of limited accessibility. Anyone at any time can have access to any proposition. But not in any way. Anyone can believe of John Perry that he is making a mess. And anyone can be in the belief state classified by the sentence "I am making a mess." But only I can have that belief by being in that state.

There is room in this scheme for *de dicto* propositions, for the characterization of one's belief states may include sentences without any indexical element. If there are any, they could appear on the exam. For this part of the structure, the hypothesis of perfect correspondence would be correct.

A more radical proposal would do away with objects of belief entirely. We would think of belief as a system of relations of various degrees between persons and other objects. Rather than saying I believed in the *de re* proposition consisting of me and the open proposition, *x is making a mess,* we would say that I stand in the relation, believing to be making a mess, to myself. There are many ways to stand in this relation to myself, that is, a variety of belief states I might be in. And these would be classified by sentences with indexicals. On this view, *de dicto* belief, already demoted from its central place in the philosophy of belief, might be seen as merely an illusion, engendered by the implicit nature of much indexicality.

To say that belief states must be distinguished from objects of belief, cannot be individuated in terms of them, and are what is crucial for the explanation of action, is not to give a full-fledged account of belief, or even a sketchy one. Similarly, to say that we must distinguish the object seen from the state of the seeing subject, and that the latter is crucial for the explanation of action guided by vision, is not to offer a full-fledged account of vision. But just as the arguments from illusion and perceptual relativity teach us that no philosophy of perception can be plausible that is not cognizant of this last distinction, the problem of the essential indexical should teach us that no philosophy of belief can be plausible that does not take account of the first.

Performative Utterances

⌇

J. L. AUSTIN

J. L. Austin (1911–1960) was an influential British philosopher who taught at Oxford University and played a crucial role in the development of linguistic philosophy. His books include *Sense and Sensibilia* and *How to Do Things with Words.*

I

You are more than entitled not to know what the word "performative" means. It is a new word and an ugly word, and perhaps it does not mean anything very much. But at any rate there is one thing in its favour, it is not a profound word. I remember once when I had been talking on this subject that somebody afterwards said: "You know, I haven't the least idea what he means, unless it could be that he simply means what he says." Well, that is what I should like to mean.

Let us consider first how this affair arises. We have not got to go very far back in the history of philosophy to find philosophers assuming more or less as a matter of course that the sole business, the sole interesting business, of any utterance—that is, of anything we say—is to be true or at least false. Of course they had always known that there are other kinds of things which we say—things like imperatives, the expressions of wishes, and exclamations—some of which had even been classified by grammarians, though it wasn't perhaps too easy to tell always which was

Reprinted from *Philosophical Papers* (Oxford: Oxford University Press, 1961).

which. But still philosophers have assumed that the only things that they are interested in are utterances which report facts or which describe situations truly or falsely. . . .

I want to discuss a kind of utterance which looks like a statement and grammatically, I suppose, would be classed as a statement, which is not nonsensical, and yet is not true or false. These are not going to be utterances which contain curious verbs like "could" or "might," or curious words like "good," which many philosophers regard nowadays simply as danger signals. They will be perfectly straightforward utterances, with ordinary verbs in the first person singular present indicative active, and yet we shall see at once that they couldn't possibly be true or false. Furthermore, if a person makes an utterance of this sort we should say that he is *doing* something rather than merely *saying* something. This may sound a little odd, but the examples I shall give will in fact not be odd at all, and may even seem decidedly dull. Here are three or four. Suppose, for example, that in the course of a marriage ceremony I say, as people will, "I do"—(sc. take this woman to be my lawful wedded wife). Or again, suppose that I tread on your toe and say "I apologize." Or again, suppose that I have the bottle of champagne in my hand and say "I name this ship the *Queen Elizabeth*." Or suppose I say "I bet you sixpence it will rain tomorrow." In all these cases it would be absurd to regard the thing that I say as a report of the performance of the action which is undoubtedly done—the action of betting, or christening, or apologizing. We should say rather that, in saying what I do, I actually perform that action. When I say "I name this ship the *Queen Elizabeth*" I do not describe the christening ceremony, I actually perform the christening; and when I say "I do" (sc. take this woman to be my lawful wedded wife), I am not reporting on a marriage, I am indulging in it.

Now these kinds of utterance are the ones that we call *performative* utterances. This is rather an ugly word, and a new word, but there seems to be no word already in existence to do the job. . . .

Now at this point one might protest, perhaps even with some alarm, that I seem to be suggesting that marrying is simply saying a few words, that just saying a few words *is* marrying. Well, that certainly is not the case. The words have to be said in the appropriate circumstances, and this is a matter that will come up again later. But the one thing we must not suppose is that what is needed in addition to the saying of the words in such cases is the performance of some internal spiritual act, of which the words then are to be the report. It's very easy to slip into this view at least in difficult, portentous cases, though perhaps not so easy in simple cases like apologizing. In the case of promising—for example, "I promise to be there tomorrow"—it's very easy to think that the utterance is simply the outward and visible (that is, verbal) sign of the performance of some inward spiritual act of promising, and this view has certainly been expressed in many classic places. There is the case of Euripides' Hippolytus, who said "My tongue swore to, but my heart did not"—perhaps it should be "mind" or "spirit" rather than "heart," but at any rate some kind of backstage artiste. Now it is clear from this sort of example that, if we slip into thinking that such utterances are reports, true or false, of the performance of inward and spiritual acts, we open a loophole to perjurers and welshers and bigamists and so on, so that there are disadvantages in being excessively solemn in this way. It is better, perhaps, to stick to the old saying that our word is our bond.

However, although these utterances do not themselves report facts and are not themselves true or false, saying these things does very often *imply* that certain things are true and not false, in some sense at least of that rather woolly word "imply." For example, when I say "I do take this woman to be my lawful wedded wife," or some other formula in the marriage ceremony, I do imply that I'm not already married, with wife living, sane, undivorced, and the rest of it. But still it is very important to realize that to imply that something or other is true, is not at all the same as saying something which is true itself.

These performative utterances are not true or false, then. But they do suffer from certain disabilities of their own. They can fail to come off in special ways, and that is what I want to consider next. The various ways in which a performative utterance may be unsatisfactory we call, for the sake of a name, the infelicities; and an infelicity arises—that is to say, the utterance is unhappy—if certain rules, transparently simple rules, are broken. I will mention some of these rules and then give examples of some infringements.

First of all, it is obvious that the conventional procedure which by our utterance we are purporting to use must actually exist. In the examples given here this procedure will be a verbal one, a verbal procedure for marrying or giving or whatever it may be; but it should be borne in mind that there are many non-verbal procedures by which we can perform exactly the same acts as we perform by these verbal means. It's worth remembering too that a great many of the things we do are at least in part of this conventional kind. Philosophers at least are too apt to assume that an action is always in the last resort the making of a physical movement, whereas it's usually, at least in part, a matter of convention.

The first rule is, then, that the convention invoked must exist and be accepted. And the second rule, also a very obvious one, is that the circumstances in which we purport to invoke this procedure must be appropriate for its invocation. If this is not observed, then the act that we purport to perform would not come off—it will be, one might say, a misfire. This will also be the case if, for example, we do not carry through the procedure—whatever it may be—correctly and completely, without a flaw and without a hitch. If any of these rules are not observed, we say that the act which we purported to perform is void, without effect. If, for example, the purported act was an act of marrying, then we should say that we 'went through a form' of marriage, but we did not actually succeed in marrying.

Here are some examples of this kind of misfire. Suppose that, living in a country like our own, we wish to divorce our wife. We may try standing her in front of us squarely in the room and saying, in a voice loud enough for all to hear, "I divorce you." Now this procedure is not accepted. We shall not thereby have succeeded in divorcing our wife, at least in this country and others like it. This is a case where the convention, we should say, does not exist or is not accepted. Again, suppose that, picking sides at a children's party, I say "I pick George." But George turns red in the face and says "Not playing." In that case I plainly, for some reason or another, have not picked George—whether because there is no convention that you can pick people who aren't playing, or because George in the circumstances is an inappropriate object for the procedure of picking. Or consider the case in which I say "I appoint you Consul," and it turns out that you have been appointed already—or perhaps it may even transpire that you are a horse; here again we have the infelicity of inappropriate circumstances, inappropriate objects, or what not. Examples of flaws and hitches are perhaps scarcely necessary—one party in the marriage ceremony says "I will," the other says "I won't"; I say "I bet sixpence," but nobody says "Done," nobody takes up the offer. In all these and other such cases, the act which we purport to perform, or set out to perform, is not achieved.

But there is another and a rather different way in which this kind of utterance may go wrong. A good many of these verbal procedures are designed for use by people who hold certain beliefs or have certain feelings or intentions. And if you use one of these formulae when you do not have the requisite thoughts or feelings or intentions then there is an abuse of the procedure, there is insincerity. Take, for example, the expression, "I congratulate you." This is designed for use by people who are glad that the person addressed has achieved a certain feat, believe that he was personally responsible for the success and so on. If I say "I congratulate you" when I'm not pleased or when I don't believe that the credit was yours, then there is insincerity. Likewise if I say I promise to do something, without having the least intention of doing it or without believing it feasible. In these cases there is something wrong certainly but it is not like a misfire. We should not say that I didn't in fact promise, but rather that I did promise but promised insincerely; I did congratulate you but the congratulations were hollow. And there may be an infelicity of a somewhat similar kind when the performative utterance commits the speaker to future conduct of a certain description and then in the future he does not in fact behave in the expected way. This is very obvious, of course, if I promise to do something and then break my promise, but there are many kinds of commitment of a rather less tangible form than that in the case of promising. For instance, I may say "I welcome you," bidding you welcome to my home or wherever it may be, but then I proceed to treat you as though you were exceedingly unwelcome. In this case the procedure of saying 'I welcome you' has been abused in a way rather different from that of simple insincerity.

Now we might ask whether this list of infelicities is complete, whether the kinds of infelicity are mutually exclusive and so forth. Well, it is not complete, and they are not mutually exclusive; they never are. Suppose that you are just about to name the ship, you have been appointed to name it, and you are just about to bang the bottle against the stem; but at that very moment some low type comes up, snatches the bottle one of your hand, breaks it on the stem, shouts out "I name this ship the *Generalissimo Stalin,*" and then for good measure kicks away the chocks. Well, we agree of course on several things. We agree that the ship certainly isn't now named the *Generalissimo Stalin,* and we agree that it's an infernal shame and so on and so forth. But we may not agree as to how we should classify the particular infelicity in this case. We might say that here is a case of a perfectly legitimate and agreed procedure which, however, has been invoked in the wrong circumstances, namely by the wrong person, this low type instead of the person appointed to do it. But on the other hand we might look at it differently and say that this is a case where the procedure has not as a whole been gone through correctly, because part of the procedure for naming a ship is that you should first of all get yourself appointed as the person to do the naming and that's what this fellow did not do. Thus the way we should classify infelicities in different cases will be perhaps rather a difficult matter, and may even in the last resort be a bit arbitrary. . . .

As for whether this list is complete, it certainly is not. One further way in which things may go wrong is, for example, through what in general may be called misunderstanding. You may not hear what I say, or you may understand me to refer to something different from what I intended to refer to, and so on. And apart from further additions which we might make to the list, there is the general over-riding consideration that, as we are performing an act when we issue these performative utterances, we may of course be doing so under duress or in some other circumstances which

make us not entirely responsible for doing what we are doing. That would certainly be an unhappiness of a kind—any kind of nonresponsibility might be called an unhappiness; but of course it is a quite different kind of thing from what we have been talking about. And I might mention that, quite differently again, we could be issuing any of these utterances, as we can issue an utterance of any kind whatsoever, in the course, for example, of acting a play or making a joke or writing a poem—in which case of course it would not be seriously meant and we shall not be able to say that we seriously performed the act concerned. If the poet says "Go and catch a falling star" or whatever it may be, he doesn't seriously issue an order Considerations of this kind apply to any utterance at all, not merely to performatives. . . .

So far we have been going along as though there was a quite clear difference between our performative utterances and what we have contrasted them with, statements or reports or descriptions. But now we begin to find that this distinction is not as clear as it might be. It's now that we begin to sink in a little. In the first place, of course, we may feel doubts as to how widely our performatives extend. If we think up some odd kinds of expression we use in odd cases, we might very well wonder whether or not they satisfy our rather vague criteria for being performative utterances. Suppose, for example, somebody says "Hurrah." Well, not true or false; he is performing the act of cheering. Does that make it a performative utterance in our sense or not? Or suppose he says "Damn"; he is performing the act of swearing, and it is not true or false. Does that make it performative? We feel that in a way it does and yet it's rather different. Again, consider cases of "suiting the action to the words"; these too may make us wonder whether perhaps the utterance should be classed as performative. Or sometimes, if somebody says "I am sorry," we wonder whether this is just the same as "I apologize"—in which case of course we have said it's a performative utterance—or whether perhaps it's to be taken as a description, true or false, of the state of his feelings. If he had said "I feel perfectly awful about it," then we should think it must be meant to be a description of the state of his feelings. If he had said "I apologize," we should feel this was clearly a performative utterance, going through the ritual of apologizing. But if he says "I am sorry" there is an unfortunate hovering between the two. This phenomenon is quite common. We often find cases in which there is an obvious pure performative utterance and obvious other utterances connected with it which are not performative but descriptive, but on the other hand a good many in between where we're not quite sure which they are. On some occasions of course they are obviously used the one way, on some occasions the other way, but on some occasions they seem positively to revel in ambiguity.

Again, consider the case of the umpire when he says "Out" or "Over," or the jury's utterance when they say that they find the prisoner guilty. Of course, we say, these are cases of giving verdicts, performing the act of appraising and so forth, but still in a way they have some connexion with the facts. They seem to have something like the duty to be true or false, and seem not to be so very remote from statements. If the umpire says "Over," this surely has at least something to do with six balls in fact having been delivered rather than seven, and so on. In fact in general we may remind ourselves that "I state that . . ." does not look so very different from "I warn you that . . ." or "I promise to. . . ." It makes clear surely that the act that we are performing is an act of stating, and so functions just like "I warn" or "I order." So isn't "I state that . . ." a performative utterance? But then one may feel that utterances beginning "I state that . . ." do have to be true or false, that they *are* statements.

Considerations of this sort, then, may well make us feel pretty unhappy. If we look back for a moment at our contrast between statements and performative utterances, we realize that we were taking statements very much on trust from, as we said, the traditional treatment. Statements, we had it, were to be true or false; performative utterances on the other hand were to be felicitous or infelicitous. They were the doing of something, whereas for all we said making statements was not doing something. Now this contrast surely, if we look back at it, is unsatisfactory. Of course statements are liable to be assessed in this matter of their correspondence or failure to correspond with the facts, that is, being true or false. But they are also liable to infelicity every bit as much as

are performative utterances. In fact some troubles that have arisen in the study of statements recently can be shown to be simply troubles of infelicity. For example, it has been pointed out that there is something very odd about saying something like this: "The cat is on the mat but I don't believe it is." Now this is an outrageous thing to say, but it is not self-contradictory. There is no reason why the cat shouldn't be on the mat without my believing that it is. So how are we to classify what's wrong with this peculiar statement? If we remember now the doctrine of infelicity we shall see that the person who makes this remark about the cat is in much the same position as somebody who says something like this: "I promise that I shall be there, but I haven't the least intention of being there." Once again you can of course perfectly well promise to be there without having the least intention of being there, but there is something outrageous about saying it, about actually avowing the insincerity of the promise you give. In the same way there is insincerity in the case of the person who says "The cat is on the mat but I don't believe it is," and he is actually avowing that insincerity—which makes a peculiar kind of nonsense.

A second case that has come to light is the one about John's children—the case where somebody is supposed to say "All John's children are bald but John hasn't got any children." Or perhaps somebody says "All John's children are bald," when as a matter of fact—he doesn't say so—John has no children. Now those who study statements have worried about this; ought they to say that the statement "All John's children are bald" is meaningless in this case? Well, if it is, it is not a bit like a great many other more standard kinds of meaninglessness; and we see, if we look back at our list of infelicities, that what is going wrong here is much the same as what goes wrong in, say, the case of a contract for the sale of a piece of land when the piece of land referred to does not exist. Now what we say in the case of this sale of land, which of course would be effected by a performative utterance, is that the sale is void—void for lack of reference or ambiguity of reference; and so we can see that the statement about all John's children is likewise void for lack of reference. And if the man actually says that John has no children in the same breath as saying they're all bald, he is making the same kind of outrageous utterance as the man who says "The cat is on the mat and I don't believe it is," or the man who says "I promise to but I don't intend to."

In this way, then, ills that have been found to afflict statements can be precisely paralleled with ills that are characteristic of performative utterances. And after all when we state something or describe something or report something, we do perform an act which is every bit as much an act as an act of ordering or warning. There seems no good reason why stating should be given a specially unique position. Of course philosophers have been wont to talk as though you or I or anybody could just go round stating anything about anything and that would be perfectly in order, only there's just a little question: is it true or false? But besides the little question, is it true or false, there is surely the question: *is* it in order? Can you go round just making statements about anything? Suppose for example you say to me "I'm feeling pretty mouldy this morning." Well, I say to you "You're not"; and you say "What the devil do you mean, I'm not?" I say "Oh nothing—I'm just stating you're not, is it true or false?" And you say "Wait a bit about whether it's true or false, the question is what did you mean by making statements about somebody else's feelings? I told you I'm feeling pretty mouldy. You're just not in a position to say, to state that I'm not." This brings out that you can't just make statements about other people's feelings (though you can make guesses if you like); and there are very many things which, having no knowledge of, not being in a position to pronounce about, you just can't state. What we need to do for the case of stating, and by the same token describing and reporting, is to take them a bit off their pedestal, to realize that they are speech-acts no less than all these other speech-acts that we have been mentioning and talking about as performative.

Then let us look for a moment at our original contrast between the performative and the statement from the other side. In handling performatives we have been putting it all the time as though the only thing that a performative utterance had to do was to be felicitous, to come off, not to be a misfire, not to be an abuse. Yes, but that's not the end of the matter.

At least in the case of many utterances which, on what we have said, we should have to class as performative—cases where we say "I warn you to . . . ," "I advise you to . . ." and so on—there will be other questions besides simply: was it in order, was it all right, as a piece of advice or a warning, did it come off? After that surely there will be the question: was it good or sound advice? Was it a justified warning? Or in the case, let us say, of a verdict or an estimate: was it a good estimate, or a sound verdict? And these are questions that can only be decided by considering how the content of the verdict or estimate is related in some way to fact, or to evidence available about the facts. This is to say that we do require to assess at least a great many performative utterances in a general dimension of correspondence with fact. It may still be said, of course, that this does not make them *very* like statements because still they are not true or false, and that's a little black and white speciality that distinguishes statements as a class apart. But actually—though it would take too long to go on about this—the more you think about truth and falsity the more you find that very few statements that we ever utter are just true or just false. Usually there is the question are they fair or are they not fair, are they adequate or not adequate, are they exaggerated or not exaggerated? Are they too rough, or are they perfectly precise, accurate, and so on? "True" and "false" are just general labels for a whole dimension of different appraisals which have something or other to do with the relation between what we say and the facts. If, then, we loosen up our ideas of truth and falsity we shall see that statements, when assessed in relation to the facts, are not so very different after all from pieces of advice, warnings, verdicts, and so on.

We see then that stating something is performing an act just as much as is giving an order or giving a warning; and we see, on the other hand, that, when we give an order or a warning or a piece of advice, there is a question about how this is related to fact which is not perhaps so very different from the kind of question that arises when we discuss how a statement is related to fact. Well, this seems to mean that in its original form our distinction between the performative and the statement is considerably weakened, and indeed breaks down.

Logic and Conversation

~

PAUL GRICE

Paul Grice (1913–1988) was a noted English philosopher of language who taught at Oxford University and then at the University of California at Berkeley.

It is a commonplace of philosophical logic that there are, or appear to be, divergences in meaning between, on the one hand, at least some of what I shall call the formal devices—$\sim$, $\wedge$, $\vee$, $\supset$, $(\forall x)$, $(\exists x)$, (ιx) (when these are given a standard two-valued interpretation)—and, on the other, what are taken to be their analogues or counterparts in natural language—such expressions as *not, and, or, if, all, some* (or *at least one*), *the*. Some logicians may at some time have wanted to claim that there are in fact no such divergences; but such claims, if made at all, have been somewhat rashly made, and those suspected of making them have been subjected to some pretty rough handling.

Those who concede that such divergences exist adhere, in the main, to one or the other of two rival groups, which I shall call the formalist and the informalist groups. An outline of a not uncharacteristic formalist position may be given as follows: Insofar as logicians are concerned with the formulation of very general patterns of valid inference, the formal devices possess a decisive advantage over their natural counterparts. For it will be possible to construct in terms of the formal devices a system of very general formulas, a considerable number of which can be regarded as, or are closely related to, patterns of inferences the expression of which involves some or all of the devices: Such a system may consist of a certain set of simple formulas that must be acceptable if the devices have the meaning that has been assigned to them, and an indefinite number of further formulas, many of which are less obviously acceptable and each of which can be shown to be acceptable if the members of the original set are acceptable. We have, thus, a way of handling dubiously acceptable patterns of inference, and if, as is sometimes possible, we can apply a decision procedure, we have an even better way. Furthermore, from a philosophical point of view, the possession by the natural counterparts of those elements in their meaning, which they do not share with the corresponding formal devices, is to be regarded as an imperfection of natural languages; the elements in question are undesirable excrescences. For the presence of these elements has the result both that the concepts within which they appear cannot be precisely or clearly defined, and that at least some statements involving them cannot, in some circumstances, be assigned a definite truth value; and the indefiniteness of these concepts not only is objectionable in itself but also leaves open the way to metaphysics—we cannot be certain that none of these natural language expressions is metaphysically "loaded." For these reasons, the expressions, as used in natural speech, cannot be regarded as finally acceptable, and may turn out to be, finally, not fully intelligible. The proper course is to conceive and begin to construct an ideal language, incorporating the formal devices, the sentences of which will be clear, determinate in truth value, and certifiably free from metaphysical implications; the foundations of

Reprinted from *Studies in the Way of Words* by Paul Grice (New York: Academic Press, 1975).

science will now be philosophically secure, since the statements of the scientist will be expressible (though not necessarily actually expressed) within this ideal language. (I do not wish to suggest that all formalists would accept the whole of this outline, but I think that all would accept at least some part of it.)

To this, an informalist might reply in the following vein. The philosophical demand for an ideal language rests on certain assumptions that should not be conceded; these are, that the primary yardstick by which to judge the adequacy of a language is its ability to serve the needs of science, that an expression cannot be guaranteed as fully intelligible unless an explication or analysis of its meaning has been provided, and that every explication or analysis must take the form of a precise definition that is the expression or assertion of a logical equivalence. Language serves many important purposes besides those of scientific inquiry; we can know perfectly well what an expression means (and so a fortiori that it is intelligible) without knowing its analysis, and the provision of an analysis may (and usually does) consist in the specification, as generalized as possible, of the conditions that count for or against the applicability of the expression being analyzed. Moreover, while it is no doubt true that the formal devices are especially amenable to systematic treatment by the logician, it remains the case that there are very many inferences and arguments, expressed in natural language and not in terms of these devices, which are nevertheless recognizably valid. So there must be a place for an unsimplified, and so more or less unsystematic, logic of the natural counterparts of these devices; this logic may be aided and guided by the simplified logic of the formal devices but cannot be supplanted by it. Indeed, not only do the two logics differ, but sometimes they come into conflict; rules that hold for a formal device may not hold for its natural counterpart.

On the general question of the place in philosophy of the reformation of natural language, I shall, in this essay, have nothing to say. I shall confine myself to the dispute in its relation to the alleged divergences. I have, moreover, no intention of entering the fray on behalf of either contestant. I wish, rather, to maintain that the common assumption of the contestants that the divergences do in fact exist is (broadly speaking) a common mistake, and that the mistake arises from inadequate attention to the nature and importance of the conditions governing conversation. I shall, therefore, inquire into the general conditions that, in one way or another, apply to conversation as such, irrespective of its subject matter. I begin with a characterization of the notion of "implicature."

IMPLICATURE

Suppose that A and B are talking about a mutual friend, C, who is now working in a bank. A asks B how C is getting on in his job, and B replies, *Oh quite well, I think; he likes his colleagues, and he hasn't been to prison yet.* At this point, A might well inquire what B was implying, what he was suggesting, or even what he meant by saying that C had not yet been to prison. The answer might be any one of such things as that C is the sort of person likely to yield to the temptation provided by his occupation, that C's colleagues are really very unpleasant and treacherous people, and so forth. It might, of course, be quite unnecessary for A to make such an inquiry of B, the answer to it being, in the context, clear in advance. It is clear that whatever B implied, suggested, meant in this example, is distinct from what B said, which was simply that C had not been to prison yet. I wish to introduce, as terms of art, the verb *implicate* and the related nouns *implicature* (cf. *implying*) and *implicatum* (cf. *what is implied*). The point of this maneuver is to avoid having, on each occasion, to choose between this or that member of the family of verbs for which *implicate* is to do general duty. I shall, for the time being at least, have to assume to a considerable extent an intuitive understanding of the meaning of *say* in such contexts, and an ability to recognize particular verbs as members of the family with which *implicate* is associated. I can, however, make one or two remarks that may help to clarify the more problematic of these assumptions, namely, that connected with the meaning of the word *say*.

In the sense in which I am using the word *say,* I intend what someone has said to be closely related to the conventional meaning of the words (the sentence) he has uttered. Suppose someone to have uttered the sentence *He is in the grip of a vice.* Given a knowledge of the English language, but no knowledge of the circumstances of the utterance, one would know something about what the speaker had said, on the assumption that he was speaking standard English, and speaking literally. One would know that he had said, about some particular male person or animal *x,* that at the time of the utterance (whatever that was), either (1) *x* was unable to rid himself of a certain kind of bad character trait or (2) some part of *x*'s person was caught in a certain kind of tool or instrument (approximate account, of course). But for a full identification of what the speaker had said, one would need to know (a) the identity of *x,* (b) the time of utterance, and (c) the meaning, on the particular occasion of utterance, of the phrase *in the grip of a vice* [a decision between (1) and (2)]. This brief indication of my use of *say* leaves it open whether a man who says (today) *Harold Wilson is a great man* and another who says (also today) *The British Prime Minister is a great man* would, if each knew that the two singular terms had the same reference, have said the same thing. But whatever decision is made about this question, the apparatus that I am about to provide will be capable of accounting for any implicatures that might depend on the presence of one rather than another of these singular terms in the sentence uttered. Such implicatures would merely be related to different maxims.

In some cases the conventional meaning of the words used will determine what is implicated, besides helping to determine what is said. If I say (smugly), *He is an Englishman; he is, therefore, brave,* I have certainly committed myself, by virtue of the meaning of my words, to its being the case that his being brave is a consequence of (follows from) his being an Englishman. But while I have said that he is an Englishman, and said that he is brave, I do not want to say that I have *said* (in the favored sense) that it follows from his being an Englishman that he is brave, though I have certainly indicated, and so implicated, that this is so. I do not want to say that my utterance of this sentence would be, *strictly speaking,* false should the consequence in question fail to hold. So *some* implicatures are conventional, unlike the one with which I introduced this discussion of implicature.

I wish to represent a certain subclass of nonconventional implicatures, which I shall call *conversa-*

tional implicatures, as being essentially connected with certain general features of discourse; so my next step is to try to say what these features are. The following may provide a first approximation to a general principle. Our talk exchanges do not normally consist of a succession of disconnected remarks, and would not be rational if they did. They are characteristically, to some degree at least, cooperative efforts; and each participant recognizes in them, to some extent, a common purpose or set of purposes, or at least a mutually accepted direction. This purpose or direction may be fixed from the start (e.g., by an initial proposal of a question for discussion), or it may evolve during the exchange; it may be fairly definite, or it may be so indefinite as to leave very considerable latitude to the participants (as in a casual conversation). But at each stage, *some* possible conversational moves would be excluded as conversationally unsuitable. We might then formulate a rough general principle which participants will be expected (ceteris paribus) to observe, namely: Make your conversational contribution such as is required, at the stage at which it occurs, by the accepted purpose or direction of the talk exchange in which you are engaged. One might label this the Cooperative Principle.

On the assumption that some such general principle as this is acceptable, one may perhaps distinguish four categories under one or another of which will fall certain more specific maxims and submaxims, the following of which will, in general, yield results in accordance with the Cooperative Principle. *Echoing Kant,* I call these categories Quantity, Quality, Relation, and Manner. The category of Quantity relates to the quantity of information to be provided, and under it fall the following maxims:

1. Make your contribution as informative as is required (for the current purposes of the exchange).
2. Do not make your contribution more informative than is required.

(The second maxim is disputable; it might be said that to be overinformative is not a transgression of the Cooperative Principle but merely a waste of time. However, it might be answered that such overinformativeness may be confusing in that it is liable to raise side issues; and there may also be an indirect effect, in that the hearers may be misled as a result of thinking that there is some particular *point* in the provision of the excess of information. However this may be, there is perhaps a different reason for doubt about the admission of this second maxim, namely, that its effect will be secured by a later maxim, which concerns relevance.)

Under the category of Quality falls a supermaxim—"Try to make your contribution one that is true"—and two more specific maxims:

1. Do not say what you believe to be false.
2. Do not say that for which you lack adequate evidence.

Under the category of Relation I place a single maxium, namely, "Be relevant." Though the maxim itself is terse, its formulation conceals a number of problems that exercise me a good deal: questions about what different kinds and focuses of relevance there may be, how these shift in the course of a talk exchange, how to allow for the fact that subjects of conversation are legitimately changed, and so on. I find the treatment of such questions exceedingly difficult, and I hope to revert to them in later work.

Finally, under the category of Manner, which I understand as relating not (like the previous categories) to what is said but, rather, to *how* what is said is to be said, I include the supermaxim—"Be perspicuous"—and various maxims such as:

1. Avoid obscurity of expression.
2. Avoid ambiguity.
3. Be brief (avoid unnecessary prolixity).
4. Be orderly.

And one might need others.

It is obvious that the observance of some of these maxims is a matter of less urgency than is the observance of others; a man who has expressed himself with undue prolixity would, in general, be open to milder comment than would a man who has said something he believes to be false. Indeed, it might be felt that the importance of at least the first maxim of Quality is such that it should not be included in a scheme of the kind I am constructing; other maxims come into operation only on the assumption that this maxim of Quality is satisfied. While this may be correct, so far as the generation of implicatures is concerned it seems to play a role not totally different from the other maxims, and it will be convenient, for the present at least, to treat it as a member of the list of maxims.

There are, of course, all sorts of other maxims (aesthetic, social, or moral in character), such as "Be polite," that are also normally observed by participants in talk exchanges, and these may also generate nonconventional implicatures. The conversational maxims, however, and the conversational implicatures connected with them, are specially connected (I hope) with the particular purposes that talk (and so, talk exchange) is adapted to serve and is primarily employed to serve. I have stated my maxims as if this purpose were a maximally effective exchange of information; this specification is, of course, too narrow, and the scheme needs to be generalized to allow for such general purposes as influencing or directing the actions of others.

As one of my avowed aims is to see talking as a special case or variety of purposive, indeed rational, behavior, it may be worth noting that the specific expectations or presumptions connected with at least some of the foregoing maxims have their analogues in the sphere of transactions that are not talk exchanges. I list briefly one such analogue for each conversational category.

1. *Quantity*. If you are assisting me to mend a car, I expect your contribution to be neither more nor less than is required. If, for example, at a particular stage I need four screws, I expect you to hand me four, rather than two or six.

2. *Quality*. I expect your contributions to be genuine and not spurious. If I need sugar as an ingredient in the cake you are assisting me to make, I do not expect you to hand me salt; if I need a spoon, I do not expect a trick spoon made of rubber.

3. *Relation*. I expect a partner's contribution to be appropriate to the immediate needs at each stage of the transaction. If I am mixing ingredients for a cake, I do not expect to be handed a good book, or even an oven cloth (though this might be an appropriate contribution at a later stage).

4. *Manner.* I expect a partner to make it clear what contribution he is making and to execute his performance with reasonable dispatch.

These analogies are relevant to what I regard as a fundamental question about the Cooperative Principle and its attendant maxims, namely, what the basis is for the assumption which we seem to make, and on which (I hope) it will appear that a great range of implicatures depends, that talkers will in general (ceteris paribus and in the absence of indications to the contrary) proceed in the manner that these principles prescribe. A dull but, no doubt at a certain level, adequate answer is that it is just a well-recognized empirical fact that people do behave in these ways; they learned to do so in childhood and have not lost the habit of doing so; and, indeed, it would involve a good deal of effort to make a radical departure from the habit. It is much easier, for example, to tell the truth than to invent lies.

I am, however, enough of a rationalist to want to find a basis that underlies these facts, undeniable though they may be; I would like to be able to think of the standard type of conversational practice not merely as something that all or most do *in fact* follow but as something that it is *reasonable* for us to follow, that we *should not* abandon. For a time, I was attracted by the idea that observance of the Cooperative Principle and the maxims, in a talk exchange, could be thought of as a quasi-contractual matter, with parallels outside the realm of discourse. If you pass by when I am struggling with my stranded car, I no doubt have some degree of expectation that you will offer help, but once you join me in tinkering under the hood, my expectations become stronger and take more specific forms (in the absence of indications that you are merely an incompetent meddler); and talk exchanges seemed to me to exhibit, characteristically, certain features that jointly distinguish cooperative transactions:

1. The participants have some common immediate aim, like getting a car mended; their ultimate aims may, of course, be independent and even in conflict—each may want to get the car mended in order to drive off, leaving the other stranded. In characteristic talk exchanges, there is a common aim even if, as in an over-the-wall chat, it is a second-order one, namely, that each party should, for the time being, identify himself with the transitory conversational interests of the other.

2. The contributions of the participants should be dovetailed, mutually dependent.

3. There is some sort of understanding (which may be explicit but which is often tacit) that, other things being equal, the transaction should continue in appropriate style unless both parties are agreeable that it should terminate. You do not just shove off or start doing something else.

But while some such quasi-contractual basis as this may apply to some cases, there are too many types of exchange, like quarreling and letter writing, that it fails to fit comfortably. In any case, one feels that the talker who is irrelevant or obscure has primarily let down not his audience but himself. So I would like to be able to show that observance of the Cooperative Principle and maxims is reasonable (rational) along the following lines: that anyone who cares about the goals that are central to conversation/communication (such as giving and receiving information, influencing and being influenced by others) must be expected to have an interest, given suitable circumstances, in participation in talk exchanges that will be profitable only on the assumption that they are conducted in general accordance with the Cooperative Principle and the maxims. Whether any such conclusion can be reached, I am uncertain; in any case, I am fairly sure that I cannot reach it until I am a good deal clearer about the nature of relevance and of the circumstances in which it is required.

It is now time to show the connection between the Cooperative Principle and maxims, on the one hand, and conversational implicature on the other.

A participant in a talk exchange may fail to fulfill a maxim in various ways, which include the following:

1. He may quietly and unostentatiously *violate* a maxim; if so, in some cases he will be liable to mislead.

2. He may *opt out* from the operation both of the maxim and of the Cooperative Principle; he may say, indicate, or allow it to become plain that he is unwilling to cooperate in the way the maxim requires. He

may say, for example, *I cannot say more; my lips are sealed.*

3. He may be faced by a *clash:* He may be unable, for example, to fulfill the first maxim of Quantity (Be as informative as is required) without violating the second maxim of Quality (Have adequate evidence for what you say).

4. He may *flout* a maxim; that is, he may blatantly fail to fulfill it. On the assumption that the speaker is able to fulfill the maxim and to do so without violating another maxim (because of a clash), is not opting out, and is not, in view of the blatancy of his performance, trying to mislead, the hearer is faced with a minor problem: How can his saying what he did say be reconciled with the supposition that he is observing the overall Cooperative Principle? This situation is one that characteristically gives rise to a conversational implicature; and when a conversational implicature is generated in this way, I shall say that a maxim is being *exploited.*

I am now in a position to characterize the notion of conversational implicature. A man who, by (in, when) saying (or making as if to say) that *p* has implicated that *q,* may be said to have conversationally implicated that *q,* provided that (1) he is to be presumed to be observing the conversational maxims, or at least the Cooperative Principle; (2) the supposition that he is aware that, or thinks that, *q* is required in order to make his saying or making as if to say *p* (or doing so in *those* terms) consistent with this presumption; and (3) the speaker thinks (and would expect the hearer to think that the speaker thinks) that it is within the competence of the hearer to work out, or grasp intuitively, that the supposition mentioned in (2) is required. Apply this to my initial example, to B's remark that C has not yet been to prison. In a suitable setting A might reason as follows: "(1) B has apparently violated the maxim 'Be relevant' and so may be regarded as having flouted one of the maxims conjoining perspicuity, yet I have no reason to suppose that he is opting out from the operation of the Cooperative Principle; (2) given the circumstances, I can regard his irrelevance as only apparent if, and only if, I suppose him to think that C is potentially dishonest; (3) B knows that I am capable of working out step (2). So B implicates that C is potentially dishonest."

The presence of a conversational implicature must be capable of being worked out; for even if it can in fact be intuitively grasped, unless the intuition is replaceable by an argument, the implicature (if present at all) will not count as a conversational implicature; it will be a conventional implicature. To work out that a particular conversational implicature is present, the hearer will reply on the following data: (1) the conventional meaning of the words used, together with the identity of any references that may be involved; (2) the Cooperative Principle and its maxims; (3) the context, linguistic or otherwise, of the utterance; (4) other items of background knowledge; and (5) the fact (or supposed fact) that all relevant items falling under the previous headings are available to both participants and both participants know or assume this to be the case. A general pattern for the working out of a conversational implicature might be given as follows: "He has said that *p;* there is no reason to suppose that he is not observing the maxims, or at least the Cooperative Principle; he could not be doing this unless he thought that *q;* he knows (and knows that I know that he knows) that I can see that the supposition that he thinks that *q* is required; he has done nothing to stop me thinking that *q;* he intends me to think, or is at least willing to allow me to think, that *q;* and so he has implicated that *q.*"

EXAMPLES OF CONVERSATIONAL IMPLICATURE

I shall now offer a number of examples, which I shall divide into three groups.

Group A: *Examples in which no maxim is violated, or at least in which it is not clear that any maxim is violated*

A is standing by an obviously immobilized car and is approached by B; the following exchange takes place:

(1) A: *I am out of petrol.*
    B: *There is a garage round the corner.*

(Gloss: B would be infringing the maxim "Be relevant" unless he thinks, or thinks it possible, that the garage is open, and has petrol to sell; so he implicates that the garage is, or at least may be open, etc.)

In this example, unlike the case of the remark *He hasn't been to prison yet,* the unstated connection between B's remark and A's remark is so obvious that, even if one interprets the supermaxim of Manner, "Be perspicuous," as applying not only to the expression of what is said but also to the connection of what is said with adjacent remarks, there seems to be no case for regarding that supermaxim as infringed in this example. The next example is perhaps a little less clear in this respect:

(2) A: *Smith doesn't seem to have a girlfriend these days.*
B: *He has been paying a lot of visits to New York lately.*

B implicates that Smith has, or may have, a girlfriend in New York. (A gloss is unnecessary in view of that given for the previous example.)

In both examples, the speaker implicates that which he must be assumed to believe in order to preserve the assumption that he is observing the maxim of Relation.

Group B: *Examples in which a maxim is violated, but its violation is to be explained by the supposition of a clash with another maxim*

A is planning with B an itinerary for a holiday in France. Both know that A wants to see his friend C, if to do so would not involve too great a prolongation of his journey:

(3) A: *Where does C live?*
B: *Somewhere in the South of France.*

(Gloss: There is no reason to suppose that B is opting out; his answer is, as he well knows, less informative than is required to meet A's needs. This infringement of the first maxim of Quantity can be explained only by the supposition that B is aware that to be more informative would be to say something that infringed the second maxim of Quality. "Don't say what you lack adequate evidence for," so B implicates that he does not know in which town C lives.)

Group C: *Examples that involve exploitation, that is, a procedure by which a maxim is flouted for the purpose of getting in a conversational implicature by means of something of the nature of a figure of speech*

In these examples, though some maxim is violated at the level of what is said, the hearer is entitled to assume that that maxim, or at least the overall Cooperative Principle, is observed at the level of what is implicated.

(1a) *A flouting of the first maxim of Quantity*

A is writing a testimonial about a pupil who is a candidate for a philosophy job, and his letter reads as follows: "Dear Sir, Mr. X's command of English is excellent, and his attendance at tutorials has been regular. Yours, etc." (Gloss: A cannot be opting out, since if he wished to be uncooperative, why write at all? He cannot be unable, through ignorance, to say more, since the man is his pupil; moreover, he knows that more information than this is wanted. He must, therefore, be wishing to impart information that he is reluctant to write down. This supposition is tenable only if he thinks Mr. X is no good at philosophy. This, then, is what he is implicating.)

Extreme examples of a flouting of the first maxim of Quantity are provided by utterances of patent tautologies like *Women are women* and *War is war.* I would wish to maintain that at the level of what is said, in my favored sense, such remarks are totally noninformative and so, at that level, cannot but infringe the first maxim of Quantity in any conversational context. They are, of course, informative at the level of what is implicated, and the hearer's identification of their informative content at this level is dependent on his ability to explain the speaker's selection of this particular patent tautology.

(1b) *An infringement of the second maxim of Quantity, "Do not give more information than is required," on the assumption that the existence of such a maxim should be admitted*

A wants to know whether *p,* and B volunteers not only the information that *p,* but information to the effect that it is certain that *p,* and that the evidence for its being the case that *p* is so-and-so and such-and-such.

B's volubility may be undesigned, and if it is so regarded by A it may raise in A's mind a doubt as to whether B is as certain as he says he is ("Methinks the lady doth protest too much"). But if it is thought of as designed, it would be an oblique way of conveying that it is to some degree controversial whether or not *p*. It is, however, arguable that such an implicature could be explained by reference to the maxim of Relation without invoking an alleged second maxim of Quantity.

(2a) *Examples in which the first maxim of Quality is flouted*

Irony. X, with whom A has been on close terms until now, has betrayed a secret of A's to a business rival. A and his audience both know this. A says *X is a fine friend.* (Gloss: It is perfectly obvious to A and his audience that what A has said or has made as if to say is something he does not believe, and the audience knows that A knows that this is obvious to the audience. So, unless A's utterance is entirely pointless, A must be trying to get across some other proposition than the one he purports to be putting forward. This must be some obviously related proposition; the most obviously related proposition is the contradictory of the one he purports to be putting forward.)

Metaphor. Examples like *You are the cream in my coffee* characteristically involve categorial falsity, so the contradictory of what the speaker has made as if to say will, strictly speaking, be a truism; so it cannot be *that* that such a speaker is trying to get across. The most likely supposition is that the speaker is attributing to his audience some feature or features in respect of which the audience resembles (more or less fancifully) the mentioned substance.

It is possible to combine metaphor and irony by imposing on the hearer two stages of interpretation. I say *You are the cream in my coffee,* intending the hearer to reach first the metaphor interpretant "You are my pride and joy" and then the irony interpretant "You are my bane."

Meiosis. Of a man known to have broken up all the furniture, one says *He was a little intoxicated.*

Hyperbole. Every nice girl loves a sailor.

(2b) Examples in which the second maxim of Quality, "Do not say that for which you lack adequate evidence," is flouted are perhaps not easy to find, but the following seems to be a specimen. I say of X's wife, *She is probably deceiving him this evening.* In a

suitable context, or with a suitable gesture or tone of voice, it may be clear that I have no adequate reason for supposing this to be the case. My partner, to preserve the assumption that the conversational game is still being played, assumes that I am getting at some related proposition for the acceptance of which I do have a reasonable basis. The related proposition might well be that she is given to deceiving her husband, or possibly that she is the sort of person who would not stop short of such conduct.

(3) *Examples in which an implicature is achieved by real, as distinct from apparent, violation of the maxim of Relation* are perhaps rare, but the following seems to be a good candidate. At a genteel tea party, A says *Mrs. X is an old bag.* There is a moment of appalled silence, and then B says *The weather has been quite delightful this summer, hasn't it?* B has blatantly refused to make what he says relevant to A's preceding remark. He thereby implicates that A's remark should not be discussed and, perhaps more specifically, that A has committed a social gaffe.

(4) *Examples in which various maxims falling under the supermaxim "Be perspicuous" are flouted*

Ambiguity. We must remember that we are concerned only with ambiguity that is deliberate, and that the speaker intends or expects to be recognized by his hearer. The problem the hearer has to solve is why a speaker should, when still playing the conversational game, go out of his way to choose an ambiguous utterance. There are two types of cases:

(a) Examples in which there is no difference, or no striking difference, between two interpretations of an utterance with respect to straightforwardness; neither interpretation is notably more sophisticated, less standard, more recondite or more far-fetched than the other. We might consider Blake's lines: "Never seek to tell thy love, Love that never told can be." To avoid the complications introduced by the presence of the imperative mood, I shall consider the related sentence, *I sought to tell my love, love that never told can be.* There may be a double ambiguity here. *My love* may refer to either a state of emotion or an object of emotion, and *love that never told can be* may mean either "Love that cannot be told" or "love that if told cannot continue to exist." Partly because of the sophistication of the poet and partly because of internal evidence (that the ambiguity is kept up), there seems to be no alternative to supposing that the ambiguities are deliberate and that the poet is conveying both what he would be saying if one interpretation were intended rather than the other, and vice versa; though no doubt the poet is not explicitly saying any one of these things but only conveying or suggesting them (cf. "Since she [nature] pricked thee out for women's pleasure, mine be thy love, and thy love's use their treasure").

(b) Examples in which one interpretation is notably less straightforward than another. Take the complex example of the British General who captured the province of Sind and sent back the message *Peccavi*. The ambiguity involved ("I have Sind"/"I have sinned") is phonemic, not morphemic; and the expression actually used is unambiguous, but since it is in a language foreign to speaker and hearer, translation is called for, and the ambiguity resides in the standard translation into native English.

Whether or not the straightforward interpretant ("I have sinned") is being conveyed, it seems that the nonstraightforward interpretant must be. There might be stylistic reasons for conveying by a sentence merely its nonstraightforward interpretant, but it would be pointless, and perhaps also stylistically objectionable, to go to the trouble of finding an expression that nonstraightforwardly conveys that *p*, thus imposing on an audience the effort involved in finding this interpretant, if this interpretant were otiose so far as communication was concerned. Whether the straightforward interpretant is also being conveyed seems to depend on whether such a supposition would conflict with other conversational requirements, for example, would it be relevant, would it be something the speaker could be supposed to accept, and so on. If such requirements are not satisfied, then the straightforward interpretant is not being conveyed. If they are, it is. If the author of *Peccavi* could naturally be supposed to think that he had committed some kind of transgression, for example, had disobeyed his orders in capturing Sind, and if reference to such a transgression would be relevant to the presumed interests of the audience, then he would have been conveying both interpretants: otherwise he would be conveying only the nonstraightforward one.

Obscurity. How do I exploit, for the purposes of communication, a deliberate and overt violation of the requirement that I should avoid obscurity? Obviously, if the Cooperative Principle is to operate, I must intend my partner to understand what I am saying despite the obscurity I import into my utterance. Suppose that A and B are having a conversation in the presence of a third party, for example, a child, then A might be deliberately obscure, though not too obscure, in the hope that B would understand and the third party not. Furthermore, if A expects B to see that A is being deliberately obscure, it seems reasonable to suppose that, in making his conversational contribution in this way, A is implicating that the contents of his communication should not be imparted to the third party.

Failure to be brief or succinct. Compare the remarks:

(a) *Miss X sang "Home Sweet Home."*
(b) *Miss X produced a series of sounds that corresponded closely with the score of "Home Sweet Home."*

Suppose that a reviewer has chosen to utter (b) rather than (a). (Gloss: Why has he selected that rigmarole in place of the concise and nearly synonymous *sang*? Presumably, to indicate some striking difference between Miss X's performance and those to which the word *singing* is usually applied. The most obvious supposition is that Miss X's performance suffered from some hideous defect. The reviewer knows that this supposition is what is likely to spring to mind, so that is what he is implicating.)

GENERALIZED CONVERSATIONAL IMPLICATURE

I have so far considered only cases of what I might call "particularized conversational implicature"—that is to say, cases in which an implicature is carried by saying that *p* on a particular occasion in virtue of special features of the context, cases in which there is no room for the the idea that an implicature of this sort is normally carried by saying that *p*. But there are cases of generalized conversational implicature. Sometimes one can say that the use of a certain form of words in an utterance would normally (in the absence of special circumstances) carry such-and-such an implicature or type of implicature. Noncontroversial examples are perhaps hard to find, since it is all too easy to treat a generalized conversational implicature as if it were a conventional implicature. I offer an example that I hope may be fairly noncontroversial.

Anyone who uses a sentence of the form *X is meeting a woman this evening* would normally implicate that the person to be met was someone other than X's wife, mother, sister, or perhaps even close platonic friend. Similarly, if I were to say *X went into a house yesterday and found a tortoise inside the front door,* my hearer would normally be surprised if some time later I revealed that the house was X's own. I could produce similar linguistic phenomena involving the expressions *a garden, a car, a college,* and so on. Sometimes, however, there would normally be no such implicature ("I have been sitting in a car all morning"), and sometimes a reverse implicature ("I broke a finger yesterday"). I am inclined to think that one would not lend a sympathetic ear to a philosopher who suggested that there are three senses of the form of expression *an X:* one in which it means roughly "something that satisfies the conditions defining the word *X,*" another in which it means approximately "an X (in the first sense) that is only remotely related in a certain way to some person indicated by the context," and yet another in which it means "an X (in the first sense) that is closely related in a certain way to some person indicated by the context." Would we not much prefer an account on the following lines (which, of course, may be incorrect in detail): When someone, by using the form of expression *an X,* implicates that the X does not belong to or is not otherwise closely connected with some identifiable person, the implicature is present because the speaker has failed to be specific in a way in which he might have been expected to be specific, with the consequence that it is likely to be assumed that he is not in a position to be specific. This is a familiar implicature situation and is classifiable as a failure, for one reason or another, to fulfill the first maxim of Quantity. The only difficult question is why it should, in certain cases, be presumed, independently of

information about particular contexts of utterance, that specification of the closeness or remoteness of the connection between a particular person or object and a further person who is mentioned or indicated by the utterance should be likely to be of interest. The answer must lie in the following region: Transactions between a person and other persons or things closely connected with him are liable to be very different as regards their concomitants and results from the same sort of transactions involving only remotely connected persons or things; the concomitants and results, for instance, of my finding a hole in my roof are likely to be very different from the concomitants and results of my finding a hole in someone else's roof. Information, like money, is often given without the giver's knowing to just what use the recipient will want to put it. If someone to whom a transaction is mentioned gives it further consideration, he is likely to find himself wanting the answers to further questions that the speaker may not be able to identify in advance; if the appropriate specification will be likely to enable the hearer to answer a considerable variety of such questions for himself, then there is a presumption that the speaker should include it in his remark; if not, then there is no such presumption.

Finally, we can now show that, conversational implicature being what it is, it must possess certain features:

1. Since, to assume the presence of a conversational implicature, we have to assume that at least the Cooperative Principle is being observed, and since it is possible to opt out of the observation of this principle, it follows that a generalized conversational implicature can be canceled in a particular case. It may be explicitly canceled, by the addition of a clause that states or implies that the speaker has opted out, or it may be contextually canceled, if the form of utterance that usually carries it is used in a context that makes it clear that the speaker is opting out.

2. Insofar as the calculation that a particular conversational implicature is present requires, besides contextual and background information, only a knowledge of what has been said (or of the conventional commitment of the utterance), and insofar as the manner of expression plays no role in the calculation, it will not be possible to find another way of

saying the same thing, which simply lacks the implicature in question, except where some special feature of the substituted version is itself relevant to the determination of an implicature (in virtue of one of the maxims of Manner). If we call this feature nondetachability, one may expect a generalized conversational implicature that is carried by a familiar, nonspecial locution to have a high degree of nondetachability.

3. To speak approximately, since the calculation of the presence of a conversational implicature presupposes an initial knowledge of the conventional force of the expression the utterance of which carries the implicature, a conversational implicatum will be a condition that is not included in the original specification of the expression's conventional force. Though it may not be impossible for what starts life, so to speak, as a conversational implicature to become conventionalized, to suppose that this is so in a given case would require special justification. So, initially at least, conversational implicata are not part of the meaning of the expressions to the employment of which they attach.

4. Since the truth of a conversational implicatum is not required by the truth of what is said (what is said may be true—what is implicated may be false), the implicature is not carried by what is said, only by the saying of what is said, or by "putting it that way."

5. Since, to calculate a conversational implicature is to calculate what has to be supposed in order to preserve the supposition that the Cooperative Principle is being observed, and since there may be various possible specific explanations, a list of which may be open, the conversational implicatum in such cases will be disjunction of such specific explanations; and if the list of these is open, the implicatum will have just the kind of indeterminacy that many actual implicata do in fact seem to possess.

PART 7

~

Ethics

Introduction

STUART RACHELS

Ethics is a broad subject. Sometimes people speak of ethics more narrowly to refer to what is mandated by professional codes of conduct. For example, someone may say that it was unethical for Stephen Jones to write a book about his client, executed Oklahoma City bomber Timothy McVeigh, since the norms of the legal profession require keeping clients' information confidential. But for philosophers, ethics concerns *every* question of right and wrong. Hence ethics is also wider than *morality,* as that term is sometimes used. When people say that Bill Clinton behaved immorally while he was president, they probably have in mind his sexual behavior, not his policies, even though his policies had enormous ethical implications. Sex needn't have special significance in ethics, however it is viewed by conventional morality.

There are three major subfields of ethics: metaethics, ethical theory, and applied ethics. Metaethics concerns the meaning of moral judgments and how "objective" or "subjective" ethical discourse is. Ethical theory is about formulating and assessing ethical principles— that is, rules for evaluating acts, agents, and outcomes. Applied ethics deals with practical issues like abortion, famine relief, and euthanasia.

The first set of readings is on metaethics. According to J. L. Mackie, there are no objective values. Ronald Dworkin disputes two of Mackie's arguments. And Renford Bambrough tries to show that there are objective values.

The second set of readings is on ethical theories. John Stuart Mill defends *utilitarianism.* Utilitarians think that happiness or pleasure is all that matters in assessing acts, agents, and outcomes. Robert Nozick disagrees. He says that values would be lost were we hooked into an "experience machine" that gave us pleasure. Utilitarianism is often contrasted with a "Kantian" approach to ethics. According to Immanuel Kant, the only thing good in itself is a good will. He thinks that our moral duties can all be derived from a single rule, the Categorical Imperative. Onora O'Neill provides a modern interpretation of Kant, focusing on Kant's idea that people should never be treated as mere means. W. D. Ross endorses a framework for ethics that can accommodate both utilitarian and Kantian ideals. Ross thinks that morality consists of a variety of prima facie, or overridable, rules. Note that none of these writers is a *cultural relativist;* each assumes that there are correct ethical principles that apply to every culture. James Rachels defends this assumption but finds some truth in cultural relativism. He also examines psychological egoism, the view that we always act in our self-interest, and ethical egoism, the view that we should always act in our self-interest. He finds neither position persuasive.

The third set of readings is on virtue and luck. Aristotle thinks that human happiness consists of being virtuous. According to his "doctrine of the golden mean," every virtue lies between two vices. Courage, for example, lies between cowardice and foolhardiness. Alasdair MacIntyre offers a contemporary version of virtue ethics. Peter Singer describes real-life examples of virtue in "Living Ethically." Jonathan Bennett explores the uncertain relationship between conscience and sympathy in "The Conscience of Huckleberry Finn".

Thomas Nagel poses the problem of moral luck. He observes that people can be lucky or unlucky in ways that affect our moral judgment of them. For example, we judge murderers more harshly than attempted murderers, even though it can be a matter of luck whether an attempt succeeds. This is paradoxical, since how good or bad one is would seem not to turn on matters of fortune. David Lewis explores whether, given moral luck, it may be just to introduce additional luck into our penal system.

The final set of readings is on starvation and animals. These are two separate topics. According to Singer, people who are financially well off have a strong obligation to assist those who live in "absolute poverty." John Arthur thinks that people have a right to their property and deserve what they earn and hence needn't turn over their money to the needy. O'Neill locates the main ills of poverty from a Kantian perspective.

Kant says we have no obligations to animals. Nozick disagrees, raising a number of provocative questions. Rachels also disagrees and hopes to change how we eat. He argues for vegetarianism, based on the cruelty of factory farming. According to Tibor Machan, animals have no moral rights—for example, they have no right to life—although we should be humane in our dealings with them.

The best way to read these essays is to struggle with the problems they raise. Make these problems your own. Those who do will find it rewarding. The problems of ethics are beautiful and deep; struggling with them is vital to developing one's own ethical perspective, and what perspective one adopts is crucial to one's way of life. It is, as Socrates said, no small matter.

The Subjectivity of Values

J. L. MACKIE

John L. Mackie (1917–1981) was born in Australia and taught at Oxford University for the last 14 years of his life. He wrote books on God, truth, Hume's moral theory, causation, and John Locke.

MORAL SCEPTICISM

There are no objective values. This is a bald statement of the thesis of this chapter, but before arguing for it I shall try to clarify and restrict it in ways that may meet some objections and prevent some misunderstanding.

The statement of this thesis is liable to provoke one of three very different reactions. Some will think it not merely false but pernicious; they will see it as a threat to morality and to everything else that is worthwhile, and they will find the presenting of such a thesis in what purports to be a book on ethics paradoxical or even outrageous. Others will regard it as a trivial truth, almost too obvious to be worth mentioning, and certainly too plain to be worth much argument. Others again will say that it is meaningless or empty, that no real issue is raised by the question whether values are or are not part of the fabric of the world. But, precisely because there can be these three different reactions, much more needs to be said.

The claim that values are not objective, are not part of the fabric of the world, is meant to include not only moral goodness, which might be most naturally equated with moral value, but also other things that could be more loosely called moral values or disvalues—rightness and wrongness, duty, obligation, an action's being rotten and contemptible, and so on. It also includes non-moral values, notably aesthetic ones, beauty and various kinds of artistic merit. I shall not discuss these explicitly, but clearly much the same considerations apply to aesthetic and to moral values, and there would be at least some initial implausibility in a view that gave the one a different status from the other.

Since it is with moral values that I am primarily concerned, the view I am adopting may be called moral scepticism. But this name is likely to be misunderstood: "moral scepticism" might also be used as a name for either of two first order views, or perhaps for an incoherent mixture of the two. A moral sceptic might be the sort of person who says "All this talk of morality is tripe," who rejects morality and will take no notice of it. Such a person may be literally rejecting all moral judgements; he is more likely to be making moral judgements of his own, expressing a positive moral condemnation of all that conventionally passes for morality; or he may be confusing these two logically incompatible views, and saying that he rejects all morality, while he is in fact rejecting only a particular morality that is current in the society in which he has grown up. But I am not at present concerned with the merits or faults of such a position. These are first order moral views, positive or negative: the person who adopts either of them is taking a certain practical, normative, stand. By contrast, what I am discussing is a second order view, a view about the status of moral values and the nature of moral valuing, about where and how they fit into the world. These first and second order views are not merely distinct but completely independent: one

Reprinted from *Ethics: Inventing Right and Wrong* (London: Penguin Books, 1977), by permission of the publisher.

could be a second order moral sceptic without being a first order one, or again the other way round. A man could hold strong moral views, and indeed ones whose content was thoroughly conventional, while believing that they were simply attitudes and policies with regard to conduct that he and other people held. Conversely, a man could reject all established morality while believing it to be an objective truth that it was evil or corrupt.

With another sort of misunderstanding moral scepticism would seem not so much pernicious as absurd. How could anyone deny that there is a difference between a kind action and a cruel one, or that a coward and a brave man behave differently in the face of danger? Of course, this is undeniable; but it is not to the point. The kinds of behaviour to which moral values and disvalues are ascribed are indeed part of the furniture of the world, and so are the natural, descriptive, differences between them; but not, perhaps, their differences in value. It is a hard fact that cruel actions differ from kind ones, and hence that we can learn, as in fact we all do, to distinguish them fairly well in practice, and to use the words 'cruel' and 'kind' with fairly clear descriptive meanings; but is it an equally hard fact that actions which are cruel in such a descriptive sense are to be condemned? The present issue is with regard to the objectivity specifically of value, not with regard to the objectivity of those natural, factual, differences on the basis of which differing values are assigned. . . .

STANDARDS OF EVALUATION

One way of stating the thesis that there are no objective values is to say that value statements cannot be either true or false. But this formulation, too, lends itself to misinterpretation. For there are certain kinds of value statements which undoubtedly can be true or false, even if, in the sense I intend, there are no objective values. Evaluations of many sorts are commonly made in relation to agreed and assumed standards. The classing of wool, the grading of apples, the awarding of prizes at sheepdog trials, flower shows, skating and diving championships, and even the marking of examination papers are carried out in relation to standards of quality or merit which are peculiar to each particular subject-matter or type of contest, which may be explicitly laid down but which, even if they are nowhere explicitly stated, are fairly well understood and agreed by those who are recognized as judges or experts in each particular field. Given any sufficiently determinate standards, it will be an objective issue, a matter of truth and falsehood, how well any particular specimen measures up to those standards. Comparative judgements in particular will be capable of truth and falsehood: it will be a factual question whether this sheepdog has performed better than that one.

The subjectivist about values, then, is not denying that there can be objective evaluations relative to standards, and these are as possible in the aesthetic and moral fields as in any of those just mentioned. More than this, there is an objective distinction which applies in many such fields, and yet would itself be regarded as a peculiarly moral one: the distinction between justice and injustice. In one important sense of the word it is a paradigm case of injustice if a court declares someone to be guilty of an offence of which it knows him to be innocent. More generally, a finding is unjust if it is at variance with what the relevant law and the facts together require, and particularly if it is known by the court to be so. More generally still, any award of marks, prizes, or the like is unjust if it is at variance with the agreed standards for the contest in question: if one diver's performance in fact measures up better to the accepted standards for diving than another's, it will be unjust if the latter is awarded higher marks or the prize. In this way the justice or injustice of decisions relative to standards can be a thoroughly objective matter, though there may still be a subjective element in the interpretation or application of standards. But the statement that a certain decision is thus just or unjust will not be objectively prescriptive: in so far as it can be simply true it leaves open the question whether there is any objective requirement to do what is just and to refrain from what is unjust, and equally leaves open the practical decision to act in either way.

Recognizing the objectivity of justice in relation to standards, and of evaluative judgements relative to standards, then, merely shifts the question of the objectivity of values back to the standards themselves. The subjectivist may try to make his point by insisting that there is no objective validity about the choice of standards. Yet he would clearly be wrong if he said that the choice of even the most basic standards in any field was completely arbitrary. The standards used in sheepdog trials clearly bear some relation to the work that sheepdogs are kept to do, the standards for grading apples bear some relation to what people generally want in or like about apples, and so on. On the other hand, standards are not as a rule strictly validated by such purposes. The appropriateness of standards is neither fully determinate nor totally indeterminate in relation to independently specifiable aims or desires. But however determinate it is, the objective appropriateness of standards in relation to aims or desires is no more of a threat to the denial of objective values than is the objectivity of evaluation relative to standards. In fact it is logically no different from the objectivity of goodness relative to desires. Something may be called good simply in so far as it satisfies or is such as to satisfy a certain desire; but the objectivity of such relations of satisfaction does not constitute in our sense an objective value. . . .

HYPOTHETICAL AND CATEGORICAL IMPERATIVES

We may make this issue clearer by referring to Kant's distinction between hypothetical and categorical imperatives, though what he called imperatives are more naturally expressed as "ought"-statements than in the imperative mood. "If you want *X,* do *Y*" (or "You ought to do *Y*") will be a hypothetical imperative if it is based on the supposed fact that *Y* is, in the circumstances, the only (or the best) available means to *X,* that is, on a causal relation between *Y* and *X.* The reason for doing *Y* lies in its causal connection with the desired end, *X;* the oughtness is contingent upon the desire. But "You ought to do *Y*" will be a categorical imperative if you ought to do *Y* irrespective of any such desire for any end to which *Y* would contribute, if the oughtness is not thus contingent upon any desire. . . .

A categorical imperative, then, would express a reason for acting which was unconditional in the sense of not being contingent upon any present desire of the agent to whose satisfaction the recommended action would contribute as a means—or more directly: "You ought to dance," if the implied reason is just that you want to dance or like dancing, is still a hypothetical imperative. Now Kant himself held that moral judgements are categorical imperatives, or perhaps are all applications of one categorical imperative, and it can plausibly be maintained at least that many moral judgements contain a categorically imperative element. So far as ethics is concerned, my thesis that there are no objective values is specifically the denial that any such categorically imperative element is objectively valid. The objective values which I am denying would be action-directing absolutely, not contingently (in the way indicated) upon the agent's desires and inclinations.

Another way of trying to clarify this issue is to refer to moral reasoning or moral arguments. In practice, of course, such reasoning is seldom fully explicit: but let us suppose that we could make explicit the reasoning that supports some evaluative conclusion, where this conclusion has some actionguiding force that is not contingent upon desires or purposes or chosen ends. Then what I am saying is that somewhere in the input to this argument—perhaps in one or more of the premisses, perhaps in some part of the form of the argument—there will be something which cannot be objectively validated—some premiss which is not capable of being simply true, or some form of argument which is not valid as a matter of general logic, whose authority or cogency is not objective, but is constituted by our choosing or deciding to think in a certain way. . . .

THE CLAIM TO OBJECTIVITY

If I have succeeded in specifying precisely enough the moral values whose objectivity I am denying, my thesis may now seem to be trivially true. Of course, some will say, valuing, preferring, choosing, recommending, rejecting, condemning, and so on, are human activities, and there is no need to look for values that are prior to and logically independent of all such activities. There may be widespread agreement in valuing, and particular value-judgements are not in general arbitrary or isolated: they typically cohere with others, or can be criticized if they do not, reasons can be given for them, and so on: but if all that the subjectivist is maintaining is that desires, ends, purposes, and the like figure somewhere in the system of reasons, and that no ends or purposes are objective as opposed to being merely intersubjective, then this may be conceded without much fuss.

But I do not think that this should be conceded so easily. As I have said, the main tradition of European moral philosophy includes the contrary claim, that there are objective values of just the sort I have denied. I have referred already to Plato, Kant, and Sidgwick. Kant in particular holds that the categorical imperative is not only categorical and imperative but objectively so: though a rational being gives the moral law to himself, the law that he thus makes is determinate and necessary. Aristotle begins the *Nicomachean Ethics* by saying that the good is that at which all things aim, and that ethics is part of a science which he calls "politics," whose goal is not knowledge but practice; yet he does not doubt that there can be *knowledge* of what is the good for man, nor, once he has identified this as well-being or happiness, *eudaimonia,* that it can be known, rationally determined, in what happiness consists; and it is plain that he thinks that this happiness is intrinsically desirable, not good simply because it is desired. The rationalist Samuel Clarke holds that

> these eternal and necessary differences of things make it *fit and reasonable* for creatures so to act . . . even separate from the consideration of these rules being the *positive will* or *command of God;* and also antecedent to any respect or regard, expectation or apprehension, of any *particular private and personal advantage or disadvantage, reward or punishment,* either present or future. . . .

Even the sentimentalist Hutcheson defines moral goodness as "some quality apprehended in actions, which procures approbation . . . ," while saying that the moral sense by which we perceive virtue and vice has been given to us (by the Author of nature) to direct our actions. Hume indeed was on the other side, but he is still a witness to the dominance of the

objectivist tradition, since he claims that when we "see that the distinction of vice and virtue is not founded merely on the relations of objects, nor is perceiv'd by reason," this "wou'd subvert all the vulgar systems of morality." And Richard Price insists that right and wrong are "real characters of actions," not "qualities of our minds," and are perceived by the understanding; he criticizes the notion of moral sense on the ground that it would make virtue an affair of taste, and moral right and wrong "nothing in the objects themselves"; he rejects Hutcheson's view because (perhaps mistakenly) he sees it as collapsing into Hume's. . . .

The prevalence of this tendency to objectify values—and not only moral ones—is confirmed by a pattern of thinking that we find in existentialists and those influenced by them. The denial of objective values can carry with it an extreme emotional reaction, a feeling that nothing matters at all, that life has lost its purpose. Of course this does not follow; the lack of objective values is not a good reason for abandoning subjective concern or for ceasing to want anything. But the abandonment of a belief in objective values can cause, at least temporarily, a decay of subjective concern and sense of purpose. That it does so is evidence that the people in whom this reaction occurs have been tending to objectify their concerns and purposes, have been giving them a fictitious external authority. A claim to objectivity has been so strongly associated with their subjective concerns and purposes that the collapse of the former seems to undermine the latter as well.

This view, that conceptual analysis would reveal a claim to objectivity, is sometimes dramatically confirmed by philosophers who are officially on the other side. Bertrand Russell, for example, says that "ethical propositions should be expressed in the optative mood, not in the indicative"; he defends himself effectively against the charge of inconsistency in both holding ultimate ethical valuations to be subjective and expressing emphatic opinions on ethical questions. Yet at the end he admits:

> Certainly there *seems* to be something more. Suppose, for example, that some one were to advocate the introduction of bullfighting in this country. In

opposing the proposal, I should *feel,* not only that I was expressing my desires, but that my desires in the matter are *right,* whatever that may mean. As a matter of argument, I can, I think, show that I am not guilty of any logical inconsistency in holding to the above interpretation of ethics and at the same time expressing strong ethical preferences. But in feeling I am not satisfied.

But he concludes, reasonably enough, with the remark: "I can only say that, while my own opinions as to ethics do not satisfy me, other people's satisfy me still less."

I conclude, then, that ordinary moral judgements include a claim to objectivity, an assumption that there are objective values in just the sense in which I am concerned to deny this. And I do not think it is going too far to say that this assumption has been incorporated in the basic, conventional, meanings of moral terms. Any analysis of the meanings of moral terms which omits this claim to objective, intrinsic, prescriptivity is to that extent incomplete; and this is true of any non-cognitive analysis, any naturalist one, and any combination of the two.

If second order ethics were confined, then, to linguistic and conceptual analysis, it ought to conclude that moral values at least are objective: that they are so is part of what our ordinary moral statements mean: the traditional moral concepts of the ordinary man as well as of the main line of western philosophers are concepts of objective value. But it is precisely for this reason that linguistic and conceptual analysis is not enough. The claim to objectivity, however ingrained in our language and thought, is not self-validating. It can and should be questioned. But the denial of objective values will have to be put forward not as the result of an analytic approach, but as an "error theory," a theory that although most people in making moral judgements implicitly claim, among other things, to be pointing to something objectively prescriptive, these claims are all false. It is this that makes the name "moral scepticism" appropriate.

But since this is an error theory, since it goes against assumptions ingrained in our thought and built into some of the ways in which language is used, since it conflicts with what is sometimes called

common sense, it needs very solid support. It is not something we can accept lightly or casually and then quietly pass on. If we are to adopt this view, we must argue explicitly for it. Traditionally it has been supported by arguments of two main kinds, which I shall call the argument from relativity and the argument from queerness, but these can, as I shall show, be supplemented in several ways.

THE ARGUMENT FROM RELATIVITY

The argument from relativity has as its premiss the well-known variation in moral codes from one society to another and from one period to another, and also the differences in moral beliefs between different groups and classes within a complex community. Such variation is in itself merely a truth of descriptive morality, a fact of anthropology which entails neither first order nor second order ethical views. Yet it may indirectly support second order subjectivism: radical differences between first order moral judgements make it difficult to treat those judgements as apprehensions of objective truths. But it is not the mere occurrence of disagreements that tells against the objectivity of values. Disagreement on questions in history or biology or cosmology does not show that there are no objective issues in these fields for investigators to disagree about. But such scientific disagreement results from speculative inferences or explanatory hypotheses based on inadequate evidence, and it is hardly plausible to interpret moral disagreement in the same way. Disagreement about moral codes seems to reflect people's adherence to and participation in different ways of life. The causal connection seems to be mainly that way round: it is that people approve of monogamy because they participate in a monogamous way of life rather than that they participate in a monogamous way of life because they approve of monogamy. Of course, the standards may be an idealization of the way of life from which they arise: the monogamy in which people participate may be less complete, less rigid, than that of which it leads them to approve. This is not to say that moral judgements are purely conventional. Of course there have been and are moral heretics and moral reformers, people who have turned against the established rules and practices of their own communities for moral reasons, and often for moral reasons that we would endorse. But this can usually be understood as the extension, in ways which, though new and unconventional, seemed to them to be required for consistency, of rules to which they already adhered as arising out of an existing way of life. In short, the argument from relativity has some force simply because the actual variations in the moral codes are more readily explained by the hypothesis that they reflect ways of life than by the hypothesis that they express perceptions, most of them seriously inadequate and badly distorted, of objective values.

But there is a well-known counter to this argument from relativity, namely to say that the items for which objective validity is in the first place to be claimed are not specific moral rules or codes but very general basic principles which are recognized at least implicitly to some extent in all society—such principles as provide the foundations of what Sidgwick has called different methods of ethics: the principle of universalizability, perhaps, or the rule that one ought to conform to the specific rules of any way of life in which one takes part, from which one profits, and on which one relies, or some utilitarian principle of doing what tends, or seems likely, to promote the general happiness. It is easy to show that such general principles, married with differing concrete circumstances, different existing social patterns or different preferences, will beget different specific moral rules; and there is some plausibility in the claim that the specific rules thus generated will vary from community to community or from group to group in close agreement with the actual variations in accepted codes.

The argument from relativity can be only partly countered in this way. To take this line the moral objectivist has to say that it is only in these principles that the objective moral character attaches immediately to its descriptively specified ground or subject: other moral judgements are objectively valid or true, but only derivatively and contingently—if things had been otherwise, quite different sorts of actions would have been right. And despite the prominence in recent philosophical ethics of universalization, utilitarian principles, and the like, these are very far from

constituting the whole of what is actually affirmed as basic in ordinary moral thought. Much of this is concerned rather with what Hare calls "ideals" or, less kindly, "fanaticism." That is, people judge that some things are good or right, and others are bad or wrong, not because—or at any rate not only because—they exemplify some general principle for which widespread implicit acceptance could be claimed, but because something about those things arouses certain responses immediately in them, though they would arouse radically and irresolvably different responses in others. "Moral sense" or "intuition" is an initially more plausible description of what supplies many of our basic moral judgements than "reason." With regard to all these starting points of moral thinking the argument from relativity remains in full force.

THE ARGUMENT FROM QUEERNESS

Even more important, however, and certainly more generally applicable, is the argument from queerness. This has two parts, one metaphysical, the other epistemological. If there were objective values, then they would be entities or qualities or relations of a very strange sort, utterly different from anything else in the universe. Correspondingly, if we were aware of them, it would have to be by some special faculty of moral perception or intuition, utterly different from our ordinary ways of knowing everything else. These points were recognized by Moore when he spoke of non-natural qualities, and by the intuitionists in their talk about a "faculty of moral intuition." Intuitionism has long been out of favour, and it is indeed easy to point out its implausibilities. What is not so often stressed, but is more important, is that the central thesis of intuitionism is one to which any objectivist view of values is in the end committed: intuitionism merely makes unpalatably plain what other forms of objectivism wrap up. Of course the suggestion that moral judgements are made or moral problems solved by just sitting down and having an ethical intuition is a travesty of actual moral thinking. But, however complex the real process, it will require (if it is to yield authoritatively prescriptive conclusions) some input of this distinctive sort, either premises or forms of argument or both. When we ask the awkward question, how we can be aware of this authoritative prescriptivity, of the truth of these distinctively ethical premises or of the cogency of this distinctively ethical pattern of reasoning, none of our ordinary accounts of sensory perception or introspection or the framing and confirming of explanatory hypotheses or inference or logical construction or conceptual analysis, or any combination of these, will provide a satisfactory answer; "a special sort of intuition" is a lame answer, but it is the one to which the clearheaded objectivist is compelled to resort.

Indeed, the best move for the moral objectivist is not to evade this issue, but to look for companions in guilt. For example, Richard Price argues that it is not moral knowledge alone that such an empiricism as those of Locke and Hume is unable to account for, but also our knowledge and even our ideas of essence, number, identity, diversity, solidity, inertia, substance, the necessary existence and infinite extension of time and space, necessity and possibility in general, power, and causation. If the understanding, which Price defines as the faculty within us that discerns truth, is also a source of new simple ideas of so many other sorts, may it not also be a power of immediately perceiving right and wrong, which yet are real characters of actions?

This is an important counter to the argument from queerness. The only adequate reply to it would be to show how, on empiricist foundations, we can construct an account of the ideas and beliefs and knowledge that we have of all these matters. I cannot even begin to do that here, though I have undertaken some parts of the task elsewhere. I can only state my belief that satisfactory accounts of most of these can be given in empirical terms. If some supposed metaphysical necessities or essences resist such treatment, then they too should be included, along with objective values, among the targets of the argument from queerness.

This queerness does not consist simply in the fact that ethical statements are "unverifiable." Although logical positivism with its verifiability theory of descriptive meaning gave an impetus to non-cognitive accounts of ethics, it is not only logical positivists but also empiricists of a much more liberal sort who should find objective values hard to accommodate.

Indeed, I would not only reject the verifiability principle but also deny the conclusion commonly drawn from it, that moral judgements lack descriptive meaning. The assertion that there are objective values or intrinsically prescriptive entities or features of some kind, which ordinary moral judgements presuppose, is, I hold, not meaningless but false.

Plato's Forms give a dramatic picture of what objective values would have to be. The form of the Good is such that knowledge of it provides the knower with both a direction and an overriding motive; something's being good both tells the person who knows this to pursue it and makes him pursue it. An objective good would be sought by anyone who was acquainted with it, not because of any contingent fact that this person, or every person, is so constituted that he desires this end, but just because the end has to-be-pursuedness somehow built into it. Similarly, if there were objective principles of right and wrong, any wrong (possible) course of action would have not-to-be-doneness somehow built into it. Or we should have something like Clarke's necessary relations of fitness between situations and actions, so that a situation would have a demand for such-and-such an action somehow built into it.

The need for an argument of this sort can be brought out by reflection on Hume's argument that "reason"—in which at this stage he includes all sorts of knowing as well as reasoning—can never be an "influencing motive of the will." Someone might object that Hume has argued unfairly from the lack of influencing power (not contingent upon desires) in ordinary objects of knowledge and ordinary reasoning, and might maintain that values differ from natural objects precisely in their power, when known, automatically to influence the will. To this Hume could, and would need to, reply that this objection involves the postulating of value-entities or value-features of quite a different order from anything else with which we are acquainted, and of a corresponding faculty with which to detect them. That is, he would have to supplement his explicit argument with what I have called the argument from queerness.

Another way of bringing out this queerness is to ask, about anything that is supposed to have some objective moral quality, how this is linked with its natural features. What is the connection between the natural fact that an action is a piece of deliberate cruelty—say, causing pain just for fun—and the moral fact that it is wrong? It cannot be an entailment, a logical or semantic necessity. Yet it is not merely that the two features occur together. The wrongness must somehow be "consequential" or "supervenient"; it is wrong because it is a piece of deliberate cruelty. But just what *in the world* is signified by this "because?" And how do we know the relation that it signifies, if this is something more than such actions being socially condemned, and condemned by us too, perhaps through our having absorbed attitudes from our social environment? It is not even sufficient to postulate a faculty which "sees" the wrongness: something must be postulated which can see at once the natural features that constitute the cruelty, and the wrongness, and the mysterious consequential link between the two. Alternatively, the intuition required might be the perception that wrongness is a higher order property belonging to certain natural properties; but what is this belonging of properties to other properties, and how can we discern it? How much simpler and more comprehensible the situation would be if we could replace the moral quality with some sort of subjective response which could be causally related to the detection of the natural features on which the supposed quality is said to be consequential.

A Critique of Mackie

RONALD DWORKIN

Ronald Dworkin is widely considered one of the world's foremost philosophers of law. He is the Quain Professor of Jurisprudence at University College London and holds joint appointments at New York University in philosophy and law. He has written books on abortion and euthanasia, equality, the American Constitution, and the notion of rights.

Mackie relied on two arguments that are now staples of austere skepticism. The first is the familiar argument from moral diversity, which insists that the fact that people disagree so much about morality, from time to time, and place to place, and even within particular cultures, shows that the face-value view must be wrong and that no moral claim could be true. Moral diversity is sometimes exaggerated: the degree of convergence over basic moral matters throughout history is both striking and predictable. But people do disagree about fundamental matters, like abortion and social justice, even within particular cultures, and this fact does give people reason to reexamine their own convictions. Why should I be so confident that I am right if others, who seem just as intelligent and sensitive, disagree with me so deeply?

It is one thing, however, to reexamine one's own views, and perhaps change them after further reflection, and another to decide, as Mackie and other[s] insist we should, that no positive moral claim is true. After all, we would not count the popularity of our moral opinions as evidence for their truth. Why should we count their controversiality as evidence against it? In any case, however, the popular argument

From *Philosophy and Public Affairs*, 25 (Spring 1996). Copyright © by Princeton University Press. Reprinted by permission of Princeton University Press.

from moral diversity is radically incomplete. Whether diversity of opinion in some intellectual domain has skeptical implications depends on a further philosophical question: it has such implications only if the best account of the content of that domain explains why it should. The best account of scientific thought does explain when and why disagreement in scientific judgments is suspicious. Suppose millions of people claimed to have seen unicorns but disagreed wildly about their size and shape. We would discount their evidence: if there were unicorns, and people had seen them, the actual properties of the beast would have caused more uniform reports. But when we have no such domain-specific account of why diversity of opinion impeaches all opinion, we draw no skeptical conclusions from that diversity. Since we do not think that philosophical opinions are caused by philosophical facts, we do not conclude from the diversity of philosophical views (which is more pronounced than moral disagreement) that no positive philosophical thesis is sound. If the moral-field thesis were true, then moral controversy would be like controversy about the properties of unicorns, and would excite similar suspicion. [According to the moral-field thesis, which Dworkin finds absurd, the universe houses some special particles—morons—whose energy and momentum establish fields that at once constitute the morality or immorality of particular human acts and also interact in some way with human nervous systems so as to make people aware of this morality or immorality.] But once we reject that thesis, we are left with no connection between diversity and skepticism. Perhaps we will discover such a connection when we turn more directly to the question of moral epistemology, as we shall in a moment. But unless we do, we can set the argument from diversity aside.

Mackie's second argument is also familiar . . . : it insists on the "queerness" of an idea that it declares is essential to morality as it is commonly understood—the idea that that moral properties are inherently motivating. The idea of an "objective good," Mackie said, is queer because it supposes that "objective good would be sought by anyone who was acquainted with it, not because of any contingent fact that this person, or every person, is so constituted that he desires this end, but just because the end has to-be-pursuedness

somehow built into it. Similarly, if there were objective principles of right and wrong, any wrong (possible) course of action would have not-to-be-doneness somehow built into it."

More metaphors! What could be meant by saying that an end has "to-be-pursuedness" or an action "not-to-be-doneness" "built into" it? That is not clear, and the popularity of the supposedly skeptical argument about morality and motivation may depend on not separating different ways in which these metaphors might be unpacked. On one reading, the proposition that morality is inherently motivating means that anyone who contemplates an end that is in fact good, or an act that is in fact wrongful, feels an emotional tug toward that end or away from that act. That could not be true unless something like the moral-field thesis were true; if it were, then the morons surrounding a genuinely good end or genuinely wrong act might have the power to suck people into an attraction or repel them into an inhibition. But the suggestion that good ends or bad acts have a built-in magnetic attraction or repulsion is plainly not essential to ordinary moral opinion or practice. We know that many of our moral opinions are controversial, and that otherwise perfectly normal people who contemplate abortion or economic equality feel very different emotions and impulses from those we feel. No one takes that obvious fact to undermine anyone's position.

The second reading supposes a connection, not between bare contemplation and impulse, but between two kinds of belief: it holds that anyone who believes that an end is good or an act wrong must also believe, on pain of contradiction, that he himself ought to behave in some indicated way. That implication fails in Mackie's first case of supposed "built-in-ness," the case of objectively good ends. If I believe that the world would be morally better if there were less suffering, then perhaps I ought to do what I can to lessen suffering. But that is a matter of moral or ethical judgment, not conceptual connection. In Mackie's second case—the objective wrongness of acts—the connection does seem more conceptual. If I acknowledged that it is morally wrong to cheat on my taxes, but denied that I had any reason not to do so, you would understandably be bewildered. There is nothing bizarre in the idea that a moral duty necessarily supplies a moral reason for action, however. That can be true only in virtue of what "duty" and "reason" mean.

A third reading of the proposition about "built-in-ness," which combines elements of the first two readings, is a more plausible interpretation of what [Mackie had] in mind. On this view, the claim that morality is inherently motivating means that no one really accepts a moral or valuational judgment unless he feels some actual motivational impulse to act in the direction that judgment points. Once again, the proposition, so understood, seems wrong in the case of beliefs about objectively good ends. Someone who thinks that the world would be better with less suffering may be defective in character, as I said, if he is

not thereby moved to action. But if he is not, it does not follow that he does not have that thought. Once again, however, the proposition does seems plausible in the case of beliefs about objectively wrongful acts. I may claim to think that cheating is wrong, but if you see that I am in no way deterred from cheating whenever I have the opportunity, and that I show no regret or hesitation or discomfort when I do, you may well think that I am either insincere or out of touch with my own real convictions. There is nothing queer in the idea that whether we ascribe a certain mental state to someone depends on more than his own opinion about that state, however. Someone may honestly think he is jealous or in love or trusting when his impulses and behavior show that he is not.

A Proof of the Objectivity of Morals

~

RENFORD BAMBROUGH

John Renford Bambrough (1926–1999) was a longtime fellow of St. John's College, Cambridge and edited the journal *Philosophy*. He wrote books on Aristotle, moral skepticism, and philosophical theology.

My proof that we have moral knowledge consists essentially in saying, "We know that this child, who is about to undergo what would otherwise be painful surgery, should be given an anaesthetic before the operation. Therefore we know at least one moral proposition to be true." I argue that no proposition that could plausibly be alleged as a reason in favour of doubting the truth of the proposition that the child should be given an anaesthetic can possibly be more certainly true than that proposition itself. If a philosopher produces an argument against my claim to *know* that the child should be given an anaesthetic, I can therefore be sure in advance that *either* at least one of the premises of his argument is false, *or* there is a mis-

take in the reasoning by which he purports to derive from his premises the conclusion that I do not know that the child should be given an anaesthetic. . . .

Those who reject the common sense account of moral knowledge, like those who reject the common sense account of our knowledge of the external world, do of course offer arguments in favour of their rejection. . . . It will be impossible in a small space to give a full treatment of any one argument, and it will also be impossible to refer to all the arguments that have been offered by moral philosophers who are consciously or unconsciously in conflict with common sense. I shall refer briefly to the most familiar and most plausible arguments, and I shall give to

Reprinted from the *American Journal of Jurisprudence* (1969), by permission of the Natural Law Institute.

each of them the outline of what I believe to be an adequate answer in defence of the common sense account.

"Moral disagreement is more widespread, more radical and more persistent than disagreement about matters of fact."

I have two main comments to make on this suggestion: the first is that it is almost certainly untrue, and the second is that it is quite certainly irrelevant.

The objection loses much of its plausibility as soon as we insist on comparing the comparable. We are usually invited to contrast our admirably close agreement that there is a glass of water on the table with the depth, vigour and tenacity of our disagreements about capital punishment, abortion, birth control and nuclear disarmament. But this is a game that may be played by two or more players. A sufficient reply in kind is to contrast our general agreement that this child should have an anaesthetic with the strength and warmth of the disagreements between cosmologists and radio astronomers about the interpretation of certain radio-astronomical observations. If the moral sceptic then reminds us of Christian Science we can offer him in exchange the Flat Earth Society.

But this is a side issue. Even if it is true that moral disagreement is more acute and more persistent than other forms of disagreement, it does not follow that moral knowledge is impossible. However long and violent a dispute may be, and however few or many heads may be counted on this side or on that, it remains possible that one party to the dispute is right and the others wrong. Galileo was right when he contradicted the Cardinals: and so was Wilberforce when he rebuked the slave owners.

There is a more direct and decisive way of showing the irrelevance of the argument from persistent disagreement. The question of whether a given type of enquiry is objective is the question whether it is *logically capable* of reaching knowledge, and is therefore an *a priori,* logical question. The question of how much agreement or disagreement there is between those who actually engage in that enquiry is a question of psychological or sociological fact. It follows that the question about the actual extent of

agreement or disagreement has no bearing on the question of the objectivity of the enquiry. If this were not so, the objectivity of every enquiry might wax and wane through the centuries as men became more or less disputatious or more or less proficient in the arts of persuasion.

"Our moral opinions are conditioned by our environment and upbringing."

It is under this heading that we are reminded of the variegated customs and beliefs of Hottentots, Eskimos, Polynesians and American Indians, which do indeed differ widely from each other and from our own. But this objection is really a special case of the general argument from disagreement, and it can be answered on the same lines. The beliefs of the Hottentots and the Polynesians about straightforwardly factual matters differs widely from our own, but that does not tempt us to say that science is subjective.

It is true that most of those who are born and bred in the stately homes of England have a different outlook on life from that of the Welsh miner or the Highland crofter, but it is also true that all these classes of people differ widely in their factual beliefs, and not least in their factual beliefs about themselves and each other.

Let us consider some of the moral sceptic's favourite examples, which are often presented as though they settled the issue beyond further argument.

(1) Herodotus reports that within the Persian Empire there were some tribes who buried their dead and some who burned them. Each group thought that the other's practice was barbarous. But (a) they agreed that respect must be shown to the dead; (b) they lived under very different climatic conditions; (c) we can now see that they were guilty of moral myopia in setting such store by what happened, for good or bad reasons, to be their own particular practice. Moral progress in this field has consisted in coming to recognize that burying-versus-burning is not an issue on which it is necessary for the whole of mankind to have a single, fixed, universal standpoint, regardless of variations of conditions in time and place.

(2) Some societies practise polygamous marriage. Others favour monogamy. Here again there need be

no absolute and unvarying rule. In societies where women heavily outnumber men, institutions may be appropriate which would be out of place in societies where the numbers of men and women are roughly equal. The moralist who insists that monogamy is right regardless of circumstances, is like the inhabitant of the northern hemisphere who insists that it is always and everywhere cold at Christmas, or the inhabitant of the southern hemisphere who cannot believe that it is ever or anywhere cold at Christmas.

(3) Some societies do not disapprove of what we condemn as "stealing." In such societies, anybody may take from anybody else's house anything he may need or want. This case serves further to illustrate that circumstances objectively alter cases, the relative is not only compatible with, but actually required by, the objective and rational determination of questions of right and wrong. I can maintain with all possible force that Bill Sykes is a rogue, and that prudence requires me to lock all my doors and windows against him, without being committed to holding that if an Eskimo takes whalemeat from the unlocked igloo of another Eskimo, then one of them is a knave and the other a fool. It is not that we disapprove of stealing and that the Eskimos do not, but that their circumstances differ so much from ours as to call for new consideration and a different judgment, which may be that in their situation stealing is innocent, or that in their situation there is no private property and therefore no possibility of *stealing* at all.

(4) Some tribes leave their elderly and useless members to die in the forest. Others, including our own, provide old age pensions and geriatric hospitals. But we should have to reconsider our arrangements if we found that the care of the aged involved for us the consequences that it might involve for a nomadic and pastoral people: general starvation because the old could not keep pace with the necessary movement to new pastures, children and domestic animals a prey to wild beasts, a life burdensome to all and destined to end with the extinction of the tribe.

"When I say that something is good or bad or right or wrong I commit myself, and reveal something of my attitudes and feelings."

This is quite true, but it is equally and analogously true that when I say that something is true or false, or even that something is red or round, I also commit myself and reveal something of my *beliefs*. Some emotivist and imperativist philosophers have sometimes failed to draw a clear enough distinction between what is said or meant by a particular form of expression and what is implied or suggested by it, and even those who have distinguished clearly and correctly between meaning and implication in the case of moral propositions have often failed to see that exactly the same distinction can be drawn in the case of nonmoral propositions. If I say "this is good" and then add "but I do not approve of it," I certainly behave oddly enough to owe you an explanation, but I behave equally oddly and owe you a comparable explanation if I say "that is true, but I don't believe it." If it is held that I contradict myself in the first case, it must be allowed that I contradict myself in the second case. If it is claimed that I do not contradict myself in the second case, then it must be allowed that I do not contradict myself in the first case. If this point can be used as an argument against the objectivity of morals, then it can also be used as an argument against the objectivity of science, logic, and of every other branch of enquiry.

The parallel between *approve* and *believe* and between *good* and *true* is so close that it provides a useful test of the paradoxes of subjectivism and emotivism. The emotivist puts the cart before the horse in trying to explain goodness in terms of approval, just as he would if he tried to explain truth in terms of belief. Belief cannot be explained without introducing the notion of truth, and approval cannot be explained without introducing the notion of goodness. To believe is (roughly) to hold to be true, and to approve is (equally roughly) to hold to be good. Hence it is as unsatisfactory to try to reduce goodness to approval, or to approval plus some other component, as it would be to try to reduce truth to belief, or to belief plus some other component.

If we are to give a correct account of the logical character of morality we must preserve the distinction between appearance and reality, between seeming and really being, that we clearly and admittedly have to preserve if we are to give a correct account of truth and belief. Just as we do and must hope that what we believe (what seems to us to be true) is and will be in fact true, so we must hope that what we approve (what seems to us to be good) is and will be in fact good.

I can say of another "He thinks it is raining, but it is not," and of myself, "I thought it was raining but it was not." I can also say of another "He thinks it is good, but it is not," and of myself "I thought it was good, but it was not."

"After every circumstance, every relation is known, the understanding has no further room to operate, nor any object on which it could employ itself."

This sentence from the first Appendix to Hume's *Enquiry Concerning the Principles of Morals* is the moral sceptic's favourite quotation, and he uses it for several purposes, including some that are alien to Hume's intentions. Sometimes it is no more than a flourish added to the argument from disagreement. Sometimes it is used in support of the claim that there comes a point in every moral dispute when further reasoning is not so much ineffective as impossible in principle. In either case the answer is once again a firm *tu quoque*. In any sense in which it is true that there may or must come a point in moral enquiry beyond which no further reasoning is possible, it is in that same sense equally true that there may or must be a point in any enquiry at which the reasoning has to stop. Nothing can be proved to a man who will accept nothing that has not been proved. Moore recognized that his proof of an external world uses premises which have not themselves been proved. Not even in pure mathematics, that paradigm of strict security of reasoning, can we *force* a man to accept our premises or our modes of inference; and therefore we cannot force him to accept our conclusions. Once again the moral sceptic counts as a reason for doubting the objectivity of morals a feature of moral enquiry which is exactly paralleled in other departments of enquiry where he does *not* count it as a reason for scepticism. If he is to be consistent, he must

either withdraw his argument against the objectivity of morals or subscribe also to an analogous argument against the objectivity of mathematics, physics, history, and every other branch of enquiry.

But of course such an argument gives no support to a sceptical conclusion about any of these enquiries. However conclusive a mode of reasoning may be, and however accurately we may use it, it always remains possible that we shall fail to convince a man who disagrees with us. There may come a point in a moral dispute when it is wiser to agree to differ than to persist with fruitless efforts to convince an opponent. But this by itself is no more a reason for doubting the truth of our premises and the validity of our arguments than the teacher's failure to convince a pupil of the validity of a proof of Pythagoras' theorem is a reason for doubting the validity of the proof and the truth of the theorem. It is notorious that even an expert physicist may fail to convince a member of the Flat Earth Society that the earth is not flat, but we nevertheless *know* that the earth is not flat. Lewis Carroll's tortoise ingeniously resisted the best efforts of Achilles to convince him of the validity of a simple deductive argument, but of course the argument *is* valid.

"A dispute which is purely moral is inconclusive in principle. The specifically moral element in moral disputes is one which cannot be resolved by investigation and reflection."

This objection brings into the open an assumption that is made at least implicitly by most of those who use Hume's remark as a subjective weapon: the assumption that whatever is a logical or factual dispute, or a mixture of logic and factual disputes, is necessarily *not* a moral dispute; that nothing is a moral dispute unless it is *purely* moral in the sense that it is a dispute between parties who agree on *all* the relevant factual and logical questions. But the *purely moral* dispute envisaged by this assumption is a pure fiction. The search for the "specifically moral elements" in moral disputes is a wild goose chase, and is the result of the initial confusion of supposing that no feature of moral reasoning is *really* a feature of moral reasoning, or is *characteristic* of moral reasoning, unless it is peculiar to moral reasoning. It is as if one insisted that a ginger cake could be fully characterized, and could only be characterized, by saying that there is ginger in it. It is true that ginger is the peculiar ingredient of a ginger cake as contrasted with other cakes, but no cake can be made entirely of ginger, and the ingredients that are combined with ginger to make ginger cakes are the same as those that are combined with chocolate, lemon, orange or vanilla to make other kinds of cakes; and ginger itself, when combined with other ingredients and treated in other ways, goes into the making of ginger puddings, ginger biscuits and ginger beer.

To the question "What is the place of reason in ethics?" why should we not answer: "The place of reason in ethics is exactly what it is in other enquiries, to enable us to find out the relevant facts and to make our judgments mutually consistent, to expose factual errors and detect logical inconsistencies"? This might seem to imply that there are some moral judgments which will serve as starting points for any moral enquiry, and will not themselves be proved, as others may be proved by being derived from them or disproved by being shown to be incompatible with them, and also to imply that we cannot engage in moral argument with a man with whom we agree on *no* moral question. In so far as these implications are correct they apply to all enquiry and not only to moral enquiry, and they do not, when correctly construed, constitute any objection to the rationality and objectivity of morality or of any other mode of enquiry. . . .

"There are recognized methods for settling factual and logical disputes, but there are no recognized methods for settling moral disputes."

This is either false, or true but irrelevant, according to how it is understood. Too often those who make this complaint are arguing in a circle, since they will count nothing as a recognized method of argument unless it is a recognized method of logical or scientific argument. If we adopt this interpretation, then it is true that there is no recognized method of moral argument, but the lack of such methods does not affect the claim that morality is objective. One

department of enquiry has not been shown to be no true department of enquiry when all that has been shown is that it cannot be carried on by exactly the methods that are appropriate to some other department of enquiry. We know without the help of the sceptic that morality is not identical with logic or science.

But in its most straightforward sense the claim is simply false. There *are* recognized methods of moral argument. Whenever we say "How would you like it if somebody did this to you?" or "How would it be if we all acted like this?" we are arguing according to recognized and established methods, and are in fact appealing to the consistency-requirement to which I have already referred. It is true that such appeals are often ineffective, but it is also true that well-founded logical or scientific arguments often fail to convince those to whom they are addressed. If the present objection is pursued beyond this point it turns into the argument from radical disagreement.

Now the moral sceptic is even more inclined to exaggerate the amount of disagreement that there is about methods of moral argument than he is inclined to exaggerate the amount of disagreement of moral belief as such. One reason for this is that he concentrates his attention on the admittedly striking and important fact that there is an enormous amount of immoral *conduct*. But most of those who *behave* immorally appeal to the very same methods of moral argument as those who condemn their immoral conduct. Hitler broke many promises, but he did not explicitly hold that promisebreaking as such and in general was justified. When others broke their promises to him he complained with the same force and in the same terms as those with whom he himself had failed to keep faith. And whenever he broke a promise he tried to *justify* his breach by claiming that other obligations overrode the duty to keep the promise. He did not simply deny that it was his duty to keep promises. He thus entered into the very process of argument by which it is possible to condemn so many of his own actions. He was *inconsistent* in requiring of other nations and their leaders standards of conduct to which he himself did not conform, and in failing to produce *convincing reasons* for his own departures from the agreed standards.

Utilitarianism

~

JOHN STUART MILL

John Stuart Mill (1806–1873), widely regarded as one of the greatest philosophers of the 19th century, wrote books about ethics, science, language, politics, and economics. He put his ideas into practice, serving in the British Parliament from 1865 to 1868.

The creed which accepts as the foundation of morals, Utility, or the Greatest Happiness Principle, holds that actions are right in proportion as they tend to promote happiness, wrong as they tend to produce the reverse of happiness. By happiness is intended pleasure, and the absence of pain; by unhappiness, pain, and the privation of pleasure. To give a clear view of the moral standard set up by the theory, much more requires to be said; in particular, what things it includes in the ideas of pain and pleasure; and to what extent this is left an open question. But these supplementary explanations do not affect the theory of life on which this theory of morality is grounded—namely, that pleasure, and freedom from pain, are the only things desirable as ends; and that all desirable things (which are as numerous in the utilitarian as in any other scheme) are desirable either for the pleasure inherent in themselves, or as means to the promotion of pleasure and the prevention of pain.

Now, such a theory of life excites in many minds, and among them in some of the most estimable in feeling and purpose, inveterate dislike. To suppose that life has (as they express it) no higher end than pleasure—no better and nobler object of desire and pursuit—they designate as utterly mean and grovelling; as a doctrine worthy only of swine, to whom the followers of Epicurus were, at a very early period, contemptuously likened; and modern holders of the doctrine are occasionally made the subject of equally polite comparisons by its German, French, and English assailants.

When thus attacked, the Epicureans have always answered, that it is not they, but their accusers, who represent human nature in a degrading light; since the accusation supposes human beings to be capable of no pleasures except those of which swine are capable. If this supposition were true, the charge could not be gainsaid, but would then be no longer an imputation; for if the sources of pleasure were precisely the same to human beings and to swine, the rule of life which is good enough for the one would be good enough for the other. The comparison of the Epicurean life to that of beasts is felt as degrading, precisely because a beast's pleasures do not satisfy a human being's conceptions of happiness. Human beings have faculties more elevated than the animal appetites, and when once made conscious of them, do not regard anything as happiness which does not include their gratification. I do not, indeed, consider the Epicureans to have been by any means faultless in drawing out their scheme of consequences from the utilitarian principle. To do this in any sufficient manner, many Stoic, as well as Christian elements require to be included. But there is no known Epicurean theory of life which does not assign to the pleasures of the intellect, of the feelings and imagination, and of the moral sentiments, a much higher value as pleasures than to those of mere sensation. It must be admitted, however, that utilitarian writers in general have placed the superiority of mental over bodily pleasures chiefly in the greater permanency, safety, uncostliness, &c., of the former—that is, in their circumstantial advantages rather than in their intrinsic nature. And on all these points utilitarians have fully proved their case; but they might have taken the other, and, as it may be called, higher ground, with entire consistency. It is quite compatible with the principle of utility to recognise the fact, that some kinds of pleasure are more desirable and more valuable than others. It would be absurd that while, in estimating all other things, quality is considered as well as quantity, the estimation of pleasures should be supposed to depend on quantity alone.

If I am asked, what I mean by difference of quality in pleasures, or what makes one pleasure more valuable than another, merely as a pleasure, except its being greater in amount, there is but one possible answer. Of two pleasures, if there be one to which all or almost all who have experience of both give a decided preference, irrespective of any feeling of moral obligation to prefer it, that is the more desirable pleasure. If one of the two is, by those who are competently acquainted with both, placed so far above the other that they prefer it, even though knowing it to be attended with a greater amount of discontent, and would not resign it for any quantity of the other pleasure which their nature is capable of, we are justified in ascribing to the preferred enjoyment a superiority in quality, so far outweighing quantity as to render it, in comparison, of small account.

Now it is an unquestionable fact that those who are equally acquainted with, and equally capable of appreciating and enjoying, both, do give a most marked preference to the manner of existence which employs their higher faculties. Few human creatures would consent to be changed into any of the lower animals, for a promise of the fullest allowance of a beast's pleasures; no intelligent human being would consent to be a fool, no instructed person would be an ignoramus, no person of feeling and conscience would be selfish and base, even though they should be persuaded that the fool, the dunce, or the rascal is better satisfied with his lot than they are with theirs. They would not resign what they possess more than he, for the most complete satisfaction of all the desires which they have in common with him. If they ever fancy they would, it is only in cases of unhappiness so extreme, that to escape from it they would exchange their lot for almost any other, however undesirable in their own eyes. A being of higher faculties requires more to make him happy, is capable probably of more acute suffering, and is certainly accessible to it at more points, than one of an inferior type; but in spite of these liabilities, he can never really wish to sink into what he feels to be a lower grade of existence. We may give what explanation we please of this unwillingness; we may attribute it to pride, a name which is given indiscriminately to some of the most and to some of the least estimable feelings of which mankind are capable: we may refer it to the love of liberty and personal independence, an appeal to which was with the Stoics one of the most effective means for the inculcation of it; to the love of power, or to the love of excitement, both of which do really enter into and contribute to it: but its most appropriate appellation is a sense of dignity, which all human beings possess in one form or other, and in some, though by no means in exact, proportion to their higher faculties, and which is so essential a part of the happiness of those in whom it is strong, that nothing which conflicts with it could be, otherwise than momentarily, an object of desire to them. Whoever supposes that this preference takes place at a sacrifice of happiness—that the superior being, in anything like equal circumstances, is not happier than the inferior—confounds the two very different ideas, of happiness, and content. It is indisputable that the being whose capacities of enjoyment are low, has the greatest chance of having them fully satisfied; and a highly-endowed being will always feel that any happiness which he can look for, as the world is constituted, is imperfect. But he can learn to bear its imperfections, if they are at all bearable; and they will not make him envy the being who is indeed unconscious of the imperfections, but only because he feels not at all the good which those imperfections qualify. It is better to be a human being dissatisfied than a pig satisfied; better to be Socrates dissatisfied than a fool satisfied. And if the fool, or the pig, is of a different opinion, it is because they only know their own side of the question. The other party to the comparison knows both sides.

It may be objected, that many who are capable of the higher pleasures, occasionally, under the influence of temptation, postpone them to the lower. But this is quite compatible with a full appreciation of the intrinsic superiority of the higher. Men often, from infirmity of character, make their election for the nearer good, though they know it to be the less valuable; and this no less when the choice is between two bodily pleasures, than when it is between bodily and mental. They pursue sensual indulgences to the injury of health, though perfectly aware that health is the greater good. It may be further objected, that many who begin with youthful enthusiasm for everything noble, as they advance in years sink into indolence and selfishness. But I do not believe that those who undergo this very common change, voluntarily choose the lower description of pleasures in preference to the higher. I believe that before they devote themselves exclusively to the one, they have already become incapable of the other. Capacity for the nobler feelings is in most natures a very tender plant, easily killed, not only by hostile influences, but by mere want of sustenance; and in the majority of young persons it speedily dies away if the occupations to which their position in life has devoted them, and the society into which it has thrown them, are not favourable to keeping that higher capacity in exercise. Men lose their high aspirations as they lose their intellectual tastes, because they have not time or opportunity for indulging them; and they addict themselves to inferior pleasures, not because they deliberately prefer them, but because they are either the only ones to which they have access, or the only ones which they are any longer capable of enjoying. It may be questioned whether any one who has remained equally susceptible to both classes of pleasures, ever knowingly and calmly preferred the lower; though many, in all ages, have broken down in an ineffectual attempt to combine both.

From this verdict of the only competent judges, I apprehend there can be no appeal. On a question which is the best worth having of two pleasures, or which of two modes of existence is the most grateful to the feelings, apart from its moral attributes and from its consequences, the judgment of those who are qualified by knowledge of both, or, if they differ, that of the majority among them, must be admitted as final. And there needs be the less hesitation to accept this judgment respecting the quality of pleasures, since there is no other tribunal to be referred to even on the question of quantity. What means are there of determining which is the acutest of two pains, or the intensest of two pleasurable sensations, except the general suffrage of those who are familiar with both? Neither pains nor pleasures are homogeneous, and pain is always heterogeneous with pleasure. What is there to decide whether a particular pleasure is worth purchasing at the cost of a particular pain, except the feelings and judgment of the experienced? When, therefore, those feelings and judgment declare the pleasures derived from the higher faculties to be preferable *in kind,* apart from the question of intensity, to those of which the animal nature, disjoined from the higher faculties, is susceptible, they are entitled on this subject to the same regard.

I have dwelt on this point, as being a necessary part of a perfectly just conception of Utility or Happiness, considered as the directive rule of human conduct. But it is by no means an indispensable condition to the acceptance of the utilitarian standard; for that standard is not the agent's own greatest happiness, but the greatest amount of happiness altogether; and if it may possibly be doubted whether a noble character is always the happier for its nobleness, there can be no doubt that it makes other people happier, and that the world in general is immensely a gainer by it. Utilitarianism, therefore, could only attain its end by the general cultivation of nobleness of character, even if each individual were only benefited by the nobleness of others, and his own, so far as happiness is concerned, were a sheer deduction from the benefit. But the bare enunciation of such an absurdity as this last, renders refutation superfluous.

According to the Greatest Happiness Principle, as above explained, the ultimate end, with reference to and for the sake of which all other things are desirable (whether we are considering our own good or that of other people), is an existence exempt as far as possible from pain, and as rich as possible in enjoyments, both in point of quantity and quality; the test of quality, and the rule for measuring it against quantity, being the preference felt by those who, in their opportunities of experience, to which must be added their habits of self-consciousness and self-observation, are best furnished with the means of comparison. This, being, according to the utilitarian opinion, the end of human action, is necessarily also the standard of morality; which may accordingly be defined, the rules and precepts for human conduct, by the observance of which an existence such as has been described might be, to the greatest extent possible, secured to all mankind; and not to them only, but, so far as the nature of things admits, to the whole sentient creation. . . .

CHAPTER FOUR • OF WHAT SORT OF PROOF THE PRINCIPLE OF UTILITY IS SUSCEPTIBLE

It has already been remarked, that questions of ultimate ends do not admit of proof, in the ordinary acceptation of the term. To be incapable of proof by reasoning is common to all first principles; to the first premises of our knowledge, as well as to those of our conduct. But the former, being matters of fact, may be the subject of a direct appeal to the faculties which judge of fact—namely, our senses, and our internal consciousness. Can an appeal be made to the same faculties on questions of practical ends? Or by what other faculty is cognizance taken of them?

Questions about ends are, in other words, questions about what things are desirable. The utilitarian doctrine is, that happiness is desirable, and the only thing desirable, as an end; all other things being only desirable as means to that end. What ought to be required of this doctrine—what conditions is it requisite that the doctrine should fulfil—to make good its claim to be believed?

The only proof capable of being given that an object is visible, is that people actually see it. The only proof that a sound is audible, is that people hear it: and so of the other sources of our experience. In like manner, I apprehend, the sole evidence it is possible to produce that anything is desirable, is that people do actually desire it. If the end which the utilitarian doctrine proposes to itself were not, in theory and in practice, acknowledged to be an end, nothing could ever convince any person that it was so. No reason can be given why the general happiness is desirable, except that each person, so far as he believes it

to be attainable, desires his own happiness. This, however, being a fact, we have not only all the proof which the case admits of, but all which it is possible to require, that happiness is a good: that each person's happiness is a good to that person, and the general happiness, therefore, a good to the aggregate of all persons. Happiness has made out its title as *one* of the ends of conduct, and consequently one of the criteria of morality.

But it has not, by this alone, proved itself to be the sole criterion. To do that, it would seem, by the same rule, necessary to show, not only that people desire happiness, but that they never desire anything else. Now it is palpable that they do desire things which, in common language, are decidedly distinguished from happiness. They desire, for example, virtue, and the absence of vice, no less really than pleasure and the absence of pain. The desire of virtue is not as universal, but it is as authentic a fact, as the desire of happiness. And hence the opponents of the utilitarian standard deem that they have a right to infer that there are other ends of human action besides happiness, and that happiness is not the standard of approbation and disapprobation.

But does the utilitarian doctrine deny that people desire virtue, or maintain that virtue is not a thing to be desired? The very reverse. It maintains not only that virtue is to be desired, but that it is to be desired disinterestedly, for itself. Whatever may be the opinion of utilitarian moralists as to the original conditions by which virtue is made virtue; however they may believe (as they do) that actions and dispositions are only virtuous because they promote another end than virtue; yet this being granted, and it having been decided, from considerations of this description, what *is* virtuous, they not only place virtue at the very head of the things which are good as means to the ultimate end, but they also recognise as a psychological fact the possibility of its being, to the individual, a good in itself, without looking to any end beyond it; and hold, that the mind is not in a right state, not in a state conformable to Utility, not in the state most conducive to the general happiness, unless it does love virtue in this manner—as a thing desirable in itself, even although, in the individual instance, it should not produce those other desirable consequences which it tends to produce, and on account of which it is held to be virtue. This opinion is not, in the smallest degree, a departure from the Happiness principle. The ingredients of happiness are very various, and each of them is desirable in itself, and not merely when considered as swelling an aggregate. The principle of utility does not mean that any given pleasure, as music, for instance, or any given exemption from pain, as for example health, are to be looked upon as means to a collective something termed happiness, and to be desired on that account. They are desired and desirable in and for themselves; besides being means, they are a part of the end. Virtue, according to the utilitarian doctrine, is not naturally and originally part of the end, but it is capable of becoming so; and in those who love it disinterestedly it has become so, and is desired and cherished, not as a means to happiness, but as a part of their happiness.

To illustrate this farther, we may remember that virtue is not the only thing, originally a means, and which if it were not a means to anything else, would be and remain indifferent, but which by association with what it is a means to, comes to be desired for itself, and that too with the utmost intensity. What, for example, shall we say of the love of money? There is nothing originally more desirable about money than about any heap of glittering pebbles. Its worth is solely that of the things which it will buy; the desires for other things than itself, which it is a means of gratifying. Yet the love of money is not only one of the strongest moving forces of human life, but money is, in many cases, desired in and for itself; the desire to possess it is often stronger than the desire to use it, and goes on increasing when all the desires which point to ends beyond it, to be compassed by it, are falling off. It may then be said truly, that money is desired not for the sake of an end, but as part of the end. From being a means to happiness, it has come to be itself a principal ingredient of the individual's conception of happiness. The same may be said of the majority of the great objects of human life—power, for example, or fame; except that to each of these there is a certain amount of immediate pleasure annexed, which has at least the semblance of being naturally inherent in them; a thing which cannot be said of money. Still, however, the strongest natural

attraction, both of power and of fame, is the immense aid they give to the attainment of our other wishes; and it is the strong association thus generated between them and all our objects of desire, which gives to the direct desire of them the intensity it often assumes, so as in some characters to surpass in strength all other desires. In these cases the means have become a part of the end, and a more important part of it than any of the things which they are means to. What was once desired as an instrument for the attainment of happiness, has come to be desired for its own sake. In being desired for its own sake it is, however, desired as part of happiness. The person is made, or thinks he would be made, happy by its mere possession; and is made unhappy by failure to obtain it. The desire of it is not a different thing from the desire of happiness, any more than the love of music, or the desire of health. They are included in happiness. They are some of the elements of which the desire of happiness is made up. Happiness is not an abstract idea, but a concrete whole; and these are some of its parts. And the utilitarian standard sanctions and approves their being so. Life would be a poor thing, very ill provided with sources of happiness, if there were not this provision of nature, by which things originally indifferent, but conducive to, or otherwise associated with, the satisfaction of our primitive desires, become in themselves sources of pleasure more valuable than the primitive pleasures, both in permanency, in the space of human existence that they are capable of covering, and even in intensity.

Virtue, according to the utilitarian conception, is a good of this description. There was no original desire of it, or motive to it, save its conduciveness to pleasure, and especially to protection from pain. But through the association thus formed, it may be felt a good in itself, and desired as such with as great intensity as any other good; and with this difference between it and the love of money, of power, or of fame, that all of these may, and often do, render the individual noxious to the other members of the society to which he belongs, whereas there is nothing which makes him so much a blessing to them as the cultivation of the disinterested love of virtue. And consequently, the utilitarian standard, while it tolerates and approves those other acquired desires, up to the point beyond which they would be more injurious to the general happiness than promotive of it, enjoins and requires the cultivation of the love of virtue up to the greatest strength possible, as being above all things important to the general happiness.

It results from the preceding considerations, that there is in reality nothing desired except happiness. Whatever is desired otherwise than as a means to some end beyond itself, and ultimately to happiness, is desired as itself a part of happiness, and is not desired for itself until it has become so.

The Experience Machine

~

ROBERT NOZICK

Robert Nozick (1938–2002) was Pellegrino University Professor at Harvard University. He wrote in a lively fashion on many philosophical topics. His books include *Philosophical Explanations, Invariances: The Structure of the Objective World,* and *The Examined Life.*

There are also substantial puzzles when we ask what matters other than how *people's* experiences feel "from the inside." Suppose there were an experience machine that would give you any experience you desired. Superduper neuropsychologists could stimulate your brain so that you would think and feel you were writing a great novel, or making a friend, or reading an interesting book. All the time you would be floating in a tank, with electrodes attached to your brain. Should you plug into this machine for life, pre-programming your life's experiences? If you are worried about missing out on desirable experiences, we can suppose that business enterprises have researched thoroughly the lives of many others. You can pick and choose from their large library or smorgasbord of such experiences, selecting your life's experiences for, say, the next two years. After two years have passed, you will have ten minutes or ten hours out of the tank, to select the experiences of your *next* two years. Of course, while in the tank you won't know that you're there; you'll think it's all actually happening. Others can also plug in to have the experiences they want, so there's no need to stay unplugged to serve them. (Ignore problems such as who will service the machines if everyone plugs in.) Would you plug in? *What else can matter to us, other than how our lives feel from the inside?* Nor should you refrain because of the few moments of distress between the moment you've decided and the moment you're plugged. What's few moments of distress compared to a lifetime of bliss (if that's what you choose), and why feel any distress at all if your decision *is* the best one?

What does matter to us in addition to our experiences? First, we want to *do* certain things, and not just have the experience of doing them. In the case of certain experiences, it is only because first we want to do the actions that we want the experiences of doing them or thinking we've done them. (But *why* do we want to do the activities rather than merely to experience them?) A second reason for not plugging in is that we want to *be* a certain way, to be a certain sort of person. Someone floating in a tank is an indeterminate blob. There is no answer to the question of what a person is like who has long been in the tank.

Is he courageous, kind, intelligent, witty, loving? It's not merely that it's difficult to tell; there's no way he is. Plugging into the machine is a kind of suicide. It will seem to some, trapped by a picture, that nothing about what we are like can matter except as it gets reflected in our experiences. But should it be surprising that what *we are* is important to us? Why should we be concerned only with how our time is filled, but not with what we are?

Thirdly, plugging into an experience machine limits us to a man-made reality, to a world no deeper or more important than that which people can construct. There is no *actual* contact with any deeper reality, though the experience of it can be simulated. Many persons desire to leave themselves open to such contact and to a plumbing of deeper significance. This clarifies the intensity of the conflict over psychoactive drugs, which some view as mere local experience machines, and others view as avenues to a deeper reality; what some view as equivalent to surrender to the experience machine, others view as following one of the reasons *not* to surrender!

We learn that something matters to us in addition to experience by imagining an experience machine and then realizing that we would not use it. We can continue to imagine a sequence of machines each designed to fill lacks suggested for the earlier machines. For example, since the experience machine doesn't meet our desire to *be* a certain way, imagine a transformation machine which transforms us into whatever sort of person we'd like to be (compatible with our staying us). Surely one would not use the transformation machine to become as one would wish, and thereupon plug into the experience machine! So something matters in addition to one's experiences *and* what one is like. Nor is the reason merely that one's experiences are unconnected with what one is like. For the experience machine might be limited to provide only experiences possible to the sort of person plugged in. Is it that we want to make a difference in the world? Consider then the result machine, which produces in the world any result you would produce and injects your vector input into any joint activity. We shall not pursue here the fascinating details of these or other machines. What is most disturbing about them is their living of our lives for us. Is it misguided to search for *particular* additional functions beyond the competence of machines to do for us? Perhaps what we desire is to live (an active verb) ourselves, in contact with reality. (And this, machines cannot do *for* us.) Without elaborating on the implications of this, which I believe connect surprisingly with issues about free will and causal accounts of knowledge, we need merely note the intricacy of the question of what matters *for people* other then their experiences. Until one finds a satisfactory answer, and determines that this answer does not *also* apply to animals, one cannot reasonably claim that only the felt experiences of animals limit what we may do to them.

Fundamental Principles of the Metaphysics of Morals

~

IMMANUEL KANT

Immanuel Kant (1724–1804) is one of the most influential of all philosophers. His works in ethics include the *Critique of Practical Reason* and *The Metaphysics of Morals.* He is said never to have traveled more than 50 miles from Königsberg, the East Prussian city of his birth.

Nothing can possibly be conceived in the world, or even out of it, which can be called good without qualification, except a *good will.* Intelligence, wit, judgment, and the other *talents* of the mind, however they may be named, or courage, resolution, perseverance, as qualities of temperament, are undoubtedly good and desirable in many respects; but these gifts of nature may also become extremely bad and mischievous if the will which is to make use of them, and which, therefore, constitutes what is called *character,* is not good. It is the same with the *gifts of fortune.* Power, riches, honor, even health, and the general well-being and contentment with one's condition which is called *happiness,* inspire pride, and often presumption, if there is not a good will to correct the influence of these on the mind, and with this also to rectify the whole principle of acting, and adapt it to its end. The sight of a being who is not adorned with a single feature of a pure and good will, enjoying unbroken prosperity, can never give pleasure to an impartial rational spectator. Thus a good will appears to constitute the indispensable condition even of being worthy of happiness.

There are even some qualities which are of service to this good will itself, and may facilitate its actions, yet which have no intrinsic unconditional value, but always presuppose a good will, and this qualifies the esteem that we justly have for them, and does not permit us to regard them as absolutely good. Moderation in the affections and passions, self-control, and calm deliberation are not only good in many respects, but even seem to constitute part of the intrinsic worth of the person; but they are far deserving to be called good without qualification, although they have been so unconditionally praised by the ancients. For without the principles of a good will, they may become extremely bad; and the coolness of a villain not only makes him far more dangerous, but also directly makes him more abominable in our eyes than he would have been without it.

A good will is good not because of what it performs or effects, not by its aptness for the attainment of some proposed end, but simply by virtue of the volition—that is, it is good in itself, and considered by itself is to be esteemed much higher than all that can be brought about by it in favor of any inclination nay, even of the sum-total of all inclinations. Even if it should happen that, owing to special disfavor of fortune, or the niggardly provision of a stepmotherly nature, this will should wholly lack power to accomplish its purpose, if with its greatest efforts it should yet achieve nothing, and there should remain only the good will (not, to be sure, a mere wish, but the summoning of all means in our power), then, like a jewel, it would still shine by its own light, as a thing which has its whole value in itself. Its usefulness or fruitlessness can neither add to nor take away anything from this value. It would be, as it were, only the set-

From the *Fundamental Principles of the Metaphysics of Morals,* translated by Thomas K. Abbott.

ting to enable us to handle it the more conveniently in common commerce, or to attract to it the attention of those who are not yet connoisseurs, but not to recommend it to true connoisseurs, or to determine its value . . .

We have then to develop the notion of a will which deserves to be highly esteemed for itself, and is good without a view to anything further, a notion which exists already in the sound natural understanding, requiring rather to be cleared up than to be taught, and which in estimating the value of our actions always takes the first place and constitutes the condition of all the rest. In order to do this, we will take the notion of duty, which includes that of a good will, although implying certain subjective restrictions and hindrances. These, however, far from concealing it or rendering it unrecognizable, rather bring it out by contrast and make it shine forth so much the brighter.

I omit here all actions which are already recognized as inconsistent with duty, although they may be useful for this or that purpose, for with these the question whether they are done *from duty* cannot arise at all, since they even conflict with it. I also set aside those actions which really conform to duty, but to which men have *no* direct *inclination,* performing them because they are impelled thereto by some other inclination. For in this case we can readily distinguish whether the action which agrees with duty is done *from duty* or from a selfish view. It is much harder to make this distinction when the action accords with duty, and the subject has besides a *direct* inclination to it. For example, it is always a matter of duty that a dealer should not overcharge an inexperienced purchaser; and wherever there is much commerce the prudent tradesman does not overcharge, but keeps a fixed price for everyone, so that a child buys of him as well as any other. Men are thus *honestly* served; but this is not enough to make us believe that the tradesman has so acted from duty and from principles of honesty; his own advantage required it; it is out of the question in this case to suppose that he might besides have a direct inclination in favor of the buyers, so that, as it were, from love he should give no advantage to one over another. Accordingly the action was done neither from duty nor from direct inclination, but merely with a selfish view.

On the other hand, it is a duty to maintain one's life; and, in addition, everyone has also a direct inclination to do so. But on this account the often anxious care which most men take for it has no intrinsic worth, and their maxim has no moral import. They preserve their life *as duty requires,* no doubt, but not *because duty requires.* On the other hand, if adversity and hopeless sorrow have completely taken away the relish for life, if the unfortunate one, strong in mind, indignant at his fate rather than desponding or dejected, wishes for death, and yet preserves his life without loving it—not from inclination or fear, but from duty—then his maxim has a moral worth.

To be beneficent when we can is a duty; and besides this, there are many minds so sympathetically constituted that, without any other motive of vanity or self-interest, they find a pleasure in spreading joy around them, and can take delight in the satisfaction of others so far as it is their own work. But I maintain that in such a case an action of this kind, however proper, however amiable it may be, has nevertheless no true moral worth, but is on a level with other inclinations, for example, the inclination to honor, which, if it is happily directed to that which is in fact of public utility and accordant with duty, and consequently honorable, deserves praise and encouragement, but not esteem. For the maxim lacks the moral import, namely, that such actions be done *from duty,* not from inclination. Put the case that the mind of that philanthropist was clouded by sorrow of his own, extinguishing all sympathy with the lot of others, and that while he still has the power to benefit others in distress, he is not touched by their trouble because he is absorbed with his own; and now suppose that he tears himself out of this dead insensibility and performs the action without any inclination to it, but simply from duty, then first has his action its genuine moral worth. Further still, if nature has put little sympathy in the heart of this or that man, if he, supposed to be an upright man, is by temperament cold and indifferent to the sufferings of others, perhaps because in respect of his own he is provided with the special gift of patience and fortitude, and supposes, or even requires, that others should have the same—and such a man would certainly not be the meanest product of nature—but if nature had not specially framed him for a philanthropist, would he not still find in himself a source from whence to give himself a far higher worth than that of a goodnatured temperament could be? Unquestionably. It is just in this that the moral worth of the character is brought out which is incomparably the highest of all, namely, that he is beneficent, not from inclination, but from duty. . . .

The second proposition is: That an action done from duty derives its moral worth, *not from the purpose* which is to be attained by it, but from the maxim by which it is determined, and therefore does not depend on the realization of the object of the action, but merely on the *principle of volition* by which the action has taken place, without regard to any object of desire. It is clear from what precedes that the purposes which we may have in view in our actions, or their effects regarded as ends and springs of the will, cannot give to actions any unconditional or moral worth. In what, then, can their worth lie if it is not to consist in the will and in reference to its expected effect? It cannot lie anywhere but in the *principle of the will* without regard to the ends which can be attained by the action. For the will stands between its *a priori* principle, which is formal, and its *a posteriori* spring, which is material, as between two roads, and as it must be determined by something, it follows that it must be determined by the formal principle of volition when an action is done from duty, in which case every material principle has been withdrawn from it.

The third proposition, which is a consequence of the two preceding, I would express thus: *Duty is the necessity of acting from respect for the law.* I may have *inclination* for an object as the effect of my proposed action, but I cannot have *respect* for it just for this reason that it is an effect and not an energy of will. Similarly, I cannot have respect for inclination, whether my own or another's; I can at most, if my own, approve it; if another's, sometimes even love it, that is, look on it as favorable to my own interest. It is only what is connected with my will as a principle, by no means as an effect—what does not subserve my inclination, but overpowers it, or at least in case of choice excludes it from its calculation—in other words, simply the law of itself, which can be an object of respect, and hence a command. Now an action done from duty must wholly exclude the influence of inclination, and with it every object of the will, so that nothing remains which can determine the will except objectively the *law,* and subjectively *pure respect* for this practical law, and consequently the maxim that I should follow this law even to the thwarting of all my inclinations.

Thus the moral worth of an action does not lie in the effect expected from it, nor in any principle of action which requires to borrow its motive from this expected effect. For all these effects—agreeableness of one's condition, and even the promotion of the happiness of others—could have been also brought about by other causes, so that for this there would have been no need of the will of a rational being; whereas it is in this alone that the supreme and unconditional good can be found. The pre-eminent good which we call moral can therefore consist in nothing else than *the conception of law* in itself, *which certainly is only possible in a rational being,* in so far as this conception, and not the expected effect, determines the will. This is a good which is already present in the person who acts accordingly, and we have not to wait for it to appear first in the result.

But what sort of law can that be the conception of which must determine the will, even without paying any regard to the effect expected from it, in order that this will may be called good absolutely and without qualification? As I have deprived the will of every impulse which could arise to it from obedience to any law, there remains nothing but the universal conformity of its actions to law in general, which alone is to serve the will as a principle, that is, I am never to act otherwise than so *that I could also will that my maxim should become a universal law.* Here, now, it is the simple conformity to law in general, without assuming any particular law applicable to certain actions, that serves the will as its principle, and must so serve it if duty is not to be a vain delusion and a chimerical notion. The common reason of men in its practical judgments perfectly coincides with this, and always has in view the principle here suggested. Let the question be, for example: May I when in distress make a promise with the intention not to keep it? I readily distinguish here between the two significations which the question may have: whether it is prudent or whether it is right to make a false promise? The former may undoubtedly often be the case. I see clearly indeed that it is not enough to extricate myself from a present difficulty by means of this subterfuge, but it must be well considered whether there may not hereafter spring from this lie much greater inconvenience than that from which I now free myself, and as, with all my supposed *cunning,* the consequences cannot be so easily foreseen but that credit once lost may be much more injurious to me than any mischief which I seek to avoid at present, it should be considered whether it would not be more *prudent* to act herein according to a universal maxim, and to make it a habit to promise nothing except with the intention of keeping it. But it is soon clear to me that such a maxim will still only be based on the fear of consequences. Now it is a wholly different thing to be truthful from duty, and to be so from apprehension of injurious consequences. In the first case, the very notion of the action already implies a law for me; in the second case, I must first look about elsewhere to see what results may be combined with it which would affect myself. For to deviate from the principle of duty is beyond all doubt wicked; but to be unfaithful to my maxim of prudence may often be very advantageous to me, although to abide by it is certainly safer. The shortest way, however, and an unerring one, to discover the answer to this question whether a lying promise is consistent with duty, is to ask myself, Should I be content that my maxim (to extricate myself from difficulty by a false promise) should hold good as a universal law, for myself as well as for others; and should I be able to say to myself, "Every one may make a deceitful promise when he finds himself in a difficulty from which he cannot otherwise extricate himself"? Then I presently become aware that, while I can will the lie, I can by no means will that lying should be a universal law. For which such a law there would be no promises at all, since it would be in vain to allege my intention in regard to my future actions to those who would not believe this allegation, or if they over-hastily did so, would pay me back in my own coin. Hence my maxim, as soon as it should be made a universal law, would necessarily destroy itself.

I do not, therefore, need any far-reaching penetration to discern what I have to do in order that my will may be morally good. Inexperienced in the course of the world, incapable of being prepared for all its contingencies, I only ask myself: Canst thou also will that thy maxim should be a universal law? If not, then it must be rejected, and that not because of a disadvantage accruing from it to myself or even to others, but because it cannot enter as a principle into a possible universal legislation, and reason extorts from me immediate respect for such legislation. I do not indeed as yet *discern* on what this respect is based (this the philosopher may inquire), but at least I understand this—that it is an estimation of the worth which far outweighs all worth of what is recommended by inclination, and that the necessity of acting from pure respect for the practical law is what constitutes duty, to which every other motive must give place because it is the condition of a will being good *in itself,* and the worth of such a will is above everything. . . .

We will now enumerate a few duties, adopting the usual division of them into duties to ourselves and to others, and into perfect and imperfect duties.

1. A man reduced to despair by a series of misfortunes feels wearied of life, but is still so far in possession of his reason that he can ask himself whether it would not be contrary to his duty to himself to take his own life. Now he inquires whether the maxim of his action could become a universal law of nature. His maxim is: From self-love I adopt it as a principle to shorten my life when its longer duration is likely to bring more evil than satisfaction. It is asked then simply whether this principle founded on self-love can become a universal law of nature. Now we see at once that a system of nature of which it should be a law to destroy life by means of the very feeling whose special nature it is to impel to the improvement of life would contradict itself, and therefore could not exist as a system of nature; hence that maxim cannot possibly exist as a universal law of nature, and consequently would be wholly inconsistent with the supreme principle of all duty.

2. Another finds himself forced by necessity to borrow money. He knows that he will not be able to

repay it, but sees also that nothing will be lent to him unless he promises stoutly to repay it in a definite time. He desires to make this promise, but he has still so much conscience as to ask himself: Is it not unlawful and inconsistent with duty to get out of a difficulty in this way? Suppose, however, that he resolves to do so, then the maxim of his action would be expressed thus: When I think myself in want of money, I will borrow money and promise to repay it, although I know that I never can do so. Now this principle of self-love or of one's own advantage may perhaps be consistent with my whole future welfare; but the question now is, Is it right? I change then the suggestion of self-love into a universal law, and state the question thus: How would it be if my maxim were a universal law? Then I see at once that it could never hold as a universal law of nature, but would necessarily contradict itself. For supposing it to be a universal law that everyone when he thinks himself in a difficulty should be able to promise whatever he pleases, with the purpose of not keeping his promise, the promise itself would become impossible, as well as the end that one might have in view in it, since no one would consider that anything was promised to him, but would ridicule all such statements as vain pretenses.

3. A third finds in himself a talent which with the help of some culture might make him a useful man in many respects. But he finds himself in comfortable circumstances and prefers to indulge in pleasure rather than to take pains in enlarging and improving his happy natural capacities. He asks, however, whether his maxim of neglect of his natural gifts, besides agreeing with his inclination to indulgence, agrees also with what is called duty. He sees then that

a system of nature could indeed subsist with such a universal law, although men (like the South Sea islanders) should let their talents rest and resolve to devote their lives merely to idleness, amusement, and propagation of their species—in a word, to enjoyment; but he cannot possibly *will* that this should be a universal law of nature, or be implanted in us as such by a natural instinct. For, as a rational being, he necessarily wills that his faculties be developed, since they serve him, and have been given him, for all sorts of possible purposes.

4. A fourth, who is in prosperity, while he sees that others have to contend with great wretchedness and that he could help them, thinks: What concern is it of mine? Let everyone be as happy as Heaven pleases, or as he can make himself; I will take nothing from him nor even envy him, only I do not wish to contribute anything to his welfare or to his assistance in distress! Now no doubt, if such a mode of thinking were a universal law, the human race might very well subsist, and doubtless even better than in a state in which everyone talks of sympathy and goodwill, or even takes care occasionally to put it into practice, but, on the other side, also cheats when he can, betrays the rights of men, or otherwise violates them. But although it is possible that a universal law of nature might exist in accordance with that maxim, it is impossible to *will* that such a principle should have the universal validity of a law of nature. For a will which resolved this would contradict itself, inasmuch as many cases might occur in which one would have the need of the love and sympathy of others, and in which, by such a law of nature, sprung from his own will, he would deprive himself of all hope of the aid he desires.

A Simplified Account of Kant's Ethics

~

ONORA O'NEILL

Onora O'Neill is principal of Newnham College, Cambridge University. Her books include *Bounds of Justice* and *Towards Justice and Virtue.* A native of Northern Ireland, O'Neill writes on political philosophy, ethics, and Kant.

Kant's moral theory has acquired the reputation of being forbiddingly difficult to understand and, once understood, excessively demanding in its requirements. I don't believe that this reputation has been wholly earned, and I am going to try to undermine it. . . .

The main method by which I propose to avoid some of the difficulties of Kant's moral theory is by explaining only one part of the theory. This does not seem to me to be an irresponsible approach in this case. One of the things that makes Kant's moral theory hard to understand is that he gives a number of different versions of the principle that he calls the Supreme Principle of Morality, and these different versions don't look at all like one another. They also don't look at all like the utilitarians' Greatest Happiness Principle. But the Kantian principle is supposed to play a similar role in arguments about what to do.

Kant calls his Supreme Principle the *Categorical Imperative;* its various versions also have sonorous names. One is called the Formula of Universal Law; another is the Formula of the Kingdom of Ends. The one on which I shall concentrate is known as the *Formula of the End in Itself.* To understand why Kant thinks that these picturesquely named principles are equivalent to one another takes quite a lot of close and detailed analysis of Kant's philosophy. I shall avoid this and concentrate on showing the implications of this version of the Categorical Imperative.

THE FORMULA OF THE END IN ITSELF

Kant states the Formula of the End in Itself as follows:

> Act in such a way that you always treat humanity, whether in your own person or in the person of any other, never simply as a means but always at the same time as an end.

To understand this we need to know what it is to treat a person as a means or as an end. According to Kant, each of our acts reflects one or more *maxims.* The maxim of the act is the principle on which one sees oneself as acting. A maxim expresses a person's policy, or if he or she has no settled policy, the principle underlying the particular intention or decision on which he or she acts. Thus, a person who decides "This year I'll give 10 percent of my income to famine relief" has as a maxim the principle of tithing his or her income for famine relief. In practice, the difference between intentions and maxims is of little importance, for given any intention, we can formulate the corresponding maxim by deleting references to particular times, places, and persons. In what follows I shall take the terms 'maxim' and 'intention' as equivalent.

Whenever we act intentionally, we have at least one maxim and can, if we reflect, state what it is. (There is of course room for self-deception here—

Reprinted from *Matters of Life and Death,* ed. Tom Regan (Philadelphia: Temple University Press, 1980).

"I'm only keeping the wolf from the door" we may claim as we wolf down enough to keep ourselves overweight, or, more to the point, enough to feed someone else who hasn't enough food.)

When we want to work out whether an act we propose to do is right or wrong, according to Kant, we should look at our maxims and not at how much misery or happiness the act is likely to produce, and whether it does better at increasing happiness than other available acts. We just have to check that the act we have in mind will not use anyone as a mere means, and, if possible, that it will treat other persons as ends in themselves.

USING PERSONS AS MERE MEANS

To use someone as a *mere means* is to involve them in a scheme of action *to which they could not in principle consent.* Kant does not say that there is anything wrong about using someone as a means. Evidently we have to do so in any cooperative scheme of action. If I cash a check I use the teller as a means, without whom I could not lay my hands on the cash; the teller in turn uses me as a means to earn his or her living. But in this case, each party consents to her or his part in the transaction. Kant would say that though they use one another as means, they do not use one another as *mere* means. Each person assumes that the other has maxims of his or her own and is not just a thing or a prop to be manipulated.

But there are other situations where one person uses another in a way to which the other could not in principle consent. For example, one person may make a promise to another with every intention of breaking it. If the promise is accepted, then the person to whom it was given must be ignorant of what the promisor's intention (maxim) really is. If one knew that the promisor did not intend to do what he or she was promising, one would, after all, not accept or rely on the promise. It would be as though there had been no promise made. Successful false promising depends on deceiving the person to whom the promise is made about what one's real maxim is. And since the person who is deceived doesn't know that real maxim, he or she can't in principle consent to his or her part in the proposed scheme of action.

The person who is deceived is, as it were, a prop or a tool—a mere means—in the false promisor's scheme. A person who promises falsely treats the acceptor of the promise as a prop or a thing and not as a person. In Kant's view, it is this that makes false promising wrong.

One standard way of using others as mere means is by deceiving them. By getting someone involved in a business scheme or a criminal activity on false pretenses, or by giving a misleading account of what one is about, or by making a false promise or a fraudulent contract, one involves another in something to which he or she in principle cannot consent, since the scheme requires that he or she doesn't know what is going on. Another standard way of using others as mere means is by coercing them. If a rich or powerful person threatens a debtor with bankruptcy unless he or she joins in some scheme, then the creditor's intention is to coerce; and the debtor, if coerced, cannot consent to his or her part in the creditor's scheme. To make the example more specific: If a moneylender in an Indian village threatens not to renew a vital loan unless he is given the debtor's land, then he uses the debtor as a mere means. He coerces the debtor, who cannot truly consent to this "offer he can't refuse." (Of course the outward form of such transactions may look like ordinary commercial dealings, but we know very well that some offers and demands couched in that form are coercive.)

In Kant's view, acts that are done on maxims that require deception or coercion of others, and so cannot have the consent of those others (for consent precludes both deception and coercion), are wrong. When we act on such maxims, we treat others as mere means, as things rather than as ends in themselves. If we act on such maxims, our acts are not only wrong but unjust: such acts wrong the particular others who are deceived or coerced.

TREATING PERSONS AS ENDS
IN THEMSELVES

Duties of justice are, in Kant's view (as in many others'), the most important of our duties. When we fail in these duties, we have used some other or others as mere means. But there are also cases where, though we do not use others as mere means, still we fail to use them as ends in themselves in the fullest possible way. To treat someone as an end in him or herself requires in the first place that one not use him or her as mere means, that one respect each as a rational person with his or her own maxims. But beyond that, one may also seek to foster others' plans and maxims by sharing some of their ends. To act beneficently is to seek others' happiness, therefore to intend to achieve some of the things that those others aim at with their maxims. If I want to make others happy, I will adopt maxims that not merely do not manipulate them but that foster some of their plans and activities. Beneficent acts try to achieve what others want. However, we cannot seek everything that others want; their wants are too numerous and diverse, and, of course, sometimes incompatible. It follows that beneficence has to be selective.

There is then quite a sharp distinction between the requirements of justice and of beneficence in Kantian ethics. Justice requires that we act on *no* maxims that use others as mere means. Beneficence requires that we act on *some* maxims that foster others' ends, though it is a matter for judgment and discretion which of their ends we foster. Some maxims no doubt ought not to be fostered because it would be unjust to do so. Kantians are not committed to working inter-minably through a list of happiness-producing and misery-reducing acts; but there are some acts whose obligatoriness utilitarians may need to debate as they try to compare total outcomes of different choices, to which Kantians are stringently bound. Kantians will claim that they have done nothing wrong if none of their acts is unjust, and that their duty is complete if in addition their life plans have in the circumstances been reasonably beneficent.

In making sure that they meet all the demands of justice, Kantians do not try to compare all available acts and see which has the best effects. They consider only the proposals for action that occur to them and check that these proposals use no other as mere means. If they do not, the act is permissible; if omitting the act would use another as mere means, the act is obligatory. Kant's theory has less scope than utilitarianism. Kantians do not claim to discover whether acts whose maxims they don't know fully are just. They may be reluctant to judge others' acts or policies that cannot be regarded as the maxim of any person or institution. They cannot rank acts in order of merit. Yet, the theory offers more precision than utilitarianism when data are scarce. One can usually tell whether one's act would use others as mere means, even when its impact on human happiness is thoroughly obscure.

The Right and the Good

W. D. ROSS

W. D. Ross (1877–1971) was a philosopher for many years at Oxford University. He is remembered as a first-rate ethicist and scholar of Aristotle.

When a plain man fulfils a promise because he thinks he ought to do so, it seems clear that he does so with no thought of its total consequences, still less with any opinion that these are likely to be the best possible. He thinks in fact much more of the past than of the future. What makes him think it right to act in a

Reprinted from *The Right and the Good* (Oxford: Oxford University Press, 1930), by permission of the publisher.

certain way is the fact that he has promised to do so—that and, usually, nothing more. . . . It may be said that besides the duty of fulfilling promises I have and recognize a duty of relieving distress, and that when I think it right to do the latter at the cost of not doing the former, it is not because I think I shall produce more good thereby but because I think it the duty which is in the circumstances more of a duty. This account surely corresponds . . . closely with what we really think in such a situation. . . .

[Utilitarianism] . . . seems to simplify unduly our relations to our fellows. It says, in effect, that the only morally significant relation in which my neighbours stand to me is that of being possible beneficiaries by my action. They do stand in this relation to me, and this relation is morally significant. But they may also stand to me in the relation of promisee to promiser, of creditor to debtor, of wife to husband, of child to parent, of friend to friend, of fellow countryman to fellow countryman, and the like; and each of these relations is the foundation of a prima facie duty, which is more or less incumbent on me according to the circumstances of the case. When I am in a situation, as perhaps I always am, in which more than one of these prima facie duties is incumbent on me, what I have to do is to study the situation as fully as I can until I form the considered opinion (it is never more) that in the circumstances one of them is more incumbent than any other; then I am bound to think that to do this prima facie duty is my duty *sans phrase* in the situation.

I suggest "prima facie duty" or "conditional duty" as a brief way of referring to the characteristic (quite distinct from that of being a duty proper) which an act has, in virtue of being of a certain kind (e.g., the keeping of a promise), of being an act which would be a duty proper if it were not at the same time of another kind which is morally significant. Whether an act is a duty proper or actual duty depends on *all* the morally significant kinds it is an instance of. . . .

There is nothing arbitrary about these prima facie duties. Each rests on a definite circumstance which cannot seriously be held to be without moral significance. Of prima facie duties I suggest, without claiming completeness or finality for it, the following division.

(1) Some duties rest on previous acts of my own. These duties seem to include two kinds, (*a*) those resting on a promise or what may fairly be called an implicit promise, such as the implicit undertaking not to tell lies which seems to be implied in the act of entering into conversation (at any rate by civilized men), or of writing books that purport to be history and not fiction. These may be called the duties of fidelity, (*b*) Those resting on a previous wrongful act. These may be called the duties of reparation. (2) Some rest on previous acts of other men, i.e. services done by them to me. These may be loosely described as the duties of gratitude. (3) Some rest on the fact or possibility of a distribution of pleasure or happiness (or of the means thereto) which is not in accordance with the merit of the persons concerned; in such cases there arises a duty to upset or prevent such a distribution. These are the duties of justice. (4) Some rest on the mere fact that there are other beings in the world whose condition we can make better in respect of virtue, or of intelligence, or of pleasure. These are the duties of beneficence. (5) Some rest on the fact that we can improve our own condition in respect of virtue or of intelligence. These are the duties of self-improvement. (6) I think that we should distinguish from (4) the duties that may be summed up under the title of 'not injuring others'. No doubt to injure others is incidentally to fail to do them good; but it seems to me clear that non-maleficence is apprehended as a duty distinct from that of beneficence, and as a duty of a more stringent character. It will be noticed that this alone among the types of duty has been stated in a negative way. An attempt might no doubt be made to state this duty, like the others, in a positive way. It might be said that it is really the duty to prevent ourselves from acting either from an inclination to harm others or from an inclination to seek our own pleasure, in doing which we should incidentally harm them. But on reflection it seems clear that the primary duty here is the duty not to harm others, this being a duty whether or not we have an inclination that if followed would lead to our harming them; and that when we have such an inclination the primary duty not to harm others gives rise to a consequential duty to resist the inclination. The recognition of this duty of non-maleficence is the first step on

the way to the recognition of the duty of beneficence; and that accounts for the prominence of the commands "thou shalt not kill," "thou shalt not commit adultery," "thou shalt not steal," "thou shalt not bear false witness," in so early a code as the Decalogue. But even when we have come to recognize the duty of beneficence, it appears to me that the duty of non-maleficence is recognized as a distinct one, and as prima facie more binding. We should not in general consider it justifiable to kill one person in order to keep another alive or to steal from one in order to give alms to another. . . .

If the objection be made, that this catalogue of the main types of duty is an unsystematic one resting on no logical principle, it may be replied, first, that it makes no claim to being ultimate. It is a prima facie classification of the duties which reflection on our moral convictions seems actually to reveal. And if these convictions are, as I would claim that they are, of the nature of knowledge, and if I have not misstated them, the list will be a list of authentic conditional duties, correct as far as it goes though not necessarily complete. . . .

It may, again, be objected that our theory that there are these various and often conflicting types of prima facie duty leaves us with no principle upon which to discern what is our actual duty in particular circumstances. But . . . [w]hy should two sets of circumstances, or one set of circumstances, *not* possess different characteristics, any one of which makes a certain act our prima facie duty? When I ask what it is that makes me in certain cases sure that I have a prima facie duty to do so and so, I find that it lies in the fact that I have made a promise; when I ask the same question in another case, I find the answer lies in the fact that I have done a wrong. And if on reflection I find (as I think I do) that neither of these reasons is reducible to the other, I must not on any a priori ground assume that such a reduction is possible. . . .

In actual experience [prima facie duties] . . . are compounded together in highly complex ways. Thus, for example, the duty of obeying the laws of one's country arises partly (as Socrates contends in the *Crito*) from the duty of gratitude for the benefits one has received from it; partly from the implicit promise to obey which seems to be involved in permanent res-

idence in a country whose laws we know we are *expected* to obey, and still more clearly involved when we ourselves invoke the protection of its laws (this is the truth underlying the doctrine of the social contract); and partly (if we are fortunate in our country) from the fact that its laws are potent instruments for the general good.

Or again, the sense of a general obligation to bring about (so far as we can) a just apportionment of happiness to merit is often greatly reinforced by the fact that many of the existing injustices are due to a social and economic system which we have, not indeed created, but taken part in and assented to; the duty of justice is then reinforced by the duty of reparation.

It is necessary to say something by way of clearing up the relation between prima facie duties and the actual or absolute duty to do one particular act in particular circumstances. If, as almost all moralists except Kant are agreed, and as most plain men think, it is sometimes right to tell a lie or to break a promise, it must be maintained that there is a difference between prima facie duty and actual or absolute duty. When we think ourselves justified in breaking, and indeed morally obliged to break, a promise in order to relieve some one's distress, we do not for a moment cease to recognize a prima facie duty to keep our promise, and this leads us to feel, not indeed shame or repentance, but certainly compunction, for behaving as we do; we recognize, further, that it is our duty to make up somehow to the promisee for the breaking of the promise. We have to distinguish from the characteristic of being our duty that of tending to be our duty. Any act that we do contains various elements in virtue of which it falls under various categories. In virtue of being the breaking of a promise, for instance, it tends to be wrong; in virtue of being an instance of relieving distress it tends to be right. Tendency to be one's duty may be called a parti-resultant attribute, i.e. one which belongs to an act in virtue of some one component in its nature. *Being* one's duty is a toti-resultant attribute, one which belongs to an act in virtue of its whole nature and of nothing less than this. . . .

Something should be said of the relation between our apprehension of the prima facie rightness of certain types of act and our mental attitude towards particular acts. It is proper to use the word "apprehen-sion" in the former case and not in the latter. That an act, qua fulfilling a promise, or *qua* effecting a just distribution of good, or *qua* returning services ren-dered, or qua promoting the good of others, or qua promoting the virtue or insight of the agent, is prima facie right, is self-evident; not in the sense that it is evident from the beginning of our lives, or as soon as we attend to the proposition for the first time, but in the sense that when we have reached sufficient men-tal maturity and have given sufficient attention to the proposition it is evident without any need of proof, or of evidence beyond itself. It is self-evident just as a mathematical axiom, or the validity of a form of inference, is evident. The moral order expressed in these propositions is just as much part of the funda-mental nature of the universe (and, we may add, of any possible universe in which there were moral agents at all) as is the spatial or numerical structure expressed in the axioms of geometry or arithmetic. In our confidence that these propositions are true there is involved the same trust in our reason that is involved in our confidence in mathematics; and we should have no justification for trusting it in the latter sphere and distrusting it in the former. In both cases we are dealing with propositions that cannot be proved, but that just as certainly need no proof. . . .

Our judgements about our actual duty in concrete situations have none of the certainty that attaches to our recognition of the general principles of duty. A statement is certain, i.e. is an expression of knowl-edge, only in one or other of two cases: when it is either self-evident, or a valid conclusion from self-evident premises. And our judgments about our par-ticular duties have neither of these characters. (1) They are not self-evident. Where a possible act is seen to have two characteristics, in virtue of one of which it is prima facie right, and in virtue of the other prima facie wrong, we are (I think) well aware that we are not certain whether we ought or ought not to do it; that whether we do it or not, we are taking a moral risk. We come in the long run, after considera-tion, to think one duty more pressing than the other, but we do not feel certain that it is so. And though we do not always recognize that a possible act has two such characteristics, and though there *may* be cases

in which it has not, we are never certain that any par-ticular possible act has not, and therefore never cer-tain that is right, nor certain that it is wrong. For, to go no further in the analysis, it is enough to point out that any particular act will in all probability in the course of time contribute to the bringing about of good or of evil for many human beings, and thus have a prima facie rightness or wrongness of which we know nothing. (2) Again, our judgments about our particular duties are not logical conclusions from self-evident premises. The only possible premises would be the general principles stating their prima facie rightness or wrongness qua having the different characteristics they do have; and even if we could (as we cannot) apprehend the extent to which an act will tend on the one hand, for example, to bring about advantages for our benefactors, and on the other hand to bring about disadvantages for fellow men who are not our benefactors, there is no principle by which we can draw the conclusion that it is on the whole right or on the whole wrong. In this respect the judgement as to the rightness of a particular act is just like the judgement as to the beauty of a—particular natural object or work of art. A poem is, for instance, in respect of certain qualities beautiful and in respect of certain others not beautiful; and our judgement as to the degree of beauty it possesses on the whole is never reached by logical reasoning from the appre-hension of its particular beauties or particular defects. Both in this and in the moral case we have more or less probable opinions which are not logi-cally justified conclusions from the general princi-ples that are recognized as self-evident.

There is therefore much truth in the description of the right act as a fortunate act. If we cannot be certain that it is right, it is our good fortune if the act we do is the right act. This consideration does not, however, make the doing of our duty a mere matter of chance. There is a parallel here between the doing of duty and the doing of what will be to our personal advantage. We never *know* what act will in the long run be to our advantage. Yet it is certain that we are more likely in general to secure our advantage if we estimate to the best of our ability the probable tendencies of our actions in this respect, than if we act on caprice. And similarly we are more likely to do our duty if we reflect to the best of our ability on the prima facie rightness or wrongness of various possible acts in virtue of the characteristics we perceive them to have, than if we act without reflection. With this greater likelihood we must be content. . . .

In what has preceded, a good deal of use has been made of 'what we really think' about moral questions . . . It might be said that this is in principle wrong; that we should not be content to expound what our present moral consciousness tells us but should aim at a criticism of our existing moral consciousness in the light of theory. Now I do not doubt that the moral consciousness of men has in detail undergone a good deal of modification as regards the things we think right, at the hands of moral theory. But . . . we have to ask ourselves . . . whether we really *can* get rid of our view that promise-keeping has a bindingness independent of productiveness of maximum good. In my own experience I find that I cannot, in spite of a very genuine attempt to do so; and I venture to think that most people will find the same, and that just because they cannot lose the sense of special obligation, they cannot accept as self-evident, or even as true, the theory which would require them to do so. . . .

I would maintain, in fact, that what we are apt to describe as "what we think" about moral questions contains a considerable amount that we do not think but know, and that this forms the standard by reference to which the truth of any moral theory has to be tested, instead of having itself to be tested by reference to any theory. I hope that I have in what precedes indicated what in my view these elements of knowledge are that are involved in our ordinary moral consciousness.

It would be a mistake to found a natural science on "what we really think," i.e. on what reasonably thoughtful and well-educated people think about the subjects of the science before they have studied them scientifically. For such opinions are interpretations, and often misinterpretations, of sense-experience; and the man of science must appeal from these to sense-experience itself, which furnishes his real data. In ethics no such appeal is possible. We have no more direct way of access to the facts about rightness and goodness and about what things are right or good, than by thinking about them; the moral convictions of thoughtful and well-educated people are the data of ethics just as sense-perceptions are the data of a natural science. Just as some of the latter have to be rejected as illusory, so have some of the former; but as the latter are rejected only when they are in conflict with other more accurate sense-perceptions, the former are rejected only when they are in conflict with other convictions which stand better the test of reflection. The existing body of moral convictions of the best people is the cumulative product of the moral reflection of many generations, which has developed an extremely delicate power of appreciation of moral distinctions; and this the theorist cannot afford to treat with anything other than the greatest respect. The verdicts of the moral consciousness of the best people are the foundation on which he must build; though he must first compare them with one another and eliminate any contradictions they may contain.

The Challenge of Cultural Relativism

~

JAMES RACHELS

James Rachels is University Professor of Philosophy at the University of Alabama at Birmingham. His books include *The End of Life,* on euthanasia and morality, and *Created from Animals,* on Darwin's relevance to ethics. This selection is from *The Elements of Moral Philosophy.*

Morality differs in every society, and is a convenient term for socially approved habits.

—*Ruth Benedict,* Patterns Of Culture (1934)

1. HOW DIFFERENT CULTURES HAVE DIFFERENT MORAL CODES

Darius, a king of ancient Persia, was intrigued by the variety of cultures he encountered in his travels. He had found, for example, that the Callatians (a tribe of Indians) customarily ate the bodies of their dead fathers. The Greeks, of course, did not do that—the Greeks practiced cremation and regarded the funeral pyre as the natural and fitting way to dispose of the dead. Darius thought that a sophisticated understanding of the world must include an appreciation of such differences between cultures. One day, to teach this lesson, he summoned some Greeks who happened to be present at his court and asked them what they would take to eat the bodies of their dead fathers. They were shocked, as Darius knew they would be, and replied that no amount of money could persuade them to do such a thing. Then Darius called in some Callatians, and while the Greeks listened asked them what they would take to burn their dead fathers' bodies. The Callatians were horrified and told Darius not even to mention such a dreadful thing.

This story, recounted by Herodotus in his *History,* illustrates a recurring theme in the literature of social science: different cultures have different moral codes. What is thought right within one group may be utterly abhorrent to the members of another group, and vice versa. Should we eat the bodies of the dead or burn them? If you were a Greek, one answer would seem obviously correct; but if you were a Callatian, the opposite would seem equally certain.

It is easy to give additional examples of the same kind. Consider the Eskimos. They are a remote and inaccessible people. Numbering only about 25,000, they live in small, isolated settlements scattered mostly along the northern fringes of North America and Greenland. Until the beginning of the 20th century, the outside world knew little about them. Then explorers began to bring back strange tales.

Eskimo customs turned out to be very different from our own. The men often had more than one wife, and they would share their wives with guests, lending them for the night as a sign of hospitality. Moreover, within a community a dominant male might demand and get regular sexual access to other men's wives. The women however, were free to break these arrangements simply by leaving their husbands and taking up with new partners—free, that is, so long as their former husbands chose not to make trouble. All in all, the Eskimo practice was a volatile

From James Rachels, *Elements of Moral Philosophy, Fourth Edition* (New York: McGraw-Hill, 2002). Reprinted with permission of the McGraw-Hill Companies.

scheme that bore little resemblance to what we call marriage.

But it was not only their marriage and sexual practices that were different. The Eskimos also seemed to have less regard for human life. Infanticide, for example, was common. Knud Rasmussen, one of the most famous early explorers, reported that he met one woman who had borne 20 children but had killed 10 of them at birth. Female babies, he found, were especially liable to be destroyed, and this was permitted simply at the parents' discretion, with no social stigma attached to it. Old people also, when they became too feeble to contribute to the family, were left out in the snow to die. So there seemed to be, in this society, remarkably little respect for life.

To the general public, these were disturbing revelations. Our own way of living seems so natural and right that for many of us it is hard to conceive of others living so differently. And when we do hear of such things, we tend immediately to categorize the other peoples as "backward" or "primitive." But to anthropologists, there was nothing particularly surprising about the Eskimos. Since the time of Herodotus, enlightened observers have been accustomed to the idea that conceptions of right and wrong differ from culture to culture. If we assume that our ethical ideas will be shared by all peoples at all times, we are merely naive.

2. CULTURAL RELATIVISM

To many thinkers, this observation—"Different cultures have different moral codes"—has seemed to be the key to understanding morality. The idea of universal truth in ethics, they say, is a myth. The customs of different societies are all that exist. These customs cannot be said to be "correct" or "incorrect," for that implies we have an independent standard of right and wrong by which they may be judged. But there is no such independent standard; every standard is culture-bound. The great pioneering sociologist William Graham Sumner, writing in 1906, put it like this:

> The "right" way is the way which the ancestors used and which has been handed down. The tradition is its own warrant. It is not held subject to verification by

experience. The notion of right is in the folkways. It is not outside of them, of independent origin, and brought to test them. In the folkways, whatever is, is right. This is because they are traditional, and therefore contain in themselves the authority of the ancestral ghosts. When we come to the folkways we are at the end of our analysis.

This line of thought has probably persuaded more people to be skeptical about ethics than any other single thing. Cultural Relativism, as it has been called, challenges our ordinary belief in the objectivity and universality of moral truth. It says, in effect, that there is no such thing as universal truth in ethics; there are only the various cultural codes, and nothing more. Moreover, our own code has no special status; it is merely one among many. As we shall see, this basic idea is really a compound of several different thoughts. It is important to separate the various elements of the theory because, on analysis, some parts turn out to be correct, while others seem to be mistaken. As a beginning, we may distinguish the following claims, all of which have been made by cultural relativists:

1. Different societies have different moral codes.
2. The moral code of a society determines what is right within that society; that is, if the moral code of a society says that a certain action is right, then that action *is* right, at least within that society.
3. There is no objective standard that can be used to judge one society's code better than another's.
4. The moral code of our own society has no special status; it is merely one among many.
5. There is no "universal truth" in ethics; that is, there are no moral truths that hold for all peoples at all times.
6. It is mere arrogance for us to try to judge the conduct of other peoples. We should adopt an attitude of tolerance toward the practices of other cultures.

Although it may seem that these six propositions go naturally together, they are independent of one another, in the sense that some of them might be false even if others are true. In what follows, we will try to identify what is correct in Cultural Relativism, but we will also be concerned to expose what is mistaken about it.

3. THE CULTURAL DIFFERENCES ARGUMENT

Cultural Relativism is a theory about the nature of morality. At first blush it seems quite plausible. However, like all such theories, it may be evaluated by subjecting it to rational analysis; and when we analyze Cultural Relativism we find that it is not so plausible as it first appears to be.

The first thing we need to notice is that at the heart of Cultural Relativism there is a certain *form of argument*. The strategy used by cultural relativists is to argue from facts about the differences between cultural outlooks to a conclusion about the status of morality. Thus we are invited to accept this reasoning:

(1) The Greeks believed it was wrong to eat the dead, whereas the Callatians believed it was right to eat the dead.
(2) Therefore, eating the dead is neither objectively right nor objectively wrong. It is merely a matter of opinion that varies from culture to culture.

Or, alternatively:

(1) The Eskimos see nothing wrong with infanticide, whereas Americans believe infanticide is immoral.
(2) Therefore, infanticide is neither objectively right nor objectively wrong. It is merely a matter of opinion, which varies from culture to culture.

Clearly, these arguments are variations of one fundamental idea. They are both special cases of a more general argument, which says:

(1) Different cultures have different moral codes.
(2) Therefore, there is no objective "truth" in morality. Right and wrong are only matters of opinion, and opinions vary from culture to culture.

We may call this the Cultural Differences Argument. To many people, it is persuasive. But from a logical point of view, is it sound?

It is not sound. The trouble is that the conclusion does not follow from the premise—that is, even if the premise is true, the conclusion still might be false. The premise concerns what people *believe*—in some societies, people believe one thing; in other societies, people believe differently. The conclusion, however, concerns what *really is the case*. The trouble is that this sort of conclusion does not follow logically from this sort of premise.

Consider again the example of the Greeks and Callatians. The Greeks believed it was wrong to eat the dead; the Callatians believed it was right. Does it follow, *from the mere fact that they disagreed,* that there is no objective truth in the matter? No, it does not follow; for it could be that the practice was objectively right (or wrong) and that one or the other of them was simply mistaken.

To make the point clearer, consider a different matter. In some societies, people believe the earth is flat. In other societies, such as our own, people believe the earth is (roughly) spherical. Does it follow, from the mere fact that people disagree, that there is no "objective truth" in geography? Of course not; we would never draw such a conclusion because we realize that, in their beliefs about the world, the members of some societies might simply be wrong. There is no reason to think that if the world is round everyone must know it. Similarly, there is no reason to think that if there is moral truth everyone must know it. The fundamental mistake in the Cultural Differences Argument is that it attempts to derive a substantive conclusion about a subject from the mere fact that people disagree about it.

This is a simple point of logic, and it is important not to misunderstand it. We are not saying (not yet, anyway) that the conclusion of the argument is false. That is still an open question. The logical point is just that the conclusion does not *follow from* the premise. This is important, because in order to determine whether the conclusion is true, we need arguments in its support. Cultural Relativism proposes this argument, but unfortunately the argument turns out to be fallacious. So it proves nothing.

4. THE CONSEQUENCES OF TAKING CULTURAL RELATIVISM SERIOUSLY

Even if the Cultural Differences Argument is invalid, Cultural Relativism might still be true. What would it be like if it were true?

In the passage quoted above, William Graham Sumner summarizes the essence of Cultural Relativism. He says that there is no measure of right and wrong other than the standards of one's society: "The notion of right is in the folkways. It is not outside of them, of independent origin, and brought to test them. In the folkways, whatever is, is right." Suppose we took this seriously. What would be some of the consequences?

1. *We could no longer say that the customs of other societies are morally inferior to our own.* This, of course, is one of the main points stressed by Cultural Relativism. We would have to stop condemning other societies merely because they are "different." So long as we concentrate on certain examples, such as the funerary practices of the Greeks and Callatians, this may seem to be a sophisticated, enlightened attitude.

However, we would also be stopped from criticizing other, less benign practices. Suppose a society waged war on its neighbors for the purpose of taking slaves. Or suppose a society was violently anti-Semitic and its leaders set out to destroy the Jews. Cultural Relativism would preclude us from saying that either of these practices was wrong. (We would not even be able to say that a society tolerant of Jews is *better* than the anti-Semitic society, for that would imply some sort of transcultural standard of comparison.) The failure to condemn *these* practices does not seem enlightened; on the contrary, slavery and anti-Semitism seem wrong wherever they occur. Nevertheless, if we took Cultural Relativism seriously, we would have to regard these social practices as immune from criticism.

2. *We could decide whether actions are right or wrong just by consulting the standards of our society.* Cultural Relativism suggests a simple test for determining what is right and what is wrong: all one need do is ask whether the action is in accordance with the code of one's society. Suppose in 1975 a resident of

South Africa was wondering whether his country's policy of apartheid—a rigidly racist system—was morally correct. All he has to do is ask whether this policy conformed to his society's moral code. If it did, there would have been nothing to worry about, at least from a moral point of view.

This implication of Cultural Relativism is disturbing because few of us think that our society's code is perfect—we can think of all sorts of ways in which it might be improved. Yet Cultural Relativism not only forbids us from criticizing the codes of *other* societies; it also stops us from criticizing our own. After all, if right and wrong are relative to culture, this must be true for our own culture just as much as for other cultures.

3. *The idea of moral progress is called into doubt.* Usually, we think that at least some social changes are for the better. (Although, of course, other changes may be for the worse.) Throughout most of Western history the place of women in society was narrowly circumscribed. They could not own property; they could not vote or hold political office; and generally they were under the almost absolute control of their husbands. Recently much of this has changed, and most people think of it as progress.

But if Cultural Relativism is correct, can we legitimately think of this as progress? Progress means replacing a way of doing things with a better way. But by what standard do we judge the new ways as better? If the old ways were in accordance with the social standards of their time, then Cultural Relativism would say it is a mistake to judge them by the standards of a different time. Eighteenth-century society was a different society from the one we have now. To say that we have made progress implies a judgment that present-day society is better, and that is just the sort of transcultural judgment that, according to Cultural Relativism, is impossible.

Our idea of social *reform* will also have to be reconsidered. Reformers such as Martin Luther King, Jr., have sought to change their societies for the better. Within the constraints imposed by Cultural Relativism, there is one way this might be done. If a society is not living up to its own ideals, the reformer may be regarded as acting for the best; the ideals of the society are the standard by which we judge his or her proposals as worthwhile. But no one may challenge the ideals themselves, for those ideals are by definition correct. According to Cultural Relativism, then, the idea of social reform makes sense only in this limited way.

These three consequences of Cultural Relativism have led many thinkers to reject it as implausible on its face. It does make sense, they say, to condemn some practices, such as slavery and anti-Semitism, wherever they occur. It makes sense to think that our own society has make some moral progress, while admitting that it is still imperfect and in need of reform. Because Cultural Relativism says that these judgments make no sense, the argument goes, it cannot be right.

5.   WHY THERE IS LESS DISAGREEMENT THAN IT SEEMS

The original impetus for Cultural Relativism comes from the observation that cultures differ dramatically in their views of right and wrong. But just how much do they differ? It is true that there are differences. However, it is easy to overestimate the extent of those differences. Often, when we examine what seems to be a dramatic difference, we find that the cultures do not differ nearly as much as it appears.

Consider a culture in which people believe it is wrong to eat cows. This may even be a poor culture, in which there is not enough food; still, the cows are not to be touched. Such a society would appear to have values very different from our own. But does it? We have not yet asked *why* these people will not eat cows. Suppose it is because they believe that after death the souls of humans inhabit the bodies of animals, especially cows, so that a cow may be someone's grandmother. Now shall we say that their values are different from ours? No; the difference lies elsewhere. The difference is in our belief systems, not in our values. We agree that we shouldn't eat Grandma; we simply disagree about whether the cow is (or could be) Grandma.

The point is that many factors work together to produce the customs of a society. The society's values are only one of them. Other matters, such as the religious and factual beliefs held by its members, and the physical circumstances in which they must live, are also important. We cannot conclude, then, merely because customs differ, that there is a disagreement about values. The difference in customs may be attributable to some other aspect of social life. Thus there may be less disagreement about values than there appears to be.

Consider again the Eskimos, who often kill perfectly normal infants, especially girls. We do not approve of such things; in our society, a parent who killed a baby would be locked up. Thus there appears to be a great difference in the values of our two cultures. But suppose we ask why the Eskimos do this. The explanation is not that they have less affection for their children or less respect for human life. An Eskimo family will always protect its babies if conditions permit. But they live in a harsh environment, where food is in short supply. A fundamental postulate of Eskimo thought is: "Life is hard, and the margin of safety small." A family may want to nourish its babies but be unable to do so.

As in many "primitive" societies, Eskimo mothers will nurse their infants over a much longer period of time than mothers in our culture. The child will take nourishment from its mother's breast for four years, perhaps even longer. So even in the best of times there are limits to the number of infants that one mother can sustain. Moreover, the Eskimos are a nomadic people—unable to farm, they must move about in search of food. Infants must be carried, and a mother can carry only one baby in her parka as she travels and goes about her outdoor work. Other family members help however they can.

Infant girls are more readily disposed of because, first, in this society the males are the primary food providers—they are the hunters, following the traditional division of labor—and it is obviously important to maintain a sufficient number of food providers. But there is an important second reason as well. Because the hunters suffer a high casualty rate, the adult men who die prematurely far outnumber the women who die early. Thus if male and female infants survived in equal numbers, the female adult population would greatly outnumber the male adult population. Examining the available statistics, one writer concluded that "were it not for female infanticide . . . there would be approximately one-and-a-half times as many females in the average Eskimo local group as there are food-producing males."

So among the Eskimos, infanticide does not signal a fundamentally different attitude toward children. Instead, it is a recognition that drastic measures are sometimes needed to ensure the family's survival. Even then, however, killing the baby is not the first option considered. Adoption is common; childless couples are especially happy to take a more fertile couple's "surplus." Killing is only the last resort. I emphasize this in order to show that the raw data of the anthropologists can be misleading; it can make the differences in values between cultures appear greater than they are. The Eskimos' values are not all that different from our values. It is only that life forces upon them choices that we do not have to make.

6. HOW ALL CULTURES HAVE SOME VALUES IN COMMON

It should not be surprising that, despite appearances, the Eskimos are protective of their children. How could it be otherwise? How could a group survive that did not value its young? It is easy to see that, in fact, all cultural groups must protect their infants. Babies are helpless and cannot survive if they are not given extensive care for a period of years. Therefore, if a group did not care for its young, the young would not survive, and the older members of the group would not be replaced. After a while the group would die out. This means that any cultural group that continues to exist must care for its young. Infants that are not cared for must be the exception rather than the rule.

Similar reasoning shows that other values must be more or less universal. Imagine what it would be like for a society to place no value at all on truth telling. When one person spoke to another, there would be no presumption that she was telling the truth, for she could just as easily be speaking falsely. Within that society, there would be no reason to pay attention to what anyone says. (I ask you what time it is, and you

say "Four o'clock." But there is no presumption that you are speaking truly; you could just as easily have said the first thing that came into your head. So I have no reason to pay attention to your answer. In fact, there was no point in my asking you in the first place.) Communication would then be extremely difficult, if not impossible. And because complex societies cannot exist without communication among their members, society would become impossible. It follows that in any complex society there must be a presumption in favor of truthfulness. There may of course be exceptions to this rule: there may be situations in which it is thought to be permissible to lie. Nevertheless, these will be exceptions to a rule that *is* in force in the society.

Here is one further example of the same type. Could a society exist in which there was no prohibition on murder? What would this be like? Suppose people were free to kill other people at will, and no one thought there was anything wrong with it. In such a "society," no one could feel safe. Everyone would have to be constantly on guard. People who wanted to survive would have to avoid other people as much as possible. This would inevitably result in individuals trying to become as self-sufficient as possible—after all, associating with others would be dangerous. Society on any large scale would collapse. Of course, people might band together in smaller groups with others that they could trust not to harm them. But notice what this means: they would be forming smaller societies that did acknowledge a rule against murder. The prohibition of murder, then, is a necessary feature of all societies.

There is a general theoretical point here, namely, that *there are some moral rules that all societies must have in common, because those rules are necessary for society to exist.* The rules against lying and murder are two examples. And in fact, we do find these rules in force in all viable cultures. Cultures may differ in what they regard as legitimate exceptions to the rules, but this disagreement exists against a background of agreement on the larger issues. Therefore, it is a mistake to over-estimate the amount of difference between cultures. Not every moral rule can vary from society to society.

7. JUDGING A CULTURAL PRACTICE TO BE UNDESIRABLE

In 1996, a 17-year-old girl named Fauziya Kassindja arrived at Newark International Airport and asked for asylum. She had fled her native country of Togo, a small west African nation, to escape what people there call "excision." Excision is a permanently disfiguring procedure that is sometimes called "female circumcision," although it bears little resemblance to the Jewish practice. More commonly, at least in Western newspapers, it is referred to as "female genital mutilation."

According to the World Health Organization, the practice is widespread in 26 African nations, and two million girls each year are "excised." In some instances, excision is part of an elaborate tribal ritual, performed in small traditional villages, and girls look forward to it because it signals their acceptance into the adult world. In other instances, the practice is carried out by families living in cities on young women who desperately resist.

Fauziya Kassindja was the youngest of five daughters in a devoutly Muslim family. Her father, who owned a successful trucking business, was opposed to excision, and he was able to defy the tradition because of his wealth. His first four daughters were married without being mutilated. But when Fauziya was 16, he suddenly died. Fauziya then came under the authority of his father, who arranged a marriage for her and prepared to have her excised. Fauziya was terrified, and her mother and oldest sister helped her to escape. Her mother, left without resources, eventually had to formally apologize and submit to the authority of the patriarch she had offended.

Meanwhile, in America, Fauziya was imprisoned for two years while the authorities decided what to do with her. She was finally granted asylum, but not before she became the center of a controversy about how foreigners should regard the cultural practices of other peoples. A series of articles in the *New York Times* encouraged the idea that excision is a barbaric practice that should be condemned. Other observers were reluctant to be so judgmental—live and let live, they said; after all, our culture probably seems just as strange to them.

Suppose we are inclined to say that excision is bad. Would we merely be imposing the standards of our own culture? If Cultural Relativism is correct, that is all we can do, for there is no culture-neutral moral standard to which we may appeal. But is that true?

Is There a Culture-Neutral Standard of Right and Wrong?

There is, of course, a lot that can be said against excision. Excision is painful and it results in the permanent loss of sexual pleasure. Its short-term effects include hemorrhage, tetanus, and septicemia. Sometimes the woman dies. Long-term effects include chronic infection, scars that hinder walking, and continuing pain.

Why, then, has it become a widespread social practice? It is not easy to say. Excision has no apparent social benefits. Unlike Eskimo infanticide, it is not necessary for the group's survival. Nor is it a matter of religion. Excision is practiced by groups with various religions, including Islam and Christianity, neither of which commend it.

Nevertheless, a number of reasons are given in its defense. Women who are incapable of sexual pleasure are said to be less likely to be promiscuous; thus there will be fewer unwanted pregnancies in unmarried women. Moreover, wives for whom sex is only a duty are less likely to be unfaithful to their husbands; and because they will not be thinking about sex, they will be more attentive to the needs of their husbands and children. Husbands, for their part, are said to enjoy sex more with wives who have been excised. (The women's own lack of enjoyment is said to be unimportant.) Men will not want unexcised women, as they are unclean and immature. And above all, it has been done since antiquity, and we may not change the ancient ways.

It would be easy, and perhaps a bit arrogant, to ridicule these arguments. But we may notice an important feature of this whole line of reasoning: it attempts to justify excision by showing that excision is beneficial—men, women, and their families are said to be better off when women are excised. Thus we might approach this reasoning, and excision itself, by asking whether this is true: is excision, on the whole, helpful or harmful?

In fact, this is a standard that might reasonably be used in thinking about any social practice whatever: we may ask *whether the practice promotes or hinders the welfare of the people whose lives are affected by it.* And, as a corollary, we may ask if there is an alternative set of social arrangements that would do a better job of promoting their welfare. If so, we may conclude that the existing practice is deficient.

But this looks like just the sort of independent moral standard that Cultural Relativism says cannot exist. It is a single standard that may be brought to bear in judging the practices of any culture, at any time, including our own. Of course, people will not usually see this principle as being "brought in from the outside" to judge them, because, like the rules against lying and homicide, the welfare of its members is a value internal to all viable cultures.

Why, Despite All This, Thoughtful People May Nevertheless Be Reluctant to Criticize Other Cultures

Although they are personally horrified by excision, many thoughtful people are reluctant to say it is wrong, for at least three reasons.

First, there is an understandable nervousness about "interfering in the social customs of other peoples." Europeans and their cultural descendents in America have a shabby history of destroying native cultures in the name of Christianity and Enlightenment. Recoiling from this record, some people refuse to make any negative judgments about other cultures, especially cultures that resemble those that have been wronged in the past. We should notice, however, that there is a difference between (a) judging a cultural practice to be deficient, and (b) thinking that we should announce the fact, conduct a campaign, apply diplomatic pressure, or send in the army. The first is just a matter of trying to see the world clearly, from a moral point of view. The second is another matter altogether. Sometimes it may be right to "do something about it," but often it will not be.

People also feel, rightly enough, that they should be tolerant of other cultures. Tolerance is, no doubt, a virtue—a tolerant person is willing to live in peaceful cooperation with those who see things differently. But there is nothing in the nature of tolerance that requires you to say that all beliefs, all religions, and all social practices are equally admirable. On the contrary, if you did not think that some were better than others, there would be nothing for you to tolerate.

Finally, people may be reluctant to judge because they do not want to express contempt for the society being criticized. But again, this is misguided: to condemn a particular practice is not to say that the culture is on the whole contemptible or that it is generally inferior to any other culture, including one's own. It could have many admirable features. In fact, we should expect this to be true of most human societies—they are mixes of good and bad practices. Excision happens to be one of the bad ones.

8. WHAT CAN BE LEARNED FROM CULTURAL RELATIVISM

At the outset, I said that we were going to identify both what is right and what is wrong in Cultural Relativism. But I have dwelled on its mistakes: I have said that it rests on an invalid argument, that it has consequences that make it implausible on its face, and that the extent of moral disagreement is far less than it implies. This all adds up to a pretty thorough repudiation of the theory. Nevertheless, it is still a very appealing idea, and the reader may have the feeling that all this is a little unfair. The theory must have something going for it, or else why has it been so influential? In fact, I think there is something right about Cultural Relativism, and now I want to say what that is. There are two lessons we should learn from the theory, even if we ultimately reject it.

First, Cultural Relativism warns us, quite rightly, about the danger of assuming that all our preferences are based on some absolute rational standard. They are not. Many (but not all) of our practices are merely peculiar to our society, and it is easy to lose sight of that fact. In reminding us of it, the theory does a service.

Funerary practices are one example. The Callatians, according to Herodotus, were "men who eat their fathers"—a shocking idea, to us at least. But eating the flesh of the dead could be understood as a sign of respect. It could be taken as a symbolic act that says: we wish this person's spirit to dwell within us. Perhaps this was the understanding of the Callatians. On such a way of thinking, burying the dead could be seen as an act of rejection, and burning the corpse as positively scornful. If this is hard to imagine, then we may need to have our imaginations stretched. Of course we may feel a visceral repugnance at the idea of eating human flesh in any circumstances. But what of it? This repugnance may be, as the relativists say, only a matter of what is customary in our particular society.

There are many other matters that we tend to think of in terms of objective right and wrong that are really nothing more than social conventions. We could make a long list. Should women cover their breasts? A publicly exposed breast is scandalous in our society, whereas in other cultures it is unremarkable. Objectively speaking, it is neither right nor wrong—there is no objective reason why either custom is better. Cultural Relativism begins with the valuable insight that many of our practices are like this; they are only cultural products. Then it goes wrong by inferring that, because some practices are like this, all must be.

The second lesson has to do with keeping an open mind. In the course of growing up, each of us has acquired some strong feelings: we have learned to think of some types of conduct as acceptable, and others we have learned to reject. Occasionally, we may find those feelings challenged. For example, we may have been taught that homosexuality is immoral, and we may feel quite uncomfortable around gay people and see them as alien and "different." Now someone suggests that this may be a mere prejudice; that there is nothing evil about homosexuality; that gay people are just people, like anyone else, who happen, through no choice of their own, to be attracted to others of the same sex. But because we feel so strongly about the matter, we may find it hard to take this seriously. Even after we listen to the arguments, we may still have the unshakable feeling that homosexuals must, somehow, be an unsavory lot.

Cultural Relativism, by stressing that our moral views can reflect the prejudices of our society, provides an antidote for this kind of dogmatism. When he tells the story of the Greeks and Callatians, Herodotus adds:

> For if anyone, no matter who, were given the opportunity of choosing from amongst all the nations of the world the set of beliefs which he thought best, he would inevitably, after careful consideration of their relative merits, choose that of his own country. Everyone without exception believes his own native customs, and the religion he was brought up in, to be the best.

Realizing this can result in our having more open minds. We can come to understand that our feelings are not necessarily perceptions of the truth—they may be nothing more than the result of cultural conditioning. Thus when we hear it suggested that some element of our social code is *not* really the best, and we find ourselves instinctively resisting the suggestion, we might stop and remember this. Then we may be more open to discovering the truth, whatever that might be.

We can understand the appeal of Cultural Relativism, then, even though the theory has serious shortcomings. It is an attractive theory because it is based on a genuine insight, that many of the practices and attitudes we think so natural are really only cultural products. Moreover, keeping this thought firmly in view is important if we want to avoid arrogance and have open minds. These are important points, not to be taken lightly. But we can accept these points without going on to accept the whole theory.

Egoism and Moral Scepticism

~

JAMES RACHELS

James Rachels is University Professor of Philosophy at the University of Alabama at Birmingham.

1. Our ordinary thinking about morality is full of assumptions that we almost never question. We assume, for example, that we have an obligation to consider the welfare of other people when we decide what actions to perform or what rules to obey; we think that we must refrain from acting in ways harmful to others, and that we must respect their rights and interests as well as our own. We also assume that people are in fact capable of being motivated by such considerations, that is, that people are not wholly selfish and that they do sometimes act in the interests of others.

Both of these assumptions have come under attack by moral sceptics, as long ago as by Glaucon in Book II of Plato's *Republic.* Glaucon recalls the legend of Gyges, a shepherd who was said to have found a magic ring in a fissure opened by an earthquake. The ring would make its wearer invisible and thus would enable him to go anywhere and do anything undetected. Gyges used the power of the ring to gain entry to the Royal Palace where he seduced the Queen, murdered the King, and subsequently seized the throne. Now Glaucon asks us to imagine that there are two such rings, one given to a man of virtue and one given to a rogue. The rogue, of course, will use his ring unscrupulously and do anything necessary to increase his own wealth and power. He will recognize no moral constraints on his conduct, and, since the cloak of invisibility will protect him from discovery, he can do anything he pleases without fear of reprisal. So, there will be no end to the mischief he will do. But how will the so called virtuous man behave? Glaucon suggests that he will behave no better than the rogue: "No one, it is commonly believed, would have such iron strength of mind as to stand fast in doing right or keep his hands off other men's goods, when he could go to the market-place and fearlessly help himself to anything he wanted, enter houses and sleep with any woman he chose, set prisoners free and kill men at his pleasure, and in a word go about among men with the powers of a god. He would behave no better than the other; both would take the same course."[1] Moreover, why shouldn't he? Once he is freed from the fear of reprisal, why shouldn't a man simply do what he pleases, or what he thinks is best for himself? What reason is there for him to continue being "moral" when it is clearly not to his own advantage to do so?

These sceptical views suggested by Glaucon have come to be known as *psychological egoism* and *ethical egoism* respectively. Psychological egoism is the view that all men are selfish in everything that they do, that is, that the only motive from which anyone ever acts is self-interest. On this view, even when men are acting in ways apparently calculated to benefit others, they are actually motivated by the belief that acting in this way is to their own advantage, and if they did not believe this, they would not be doing that action. Ethical egoism is, by contrast, a normative view about how men *ought* to act. It is the view

From *A New Introduction to Philosophy* (New York: Harper & Row, 1971), ed. Steven M. Cahn. Reprinted by permission of Steven M. Cahn.

that, regardless of how men do in fact behave, they have no obligation to do anything except what is in their own interests. According to the ethical egoist, a person is always justified in doing whatever is in his own interests, regardless of the effect on others.

Clearly, if either of these views is correct, then "the moral institution of life" (to use Butler's well-turned phrase) is very different than what we normally think. The majority of mankind is grossly deceived about what is, or ought to be, the case, where morals are concerned.

2. Psychological egoism seems to fly in the face of the facts. We are tempted to say: "Of course people act unselfishly all the time. For example, Smith gives up a trip to the country, which he would have enjoyed very much, in order to stay behind and help a friend with his studies, which is a miserable way to pass the time. This is a perfectly clear case of unselfish behavior, and if the psychological egoist thinks that such cases do not occur, then he is just mistaken." Given such obvious instances of "unselfish behavior," what reply can the egoist make? There are two general arguments by which he might try to show that all actions, including those such as the one just outlined, are in fact motivated by self-interest. Let us examine these in turn:

A. The first argument goes as follows. If we describe one person's action as selfish, and another person's action as unselfish, we are overlooking the crucial fact that in both cases, assuming that the action is done voluntarily, *the agent is merely doing what he most wants to do.* If Smith stays behind to help his friend, that only shows that he wanted to help his friend more than he wanted to go to the country. And why should he be praised for his "unselfishness" when he is only doing what he most wants to do? So, since Smith is only doing what he wants to do, he cannot be said to be acting unselfishly.

This argument is so bad that it would not deserve to be taken seriously except for the fact that so many otherwise intelligent people have been taken in by it. First, the argument rests on the premise that people never voluntarily do anything except what they want to do. But this is patently false; there are at least two classes of actions that are exceptions to this generalization. One is the set of actions which we may not want to do, but which we do anyway as a means to an end which we want to achieve; for example, going to the dentist in order to stop a toothache, or going to work every day in order to be able to draw our pay at the end of the month. These cases may be regarded as consistent with the spirit of the egoist argument, however, since the ends mentioned are wanted by the agent. But the other set of actions are those which we do, not because we want to, nor even because there is an end which we want to achieve, but because we feel ourselves *under an obligation* to do them. For example, someone may do something because he has promised to do it, and thus feels obligated, even though he does not want to do it. It is sometimes suggested that in such cases we do the action because, after all, we want to keep our promises; so, even here, we are doing what we want. However, this dodge will not work: if I have promised to do something, and if I do not want to do it, then it is simply false to say that I want to keep my promise. In such cases we feel a conflict precisely because we do *not* want to do what we feel obligated to do. It is reasonable to think that Smith's action falls roughly into this second category: he might stay behind, not because he wants to, but because he feels that his friend needs help.

But suppose we were to concede, for the sake of the argument, that all voluntary action is motivated by the agent's wants, or at least that Smith is so motivated. Even if this were granted, it would not follow that Smith is acting selfishly or from self-interest. For if Smith wants to do something that will help his friend, even when it means forgoing his own enjoyments, that is precisely what makes him *un*selfish. What else could unselfishness be, if not wanting to help others? Another way to put the same point is to say that it is the *object* of a want that determines whether it is selfish or not. The mere fact that I am acting on *my* wants does not mean that I am acting selfishly; that depends on *what it is* that I want. If I want only my own good, and care nothing for others, then I am selfish; but if I also want other people to be well-off and happy, and if I act on *that* desire, then my action is not selfish. So much for this argument.

B. The second argument for psychological egoism is this. Since so-called unselfish actions always produce a sense of self-satisfaction in the agent,[2] and since this sense of satisfaction is a pleasant state of consciousness, it follows that the point of the action is really to achieve a pleasant state of consciousness, rather than to bring about any good for others. Therefore, the action is "unselfish" only at a superficial level of analysis. Smith will feel much better with himself for having stayed to help his friend—if he had gone to the country, he would have felt terrible about it—and that is the real point of the action. According to a well-known story, this argument was once expressed by Abraham Lincoln:

> Mr. Lincoln once remarked to a fellow-passenger on an old-time mud-coach that all men were prompted by selfishness in doing good. His fellow-passenger was antagonizing this position when they were passing over a corduroy bridge that spanned a slough. As they crossed this bridge they espied an old razor-backed sow on the bank making a terrible noise because her pigs had got into the slough and were in danger of drowning. As the old coach began to climb the hill, Mr. Lincoln called out, "Driver, can't you stop just a moment?" Then Mr. Lincoln jumped out, ran back, and lifted the little pigs out of the mud and water and placed them on the bank. When he returned, his companion remarked: "Now, Abe, where does selfishness come in on this little episode?" "Why, bless your soul, Ed, that was the very essence of selfishness. I should have had no peace of mind all day had I gone on and left that suffering old sow worrying over those pigs. I did it to get peace of mind, don't you see?"[3]

This argument suffers from defects similar to the previous one. Why should we think that merely because someone derives satisfaction from helping others this makes him selfish? Isn't the unselfish man precisely the one who *does* derive satisfaction from helping others, while the selfish man does not? If Lincoln "got peace of mind" from rescuing the piglets, does this show him to be selfish, or, on the contrary, doesn't it show him to be compassionate and good-hearted? (If a man were truly selfish, why should it bother his conscience that *others* suffer—much less pigs?) Similarly, it is nothing more than shabby sophistry to say, because Smith takes satisfaction in helping his friend, that he is behaving self-

ishly. If we say this rapidly, while thinking about something else, perhaps it will sound all right; but if we speak slowly, and pay attention to what we are saying, it sounds plain silly.

Moreover, suppose we ask *why* Smith derives satisfaction from helping his friend. The answer will be, it is because Smith cares for him and wants him to succeed. If Smith did not have these concerns, then he would take no pleasure in assisting him; and these concerns, as we have already seen, are the marks of unselfishness, not selfishness. To put the point more generally: if we have a positive attitude toward the attainment of some goal, then we may derive satisfaction from attaining that goal. But the *object* of our attitude is *the attainment of that goal;* and we must want to attain the goal *before* we can find any satisfaction in it. We do not, in other words, desire some sort of "pleasurable consciousness" and then try to figure out how to achieve it; rather, we desire all sorts of different things—money, a new fishing-boat, to be a better chess-player, to get a promotion in our work, etc.—and because we desire these things, we derive satisfaction from attaining them. And so, if someone desires the welfare and happiness of another person, he will derive satisfaction from that; but this does not mean that this satisfaction is the object of his desire, or that he is in any way selfish on account of it.

It is a measure of the weakness of psychological egoism that these insupportable arguments are the ones most often advanced in its favor. Why, then, should anyone ever have thought it a true view? Perhaps because of a desire for theoretical simplicity: In thinking about human conduct, it would be nice if there were some simple formula that would unite the diverse phenomena of human behavior under a single explanatory principle, just as simple formulae in physics bring together a great many apparently different phenomena. And since it is obvious that self-regard is an overwhelmingly important factor in motivation, it is only natural to wonder whether all motivation might not be explained in these terms. But the answer is clearly No; while a great many human actions are motivated entirely or in part by self-interest, only by a deliberate distortion of the facts can we say that all conduct is so motivated. This will be clear, I think, if we correct three confusions which are common-place. The exposure of these confusions will remove the last traces of plausibility from the psychological egoist thesis.

The first is the confusion of selfishness with self-interest. The two are clearly not the same. If I see a physician when I am feeling poorly, I am acting in my own interest but no one would think of calling me "selfish" on account of it. Similarly, brushing my teeth, working hard at my job, and obeying the law are all in my self-interest but none of these are examples of selfish conduct. This is because selfish behavior is behavior that ignores the interests of others, in circumstances in which their interests ought not to be ignored. This concept has a definite evaluative flavor; to call someone "selfish" is not just to describe his action but to condemn it. Thus, you would not call me selfish for eating a normal meal in normal circumstances (although it may surely be in my self-interest); but you would call me selfish for hoarding food while others about are starving.

The second confusion is the assumption that every action is done *either* from self-interest or from other-regarding motives. Thus, the egoist concludes that if there is no such thing as genuine altruism then all actions must be done from self-interest. But this is certainly a false dichotomy. The man who continues to smoke cigarettes, even after learning about the connection between smoking and cancer, is surely not acting from self-interest, not even by his own standards—self-interest would dictate that he quit smoking at once—and he is not acting altruistically either. He *is,* no doubt, smoking for the pleasure of it, but all that this shows is that undisciplined pleasure-seeking and acting from self-interest are very different. This is what led Butler to remark that "The thing to be lamented is, not that men have so great regard to their own good or interest in the present world, for they have not enough."[4]

The last two paragraphs show (*a*) that it is false that all actions are selfish, and (*b*) that it is false that all actions are done out of self-interest. And it should be noted that these two points can be made, and were, without any appeal to putative examples of altruism.

The third confusion is the common but false assumption that a concern for one's own welfare is incompatible with any genuine concern for the welfare of others. Thus, since it is obvious that everyone (or very nearly everyone) does desire his own well-being, it might be thought that no one can really be concerned with others. But again, this is false. There is no inconsistency in desiring that everyone, including oneself *and* others, be well-off and happy. To be sure, it may happen on occasion that our own interests conflict with the interests of others, and in these cases we will have to make hard choices. But even in these cases we might sometimes opt for the interests of others, especially when the others involved are our family or friends. But more importantly, not all cases are like this: sometimes we are able to promote the welfare of others when our own interests are not involved at all. In these cases not even the strongest self-regard need prevent us from acting considerately toward others.

Once these confusions are cleared away, it seems to me obvious enough that there is no reason whatever to accept psychological egoism. On the contrary, if we simply observe people's behavior with an open mind, we may find that a great deal of it is motivated by self-regard, but by no means all of it; and that there is no reason to deny that "the moral institution of life" can include a place for the virtue of beneficence.[5]

3. The ethical egoist would say at this point, "Of course it is possible for people to act altruistically, and perhaps many people do act that way—but there is no reason why they *should* do so. A person is under no obligation to do anything except what is in his own interests."[6] This is really quite a radical doctrine. Suppose I have an urge to set fire to some public building (say, a department store) just for the fascination of watching the spectacular blaze: according to this view, the fact that several people might be burned to death provides no reason whatever why I should not do it. After all, this only concerns *their* welfare, not my own, and according to the ethical egoist the only person I need think of is myself.

Some might deny that ethical egoism has any such monstrous consequences. They would point out that it is really to my own advantage not to set the fire—for, if I do that I may be caught and put into prison (unlike Gyges, I have no magic ring for protection). Moreover, even if I could avoid being caught it is still to my advantage to respect the rights and interests of others, for it is to my advantage to live in a society in which people's rights and interests are respected. Only in such a society can I live a happy and secure life; so, in acting kindly toward others, I would merely be doing my part to create and maintain the sort of society which it is to my advantage to have.[7] Therefore, it is said, the egoist would not be such a bad man; he would be as kindly and considerate as anyone else, because he would see that it is to his own advantage to be kindly and considerate.

This is a seductive line of thought, but it seems to me mistaken. Certainly it is to everyone's advantage (including the egoist's) to preserve a stable society where people's interests are generally protected. But there is no reason for the egoist to think that merely because *he* will not honor the rules of the social game, decent society will collapse. For the vast majority of people are not egoists, and there is no reason to think that they will be converted by his example—especially if he is discreet and does not unduly flaunt his style of life. What this line of reasoning shows is not that the egoist himself must act benevolently, but that he must encourage *others* to do so. He must take care to conceal from public view his own self-centered method of decision-making, and urge others to act on precepts very different from those on which he is willing to act.

The rational egoist, then, cannot advocate that egoism be universally adopted by everyone. For he wants a world in which his own interests are maximized; and if other people adopted the egoistic policy of pursuing their own interests to the exclusion of his interests, as he pursues his interests to the exclusion of theirs, then such a world would be impossible. So he himself will be an egoist, but he will want others to be altruists.

This brings us to what is perhaps the most popular "refutation" of ethical egoism current among philosophical writers—the argument that ethical egoism is at bottom inconsistent because it cannot be universalized.[8] The argument goes like this:

To say that any action or policy of action is *right* (or that it *ought* to be adopted) entails that it is right for *anyone* in the same sort of circumstances. I cannot, for example, say that it is right for me to lie to you, and yet object when you lie to me (provided, of course, that the circumstances are the same). I cannot hold that it is all right for me to drink your beer and then complain when you drink mine. This is just the requirement that we be consistent in our evaluations; it is a requirement of logic. Now it is said that ethical egoism cannot meet this requirement because, as we have already seen, the egoist would not want others to act in the same way that he acts. Moreover, suppose he *did* advocate the universal adoption of egoistic policies: he would be saying to Peter, "You ought to pursue your own interests even if it means destroying Paul"; and he would be saying to Paul, "You ought to pursue your own interests even if it means destroying Peter." The attitudes expressed in these two recommendations seem clearly inconsistent—he is urging the advancement of Peter's interest at one moment, and countenancing their defeat at the next. Therefore, the argument goes, there is no way to maintain the doctrine of ethical egoism as a consistent view about how we ought to act. We will fall into inconsistency whenever we try.

What are we to make of this argument? Are we to conclude that ethical egoism has been refuted? Such a conclusion, I think, would be unwarranted; for I think that we can show, contrary to this argument, how ethical egoism can be maintained consistently. We need only to interpret the egoist's position in a sympathetic way: we should say that he has in mind a certain kind of world which he would prefer over all others; it would be a world in which his own interests were maximized, regardless of the effects on other people. The egoist's primary policy of action, then, would be to act in such a way as to bring about, as nearly as possible, this sort of world. Regardless of however morally reprehensible we might find it, there is nothing *inconsistent* in someone's adopting this as his ideal and acting in a way calculated to bring it about. And if someone did adopt this as his ideal, then he would not advocate universal egoism; as we have already seen, he would want other people to be altruists. So, if he advocates any principles of conduct for the general public, they will be altruistic principles. This would not be inconsistent; on the contrary, it would be perfectly consistent with his goal of creating a world in which his own interests are maximized.

To be sure, he would have to be deceitful; in order to secure the good will of others, and a favorable hearing for his exhortations to altruism, he would have to pretend that he was himself prepared to accept altruistic principles. But again, that would be all right; from the egoist's point of view, this would merely be a matter of adopting the necessary means to the achievement of his goal—and while we might not approve of this, there is nothing inconsistent about it. Again, it might be said: "He advocates one thing, but does another. Surely *that's* inconsistent." But it is not; for what he advocates and what he does are both calculated as means to an end (the *same* end, we might note); and as such, he is doing what is rationally required in each case. Therefore, contrary to the previous argument, there is nothing inconsistent in the ethical egoist's view. He cannot be refuted by the claim that he contradicts himself.

Is there, then, no way to refute the ethical egoist? If by "refute" we mean show that he has made some *logical* error, the answer is that there is not. However, there is something more that can be said. The egoist challenge to our ordinary moral convictions amounts to a demand for an explanation of why we should adopt certain policies of action, namely policies in which the good of others is given importance. We can give an answer to this demand, albeit an indirect one. The reason one ought not to do actions that would hurt other people is: other people would be hurt. The reason one ought to do actions that would benefit other people is: other people would be benefited. This may at first seem like a piece of philosophical sleight-of-hand, but it is not. The point is that the welfare of human beings is something that most of us value *for its own sake,* and not merely for the sake of something else. Therefore, when *further* reasons are demanded for valuing the welfare of human beings, we cannot point to anything further to satisfy this demand. It is not that we have no reason for pursuing these policies, but that our reason *is* that these policies are for the good of human beings.

So: if we are asked "Why shouldn't I set fire to this department store?" one answer would be "Because if you do, people may be burned to death." This is a complete, sufficient reason which does not require qualification or supplementation of any sort. If someone seriously wants to know why this action shouldn't be done, that's the reason. If we are pressed further and asked the sceptical question "But why shouldn't I do actions that will harm others?" we may not know what to say—but this is because the questioner has included in his question the very answer we would like to give: "Why shouldn't you do actions that will harm others? Because, doing those actions would harm others."

The egoist, no doubt, will not be happy with this. He will protest that *we* may accept this as a reason, but *he* does not. And here the argument stops: there are limits to what can be accomplished by argument, and if the egoist really doesn't care about other people—if he honestly doesn't care whether they are helped or hurt by his actions—then we have reached those limits. If we want to persuade him to act decently toward his fellow humans, we will have to make our appeal to such other attitudes as he does possess, by threats, bribes, or other cajolery. That is all that we can do.

Though some may find this situation distressing (we would like to be able to show that the egoist is just *wrong*), it holds no embarrassment for common morality. What we have come up against is simply a fundamental requirement of rational action, namely, that the existence of reasons for action always depends on the prior existence of certain attitudes in the agent. For example, the fact that a certain course of action would make the agent a lot of money is a reason for doing it only if the agent wants to make money; the fact that practicing at chess makes one a better player is a reason for practicing only if one wants to be a better player; and so on. Similarly, the fact that a certain action would help the agent is a reason for doing the action only if the agent cares about his own welfare, and the fact that an action would help others is a reason for doing it only if the agent cares about others. In this respect ethical egoism and what we might call ethical altruism are in exactly the same fix: both require that the agent *care* about himself, or about other people, before they can get started.

So a nonegoist will accept "It would harm another person" as a reason not to do an action simply because he cares about what happens to that other person. When the egoist says that he does *not* accept that as a reason, he is saying something quite extraordinary. He is saying that he has no affection for friends or family, that he never feels pity or compassion, that he is the sort of person who can look on scenes of human misery with complete indifference, so long as he is not the one suffering. Genuine egoists, people who really don't care at all about anyone other than themselves, are rare. It is important to keep this in mind when thinking about ethical egoism; it is easy to forget just how fundamental to human psychological makeup the feeling of sympathy is. Indeed, a man without any sympathy at all would scarcely be recognizable as a man; and that is what makes ethical egoism such a disturbing doctrine in the first place.

4. There are, of course, many different ways in which the sceptic might challenge the assumptions underlying our moral practice. In this essay I have discussed only two of them, the two put forward by Glaucon in the passage that I cited from Plato's *Republic*. It is important that the assumptions underlying our moral practice should not be confused with particular judgments made within that practice. To defend one is not to defend the other. We may assume—quite properly, if my analysis has been correct—that the virtue of beneficence does, and indeed should, occupy an important place in "the moral institution of life"; and yet we may make constant and miserable errors when it comes to judging when and in what ways this virtue is to be exercised. Even worse, we may often be able to make accurate moral judgments, and know what we ought to do, but not do it. For these ills, philosophy alone is not the cure.

NOTES

1. *The Republic of Plato,* translated by F. M. Cornford (Oxford, 1941), p. 45.

2. Or, as it is sometimes said, "It gives him a clear conscience," or "He couldn't sleep at night if he had done otherwise," or "He would have been ashamed of himself for not doing it," and so on.

3. Frank C. Sharp, *Ethics* (New York, 1928), pp. 74–75. Quoted from the Springfield (Ill.) *Monitor* in the *Outlook,* vol. 56, p. 1059.

4. *The Works of Joseph Butler,* edited by W. E. Gladstone (Oxford, 1896), vol. II, p. 26. It should be noted that most of the points I am making against psychological egoism were first made by Butler. Butler made all the important points; all that is left for us is to remember them.

5. The capacity for altruistic behavior is not unique to human beings. Some interesting experiments with rhesus monkeys have shown that these animals will refrain from operating a device for securing food if this causes other animals to suffer pain. See Masserman, Wechkin, and Terris, "'Altruistic' Behavior in Rhesus Monkeys," *The American Journal of Psychiatry,* vol. 121 (1964), 584–585.

6. I take this to be the view of Ayn Rand, in so far as I understand her confusing doctrine.

7. Cf. Thomas Hobbes, *Leviathan* (London, 1651), chap. 17.

8. See, for example, Brian Medlin, "Ultimate Principles and Ethical Egoism," *Australasian Journal of Philosophy,* vol. 35 (1957), 111–118; and D. H. Monro, *Empiricism and Ethics* (Cambridge, 1967), chap. 16.

Nicomachean Ethics

~

ARISTOTLE

Aristotle (384–322 B.C.), a student of Plato and tutor to Alexander the Great, had an enormous impact on the development of thought. His theory of physics reigned for a thousand years, his system of logic was dominant until the 19th century, Darwin called him "the greatest biologist of all time," and his work in ethics still has many followers.

BOOK I

1. Every art and every inquiry, and similarly every action and choice, is thought to aim at some good; and for this reason the good has rightly been declared to be that at which all things aim. . . .

2. If, then, there is some end of the things we do, which we desire for its own sake (everything else being desired for the sake of this), and if we do not choose everything for the sake of something else (for at that rate the process would go on to infinity, so that our desire would be empty and vain), clearly this must be the good and the chief good. Will not the knowledge of it, then, have a great influence on life? Shall we not, like archers who have a mark to aim at, be more likely to hit upon what we should? If so, we must try, in outline at least, to determine what it is. . . .

4. Let us resume our inquiry and state, in view of the fact that all knowledge and choice aims at some good, what it is that we say political science aims at and what is the highest of all goods achievable by action. Verbally there is very general agreement; for both the general run of men and people of superior refinement say that it is happiness, and identify living well and faring well with being happy; but with regard to what happiness is they differ, and the many do not give the same account as the wise. For the for-mer think it is some plain and obvious thing, like pleasure, wealth, or honour; they differ, however, from one another—and often even the same man identifies it with different things, with health when he is ill, with wealth when he is poor. . . .

5. . . . To judge from the lives that men lead, most men, and men of the most vulgar type, seem (not without some reason) to identify the good, or happiness, with pleasure; which is the reason why they love the life of enjoyment. For there are, we may say, three prominent types of life—that just mentioned, the political, and thirdly the contemplative life. Now the mass of mankind are evidently quite slavish in their tastes, preferring a life suitable to beasts. . . . But people of superior refinement and of active disposition identify happiness with honour; for this is, roughly speaking, the end of the political life. But it seems too superficial to be what we are looking for, since it is thought to depend on those who bestow honour rather than on him who receives it, but the good we divine to be something of one's own and not easily taken from one. . . .

Third comes the contemplative life, which we shall consider later.

The life of money-making is one undertaken under compulsion, and wealth is evidently not the good we are seeking; for it is merely useful and for the sake of something else. . . .

From *The Nicomachean Ethics,* translated by David Ross, revised by J. L. Ackrill and J. O. Urmson. Reprinted by permission of Oxford University Press.

7. Let us again return to the good we are seeking, and ask what it can be. It seems different in different actions and arts; it is different in medicine, in strategy, and in the other arts likewise. What then is the good of each? Surely that for whose sake everything else is done. In medicine this is health, in strategy victory, in architecture a house, in any other sphere something else, and in every action and choice the end; for it is for the sake of this that all men do whatever else they do. Therefore, if there is an end for all that we do, this will be the good achievable by action, and if there are more than one, these will be the goods achievable by action.

So the argument has by a different course reached the same point; but we must try to state this even more clearly. Since there are evidently more than one end, and we choose some of these (e.g. wealth, flutes, and in general instruments) for the sake of something else, clearly not all ends are complete ends; but the chief good is evidently something complete. Therefore, if there is only one complete end, this will be what we are seeking, and if there are more than one, the most complete of these will be what we are seeking. Now we call that which is in itself worthy of pursuit more complete than that which is worthy of pursuit for the sake of something else, and that which is never desirable for the sake of something else more complete than the things that are desirable both in themselves and for the sake of that other thing, and therefore we call complete without qualification that which is always desirable in itself and never for the sake of something else.

Now such a thing happiness, above all else, is held to be; for this we choose always for itself and never for the sake of something else, but honour, pleasure, reason, and every excellence we choose indeed for themselves (for if nothing resulted from them we should still choose each of them), but we choose them also for the sake of happiness, judging that through them we shall be happy. Happiness, on the other hand, no one chooses for the sake of these, nor, in general, for anything other than itself.

From the point of view of self-sufficiency the same result seems to follow; for the complete good is thought to be self-sufficient. Now by self-sufficient we do not mean that which is sufficient for a man by himself, for one who lives a solitary life, but also for parents, children, wife, and in general for his friends and fellow citizens, since man is sociable by nature. . . . [T]he self-sufficient we now define as that which when isolated makes life desirable and lacking in nothing; and such we think happiness to be; and further we think it most desirable of all things, without being counted as one good thing among others—if it were so counted it would clearly be made more desirable by the addition of even the least of goods; for that which is added becomes an excess of goods, and of goods the greater is always more desirable. Happiness, then, is something complete and self-sufficient, and is the end of action.

Presumably, however, to say that happiness is the chief good seems a platitude, and a clearer account of what it is is still desired. This might perhaps be given, if we could first ascertain the function of man. For just as for a flute-player, a sculptor, or any artist, and, in general, for all things that have a function or activity, the good and the 'well' is thought to reside in the function, so would it seem to be for man, if he has a function. Have the carpenter, then, and the tanner certain functions or activities, and has man none? Is he naturally functionless? Or as eye, hand, foot, and in general each of the parts evidently has a function, may one lay it down that man similarly has a function apart from all these? What then can this be? Life seems to be common even to plants, but we are seeking what is peculiar to man. Let us exclude, therefore, the life of nutrition and growth. Next there would be a life of perception, but *it* also seems to be common even to the horse, the ox, and every animal. There remains, then, an active life of the element that has a rational principle (of this, one part has such a principle in the sense of being obedient to one, the other in the sense of possessing one and exercising thought); and as this too can be taken in two ways, we must state that life in the sense of activity is what we mean; for this seems to be the more proper sense of the term. Now if the function of man is an activity of soul in accordance with, or not without, rational principle, and if we say a so-and-so and a good so-and-so have a function which is the same in kind, e.g. a lyre-player and a good lyre-player, and so without qualification in all cases, eminence in respect of excellence being added to the function (for the function of a lyre-player is to play the lyre, and that of a good lyre-player is to do so well): if this is the case, [and we state the function of man to be a certain kind of life, and this to be an activity or actions of the soul implying a rational principle, and the function of a good man to be the good and noble performance of these, and if any action is well performed when it is performed in accordance with the appropriate excellence: if this is the case,] human good turns out to be activity of soul in conformity with excellence, and if there are more than one excellence, in conformity with the best and most complete. . . .

BOOK II

1. Excellence, then, being of two kinds, intellectual and moral, intellectual excellence in the main owes both its birth and its growth to teaching (for which reason it requires experience and time), while moral excellence comes about as a result of habit, whence also its name is one that is formed by a slight variation from the word for "habit." From this it is also plain that none of the moral excellences arises in us by nature; for nothing that exists by nature can form a habit contrary to its nature. For instance the stone which by nature moves downwards cannot be habituated to move upwards, not even if one tries to train it by throwing it up ten thousand times; nor can fire be habituated to move downwards, nor can anything else that by nature behaves in one way be trained to behave in another. Neither by nature, then, nor contrary to nature do excellences arise in us; rather we are adapted by nature to receive them, and are made perfect by habit.

Again, of all the things that come to us by nature we first acquire the potentiality and later exhibit the activity (this is plain in the case of the senses; for it was not by often seeing or often hearing that we got these senses, but on the contrary we had them before we used them, and did not come to have them by using them); but excellences we get by first exercising them, as also happens in the case of the arts as well. For the things we have to learn before we can do, we learn by doing, e.g. men become builders by building and lyre-players by playing the lyre; so too

we become just by doing just acts, temperate by doing temperate acts, brave by doing brave acts.

This is confirmed by what happens in states; for legislators make the citizens good by forming habits in them, and this is the wish of every legislator; and those who do not effect it miss their mark, and it is in this that a good constitution differs from a bad one.

Again, it is from the same causes and by the same means that every excellence is both produced and destroyed, and similarly every art; for it is from playing the lyre that both good and bad lyre-players are produced. And the corresponding statement is true of builders and of all the rest; men will be good or bad builders as a result of building well or badly. For if this were not so, there would have been no need of a teacher, but all men would have been born good or bad at their craft. This, then, is the case with the excellences also; by doing the acts that we do in our transactions with other men we become just or unjust, and by doing the acts that we do in the presence of danger, and being habituated to feel fear or confidence, we become brave or cowardly. The same is true of appetites and feelings of anger; some men become temperate and good-tempered, others self-indulgent and irascible, by behaving in one way or the other in the appropriate circumstances. Thus, in one word, states arise out of like activities. This is why the activities we exhibit must be of a certain kind; it is because the states correspond to the differences between these. It makes no small difference, then, whether we form habits of one kind or of another from our very youth; it makes a very great difference, or rather *all* the difference. . . .

3. We must take as a sign of states the pleasure or pain that supervenes on acts; for the man who abstains from bodily pleasures and delights in this very fact is temperate, while the man who is annoyed at it is self-indulgent, and he who stands his ground against things that are terrible and delights in this or at least is not pained is brave, while the man who is pained is a coward. For moral excellence is concerned with pleasures and pains; it is on account of pleasure that we do bad things, and on account of pain that we abstain from noble ones. . . .

The following facts also may show us that they are concerned with these same things. There being three objects of choice and three of avoidance, the noble, the advantageous, the pleasant, and their contraries, the base, the injurious, the painful, about all of these the good man tends to go right and the bad man to go wrong, and especially about pleasure; for this is common to the animals, and also it accompanies all objects of choice; for even the noble and the advantageous appear pleasant. . . .

4. The question might be asked, what we mean by saying that we must become just by doing just acts, and temperate by doing temperate acts; for if men do just and temperate acts, they are already just and temperate, exactly as, if they do what is grammatical or musical they are proficient in grammar and music.

Or is this not true even of the arts? It is possible to do something grammatical either by chance or under the guidance of another. A man will be proficient in grammar, then, only when he has both done something grammatical and done it grammatically; and this means doing it in accordance with the grammatical knowledge in himself.

Again, the case of the arts and that of the excellences are not similar; for the products of the arts have their goodness in themselves, so that it is enough that they should have a certain character, but if the acts that are in accordance with the excellences have themselves a certain character it does not follow that they are done justly or temperately. The agent also must be in a certain condition when he does them; in the first place he must have knowledge, secondly he must choose the acts, and choose them for their own sakes, and thirdly his action must proceed from a firm and unchangeable character. . . .

Actions, then, are called just and temperate when they are such as the just or the temperate man would do; but it is not the man who does these that is just and temperate, but the man who also does them *as* just and temperate men do them. It is well said, then, that it is by doing just acts that the just man is produced, and by doing temperate acts the temperate man; without doing these no one would have even a prospect of becoming good. . . .

5. Next we must consider what excellence is. Since things that are found in the soul are of three kinds— passions, faculties, states—excellence must be one of these. By passions I mean appetite, anger, fear, confi-

dence, envy, joy, love, hatred, longing, emulation, pity, and in general the feelings that are accompanied by pleasure or pain; by faculties the things in virtue of which we are said to be capable of feeling these, e.g. of becoming angry or being pained or feeling pity; by states the things in virtue of which we stand well or badly with reference to the passions, e.g. with reference to anger we stand badly if we feel it violently or too weakly, and well if we feel it moderately; and similarly with reference to the other passions.

Now neither the excellences nor the vices are *passions,* because we are not called good or bad on the ground of our passions, but are so called on the ground of our excellences and our vices, and because we are neither praised nor blamed for our passions (for the man who feels fear or anger is not praised, nor is the man who simply feels anger blamed, but the man who feels it in a certain way), but for our excellences and our vices we *are* praised or blamed.

Again, we feel anger and fear without choice, but the excellences are choices or involve choice. Further, in respect of the passions we are said to be moved, but in respect of the excellences and the vices we are said not to be moved but to be disposed in a particular way.

For these reasons also they are not *faculties;* for we are neither called good nor bad, nor praised nor blamed, for the simple capacity of feeling the passions; again, we have the faculties by nature, but we are not made good or bad by nature; we have spoken of this before.

If, then, the excellences are neither passions nor faculties, all that remains is that they should be *states.*

Thus we have stated what excellence is in respect of its genus.

6. We must, however, not only describe it as a state, but also say what sort of state it is. We may remark, then, that every excellence both brings into good condition the thing of which it is the excellence and makes the work of that thing be done well; e.g. the excellence of the eye makes both the eye and its work good; for it is by the excellence of the eye that we see well. Similarly the excellence of the horse makes a horse both good in itself and good at running and at carrying its rider and at awaiting the attack of the enemy. Therefore, if this is true in every case, the

excellence of man also will be the state which makes a man good and which makes him do his own work well.

How this is to happen we have stated already, but it will be made plain also by the following consideration of the nature of excellence. In everything that is continuous and divisible it is possible to take more, less, or an equal amount, and that either in terms of the thing itself or relatively to us; and the equal is an intermediate between excess and defect. By the intermediate in the object I mean that which is equidistant from each of the extremes, which is one and the same for all men; by the intermediate relatively to us that which is neither too much nor too little—and this is not one, nor the same for all. For instance, if ten is many and two is few, six is intermediate, taken in terms of the object; for it exceeds and is exceeded by an equal amount; this is intermediate according to arithmetical proportion. But the intermediate relatively to us is not to be taken so; if ten pounds are too much for a particular person to eat and two too little, it does not follow that the trainer will order six pounds; for this also is perhaps too much for the person who is to take it, or too little—too little for Milo, too much for the beginner in athletic exercises. The same is true of running and wrestling. Thus a master of any art avoids excess and defect, but seeks the intermediate and chooses this—the intermediate not in the object but relatively to us.

If it is thus, then, that every art does its work well—by looking to the intermediate and judging its works by this standard (so that we often say of good works of the art that it is not possible either to take away or to add anything, implying that excess and defect destroy the goodness of works of art, while the mean preserves it; and good artists, as we say, look to this in their work), and if, further, excellence is more exact and better than any art, as nature also is, then it must have the quality of aiming at the intermediate. I mean moral excellence; for it is this that is concerned with passions and actions, and in these there is excess, defect, and the intermediate. For instance, both fear and confidence and appetite and anger and pity and in general pleasure and pain may be felt both too much and too little, and in both cases not well; but to feel them at the right times, with reference to

the right objects, towards the right people, with the right aim, and in the right way, is what is both intermediate and best, and this is characteristic of excellence. Similarly with regard to actions also there is excess, defect, and the intermediate. Now excellence is concerned with passions and actions, in which excess is a form of failure, and so is defect, while the intermediate is praised and is a form of success; and both these things are characteristics of excellence. Therefore excellence is a kind of mean, since it aims at what is intermediate.

Again, it is possible to fail in many ways (for evil belongs to the class of the unlimited, as the Pythagoreans conjectured, and good to that of the limited), while to succeed is possible only in one way (for which reason one is easy and the other difficult—to miss the mark easy, to hit it difficult); for these reasons also, then, excess and defect are characteristic of vice, and the mean of excellence;

For men are good in but one way, but bad in many.

Excellence, then, is a state concerned with choice, lying in a mean relative to us, this being determined by reason and in the way in which the man of practical wisdom would determine it. Now it is a mean between two vices, that which depends on excess and that which depends on defect; and again it is a mean because the vices respectively fall short of or exceed what is right in both passions and actions, while excellence both finds and chooses that which is intermediate. Hence in respect of its substance and the account which states its essence is a mean, with regard to what is best and right it is an extreme.

But not every action nor every passion admits of a mean; for some have names that already imply badness, e.g., spite, shamelessness, envy, and in the case of actions adultery, theft, murder; for all of these and suchlike things imply by their names that they are themselves bad, and not the excesses or deficiencies of them. It is not possible, then, ever to be right with regard to them; one must always be wrong. Nor does goodness or badness with regard to such things depend on committing adultery with the right woman, at the right time, and in the right way, but simply to do any of them is to go wrong. It would be equally absurd, then, to expect that in unjust, cowardly, and self-indulgent action there should be a mean, an excess, and a deficiency; for at that rate there would be a mean of excess and of deficiency, an excess of excess, and a deficiency of deficiency. But as there is no excess and deficiency of temperance and courage because what is intermediate is in a sense an extreme, so too of the actions we have mentioned there is no mean nor any excess and deficiency, but however they are done they are wrong; for in general there is neither a mean of excess and deficiency, nor excess and deficiency of a mean.

7. . . . With regard to feelings of fear and confidence courage is the mean; of the people who exceed, he who exceeds in fearlessness has no name (many of the states have no name), while the man who exceeds in confidence is rash, and he who exceeds in fear and falls short in confidence is a coward. With regard to pleasures and pains—not all of them, and not so much with regard to the pains—the mean is temperance, the excess self-indulgence. Persons deficient with regard to the pleasures are not often found; hence such persons also have received no name. But let us call them 'insensible'.

With regard to giving and taking of money the mean is liberality, the excess and the defect prodigality and meanness. They exceed and fall short in contrary ways to one another: the prodigal exceeds in spending and falls short in taking, while the mean man exceeds in taking and falls short in spending. . . . With regard to money there are also other dispositions—a mean, magnificence (for the magnificent man differs from the liberal man; the former deals with large sums, the latter with small ones), an excess, tastelessness and vulgarity, and a deficiency, niggardliness; these differ from the states opposed to liberality, and the mode of their difference will be stated later.

With regard to honour and dishonour the mean is proper pride, the excess is known as a sort of empty vanity, and the deficiency is undue humility; and as we said liberality was related to magnificence, differing from it by dealing with small sums, so there is a state similarly related to proper pride, being concerned with small honours while that is concerned with great. For it is possible to desire small honours as one ought, and more than one ought, and less, and the man who exceeds in his desires is called ambitious, the man who falls short unambitious, while the

intermediate person has no name. The dispositions also are nameless, except that that of the ambitious man is called ambition. Hence the people who are at the extremes lay claim to the middle place; and we ourselves sometimes call the intermediate person ambitious and sometimes unambitious, and sometimes praise the ambitious man and sometimes the unambitious. The reason of our doing this will be stated in what follows; but now let us speak of the remaining states according to the method which has been indicated.

With regard to anger also there is an excess, a deficiency, and a mean. Although they can scarcely be said to have names, yet since we call the intermediate person good-tempered let us call the mean good temper; of the persons at the extremes let the one who exceeds be called irascible, and his vice irascibility, and the man who falls short an inirascible sort of person, and the deficiency inirascibility.

There are also three other means, which have a certain likeness to one another, but differ from one another: for they are all concerned with intercourse in words and actions, but differ in that one is concerned with truth in this sphere, the other two with pleasantness; and of this one kind is exhibited in giving amusement, the other in all the circumstances of life. We must therefore speak of these too, that we may the better see that in all things the mean is praiseworthy, and the extremes neither praiseworthy nor right, but worthy of blame. Now most of these states also have no names, but we must try, as in the other cases, to invent names ourselves so that we may be clear and easy to follow. With regard to truth, then, the intermediate is a truthful sort of person and the mean may be called truthfulness, while the pretence which exaggerates is boastfulness and the person characterized by it a boaster, and that which understates is mock modesty and the person characterized by it mock-modest. With regard to pleasantness in the giving of amusement the intermediate person is ready-witted and the disposition ready wit, the excess is buffoonery and the person characterized by it a buffoon, while the man who falls short is a sort of boor and his state is boorishness. With regard to the remaining kind of pleasantness, that which is exhibited in life in general, the man who is pleasant in the right way is friendly and the mean is friendliness, while the man who exceeds is an obsequious person if he has no end in view, a flatterer if he is aiming at his own advantage, and the man who falls short and is unpleasant in all circumstances is a quarrelsome and surly sort of person.

There are also means in the passions and concerned with the passions; since shame is not an excellence, and yet praise is extended to the modest man. For even in these matters one man is said to be intermediate, and another to exceed, as for instance the bashful man who is ashamed of everything; while he who falls short or is not ashamed of anything at all is shameless, and the intermediate person is modest. Righteous indignation is a mean between envy and spite, and these states are concerned with the pain and pleasure that are felt at the fortunes of our neighbours; the man who is characterized by righteous indignation is pained at undeserved good fortune, the envious man, going beyond him, is pained at all good fortune, and the spiteful man falls so far short of being pained that he even rejoices. But these states there will be an opportunity of describing elsewhere; with regard to justice, since it has not one simple meaning, we shall, after describing the other states, distinguish its two kinds and say how each of them is a mean; and similarly we shall treat also of the rational excellences.

8. There are three kinds of disposition, then, two of them vices, involving excess and deficiency and one an excellence, viz. the mean. . . .

To the mean in some cases the deficiency, in some the excess is more opposed; e.g. it is not rashness, which is an excess, but cowardice, which is a deficiency, that is more opposed to courage, and not insensibility, which is a deficiency, but self-indulgence, which is an excess, that is more opposed to temperance. This happens from two reasons, one being drawn from the thing itself; for because one extreme is nearer and liker to the intermediate, we oppose not this but rather its contrary to the intermediate. E.g., since rashness is thought liker and nearer to courage, and cowardice more unlike, we oppose rather the latter to courage; for things that are further from the intermediate are thought more contrary to it. This, then, is one cause, drawn from the thing itself; another is drawn from ourselves; for the things to which we

ourselves more naturally tend seem more contrary to the intermediate. For instance, we ourselves tend more naturally to pleasures, and hence are more easily carried away towards self-indulgence than towards propriety. We describe as contrary to the mean, then, the states into which we are more inclined to lapse; and therefore self-indulgence, which is an excess, is the more contrary to temperance.

9. . . . [I]t is no easy task to be good. For in everything it is no easy task to find the middle, e.g. to find the middle of a circle is not for every one but for him who knows; so, too, any one can get angry—that is easy—or give or spend money; but to do this to the right person, to the right extent, at the right time, with the right aim, and in the right way, *that* is not for every one, nor is it easy; that is why goodness is both rare and laudable and noble. . . .

Now in everything the pleasant or pleasure is most to be guarded against; for we do not judge it impartially. . . .

But [hitting the mean] . . . is no doubt difficult, and especially in individual cases; for it is not easy to determine both how and with whom and on what provocation and how long one should be angry; for we too sometimes praise those who fall short and call them good-tempered, but sometimes we praise those who get angry and call them manly. The man, however who deviates little from goodness is not blamed, whether he do so in the direction of the more or of the less, but only the man who deviates more widely; for *he* does not fail to be noticed. But up to what point and to what extent a man must deviate before he becomes blameworthy it is not easy to determine by reasoning, any more than anything else that is perceived by the senses; such things depend on particular facts, and the decision rests with perception. So much, then, makes it plain that the intermediate state is in all things to be praised, but that we must incline sometimes towards the excess, sometimes towards the deficiency; for so shall we most easily hit the mean and what is right.

BOOK III

2. . . . [W]e must next discuss choice; for it is thought to be most closely bound up with excellence and to discriminate characters better than actions do. . . .

Is it, then, what has been decided on by previous deliberation? For choice involves reason and thought. Even the name seems to suggest that it is what is chosen before other things.

3. . . . We deliberate about things that are in our power and can be done . . . [E]very class of men deliberates about the things that can be done by their own efforts . . .

Deliberation is concerned with things that happen in a certain way for the most part, but in which the event is obscure, and with things in which it is indeterminate. We call in others to aid us in deliberation on important questions, distrusting ourselves as not being equal to deciding.

We deliberate not about ends but about what contributes to ends. For a doctor does not deliberate whether he shall heal, nor an orator whether he shall convince, nor a statesman whether he shall produce law and order, nor does any one else deliberate about his end. Having set the end they consider how and by what means it is to be attained; and if it seems to be produced by several means they consider by which it is most easily and best produced, while if it is achieved by one only they consider how it will be achieved by this and by what means *this* will be achieved, till they come to the first cause, which in the order of discovery is last. . . .

The same thing is deliberated upon and is chosen, except that the object of choice is already determinate, since it is that which has been decided upon as a result of deliberation that is the object of choice.

The object of choice being one of the things in our own power which is desired after deliberation, choice will be deliberate desire of things in our own power; for when we have decided as a result of deliberation, we desire in accordance with our deliberation. . . .

BOOK VI

1. Since we have previously said that one ought to choose that which is intermediate, not the excess nor the defect, and that the intermediate is determined by the dictates of reason, let us discuss this. In all the states we have mentioned, as in all other matters, there is a mark to which the man who possesses reason looks, and heightens or relaxes his activity accordingly, and there is a standard which determines the mean states which we say are intermediate between excess and defect, being in accordance with right reason. . . .

2. What affirmation and negation are in thinking, pursuit and avoidance are in desire; so that since moral excellence is a state concerned with choice, and choice is deliberate desire, therefore both the reasoning must be true and the desire right, if the choice is to be good, and the latter must pursue just what the former asserts. Now this kind of intellect and of truth is practical; . . . the good state is truth in agreement with right desire.

The origin of action—its efficient, not its final cause—is choice, and that of choice is desire and reasoning with a view to an end. This is why choice cannot exist either without thought and intellect or without a moral state; for good action and its opposite cannot exist without a combination of intellect and character. Intellect itself, however, moves nothing, but only the intellect which aims at an end and is practical . . .

5. Regarding *practical wisdom* we shall get at the truth by considering who are the persons we credit with it. Now it is thought to be a mark of a man of practical wisdom to be able to deliberate well about what is good and expedient for himself, not in some particular respect, e.g. about what sorts of thing conduce to health or to strength, but about what sorts of thing conduce to the good life in general. . . .

Practical wisdom, then, must be a reasoned and true state of capacity to act with regard to human goods. . . . But yet it is not only a reasoned state; this is shown by the fact that a state of that sort may be forgotten but practical wisdom cannot.

12. . . . Practical wisdom is the quality of mind concerned with things just and noble and good for man, but . . . the function of man is achieved only in accordance with practical wisdom as well as with moral excellence; for excellence makes the aim right, and practical wisdom the things leading to it. . . .

As we say that some people who do just acts are not necessarily just, i.e. those who do the acts ordained by the laws either unwillingly or owing to ignorance or for some other reason and not for the sake of the acts themselves (though, to be sure, they do what they should and all the things that the good man ought), so is it, it seems, that in order to be good one must be in a certain state when one does the several acts, i.e. one must do them as a result of choice and for the sake of the acts themselves. Now excellence makes the choice right, but the question of the things which should naturally be done to carry out our choice belongs not to excellence but to another faculty. We must devote our attention to these matters and give a clearer statement about them. There is a faculty which is called cleverness; and this is such as to be able to do the things that tend towards the mark we have set before ourselves, and to hit it. Now if the mark be noble, the cleverness is laudable, but if the mark be bad, the cleverness is mere villainy; hence we call clever both men of practical wisdom and villains. Practical wisdom is not the faculty, but it does not exist without this faculty. And this eye of the soul acquires its formed state not without the aid of excellence as has been said and is plain; for inferences which deal with acts to be done are things which involve a starting-point, viz. "since the end, i.e. what is best, is of such and such a nature," whatever it may be (let it for the sake of argument be what we please); and this is not evident except to the good man; for wickedness perverts us and causes us to be deceived about the starting-points of action. Therefore it is evident that it is impossible to be practically wise without being good.

13. We must therefore consider excellence also once more; for virtue too is similarly related; as practical wisdom is to cleverness—not the same, but like it—so is natural excellence to excellence in the strict sense. For all men think that each type of character belongs to its possessors in some sense by nature; for from the very moment of birth we are just or fitted for self-control or brave or have the other moral qualities; but yet we seek something else as that which is good in the strict sense—we seek for the presence of such qualities in another way. For both children and brutes have the natural dispositions to these qualities, but without thought these are evidently hurtful. Only we seem to see this much, that, while one may be led astray by them, as a strong body which moves without sight may stumble badly because of its lack of sight, still, if a man once acquires thought that makes a difference in action; and his state, while still like what it was, will then be excellence in the strict sense. Therefore, as in the part of us which forms opinions there are two types, cleverness and practical wisdom, so too in the moral part there are two types, natural excellence and excellence in the strict sense, and of these the latter involves practical wisdom. This is why some say that all the excellences are forms of practical wisdom, and why Socrates in one respect was on the right track while in another he went astray; in thinking that all the excellences were forms of practical wisdom he was wrong, but in saying they implied practical wisdom he was right. This is confirmed by the fact that even now all men, when they define excellence, after naming the state and its objects add 'that (state) which is in accordance with the right reason'; now the right reason is that which is in accordance with practical wisdom. All men, then, seem somehow to divine that this kind of state is excellence, viz. that which is in accordance with practical wisdom. But we must go a little further. For it is not merely the state in accordance with right reason, but the state that implies the *presence* of right reason, that is excellence; and practical wisdom is right reason about such matters. Socrates, then, thought the excellences were forms of reason (for he thought they were, all of them, forms of knowledge), while we think they *involve* reason.

It is clear, then, from what has been said, that it is not possible to be good in the strict sense without practical wisdom, nor practically wise without moral excellence.

After Virtue

～

ALASDAIR MACINTYRE

Alasdair MacIntyre is professor of philosophy at the University of Notre Dame. Among his numerous books are *A Short History of Ethics, Three Rival Versions of Moral Enquiry,* and *Common Truths.*

One response to the history which I have narrated so far might well be to suggest that even within the relatively coherent tradition of thought which I have sketched there are just too many different and incompatible conceptions of a virtue for there to be any real unity to the concept or indeed to the history. Homer, Sophocles, Aristotle, the New Testament and medieval thinkers differ from each other in too many ways. They offer us different and incompatible lists of the virtues; they give a different rank order of importance to different virtues; and they have different and incompatible theories of the virtues. If we were to consider later Western writers on the virtues, the list of differences and incompatibilities would be enlarged still further; and if we extended our enquiry to Japanese, say, or American Indian cultures, the differences would become greater still. It would be all too easy to conclude that there are a number of rival and alternative conceptions of the virtues, but, even within the tradition which I have been delineating, no single core conception.

The case for such a conclusion could not be better constructed than by beginning from a consideration of the very different lists of items which different authors in different times and places have included in their catalogues of virtues. Some of these catalogues—Homer's, Aristotle's and the New Testament's—I have already noticed at greater or lesser length. Let me at the risk of some repetition recall some of their key features and then introduce for further comparison the catalogues of two later Western writers, Benjamin Franklin and Jane Austen.

The first example is that of Homer. At least some of the items in a Homeric list of the *aretai* would clearly not be counted by most of us nowadays as virtues at all, physical strength being the most obvious example. To this it might be replied that perhaps we ought not to translate the word *aretê* in Homer by our word "virtue," but instead by our word "excellence"; and perhaps, if we were so to translate it, the apparently surprising difference between Homer and ourselves would at first sight have been removed. For we could allow without any kind of oddity that the possession of physical strength is the possession of an excellence. But in fact we would not have removed, but instead would merely have relocated, the difference between Homer and ourselves. For we would now seem to be saying that Homer's concept of an *aretê,* an excellence, is one thing and that our concept of a virtue is quite another since a particular quality can be an excellence in Homer's eyes, but not a virtue in ours and *vice versa.*

But of course it is not that Homer's list of virtues differs only from our own; it also notably differs from Aristotle's. And Aristotle's of course also differs from our own. For one thing, as I noticed earlier, some Greek virtue-words are not easily translatable into English or rather out of Greek. Moreover consider the importance of friendship as a virtue in Aristotle's list—how different from us! Or the place of *phronêsis*—how different from Homer and from us! The mind receives from Aristotle the kind of tribute which the body receives from Homer. But it is not just the case that the difference between Aristotle and Homer lies in the inclusion of some items and the omission of others in their respective catalogues. It turns out also in the way in which those catalogues are ordered, in which items are ranked as relatively central to human excellence and which marginal.

Moreover the relationship of virtues to the social order has changed. For Homer the paradigm of human excellence is the warrior; for Aristotle it is the Athenian gentleman. Indeed according to Aristotle certain virtues are only available to those of great riches and of high social status; there are virtues which are unavailable to the poor man, even if he is a free man. And those virtues are on Aristotle's view ones central to human life; magnanimity—and once again, any translation of *megalopsuchia* is unsatisfactory—and munificence are not just virtues, but important virtues within the Aristotelian scheme.

At once it is impossible to delay the remark that the most striking contrast with Aristotle's catalogue is to be found neither in Homer's nor in our own, but in the New Testament's. For the New Testament not only praises virtues of which Aristotle knows nothing—faith, hope and love—and says nothing about virtues such as *phronêsis* which are crucial for Aristotle, but it praises at least one quality as a virtue which Aristotle seems to count as one of the vices relative to magnanimity, namely humility. Moreover since the New Testament quite clearly sees the rich as destined for the pains of Hell, it is clear that the key values cannot be available to them; yet they *are* available to slaves. And the New Testament of course differs from both Homer and Aristotle not only in the items included in its catalogue, but once again in its rank ordering of the virtues.

Turn now to compare all three lists of virtues considered so far—the Homeric, the Aristotelian, and the New Testament's—with two much later lists, one which can be compiled from Jane Austen's novels and the other which Benjamin Franklin constructed for himself. Two features stand out in Jane Austen's

list. The first is the importance that she allots to the virtue which she calls "constancy." In some ways constancy plays a role in Jane Austen analogous to that of *phronêsis* in Aristotle; it is a virtue the possession of which is a prerequisite for the possession of other virtues. The second is the fact that what Aristotle treats as the virtue of agreeableness (a virtue for which he says there is no name) she treats as only the simulacrum of a genuine virtue—the genuine virtue in question is the one she calls amiability. For the man who practices agreeableness does so from considerations of honour and expediency, according to Aristotle; whereas Jane Austen thought it possible and necessary for the possessor of that virtue to have a certain real affection for people as such. (It matters here that Jane Austen is a Christian.) Remember that Aristotle himself had treated military courage as a simulacrum of true courage. Thus we find here yet another type of disagreement over the virtues; namely, one as to which human qualities are genuine virtues and which mere simulacra.

In Benajmin Franklin's list we find almost all the types of difference from at least one of the other catalogues we have considered and one more. Franklin includes virtues which are new to our consideration such as cleanliness, silence and industry; he clearly considers the drive to acquire itself a part of virtue, whereas for most ancient Greeks this is the vice of *pleonexia;* he treats some virtues which earlier ages had considered minor as major; but he also redefines some familiar virtues. In the list of thirteen virtues which Franklin compiled as part of his system of private moral accounting, he elucidates each virtue by citing a maxim obedience to which *is* the virtue in question. In the case of chastity the maxim is "Rarely use venery but for health or offspring—never to dullness, weakness or the injury of your own or another's peace or reputation." This is clearly not what earlier writers had meant by "chastity."

We have therefore accumulated a startling number of differences and incompatibilities in the five stated and implied accounts of the virtues. So the question which I raised at the outset becomes more urgent. If different writers in different times and places, but all within the history of Western culture, include such different sets and types of items in their lists, what grounds have we for supposing that they do indeed aspire to list items of one and the same kind, that there is any shared concept at all? A second kind of consideration reinforces the presumption of a negative answer to this question. It is not just that each of these five writers lists different and differing kinds of items; it is also that each of these lists embodies, is the expression of a different theory about what a virtue is.

In the Homeric poems a virtue is a quality the manifestation of which enables someone to do exactly what their well-defined social role requires. The primary role is that of the warrior king and that Homer lists those virtues which he does becomes intelligible at once when we recognise that the key virtues therefore must be those which enable a man to excel in combat and in the games. It follows that we cannot identify the Homeric virtues until we have first identified the key social roles in Homeric society and the requirements of each of them. The concept of *what anyone filling such-and-such a role ought to do* is prior to the concept of a virtue; the latter concept has application only via the former.

On Aristotle's account matters are very different. Even though some virtues are available only to certain types of people, none the less virtues attach not to men as inhabiting social roles, but to man as such. It is the *telos* of man as a species which determines what human qualities are virtues. We need to remember however that although Aristotle treats the acquisition and exercise of the virtues as means to an end, the relationship of means to end is internal and not external. I call a means internal to a given end when the end cannot be adequately characterised independently of a characterisation of the means. So it is with the virtues and the *telos* which is the good life for man on Aristotle's account. The exercise of the virtues is itself a crucial component of the good life for man. This distinction between internal and external means to an end is not drawn by Aristotle himself in the *Nicomachean Ethics,* as I noticed earlier, but it is an essential distinction to be drawn if we are to understand what Aristotle intended. The distinction *is* drawn explicitly by Aquinas in the course of his defence of St Augustine's definition of a virtue, and it is clear that Aquinas understood that in drawing it he was maintaining an Aristotelian point of view.

The New Testament's account of the virtues, even if it differs as much as it does in content from Aristotle's—Aristotle would certainly not have admired Jesus Christ and he would have been horrified by St Paul—does have the same logical and conceptual structure as Aristotle's account. A virtue is, as with Aristotle, a quality the exercise of which leads to the achievement of the human telos. *The* good for man is of course a supernatural and not only a natural good, but supernature redeems and completes nature. Moreover the relationship of virtues as means to the end which is human incorporation in the divine kingdom of the age to come is internal and not external, just as it is in Aristotle. It is of course this parallelism which allows Aquinas to synthesise Aristotle and the New Testament. A key feature of this parallelism is the way in which the concept of *the good life for man* is prior to the concept of a virtue in just the way in which on the Homeric account the concept of a social role was prior. Once again it is the way in which the former concept is applied which determines how the latter is to be applied. In both cases the concept of a virtue is a secondary concept.

The intent of Jane Austen's theory of the virtues is of another kind. C. S. Lewis has rightly emphasised how profoundly Christian her moral vision is and Gilbert Ryle has equally rightly emphasised her inheritance from Shaftesbury and from Aristotle. In fact her views combine elements from Homer as well, since she is concerned with social roles in a way that neither the New Testament nor Aristotle are. She is therefore important for the way in which she finds it possible to combine what are at first sight disparate theoretical accounts of the virtues. But for the moment any attempt to assess the significance of Jane Austen's synthesis must be delayed. Instead we must notice the quite different style of theory articulated in Benjamin Franklin's account of the virtues.

Franklin's account, like Aristotle's, is teleological; but unlike Aristotle's, it is utilitarian. According to Franklin in his *Autobiography* the virtues are means to an end, but he envisages the means-ends relationship as external rather than internal. The end to which the cultivation of the virtues ministers is happiness, but happiness understood as success, prosperity in Philadelphia and ultimately in heaven. The virtues are to be useful and Franklin's account continuously stresses utility as a criterion in individual cases: "Make no expence but to do good to others or yourself; i.e. waste nothing," "Speak not but what may benefit others or yourself. Avoid trifling conversation" and, as we have already seen, "Rarely use venery but for health or offspring . . ." When Franklin was in Paris he was horrified by Parisian architecture: "Marble, porcelain and gilt are squandered without utility."

We thus have at least three very different conceptions of a virtue to confront: a virtue is a quality which enables an individual to discharge his or her social role (Homer); a virtue is a quality which enables an individual to move towards the achievement of the specifically human *telos,* whether natural or supernatural (Aristotle, the New Testament and Aquinas); a virtue is a quality which has utility in achieving earthly and heavenly success (Franklin). Are we to take these as three rival accounts of the same thing? Or are they instead accounts of three different things? Perhaps the moral structures in archaic Greece, in fourth-century Greece, and in eighteenth-century Pennsylvania were so different from each other that we should treat them as embodying quite different concepts, whose difference is initially disguised from us by the historical accident of an inherited vocabulary which misleads us by linguistic resemblance long after conceptual identity and similarity have failed. Our initial question has come back to us with redoubled force.

Yet although I have dwelt upon the prima facie case for holding that the differences and incompatibilities between different accounts at least suggest that there is no single, central, core conception of the virtues which might make a claim for universal allegiance, I ought also to point out that each of the five moral accounts which I have sketched so summarily does embody just such a claim. It is indeed just this feature of those accounts that makes them of more than sociological or antiquarian interest. Every one of these accounts claims not only theoretical, but also an institutional hegemony. For Odysseus the Cyclopes stand condemned because they lack agriculture, on *agora* and *themis.* For Aristotle the barbarians stand condemned because they lack the *polis* and are therefore incapable of politics. For New Testament Christians there is no salvation outside the apostolic

church. And we know that Benjamin Franklin found the virtues more at home in Philadelphia than in Paris and that for Jane Austen the touchstone of the virtues is a certain kind of marriage and indeed a certain kind of naval officer (that is, a certain kind of *English* naval officer).

The question can therefore now be posed directly: are we or are we not able to disentangle from these rival and various claims a unitary core concept of the virtues of which we can give a more compelling account than any of the other accounts so far? I am going to argue that we can in fact discover such a core concept and that it turns out to provide the tradition of which I have written the history with its conceptual unity. It will indeed enable us to distinguish in a clear way those beliefs about the virtues which genuinely belong to the tradition from those which do not. Unsurprisingly perhaps it is a complex concept, different parts of which derive from different stages in the development of the tradition. Thus the concept itself in some sense embodies the history of which it is the outcome.

One of the features of the concept of a virtue which has emerged with some clarity from the argument so far is that it always requires for its application the acceptance of some prior account of certain features of social and moral life in terms of which it has to be defined and explained. So in the Homeric account the concept of a virtue is secondary to that of *a social role,* in Aristotle's account it is secondary to that of *the good life for man* conceived as the *telos* of human action and in Franklin's much later account it is secondary to that of utility. What is it in the account which I am about to give which provides in a similar way the necessary background against which the concept of a virtue has to be made intelligible? It is in answering this question that the complex, historical, multilayered character of the core concept of virtue becomes clear. For there are no less than three stages in the logical development of the concept which have to be identified in order, if the core conception of a virtue is to be understood, and each of these stages has its own conceptual background. The first stage requires a background account of what I shall call a practice, the second an account of what I have already characterised as the narrative order of a single human life and the third an account a good deal fuller than I have given up to now of what constitutes a moral tradition. Each later stage presupposes the earlier, but not vice versa. Each earlier stage is both modified by and reinterpreted in the light of, but also provides an essential constituent of each later stage. The progress in the development of the concept is closely related to, although it does not recapitulate in any straightforward way, the history of the tradition of which it forms the core.

In the Homeric account of the virtues—and in heroic societies more generally—the exercise of a virtue exhibits qualities which are required for sustaining a social role and for exhibiting excellence in some well-marked area of social practice: to excel is to excel at war or in the games, as Achilles does, in sustaining a household, as Penelope does, in giving counsel in the assembly, as Nestor does, in the telling of a tale, as Homer himself does. When Aristotle speaks of excellence in human activity, he sometimes though not always, refers to some well-defined type of human practice: flute-playing, or war, or geometry. I am going to suggest that this notion of a particular type of practice as providing the arena in which the virtues are exhibited and in terms of which they are to receive their primary, if incomplete, definition is crucial to the whole enterprise of identifying a core concept of the virtues. I hasten to add two caveats however.

The first is to point out that my argument will not in any way imply that virtues are *only* exercised in the course of what I am calling practices. The second is to warn that I shall be using the word 'practice' in a specially defined way which does not completely agree with current ordinary usage, including my own previous use of that word. What am I going to mean by it?

By a "practice" I am going to mean any coherent and complex form of socially established cooperative human activity through which goods internal to that form of activity are realised in the course of trying to achieve those standards of excellence which are appropriate to, and partially definitive of, that form of activity, with the result that human powers to achieve excellence, and human conceptions of the ends and goods involved, are systematically extended. Tic-tac-toe is not an example of a practice in this sense, nor is throwing a football with skill; but the game of football is, and so is chess. Bricklaying is not a practice; architecture is. Planting turnips is not a practice; farming is. So are the enquiries of physics, chemistry and biology, and so is the work of the historian, and so are painting and music. In the ancient and medieval worlds the creation and sustaining of human communities—of households, cities, nations—is generally taken to be a practice in the sense in which I have defined it. Thus the range of practices is wide: arts, sciences, games, politics in the Aristotelian sense, the making and sustaining of family life, all fall under the concept. But the question of the precise range of practices is not at this stage of the first importance. Instead let me explain some of the key terms involved in my definition, beginning with the notion of goods internal to a practice.

Consider the example of a highly intelligent seven-year-old child whom I wish to teach to play chess, although the child has no particular desire to learn the game. The child does however have a very strong desire for candy and little chance of obtaining it. I therefore tell the child that if the child will play chess with me once a week I will give the child 50¢ worth of candy; moreover I tell the child that I will always play in such a way that it will be difficult, but not impossible, for the child to win and that, if the child wins, the child will receive an extra 50¢ worth of candy. Thus motivated the child plays and plays to win. Notice however that, so long as it is the candy alone which provides the child with a good reason for playing chess, the child has no reason not to cheat and every reason to cheat, provided he or she can do so successfully. But, so we may hope, there will come a time when the child will find in those goods specific to chess, in the achievement of a certain highly particular kind of analytical skill, strategic imagination and competitive intensity, a new set of reasons, reasons now not just for winning on a particular occasion, but for trying to excel in whatever way the game of chess demands. Now if the child cheats, he or she will be defeating not me, but himself or herself.

There are thus two kinds of good possibly to be gained by playing chess. On the one hand there are those goods externally and contingently attached to chess-playing and to other practices by the accidents of social circumstance—in the case of the imaginary child candy, in the case of real adults such goods as prestige, status and money. There are always alternative ways for achieving such goods, and their achievement is never to be had *only* by engaging in some particular kind of practice. On the other hand there are the goods internal to the practice of chess which cannot be had in any way but by playing chess or some other game of that specific kind. We call them internal for two reasons: first, as I have already suggested, because we can only specify them in terms of chess or some other game of that specific kind and by means of examples from such games (otherwise the meagerness of our vocabulary for speaking of such goods forces us into such devices as my own resort to writing of "a certain highly particular kind of"); and secondly because they can only be identified and recognised by the experience of participating in the practice in question. Those who lack the relevant experience are incompetent thereby as judges of internal goods.

This is clearly the case with all the major examples of practices: consider for example—even if briefly and inadequately—the practice of portrait painting as it developed in Western Europe from the late middle ages to the eighteenth century. The successful portrait painter is able to achieve many goods which are in the sense just defined external to the practice of portrait painting—fame, wealth, social status, even a measure of power and influence at courts upon occasion. But those external goods are not to be confused with the goods which are internal to the practice. The internal goods are those which result from an extended attempt to show how Wittgenstein's dictum "The human body is the best picture of the human soul" (*Investigations,* p. 178e) might be made to become true by teaching us "to regard . . . the picture on our wall as the object itself (the men, landscape and so on) depicted there" (p. 205e) in a quite new way. What is misleading about Wittgenstein's dictum as it stands is its neglect of the truth in George Orwell's thesis "At 50 everyone has the face he deserves." What painters from Giotto to Rembrandt learnt to show was how the face at any age may be revealed as the face that the subject of a portrait deserves.

Originally in medieval paintings of the saints the face was an icon; the question of a resemblance between the depicted face of Christ or St. Peter and the face that Jesus or Peter actually possessed at some particular age did not even arise. The antithesis to this iconography was the relative naturalism of certain fifteenth-century Flemish and German painting. The heavy eyelids, the coifed hair, the lines around the mouth undeniably represent some particular woman, either actual or envisaged. Resemblance has usurped the iconic relationship. But with Rembrandt there is, so to speak, synthesis: the naturalistic portrait is now rendered as an icon, but an icon of a new and hitherto inconceivable kind. Similarly in a very different kind of sequence mythological faces in a certain kind of seventeenth-century French painting become aristocratic faces in the eighteenth century. Within each of these sequences at least two different kinds of good internal to the painting of human faces and bodies are achieved.

There is first of all the excellence of the products, both the excellence in performance by the painters and that of each portrait itself. This excellence—the very verb "excel" suggests it—has to be understood historically. The sequences of development find their point and purpose in a progress towards and beyond a variety of types and modes of excellence. There are of course sequences of decline as well as of progress, and progress is rarely to be understood as straightforwardly linear. But it is in participation in the attempts to sustain progress and to respond creatively to moments that the second kind of good internal to the practices of portrait painting is to be found. For what the artist discovers within the pursuit of excellence in portrait painting—and what is true of portrait painting is true of the practice of the fine arts in general—is the good of a certain kind of life. That life may not constitute the whole of life for someone who is a painter by a very long way or it may at least for a period, Gauguin-like, absorb him or her at the expense of almost everything else. But it is the painter's living out of a greater or lesser part of his or her life *as a painter* that is the second kind of good internal to painting. And judgment upon these goods requires at the very least the kind of competence that is only to be acquired either as a painter or as someone willing to learn systematically what the portrait painter has to teach.

A practice involves standards of excellence and obedience to rules as well as the achievement of goods. To enter into a practice is to accept the authority of those standards and the inadequacy of my own performance as judged by them. It is to subject my own attitudes, choices, preferences and tastes to the standards which currently and partially define the practice. Practices of course, as I have just noticed, have a history: games, sciences and arts all have histories. Thus the standards are not themselves immune from criticism, but none the less we cannot be initiated into a practice without accepting the authority of the best standards realised so far. If, on starting to listen to music, I do not accept my own incapacity to judge correctly, I will never learn to hear, let alone to appreciate, Bartok's last quartets. If, on starting to play baseball, I do not accept that others know better than I when to throw a fast ball and when not, I will never learn to appreciate good pitching let alone to pitch. In the realm of practices the authority of both goods and standards operates in such a way as to rule out all subjectivist and emotivist analyses of judgment. De gustibus *est* disputandum.

We are now in a position to notice an important difference between what I have called internal and what I have called external goods. It is characteristic of what I have called external goods that when achieved they are always some individual's property and possession. Moreover characteristically they are such that the more someone has of them, the less there is for other people. This is sometimes necessarily the case, as with power and fame, and sometimes the case by reason of contingent circumstance as with money. External goods are therefore characteristically objects of competition in which there must be losers as well as sinners. Internal goods are indeed the outcome of competition to excel, but it is characteristic of them that their achievement is a good for the whole community who participate in the practice. So when Turner transformed the seascape in painting or W. G. Grace advanced the art of batting in cricket in a quite new way their achievement enriched the whole relevant community.

But what does all or any of this have to do with the concept of the virtues? It turns out that we are now in a position to formulate a first, even if partial and tentative definition of a virtue: *A virtue is an acquired human quality the possession and exercise of which tends to enable us to achieve those goods which are internal to practices and the lack of which effectively prevents us from achieving any such goods.* Later this definition will need amplification and amendment. But as a first approximation to an adequate definition it already illuminates the place of the virtues in human life. For it is not difficult to show for a whole range of key virtues that without them the goods internal to practices are barred to us, but not just barred to us generally, barred in a very particular way.

It belongs to the concept of a practice as I have outlined it—and as we are all familiar with it already in our actual lives, whether we are painters or physicists or quarterbacks or indeed just lovers of good painting or first-rate experiments or a well-thrown pass—that its goods can only be achieved by subordinating ourselves to the best standard so far achieved, and that entails subordinating ourselves within the practice in our relationship to other practitioners. We have to learn to recognise what is due to whom; we have to be prepared to take whatever self-endangering risks are demanded along the way; and we have to listen carefully to what we are told about our own inadequacies and to reply with the same carefulness for the facts. In other words we have to accept as necessary components of any practice with internal goods and standards of excellence the virtues of justice, courage and honesty. For not to accept these, to be willing to cheat as our imagined child was willing to cheat in his or her early days at chess, so far bars us from achieving the standards of excellence or the goods internal to the practice that it renders the practice pointless except as a device for achieving external goods.

We can put the same point in another way. Every practice requires a certain kind of relationship between those who participate in it. Now the virtues are those goods by reference to which, whether we like it or not, we define our relationships to those other people with whom we share the kind of purposes and standards which inform practices. Consider an example of how reference to the virtues has to be made in certain kinds of human relationship.

A, B, C, and D are friends in that sense of friend-ship which Aristotle takes to be primary: they share in the pursuit of certain goods. In my terms they share in a practice. D dies in obscure circumstances, A dis-covers how D died and tells the truth about it to B while lying to C. C discovers the lie. What A cannot then intelligibly claim is that he stands in the same relationship of friendship to both B and C. By telling the truth to one and lying to the other he has partially defined a difference in the relationship. Of course it is open to A to explain this difference in a number of ways; perhaps he was trying to spare C pain or per-haps he is simply cheating C. But some difference in the relationship now exists as a result of the lie. For their allegiance to each other in the pursuit of com-mon goods has been put in question.

Just as, so long as we share the standards and pur-poses characteristic of practices, we define our rela-tionships to each other, whether we acknowledge it or not, by reference to standards of truthfulness and trust, so we define them too by reference to standards of justice and of courage. If A, a professor, gives B and C the grades that their papers deserve, but grades D because he is attracted by D's blue eyes or is repelled by D's dandruff, he has defined his relation-ship to D differently from his relationship to the other members of the class, whether he wishes it or not. Justice requires that we treat others in respect of merit or desert according to uniform and impersonal standards; to depart from the standards of justice in some particular instance defines our relationship with the relevant person as in some way special or distinctive.

The case with courage is a little different. We hold courage to be a virtue because the care and concern for individuals, communities and causes which is so crucial to so much in practices requires the existence of such a virtue. If someone says that he cares for some individual, community or cause, but is unwill-ing to risk harm or danger on his, her or its own behalf, he puts in question the genuineness of his care and concern. Courage, the capacity to risk harm or danger to oneself, has its role in human life because of this connection with care and concern. This is not to say that a man cannot genuinely care and also be a coward. It is in part to say that a man who genuinely

cares and has not the capacity for risking harm or danger has to define himself, both to himself and to others, as a coward.

I take it then that from the standpoint of those types of relationship without which practices cannot be sustained truthfulness, justice and courage—and perhaps some others—are genuine excellences, are virtues in the light of which we have to characterise ourselves and others, whatever our private moral standpoint or our society's particular codes may be. For this recognition that we cannot escape the defini-tion of our relationships in terms of such goods is perfectly compatible with the acknowledgment that different societies have and have had different codes of truthfulness, justice and courage. Lutheran pietists brought up their children to believe that one ought to tell the truth to everybody at all times, whatever the circumstances or consequences, and Kant was one of their children. Traditional Bantu parents brought up their children not to tell the truth to unknown strangers, since they believed that this could render the family vulnerable to witchcraft. In our culture many of us have been brought up not to tell the truth to elderly great-aunts who invite us to admire their new hats. But each of these codes embodies an acknowledgment of the virtue of truthfulness. So it is also with varying codes of justice and of courage.

Practices then might flourish in societies with very different codes; what they could not do is flourish in societies in which the virtues were not valued, although institutions and technical skills serving uni-fied purposes might well continue to flourish. (I shall have more to say about the contrast between institu-tions and technical skills mobilised for a unified end, on the one hand, and practices on the other, in a moment.) For the kind of cooperation, the kind of recognition of authority and of achievement, the kind of respect for standards and the kind of risk-taking which are characteristically involved in practices demand for example fairness in judging oneself and others—the kind of fairness absent in my example of the professor, a ruthless truthfulness without which fairness cannot find application—the kind of truth-fulness absent in my example of A, B, C and D—and willingness to trust the judgments of those whose achievement in the practice give them an authority to judge which presupposes fairness and truthfulness in those judgments, and from time to time the taking of self-endangering, reputation-endangering and even achievement-endangering risks. It is no part of my thesis that great violinists cannot be vicious or great chess-players mean-spirited. Where the virtues are required, the vices also may flourish. It is just that the vicious and mean-spirited necessarily rely on the virtues of others for the practices in which they engage to flourish and also deny themselves the experience of achieving those internal goods which may reward even not very good chess-players and violinists.

To situate the virtues any further within practices it is necessary now to clarify a little further the nature of a practice by drawing two important contrasts. The discussion so far I hope makes it clear that a practice, in the sense intended, is never just a set of technical skills, even when directed towards some unified purpose and even if the exercise of those skills can on occasion be valued or enjoyed for their own sake. What is distinctive of a practice is in part the way in which conceptions of the relevant goods and ends which the technical skills serve—and every practice does require the exercise of technical skills—are transformed and enriched by these extensions of human powers and by that regard for its own internal goods which are partially definitive of each particular practice or type of practice. Practices never have a goal or goals fixed for all time—painting has no such goal nor has physics—but the goals themselves are transmuted by the history of the activity. It therefore turns out not to be accidental that every practice has its own history and a history which is more and other than that of the improvement of the relevant technical skills. This historical dimension is crucial in relation to the virtues.

To enter into a practice is to enter into a relationship not only with its contemporary practitioners, but also with those who have preceded us in the practice, particularly those whose achievements extended the reach of the practice to its present point. It is thus the achievement, and a fortiori the authority, of a tradition which I then confront and from which I have to learn. And for this learning and the relationship to the past which it embodies the virtues of justice, courage and truthfulness are prerequisite in precisely the same way and for precisely the same reason as they are in sustaining present relationships within practices.

It is not only of course with sets of technical skills that practices ought to be contrasted. Practices must not be confused with institutions. Chess, physics and medicine are practices; chess clubs, laboratories, universities and hospitals are institutions. Institutions are characteristically and necessarily concerned with what I have called external goods. They are involved in acquiring money and other material goods; they are structured in terms of power and status, and they distribute money, power and status as rewards. Nor could they do otherwise if they are to sustain not only themselves, but also the practices of which they are the bearers. For no practices can survive for any length of time unsustained by institutions. Indeed so intimate is the relationship of practices to institutions—and consequently of the goods external to the goods internal to the practices in question—that institutions and practices characteristically form a single causal order in which the ideals and the creativity of the practice are always vulnerable to the acquisitiveness of the institution, in which the cooperative care for common goods of the practice is always vulnerable to the competitiveness of the institution. In this context the essential function of the virtues is clear. Without them, without justice, courage and truthfulness, practices could not resist the corrupting power of institutions.

Yet if institutions do have corrupting power, the making and sustaining of forms of human community—and therefore of institutions—itself has all the characteristics of a practice, and moreover of a practice which stands in a peculiarly close relationship to the exercise of the virtues in two important ways. The exercise of the virtues is itself apt to require a highly determinate attitude to social and political issues; and it is always within some particular community with its own specific institutional forms that we learn or fail to learn to exercise the virtues. There is of course a crucial difference between the way in which the relationship between moral character and political community is envisaged from the standpoint of liberal individualist modernity and the way in which that relationship was envisaged from the standpoint of the type of ancient and medieval tradition of the virtues which I have sketched. For liberal individualism a community is simply an arena in which individuals each pursue their own self-chosen conception of the good life, and political institutions exist to provide that degree of order which makes such self-determined activity possible. Government and law are, or ought to be, neutral between rival conceptions of the good life for man, and hence, although it is the task of government to promote law-abidingness, it is on the liberal view no part of the legitimate function of government to inculcate any one moral outlook.

By contrast, on the particular ancient and medieval view which I have sketched political community not only requires the exercise of the virtues for its own sustenance, but it is one of the tasks of government to make its citizens virtuous, just as it is one of the tasks of parental authority to make children grow up so as to be virtuous adults. The classical statement of this analogy is by Socrates in the *Crito*. It does not of course follow from an acceptance of the Socratic view of political community and political authority that we ought to assign to the modern state the moral function which Socrates assigned to the city and its laws. Indeed the power of the liberal individualist standpoint partly derives from the evident fact that the modern state is indeed totally unfitted to act as moral educator of any community. But the history of how the modern state emerged is of course itself a moral history. If my account of the complex relationship of virtues to practices and to institutions is correct, it follows that we shall be unable to write a true history of practices and institutions unless that history is also one of the virtues and vices. For the ability of a practice to retain its integrity will depend on the way in which the virtues can be and are exercised in sustaining the institutional forms which are the social bearers of the practice. The integrity of a practice causally requires the exercise of the virtues by at least some of the individuals who embody it in their activities; and conversely the corruption of institutions is always in part at least an effect of the vices.

The virtues are of course themselves in turn fostered by certain types of social institution and endangered by others. Thomas Jefferson thought that only in a society of small farmers could the virtues flourish; and Adam Ferguson with a good deal more sophistication saw the institutions of modern commercial society as endangering at least some traditional virtues. It is Ferguson's type of sociology which is the empirical counterpart of the conceptual account of the virtues which I have given, a sociology which aspires to lay bare the empirical, causal connection between virtues, practices and institutions. For this kind of conceptual account has strong empirical implications; it provides an explanatory scheme which can be tested in particular cases. Moreover my thesis has empirical content in another way; it does entail that without the virtues there could be a recognition only of what I have called external goods and not at all of internal goods in the context of practices. And in any society which recognized only external goods competitiveness would be the dominant and even exclusive feature. We have a brilliant portrait of such a society in Hobbes's account of the state of nature; and Professor Turnbull's report of the fate of the Ik suggests that social reality does in the most horrifying way confirm both my thesis and Hobbes's.

Virtues then stand in a different relationship to external and to internal goods. The possession of the virtues—and not only of their semblance and simulacra—is necessary to achieve the latter; yet the possession of the virtues may perfectly well hinder us in achieving external goods. I need to emphasise at this point that external goods genuinely are goods. Not only are they characteristic objects of human desire, whose allocation is what gives point to the virtues of justice and of generosity, but no one can despise them altogether without a certain hypocrisy. Yet notoriously the cultivation of truthfulness, justice and courage will often, the world being what it contingently is, bar us from being rich or famous or powerful. Thus although we may hope that we can not only achieve the standards of excellence and the internal goods of certain practices by possessing the virtues *and* become rich, famous and powerful, the virtues are always a potential stumbling block to this comfortable ambition. We should therefore expect that, if in a particular society the pursuit of external goods were to become dominant, the concept of the virtues might suffer first attrition and then perhaps something near total effacement, although simulacra might abound.

The time has come to ask the question of how far this partial account of a core conception of the virtues—and I need to emphasise that all that I have offered so far is the first stage of such an account—is faithful to the tradition which I delineated. How far, for example, and in what ways is it Aristotelian? It is—happily—not Aristotelian in two ways in which a good deal of the rest of the tradition also dissents from Aristotle. First, although this account of the virtues is teleological, it does not require the identification of any teleology in nature, and hence it does not require any allegiance to Aristotle's metaphysical biology. And secondly, just because of the multiplicity of human practices and the consequent multiplicity of goods in the pursuit of which the virtues may be exercised—goods which will often be contingently incompatible and which will therefore make rival claims upon our allegiance—conflict will not spring solely from flaws in individual character. But it was just on these two matters that Aristotle's account of the virtues seemed most vulnerable; hence if it turns out to be the case that this socially teleological account can support Aristotle's general account of the virtues as well as does his own biologically teleological account, these differences from Aristotle himself may well be regarded as strengthening rather than weakening the case for a generally Aristotelian standpoint.

There are at least three ways in which the account that I have given *is* clearly Aristotelian. First it requires for its completion a cogent elaboration of just those distinctions and concepts which Aristotle's account requires: voluntariness, the distinction between the intellectual virtues and the virtues of character, the relationship of both to natural abilities and to the passions and the structure of practical reasoning. On every one of these topics something very like Aristotle's view has to be defended, if my own account is to be plausible.

Secondly my account can accommodate an Aristotelian view of pleasure and enjoyment, whereas it is interestingly irreconcilable with any utilitarian view and more particularly with Franklin's account of the virtues. We can approach these questions by considering how to reply to someone who, having considered my account of the differences between goods internal to and goods external to a practice required into which class, if either, does pleasure or enjoyment fall? The answer is, 'Some types of pleasure into one, some into the other.'

Someone who achieves excellence in a practice, who plays chess or football well or who carries through an enquiry in physics or an experimental mode in painting with success, characteristically enjoys his achievement and his activity in achieving. So does someone who, although not breaking the limit of achievement, plays or thinks or acts in a way that leads towards such a breaking of limit. As Aristotle says, the enjoyment of the activity and the enjoyment of achievement are not the ends at which the agent aims, but the enjoyment supervenes upon the successful activity in such a way that the activity achieved and the activity enjoyed are one and the same state. Hence to aim at the one is to aim at the other; and hence also it is easy to confuse the pursuit of excellence with the pursuit of enjoyment *in this specific sense.* This particular confusion is harmless enough; what is not harmless is the confusion of enjoyment *in this specific sense* with other forms of pleasure.

For certain kinds of pleasure are of course external goods along with prestige, status, power and money. Not all pleasure is the enjoyment supervening upon achieved activity; some is the pleasure of psychological or physical states independent of all activity. Such states—for example that produced on a normal palate by the closely successive and thereby blended sensations of Colchester oyster, cayenne pepper and Veuve Cliquot—may be sought as external goods, as external rewards which may be purchased by money or received in virtue of prestige. Hence the pleasures are categorised neatly and appropriately by the classification into internal and external goods.

It is just this classification which can find no place within Franklin's account of the virtues which is formed entirely in terms of external relationships and external goods. Thus although by this stage of the argument it is possible to claim that my account does capture a conception of the virtues which is at the core of the particular ancient and medieval tradition which I have delineated, it is equally clear that there is more than one possible conception of the virtues and that Franklin's standpoint and indeed any utilitarian standpoint is such that to accept it will entail rejecting the tradition and vice versa.

One crucial point of incompatibility was noted long ago by D. H. Lawrence. When Franklin asserts, "Rarely use venery but for health or offspring . . . ," Lawrence replies. "Never *use* venery." It is of the character of a virtue that in order that it be effective in producing the internal goods which are the rewards of the virtues it should be exercised without regard to consequences. For it turns out to be the case that—and this is in part at least one more empirical factual claim—although the virtues are just those qualities which tend to lead to the achievement of a certain class of goods, none the less unless we practice them irrespective of whether in any particular set of contingent circumstances they will produce those goods or not, we cannot possess them at all. We cannot be genuinely courageous or truthful and be so only on occasion. Moreover, as we have seen, cultivation of the virtues always may and often does hinder the achievement of those external goods which are the mark of worldly success. The road to success in Philadelphia and the road to heaven may not coincide after all.

Furthermore we are now able to specify one crucial difficulty for *any* version of utilitarianism—in addition to those which I noticed earlier. Utilitarianism cannot accommodate the distinction between goods internal to and goods external to a practice. Not only is that distinction marked by none of the classical utilitarians—it cannot be found in Bentham's writings nor in those of either of the Mills or of Sidgwick—but internal goods and external goods are not commensurable with each other. Hence the notion of summing goods—and a fortiori in the light of what I have said about kinds of pleasure and enjoyment the notion of summing happiness—in terms of one single formula or conception of utility, whether it is Franklin's or Bentham's or Mill's, makes no sense. None the less we ought to note that although *this* distinction is alien to J. S. Mill's thought, it is plausible and in no way patronising to suppose that something

like this is the distinction which he was trying to make in *Utilitarianism* when he distinguished between "higher" and "lower" pleasures. At the most we can say "something like this": for J. S. Mill's upbringing had given him a limited view of human life and powers, had unfitted him, for example, for appreciating games just because of the way it had fitted him for appreciating philosophy. None the less the notion that the pursuit of excellence in a way that extends human powers is at the heart of human life is instantly recognisable as at home in not only J. S. Mill's political and social thought, but also in his and Mrs Taylor's life. Were I to choose human exemplars of certain of the virtues as I understand them, there would of course be many names to name, those of St Benedict and St Francis of Assisi and St Theresa *and* those of Frederick Engels and Eleanor Marx and Leon Trotsky among them. But that of John Stuart Mill would have to be there as certainly as any other.

Thirdly my account is Aristotelian in that it links evaluation and explanation in a characteristically Aristotelian way. From an Aristotelian standpoint to identify certain actions as manifesting or failing to manifest a virtue or virtues is never only to evaluate; it is also to take the first step towards explaining why those actions rather than some others were performed. Hence for an Aristotelian quite as much as for a Platonist the fate of a city or an individual can be explained by citing the injustice of a tyrant or the courage of its defenders. Indeed without allusion to the place that justice and injustice, courage and cowardice play in human life very little will be genuinely explicable. It follows that many of the explanatory projects of the modern social sciences, a methodological canon of which is the separation of "the facts"—this conception of "the facts" is the one which I delineated in Chapter 7—from all evaluation, are bound to fail. For the fact that someone was or failed to be courageous or just cannot be recognised as "a fact" by those who accept that methodological canon. The account of the virtues which I have given is completely at one with Aristotle's on this point. But now the question may be raised: your account may be in many respects Aristotelian, but is it not in some respects false? Consider the following important objection.

I have defined the virtues partly in terms of their place in practices. But surely, it may be suggested, some practices—that is, some coherent human activities which answer to the description of what I have called a practice—are evil. So in discussions by some moral philosophers of this type of account of the virtues it has been suggested that torture and sado-masochistic sexual activities might be examples of practices. But how can a disposition be a virtue if it is the kind of disposition which sustains practices and some practices issue in evil? My answer to this objection falls into two parts.

First I want to allow that there *may* be practices—in the sense in which I understand the concept—which simply *are* evil. I am far from convinced that there are, and I do not in fact believe that either torture or sado-masochistic sexuality answer to the description of a practice which my account of the virtues employs. But I do not want to rest my case on this lack of conviction, especially since it is plain that as a matter of contingent fact many types of practice may on particular occasions be productive of evil. For the range of practices includes the arts, the sciences and certain types of intellectual and athletic game. And it is at once obvious that any of these may under certain conditions be a source of evil: the desire to excel and to win can corrupt, a man may be so engrossed by his painting that he neglects his family, what was initially an honourable resort to war can issue in savage cruelty. But what follows from this?

It certainly is not the case that my account entails *either* that we ought to excuse or condone such evils *or* that whatever flows from a virtue is right. I do have to allow that courage sometimes sustains injustice, that loyalty has been known to strengthen a murderous aggressor and that generosity has sometimes weakened the capacity to do good. But to deny this would be to fly in the face of just those empirical facts which I invoked in criticising Aquinas' account of the unity of the virtues. That the virtues need initially to be defined and explained with reference to the notion of a practice thus in no way entails approval of all practices in all circumstances. That the virtues—as the objection itself presupposed—*are* defined not in terms of good and right practices, but of practices, does not entail or imply that practices as

actually carried through at particular times and places do not stand in need of moral criticism. And the resources for such criticism are not lacking. There is in the first place no inconsistency in appealing to the requirements of a virtue to criticise a practice. Justice may be initially defined as a disposition which in its particular way is necessary to sustain practices; it does not follow that in pursuing the requirements of a practice violations of justice are not to be condemned. Moreover I already pointed out . . . that a morality of virtues requires as its counterpart a conception of moral law. Its requirements too have to be met by practices. But, it may be asked, does not all this imply that more needs to be said about the place of practices in some larger moral context? Does not this at least suggest that there is more to the core concept of a virtue than can be spelled out in terms of practices? I have after all emphasised that the scope of any virtue in human life extends beyond the practices in terms of which it is initially defined. What then is the place of the virtues in the larger arenas of human life?

I stressed earlier that any account of the virtues in terms of practices could only be a partial and first account. What is required to complement it? The most notable difference so far between my account and any account that could be called Aristotelian is that although I have in no way restricted the exercise of the virtues to the context of practices, it is in terms of practices that I have located their point and function. Whereas Aristotle locates that point and function in terms of the notion of a type of whole human life which can be called good. And it does seem that the question "What would a human being lack who lacked the virtues?" must be given a kind of answer which goes beyond anything which I have said so far. For such an individual would not merely fail *in a variety of particular ways* in respect of the kind of excellence which can be achieved through participation in practices and in respect of the kind of human relationship required to sustain such excellence. His own life *viewed as a whole* would perhaps be defective; it would not be the kind of life which someone would describe in trying to answer the question "What is the best kind of life for this kind of man or woman to live?" And that question cannot be answered without at least raising Aristotle's own question, "What is the good life for man?" Consider three ways in which a human life informed only by the conception of the virtues sketched so far would be defective.

It would be pervaded, first of all, by *too many* conflicts and *too much* arbitrariness. I argued earlier that it is a merit of an account of the virtues in terms of a multiplicity of goods that it allows for the possibility of tragic conflict in a way in which Aristotle's does not. But it may also produce even in the life of someone who is virtuous and disciplined too many occasions when one allegiance points in one direction, another in another. The claims of one practice may be incompatible with another in such a way that one may find oneself oscillating in an arbitrary way, rather than making rational choices. So it seems to have been with T. E. Lawrence. Commitment to sustaining the kind of community in which the virtues can flourish may be incompatible with the devotion which a particular practice—of the arts, for example—requires. So there may be tensions between the claims of family life and those of the arts—the problem that Gauguin solved or failed to solve by fleeing to Polynesia, or between the claims of politics and those of the arts—the problem that Lenin solved or failed to solve by refusing to listen to Beethoven.

If the life of the virtues is continuously fractured by choices in which one allegiance entails the apparently arbitrary renunciation of another, it may seem that the goods internal to practices do after all derive their authority from our individual choices; for when different goods summon in different and in incompatible directions. "I" have to choose between their rival claims. The modern self with its criterionless choices apparently reappears in the alien context of what was claimed to be an Aristotelian world. This accusation might be rebutted in part by returning to the question of why both goods and virtues do have authority in our lives and repeating what was said earlier in this chapter. But this reply would only be partly successful: the distinctively modern notion of choice would indeed have reappeared, even if with a more limited scope for its exercise than it has usually claimed.

Secondly without an overriding conception of the *telos* of a whole human life, conceived as a unity, our conception of certain individual virtues has to remain partial and incomplete. Consider two examples. Justice, on an Aristotelian view, is defined in terms of giving each person his or her due or desert. To deserve well is to have contributed in some substantial way to the achievement of those goods, the sharing of which and the common pursuit of which provide foundations for human community. But the goods internal to practices, including the goods internal to the practice of making and sustaining forms of community, need to be ordered and evaluated in some way if we are to assess relative desert. Thus only substantive application of an Aristotelian concept of justice requires an understanding of goods and of the good that goes beyond the multiplicity of goods which inform practices. As with justice, so also with patience. Patience is the virtue of waiting attentively without complaint, but not of waiting thus for anything at all. To treat patience as a virtue presupposes some adequate answer to the question: waiting for what? Within the context of practices a partial, although for many purposes adequate, answer can be given: the patience of a craftsman with refractory material, of a teacher with a slow pupil, of a politician in negotiations, are all species of patience. But what if the material is just too refractory, the pupil too slow, the negotiations too frustrating? Ought we always at a certain point just to give up in the interests of the practice itself? The medieval exponents of the virtue of patience claimed that there are certain types of situation in which the virtue of patience requires that I do not ever give up on some person or task, situations in which, as they would have put it, I am required to embody in my attitude to that person or task something of the patient attitude of God towards his creation. But this could only be so if patience served some overriding good, some *telos* which warranted putting other goods in a subordinate place. Thus it turns out that the content of the virtue of patience depends upon how we order various goods in a hierarchy and a fortiori on whether we are able rationally so to order these particular goods.

I have suggested so far that unless there is a *telos* which transcends the limited goods of practices by constituting the good of a whole human life, the good of a human life conceived as a unity, it will *both* be the case that a certain subversive arbitrariness will invade the moral life *and* that we shall be unable to specify the context of certain virtues adequately. These two considerations are reinforced by a third: that there is at least one virtue recognised by the tradition which cannot be specified at all except with reference to the wholeness of a human life—the virtue of integrity or constancy. "Purity of heart," said Kierkegaard, "is to will one thing." This notion of singleness of purpose in a whole life can have no application unless that of a whole life does.

It is clear therefore that my preliminary account of the virtues in terms of practices captures much, but very far from all, of what the Aristotelian tradition taught about the virtues. It is also clear that to give an account that is at once more fully adequate to the tradition and rationally defensible, it is necessary to raise a question to which the Aristotelian tradition presupposed an answer, an answer so widely shared in the pre-modern world that it never had to be formulated explicitly in any detailed way. This question is: is it rationally justifiable to conceive of each human life as a unity, so that we may try to specify each such life as having its good and so that we may understand the virtues as having their function in enabling an individual to make of his or her life one kind of unity rather than another?

Living Ethically

PETER SINGER

Peter Singer is Ira W. DeCamp Professor of Bioethics at the University Center for Human Values at Princeton University. A native of Australia, he has written numerous books, including *Animal Liberation* and *Practical Ethics*.

HEROES

Yad Vashem is situated on a hilltop outside Jerusalem. Established by the Israeli Government to commemorate the victims of the Holocaust and those who came to their aid, it is a shrine, a museum, and a research centre. Leading toward the museum is a long, tree-lined avenue, the Allee des Justes, or Avenue of the Righteous. Each tree commemorates a non-Jewish person who risked her or his life in order to save a Jew during the Nazi period. Only those who gave help without expectation of reward or benefit are deemed worthy of inclusion among the Righteous. Before a tree is planted a special committee, headed by a Judge, scrutinizes all the available evidence concerning the individual who has been sug-

gested for commemoration. Notwithstanding this strict test, the Avenue of the Righteous is not long enough to contain all the trees that need to be planted. The trees overflow onto a nearby hillside. There are now more than 6,000 of them. There must be many more rescuers of Jews from the Nazis who have never been identified. Estimates range from 50,000 to 500,000, but we will never really know. Harold Schulweis, who started a foundation that honours and assists such people, has pointed out that there are no Simon Wiesenthals to search out those who hid, fed and saved the hunted. Yad Vashem, with a limited budget, can play only a passive role in reviewing evidence about people nominated by survivors. Many who were helped did not, in the end, survive; others prefer not to relive painful memories, and have not

Reprinted from *How Are We to Live?* (Amherst, NY: Prometheus Books, 1995), by permission of the publisher.

come forward, or in any case could not identify their rescuers.

Perhaps the most famous of those commemorated at Yad Vashem is Raoul Wallenberg. In the early years of World War II, as the Nazis extended their rule across Europe, Wallenberg was leading a comfortable life as a Swedish businessman. Since Sweden was neutral, Wallenberg travelled extensively throughout Germany and to its ally, Hungary, in order to sell his firm's line of specialty foods. But he was disturbed at what he saw and heard of the persecution of the Jews. One of his friends described him as depressed, and added, "I had the feeling he wanted to do something more worthwhile with his life." In 1944, the scarcely credible news of the systematic extermination of the Jews began to build up to such a degree that it could no longer be ignored. The American Government asked the Swedish Government if, as a neutral nation, it could expand its diplomatic staff in Hungary, where there were still 750,000 Jews. It was thought that a strong diplomatic staff might somehow put pressure on the nominally independent Hungarian government to resist the deportation of Hungarian Jews to Auschwitz. The Swedish Government agreed. Wallenberg was asked to go. In Budapest he found that Adolf Eichmann, who had been appointed by Himmler to administer the "Final Solution," was determined to show his superiors just how ruthlessly efficient he could be in wiping out the Hungarian Jewish community. Wallenberg succeeded in persuading the Hungarian Government to refuse Nazi pressure for further deportations of Jews, and for a brief interlude it seemed that he could return to Sweden, his mission accomplished. Then the Nazis overthrew the Hungarian government and installed in its place a puppet regime led by the Hungarian "Arrow Cross" Nazi party. The deportations began again. Wallenberg issued "Swedish Protective Passes" to thousands of Jews, declaring them to have connections with Sweden, and to be under the protective custody of the Swedish Government. At times he stood between the Nazis and their intended victims, saying that the Jews were protected by the Swedish Government, and the Nazis would have to shoot him first if they wanted to take them away. As

the Red Army advanced on Budapest, the situation began to disintegrate. Other neutral diplomats left, but the danger remained that the Nazis and their Arrow Cross puppets would carry out a final massacre of the Jewish ghetto. Wallenberg remained in Budapest, risking falling bombs and the hatred of trigger-happy German SS and Hungarian Arrow Cross officers. He worked to get Jews to safer hiding places, and then to let the Nazi leaders know that if a massacre took place, he would personally see to it that they were hanged as war criminals. At the end of the war, 120,000 Jews were still alive in Budapest; directly or indirectly, most of them owed their lives to Wallenberg. Tragically, when the fighting in Hungary was over, Wallenberg himself disappeared and is presumed to have been killed, not by the Germans or the Arrow Cross, but by the Soviet secret police.[1]

Oskar Schindler was, like Wallenberg, a businessman, but of very different character and background. Schindler was an ethnic German from Moravia, in Czechoslovakia. Initially enthusiastic for the Nazi cause and the incorporation of the Czech provinces into Germany, he moved into Poland after the invading Nazi armies, and took over a factory in Cracow, formerly Jewish-owned, that made enamel ware. As the Nazis began taking the Jews of Cracow to the death camps, Schindler protected his Jewish workers, using as a justification the claim that his factory was producing goods essential for the war effort. On the railway platforms, as Jews were being herded into the cattle-trucks that would take them to the extermination camps, he would bribe or intimidate SS officials into releasing some that he said belonged to, or had skills that were needed for, his factory. He used his own money on the black market, buying food to supplement the inadequate rations his workers received. He even travelled secretly to Budapest in order to meet with members of an underground network who could get news of the Nazi genocide to the outside world. Near the end of the war, as the Russian army advanced across Poland, he moved his factory and all his workers to a new "labour camp" he constructed at Brinnlitz in Moravia. It was the only labour camp in Nazi Europe where Jews were not beaten, shot, or worked or starved to death. All of this was very risky;

twice Schindler was arrested by the Gestapo, but bluffed his way out of their cells. By the end of the war, at least 1,200 of Schindler's Jewish workers had survived; without Schindler they would almost certainly have died.

Schindler exemplifies the way in which people who otherwise show no signs of special distinction prove capable of heroic altruism under the appropriate circumstances. Schindler drank heavily and liked to gamble. (Once, playing cards with the brutal Nazi commandant of a forced labour camp, he wagered all his evening's winnings for the commandant's Jewish servant, saying that he needed a well-trained maid. He won, and thus saved the woman's life.) After the war Schindler had an undistinguished career, failing in a succession of business ventures, from fur breeding to running a cement works.[2]

The stories of Wallenberg and Schindler are now well known, but there are thousands of other cases of people who took risks and made sacrifices to help strangers. Those documented at Yad Vashem include: a Berlin couple with three children who moved out of one of the two rooms of their apartment, so that a Jewish family could live in the other room; a wealthy German who lost most of his money through his efforts to help Jews; and a Dutch mother of eight who, during the winter of 1944, when food was scarce, often went hungry, and rationed her children's food too, so that their Jewish guests could survive. Samuel Oliner was a twelve-year-old boy when the Nazis decided to liquidate the ghetto of Bobowa, the Polish town in which he was living. His mother told him to run away; he escaped from the ghetto, and was befriended by a Polish peasant woman who had once done some business with his father. She helped him assume a Polish identity, and arranged for him to work as an agricultural labourer. Forty-five years later Oliner, then a professor at Humboldt State University in California, co-authored *The Altruistic Personality,* a study of the circumstances and characteristics of those who rescued Jews.[3]

I know from my own parents, Jews who lived in Vienna until 1938, that for each of these heroic stories there are many more that show less dramatic, but still significant, instances of altruism. In my parents'

escape from Nazi Europe, the altruism of a virtual stranger proved more effective than ties of kinship. When Hitler marched into Vienna my newly-wedded parents sought to emigrate; but where could they go? To obtain an entry visa, countries like the United States and Australia required that one be sponsored by a resident, who would guarantee that the new immigrants would be of good behaviour and would not be a burden on the state. My father had an uncle who, several years earlier, had emigrated to the United States. He wrote seeking sponsorship. The uncle replied that he was very willing to sponsor my father, but since he had never met my mother, he was not willing to extend the sponsorship to her! In desperation my mother turned to an Australian whom she had met only once, through a mutual acquaintance, when he was a tourist in Vienna. He had not met my father at all; but he responded immediately to my mother's request, arranged the necessary papers, met my parents on the wharf when their ship arrived, and did everything he could to make them feel welcome in their new country.

Sadly, my parents' efforts to persuade their own parents to leave Vienna were not heeded with sufficient speed. My mother's father, for example, was a teacher at Vienna's leading academic high school, until the school was ordered to dismiss all Jewish teachers. Despite the loss of employment, he believed that as a veteran of the World War I, wounded in battle and decorated for gallantry, he and his wife would be safe from any attack on their person or lives. Until 1943 my grandparents continued to live in Vienna, under increasingly difficult conditions, until they were sent to concentration camps, which only my maternal grandmother survived. Even during the grim years of the war prior to 1943, however, we know from letters that my parents received that some non-Jews visited them, to bring news and comfort. When my grandfather became nervous about possessing his ceremonial sword (because Jews had for some time been forbidden to keep weapons), a friend of my mother hid the sword under her coat and threw it into a canal. This woman was also a schoolteacher; her refusal to join the Nazi Party cost her any chance of promotion. Non-Jewish former pupils of my grandfather continued to visit him in his flat, and one refused to accept a university chair because he would then have been compelled to support Nazi doctrines. These were not heroic, life-saving acts, but they were also not without a certain risk. The important point, for our purposes, is that all the social pressure on these people was pushing them in the opposite direction: to have nothing to do with Jews, and certainly not to help them in any way. Yet they did what they thought right, not what was easiest to do, or would bring them the most benefit.

Primo Levi was an Italian chemist who was sent to Auschwitz because he was Jewish. He survived, and wrote *If This Is a Man,* an extraordinarily telling account of his life as a slave on rations that were not sufficient to sustain life. He was saved from death by Lorenzo, a non-Jewish Italian who was working for the Germans as a civilian on an industrial project for which the labour of the prisoners was being used. I cannot do better than close this section with Levi's reflections on what Lorenzo did for him:

> In concrete terms it amounts to little: an Italian civilian worker brought me a piece of bread and the remainder of his ration every day for six months; he gave me a vest of his, full of patches; he wrote a postcard on my behalf and brought me the reply. For all this he neither asked nor accepted any reward, because he was good and simple and did not think that one did good for a reward.
>
> . . . I believe that it was really due to Lorenzo that I am alive today; and not so much for his material aid, as for his having constantly reminded me by his presence, by his natural and plain manner of being good, that there still existed a just world outside our own, something and someone still pure and whole, not corrupt, not savage, extraneous to hatred and terror; something difficult to define, a remote possibility of good, but for which it was worth surviving.
>
> The personages in these pages are not men. Their humanity is buried, or they themselves have buried it, under an offence received or inflicted on someone else. The evil and insane SS men, the Kapos, the politicals, the criminals, the prominents, great and small, down to the indifferent slave Haftlinge [prisoners], all the grades of the mad hierarchy created by the Germans paradoxically fraternized in a uniform internal desolation.

> But Lorenzo was a man; his humanity was pure and uncontaminated, he was outside this world of negation. Thanks to Lorenzo, I managed not to forget that I myself was a man.[4]

A GREEN SHOOT

We must, of course, be thankful for the fact that today we can help strangers without dreading the knock of the Gestapo on our door. We should not imagine, however, that the era of heroism is over. Those who took part in the "velvet revolution" that overthrew communism in Czechoslovakia, and in the parallel movement for democracy in East Germany, took great personal risks and were not motivated by thoughts of personal gain. The same can be said of the thousands who turned out to surround the Russian Parliament in defence of Boris Yeltsin in his resistance to the hard-liners' coup that deposed Mikhail Gorbachev. The supreme contemporary image of this kind of courage, however, comes not from Europe, but from China. It is a picture that appeared on television and in newspapers around the world: a lone Chinese student standing in front of a column of tanks rolling towards Tiananmen Square.

In liberal democracies, living an ethical life does not involve this kind of risk, but there is no shortage of opportunities for ethical commitment to worthwhile causes. My involvement in the animal liberation movement has brought me into contact with thousands of people who have made a fundamental decision on ethical grounds: they have changed their diet, given up meat, or, in some cases, abstained from *all* animal products. This is a decision that affects your life every day. Moreover, in a society in which most people continue to eat meat, becoming a vegetarian inevitably has an impact on how others think about you. Yet thousands of people have done this, not because they believe that they will be healthier or live longer on such a diet—although this may be the case—but because they became convinced that there is no ethical justification for the way in which animals are treated when they are raised for food. For example, Mrs A. Cardoso wrote from Los Angeles:

> I received your book, *Animal Liberation,* two weeks ago . . . I thought you would like to know that

overnight it changed my thinking and I instantly changed my eating habits to that of the vegetarian . . . Thank you for making me aware of our selfishness.

There have been many letters like this. Some of the writers had no particular interest in the treatment of animals before they more or less accidentally came into contact with the issue. Typical of these is Alan Skelly, a high school teacher from the Bahamas:

> As a high school teacher I was asked to become involved in the general studies taught to grade eleven. I was asked to prepare three consecutive lessons on any social topic. My wife had been given a small leaflet, "Animal Rights," by a child in her class. I wrote to the organization, People for the Ethical Treatment of Animals, in Washington, DC and received on hire the video "Animal Rights." This video has had such an impact upon my wife and I that we are now vegetarians and committed to animal liberation. They also sent me a copy of your book, *Animal Liberation* . . . Please be aware that fourteen years after the publication of your book you are responsible for the radicalization and commitment of my wife and I to animal liberation. Perhaps next month when I show PETA's video to 100 eleventh grade students I may also extend others' moral boundaries.

Some of the people who write tell me of particular difficulties they may have; how they can't get non-leather hiking boots, or see no practical alternative to killing mice that get into their house. One had a retail fur and leather shop when he became convinced that we ought not to be killing animals for their skins—he has had problems convincing his partner to change the nature of the business! Others want to know what to feed their dogs and cats, or whether I think prawns can feel pain. Some practise their new diets alone, others work together with groups trying to change the way animals are treated. A few risk their own freedom, breaking into laboratories in order to document the pain and suffering occurring there, and perhaps to release a few animals from it. Wherever they draw the line, they all provide significant evidence that ethical argument can change people's lives. Once they were convinced that it is wrong to rear hens in small wire cages to produce eggs more cheaply, or to put pigs in stalls too narrow for them to turn around, these people decided that they had to bring about a moral revolution in their own lives.

Animal liberation is one of many causes that rely on the readiness of people to make an ethical commitment. For two gay Americans, the cause was the outbreak of AIDS. Jim Corti, a medical nurse, and Martin Delaney, a corporate consultant, were horrified to discover that American regulations prevented their HIV-positive friends from receiving novel drugs that appeared to offer some hope for people with AIDS. They drove to Mexico, where the drugs were available, and smuggled them back into the USA. Soon they found themselves running an illegal worldwide operation, smuggling drugs and fighting government bureaucracies that sought to protect people dying from an incurable disease against drugs that were not proven safe and effective. Eventually, after taking considerable risks and doing a lot of hard work, they succeeded in changing government policies so that AIDS patients—and all those with terminal diseases—have quicker access to experimental treatments.[5]

Australia's most memorable wilderness struggle took place in 1982 and 1983, when 2,600 people sat in front of bulldozers that were being used to begin construction of a dam on the Franklin river, in southwest Tasmania. The Franklin was Tasmania's last wild river, and the dam, to be built to generate electricity, would flood dramatic gorges and rapids, obliterate Aboriginal heritage sites, destroy Huon Pines that had taken 2,000 years to grow, and drown the animals that lived in the forests. The blockaders came from all over Australia, some travelling thousands of kilometres at their own expense from Queensland and Western Australia. They included teachers, doctors, public servants, scientists, farmers, clerks, engineers and taxi drivers. Almost half were arrested by police, mostly charged with trespass. A team of twenty lawyers, all volunteers, helped with court proceedings. Nearly 450 people refused to accept bail conditions, and spent between two and twenty-six days in gaol. Professor David Bellamy, the world-renowned English botanist, travelled around the world to take part in the blockade, and was duly arrested. Interviewed later in the local police lock-up, he said:

> It was the most uplifting thing I have ever been part of, to see such a broad cross-section of society peacefully demonstrating in quite inhospitable weather against the destruction of something they all believed in.[6]

Ethical commitment, no matter how strong, is not always rewarded; but this time it was. The blockade made the Franklin dam a national issue, and contributed to the election of a federal Labor government pledged to stop it. The Franklin still runs free.

These exciting struggles exemplify one aspect of a commitment to living ethically; but to focus too much on them can be misleading. Ethics appears in our lives in much more ordinary, everyday ways. As I was writing this chapter, my mail brought me the newsletter of the Australian Conservation Foundation, Australia's leading conservation lobby group. It included an article by the Foundation's fund-raising co-ordinator, in which he reported on a trip to thank a donor who had regularly sent donations of $1,000 or more. When he reached the address he thought something must be wrong; he was in front of a very modest suburban home. But there was no mistake: David Allsop, an employee of the state department of public works, donates 50 percent of his income to environmental causes. David had previously worked as a campaigner himself, and said he found it deeply satisfying now to be able to provide the financial support for others to campaign.[7]

There is something uplifting about ethical commitment, whether or not we share the objectives. No doubt some who read these pages will think that it is wrong to release animals from laboratories, no matter what the animals might suffer; others will think that everyone ought to abide by the decisions of the state's planning procedures on whether or not a new dam should go ahead. They may think that those who take the opposite view are not acting ethically at all. Yet they should be able to recognize the unselfish commitment of those who took part in these actions. In the abortion controversy, for example, I can acknowledge the actions of opponents of abortion as ethically motivated, even while I disagree with them

about the point from which human life ought to be protected, and deplore their insensitivity to the feelings of young pregnant women who are harassed when going to clinics that provide abortions.

In contrast to most of the examples given so far, I shall now consider some in which unselfish, ethical action is a much quieter, more ordinary event, but no less significant for that. Maimonides, the greatest Jewish moral thinker of the medieval period, drew up a "Golden Ladder of Charity." The lowest level of charity, he said, is to give reluctantly; the second lowest is to give cheerfully but not in proportion to the distress of the person in need; the third level is to give cheerfully and proportionately, but only when asked; the fourth to give cheerfully, proportionately, without being asked, but to put the gift into the poor person's hand, thus causing him to feel shame; the fifth is to give so that one does not know whom one benefits, but they know who their benefactor is; the sixth is to know whom we benefit, but to remain unknown to them; and the seventh is to give so that one does not know whom one benefits and they do not know who benefits them. Above this highly meritorious seventh level Maimonides placed only the anticipation of the need for charity, and its prevention by assisting others to earn their own livelihood so as not to need charity at all.[8] It is striking that, 800 years after Maimonides graded charity in this way, many ordinary citizens take part in what he would classify as the highest possible level of charity, at least where prevention is not possible. This happens at the voluntary blood banks that are—in Britain, Australia, Canada and many European countries—the only source of supply for the very large amount of human blood needed for medical purposes. . . . The gift of blood is in one sense a very intimate one (the blood that is flowing in my body will later be inside the body of another); and in another sense a very remote one (I will never know who receives my blood, nor will they know from whom the blood came). It is relatively easy to give blood. Every healthy person, rich or poor, can give it, without risk. Yet to the recipient, the gift can be as precious as life itself.

It is true that only a minority of the population (in Britain, about 6 percent of people eligible to donate) actually do donate.[9] It is also true that to give blood is not much of a sacrifice. It takes an hour or so, involves a slight prick, and may make you feel a little weak for the next few hours, but that is all. How many people, a sceptic might ask, would be prepared to make a *real* sacrifice so that a stranger could live?

If the willingness to undergo anaesthesia and stay overnight in hospital is enough of a real sacrifice, we now know that hundreds of thousands of people *are* prepared to do this. In recent years, bone marrow donor registries have been established in about twenty-five countries. In the USA, about 650,000 people have registered and 1,300 have donated. Figures in some other countries are comparable. For instance, in France, 63,000 have registered, and 350 have donated; England has had 180,000 registrations and 700 donations to date; in Canada, 36,000 have registered, and 83 have donated; while Denmark's registrations total 10,000, with five donations. Approximately 25,000 Australians have registered on the Australian Bone Marrow Donor Registry, and at the time of writing, ten have already donated bone marrow.[10] With clam deliberation, in a situation untouched by nationalism or the hysteria of war, and with no prospect of any tangible reward, a number of ordinary citizens are prepared to go to considerable lengths to help a stranger.

We should not be surprised about this willingness to help. As the American author Alfie Kohn puts it in a cheery book called *The Brighter Side of Human Nature:*

> It is the heroic acts that turn up in the newspaper ("Man Dives into Pond to Save Drowning Child") and upstage the dozens of less memorable prosocial behaviors that each of us witnesses and performs in a given week. In my experience, cars do not spin their wheels on the ice for very long before someone stops to give a push. We disrupt our schedules to visit sick friends, stop to give directions to lost travelers, ask crying people if there is anything we can do to help . . . All of this, it should be stressed, is particularly remarkable in light of the fact that we are socialized in an ethic of competitive individualism. Like a green shoot forcing its way up between the concrete slabs of a city sidewalk, evidence of human caring and helping defies this culture's ambivalence about—if not outright discouragement of—such activity.[11]

Countless voluntary charities depend on public donations; and most also rely on something that, for many of us, is even harder to give: our own time. American surveys indicate that nearly 90 percent of Americans give money to charitable causes, including 20 million families who give at least 5 percent of their income to charity. Eighty million Americans—nearly half the adult population—volunteer their time, contributing a total of 15 billion hours of volunteer work in 1988.[12]

We act ethically as consumers, too. When the public learnt that the use of aerosols containing CFCs damages the ozone layer, the sale of those products fell significantly, before any legal phase-out had come into effect. Consumers had gone to the trouble of reading the labels, and choosing products without the harmful chemicals, even though each of them could have chosen not to be bothered. Leading advertising agency J. Walter Thompson surveyed American consumers in 1990 and found that 82 percent indicated that they were prepared to pay more for environmentally-friendly products. Between a third and half said that they had already made some environmental choices with their spending dollars. For example, 54 percent said that they had already stopped using aerosol sprays.[13]

The Council on Economic Priorities is a United States organization that rates companies on their corporate citizenship records. The aspects rated are giving to charity, supporting the advancement of women and members of minority groups, animal testing, military contracts, community outreach, nuclear power, involvement with South Africa, environmental impact, and family benefits. The results are published annually in a paperback that has sold 800,000 copies. Presumably many of those who buy the book are interested in supporting companies that have a good record on ethical issues.

Many of the millions of customers who have helped to make The Body Shop a successful international cosmetics chain go there because they want to make sure that when they buy cosmetics, they are not supporting animal testing or causing damage to the environment. From small beginnings, the organization has grown at an average rate of 50 percent per annum, and sales are now around $150 million a year.

Similarly, mutual investment funds that restrict their investments to corporations that satisfy ethical guidelines have become much more significant in the last decade, as people become concerned about the ethical impact of their investments and not only about the financial return they may gain.[14]

These examples of ethical conduct have focused on ethical acts that help strangers, or the community as a whole, or nonhuman animals, or the preservation of wilderness, because these are the easiest to identify as altruistic, and therefore as ethical. But most of our daily lives, and hence most of our ethical choices, involve people with whom we have some relationship. The family is the setting for much of our ethical decision-making; so is the workplace. When we are in long-standing relationships with people it is less easy to see clearly whether we do what we do because it is right, or because we want, for all sorts of reasons, to preserve the relationship. We may also know that the other person will have opportunities to pay us back—to assist us, or to make life difficult for us—according to how we behave toward him or her. In such relationships, ethics and self-interest are inextricably mingled, along with love, affection, gratitude and many other central human feelings. The ethical aspect may still be significant.

WHY DO PEOPLE ACT ETHICALLY?

In [a previous chapter] I referred . . . to the cynical view that if only we probe deeply enough, we will find that self-interest lurks somewhere beneath the surface of every ethical action. In contrast to this view, we saw that evolutionary theory, properly understood predicts that we will be concerned for the welfare of our kin, members of our group, and those with whom we may enter into reciprocal relationships. Now we have seen that many people act ethically in circumstances that cannot be explained in any of these ways. Oskar Schindler was not furthering his own interests, nor those of his kin or of his group, when he bribed and cajoled SS officers to protect Jewish prisoners from deportation to the death camps. To a successful non-Jewish German businessman, the abject and helpless Jewish prisoners of the

SS would hardly have been promising subjects with whom to begin a reciprocal relationship. (Real life has unpredictable twists; as it happened, many years after the war, when Schindler was struggling to find a career for himself, some of those whose lives he had saved were able to help him; but in 1942, as far as anyone could possibly tell, the prudent thing for Schindler to do would have been to keep his mind on his business, or relax with the wine, women and gambling that he obviously enjoyed.) Similar things can be said about other rescuers in thousands of well-documented cases. The point is sufficiently established, though, by the more humdrum example of blood donation. Since this is an institution that continues to thrive, it is easier to investigate.

Richard Titmuss, a distinguished British social researcher, published the results of a study of nearly 4,000 British blood donors in a splendid book called *The Gift Relationship*. He asked his sample of donors why they first gave blood, and why they continued to give. Overwhelmingly, people from all levels of education and income answered that they were trying to help others. Here is one example, from a young married woman who worked as a machine operator:

> You can't get blood from supermarkets and chain stores. People themselves must come forward, sick people can't get out of bed to ask you for a pint to save their life, so I came forward in hope to help somebody who needs blood.

A maintenance fitter said simply:

> No man is an island.

A bank manager wrote:

> I felt it was a small contribution that I could make to the welfare of humanity.

And a widow on a pension answered:

> Because I am fortunate in having good health myself and like to think my blood can help someone else back to health, and I felt this was a wonderful service I wanted to be part of.[15]

Aristotle suggested that we become virtuous by practising virtue, in much the same way as we become players of the lyre, a kind of ancient harp, by playing the lyre. In some respects this seems a strange idea, but it is supported by further research on the motivation of blood donors. Professor Ernie Lightman, of the University of Toronto, surveyed 2,000 voluntary blood donors, and found that their first donation was prompted by some outside event, such as an appeal from a blood bank for more donors, the fact that friends or colleagues were donating, or the convenience of a place to donate. As time passed, however, these external motivators became less significant, and "ideas such as a sense of duty and support for the work of the Red Cross, along with a general desire to help" became more important. Lightman concludes that "with repeated performance of a voluntary act over time, the sense of personal, moral obligation assumed increasing importance." Researchers at the University of Wisconsin have also studied the motivation of blood donors, and found that the greater the number of donations the donors have made, the less likely they were to say that they were prompted to give by the expectations of others, and the more likely to say that they were motivated by a sense of moral obligation and responsibility to the community. So maybe Aristotle was right: the more we practise virtue, for whatever reason, the more likely we are to become virtuous in an inner sense as well.[16]

Altruistic action is easy to recognize as ethical, but much ethical behaviour is quite compatible with regard for one's own interests. Here is one last example, this time from my own experience. As a teenager, I worked during the summer holidays in my father's office. It was a small family business, importing coffee and tea. Among the correspondence I had to read were, occasionally, letters that my father sent out to the exporters from whom he had purchased goods, reminding them that they had not yet sent him invoices for goods dispatched a considerable time ago. Sometimes it was clear, from the length of time that had elapsed, that something had slipped through the system in the "accounts payable" section of the exporter's business. If the exporters were large firms, they might never have noticed their mistake; for us, on the other hand, since we worked on gross profit

margins of 3 percent, one or two "free" consignments would have made more profit than a month's normal trading. So why not, I asked my father, let the exporters look after their own problems? If they remembered to ask for their money, well and good, if they did not, better still! His reply was that that was not how decent people did business; and anyway, to send these reminders built up trust, which was vital for any business relationship, and would in the long run rebound to our profit. The answer, in other words, hovered between references to an ethical ideal of how one ought to behave (what it is to be virtuous in business, one might say) and a justification in terms of long-term self-interest. Despite this ambivalence, my father was clearly acting ethically.

Ethics is everywhere in our daily lives. It lies behind many of our choices, whether personal or political, or bridging the division between the two. Sometimes it comes easily and naturally to us; in other circumstances, it can be very demanding. But ethics intrudes into our conscious lives only occasionally, and often in a confused way. If we are to make properly considered ultimate choices, we must first become more aware of the ethical ramifications of the way we live. Only then is it possible to make ethics a more conscious and coherent part of everyday life.

NOTES

1. For details on Wallenberg's life, see John Bierman, *The Righteous Gentile,* Viking Press, New York, 1981.

2. See Thomas Kenneally, *Schindler's Ark,* Hodder and Stoughton, London, 1982.

3. Samuel and Pearl Oliner, *The Altruistic Personality: Rescuers of Jews in Nazi Europe,* Free Press, New York, 1988. The cases mentioned earlier in the paragraph are taken from Kristen R. Monroe, Michael C. Barton and Ute Klingemann, "Altruism and the Theory of Rational Action: Rescuers of Jews in Nazi Europe," *Ethics,* Oct. 1990, vol. 101, no. 1, pp. 103–123. See also Perry London, "The Rescuers: motivational hypotheses about Christians who saved Jews from the Nazis," in J. Macaulay and L. Berkowitz, eds., *Altruism and Helping Behavior,* Academic Press, New York, 1970; Carol Rittner and Gordon Myers, eds., *The Courage to Care—Rescuers of Jews During the Holocaust,* New York University Press, New York, 1986;

Nehama Tec, *When Light Pierced the Darkness—Christian Rescuers of Jews in Nazi-Occupied Poland,* Oxford University Press, New York, 1986; and Gay Block and Malka Drucker, *Rescuers—Portraits of Moral Courage in the Holocaust,* Holmes and Meier, New York, 1992.

4. Primo Levi, *If This Is a Man,* trans. Stuart Woolf, Abacus, London, 1987, pp. 125, 127–8.

5. The story of Corti and Delaney is the subject of Jonathan Kwitny's *Acceptable Risks,* Poseidon Press, New York, 1992.

6. The Blockaders, *The Franklin Blockade,* The Wilderness Society, Hobart, 1983, p. 72.

7. *Conservation News,* vol. 24, no. 2, April/May 1992.

8. Maimonides, *Mishneh Torah,* Book 7, ch. 10, reprinted in Isadore Twersky, *A Maimonides Reader,* Behrman House, New York, 1972, pp. 136–7.

9. R. M. Titmuss, *The Gift Relationship,* Allen & Unwin, London, 1971, p. 44.

10. These figures were obtained from correspondence received from the relevant bone marrow registries during June/July 1992.

11. Alfie Kohn, *The Brighter Side of Human Nature,* Basic Books, New York, 1990, p. 64.

12. B. O'Connell, "Already 1,000 Points of Light," *New York Times,* Jan. 25, 1989, A23. (I owe this reference to Alfie Kohn, *The Brighter Side of Human Nature,* p. 290.) See also *Time,* April 8, 1991.

13. Aerosol production of personal care products in 1989 declined 11 percent from 1988 levels, according to the Chemical Specialty Manufacturers Association, *The Rose Sheet,* Federal Department of Conservation Reports, Chevy Chase, Maryland, vol. 11, no. 50, Dec. 10, 1990.

14. "Doing the Right Thing," *Newsweek,* Jan. 7, 1991, pp. 42–3.

15. The quotations are taken from R. M. Titmuss, *The Gift Relationship,* pp. 227–8.

16. E. Lightman, "Continuity in social policy behaviors: The case of voluntary blood donorship," *Journal of Social Policy,* 1981, vol. 10, no. 1, pp. 53–79; J. A. Piliavin, D. E. Evans and P. Callero, "Learning to 'give to unnamed strangers': The process of commitment to regular blood donation," in E. Staub et al, eds., *Development and Maintenance of Prosocial Behavior: International Perspectives on Positive Morality,* Plenum Press, New York, 1984, pp. 471–491; J. Piliavin, "Why do they give the gift of life? A review of research on blood donors since 1977," *Transfusion,* 1990, vol. 30, no. 5, pp. 444–459. For Aristotle's views on virtue, see his *Nicomachean Ethics,* trans. W. D. Ross, World Classics, Oxford University Press, London, 1959. I take the point made in this paragraph from "Giving Blood: The Development of Generosity," an unsigned article in *Issues in Ethics,* 1992, vol. 5, no. 1, published by the Santa Clara University Center for Applied Ethics, Calif.

The Conscience of Huckleberry Finn

~

JONATHAN BENNETT

Jonathan Bennett, who now lives in Canada, is professor emeritus of philosophy at Syracuse University. He has written numerous books, including *The Act Itself,* about ethics, and *Learning from Six Philosophers,* about Descartes, Spinoza, Leibniz, Locke, Berkeley, and Hume.

In this paper, I shall present not just the conscience of Huckleberry Finn but two others as well. One of them is the conscience of Heinrich Himmler. He became a Nazi in 1923; he served drably and quietly, but well, and was rewarded with increasing responsibility and power. At the peak of his career he held many offices and commands, of which the most powerful was that of leader of the S.S.—the principal

Reprinted from *Philosophy, 49* (1974), by permission of Cambridge University Press and the author.

police force of the Nazi regime. In this capacity, Himmler commanded the whole concentration-camp system, and was responsible for the execution of the so-called "final solution of the Jewish problem." It is important for my purposes that this piece of social engineering should be thought of not abstractly but in concrete terms of Jewish families being marched to what they think are bath-houses, to the accompaniment of loud-speaker renditions of extracts from *The Merry Widow* and *Tales of Hoffman,* there to be choked to death by poisonous gases. Altogether, Himmler succeeded in murdering about four and a half million of them, as well as several million gentiles, mainly Poles and Russians.

The other conscience to be discussed is that of the Calvinist theologian and philosopher Jonathan Edwards. He lived in the first half of the eighteenth century, and has a good claim to be considered America's first serious and considerable philosophical thinker. He was for many years a widely-renowned preacher and Congregationalist minister in New England; in 1748 a dispute with his congregation led him to resign (he couldn't accept their view that unbelievers should be admitted to the Lord's Supper in the hope that it would convert them); for some years after that he worked as a missionary, preaching to Indians through an interpreter; then in 1758 he accepted the presidency of what is now Princeton University, and within two months died from a smallpox inoculation. Along the way he wrote some first-rate philosophy: his book attacking the notion of free will is still sometimes read. Why I should be interested in Edwards' *conscience* will be explained in due course.

I shall use Heinrich Himmler, Jonathan Edwards and Huckleberry Finn to illustrate different aspects of a single theme, namely the relationship between *sympathy* on the one hand and *bad morality* on the other.

All that I can mean by a "bad morality" is a morality whose principles I deeply disapprove of. When I call a morality bad, I cannot prove that mine is better; but when I here call any morality bad, I think you will agree with me that it is bad; and that is all I need.

There could be dispute as to whether the springs of someone's actions constitute a *morality*. I think, though, that we must admit that someone who acts in ways which conflict grossly with our morality may

nevertheless have a morality of his own—a set of principles of action which he sincerely assents to, so that for him the problem of acting well or rightly or in obedience to conscience is the problem of conforming to *those* principles. The problem of conscientiousness can arise as acutely for a bad morality as for any other: rotten principles may be as difficult to keep as decent ones.

As for "sympathy": I use this term to cover every sort of fellow-feeling, as when one feels pity over someone's loneliness, or horrified compassion over his pain, or when one feels a shrinking reluctance to act in a way which will bring misfortune to someone else. These *feelings* must not be confused with *moral judgments*. My sympathy for someone in distress may lead me to help him, or even to think that I ought to help him; but in itself it is not a judgment about what I ought to do but just a *feeling* for him in his plight. We shall get some light on the difference between feelings and moral judgments when we consider Huckleberry Finn.

Obviously, feelings can impel one to action, and so can moral judgments; and in a particular case sympathy and morality may pull in opposite directions. This can happen not just with bad moralities, but also with good ones like yours and mine. For example, a small child, sick and miserable, clings tightly to his mother and screams in terror when she tries to pass him over to the doctor to be examined. If the mother gave way to her sympathy, that is to her feeling for the child's misery and fright, she would hold it close and not let the doctor come near; but don't we agree that it might be wrong for her to act on such a feeling? Quite generally, then, anyone's moral principles may apply to a particular situation in a way which runs contrary to the particular thrusts of fellow-feeling that he has in that situation. My immediate concern is with sympathy in relation to bad morality, but not because such conflicts occur only when the morality is bad.

Now, suppose that someone who accepts a bad morality is struggling to make himself act in accordance with it in a particular situation where his sympathies pull him another way. He sees the struggle as one between doing the right, conscientious thing, and acting wrongly and weakly, like the mother who won't let the doctor come near her sick, frightened baby. Since we don't accept this person's morality, we may see the situation very differently, thoroughly disapproving of the action he regards as the right one, and endorsing the action which from his point of view constitutes weakness and backsliding.

Conflicts between sympathy and bad morality won't always be like this, for we won't disagree with every single dictate of a bad morality. Still, it can happen in the way I have described, with the agent's right action being our wrong one, and vice versa. That is just what happens in a certain episode in chapter 16 of *The Adventures of Huckleberry Finn,* an episode which brilliantly illustrates how fiction can be instructive about real life.

Huck Finn has been helping his slave friend Jim to run away from Miss Watson, who is Jim's owner. In their raft-journey down the Mississippi river, they are near to the place at which Jim will become legally free. Now let Huck take over the story:

> Jim said it made him all over trembly and feverish to be so close to freedom. Well, I can tell you it made me all over trembly and feverish, too, to hear him, because I begun to get it through my head that he *was* most free—and who was to blame for it? Why, *me.* I couldn't get that out of my conscience, no how nor no way.... It hadn't ever come home to me, before, what this thing was that I was doing. But now it did; and it stayed with me, and scorched me more and more. I tried to make out to myself that *I* warn't to blame, because *I* didn't run Jim off from his rightful owner; but it warn't no use, conscience up and say, every time: "But you knowed he was running for his freedom, and you could a paddled ashore and told somebody." That was so—I couldn't get around that, no way. That was where it pinched. Conscience says to me: "What had poor Miss Watson done to you, that you could see her nigger go off right under your eyes and never say one single word? What did that poor old woman do to you, that you could treat her so mean? . . ." I got to feeling so mean and so miserable I most wished I was dead.

Jim speaks of his plan to save up to buy his wife, and then his children, out of slavery; and he adds that if the children cannot be bought he will arrange to steal them. Huck is horrified:

> Thinks I, this is what comes of my not thinking. Here was this nigger which I had as good as helped

to run away, coming right out flat-footed and saying he would steal his children—children that belonged to a man I didn't even know; a man that hadn't ever done me no harm.

> I was sorry to hear Jim say that, it was such a lowering of him. My conscience got to stirring me up hotter than ever, until at last I says to it: "Let up on me—it ain't too late, yet—I'll paddle ashore at first light, and tell." I felt easy, and happy, and light as a feather, right off. All my troubles was gone.

This is bad morality all right. In his earliest years Huck wasn't taught any principles, and the only ones he has encountered since then are those of rural Missouri, in which slave-owning is just one kind of ownership and is not subject to critical pressure. It hasn't occurred to Huck to question those principles. So the action, to us abhorrent, of turning Jim in to the authorities presents itself *clearly* to Huck as the right thing to do.

For us, morality and sympathy would both dictate helping Jim to escape. If we felt any conflict, it would have both these on one side and something else on the other—greed for a reward, or fear of punishment. But Huck's morality conflicts with his sympathy, that is, with his unargued, natural feeling for his friend. The conflict starts when Huck sets off in the canoe towards the shore, pretending that he is going to reconnoitre, but really planning to turn Jim in:

> As I shoved off, [Jim] says: "Pooty soon I'll be a-shout'n for joy, en I'll say, it's all on accounts o' Huck I's a free man . . . Jim won't ever forgit you, Huck; you's de bes' fren' Jim's ever had; en you's de *only* fren' old Jim's got now."

> I was paddling off, all in a sweat to tell on him; but when he says this, it seemed to kind of take the tuck all out of me. I went along slow then, and I warn't right down certain whether I was glad I started or whether I warn't. When I was fifty yards off, Jim says:

> "Dah you goes, de ole true Huck; de on'y white genlman dat ever kep' his promise to ole Jim." Well, I just felt sick. But I says, I *got* to do it—I can't get *out* of it.

In the upshot, sympathy wins over morality. Huck hasn't the strength of will to do what he sincerely thinks he ought to do. Two men hunting for runaway slaves ask him whether the man on his raft is black or white:

> I didn't answer up prompt. I tried to, but the words wouldn't come. I tried, for a second or two, to brace up and out with it, but I warn't man enough—hadn't the spunk of a rabbit. I see I was weakening; so I just give up trying, and up and says: "He's white."

So Huck enables Jim to escape, thus acting weakly and wickedly—he thinks. In this conflict between sympathy and morality, sympathy wins.

One critic has cited this episode in support of the statement that Huck suffers "excruciating moments of wavering between honesty and respectability." That is hopelessly wrong, and I agree with the perceptive comment on it by another critic, who says:

> The conflict waged in Huck is much more serious: he scarcely cares for respectability and never hesitates to relinquish it, but he does care for honesty and gratitude—and both honesty and gratitude require that he should give Jim up. It is not, in Huck, honesty at war with respectability but love and compassion for Jim struggling against his conscience. His decision is for Jim and hell: a right decision made in the mental chains that Huck never breaks. His concern for Jim is and remains *irrational*. Huck finds many reasons for giving Jim up and none for stealing him. To the end Huck sees his compassion for Jim as a weak, ignorant, and wicked felony.

That is precisely correct—and it can have that virtue only because Mark Twain wrote the episode with such unerring precision. The crucial point concerns *reasons,* which all occur on one side of the conflict. On the side of conscience we have principles, arguments, considerations, ways of looking at things:

> "It hadn't ever come home to me before what I was doing"
> "I tried to make out that I warn't to blame"
> "Conscience said 'But you knowed . . .'—I couldn't get around that"
> 'What had poor Miss Watson done to you?'
> "This is what comes of my not thinking"
> " . . . children that belonged to a man I didn't even know."

On the other side, the side of feeling, we get nothing like that. When Jim rejoices in Huck, as his only

friend, Huck doesn't consider the claims of friendship or have the situation "come home" to him in a different light. All that happens is: "When he says this, it seemed to kind of take the tuck all out of me. I went along slow then, and I warn't right down certain whether I was glad I started or whether I warn't." Again, Jim's words about Huck's "promise" to him don't give Huck any *reason* for changing his plan: in his morality promises to slaves probably don't count. Their effect on him is of a different kind: "Well, I just felt sick." And when the moment for final decision comes, Huck doesn't weigh up pros and cons: he simply *fails* to do what he believes to be right—he isn't strong enough, hasn't "the spunk of a rabbit." This passage in the novel is notable not just for its finely wrought irony, with Huck's weakness of will leading him to do the right thing, but also for its masterly handling of the difference between general moral principles and particular unreasoned emotional pulls.

Consider now another case of bad morality in conflict with human sympathy the case of the odious Himmler. Here, from a speech he made to some S.S. generals, is an indication of the content of his morality:

> What happens to a Russian, to a Czech, does not interest me in the slightest. What the nations can offer in the way of good blood of our type, we will take, if necessary by kidnapping their children and raising them here with us. Whether nations live in prosperity or starve to death like cattle interests me only in so far as we need them as slaves to our *Kultur;* otherwise it is of no interest to me. Whether 10,000 Russian females fall down from exhaustion while digging an antitank ditch interests me only in so far as the antitank ditch for Germany is finished.

But has this a moral basis at all? And if it has, was there in Himmler's own mind any conflict between morality and sympathy? Yes there was. Here is more from the same speech:

> . . . I also want to talk to you quite frankly on a very grave matter . . . I mean . . . the extermination of the Jewish race. . . . Most of you must know what it means when 100 corpses are lying side by side, or 500, or 1,000. To have stuck it out and at the same time—apart from exceptions caused by human

weakness—to have remained decent fellows, that is what has made us hard. This is a page of glory in our history which has never been written and is never to be written.

Himmler saw his policies as being hard to implement while still retaining one's human sympathies—while still remaining a "decent fellow." He is saying that only the weak take the easy way out and just squelch their sympathies, and is praising the stronger and more glorious course of retaining one's sympathies while acting in violation of them. In the same spirit, he ordered that when executions were carried out in concentration camps, those responsible "are to be influenced in such a way as to suffer no ill effect in their character and mental attitude." A year later he boasted that the S.S. had wiped out the Jews

> without our leaders and their men suffering any damage in their minds and souls. The danger was considerable, for there was only a narrow path between the Scylla of their becoming heartless ruffians unable any longer to treasure life, and the Charybdis of their becoming soft and suffering nervous breakdowns.

And there really can't be any doubt that the basis of Himmler's policies was a set of principles which constituted his morality—a sick, bad, wicked *morality*. He described himself as caught in "the old tragic conflict between will and obligation." And when his physician Kersten protested at the intention to destroy the Jews, saying that the suffering involved was "not to be contemplated," Kersten reports that Himmler replied:

> He knew that it would mean much suffering for the Jews. . . . "It is the curse of greatness that it must step over dead bodies to create new life. Yet we must . . . cleanse the soil or it will never bear fruit. It will be a great burden for me to bear."

This, I submit, is the language of morality.

So in this case, tragically, bad morality won out over sympathy. I am sure that many of Himmler's killers did extinguish their sympathies, becoming "heartless ruffians" rather than "decent fellows"; but

not Himmler himself. Although his policies ran against the human grain to a horrible degree, he did not sandpaper down his emotional surfaces so that there was no grain there, allowing his actions to slide along smoothly and easily. He did, after all, bear his hideous burden, and even paid a price for it. He suffered a variety of nervous and physical disabilities, including nausea and stomach-convulsions, and Kersten was doubtless right in saying that these were "the expression of a psychic division which extended over his whole life."

This same division must have been present in some of those officials of the Church who ordered heretics to be tortured so as to change their theological opinions. Along with the brutes and the cold careerists, there must have been some who cared, and who suffered from the conflict between their sympathies and their bad morality.

In the conflict between sympathy and bad morality, then, the victory may go to sympathy as in the case of Huck Finn, or to morality as in the case of Himmler.

Another possibility is that the conflict may be avoided by giving up, or not ever having, those sympathies which might interfere with one's principles. That seems to have been the case with Jonathan Edwards. I am afraid that I shall be doing an injustice to Edwards' many virtues, and to his great intellectual energy and inventiveness; for my concern is only with the worst thing about him—namely his morality, which was worse than Himmler's.

According to Edwards, God condemns some men to an eternity of unimaginably awful pain, though he arbitrarily spares others—"arbitrarily" because none deserve to be spared:

> Natural men are held in the hand of God over the pit of hell; they have deserved the fiery pit, and are already sentenced to it; and God is dreadfully provoked, his anger is as great towards them as to those that are actually suffering the executions of the fierceness of his wrath in hell . . . ; the devil is waiting for them, hell is gaping for them, the flames gather and flash about them, and would fain lay hold on them . . . ; and . . . there are no means within reach that can be any security to them. . . . All that preserves them is the mere arbitrary will,

and uncovenanted unobliged forebearance of an incensed God.

Notice that he says "they have deserved the fiery pit." Edwards insists that men *ought* to be condemned to eternal pain; and his position isn't that this is right because God wants it, but rather that God wants it because it is right. For him, moral standards exist independently of God, and God can be assessed in the light of them (and of course found to be perfect). For example, he says:

They deserve to be cast into hell; so that . . . justice never stands in the way, it makes no objection against God's using his power at any moment to destroy them. Yea, on the contrary, justice calls aloud for an infinite punishment of their sins.

Elsewhere, he gives elaborate arguments to show that God is acting justly in damning sinners. For example, he argues that a punishment should be exactly as bad as the crime being punished; God is infinitely excellent; so any crime against him is infinitely bad; and so eternal damnation is exactly right as a punishment— it is infinite, but, as Edwards is careful also to say, it is "no more than infinite."

Of course, Edwards himself didn't torment the damned; but the question still arises of whether his sympathies didn't conflict with his *approval* of eternal torment. Didn't he find it painful to contemplate any fellow-human's being tortured for ever? Apparently not:

The God that holds you over the pit of hell, much as one holds a spider or some loathsome insect over the fire, abhors you, and is dreadfully provoked; . . . he is of purer eyes than to bear to have you in his sight; you are ten thousand times so abominable in his eyes as the most hateful venomous serpent is in ours.

When God is presented as being as misanthropic as that, one suspects misanthropy in the theologian. This suspicion is increased when Edwards claims that "the saints in glory will . . . understand how terrible the sufferings of the damned are; yet . . . will not be sorry for [them]." He bases this partly on a view of human nature whose ugliness he seems not to notice:

The seeing of the calamities of others tends to heighten the sense of our own enjoyments. When the saints in glory, therefore, shall see the doleful state of the damned, how will this heighten their sense of the blessedness of their own state. . . . When they shall see how miserable others of their fellow-creatures are . . . ; when they shall see the smoke of their torment, . . . and hear their dolorous shrieks and cries, and consider that they in the mean time are in the most blissful state, and shall surely be in it to all eternity; how they will rejoice!

I hope this is less than the whole truth! His other main point about why the saints will rejoice to see the torments of the damned is that it is *right* that they should do so:

The heavenly inhabitants . . . will have no love nor pity to the damned. . . . [This will not show] a want of a spirit of love in them . . . ; for the heavenly inhabitants will know that it is not fit that they should love [the damned] because they will know then, that God has no love to them, nor pity for them.

The implication that *of course* one can adjust one's feelings of pity so that they conform to the dictates of some authority—doesn't this suggest that ordinary human sympathies played only a small part in Edwards' life?

Huck Finn, whose sympathies are wide and deep, could never avoid the conflict in that way; but he is determined to avoid it, and so he opts for the only other alternative he can see—to give up morality altogether. After he has tricked the slave-hunters, he returns to the raft and undergoes a peculiar crisis:

I got aboard the raft, feeling bad and low, because I knowed very well I had done wrong, and I see it warn't no use for me to try to learn to do right; a body that don't get *started* right when he's little, ain't got no show—when the pinch comes there ain't nothing to back him up and keep him to his work, and so he gets beat. Then I thought a minute, and says to myself, hold on—s'pose you'd a done right and give Jim up; would you feel better than what you do now? No, says I, I'd feel bad—I'd feel just the same way I do now. Well, then, says I, what's the use you learning to do right, when it's troublesome to do right and ain't no trouble to do wrong, and the wages is just the same? I was stuck. I couldn't answer that. So I reckoned I wouldn't bother no more about it, but after this always do whichever come handiest at the time.

Huck clearly cannot conceive of having any morality except the one he has learned—too late, he thinks—from his society. He is not entirely a prisoner of that morality, because he does after all reject it; but for him that is a decision to relinquish morality as such; he cannot envisage revising his morality, altering its content in face of the various pressures to which it is subject, including pressures from his sympathies. For example, he does not begin to approach the thought that slavery should be rejected on moral grounds, or the thought that what he is doing is not theft because a person cannot be owned and therefore cannot be stolen.

The basic trouble is that he cannot or will not engage in abstract intellectual operations of any sort. In chapter 33 he finds himself "feeling to blame, somehow" for something he knows he had no hand in; he assumes that this feeling is a deliverance of conscience; and this confirms him in his belief that conscience shouldn't be listened to:

> It don't make no difference whether you do right or wrong, a person's conscience ain't got no sense, and just goes for him *anyway*. If I had a yaller dog that didn't know no more than a person's conscience does, I would pison him. It takes up more room than all the rest of a person's insides, and yet ain't no good, nohow.

That brisk, incurious dismissiveness fits well with the comprehensive rejection of morality back on the raft. But this is a digression.

On the raft, Huck decides not to live by principles, but just to do whatever "comes handiest at the time"—always acting according to the mood of the moment. Since the morality he is rejecting is narrow and cruel, and his sympathies are broad and kind, the results will be good. But moral principles are good to have, because they help to protect one from acting badly at moments when one's sympathies happen to be in abeyance. On the highest possible estimate of the role one's sympathies should have, one can still

allow for principles as embodiments of one's best feelings, one's broadest and keenest sympathies. On that view, principles can help one across intervals when one's feelings are at less than their best, i.e. through periods of misanthropy or meanness or self-centredness or depression or anger.

What Huck didn't see is that one can live by principles and yet have ultimate control over their content. And one way such control can be exercised is by checking of one's principles in the light of one's sympathies. This is sometimes a pretty straightforward matter. It can happen that a certain moral principle becomes untenable—meaning literally that one cannot hold it any longer—because it conflicts intolerably with the pity or revulsion or whatever that one feels when one sees what the principle leads to. One's experience may play a large part here: experiences evoke feelings, and feelings force one to modify principles. Something like this happened to the English poet Wilfred Owen, whose experiences in the First World War transformed him from an enthusiastic soldier into a virtual pacifist. I can't document his change of conscience in detail; but I want to present something which he wrote about the way experience can put pressure on morality.

The Latin poet Horace wrote that it is sweet and fitting (or right) to die for one's country—*dulce et decorum est pro patria mori*—and Owen wrote a fine poem about how experience could lead one to relinquish that particular moral principle. He describes a man who is too slow donning his gas mask during a gas attack—"As under a green sea I saw him drowning," Owen says. The poem ends like this:

> *In all my dreams before my helpless sight*
> *He plunges at me, guttering, choking, drowning.*
> *If in some smothering dreams, you too could pace*
> *Behind the wagon that we flung him in,*
> *And watch the white eyes writhing in his face,*
> *His hanging face, like a devil's sick of sin;*
> *If you could hear, at every jolt, the blood*
> *Come gargling from the froth-corrupted lungs,*
> *Bitter as the cud*
> *Of vile, incurable sores on innocent tongues,—*
> *My friend, you would not tell with such high zest*
> *To children ardent for some desperate glory,*
> *The old Lie: Dulce et decorum est*
> *Pro patria mori.*

There is a difficulty about drawing from all this a moral for ourselves. I imagine that we agree in our rejection of slavery, eternal damnation, genocide, and uncritical patriotic self-abnegation; so we shall agree that Huck Finn, Jonathan Edwards, Heinrich Himmler, and the poet Horace would all have done well to bring certain of their principles under severe pressure from ordinary human sympathies. But then we can say this because we can say that all those are bad moralities, whereas we cannot look at our own moralities and declare them bad. This is not arrogance: it is obviously incoherent for someone to declare the system of moral principles that he *accepts* to be *bad,* just as one cannot coherently say of anything that one *believes* it but it is *false.*

Still, although I can't point to any of my beliefs and say "That is false," I don't doubt that some of my beliefs *are* false; and so I should try to remain open to correction. Similarly, I accept every single item in my morality—that is inevitable—but I am sure that my morality could be improved, which is to say that it could undergo changes which I should be glad of once I had made them. So I must try to keep my morality open to revision, exposing it to whatever valid pressures there are—including pressures from my sympathies.

I don't give my sympathies a blank cheque in advance. In a conflict between principle and sympathy, principles ought sometimes to win. For example, I think it was right to take part in the Second World War on the allied side; there were many ghastly individual incidents which might have led someone to doubt the rightness of his participation in that war; and I think it would have been right for such a person to keep his sympathies in a subordinate place on those occasions, not allowing them to modify his principles in such a way as to make a pacifist of him.

Still, one's sympathies should be kept as sharp and sensitive and aware as possible, and not only because they can sometimes affect one's principles or one's conduct or both. Owen, at any rate, says that feelings and sympathies are vital even when they can do nothing but bring pain and distress. In another poem he speaks of the blessings of being numb in one's feelings: "Happy are the men who yet before they are killed/Can let their veins run cold," he says. These are the ones who do not suffer from any compassion which, as Owen puts it, "makes their feet/Sore on the alleys cobbled with their brothers." He contrasts these "happy" ones, who "lose all imagination," with himself and others "who with a thought besmirch/Blood over all our soul." Yet the poem's verdict goes against the "happy" ones. Owen does not say that they will act worse than the others whose souls are besmirched with blood because of their keen awareness of human suffering. He merely says that they are the losers because they have cut themselves off from the human condition:

> *By choice they made themselves immune*
> *To pity and whatever moans in man*
> *Before the last sea and the hapless stars;*
> *Whatever mourns when many leave these shores;*
> *Whatever shares*
> *The eternal reciprocity of tears.*

Moral Luck

~

THOMAS NAGEL

Thomas Nagel is professor of philosophy and law at New York University. His books include *The Possibility of Altruism: The View from Nowhere,* and *Equality and Partiality.* Among the numerous topics he has addressed are privacy, consciousness, and sexual perversion.

Kant believed that good or bad luck should influence neither our moral judgment of a person and his actions, nor his moral assessment of himself.

> The good will is not good because of what it effects or accomplishes or because of its adequacy to achieve some proposed end; it is good only because of its willing, i.e., it is good of itself. And, regarded for itself, it is to be esteemed incomparably higher than anything which could be brought about by it in favor of any inclination or even of the sum total of all inclinations. Even if it should happen that, by a particularly unfortunate fate or by the niggardly provision of a stepmotherly nature, this will should be wholly lacking in power to accomplish its purpose, and if even the greatest effort should not avail it to achieve anything of its end, and if there remained only the good will (not as a mere wish but as the summoning of all the means in our power), it would sparkle like a jewel in its own right, as something that had its full worth in itself. Usefulness or fruitlessness can neither diminish nor augment this worth.

He would presumably have said the same about a bad will: whether it accomplishes its evil purposes is morally irrelevant. And a course of action that would be condemned if it had a bad outcome cannot be vindicated if by luck it turns out well. There cannot be moral risk. This view seems to be wrong, but it arises in response to a fundamental problem about moral responsibility to which we possess no satisfactory solution.

The problem develops out of the ordinary conditions of moral judgment. Prior to reflection it is intuitively plausible that people cannot be morally assessed for what is not their fault, or for what is due to factors beyond their control. Such judgment is different from the evaluation of something as a good or bad thing, or state of affairs. The latter may be present in addition to moral judgment, but when we blame someone for his actions we are not merely saying it is bad that they happened, or bad that he exists: we are judging *him,* saying he is bad, which is different from his being a bad thing. This kind of judgment takes only a certain kind of object. Without being able to explain exactly why, we feel that the appropriateness of moral assessment is easily undermined by the discovery that the act or attribute, no matter how good or bad, is not under the person's control. While other evaluations remain, this one seems to lose its footing. So a clear absence of control, produced by involuntary movement, physical force, or ignorance of the circumstances, excuses what is done from moral judgment. But what we do depends in many more ways than these on what is not under our control—what is not produced by a good or a bad will, in Kant's phrase. And external influences in this broader range are not usually thought to excuse what is done from moral judgment, positive or negative.

Let me give a few examples, beginning with the type of case Kant has in mind. Whether we succeed or fail in what we try to do nearly always depends to some extent on factors beyond our control. This is true of murder, altruism, revolution, the sacrifice of certain interests for the sake of others—almost any morally important act. What has been done, and what is morally judged, is partly determined by external factors. However jewel-like the good will may be in its own right, there is a morally significant difference between rescuing someone from a burning building and dropping him from a twelfth-storey window while trying to rescue him. Similarly, there is a morally significant difference between reckless driving and manslaughter. But whether a reckless driver hits a pedestrian depends on the presence of the pedestrian at the point where he recklessly passes a red light. What we do is also limited by the opportunities and choices with which we are faced, and these are largely determined by factors beyond our control. Someone who was an officer in a concentration camp might have led a quiet and harmless life if the Nazis had never come to power in Germany. And someone who led a quiet and harmless life in Argentina might have become an officer in a concentration camp if he had not left Germany for business reasons in 1930.

I shall say more later about these and other examples. I introduce them here to illustrate a general point. Where a significant aspect of what someone does depends on factors beyond his control, yet we continue to treat him in that respect as an object of moral judgment, it can be called moral luck. Such luck can be good or bad. And the problem posed by this phenomenon, which led Kant to deny its possibility, is that the broad range of external influences here identified seems on close examination to undermine moral assessment as surely as does the narrower range of familiar excusing conditions. If the condition of control is consistently applied, it threatens to erode most of the moral assessments we find it natural to make. The things for which people are morally judged are determined in more ways than we at first realize by what is beyond their control. And when the seemingly natural requirement of fault or responsibility is applied in light of these facts, it leaves few pre-reflective moral judgments intact.

Ultimately, nothing or almost nothing about what a person does seems to be under his control.

Why not conclude, then, that the condition of control is false—that it is an initially plausible hypothesis refuted by clear counter-examples? One could in that case look instead for a more refined condition which picked out the *kinds* of lack of control that really undermine certain moral judgments, without yielding the unacceptable conclusion derived from the broader condition, that most or all ordinary moral judgments are illegitimate.

What rules out this escape is that we are dealing not with a theoretical conjecture but with a philosophical problem. The condition of control does not suggest itself merely as a generalization from certain clear cases. It seems *correct* in the further cases to which it is extended beyond the original set. When we undermine moral assessment by considering new ways in which control is absent, we are not just discovering what *would* follow given the general hypothesis, but are actually being persuaded that in itself the absence of control is relevant in these cases too. The erosion of moral judgment emerges not as the absurd consequence of an over-simple theory, but as a natural consequence of the ordinary idea of moral assessment, when it is applied in view of a more complete and precise account of the facts. It would therefore be a mistake to argue from the unacceptability of the conclusions to the need for a different account of the conditions of moral responsibility. The view that moral luck is paradoxical is not a *mistake,* ethical or logical, but a perception of one of the ways in which the intuitively acceptable conditions of moral judgment threaten to undermine it all.

It resembles the situation in another area of philosophy, the theory of knowledge. There too conditions which seem perfectly natural, and which grow out of the ordinary procedures for challenging and defending claims to knowledge, threaten to undermine all such claims if consistently applied. Most skeptical arguments have this quality: they do not depend on the imposition of arbitrarily stringent standards of knowledge, arrived at by misunderstanding, but appear to grow inevitably from the consistent application of ordinary standards. There is a substantive parallel as well, for epistemological skepticism arises from consideration of the respects in which our beliefs and their relation to reality depend on factors beyond our control. External and internal causes produce our beliefs. We may subject these processes to scrutiny in an effort to avoid error, but our conclusions at this next level also result, in part, from influences which we do not control directly. The same will be true no matter how far we carry the investigation. Our beliefs are always, ultimately, due to factors outside our control, and the impossibility of encompassing those factors without being at the mercy of others leads us to doubt whether we know anything. It looks as though, if any of our beliefs are true, it is pure biological luck rather than knowledge.

Moral luck is like this because while there are various respects in which the natural objects of moral assessment are out of our control or influenced by what is out of our control, we cannot reflect on these facts without losing our grip on the judgments.

There are roughly four ways in which the natural objects of moral assessment are disturbingly subject to luck. One is the phenomenon of constitutive luck—the kind of person you are, where this is not just a question of what you deliberately do, but of your inclinations, capacities, and temperament. Another category is luck in one's circumstances—the kind of problems and situations one faces. The other two have to do with the causes and effects of action: luck in how one is determined by antecedent circumstances, and luck in the way one's actions and projects turn out. All of them present a common problem. They are all opposed by the idea that one cannot be more culpable or estimable for anything than one is for that fraction of it which is under one's control. It seems irrational to take or dispense credit or blame for matters over which a person has no control, or for their influence on results over which he has partial control. Such things may create the conditions for action, but action can be judged only to the extent that it goes beyond these conditions and does not just result from them.

Let us first consider luck, good and bad, in the way things turn out. Kant, in the above-quoted passage, has one example of this in mind, but the category covers a wide range. It includes the truck driver who accidentally runs over a child, the artist who abandons his wife and five children to devote himself

to painting, and other cases in which the possibilities of success and failure are even greater. The driver, if he is entirely without fault, will feel terrible about his role in the event, but will not have to reproach himself. Therefore this example of agent-regret is not yet a case of *moral* bad luck. However, if the driver was guilty of even a minor degree of negligence—failing to have his brakes checked recently, for example— then if that negligence contributes to the death of the child, he will not merely feel terrible. He will blame himself for the death. And what makes this an example of moral luck is that he would have to blame himself only slightly for the negligence itself if no situation arose which required him to brake suddenly and violently to avoid hitting a child. Yet the *negligence* is the same in both cases, and the driver has no control over whether a child will run into his path.

The same is true at higher levels of negligence. If someone has had too much to drink and his car swerves on to the sidewalk, he can count himself morally lucky if there are no pedestrians in its path. If there were, he would be to blame for their deaths, and would probably be prosecuted for manslaughter. But if he hurts no one, although his recklessness is exactly the same, he is guilty of a far less serious legal offence and will certainly reproach himself and be reproached by others much less severely. To take another legal example, the penalty for attempted murder is less than that for successful murder—however similar the intentions and motives of the assailant may be in the two cases. His degree of culpability can depend, it would seem, on whether the victim happened to be wearing a bullet-proof vest, or whether a bird flew into the path of the bullet—matters beyond his control.

Finally, there are cases of decision under uncertainty—common in public and in private life. Anna Karenina goes off with Vronsky, Gauguin leaves his family, Chamberlain signs the Munich agreement, the Decembrists persuade the troops under their command to revolt against the czar, the American colonies declare their independence from Britain, you introduce two people in an attempt at match-making. It is tempting in all such cases to feel that some decision must be possible, in the light of what is known at the time, which will make reproach unsuitable no matter how things turn out. But this is not true; when someone acts in such ways he takes his life, or his moral position, into his hands, because how things turn out determines what he has done. It is possible *also* to assess the decision from the point of view of what could be known at the time, but this is not the end of the story. If the Decembrists had succeeded in overthrowing Nicholas I in 1825 and establishing a constitutional regime, they would be heroes. As it is, not only did they fail and pay for it, but they bore some responsibility for the terrible punishments meted out to the troops who had been persuaded to follow them. If the American Revolution had been a bloody failure resulting in greater repression, then Jefferson, Franklin and Washington would still have made a noble attempt, and might not even have regretted it on their way to the scaffold, but they would also have had to blame themselves for what they had helped to bring on their compatriots. (Perhaps peaceful efforts at reform would eventually have succeeded.) If Hitler had not overrun Europe and exterminated millions, but instead had died of a heart attack after occupying the Sudetenland, Chamberlain's action at Munich would still have utterly betrayed the Czechs, but it would not be the great moral disaster that has made his name a household word.

In many cases of difficult choice the outcome cannot be foreseen with certainty. One kind of assessment of the choice is possible in advance, but another kind must await the outcome, because the outcome determines what has been done. The same degree of culpability or estimability in intention, motive, or concern is compatible with a wide range of judgments, positive or negative, depending on what happened beyond the point of decision. The *mens rea* which could have existed in the absence of any consequences does not exhaust the grounds of moral judgment. Actual results influence culpability or esteem in a large class of unquestionably ethical cases ranging from negligence through political choice.

That these are genuine moral judgments rather than expressions of temporary attitude is evident from the fact that one can say *in advance* how the moral verdict will depend on the results. If one negligently leaves the bath running with the baby in it, one will realize, as one bounds up the stairs toward the bathroom, that if the baby has drowned one has done something awful, whereas if it has not one has

merely been careless. Someone who launches a violent revolution against an authoritarian regime knows that if he fails he will be responsible for much suffering that is in vain, but if he succeeds he will be justified by the outcome. I do not mean that *any* action can be retroactively justified by history. Certain things are so bad in themselves, or so risky, that no results can make them all right. Nevertheless, when moral judgment does depend on the outcome, it is objective and timeless and not dependent on a change of standpoint produced by success or failure. The judgment after the fact follows from an hypothetical judgment that can be made beforehand, and it can be made as easily by someone else as by the agent.

From the point of view which makes responsibility dependent on control, all this seems absurd. How is it possible to be more or less culpable depending on whether a child gets into the path of one's car, or a bird into the path of one's bullet? Perhaps it is true that what is done depends on more than the agent's state of mind or intention. The problem then is, why is it not irrational to base moral assessment on what people do, in this broad sense? It amounts to holding them responsible for the contributions of fate as well as for their own—provided they have made some contribution to begin with. If we look at cases of negligence or attempt, the pattern seems to be that overall culpability corresponds to the product of mental or intentional fault and the seriousness of the outcome. Cases of decision under uncertainty are less easily explained in this way, for it seems that the overall judgment can even shift from positive to negative depending on the outcome. But here too it seems rational to subtract the effects of occurrences subsequent to the choice, that were merely possible at the time, and concentrate moral assessment on the actual decision in light of the probabilities. If the object of moral judgment is the *person,* then to hold him accountable for what he has done in the broader sense is akin to strict liability, which may have its legal uses but seems irrational as a moral position.

The result of such a line of thought is to pare down each act to its morally essential core, an inner act of pure will assessed by motive and intention. Adam Smith advocates such a position in *The Theory of Moral Sentiments,* but notes that it runs contrary to our actual judgments.

But how well soever we may seem to be persuaded of the truth of this equitable maxim, when we consider it after this manner, in abstract, yet when we come to particular cases, the actual consequences which happen to proceed from any action, have a very great effect upon our sentiments concerning its merit or demerit, and almost always either enhance or diminish our sense of both. Scarce, in any one instance, perhaps, will our sentiments be found, after examination, to be entirely regulated by this rule, which we all acknowledge ought entirely to regulate them.

Joel Feinberg points out further that restricting the domain of moral responsibility to the inner world will not immunize it to luck. Factors beyond the agent's control, like a coughing fit, can interfere with his decisions as surely as they can with the path of a bullet from his gun. Nevertheless the tendency to cut down the scope of moral assessment is pervasive, and does not limit itself to the influence of effects. It attempts to isolate the will from the other direction, so to speak, by separating out constitutive luck. Let us consider that next.

Kant was particularly insistent on the moral irrelevance of qualities of temperament and personality that are not under the control of the will. Such qualities as sympathy or coldness might provide the background against which obedience to moral requirements is more or less difficult, but they could not be objects of moral assessment themselves, and might well interfere with confident assessment of its proper object—the determination of the will by the motive of duty. This rules out moral judgment of many of the virtues and vices, which are states of character that influence choice but are certainly not exhausted by dispositions to act deliberately in certain ways. A person may be greedy, envious, cowardly, cold, ungenerous, unkind, vain, or conceited, but *behave* perfectly by a monumental effort of will. To possess these vices is to be unable to help having certain feelings under certain circumstances, and to have strong spontaneous impulses to act badly. Even if one controls the impulses, one still has the vice. An envious person hates the greater success of others. He can be morally condemned as envious even if he congratulates them cordially and does nothing to denigrate or spoil their success. Conceit, likewise, need not be displayed. It is fully present in someone who cannot help dwelling with secret satisfaction on the superiority of his own achievements, talents, beauty, intelligence, or virtue. To some extent such a quality may be the product of earlier choices; to some extent it may be amenable to change by current actions. But it is largely a matter of constitutive bad fortune. Yet people are morally condemned for such qualities, and esteemed for others equally beyond control of the will: they are assessed for what they are *like*.

To Kant this seems incoherent because virtue is enjoined on everyone and therefore must in principle be possible for everyone. It may be easier for some than for others, but it must be possible to achieve it by making the right choices, against whatever temperamental background. One may want to have a generous spirit, or regret not having one, but it makes no sense to condemn oneself or anyone else for a quality which is not within the control of the will. Condemnation implies that you should not be like that, not that it is unfortunate that you are.

Nevertheless, Kant's conclusion remains intuitively unacceptable. We may be persuaded that these moral judgments are irrational, but they reappear involuntarily as soon as the argument is over. This is the pattern throughout the subject.

The third category to consider is luck in one's circumstances, and I shall mention it briefly. The things we are called upon to do, the moral tests we face, are importantly determined by factors beyond our control. It may be true of someone that in a dangerous situation he would behave in a cowardly or heroic fashion, but if the situation never arises, he will never have the chance to distinguish or disgrace himself in this way, and his moral record will be different.

A conspicuous example of this is political. Ordinary citizens of Nazi Germany had an opportunity to behave heroically by opposing the regime. They also had an opportunity to behave badly, and most of them are culpable for having failed this test. But it is a test to which the citizens of other countries were not subjected, with the result that even if they, or some of them, would have behaved as badly as the Germans in like circumstances, they simply did not and therefore are not similarly culpable. Here again one is morally at the mercy of fate, and it may seem irrational upon reflection, but our ordinary moral attitudes would be unrecognizable without it. We judge people for what they actually do or fail to do, not just for what they would have done if circumstances had been different.

This form of moral determination by the actual is also paradoxical, but we can begin to see how deep in the concept of responsibility the paradox is embedded. A person can be morally responsible only for what he does; but what he does results from a great deal that he does not do; therefore he is not morally responsible for what he is and is not responsible for. (This is not a contradiction, but it is a paradox.)

It should be obvious that there is a connection between these problems about responsibility and control and an even more familiar problem, that of freedom of the will. That is the last type of moral luck I want to take up, though I can do no more within the scope of this essay than indicate its connection with the other types.

If one cannot be responsible for consequences of one's acts due to factors beyond one's control, or for antecedents of one's acts that are properties of temperament not subject to one's will, or for the circumstances that pose one's moral choices, then how can one be responsible even for the stripped-down acts of the will itself, if *they* are the product of antecedent circumstances outside of the will's control?

The area of genuine agency, and therefore of legitimate moral judgment, seems to shrink under this scrutiny to an extensionless point. Everything seems to result from the combined influence of factors, antecedent and posterior to action, that are not within the agent's control. Since he cannot be responsible for them, he cannot be responsible for their results— though it may remain possible to take up the aesthetic or other evaluative analogues of the moral attitudes that are thus displaced.

It is also possible, of course, to brazen it out and refuse to accept the results, which indeed seem unacceptable as soon as we stop thinking about the arguments. Admittedly, if certain surrounding circumstances had been different, then no unfortunate consequences would have followed from a wicked intention, and no seriously culpable act would have been performed; but since the circumstances were *not* different, and the agent *in fact* succeeded in perpetrating a particularly cruel murder, *that* is what he did, and that is what he is responsible for. Similarly,

we may admit that if certain antecedent circumstances had been different, the agent would never have developed into the sort of person who would do such a thing; but since he *did* develop (as the inevitable result of those antecedent circumstances) into the sort of swine he is, and into the person who committed such a murder, *that* is what he is blameable for. In both cases one is responsible for what one actually does—even if what one actually does depends in important ways on what is not within one's control. This compatibilist account of our moral judgments would leave room for the ordinary conditions of responsibility—the absence of coercion, ignorance, or involuntary movement—as part of the determination of what someone has done—but it is understood not to exclude the influence of a great deal that he has not done.

The only thing wrong with this solution is its failure to explain how skeptical problems arise. For they arise not from the imposition of an arbitrary external requirement, but from the nature of moral judgment itself. Something in the ordinary idea of what someone does must explain how it can seem necessary to subtract from it anything that merely happens—even though the ultimate consequence of such subtraction is that nothing remains. And something in the ordinary idea of knowledge must explain why it seems to be undermined by any influences on belief not within the control of the subject—so that knowledge seems impossible without an impossible foundation in autonomous reason. But let us leave epistemology aside and concentrate on action, character, and moral assessment.

The problem arises, I believe, because the self which acts and is the object of moral judgment is threatened with dissolution by the absorption of its acts and impulses into the class of events. Moral judgment of a person is judgment not of what happens to him, but of him. It does not say merely that a certain event or state of affairs is fortunate or unfortunate or even terrible. It is not an evaluation of a state of the world, or of an individual as part of the world. We are not thinking just that it would be better if he were different, or did not exist, or had not done some of the things he has done. We are judging *him,* rather than his existence or characteristics. The effect of concentrating on the influence of what is not under his control is to make this responsible self seem to disappear, swallowed up by the order of mere events.

What, however, do we have in mind that a person must *be* to be the object of these moral attitudes? While the concept of agency is easily undermined, it is very difficult to give it a positive characterization. That is familiar from the literature on Free Will.

I believe that in a sense the problem has no solution, because something in the idea of agency is incompatible with actions being events, or people being things. But as the external determinants of what someone has done are gradually exposed, in their effect on consequences, character, and choice itself, it becomes gradually clear that actions are events and people things. Eventually nothing remains which can be ascribed to the responsible self, and we are left with nothing but a portion of the larger sequence of events, which can be deplored or celebrated, but not blamed or praised.

Though I cannot define the idea of the active self that is thus undermined, it is possible to say something about its sources. There is a close connexion between our feelings about ourselves and our feelings about others. Guilt and indignation, shame and contempt, pride and admiration are internal and external sides of the same moral attitudes. We are unable to view ourselves simply as portions of the world, and from inside we have a rough idea of the boundary between what is us and what is not, what we do and what happens to us, what is our personality and what is an accidental handicap. We apply the same essentially internal conception of the self to others. About ourselves we feel pride, shame, guilt, remorse—and agent-regret. We do not regard our actions and our characters merely as fortunate or unfortunate episodes—though they may also be that. We cannot *simply* take an external evaluative view of ourselves—of what we most essentially are and what we do. And this remains true even when we have seen that we are not responsible for our own existence, or our nature, or the choices we have to make, or the circumstances that give our acts the consequences they have. Those acts remain ours and we remain ourselves, despite the persuasiveness of the reasons that seem to argue us out of existence.

It is this internal view that we extend to others in moral judgment—when we judge *them* rather than their desirability or utility. We extend to others the refusal to limit ourselves to external evaluation, and we accord to them selves like our own. But in both cases this comes up against the brutal inclusion of humans and everything about them in a world from which they cannot be separated and of which they are nothing but contents. The external view forces itself on us at the same time that we resist it. One way this occurs is through the gradual erosion of what we do by the subtraction of what happens.

The inclusion of consequences in the conception of what we have done is an acknowledgment that we are parts of the world, but the paradoxical character of moral luck which emerges from this acknowledgment shows that we are unable to operate with such a view, for it leaves us with no one to be. The same thing is revealed in the appearance that determinism obliterates responsibility. Once we see an aspect of what we or someone else does as something that happens, we lose our grip on the idea that it has been done and that we can judge the doer and not just the happening. This explains why the absence of determinism is no more hospitable to the concept of agency than is its presence—a point that has been noticed often. Either way the act is viewed externally, as part of the course of events.

The problem of moral luck cannot be understood without an account of the internal conception of agency and its special connection with the moral attitudes as opposed to other types of value. I do not have such an account. The degree to which the problem has a solution can be determined only by seeing whether in some degree the incompatibility between this conception and the various ways in which we do not control what we do is only apparent. I have nothing to offer on that topic either. But it is not enough to say merely that our basic moral attitudes toward ourselves and others are determined by what is actual; for they are also threatened by the sources of that actuality, and by the external view of action which forces itself on us when we see how everything we do belongs to a world that we have not created.

The Punishment That Leaves Something to Chance

DAVID LEWIS

David Lewis (1941–2001) was professor of philosophy at Princeton University. A leading figure in contemporary philosophy, he wrote numerous influential papers in a variety of fields, including metaphysics, epistemology, and ethics. One of his best-known books is *On the Plurality of Worlds.*

I

We are accustomed to punish criminal attempts much more severely if they succeed than if they fail. We are also accustomed to wonder why. It is hard to find any rationale for our leniency toward the unsuccessful. Leniency toward aborted attempts, or mere preparation, might be easier to understand. (And whether easy or hard, it is not my present topic.) But what sense can we make of leniency toward a completed attempt—one that puts a victim at risk of harm, and fails only by luck to do actual harm?

Dee takes a shot at his enemy, and so does Dum. They both want to kill; they both try, and we may suppose they try equally hard. Both act out of malice, without any shred of justification or excuse. Both give us reason to fear that they might be ready to kill in the future. The only difference is that Dee hits and Dum misses. So Dee has killed, he is guilty of murder, and we put him to death. Dum has not killed, he is guilty only of attempted murder, and he gets a short prison sentence.

Why? Dee and Dum were equally wicked in their desires. They were equally uninhibited in pursuing their wicked desires. Insofar as the wicked deserve to be punished, they deserve it equally. Their conduct was equally dangerous: they inflicted equal risks of death on their respective victims. Insofar as those who act dangerously deserve to be punished, again they deserve it equally. Maybe Dee's act was worse than Dum's act, just because of Dee's success; but it is not the act that suffers punishment, it is the agent. Likewise, if we want to express our abhorrence of wickedness or of dangerous conduct, either exemplar of what we abhor is fit to star in the drama of crime and punishment. Further, Dee and Dum have equally engaged in conduct we want to prevent by deterrence. For we prevent successful attempts by preventing attempts generally. We cannot deter success separately from deterring attempts, since attempters make no separate choice about whether to succeed. Further, Dee and Dum have equally shown us that we might all be safer if we defended ourselves against them; and one function of punishment (at any rate if it is death, imprisonment, or transportation) is to get dangerous criminals off the streets before they do more harm. So how does their different luck in hitting or missing make any difference to considerations of desert, expression, deterrence, or defense? How can it be just, on any credible theory of just punishment, to punish them differently?

A purely conservative rationale is open to the same complaint. Maybe it is a good idea to stay with the practice we have learned how to operate, lest a reform cause unexpected problems. Maybe it is good for people to see the law go on working as they are

From *Philosophy & Public Affairs, 18.* Copyright © 1989 by Princeton University Press. Reprinted by permission of Princeton University Press.

accustomed to expect it to. Maybe a reform would convey unintended and disruptive messages: as it might be, that we have decided to take murder less seriously than we used to. These considerations may be excellent reasons why it is prudent to leave well enough alone, and condone whatever injustice there may be in our present practice. They do nothing at all to defend our practice as just.

Another rationale concerns the deterrence of second attempts. If at first you don't succeed, and if success would bring no extra punishment, then you have nothing left to lose if you try, try again. "If exactly the same penalty is prescribed for successes as for attempts, there will be every reason to make sure that one is successful." It cannot hurt to have some deterrence left after deterrence has failed. Maybe the experience of having tried once will make the criminal more deterrable than he was at first.—But why is this any reason for punishing successful attempts more severely? It might as well just be a reason for punishing two attempts more severely than one, which we could do regardless of success. If each separate attempt is punished, and if one share of punishment is not so bad that a second share would be no worse, then we have some deterrence against second attempts.

Another rationale invokes the idea of "moral luck." Strange to say, it can happen by luck alone that one person ends up more wicked than another. Perhaps that is why the successful attempter, by luck alone, ends up deserving more severe punishment?— I reply, first, that to some extent this suggestion merely names our problem. We ask how Dee can deserve more severe punishment just because his shot hits the mark. Call that "moral luck" if you will; then we have been asking all along how this sort of moral luck is possible. But, second, it may be misleading to speak of the moral luck of the attempter, since it may tend to conflate this case with something quite different. The most intelligible cases of moral luck are those in which the lucky and the unlucky alike are disposed to become wicked if tempted, and only the unlucky are tempted. But then, however alike they may have been originally, the lucky and the unlucky do end up different in how they are and in how they act. Not so for the luck of hitting or missing. It makes no difference to how the lucky and the unlucky are, and no difference to how they act.

Finally, another rationale invokes the difference between wholehearted and halfhearted attempts. Both are bad, but wholehearted attempts are worse. A wholehearted attempt involves more careful planning, more precautions against failure, more effort, more persistence, and perhaps repeated tries. Ceteris paribus, a wholehearted attempt evinces more wickedness—stronger wicked desires, or less inhibition about pursuing them. Ceteris paribus, a wholehearted attempt is more dangerous. It is more likely to succeed; it subjects the victim, knowingly and wrongfully, to a greater risk. Therefore it is more urgently in need of prevention by deterrence. Ceteris paribus, the perpetrator of a wholehearted attempt is more of a proven danger to us all, so it is more urgent to get him off the streets. So from every standpoint— desert, expression, deterrence, defense—it makes good sense to punish attempts more severely when they are wholehearted. Now, since wholehearted attempts are more likely to succeed, success is some evidence that the attempt was wholehearted. Punishing success, then, is a rough and ready way of punishing wholeheartedness.

I grant that it is just to punish wholehearted attempts more severely—or better, since "heartedness" admits of degrees, to proportion the punishment to the heartedness of the attempt. And I grant that in so doing we may take the probability of success—in other words, the risk inflicted on the victim—as our measure of heartedness. That means not proportioning the punishment simply to the offender's wickedness, because two equally wicked attempters may not be equally likely to succeed. One may be more dangerous than the other because he has the advantage in skill or resources or information or opportunity. Then if we proportion punishment to heartedness measured by risk, we may punish one attempter more severely not because he was more wicked, but because his conduct was more dangerous. From a purely retributive standpoint, wickedness might seem the more appropriate measure; but from the expressive standpoint, we may prefer to dramatize our abhorrence not of wickedness per se but of dangerous wickedness; and from the standpoint of deterrence or defense, clearly it is dangerous conduct that matters.

So far, so good; but I protest that it is unjust to punish success as a rough and ready way of punishing wholeheartedness. It's just too rough and ready. Success is some evidence of wholeheartedness, sure enough. But it is very unreliable evidence: the whole-hearted attempt may very well be thwarted, the half- or quarterhearted attempt may succeed. And we can have other evidence that bears as much or more on whether the attempt was wholehearted. If what we really want is to punish wholeheartedness, we have no business heeding only one unreliable fragment of the total evidence, and then treating that fragment as if it were conclusive. Suppose we had reason—*good* reason—to think that on average the old tend to be more wholehearted than the young in their criminal attempts. Suppose even that we could infer whole-heartedness from age somewhat more reliably than we can infer it from success. Then if we punished attempters more severely in proportion to their age, that would be another rough and ready way of pun-ishing wholeheartedness. *Ex hypothesi,* it would be less rough and ready than what we do in punishing success. It would still fall far short of our standards of justice.

II

In what follows, I shall propose a new rationale. *I do not say that it works.* I do say that the new rationale works better than the old ones. It makes at least a prima facie case that our peculiar practice is just, and I do not see any decisive rebuttal. All the same, I think that the prima facie case is probably not good enough, and probably there is no adequate justification for punishing attempts more severely when they succeed.

Our present practice amounts to a disguised form of *penal lottery*—a punishment that leaves some-thing to chance. Seen thus, it *does* in some sense pun-ish all attempts alike, regardless of success. It is no less just, and no more just, than an undisguised penal lottery would be. Probably any penal lottery is seri-ously unjust, but it is none too easy to explain why.

By a penal lottery, I mean a system of punishment in which the convicted criminal is subjected to a risk of punitive harm. If he wins the lottery, he escapes the harm. If he loses, he does not. A pure penal lottery is one in which the winners suffer no harm at all; an impure penal lottery is one in which winners and los-ers alike suffer some harm, but the losers suffer more

harm. It is a mixture: part of the punishment is certain harm, part is the penal lottery.

An overt penal lottery is one in which the punish-ment is announced explicitly as a risk—there might be ways of dramatizing the fact, such as a drawing of straws on the steps of the gallows. A covert penal lot-tery is one in which the punishment is not announced as a risk, but it is common knowledge that it brings risk with it. (A covert lottery must presumably be impure.)

A historical example of an overt penal lottery is the decimation of a regiment as punishment for mutiny. Each soldier is punished for his part in the mutiny by a one-in-ten risk of being put to death. It is a fairly pure penal lottery, but not entirely pure: the terror of waiting to see who must die is part of the punishment, and this part falls with certainty on all the mutineers alike.

Covert and impure penal lotteries are common-place in our own time. If one drawback of prison is that it is a place where one is exposed to capricious violence, or to a serious risk of catching AIDS, then a prison sentence is in part a penal lottery. If the gulag is noted for its abysmal standards of occupational health and safety, then a sentence of forced labor is in part a penal lottery.

III

What do we think, and what should we think, of penal lotteries? Specifically, what should we think of a penal lottery, with death for the losers, as the pun-ishment for all attempts at murder, regardless of suc-cess? Successful or not, the essence of the crime is to subject the victim, knowingly and wrongfully, to a serious risk of death. The proposed punishment is to be subjected to a like risk of death.

We need a standard of comparison. Our present system of leniency toward the unsuccessful is too problematic to make a good standard, so let us instead compare the penal lottery with a hypothetical reformed system. How does the lottery compare with a system that punishes all attempts regardless of suc-cess, by the certain harm of a moderate prison term? A moderate term, because if we punished successful and unsuccessful attempts alike, we would presum-ably set the punishment somewhere between our present severe punishment of the one and our lenient punishment of the other. (Let the prison be a safe one, so that in the comparison case we have no trace of a penal lottery.) Both for the lottery and for the comparison case, I shall assume that we punish regardless of success. In the one case, success per se makes no difference to the odds; in the other case, no difference to the time in prison. This is not to say that every convicted criminal gets the very same sentence. Other factors might still make a difference. In particular, heartedness (measured by the risk inflicted) could make a difference, and success could make a difference to the extent that it is part of our evidence about heartedness.

Now, how do the two alternatives compare?

The penal lottery may have some practical advantages. It gets the case over and done with quickly. It is not a crime school. A prison costs a lot more than a gallows plus a supply of long and short straws.

(Likewise a prison with adequate protection against random brutality by guards and fellow inmates costs more than a prison without. So it seems that we have already been attracted by the economy of a system that has at least some covert admixture of lottery.)

Like a prison term (or fines, or flogging) and unlike the death penalty *simpliciter,* the penal lottery can be graduated as finely as we like. When we take the crime to be worse, we provide fewer long straws to go with the fatal short straws. In particular, that is how we can provide a more severe punishment for the more wholehearted attempt that subjected the victim to a greater risk.

From the standpoint of dramatizing our abhorrence of wicked and dangerous conduct, a penal lottery seems at least as good as a prison sentence. Making the punishment fit the crime, Mikado-fashion, is *poetic* justice. The point we want to dramatize, both to the criminal and to the public, is that what we think of the crime is just like what the criminal thinks of his punishment. If it's a risk for a risk, how can anybody miss the point?

From the standpoint of deterrence, there is no doubt that we are sometimes well deterred by the prospect of risk. It happens every time we wait to cross the street. It is an empirical question how effective a deterrent the penal lottery might be. Compared with the alternative punishment of a certain harm, such as a moderate prison term, the lottery might give us more deterrence for a given amount of penal harm, or it might give us less. Whether it gives us more or less might depend a lot on the details of how the two systems operate. If the lottery gave us more, that would make it preferable from the standpoint of deterrence.

From the standpoint of defense, the penal lottery gets some dangerous criminals off the streets forever, while others go free at once. Moderate prison terms would let all go free after a longer time, some of them perhaps reformed and some of them hardened and embittered. It is another empirical question which alternative is the more effective system of defense. Again, the answer may depend greatly on the details of the two systems, and on much else that we cannot easily find out.

IV

So far we have abundant uncertainties, but no clear-cut case against the penal lottery. If anything, the balance may be tipping in its favor. So let us turn finally to the standpoint of desert. Here it is a bit hard to know what to make of the penal lottery. If the court has done its job correctly, then all who are sentenced to face the same lottery, with the same odds, are equally guilty of equally grave crimes. They deserve equal treatment. Do they get it?—Yes and no.

Yes. We treat them alike because we subject them all to the very same penal lottery, with the very same odds. And when the lots are drawn, we treat them alike again, because we follow the same predetermined contingency plan—death for losers, freedom for winners—for all of them alike.

> *No.* Some of them are put to death, some are set free, and what could be more unequal than that?

Yes. Their fates are unequal, of course. But that is not our doing. They are treated unequally by Fortune, not by us.

> *No.* But it is we who hand them over to the inequity of Fortune. We are Fortune's accomplices.

Yes. Everyone is exposed to the inequity of Fortune, in ever so many ways. However nice it may be to undo some of these inequities, we do not ordinarily think of this as part of what is required for equal treatment.

No. It's one thing not to go out of our way to undo the inequities of Fortune; it's another thing to go out of our way to increase them.

Yes. We do that too, and think it not at all contrary to equal treatment. When we hire astronauts, or soldiers or sailors or firemen or police, we knowingly subject these people to more of the inequities of Fortune than are found in ordinary life.

No. But the astronauts are volunteers . . .

Yes . . . and so are the criminals, when they commit the crimes for which they know they must face the lottery. The soldiers, however, sometimes are not.

No. Start over. We agreed that the winners and losers deserve equal punishment. That is because they are equally guilty. Then they deserve to suffer equally. But they do not.

Yes. They do not suffer equally; but if they deserve to, that is not our affair. We seldom think that equal punishment means making sure of equal suffering. Does the cheerful man get a longer prison sentence than the equally guilty morose man, to make sure of equal suffering? If one convict gets lung cancer in prison, do we see to it that the rest who are equally guilty suffer equally? When we punish equally, what we equalize is not the suffering itself. What we equalize is our contribution to expected suffering.

No. This all seems like grim sophistry. Surely, equal treatment has to mean more than just treating people so that *some* common description of what we are doing will apply to them all alike.

Yes. True. But we have made up our minds already, in other connections, that lotteries count as equal treatment, or near enough. When we have an indivisible benefit or burden to hand out (or even one that is divisible at a significant cost) we are very well content to resort to a lottery. We are satisfied that all who have equal chances are getting equal treatment—and not in some queer philosophers' sense, but in the sense that matters to justice.

It seems to me that "Yes" is winning this argument, but that truth and justice are still somehow on the side of "No." The next move, dear readers, is up to you. I shall leave it unsettled whether a penal lottery would be just.

Rich and Poor

PETER SINGER

Peter Singer is Ira W. Decamp Professor of Bioethics at the University Center for Human Values at Princeton University.

SOME FACTS ABOUT POVERTY

Consider these facts: by the most cautious estimates, 400 million people lack the calories, protein, vitamins and minerals needed to sustain their bodies and minds in a healthy state. Millions are constantly hungry; others suffer from deficiency diseases and from infections they would be able to resist on a better diet. Children are the worst affected. According to one study, 14 million children under five die every year

Reprinted from *Practical Ethics,* 2nd ed. (Cambridge, England: Cambridge University Press, 1993) by permission of the publisher.

from the combined effects of malnutrition and infection. In some districts half the children born can be expected to die before their fifth birthday.

Nor is lack of food the only hardship of the poor. To give a broader picture, Robert McNamara, when president of the World Bank, suggested the term "absolute poverty." The poverty we are familiar with in industrialised nations is relative poverty—meaning that some citizens are poor, relative to the wealth enjoyed by their neighbours. People living in relative poverty in Australia might be quite comfortably off by comparison with pensioners in Britain, and British pensioners are not poor in comparison with the poverty that exists in Mali or Ethiopia. Absolute poverty, on the other hand, is poverty by any standard. In McNamara's words:

> Poverty at the absolute level . . . is life at the very margin of existence. The absolute poor are severely deprived human beings struggling to survive in a set of squalid and degraded circumstances almost beyond the power of our sophisticated imaginations and privileged circumstances to conceive.

> Compared to those fortunate enough to live in developed countries, individuals in the poorest nations have:

> An infant mortality rate eight times higher
> A life expectancy one-third lower
> An adult literacy rate 60 per cent less
> A nutritional level, for one out of every two in the population, below acceptable standards;
> And for millions of infants, less protein than is sufficient to permit optimum development of the brain.

McNamara has summed up absolute poverty as "a condition of life so characterised by malnutrition, illiteracy, disease, squalid surroundings, high infant mortality and low life expectancy as to be beneath any reasonable definition of human decency."

Absolute poverty is, as McNamara has said, responsible for the loss of countless lives, especially among infants and young children. When absolute poverty does not cause death, it still causes misery of a kind not often seen in the affluent nations. Malnutrition in young children stunts both physical and mental development. According to the United Nations

Development Programme, 180 million children under the age of five suffer from serious malnutrition. Millions of people on poor diets suffer from deficiency diseases, like goitre, or blindness caused by a lack of vitamin A. The food value of what the poor eat is further reduced by parasites such as hookworm and ringworm, which are endemic in conditions of poor sanitation and health education.

Death and disease apart, absolute poverty remains a miserable condition of life, with inadequate food, shelter, clothing, sanitation, health services and education. The Worldwatch Institute estimates that as many as 1.2 billion people—or 23 per cent of the world's population—live in absolute poverty. For the purposes of this estimate, absolute poverty is defined as "the lack of sufficient income in cash or kind to meet the most basic biological needs for food, clothing, and shelter." Absolute poverty is probably the principal cause of human misery today.

SOME FACTS ABOUT WEALTH

This is the background situation, the situation that prevails on our planet all the time. It does not make headlines. People died from malnutrition and related diseases yesterday, and more will die tomorrow. The occasional droughts, cyclones, earthquakes, and floods that take the lives of tens of thousands in one place and at one time are more newsworthy. They add greatly to the total amount of human suffering; but it is wrong to assume that when there are no major calamities reported, all is well.

The problem is not that the world cannot produce enough to feed and shelter its people. People in the poor countries consume, on average, 180 kilos of grain a year, while North Americans average around 900 kilos. The difference is caused by the fact that in the rich countries we feed most of our grain to animals, converting it into meat, milk, and eggs. Because this is a highly inefficient process, people in rich countries are responsible for the consumption of far more food than those in poor countries who eat few animal products. If we stopped feeding animals on grains and soybeans, the amount of food saved would—if distributed to those who need it—be more than enough to end hunger throughout the world.

These facts about animal food do not mean that we can easily solve the world food problem by cutting down on animal products, but they show that the problem is essentially one of distribution rather than production. The world does produce enough food. Moreover, the poorer nations themselves could produce far more if they made more use of improved agricultural techniques.

So why are people hungry? Poor people cannot afford to buy grain grown by farmers in the richer nations. Poor farmers cannot afford to buy improved seeds, or fertilisers, or the machinery needed for drilling wells and pumping water. Only by transferring some of the wealth of the rich nations to the poor can the situation be changed.

That this wealth exists is clear. Against the picture of absolute poverty that McNamara has painted, one might pose a picture of "absolute affluence." Those who are absolutely affluent are not necessarily affluent by comparison with their neighbours, but they are affluent by any reasonable definition of human needs. This means that they have more income than they need to provide themselves adequately with all the basic necessities of life. After buying (either directly or through their taxes) food, shelter, clothing, basic health services, and education, the absolutely affluent are still able to spend money on luxuries. The absolutely affluent choose their food for the pleasures of the palate, not to stop hunger; they buy new clothes to look good, not to keep warm; they move house to be in a better neighbourhood or have a playroom for the children, not to keep out the rain; and after all this there is still money to spend on stereo systems, video-cameras, and overseas holidays.

At this stage I am making no ethical judgments about absolute affluence, merely pointing out that it exists. Its defining characteristic is a significant amount of income above the level necessary to provide for the basic human needs of oneself and one's dependents. By this standard, the majority of citizens of Western Europe, North America, Japan, Australia, New Zealand, and the oil-rich Middle Eastern states are all absolutely affluent. To quote McNamara once more:

"The average citizen of a developed country enjoys wealth beyond the wildest dreams of the one billion people in countries with per capita incomes under $200." These, therefore, are the countries—and individuals—who have wealth that they could, without threatening their own basic welfare, transfer to the absolutely poor.

At present, very little is being transferred. Only Sweden, the Netherlands, Norway, and some of the oil-exporting Arab states have reached the modest target, set by the United Nations, of 0.7 per cent of gross national product (GNP). Britain gives 0.31 per cent of its GNP in official development assistance and a small additional amount in unofficial aid from voluntary organisations. The total comes to about £2 per month per person, and compares with 5.5 per cent of GNP spent on alcohol, and 3 per cent on tobacco. Other, even wealthier nations, give little more: Germany gives 0.41 per cent and Japan 0.32 per cent. The United States gives a mere 0.15 per cent of its GNP.

THE MORAL EQUIVALENT OF MURDER?

If these are the facts, we cannot avoid concluding that by not giving more than we do, people in rich countries are allowing those in poor countries to suffer from absolute poverty, with consequent malnutrition, ill health, and death. This is not a conclusion that applies only to governments. It applies to each absolutely affluent individual, for each of us has the opportunity to do something about the situation; for instance, to give our time or money to voluntary organisations like Oxfam, Care, War on Want, Freedom from Hunger, Community Aid Abroad, and so on. If, then, allowing someone to die is not intrinsically different from killing someone, it would seem that we are all murderers.

Is this verdict too harsh? Many will reject it as self-evidently absurd. They would sooner take it as showing that allowing to die cannot be equivalent to killing than as showing that living in an affluent style without contributing to an overseas aid agency is ethically equivalent to going over to Ethiopia and shooting a few peasants. And no doubt, put as bluntly as that, the verdict is too harsh.

There are several significant differences between spending money on luxuries instead of using it to save lives, and deliberately shooting people.

First, the motivation will normally be different. Those who deliberately shoot others go out of their way to kill; they presumably want their victims dead, from malice, sadism, or some equally unpleasant motive. A person who buys a new stereo system presumably wants to enhance her enjoyment of music—not in itself a terrible thing. At worst, spending money on luxuries instead of giving it away indicates selfishness and indifference to the sufferings of others, characteristics that may be undesirable but are not comparable with actual malice or similar motives.

Second, it is not difficult for most of us to act in accordance with a rule against killing people: it is, on the other hand, very difficult to obey a rule that commands us to save all the lives we can. To live a comfortable, or even luxurious life it is not necessary to kill anyone; but it is necessary to allow some to die whom we might have saved, for the money that we need to live comfortably could have been given away. Thus the duty to avoid killing is much easier to discharge completely than the duty to save. Saving every life we could would mean cutting our standard of living down to the bare essentials needed to keep us alive.[1] To discharge this duty completely would require a degree of moral heroism utterly different from that required by mere avoidance of killing.

A third difference is the greater certainty of the outcome of shooting when compared with not giving aid. If I point a loaded gun at someone at close range and pull the trigger, it is virtually certain that the person will be killed; whereas the money that I could give might be spent on a project that turns out to be unsuccessful and helps no one.

Fourth, when people are shot there are identifiable individuals who have been harmed. We can point to them and to their grieving families. When I buy my stereo system, I cannot know who my money would have saved if I had given it away. In a time of famine I may see dead bodies and grieving families on television reports, and I might not doubt that my money would have saved some of them; even then it is impossible to point to a body and say that had I not bought the stereo, that person would have survived.

Fifth, it might be said that the plight of the hungry is not my doing, and so I cannot be held responsible for it. The starving would have been starving if I had never existed. If I kill, however, I am responsible for my victims' deaths, for those people would not have died if I had not killed them.

These differences need not shake our previous conclusion that there is no intrinsic difference between killing and allowing to die. They are extrinsic differences, that is, differences normally but not necessarily associated with the distinction between killing and allowing to die. We can imagine cases in which someone allows another to die for malicious or sadistic reasons; we can imagine a world in which there are so few people needing assistance, and they are so easy to assist, that our duty not to allow people to die is as easily discharged as our duty not to kill; we can imagine situations in which the outcome of not helping is as sure as shooting; we can imagine cases in which we can identify the person we allow to die. We can even imagine a case of allowing to die in which, if I had not existed, the person would not have died—for instance, a case in which if I had not been in a position to help (though I don't help) someone else would have been in my position and would have helped.

Our previous discussion of euthanasia illustrates the extrinsic nature of these differences, for they do not provide a basis for distinguishing active from passive euthanasia. If a doctor decides, in consultation with the parents, not to operate on—and thus to allow to die—a Down's syndrome infant with an intestinal blockage, her motivation will be similar to that of a doctor who gives a lethal injection rather than allow the infant to die. No extraordinary sacrifice or moral heroism will be required in either case. Not operating will just as certainly end in death as administering the injection. Allowing to die does have an identifiable victim. Finally, it may well be that the doctor is personally responsible for the death of the infant she decides not to operate upon, since she may know that if she had not taken this case, other doctors in the hospital would have operated.

Nevertheless, euthanasia is a special case, and very different from allowing people to starve to death. (The major difference being that when euthanasia is justifiable, death is a good thing.) The extrinsic differences that *normally* mark off killing and allowing to die do explain why we *normally* regard killing as much worse than allowing to die.

To explain our conventional ethical attitudes is not to justify them. Do the five differences not only explain, but also justify, our attitudes? Let us consider them one by one:

1. Take the lack of an identifiable victim first. Suppose that I am a travelling salesperson, selling tinned food, and I learn that a batch of tins contains a contaminant, the known effect of which, when consumed, is to double the risk that the consumer will die from stomach cancer. Suppose I continue to sell the tins. My decision may have no identifiable victims. Some of those who eat the food will die from cancer. The proportion of consumers dying in this way will be twice that of the community at large, but who among the consumers died because they ate what I sold, and who would have contracted the disease anyway? It is impossible to tell; but surely this impossibility makes my decision no less reprehensible than it would have been had the contaminant had more readily detectable, though equally fatal, effects.

2. The lack of certainty that by giving money I could save a life does reduce the wrongness of not giving, by comparison with deliberate killing; but it is insufficient to show that not giving is acceptable conduct. The motorist who speeds through pedestrian crossings, heedless of anyone who might be on them, is not a murderer. She may never actually hit a pedestrian; yet what she does is very wrong indeed.

3. The notion of responsibility for acts rather than omissions is more puzzling. On the one hand, we feel ourselves to be under a greater obligation to help those whose misfortunes we have caused. (It is for this reason that advocates of overseas aid often argue that Western nations have created the poverty of third world nations, through forms of economic exploitation that go back to the colonial system.) On the other hand, any consequentialist would insist that we are responsible for all the consequences of our actions, and if a consequence of my spending money on a luxury item is that someone dies, I am responsible for that death. It is true that the person would have died even if I had never existed, but what is the relevance of that? The fact is that I do exist, and the consequentialist will say that our responsibilities derive from the world as it is, not as it might have been.

One way of making sense of the non-consequentialist view of responsibility is by basing it on a theory of rights of the kind proposed by John Locke or, more recently, Robert Nozick. If everyone has a right to life, and this right is a right *against* others who might threaten my life, but not a right to assistance from others when my life is in danger, then we can understand the feeling that we are responsible for acting to kill but not for omitting to save. The former violates the rights of others, the latter does not.

Should we accept such a theory of rights? If we build up our theory of rights by imagining, as Locke and Nozick do, individuals living independently from each other in a 'state of nature', it may seem natural to adopt a conception of rights in which as long as each leaves the other alone, no rights are violated. I might, on this view, quite properly have maintained my independent existence if I had wished to do so. So if I do not make you any worse off than you would have been if I had had nothing at all to do with you, how can I have violated your rights? But why start from such an unhistorical, abstract and ultimately inexplicable idea as an independent individual? Our ancestors were—like other primates—social beings long before they were human beings, and could not have developed the abilities and capacities of human beings if they had not been social beings first. In any case, we are not, now, isolated individuals. So why should we assume that rights must be restricted to rights against interference? We might, instead, adopt the view that taking rights to life seriously is incompatible with standing by and watching people die when one could easily save them.

4. What of the difference in motivation? That a person does not positively wish for the death of another lessens the severity of the blame she deserves; but not by as much as our present attitudes to giving aid suggest. The behaviour of the speeding motorist is again comparable, for such motorists usually have no desire at all to kill anyone. They merely enjoy speeding and are indifferent to the consequences. Despite their lack of malice, those who kill with cars deserve not only blame but also severe punishment.

5. Finally, the fact that to avoid killing people is normally not difficult, whereas to save all one possibly could save is heroic, must make an important difference to our attitude to failure to do what the respective principles demand. Not to kill is a min- moral significance to the bad thing that is to be prevented, they will automatically regard the principle as not applying in those cases in which the bad thing can only be prevented by violating rights, doing injustice, breaking promises, or whatever else is at stake. Most non-consequentialists hold that we ought to prevent what is bad and promote what is good. Their dispute with consequentialists lies in their insistence that this is not the sole ultimate ethical principle: that it is an ethical principle is not denied by any plausible ethical theory.

Nevertheless the uncontroversial appearance of the principle that we ought to prevent what is bad when we can do so without sacrificing anything of comparable moral significance is deceptive. If it were taken seriously and acted upon, our lives and our world would be fundamentally changed. For the principle applies, not just to rare situations in which one can save a child from a pond, but to the everyday situation in which we can assist those living in absolute poverty. In saying this I assume that absolute poverty, with its hunger and malnutrition, lack of shelter, illiteracy, disease, high infant mortality, and low life expectancy, is a bad thing. And I assume that it is within the power of the affluent to reduce absolute poverty, without sacrificing anything of comparable moral significance. If these two assumptions and the principle we have been discussing are correct, we have an obligation to help those in absolute poverty that is no less strong than our obligation to rescue a drowning child from a pond. Not to help would be wrong, whether or not it is intrinsically equivalent to killing. Helping is not, as conventionally thought, a charitable act that it is praiseworthy to do, but not wrong to omit; it is something that everyone ought to do.

This is the argument for an obligation to assist. Set out more formally, it would look like this.

First premise: If we can prevent something bad without sacrificing anything of comparable significance, we ought to do it.

Second premise: Absolute poverty is bad.

Third premise: There is some absolute poverty we can prevent without sacrificing anything of comparable moral significance.

Conclusion: We ought to prevent some absolute poverty.

The first premise is the substantive moral premise on which the argument rests, and I have tried to show that it can be accepted by people who hold a variety of ethical positions.

The second premise is unlikely to be challenged. Absolute poverty is, as McNamara put it, "beneath any reasonable definition of human decency" and it would be hard to find a plausible ethical view that did not regard it as a bad thing.

The third premise is more controversial, even though it is cautiously framed. It claims only that some absolute poverty can be prevented without the sacrifice of anything of comparable moral significance. It thus avoids the objection that any aid I can give is just "drops in the ocean" for the point is not whether my personal contribution will make any noticeable impression on world poverty as a whole (of course it won't) but whether it will prevent some poverty. This is all the argument needs to sustain its conclusion, since the second premise says that any absolute poverty is bad, and not merely the total amount of absolute poverty. If without sacrificing anything of comparable moral significance we can provide just one family with the means to raise itself out of absolute poverty, the third premise is vindicated.

I have left the notion of moral significance unexamined in order to show that the argument does not depend on any specific values or ethical principles. I think the third premise is true for most people living in industrialised nations, on any defensible view of what is morally significant. Our affluence means that we have income we can dispose of without giving up the basic necessities of life, and we can use this income to reduce absolute poverty. Just how much we will think ourselves obliged to give up will depend on what we consider to be of comparable moral imum standard of acceptable conduct we can require of everyone; to save all one possibly could is not something that can realistically be required, especially not in societies accustomed to giving as little as ours do. Given the generally accepted standards, people who give, say, $1,000 a year to an overseas aid organisation are more aptly praised for above average generosity than blamed for giving less than they might. The appropriateness of praise and blame is, however, a separate issue from the rightness or wrongness of actions. The former evaluates the agent: the latter evaluates the action. Perhaps many people who give $1,000 really ought to give at least $5,000, but to blame them for not giving more could be counterproductive. It might make them feel that what is required is too demanding, and if one is going to be blamed anyway, one might as well not give anything at all.

(That an ethic that put saving all one possibly can on the same footing as not killing would be an ethic for saints or heroes should not lead us to assume that the alternative must be an ethic that makes it obligatory not to kill, but puts us under no obligation to save anyone. There are positions in between these extremes, as we shall soon see.)

Here is a summary of the five differences that normally exist between killing and allowing to die, in the context of absolute poverty and overseas aid. The lack of an identifiable victim is of no moral significance, though it may play an important role in explaining our attitudes. The idea that we are directly responsible for those we kill, but not for those we do not help, depends on a questionable notion of responsibility and may need to be based on a controversial theory of rights. Differences in certainty and motivation are ethically significant, and show that not aiding the poor is not to be condemned as murdering them; it could, however, be on a par with killing someone as a result of reckless driving, which is serious enough. Finally the difficulty of completely discharging the duty of saving all one possibly can makes it inappropriate to blame those who fall short of this target as we blame those who kill; but this does not show that the act itself is less serious. Nor does it indicate anything about those who, far from saving all they possibly can, make no effort to save anyone.

These conclusions suggest a new approach. Instead of attempting to deal with the contrast between affluence and poverty by comparing not saving with deliberate killing, let us consider afresh whether we have an obligation to assist those whose lives are in danger, and if so, how this obligation applies to the present world situation.

THE OBLIGATION TO ASSIST

The Argument for an Obligation to Assist

The path from the library at my university to the humanities lecture theatre passes a shallow ornamental pond. Suppose that on my way to give a lecture I notice that a small child has fallen in and is in danger of drowning. Would anyone deny that I ought to wade in and pull the child out? This will mean getting my clothes muddy and either cancelling my lecture or delaying it until I can find something dry to change into; but compared with the avoidable death of a child this is insignificant.

A plausible principle that would support the judgment that I ought to pull the child out is this: if it is in our power to prevent something very bad from happening, without thereby sacrificing anything of comparable moral significance, we ought to do it. This principle seems uncontroversial. It will obviously win the assent of consequentialists; but non-consequentialists should accept it too, because the injunction to prevent what is bad applies only when nothing comparably significant is at stake. Thus the principle cannot lead to the kinds of actions of which non-consequentialists strongly disapprove—serious violations of individual rights, injustice, broken promises, and so on. If non-consequentialists regard any of these as comparable in significance to the poverty we could prevent: stylish clothes, expensive dinners, a sophisticated stereo system, overseas holidays, a (second?) car, a larger house, private schools for our children, and so on. For a utilitarian, none of these is likely to be of comparable significance to the reduction of absolute poverty; and those who are not utilitarians surely must, if they subscribe to the principle of universalisability, accept that at least some of these things are of far less moral significance than the absolute poverty that could be prevented by the money they cost. So the third premise seems to be true on any plausible ethical view—although the precise amount of absolute poverty that can be prevented before anything of moral significance is sacrificed will vary according to the ethical view one accepts.

Objections to the Argument

Taking Care of Our Own

Anyone who has worked to increase overseas aid will have come across the argument that we should look after those near us, our families, and then the poor in our own country, before we think about poverty in distant places.

No doubt we do instinctively prefer to help those who are close to us. Few could stand by and watch a child drown; many can ignore a famine in Africa. But the question is not what we usually do, but what we ought to do, and it is difficult to see any sound moral justification for the view that distance, or community membership, makes a crucial difference to our obligations.

Consider, for instance, racial affinities. Should people of European origin help poor Europeans before helping poor Africans? Most of us would reject such a suggestion out of hand, and our discussion of the principle of equal consideration of interests in Chapter 2 has shown why we should reject it: people's need for food has nothing to do with their race, and if Africans need food more than Europeans, it would be a violation of the principle of equal consideration to give preference to Europeans.

The same point applies to citizenship or nationhood. Every affluent nation has some relatively poor citizens, but absolute poverty is limited largely to the poor nations. Those living on the streets of Calcutta, or in the drought-prone Sahel region of Africa, are experiencing poverty unknown in the West. Under these circumstances it would be wrong to decide that only those fortunate enough to be citizens of our own community will share our abundance.

We feel obligations of kinship more strongly than those of citizenship. Which parents could give away their last bowl of rice if their own children were starving? To do so would seem unnatural, contrary to our nature as biologically evolved beings —although whether it would be wrong is another question altogether. In any case, we are not faced with that situation, but with one in which our own children are well-fed, well-clothed, well-educated, and would now like new bikes, a stereo set, or their own car. In these circumstances any special obligations we might have to our children have been fulfilled, and the needs of strangers make a stronger claim upon us.

The element of truth in the view that we should first take care of our own, lies in the advantage of a recognised system of responsibilities. When families and local communities look after their own poorer members, ties of affection and personal relationships achieve ends that would otherwise require a large, impersonal bureaucracy. Hence it would be absurd to propose that from now on we all regard ourselves as equally responsible for the welfare of everyone in the world; but the argument for an obligation to assist does not propose that. It applies only when some are in absolute poverty, and others can help without sacrificing anything of comparable moral significance. To allow one's own kin to sink into absolute poverty would be to sacrifice something of comparable significance; and before that point had been reached, the breakdown of the system of family and community responsibility would be a factor to weigh the balance in favour of a small degree of preference for family and community. This small degree of preference is, however, decisively outweighed by existing discrepancies in wealth and property.

Property Rights

Do people have a right to private property, a right that contradicts the view that they are under an obligation to give some of their wealth away to those in absolute poverty? According to some theories of rights (for instance, Robert Nozick's), provided one has acquired one's property without the use of unjust means like force and fraud, one may be entitled to enormous wealth while others starve. This individualistic conception of rights is in contrast to other views, like the early Christian doctrine to be found in the works of Thomas Aquinas, which holds that since property exists for the satisfaction of human needs, "whatever a man has in superabundance is owed, of natural right, to the poor for their sustenance." A socialist would also, of course, see wealth as belonging to the community rather than the individual, while utilitarians, whether socialist or not, would be prepared to override property rights to prevent great evils.

Does the argument for an obligation to assist others therefore presuppose one of these other theories of property rights, and not an individualistic theory like Nozick's? Not necessarily. A theory of property rights can insist on our *right* to retain wealth without pronouncing on whether the rich *ought* to give to the poor. Nozick, for example, rejects the use of compulsory means like taxation to redistribute income, but suggests that we can achieve the ends we deem morally desirable by voluntary means. So Nozick would reject the claim that rich people have an 'obligation' to give to the poor, in so far as this implies that the poor have a right to our aid, but might accept that giving is something we ought to do and failing to give, though within one's rights, is wrong—for there is more to an ethical life than respecting the rights of others.

The argument for an obligation to assist can survive, with only minor modifications, even if we accept an individualistic theory of property rights. In any case, however, I do not think we should accept such a theory. It leaves too much to chance to be an acceptable ethical view. For instance, those whose forefathers happened to inhabit some sandy wastes around the Persian Gulf are now fabulously wealthy, because oil lay under those sands; while those whose forefathers settled on better land south of the Sahara live in absolute poverty, because of drought and bad harvests. Can this distribution be acceptable from an impartial point of view? If we imagine ourselves about to begin life as a citizen of either Bahrein or Chad—but we do not know which—would we accept the principle that citizens of Bahrein are under no obligation to assist people living in Chad?

Population and the Ethics of Triage

Perhaps the most serious objection to the argument that we have an obligation to assist is that since the major cause of absolute poverty is overpopulation, helping those now in poverty will only ensure that yet more people are born to live in poverty in the future.

In its most extreme form, this objection is taken to show that we should adopt a policy of "triage." The term comes from medical policies adopted in wartime. With too few doctors to cope with all the casualties, the wounded were divided into three categories: those who would probably survive without medical assistance, those who might survive if they received assistance, but otherwise probably would

not, and those who even with medical assistance probably would not survive. Only those in the middle category were given medical assistance. The idea, of course, was to use limited medical resources as effectively as possible. For those in the first category, medical treatment was not strictly necessary; for those in the third category, it was likely to be useless. It has been suggested that we should apply the same policies to countries, according to their prospects of becoming self-sustaining. We would not aid countries that even without our help will soon be able to feed their populations. We would not aid countries that, even with our help, will not be able to limit their population to a level they can feed. We would aid those countries where our help might make the difference between success and failure in bringing food and population into balance.

Advocates of this theory are understandably reluctant to give a complete list of the countries they would place into the 'hopeless' category; Bangladesh has been cited as an example, and so have some of the countries of the Sahel region of Africa. Adopting the policy of triage would, then, mean cutting off assistance to these countries and allowing famine, disease, and natural disasters to reduce the population of those countries to the level at which they can provide adequately for all.

In support of this view Garrett Hardin has offered a metaphor: we in the rich nations are like the occupants of a crowded lifeboat adrift in a sea full of drowning people. If we try to save the drowning by bringing them aboard, our boat will be overloaded and we shall all drown. Since it is better that some survive than none, we should leave the others to drown. In the world today, according to Hardin, "lifeboat ethics" apply. The rich should leave the poor to starve, for otherwise the poor will drag the rich down with them.

Against this view, some writers have argued that overpopulation is a myth. The world produces ample food to feed its population, and could, according to some estimates, feed ten times as many. People are hungry not because there are too many but because of inequitable land distribution, the manipulation of third world economies by the developed nations, wastage of food in the West, and so on.

Putting aside the controversial issue of the extent to which food production might one day be increased, it is true, as we have already seen, that the world now produces enough to feed its inhabitants—the amount lost by being fed to animals itself being enough to meet existing grain shortages. Nevertheless population growth cannot be ignored. Bangladesh could, with land reform and using better techniques, feed its present population of 115 million; but by the year 2000, according to United Nations Population Division estimates, its population will be 150 million. The enormous effort that will have to go into feeding an extra 35 million people, all added to the population within a decade, means that Bangladesh must develop at full speed to stay where it is. Other low-income countries are in similar situations. By the end of the century, Ethiopia's population is expected to rise from 49 to 66 million; Somalia's from 7 to 9 million, India's from 853 to 1041 million, Zaire's from 35 to 49 million.[2]

What will happen if the world population continues to grow? It cannot do so indefinitely. It will be checked by a decline in birth rates or a rise in death rates. Those who advocate triage are proposing that we allow the population growth of some countries to be checked by a rise in death rates—that is, by increased malnutrition, and related diseases; by widespread famines; by increased infant mortality; and by epidemics of infectious diseases.

The consequences of triage on this scale are so horrible that we are inclined to reject it without further argument. How could we sit by our television sets, watching millions starve while we do nothing? Would not that be the end of all notions of human equality and respect for human life? (Those who attack the proposals for legalising euthanasia discussed in Chapter 7, saying that these proposals will weaken respect for human life, would surely do better to object to the idea that we should reduce or end our overseas aid programs, for that proposal, if implemented, would be responsible for a far greater loss of human life.) Don't people have a right to our assistance, irrespective of the consequences?

Anyone whose initial reaction to triage was not one of repugnance would be an unpleasant sort of person.

Yet initial reactions based on strong feelings are not always reliable guides. Advocates of triage are rightly concerned with the long-term consequences of our actions. They say that helping the poor and starving now merely ensures more poor and starving in the future. When our capacity to help is finally unable to cope—as one day it must be—the suffering will be greater than it would be if we stopped helping now. If this is correct, there is nothing we can do to prevent absolute starvation and poverty, in the long run, and so we have no obligation to assist. Nor does it seem reasonable to hold that under these circumstances people have a right to our assistance. If we do accept such a right, irrespective of the consequences, we are saying that, in Hardin's metaphor, we should continue to haul the drowning into our lifeboat until the boat sinks and we all drown.

If triage is to be rejected it must be tackled on its own ground, within the framework of consequentialist ethics. Here it is vulnerable. Any consequentialist ethics must take probability of outcome into account. A course of action that will certainly produce some benefit is to be preferred to an alternative course that may lead to a slightly larger benefit, but is equally likely to result in no benefit at all. Only if the greater magnitude of the uncertain benefit outweighs its uncertainty should we choose it. Better one certain unit of benefit than a 10 per cent chance of five units; but better a 50 per cent chance of three units than a single certain unit. The same principle applies when we are trying to avoid evils.

The policy of triage involves a certain, very great evil: population control by famine and disease. Tens of millions would die slowly. Hundreds of millions would continue to live in absolute poverty, at the very margin of existence. Against this prospect, advocates of the policy place a possible evil that is greater still: the same process of famine and disease, taking place in, say, fifty years' time, when the world's population may be three times its present level, and the number who will die from famine, or struggle on in absolute poverty, will be that much greater. The question is: how probable is this forecast that continued assistance now will lead to greater disasters in the future?

Forecasts of population growth are notoriously

fallible, and theories about the factors that affect it remain speculative. One theory, at least as plausible as any other, is that countries pass through a "demographic transition" as their standard of living rises. When people are very poor and have no access to modern medicine their fertility is high, but population is kept in check by high death rates. The introduction of sanitation, modern medical techniques, and other improvements reduces the death rate, but initially has little effect on the birth rate. Then population grows rapidly. Some poor countries, especially in sub-Saharan Africa, are now in this phase. If standards of living continue to rise, however, couples begin to realise that to have the same number of children surviving to maturity as in the past, they do not need to give birth to as many children as their parents did. The need for children to provide economic support in old age diminishes. Improved education and the emancipation and employment of women also reduce the birth-rate, and so population growth begins to level off. Most rich nations have reached this stage, and their populations are growing only very slowly, if at all.

If this theory is right, there is an alternative to the disasters accepted as inevitable by supporters of triage. We can assist poor countries to raise the living standards of the poorest members of their population. We can encourage the governments of these countries to enact land reform measures, improve education, and liberate women from a purely child-bearing role. We can also help other countries to make contraception and sterilisation widely available. There is a fair chance that these measures will hasten the onset of the demographic transition and bring population growth down to a manageable level. According to United Nations estimates, in 1965 the average woman in the third world gave birth to six children, and only 8 per cent were using some form of contraception; by 1991 the average number of children had dropped to just below four, and more than half the women in the third world were taking contraceptive measures. Notable successes in encouraging the use of contraception had occurred in Thailand, Indonesia, Mexico, Colombia, Brazil, and Bangladesh. This achievement reflected a relatively low expenditure in developing countries—considering the size and significance of the problem—of $3 billion annually, with only 20 per cent of this sum coming from developed nations. So expenditure in this area seems likely to be highly cost-effective. Success cannot be guaranteed; but the evidence suggests that we can reduce population growth by improving economic security and education, and making contraceptives more widely available. This prospect makes triage ethically unacceptable. We cannot allow millions to die from starvation and disease when there is a reasonable probability that population can be brought under control without such horrors.

Population growth is therefore not a reason against giving overseas aid, although it should make us think about the kind of aid to give. Instead of food handouts, it may be better to give aid that leads to a slowing of population growth. This may mean agricultural assistance for the rural poor, or assistance with education, or the provision of contraceptive services. Whatever kind of aid proves most effective in specific circumstances, the obligation to assist is not reduced.

One awkward question remains. What should we do about a poor and already overpopulated country that, for religious or nationalistic reasons, restricts the use of contraceptives and refuses to slow its population growth? Should we nevertheless offer development assistance? Or should we make our offer conditional on effective steps being taken to reduce the birthrate? To the latter course, some would object that putting conditions on aid is an attempt to impose our own ideas on independent sovereign nations. So it is—but is this imposition unjustifiable? If the argument for an obligation to assist is sound, we have an obligation to reduce absolute poverty; but we have no obligation to make sacrifices that, to the best of our knowledge, have no prospect of reducing poverty in the long run. Hence we have no obligation to assist countries whose governments have policies that will make our aid ineffective. This could be very harsh on poor citizens of these countries—for they may have no say in the government's policies—but we will help more people in the long run by using our resources where they are most effective. (The same principles may apply, incidentally, to countries that refuse to take other steps that could make assistance effective—like refusing to reform systems of land holding that impose intolerable burdens on poor tenant farmers.)

Leaving It to the Government

We often hear that overseas aid should be a government responsibility, not left to privately run charities. Giving privately, it is said, allows the government to escape its responsibilities.

Since increasing government aid is the surest way of making a significant increase to the total amount of aid given, I would agree that the governments of affluent nations should give much more genuine, no-strings-attached, aid than they give now. Less than one-sixth of one per cent of GNP is a scandalously small amount for a nation as wealthy as the United States to give. Even the official UN target of 0.7 per cent seems much less than affluent nations can and should give—though it is a target few have reached. But is this a reason against each of us giving what we can privately, through voluntary agencies? To believe that it is seems to assume that the more people there are who give through voluntary agencies, the less likely it is that the government will do its part. Is this plausible? The opposite view—that if no one gives voluntarily the government will assume that its citizens are not in favour of overseas aid, and will cut its programme accordingly—is more reasonable. In any case, unless there is a definite probability that by refusing to give we would be helping to bring about an increase in government assistance, refusing to give privately is wrong for the same reason that triage is wrong: it is a refusal to prevent a definite evil for the sake of a very uncertain gain. The onus of showing how a refusal to give privately will make the government give more is on those who refuse to give.

This is not to say that giving privately is enough. Certainly we should campaign for entirely new standards for both public and private overseas aid. We should also work for fairer trading arrangements between rich and poor countries, and less domination of the economies of poor countries by multinational corporations more concerned about producing profits for shareholders back home than food for the local poor. Perhaps it is more important to be politically active in the interests of the poor than to give to them oneself—but why not do both? Unfortunately, many use the view that overseas aid is the government's responsibility as a reason against giving, but not as a reason for being politically active.

Too High a Standard?

The final objection to the argument for an obligation to assist is that it sets a standard so high that none but a saint could attain it. This objection comes in at least three versions. The first maintains that, human nature being what it is, we cannot achieve so high a standard, and since it is absurd to say that we ought to do what we cannot do, we must reject the claim that we ought to give so much. The second version asserts that even if we could achieve so high a standard, to do so would be undesirable. The third version of the objection is that to set so high a standard is undesirable because it will be perceived as too difficult to reach, and will discourage many from even attempting to do so.

Those who put forward the first version of the objection are often influenced by the fact that we have evolved from a natural process in which those with a high degree of concern for their own interests, or the interests of their offspring and kin, can be expected to leave more descendants in future generations, and eventually to completely replace any who are entirely altruistic. Thus the biologist Garrett Hardin has argued, in support of his "lifeboat ethics," that altruism can only exist "on a small scale, over the short term, and within small, intimate groups"; while Richard Dawkins has written, in his provocative book *The Selfish Gene:* "Much as we might wish to believe otherwise, universal love and the welfare of the species as a whole are concepts which simply do not make evolutionary sense." I have already noted, in discussing the objection that we should first take care of our own, the very strong tendency for partiality in human beings. We naturally have a stronger desire to further our own interests, and those of our close kin, than we have to further the interests of strangers. What this means is that we would be foolish to expect widespread conformity to a standard that demands impartial concern, and for that reason it would scarcely be appropriate or feasible to condemn all those who fail to reach such a standard. Yet to act impartially, though it might be very difficult, is not impossible. The commonly quoted assertion that "ought" implies "can" is a reason for rejecting such moral judgments as "You ought to have saved all the people from the sinking ship," when in fact if you had taken one more person into the lifeboat, it would have sunk and you would not have saved any. In that situation, it is absurd to say that you ought to have done what you could not possibly do. When we have money to spend on luxuries and others are starving, however, it is clear that we can all give much more than we do give, and we can therefore all come closer to the impartial standard proposed in this chapter. Nor is there, as we approach closer to this standard, any barrier beyond which we cannot go. For that reason there is no basis for saying that the impartial standard is mistaken because "ought" implies "can" and we cannot be impartial.

The second version of the objection has been put by several philosophers during the past decade, among them Susan Wolf in a forceful article entitled "Moral Saints." Wolf argues that if we all took the kind of moral stance defended in this chapter, we would have to do without a great deal that makes life interesting: opera, gourmet cooking, elegant clothes, and professional sport, for a start. The kind of life we come to see as ethically required of us would be a single-minded pursuit of the overall good, lacking that broad diversity of interests and activities that, on a less demanding view, can be part of our ideal of a good life for a human being. To this, however, one can respond that while the rich and varied life that Wolf upholds as an ideal may be the most desirable form of life for a human being in a world of plenty, it is wrong to assume that it remains a good life in a world in which buying luxuries for oneself means accepting the continued avoidable suffering of others. A doctor faced with hundreds of injured victims of a train crash can scarcely think it defensible to treat fifty of them and then go to the opera, on the grounds that going to the opera is part of a well-rounded human life. The life-or-death needs of others must take priority. Perhaps we are like the doctor in that we live in a time when we all have an opportunity to help to mitigate a disaster.

Associated with this second version of the objection is the claim that an impartial ethic of the kind advocated here makes it impossible to have serious personal relationships based on love and friendship; these relationships are, of their nature, partial. We put the interests of our loved ones, our family, and our friends ahead of those of strangers; if we did not do so, would these relationships survive? I have already indicated, in the response I gave when considering the objection that we should first take care of our own, that there is a place, within an impartially grounded moral framework, for recognising some degree of partiality for kin, and the same can be said for other close personal relationships. Clearly, for most people, personal relationships are among the necessities of a flourishing life, and to give them up would be to sacrifice something of great moral significance. Hence no such sacrifice is required by the principle for which I am here arguing.

The third version of the objection asks: might it not be counterproductive to demand that people give up so much? Might not people say: "As I can't do what is morally required anyway, I won't bother to give at all." If, however, we were to set a more realistic standard, people might make a genuine effort to reach it. Thus setting a lower standard might actually result in more aid being given.

It is important to get the status of this third version of the objection clear. Its accuracy as a prediction of human behaviour is quite compatible with the argument that we are obliged to give to the point at which by giving more we sacrifice something of comparable moral significance. What would follow from the objection is that public advocacy of this standard of giving is undesirable. It would mean that in order to do the maximum to reduce absolute poverty, we should advocate a standard lower than the amount we think people really ought to give. Of course we ourselves—those of us who accept the original argument, with its higher standard—would know that we ought to do more than we publicly propose people ought to do, and we might actually give more than we urge others to give. There is no inconsistency here, since in both our private and our public behaviour we are trying to do what will most reduce absolute poverty.

For a consequentialist, this apparent conflict between public and private morality is always a possibility, and not in itself an indication that the underlying principle is wrong. The consequences of a principle are one thing, the consequences of publicly advocating it another. A variant of this idea is already acknowledged by the distinction between the intuitive and critical levels of morality, of which I have made use in previous chapters. If we think of principles that are suitable for the intuitive level of morality as those that should be generally advocated, these are the principles that, when advocated, will give rise to the best consequences. Where overseas aid is concerned, those will be the principles that lead to largest amount being given by the affluent to the poor.

Is it true that the standard set by our argument is so high as to be counterproductive? There is not much evidence to go by, but discussions of the argument, with students and others have led me to think it might be. Yet, the conventionally accepted standard—a few coins in a collection tin when one is waved under your nose—is obviously far too low. What level should we advocate? Any figure will be arbitrary, but there may be something to be said for a round percentage of one's income like, say, 10 per cent—more than a token donation, yet not so high as to be beyond all but saints. (This figure has the additional advantage of being reminiscent of the ancient tithe, or tenth, that was traditionally given to the church, whose responsibilities included care of the poor in one's local community. Perhaps the idea can be revived and applied to the global community.) Some families, of course, will find 10 per cent a considerable strain on their finances. Others may be able to give more without difficulty. No figure should be advocated as a rigid minimum or maximum; but it seems safe to advocate that those earning average or above average incomes in affluent societies, unless they have an unusually large number of dependents or other special needs, ought to give a tenth of their income to reducing absolute poverty. By any reasonable ethical standards this is the minimum we ought to do, and we do wrong if we do less.

NOTES

1. Strictly, we would need to cut down to the minimum level compatible with earning the income which, after providing for our needs, left us most to give away. Thus if my present position earns me, say, $40,000 a year, but requires me to spend $5,000 a year on dressing respectably and maintaining a car, I cannot save more people by giving away the car and clothes if that will mean taking a job that, although it does not involve me in these expenses, earns me only $20,000.

2. Ominously, in the twelve years that have passed between editions of this book, the signs are that the situation is becoming even worse than was then predicted. In 1979 Bangladesh had a population of 80 million and it was predicted that by 2000 its population would reach 146 million; Ethiopia's was only 29 million, and was predicted to reach 54 million; and India's was 620 million and predicted to reach 958 million.

Equality, Entitlements, and the Distribution of Income

⁓

JOHN ARTHUR

John Arthur is professor of philosophy at Binghamton University, State University of New York. Among his fields of specialization are political philosophy and the philosophy of law.

INTRODUCTION

My guess is that everyone who reads these words is wealthy by comparison with the poorest millions of people on our planet. Not only do we have plenty of money for food, clothing, housing, and other necessities, but a fair amount is left over for far less important purchases like phonograph records, fancy clothes, trips, intoxicants, movies, and so on. And what's more, we don't usually give thought to whether or not we ought to spend our money on such luxuries rather than to give it to those who need it more; we just assume it's ours to do with as we please.

Peter Singer . . . argue[s] that our assumption is wrong, that we should not buy luxuries when others are in severe need. But are they correct? In the first two sections of this paper my aim is to get into focus just what their arguments are, and to evaluate them. Both Singer and Watson, it seems to me, ignore an important feature of our moral code, namely that it allows people who deserve or have rights to their earnings to keep them.

But the fact that our code encourages a form of behavior is not a complete defense, for it is possible that our current moral attitudes are mistaken. Sections 3 and 4 consider this possibility from two angles: universalizability and the notion of an ideal moral code. Neither of these approaches, I argue, requires that desert and rights be sacrificed in the name of redistribution.

1. EQUALITY AND THE DUTY TO AID

What does our moral code have to say about helping people in need? Watson emphasizes what he calls the "principle of equity." Since "all human life is of equal value," and difference in treatment should be "based on freely chosen actions and not accidents of birth or environment," he thinks that we have "equal rights to the necessities of life." To distribute food unequally assumes that some lives are worth more than others, an assumption which, he says, we do not accept. Watson believes, in fact, that we put such importance on the "equity principle" that it should not be violated even if unequal distribution is the only way for anybody to survive. (Leaving aside for the moment whether or not he is correct about our code, it seems to me that if it really did require us to commit mass suicide rather than allow inequality in wealth, then we would want to abandon it for a more suitable set of rules. But more on that later.)

Is Watson correct in assuming that all life is of equal value? Did Adolph Hitler and Martin Luther King, for example, lead two such lives? Clearly one did far more good and less harm than the other. Nor are moral virtues like courage, kindness, and trustworthiness equally distributed among people. So there are at least two senses in which people are not morally equal.

Yet the phrase "All men are equal" has an almost

platitudinous ring, and many of us would not hesitate to say that equality is a cornerstone of our morality. But what does it mean? It seems to me that we might have in mind one of two things. First is an idea that Thomas Jefferson expressed in the *Declaration of Independence.* "All men are created equal" meant, for him, that no man is the moral inferior of another, that, in other words, there are certain rights which all men share equally, including life and liberty. We are entitled to pursue our own lives with a minimum of interference from others, and no person is the natural slave of another. But, as Jefferson also knew, equality in that sense does not require equal distribution of the necessities of life, only that we not interfere with one another, allowing instead every person the liberty to pursue his own affairs, so long as he does not violate the rights of his fellows.

Others, however, have something different in mind when they speak of human equality. I want to develop this second idea by recounting briefly the details of Singer's argument in "Famine, Affluence, and Morality." He first argues that two general moral principles are widely accepted, and then that those principles imply an obligation to eliminate starvation.

The first principle is simply that "suffering and death from lack of food, shelter and medical care are bad." Some may be inclined to think that the mere existence of such an evil in itself places an obligation on others, but that is, of course, the problem which Singer addresses. I take it that he is not begging the question in this obvious way and will argue from the existence of evil to the obligation of others to eliminate it. But how, exactly, does he establish this? The second principle, he thinks, shows the connection, but it is here that controversy arises.

This principle, which I will call the greater moral evil rule, is as follows:

> If it is in our power to prevent something bad from happening, without thereby sacrificing anything of comparable moral importance, we ought, morally, to do it.

In other words, people are entitled to keep their earnings only if there is no way for them to prevent a greater evil by giving them away. Providing others with food, clothing, and housing would generally be of more importance than buying luxuries, so the greater moral evil rule now requires substantial redistribution of wealth.

Certainly there are few, if any, of us who live by that rule, although that hardly shows we are *justified* in our way of life; we often fail to live up to our own standards. Why does Singer think our shared morality requires that we follow the greater moral evil rule? What arguments does he give for it?

He begins with an analogy. Suppose you came across a child drowning in a shallow pond. Certainly we feel it would be wrong not to help. Even if saving the child meant we must dirty our clothes, we would emphasize that those clothes are not of comparable significance to the child's life. The greater moral evil rule thus seems a natural way of capturing why we think it would be wrong not to help.

But the argument for the greater moral evil rule is not limited to Singer's claim that it explains our feelings about the drowning child or that it appears "uncontroversial." Moral equality also enters the picture. Besides the Jeffersonian idea that we share certain rights equally, most of us are also attracted to another type of equality, namely that like amounts of suffering (or happiness) are of equal significance, no matter who is experiencing them. I cannot reasonably say that, while my pain is no more severe than yours, I am somehow special and it's more important that mine be alleviated. Objectivity requires us to admit the opposite, that no one has a unique status which warrants such special pleading. So equality demands equal consideration of interests as well as respect for certain rights.

But if we fail to give to famine relief and instead purchase a new car when the old one will do, or buy fancy clothes for a friend when his or her old ones are perfectly good, are we not assuming that the relatively minor enjoyment we or our friends may get is as important as another person's life? And that is a form of prejudice; we are acting as if people were not equal in the sense that their interests deserve equal consideration. We are giving special consideration to ourselves or to our group, rather like a racist does. Equal consideration of interests thus leads naturally to the greater moral evil rule.

2. RIGHTS AND DESERT

Equality, in the sense of giving equal consideration to equally serious needs, is part of our moral code. And so we are led, quite rightly I think, to the conclusion that we should prevent harm to others if in doing so we do not sacrifice anything of comparable moral importance. But there is also another side to the coin, one which Singer and Watson ignore. This can be expressed rather awkwardly by the notion of entitlements. These fall into two broad categories, rights and desert. A few examples will show what I mean.

All of us could help others by giving away or allowing others to use our bodies. While your life may be shortened by the loss of a kidney or less enjoyable if lived with only one eye, those costs are probably not comparable to the loss experienced by a person who will die without any kidney or who is totally blind. We can even imagine persons who will actually be harmed in some way by your not granting sexual favors to them. Perhaps the absence of a sexual partner would cause psychological harm or even rape. Now suppose that you can prevent this evil without sacrificing anything of comparable importance. Obviously such relations may not be pleasant, but according to the greater moral evil rule, that is not enough; to be justified in refusing, you must show that the unpleasantness you would experience is of equal importance to the harm you are preventing. Otherwise, the rule says you must consent.

If anything is clear, however, it is that our code does not *require* such heroism; you are entitled to keep your second eye and kidney and not bestow sexual favors on anyone who may be harmed without them. The reason for this is often expressed in terms of rights; it's your body, you have a right to it, and that weighs against whatever duty you have to help. To sacrifice a kidney for a stranger is to do more than is required, it's heroic.

Moral rights are normally divided into two categories. Negative rights are rights of noninterference. The right to life, for example, is a right not to be killed. Property rights, the right to privacy, and the right to exercise religious freedom are also negative, requiring only that people leave others alone and not interfere.

Positive rights, however, are rights of recipience. By not putting their children up for adoption, parents give them various positive rights, including the rights to be fed, clothed, and housed. If I agree to share in a business venture, my promise creates a right of recipience, so that when I back out of the deal, I've violated your right.

Negative rights also differ from positive in that the former are natural; the ones you have depend on what you are. If lower animals lack rights to life or liberty it is because there is a relevant difference between them and us. But the positive rights you may have are not natural; they arise because others have promised, agreed, or contracted to give you something.

Normally, then, a duty to help a stranger in need is not the result of a right he has. Such a right would be positive, and since no contract or promise was made, no such right exists. An exception to this would be a lifeguard who contracts to watch out for someone's children. The parent whose child drowns would in this case be doubly wronged. First, the lifeguard should not have cruelly or thoughtlessly ignored the child's interests, and second, he ought not to have violated the rights of the parents that he help. Here, unlike Singer's case, we can say there are rights at stake. Other bystanders also act wrongly by cruelly ignoring the child, but unlike the lifeguard they do not violate anybody's rights. Moral rights are one factor to be weighed, but we also have other obligations; I am not claiming that rights are all we need to consider. That view, like the greater moral evil rule, trades simplicity for accuracy. In fact, our code expects us to help people in need as well as to respect negative and positive rights. But we are also entitled to invoke our own rights as justification for not giving to distant strangers or when the cost to us is substantial, as when we give up an eye or a kidney.

Rights come in a variety of shapes and sizes, and people often disagree about both their shape and size. Can a woman kill an unborn child because of her right to control her body? Does mere inheritance transfer rights to property? Do dolphins have a right to live? While some rights are widely accepted, others are controversial.

One more comment about rights, then we'll look at desert. Watson's position, which I criticized for other reasons earlier, is also mistaken because he ignores important rights. He claims that we must pay no attention to "accidents of birth and environment" and base our treatment of people on "what they freely choose." But think about how you will (or did) select a spouse or lover. Are you not entitled to consider such "accidents of birth and environment" as attractiveness, personality, and intelligence? It is, after all, your future, and it is certainly a part of our shared moral code that you have a right to use those (or whatever) criteria you wish in selecting a mate. It is at best an exaggeration to say we must always "ignore accidents of birth and environment" in our treatment of people.

Desert is a second form of entitlement. Suppose, for example, an industrious farmer manages through hard work to produce a surplus of food for the winter while a lazy neighbor spends his summer fishing. Must our industrious farmer ignore his hard work and give the surplus away because his neighbor or his family will suffer? What again seems clear is that we have more than one factor to weigh. Not only should we compare the consequences of his keeping it with his giving it away; we also should weigh the fact that one farmer deserves the food, he earned it through his hard work. Perhaps his deserving the product of his labor is outweighed by the greater need of his lazy neighbor, or perhaps it isn't, but being outweighed is in any case not the same as weighing nothing!

Desert can be negative, too. The fact that the Nazi war criminal did what he did means he deserves punishment, that we have a reason to send him to jail. Other considerations, for example the fact that nobody will be deterred by his suffering, or that he is old and harmless, may weigh against punishment and so we may let him go; but again that does not mean he doesn't still deserve to be punished.

Our moral code gives weight to both the greater moral evil principle and entitlements. The former emphasizes equality, claiming that from an objective point of view all comparable suffering, whoever its victim, is equally significant. It encourages us to take an impartial look at all the various effects of our actions; it is thus forward-looking. When we consider matters of entitlement, however, our attention is directed to the past. Whether we have rights to money, property, eyes, or whatever, depends on how we came to possess them. If they were acquired by theft rather than from birth or through gift exchange, then the right is suspect. Desert, like rights, is also backward-looking, emphasizing past effort or past transgressions which now warrant reward or punishment.

Our commonly shared morality thus requires that we ignore neither consequences nor entitlements, neither the future results of our action nor relevant events in the past. It encourages people to help others in need, especially when it's a friend or someone we are close to geographically, and when the cost is not significant. But it also gives weight to rights and desert, so that we are not usually obligated to give to strangers.

One path is still open as a defense of the greater moral evil rule, and it deserves comment. I have assumed throughout that Singer wants to emphasize the great disparity in the amount of enjoyment someone may get from, say, a new car, as compared with the misery that could be prevented by using the money to save another's life. The fact that the two are not comparable means that the money should not be spent on the car. It is possible to interpret the rule differently, however. By admitting that having rights and deserving things are also of moral significance, Singer could accept what I have said so that the greater moral evil rule would survive intact.

The problem with this response, however, is that the greater moral evil rule has now become an almost empty platitude, urging nothing more than that we should prevent something bad unless we have adequate moral reason not to do so. Since rights and desert often provide such reasons, the rule would say nothing useful about our obligation to help others, and it certainly would not require us to "reduce ourselves to the level of marginal utility" so that the "consumer society" would "slow down and perhaps disappear" as Singer claims. I will therefore assume he would not accept such an interpretation of his view, that entitlements are not among the sacrifices which could balance off the suffering caused by failing to help people in need.

But unless we are moral relativists, the mere fact that entitlements are an important part of our moral code does not in itself justify such a role. Singer and Watson can perhaps best be seen as moral reformers, advocating the rejection of rules which provide for distribution according to rights and desert. Certainly the fact that in the past our moral code condemned suicide and racial mixing while condoning slavery should not convince us that a more enlightened moral code, one which we would want to support, would take such positions. Rules which define acceptable behavior are continually changing, and we must allow for the replacement of inferior ones.

Why should we not view entitlements as examples of inferior rules we are better off without? What could justify our practice of evaluating actions by looking backward to rights and desert instead of just to their consequences? One answer is that more fundamental values than rights and desert are at stake, namely fairness, justice, and respect. Failure to reward those who earn good grades or promotions is wrong because it's *unfair;* ignoring past guilt shows a lack of regard for *justice;* and failure to respect rights to life, privacy, or religious choice suggests a lack of *respect for other persons.*

Some people may be persuaded by those remarks, feeling that entitlements are now on an acceptably firm foundation. But an advocate of equality may well want to question why fairness, justice, and respect for persons should matter. But since it is no more obvious that preventing suffering matters than that fairness, respect, and justice do, we again seem to have reached an impasse.

3. UNIVERSALIZABILITY

It is sometimes thought that we can choose between competing moral rules by noting which ones are compatible with some more fundamental rule. One such fundamental standard is attributed to Kant, though it is also rooted in traditional Christian thought. "Do unto others as you would have them do unto you" and the Kantian categorical imperative, "Act only on maxims that you can will would become universal laws," express an idea some think is basic to *all* moral rules. The suggestion is that if you think what you're doing is right, then you have got to be willing to universalize your judgment, that is, to acknowledge that anyone in similar circumstances would be correct if he were to follow the same rule.

Such familiar reasoning can be taken in two very different ways. The first requires only that a person not make himself an exception, that he live up to his own standard. This type of universalizability, however, cannot help choose between the two rules. An advocate of rights and desert would surely agree that whether he were the deserving or undeserving one, whether he had the specific right or did not have it, entitlements still should not be ignored. Nothing about the position of those supporting rights and desert suggests that they must make exceptions for themselves; such rules are in that sense universalizable. But the advocate of the greater moral evil rule can also be counted on to claim that he too should not be made an exception, and that *ignoring* entitlements in favor of the greater moral evil rule is the proper course whether or not he would benefit from the policy. Both views, then, could be universalized in the first sense.

But if we understand universalizability in another sense, neither of the rules passes the test. If being "willing to universalize the judgment" means that a supporter of a particular moral rule would be equally happy with the result were the roles reversed, then there is doubt whether either is universalizable. The rights advocate cannot promise always to like the outcome; he probably would *prefer,* were the tables turned and his life depended on somebody not keeping his rightfully owned income, that entitlements be ignored in that instance. But his opponent cannot pass the test either, since he would likely prefer that rights and desert *not* be ignored were he in a position to benefit from them. But in any case it is not at all clear why we should expect people who make moral judgments to be neutral as to which position they occupy. Must a judge who thinks justice requires that a murderer go to jail agree that he would prefer jail if he were the murderer? It seems that all he must do to universalize his judgment is agree that it would be *right* that he go to jail if the tables were turned, that, in other words, he is not exempt from the rules. But that is a test, as I said, which supporters of entitlements can pass.

So the test of universalizability does not provide grounds for rejecting entitlement rules, and we are once again at an impasse. A second possibility is to view the egalitarian as a moral reformer. Then, perhaps, the criticism of entitlements can be defended as part of a more reasonable and effective moral system. In the final section I look in detail at the idea that rights and desert would not be part of a such ideal moral code, one which we would support if we were fully rational.

4. ENTITLEMENTS AND THE IDEAL MORAL CODE

The idea I want now to consider is that part of our code should be dropped, so that people could no longer invoke rights and desert as justification for not making large sacrifices for strangers. In place of entitlements would be a rule requiring that any time we can prevent something bad without sacrificing anything of comparable moral significance we ought to do it. Our current code, however, allows people to say that while they would do more good with their earnings, still they have rights to the earnings, the earnings are deserved, and so need not be given away. The crucial question is whether we want to have such entitlement rules in our code, or whether we should reject them in favor of the greater moral evil rule.

Universalizability, I argued, gives no clear answer to this. Each position also finds a certain amount of support within our code, either from the idea of equal consideration of interests or from our concerns about fairness, justice, and respect for other persons. The problem to be resolved, then, is whether there are other reasons to drop entitlement rules in favor of the greater moral evil rule.

I believe that our best procedure is not to think about this or that specific rule, drawing analogies, refining it, and giving counterexamples, but to focus instead on the nature of morality as a whole. What is a moral code? What do we want it to do? What type of code do we want to support? These questions will give us a fresh perspective from which to consider the merits of rules which allow people to appeal to rights and desert and to weigh the issue of whether our present code should be reformed.

We can begin with the obvious: A moral code is a system of rules designed to guide people's conduct. As such, it has characteristics in common with other systems of rules. Virtually every organization has rules which govern the conduct of members; clubs, baseball leagues, corporations, bureaucracies, profession associations, even *The* Organization all have rules. Another obvious point is this: What the rules are depends on why the organization exists. Rules function to enable people to accomplish goals which lead them to organize in the first place. Some rules, for example, "Don't snitch on fellow mafioso," "Pay dues to the fraternity," and "Don't give away trade secrets to competing companies," serve in obvious ways. Other times the real purposes of rules are controversial, as when doctors do not allow advertising by fellow members of the AMA.

Frequently rules reach beyond members of a specific organization, obligating everyone who is capable of following them to do so. These include costs of civil and criminal law, etiquette, custom, and morality. But before discussing the specific purposes of moral rules, it will be helpful to look briefly at some of the similarities and differences between these more universal codes.

First, the sanctions imposed on rule violators vary among different types of codes. While in our legal code, transgressions are punished by fines, jail, or repayment of damages, informal sanctions of praise, blame, or guilt encourage conformity to the rules of morality and etiquette. Another difference is that while violation of a moral rule is always a serious affair, this need not be so for legal rules of etiquette and custom. Many of us think it unimportant whether a fork is on the left side of a plate or whether an outmoded and widely ignored Sunday closing law is violated, but violation of a moral rule is not ignored. Indeed, that a moral rule has lost its importance is often shown by its demotion to status of mere custom.

A third difference is that legal rules, unlike rules of morality, custom, and etiquette, provide for a specific person or procedure that is empowered to alter the rules. If Congress acts to change the tax laws, then as of the date stated in the statute the rules are changed. Similarly for the governing rules of social clubs, government bureaucracies, and the AMA. Rules of custom, morals, and etiquette also change, of course, but they do so in a less precise and much more gradual fashion, with no person or group specifically empowered to make changes.

This fact, that moral rules are *in a sense* beyond the power of individuals to change, does not show that rules of morality, any more than those of etiquette, are objective in the same sense that scientific laws are. All that needs to happen for etiquette or morality to change is for people to change certain practices, namely the character traits they praise and blame, or the actions they approve and disapprove. Scientific laws, however, are discovered, not invented by society, and so are beyond human control. The law that the boiling point of water increases as its pressure increases cannot be changed by humans, either individually or collectively. Such laws are a part of the fabric of nature.

But the fact that moral rules, like legal ones, are not objective in the same sense as scientific ones does not mean that there is no objective standard of right or wrong, that one code is as good as another, or even that the "right thing to do" is just what the moral code currently followed in our society teaches is right. Like the rules of a fraternity or corporation, legal and moral rules can serve their purposes either well or poorly, and whether they do is a matter of objective fact. Further, if a moral code doesn't serve its purpose, we have good reason to criticize all or part of it, to ignore it, and to think of a way to change it, just as its serving us well provides a good reason to obey. In important respects morality is not at all subjective.

Take, for example, a rule which prohibits homosexual behavior. Suppose it serves no useful purpose, but only increases the burdens of guilt, shame, and social rejection borne by 10% of our population. If this is so, we have good reason to ignore the rule. On the other hand, if rules against killing and lying help us to accomplish what we want from a moral code, we have good reason to support those rules. Morality is created, and as with other systems of rules which we devise, a particular rule may or may not further the shared human goals and interests which motivated its creation. There is thus a connection between what we ought to do and how well a code serves its purposes. If a rule serves well the general purposes of a moral code, then we have reason to support it, and if we have reason to support it, we also have reason to obey it. But if, on the other hand, a rule is useless, or if it frustrates the purposes of morality, we have

reason neither to support nor to follow it. All of this suggests the following conception of a right action: Any action is right which is approved by an ideal moral code, one which it is rational for us to support. Which code we would want to support would depend, of course, on which one is able to accomplish the purposes of morality.

If we are to judge actions in this way, by reference to what an ideal moral code would require, we must first have a clear notion of just what purposes morality is meant to serve. And here again the comparison between legal and moral rules is instructive. Both systems discourage certain types of behavior—killing, robbing, and beating—while encouraging others—repaying debts, keeping important agreements, and providing for one's children. The purpose which both have in discouraging various behaviors is obvious. Such negative rules help keep people from causing harm. Think, for example, of how we are first taught it is wrong to hit a baby brother or sister. Parents explain the rule by emphasizing that it hurts the infant when we hit him. Promoting the welfare of ourselves, our friends and family, and to a lesser degree all who have the capacity to be harmed is the primary purpose of negative moral rules. It's how we learn them as children and why we support them as adults.

The same can be said of positive rules, rules which encourage various types of behavior. Our own welfare, as well as that of friends, family, and others, depends on general acceptance of rules which encourage keeping promises, fulfilling contracts, and meeting the needs of our children. Just try to imagine a society in which promises or agreements mean nothing, or where family members took no concern for one another. A life without positive or negative rights would be as Thomas Hobbes long ago observed: nasty, brutish, and short.

Moral rules thus serve two purposes. They promote our own welfare by discouraging acts of violence and promoting social conventions like promising and paying debts, and second, they perform the same service for our family, friends, and others. We have reason to support a moral code because we care about our own welfare, and because we care about the well-being of others. For most of us the ideal moral code, the one we would support because it best fulfills these purposes, is the code which is most effective in promoting general welfare.

But can everyone be counted on to share these concerns? Think, for example, of an egoist, who only desires that *he* be happy. Such a person, if he existed, would obviously like a code which maximizes his own welfare. How can we hope to get agreement about which code it is rational to support, if different people expect different things from moral rules?

Before considering these questions, I want to mention two preliminary points. First, the problem with egoism is that it tends to make morality relative. If we are going to decide moral disputes by considering what would be required by the code which it is rational for people to support, then we must reach agreement about what that code is. Otherwise the right action for an altruist, the one which is required by the code which it's rational for him to support, may be the wrong act for the egoist. Yet how can the very same act done in identical circumstances be wrong for one person yet right for another? Maybe morality is relative in that way, but if so the prospects for peaceful resolution of important disputes is lessened, a result not to be hoped for.

My second point is that while we certainly do not want to assume people are perfect altruists, we also do not want to give people less credit than they deserve. There is some evidence, for example, that concern for others in our species is part of our biological heritage. Some geneticists think that many animals, particularly higher ones, take an innate interest in the welfare of other members of their species. Other researchers argue that feelings of benevolence originate naturally, through classical conditioning; we develop negative associations with our own pain behavior (since we are then in pain) and this attitude becomes generalized to the pain behavior of others. If either of these is true, egoism might be far more unusual than is commonly supposed, perhaps rare enough that it can be safely ignored.

There is also a line of reasoning which suggests that disagreement about which moral code to support need not be as deep as is often thought. What sort of code in fact *would* a rational egoist support? He would first think of proposing one which allows him to do anything whatsoever that he desires, while requiring that others ignore their own happiness and do what is in his interests. But here enters a family of considerations which will bring us back to the merits of entitlements versus the greater moral evil rule. Our egoist is contemplating what code to *support,* which means going before the public and trying to win general acceptance of his proposed rules. Caring for nobody else, he might secretly prefer the code I mentioned, yet it would hardly make sense for him to work for its public adoption since others are unlikely to put his welfare above the happiness of themselves and their families. So it looks as if the code an egoist would actually support might not be all that different from the ideal (welfare maximizing) code; he would be wasting his time to advocate rules that serve only his own interests because they have no chance of public acceptance.

The lesson to be learned here is a general one: The moral code it is rational for us to support must be practical; it must actually work. This means, among other things, that it must be able to gain the support of almost everyone.

But the code must be practical in other respects as well. I have emphasized that it is wrong to ignore the possibilities of altruism, but it is also important that a code not assume people are more unselfish than they are. Rules that would work only for angels are not the ones it is rational to support for humans. Second, an ideal code cannot assume we are more objective than we are; we often tend to rationalize when our own interests are at stake, and a rational person will also keep that in mind when choosing a moral code. Finally, it is not rational to support a code which assumes we have perfect knowledge. We are often mistaken about the consequences of what we do, and a workable code must take that into account as well.

I want now to bring these various considerations together in order to decide whether or not to reject entitlements in favor of the greater moral evil rule. I will assume that the egoist is not a serious obstacle to acceptance of a welfare maximizing code, either because egoists are, like angels, merely imaginary, or because a practical egoist would only support a code which can be expected to gain wide support. We still have to ask whether entitlements would be included in a welfare maximizing code. The initial temptation is to substitute the greater moral evil rule for entitlements, requiring people to prevent something bad whenever the cost to them is less significant than the benefit to another. Surely, we might think, total welfare would be increased by a code requiring people to give up their savings if a greater evil can be prevented.

I think, however, that this is wrong, that an ideal code would provide for rights and would encourage rewarding according to desert. My reasons for thinking this stem from the importance of insuring that a moral code really does, in fact, work. Each of the three practical considerations mentioned above now enters the picture. First, it will be quite difficult to get people to accept a code which requires that they give away their savings, extra organs, or anything else merely because they can avoid a greater evil for a stranger. Many people simply wouldn't do it: they aren't that altruistic. If the code attempts to require it anyway, two results would likely follow. First, because many would not live up to the rules, there would be a tendency to create feelings of guilt in those who keep their savings in spite of having been taught it is wrong, as well as conflict between those who meet their obligations and those who do not. And, second, a more realistic code, one which doesn't expect more than can be accomplished, may actually result in more giving. It's a bit like trying to influence how children spend their money. Often they will buy less candy if rules allow them to do so occasionally but they are praised for spending on other things than if its purchase is prohibited. We cannot assume that making a charitable act a requirement will always encourage such behavior. Impractical rules not only create guilt and social conflict, they often tend to encourage the opposite of the desired result. By giving people the right to use their savings for themselves, yet praising those who do not exercise the right but help others instead, we have struck a good balance; the rules are at once practical yet reasonably effective.

Similar practical considerations would also influence our decision to support rules that allow people to keep what they deserve. For most people, working is not their favorite activity. If we are to prosper, however, goods and services must be produced. Incentives are therefore an important motivation, and one such incentive for work is income. Our code encourages work by allowing people to keep a large part of what they earn, indeed that's much the point of entitlements. "I worked hard for it, so I can keep it" is an oft-heard expression. If we eliminate this rule from our code and ask people to follow the greater moral evil rule instead, the result would likely be less work done and so less total production. Given a choice between not working and continuing to work knowing the efforts should go to benefit others, many would choose not to work.

Moral rules should be practical in a third sense, too. They cannot assume people are either more unbiased or more knowledgeable than they are. This fact has many implications for the sorts of rules we would want to include in a welfare maximizing code. For example, we may be tempted to avoid slavish conformity to counterproductive rules by allowing people to break promises whenever they think doing so would increase total welfare. But again we must not ignore human nature, in this case our tendency to give special weight to our own welfare and our inability to be always objective in tracing the effects of our actions. While we would not want to teach that promises must never be broken no matter what the consequences, we also would not want to encourage breaking promises any time a person can convince himself the results of doing so would be better than if he kept his word.

Similar considerations apply to the greater moral evil rule. Imagine a situation where someone feels he can prevent an evil befalling himself by taking what he needs from a large store. The idea that he's preventing something bad from happening (to himself) without sacrificing anything of comparable moral significance (the store won't miss the goods) would justify robbery. Although sometimes a particular act of theft really is welfare maximizing, it does not follow that we should support a *rule* which allows theft whenever the robber is preventing a greater evil. Such a rule, to work, would require more objectivity and more knowledge of long-term consequences than we have. Here again, including rights in our moral code serves a useful role, discouraging the tendency to rationalize our behavior by underestimating the harm we may cause to others or exaggerating the benefits that may accrue to ourselves.

The first sections of this paper attempted to show that our moral code is a bit schizophrenic. It seems to pull us in opposite directions, sometimes toward helping people who are in need, other times toward the view that rights and desert justify keeping things we have even if greater evil could be avoided were we to give away our extra eye or our savings account. This apparent inconsistency led us to a further question: Is the emphasis on entitlements really defensible, or should we try to resolve the tension in our own code by adopting the greater moral evil rule and ignoring entitlements? In this section I considered the idea that we might choose between entitlements and the greater moral evil rule by paying attention to the general nature of a moral code; and in particular to the sort of code we might want to support. I argued that all of us, including egoists, have reason to support a code which promotes the welfare of everyone who lives under it. That idea, of an ideal moral code which it is rational for everyone to support, provides a criterion for deciding which rules are sound and which ones we should support.

My conclusion is a conservative one: Concern that our moral code encourages production and not fail because it unrealistically assumes people are more altruistic or objective than they are means that our rules giving people rights to their possessions and encouraging distribution according to desert should be part of an ideal moral code. And since this is so, it is not always wrong to invoke rights or claim that money is deserved as justification for not giving aid, even when something worse could be prevented by offering help. The welfare maximizing moral code would not require us to maximize welfare in each individual case.

I have not yet discussed just how much weight should be given to entitlements, only that they are important and should not be ignored as Singer and Watson suggest. Certainly an ideal moral code would not allow people to overlook those in desperate need by making entitlements absolute, any more than it would ignore entitlements. But where would it draw the line?

It's hard to know, of course, but the following seems to me to be a sensible stab at an answer. Concerns about discouraging production and the general adherence to the code argue strongly against expecting too much; yet on the other hand, to allow extreme wealth in the face of grinding poverty would seem to put too much weight on entitlements. It seems to me, then, that a reasonable code would require people to help when there is no substantial cost to themselves, that is, when what they are sacrificing would not mean *significant* reduction in their own or their families' level of happiness. Since most people's savings accounts and nearly everybody's second kidney are not insignificant, entitlements would in those cases outweigh another's need. But if what is at stake is trivial, as dirtying one's clothes would normally be, then an ideal moral code would not allow rights to override the greater evil that can be prevented. Despite our code's unclear and sometimes schizophrenic posture, it seems to me that these judgments are not that different from our current moral attitudes. We tend to blame people who waste money on trivia when they could help others in need, yet not to expect people to make large sacrifices to distant strangers. An ideal moral code thus might not be a great deal different from our own.

Kantian Deliberations on Famine Problems

~

ONORA O'NEILL

Onora O'Neill is principal of Newnham College, Cambridge University.

KANTIAN DELIBERATIONS ON FAMINE PROBLEMS

The theory I have just sketched may seem to have little to say about famine problems. For it is a theory that forbids us to use others as mere means but does not require us to direct our benevolence first to those who suffer most. A conscientious Kantian, it seems, has only to avoid being unjust to those who suffer famine and can then be beneficent to those nearer home. He or she would not be obliged to help the starving, even if no others were equally distressed.

Kant's moral theory does make less massive demands on moral agents than utilitarian moral theory. On the other hand, it is somewhat clearer just what the more stringent demands are, and they are not negligible. We have here a contrast between a theory that makes massive but often indeterminate demands and a theory that makes fewer but less unambiguous demands and leaves other questions, in particular the allocation of beneficence, unresolved. We have also a contrast between a theory whose scope is comprehensive and one that is applicable only to persons acting intentionally and to those institutions that adopt policies, and so maxims. Kantian ethics is silent about the moral status of unintentional action; utilitarians seek to assess all consequences regardless of the intentions that led to them.

KANTIAN DUTIES OF JUSTICE IN TIMES OF FAMINE

In famine situations, Kantian moral theory requires unambiguously that we do no injustice. We should not act on any maxim that uses another as mere means, so we should neither deceive nor coerce others. Such a requirement can become quite exacting when the means of life are scarce, when persons can more easily be coerced, and when the advantage of gaining more than what is justly due to one is great. I shall give a list of acts that on Kantian principles it would be unjust to do, but that one might be strongly tempted to do in famine conditions.

I will begin with a list of acts that one might be tempted to do as a member of a famine-stricken population. First, where there is a rationing scheme, one ought not to cheat and seek to get more than one's share—any scheme of cheating will use someone as mere means. Nor may one take advantage of others' desperation to profiteer or divert goods onto the black market or to accumulate a fortune out of others' misfortunes. Transactions that are outwardly sales and purchases can be coercive when one party is desperate. All the forms of corruption that deceive or put pressure on others are also wrong: hoarding unallocated food, diverting relief supplies for private use, corruptly using one's influence to others' disadvan-

Reprinted from *Matters of Life and Death,* ed. Tom Regan (Philadelphia: Temple University Press, 1980).

tage. Such requirements are far from trivial and frequently violated in hard times. In severe famines, refraining from coercing and deceiving may risk one's own life and require the greatest courage.

Second, justice requires that in famine situations one still try to fulfill one's duties to particular others. For example, even in times of famine, a person has duties to try to provide for dependents. These duties may, tragically, be unfulfillable. If they are, Kantian ethical theory would not judge wrong the acts of a person who had done her or his best. There have no doubt been times in human history where there was nothing to be done except abandon the weak and old or to leave children to fend for themselves as best they might. But providing the supporter of dependents acts on maxims of attempting to meet their claims, he or she uses no others as mere means to his or her own survival and is not unjust. A conscientious attempt to meet the particular obligations one has undertaken may also require of one many further maxims of self-restraint and of endeavor—for example, it may require a conscientious attempt to avoid having (further) children; it may require contributing one's time and effort to programs of economic development. Where there is no other means to fulfill particular obligations, Kantian principles may require a generation of sacrifice. They will not, however, require one to seek to maximize the happiness of later generations but only to establish the modest security and prosperity needed for meeting present obligations.

The obligations of those who live with or near famine are undoubtedly stringent and exacting; for those who live further off it is rather harder to see what a Kantian moral theory demands. Might it not, for example, be permissible to do nothing at all about those suffering famine? Might one not ensure that one does nothing unjust to the victims of famine by adopting no maxims whatsoever that mention them? To do so would, at the least, require one to refrain from certain deceptive and coercive practices frequently employed during the European exploration and economic penetration of the now underdeveloped world and still not unknown. For example, it would be unjust to "purchase" valuable lands and resources from persons who don't understand commercial transactions or exclusive property rights or mineral rights, so do not understand that their acceptance of trinkets destroys their traditional economic pattern and way of life. The old adage "trade follows the flag" reminds us to how great an extent the economic penetration of the less-developed countries involved elements of coercion and deception, so was on Kantian principles unjust (regardless of whether or not the net effect has benefited the citizens of those countries).

Few persons in the developed world today find themselves faced with the possibility of adopting on a grand scale maxims of deceiving or coercing persons living in poverty. But at least some people find that their jobs require them to make decisions about investment and aid policies that enormously affect the lives of those nearest to famine. What does a commitment to Kantian moral theory demand of such persons?

It has become common in writings in ethics and social policy to distinguish between one's *personal responsibilities* and one's *role responsibilities.* So a person may say, "As an individual I sympathize, but in my official capacity I can do nothing"; or we may excuse persons' acts of coercion because they are acting in some particular capacity—e.g., as a soldier or a jailer. On the other hand, this distinction isn't made or accepted by everyone. At the Nuremberg trials of war criminals, the defense "I was only doing my job" was disallowed, at least for those whose command position meant that they had some discretion in what they did. Kantians generally would play down any distinction between a person's own responsibilities and his or her role responsibilities. They would not deny that in any capacity one is accountable for certain things for which as a private person one is not accountable. For example, the treasurer of an organization is accountable to the board and has to present periodic reports and to keep specified records. But if she fails to do one of these things for which she is held accountable she will be held responsible for that failure—it will be imputable to her as an individual. When we take on positions, we *add* to our responsibilities those that the job requires; but we do not lose those that are already required of us. Our social role or job gives us, on Kant's view, no license to use others as mere means; even business executives and aid officials and social revolutionaries will act unjustly, so wrongly, if they deceive or coerce—however benevolent their motives.

If persons are responsible for all their acts, it follows that it would be unjust for aid officials to coerce persons into accepting sterilization, wrong for them to use coercive power to achieve political advantages (such as military bases) or commercial advantages (such as trade agreements that will harm the other country). It would be wrong for the executives of large corporations to extort too high a price for continued operation employment and normal trading. Where a less-developed country is pushed to exempt a multinational corporation from tax laws, or to construct out of its meager tax revenues the infrastructure of roads, harbors, or airports (not to mention executive mansions) that the corporation—but perhaps not the country—needs, then one suspects that some coercion has been involved.

The problem with such judgments—and it is an immense problem—is that it is hard to identify coercion and deception in complicated institutional settings. It is not hard to understand what is coercive about one person threatening another with serious injury if he won't comply with the first person's suggestion. But it is not at all easy to tell where the outward forms of political and commercial negotiation—which often involve an element of threat—have become coercive. I can't here explore this fascinating question. But I think it is at least fairly clear that the preservation of the outward forms of negotiation, bargaining, and voluntary consent do *not* demonstrate that there is no coercion, especially when one party is vastly more powerful or the other in dire need. Just as our judiciary has a long tradition of voiding contracts and agreements on grounds of duress or incompetence of one of the parties, so one can imagine a tribunal of an analogous sort rejecting at least some treaties and agreements as coercive, despite the fact that they were negotiated between "sovereign" powers or their representatives. In particular, where such agreements were negotiated with some of the cruder deceptions and coercion of the early days of European economic expansion or the subtler coercions and deceptions of contemporary superpowers, it seems doubtful that the justice of the agreement could be sustained.

Justice, of course, is not everything, even for Kantians. But its demands are ones that they can reasonably strive to fulfill. They may have some uncertain moments—for example, does advocating cheap raw materials mean advocating an international trade system in which the less developed will continue to suffer the pressures of the developed world—or is it a benevolent policy that will maximize world trade and benefit all parties, while doing no one an injustice? But for Kantians, the important moral choices are above all those in which one acts directly, not those in which one decides which patterns of actions to encourage in others or in those institutions that one can influence. And such moral decisions include decisions about the benevolent acts that one will or will not do.

KANTIAN DUTIES OF BENEFICENCE IN TIMES OF FAMINE

The grounds of duties of beneficence are that such acts not merely don't use others as mere means but are acts that develop or promote others' ends and that, in particular, foster others' capacities to pursue ends, to be autonomous beings.

Clearly there are many opportunities for beneficence. But one area in which the *primary* task of developing others' capacity to pursue their own ends is particularly needed is in the parts of the world where extreme poverty and hunger leave people unable to pursue *any* of their other ends. Beneficence directed at putting people in a position to pursue whatever ends they may have has, for Kant, a stronger claim on us than beneficence directed at sharing ends with those who are already in a position to pursue varieties of ends. It would be nice if I bought a tennis racquet to play with my friend who is tennis mad and never has enough partners; but it is more important to make people able to plan their own lives to a minimal extent. It is nice to walk a second mile with someone who requests one's company; better to share a cloak with someone who may otherwise be too cold to make any journey. Though these suggestions are not a detailed set of instructions for the allocation of beneficence by Kantians, they show that relief of famine must stand very high among duties of beneficence.

Why We Have No Obligations to Animals

⁓

IMMANUEL KANT

Immanuel Kant (1724–1804) played a central role in the development of modern philosophy.

Baumgarten speaks of duties towards beings which are beneath us and beings which are above us. But so far as animals are concerned, we have no direct duties. Animals are not self-conscious and are there merely as a means to an end. That end is man. We can ask, "Why do animals exist?" But to ask, "Why does man exist?" is a meaningless question. Our duties towards animals are merely indirect duties towards humanity. Animal nature has analogies to human nature, and by doing our duties to animals in respect of manifestations which correspond to manifestations of human nature, we indirectly do our duty towards humanity. Thus, if a dog has served his master long and faithfully, his service, on the analogy of human service, deserves reward, and when the dog has grown too old to serve, his master ought to keep him until he dies. Such action helps to support us in our duties towards human beings, where they are bounden duties. If then any acts of animals are analogous to human acts and spring from the same principles, we have duties towards the animals because thus we cultivate the corresponding duties towards human beings. If a man shoots his dog because the animal is no longer capable of service, he does not fail in his duty to the dog, for the dog cannot judge, but his act is inhuman and damages in himself that humanity which it is his duty to show towards mankind. If he is not to stifle his human feelings, he must practise kindness towards animals, for he who is cruel to animals becomes hard also in his dealings with men. We can judge the heart of a man by his treatment of animals. Hogarth depicts this in his engravings. He shows how cruelty grows and develops. He shows the child's cruelty to animals, pinching the tail of a dog or a cat; he then depicts the grown man in his cart running over a child; and lastly, the culmination of cruelty in murder. He thus brings home to us in a terrible fashion the rewards of cruelty, and this should be an impressive lesson to children. The more we come in contact with animals and observe their behavior, the more we love them, for we see how great is their care for their young. It is then difficult for us to be cruel in thought even to a wolf. Leibnitz used a tiny worm for purposes of observation, and then carefully replaced it with its leaf on the tree so that it should not come to harm through any act of his. He would have been sorry—a natural feeling for a humane man—to destroy such a creature for no reason. Tender feelings towards dumb animals develop humane feelings toward mankind. In England butchers and doctors do not sit on a jury because they are accustomed to the sight of death and hardened. Vivisectionists, who use living animals for their experiments, certainly act cruelly, although their aim is praiseworthy, and they can justify their cruelty, since animals must be regarded as man's instruments; but any such cruelty for sport cannot be justified. A master who turns out his ass or his dog because the animal can no longer earn its keep manifests a small mind. The Greeks' ideas in this respect were high-minded, as can be seen from the fable of the ass and the bell of ingratitude. Our duties towards animals, then, are indirect duties towards mankind.

Reprinted from Immanuel Kant, *Lectures on Ethics,* translated by Louis Infield (London: Methuen, 1930).

Constraints and Animals

~

ROBERT NOZICK

Robert Nozick (1938–2002) was Pellegrino University Professor at Harvard University. His book, *Anarchy, State, and Utopia,* from which this selection is taken, won the 1975 National Book Award.

Animals count for something. Some higher animals, at least, ought to be given some weight in people's deliberations about what to do. It is difficult to *prove* this. (It is also difficult to prove that people count for something!) We first shall adduce particular examples, and then arguments. If you felt like snapping your fingers, perhaps to the beat of some music, and you knew that by some strange causal connection your snapping your fingers would cause 10,000 contented, unowned cows to die after great pain and suffering, or even painlessly and instantaneously, would it be perfectly all right to snap your fingers? Is there some reason why it would be morally wrong to do so?

Some say people should not do so because such acts brutalize them and make them more likely to take the lives of *persons,* solely for pleasure. These acts that are morally unobjectionable in themselves, they say, have an undesirable moral spillover. (Things then would be different if there were no possibility of such spillover—for example, for the person who knows himself to be the last person on earth.) But why *should* there be such a spillover? If it is, in itself, perfectly all right to do anything at all to animals for any reason whatsoever, then provided a person realizes the clear line between animals and persons and keeps it in mind as he acts, why should killing animals tend to brutalize him and make him more likely to harm or kill persons? Do butchers commit more murders? (Than other persons who have knives around?) If I enjoy hitting a baseball

squarely with a bat, does this significantly increase the danger of my doing the same to someone's head? Am I not capable of understanding that people differ from baseballs, and doesn't this understanding stop the spillover? Why should things be different in the case of animals? To be sure, it is an empirical question whether spillover does take place or not; but there *is* a puzzle as to why it should, at least among readers of this essay, sophisticated people who are capable of drawing distinctions and differentially acting upon them.

If some animals count for something, which animals count, how much do they count, and how can this be determined? Suppose (as I believe the evidence supports) that *eating* animals is not necessary for *health* and is not less expensive than alternate equally healthy diets available to people in the United States. The gain, then from the eating of animals is pleasures of the palate, gustatory delights, varied tastes. I would not claim that these are not truly the pleasant, delightful, and interesting. The question is: do they, or rather does the marginal addition in them gained by eating animals rather than only nonanimals, *outweigh* the moral weight to be given to animals' lives and pain? Given that animals are to count for *something,* is the *extra* gain obtained by eating them rather than nonanimal products greater than the moral cost? How might these questions be decided?

We might try looking at comparable cases, extending whatever judgments we make on those

Reprinted from Robert Nozick, *Anarchy, State, and Utopia* (New York: Basic Books, 1974), by permission of the publisher.

cases to the one before us. For example, we might look at the case of hunting, where I assume that it's not all right to hunt and kill animals merely for the fun of it. Is hunting a special case, because its *object* and what provides the fun is the chasing and maiming and death of animals? Suppose then that I enjoy swinging a baseball bat. It happens that in front of the only place to swing it stands a cow. Swinging the bat unfortunately would involve smashing the cow's head. But I wouldn't get fun from doing *that;* the pleasure comes from exercising my muscles, swinging well, and so on. It's unfortunate that as a side effect (not a means) of my doing this, the animal's skull gets smashed. To be sure, I could forego swinging the bat, and instead bend down and touch my toes or do some other exercise. But this wouldn't be as enjoyable as swinging the bat; I won't get as much fun, pleasure, or delight out of it. So the question is: would it be all right for me to swing the bat in order to get the *extra* pleasure of swinging it as compared to the best available alternative activity that does not involve harming the animal? Suppose that it is not merely a question of foregoing today's special pleasures of bat swinging; suppose that each day the

same situation arises with a different animal. Is there some principle that would allow killing and eating animals for the additional pleasure this brings, yet would not allow swinging the bat for the extra pleasure it brings? What could that principle be like? (Is this a better parallel to eating meat? The animal is killed to get a bone out of which to make the best sort of bat to use; bats made out of other material don't give quite the same pleasure. Is it all right to kill the animal to obtain the *extra* pleasure that using a bat made out of its bone would bring? Would it be morally more permissible if you could hire someone to do the killing for you?)

Such examples and questions might help someone to see what sort of line *he* wishes to draw, what sort of position he wishes to take. They face, however, the usual limitations of consistency arguments; they do not say, once a conflict is shown, which view to change. After failing to devise a principle to distinguish swinging the bat from killing and eating an animal, you might decide that it's really all right, after all, to swing the bat. Furthermore, such appeal to similar cases does not greatly help us to assign precise moral weight to different sorts of animals.

The Moral Argument for Vegetarianism

JAMES RACHELS

James Rachels is University Professor of Philosophy at the University of Alabama at Birmingham.

The idea that it is morally wrong to eat meat may seem faintly ridiculous. After all, eating meat is a normal, well-established part of our lives; people have always eaten meat; and many find it difficult even to conceive of what an alternative diet would be like. So it is not

easy to take seriously the possibility that it might be wrong. Moreover, vegetarianism is commonly associated with Eastern religions whose tenets we do not accept and with extravagant, unfounded claims about health. A quick perusal of vegetarian literature might

From *Can Ethics Provide Answers?* (Lanham, MD: Rowman & Littlefield, 1997), by permission of the author.

confirm the impression that it is all a crackpot business; tracts have titles like "Victory through Vegetables" and promise that if we will only keep to a meatless diet, we will have perfect health and be filled with wisdom. Of course we can ignore this kind of nonsense. However, there are other arguments for vegetarianism that must be taken seriously. The most powerful argument appeals to the principle that it is wrong to cause unnecessary suffering.

The wrongness of cruelty to animals is often explained in terms of its effects on human beings. The idea seems to be that although the animals themselves are not morally important, cruelty has bad consequences for humans, and so it is wrong for that reason. In legal writing, cruelty to animals has been included among the "victimless crimes," and the problem of justifying legal prohibitions has been viewed as comparable to justifying the prohibition of other behavior, such as prostitution or the distribution of pornography, where no one is hurt. In 1963 the distinguished legal scholar Louis Schwartz wrote that, in prohibiting the torturing of animals, "It is not the mistreated dog who is the ultimate object of concern. . . . Our concern is for the feelings of other human beings, a large proportion of whom, although accustomed to the slaughter of animals for food, readily identify themselves with a tortured dog or horse and respond with great sensitivity to its sufferings."[1]

Philosophers have also adopted this attitude. Kant, for example, held that we have no direct duties to nonhuman animals. "The Categorical Imperative," the ultimate principle of morality, applies only to our dealings with people: "The practical imperative, therefore, is the following: Act so that you treat humanity, whether in your own person or in that of another, always as an end and never as a means only."[2] And of other animals, Kant says: "But so far as animals are concerned, we have no direct duties. Animals are not self-conscious, and are there merely as means to an end. That end is man."[3] He adds that we should not be cruel to animals only because "he who is cruel to animals becomes hard also in his dealings with men."[4]

Surely, this is unacceptable. Cruelty to animals ought to be opposed, not only because of the ancillary effects on humans, but also because of the direct effects on the animals themselves. Animals that are tortured suffer, just as tortured humans suffer, and that is the primary reason it is wrong. We object to torturing humans on a number of grounds, but the main one is that the victims suffer so. Insofar as nonhuman animals also suffer, we have the same reason to oppose torturing them, and it is indefensible to take the one suffering but not the other as grounds for objection.

Although cruelty to animals is wrong, it does not follow that we are never justified in inflicting pain on an animal. Sometimes we are justified in doing this, just as we are sometimes justified in inflicting pain on humans. It does follow, however, that there must be a good reason for causing the suffering, and if the suffering is great, the justifying reason must be correspondingly powerful. As an example, consider the treatment of the civet cat, a highly intelligent and sociable animal. Civet cats are trapped and placed in small cages inside darkened sheds, where fires keep the temperature up to 110 degrees Fahrenheit.[5] They are confined in this way until they die. What justifies this extraordinary mistreatment? These animals have the misfortune to produce a substance that is useful in the manufacture of perfume. Musk, which is scraped from their genitals once a day for as long as they can survive, makes the scent of perfume last a bit longer after each application. (The heat increases their "production" of musk.) Here Kant's rule—"Animals are merely means to an end; that end is man"—is applied with a vengeance. To promote one of the most trivial interests we have, animals are tormented for their whole lives.

It is usually easy to persuade people that this use of animals is not justified and that we have a moral duty not to support such cruelties by consuming their products. The argument is simple: Causing suffering is not justified unless there is a good reason; the production of perfume made with musk causes suffering; our enjoyment of this product is not a good enough reason to justify causing that suffering; therefore, the use of animals in this way is wrong. Once people learn the facts about musk production, they come to regard using such products as morally objectionable. They are surprised to discover, however, that an exactly analogous argument can be given in connection with the use of animals as food. Animals that are raised and slaughtered for food also suffer, and our enjoyment of the way they taste is not a sufficient justification for mistreating them.

Most people radically underestimate the amount of suffering that is caused to animals who are raised and slaughtered for food.[6] They believe, in a vague way, that slaughterhouses are cruel and perhaps that methods of slaughter ought to be made more humane. But after all, the visit to the slaughterhouse is a relatively brief episode in the animal's life; and beyond that, people imagine that the animals are treated well enough. Nothing could be further from the truth. Today the production of meat is big business, and the helpless animals are treated more as machines in a factory than as living creatures.

Veal calves, for example, spend their lives in pens too small to allow them to turn around or even to lie down comfortably—exercise toughens the muscles, which reduces the quality of the meat; and besides, allowing the animals adequate living space would be prohibitively expensive. In these pens the calves cannot perform such basic actions as grooming themselves, which they naturally desire to do, because there is not room for them to twist their heads around. It is clear that the calves miss their mothers, and like human infants they want something to suck; they can be seen trying vainly to suck the sides of their stalls. In order to keep their meat pale and tasty, they are fed a liquid diet deficient in iron and roughage. Naturally, they develop cravings for these things, because they need them. The calf's craving for iron is so strong that if it is allowed to turn around, it will lick at its own urine, although calves normally find this repugnant. The tiny stall, which prevents the animal from turning, solves this problem. The craving for roughage is especially strong since without it the animal cannot form a cud to chew. It cannot be given any straw for bedding, since the animal would be driven to eat it and that would spoil the meat. For these animals the slaughterhouse is not an unpleasant end to an otherwise contented life. As terrifying as the process of slaughter is, for them it may actually be a merciful release.

Similar stories can be told about the treatment of other animals on which we dine. In order to produce animals by the millions, it is necessary to keep them crowded together in small spaces. Chickens are commonly kept four or five to a space smaller than a newspaper page. Unable to walk around or even stretch their wings—much less build a nest—the birds become vicious and attack one another. The problem is exacerbated because the birds are so crowded that because they are unable to move, their feet sometimes grow around the wire floors of the cages, anchoring them to the spot. An anchored bird cannot escape attack no matter how desperate it becomes. Mutilation of the animals is an efficient solution. To minimize the damage they can do to one another, poultry farmers cut off their beaks. The mutilation is painful but probably not as painful as other sorts of mutilations that are routinely practiced. Cows are castrated, not to prevent the unnatural "vices" to which overcrowded chickens are prone, but because castrated cows put on more weight and there is less danger of meat being tainted by male hormones.

> In Britain an anesthetic must be used, unless the animal is very young, but in America anesthetics are not in general use. The procedure is to pin the animal down, take a knife and slit the scrotum, exposing the testicles. You then grab each testicle in turn and pull on it, breaking the cord that attaches it; on older animals it may be necessary to cut the cord.[7]

It must be emphasized that such treatment is not out of the ordinary. It is typical of the way that animals raised for food are treated, now that meat production is big business. As Peter Singer puts it, these are the sorts of things that happened to your dinner when it was still an animal.

What accounts for such cruelties? As for the meat producers, there is no reason to think they are unusually cruel people. They simply accept the common attitude expressed by Kant: "Animals are merely means to an end; that end is man." The cruel practices are adopted not because they are cruel but because they are efficient, given that one's only concern is to produce meat (and eggs) for humans as cheaply as possible. But clearly this use of animals is immoral if anything is. Since we can nourish ourselves very well without eating them, our only reason for doing all this to the animals is our enjoyment of the way they taste. And this will not even come close to justifying the cruelty.

Does this mean that we should stop eating meat? It is tempting to say: "What is objectionable is not *eating* the animals, but only making them suffer. Perhaps we ought to protest the way they are treated and even work for better treatment of them. But it doesn't follow that we must stop eating them." This sounds plausible until we realize that it would be impossible to treat the animals decently and still produce meat in sufficient quantities to make it a normal part of our diets. Cruel methods are used in the meat-production industry because such methods are economical; they enable the producers to market a product that people can afford. Humanely produced chicken, beef, and pork would be so expensive that only the very rich could afford them. (Some of the cruelties might be eliminated without too much expense—the cows could be given an anesthetic before castration, for example, even though this alone would mean a slight increase in the cost of beef. But others, such as overcrowding, could not be eliminated without really prohibitive cost.) So to work for better treatment for the animals would be to work for a situation in which most of us would have to adopt a vegetarian diet.

Still, there remains the interesting theoretical question: If meat could be produced humanely, without mistreating the animals before killing them painlessly, would there be anything wrong with it? The question has only theoretical interest, because the actual choice we face in the supermarket is whether to buy the remains of animals that were not treated humanely. Still, the question has some interest, and we may take a quick look at it.

First, it is a vexing issue whether animals have a "right to life" that is violated when we kill them for trivial purposes; but we should not simply assume until it is proved otherwise that they don't have such a right. We assume that humans have a right to life—it would be wrong to murder a normal, healthy human even if it were done painlessly—and it is hard to think of any plausible rationale for granting this right to humans that does not also apply to other animals. Other animals live in communities, as do humans; they communicate with one another and have ongoing social relationships; killing them disrupts lives that are perhaps not as complex emotionally and intellectually as our own but that are nevertheless quite com-

plicated. They suffer and are capable of happiness as well as fear and distress, as we are. So what could be the rational basis for saying that we have a right to life but that they don't? Or even more pointedly, what could be the rational basis for saying that a severely retarded human, who is inferior in every important respect to an intelligent animal, has a right to life but that the animal doesn't? Philosophers often treat such questions as "puzzles," assuming that there must be answers even if we are not clever enough to find them. But perhaps there are no acceptable answers to this question. If it seems, intuitively, that there must be some difference between us and the other animals that confers on us, but not on them, a right to life, perhaps this intuition is mistaken. At the very least, the difficulty of answering such questions should make us hesitant about asserting that it is all right to kill animals so long as we don't make them suffer, unless we are also willing to take seriously the possibility that it is all right to kill people so long as we don't make them suffer.

But let me make a more definite suggestion about this. If we want to know whether animals have a right to life, we should start by asking why humans have such a right. What is it about humans that gives them a right to life? If humans have a right to life, but plants, say, do not, then there must be some difference between them that explains why one has a right the other lacks. There must be characteristics possessed by humans but not by plants that qualify the humans for this right. Therefore, one way to approach our question is by trying to identify those characteristics. Then we can ask whether any nonhuman animals have those characteristics.

With respect to the characteristics that qualify one for a right to life, my suggestion is that an individual has a right to life if that individual has a life. Like many philosophical ideas, this one is more complicated than it first appears.

Having a life is different from merely being alive. The latter is a biological notion—to be alive is just to be a functioning biological organism. It is the opposite of being dead. But "a life," in the sense that concerns us here, is a notion of biography rather than of biology. "The life of Babe Ruth" will be concerned not with the biological facts of Ruth's existence—he had a heart and liver and blood and kidneys—but with facts about his history, beliefs, actions, and relationships:

> He was born George Herman Ruth in Baltimore in 1895, the troubled child of a poor family. He was sent to live at St. Mary's School when he was eight; he learned baseball there and started pitching for the Red Sox at nineteen. Babe was an outstanding pitcher for six seasons before switching to the Yankee outfield and going on to become the most idolized slugger in the history of the game. He hit 60 home runs in a single season and 714 overall. He was the beer-guzzling friend of Lou Gehrig and was married to Claire. He died of cancer at age fifty-three.

These are some of the facts of his life. They are not biological facts.

Death is an evil when it puts an end not simply to being alive but to a life. Some humans, tragically, do not have lives and never will. An infant with Tay-Sachs disease will never develop beyond about six months of age, there may be some regression at that point, and it will die. Suppose such an infant contracts pneumonia; the decision might be made not to treat the pneumonia and to allow the baby to die. The decision seems justified because in the absence of any possibility of a life in the biographical sense, life in the biological sense has little value. The same sort of consideration explains why it seems so pointless to maintain persons in irreversible coma. The families of such patients are quick to realize that merely being alive is unimportant. The mother of a man who died after six years in a coma told a newspaper reporter, "My son died at age 34 after having lived for 28 years."[8] It was a melodramatic remark, and on the surface a paradoxical one—how can one die at 34 and have lived only 28 years?—yet what she meant is clear enough. The man's life was over when he entered the coma, even though he was alive for 6 years longer. The temporal boundaries of one's being alive need not be the same as the temporal boundaries of one's life.

Therefore, it is unwise to insist that any animal, human or nonhuman, has a right to life simply because it is a living being. The doctrine of the sanctity of life, interpreted as applying merely to biological life, has little to recommend it. My suggestion about the right to life is that an individual has a right to life if that individual has a life in the biographical sense. By this criterion, at least some nonhuman animals would have such a right. Monkeys, to take the most obvious example, have lives that are quite complex. They are remarkably intelligent, they have families and live together in social groups, and they apparently have forward-looking and backward-looking attitudes. Their lives do not appear to be as emotionally or intellectually complex as the lives of humans; but the more we learn about them, the more impressed we are with the similarities between them and us.

Of course we do not know a great deal about the lives of the members of most other species. To make intelligent judgments about them, we need the sort of information that could be gained by observing animals in their natural homes rather than in the laboratory—although laboratory-acquired information can be helpful. When baboons, dogs, and wolves have been studied in the wild, it has been found that the lives of individual animals, carried out within pack societies, are surprisingly diverse. But we are only beginning to appreciate the richness of the animal kingdom.

In our present state of semi-ignorance about other species, the situation seems to be this. When we consider the mammals with which we are most familiar, it is reasonable to believe that they do have lives in the biographical sense. They have emotions and cares and social systems and the rest, although perhaps not in just the way that humans do. Then the further down the old phylogenetic scale we go, the less confidence we have that there is anything resembling a life. When we come to bugs, or shrimp, the animals pretty clearly lack the mental capacities necessary for a life, although they certainly are alive. Most of us already have an intuitive sense of the importance of these gradations—we think that killing a human is worse than killing a monkey, but we also think that killing a monkey is a more morally serious matter than swatting a fly. And when we come to plants, which are alive but to which the notion of a biographical life is not applicable at all, our moral qualms about killing vanish altogether. If my suggestion about the right to life is correct, these feelings have a rational basis: insofar as we have reason to view other creatures as having lives, as we do, we have reason to view them as having a right to life, if we do.

Finally, it is important to see the slaughter of animals for food as part of a larger pattern that characterizes our whole relationship with the nonhuman world. Animals are taken from their natural homes to be made objects of our entertainment in zoos, circuses, and rodeos. They are used in laboratories, not only for experiments that are themselves morally questionable, but also in testing everything from shampoo to chemical weapons. They are killed so that their heads can be used as wall decorations or their skins as ornamental clothing or rugs. Indeed, simply killing them for the fun of it is thought to be sport. This pattern of cruel exploitation flows naturally from the Kantian attitude that animals are nothing more than things to be used for our purposes. It is this whole attitude that must be opposed, and not merely its manifestation in our willingness to hurt the animals we eat. Once one rejects this attitude and no longer regards the animals as disposable at one's whim, one ceases to think it all right to kill them, even painlessly, just for a snack.

But for those of us who do not live on old-fashioned family farms, the question of whether it would be permissible to eat humanely treated, painlessly slaughtered animals is merely theoretical. The meat available to us at the supermarket was not produced by humane methods. To provide this meat, animals were abused in ways similar to the ones we have described; and millions of other animals are being treated in these ways now, with their flesh to appear soon in the markets. The practical issue is, should we support such practices by purchasing and consuming their products?

It is discouraging to realize that no animals will actually be helped simply by one person ceasing to eat meat. One consumer's behavior, by itself, cannot have a noticeable impact on an industry as vast as the meat business. However, it is important to see one's behavior in a larger context. There are already millions of vegetarians, and because they don't eat meat, there *is* less cruelty than there otherwise would be. The question is whether one ought to side with that group or with the people whose practices cause the suffering. Compare the position of someone thinking about whether to buy slaves in 1820. He might reason as follows: "The whole practice of slavery is immoral, but I cannot help any of the poor slaves by keeping clear of it. If I don't buy these slaves, someone else will. One person's decision can't by itself have any impact on such a vast business. So I may as well own slaves like everyone else." The first thing we notice is that this fellow was too pessimistic about the possibilities of a successful movement; but beyond that, there is something else wrong with his reasoning. If one really thinks that a social practice is immoral, that is sufficient grounds for refusing to participate in it. In 1848 Henry David Thoreau remarked that even if someone did not want to devote himself to the abolition movement and actively oppose slavery, "it is his duty, at least, to wash his hands of it, and, if he gives it no thought longer, not to give it practically his support."[9] In the case of slavery, this seems clear. If it seems less clear in the case of the cruel exploitation of nonhuman animals, perhaps it is because the Kantian attitude has so tenacious a hold on us.

NOTES

1. Louis B. Schwartz, "Morals Offenses and the Model Penal Code," in *Philosophy of Law,* ed. Joel Feinberg and Hyman Gross (Encino, Calif.: Dickenson, 1975), 156. First published in *Columbia Law Review* 63 (1963):669–84.

2. Immanuel Kant, *Foundations of the Metaphysics of Morals,* trans. Lewis White Beck (Indianapolis: Bobbs-Merrill, 1959), 47.

3. Immanuel Kant, *Lectures on Ethics,* trans. Louis Infield (New York: Harper, 1963), 239.

4. Kant, *Lectures on Ethics,* 240.

5. Muriel the Lady Dowding, "Furs and Cosmetics: Too High a Price?" in *Animals, Men, and Morals,* ed. Stanley Godlovitch, Roslind Godlovitch, and John Harris (New York: Taplinger, 1972), 36.

6. The best account is chap. 3 of Peter Singer's *Animal Liberation* (New York: New York Review Books, 1975). I have drawn on Singer's work for the factual material in the following two paragraphs.

7. Singer, *Animal Liberation,* 152.

8. *Miami Herald,* 26 August 1972, sec. A, p. 3.

9. Henry David Thoreau, *Walden and Civil Disobedience,* ed. Owen Thomas (New York: W. W. Norton & Co., 1966), 229–30. First published in 1848.

Do Animals Have Rights?

~

TIBOR R. MACHAN

Tibor R. Machan is professor emeritus of philosophy at Auburn University. His books include *The Virtue of Liberty* and *Individuals and Their Rights*.

Although the idea that animals have rights goes back to the 18th century, at least, it has only recently become something of a cause celebre among numerous serious and well-placed intellectuals, including moral and political philosophers. Although Jeremy Bentham seems to have suggested legislation requiring humane treatment of animals, he didn't defend animal rights, per se—not surprisingly, since Bentham himself had not been impressed with the more basic (Lockean) doctrine of natural rights—calling them "nonsense upon stilts." John Locke's idea of individual rights has had enormous influence and even where it is not respected, it is ultimately invoked as some kind of model for what it would take for something to have rights.

In recent years the doctrine of animals rights has found champions in important circles where the general doctrine of rights is itself well respected. For example, Professor Tom Regan, in his important book *The Case for Animal Rights* (UC Press, 1983), finds the idea of natural rights intellectually congenial but then extends this idea to cover animals near humans on the evolutionary scale. The tradition from within which Regan works is clearly Lockean, only he does not agree that human nature is distinctive enough, in relevant respects, to restrict the scope of natural rights to human beings alone.

Following a different tradition, namely, utilitarianism, the idea of animal liberation has emerged. And this idea comes to roughly the same thing, practically speaking. Only the argument is different because for utilitarians what is important is not that someone or something must have a specific sphere of dominion but that they be well off in their lives. So long as the bulk of the relevant creatures enjoy a reasonably high living standard, the moral and political objectives for us will have been met. But if this goal is neglected, moral and political steps are required to improve on the situation. Animal liberation is such a step.

This essay will maintain that animals have no rights and need no liberation. I will argue that to think they do is a category mistake—it is, to be blunt, to unjustifiably anthropomorphize animals, to treat them as if they were what they are not, namely, human beings. Rights and liberty are political concepts applicable to human beings because human beings are moral agents, in need of what Harvard philosopher Robert Nozick calls "moral space," that is, a definite sphere of moral jurisdiction where their authority to act is respected and protected so it is they, not intruders, who govern themselves and either succeed or fail in their moral tasks.

Oddly, it is clearly admitted by most animal rights or liberation theorists that only human beings are moral agents—for example, they never urge animals to behave morally (by, e.g., standing up for their rights, by leading a political revolution). No animal rights theorist proposes that animals be tried for crimes and blamed for moral wrongs.

If it is true that the moral nature of human beings gives rise to the conception of basic rights and liber-

Reprinted from *Public Affairs Quarterly, 5* (1991), by permission of *Public Affairs Quarterly*.

ties, then by this alone animal rights and liberation theorists have made an admission fatal to their case.

Before getting under way I want to note that rights and liberty are certainly not the whole of moral concern to us. There are innumerable other moral issues one can raise, including about the way human beings relate to animals. In particular, there is the question how should people treat animals. Should they be hunted even when this does not serve any vital human purpose? Should they be utilized in hurtful—indeed, evidently agonizing—fashion even for trivial human purposes? Should their pain and suffering be ignored in the process of being made use of for admittedly vital human purposes?

It is clear that once one has answered the question of whether animals have rights (or ought to be liberated from human beings) in the negative, one has by no means disposed of these other issues. In this essay I will be dealing mostly with the issue of animal rights and liberation. Yet I will also touch briefly on the other moral issues just raised. I will indicate why they may all be answered in the negative without it being the case that animals have rights or should be liberated—i.e., without raising any serious political issues.

WHY MIGHT ANIMALS HAVE RIGHTS?

To have a right amounts to having those around one who have the choice to abstain from intruding on one within a given sphere of jurisdiction. If I have the right to the use of our community swimming pool, no one may prevent me from making the decision as to whether I do or do not use the pool. Someone's having a right is a kind of freedom from the unavoidable interference of moral agents, beings who are capable of choosing whether they will interfere or not interfere with the rights holder.

When a right is considered natural, the freedom involved in having this right is supposed to be justified by reference to the kind of being one is, one's nature as a certain kind of entity. The idea of natural rights was formulated in connection with the issue of the proper relationship between human beings, especially citizens and governments. The idea goes back many centuries . . .

The major political thinker with an influential doctrine of natural rights was John Locke. In his *Second Treatise on Government* he argued that each human being is responsible to follow the Law of Nature, the source of morality. But to do so, each also requires a sphere of personal authority, which is identified by the principle of the natural right to property—including one's person and estate. In other words, to be a morally responsible being in the company of other persons one needs what Robert Nozick has called "moral space," i.e., a sphere of sovereignty or personal jurisdiction so that one can engage in self-government—for better or for worse.

Locke made it a provision of having such a right that there be sufficient and good enough of whatever one may have a right to left for others—i.e., the Lockean proviso against absolute monopoly. For Locke the reason government is necessary is "that though in the state of Nature [every human being] hath such a right [to absolute freedom], yet the enjoyment of it is very uncertain and constantly exposed to the invasion of others."[1] So we establish government to make us secure in the enjoyment of our rights.

Since Locke's time the doctrine of natural rights has undergone a turbulent intellectual history, falling into disrepute at the hands of empiricism and positivism but gaining a revival at the hands of some influential political philosophers of the second half of the twentieth century.

Ironically, at a time in recent intellectual history when natural rights theory had not been enjoying much support, the idea that animals might also have rights came under increasing discussion. Most notable among those who proposed such a notion was Thomas Taylor, whose anonymous work, *Vindication of the Rights of Brutes* was published in 1792 but discussed animal rights only in the context of demeaning human rights. More positive (though brief) was the contribution of Jeremy Bentham, who in his *An Introduction to The Principles of Morals and Legislation* (1789), argued that those animals that can suffer are owed moral consideration, even if those that molest us or those we may make good use of may be killed—but not "tormented."

In the latter part of the 19th century an entire work was devoted to the idea by Henry S. Salt, entitled

Animals' Rights.[2] And in our time numerous philosophers and social commentators have made the attempt to demonstrate that if we are able to ascribe basic rights to life, liberty and property to human beings, we can do the same for many of the higher animals. In essentials their arguments can be broken down into two parts. First, they subscribe to Darwin's thesis that no difference of kind, only a difference of degree, can be found between other animals and human beings.[3] Second, even if there were a difference in kind between other animals—especially mammals—and human beings, since they both can be shown to have interests (e.g., the avoidance of pain or suffering), for certain moral and legal purposes the difference does not matter, only the similarity does. In connection with both of these arguments the central conclusion is that if human beings can be said to have certain basic rights—e.g., to life, liberty or consideration for their capacity to suffer—then so do (higher) animals.[4]

Now I do not wish to give the impression that no diversity exists among those who defend animal rights. Some do so from the viewpoint of natural rights, treating animal's rights as basic limiting principles which may not be ignored except when it would also make sense to disregard the rights of human beings. Even on this matter are there serious differences among defenders of animals rights—some do not allow any special regard for human beings,[5] some hold that when it comes to a choice between a person and a dog, it is ordinarily the person who should be given protection.[6] But others choose to defend animal rights on utilitarian grounds—to the extent that it amounts to furthering overall pleasure or happiness in the world, animals must be given equal consideration to what human beings receive. Thus only if there really is demonstrable contribution to the overall pleasure or happiness on earth, may an animal capable of experiencing pleasure or happiness be sacrificed for the sake of some human purpose. Barring such demonstrable contribution, animals and humans enjoy equal rights.[7]

At times the argument for animal rights begins with the rather mild point that "reason requires that other animals are as much within the scope of moral concern as are men" but then moves on to the more radical claim that therefore "we must view our entire history as well as all aspects of our daily lives from a new perspective."[8]

Of course, people have generally invoked some moral considerations as they treated animals—I can recall living on a farm in Hungary when I was 11 and getting all kinds of lectures about how I ought to treat the animals, receiving severe rebuke when I mistreated a cat and lots of praise when I took the favorite cow grazing every day and established a close bond with it over time. Hardly anyone can have escaped one or another moral lecture from parents or neighbors concerning the treatment of pets, household animals, or birds. When a young boy once tried out an air gun by shooting a pigeon sitting on a telephone wire before the apartment house in which he lived, I recall that there was no end of rebuke in response to his wanton callousness. Yet none of those who engaged in the moralizing ever entertained the need to "view our entire history as well as all aspects of our daily lives from a new perspective." Rather they seemed to have understood that reckless disregard for the life or well being of animals shows a defect of character, lack of sensitivity, callousness—realizing, at the same time, that numerous human purposes justify our killing and using animals in the various ways most of us do use them.

And this really is the crux of the matter. But why? Why is it more reasonable to think of animals as available for our sensible use rather than owed the kind of respect and consideration we ought to extend to other human beings? It is one thing to have this as a common sense conviction, it is another to know it as a sound viewpoint, in terms of which we may confidently conduct ourselves.

WHY WE MAY USE ANIMALS

While I will return to the arguments for animal rights, let me first place on record the case for the use of animals for human purposes. Without this case reasonably well established, it will not be possible to critically assess the case for animal rights. After all, this is a comparative matter—which viewpoint makes better sense, which is, in other words, more likely to be true?

One reason for the propriety of our use of animals is that we are more important or valuable than other animals and some of our projects may require animals for them to be successful. Notice that this is different from saying that human beings are "uniquely important," a position avidly ridiculed by Stephen R. L. Clark, who claims that "there seems no decent ground in reason or revelation to suppose that man is uniquely important or significant."[9] If man were uniquely important, that would mean that one could not assign any value to plants or non-human animals apart from their relationship to human beings. That is not the position I am defending. I argue that there is a scale of importance in nature, and among all the various kinds of being, human beings are the most important—even while it is true that some members of the human species may indeed prove themselves to be the most vile and worthless, as well.

How do we establish that we are more important or valuable? By considering whether the idea of lesser or greater importance or value in the nature of things makes clear sense and applying it to an understanding of whether human beings or other animals are more important. If it turns out that ranking things in nature as more or less important makes sense, and if we qualify as more important than other animals, there is at least the beginning of a reason why we may make use of other animals for our purposes.

That there are things of different degree of value in nature is admitted by animal rights advocates, so there is no great need here to argue about that. When they insist that we treat animals diffe rently from the way we treat, say, rocks or iron ore—so that while we may not use the former as we choose, we may use the latter—they testify, at least by implication, that animals are more important than, say, iron ore. Certainly they invoke some measure of importance or value and place animals higher in line with this measure than they place other aspects of nature. They happen, also, to deny that human beings rank higher than animals, or least they do not admit that human beings' higher ranking warrants their using animals for their purposes. But that is a distinct issue which we can consider later.

Quite independently of the implicit acknowledgment by animal rights advocates of the hierarchy of nature, there simply is evidence through the natural world of the existence of beings of greater complexity and of higher value. For example, while it makes no sense to evaluate as good or bad such things as planets or rocks or pebbles—except as they may relate to human purposes—when it comes to plants and animals the process of evaluation commences very naturally indeed. We can speak of better or worse trees, oaks, redwoods, or zebras, foxes or chimps. While at this point we confine our evaluation to the condition or behavior of such beings without any intimation of their responsibility for being better or worse, when we start discussing human beings our evaluation takes on a moral component. Indeed, none are more ready to testify to this than animal rights advocates who, after all, do not demand any change of behavior on the part of non-human animals and yet insist that human beings conform to certain moral edicts as a matter of their own choice. This means that even animal rights advocates admit outright that to the best of our knowledge it is with human beings that the idea of moral goodness and moral responsibility enters the universe.

Clearly this shows a hierarchical structure in nature: some things do not invite evaluations at all—it is a matter of no significance or of indifference whether they are or are not or what they are or how they behave. Some things invite evaluation but without implying any moral standing with reference to whether they do well or badly. And some things—namely, human beings—invite moral evaluation. The level of importance or value may be noted to move from the inanimate to the animate world, culminating, as far as we now know, with human life. Normal human life involves moral tasks, and that is why we are more important than other beings in nature—we are subject to moral appraisal, it is a matter of our doing whether we succeed or fail in our lives.

Now when it comes to our moral task, namely, to succeed as human beings, we are dependent upon reaching sensible conclusions about what we should do. We can fail to do this and too often do so. But we can also succeed. The process that leads to our success involves learning, among other things, what it is that nature avails us with to achieve our highly varied tasks in life. Clearly among these highly varied tasks could be some that make judicious use of animals— for example, to find out whether some medicine is safe for human use, we might wish to use animals. To do this is the rational thing for us to do, so as to make the best use of nature for our success in living our lives. That does not mean there need be no guidelines involved in how we might make use of animals—any more than there need be no guidelines involved in how we use anything else.

WHY INDIVIDUAL HUMAN RIGHTS?

Where do individual *human* rights come into this picture? The rights being talked of in connection with human beings have as their source, as we have noted earlier, the human capacity to make moral choices. We have the right to life, liberty and property—as well as more specialized rights connected with politics, the press, religion—because we have as our central task in life to act morally. And in order to be able to do this throughout the scope of our lives, we require a reasonably clear sphere of personal jurisdiction—a dominion where we are sovereign and can either succeed or fail to live well, to do right, to act properly.

If we did not have rights, we would not have such a sphere of personal jurisdiction and there would be no clear idea as to whether we are acting in our own behalf or those of other persons. No one could be blamed or praised for we would not know clearly enough whether what the person is doing is in his or her authority to do or in someone else's. This is precisely the problem that arises in communal living and, especially, in totalitarian countries where everything is under forced collective governance. The reason moral distinctions are still possible to make under such circumstances is that in fact—as distinct from law—there is always some sphere of personal jurisdiction wherein people may exhibit courage, prudence, justice, honesty, and other virtues. But where collectivism has been success fully enforced, there is no individual responsibility at play and people's morality and immorality is submerged within the group.

Indeed the main reason for governments has for some time been recognized to be nothing other than that our individual human rights should be protected. In the past—and in many places even today—it was thought that government (or the State) has some kind of leadership role in human communities. This belief fallowed the view that human beings differ amongst themselves radically, some being lower, some higher class, some possessing divine rights, other lacking them, some having a personal communion with God, other lacking this special advantage.

With such views in place, it made clear enough sense to argue that government should have a patriarchal role in human communities—the view against which John Locke forcefully argued his theory of natural individual human rights.[10]

WHERE IS THERE ROOM FOR ANIMAL RIGHTS?

We have seen that the most sensible and influential doctrine of human rights rests on the fact that human beings are indeed members of a discernibly different species—the members of which have a moral life to aspire to and must have principles upheld for them in communities that make their aspiration possible. Now there is plainly no valid intellectual place for rights in the non-human world, the world in which moral responsibility is for all practical purposes absent. Some would want to argue that some measure of morality can be found within the world of at least higher animals—e.g., dogs. For example, Rollin holds that "In actual fact, some animals even seem to exhibit behavior that bespeaks something like moral agency or moral agreement."[11] His argument for this is rather anecdotal but it is worth considering:

> Canids, including the domesticated dog, do not attack another when the vanquished bares its threat, showing a sign of submission. Animals typically do not prey upon members of their own species. Elephants and porpoises will and do feed injured members of their species. Porpoises will help humans, even at risk to themselves. Some animals will adopt orphaned young of other species. (Such cross-species "morality" would certainly not be explainable by simple appeal to mechanical evolution, since there is no advantage whatever to one's own

species.) Dogs will act "guilty" when they break a rule such as one against stealing food from a table and will, for the most part, learn not to take it.[12]

Animal rights advocates such as Rollin maintain that it is impossible to clearly distinguish between human and non-human animals, including on the grounds of the former's characteristic as a moral agent. Yet what they do to defend this point is to invoke borderline cases, imaginary hypothesis, and anecdotes.

In contrast, in his book *The Difference of Man and the Difference it Makes,* Mortimer Adler undertakes the painstaking task of showing that even with the full acknowledgment of the merits of Darwinian and, especially, post-Darwinian evolutionary theory, there is ample reason to uphold the doctrine of specie-distinction—a distinction, incidentally, that is actually presupposed within Darwin's own work.[13] Adler shows that although the theistic doctrine of radical species differences is incompatible with current evolutionary theory, the more naturalistic view that species are superficially (but non-negligibly) different is indeed necessary to it. The fact of occasional borderline cases is simply irrelevant—what is crucial is that the generalization is true that human beings are basically different from other animals—by virtue of "a crucial threshold in a continuum of degrees." As Adler explains:

> . . . distinct species are genetically isolated populations between which interbreeding is impossible, arising (except in the case of polyploidy) from varieties between which interbreeding was not impossible, but between which it was prevented. Modern theorists, with more assurance than Darwin could manage, treat distinct species as natural kinds, not as man-made class distinctions.[14]

Adler adds that "Without the critical insight provided by the distinction between superficial and radical differences in kind, biologists [as well as animal rights advocates, one should add] might be tempted to follow Darwin in thinking that all differences in kind must be apparent, not real."[15]

Since Locke's admittedly incomplete—sometimes even confusing—theory had gained respect and, especially, practical import (e.g., in British and American political history), it became clear enough that the only justification for the exercise of state power—namely the force of the law—is that the rights of individuals are being or have been violated. But as with all successful doctrines, Locke's idea became corrupted by innumerable efforts to concoct rights that government must protect, rights that were actually disguised special interest objectives—values that some people, perhaps quite legitimately, wanted very badly to have secured for them.

While it is no doubt true that many animal rights advocates sincerely believe that they have found a justification for the actual existence of animal rights, it is equally likely that if the Lockean doctrine of rights had not become so influential, they would now be putting their point differently—in a way, namely, that would secure for them what they, as a special interest group, want: the protection of animals they have such love and sympathy for.

CLOSING REFLECTIONS

As with most issues on the minds of many intelligent people as well as innumerable crackpots, a discussion of whether there are animals rights and how we ought to treat animals cannot be concluded with dogmatic certainty one way or the other. Even though those who defend animal rights are certain almost beyond a shadow of doubt, all I can claim is to being certain beyond a reasonable doubt. Animals are not the sort of beings with basic rights to life, liberty and property, whereas human beings, in the main, are just such beings. Yet we know that animals can feel pain and can enjoy themselves and this must give us pause when we consider using them for our legitimate purposes. We ought to be humane, we ought to kill them and rear them and train them and hunt them in a fashion consistent with such care about them as sentient beings.

In a review of Tom Regan's provocative book already mentioned, *The Case for Animal Rights,* John Hospers makes the following observations that I believe put the matter into the best light we can shed on our topic:

> As one reads page after page of Regan's book, one has the growing impression that his thesis is in an

important way "going against nature." It is a fact of nature that living things have to live on other living things in order to stay alive themselves. It is a fact of nature that carnivores must consume, not plants (which they can't digest), but other sentient beings capable of intense pain and suffering, and that they can survive in no other way. It is a fact of nature that animal reproduction is such that far more creatures are born or hatched than can possibly survive. It is a fact of nature that most creatures die slow lingering tortuous deaths, and that few animals in the wild ever reach old age. It is a fact of nature that we cannot take one step in the woods without killing thousands of tiny organisms whose lives we thereby extinguish. This has been the order of nature for millions of years before man came on the scene, and has indeed been the means by which any animal species has survived to the present day; to fight it is like trying to fight an atomic bomb with a dartgun. . . . This is the world as it is, nature in the raw, unlike the animals in Disney cartoons.[16]

Of course, one might then ask, why should human beings make any attempt to behave differently among themselves, why bother with morality at all?

The fact is that with human nature a problem arose in nature that had not been there before—basic choices had to be confronted, which other animals do not have to confront. The question "How should I live?" faces each human being. And that is what makes it unavoidable for human beings to dwell on moral issues as well as to see other human beings as having the same problem to solve, the same question to dwell on. For this reason we are very different from other animals—we also do terrible, horrible, awful things to each other as well as to nature, but we can also do much, much better and achieve incredible feats nothing else in nature can come close to.

Indeed, then, the moral life is the exclusive province of human beings, so far as we can tell for now. Other—lower(!)—animals simply cannot be accorded the kind of treatment that such a moral life demands, namely, respect for and protection of basic rights.

NOTES

1. John Locke, *Two Treatises on Government,* Par. 123.

2. Henry S. Salt, *Animals' Rights* (London: George Bell & Sons, Ltd., 1892; Clark Summit, PA: Society for Animals Rights, Inc., 1980). This is perhaps *the* major philosophical effort to defend animals rights prior to Tom Regan's treaties on the same topic.

3. Charles Darwin, *The Descent of Man,* Chpts. 3 and 4. Reprinted in Tom Regan and Peter Singer, eds., *Animal Rights and Human Obligations* (Englewood Cliffs, NJ: Prentice-Hall, 1976), pp. 72–81.

4. On these points both the deontologically oriented Tom Regan and the utilitarian Peter Singer tend to agree, although they differ considerably in their arguments.

5. Peter Singer holds that "we would be on shaky grounds if we were to demand equality for blacks, women, and other groups of oppressed humans while denying equal consideration to nonhumans." "All Animals Are Equal," op. cit., Regan & Singer, *Animal Rights,* p. 150.

6. Tom Regan contends that "[it] is not to say that practices that involve taking the lives of animals cannot possibly be justified. . . . in order to seriously consider approving such a practice [it] would [have to] prevent, reduce, or eliminate a much greater amount of evil . . . there is no other way to bring about these consequences . . . and . . . we have very good reason to believe that these consequences will obtain." "Do Animals Have a Right to Life?" Op cit., Regan & Singer, *Animal Rights,* pp. 205–4.

7. This is the gist of Singer's thesis.

8. Bernard E. Rollin, *Animal Rights and Human Morality* (Buffalo, NY: Prometheus Books, 1981), p. 4.

9. Stephen R. L. Clark, *The Moral Status of Animals* (Oxford, England: Clarendon Press, 1977), p. 13.

10. John Locke, *Two Treatises.*

11. Rollin, *Animal Rights,* p. 14.

12. Ibid.

13. See a discussion of this in Mortimer Adler, *The Difference of Man and the Difference It Makes* (New York: World Publishing Co., 1968), pp. 73ff.

14. Ibid.

15. Ibid., p. 75.

16. John Hospers, "Review of The Case for Animal Rights," *Reason Papers,* No. 10, p. 123.

PART 8

~

Political Philosophy

Introduction

CYNTHIA STARK

Political philosophers aim to justify institutions and practices that structure and define our collective life. In so doing, they address such questions as Can state authority be justified? If so, what form of government is best? How should a society's resources be distributed among its members? What part should the state play in this distribution? What part should markets play? What do we owe our fellow citizens?

Thomas Hobbes addresses the first two of these questions, arguing that political authority can be justified in the form of absolute monarchy. To support this idea, he asks us to imagine what life would be like in a "state of nature"—a condition absent of political authority. He concludes that people in such a condition would be perpetually at war, living in constant fear for their safety. This lack of security makes it rational, in Hobbes's view, for individuals to enter into a "social contract" with one other, agreeing to transfer their power to a single sovereign who will provide safety and security by invoking and enforcing laws. According to Hobbes, a sovereign's authority is justified because rational people, given the choice, would rather be under a sovereign's authority than not.

Like Hobbes, John Locke believes that people in the state of nature would consent to live under a political authority. But, unlike Hobbes, he does not think that they would choose subjection to an absolute sovereign. He argues instead that individuals in a state of nature would agree to form a representative democracy characterized by majority rule.

John Rawls works within the social contract tradition established by Hobbes and Locke. Yet he is largely concerned, not with sovereignty, but with economic arrangements. His aim is to arrive at principles for justly distributing "primary goods"—goods anyone would want, regardless of their particular goals, outlook, or abilities. He does so by asking which principles people would agree to if they were behind a "veil of ignorance," where they would lack knowledge of their talents, values, sex, race, or class. Rawls concludes that such people would adopt two principles. The first principle states that citizens should have as many liberties as possible, compatible with liberty for all. The second principle states that an inequality in primary goods is justified only under two conditions: it maximally benefits the least advantaged members of society, and it results from a career that citizens have an equal opportunity to undertake. An inequality in primary goods that does not meet these conditions is unjust and must be redressed through redistributive taxation.

Against Rawls, Robert Nozick argues that justice does not require that goods be distributed in any particular way. It is enough, he says, if a system of private property is established in which goods are acquired and transferred by private individuals according to just procedures, for example, through contracts or gifts. The state is permitted to redistribute goods among people only when the just procedures for acquiring and transferring goods have been violated, as when someone who breaches a contract is forced to provide compensation. Nonvoluntary redistribution to promote equality, however, is not permitted. In other words, Nozick opposes the government's taking money from some people, through taxation, and using it to make others better off. By limiting government-sponsored redistribution, Nozick says, a society preserves people's freedom to dispose of their property as they choose.

G. A. Cohen challenges Nozick's claim that a system of private property best preserves individual freedom. Suppose something—say, a park—is commonly owned. In this case, everyone is free to use it. If it becomes privately owned, then while the freedom of the owner to use it increases, the freedom of everyone else to use it decreases. So, Cohen claims, ownership both extends and restricts freedom. It increases the freedom of owners with respect to a particular good, and it decreases the freedom of nonowners with respect to that good. Cohen concludes that common property is therefore sometimes more conducive to freedom than private property. It can give more people the opportunity to use a good.

The classical liberal vision of the good society is of a collection of independent individuals equipped with the right to pursue their own ends within the bounds of justice. Though they relate to others in this pursuit, their bonds to those others are seen as voluntary. This vision is endorsed by egalitarian liberals, such as Rawls, and by libertarians, such as Nozick. Michael Sandel rejects this liberal ideal. He claims that it expresses a faulty conception of the individual. Individuals are not independent of one another, Sandel says, but rather have significant, nonvoluntary attachments to family members, friends, and neighbors. Furthermore, individuals are not free to pursue their ends, provided they do not commit any injustice, for they have moral obligations to others that result from their relationships to those others.

Whereas Rawls, Nozick, and Cohen are concerned with the distribution and exchange of goods generally, Debra Satz addresses the justice of a particular kind of exchange, namely, the prostitute's exchange of sex for money. Against those who argue that prostitution is wrong because of its harmful effects on society and those who argue that it is wrong in itself, Satz argues that prostitution is objectionable because of its contribution to women's subordinate social status. Prostitution upholds women's lower status by representing women as the sexual servants of men and reinforcing false beliefs about male and female sexuality. She concludes that if prostitution were sufficiently regulated and if it took place under conditions of gender equality, it may not be morally troubling.

Leviathan

~

THOMAS HOBBES

Thomas Hobbes (1588–1679), a crucial figure in the history of political philosophy, was a leading exponent of social contract theory.

CHAPTER 13 • OF THE NATURAL CONDITION OF MANKIND AS CONCERNING THEIR FELICITY, AND MISERY

Nature hath made men so equal, in the faculties of body, and mind; as that though there be found one man sometimes manifestly stronger in body, or of quicker mind than another; yet when all is reckoned together, the difference between man, and man, is not so considerable, as that one man can thereupon claim to himself any benefit, to which another may not pretend, as well as he. For as to the strength of body, the weakest has strength enough to kill the strongest, either by secret machination, or by confederacy with others, that are in the same danger as himself.

And as to the faculties of the mind, (setting aside the arts grounded upon words, and especially that skill of proceeding upon general, and infallible rules, called science; which very few have, and but in few things; as being not a native faculty, born with us; nor attained, (as prudence,) while we look after someone else,) I find yet a greater equality amongst men, than that of strength. For prudence, is but experience; which equal time, equally bestows on all men, in those things they equally apply themselves unto. That which may perhaps make such equality incredible, is but a vain conceit of one's own wisdom, which almost all men think they have in a greater degree, than the vulgar; that is, than all men but themselves, and a few others, whom by fame, or for concurring with them-selves, they approve. For such is the nature of men, that howsoever they may acknowledge many others to be more witty, or more eloquent, or more learned; yet they will hardly believe there be many so wise as themselves: For they see their own wit at hand, and other men's at a distance. But this proveth rather that men are in that point equal, than unequal. For there is not ordinarily a greater sign of the equal distribution of any thing, than that every man is contented with his share.

From this equality of ability, ariseth equality of hope in the attaining of our ends. And therefore if any two men desire the same thing, which nevertheless they cannot both enjoy, they become enemies; and in the way to their end, (which is principally their own conservation, and sometimes their delectation only,) endeavour to destroy, or subdue one another. And from hence it comes to pass, that where an invader hath no more to fear, than another man's single power; if one plant, sow, build, or possess a convenient seat, others may probably be expected to come prepared with forces united, to dispossess, and deprive him, not only of the fruit of his labour, but also of his life, or liberty. And the invader again is in the like danger of another.

And from this diffidence of one another, there is no way for any man to secure himself, so reasonable, as anticipation; that is, by force, or wiles, to master the persons of all men he can, so long, till he see no other power great enough to endanger him: and this is no more than his own conservation requireth, and is gen-

From Thomas Hobbes, *Leviathan*.

erally allowed. Also because there be some, that taking pleasure in contemplating their own power in the acts of conquest, which they pursue farther than their security requires; if others, that otherwise would be glad to be at ease within modest bounds, should not by invasion increase their power, they would not be able, long time, by standing only on their defence, to subsist. And by consequence, such augmentation of dominion over men, being necessary to a man's conservation, it ought to be allowed him.

Again, men have no pleasure, (but on the contrary a great deal of grief) in keeping company, where there is no power able to over-awe them all. For every man looketh that his companion should value him, at the same rate he sets upon himself: and upon all signs of contempt, or undervaluing, naturally endeavours, as far as he dares (which amongst them that have no common power to keep them in quiet, is far enough to make them destroy each other,) to extort a greater value from his contemners, by damage; and from others, by the example.

So that in the nature of man, we find three principal causes of quarrel. First, competition; secondly, diffidence; thirdly, glory.

The first, maketh man invade for gain; the second, for safety; and the third, for reputation. The first use violence, to make themselves masters of other men's persons, wives, children, and cattle; the second, to defend them; the third, for trifles, as a word, a smile, a different opinion, and any other sign of undervalue, either direct in their persons, or by reflection in their kindred, their friends, their nation, their profession, or their name.

Hereby it is manifest, that during the time men live without a common power to keep them all in awe, they are in that condition which is called war; and such a war, as is of every man, against every man. For WAR, consisteth not in battle only, or the act of fighting; but in a tract of time, wherein the will to contend by battle is sufficiently known: and therefore the notion of *time,* is to be considered in the nature of war; as it is in the nature of weather. For as the nature of foul weather, lieth not in a shower or two of rain; but in an inclination thereto of many days together: so the nature of war, consisteth not in actual fighting;

but in the known disposition thereto, during all the time there is no assurance to the contrary. All other time is PEACE.

Whatsoever therefore is consequent to a time of war, where every man is enemy to every man; the same is consequent to the time, wherein men live without other security, than what their own strength, and their own invention shall furnish them withal. In such condition, there is no place for industry; because the fruit thereof is uncertain: and consequently no culture of the earth; no navigation, nor use of the commodities that may be imported by sea; no commodious building; no instruments of moving, and removing such things as require much force; no knowledge of the face of the earth; no account of time; no arts; no letters; no society; and which is worst of all, continual fear, and danger of violent death; and the life of man, solitary, poor, nasty, brutish, and short.

It may seem strange to some man, that has not well weighted these things; that nature should thus dissociate, and render men apt to invade, and destroy one another: and he may therefore, not trusting to this inference, made from the passions, desire perhaps to have the same confirmed by experience. Let him therefore consider with himself, when taking a journey, he arms himself, and seeks to go well accompanied; when going to sleep, he locks his doors; when even in his house he locks his chests; and this when he knows there be laws, and public officers, armed, to revenge all injuries shall be done him; what opinion he has of his fellow subjects, when he rides armed; of his fellow citizens, when he locks his doors; and of his children, and servants, when he locks his chests. Does he not there as much accuse mankind by his actions, as I do by my words? But neither of us accuse man's nature in it. The desires, and other passions of man, are in themselves no sin. No more are the actions, that proceed from those passions, till they know a law that forbids them: which till laws be made they cannot know: nor can any law be made, till they have agreed upon the person that shall make it.

It may peradventure be thought, there was never such a time, nor condition of war as this; and I believe it was never generally so, over all the world: but there are many places, where they live so now. For the savage people in many places of *America,* except the government of small families, the concord whereof dependeth on natural lust, have no government at all; and live at this day in that brutish manner, as I said before. Howsoever, it may be perceived what manner of life there would be, where there were no common power to fear; by the manner of life, which men that have formerly lived under a peacefull government, use to degenerate into, in a civil war.

But though there had never been any time, wherein particular men were in a condition of war one against another; yet in all times, kings, and persons of sovereign authority, because of their independency, are in continual jealousies, and in the state and posture of gladiators; having their weapons pointing, and their eyes fixed on one another; that is, their forts, garrisons, and guns upon the frontiers of their kingdoms; and continual spies upon their neighbours; which is a posture of war. But because they uphold thereby, the industry of their subjects; there does not follow from it, that misery, which accompanies the liberty of particular men.

To this war of every man against every man, this also is consequent; that nothing can be unjust. The notions of right and wrong, justice and injustice have there no place. Where there is no common power, there is no law: where no law, no injustice. Force, and fraud, are in war the two cardinal virtues. Justice, and injustice are none of the faculties neither of the body, nor mind. If they were, they might be in a man that were alone in the world, as well as his senses, and passions. They are qualities, that relate to men in society, not in solitude. It is consequent also to the same condition, that there be no propriety, no dominion, no *mine* and *thine* distinct; but only that to be every man's, that he can get; and for so long, as he can keep it. And thus much for the ill condition, which many by mere nature is actually placed in; though with a possibility to come out of it, consisting partly in the passions, partly in his reason.

The passions that incline men to peace, are fear of death; desire of such things as are necessary to commodious living; and a hope by their industry to obtain them. And reason suggesteth convenient articles of peace, upon which men may be drawn to agreement. These articles, are they, which otherwise are called the Laws of Nature; whereof I shall speak more particularly, in the two following chapters.

CHAPTER 14 • OF THE FIRST AND SECOND NATURAL LAWS, AND OF CONTRACTS

The RIGHT OF NATURE, which writers commonly call *jus naturale,* is the liberty each man hath, to use his own power, as he will himself, for the preservation of his own nature; that is to say, of his own life; and consequently, of doing any thing, which in his own judgment, and reason, he shall conceive to be the aptest means thereunto.

By LIBERTY, is understood, according to the proper signification of the word, the absence of external impediments: which impediments, may oft take away part of a man's power to do what he would; but cannot hinder him from using the power left him, according as his judgment, and reason shall dictate to him.

A LAW OF NATURE, (*lex naturalis,*) is a precept, or general rule, found out by reason, by which a man is forbidden to do that, which is destructive of his life, or taketh away the means of preserving the same; and to omit that, by which he thinketh it may be best preserved. For though they that speak of this subject, use to confound *jus,* and *lex, right* and *law;* yet they ought to be distinguished; because RIGHT, consisteth in liberty to do, or to forbear; whereas LAW, determineth, and bindeth to one of them: so that law, and right, differ as much, as obligation, and liberty; which in one and the same matter are inconsistent.

And because the condition of man, (as hath been declared in the precedent chapter) is a condition of war of every one against every one; in which case every one is governed by his own reason; and there is nothing he can make use of, that may not be a help unto him, in preserving his life against his enemies; it followeth, that in such a condition, every man has a right to every thing: even to one another's body. And therefore, as long as this natural right of every man to every thing endureth, there can be no security to any man, (how strong or wise soever he be,) of living out the time, which nature ordinarily alloweth men to live. And consequently it is a precept, or general rule of reason, *that every man, ought to endeavour peace, as far as he has hope of obtaining it; and when he cannot obtain it, that he may seek, and use, all helps, and advantages of war.* The first branch of which rule, containeth the first, and fundamental law of nature; which is, *to seek peace, and follow it.* The second, the sum of the right of nature; which is, *by all means we can, to defend ourselves.*

From this fundamental law of nature, by which men are commanded to endeavor peace, is derived this second law; *that a man be willing, when others are so too, as farforth, as for peace, and defence of himself he shall think it necessary, to lay down this right to all things; and be contented with so much liberty against other men, as he would allow other men against himself.* For as long as every man holdeth this right, of doing any thing he liketh; so long are all men in the condition of war. But if other men will not lay down their right, as well as he; then there is no reason for any one, to divest himself of his: for that were to expose himself to prey, (which no man is bound to) rather than to dispose himself to peace. This is that law of the Gospel; *whatsoever you require that others should do for you, that do ye to them.* And that law of all men, *quod tibi fieri non vis, alteri ne feceris.*

To *lay down* a man's *right* to any thing, is to *divest* himself of the *liberty,* of hindering another of the benefit of his own right to the same. For he that renounceth, or passeth away his right, giveth not to any other man a right which he had not before; because there is nothing to which every man had not right by nature: but only standeth out of his way, that he may enjoy his own original right, without hindrance from him; not without hindrance from another. So that the effect which redoundeth to one man, by another man's defect of right, is but so much diminution of impediments to the use of his own right original.

Right is laid aside, either by simply renouncing it; or by transferring it to another. By *simply* RENOUNCING; when he cares not to whom the benefit thereof redoundeth. By TRANSFERRING; when he intendeth the benefit thereof to some certain person, or persons. And when a man hath in either manner abandoned, or granted away his right; then is he said to be OBLIGED, or BOUND, not to hinder those, to whom such right is granted, or abandoned, from the benefit of it: and that he *ought,* and it is his DUTY, not to make void that voluntary act of his own: and that such hindrance is INJUSTICE, and INJURY, as being *sine jure;* the right being before renounced, or transferred. So that *injury,* or *injustice,* in the controversies of the world, is somewhat like to that, which in the disputations of scholars is called *absurdity.* For as it is there called an absurdity, to contradict what one maintained in the beginning: so in the world, it is called injustice, and injury, voluntarily to undo that, which from the beginning he had voluntarily done. The way by which a man either simply renounceth, or transferreth his right, is a declaration, or signification, by some voluntary and sufficient sign, or signs, that he doth so renounced, or transfer; or hath so renounced, or transferred the same, to him that accepteth it. And these signs are either words only, or actions only; or (as it happeneth most often) both words, and actions. And the same are the BONDS, by which men are bound, and obliged: bonds, that have their strength, not from their own nature, (for nothing is more easily broken than a man's word,) but from fear of some evil consequence upon the rupture.

Whensoever a man transferreth his right, or renounceth it; it is either in consideration of some right reciprocally transferred to himself; or for some other good he hopeth for thereby. For it is a voluntary act: and of the voluntary acts of every man, the object is some *good to himself.* And therefore there be some rights, which no man can be understood by any words, or other signs, to have abandoned, or transferred. As first a man cannot lay down the right of resisting them, that assault him by force, to take away his life; because he cannot be understood to aim thereby, at any good to himself. The same may be said of wounds, and chains, and imprisonment; both because there is no benefit consequent to such patience; as there is to the patience of suffering another to be wounded, or imprisoned: as also because a man cannot tell, when he seeth men proceed against him by violence, whether they intend his death or not. And lastly the motive, and end for which this renouncing, and transferring of right is introduced, is nothing else but the security of a man's person, in his life, and in the means of so preserving life, as not to be weary of it. And therefore if a man by words, or other signs, seem to despoil himself of the end, for which those signs were intended; he is not to be understood as if he meant it, or that it was his will; but that he was ignorant of how such words and actions were to be interpreted.

The mutual transferring of right, is that which men call CONTRACT.

There is difference between transferring of right to the thing; and transferring, or tradition, that is, delivery of the thing it self. For the thing may be delivered together with the translation of the right; as in buying and selling with ready money; or exchange of goods, or lands: and it may be delivered some time after.

Again, one of the contractors, may deliver the thing contracted for on his part, and leave the other to perform his part at some determinate time after, and in the mean time be trusted; and then the contract on his part, is called PACT, or COVENANT: or both parts may contract now, to perform hereafter: in which cases, he that is to perform in time to come, being trusted, his performance is called *keeping of promise,* or faith; and the failing of performance (if it be voluntary) *violation of faith.*

When the transferring of right, is not mutual; but one of the parties transferreth, in hope to gain thereby friendship, or service from another, or from his friends; or in hope to gain the reputation of charity, or magnanimity; or to deliver his mind from the pain of compassion; or in hope of reward in heaven; this is not contract, but GIFT, FREE-GIFT, GRACE: which words signify one and the same thing. . . .

If a covenant be made, wherein neither of the parties perform presently, but trust one another; in the condition of mere nature, (which is a condition of war of every man against every man,) upon any reasonable suspicion, it is void: but if there be a common power set over them both, with right and force sufficient to compel performance, it is not void. For he that performeth first, has no assurance the other will perform after; because the bonds of words are too

weak to bridle men's ambition, avarice, anger, and other passions, without the fear of some coercive power; which in the condition of mere nature, where all men are equal, and judges of the justness of their own fears, cannot possibly be supposed. And therefore he which performeth first, does but betray himself to his enemy; contrary to the right (he can never abandon) of defending his life, and means of living.

But in a civil estate, where there is a power set up to constrain those that would otherwise violate their faith, that fear is no more reasonable; and for that cause, he which by the covenant is to perform first, is obliged so to do.

The cause of fear, which maketh such a covenant invalid, must be always something arising after the covenant made; as some new fact, or other sign of the will not to perform: else it cannot make the covenant void. For that which could not hinder a man from promising, ought not to be admitted as a hindrance of performing. . . .

The matter, or subject of a covenant, is always something that falleth under deliberation; (for to covenant, is an act of the will; that is to say an act, and the last act, of deliberation;) and is therefore always understood to be something to come; and which is judged possible for him that covenanteth, to perform.

And therefore, to promise that which is known to be impossible, is no covenant. But if that prove impossible afterwards, which before was thought possible, the covenant is valid, and bindeth, (though not to the thing it self,) yet to the value, or if that also be impossible, to the unfeigned endeavour of performing as much as is possible: for to more no man can be obliged.

Men are freed of their covenants two ways; by performing; or by being forgiven. For performance, is the natural end of obligation; and forgiveness, the restitution of liberty; as being a retransferring of that right, in which the obligation consisted.

Covenants entered into by fear, in the condition of mere nature, are obligatory. For example, if I covenant to pay a ransom, or service for my life, to an enemy; I am bound by it. For it is a contract, wherein one receiveth the benefit of life; the other is to receive money, or service for it; and consequently, where no other law (as in the condition, of mere nature) forbiddeth the performance, the covenant is valid. There are prisoners of war, if trusted with the payment of their ransom, are obliged to pay it, and if a weaker prince, make a disadvantageous peace with a stronger, for fear; he is bound to keep it; unless (as hath been said before) there ariseth some new, and just cause of fear, to renew the war. And even in commonwealths, if I be forced to redeem myself from a thief by promising him money, I am bound to pay it, till the civil law discharge me. For whatsoever I may lawfully do without obligation, the same I may lawfully covenant to do through fear: and what I lawfully covenant, I cannot lawfully break.

A former covenant, makes void a later. For a man that hath passed away his right to one may today, hath it not to pass tomorrow to another: and therefore the later promise passeth no right, but is null.

A covenant not to defend myself from force, by force, is always void. For (as I have showed before) no man can transfer, or lay down his right to save himself from death, wounds, and imprisonment, (the avoiding whereof is the only end of laying down any right, and therefore the promise of not resisting force, in no covenant transferreth any right; nor is obliging. For though a man may covenant thus, *unless I do so, or so, kill me;* he cannot covenant thus, *unless I do so, or so, I will not resist you, when you come to kill me.* For man by nature chooseth the lesser evil, which is danger of death in resisting; rather than the greater, which is certain and present death in not resisting. And this is granted to be true by all men, in that they lead criminals to execution, and prison, with armed men, notwithstanding that such criminals have consented to the law, by which they are condemned.

A covenant to accuse one self, without assurance of pardon, is likewise invalid. For in the condition of nature, where every man is judge, there is no place for accusation: and in the civil state, the accusation is followed with punishment; which being force, a man is not obliged not to resist. The same is also true, of the accusation of those, by whose condemnation a man falls into misery; as of a father, wife, or benefactor. For the testimony of such an accuser, if it be not willingly given, is presumed to be corrupted by nature; and therefore not to be received: and where a man's testimony is not to be credited, he is not bound to give it. Also accusations upon torture, are not to be reputed as testimonies. For torture is to be used but as means of conjecture, and light, in the further examination, and search of truth: and what is in that case confessed, tendeth to the ease of him that is tortured, not to the informing of the torturers: and therefore ought not to have the credit of a sufficient testimony: for whether he deliver himself by true, or false accusation, he does it by the right of preserving his own life.

The force of words, being (as I have formerly noted) too weak to hold men to the performance of their covenants; there are in man's nature, but two imaginable helps to strengthen it. And those are either a fear of the consequence of breaking their word; or a glory, or pride in appearing not to need to break it. This latter is a generosity too rarely found to be presumed on, especially in the pursuers of wealth, command, or sensual pleasure; which are the greatest part of mankind. The passion to be reckoned upon, is fear; whereof there be two very general objects: one, the power of spirits invisible; the other, the power of those men they shall therein offend. Of these two, though the former be the greater power, yet the fear of the latter is commonly the greater fear. The fear of the former is in every man, his own religion: which hath place in the nature of man before civil society. The latter hath not so; at least not place enough, to keep men to their promises; because in the condition of mere nature, the inequality of power is not discerned, but by the event of battle. So that before the time of civil society, or in the interruption thereof by war, there is nothing can strengthen a covenant of peace agreed on, against the temptations of avarice, ambition, lust, or other strong desire, but the fear of that invisible power, which they every one worship as God; and fear as a revenger of their perfidy. All therefore that can be done between two men not subject to civil power, is to put one another to swear by the God he feareth: which *swearing,* or OATH, is a *form of speech, added to a promise; by which he that promiseth, signifieth, that unless he perform, he renounceth the mercy of his God, or calleth to him for vengeance on himself.* Such was the heathen form, *Let* Jupiter *kill me else, as I kill this beast.* So is our form, *I shall do thus, and thus, so help me God.* And this, with the rites and ceremonies, which every one useth in his own religion, that the fear of breaking faith might be the greater.

By this it appears, that an oath taken according to any other form, or rite, than his, that sweareth, is in vain; and no oath: and that there is no swearing by any thing which the swearer thinks not God. For though men have sometimes used to swear by their kings, for fear, or flattery; yet they would have it thereby understood, they attributed to them divine honour. And that swearing unnecessarily by God, is but prophaning of his name: and swearing by other things, as men do in common discourse, is not swearing, but an impious custom, gotten by too much vehemence of talking.

It appears also, that the oath adds nothing to the obligation. For a covenant, if lawful, binds in the sight of God, without the oath, as much as with it: if unlawful, bindeth not at all; though it be confirmed with an oath.

CHAPTER 15 • OF OTHER LAWS OF NATURE

From that law of nature, by which we are obliged to transfer to another, such rights, as being retained, hinder the peace of mankind, there followeth a third; which is this, *that men perform their covenants made:* without which, covenants are in vain, and but empty words; and the right of all men to all things remaining, we are still in the condition of war.

And in this law of nature, consisteth the fountain and original of JUSTICE. For where no covenant hath preceded, there hath no right been transferred, and every man has right to every thing; and consequently, no action can be unjust. But when a covenant is made, then to break it is *unjust;* and the definition of INJUSTICE, is no other than *the not performance of covenant.* And whatsoever is not unjust, is *just.*

But because covenants of mutual trust, where there is fear of not performance on either part, (as hath been said in the former chapter,) are invalid; though the original of justice be the making of covenants; yet injustice actually there can be none, till the cause of such fear be taken away; which while men are in the

natural condition of war, cannot be done. Therefore before the names of just, and unjust can have place, there must be some coercive power, to compel men equally to the performance of their covenants, by the terror of some punishment, greater than the benefit they expect by the breach of their covenant; and to make good that propriety, which by mutual contract men acquire, in recompense of the universal right they abandon: and such power there is none before the erection of a commonwealth. And this is also to be gathered out of the ordinary definition of justice in the Schools: for they say, that *justice is the constant will of giving to every man his own.* And therefore where there is no *own,* that is, no propriety, there is no injustice; and where there is no coercive power erected, that is, where there is no comonwealth, there is no propriety; all men having right to all things: therefore where there is no commonwealth, there nothing is unjust. So that the nature of justice, consisteth in keeping of valid covenants: but the validity of covenants begins not but with the constitution of a civil power, sufficient to compel men to keep them: and then it is also that propriety begins.

The fool hath said in his heart, there is no such thing as justice; and sometimes also with his tongue; seriously alleging, that every man's conservation, and contentment, being committed to his own care, there could be no reason, why every man might not do what he thought conducted thereunto: and therefore also to make, or not make; keep, or not keep covenants, was not against reason, when it conduced to one's benefit. He does not therein deny, that there be covenants; and that they are sometimes broken, sometimes kept; and that such breach of them may be called injustice, and the observance of them justice: but he questioneth, whether injustice, taking away the fear of God, (for the same fool hath said in his heart there is no God,) may not sometimes stand with that reason, which dictateth to every man his own good; and particularly then, when it conduceth to such a benefit, as shall put a man in a condition, to neglect not only the dispraise, and revilings, but also the power of other men. The kingdom of God is gotten by violence: but what if it could be gotten by unjust violence? were it against reason so to get it, when it is impossible to receive hurt by it? and if it be not against reason, it is not against justice; or else justice is not to be approved for good. From such reasoning as this, successful wickedness hath obtained the name of virtue: and some that in all other things have disallowed the violation of faith; yet have allowed it, when it is for the getting of a kingdom. And the heathen that believed, that *Saturn* was deposed by his son *Jupiter,* believed nevertheless the same *Jupiter* to be the avenger of injustice: somewhat like to a piece of law in *Coke's Commentaries on Littleton;* where he says, if the right heir of the crown be attainted of treason; yet the crown shall descend to him, and *eo instante* the attainder be void: from which instances a man will be very prone to infer; that when the heir apparent of a kingdom, shall kill him that is in possession, though his father; you may call it injustice, or by what other name you will; yet it can never be against reason, seeing all the voluntary actions of men tend to the benefit of themselves; and those actions are most reasonable, that conduce most to their ends. This specious reasoning is nevertheless false.

For the question is not of promises mutual, where there is no security of performance on either side; as when there is no civil power erected over the parties promising; for such promises are no covenants: but either where one of the parties has performed already; or where there is a power to make him perform; there is the question whether it be against reason, that is, against the benefit of the other to perform, or not. And I say it is not against reason. For the manifestation whereof, we are to consider; first, that when a man doth a thing, which notwithstanding any thing can be foreseen, and reckoned on, tendeth to his own destruction, howsoever some accident which he could not expect, arriving may turn it to his benefit; yet such events do not make it reasonably or wisely done. Secondly, that in a condition of war, wherein every man to every man, for want of a common power to keep them all in awe, is an enemy, there is no man can hope by his own strength, or wit, to defend himself from destruction, without the help of confederates; where every one expects the same defence by the confederation, that any one else does: and therefore he which declares he thinks it reason to deceive those that help him, can in reason expect no other means of safety, than what can be had from his own single power. He therefore that breaketh his covenant, and consequently declareth that he thinks he may with reason do so, cannot be received into any society, that unite themselves for peace and defence, but by the error of them that receive him; nor when he is received, be retained in it, without seeing the danger of their error; which errors a man cannot reasonably reckon upon as the means of his security: and therefore if he be left, or cast out of society, he perisheth; and if he live in society, it is by the errors of other men, which he could not foresee, nor reckon upon; and consequently against the reason of his preservation; and so, as all men that contribute not to his destruction, forbear him only out of ignorance of what is good for themselves.

As for the instance of gaining the secure and perpetual felicity of heaven, by any way; it is frivolous: there being but one way imaginable; and that is not breaking, but keeping of covenant.

And for the other instances of attaining sovereignty by rebellion; it is manifest, that though the event follow, yet because it cannot reasonably be expected, but rather the contrary; and because by gaining it so, others are taught to gain the same in like manner, the attempt thereof is against reason. Justice therefore, that is to say, keeping of covenant, is a rule of reason, by which we are forbidden to do any thing destructive to our life; and consequently a law of nature.

There be some that proceed further; and will not have the law of nature to be those rules which conduce to the preservation of man's life on earth; but to the attaining of an eternal felicity after death; to which they think the breach of covenant may conduce; and consequently be just and reasonable; (such are they that think it a work of merit to kill, or depose, or rebel against, the sovereign power constituted over them by their own consent.) But because there is no natural knowledge of man's estate after death; much less of the reward that is then to be given to breach of faith; but only a belief grounded upon other men's saying, that they know it supernaturally, or that they know those, that knew them, that knew others, that knew it supernaturally; breach of faith cannot be called a precept of reason, or nature.

Second Treatise of Government

~

JOHN LOCKE

John Locke (1632–1704) made important contributions in metaphysics, epistemology, and political philosophy. His ardent defense of liberty is reflected in the words of the Declaration of Independence.

CHAPTER II • OF THE STATE OF NATURE

4. To understand political power, right, and derive it from its original, we must consider what state all men are naturally in, and that is, *a state of perfect freedom* to order their actions, and dispose of their possessions and persons, as they think fit, within the bounds of the law of nature; without asking leave, or depending upon the will of any other man.

A *state also of equality,* wherein all the power and jurisdiction is reciprocal, no one having more than another; there being nothing more evident, than that creatures of the same species and rank, promiscuously born to all the same advantages of nature, and the use of the same faculties, should also be equal one amongst another without subordination or subjection; unless the lord and master of them all should, by any manifest declaration of his will, set one above another, and confer on him, by an evident and clear appointment, an undoubted right to dominion and sovereignty.

5. This *equality* of men by nature, the judicious Hooker looks upon as so evident in itself, and beyond all question, that he makes it the foundation of that obligation to mutual love amongst men, on which he builds the duties we owe one another, and from whence he derives the great maxims of *justice* and *charity.* His words are, "The like natural inducement hath brought men to know, that it is no less their duty to love others than themselves; for seeing those things which are equal, must needs all have one measure; if I cannot but wish to receive good, even as much at every man's hands, as any man can wish unto his own soul, how should I look to have any part of my desire herein satisfied, unless myself be careful to satisfy the like desire, which is undoubtedly in other men, being of one and the same nature? To have any thing offered them repugnant to this desire, must needs in all respects grieve them as much as me; so that if I do harm, I must look to suffer, there being no reason that others should shew greater measure of love to me, than they have by me shewed unto them: my desire therefore to be loved of my equals in nature, as much as possibly may be, imposeth upon me a natural duty of bearing to them-ward fully the like affection: From which relation of equality between ourselves and them that are as ourselves, what several rules and canons natural reason hath drawn, for direction of life, no man is ignorant."

6. But though this be *a state of liberty,* yet *it is not a state of licence:* though man in that state have an uncontrollable liberty to dispose of his person or possessions, yet he has not liberty to destroy himself, or so much as any creature in his possession, but where some nobler use than its bare preservation calls for it. The *state of nature* has a law of nature to govern it, which obliges every one: And reason, which is that law, teaches all mankind, who will but consult it, that being all *equal and independent,* no one ought to

From John Locke, *Second Treatise of Government.*

harm another in his life, health, liberty, or possessions. For men being all the workmanship of one omnipotent and infinitely wise Maker; all the servants of one sovereign master, sent into the world by his order, and about his business; they are his property, whose workmanship they are, made to last during his, not another's pleasure. And being furnished with like faculties, sharing all in one community of nature, there cannot be supposed any such subordination among us, that may authorize us to destroy another, as if we were made for one another's uses, as the inferior ranks of creatures are for ours. Every one, as he is *bound to preserve himself,* and not to quit his station willfully, so by the like reason, when his own preservation comes not in competition, ought he, as much as he can, *to preserve the rest of mankind,* and may not, unless it be to do justice to an offender, take away or impair the life, or what tends to the preservation of life, the liberty, health, limb, or goods of another.

7. And that all men may be restrained from invading others rights, and from doing hurt to one another, and the law of nature be observed, which willeth the peace and *preservation of all mankind,* the *execution* of the law of nature is, in that state, put into every man's hands, whereby every one has a right to punish the transgressors of that law to such a degree as may hinder its violation. For the *law of nature* would, as all other laws that concern men in this world, be in vain, if there were no body that in the state of nature had a *power to execute* that law, and thereby preserve the innocent and restrain offenders. And if any one in the state of nature may punish another for any evil he has done, every one may do so. For in that *state of perfect equality,* where naturally there is no superiority or jurisdiction of one over another, what any may do in prosecution of that law, every one must needs have a right to do.

8. And thus, in the state of nature, *one man comes by a power over another;* but yet no absolute or arbitrary power, to use a criminal, when he has got him in his hands, according to the passionate heats, or boundless extravagancy of his own will; but only to retribute to him, so far as calm reason and conscience dictate, what is proportionate to his *transgression;* which is so much as may serve for reparation and

restraint. For these two are the only reasons, why one man may lawfully do harm to another, which is that we call *punishment.* In transgressing the law of nature, the offender declares himself to live by another rule than that of reason and common equity, which is that measure God has set to the actions of men, for their mutual security; and so he becomes dangerous to mankind, the tye, which is to secure them from injury and violence, being slighted and broken by him. Which being a trespass against the whole species, and the peace and safety of it, provided for by the law of nature; every man upon this score, by the right he hath to preserve mankind in general, may restrain, or, where it is necessary, destroy things noxious to them, and so may bring such evil on any one, who hath transgressed that law, as may make him repent the doing of it, and thereby deter him, and by his example others, from doing the like mischief. And in this case, and upon this ground, *every man hath a right to punish the offender, and be executioner of the law of nature.*

9. I doubt not but this will seem a very strange doctrine to some men: but before they condemn it, I desire them to resolve me, by what right any prince or state can put to death, or *punish an alien,* for any crime he commits in their country. It is certain their laws, by virtue of any sanction they receive from the promulgated will of the legislative, reach not a stranger. They speak not to him, nor, if they did, is he bound to hearken to them. The legislative authority, by which they are in force over the subjects of that commonwealth, hath no power over him. Those who have the supreme power of making laws in England, France, or Holland, are to an Indian but like the rest of the world, men without authority: And therefore, if by the law of nature every man hath not a power to punish offences against it, as he soberly judges the case to require, I see not how the magistrates of any community can *punish an alien* of another country; since in reference to him, they can have no more power, than what every man naturally may have over another.

10. Besides the crime which consists in violating the law, and varying from the right rule of reason, whereby a man so far becomes degenerate, and declares himself to quit the principles of human

nature, and to be a noxious creature, there is commonly injury done to some person or other, and some other man receives damage by his transgression, in which case he who hath received any damage, has besides the right of punishment common to him with other men, a particular right to seek *reparation* from him that has done it. And any other person who finds it just, may also join with him that is injured, and assist him in recovering from the offender so much as may make satisfaction for the harm he has suffered.

11. From these *two distinct rights,* the one of *punishing* the *crime for restraint,* and preventing the like offence, which right of punishing is in every body; the other of taking reparation, which belongs only to the injured party; comes it to pass that the magistrate, who by being magistrate, hath the common right of punishing put into his hands, can often, where the public good demands not the execution of the law, *remit* the punishment of criminal offences by his own authority, but yet cannot *remit* the satisfaction due to any private man, for the damage he has received. That, he who has suffered the damage has a right to demand in his own name, and he alone can remit: The damnified person has this power of appropriating to himself the goods or service of the offender, *by right of self-preservation,* as every man has a power to punish the crime, to prevent its being committed again, *by the right he has of preserving all mankind;* and doing all reasonable things he can in order to that end: And thus it is, that every man, in the state of nature, has a power to kill a murderer, both to deter others from doing the like injury, which no reparation can compensate, by the example of the punishment that attends it from every body, and also *to secure* men from the attempts of a criminal, who having renounced reason, the common rule and measure, God hath given to mankind, hath by the unjust violence and slaughter he hath committed upon one, declared war against all mankind; and therefore may be destroyed as a *lion* or a *tiger,* one of those wild savage beasts, with whom men can have no society nor security: And upon this is grounded the great law of nature, "Whoso sheddeth mans blood, by man shall his blood be shed." And Cain was so fully convinced, that every one had a right to destroy such a criminal, that after the murder of his brother, he cries out, "Every one that findeth me, shall slay me;" so plain was it writ in the hearts of all mankind.

12. By the same reason may a man in the state of nature *punish the lesser breaches* of that law. It will perhaps be demanded, with death? I answer, each transgression may be *punished* to that *degree,* and with so much *severity,* as will suffice to make it an ill bargain to the offender, give him cause to repent, and terrify others from doing the like. Every offence that can be committed in the state of nature, may in the state of nature be also punished equally, and as far forth as it may, in a commonwealth: for though it would be besides my present purpose, to enter here into the particulars of the law of nature, or its *measures of punishment;* yet it is certain there is such a law, and that too, as intelligible and plain to a rational creature, and a studier of that law, as the positive laws of commonwealths, nay possibly plainer; as much as reason is easier to be understood, than the fancies and intricate contrivances of men, following contrary and hidden interests put into words; for so truly are a great part of the *municipal laws* of countries, which are only so far right, as they are founded on the law of nature, by which they are to be regulated and interpreted.

13. To this strange doctrine, viz. That *in the state of nature every one has the executive power* of the law of nature, I doubt not but it will be objected, that it is unreasonable for men to be judges in their own cases, that self-love will make men partial to themselves and their friends: And on the other side, that ill nature, passion and revenge will carry them too far in punishing others; and hence nothing but confusion and disorder will follow, and that therefore God hath certainly appointed government to restrain the partiality and violence of men. I easily grant, that civil government is the proper remedy for the inconveniencies of the state of nature, which must certainly be great, where men may be judges in their own case, since it is easy to be imagined, that he who was so unjust as to do his brother an injury, will scarce be so just as to condemn himself for it: But I shall desire those who make this objection to remember, that *absolute monarchs* are but men, and if government is to be the remedy of those evils, which necessarily follow from men's being judges in their own cases, and the state of nature is therefore not to be endured,

I desire to know what kind of government that is, and how much better it is than the state of nature, where one man commanding a multitude, has the liberty to be judge in his own case, and may do to all his subjects whatever he pleases, without the least liberty to any one to question or control those who execute his pleasure? and in whatsoever he doth, whether led by reason, mistake or passion, must be submitted to? Much better it is in the state of nature, wherein men are not bound to submit to the unjust will of another: And if he that judges, judges amiss in his own, or any other case, he is answerable for it to the rest of mankind. . . .

CHAPTER III • OF THE STATE OF WAR

16. The *state of war* is a state of *enmity* and *destruction:* And therefore declaring by word or action, not a passionate and hasty, but a sedate settled design upon another man's life, *puts him in a state of war* with him against whom he has declared such an intention, and so has exposed his life to the other's power to be taken away by him, or any one that joins with him in his defence, and espouses his quarrel: it being reasonable and just I should have a right to destroy that which threatens me with destruction. For *by the fundamental law of nature, man being to be preserved* as much as possible, when all cannot be preserved, the safety of the innocent is to be preferred: And one may destroy a man who makes war upon him, or has discovered an enmity to his being, for the same reason that he may kill a *wolf* or a *lion;* because such men are not under the ties of the common law of reason, have no other rule, but that of force and violence, and so may be treated as beasts of prey, those dangerous and noxious creatures, that will be sure to destroy him whenever he falls into their power.

17. And hence it is, that he who attempts to get another man into his absolute power, does thereby *put himself into a state of war* with him; it being to be understood as a declaration of a design upon his life. For I have reason to conclude, that he who would get me into his power without my consent, would use me as he pleased when he got me there, and destroy me too when he had a fancy to it; for no body can desire to *have me in his absolute power* unless it be to compel me by force to that which is against the right of my freedom, i.e. make me a slave. To be free from such force is the only security of my preservation; and reason bids me look on him, as an enemy to my preservation, who would take away that freedom which is the fence to it; so that he who makes an *attempt to enslave* me, thereby puts himself into a state of war with me. He that, in the state of nature, *would take away the freedom* that belongs to any one in that state, must necessarily be supposed to have a design to take away every thing else, that *freedom* being the foundation of all the rest: As he that, in the state of society, would take away the freedom belonging to those of that society or commonwealth, must be supposed to design to take away from them every thing else, and so be looked on as *in a state of war.*

18. This makes it lawful for a man to *kill a thief,* who has not in the least hurt him, nor declared any design upon his life, any farther, than by the use of force, so to get him in his power, as to take away his money, or what he pleases, from him; because using force, where he has no right, to get me into his power, let his pretence be what it will, I have no reason to suppose, that he, who would *take away my liberty,* would not, when he had me in his power, take away every thing else. And therefore it is lawful for me to treat him as one who has put *himself into a state of war* with me, i.e. kill him if I can; for to that hazard does he justly expose himself, whoever introduces a state of war, and is aggressor in it.

19. And here we have the plain *difference between the state of nature and the state of war;* which however some men have confounded, are as far distant, as a state of peace, good will, mutual assistance and preservation, and a state of enmity, malice, violence and mutual destruction, are one from another. Men living together according to reason, without a common superior on earth, with authority to judge between them, is *properly the state of nature.* But force, or a declared design of force, upon the person of another, where there is no common superior on earth to appeal to for relief, *is the state of war:* And it is the want of such an appeal gives a man the right of war

even against an aggressor, though he be in society and a fellow subject. Thus a *thief,* whom I cannot harm, but by appeal to the law, for having stolen all that I am worth, I may kill, when he sets on me to rob me but of my horse or coat; because the law, which was made for my preservation, where it cannot interpose to secure my life from present force, which, if lost, is capable of no reparation, permits me my own defence, and the right of war, a liberty to kill the aggressor, because the aggressor allows not time to appeal to our common judge, nor the decision of the law, for remedy in a case where the mischief may be irreparable. *Want of a common judge with authority, puts all men in a state of nature: Force without right, upon a man's person, makes a state of war,* both where there is, and is not, a common judge.

20. But when the actual force is over, the *state of war ceases* between those that are in society, and are equally on both sides subjected to the fair determination of the law; because then there lies open the remedy of appeal for the past injury, and to prevent future harm: but where no such appeal is, as in the state of nature, for want of positive laws, and judges with authority to appeal to, *the state of war once begun, continues* with a right to the innocent party to destroy the other whenever he can, until the aggressor offers peace, and desires reconciliation on such terms as may repair any wrongs he has already done, and secure the innocent for the future: nay, where an appeal to the law, and constituted judges, lies open, but the remedy is denied by a manifest perverting of justice, and a barefaced wresting of the laws to protect or indemnify the violence or injuries of some men, or party of men, *there* it is hard to imagine any thing but *a state of war.* For wherever violence is used, and injury done, though by hands appointed to administer justice, it is still violence and injury, however coloured with the name, pretences, or forms of law, the end whereof being to protect and redress the innocent, by an unbiassed application of it, to all who are under it; wherever that is not *bona fide* done, *war is made* upon the sufferers, who having no appeal on earth to right them, they are left to the only remedy in such cases, an appeal to heaven.

21. To avoid this *state of war* (wherein there is no appeal but to heaven, and wherein every the least dif-ference is apt to end, where there is no authority to decide between the contenders) is one *great reason of men's putting themselves into society,* and quitting the state of nature. For where there is an authority, a power on earth, from which relief can be had by *appeal,* there the continuance of the *state of war* is excluded, and the controversy is decided by that power. Had there been any such court, any superior jurisdiction on earth, to determine the right between Jephthah and the Ammonites, they had never come to *a state of war:* But we see he was forced to appeal to heaven. "The Lord the Judge," says he, "be judge this day, between the children of Israel and the children of Ammon," *Judg.* xi. 27, and then prosecuting, and relying on his appeal, he leads out his army to battle: and therefore in such controversies, where the question is put, *who shall be judge?* it cannot be meant, who shall decide the controversy; every one knows what Jephthah here tells us, that "the Lord the Judge" shall judge. Where there is no judge on earth, the appeal lies to God in heaven. That question then cannot mean, who shall judge? whether another hath put himself in a *state of war* with me, and whether I may, as Jephthah did, *appeal to heaven* in it? of that I myself can only be judge in my own conscience, as I will answer it, at the great day, to the supreme judge of all men. . . .

CHAPTER VIII • OF THE BEGINNING OF POLITICAL SOCIETIES

95. Men being, as has been said, by nature, all free, equal, and independent, no one can be put out of this estate, and subjected to the political power of another, without his own consent. The only way, whereby any one divests himself of his natural liberty, and puts on the *bonds of civil society,* is by agreeing with other men to join and unite into a community, for their comfortable, safe, and peaceable living one amongst another, in a secure enjoyment of their properties, and a greater security against any, that are not of it. This any number of men may do, because it injures not the freedom of the rest; they are left as they were in the liberty of the state of nature. When any number of men have so *consented to make one community or government,* they are thereby

presently incorporated, and make *one body politic,* wherein the *majority* have a right to act and conclude the rest.

96. For when any number of men have, by the consent of every individual, made a *community,* they have thereby made that *community* one body, with a power to act as one body, which is only by the will and determination of the majority. For that which acts any community, being only the *consent* of the individuals of it, and it being necessary to that which greater force carries it, which is the *consent of the majority:* or else it is impossible it should act or continue one body, one community, which the consent of every individual that united into it, agreed that it should; and so every one is bound by that consent to be concluded by the majority. And therefore we see, that in assemblies, impowered to act by positive laws, where no number is set by that positive law which impowers them, the *act of the majority* passes for the act of the whole, and of course determines, as having, by the law of nature and reason, the power of the whole.

97. And thus every man, by consenting with others to make one body politic under one government, puts himself under an obligation, to every one of that society, to submit to the determination of the majority, and to be concluded by it; or else this *original compact,* whereby he with others incorporate into one society, would signify nothing, and be no compact, if he be left free, and under no other ties than he was in before in the state of nature. For what appearance would there be of any compact? What new engagement if he were no farther tied by any decrees of the society, than he himself thought fit, and did actually consent to? This would be still as great a liberty, as he himself had before his compact, or any one else in the state of nature hath, who may submit himself, and consent to any acts of it if he thinks fit.

98. For if *the consent of the majority* shall not, in reason, be received as *the act of the whole,* and conclude every individual; nothing but the consent of every individual can make any thing to be the act of the whole: But such a consent is next to impossible ever to be had, if we consider the infirmities of health, and avocations of business, which in a number, though much less than that of a commonwealth, will

necessarily keep many away from the public assembly. To which if we add the variety of opinions, and contrariety of interests, which unavoidably happen in all collections of men, the coming into society upon such terms would be only like Cato's coming into the theatre, only to go out again. Such a constitution as this would make the mighty *leviathan* of a shorter duration than the feeblest creatures, and not let it outlast the day it was born in: which cannot be supposed, till we can think, that rational creatures should desire and constitute societies only to be dissolved. For where the majority cannot conclude the rest, there they cannot act as one body, and consequently will be immediately dissolved again.

99. Whosoever therefore out of a state of nature unite into a community, must be understood to give up all the power, necessary to the ends for which they unite into society, to the majority of the community, unless they expressly agreed in any number greater than the majority. And this is done by barely agreeing to *unite into one political society,* which is *all the compact* that is, or needs be, between the individuals, that enter into, or make up a commonwealth. And, thus that, which begins and actually *constitutes any political society,* is nothing, but the consent of any number of freemen capable of a majority, to unite and incorporate into such a society. And this is that, and that only, which did, or could give beginning to any lawful government in the world. . . .

119. Every man being, as has been shewed, naturally free, and nothing being able to put him into subjection to any earthly power, but only his own consent; it is to be considered, what shall be understood to be a *sufficient declaration of* a man's *consent, to make him subject* to the laws of any government. There is a common distinction of an express and a tacit consent, which will concern our present case. No body doubts but an express consent, of any man entering into any society, makes him a perfect member of that society, a subject of that government. The difficulty is, what ought to be looked upon as a *tacit consent,* and how far it binds, i.e. how far any one shall be looked on to have consented, and thereby submitted to any government, where he has made no expressions of it at all. And to this I say, that every man, that hath any possessions, or enjoyment of any

part of the dominions of any government, doth thereby give his *tacit consent,* and is as far forth obliged to obedience to the laws of that government, during such enjoyment, as any one under it; whether this his possession be of land, to him and his heirs for ever, or a lodging only for a week; or whether it be barely travelling freely on the highway: and, in effect, it reaches as far as the very being of any one within the territories of that government.

120. To understand this the better, it is fit to consider, that every man, when he at first incorporates himself into any commonwealth, he, by his uniting himself thereunto, annexed also, and submits to the community, those possessions which he has, or shall acquire, that do not already belong to any other government. For it would be a direct contradiction, for any one to enter into society with others for the securing and regulating of property, and yet to suppose, his land, whose property is to be regulated by the laws of the society, should be exempt from the jurisdiction of that government, to which he himself, the proprietor of the land, is a subject. By the same act therefore, whereby any one unites his person, which was before free, to any commonwealth; by the same he unites his possessions, which were before free, to it also: and they become, both of them, person and possession, subject to the government and dominion of that commonwealth, as long as it hath a being. Whoever therefore, from thenceforth, by inheritance, purchase, permission, or otherways, *enjoys any part of the land* so annexed to, and under the government *of that commonwealth, must take it with the condition* it is under; that is, *of submitting to the government of the commonwealth,* under whose jurisdiction it is, as far forth as any subject of it.

121. But since the government has a direct jurisdiction only over the land, and reaches the possessor of it, (before he has actually incorporated himself in the society) only as he dwells upon, and enjoys that; the obligation any one is under, by virtue of such enjoyment, to *submit to the government, begins and ends with the enjoyment:* so that whenever the owner, who has given nothing but such a tacit consent to the government, will, by donation, sale, or otherwise, quit the said possession, he is at liberty to go and incorporate himself into any other commonwealth; or to agree with others to begin a new one, *in vacuis locis,* in any part of the world they can find free and unpossessed: whereas he, that has once, by actual agreement, and any express declaration, given his *consent* to be of any commonwealth, is perpetually and indispensably obliged to be, and remain unalterably a subject to it, and can never be again in the liberty of the state of nature; unless, by any calamity, the government he was under comes to be dissolved, or else by some public act cuts him off from being any longer a member of it.

122. But submitting to the laws of any country, living quietly, and enjoying privileges and protection under them, *makes not a man a member of that society:* this is only a local protection and homage due to and from all those, who, not being in a state of war, come within the territories belonging to any government, to all parts whereof the force of its laws extends. But this no more *makes a man a member of that society,* a perpetual subject of that commonwealth, than it would make a man a subject to another, in whose family he found it convenient to abide for some time, though, whilst he continued in it, he were obliged to comply with the laws, and submit to the government he found there. And thus we see, that foreigners, by living all their lives under another government, and enjoying the privileges and protection of it, though they are bound, even in conscience, to submit to its administration, as far forth as any denison; yet do not thereby come to be *subjects or members of that commonwealth.* Nothing can make any man so, but his actually entering into it by positive engagement, and express promise and compact. This is that, which I think concerning the beginning of political societies, and that *consent which makes any one a member of any commonwealth.*

A Theory of Justice

~

JOHN RAWLS

John Rawls is James B. Conant University Professor, Emeritus, at Harvard University. After publishing *A Theory of Justice* in 1971 he continued to rethink his views on justice, resulting in his later books *Political Liberalism* and *The Law of Peoples*.

THE MAIN IDEA OF THE THEORY OF JUSTICE

My aim is to present a conception of justice which generalizes and carries to a higher level of abstraction the familiar theory of the social contract as found, say, in Locke, Rousseau, and Kant.[1] In order to do this we are not to think of the original contract as one to enter a particular society or to set up a particular form of government. Rather, the guiding idea is that the principles of justice for the basic structure of society are the object of the original agreement. They are the principles that free and rational persons concerned to further their own interests would accept in an initial position of equality as defining the fundamental terms of their association. These principles are to regulate all further agreements; they specify the kinds of social cooperation that can be entered into and the forms of government that can be established. This way of regarding the principles of justice I shall call justice as fairness.

Thus we are to imagine that those who engage in social cooperation choose together, in one joint act, the principles which are to assign basic rights and duties and to determine the division of social benefits. Men are to decide in advance how they are to regulate their claims against one another and what is to be the foundation charter of their society. Just as each person must decide by rational reflection what con-

stitutes his good, that is, the system of ends which it is rational for him to pursue, so a group of persons must decide once and for all what is to count among them as just and unjust. The choice which rational men would make in this hypothetical situation of equal liberty, assuming for the present that this choice problem has a solution, determines the principles of justice.

In justice as fairness the original position of equality corresponds to the state of nature in the traditional theory of the social contract. This original position is not, of course, thought of as an actual historical state of affairs, much less as a primitive condition of culture. It is understood as a purely hypothetical situation characterized so as to lead to a certain conception of justice.[2] Among the essential features of this situation is that no one knows his place in society, his class position or social status, nor does any one know his fortune in the distribution of natural assets and abilities, his intelligence, strength, and the like. I shall even assume that the parties do not know their conceptions of the good or their special psychological propensities. The principles of justice are chosen behind a veil of ignorance. This ensures that no one is advantaged or disadvantaged in the choice of principles by the outcome of natural chance or the contingency of social circumstances. Since all are similarly situated and no one is able to design principles to favor his particular condition, the principles of justice are the result of a fair agreement or bargain. For given the circumstances of the original position, the symmetry of everyone's relations to each other, this initial situation is fair between individuals as moral persons, that is, as rational beings with their own ends and capable, I shall assume, of a sense of justice. The original position is, one might say, the appropriate initial status quo, and thus the fundamental agreements reached in it are fair. This explains the propriety of the name "justice as fairness." . . .

FURTHER CASES OF PRIORITY

I now wish to give the final statement of the two principles of justice for institutions. . . .

First Principle

Each person is to have an equal right to the most extensive total system of equal basic liberties compatible with a similar system of liberty for all.

Second Principle

Social and economic inequalities are to be arranged so that they are both:

  (a) to the greatest benefit of the least advantaged, consistent with the just savings principle, and
  (b) attached to offices and positions open to all under conditions of fair equality of opportunity.

First Priority Rule (the Priority of Liberty)

The principles of justice are to be ranked in lexical order and therefore the basic liberties can be restricted only for the sake of liberty. There are two cases:

  (a) a less extensive liberty must strengthen the total system of liberties shared by all;
  (b) a less than equal liberty must be acceptable to those with the lesser liberty.

Second Priority Rule (the Priority of Justice over Efficiency and Welfare)

The second principle of justice is lexically prior to the principle of efficiency and to that of maximizing the sum of advantages; and fair opportunity is prior to the difference principle. There are two cases:

  (a) an inequality of opportunity must enhance the opportunities of those with the lesser opportunity;
  (b) an excessive rate of saving must on balance mitigate the burden of those bearing this hardship.

THE VEIL OF IGNORANCE

The idea of the original position is to set up a fair procedure so that any principles agreed to will be just. The aim is to use the notion of pure procedural justice as a basis of theory. Somehow we must nullify the effects of specific contingencies which put men at odds and tempt them to exploit social and natural circumstances to their own advantage. Now in order to do this I assume that the parties are situated behind a veil of ignorance. They do not know how the various alternatives will affect their own particular case and they are obliged to evaluate principles solely on the basis of general considerations.[3]

It is assumed, then, that the parties do not know certain kinds of particular facts. First of all, no one knows his place in society, his class position or social status; nor does he know his fortune in the distribution of natural assets and abilities, his intelligence and strength, and the like. Nor, again, does anyone know his conception of the good, the particulars of his rational plan of life, or even the special features of his psychology such as his aversion to risk or liability to optimism or pessimism. More than this, I assume that the parties do not know the particular circumstances of their own society. That is, they do not know its economic or political situation, or the level of civilization and culture it has been able to achieve. The persons in the original position have no information as to which generation they belong. These broader restrictions on knowledge are appropriate in part because questions of social justice arise between generations as well as within them, for example, the question of the appropriate rate of capital saving and of the conservation of natural resources and the environment of nature. There is also, theoretically anyway, the question of a reasonable genetic policy. In these cases too, in order to carry through the idea of the original position, the parties must not know the contingencies that set them in opposition. They must choose principles the consequences of which they are prepared to live with whatever generation they turn out to belong to.

As far as possible, then, the only particular facts which the parties know is that their society is subject to the circumstances of justice and whatever this implies. It is taken for granted, however, that they know the general facts about human society. They understand political affairs and the principles of economic theory; they know the basis of social organization and the laws of human psychology. Indeed, the parties are presumed to know whatever general facts affect the choice of the principles of justice. There are no limitations on general information, that is, on general laws and theories, since conceptions of justice must be adjusted to the characteristics of the systems of social cooperation which they are to regulate, and there is no reason to rule out these facts. It is, for example, a consideration against a conception of justice that, in view of the laws of moral psychology, men would not acquire a desire to act upon it even when the institutions of their society satisfied it. For in this case there would be difficulty in securing the stability of social cooperation. An important feature of a conception of justice is that it should generate its own support. Its principles should be such that when they are embodied in the basic structure of society men tend to acquire the corresponding sense of justice and develop a desire to act in accordance with its principles. In this case a conception of justice is stable. This kind of general information is admissible in the original position.

The notion of the veil of ignorance raises several difficulties. Some may object that the exclusion of nearly all particular information makes it difficult to grasp what is meant by the original position. Thus it may be helpful to observe that one or more persons

can at any time enter this position, or perhaps better, simulate the deliberations of this hypothetical situation, simply by reasoning in accordance with the appropriate restrictions. In arguing for a conception of justice we must be sure that it is among the permitted alternatives and satisfies the stipulated formal constraints. No considerations can be advanced in its favor unless they would be rational ones for us to urge were we to lack the kind of knowledge that is excluded. The evaluation of principles must proceed in terms of the general consequences of their public recognition and universal application, it being assumed that they will be complied with by everyone. To say that a certain conception of justice would be chosen in the original position is equivalent to saying that rational deliberation satisfying certain conditions and restrictions would reach a certain conclusion. If necessary, the argument to this result could be set out more formally. I shall, however, speak throughout in terms of the notion of the original position. It is more economical and suggestive, and brings out certain essential features that otherwise one might easily overlook.

These remarks show that the original position is not to be thought of as a general assembly which includes at one moment everyone who will live at some time; or, much less, as an assembly of everyone who could live at some time. It is not a gathering of all actual or possible persons. If we conceived of the original position in either of these ways, the conception would cease to be a natural guide to intuition and would lack a clear sense. In any case, the original position must be interpreted so that one can at any time adopt its perspective. It must make no difference when one takes up this viewpoint, or who does so: the restrictions must be such that the same principles are always chosen. The veil of ignorance is a key condition in meeting this requirement. It insures not only that the information available is relevant, but that it is at all times the same.

It may be protested that the condition of the veil of ignorance is irrational. Surely, some may object, principles should be chosen in the light of all the knowledge available. There are various replies to this contention. Here I shall sketch those which emphasize the simplifications that need to be made if one is to have any theory at all. . . . To begin with, it is clear that since the differences among the parties are unknown to them, and everyone is equally rational and similarly situated, each is convinced by the same arguments. Therefore, we can view the agreement in the original position from the standpoint of one person selected at random. If anyone after due reflection prefers a conception of justice to another, then they all do, and a unanimous agreement can be reached. We can, to make the circumstances more vivid, imagine that the parties are required to communicate with each other through a referee as intermediary, and that he is to announce which alternatives have been suggested and the reasons offered in their support. He forbids the attempt to form coalitions, and he informs the parties when they have come to an understanding. But such a referee is actually superfluous, assuming that the deliberations of the parties must be similar.

Thus there follows the very important consequence that the parties have no basis for bargaining in the usual sense. No one knows his situation in society nor his natural assets, and therefore no one is in a position to tailor principles to his advantage. We might imagine that one of the contractees threatens to hold out unless the others agree to principles favorable to him. But how does he know which principles are especially in his interests? The same holds for the formation of coalitions: if a group were to decide to band together to the disadvantage of the others, they would not know how to favor themselves in the choice of principles. Even if they could get everyone to agree to their proposal, they would have no assurance that it was to their advantage, since they cannot identify themselves either by name or description. The one case where this conclusion fails is that of saving. Since the persons in the original position know that they are contemporaries (taking the present time of entry interpretation), they can favor their generation by refusing to make any sacrifices at all for their successors; they simply acknowledge the principle that no one has a duty to save for posterity. Previous generations have saved or they have not; there is nothing the parties can now do to affect that. So in this instance the veil of ignorance fails to secure the desired result. Therefore, to handle the question of justice between generations, I modify the motiva-tion assumption and add a further constraint. With these adjustments, no generation is able to formulate principles especially designed to advance its own cause and some significant limits on savings principles can be derived. Whatever a person's temporal position, each is forced to choose for all.[4]

The restrictions on particular information in the original position are, then, of fundamental importance. Without them we would not be able to work out any definite theory of justice at all. We would have to be content with a vague formula stating that justice is what would be agreed to without being able to say much, if anything, about the substance of the agreement itself. The formal constraints of the concept of right, those applying to principles directly, are not sufficient for our purpose. The veil of ignorance makes possible a unanimous choice of a particular conception of justice. Without these limitations on knowledge the bargaining problem of the original position would be hopelessly complicated. Even if theoretically a solution were to exist, we would not, at present anyway, be able to determine it.

The notion of the veil of ignorance is implicit, I think, in Kant's ethics. Nevertheless the problem of defining the knowledge of the parties and of characterizing the alternatives open to them has often been passed over, even by contract theories. Sometimes the situation definitive of moral deliberation is presented in such an indeterminate way that one cannot ascertain how it will turn out. Thus Perry's doctrine is essentially contractarian: he holds that social and personal integration must proceed by entirely different principles, the latter by rational prudence, the former by the concurrence of persons of good will. He would appear to reject utilitarianism on much the same grounds suggested earlier: namely, that it improperly extends the principle of choice for one person to choices facing society. The right course of action is characterized as that which best advances social aims as these would be formulated by reflective agreement, given that the parties have full knowledge of the circumstances and are moved by a benevolent concern for one another's interests. No effort is made, however, to specify in any precise way the possible outcomes of this sort of agreement. Indeed, without a far more elaborate account, no conclusions can be drawn.[5] I do not wish here to criticize others; rather, I want to explain the necessity for what may seem at times like so many irrelevant details.

Now the reasons for the veil of ignorance go beyond mere simplicity. We want to define the original position so that we get the desired solution. If a knowledge of particulars is allowed, then the outcome is biased by arbitrary contingencies. As already observed, to each according to his threat advantage is not a principle of justice. If the original position is to yield agreements that are just, the parties must be fairly situated and treated equally as moral persons. The arbitrariness of the world must be corrected for by adjusting the circumstances of the initial contractual situation. Moreover, if in choosing principles we required unanimity even when there is full information, only a few rather obvious cases could be decided. A conception of justice based on unanimity in these circumstances would indeed be weak and trivial. But once knowledge is excluded, the requirement of unanimity is not out of place and the fact that it can be satisfied is of great importance. It enables us to say of the preferred conception of justice that it represents a genuine reconciliation of interests.

A final comment. For the most part I shall suppose that the parties possess all general information. No general facts are closed to them. I do this mainly to avoid complications. Nevertheless a conception of justice is to be the public basis of the terms of social cooperation. Since common understanding necessitates certain bounds on the complexity of principles, there may likewise be limits on the use of theoretical knowledge in the original position. Now clearly it would be very difficult to classify and to grade the complexity of the various sorts of general facts. I shall make no attempt to do this. We do however recognize an intricate theoretical construction when we meet one. Thus it seems reasonable to say that other things equal one conception of justice is to be preferred to another when it is founded upon markedly simpler general facts, and its choice does not depend upon elaborate calculations in the light of a vast array of theoretically defined possibilities. It is desirable that the grounds for a public conception of justice should be evident to everyone when circumstances permit. This consideration favors, I believe, the two principles of justice over the criterion of utility.

THE RATIONALITY OF THE PARTIES

I have assumed throughout that the persons in the original position are rational. But I have also assumed that they do not know their conception of the good. This means that while they know that they have some rational plan of life, they do not know the details of this plan, the particular ends and interests which it is calculated to promote. How, then, can they decide which conceptions of justice are most to their advantage? Or must we suppose that they are reduced to mere guessing? To meet this difficulty, I postulate that they accept the account of the good touched upon in the preceding chapter: they assume that they normally prefer more primary social goods rather than less. Of course, it may turn out, once the veil of ignorance is removed, that some of them for religious or other reasons may not, in fact, want more of these goods. But from the standpoint of the original position, it is rational for the parties to suppose that they do want a larger share, since in any case they are not compelled to accept more if they do not wish to. Thus even though the parties are deprived of information about their particular ends, they have enough knowledge to rank the alternatives. They know that in general they must try to protect their liberties, widen their opportunities, and enlarge their means for promoting their aims whatever these are. Guided by the theory of the good and the general facts of moral psychology, their deliberations are no longer guesswork. They can make a rational decision in the ordinary sense.

The concept of rationality invoked here, with the exception of one essential feature, is the standard one familiar in social theory.[6] Thus in the usual way, a rational person is thought to have a coherent set of preferences between the options open to him. He ranks these options according to how well they further his purposes; he follows the plan which will satisfy more of his desires rather than less, and which has the greater chance of being successfully executed. The special assumption I make is that a rational individual does not suffer from envy. He is not ready to accept a loss for himself if only others have less as well. He is not downcast by the knowledge or perception that others have a larger index of primary social goods. Or at least this is true as long as the differences between himself and others do not exceed certain limits, and he does not believe that the existing inequalities are founded on injustice or are the result of letting chance work itself out for no compensating social purpose.

The assumption that the parties are not moved by envy raises certain questions. Perhaps we should also assume that they are not liable to various other feelings such as shame and humiliation. Now a satisfactory account of justice will eventually have to deal with these matters too, but for the present I shall leave these complications aside. Another objection to our procedure is that it is too unrealistic. Certainly men are afflicted with these feelings. How can a conception of justice ignore this fact? I shall meet this problem by dividing the argument for the principles of justice into two parts. In the first part, the principles are derived on the supposition that envy does not exist; while in the second, we consider whether the conception arrived at is feasible in view of the circumstances of human life.

One reason for this procedure is that envy tends to make everyone worse off. In this sense it is collectively disadvantageous. Presuming its absence amounts to supposing that in the choice of principles men should think of themselves as having their own plan of life which is sufficient for itself. They have a secure sense of their own worth so that they have no desire to abandon any of their aims provided others have less means to further theirs. I shall work out a conception of justice on this stipulation to see what happens. Later I shall try to show that when the principles adopted are put into practice, they lead to social arrangements in which envy and other destructive feelings are not likely to be strong. The conception of justice eliminates the conditions that give rise to disruptive attitudes. It is, therefore, inherently stable.

The assumption of mutually disinterested rationality, then, comes to this: the persons in the original position try to acknowledge principles which advance their system of ends as far as possible. They do this by attempting to win for themselves the highest index of primary social goods, since this enables them to promote their conception of the good most effectively whatever it turns out to be. The parties do not seek to confer benefits or to impose injuries on one another; they are not moved by affection or rancor. Nor do they try to gain relative to each other; they are not envious or vain. Put in terms of a game, we might say: they strive for as high an absolute score as possible. They do not wish a high or a low score for their opponents, nor do they seek to maximize or minimize the difference between their successes and those of others. The idea of a game does not really apply, since the parties are not concerned to win but to get as many points as possible judged by their own system of ends.

There is one further assumption to guarantee strict compliance. The parties are presumed to be capable of a sense of justice and this fact is public knowledge among them. This condition is to insure the integrity of the agreement made in the original position. It does not mean that in their deliberations the parties apply some particular conception of justice, for this would defeat the point of the motivation assumption. Rather, it means that the parties can rely on each other to understand and to act in accordance with whatever principles are finally agreed to. Once principles are acknowledged the parties can depend on one another to conform to them. In reaching an agreement, then, they know that their undertaking is not in vain: their capacity for a sense of justice insures that the principles chosen will be respected. It is essential to observe, however, that this assumption still permits the consideration of men's capacity to act on the various conceptions of justice. The general facts of human psychology and the principles of moral learning are relevant matters for the parties to examine. If a conception of justice is unlikely to generate its own support, or lacks stability, this fact must not be overlooked. For then a different conception of justice might be preferred. The assumption only says that the parties have a capacity for justice in a purely formal sense: taking everything relevant into account, including the general facts of moral psychology, the parties will adhere to the principles eventually chosen. They are rational in that they will not enter into agreements they know they cannot keep, or can do so only with great difficulty. Along with other considerations, they count the strains of commitment. Thus in assessing conceptions of justice the persons in the original position are to assume that the one they adopt will be strictly complied with. The consequences of their agreement are to be worked out on this basis. . . .

We can turn now to the choice of principles. But first I shall mention a few misunderstandings to be avoided. First of all, we must keep in mind that the parties in the original position are theoretically defined individuals. The grounds for their consent are set out by the description of the contractual situation and their preference for primary goods. Thus to say that the principles of justice would be adopted is to say how these persons would decide being moved in ways our account describes. Of course, when we try to simulate the original position in everyday life, that is, when we try to conduct ourselves in moral argument as its constraints require, we will presumably find that our deliberations and judgments are influenced by our special inclinations and attitudes. Surely it will prove difficult to correct for our various propensities and aversions in striving to adhere to the conditions of this idealized situation. But none of this affects the contention that in the original position rational persons so characterized would make a certain decision. This proposition belongs to the theory of justice. It is another question how well human beings can assume this role in regulating their practical reasoning.

Since the persons in the original position are assumed to take no interest in one another's interests (although they may have a concern for third parties), it may be thought that justice as fairness is itself an egoistic theory. It is not, of course, one of the three forms of egoism mentioned earlier, but some may think, as Schopenhauer thought of Kant's doctrine, that it is egoistic nevertheless.[7] Now this is a misconception. For the fact that in the original position the parties are characterized as mutually disinterested does not entail that persons in ordinary life, or in a well-ordered society, who hold the principles that would be agreed to are similarly disinterested in one another. Clearly the two principles of justice and the

principles of obligation and natural duty require us to consider the rights and claims of others. And the sense of justice is a normally effective desire to comply with these restrictions. The motivation of the persons in the original position must not be confused with the motivation of persons in everyday life who accept the principles of justice and who have the corresponding sense of justice. In practical affairs an individual does have a knowledge of his situation and he can, if he wishes, exploit contingencies to his advantage. Should his sense of justice move him to act on the principles of right that would be adopted in the original position, his desires and aims are surely not egoistic. He voluntarily takes on the limitations expressed by this interpretation of the moral point of view. Thus, more generally, the motivation of the parties in the original position does not determine directly the motivation of people in a just society. For in the latter case, we assume that its members grow up and live under a just basic structure, as the two principles require; and then we try to work out what kind of conception of the good and moral sentiments people would acquire. Therefore the mutual disinterestedness of the parties determines other motivations only indirectly, that is, via its effects on the agreement on principles. It is these principles, together with the laws of psychology (as these work under the conditions of just institutions), which shape the aims and moral sentiments of citizens of a well-ordered society.

Once we consider the idea of a contract theory it is tempting to think that it will not yield the principles we want unless the parties are to some degree at least moved by benevolence, or an interest in one another's interests. Perry, as I mentioned before, thinks of the right standards and decisions as those promoting the ends reached by reflective agreement under circumstances making for impartiality and good will. Now the combination of mutual disinterest and the veil of ignorance achieves much the same purpose as benevolence. For this combination of conditions forces each person in the original position to take the good of others into account. In justice as fairness, then, the effects of good will are brought about by several conditions working jointly. The feeling that this conception of justice is egoistic is an illusion fostered by looking at but one of the elements of the original position. Furthermore, this pair of assumptions has enormous advantages over that of benevolence plus knowledge. As I have noted, the latter is so complex that no definite theory at all can be worked out. Not only are the complications caused by so much information insurmountable, but the motivational assumption requires clarification. For example, what is the relative strength of benevolent desires? In brief, the combination of mutual disinterestedness plus the veil of ignorance has the merits of simplicity and clarity while at the same time insuring the effects of what are at first sight morally more attractive assumptions.

Finally, if the parties are conceived as themselves making proposals, they have no incentive to suggest pointless or arbitrary principles. For example, none would urge that special privileges be given to those exactly six feet tall or born on a sunny day. Nor would anyone put forward the principle that basic rights should depend on the color of one's skin or the texture of one's hair. No one can tell whether such principles would be to his advantage. Furthermore, each such principle is a limitation of one's liberty of action, and such restrictions are not to be accepted without a reason. Certainly we might imagine peculiar circumstances in which these characteristics are relevant. Those born on a sunny day might be blessed with a happy temperament, and for some positions of authority this might be a qualifying attribute. But such distinctions would never be proposed in first principles, for these must have some rational connection with the advancement of human interests broadly defined. The rationality of the parties and their situation in the original position guarantees that ethical principles and conceptions of justice have this general content.[8] Inevitably, then, racial and sexual discrimination presupposes that some hold a favored place in the social system which they are willing to exploit to their advantage. From the standpoint of persons similarly situated in an initial situation which is fair, the principles of explicit racist doctrines are not only unjust. They are irrational. For this reason we could say that they are not moral conceptions at all, but simply means of suppression. They have no place on a reasonable list of traditional conceptions of justice.[9] Of course, this contention is not at all a

matter of definition. It is rather a consequence of the conditions characterizing the original position, especially the conditions of the rationality of the parties and the veil of ignorance. That conceptions of right have a certain content and exclude arbitrary and pointless principles is, therefore, an inference from the theory.

THE REASONING LEADING TO THE TWO PRINCIPLES OF JUSTICE

In this and the next two sections I take up the choice between the two principles of justice and the principle of average utility. Determining the rational preference between these two options is perhaps the central problem in developing the conception of justice as fairness as a viable alternative to the utilitarian tradition. I shall begin in this section by presenting some intuitive remarks favoring the two principles. I shall also discuss briefly the qualitative structure of the argument that needs to be made if the case for these principles is to be conclusive.

Now consider the point of view of anyone in the original position. There is no way for him to win special advantages for himself. Nor, on the other hand, are there grounds for his acquiescing in special disadvantages. Since it is not reasonable for him to expect more than an equal share in the division of social primary goods, and since it is not rational for him to agree to less, the sensible thing is to acknowledge as the first step a principle of justice requiring an equal distribution. Indeed, this principle is so obvious given the symmetry of the parties that it would occur to everyone immediately. Thus the parties start with a principle requiring equal basic liberties for all, as well as fair equality of opportunity and equal division of income and wealth.

But even holding firm to the priority of the basic liberties and fair equality of opportunity, there is no reason why this initial acknowledgment should be final. Society should take into account economic efficiency and the requirements of organization and technology. If there are inequalities in income and wealth, and differences in authority and degrees of responsibility, that work to make everyone better off in comparison with the benchmark of equality, why not permit them? One might think that ideally individuals should want to serve one another. But since the parties are assumed to be mutually disinterested, their acceptance of these economic and institutional inequalities is only the recognition of the relations of opposition in which men stand in the circumstances of justice. They have no grounds for complaining of one another's motives. Thus the parties would agree to these differences only if they would be dejected by the bare knowledge or perception that others are better situated; but I suppose that they decide as if they are not moved by envy. Thus the basic structure should allow these inequalities so long as these improve everyone's situation, including that of the least advantaged, provided that they are consistent with equal liberty and fair opportunity. Because the parties start from an equal division of all social primary goods, those who benefit least have, so to speak, a veto. Thus we arrive at the difference principle. Taking equality as the basis of comparison, those who have gained more must do so on terms that are justifiable to those who have gained the least.

By some such reasoning, then, the parties might arrive at the two principles of justice in serial order. I shall not try to justify this ordering here, but the following remarks may convey the intuitive idea. I assume that the parties view themselves as free persons who have fundamental aims and interests in the name of which they think it legitimate for them to make claims on one another concerning the design of the basic structure of society. The religious interest is a familiar historical example; the interest in the integrity of the person is another. In the original position the parties do not know what particular forms these interests take; but they do assume that they have such interests and that the basic liberties necessary for their protection are guaranteed by the first principle. Since they must secure these interests, they rank the first principle prior to the second. The case for the two principles can be strengthened by spelling out in more detail the notion of a free person. Very roughly the parties regard themselves as having a highest-order interest in how all their other interests, including even their fundamental ones, are shaped and regulated by social institutions. They do not think of themselves as inevitably bound to, or as identical

with, the pursuit of any particular complex of fundamental interests that they may have at any given time, although they want the right to advance such interests (provided they are admissible). Rather, free persons conceive of themselves as beings who can revise and alter their final ends and who give first priority to preserving their liberty in these matters. Hence, they not only have final ends that they are in principle free to pursue or to reject, but their original allegiance and continued devotion to these ends are to be formed and affirmed under conditions that are free. Since the two principles secure a social form that maintains these conditions, they would be agreed to rather than the principle of utility. Only by this agreement can the parties be sure that their highest-order interest as free persons is guaranteed.

The priority of liberty means that whenever the basic liberties can be effectively established, a lesser or an unequal liberty cannot be exchanged for an improvement in economic well-being. It is only when social circumstances do not allow the effective establishment of these basic rights that one can concede their limitation; and even then these restrictions can be granted only to the extent that they are necessary to prepare the way for the time when they are no longer justified. The denial of the equal liberties can be defended only when it is essential to change the conditions of civilization so that in due course these liberties can be enjoyed. Thus in adopting the serial order of the two principles, the parties are assuming that the conditions of their society, whatever they are, admit the effective realization of the equal liberties. Or that if they do not, circumstances are nevertheless sufficiently favorable so that the priority of the first principle points out the most urgent changes and identifies the preferred path to the social state in which all the basic liberties can be fully instituted. The complete realization of the two principles in serial order is the long-run tendency of this ordering, at least under reasonably fortunate conditions.

It seems from these remarks that the two principles are at least a plausible conception of justice. The question, though, is how one is to argue for them more systematically. Now there are several things to do. One can work out their consequences for institutions and note their implications for fundamental social policy. In this way they are tested by a comparison with our considered judgments of justice. . . . But one can also try to find arguments in their favor that are decisive from the standpoint of the original position. In order to see how this might be done, it is useful as a heuristic device to think of the two principles as the maximin solution to the problem of social justice. There is a relation between the two principles and the maximin rule for choice under uncertainty.[10] This is evident from the fact that the two principles are those a person would choose for the design of a society in which his enemy is to assign him his place. The maximin rule tells us to rank alternatives by their worst possible outcomes: we are to adopt the alternative the worst outcome of which is superior to the worst outcomes of the others.[11] The persons in the original position do not, of course, assume that their initial place in society is decided by a malevolent opponent. As I note below, they should not reason from false premises. The veil of ignorance does not violate this idea, since an absence of information is not misinformation. But that the two principles of justice would be chosen if the parties were forced to protect themselves against such a contingency explains the sense in which this conception is the maximin solution. And this analogy suggests that if the original position has been described so that it is rational for the parties to adopt the conservative attitude expressed by this rule, a conclusive argument can indeed be constructed for these principles. Clearly the maximum rule is not, in general, a suitable guide for choices under uncertainty. But it holds only in situations marked by certain special features. My aim, then, is to show that a good case can be made for the two principles based on the fact that the original position has these features to a very high degree.

NOTES

1. As the text suggests, I shall regard Locke's *Second Treatise of Government,* Rousseau's *The Social Contract,* and Kant's ethical works beginning with *The Foundations of the Metaphysics of Morals* as definitive of the contract tradition. For all of its greatness, Hobbes's *Leviathan* raises, special problems. A general historical survey is provided by J. W. Gough, *The Social Contract,* 2nd ed. (Oxford, The Clarendon Press, 1957), and Otto Gierke, *Natural Law and the Theory of Society,* trans. with an introduction by Ernest Barker (Cambridge, The University Press, 1934). A presentation of the contract view as primarily an ethical theory is to be found in G. R. Grice, *The Grounds of Moral Judgment* (Cambridge, The University Press, 1967).

2. Kant is clear that the original agreement is hypothetical. See *The Metaphysics of Morals,* pt. I (*Rechtslehre*), especially §§47, 52; and pt: II of the essay "Concerning the Common Saying: This May Be True in Theory but It Does Not Apply in Practice," in *Kant's Political Writings,* ed. Hans Reiss and trans. by H. B. Nisbet (Cambridge, The University Press, 1970), pp. 73–87. See Georges Vlachos, *La Pensée politique de Kant* (Paris, Presses Universitaires de France, 1962), pp. 326–335; and J. G. Murphy, *Kant: The Philosophy of Right* (London, Macmillan, 1970), pp. 109–112, 133–136, for a further discussion.

3. The veil of ignorance is so natural a condition that something like it must have occurred to many. The formulation in the text is implicit, I believe, in Kant's doctrine of the categorical imperative, both in the way this procedural criterion is defined and the use Kant makes of it. Thus when Kant tells us to test our maxim by considering what would be the case were it a universal law of nature, he must suppose that we do not know our place within this imagined system of nature. See, for example, his discussion of the topic of practical judgment in *The Critique of Practical Reason,* Academy Edition, vol. 5, pp. 68–72. A similar restriction on information is found in J. C. Harsanyi, "Cardinal Utility in Welfare Economics and in the Theory of Risk-taking," *Journal of Political Economy,* vol. 61 (1953). However, other aspects of Harsanyi's view are quite different, and he uses the restriction to develop a utilitarian theory. . . .

4. Rousseau, *The Social Contract,* bk. II, ch. IV, par. 5.

5. See R. B. Perry, *The General Theory of Value* (New York, Longmans, Green and Company, 1926), pp. 674–682.

6. For this notion of rationality, [see the references to Sen and Arrow above, §23, note 9.] The discussion in I. M. D. Little, *The Critique of Welfare Economics,* 2nd ed. (Oxford, Clarendon Press, 1957), ch. II, is also relevant here. . . . H. A. Simon discusses the limitations of the classical conceptions of rationality and the need for a more realistic theory in "A Behavioral Model of Rational Choice," *Quarterly Journal of Economics,* vol. 69 (1955). See also his essay in *Surveys of Economic Theory,* vol. 3 (London, Macmillan, 1967). For philosophical discussions see Donald Davidson, "Actions, Reasons, and Causes,"

Journal of Philosophy, vol. 60 (1963); C. G. Hempel, *Aspects of Scientific Explanation* (New York, The Free Press, 1965), pp. 463–486; Jonathan Bennett, *Rationality* (London, Routledge and Kegan Paul, 1964), and J. D. Mabbott, "Reason and Desire," *Philosophy,* vol. 28 (1953).

7. See *On the Basis of Ethics* (1840), trans. E. F. J. Payne (New York, The Liberal Arts Press, Inc., 1965), pp. 89–92.

8. For a different way of reaching this conclusion, see Philippa Foot, "Moral Arguments," *Mind,* vol. 67 (1958), and "Moral Beliefs," *Proceedings of the Aristotelian Society,* vol. 59 (1958–1959); and R. W. Beardsmore, *Moral Reasoning* (New York, Schocken Books, 1969), especially ch. IV. The problem of content is discussed briefly in G. F. Warnock, *Contemporary Moral Philosophy* (London, Macmillan, 1967), pp. 55–61.

9. For a similar view, see B. A. O. Williams, "The Idea of Equality," *Philosophy, Politics, and Society,* Second Series, ed. Peter Laslett and W. G. Runciman (Oxford, Basil Blackwell, 1962), p. 113.

10. An accessible discussion of this and other rules of choice under uncertainty can be found in W. J. Baumol, *Economic Theory and Operations Analysis,* 2nd ed. (Englewood Cliffs, N.J., Prentice-Hall Inc., 1965), ch. 24. Baumol gives a geometric interpretation of these rules. . . . See pp. 558–562. See also R. D. Luce and Howard Raiffa, *Games and Decisions* (New York, John Wiley and Sons, Inc., 1957), ch. XIII, for a fuller account.

11. Consider the gain-and-loss table below. It represents the gains and losses for a situation which is not a game of strategy. There is no one playing against the person making the decision; instead he is faced with several possible circumstances which may or may not obtain. Which circumstances happen to exist does not depend upon what the person choosing decides or whether he announces his moves in advance. The numbers in the table are monetary values (in hundreds of dollars) in comparison with some initial situation. The gain (g) depends upon the individual's decision (d) and the circumstances (c). Thus $g = f(d, c)$. Assuming that there are three possible decisions and three possible circumstances, we might have this gain-and-loss table.

	Circumstances		
Decisions	c_1	c_2	c_3
d_1	−7	8	12
d_2	−8	7	14
d_3	5	6	8

The maximin rule requires that we make the third decision. For in this case the worst that can happen is that one gains five hundred dollars, which is better than the worst for the other actions. If we adopt one of these we may lose either eight or seven hundred dollars. Thus, the choice of d_3 maximizes $f(d,c)$ for that value of c, which for a given d, minimizes f. The term "maximin" means the *maximum minimorum;* and the rule directs our attention to the worst that can happen under any proposed course of action, and to decide in the light of that.

Anarchy, State, and Utopia

~

ROBERT NOZICK

Robert Nozick (1938–2002) was Pellegrino University Professor at Harvard University. The book from which this selection is taken won the National Book Award in 1975.

SECTION I

The Entitlement Theory

The subject of justice in holdings consists of three major topics. The first is the *original acquisition of holdings,* the appropriation of unheld things. This includes the issues of how unheld things may come to be held, the process, or processes, by which unheld things may come to be held, the things that may come to be held by these processes, the extent of what comes to be held by a particular process, and so on. We shall refer to the complicated truth about this topic, which we shall not formulate here, as the principle of justice in acquisition. The second topic concerns the *transfer of holdings* from one person to another. By what processes may a person transfer holdings to another? How may a person acquire a holding from another who holds it? Under this topic come general descriptions of voluntary exchange, and gift and (on the other hand) fraud, as well as reference to particular conventional details fixed upon in a given society. The complicated truth about this subject (with placeholders for conventional details) we shall call the principle of justice in transfer. (And we shall suppose it also includes principles governing how a person may divest himself of a holding, passing it into an unheld state.)

If the world were wholly just, the following inductive definition would exhaustively cover the subject of justice in holdings.

1. A person who acquires a holding in accordance with the principle of justice in acquisition is entitled to that holding.
2. A person who acquires a holding in accordance with the principle of justice in transfer, from someone else entitled to the holding, is entitled to the holding.
3. No one is entitled to a holding except by (repeated) applications of 1 and 2.

The complete principle of distributive justice would say simply that a distribution is just if everyone is entitled to the holdings they possess under the distribution.

A distribution is just if it arises from another just distribution by legitimate means. The legitimate means of moving from one distribution to another are specified by the principle of justice in transfer. The legitimate first "moves" are specified by the principle of justice in acquisition.[1] Whatever arises from a just situation by just steps is itself just. The means of change specified by the principle of justice in transfer preserve justice. As correct rules of inference are truth-preserving, and any conclusion deduced via repeated application of such rules from only true premises is itself true, so the means of transition from one situation to another specified by the principle of justice in transfer are justice-preserving, and any situation actually arising from repeated transitions in accordance with the principle from a just situation is itself just. The parallel between justice-preserving transformations and truth-preserving transformations illuminates where it fails as well as where it holds. That a conclusion could have been deduced by truth-preserving means from premises that are true suffices to show its truth. That from a just situation a situation *could* have arisen via justice-preserving means does *not* suffice to show its justice. The fact that a thief's victims voluntarily *could* have presented him with gifts does not entitle the thief to his ill-gotten gains. Justice in holdings is historical; it depends upon what actually has happened. We shall return to this point later.

Not all actual situations are generated in accordance with the two principles of justice in holdings: the principle of justice in acquisition and the principle of justice in transfer. Some people steal from others, or defraud them, or enslave them, seizing their product and preventing them from living as they choose, or forcibly exclude others from competing in exchanges. None of these are permissible modes of transition from one situation to another. And some persons acquire holdings by means not sanctioned by the principle of justice in acquisition. The existence of past injustice (previous violations of the first two principles of justice in holdings) raises the third major topic under justice in holdings: the rectification of injustice in holdings. If past injustice has shaped present holdings in various ways, some identifiable and some not, what now, if anything, ought to be done to rectify these injustices? What obligations do the performers of injustice have toward those whose position is worse than it would have been had the injustice not been done? . . .

The general outlines of the theory of justice in holdings are that the holdings of a person are just if he is entitled to them by the principles of justice in acquisition and transfer, or by the principle of rectification of injustice (as specified by the first two principles). If each person's holdings are just, then the total set (distribution) of holdings is just. To turn these general outlines into a specific theory we would have to specify the details of each of the three principles of justice in holdings: the principle of acquisition of holdings, the principle of transfer of holdings, and the principle of rectification of viola-

tions of the first two principles. I shall not attempt that task here.

Historical Principles and End-Result Principles

The general outlines of the entitlement theory illuminate the nature and defects of other conceptions of distributive justice. The entitlement theory of justice in distribution is *historical;* whether a distribution is just depends upon how it came about. In contrast, *current time-slice principles* of justice hold that the justice of a distribution is determined by how things are distributed (who has what) as judged by some *structural* principle(s) of just distribution. A utilitarian who judges between any two distributions by seeing which has the greater sum of utility and, if the sums tie, applies some fixed equality criterion to choose the more equal distribution, would hold a current time-slice principle of justice. As would someone who had a fixed schedule of trade-offs between the sum of happiness and equality. According to a current time-slice principle, all that needs to be looked at, in judging the justice of a distribution, is who ends up with what; in comparing any two distributions one need look only at the matrix presenting the distributions. No further information need be fed into a principle of justice. It is a consequence of such principles of justice that any two structurally identical distributions are equally just. (Two distributions are structurally identical if they present the same profile, but perhaps have different persons occupying the particular slots. My having ten and your having five, and my having five and your having ten are structurally identical distributions.) Welfare economics is the theory of current time-slice principles of justice. The subject is conceived as operating on matrices representing only current information about distribution. This, as well as some of the usual conditions (for example, the choice of distribution is invariant under relabeling of columns), guarantees that welfare economics will be a current time-slice theory, with all of its inadequacies.

Most persons do not accept current time-slice principles as constituting the whole story about distributive shares. They think it relevant in assessing the justice of a situation to consider not only the distribution it embodies, but also how that distribution came about. If some persons are in prison for murder or war crimes, we do not say that to assess the justice of the distribution in the society we must look only at what this person has, and that person has, and that person has, . . . at the current time. We think it relevant to ask whether someone did something so that he *deserved* to be punished, deserved to have a lower share. Most will agree to the relevance of further information with regard to punishments and penalties. Consider also desired things. One traditional socialist view is that workers are entitled to the product and full fruits of their labor; they have earned it; a distribution is unjust if it does not give the workers what they are entitled to. Such entitlements are based upon some past history. No socialist holding this view would find it comforting to be told that because the actual distribution *A* happens to coincide structurally with the one he desires *D, A* therefore is no less just than *D;* it differs only in that the "parasitic" owners of capital receive under *A* what the workers are entitled to under *D,* and the workers receive under *A* what the owners are entitled to under *D,* namely very little. This socialist rightly, in my view, holds onto the notions of earning, producing, entitlement, desert, and so forth, and he rejects current time-slice principles that look only to the structure of the resulting set of holdings. (The set of holdings resulting from what? Isn't it implausible that how holdings are produced and come to exist has no effect at all on who should hold what?) His mistake lies in his view of what entitlements arise out of what sorts of productive processes.

We construe the position we discuss too narrowly by speaking of *current* time-slice principles. Nothing is changed if structural principles operate upon a time sequence of current time-slice profiles and, for example, give someone more now to counterbalance the less he has had earlier. A utilitarian or an egalitarian or any mixture of the two over time will inherit the difficulties of his more myopic comrades. He is not helped by the fact that *some* of the information others consider relevant in assessing a distribution is reflected, unrecoverably, in past matrices. Henceforth, we shall refer to such unhistorical principles of distributive justice, including the current time-slice principles, as *end-result principles* or *end-state principles.*

In contrast to end-result principles of justice, *historical principles* of justice hold that past circumstances or actions of people can create differential entitlements or differential deserts to things. An injustice can be worked by moving from one distribution to another structurally identical one, for the second, in profile the same, may violate people's entitlements or deserts; it may not fit the actual history.

Patterning

The entitlement principles of justice in holdings that we have sketched are historical principles of justice. To better understand their precise character, we shall distinguish them from another subclass of the historical principles. Consider, as an example, the principle of distribution according to moral merit. This principle requires that total distributive shares vary directly with moral merit; no person should have a greater share than anyone whose moral merit is greater. (If moral merit could be not merely ordered but measured on an interval or ratio scale, stronger principles could be formulated.) Or consider the principle that results by substituting "usefulness to society" for "moral merit" in the previous principle. Or instead of "distribute according to moral merit," or "distribute according to usefulness to society," we might consider "distribute according to the weighted sum of moral merit, usefulness to society, and need," with the weights of the different dimensions equal. Let us call a principle of distribution *patterned* if it specifies that a distribution is to vary along with some natural dimension, weighted sum of natural dimensions, or lexicographic ordering of natural dimensions. And let us say a distribution is patterned if it accords with some patterned principle. (I speak of natural dimensions, admittedly without a general criterion for them, because for any set of holdings some artificial dimensions can be gimmicked up to vary along with the distribution of the set.) The principle of distribution in accordance with moral merit is a patterned historical principle, which specifies a patterned distribution. "Distribute according to I.Q." is a patterned principle that looks to information not contained in distributional matrices. It is not historical, however, in that it does not look to any past actions creating differential entitlements to evaluate a distribution; it requires only distributional matrices whose columns are labeled by I.Q. scores. The distribution in a society, however, may be composed of such simple patterned distributions, without itself being simply patterned. Different sectors may operate different patterns, or some combination of patterns may operate in different proportions across a society. A distribution composed in this manner, from a small number of patterned distributions, we also shall term "patterned." And we extend the use of "pattern" to include the overall designs put forth by combinations of end-state principles.

Almost every suggested principle of distributive justice is patterned: to each according to his moral merit, or needs, or marginal product, or how hard he tries, or the weighted sum of the foregoing, and so on. The principle of entitlement we have sketched is *not* patterned.[2] There is no one natural dimension or weighted sum or combination of a small number of natural dimensions that yields the distributions generated in accordance with the principle of entitlement. The set of holdings that results when some persons receive their marginal products, others win at gambling, others receive a share of their mate's income, others receive gifts from foundations, others receive interest on loans, others receive gifts from admirers, others receive returns on investment, others make for themselves much of what they have, others find things, and so on, will not be patterned. Heavy strands of patterns will run through it; significant portions of the variance in holdings will be accounted for by pattern-variables. If most people most of the time choose to transfer some of their entitlements to others only in exchange for something from them, then a large part of what many people hold will vary with what they held that others wanted. More details are provided by the theory of marginal productivity. But gifts to relatives, charitable donations, bequests to children, and the like, are not best conceived, in the first instance, in this manner. Ignoring the strands of pattern, let us suppose for the moment that a distribution actually arrived at by the operation of the principle of entitlement is random with respect to any pattern. Though the resulting set of holdings will be unpatterned, it will not be incomprehensible, for it can be seen as arising from the operation of a small number of principles. These principles specify how an initial distribution may arise (the principle of acquisition of holdings) and how distributions may be transformed into others (the principle of transfer of holdings). The process whereby the set of holdings is generated will be intelligible, though the set of holdings itself that results from this process will be unpatterned . . .

How Liberty Upsets Patterns

It is not clear how those holding alternative conceptions of distributive justice can reject the entitlement conception of justice in holdings. For suppose a distribution favored by one of these nonentitlement conceptions is realized. Let us suppose it is your favorite one and let us call this distribution D_1; perhaps everyone has an equal share, perhaps shares vary in accordance with some dimension you treasure. Now suppose that Wilt Chamberlain is greatly in demand by basketball teams, being a great gate attraction. (Also suppose contracts run only for a year, with players being free agents.) He signs the following sort of contract with a team: In each home game, twenty-five cents from the price of each ticket of admission goes to him. (We ignore the question of whether he is "gouging" the owners, letting them look out for themselves.) The season starts, and people cheerfully attend his team's games; they buy their tickets, each time dropping a separate twenty-five cents of their admission price into a special box with Chamberlain's name on it. They are excited about seeing him play; it is worth the total admission price to them. Let us suppose that in one season one million persons attend his home games, and Wilt Chamberlain winds up with $250,000, a much larger sum than the average income and larger even than anyone else has. Is he entitled to this income? Is this new distribution D_2, unjust? If so, why? There is *no* question about whether each of the people was entitled to the control over the resources they held in D_1; because that was the distribution (your favorite) that (for the purposes of argument) we assumed was acceptable. Each of these persons *chose* to give twenty-five cents of their money to Chamberlain. They could have spent it on going to the movies, or on candy bars, or on copies of *Dissent* magazine, or of *Monthly Review*. But they all, at least one million of them, converged on giving it to Wilt Chamberlain in exchange for watching him play basketball. If D_1 was a just distribution, and people voluntarily moved from it to D_2, transferring parts of their shares they were given under D_1 (what was it for if not to do something with?), isn't D_2 also just? If the people were entitled to dispose of the resources to which they were entitled (under D_1), didn't this include their being entitled to give it to, or exchange it with, Wilt Chamberlain? Can anyone else complain on grounds of justice? Each other person already has his legitimate share under D_1. Under D_1, there is nothing that anyone has that anyone else has a claim of justice against. After someone transfers something to Wilt Chamberlain, third parties *still* have their legitimate shares; *their* shares are not changed. By what process could such a transfer among two persons give rise to a legitimate claim of distributive justice on a portion of what was transferred, by a third party who had no claim of justice on any holding of the others *before* the transfer?[3] . . .

The general point illustrated by the Wilt Chamberlain example and the example of the entrepreneur in a socialist society is that no end-state principle or distributional patterned principle of justice can be continuously realized without continuous interference with people's lives. Any favored pattern would be transformed into one unfavored by the principle, by people choosing to act in various ways; for example, by people exchanging goods and services with other people, or giving things to other people, things the transferrers are entitled to under the favored distributional pattern. To maintain a pattern one must either continually interfere to stop people from transferring resources as they wish to, or continually (or periodically) interfere to take from some persons resources that others for some reason chose to transfer to them. (But if some time limit is to be set on how long people may keep resources others voluntarily

transfer to them, why let them keep these resources for *any* period of time? Why not have immediate confiscation?) It might be objected that all persons voluntarily will choose to refrain from actions which would upset the pattern. This presupposes unrealistically (1) that all will most want to maintain the pattern (are those who don't, to be "reeducated" or forced to undergo "self-criticism"?), (2) that each can gather enough information about his own actions and the ongoing activities of others to discover which of his actions will upset the pattern, and (3) that diverse and far-flung persons can coordinate their actions to dovetail into the pattern. Compare the manner in which the market is neutral among persons' desires, as it reflects and transmits widely scattered information via prices, and coordinates persons' activities.

Redistribution and Property Rights

. . . Patterned principles of distributive justice necessitate *re*distributive activities. The likelihood is small that any actual freely-arrived-at set of holdings fits a given pattern; and the likelihood is nil that it will continue to fit the pattern as people exchange and give. From the point of view of an entitlement theory, redistribution is a serious matter indeed, involving, as it does, the violation of people's rights. (An exception is those takings that fall under the principle of the rectification of injustices.) From other points of view, also, it is serious.

Taxation of earnings from labor is on a par with forced labor.[4] Some persons find this claim obviously true: taking the earnings of n hours labor is like taking n hours from the person; it is like forcing the person to work n hours for another's purpose. Others find the claim absurd. But even these, *if* they object to forced labor, would oppose forcing unemployed hippies to work for the benefit of the needy.[5] And they would also object to forcing each person to work five extra hours each week for the benefit of the needy. But a system that takes five hours' wages in taxes does not seem to them like one that forces someone to work five hours, since it offers the person forced a wider range of choice in activities than does taxation in kind with the particular labor specified. (But we can imagine a gradation of systems of forced labor, from one that specifies a particular activity, to one that gives a choice among two activities, to . . . ; and so on up.) Furthermore, people envisage a system with something like a proportional tax on everything above the amount necessary for basic needs. Some think this does not force someone to work extra hours, since there is no fixed number of extra hours he is forced to work, and since he can avoid the tax entirely by earning only enough to cover his basic needs. This is a very uncharacteristic view of forcing for those who *also* think people are forced to do something *whenever* the alternatives they face are considerably worse. However, *neither* view is correct. The fact that others intentionally intervene, in violation of a side constraint against aggression, to threaten force to limit the alternatives, in this case to paying taxes or (presumably the worse alternative) bare subsistence, makes the taxation system one of forced labor and distinguishes it from other cases of limited choices which are not forcings.[6] . . .

Locke's Theory of Acquisition

. . . [W]e must introduce an additional bit of complexity into the structure of the entitlement theory. This is best approached by considering Locke's attempt to specify a principle of justice in acquisition. Locke views property rights in an unowned object as originating through someone's mixing his labor with it. This gives rise to many questions. What are the boundaries of what labor is mixed with? If a private astronaut clears a place on Mars, has he mixed his labor with (so that he comes to own) the whole planet, the whole uninhabited universe, or just a particular plot? Which plot does an act bring under ownership? The minimal (possibly disconnected) area such that an act decreases entropy in that area, and not elsewhere? Can virgin land (for the purposes of ecological investigation by high-flying airplane) come under ownership by a Lockean process? Building a fence around a territory presumably would make one the owner of only the fence (and the land immediately underneath it).

Why does mixing one's labor with something make one the owner of it? Perhaps because one owns one's labor, and so one comes to own a previously unowned thing that becomes permeated with what one owns. Ownership seeps over into the rest. But why isn't mixing what I own with what I don't own a way of losing what I own rather than a way of gaining what I don't ? If I own a can of tomato juice and spill it in the sea so that its molecules (made radioactive, so I can check this) mingle evenly throughout the sea, do I thereby come to own the sea, or have I foolishly dissipated my tomato juice? Perhaps the idea, instead, is that laboring on something improves it and makes it more valuable; and anyone is entitled to own a thing whose value he has created. (Reinforcing this, perhaps, is the view that laboring is unpleasant. If some people made things effortlessly, as the cartoon characters in *The Yellow Submarine* trail flowers in their wake, would they have lesser claim to their own products whose making didn't *cost* them anything?) Ignore the fact that laboring on something may make it less valuable (spraying pink enamel paint on a piece of driftwood that you have found). Why should one's entitlement extend to the whole object rather than just to the *added value* one's labor has produced? (Such reference to value might also serve to delimit the extent of ownership; for example, substitute "increases the value of" for "decreases entropy in" in the above entropy criterion.) No workable or coherent value-added property scheme has yet been devised, and any such scheme presumably would fall to objections (similar to those) that fell the theory of Henry George.

It will be implausible to view improving an object as giving full ownership to it, if the stock of unowned objects that might be improved is limited. For an object's coming under one person's ownership changes the situation of all others. Whereas previously they were at liberty (in Hohfeld's sense) to use the object, they now no longer are. This change in the situation of others (by removing their liberty to act on a previously unowned object) need not worsen their situation. If I appropriate a grain of sand from Coney Island, no one else may now do as they will with *that* grain of sand. But there are plenty of other grains of sand left for them to do the same with. Or if not grains of sand, then other things. Alternatively, the things I do with the grain of sand I appropriate might improve the position of others, counterbalancing their loss of the liberty to use that grain. The crucial point is whether appropriation of an unowned object worsens the situation of others.

Locke's proviso that there be "enough and as good left in common for others" (sect. 27) is meant to ensure that the situation of others is not worsened. (If this proviso is met is there any motivation for his further condition of nonwaste?) It is often said that this proviso once held but now no longer does. But there appears to be an argument for the conclusion that if the proviso no longer holds, then it cannot ever have held so as to yield permanent and inheritable property rights. Consider the first person Z for whom there is not enough and as good left to appropriate. The last person Y to appropriate left Z without his previous liberty to act on an object, and so worsened Z's situation. So Y's appropriation is not allowed under Locke's proviso. Therefore the next to last person X to appropriate left Y in a worse position, for X's act ended permissible appropriation. Therefore X's appropriation wasn't permissible. But then the appropriator two from last, W, ended permissible appropriation and so, since it worsened X's position, W's appropriation wasn't permissible. And so on back to the first person A to appropriate a permanent property right.

This argument, however, proceeds too quickly. Someone may be made worse off by another's appropriation in two ways: first, by losing the opportunity to improve his situation by a particular appropriation or any one; and second, by no longer being able to use freely (without appropriation) what he previously could. A *stringent* requirement that another not be made worse off by an appropriation would exclude the first way if nothing else counterbalances the diminution in opportunity, as well as the second. A *weaker* requirement would exclude the second way, though not the first. With the weaker requirement, we cannot zip back so quickly from Z to A, as in the above argument; for though person Z can no longer *appropriate*, there may remain some for him to *use* as before. In this case Y's appropriation would not violate the weaker Lockean condition. (With less remaining that people are at liberty to use, users might face more inconvenience, crowding, and so on; in that way the situation of others might be worsened,

unless appropriation stopped far short of such a point.) It is arguable that no one legitimately can complain if the weaker provision is satisfied. However, since this is less clear than in the case of the more stringent proviso, Locke may have intended this stringent proviso by "enough and as good" remaining, and perhaps he meant the nonwaste condition to delay the end point from which the argument zips back.

Is the situation of persons who are unable to appropriate (there being no more accessible and useful unowned objects) worsened by a system allowing appropriation and permanent property? Here enter the various familiar social considerations favoring private property: it increases the social product by putting means of production in the hands of those who can use them most efficiently (profitably); experimentation is encouraged, because with separate persons controlling resources, there is no one person or small group whom someone with a new idea must convince to try it out; private property enables people to decide on the pattern and types of risks they wish to bear, leading to specialized types of risk bearing; private property protects future persons by leading some to hold back resources from current consumption for future markets; it provides alternate sources of employment for unpopular persons who don't have to convince any one person or small group to hire them, and so on. These considerations enter a Lockean theory to support the claim that appropriation of private property satisfies the intent behind the "enough and as good left over" proviso, *not* as a utilitarian justification of property. They enter to rebut the claim that because the proviso is violated no natural right to private property can arise by a Lockean process. The difficulty in working such an argument to show that the proviso is satisfied is in fixing the appropriate base line for comparison. Lockean appropriation makes people no worse off than they would be *how?* This question of fixing the baseline needs more detailed investigation than we are able to give it here. It would be desirable to have an estimate of the general economic importance of original appropriation in order to see how much leeway there is for differing theories of appropriation and of the location of the baseline. Perhaps this importance can be measured by the percentage of all income that is based upon untransformed raw materials and given resources (rather than upon human actions), mainly rental income representing the unimproved value of land, and the price of raw material *in situ,* and by the percentage of current wealth which represents such income in the past.[7]

We should note that it is not only persons favoring *private* property who need a theory of how property rights legitimately originate. Those believing in collective property, for example those believing that a group of persons living in an area jointly own the territory, or its mineral resources, also must provide a theory of how such property rights arise; they must show why the persons living there have rights to determine what is done with the land and resources there that persons living elsewhere don't have (with regard to the same land and resources).

The Proviso

Whether or not Locke's particular theory of appropriation can be spelled out so as to handle various difficulties, I assume that any adequate theory of justice in acquisition will contain a proviso similar to the weaker of the ones we have attributed to Locke. A process normally giving rise to a permanent bequeathable property right in a previously unowned thing will not do so if the position of others no longer at liberty to use the thing is thereby worsened. It is important to specify *this* particular mode of worsening the situation of others, for the proviso does not encompass other modes. It does not include the worsening due to more limited opportunities to appropriate (the first way above, corresponding to the more stringent condition), and it does not include how I "worsen" a seller's position if I appropriate materials to make some of what he is selling, and then enter into competition with him. Someone whose appropriation otherwise would violate the proviso still may appropriate provided he compensates the others so that their situation is not thereby worsened; unless he does compensate these others, his appropriation will violate the proviso of the principle of justice in acquisition and will be an illegitimate one.[8] A theory of appropriation incorporating this Lockean proviso

will handle correctly the cases (objections to the theory lacking the proviso) where someone appropriates the total supply of something necessary for life.[9]

A theory which includes this proviso in its principle of justice in acquisition must also contain a more complex principle of justice in transfer. Some reflection of the proviso about appropriation constrains later actions. If my appropriating all of a certain substance violates the Lockean proviso, then so does my appropriating some and purchasing all the rest from others who obtained it without otherwise violating the Lockean proviso. If the proviso excludes someone's appropriating all the drinkable water in the world, it also excludes his purchasing it all. (More weakly, and messily, it may exclude his charging certain prices for some of his supply.) This proviso (almost?) never will come into effect; the more someone acquires of a scarce substance which others want, the higher the price of the rest will go, and the more difficult it will become for him to acquire it all. But still, we can imagine, at least, that something like this occurs: someone makes simultaneous secret bids to the separate owners of a substance, each of whom sells assuming he can easily purchase more from the other owners; or some natural catastrophe destroys all of the supply of something except that in one person's possession. The total supply could not be permissibly appropriated by one person at the beginning. His later acquisition of it all does not show that the original appropriation violated the proviso (even by a reverse argument similar to the one above that tried to zip back from Z to A). Rather, it is the combination of the original appropriation *plus* all the later transfers and actions that violates the Lockean proviso.

Each owner's title to his holding includes the historical shadow of the Lockean proviso on appropriation. This excludes his transferring it into an agglomeration that does violate the Lockean proviso and excludes his using it in a way, in coordination with others or independently of them, so as to violate the proviso by making the situation of others worse than their baseline situation. Once it is known that someone's ownership runs afoul of the Lockean proviso, there are stringent limits on what he may do with (what it is difficult any longer unreservedly to call) "his property." Thus a person may not appropriate the only water hole in a desert and charge what he will. Nor may he charge what he will if he possesses one, and unfortunately it happens that all the water holes in the desert dry up, except for his. This unfortunate circumstance, admittedly no fault of his, brings into operation the Lockean proviso and limits his property rights.[10] Similarly, an owner's property right in the only island in an area does not allow him to order a castaway from a shipwreck off his island as a trespasser, for this would violate the Lockean proviso.

Notice that the theory does not say that owners do have these rights, but that the rights are overridden to avoid some catastrophe. (Overridden rights do not disappear; they leave a trace of a sort absent in the cases under discussion.)[11] There is no such external (and ad hoc?) overriding. Considerations internal to the theory of property itself, to its theory of acquisition and appropriation, provide the means for handling such cases. The results, however, may be coextensive with some condition about catastrophe, since the baseline for comparison is so low as compared to the productiveness of a society with private appropriation that the question of the Lockean proviso being violated arises only in the case of catastrophe (or a desert-island situation).

The fact that someone owns the total supply of something necessary for others to stay alive does *not* entail that his (or anyone's) appropriation of anything left some people (immediately or later) in a situation worse than the baseline one. A medical researcher who synthesizes a new substance that effectively treats a certain disease and who refuses to sell except on his terms does not worsen the situation of others by depriving them of whatever he has appropriated. The others easily can possess the same materials he appropriated; the researcher's appropriation or purchase of chemicals didn't make those chemicals scarce in a way so as to violate the Lockean proviso. Nor would someone else's purchasing the total supply of the synthesized substance from the medical researcher. The fact that the medical researcher uses easily available chemicals to synthesize the drug no more violates the Lockean proviso than does the fact that the only surgeon able to perform a particular operation eats easily obtainable food in order to stay alive and to have the energy to work. This shows that the Lockean proviso is not an "end-state principle"; it focuses on a particular way that appropriative actions affect others, and not on the structure of the situation that results.

Intermediate between someone who takes all of the public supply and someone who makes the total supply out of easily obtainable substances is someone who appropriates the total supply of something in a way that does not deprive the others of it. For example, someone finds a new substance in an out-of-the-way place. He discovers that it effectively treats a certain disease and appropriates the total supply. He does not worsen the situation of others; if he did not stumble upon the substance no one else would have, and the others would remain without it. However, as time passes, the likelihood increases that others would have come across the substance; upon this fact might be based a limit to his property right in the substance so that others are not below their baseline position; for example, its bequest might be limited. The theme of someone worsening another's situation by depriving him of something he otherwise would possess may also illuminate the example of patents. An inventor's patent does not deprive others of an object which would not exist if not for the inventor. Yet patents would have this effect on others who independently invent the object. Therefore, these independent inventors, upon whom the burden of proving independent discovery may rest, should not be excluded from utilizing their own invention as they wish (including selling it to others). Furthermore, a known inventor drastically lessens the chances of actual independent invention. For persons who know of an invention usually will not try to reinvent it, and the notion of independent discovery here would be murky at best. Yet we may assume that in the absence of the original invention, sometime later someone else would have come up with it. This suggests placing a time limit on patents, as a rough rule of thumb to approximate how long it would have taken, in the absence of knowledge of the invention, for independent discovery.

I believe that the free operation of a market system will not actually run afoul of the Lockean proviso. . . . If this is correct, the proviso will not play a very important role in the activities of protective agencies and will not provide a significant opportunity for future state action. Indeed, were it not for the effects of previous *illegitimate* state action, people would not think the possibility of the proviso's being violated as of more interest than any other logical possibility. (Here I make an empirical historical claim; as does someone who disagrees with this.) This completes our indication of the complication in the entitlement theory introduced by the Lockean proviso.

NOTES

1. Applications of the principle of justice in acquisition may also occur as part of the move from one distribution to another. You may find an unheld thing now and appropriate it. Acquisitions also are to be understood as included when, to simplify, I speak only of transitions by transfers.

2. One might try to squeeze a patterned conception of distributive justice into the framework of the entitlement conception, by formulating a gimmicky obligatory "principle of transfer" that would lead to the pattern. For example, the principle that if one has more than the mean income one must transfer everything one holds above the mean to persons below the mean so as to bring them up to (but not over) the mean. We can formulate a criterion for a "principle of transfer" to rule out such obligatory transfers, or we can say that no correct principle of transfer, no principle of transfer in a free society will be like this. The former is probably the better course, though the latter also is true.

Alternatively, one might think to make the entitlement conception instantiate a pattern, by using matrix entries that express the relative strength of a person's entitlements as measured by some real-valued function. But even if the limitation to natural dimensions failed to exclude this function, the resulting edifice would *not* capture our system of entitlements to *particular* things.

3. Might not a transfer have instrumental effects on a third party, changing his feasible options? (But what if the two parties to the transfer independently had used their holdings in this fashion?) I discuss this question below, but note here that this question concedes the point for distributions of ultimate intrinsic noninstrumental goods (pure utility experiences, so to speak) that are transferrable. It also might be objected that the transfer might make a third party more envious because it worsens his position relative to someone else. I find it incomprehensible how this can be thought to involve a claim of justice. . . .

Here and elsewhere in this chapter, a theory which incorporates elements of pure procedural justice might find what I say acceptable, *if* kept in its proper place; that is, if background institutions exist to ensure the satisfaction of certain conditions on distributive shares. But if these institutions are not themselves the sum or invisible-hand result of people's voluntary (nonaggressive) actions, the constraints they impose require justification. At no point does *our* argument assume any background institutions more extensive than those of the minimal night-watchman state, a state limited to protecting persons against murder, assault, theft, fraud, and so forth.

4. I am unsure as to whether the arguments I present below show that such taxation merely *is* forced labor; so that "is on a par with" means "is one kind of." Or alternatively, whether the arguments emphasize the great similarities between such taxation and forced labor, to show it is plausible and illuminating to view such taxation in the light of forced labor. This latter approach would remind one of how John Wisdom conceives of the claims of metaphysicians.

5. Nothing hangs on the fact that here and elsewhere I speak loosely of *needs,* since I go on, each time, to reject the criterion of justice which includes it. If, however, something did depend upon the notion, one would want to examine it more carefully. For a skeptical view, see Kenneth Minogue, *The Liberal Mind,* (New York: Random House, 1963), pp. 103–112.

6. Further details which this statement should include are contained in my essay "Coercion," in *Philosophy, Science, and Method,* ed. S. Morgenbesser, P. Suppes, and M. White (New York: St. Martin, 1969).

7. I have not seen a precise estimate. David Friedman. *The Machinery of Freedom* (N.Y.: Harper & Row, 1973), pp. XIV, XV, discusses this issue and suggests 5 percent of U.S. national income as an upper limit for the first two factors mentioned. However he does not attempt to estimate the percentage of current wealth which is based upon such income in the past. (The vague notion of "based upon" merely indicates a topic needing investigation.)

8. Fourier held that since the process of civilization had deprived the members of society of certain liberties (to gather, pasture, engage in the chase), a socially guaranteed minimum provision for persons was justified as compensation for the loss (Alexander Gray, *The Socialist Tradition* (New York: Harper & Row, 1968), p. 188). But this puts the point too strongly. This compensation would be due those persons, if any, for whom the process of civilization was a *net loss,* for whom the benefits of civilization did not counterbalance being deprived of these particular liberties.

9. For example, Rashdall's case of someone who comes upon the only water in the desert several miles ahead of others who also will come to it and appropriates it all. Hastings Rashdall, "The Philosophical Theory of Property," in *Property, its Duties and Rights* (London: MacMillan, 1915).

We should not Ayn Rand's theory of property rights ("Man's Rights" in *The Virtue of Selfishness* (New York: New American Library, 1964), p. 94), wherein these follow from the right to life, since people need physical things to live. But a right to life is not a right to whatever one needs to live; other people may have rights over these other things (see Chapter 3 of this book). At most, a right to life would be a right to have or strive for whatever one needs to live, provided that having it does not violate anyone else's rights. With regard to material things, the question is whether having it does violate any right of others. (Would appropriation

of all unowned things do so? Would appropriating the water hole in Rashdall's example?) Since special considerations (such as the Lockean proviso) may enter with regard to material property, one *first* needs a theory of property rights before one can apply any supposed right to life (as amended above). Therefore the right to life cannot provide the foundation for a theory of property rights.

10. The situation would be different if his water hole didn't dry up, due to special precautions he took to prevent this. Compare our discussion of the case in the text with Hayek, *The Constitution of Liberty*, p. 136; and also with Ronald Hamowy, "Hayek's Concept of Freedom; A Critique," *New Individualist Review*, April 1961, pp. 28–31.

11. I discuss overriding and its moral traces in "Moral Complications and Moral Structures," *Natural Law Forum*, 1968, pp. 1–50.

Illusions About Private Property and Freedom

~

G. A. COHEN

G. A. Cohen is Chichele Professor of Social and Political Theory and Fellow of All Souls College, Oxford University. Among his books are *If You're An Egalitarian, How Come You're So Rich?*, *Karl Marx's Theory of History: A Defense*, and *Labor and Freedom*.

1. In capitalist societies everyone owns something, be it only his own labour power, and each is free to sell what he owns and to buy whatever the sale of it enables him to buy.[1] Many claims made on capitalism's behalf may reasonably be doubted, but here is a freedom which it certainly bestows.

It is clear that under capitalism everyone has this freedom, unless being free to sell something is incompatible with being forced to sell it: but I do not think it is. For one is in general free to do anything which one is forced to do.

There are several reasons for affirming this possibly surprising thesis. The most direct argument in

favour of it is as follows: you cannot be forced to do what you are not able to do, and you are not able to do what you are not free to do. Hence you are free to do what you are forced to do.

I am not, in the foregoing argument, equating being free to do something with being able to do it.[2] Being free to do *A* is a necessary but not a sufficient condition of being able to do *A*. I may be unable to do something not because I am unfree to, but because I lack the relevant capacity. Thus I am no doubt free to swim across the English Channel, but I am nevertheless unable to. If I were a much better swimmer, but forbidden by well-enforced law to swim it, then,

Reprinted from *Issues in Marxist Philosophy, IV,* eds. John Mepham and David-Hillel Rubin (Atlantic Highlands, N.J.: Humanities Press, 1979), by permission of the author.

again, I would be unable to swim it. The argument of the last paragraph goes through on what is often called the "negative" or "social" conception of freedom, according to which I am free to do whatever nobody would prevent me from doing. I have no quarrel with that conception in this paper.

A second argument for the claim that I am free to do what I am forced to do is that one way of frustrating someone who would force me to do something is by rendering myself not free to do it: it follows, by contraposition, that if I am forced to do it, I am free to do it. To illustrate: I commit a crime, thereby causing myself to be gaoled, so that I cannot be forced by you to do something I abhor. If you still hope to force me to do it you will have to make me free to do it (by springing me from jail).

Look at it this way: before you are forced to do *A*, you are, at least in standard cases, free to do *A* and free not to do *A*. The force removes the second freedom, but why suppose that it removes the first? It puts no obstacle in the path of your doing *A*, and you therefore remain free to do it.

We may conclude, not only that being free to do *A* is compatible with being forced to do *A*, but that being forced to do *A entails* being free to do *A*. Resistance to this odd-sounding but demonstrable result reflects failure to distinguish the idea of *being free to do something* from other ideas, such as the idea of *doing something freely*. I am free to do what I am forced to do even if, as is usually true,[3] I do not do it freely, and even though, as is always true, I am not free with respect to whether or not I do it.

I labour this truth—that one is free to do what one is forced to do—because it, and failure to perceive it, help to explain the character and the persistence of a certain ideological disagreement. Marxists say that working class people are forced to sell their labour power. Bourgeois thinkers celebrate the freedom of contract manifest not only in the capitalist's purchase of labour power but also in the worker's sale of it. If Marxists are right[4] working class people are importantly unfree: they are not free not to sell their labour power. But it remains true that (unlike chattel slaves) they are free to sell their labour power. The unfreedom asserted by Marxists is compatible with the freedom asserted by bourgeois thinkers. Indeed: if the

Marxists are right the bourgeois thinkers are right, unless they also think, as characteristically they do, that the truth they emphasise refutes the Marxist claim. The bourgeois thinkers go wrong not when they say that the worker is free to sell his labour power, but when they infer that the Marxist cannot therefore be right in his claim that the worker is forced to. And Marxists[5] share the bourgeois thinkers' error when they think it necessary to deny what the bourgeois thinkers say. If the worker is not free to sell his labour power, of what freedom is a foreigner whose work permit is removed deprived?

2. Freedom to buy and sell is one freedom, of which in capitalism there is a great deal. It belongs to capitalism's essential nature. But many think that capitalism is, quite as essentially, a more comprehensively free society. Very many people, including philosophers, who try to speak carefully, use the phrase "free society" as an alternative name for societies which are capitalist.[6] And many contemporary English-speaking philosophers and economists call the doctrine which recommends a purely capitalist society "libertarianism," not, as might be thought more apt, "libertarianism with respect to buying and selling."

It is not only the libertarians themselves who think that is the right name for their party. Many who reject their aims concede the name to them: they agree that unmodified capitalism is comprehensively a realm of freedom. This applies to *some* of those who call themselves "liberals."

These liberals assert, plausibly, that liberty is a good thing, but they say that it is not the only good thing. So far, libertarians will agree. But liberals also believe that libertarians wrongly sacrifice other good things in too total defence of the one good of liberty. They agree with libertarians that pure capitalism is liberty pure and simple, or anyway *economic*[7] liberty pure and simple, but they think the various good things lost when liberty pure and simple is the rule justify restraints on liberty. They want a capitalism modified by welfare legislation and state intervention in the market. They advocate, they say, not unrestrained liberty, but liberty restrained by the demands of social and economic security. They think that what they call a free economy is too damaging to those, who, by nature or circumstance, are ill placed to achieve a minimally proper standard of life within it, so they favour, within limits, taxing the better off for the sake of the worse off, although they believe that such taxation reduces liberty. They also think that what they call a free economy is subject to fluctuations in productive activity and misallocations of resources which are potentially damaging to everyone, so they favour measures of interference in the market, although, again, they believe that such interventions diminish liberty. They do not question the libertarian's description of capitalism as the (economically) free society. But they believe that economic freedom may rightly and reasonably be abridged. They believe in a compromise between liberty and other values, and that what is known as the welfare state mixed economy achieves the right compromise.

I shall argue that libertarians, and liberals of the kind described, misuse the concept of freedom. This is not a comment on the attractiveness of the institutions they severally favour, but on the rhetoric they use to describe them. If, however, as I contend, they misdescribe those institutions, then that is surely because the correct description of them would make them less attractive, so my critique of the defensive rhetoric is indirectly a critique of the institutions the rhetoric defends.

My central contention is that liberals and libertarians see the freedom which is intrinsic to capitalism, but do not give proper notice to the unfreedom which necessarily accompanies it.

To expose this failure of perception, I shall criticise a description of the libertarian position provided by Antony Flew in his *Dictionary of Philosophy*. It is there said to be "whole-hearted political and economic liberalism, opposed to any social or legal constraints on individual freedom."[8] Liberals of the kind I described above would avow themselves unwholehearted in the terms of this definition. For they would say that they support certain (at any rate) legal constraints on individual freedom.

Now a society in which there are *no* "social and legal constraints on individual freedom" is perhaps imaginable, at any rate by people who have highly anarchic imaginations. But, be that as it may, the Flew definition misdescribes libertarians, since it does not apply to defenders of capitalism, which is what libertarians profess to be, and are.

For consider. If the state prevents me from doing something I want to do, it evidently places a constraint on my freedom. Suppose, then, that I want to perform an action which involves a legally prohibited use of your property. I want, let us say, to pitch a tent in your large back garden, because I have no home or land of my own, but I have got hold of a tent, legitimately or otherwise. If I now try to do what I want to do, the chances are that the state will intervene on your behalf. If it does, I shall suffer a constraint on my freedom. The same goes for all unpermitted uses of a piece of private property by those who do not own it, and there are always those who do not own it, since "private ownership by one person . . . presupposes non-ownership on the part of other persons."[9] But the free enterprise economy advocated by libertarians rests upon private property: you can sell and buy only what you respectively own and come to own. It follows that the Flew definition is untrue to its *definiendum,* and that 'libertarianism' is a questionable name for the position it now standardly denotes.

How could Flew publish the definition I have criticised? I do not think he was being dishonest. I would not accuse him of appreciating the truth of this particular matter and deliberately falsifying it. Why then is it that Flew, and libertarians like him,[10] see the unfreedom in prospective state interference with your use of your property, but do not see the unfreedom in the standing intervention against my use of it entailed by the fact that it *is* your private property? What explains their monocular vision?

One explanation is a tendency to take as part of the structure of human existence in general, and therefore as no "social or legal constraint" on freedom, any structure around which, *merely as things are,* much of our activity is organised. In capitalist society the institution of private property is such a structure. It is treated as so *given* that the obstacles it puts on freedom are not perceived, while any impingement on private property itself is immediately noticed. Yet private property pretty well *is* a distribution of freedom *and* unfreedom. It is necessarily associated with the liberty of private owners to do as they wish with what they own, but it no less necessarily withdraws liberty from those who do not own it. To think of capitalism as a realm of freedom is to overlook half of its nature. (I am aware that the tendency to this failure of perception is stronger, other things being equal, the more private property a person has. I do not think really poor people need to have their eyes opened to the simple conceptual truth I emphasise. I also do not claim that anyone of sound mind will for long deny that private property places restrictions on freedom, once the point has been made. What is striking is that the point so often needs to be made, against what should be *obvious* absurdities, such as Flew's definition of "libertarianism").

I have supposed that to prevent someone from doing something he wants to do is to make him, in that respect, unfree: I am unfree whenever someone interferes, *justifiably or otherwise,* with my actions. But there is a definition of freedom which is implicit in much libertarian writing,[11] and which entails that interference is *not* a sufficient condition of unfreedom. On that definition, which I shall call the *moralised* definition, I am unfree only when someone does or would *unjustifiably* interfere with me. If one now combines this moralised definition of freedom with a moral endorsement of private property, one reaches the result that the protection of legitimate private property cannot restrict anyone's freedom. It will follow from the moral endorsement of private property that you and the police are justified in preventing me from pitching my tent on your land, and, because of the moralised definition of freedom, it will then further follow that you and the police do not thereby restrict my freedom. So here we have another explanation of how intelligent philosophers are able to say what they do about capitalism, private property and freedom. But the characterisation of freedom which figures in the explanation is unacceptable. For it entails that a properly convicted murderer is not rendered unfree when he is justifiably imprisoned.

Even justified interference reduces freedom. But suppose for a moment that, as libertarians say or imply, it does not. On that supposition one cannot readily argue that interference with private property is wrong *because* it reduces freedom. For one can no longer take for granted, what is evident on a morally neutral account of freedom, that interference with private property *does* reduce freedom. Under a moralised account of freedom one must abstain from that assertion until one has shown that private property is morally defensible. Yet libertarians tend *both* to use a moralised definition *and* to take it for granted that interference with private property diminishes the owner's freedom. Yet they can take that for granted only on an account of freedom in which it is equally obvious that the protection of private property diminishes the freedom of nonowners, to avoid which consequence they retreat to a moralised definition of the concept.

Still, libertarians who embrace the moralised definition of freedom need not occupy this inconsistent position. They can escape it by justifying private property on grounds other than considerations of freedom. They can contrive, for example, to represent interference with rightfully held private property as unjust, and *therefore,* by virtue of the moralised definition, invasive of freedom. This is a consistent position.[12] But it still incorporates an unacceptable definition of freedom, and the position is improved[13] if that is eliminated. We then have a defence of private property on grounds of justice. Freedom falls out of the picture.[14]

3. I now want to consider a possible response to what I said about pitching a tent on your land. It might be granted that the prohibition on my doing so restricts my freedom, but not, so it might be said, my *economic* freedom. If the connection between capitalism and freedom is overstated by libertarians and others, the possibility that capitalism is *economic* freedom still requires consideration.

The resurrected identification will survive only if the unavailability to me of your garden is no restriction on my economic freedom. I can think of only one reason for saying so. It is that I am not here restricted with respect to whether I may sell something I own, or buy something in exchange for what I own. If that is economic freedom, then my lack of access to your garden does not limit my economic freedom.

A different definition of economic freedom would include in it freedom to use goods and services. It is hard to say whether such a definition is superior to the less inclusive one just considered, since "neither the tradition of political philosophy nor common understanding provides us with a . . . set of categories of economic liberty" comparable to the acknowledged set of categories of political liberty,[15] perhaps because the boundary of the economic domain is unclear.[16] A reasoned attempt to construct a clear concept of economic freedom might be a valuable exercise, but it is not one which I can report having completed. I am accordingly unable to recommend any particular characterisation of economic freedom.

I can nevertheless reply to the present claim, as follows: either economic freedom includes the freedom to use goods and services, or it does not. If it does, then capitalism withholds economic freedom wherever it grants it, as the tent case shows. If, on the other hand, economic freedom relates only to buying and selling, then the case for identifying economic freedom and free enterprise looks better. But we have to define "economic freedom" narrowly to obtain this result. On a wide but eligible definition of economic freedom, capitalism offers a particular limited form of it. On a narrow definition, the limitations recede, but we are now talking about a much narrower freedom.

To those who do not think this freedom is narrow, I offer three comments, which may move them a little:

(i) The freedom in question is, fully described, freedom to sell what I own and to buy whatever the sale of what I own enables me to buy. Importantly, that freedom is not identical with freedom to buy and sell just anything at all, which is much broader, and which is not granted by capitalism. For first, one is evidently not free to sell what belongs to somebody else. This is, to be sure, true by definition: there logically *could* not be that freedom, in any society. But this does not diminish the importance of noticing that capitalism does not offer it.[17] And secondly, one is free to buy, not anything at all, but only that which the sale of what one owns enables one to buy. A poor man is not free to buy a grand piano, even if one necessary condition of that freedom—he is not legally forbidden to do so—is satisfied.

(ii) It is an important fact about freedom in general, and hence about the freedom under discussion,

that it comes in degrees. That I am free to do something does not say *how* free I am to do that thing, which might be more or less. To cite just one dimension in which freedom's degree varies, my freedom to do A is, other things equal, smaller, the greater is the cost to me of doing A. It might be true of both a poor man and a rich man that each is free to buy an £8 ticket to the opera, yet the rich man's freedom to do so is greater, since, unlike the poor man, he will not have to give up a few decent meals, for example, in order to buy the ticket. Since it is consistent with the capitalist character of a society that it should contain poor people, the buying and selling freedom which capitalism grants universally can be enjoyed in very limited degrees.

Now some will disagree with my claim that freedom varies in degree in the manner just described. They will deny that some people have a higher degree of a certain freedom than others (who also have that freedom), and will say, instead, that for some people it is relatively easy to exercise a freedom which others, who also have it, find it difficult to exercise. But even if they are right, the substance of my case is unweakened. For it is scarcely intelligible that one should be interested in how much freedom people have in a certain form of society without being interested in how readily they are able to exercise it.

(iii) Finally, we should consider the *point* of the freedom to buy and sell, as far as the individual who has it is concerned. For most citizens, most of the time, that point is to obtain goods and services of various sorts. When, therefore, goods and services are available independently of the market, the individual might not feel that his lack of freedom to *buy* them is a particularly significant lack. A lack of freedom to buy medical services is no serious restriction on liberty in a society which makes them publicly available on a decent scale. In a socialist society certain things will be unbuyable, and, consequently, unsellable. But, as long as they are obtainable by other means, one should not exaggerate the gravity of the resulting restrictions on freedom.

Still, restrictions on freedom do result. I may not *want* to buy a medical or an educational service, but I am nevertheless unfree to, if the transaction is forbidden. Note that I would not be unfree to if a certain popular account of freedom were correct, according to which I am unfree only when what I *want* to do is something I shall or would be prevented from doing. But that account is false.[18] There are important connections between freedom and desire, but the straightforward one maintained in the popular account is not among them. Reference to a man's desires is irrelevant to the question "What is he free to do?" but it is, I believe, relevant to the question "How much freedom (comprehensively) does he have?" and consequently to the politically crucial question of comparing the amounts of freedom enjoyed in different societies. As far as I know, the vast philosophical literature on freedom contains no sustained attempt to formulate criteria for answering questions about quantity of freedom. I attempted a discussion of such criteria in an earlier draft of this paper, but the response to it from many friends was so skeptical that I decided to abandon it. I hope to return to it one day, and I hope that others will address it too.

4. I have wanted to show that private property, and therefore capitalist society, limit liberty, but I have not shown that they do so more than communal property and socialist society. Each *form* of society is by its nature congenial and hostile to various sorts of liberty, for variously placed people. And *concrete* societies exemplifying either form will offer and withhold additional liberties whose presence or absence may not be inferred from the nature of the form itself. Which form is better for freedom, all things considered, is a question which may have no answer in the abstract: it may be that which form is better for freedom depends entirely on the historical circumstances.

I am here separating two questions about capitalism, socialism, and freedom. The first, or *abstract* question, is which form of society is, just as such, better for freedom, not, and this is the second, and *concrete* question, which form is better for freedom in the conditions of a particular place and time.[19] The first question is interesting, but difficult and somewhat obscure. I shall try to clarify it presently. I shall then indicate that two distinct ranges of consideration bear on the second question, about freedom in a particular case, considerations which must be distinguished not only for theoretical but also for political reasons.

Though confident that the abstract interpretation of the question, which form, if any, offers more liberty, is meaningful, I am not at all sure what its meaning is. I do not think we get an answer to it favouring one form if and only if that form would in all circumstances provide more freedom than the other. For I can understand the claim that socialism is by nature a freer society than capitalism even though it would be a less free society under certain conditions.

Consider a possible analogy. It will be agreed that sports cars are faster than jeeps, even though jeeps are faster on certain kinds of terrain. Does the abstract comparison, in which sports cars outclass jeeps, mean, therefore, that sports cars are faster on *most* terrains? I think not. It seems sufficient for sports cars to be faster in the abstract that there is some unbizarre terrain on which their maximum speed exceeds the maximum speed of jeeps on any terrain. Applying the analogy, if socialism is said to be freer than capitalism in the abstract, this would mean that there are realistic concrete conditions under which a socialist society would be freer than *any* concrete capitalist society would be. This, perhaps, is what some socialists mean when they say that socialism is a freer society, for some who say that would acknowledge that in some conditions socialism, or what would pass for it,[20] would be less free than at any rate some varieties of capitalism.

There are no doubt other interesting abstract questions, which do not yield to the analysis just given. Perhaps, for example, the following intractably rough prescription could be made more useable: consider, with respect to each form of society, the sum of liberty which remains when the liberties it withholds by its very nature are subtracted from the liberties it guarantees by its very nature. The society which is freer in the abstract is the one where that sum is larger.

So much for the abstract issue. I said that two kinds of consideration bear on the answer to concrete questions, about which form of society would provide more freedom in a particular here and now. We may look upon each form of society as a set of rules which generates, in particular cases, particular enjoyments and deprivations of freedom. Now the effect of the rules in a particular case will depend, in the first place, on the resources and traditions which prevail in the society in question. But secondly, and distinctly, it will also depend on the ideological and political views of the people concerned. (This distinction is not always easy to make, but it is never impossible to make it). To illustrate the distinction, it could be that in a given case collectivisation of agriculture would provide more freedom on the whole for rural producers, were it not for the fact that they do not *believe* it would, and would therefore resist collectivisation so strongly that it could be introduced only at the cost of enormous repression. It could be that though socialism might distribute more liberty in Britain now, capitalist ideology is now here so powerful, and the belief that socialism would reduce liberty is, accordingly, so strong, that conditions *otherwise* propitious for realising a socialism with a great deal of liberty are not favourable in the final reckoning, since the final reckoning must take account of the present views of people about how free a socialist society would be.

I think it is theoretically and politically important to attempt a reckoning independent of that final reckoning.

It is theoretically important because there exists a clear question about whether a socialist revolution would expand freedom whose answer is not determined by people's beliefs about what its answer is. *Its* answer might be "yes," even though most people think its answer is "no," and even though, as a result, "no" is the correct answer to the further, "final reckoning" question, for whose separateness I am arguing. Unless one separates the questions, one cannot coherently evaluate the ideological answers to the penultimate question which help to cause the ultimate question to have the answer it does.

It is also politically necessary to separate the questions, because it suits our rulers not to distinguish the two levels of assessment. The Right can often truly say that, all things considered, socialism would diminish liberty, where, however, the chief reason why this is so is that the Right, with its powerful ideological arsenal, have convinced enough people that it is so. Hence one needs to argue for an answer which does not take people's conviction into account,

partly, of course, in order to combat and transform those convictions. If, on the other hand, you want to defend the status quo, then I recommend that you confuse the questions I have distinguished.

The distinction between concrete questions enables me to make a further point about the abstract question, which *form* of society provides more freedom. We saw above that a plausible strategy for answering it involves asking concrete questions about particular cases. We may now add that the concrete questions relevant to the abstract one are those which prescind from people's beliefs about their answers.

I should add, finally, that people's beliefs about socialism and freedom affect not only how free an achieved socialist society would be, but also how much restriction on freedom would attend the process of achieving it. (Note that there is a somewhat analogous distinction between how much freedom we have in virtue of the currently maintained capitalist arrangements, and how much we have, or lose, because of the increasingly repressive measures used to maintain them). Refutation of bourgeois ideology is an imperative task for socialists, not as an alternative to the struggle for socialism, but as part of the struggle for a socialism which will justify the struggle which led to it.

5. I said above that capitalism and socialism offer different sets of freedoms, but I emphatically do not say that they provide freedom in two different senses of that term. To the claim that capitalism gives people freedom some socialists respond that what they get is *merely bourgeois* freedom. Good things can be meant by that response: that there are important particular liberties which capitalism does not confer; and/or that I do not have freedom, but only a necessary condition of it, when a course of action (for example, skiing) is, though not *itself* against the law, unavailable to me anyway, because other laws (for example, those of private property, which prevent a poor man from using a rich man's unused skis) forbid me the means to perform it. But when socialists suggest that there is no "real" freedom under capitalism, at any rate for the workers, or that socialism promises freedom of a higher and as yet unrealised kind, then I

think their line is theoretically incorrect and politically disastrous. For there is freedom under capitalism, in a plain, good sense, and if socialism will not give us more of it, we shall rightly be disappointed. If the socialist says he is offering a new variety of freedom, the advocate of capitalism will carry the day with his reply that he prefers freedom of the known variety to an unexplained and unexemplified rival. But if, as I would recommend, the socialist argues that capitalism is, all things considered, inimical to freedom *in the very sense* of "freedom" in which, as he should concede, a person's freedom is diminished when his private property is tampered with, then he presents a challenge which the advocate of capitalism, by virtue of his own commitment, cannot ignore.

For it is a contention of socialist thought that capitalism does not live up to its own professions. A fundamental socialist challenge to the libertarian is that pure capitalism does not protect liberty in general, but rather those liberties which are built into private property, an institution which also limits liberty. And a fundamental socialist challenge to the liberal is that the modifications of modified capitalism modify not liberty, but private property, often in the interest of liberty itself. Consequently, transformations far more revolutionary than a liberal would contemplate might be justified on the very same grounds as those which support liberal reform.

A homespun example shows how communal property offers a differently shaped liberty, in no different sense of that term, and, in certain circumstances, more liberty than the private property alternative. Neighbours *A* and *B* own sets of household tools. Each has some tools which the other lacks. If *A* needs tools of a kind which only *B* has, then, private property being what it is, he is not free to take *B*'s one for a while, even if *B* does not need it during that while. Now imagine that the following rule is imposed, bringing the tools into partly common ownership: each may take and use a tool belonging to the other without permission provided that the other is not using it and that he returns it when he no longer needs it, or when the other needs it, whichever comes first. *Things being what they are* (a substantive qualification: we are talking, as often we should, about the real world, not about remote possibilities) the communising rule would, I contend, increase tool-

using freedom, on any reasonable view. To be sure, some freedoms are removed by the new rule. Neither neighbour is as assured of the same easy access as before to the tools that were wholly his. Sometimes he has to go next door to retrieve one of them. Nor can either now charge the other for use of a tool he himself does ·not then require. But these restrictions probably count for less than the increase in the range of tools available. No one is as sovereign as before over any tool, so the privateness of the property is reduced. But freedom is probably expanded.

It is true that each would have more freedom still if he were the sovereign owner of *all* the tools. But that is not the relevant comparison. I do not deny that full ownership of a thing gives greater freedom than shared ownership of that thing. But no one did own all the tools before the modest measure of communism was introduced. The kind of comparison we need to make is between, for example, sharing ownership with ninety-nine others in a hundred things and fully owning just one of them. I submit that which arrangement nets more freedom is a matter of cases. There is little sense in one hundred people sharing control over one hundred toothbrushes. There is an overwhelming case, from the point of view of freedom, in favour of our actual practice of public ownership of street pavements. Denationalising the pavements in favour of private ownership of each piece by the residents adjacent to it would be bad for freedom of movement.

But someone will say: ownership of private property is the only example of *full* freedom. Our practice with pavements may be a good one, but no one has full freedom with respect to any part of the pavement, since he cannot, for instance, break it up and put the result to a new use, and he cannot prevent others from using it (except, perhaps, by the costly means of indefinitely standing on it himself, and he cannot even do that when laws against obstruction are enforced). The same holds for all communal possessions. No one is fully free with respect to anything in which he enjoys a merely shared ownership. Hence even if private property entails unfreedom, and even if there is freedom without private property, *there is no case of full freedom which is not a case of private property.* The underlined thesis is unaffected by the arguments against libertarianism in sections 2 and 3 of this paper.

There are two things wrong with this fresh attempt to associate freedom and private property. First, even if it is true that every case of full freedom is a case of private property, a certain number of full freedoms need not add up to more freedom overall than a larger number of partial freedoms: so it is not clear that the underlined thesis supports any interesting conclusion.

The thesis is, moreover, questionable in itself. It is a piece of bourgeois ideology masquerading as a conceptual insight. The argument for the thesis treats freedom fetishistically, as control over *material things*. But freedom, in the central sense of the term with which we have been occupied, is freedom to *act*, and if there is a concept of full freedom in that central sense, then it is inappropriate, if we want to identify it, to focus, from the start, on control over *things*. I can be fully free to walk to your home when and because the pavement is communally owned, even though I am not free to destroy or to sell a single square inch of that pavement. To be sure, action requires the use of matter, or at least space,[21] but it does not follow that to be fully free to perform an action with certain pieces of matter in a certain portion of space I need full control over the matter and the space, since some forms of control will be unnecessary to the action in question. The rights I need over things to perform a given action depend on the nature of that action.

The thesis under examination is, then, either false, or reducible to the truism that one has full freedom *with respect to a thing* only if one privately owns that thing. But why should we be especially interested in full freedom with respect to a *thing*, unless, of course, we are already ideologically committed to the overriding importance of private property?

6. Recall the example of the tools, described above. An opponent might say: the rules of private property allow neighbours to *contract* in favour of the stated arrangement. If both would gain from the change, and they are rational, they will agree to it. No communist property rule, laid down independently of contract, is needed.

This is a good reply with respect to the case at hand. For that case my only counter is the weakish one that life under capitalism tends to generate an irrationally strong attachment to purely private use of purely private property, which can lead to neglect of mutually gainful and freedom-expanding options.

That point aside, it must be granted that contracts often establish desirably communal structures, sometimes with transaction costs which communist rules would not impose, but also without the administrative costs which often attach to public regulation.

But the stated method of achieving communism cannot be generalised. We could not by contract bring into shared ownership those non-household tools and resources which Marxists call means of production. They will never be won for socialism by contract,[22] since they belong to a small minority, to whom the rest can offer no quid pro quo. Most of the rest must lease their labour power to members of that minority, in exchange for some of the proceeds of their labour on facilities in whose ownership they do not share.

So we reach, at length, a central charge with respect to freedom which Marxists lay against capitalism, and which is, in my view, well founded: that in capitalist society the great majority of people are forced, because of the character of the society, to sell their labour power to others. In properly refined form, this important claim about capitalism and liberty is, I am sure, correct. I have attempted to refine it elsewhere.[23]

NOTES

1. The present paper rewrites and extends arguments first presented on pp. 9–17 of "Capitalism, Freedom and the Proletariat," which appeared in Alan Ryan (ed.), *The Idea of Freedom: Essays in Honour of Isaiah Berlin,* Oxford, 1979. The position of the proletariat with respect to freedom, discussed on pp. 17–25 of that paper, is not treated here. I return to that issue in a forthcoming article on "The Structure of Proletarian Unfreedom").

2. I point this out because the argument was thus misinterpreted by Galen Strawson in a review of *The Idea of Freedom* which appeared in *Lycidas,* the journal of Wolfson College, Oxford. See *Lycidas,* 7, 1978–9, pp. 35–6.

3. It is not true that whenever I am forced to do something I act unfreely, not, at any rate, if we accept Gerald Dworkin's well-defended claim that "A does X freely if . . . A does X for reasons which he doesn't mind acting from" ("Acting Freely," *Nous,* 1970, p. 381). On this view some forced action is freely performed: if, for example, I

am forced to do something which I had wanted to do and had fully intended to do, then, unless I resent the supervenient coercion, I do it freely.

4. I consider whether they are right in the latter half of "Capitalism, Freedom and the Proletariat," and in "The Structure of Proletarian Unfreedom."

5. Such as Ziyad Husami, if he is a Marxist, who says of the wage worker: "Deprived of the ownership of means of production and means of livelihood, he is forced (not free) to sell his labour power to the capitalist." ("Marx on Distributive Justice," *Philosophy and Public Affairs,* Fall, 1978, pp. 51–2). I contend that the phrase in parentheses introduces a falsehood into Husami's sentence, a falsehood which Karl Marx avoided when he said of the worker that "the time for which he is free to sell his labour power is the time for which he is forced to sell it." (*Capital,* I, Moscow, 1961, p. 302).

6. See, for example, Jan Narveson, "A Puzzle about Economic Justice in Rawls' Theory," *Social Theory and Practice,* 1976, p. 3; James Rachels, "What People Deserve," in J. Arthur and W. Shaw (eds.), *Justice and Economic Distribution,* Englewood Cliffs, 1978, p. 151.

7. See p. 229 below on what might be meant by *economic* liberty.

8. *A Dictionary of Philosophy,* London 1979, p. 188.

9. Karl Marx, *Capital,* III, Moscow, 1970, p. 812.

10. The question also applies to anti-libertarian liberals of the kind described on pp. 225–226, such as Isaiah Berlin and H. L. A. Hart. See "Capitalism, Freedom and the Proletariat," p. 13, on Berlin, and my forthcoming essay "Respecting Private Property," on Hart.

11. And sometimes also explicit: see Robert Nozick, *Anarchy, State and Utopia,* New York, 1974, p. 262.

12. I argued elsewhere that, unlike libertarians, liberals of the kind described on pp. 225–226 *necessarily* proceed inconsistently, that their idea of compromise between freedom and other values requires vacillation between neutral and moralised versions of freedom. But Bill Shaw and Tim Scanlon have convinced me that my argument is inconclusive. See "Capitalism, Freedom and the Proletariat," p. 13.

13. It is improved intellectually in that a certain objection to it no longer applies, but ideologically speaking it is weakened, since there is more ideological power in a recommendation of private property on grounds of justice *and* freedom—however confused the relationship between them may be—than in a recommendation of private property on grounds of justice alone.

14. The justice argument for private property is not examined in what follows. I deal with it at length in "Respecting Private Property."

15. Thomas Scanlon, "Liberty, Contract and Contribution," in G. Dworkin et al. (eds.), *Markets and Morals,* Washington, 1977, p. 54; and see also p. 57.

16. This suggestion is due to Chris Provis.

17. Cheyney Ryan's discussion of "capacity rights" is relevant here. See his "The Normative Concept of Coercion," *Mind,* forthcoming.

18. See Isaiah Berlin, *Four Essays on Liberty,* Oxford, 1969, pp. xxxviii ff., 139–40. The point was originally made by Richard Wollheim, in a review of Berlin's *Two Concepts of Liberty.* See too Hillel Steiner, "Individual Liberty," *Proceedings of the Aristotelian Society,* 1974–5, p. 34.

19. One may also distinguish not, as above, between the capitalist form of society and a particular capitalist society, but between the capitalist form in general and specific forms of capitalism, such as competitive capitalism, monopoly capitalism, and so on (I provide a systematic means of generating specific forms in *Karl Marx's Theory of History,* Oxford, 1978, Chapter III, sections (6) and (8)). This further distinction is *at* the abstract level, rather than between abstract and concrete. I prescind from it here to keep my discussion relatively uncomplicated. The distinction would have to be acknowledged, and employed, in any treatment which pretended to be definitive.

20. Which way they would put it depends on how they would define socialism. If it is defined as public ownership of the means of production, and this is taken in a narrowly juridical sense, then it is compatible with severe restrictions on freedom. But if, to go to other extreme, it is defined as a condition in which the free development of each promotes, and is promoted by, the free development of all, then only the attempt to institute socialism, not socialism, could have negative consequences for freedom.

21. This fact is emphasised by Hillel Steiner in section III of his "Individual Liberty," but he goes too far when he says: "My theorem is . . . that *freedom is the personal possession of physical objects*" (p. 48). I claim that the "theorem" is just bourgeois ideology. For further criticism of Steiner, see Onora O'Neill, "The Most Extensive Liberty," *Proceedings of the Aristotelian Society,* 1979–80, p. 48.

22. Unless the last act of this scenario qualifies as a contract: in the course of a general strike a united working class demands that private property in major means of production be socialised, as a condition of resumption of work, and a demoralised capitalist class meets the demand. (How, by the way, could "libertarians" object to such a revolution? For hints see Robert Nozick, "Coercion," in P. Laslett *et al.,* (eds.) *Philosophy, Politics and Society,* Fourth Series, Oxford, 1972). .

23. See note 1 above.

The Procedural Republic and the Unencumbered Self

~

MICHAEL SANDEL

Michael Sandel is professor of government at Harvard University. He is the author of
Liberalism and the Limits of Justice and *Democracy's Discontent: America's Search for
a Public Philosophy.*

Political philosophy seems often to reside at a distance from the world. Principles are one thing, politics another, and even our best efforts to "live up" to our ideals typically founder on the gap between theory and practice.[1]

But if political philosophy is unrealizable in one sense, it is unavoidable in another. This is the sense in which philosophy inhabits the world from the start; our practices and institutions are embodiments of theory. To engage in a political practice is already to stand in relation to theory.[2] For all our uncertainties about ultimate questions of political philosophy—of justice and value and the nature of the good life—the one thing we know is that we live *some* answer all the time.

In this essay I will try to explore the answer we live now, in contemporary America. What is the political philosophy implicit in our practices and institutions? How does it stand, as philosophy? And how do tensions in the philosophy find expression in our present political condition?

It may be objected that it is a mistake to look for a single philosophy, that we live no "answer," only answers. But a plurality of answers is itself a kind of answer. And the political theory that affirms this plurality is the theory I propose to explore.

THE RIGHT AND THE GOOD

We might begin by considering a certain moral and political vision. It is a liberal vision, and like most liberal visions gives pride of place to justice, fairness, and individual rights. Its core thesis is this: a just society seeks not to promote any particular ends, but enables its citizens to pursue their own ends, consistent with a similar liberty for all; it therefore must govern by principles that do not presuppose any particular conception of the good. What justifies these regulative principles above all is not that they maximize the general welfare, or cultivate virtue, or otherwise promote the good, but rather that they conform to the concept of *right,* a moral category given prior to the good, and independent of it.

This liberalism says, in other words, that what makes the just society just is not the *telos* or purpose or end at which it aims, but precisely its refusal to choose in advance among competing purposes and ends. In its constitution and its laws, the just society seeks to provide a framework within which its citizens can pursue their own values and ends, consistent with a similar liberty for others.

The ideal I've described might be summed up in the claim that the right is prior to the good, and in two senses: The priority of the right means first, that individual rights cannot be sacrificed for the sake of the general good (in this it opposes utilitarianism), and second, that the principles of justice that specify these rights cannot be premised on any particular vision of the good life. (In this it opposes teleological conceptions in general.)

This is the liberalism of much contemporary

moral and political philosophy, most fully elaborated by Rawls, and indebted to Kant for its philosophical foundations.[3] But I am concerned here less with the lineage of this vision than with what seem to me three striking facts about it.

First, it has a deep and powerful philosophical appeal. Second, despite its philosophical force, the claim for the priority of the right over the good ultimately fails. And third, despite its philosophical failure, this liberal vision is the one by which we live. For us in late twentieth century America, it is our vision, the theory most thoroughly embodied in the practices and institutions most central to our public life. And seeing how it goes wrong as philosophy may help us to diagnose our present political condition. So first, its philosophical power; second, its philosophical failure; and third, however briefly, its uneasy embodiment in the world.

But before taking up these three claims, it is worth pointing out a central theme that connects them. And that is a certain conception of the person, of what it is to be a moral agent. Like all political theories, the liberal theory I have described is something more than a set of regulative principles. It is also a view about the way the world is, and the way we move within it. At the heart of this ethic lies a vision of the person that both inspires and undoes it. As I will try to argue now, what make this ethic so compelling, but also, finally, vulnerable, are the promise and the failure of the unencumbered self.

KANTIAN FOUNDATIONS

The liberal ethic asserts the priority of right, and seeks principles of justice that do not presuppose any particular conception of the good.[4] This is what Kant means by the supremacy of the moral law, and what Rawls means when he writes that "justice is the first virtue of social institutions."[5] Justice is more than just another value. It provides the framework that *regulates* the play of competing values and ends; it must therefore have a sanction independent of those ends. But it is not obvious where such a sanction could be found.

Theories of justice, and for that matter, ethics, have typically founded their claims on one or another

conception of human purposes and ends. Thus Aristotle said the measure of a *polis* is the good at which it aims, and even J. S. Mill, who in the nineteenth century called "justice the chief part, and incomparably the most binding part of all morality," made justice an instrument of utilitarian ends.[6]

This is the solution Kant's ethic rejects. Different persons typically have different desires and ends, and so any principle derived from them can only be contingent. But the moral law needs a *categorical* foundation, not a contingent one. Even so universal a desire as happiness will not do. People still differ in what happiness consists of, and to install any particular conception as regulative would impose on some the conceptions of others, and so deny at least to some the freedom to choose their *own* conceptions. In any case, to govern ourselves in conformity with desires and inclinations, given as they are by nature or circumstance, is not really to be *self*-governing at all. It is rather a refusal of freedom, a capitulation to determinations given outside us.

According to Kant, the right is "derived entirely from the concept of freedom in the external relationships of human beings, and has nothing to do with the end which all men have by nature [i.e., the aim of achieving happiness] or with the recognized means of attaining this end."[7] As such, it must have a basis prior to all empirical ends. Only when I am governed by principles that do not presuppose any particular ends am I free to pursue my own ends consistent with a similar freedom for all.

But this still leaves the question of what the basis of the right could possibly be. If it must be a basis prior to all purposes and ends, unconditioned even by what Kant calls "the special circumstances of human nature,"[8] where could such a basis conceivably be found? Given the stringent demands of the Kantian ethic, the moral law would seem almost to require a foundation in nothing, for any empirical precondition would undermine its priority. "Duty!" asks Kant at his most lyrical, "What origin is there worthy of thee, and where is to be found the root of thy noble descent which proudly rejects all kinship with the inclinations?"[9]

His answer is that the basis of the moral law is to be found in the *subject,* not the object of practical reason, a subject capable of an autonomous will. No empirical end, but rather "a subject of ends, namely a rational being himself, must be made the ground for all maxims of action."[10] Nothing other than what Kant calls "the subject of all possible ends himself" can give rise to the right, for only this subject is also the subject of an autonomous will. Only this subject could be that "something which elevates man above himself as part of the world of sense" and enables him to participate in an ideal, unconditioned realm wholly independent of our social and psychological inclinations. And only this thoroughgoing independence can afford us the detachment we need if we are ever freely to choose for ourselves, unconditioned by the vagaries of circumstance.[11]

Who or what exactly *is* this subject? It is, in a certain sense, *us.* The moral law, after all, is a law we give *ourselves;* we don't *find* it, we *will* it. That is how it (and we) escape the reign of nature and circumstance and merely empirical ends. But what is important to see is that the "we" who do the willing are not "we" qua particular persons, you and me, each for ourselves—the moral law is not up to us as individuals—but "we" qua participants in what Kant calls "pure practical reason," "we" qua participants in a transcendental subject.

Now what is to guarantee that I *am* a subject of this kind, capable of exercising pure practical reason? Well, strictly speaking, there *is* no guarantee; the transcendental subject is only a possibility. But it is a possibility I must *presuppose* if I am to think of myself as a free moral agent. Were I wholly an empirical being, I would not be capable of freedom, for every exercise of will would be conditioned by the desire for some object. All choice would be heteronomous choice, governed by the pursuit of some end. My will could never be a first cause, only the effect of some prior cause, the instrument of one or another impulse or inclination. "When we think of ourselves as free," writes Kant, "we transfer ourselves into the intelligible world as members and recognize the autonomy of the will."[12] And so the notion of a subject prior to and independent of experience, such as the Kantian ethic requires, appears not only possible but indispensable, a necessary presupposition of the possibility of freedom.

How does all of this come back to politics? As the subject is prior to its ends, so the right is prior to the good. Society is best arranged when it is governed by principles that do not presuppose any particular conception of the good, for any other arrangement would fail to respect persons as being capable of choice; it would treat them as objects rather than subjects, as means rather than ends in themselves.

We can see in this way how Kant's notion of the subject is bound up with the claim for the priority of right. But for those in the Anglo-American tradition, the transcendental subject will seem a strange foundation for a familiar ethic. Surely, one may think, we can take rights seriously and affirm the primacy of justice without embracing the *Critique of Pure Reason.* This, in any case, is the project of Rawls.

He wants to save the priority of right from the obscurity of the transcendental subject. Kant's idealist metaphysic, for all its moral and political advantage, cedes too much to the transcendent, and wins for justice its primacy only by denying it its human situation. "To develop a viable Kantian conception of justice," Rawls writes, "the force and content of Kant's doctrine must be detached from its background in transcendental idealism" and recast within the "canons of a reasonable empiricism."[13] And so Rawls' project is to preserve Kant's moral and political teaching by replacing Germanic obscurities with a domesticated metaphysic more congenial to the Anglo-American temper. This is the role of the original position.

FROM TRANSCENDENTAL SUBJECT TO UNENCUMBERED SELF

The original position tries to provide what Kant's transcendental argument cannot—a foundation for the right that is prior to the good, but still situated in the world. Sparing all but essentials, the original position works like this: It invites us to imagine the principles we would choose to govern our society if we were to choose them in advance, before we knew the particular persons we would be—whether rich or poor, strong or weak, lucky or unlucky—before we knew even our interests or aims or conceptions of the good. These principles—the ones we would choose in that imaginary situation—are the principles of justice. What is more, if it works, they are principles that do not presuppose any particular ends.

What they *do* presuppose is a certain picture of the person, of the way we must be if we are beings for whom justice is the first virtue. This is the picture of the unencumbered self, a self understood as prior to and independent of purposes and ends.

Now the unencumbered self describes first of all the way we stand toward the things we have, or want, or seek. It means there is always a distinction between the values I *have* and the person I *am.* To identify any characteristics as *my* aims, ambitions, desires, and so on, is always to imply some subject "me" standing behind them, at a certain distance, and the shape of this "me" must be given prior to any of the aims or attributes I bear. One consequence of this distance is to put the self *itself* beyond the reach of its experience, to secure its identity once and for all. Or to put the point another way, it rules out the possibility of what we might call *constitutive* ends. No role or commitment could define me so completely that I could not understand myself without it. No project could be so essential that turning away from it would call into question the person I am.

For the unencumbered self, what matters above all, what is most essential to our personhood, are not the ends we choose but our capacity to choose them. The original position sums up this central claim about us. "It is not our aims that primarily reveal our nature," writes Rawls, "but rather the principles that we would acknowledge to govern the background conditions under which these aims are to be formed . . . We should therefore reverse the relation between the right and the good proposed by teleological doctrines and view the right as prior."[14]

Only if the self is prior to its ends can the right be prior to the good. Only if my identity is never tied to the aims and interests I may have at any moment can I think of myself as a free and independent agent, capable of choice.

This notion of independence carries consequences for the kind of community of which we are capable. Understood as unencumbered selves, we are of course free to join in voluntary association with others, and so are capable of community in the cooperative sense. What is denied to the unencumbered self

is the possibility of membership in any community bound by moral ties antecedent to choice; he cannot belong to any community where the self *itself* could be at stake. Such a community—call it constitutive as against merely cooperative—would engage the identity as well as the interests of the participants, and so implicate its members in a citizenship more thoroughgoing than the unencumbered self can know.

For justice to be primary, then, we must be creatures of a certain kind, related to human circumstance in a certain way. We must stand to our circumstance always at a certain distance, whether as transcendental subject in the case of Kant, or as unencumbered selves in the case of Rawls. Only in this way can we view ourselves as subjects as well as objects of experience, as agents and not just instruments of the purposes we pursue.

The unencumbered self and the ethic it inspires, taken together, hold out a liberating vision. Freed from the dictates of nature and the sanction of social roles, the human subject is installed as sovereign, cast as the author of the only moral meanings there are. As participants in pure practical reason, or as parties to the original position, we are free to construct principles of justice unconstrained by an order of value antecedently given. And as actual, individual selves, we are free to choose our purposes and ends unbound by such an order, or by custom or tradition or inherited status. So long as they are not unjust, our conceptions of the good carry weight, whatever they are, simply in virtue of our having chosen them. We are, in Rawls' words, "self-originating sources of valid claims."[15]

This is an exhilarating promise, and the liberalism it animates is perhaps the fullest expression of the Enlightenment's quest for the self-defining subject. But is it true? Can we make sense of our moral and political life by the light of the self-image it requires? I do not think we can, and I will try to show why not by arguing first within the liberal project, then beyond it.

JUSTICE AND COMMUNITY

We have focused so far on the foundations of the liberal vision, on the way it derives the principles it defends. Let us turn briefly now to the substance of those principles, using Rawls as our example. Sparing all but essentials once again, Rawls' two principles of justice are these: first, equal basic liberties for all, and second, only those social and economic inequalities that benefit the least-advantaged members of society (the difference principle).

In arguing for these principles, Rawls argues against two familiar alternatives—utilitarianism and libertarianism. He argues against utilitarianism that it fails to take seriously the distinction between persons. In seeking to maximize the general welfare, the utilitarian treats society as a whole as if it were a single person; it conflates our many, diverse desires into a single system of desires, and tries to maximize. It is indifferent to the distribution of satisfactions among persons, except insofar as this may affect the overall sum. But this fails to respect our plurality and distinctness. It uses some as means to the happiness of all, and so fails to respect each as an end in himself. While utilitarians may sometimes defend individual rights, their defense must rest on the calculation that respecting those rights will serve utility in the long run. But this calculation is contingent and uncertain. So long as utility is what Mill said it is, "the ultimate appeal on all ethical questions,"[16] individual rights can never be secure. To avoid the danger that their life prospects might one day be sacrificed for the greater good of others, the parties to the original position therefore insist on certain basic liberties for all, and make those liberties prior.

If utilitarians fail to take seriously the distinctness of persons, libertarians go wrong by failing to acknowledge the arbitrariness of fortune. They define as just whatever distribution results from an efficient market economy, and oppose all redistribution on the grounds that people are entitled to whatever they get, so long as they do not cheat or steal or otherwise violate someone's rights in getting it. Rawls opposes this principle on the ground that the distribution of talents and assets and even efforts by which some get more and others get less is arbitrary from a moral point of view, a matter of good luck. To distribute the good things in life on the basis of these differences is not to do justice, but simply to carry over into human arrangements the arbitrariness of social and natural contingency. We deserve, as individuals, neither the talents our good fortune may have brought, nor the benefits that flow from them. We should therefore regard these talents as common assets, and regard one another as common beneficiaries of the rewards they bring. "Those who have been favored by nature, whoever they are, may gain from their good fortune only on terms that improve the situation of those who have lost out . . . In justice as fairness, men agree to share one another's fate."[17]

This is the reasoning that leads to the difference principle. Notice how it reveals, in yet another guise, the logic of the unencumbered self. I cannot be said to deserve the benefits that flow from, say, my fine physique and good looks, because they are only accidental, not essential facts about me. They describe attributes I *have,* not the person I *am,* and so cannot give rise to a claim of desert. Being an unencumbered self, this is true of *everything* about me. And so I cannot, as an individual, deserve anything at all.

However jarring to our ordinary understandings this argument may be, the picture so far remains intact; the priority of right, the denial of desert, and the unencumbered self all hang impressively together.

But the difference principle requires more, and it is here that the argument comes undone. The difference principle begins with the thought, congenial to the unencumbered self, that the assets I have are only accidentally mine. But it ends by assuming that these assets are therefore *common* assets and that society has a prior claim on the fruits of their exercise. But this assumption is without warrant. Simply because I, as an individual, do not have a privileged claim on the assets accidentally residing "here," it does not follow that everyone in the world collectively does. For there is no reason to think that their location in society's province or, for that matter, within the province of humankind, is any *less* arbitrary from a moral point of view. And if their arbitrariness within *me* makes them ineligible to serve *my* ends, there seems no obvious reason why their arbitrariness within any particular society should not make them ineligible to serve that society's ends as well.

To put the point another way, the difference principle, like utilitarianism, is a principle of sharing. As such, it must presuppose some prior moral tie among those whose assets it would deploy and whose efforts it would enlist in a common endeavor. Otherwise, it is simply a formula for using some as means to others' ends, a formula this liberalism is committed to reject.

But on the cooperative vision of community alone, it is unclear what the moral basis for this sharing could be. Short of the constitutive conception, deploying an individual's assets for the sake of the common good would seem an offense against the "plurality and distinctness" of individuals this liberalism seeks above all to secure.

If those whose fate I am required to share really are, morally speaking, *others,* rather than fellow participants in a way of life with which my identity is bound, the difference principle falls prey to the same objections as utilitarianism. Its claim on me is not the claim of a constitutive community whose attachments I acknowledge, but rather the claim of a concatenated collectivity whose entanglements I confront.

What the difference principle requires, but cannot provide, is some way of identifying those *among* whom the assets I bear are properly regarded as common, some way of seeing ourselves as mutually indebted and morally engaged to begin with. But as we have seen, the constitutive aims and attachments that would save and situate the difference principle are precisely the ones denied to the liberal self; the moral encumbrances and antecedent obligations they imply would undercut the priority of right.

What, then, of those encumbrances? The point so far is that we cannot be persons for whom justice is primary, and also be persons for whom the difference principle is a principle of justice. But which must give way? Can we view ourselves as independent selves, independent in the sense that our identity is never tied to our aims and attachments?

I do not think we can, at least not without cost to those loyalties and convictions whose moral force consists partly in the fact that living by them is inseparable from understanding ourselves as the particular persons we are—as members of this family or community or nation or people, as bearers of that history, as citizens of this republic. Allegiances such as these are more than values I happen to have, and to hold, at a certain distance. They go beyond the obligations I voluntarily incur and the "natural duties" I owe to human beings as such. They allow that to some I owe more than justice requires or even permits, not by reason of agreements I have made but instead in

virtue of those more or less enduring attachments and commitments that, taken together, partly define the person I am.

To imagine a person incapable of constitutive attachments such as these is not to conceive an ideally free and rational agent, but to imagine a person wholly without character, without moral depth. For to have character is to know that I move in a history I neither summon nor command, which carries consequences nonetheless for my choices and conduct. It draws me closer to some and more distant from others; it makes some aims more appropriate, others less so. As a self-interpreting being, I am able to reflect on my history and in this sense to distance myself from it, but the distance is always precarious and provisional, the point of reflection never finally secured outside the history itself. But the liberal ethic puts the self beyond the reach of its experience, beyond deliberation and reflection. Denied the expansive self-understandings that could shape a common life, the liberal self is left to lurch between detachment on the one hand, and entanglement on the other. Such is the fate of the unencumbered self, and its liberating promise.

THE PROCEDURAL REPUBLIC

But before my case can be complete, I need to consider one powerful reply. While it comes from a liberal direction, its spirit is more practical than philosophical. It says, in short, that I am asking too much. It is one thing to seek constitutive attachments in our private lives; among families and friends, and certain tightly knit groups, there may be found a common good that makes justice and rights less pressing. But with public life—at least today, and probably always—it is different. So long as the nation-state is the primary form of political association, talk of constitutive community too easily suggests a darker politics rather than a brighter one; amid echoes of the moral majority, the priority of right, for all its philosophical faults, still seems the safer hope.

This is a challenging rejoinder, and no account of political community in the twentieth century can fail to take it seriously. It is challenging not least because it calls into question the status of political philosophy and its relation to the world. For if my argument is correct, if the liberal vision we have considered is not morally self-sufficient but parasitic on a notion of community it officially rejects, then we should expect to find that the political practice that embodies this vision is not *practically* self-sufficient either—that it must draw on a sense of community it cannot supply and may even undermine. But is that so far from the circumstance we face today? Could it be that through the original position darkly, on the far side of the veil of ignorance, we may glimpse an intimation of our predicament, a refracted vision of ourselves?

How does the liberal vision—and its failure— help us make sense of our public life and its predicament? Consider, to begin, the following paradox in the citizen's relation to the modern welfare state. In many ways, we in the 1980s stand near the completion of a liberal project that has run its course from the New Deal through the Great Society and into the present. But notwithstanding the extension of the franchise and the expansion of individual rights and entitlements in recent decades, there is a widespread sense that, individually and collectively, our control over the forces that govern our lives is receding rather than increasing. This sense is deepened by what appear simultaneously as the power and the powerlessness of the nation-state. On the one hand, increasing numbers of citizens view the state as an overly intrusive presence, more likely to frustrate their purposes than advance them. And yet, despite its unprecedented role in the economy and society, the modern state seems itself disempowered, unable effectively to control the domestic economy, to respond to persisting social ills, or to work America's will in the world.

This is a paradox that has fed the appeals of recent politicians (including Carter and Reagan), even as it has frustrated their attempts to govern. To sort it out, we need to identify the public philosophy implicit in our political practice, and to reconstruct its arrival. We need to trace the advent of the procedural republic, by which I mean a public life animated by the liberal vision and self-image we've considered.

The story of the procedural republic goes back in some ways to the founding of the republic, but its central drama begins to unfold around the turn of the century. As national markets and large-scale enterprise displaced a decentralized economy, the decen-

tralized political forms of the early republic became outmoded as well. If democracy was to survive, the concentration of economic power would have to be met by a similar concentration of political power. But the Progressives understood, or some of them did, that the success of democracy required more than the centralization of government; it also required the nationalization of politics. The primary form of political community had to be a recast on a national scale. For Herbert Croly, writing in 1909, the "nationalizing of American political, economic, and social life" was "an essentially formative and enlightening political transformation." We would become more of a democracy only as we became "more of a nation . . . in ideas, in institutions, and in spirit."[18]

This nationalizing project would be consummated in the New Deal, but for the democratic tradition in America, the embrace of the nation was a decisive departure. From Jefferson to the populists, the party of democracy in American political debate had been, roughly speaking, the party of the provinces, of decentralized power, of small-town and small-scale America. And against them had stood the party of the nation—first Federalists, then Whigs, then the Republicans of Lincoln—a party that spoke for the consolidation of the union. It was thus the historic achievement of the New Deal to unite, in a single party and political program, what Samuel Beer has called "liberalism and the national idea."[19]

What matters for our purpose is that, in the twentieth century, liberalism made its peace with concentrated power. But it was understood at the start that the terms of this peace required a strong sense of national community, morally and politically to underwrite the extended involvements of a modern industrial order. If a virtuous republic of small-scale, democratic communities was no longer a possibility, a national republic seemed democracy's next best hope. This was still, in principle at least, a politics of the common good. It looked to the nation, not as a neutral framework for the play of competing interests, but rather as a formative community, concerned to shape a common life suited to the scale of modern social and economic forms.

But this project failed. By the mid- or late twentieth century, the national republic had run its course. Except for extraordinary moments, such as war, the nation proved too vast a scale across which to cultivate the shared self-understandings necessary to community in the formative, or constitutive sense. And so the gradual shift, in our practices and institutions, from a public philosophy of common purposes to one of fair procedures, from a politics of good to a politics of right, from the national republic to the procedural republic.

OUR PRESENT PREDICAMENT

A full account of this transition would take a detailed look at the changing shape of political institutions, constitutional interpretation, and the terms of political discourse in the broadest sense. But I suspect we would find in the *practice* of the procedural republic two broad tendencies foreshadowed by its philosophy: first, a tendency to crowd out democratic possibilities; second, a tendency to undercut the kind of community on which it nonetheless depends.

Where liberty in the early republic was understood as a function of democratic institutions and dispersed power,[20] liberty in the procedural republic is defined in opposition to democracy, as an individual's guarantee against what the majority might will. I am free insofar as I am the bearer of rights, where rights are trumps.[21] Unlike the liberty of the early republic, the modern version permits—in fact even requires—concentrated power. This has to do with the universalizing logic of rights. Insofar as I have a right, whether to free speech or a minimum income, its provision cannot be left to the vagaries of local preferences but must be assured at the most comprehensive level of political association. It cannot be one thing in New York and another in Alabama. As rights and entitlements expand, politics is therefore displaced from smaller forms of association and relocated at the most universal form—in our case, the nation. And even as politics flows to the nation, power shifts away from democratic institutions (such as legislatures and political parties) and toward institutions designed to be insulated from democratic pressures, and hence better equipped to dispense and defend individual rights (notably the judiciary and bureaucracy).

These institutional developments may begin to account for the sense of powerlessness that the welfare state fails to address and in some ways doubtless deepens. But it seems to me a further clue to our condition that recalls even more directly the predicament of the unencumbered self—lurching, as we left it, between detachment on the one hand, the entanglement on the other. For it is a striking feature of the welfare state that it offers a powerful promise of individual rights, and also demands of its citizens a high measure of mutual engagement. But the self-image that attends the rights cannot sustain the engagement.

As bearers of rights, where rights are trumps, we think of ourselves as freely choosing, individual selves, unbound by obligations antecedent to rights, or to the agreements we make. And yet, as citizens of the procedural republic that secures these rights, we find ourselves implicated willy-nilly in a formidable array of dependencies and expectations we did not choose and increasingly reject.

In our public life, we are more entangled, but less attached, than ever before. It is as though the unencumbered self presupposed by the liberal ethic had begun to come true—less liberated than disempowered, entangled in a network of obligations and involvements unassociated with any act of will, and yet unmediated by those common identifications or expansive self-definitions that would make them tolerable. As the scale of social and political organization has become more comprehensive, the terms of our collective identity have become more fragmented, and the forms of political life have outrun the common purpose needed to sustain them.

Something like this, it seems to me, has been unfolding in America for the past half-century or so. I hope I have said at least enough to suggest the shape a fuller story might take. And I hope in any case to have conveyed a certain view about politics and philosophy and the relation between them—that our practices and institutions are themselves embodiments of theory, and to unravel their predicament is, at least in part, to seek after the self-image of the age.

NOTES

1. An excellent example of this view can be found in Samuel Huntington, *American Politics: The Promise of Disharmony* (Cambridge: Harvard University Press, 1981).

See especially his discussion of the "ideals versus institutions" gap, pp. 10–12, 39–41, 61–84, 221–262.

2. See, for example, the conceptions of a "practice" advanced by Alasdair MacIntyre and Charles Taylor. MacIntyre, *After Virtue* (Notre Dame: University of Notre Dame Press, 1981), pp. 175–209. Taylor, "Interpretation and the Sciences of Man," *Review of Metaphysics* 25, (1971) pp. 3–51.

3. John Rawls, *A Theory of Justice* (Oxford: Oxford University Press, 1972). Immanuel Kant, *Groundwork of the Metaphysics of Morals,* trans. H. J. Paton. (1785; New York: Harper and Row, 1956). Kant, *Critique of Pure Reason,* trans. Norman Kemp Smith (1781, 1787; London: Macmillan, 1929). Kant, *Critique of Practical Reason,* trans. L. W. Beck (1788; Indianapolis: Bobbs-Merrill, 1956). Kant, "On the Common Saying: 'This May Be True in Theory, But It Does Not Apply in Practice,'" in Hans Reiss, ed., *Kant's Political Writings* (1793; Cambridge: Cambridge University Press, 1970). Other recent versions of the claim for the priority of the right over good can be found in Robert Nozick, *Anarchy, State and Utopia* (New York: Basic Books, 1974); Ronald Dworkin, *Taking Rights Seriously* (London: Duckworth, 1977); Bruce Ackerman, *Social Justice in the Liberal State* (New Haven: Yale University Press, 1980).

4. This section, and the two that follow, summarize arguments developed more fully in Michael Sandel, *Liberalism and the Limits of Justice* (Cambridge: Cambridge University Press, 1982).

5. Rawls (1971), p. 3.

6. John Stuart Mill, *Utilitarianism,* in *The Utilitarians* (1893; Garden City: Doubleday, 1973), p. 465. Mill, *On Liberty,* in *The Utilitarians,* p. 485 (Originally published 1849).

7. Kant (1793), p. 73.

8. Kant (1785), p. 92.

9. Kant (1788), p. 89.

10. Kant (1785), p. 105.

11. Kant (1788), p. 89.

12. Kant (1785), p. 121.

13. Rawls, "The Basic Structure as Subject," *American Philosophical Quarterly* (1977), p. 165.

14. Rawls (1971), p. 560.

15. Rawls, "Kantian Constructivism in Moral Theory," *Journal of Philosophy* 77 (1980), p. 543.

16. Mill (1849), p. 485.

17. Rawls (1971), pp. 101–102.

18. Croly, *The Promise of American Life* (Indianapolis: Bobbs-Merrill, 1965), pp. 270–273.

19. Beer, "Liberalism and the National Idea," *The Public Interest,* Fall (1966), pp. 70–82.

20. See, for example, Laurence Tribe, *American Constitutional Law* (Mineola: The Foundation Press, 1978), pp. 2–3.

21. See Ronald Dworkin, "Liberalism," in Stuart Hampshire, ed., *Public and Private Morality* (Cambridge: Cambridge University Press, 1978), p. 136.

Markets in Women's Sexual Labor

DEBRA SATZ

Debra Satz is associate professor of philosophy at Stanford University. Her articles on topics such as reproduction, rational choice theory, and prostitution have appeared in *Philosophy and Public Affairs, The Journal of Philosophy,* and *Ethics.*

There is a widely shared intuition that markets are inappropriate for some kinds of human endeavor: that some things simply should not be bought and sold. For example, virtually everyone believes that love and friendship should have no price. The sale of other human capacities is disputed, but many people believe that there is something about sexual and reproductive activities that makes their sale inappropriate. I have called the thesis supported by this intuition the asymmetry thesis.[1] Those who hold the asymmetry thesis believe that markets in reproduction and sex are asymmetric to other labor markets. They think that treating sexual and reproductive capacities as commodities, as goods to be developed and exchanged for a price, is worse than treating our other capacities as commodities. They think that there is something wrong with commercial surrogacy and prostitution that is not wrong with teaching and professional sports.

The intuition that there is a distinction between markets in different human capacities is a deep one, even among people who ultimately think that the distinction does not justify legally forbidding sales of reproductive capacity and sex. I accept this intuition, which I continue to probe in this article. In particular, I ask: What justifies taking an asymmetric attitude toward markets in our sexual capacities? What, if anything, is problematic about a woman selling her sexual as opposed to her secretarial labor? And, if the apparent asymmetry can be explained and justified, what implications follow for public policy?

In this article, I sketch and criticize two popular approaches to these questions. The first, which I call the economic approach, attributes the wrongness of prostitution to its consequences for efficiency or welfare. The important feature of this approach is its treatment of sex as a morally indifferent matter: sexual labor is not to be treated as a commodity if and only if such treatment fails to be efficient or welfare maximizing. The second, the "essentialist" approach, by contrast, stresses that sales of sexual labor are wrong because they are inherently alienating or damaging to human happiness. In contrast to these two ways of thinking about the immorality of prostitution, I will argue that the most plausible support for the asymmetry thesis stems from the role of commercialized sex and reproduction in sustaining a social world in which women form a subordinated group. Prostitution is wrong insofar as the sale of women's sexual labor reinforces broad patterns of sex discrimination. My argument thus stresses neither efficiency nor sexuality's intrinsic value but, rather, equality. In particular, I argue that contemporary prostitution contributes to, and also instantiates, the perception of women as socially inferior to men.

On the basis of my analysis of prostitution's wrongness, there is no simple conclusion as to what its legal status ought to be. Both criminalization and decriminalization may have the effect of exacerbating the inequalities in virtue of which I claim that prostitution is wrong. Nonetheless, my argument does have implications for the form of prostitution's regulation, if legal, and its prohibition and penalties, if illegal. Overall, my argument tends to support decriminalization.

The argument I will put forward here is qualified and tentative in its practical conclusions, but its theoretical point is not. I will argue that the most plausible account of prostitution's wrongness turns on its relationship to the pervasive social inequality between men and women. If, in fact, no causal relationship obtains between prostitution and gender inequality, then I do not think that prostitution is morally troubling.[2] This a controversial claim. In my evaluation of prostitution, consideration of the actual social conditions which many, if not most, women face plays a crucial role. It will follow from my analysis that male prostitution raises distinct issues and is not connected to injustice in the same way as female prostitution.

On my view, prostitution is not wrong irrespective of its cultural and economic context. Moreover, prostitution is a complex phenomenon. I begin, accordingly, with the question, Who is a prostitute?

WHO IS A PROSTITUTE?

While much has been written on the history of prostitution, and some empirical studies of prostitutes themselves have been undertaken, the few philosophers writing on this subject have tended to treat prostitution as if the term referred to something as obvious as "table."[3] But it does not. Not only is it hard to draw a sharp line between prostitution and practices which look like prostitution, but as historians of the subject have emphasized, prostitution today is also a very different phenomenon from earlier forms of commercial sex.[4] In particular, the idea of prostitution as a specialized occupation of an outcast and stigmatized group is of relatively recent origin.[5]

While all contemporary prostitutes are stigmatized as outsiders, prostitution itself has an internal hierarchy based on class, race, and gender. The majority of prostitutes—and all those who walk the streets—are poor. The majority of streetwalkers in the United States are poor black women. These women are a world apart from prostitution's upper tier. Consider three cases: a streetwalker in Boston, a call girl on Park Avenue, and a male prostitute in San Francisco's tender-loin district. In what way do these three lives resemble one another? Consider the three cases:

1. A fourteen-year-old girl prostitutes herself to support her boyfriend's heroin addiction. Later, she works the streets to support her own habit. She begins, like most teenage streetwalkers, to rely on a pimp for protection. She is uneducated and is frequently subjected to violence in her relationships and with her customers. She also receives no social security, no sick leave or maternity leave, and—most important—no control as to whether or not she has sex with a man. The latter is decided by her pimp.

2. Now imagine the life of a Park Avenue call girl. Many call girls drift into prostitution after "run of the mill promiscuity," led neither by material want nor lack of alternatives.[6] Some are young college graduates, who upon graduation earn money by prostitution while searching for other jobs. Call girls can earn between $30,000 and $100,000 annually. These women have control over the entire amount they earn as well as an unusual degree of independence, far greater than in most other forms of work. They can also decide who they wish to have sex with and when they wish to do so.[7] There is little resemblance between their lives and that of the Boston streetwalker.

3. Finally, consider the increasing number of male prostitutes. Most male prostitutes (but not all) sell sex to other men.[8] Often the men who buy such sex are themselves married. Unfortunately, there is little information on male prostitutes; it has not been well studied as either a historical or a contemporary phenomenon.[9] What we do know suggests that like their female counterparts, male prostitutes cover the economic spectrum. Two important differences between male and female prostitutes are that men are more likely to work only part time and that they are not generally subject to the violence of male pimps; they tend to work on their own.

Are these three cases distinct? Many critics of prostitution have assumed that all prostitutes were women who entered the practice under circumstances which included abuse and economic desperation. But that is a false assumption: the critics have mistaken a part of the practice for the whole.[10] For example, although women who walk the streets are the most visible, they constitute only about 20 percent of the prostitute population in the United States.[11]

The varying circumstances of prostitution are important because they force us to consider carefully what we think may be wrong with prostitution. For example, in the first case, the factors which seem crucial to our response of condemnation are the miserable background conditions, the prostitute's vulnerability to violence at the hands of her pimp or client, her age, and her lack of control over whether she has sex with a client. These conditions could be redressed through regulation without forbidding commercial sexual exchanges between consenting adults.[12] The second class of prostitution stands in sharp contrast. These women engage in what seems to be a voluntary activity, chosen among a range of decent alternatives. Many of these women sell their sexual capacities without coercion or regret. The third case rebuts arguments that prostitution has no other purpose than to subordinate women.

In the next section, I explore three alternative explanations of prostitution's wrongness, which I refer to respectively as economic, essentialist, and egalitarian.

WHAT IS WRONG WITH PROSTITUTION?

The Economic Approach

Economists generally frame their questions about the best way to distribute a good without reference to its intrinsic qualities. They tend to focus on the quantitative features of a good and not its qualities.[13] Economists tend to endorse interference with a market in some good only when the results of that market are inefficient or have adverse effects on welfare.

An economic approach to prostitution does not specify a priori that certain sales are wrong: no act of commodification is ruled out in advance.[14] Rather, this approach focuses on the costs and benefits that accompany such sales. An economic approach to contracts will justify inalienability rules—rules which forbid individuals from entering into certain transactions—in cases where there are costly externalities to those transactions and in general where such transactions are inefficient. The economic approach thus supports the asymmetry thesis when the net social costs of prostitution are greater than the net social costs incurred by the sale of other human capacities.

What are the costs of prostitution? In the first place, the parties to a commercial sex transaction share possible costs of disease and guilt.[15] Prostitution also has costs to third parties: a man who frequents a prostitute dissipates financial resources which might otherwise be directed to his family; in a society which values intimate marriage, infidelity costs a man's wife or companion in terms of mistrust and suffering (and therefore prostitution may sometimes lead to marital instability); and prostitutes often have diseases which can be spread to others. Perhaps the largest third-party costs to prostitution are "moralisms":[16] many people find the practice morally offensive and are pained by its existence. (Note that "moralisms" refers to people's preferences about moral issues and not to morality as such.)

The economic approach generates a contingent case for the asymmetry thesis, focusing on prostitution's "moral" costs in terms of public opinion or the welfare costs to prostitutes or the population as a whole (e.g., through the spread of diseases). Consideration of the limitations on sexual freedom which can be justified from a welfare standpoint can be illuminating and forces us to think about the actual effects of sexual regulations.[17] Nevertheless, I want to register three objections to this approach to justifying the asymmetry thesis.

First, and most obvious, both markets and contractual exchanges function within a regime of property rights and legal entitlements. The economic approach ignores the background system of distribution within which prostitution occurs. Some background systems, however, are unjust. How do we know whether prostitution itself is part of a morally acceptable system of property rights and entitlements?

Second, this type of approach seems disabled from making sense of distinctions between goods in cases where these distinctions do not seem to reflect mere differences in the net sum of costs and benefits. The sale of certain goods seems to many people simply unthinkable—human life, for example. While it may be possible to justify prohibitions on slavery by appeal to costs and benefits (and even count moralisms in the sum), the problem is that such justification makes contingent an outcome which reasonable people do not hold contingently. It also makes little sense, phenomenologically, to describe the moral repugnance people feel toward slavery as "just a cost."[18]

Let me elaborate this point. There seems to be a fundamental difference between the "goods" of my person and my external goods, a difference whose nature is not completely explained by appeal to information failures and externalities. "Human capital" is not just another form of capital. For example, my relationship with my body and my capacities is more intimate than my relationship with most external things. The economic approach fails to capture this distinction.

Richard Posner—one of the foremost practitioners of the economic approach to law—illustrates the limits of the economic approach when he views a rapist as a "sex thief."[19] He thus overlooks the fact that rape is a crime of violence and assault.[20] He also ignores the qualitative differences between my relationship with my body and my car. But that there are such differences is obvious. The circumstances in which I sell my capacities have a much more profound effect on who I am and who I become—through effects on my desires, capacities, and values—than the circumstances in which I sell my Honda Civic. Moreover, the idea of sovereignty over body and mind is closely related to the idea of personal integrity, which is a crucial element of any reasonable scheme of liberty. The liberty to exercise sovereignty over my car has a lesser place in any reasonable scheme of liberties than the liberty to be sovereign over my body and mind.[21]

Third, some goods seem to have a special status which requires that they be shielded from the market if their social meaning or role is to be preserved. The sale of citizenship rights or friendship does not simply produce costs and benefits: it transforms the nature of the goods sold. In this sense, the market is not a neutral mechanism of exchange: there are some goods whose sale transforms or destroys their initial meaning.

These objections resonate with objections to prostitution for which its wrongness is not adequately captured by summing up contingent welfare costs and benefits. These objections resonate with moralist and egalitarian concerns. Below I survey two other types of arguments which can be used to support the asymmetry thesis: (1) essentialist arguments that the sale of sexual labor is intrinsically wrong because it is alienating or contrary to human flourishing and happiness; and (2) my own egalitarian argument that the sale of sex is wrong because, given the background conditions within which it occurs, it tends to reinforce gender inequality. I thus claim that contemporary prostitution is wrong because it promotes injustice, and not because it makes people less happy.

The Essentialist Approach

Economists abstract from the qualities of the goods that they consider. By contrast essentialists hold that there is something intrinsic to the sphere of sex and intimacy that accounts for the distinction we mark between it and other types of labor. Prostitution is not wrong simply because it causes harm; prostitution constitutes a harm. Essentialists hold that there is some intrinsic property of sex which makes its commodification wrong. Specific arguments differ, however, in what they take this property to be. I will consider two popular versions of essentialism: the first stresses the close connection between sex and the self; the second stresses the close connection between sex and human flourishing.[22]

Some feminist critics of prostitution have argued that sexual and reproductive capacities are more cru-cially tied to the nature of our selves than our other capacities.[23] The sale of sex is taken to cut deeper into the self, to involve a more total alienation from the self. As Carole Pateman puts it, "When a prostitute contracts out use of her body she is thus selling *herself* in a very real sense. Women's selves are involved in prostitution in a different manner from the involvement of the self in other occupations."[24] The realization of women's selfhood requires, on this view, that some of the capacities embodied in their persons, including their sexuality, remain "market-inalienable."[25]

Consider an analogous strategy for accounting for the value of bodily integrity in terms of its relationship to our personhood. It seems right to say that a world in which the boundaries of our bodies were not (more or less) secure would be a world in which our sense of self would be fundamentally shaken. Damage to, and violation of, our bodies affects us in a "deeper" way, a more significant way, than damage to our external property. Robbing my body of a kidney is a violation different in kind than robbing my house of a stereo, however expensive. Distributing kidneys from healthy people to sick people through a lottery is a far different act than using a lottery to distribute door prizes.[26]

But this analogy can only be the first step in an argument in favor of treating either our organs or sexual capacities as market-inalienable. Most liberals think that individual sovereignty over mind and body is crucial for the exercise of fundamental liberties. Thus, in the absence of clear harms, most liberals would reject legal bans on voluntary sales of body parts or sexual capacities. Indeed, the usual justification of such bans is harm to self: such sales are presumed to be "desperate exchanges" that the individual herself would reasonably want to fore-close. American law blocks voluntary sales of individual organs and body parts but not sales of blood on the assumption that only the former sales are likely to be so harmful to the individual that given any reasonable alternative, she herself would refrain from such sales.

Whatever the plausibility of such a claim with respect to body parts, it is considerably weaker when applied to sex (or blood). There is no strong evidence that prostitution is, at least in the United States, a desperate exchange. In part this reflects the fact that the relationship people have with their sexual capacities is far more diverse than the relationship they have with their body parts. For some people, sexuality is a realm of ecstatic communion with another, for others it is little more than a sport or distraction. Some people will find consenting to be sexually used by another person enjoyable or adequately compensated by a wage. Even for the same person, sex can be the source of a range of experiences.

Of course, the point cannot simply be that, as an empirical matter, people have differing conceptions of sexuality. The critics of prostitution grant that. The point is whether, and within what range, this diversity is desirable.[27]

Let us assume, then, in the absence of compelling counterargument, that an individual can exercise sovereignty through the sale of her sexual capacities. Margaret Radin raises a distinct worry about the effects of widespread prostitution on human flourishing. Radin's argument stresses that widespread sex markets would promote inferior forms of personhood. She says that we can see this is the case if we "reflect on what we know now about human life and choose the best from among the conceptions available to us."[28] If prostitution were to become common, Radin argues, it would have adverse effects on a form of personhood which itself is intrinsically valuable. For example, if the signs of affection and intimacy were frequently detached from their usual meaning, such signs might well become more ambiguous and easy to manipulate. The marks of an intimate relationship (physical intimacy, terms of endearment, etc.) would no longer signal the existence of intimacy. In that case, by obscuring the nature of sexual relationships, prostitution might undermine our ability to apply the criteria for coercion and informational failure.[29] Individuals might more easily enter into damaging relationships and lead less fulfilling lives as a result.

Radin is committed to a form of perfectionism which rules out the social practice of prostitution as incompatible with the highest forms of human development and flourishing. But why should perfectionists condemn prostitution while tolerating practices such as monotonous assembly line work where human beings are often mere appendages to machines? Monotonous wage labor, moreover, is far more widespread than prostitution.[30] Can a consistent perfectionist give reasons for differentiating sexual markets from other labor markets?

It is difficult to draw a line between our various capacities such that only sexual and reproductive capacities are essential to the flourishing self. In a money economy like our own, we each sell the use of many human capacities. Writers sell the use of their ability to write, advertisers sell the use of their ability to write jingles, and musicians sell the use of their ability to write and perform symphonies. Aren't these capacities also closely tied to our personhood and its higher capacities?[31] Yet the mere alienation of the use of these capacities, even when widespread, does not seem to threaten personal flourishing.

An alternative version of the essentialist thesis views the commodification of sex as an assault on personal dignity.[32] Prostitution degrades the prostitute. Elizabeth Anderson, for example, discusses the effect of commodification on the nature of sex as a shared good, based on the recognition of mutual attraction. In commercial sex, each party now values the other only instrumentally, not intrinsically. And, while both parties are thus prevented from enjoying a shared good, it is worse for the prostitute. The customer merely surrenders a certain amount of cash; the prostitute cedes her body: the prostitute is thus degraded to the status of a thing. Call this the degradation objection.

I share the intuition that the failure to treat others as persons is morally significant; it is wrong to treat people as mere things. But I am skeptical as to whether this intuition supports the conclusion that prostitution is wrong. Consider the contrast between slavery and prostitution. Slavery was, in Orlando Patterson's memorable phrase, a form of "social death": it denied to enslaved individuals the ability to press claims, to be—in their own right—sources of value and interest. But the mere sale of the use of someone's capacities does not necessarily involve a failure of this kind, on the part of either the buyer or the seller.[33] Many forms of labor, perhaps most, cede some control of a person's body to others. Such control can range from requirements to be in a certain place at a certain time (e.g., reporting to the office), to require-ments that a person (e.g., a professional athlete) eat certain foods and get certain amounts of sleep, or maintain good humor in the face of the offensive behavior of others (e.g., airline stewardesses). Some control of our capacities by others does not seem to be ipso facto destructive of our dignity.[34] Whether the purchase of a form of human labor power will have this negative consequence will depend on background social macrolevel and microlevel institutions. Mini-mum wages, worker participation and control, health and safety regulations, maternity and paternity leave, restrictions on specific performance, and the right to "exit" one's job are all features which attenuate the objectionable aspects of treating people's labor as a mere economic input. The advocates of prostitution's wrongness in virtue of its connection to self-hood, flourishing and degradation have not shown that a sys-tem of regulated prostitution would be unable to respond to their worries. In particular, they have not established that there is something wrong with pros-titution irrespective of its cultural and historical context.

There is, however, another way of interpreting the degradation objection which draws a connection between the current practice of prostitution and the lesser social status of women.[35] This connection is not a matter of the logic of prostitution per se but of the fact that contemporary prostitution degrades women by treating them as the sexual servants of men. In cur-rent prostitution, prostitutes are over-whelmingly women and their clients are almost exclusively men. Prostitution, in conceiving of a class of women as needed to satisfy male sexual desire, represents women as sexual servants to men. The degradation objection, so understood, can be seen as a way of expressing an egalitarian concern since there is no reciprocal ideology which represents men as servic-ing women's sexual needs. It is to this egalitarian understanding of prostitution's wrongness that I turn in the next section.

The Egalitarian Approach

While the essentialists rightly call our attention to the different relation we have with our capacities and

external things, they overstate the nature of the dif-ference between our sexual capacities and our other capacities with respect to our personhood, flourish-ing, and dignity.[36] They are also insufficiently atten-tive to the background conditions in which commer-cial sex exchanges take place. A third account of prostitution's wrongness stresses its causal relation-ship to gender inequality. I have defended this line of argument with respect to markets in women's repro-ductive labor.[37] Can this argument be extended to cover prostitution as well?

The answer hinges in part on how we conceive of gender inequality. On my view, there are two impor-tant dimensions of gender inequality, often conflated. The first dimension concerns inequalities in the dis-tribution of income, wealth, and opportunity. In most nations, including the United States, women form an economically and socially disadvantaged group. The statistics regarding these disadvantages, even in the United States, are grim.

1. *Income inequality.*—In 1992, given equal hours of work, women in the United States earned on aver-age sixty-six cents for every dollar earned by a man.[38] Seventy-five percent of full-time working women (as opposed to 37 percent of full-time work-ing men) earn less than twenty thousand dollars.[39]

2. *Job segregation.*—Women are less likely than men to fill socially rewarding, high-paying jobs. Despite the increasing entrance of women into previ-ously gender-segregated occupations, 46 percent of all working women are employed in service and administrative support jobs such as secretaries, wait-resses, and health aides. In the United States and Canada, the extent of job segregation in the lowest-paying occupations is increasing.[40]

3. *Poverty.*—In 1989, one out of five families were headed by women. One-third of such women-headed families live below the poverty line, which was $13,359 for a family of four in 1990.[41] In the United States, fathers currently owe mothers 24 billion dol-lars in unpaid child support.[42]

4. *Unequal division of labor in the family.*— Within the family, women spend disproportionate amounts of time on housework and rearing children. According to one recent study, wives employed full time outside the home do 70 percent of the house-

work; full-time housewives do 83 percent.[43] The unequal family division of labor is itself caused by and causes labor market inequality: given the lower wages of working women, it is more costly for men to participate in household labor.

Inequalities in income and opportunity form an important part of the backdrop against which prostitution must be viewed. While there are many possible routes into prostitution, the largest number of women who participate in it are poor, young, and uneducated. Labor market inequalities will be part of any plausible explanation of why many women "choose" to enter into prostitution.

The second dimension of gender inequality does not concern income and opportunity but status.[44] In many contemporary contexts, women are viewed and treated as inferior to men. This inferior treatment proceeds via several distinct mechanisms.

1. *Negative stereotyping.*—Stereotypes persist as to the types of jobs and responsibilities a woman can assume. Extensive studies have shown that people typically believe that men are more dominant, assertive, and instrumentally rational than women. Gender shapes beliefs about a person's capacities: women are thought to be less intelligent than their male equals.[45]

2. *Unequal power.*—Men are able to asymmetrically sanction women. The paradigm case of this is violence. Women are subjected to greater amounts of violence by men than is the reverse: every fifteen seconds a woman is battered in the United States. Battering causes more injury (excluding deaths) to women than car accidents, rape, and muggings combined.[46] Four million women a year are physically assaulted by their male partners.[47]

3. *Marginalization.*—People who are marginalized are excluded from, or absent from, core productive social roles in society—roles which convey self-respect and meaningful contribution.[48] At the extremes, marginalized women lack the means for their basic survival: they are dependent on state welfare or male partners to secure the basic necessities of life. Less severely marginalized women lack access to central and important social roles. Their activities are confined to peripheral spheres of social organization. For example, the total number of women who have

served in Congress since its inception through 1992 is 134. The total number of men is 11,096. In one-third of governments worldwide, there are no women in the decision-making bodies of the country.[49]

4. *Stigma.*—A woman's gender is associated, in some contexts, with stigma, a badge of dishonor. Consider rape. In crimes of rape, the complainant's past behavior and character are central in determining whether a crime has actually occurred. This is not true of other crimes: "mail fraud" (pun intended) is not dismissed because of the bad judgment or naïveté of the victims. Society views rape differently, I suggest, because many people think that women really want to be forced into sex. Women's lower status thus influences the way that rape is seen.

Both forms of inequality—income inequality and status inequality—potentially bear on the question of prostitution's wrongness. Women's decisions to enter into prostitution must be viewed against the background of their unequal life chances and their unequal opportunities for income and rewarding work. The extent to which women face a highly constrained range of options will surely be relevant to whether, and to what degree, we view their choices as autonomous. Some women may actually loathe or judge as inferior the lives of prostitution they "choose." Economic inequality may thus shape prostitution.

We can also ask, Does prostitution itself shape employment inequalities between men and women? In general, whenever there are significant inequalities between groups, those on the disadvantageous side will be disproportionately allocated to subordinate positions. What they do, the positions they occupy, will serve to reinforce negative and disempowering images of themselves. In this sense, prostitution can have an effect on labor-market inequality, associating women with certain stereotypes. For example, images reinforced by prostitution may make it less likely for women to be hired in certain jobs. Admittedly the effect of prostitution on labor-market inequality, if it exists at all, will be small. Other roles which women disproportionately occupy—secretaries, housecleaners, babysitters, waitresses, and saleswomen—will be far more significant in reinforcing (as well as constituting) a gender-segregated division of labor.

I do not think it is plausible to attribute to prostitution a direct causal role in income inequality between men and women. But I believe that it is plausible to maintain that prostitution makes an important and direct contribution to women's inferior social status. Prostitution shapes and its itself shaped by custom and culture, by cultural meanings about the importance of sex, about the nature of women's sexuality and male desire.[50]

If prostitution is wrong it is because of its effects on how men perceive women and on how women perceive themselves. In our society, prostitution represents women as the sexual servants of men. It supports and embodies the widely held belief that men have strong sex drives which must be satisfied—largely through gaining access to some woman's body. This belief underlies the mistaken idea that prostitution is the "oldest" profession, since it is seen as a necessary consequence of human (i.e., male) nature. It also underlies the traditional conception of marriage, in which a man owned not only his wife's property but her body as well. It should not fail to startle us that until recently, most states did not recognize the possibility of "real rape" in marriage.[51] (Marital rape remains legal in two states: North Carolina and Oklahoma.)

Why is the idea that women must service men's sexual needs an image of inequality and not mere difference? My argument suggests that there are two primary, contextual reasons:

First, in our culture, there is no reciprocal social practice which represents men as serving women's sexual needs. Men are gigolos and paid escorts—but their sexuality is not seen as an independent capacity whose use women can buy. It is not part of the identity of a class of men that they will service women's sexual desires. Indeed, male prostitutes overwhelmingly service other men and not women. Men are not depicted as fully capable of commercially alienating their sexuality to women; but prostitution depicts women as sexual servants of men.

Second, the idea that prostitution embodies an idea of women as inferior is strongly suggested by the high incidence of rape and violence against prostitutes, as well as the fact that few men seek out or even contemplate prostitutes as potential marriage partners. While all women in our society are potential targets of rape and violence, the mortality rates for women engaged in streetwalking prostitution are roughly forty times higher than that of nonprostitute women.[52]

My suggestion is that prostitution depicts an image of gender inequality, by constituting one class of women as inferior. Prostitution is a "theater" of inequality—it displays for us a practice in which women are subordinated to men. This is especially the case where women are forcibly controlled by their (male) pimps. It follows from my conception of prostitution that it need not have such a negative effect when the prostitute is male. More research needs to be done on popular images and conceptions of gay male prostitutes, as well as on the extremely small number of male prostitutes who have women clients.

The negative image of women who participate in prostitution, the image of their inferior status, is objectionable in itself. It constitutes an important form of inequality—unequal status—based on attitudes of superiority and disrespect. Unfortunately, this form of inequality has largely been ignored by political philosophers and economists who have focused instead on inequalities in income and opportunity. Moreover, this form of inequality is not confined to prostitutes. I believe that the negative image of women prostitutes has third party effects: it shapes and influences the way women as a whole are seen. This hypothesis is, of course, an empirical one. It has not been tested largely because of the lack of studies of men who go to prostitutes. Most extant studies of prostitution examine the behavior and motivations of the women who enter into the practice, a fact which itself raises the suspicion that prostitution is viewed as "a problem about the women who are prostitutes . . . [rather than] a problem about the men who demand to buy them."[53] In these studies, male gender identity is taken as a given.

To investigate prostitution's negative image effects on female prostitutes and on women generally we need research on the following questions: (1) What are the attitudes of men who visit women prostitutes toward prostitutes? How do their attitudes compare with the attitudes of men who do not visit prostitutes toward women prostitutes? (2) What are the attitudes of men who visit women prostitutes toward women generally? What are the attitudes of men who do not visit women prostitutes toward women generally? (3) What are the attitudes of women toward women prostitutes? (4) What are the attitudes of the men and women involved in prostitution toward themselves? (5) Given the large proportion of African-American women who participate in prostitution, in what ways does prostitution contribute to male attitudes toward these women? (6) Does prostitution contribute to or diminish the likelihood of crimes of sexual violence? (7) What can we learn about these questions through cross-national studies? How do attitudes in the United States about women prostitutes compare with those in countries with more egalitarian wage policies or less status inequality between men and women?

The answers to these questions will reflect social facts about our culture. Whatever plausibility there is to the hypothesis that prostitution causally contributes to gender status inequality, it gains this plausibility from its surrounding cultural context.

I can imagine hypothetical circumstances in which prostitution would not have a negative image effect, where it could mark a reclaiming of women's sexuality. Margo St. James and other members of Call Off Your Old Tired Ethics (COYOTE) have argued that prostitutes can function as sex therapists, fulfilling a legitimate social need as well as providing a source of experiment and alternative conceptions of sexuality and gender.[54] I agree that in a different culture, with different assumptions about men's and women's gender identities, prostitution might not have unequalizing effects. But I think that St. James and others have minimized the cultural stereotypes that surround contemporary prostitution and their power over the shape of the practice. Prostitution, as we know it, is not separable from the larger surrounding culture which marginalizes, stereotypes, and stigmatizes women. Rather than providing an alternative conception of sexuality, I think that we need to look carefully at what men and women actually learn in prostitution. I do not believe that ethnographic studies of prostitution would support COYOTE's claim that prostitution contributes to images of women's dignity and equal standing.

If, through its negative image of women as sexual servants of men, prostitution reinforces women's inferior status in society, then it is wrong. Even though men can be and are prostitutes, I think that it is unlikely that we will find such negative image effects on men as a group. Individual men may be degraded in individual acts of prostitution: men as a group are not.

Granting all of the above, one objection to the equality approach to prostitution's wrongness remains. Is prostitution's negative image effect greater than that produced by other professions in which women largely service men, for example, secretarial labor? What is special about prostitution?

The negative image effect undoubtedly operates outside the domain of prostitution. But there are two significant differences between prostitution and other gender-segregated professions.

First, most people believe that prostitution, unlike secretarial work, is especially objectionable. Holding such moral views of prostitution constant, if prostitution continues to be primarily a female occupation, then the existence of prostitution will disproportionately fuel negative images of women.[55] Second, and relatedly, the particular image of women in prostitution is more of an image of inferiority than that of a secretary. The image embodies a greater amount of objectification, of representing the prostitute as an object without a will of her own. Prostitutes are far more likely to be victims of violence than are secretaries: as I mentioned, the mortality rate of women in prostitution is forty times that of other women. Prostitutes are also far more likely to be raped: a prostitute's "no" does not, to the male she services, mean no.

My claim is that, unless such arguments about prostitution's causal role in sustaining a form of gender inequality can be supported, I am not persuaded that something is morally wrong with markets in sex. In particular, I do not find arguments about the necessary relationship between commercial sex and diminished flourishing and degradation convincing. If prostitution is wrong, it is not because of its effects on happiness or personhood (effects which are shared with other forms of wage-labor); rather, it is because the sale of women's sexual labor may have adverse consequences for achieving a significant form of equality between men and women. My argument for the asymmetry thesis, if correct, connects prostitution to injustice. I now turn to the question of whether, even if we assume that prostitution is wrong under current conditions, it should remain illegal.

SHOULD PROSTITUTION BE LEGALIZED?

It is important to distinguish between prostitution's wrongness and the legal response that we are entitled to make to that wrongness. Even if prostitution is wrong, we may not be justified in prohibiting it if that prohibition makes the facts in virtue of which it is wrong worse, or if its costs are too great for other important values, such as autonomy and privacy. For example, even if someone accepts that the contemporary division of labor in the family is wrong, they may still reasonably object to government surveillance of the family's division of household chores. To determine whether such surveillance is justified, we need know more about the fundamental interests at stake, the costs of surveillance and the availability of alternative mechanisms for promoting equality in families. While I think that there is no acceptable view which would advocate government surveillance of family chores, there remain a range of plausible views about the appropriate scope of state intervention and, indeed, the appropriate scope of equality considerations.[56]

It is also important to keep in mind that in the case of prostitution, as with pornography and hate speech, narrowing the discussion of solutions to the single question of whether to ban or not to ban shows a poverty of imagination. There are many ways of challenging existing cultural values about the appropriate division of labor in the family and the nature of women's sexual and reproductive capacities—for example, education, consciousness-raising groups, changes in employee leave policies, comparable worth programs, etc. The law is not the only way to provide women with incentives to refrain from participating in prostitution. Nonetheless, we do need to decide what the best legal policy toward prostitution should be.

I begin with an assessment of the policy which we now have. The United States is one of the few developed Western countries which criminalizes prostitution.[57] Denmark, the Netherlands, West Germany, Sweden, Switzerland, and Austria all have legalized prostitution, although in some of these countries it is restricted by local ordinances.[58] Where prostitution is permitted, it is closely regulated.

Suppose that we accept that gender equality is a legitimate goal of social policy. The question is whether the current legal prohibition on prostitution in the United States promotes gender equality. The answer I think is that it clearly does not. The current legal policies in the United States arguably exacerbate the factors in virtue of which prostitution is wrong.

The current prohibition on prostitution renders the women who engage in the practice vulnerable. First, the participants in the practice seek assistance from pimps in lieu of the contractual and legal remedies which are denied them. Male pimps may protect women prostitutes from their customers and from the police, but the system of pimp-run prostitution has enormous negative effects on the women at the lowest rungs of prostitution. Second, prohibition of prostitution raises the dilemma of the "double bind": if we prevent prostitution without greater redistribution of income, wealth, and opportunities, we deprive poor women of one way—in some circumstances the only way—of improving their condition.[59] Analogously, we do not solve the problem of homelessness by criminalizing it.

Furthermore, women are disproportionately punished for engaging in commercial sex acts. Many state laws make it a worse crime to sell sex than to buy it. Consequently, pimps and clients ("johns") are rarely prosecuted. In some jurisdictions, patronizing a prostitute is not illegal. The record of arrests and convictions is also highly asymmetric. Ninety percent of all convicted prostitutes are women. Studies have shown that male prostitutes are arrested with less frequency than female prostitutes and receive shorter sentences. One study of the judicial processing of 2,859 male and female prostitutes found that judges were more likely to find defendants guilty if they were female.[60]

Nor does the current legal prohibition on prostitution unambiguously benefit women as a class because the cultural meaning of current governmental prohibition of prostitution is unclear. While an unrestricted regime of prostitution—a pricing system in women's sexual attributes—could have negative external consequences on women's self-perceptions and perceptions by men, state prohibition can also reflect a view of women which contributes to their inequality. For example, some people support state regulation because they believe that women's sexuality is for purposes of reproduction, a claim tied to traditional ideas about women's proper role.

There is an additional reason why banning prostitution seems an inadequate response to the problem of gender inequality and which suggests a lack of parallel with the case of commercial surrogacy. Banning prostitution would not by itself—does not—eliminate it. While there is reason to think that making commercial surrogacy arrangements illegal or unenforceable would diminish their occurrence, no such evidence exists about prostitution. No city has eliminated prostitution merely through criminalization. Instead, criminalized prostitution thrives as a black market activity in which pimps substitute for law as the mechanism for enforcing contracts. It thereby makes the lives of prostitutes worse than they might otherwise be and without clearly counteracting prostitution's largely negative image of women.

If we decide to ban prostitution, these problems must be addressed. If we decide not to ban prostitution (either by legalizing it or decriminalizing it), then we must be careful to regulate the practice to address its negative effects. Certain restrictions on advertising and recruitment will be needed in order to address the negative image effects that an unrestricted regime of prostitution would perpetuate. But the current regime of prostitution has negative effects on the prostitutes themselves. It places their sexual capacities largely under the control of men. In order to promote women's autonomy, the law needs to ensure that certain restrictions—in effect, a Bill of Rights for Women—are in place.[61]

1. No woman should be forced, either by law or by private persons, to have sex against her will. (Recall that it is only quite recently that the courts have recognized the existence of marital rape.) A woman who sells sex must be able to refuse to give it; she must not be coerced by law or private persons to perform.

2. No woman should be denied access, either by law or by private persons, to contraception or to treatment for sexually transmitted diseases, particularly AIDS, or to abortion (at least in the first trimester).

3. The law should ensure that a woman has adequate information before she agrees to sexual intercourse. The risks of venereal and other sexually transmitted diseases, the risks of pregnancy, and the laws protecting a woman's right to refuse sex should all be generally available.

4. Minimum age of consent laws for sexual intercourse should be enforced. These laws should ensure that woman (and men) are protected from coercion and do not enter into sexual relationships until they are in a position to understand what they are consenting to.

5. The law should promote women's control over their own sexuality by prohibiting brokerage. If what is wrong with prostitution is its relation to gender inequality, then it is crucial that the law be brought to bear primarily on the men who profit from the use of women's sexual capacities.

Each of these principles is meant to establish and protect a woman's right to control her sexual and reproductive capacities and not to give control of these capacities to others. Each of these principles is meant to protect the conditions for women's consent to sex, whether commercial or not. Each of these principles also seeks to counter the degradation of women in prostitution by mitigating its nature as a form of female servitude. In addition, given that a woman's choices are shaped both by the range of available opportunities and by the distribution of entitlements in society, it is crucial to attend to the inferior economic position of women in American society and those social and economic factors which produce the unequal life chances of men and women.

CONCLUSION

If the arguments I have offered here are correct, then prostitution is wrong in virtue of its contributions to perpetuating a pervasive form of inequality. In different circumstances, with different assumptions about women and their role in society, I do not think that prostitution would be especially troubling—no more troubling than many other labor markets currently allowed. It follows, then, that in other circumstances, the asymmetry thesis would be denied or less strongly felt. While the idea that prostitution is intrinsically degrading is a powerful intuition (and like many such intuitions, it persists even after its proponents undergo what Richard Brandt has termed "cognitive therapy," in which errors of fact and inference are corrected), I believe that this intuition is itself bound up with well-entrenched views of male gender identity and women's sexual role in the context of that identity.[62] If we are troubled by prostitution, as I think we should be, then we should direct much of our energy to putting forward alternative models of egalitarian relations between men and women.

NOTES

1. Debra Satz, "Markets in Women's Reproductive Labor," *Philosophy and Public Affairs* 21 (1992): 107–31.

2. What would remain troubling would be the miserable and unjust background circumstances in which much prostitution occurs. That is, if there were gender equality between the sexes but a substantial group of very poor men and women were selling sex, this would indeed be troubling. We should be suspicious of any labor contract entered into under circumstances of desperation.

3. Laurie Shrage, "Should Feminists Oppose Prostitution?" *Ethics* 99 (1989): 347–61, is an important exception. See also her new book, *Moral Dilemmas of Feminism: Prostitution, Adultery and Abortion* (New York: Routledge, 1994).

4. The fact that monetary exchange plays a role in maintaining many intimate relationships is a point underscored by George Bernard Shaw in *Mrs. Warren's Profession* (New York: Garland, 1981).

5. Compare Judith Walkowitz, *Prostitution and Victorian Society* (Cambridge: Cambridge University Press, 1980); Ruth Rosen, *Prostitution in America: 1900–1918* (Baltimore: Johns Hopkins University Press, 1982); B. Hobson, *Uneasy Virtue: The Politics of Prostitution and the American Reform Tradition* (Chicago: University of Chicago Press, 1990).

6. John Decker, *Prostitution: Regulation and Control* (Littleton, Colo.: Rothman, 1979), p. 191.

7. Compare Harold Greenwald, *The Elegant Prostitute: A Social and Psychoanalytic Study* (New York: Walker, 1970), p. 10.

8. For discussion of male prostitutes who sell sex to women, see H. Smith and B. Van der Horst, "For Women Only—How It Feels to Be a Male Hooker," *Village Voice* (March 7, 1977). Dictionary and common usage tends to identify prostitutes with women. Men who sell sex to women are generally referred to as "gigolos," not "prostitutes." The former term encompasses the sale of companionship as well as sex.

9. Male prostitutes merit only a dozen pages in John Decker's monumental study of prostitution. See also D. Drew and J. Drake, *Boys for Sale: A Sociological Study of Boy Prostitution* (Deer Park, N.Y.: Brown Book Co., 1969); D. Deisher, "Young Male Prostitutes," *Journal of American Medical Association* 212 (1970): 1661–66; Gita Sereny, *The Invisible Children: Child Prostitution in America, West Germany and Great Britain* (London: Deutsch, 1984). I am grateful to Vincent DiGirolamo for bringing these works to my attention.

10. Compare Kathleen Barry, *Female Sexual Slavery* (New York: Avon, 1979). If we consider prostitution as an international phenomenon, then a majority of prostitutes are desperately poor and abused women. Nevertheless, there is a significant minority who are not. Furthermore, if prostitution were legalized, it is possible that the minimum condition of prostitutes in at least some countries would be raised.

11. Priscilla Alexander, "Prostitution: A Difficult Issue for Feminists," in *Sex Work: Writings by Women in the Sex Industry,* ed. P. Alexander and F. Delacoste (Pittsburgh: Cleis, 1987).

12. Moreover, to the extent that the desperate background conditions are the problem it is not apparent that outlawing prostitution is the solution. Banning prostitution may only remove a poor woman's best option: it in no way eradicates the circumstances which led her to such a choice. See M. Radin, "Market-Inalienability," *Harvard Law Review* 100 (1987): 1849–1937, on the problem of the "double bind."

13. Sometimes the qualitative aspects of a good have quantitative effects and so for that reason need to be taken into account. It is difficult, e.g., to establish a market in used cars given the uncertainties of ascertaining their qualitative condition. Compare George Akerlof, "The Market for Lemons: Qualitative Uncertainty and the Market Mechanism," *Quarterly Journal of Economics* 84 (1970): 488–500.

14. For an attempt to understand human sexuality as a whole through the economic approach, see Richard Posner, *Sex and Reason* (Cambridge, Mass.: Harvard University Press, 1992).

15. Although two-thirds of prostitutes surveyed say that they have no regrets about choice of work. Compare Decker, pp. 165–66. This figure is hard to interpret, given the high costs of thinking that one has made a bad choice of occupation and the lack of decent employment alternatives for many prostitutes.

16. See Guido Calabresi and A. Douglas Melamed, "Property Rules, Liability Rules and Inalienability: One View of the Cathedral," *Harvard Law Review* 85 (1972): 1089–1128.

17. Economic analysis fails to justify the laws we now have regarding prostitution. See below.

18. See Radin, pp. 1884 ff.

19. Posner, *Sex and Reason,* p. 182. See also R. Posner, "An Economic Theory of the Criminal Law," *Columbia Law Review* 85 (1985): 1193–1231. "The prohibition against rape is to the sex and marriage 'market' as the prohibition against theft is to explicit markets in goods and services" (p. 1199).

20. His approach in fact suggests that rape be seen as a "benefit" to the rapist, a suggestion that I think we should be loathe to follow.

21. I do not mean to claim however that such sovereignty over the body is absolute.

22. This section draws from and enlarges upon Satz.

23. Prostitution is, however, an issue which continues to divide feminists as well as prostitutes and former prostitutes. On the one side, some feminists see prostitution as dehumanizing and alienating and linked to male domination. This is the view taken by the prostitute organization Women Hurt in Systems of Prostitution Engaged in Revolt (WHISPER). On the other side, some feminists see sex markets as affirming a woman's right to autonomy, sexual pleasure, and economic welfare. This is the view taken by the prostitute organization COYOTE.

24. Carole Pateman, *The Sexual Contract* (Stanford, Calif.: Stanford University Press, 1988), p. 207; emphasis added.

25. The phrase is Radin's.

26. J. Harris, "The Survival Lottery," *Philosophy* 50 (1975): 81–87.

27. As an example of the ways in which the diversity of sexual experience has been culturally productive, see Lynn Hunt, ed., *The Invention of Pornography* (New York: Zone, 1993). Many of the essays in this volume illustrate the ways in which pornography has historically contributed to broader social criticism.

28. Radin, p. 1884.

29. An objection along these lines is raised by Margaret Baldwin ("Split at the Root: Feminist Discourses of Law Reform," *Yale Journal of Law and Feminism* 5 [1992]: 47–120). Baldwin worries that prostitution undermines our ability to understand a woman's capacity to consent to sex. Baldwin asks, Will a prostitute's consent to sex be seen as consent to a twenty dollar payment? Will courts determine sentences in rape trials involving prostitutes as the equiva-

lent of parking fine violations (e.g., as another twenty dollar payment)? Aren't prostitutes liable to have their fundamental interests in bodily integrity discounted? I think Baldwin's worry is a real one, especially in the context of the current stigmatization of prostitutes. It could be resolved, in part, by withholding information about a woman's profession from rape trials.

30. Radin is herself fairly consistent in her hostility to many forms of wage labor. She has a complicated view about decommodification in nonideal circumstances which I cannot discuss here.

31. Also notice that many forms of labor we make inalienable—e.g., bans on mercenaries—cannot be justified by that labor's relationship to our personhood.

32. Elizabeth Anderson, *Value in Ethics and Economics* (Cambridge, Mass.: Harvard University Press, 1993), p. 45.

33. Actually, the prostitute's humanity is a part of the sex transaction itself. Whereas Posner's economic approach places sex with another person on the same scale as sex with a sheep, for many people the latter is not a form of sex at all (*Sex and Reason*). Moreover, in its worst forms, the prostitute's humanity (and gender) may be crucial to the john's experience of himself as superior to her. See Catherine MacKinnon, *Toward a Feminist Theory of the State* (Cambridge, Mass.: Harvard University Press, 1989).

34. Although this statement might have to be qualified in the light of empirical research. Arlie Hochschild, e.g., has found that the sale of "emotional labor" by airline stewardesses and insurance salesmen distorts their responses to pain and frustration (*The Managed Heart: The Commercialization of Human Feeling* [New York: Basic, 1983]).

35. I owe this point to Elizabeth Anderson, who stressed the need to distinguish between different versions of the degradation objection and suggested some lines of interpretation (conversation with author, Oxford University, July 1994).

36. More generally, they raise questions about the desirability of a world in which people use and exploit each other as they use and exploit other natural objects, insofar as this is compatible with Pareto improvements.

37. See Satz.

38. U.S. Department of Labor, Women's Bureau (Washington, D.C.: Government Printing Office, 1992).

39. D. Taylor, "Women: An Analysis," in *Women: A World Report* (London: Methuen, 1985). Taylor reports that while on a world scale women "perform nearly two-thirds of all working hours [they] receive only one tenth of the world income and own less than one percent of world resources."

40. J. David-McNeil, "The Changing Economic Status of the Female Labor Force in Canada," in *Towards Equity: Proceedings of a Colloquium on the Economic Status of Women in the Labor Market*," ed. Economic Council of Canada (Ottawa: Canadian Government Publication Centre, 1985).

41. S. Rix, ed., *The American Woman, 1990–91* (New York: Norton, 1990), cited in Woman's Action Coalition, ed., *WAC Stats: The Facts about Women* (New York: New Press, 1993), p. 41.

42. Report of the Federal Office of Child Support Enforcement, 1990.

43. Rix, ed. Note also that the time women spend doing housework has not declined since the 1920s despite the invention of labor saving technologies (e.g., laundry machines and dishwashers).

44. My views about this aspect of gender inequality have been greatly clarified in discussions and correspondence with Elizabeth Anderson and Elizabeth Wood during 1994.

45. See Paul Rosenkrantz, Susan Vogel, Helen Bees, Inge Broverman, and David Broverman, "Sex-Role Stereotypes and Self-Concepts in College Students," *Journal of Consulting and Clinical Psychology* 32 (1968): 286–95.

46. L. Heise, "Gender Violence as a Health Issue" (Violence, Health and Development Project, Center for Women's Global Leadership, Rutgers University, New Brunswick, N.J., 1992).

47. L. Heise, "Violence against Women: The Missing Agenda," in *Women's Health: A Global Perspective* (New York: Westview, 1992), cited in Woman's Action Coalition, ed., p. 55. More than one-third of female homicide victims are killed by their husbands or boyfriends.

48. I am indebted here to the discussion of Iris Young in *Justice and the Politics of Difference* (Princeton, N.J.: Princeton University Press, 1990).

49. Ruth Leger Sivard, *Women . . . a World Survey* (Washington, D.C.: World Priorities, 1985).

50. Shrage ("Should Feminists Oppose Prostitution?") argues that prostitution perpetuates the following beliefs which oppress women: (1) the universal possession of a potent sex drive; (2) the "natural" dominance of men; (3) the pollution of women by sexual contact; and (4) the reification of sexual practice.

51. Susan Estrich, *Real Rape* (Cambridge, Mass.: Harvard University Press, 1987).

52. Baldwin, p. 75. Compare the Canadian Report on Prostitution and Pornography; also M. Silbert, "Sexual Assault on Prostitutes," research report to the *National Center for the Prevention and Control of Rape*, November 1980, for a study of street prostitutes in which 70 percent of those surveyed reported that they had been raped while walking the streets.

53. Carole Pateman, "Defending Prostitution: Charges against Ericsson," *Ethics* 93 (1983): 561–65, p. 563.

54. See also, S. Schwartzenbach, "Contractarians and Feminists Debate Prostitution," *New York University Review of Law and Social Change* 18 (1990–91): 103–30.

55. I owe this point to Arthur Kuflik.

56. For example, does the fact that racist joke telling reinforces negative stereotypes and perpetuates racial prejudice and inequality justify legal bans on such joke telling? What are the limits on what we can justifiably use the state to do in the name of equality? This is a difficult question. I only note here that arguments which justify state banning of prostitution can be consistent with the endorsement of stringent protections for speech. This is because speech and expression are arguably connected with basic fundamental human interests—with forming and articulating conceptions of value, with gathering information, with testifying on matters of conscience—in a way that prostitution (and some speech, e.g., commercial speech) is not. Even if we assume, as I think we should, that people have fundamental interests in having control over certain aspects of their bodies and lives, it does not follow that they have a fundamental interest in being free to sell themselves, their body parts, or any of their particular capacities.

57. Prostitution is legalized only in several jurisdictions in Nevada.

58. These countries have more pay equity between men and women than does the United States. This might be taken to undermine an argument about prostitution's role in contributing to income inequality. Moreover, women's status is lower in some societies which repress prostitution (such as those of the Islamic nations) than in those which do not (such as those of the Scandinavian nations). But given the variety of cultural, economic, and political factors and mechanisms which need to be taken into account, we need to be very careful in drawing hasty conclusions. Legalizing prostitution might have negative effects on gender equality in the United States, even if legal prostitution does not correlate with gender inequality in other countries. There are many differences between the United States and European societies which make it implausible to think that one factor can alone be explanatory with respect to gender inequality.

59. Radin, pp. 1915 ff.

60. J. Lindquist et al., "Judicial Processing of Males and Females Charged with Prostitution," *Journal of Criminal Justice* 17 (1989): 277–91. Several state laws banning

prostitution have been challenged on equal protection grounds. These statistics support the idea that prostitution's negative image effect has disproportionate bearing on male and female prostitutes.

61. In this section, I have benefited from reading Cass Sunstein, "Gender Difference, Reproduction and the Law" (University of Chicago Law School, 1992, unpublished manuscript). Sunstein believes that someone committed to gender equality will, most likely, advocate a legal ban on prostitution.

62. Richard B. Brandt, *A Theory of the Good and the Right* (Oxford: Clarendon, 1979).

PART 9

~

Philosophy of Art

Introduction

GABRIELA SAKAMOTO

The philosophy of art is a branch of inquiry that seeks to explore the nature of artworks and our relationship to them. Work in the philosophy of art is as diverse as art itself, and it would be inaccurate to say that there is presently a single set of issues or concepts defining this field. Rather than attempt to capture such diversity, the readings in this section focus on two central questions in the philosophy of art: can art be defined? Are aesthetic responses and judgments merely subjective?

Although most of us can cite examples of paintings, movies, pieces of music, works of literature, etc. that we would consider to be works of art, specifying what makes these things art is extremely difficult. Attempts to define this category of objects have ranged from appeals to imitation, to expression, and to formal properties of the work. According to Morris Weitz, however, any attempt to define art is misconceived. The very nature of art and of creativity, Weitz argues, demands that art is an "open concept," that there be no necessary and sufficient conditions for its application.

In opposition to Weitz, George Dickie contends that art can be defined and, moreover, defined in such a way that does not undermine "the expansive, adventurous character of art." For Dickie, an artwork is any artifact that an art-world public (audiences, critics, curators, artists, etc.) deems a candidate of appreciation. Arthur Danto has a similar approach toward understanding the nature of art. For Danto, it is an object's place in a specific historical and theoretical context that gives it the status of art. It is this kind of "art world" that gives artworks their meaning. Once this history has run its course, Danto suggests, the notion of art will also come to an end. Theories of art that rely on the importance of history and social context to define art, however, may not be without problems. As Peg Zeglin Brand argues in her essay, such theories may, in fact, perpetrate traditional prejudices against certain kinds of art and artists by relying on male-dominated paradigms of aesthetic production and reception.

Brand's skepticism that our understanding of what art is may not have a basis in objective fact raises a more general question concerning the ground for any judgment of aesthetic value and significance. Can aesthetic judgments ever be correct or incorrect? Or are art and beauty, as the saying goes, merely in the eye of the beholder? The selections by David Hume and Immanuel Kant represent two of the most important discussions on this issue. Both Hume and Kant hold that judgments of taste are grounded in feelings of pleasure. Yet for neither thinker does it follow that there are no norms for such judgments, that our feelings cannot be said to be proper or improper or that we can never demand agreement from others. For Hume, widespread differences of feeling in matters of taste are generally a result of prejudice, lack of sensibility, or lack of knowledge. Only those immune to such defects can be said to be "true judges," and for Hume, it is precisely in the "joint verdict" of a community of such judges that we find standards of correctness.

Kant, on the other hand, locates the basis for agreement in the nature of aesthetic judgments themselves. For Kant, true judgments of taste or beauty are "disinterested," completely free of any desire for or interest in the object perceived. So, while aesthetic judgments are grounded on individual feeling, there is nothing in them that accounts for one person's judgment differing from another's. This is why a person making such a judgment can insist that his or her pleasure in an object is of universal assent, that others ought to feel and thus judge the object in the same way.

Kendall Walton's essay "Categories of Art" is a contemporary reflection on issues raised by Hume and Kant. For Walton, our interpretations of a work are dependent on the categories in which we see it. In order to make adequate judgments of aesthetic value, we need to know whether the work is a painting, a poem, a symphony, etc. Of course, there can be much debate as to what the defining essence, and thus value, of a particular medium is. Ted Cohen argues, for example, that it may be misleading to place too much aesthetic significance on the idea that photographs, unlike other forms of pictorial representation, stand in a direct relationship to reality or that they are produced by a mechanical process.

For Walton, insofar as there exist criteria for belonging to a certain category, only persons who see the work in the appropriate category are in a position to make correct judgments about it. While this is Walton's way of solving the problem that faced both Hume and Kant, the implications of Walton's view are different. First, aesthetic judgments require specialized knowledge. Understanding art involves more than just developing a keen perceptual sensibility—we must also know about the conditions and history of particular media. Second, contrary to Kant's view, responding appropriately to an artwork demands some degree of conceptualization or even guided interest, for without some prior idea as to what category the artwork belongs, in what way it fits or fails to fit with the history and conditions of its medium, no aesthetic judgment can get off the ground.

In the end, this suggests that it may be wrong to think there exists a philosophy of art at all. Rather, it may be better to think in terms of philosophies of art. Yet whether one chooses to think of the individual arts as connected by a common essence or as largely independent categories, what matters, of course, is that our debates over art continue. If Morris Weitz is right, the very possibility of art and our enduring interest in it is a direct consequence of art always changing. To a large extent, it is philosophical inquiry and reflection that keep it so.

The Role of Theory in Aesthetics

~

MORRIS WEITZ

Morris Weitz (1916–1981) was Richard Koret Professor of Philosophy at Brandeis University. He was one of the first to apply the methods of analytic philosophy to problems in aesthetics. Among his numerous writings in the philosophy of art are *Hamlet and the Philosophy of Literary Criticism* and *The Opening Mind.*

Theory has been central in aesthetics and is still the preoccupation of the philosophy of art. Its main avowed concern remains the determination of the nature of art which can be formulated into a definition of it. It construes definition as the statement of the necessary and sufficient properties of what is being defined, where the statement purports to be a true or false claim about the essence of art, what characterizes and distinguishes it from everything else. Each of the great theories of art—Formalism, Voluntarism, Emotionalism, Intellectualism, Intuitionism, Organicism—converges on the attempt to state the defining properties of art. Each claims that it is the true theory because it has formulated correctly into a real definition the nature of art; and that the others are false because they have left out some necessary or sufficient property. Many theorists contend that their enterprise is no mere intellectual exercise but an absolute necessity for any understanding of art and our proper evaluation of it. Unless we know what art is, they say, what are its necessary and sufficient properties, we cannot begin to respond to it adequately or to say why one work is good or better than another. Aesthetic theory, thus, is important not only in itself but for the foundations of both appreciation and criticism. Philosophers, critics, and even artists who have written on art agree that what is primary in aesthetics is a theory about the nature of art.

Is aesthetic theory, in the sense of a true definition or set of necessary and sufficient properties of art, possible? If nothing else does, the history of aesthetics itself should give one enormous pause here. For, in spite of the many theories, we seem no nearer our goal today than we were in Plato's time. Each age, each art-movement, each philosophy of art, tries over and over again to establish the stated ideal only to be succeeded by a new or revised theory, rooted, at least in part, in the repudiation of preceding ones. Even today, almost everyone interested in aesthetic matters is still deeply wedded to the hope that the correct theory of art is forthcoming. We need only examine the numerous new books on art in which new definitions are proffered; or, in our own country especially, the basic textbooks and anthologies to recognize how strong the priority of a theory of art is.

In this essay I want to plead for the rejection of this problem. I want to show that theory—in the requisite classical sense—is *never* forthcoming in aesthetics, and that we would do much better as philosophers to supplant the question, "What is the nature of art?" by other questions, the answers to which will provide us with all the understanding of the arts there can be. I want to show that the inadequacies of the theories are not primarily occasioned by any legitimate difficulty such as, e.g., the vast complexity of art, which might be corrected by further probing and research. Their basic inadequacies reside instead in a fundamental misconception of art. Aesthetic the-

Reprinted from *The Journal of Aesthetics and Art Criticism, 15* (1956), by permission of the American Society for Aesthetics.

ory—all of it—is wrong in principle in thinking that a correct theory is possible because it radically misconstrues the logic of the concept of art. Its main contention that "art" is amenable to real or any kind of true definition is false. Its attempt to discover the necessary and sufficient properties of art is logically misbegotten for the very simple reason that such a set and, consequently, such a formula about it, is never forthcoming. Art, as the logic of the concept shows, has no set of necessary and sufficient properties; hence a theory of it is logically impossible and not merely factually difficult. Aesthetic theory tries to define what cannot be defined in its requisite sense. But in recommending the repudiation of aesthetic theory I shall not argue from this, as too many others have done, that its logical confusions render it meaningless or worthless. On the contrary, I wish to reassess its role and its contribution primarily in order to show that it is of the greatest importance to our understanding of the arts.

Let us now survey briefly some of the more famous extant aesthetic theories in order to see if they do incorporate correct and adequate statements about the nature of art. In each of these there is the assumption that it is the true enumeration of the defining properties of art, with the implication that previous theories have stressed wrong definitions. Thus, to begin with, consider a famous version of Formalist theory, that propounded by Bell and Fry. It is true that they speak mostly of painting in their writings but both assert that what they find in that art can be generalized for what is "art" in the others as well. The essence of painting they maintain, is the plastic elements in relation. Its defining property is significant form, i.e., certain combinations of lines, colors, shapes, volumes—everything on the canvas except the representational elements—which evoke a unique response to such combinations. Painting is definable as plastic organization. The nature of art, what it *really* is, so their theory goes, is a unique combination of certain elements (the specifiable plastic ones) in their relations. Anything which is art is an instance of significant form; and anything which is not art has no such form.

To this the Emotionalist replies that the truly essential property of art has been left out. Tolstoy, Ducasse, or any of the advocates of this theory, find that the requisite defining property is not significant

form but rather the expression of emotion in some sensuous public medium. Without projection of emotion into some piece of stone or words or sounds, etc., there can be no art. Art is really such embodiment. It is this that uniquely characterizes art, and any true, real definition of it contained in some adequate theory of art, must so state it.

The Intuitionist disclaims both emotion and form as defining properties. In Croce's version, for example, art is identified not with some physical, public object but with a specific creative, cognitive, and spiritual art. Art is really a first stage of knowledge in which certain human beings (artists) bring their images and intuitions into lyrical clarification or expression. As such, it is an awareness, nonconceptual in character, of the unique individuality of things; and since it exists below the level of conceptualization or action, it is without scientific or moral content. Croce singles out as the defining essence of art this first stage of spiritual life and advances its identification with art as a philosophically true theory or definition.

The Organicist says to all of this that art is really a class of organic wholes consisting of distinguishable, albeit inseparable, elements in their causally efficacious relations which are presented in some sensuous medium. In A. C. Bradley, in piecemeal versions of it in literary criticism, or in my own generalized adaptation of it in my *Philosophy of the Arts,* what is claimed is that anything which is a work of art is in its nature a unique complex of interrelated parts—in painting, for example, lines, colors, volumes, subjects, etc., all interacting upon one another on a paint surface of some sort. Certainly, at one time at least it seemed to me that this organic theory constituted the one true and real definition of art.

My final example is the most interesting of all, logically speaking. This is the Voluntarist theory of Parker. In his writings on art, Parker persistently calls into question the traditional simpleminded definitions of aesthetics. "The assumption underlying every philosophy of art is the existence of some common nature present in all the arts."[1] "All the so popular brief definitions of art—'significant form,' 'expression,' 'intuition,' 'objectified pleasure'—all fallacious, either because, while true of art, they are also true of much that is not art, and hence fail to differentiate art from other things; or else because they neglect some essential aspect of art."[2] But instead of inveighing against the attempt at definition of art itself, Parker insists that what is needed is a complex definition rather than a simple one. "The definition of art must therefore be in terms of a complex of characteristics. Failure to recognize this has been the fault of all the well-known definitions."[3] His own version of Voluntarism is the theory that art is essentially three things: embodiment of wishes and desires imaginatively satisfied, language, which characterizes the public medium of art, and harmony, which unifies the language with the layers of imaginative projections. Thus, for Parker, it is a true definition to say of art that it is "the provision of satisfaction through the imagination, social significance, and harmony. I am claiming that nothing except works of art possesses all three of these marks."[4]

Now, all these sample theories are inadequate in many different ways. Each purports to be in a complete statement about the defining features of all works of art and yet each of them leaves out something which the others take to be central. Some are circular, e.g., the Bell-Fry theory of art as significant form which is defined in part in terms of our response to significant form. Some of them, in their search for necessary and sufficient properties, emphasize too few properties, like (again) the Bell-Fry definition, which leaves out subject-representation in painting, or the Croce theory, which omits inclusion of the very important feature of the public, physical character, say, of architecture. Others are too general and cover objects that are not art as well as works of art. Organicism is surely such a view since it can be applied to *any* causal unity in the natural world as well as to art.[5] Still others rest on dubious principles, e.g., Parker's claim that art embodies imaginative satisfactions, rather than real ones; or Croce's assertion that there is nonconceptual knowledge. Consequently, even if art has one set of necessary and sufficient properties, none of the theories we have noted or, for that matter, no aesthetic theory yet proposed has enumerated that set to the satisfaction of all concerned.

Then there is a different sort of difficulty. As real definitions, these theories are supposed to be factual reports on art. If they are, may we not ask, Are they empirical and open to verification or falsification? For example, what would confirm or disconfirm the theory that art is significant form or embodiment of emotion or creative synthesis of images? There does not even seem to be a hint of the kind of evidence which might be forthcoming to test these theories; and indeed one wonders if they are perhaps honorific definitions of "art," that is, proposed redefinitions in terms of some *chosen* conditions for applying the concept of art, and not true or false reports on the essential properties of art at all.

But all these criticisms of traditional aesthetic theories—that they are circular, incomplete, untestable, pseudo-factual, disguised proposals to change the meaning of concepts—have been made before. My intention is to go beyond these to make a much more fundamental criticism, namely, that aesthetic theory is a logically vain attempt to define what cannot be defined, to state the necessary and sufficient properties of that which has no necessary and sufficient properties, to conceive the concept of art as closed when its very use reveals and demands its openness.

The problem with which we must begin is not "What is art?" but "What sort of concept is 'art'?" Indeed, the root problem of philosophy itself is to explain the relation between the employment of certain kinds of concepts and the conditions under which they can be correctly applied. If I may paraphrase Wittgenstein, we must not ask, What is the nature of any philosophical x? or even, according to the semanticist, What does "x" mean?, a transformation that leads to the disastrous interpretation of "art" as a name for some specifiable class of objects; but rather, What is the use or employment of "x"? What does "x" do in the language? This, I take it, is the initial question, the begin-all if not the end-all of any philosophical problem and solution. Thus, in aesthetics, our first problem is the elucidation of the actual employment of the concept of art, to give a logical description of the actual functioning of the concept, including a description of the conditions under which we correctly use it or its correlates.

My model in this type of logical description or philosophy derives from Wittgenstein. It is also he who, in his refutation of philosophical theorizing in the sense of constructing definitions of philosophical entities, has furnished contemporary aesthetics with a starting point for any future progress. In his new work,

Philosophical Investigations,[6] Wittgenstein raises as an illustrative question, What is a game? The traditional philosophical, theoretical answer would be in terms of some exhaustive set of properties common to all games. To this Wittgenstein says, let us consider what we call "games": "I mean board-games, card-games, ball-games, Olympic games, and so on. What is common to them all?—Don't say: 'there *must* be something common, or they would not be called "games"' but *look and see* whether there is anything common to all. For if you look at them you will not see something that is common to *all,* but similarities, relationships, and a whole series of them at that. . . ."

Card games are like board games in some respects but not in others. Not all games are amusing, nor is there always winning or losing or competition. Some games resemble others in some respects—that is all. What we find is no necessary and sufficient properties, only "a complicated network of similarities overlapping and crisscrossing," such that we can say of games that they form a family with family resemblances and no common trait. If one asks what a game is, we pick out sample games, describe these, and add, "This and *similar things* arc called 'games.'" This is all we need to say and indeed all any of us knows about games. Knowing what a game is is not knowing some real definition or theory but being able to recognize and explain games and to decide which among imaginary and new examples would or would not be called "games."

The problem of the nature of art is like that of the nature of games, at least in these respects: If we actually look and see what it is that we call "art," we will also find no common properties—only strands of similarities. Knowing what art is is not apprehending some manifest or latent essence but being able to recognize, describe, and explain those things we call "art" in virtue of these similarities.

But the basic resemblance between these concepts is their open texture. In elucidating them, certain (paradigm) cases can be given, about which there can be no question as to their being correctly described as "art" or "game," but no exhaustive set of cases can be given. I can list some cases and some conditions under which I can apply correctly the concept of art but I cannot list all of them, for the all-important rea-

son that unforeseeable or novel conditions are always forthcoming or envisageable.

A concept is open if its conditions of application are emendable and corrigible; i.e., if a situation or case can be imagined or secured which would call for some sort of *decision* on our part to extend the use of the concept to cover this, or to close the concept and invent a new one to deal with the new case and its new property. If necessary and sufficient conditions for the application of a concept can be stated, the concept is a closed one. But this can happen only in logic or mathematics where concepts are constructed and completely defined. It cannot occur with empirically descriptive and normative concepts unless we arbitrarily close them by stipulating the ranges of their uses.

I can illustrate this open character of "art" best by examples drawn from its sub-concepts. Consider questions like "Is Dos Passos' *U.S.A.* a novel?" "Is V. Woolf's *To the Lighthouse* a novel?" "Is Joyce's *Finnegans Wake* a novel?" On the traditional view, these are construed as factual problems to be answered yes or no in accordance with the presence or absence of defining properties. But certainly this is not how any of these questions is answered. Once it arises, as it has many times in the development of the novel from Richardson to Joyce (e.g., "Is Gide's *The School for Wives* a novel or a diary?"), what is at stake is no factual analysis concerning necessary and sufficient properties but a decision as to whether the work under examination is similar in certain respects to other works, already called "novels," and consequently warrants the extension of the concept to cover the new case. The new work is narrative, fictional, contains character delineation and dialogue but (say) it has no regular time-sequence in the plot or is interspersed with actual newspaper reports. It is like recognized novels, A, B, C . . . , in some respects but not like them in others. But then neither were B and C like A in some respects when it was decided to extend the concept applied to A to B and C. Because work N + 1 (the brand new work) is like A, B, C, . . . N in certain respects—has strands of similarity to them—the concept is extended and a new phase of the novel engendered. "Is N + 1 a novel?," then, is no factual, but rather a decision problem, where the verdict turns on whether or not we enlarge our set of conditions for applying the concept.

What is true of the novel is, I think, true of every sub-concept of art: "tragedy," "comedy," "painting," "opera," etc., of "art" itself. No "Is X a novel, painting, opera, work of art, etc.?" question allows of a definitive answer in the sense of a factual yes or no report. "Is this *collage* a painting or not?" does not rest on any set of necessary and sufficient properties of painting but on whether we decide—as we did!—to extend "painting" to cover this case.

"Art," itself, is an open concept. New conditions (cases) have constantly arisen and will undoubtedly constantly arise; new art forms, new movements will emerge, which will demand decisions on the part of those interested, usually professional critics, as to whether the concept should be extended or not. Aestheticians may lay down similarity conditions but never necessary and sufficient ones for the correct application of the concept. With "art" its conditions of application can never be exhaustively enumerated since new cases can always be envisaged or created by artists, or even nature, which would call for a decision on someone's part to extend or to close the old or to invent a new concept. (E.g., "It's not a sculpture, it's a mobile.")

What I am arguing, then, is that the very expansive, adventurous character of art, its ever-present changes and novel creations, make it logically impossible to ensure any set of defining properties. We can, of course, choose to close the concept. But to do this with "art" or "tragedy" or "portraiture," etc., is ludicrous since it forecloses on the very conditions of creativity in the arts.

Of course there are legitimate and serviceable closed concepts in art. But these are always those whose boundaries of conditions have been drawn for a *special* purpose. Consider the difference, for example, between "tragedy" and "(extant) Greek tragedy." The first is open and must remain so to allow for the possibility of new conditions, e.g., a play in which the hero is not noble or fallen or in which there is no hero but other elements that are like those of plays we already call "tragedy." The second is closed. The plays it can be applied to, the conditions under which it can be correctly used are all in, once the boundary,

"Greek," is drawn. Here the critic can work out a theory or real definition in which he lists the common properties at least of the extant Greek tragedies. Artistotle's definition, false as it is as a theory of all the plays of Aeschylus, Sophocles, and Euripides, since it does not cover some of them,[7] properly called "tragedies," can be interpreted as a real (albeit incorrect) definition of this closed concept; although it can also be, as it unfortunately has been conceived as a purported real definition of "tragedy," in which case it suffers from the logical mistake of trying to define what cannot be defined—of trying to squeeze what is an open concept into an honorific formula for a closed concept.

What is supremely important, if the critic is not to become muddled, is to get absolutely clear about the way in which he conceives his concepts; otherwise he goes from the problem of trying to define "tragedy," etc., to an arbitrary closing of the concept in terms of certain preferred conditions or characteristics which he sums up in some linguistic recommendation that he mistakenly thinks is a real definition of the open concept. Thus, many critics and aestheticians ask, "What is tragedy?," choose a class of samples for which they may give a true account of its common properties, and then go on to construe this account of the chosen closed class as a true definition or theory of the whole open class of tragedy. This, I think, is the logical mechanism of most of the so-called theories of the sub-concepts of art: "tragedy," "comedy," "novel," etc. In effect, this whole procedure, subtly deceptive as it is, amounts to a transformation of correct criteria for *recognizing* members of certain legitimately closed classes of works of art into recommended criteria for *evaluating* any putative member of the class.

The primary task of aesthetics is not to seek a theory but to elucidate the concept of art. Specifically, it is to describe the conditions under which we employ the concept correctly. Definition, reconstruction, patterns of analysis are out of place here since they distort and add nothing to our understanding of art. What, then, is the logic of "X is a work of art"?

As we actually use the concept, "Art" is both descriptive (like "chair") and evaluative (like "good"); i.e., we sometimes say, "This is a work of art," to describe something and we sometimes say it to evaluate something Neither use surprises anyone.

What, first, is the logic of "X is a work of art," when it is a descriptive utterance? What are the conditions under which we would be making such an utterance correctly? There are no necessary and sufficient conditions but there are the strands of similarity conditions, i.e., bundles of properties, none of which need be present but most of which are, when we describe things as works of art. I shall call these the "criteria of recognition" of works of art. All these have served as the defining criteria of the individual traditional theories of art; so we are already familiar with them. Thus, mostly, when we describe something as a work of art, we do so under the conditions of there being present some sort of artifact, made by human skill, ingenuity, and imagination, which embodies in its sensuous, public medium—stone, wood, sounds, words, etc.—certain distinguishable elements and relations. Special theorists would add conditions like satisfaction of wishes, objectification or expression of emotion, some act of empathy, and so on; but these latter conditions seem to be quite adventitious, present to some but not to other spectators when things are described as works of art. "X is a work of art and contains *no* emotion, expression, act of empathy, satisfaction, etc.," is perfectly good sense and may frequently be true. "X is a work of art and . . . was made by no one," or " . . . exists only in the mind and not in any publicly observable thing," or " . . . was made by accident when he spilled the paint on the canvas," in each case of which a normal condition is denied, are also sensible and capable of being true in certain circumstances. None of the criteria of recognition is a defining one, either necessary or sufficient, because we can sometimes assert of something that it is a work of art and go on to deny any one of these conditions, even the one which has traditionally been taken to be basic, namely, that of being an artifact: Consider, "This piece of driftwood is a lovely piece of sculpture." Thus, to say of anything that it is a work of art is to commit oneself to the presence of *some* of these conditions. One would scarcely describe X as a work of art if X were not an artifact, or a collection of elements sensuously pre-

sented in a medium, or a product of human skill, and so on. If none of the conditions was present, if there were no criteria present for recognizing something as a work of art, we would not describe it as one. But, even so, no one of these or any collection of them is either necessary or sufficient.

The elucidation of the descriptive use of "Art" creates little difficulty. But the elucidation of the evaluative use does. For many, especially theorists, "This is a work of art" does more than describe; it also praises. Its conditions of utterance, therefore, include certain preferred properties or characteristics of art. I shall call these "criteria of evaluation." Consider a typical example of this evaluative use, the view according to which to say of something that it is a work of art is to imply that it is a *successful* harmonization of elements. Many of the honorific definitions of art and its sub-concepts are of this form. What is at stake here is that "Art" is construed as an evaluative term which is either identified with its criterion or justified in terms of it. "Art" is defined in terms of its evaluative property, e.g., successful harmonization. On such a view, to say "X is a work of art" is (1) to say something which is taken *to mean* "X is a successful harmonization" (e.g., "Art *is* significant form") or (2) to say something praiseworthy *on the basis* of its successful harmonization. Theorists are never clear whether it is (1) or (2) which is being put forward. Most of them, concerned as they are with this evaluative use, formulate (2), i.e., that feature of art that *makes* it art in the praise-sense, and then go on to state (1), i.e., the definition of "Art" in terms of its art-making feature. And this is clearly to confuse the conditions under which we say something evaluatively with the meaning of what we say. "This is a work of art," said evaluatively, cannot mean "This is a successful harmonization of elements"—except by stipulation—but at most is said in virtue of the art-making property, which is taken as a (the) criterion of "Art," when "Art" is employed to assess. "This is a work of art," used evaluatively, serves to praise and not to affirm the reason that it is said.

The evaluative use of "Art," although distinct from the conditions of its use, relates in a very intimate way to these conditions. For, in every instance of "This is a work of art" (used to praise), what happens is that the criterion of evaluation (e.g., successful harmonization) for the employment of the concept of art is converted into a criterion of recognition. This is why, on its evaluative use, "This is a work of art" implies "This has P," where "P" is some chosen art-making property. Thus, if one chooses to employ "Art" evaluatively, as many do, so that "This is a work of art and not (aesthetically) good" makes no sense, he uses "Art" in such a way that he refuses to *call* anything a work of art unless it embodies his criterion of excellence.

There is nothing wrong with the evaluative use; in fact, there is good reason for using "Art" to praise. But what cannot be maintained is that theories of the evaluative use of "Art" are true and real definitions of the necessary and sufficient properties of art. Instead they are honorific definitions, pure and simple, in which "Art" has been redefined in terms of chosen criteria.

But what makes them—these honorific definitions—so supremely valuable is not their disguised linguistic recommendations; rather it is the *debates* over the reasons for changing the criteria of the concept of art which are built into the definitions. In each of the great theories of art, whether correctly understood as honorific definitions or incorrectly accepted as real definitions, what is of the utmost importance is the reasons proffered in the argument for the respective theory, that is, the reasons given for the chosen or preferred criterion of excellence and evaluation. It is this perennial debate over these criteria of evaluation which makes the history of aesthetic theory the important study it is. The value of each of the theories resides in its attempt to state and to justify certain criteria which are either neglected or distorted by previous theories. Look at the Bell-Fry theory again. Of course, "Art is significant form" cannot be accepted as a true, real definition of art; and most certainly it actually functions in their aesthetics as a redefinition of art in terms of the chosen condition of significant form. But what gives it its aesthetic importance is what lies behind the formula: In an age in which literary and representational elements have become paramount in painting, *return* to the plastic ones since these are indigenous to painting. Thus, the role of theory is not to define anything but to use the

definitional form, almost epigrammatically, to pinpoint a crucial recommendation to turn our attention once again to the plastic elements in painting.

Once we, as philosophers, understand this distinction between the formula and what lies behind it, it behooves us to deal generously with the traditional theories of art; because incorporated in every one of them is a debate over and argument for emphasizing or centering upon some particular feature of art which has been neglected or perverted. If we take the aesthetic theories literally, as we have seen, they all fail; but if we reconstrue them, in terms of their function and point, as serious and argued-for recommendations to concentrate on certain criteria of excellence in art, we shall see that aesthetic theory is far from worthless. Indeed, it becomes as central as anything in aesthetics, in our understanding of art, for it teaches us what to look for and how to look at it in art. What is central and must be articulated in all the theories are their debates over the reasons for excellence in art—debates over emotional depth, profound truths, natural beauty, exactitude, freshness of treatment, and so on, as criteria of evaluation—the whole of which converges on the perennial problem of what makes a work of art good. To understand the role of aesthetic theory is not to conceive it as definition, logically doomed to failure, but to read it as summaries of seriously made recommendations to attend in certain ways to certain features of art.

NOTES

1. D. Parker, "The Nature of Art," reprinted in E. Vivas and M. Krieger, *The Problems of Aesthetics* (New York, 1953), p. 90.

2. Ibid., pp. 93–94.

3. Ibid., p. 94.

4. Ibid., p. 104.

5. See M. Macdonald's review of my *Philosophy of the Arts, Mind,* October 1951, pp. 561–564, for a brilliant discussion of this objection to the Organic theory.

6. L. Wittgenstein, *Philosophical Investigations,* tr. E. Anscombe (Oxford, 1953); see especially part 1, sec. 65–75. All quotations are from these sections.

7. See H. D. F. Kitto, *Greek Tragedy* (London, 1939), on this point.

Defining Art

∽

GEORGE DICKIE

George Dickie is Professor Emeritus at the University of Illinois, Chicago Circle campus. Best known for developing an institutional theory of art, his works include *Art and the Aesthetic: An Institutional Analysis, The Art Circle,* and *Evaluating Art.*

In recent years it has been argued that the expression "work of art" cannot be defined and Morris Weitz has even argued that *being an artifact* is not a necessary condition for being a work of art.[1] More recently, however, Joseph Margolis has offered a definition[2] and Maurice Mandelbaum has made tentative suggestions about defining "art."[3]

I shall not repeat the well-known argument of Weitz, whose views I take to be representative of those who maintain that "art" cannot be defined, but shall state his main conclusion and comment on one of his arguments. Neither shall I repeat the arguments of Margolis or Mandelbaum, but I do want to note (1) that they agree that artifactuality is a necessary condition of art, and (2) that Mandelbaum points out the significance of the *non-exhibited* characteristics of art for the definition of "art."

Weitz's main conclusion is that there are no necessary and sufficient conditions for the definition of "art" or for any of the subconcepts of art, such as "novel," "tragedy," "painting," and so on. All of these notions are open concepts and their instances have "family resemblances."

Weitz rejects artifactuality as a necessary condition of art because we sometimes make statements such as "This driftwood is a lovely piece of sculpture."[4] We do sometimes speak this way of natural objects, but nothing follows from this fact. Weitz is confused because he takes the driftwood remark to be

a descriptive statement and it is not. Weitz himself, quite correctly, distinguishes between an evaluative use and a descriptive use of "work of art,"[5] and once this distinction is understood it can be seen that the driftwood remark is an evaluation of the driftwood. But it is, of course, the descriptive sense of "work of art" which is at issue when the question of whether "art" can be defined is raised. I maintain that the descriptive use of "work of art" is used to indicate that a thing belongs to a certain category of artifacts. By the way, the evaluative sense can be applied to artifacts as well as nonartifacts, as when we say, "That painting is a work of art." Such remarks are not intended as tautologies.

Before going on to discuss the second condition of the definition of the descriptive sense of "art," it will be helpful to distinguish the generic concept of art from the various subconcepts which fall under it. It may very well be the case that all or some of the subconcepts of art, such as novel, tragedy, ceramics, sculpture, painting, and so on, may lack necessary and sufficient conditions for their application as subconcepts and it still be the case that "work of art," which is the germs of all these subconcepts, can be defined. For example, there may not be any characteristics which all tragedies have which would distinguish them from comedies, satyr plays, happenings, and the like within the domain of art. Even if this were the case, in the light of the foregoing, tragedies and all other works of art would have at least one characteristic in common, namely, artifactuality. Perhaps artifactuality and some one or more other features of works of art distinguish them from nonart. If all or some of the subconcepts of art cannot be defined and, as I think is the case, "art" can be, then Weitz is right in part.

Assuming that artifactuality is the genus of art, the differentia is still lacking. This second condition will be a social property of art. Furthermore, this social propety will, in Mandelbaum's terminology, be a nonexhibited, relational property.

W. E. Kennick contends that such an approach to the definition of "art" is futile. He argues from such facts as that the ancient Egyptians sealed up paintings and sculptures in tombs to the conclusion that "The attempt to define Art in terms of what we do with certain objects is as doomed as any other."[6] There are several difficulties with Kennick's argument. First, the fact that the Egyptians sealed up paintings and sculptures in tombs does not entail that they generally regarded them differently from the way in which we regard them. Indeed, they might have put them there for the dead to appreciate, or simply because they belonged to the dead person, or for some other reason. The Egyptian practice does not prove a radical difference between their conception of art and ours such that a definition which subsumes both is impossible. Secondly, there is no need to assume that we and the ancient Egyptians (or any other group) share a common conception of art. I would be happy to be able to specify the necessary and sufficient conditions for the concept of art which we have (we present-day Americans, we present-day Westerners, we Westerners since the organization of the system of the arts in or about the 18th century—I am not sure of the exact limits of the "we"). Kennick notwithstanding, we are most likely to discover the differentia of art by considering "what we do with certain objects," that is, "works of art." But, of course, there is no guarantee that any given thing we or an ancient Egyptian might possibly do with a work of art will throw light on the concept af art. Not every *doing* will reveal what is required.

Arthur Danto's stimulating article, "The Art-

world,"[7] is helpful here. In speaking of Warhol's Brillo Carton and Rauschenberg's Bed, he writes, "To see something as art requires something the eye cannot de[s]cry—an atmosphere of artistic theory, a knowledge of history of art: an artworld."[8] What the eye cannot descry is a complicated non-exhibited characteristic of the artifacts in question. The "atmosphere" of which Danto speaks is elusive, but it has a substantial content. Perhaps this content can be captured in a definition. I shall first state the definition and then go on to defend it. *A work of art in the descriptive sense is (1) an artifact (2) upon which some society or some sub-group of a society has conferred the status of candidate for appreciation.*

The definition speaks of the conferring of the status of *candidate* for appreciation: nothing is said about actual appreciation and this leaves open the possibility of works of art which, for whatever reason, are not appreciated. Also, not every aspect of a work is included in the candidacy for appreciation, for example, the color of the back of a painting is not ordinarily an object of appreciation. The problem of *which* aspects of a work of art are to be included within the candidacy for appreciation is a question which I have pursued elsewhere.[9]

Just how is the status of candidate for appreciation conferred? An artifact's hanging in an art museum, a performance at a theater, and the like are sure signs that the status *has been conferred*. But many works of art never reach museum walls and some are never seen by anyone but the artist himself. The status, therefore, must be conferrable by a single person's treating an artifact as a candidate for appreciation, usually the artist himself, although not always, because someone might create an artifact without ever considering it as a candidate for appreciation and the status be conferred by some other person or persons. But can status be conferred so easily? We associate status with ceremony—the wedding ceremony and the status of being married, for example. However, ceremony is not the only way of getting married, in some jurisdictions common-law marriage is possible—a status acquired without ceremony. What I want to suggest is that, just as two persons can acquire the status of common-law marriage within a legal system, an artifact can acquire the status of a candidate for appreciation within the system which Danto has called "the artworld."

A number of questions arise about this notion of status of candidate for appreciation and perhaps the whole matter can best be clarified by stating them and trying to answer them. Probably the first question is: what *kind* of appreciation? Surely the definition does seem to suggest that there is a special kind of "aesthetic" appreciation. Appreciation is not crucial, but something should be said about it to prepare the way for the crucial point. The kind of appreciation I have in mind is simply the kind characteristic of our experiences of paintings, poetry, novels, and the like. This remark seems to collapse the definition into circularity, but it does not because "work of art" (the term defined) does not appear in the explanation of appreciation, only subconcept terms appear. Another apparent problem is that works of art differ so much from one another—for example, comedies are very different from tragedies—that it seems unlikely that the appreciation characteristic of our experience of one kind of work has something in common with the appreciation characteristic of our experience of another kind of work. But paintings, poems, and plays are the *objects* of our appreciation and the fact that the objects differ considerably does not mean that the various appreciations differ. Indeed, if we mean by "appreciation" something like "in experiencing the qualities of a thing one finds them worthy or valuable," then there is no problem about the similarity of the various appreciations.

It can now be seen that appreciation will not serve to pick out the subclass of works of art from the class of artifacts—it is too broad: many artifacts which are obviously not works of art are appreciated. To pick out the class of works of art one must stress the conferring of the status of candidate rather than appreciation. When, for example, a salesman of plumbing supplies spreads his wares before us, he presents them for our appreciation all right, but the presenting is not a conferring of status of candidate, it is simply a placing before us. But what is the difference between "placing before" and "conferring the status of candidate?" The difference is analogous to the difference between my uttering "I declare this man to be a candidate for alderman" and the head of the election board uttering

the same sentence while acting in his official capacity. When I utter the sentence it has no effect because I have not been vested with any authority in this regard. Of course the analogy is not a complete one—lines of authority in the politico-legal world are by and large explicitly defined and incorporated into law, while lines of authority (or something like authority) in the art-world are nowhere codified. The artworld carries on its business at the level of customary practice. Still there *is* a practice and this defines a social institution. To return to the plumbing line, the salesman's presentation is different from Duchamp's superficially similar act of placing a urinal which he christened "Fountain" in that now famous art show. The point is that Duchamp's act took place within a certain institutional setting and that makes all the difference. Our salesman of plumbing supplies could do what Duchamp did, that is, convert a urinal into a work of art, but he probably would not—such weird ideas seem to occur only to artists with bizarre senses of humor. Please remember that when I say "Fountain" is a work of art, I am not saying it is a good one. And in making this last remark I am not insinuating that it is a bad one either.

Duchamp's "ready-mades" raise the question—"If urinals, snowshovels, and hatracks can become works of art, why can't natural objects such as driftwood become works of art?" and, of course, driftwood and other natural objects can become works of art if any one of a number of things is done to them. One thing which would do the trick would be to pick it up, take it home, and hang it on the wall. Another thing which would do the trick would be to pick it up and enter it in an exhibition. (I was, by the way, assuming that Weitz's sentence about driftwood referred to a piece of driftwood in its ordinary situation on a beach and untouched by human hand.) This means that natural objects which become works of art acquire their artifactuality (are artifactualized) at the same time that the status of candidate for appreciation is conferred on them. But perhaps a similar thing ordinarily happens with paintings, poems, and such; they come to exist as artifacts at the same time that they have conferred on them the status of candidate for appreciation. (Of course, being an artifact and being a candidate for appreciation are not the same thing—they are two properties of a single thing which may be acquired at the same time.) A somewhat more complicated case would be an artifact from a primitive culture which played a role in a religious system and which had no artistic function in the sense developed here. Such an artifact might become a work of art in our culture in a way similar to that in which driftwood might become a work of art. However, such a religious object which becomes a work of art would be an artifact in two senses, but the driftwood in only one. (I am not suggesting that something cannot be a religious object and work of art at the same time—there are many counter-instances to this in our own culture.)

A question which frequently arises in connection with discussions of the concept of art is "How are we to conceive of paintings done by individuals such as Betsy the chimpanzee from the Baltimore Zoo?" It all depends on what is done with the paintings. (Note that I unhesitatingly call the objects paintings, although I am uncertain about their status as works of art.) For example, The Field Natural History Museum in Chicago recently exhibited some chimpanzee paintings. In the case of these paintings we must say that they are not works of art. However, if they had been exhibited a few miles away at the Chicago Art Institute they would have been works of art. (If, so to speak, the director of the Art Institute had gone out on a limb.) It all depends on the institutional setting.

In concluding, it may be worthwhile to consider in what ways the definition offered here differs from some traditional definitions. (1) It does not attempt to smuggle a conception of good art into the definition of "art." (2) It is not, to use Margolis' term, "overloaded," as is the one Margolis cites as a horrible example: "Art is a human activity which explores, and hereby creates, new reality in a suprarational, visional manner and presents it symbolically or metaphoncally,[10] as a microcosmic whole signifying a macrocosmic whole."[11] (3) It does not contain any commitment to any metaphysical or unempirical theory, as contrasted with, for example, the view that art is unreal. (4) It is broad enough so that those things generally recognized as art can be brought under it without undue strain, as contrasted with, for example, the imitation definition which involves enormous

strain in trying to show that every work of art is an imitation of something or other. (5) It takes into account (or at least attempts to) the actual practices of the artworld of the past and of the present day.

Now what I have been saying may sound like saying, "a work of art is an object of which someone has said, 'I christen this object a work of art.'" And I think it is rather like that. So one *can* make a work of art out of a sow's ear, but of course that does not mean that it is a silk purse.

NOTES

1. Morris Weitz, "The Role of Theory in Aesthetics," *The Journal of Aesthetics and Art Criticism,* vol. 15 (1956), pp. 27–35; reprinted in *Philosophy Looks at the Arts,* ed. by Joseph Margolis (New York, 1962); Paul Ziff, "The Task of Defining a Work of Art," reprinted in *Aesthetics and the Philosophy of Criticism,* ed. by Marvin Levich (New York, 1963); William Kennick, "Does Traditional Aesthetics Rest on a Mistake," *Mind,* vol. 66 (1958), pp. 317–334.

2. *The Language of Art and Art Criticism* (Detroit, 1965), pp. 37–47. Margolis' definition is not satisfactory, however; see Andrew Harrison's review in *Philosophical Books,* vol. 7 (1966), p. 19.

3. "Family Resemblances and Generalization Concerning the Arts," *American Philosophical Quarterly,* vol. 2 (1965), pp. 219–228.

4. Op. cit., p. 57.

5. Ibid., p. 56.

6. Kennick, op. cit., p. 330.

7. *The Journal of Philosophy,* vol. 61 (1964), pp. 571–584.

8. Ibid., p. 580.

9. In my "Art Narrowly and Broadly Speaking," *American Philosophical Quarterly,* vol. 5 (1968), pp. 71–77, where I analyze the notion of *aesthetic object.* The subject of the present essay is the concept of *art* which, although related to the notion of aesthetic object, is distinct from it.

10. There are apparently two typographical errors here. Margolis quotes the word as "metaphonically" and the original text reads "metaphoncally." A reading of the original text indicates that it should have been "metaphorically."

11. Op. cit., p. 44. The passage is quoted from Erick Kahler's "What is Art?," in *Problems in Aesthetics,* ed. by Morris Weitz (New York, 1959).

The End of Art

ARTHUR C. DANTO

Arthur Danto is the Johnsonian Professor of Philosophy Emeritus at Columbia University. He is the author of numerous books in philosophy, including *The Transfiguration of the Commonplace* and *The Philosophical Disenfranchisement of Art.* He has also written extensively on aesthetics and the arts in his role as art critic for *The Nation.*

Art is dead.

Its present movements are not at all indications of vitality; they are not even the convulsions of agony prior to death; they are the mechanical reflex actions of a corpse submitted to galvanic force.

—*Marius de Zayas, "The Sun Has Set,"*
Camera Work *(July 1912), 39:17.*

There are philosophical visions of history which allow, or even demand, a speculation regarding the future of art. Such a speculation concerns the question of whether art has a future, and must be distinguished from one which merely concerns the art of the future, if we suppose art will go on and on. Indeed, the latter speculation is more difficult in a way, just because of the difficulties which go with trying to imagine what the artworks of the future will look like or how they will be appreciated. Just think how out of the question it would have been, in 1865, to predict the forms of Post-Impressionist painting, or to have anticipated, as late as 1910, that there would be, only five years in the future, a work such as Duchamp's *In Advance of the Broken Arm,* which, even when accepted as a work of art, retained its identity as a quite ordinary snow shovel. Comparable examples can be drawn from the other arts, especially as we approach our own century, when music and poetry and dance have yielded exemplars which could not have been perceived as art had anything like them appeared in earlier times, as sets of words or sounds or movements. The visionary artist Albert Robida began in 1882 the serial publication of *Le vingtième siècle.* It meant to show the world as it would be in 1952. His pictures are filled with wonders to come: *le téléphonoscope,* flying machines, television, underwater metropolises, but the pictures themselves are unmistakably of their own era, as is the way much of what they show is shown. Robida imagined there would be restaurants in the sky to which customers would come in airborne vehicles. But the boldly anticipated eating places are put together of ornamental ironworks of the sort we associate with Les Halles and the Gare St. Lazare, and look a lot like the steamboats that floated the Mississippi at that time, in proportion and in decorative fretwork. They are patronized by gentlemen in top hats and ladies in bustles, served by waiters wearing long aprons from the Belle Epoque, and they arrive in balloons Montgolfier would recognize. We may be certain that were Robida to have depicted an underwater art museum, its most advanced works would be Impressionist paintings, if Robida had eyes even for those. In 1952, the most advanced galleries were showing Pollack, De Kooning, Gottlieb, and Klein, which would have been temporally unimaginable in

Reprinted from *The Philosophical Disenfranchisement of Art* (New York: Columbia University Press, 1986), by permission of the publisher.

1882. Nothing so much belongs to its own time as an age's glimpses into the future: Buck Rogers carries the decorative idioms of the 1930s into the twenty-first century, and *now* looks at home with Rockefeller Center and the Cord automobile; the science fiction novels of the 1950s project the sexual moralities of the Eisenhower era, along with the dry martini, into distant eons, and the technical clothing worn by its spacemen belong to that era's haberdashery. So were *we* to depict an interplanetary art gallery, it would display works which, however up to the minute they look to us, will belong to the history of art by the time there are such galleries, just as the mod clothing we put on the people we show will belong to the history of costume in no time at all. The future is a kind of mirror in which we can show only ourselves, though it seems to us a window through which we may see things to come. Leonardo's wonderful saying, that *ogni dipintore dipinge se,* implies an unintended historical limitation, as may be seen from Leonardo's own visionary drawings, so profoundly part of their own time. We may imagine *that* all sorts of things will come to be. But when we seek to *imagine* those things, they inevitably will look like things that *have* come to be, for we have only the forms we know to give them.

Even so, we may speculate historically on the future of art without committing ourselves on what the artworks of the future are to be like, if there are to be any; and it is even possible to suppose that art itself has no future, though art-works may still be produced post-historically, as it were, in the after-shock of a vanished vitality. Such indeed was a thesis of Hegel, certain of whose views have inspired the present essay, for Hegel said quite unequivocally that art as such, or at least at its highest vocation, is quite finished with as a historical moment, though he did not commit himself to the prediction that there would be no more works of art. He might have argued that, certain as he was that his astonishing thesis was true, he had nothing to say about those works to come, which might, perhaps must, be produced in ways he could not anticipate and enjoyed in ways he could not understand. I find it an extraordinary thought that the world should have gone through what one might term the Age of Art, parallel to the way in which, accord-

ing to a theological speculation of the Christian theorist Joachim of Flores, the Age of the Father came to an end with the birth of His Son, and the Age of the Son with the Age of the Holy Spirit. Joachim did not claim that those whose historical fulfillment lay in the Age of the Father will become extinct or that their forms of life will abruptly disappear in the Age of the Son: they may continue to exist past the moment of their historical mission, historical fossils, so to speak, as Joachim would have supposed the Jews to be, whose time on the stage of history he believed over with. So though there will be Jews in time to come, whose forms of life may evolve in unforeseeable ways, still, their history will no longer be coincident with the history of History itself, conceived of as Joachim did, in the grandest philosophical manner.

In almost precisely this way, Hegel's thought was that for a period of time the energies of history coincided with the energies of art, but now history and art must go in different directions, and though art may continue to exist in what I have termed a post-historical fashion, its existence carries no historical significance whatever. Now such a thesis can hardly be pondered outside the framework of a philosophy of history it would be difficult to take seriously were the urgency of art's future not somehow raised from within the artworld itself, which can be seen today as having lost any historical direction, and we have to ask whether this is temporary, whether art will regain the path of history—or whether this destructured condition *is* its future: a kind of cultural entropy. So whatever comes next will not matter because the concept of art is internally exhausted. Our institutions—museums, galleries, collectors, art journals, and the like—exist against the assumption of a significant, even a brilliant, future. There is an inevitable commercial interest in what is to come now, and who are to be the important practitioners in movements next to come. It is very much in the spirit of Joachim that the English sculptor William Tucker has said, "The 60's was the age of the critic. Now it's the age of the dealer." But suppose it *has* really all come to an end, and that a point has been reached where there can be change without development, where the engines of artistic production can only combine and recombine known forms, though external pressures may favor this or that combination? Suppose it is no longer a historical possibility that art should continue to astonish us, that in this sense the Age of Art is internally worn out, and that in Hegel's stunning and melancholy phrase, a form of life has grown old?

Is it possible that the wild effervescence of the art-world in the past seven or eight decades has been a terminal fermentation of something the historical chemistry of which remains to be understood? I want to take Hegel quite seriously, and to sketch a model of the history of art in which something like it may even be said to make sense. Better to appreciate the sense it does make, I shall first sketch two rather more familiar models of art history, for the model which will finally interest me presupposes them in a striking and almost dialectical way. It is an interesting fact that though the first model has application primarily to mimetic art, to painting and sculpture and moving pictures, the second model will include them and include a great deal more of art than mimesis can easily characterize. The final model will apply to art in so comprehensive a way that the question of whether art has come to an end will have as wide a reference as the term "art" itself has, though its most dramatic reference will be to the objects purveyed in what is narrowly known as "the artworld." Indeed, part of the explanation lies in the fact that the boundaries between painting and the other arts—poetry and performance, music and dance—have become radically unstable. It is an instability induced by the factors which make my final model historically possible, and which enables the dismal question to be put. I will conclude by asking how we are to adapt to the fact that the question has an affirmative answer, that art really is over with, having become transmuted into philosophy. . . .

Whatever the case, it has always been possible to imagine, at least grossly, the future of art construed in terms of representational progress. One knew in principle what the agenda was, and hence what progress would have to be if there was to be progress. Visionaries could say such things as "Someday pictures will move," without knowing how it was to be achieved, just as not long ago they could say, "Someday men will walk on the moon," without knowing, again, quite how *this* was to be achieved. But then, and this has been the main reason for canvassing this entire theory, it would be possible to speak of the end of art, at least as a progressive discipline. When, for every perceptual range R, an equivalent could be technically generated, then art would be over with, just as science would be over with when, as was thought to be a genuine possibility in the nineteenth century, everything was known. In the nineteenth century, for example, it was believed that logic was a finished science, and even that physics was, with a few nagging details to mop up. But there is no internal reason for us to think that science, or art, has be be endless, and so there was always a question that would have to be faced, as to what post-progressive life would be like. To be sure, we have more or less abandoned this model in art, since the production of perceptual equivalence no longer much dazzles us, and in any case there are certain definite limits set when narrativization becomes an artistic fact. Even so, as we shall see, the model has an oblique pertinence even today.

Before coming to that, however, I want to raise a philosophical point. So long as the philosophy of art was articulated in terms of success or failure in technologies of perceptual equivalence, it would have been difficult to get an interestingly general definition of art. Aristotle widened the notion of imitation to include the imitation of an action, in order to bring narrative drama into the scope of that concept, but at that point the theory of mimesis parts company with the concept of perceptual equivalences, since it is far from plain that drama presents us with merely perceptual equivalences to what a sort of eyewitness to the action would perceive. And while this is, in the case of dramatic presentations, a mistakenly entertainable ideal, it is not so at all when we consider *fiction* as the description of an action. And when we think of description as against mimesis, we may immediately notice that it is not at all clear that there is any room for the concept of progress or of technological transformations at all. Let me explain this.

Thinkers have, from Lao Tzu to the present, lamented or celebrated the inadequacies of language. It is felt that there are descriptive limits, and then important things beyond these limits which language cannot express. But to the degree that this is true, no expansion of representational possibilities, say by introducing new terms into the language, will remedy the situation, largely because the complaint is against descriptivity itself, which simply is too distant from reality to give us the experience reality itself affords. And it is a mark of the natural languages that whatever can be said in one can be said in any (and what *cannot* be said in one cannot be said in any), allowing always for differences of felicity and degrees of roundaboutness. So there cannot ever have been a technological problem of expanding the descriptive resources of the natural languages: they are equivalently universal.

I do not mean to imply that there are no limits to language, but only that whatever they are, nothing is going to count as progress toward their overcoming, since this would still be within language as a representational system. So there is no logical room for the concept of progress. At no point in the history of literature, for example, would visionaries have been able to prophesy that someday men will be able to say certain things—in part perhaps because in saying what men will be able to say, it is *already* said. Of course someone might have been able to say that someday men will be able to talk about things then forbidden, sex perhaps, or be able to use language to criticize institutions which they are not able to do now. But this would be a matter of moral progress, or political progress, if it is that, and would have as much application to pictures as to words. Whatever the value of doing so, we can today see things in movies it would have been unthinkable to show a generation ago—the star's breasts, say. But this is not *technological* advance.

The linear or progressive model of the history of art thus finds its best examples in painting and sculpture, then in movies and talkies and, if you wish, feelies. There has never been a problem of *describing* motion, or depth, or for that matter palpability. "Her soft and yielding flesh" describes a perceptual experience for which there is no mimetic equivalent. Our next model will make a more general definition possible, since it is not thwarted by the differences between words and pictures. But then it eliminates those factors from the essence of art which made it possible to think of art as a progressive discipline.

I like to surmise that a confirmation of my historical thesis—that the task of art to produce equivalences to perceptual experiences passed, in the late nineteenth and early twentieth centuries, from the activities of painting and sculpture to those of cinematography—in the fact that painters and sculptors began conspicuously to abandon this goal at just about the same time that all the basic strategies for narrative cinema were in place. By about 1905, almost every cinematic strategy since employed had been discovered, and it was just about then that painters and sculptors began asking, if only through their actions, the question of what could be left for *them* to do, now that the torch had, as it were, been taken up by other technologies. I suppose that the history of artistic progress could be run backward: we can imagine the projected end state as having been achieved, but now it seems a good idea, for whatever reason, to replace perceptual equivalences with cues to inference—perhaps because a greater value gets put on inference (= Reason) than on perception. Bit by bit cinematography gets replaced with the cues to kinematic motion of the sort we find in Rosa Bonheur or Rodin, and so on, until, I suppose, perceptual equivalence disappears from art altogether and we get an art of pure descriptivity, where words replace perceptual stimuli. And who knows, this may seem too closely tied to experience and the next move might be music. But given the way progress itself *was* conceived, about 1905 it appeared that painters and sculptors could only justify their activities by redefining art in ways which had to be shocking indeed to those who continued to judge painting and sculpture by the criteria of the progressive paradigm, not realizing that a transformation in technology now made practices appropriate to those critera more and more archaic.

The Fauves are good examples. Consider the portrait by Matisse of his wife done in 1906, in which Madame Matisse is shown with a green stripe down her nose (indeed, the title of the painting is *The Green Stripe*). Chiang Yee told me of a painting done by a Jesuit artist of a Chinese emperor's favorite concubine, which shocked her, since she knew her face was not half black and *he* used shadows. Instruction on how the world really looks would have made her recognize that *she* really looked the way he had shown her, given the realities of light and shade. But nothing of that sort is going to redeem Matisse's painting for the history of perceptual equivalences, not even if there happened to be a greenish shadow along his subject's nose—for it would not have been *that* particular green. Nor were ladies at that time using nose shadow as those of our time use eye shadow. Nor was she suffering nasal gangrene. So one could only conclude (as people did) that Matisse had forgotten how to paint, had remembered how to paint but had gone crazy, was sane but was perverting his skills to the end of shocking the bourgeoisie, or trying to put something over on the collectors, critics, and curators (who are the three C's of the artworld).

These would have been standard rationalizations of objects, beginning to appear in epidemic quantity just then, which were unquestionably *paintings,* but which fell short by so considerable a degree of perceptual equivalence to anything in either the real world or the artworld, that some explanation of their existence seemed imperative. Until, that is, it began to be grasped that only relative to a theory which may have been put to a challenge was there any discrepancy at all, and that if there was one, well, it might be the fault of the theory. In science, ideally at least, we don't blame the world when our theories don't work—we change the theories until they do work. And so it was with Post-Impressionist painting. It became increasingly clear that a new theory was urgently required, that the artists were not failing to yield up perceptual equivalences but were after something not to be understood in those terms primarily or at all. It is to the credit of aesthetics that its practitioners responded to this with theories which, however inadequate, recognized the need, and a good example of at least a suitable theory was that painters were not so much representing as expressing. Croce's *Estetica come scienza dell'espressione* appeared in 1902. Suppose then that *The Green Stripe* tries to get us to see how Matisse felt about the subject shown, his own wife, calling for a complex act of interpretation on the part of the viewer.

This account is remarkable for the fact that it incorporates the theory of perceptual equivalences in the sense that it presupposes the discrepancies, which it then explains as due to feelings. It acknowledges, as it were, the intentional character of emotional states, that feelings are *about,* or *toward,* some object or state of affairs; and since Croce supposes art to be a kind of language, and language a form of communication, the communication of feeling will succeed to just the extent that the work can show what object it is toward which the feeling is expressed—e.g., the artist's wife. Then the discrepancies between the way this object is in fact shown and the way it would be shown were mere perceptual equivalence aimed at, no longer marks a distance to be covered by the progress of art or by the artist's mastery of illusionist technique, but rather consists in the externalization or objectification of the artist's feelings toward what he shows. The feeling is then communicated to the viewer to just the degree that the viewer can infer it on the basis of the discrepancies. Indeed, the viewer must generate some hypothesis to the effect that the object is shown the way it is because the artist feels about the object the way he does. Thus De Kooning paints a woman as the locus of slashes, El Greco paints saints as stretched verticalities, Giacometti molds figures as impossibly emaciated, not for optical reasons nor because there really are women, saints, or persons like these, but because the artists respectively reveal feelings of aggressiveness, spiritual longing, or compassion. It would be very difficult to suppose De Kooning is expressing compassion, let alone spirituality, or that El Greco is expressing aggression. But of course the ascription of feelings is always epistemologically delicate.

It becomes particularly delicate when the theory recommends the view that the object represented by the work becomes the occasion for expressing something about it, and we then begin to reconstitute the history of art along these new lines. For we now have to decide to what degree the discrepancies with an ideal perceptual equivalence are a matter of technical shortfall, and to what degree a matter of expression. Obviously we are not to read all discrepancies as expressive, for then the concept of progress no longer applies: we must assume that in a great many cases an artist would eliminate discrepancies if he but knew how. Even so, certain discrepancies which would be laughable from the point of view of representation become artistically fundamental from that of expres-

sion. At the time of the Fauves, the deviations emphasized by apologists of the new art and subscribers to
the new theory were made acceptable by pointing to
the fact that the artist after all could *draw:* one
pointed in evidence to Matisse's academic exercises,
or to Picasso's amazing canvases of his sixteenth
year. But these anxious questions lost their force after
a time as expression seemed more and more to carry
the definitional properties of art. Objects became less
and less recognizable and finally disappeared altogether in Abstract Expressionism, which of course
meant that interpretation of purely expressionist
work required reference to objectless feelings: joy,
depression, generalized excitement, etc. What was
interesting was the fact that since there could be
paintings which were purely expressive and hence
not explicitly representational at all, representation-
ality must disappear from the definition of art. But
even *more* interesting from our perspective is the fact
that the *history* of art acquires a totally different
structure.

It does so because there is no longer any reason to
think of art as having a progressive history: there
simply is not the possibility of a developmental
sequence with the concept of expression as there is
with the concept of mimetic representation. There is
not because there is no mediating technology of
expression. I do not mean to imply that novel technologies of representation may not admit novel
modes of expression: beyond question there are
expressive possibilities in cinema that simply had no
parallel in the kind of art cinema transformed. But
these new possibilities would not constitute a progressive development—viz., there would be no basis
for saying that we now can express what we could
express badly or not at all before, as we could say that
we now can show things we could only show badly
or not at all before. So the history of art has no future
of the sort that can be extrapolated as it can against
the paradigm of progress: it sunders into a sequence
of individual acts, one after another. Of course there
may be feelings one dare not express at a given time
but which in time one can express, but the raising or
lowering of the thresholds of expressive inhibition
belong to the history of morality. And of course there
may be a history of *learning* to express feelings, as

through a kind of therapy, but then this would belong
to the general history of freedom, with no particular
application to art. Heidegger has said that not one
step has been taken since Aristotle's *Rhetoric* in the
philosophical analysis of feelings—but this surely is
because the range of human feelings can be very little different from what it was in ancient times. There
may be new objects for these feelings, even new ways
of expressing them—but once more this is not a
development history.

There is a further point. Once art becomes construed as expression, the work of art must send us
ultimately to the state of mind of its maker, if we are
to interpret it. Realistically speaking, artists of a
given period share a certain expressive vocabulary,
which is why, right or wrong, my casual interpretations of De Kooning, El Greco, and Giacometti seem
at least natural. Even so, this seems to me a quite
external fact, not at all necessary to the concept of
expression, and conceivably each artist could express
himself in his own way, so that one vocabulary, as it
were, would be incommensurable with another,
which makes possible a radically discontinuous view
of the history of art, in which one style of art follows
another, as in an archipelago, and we might in principle imagine any sequence we choose. In any case we
must understand each work, each corpus, in the terms
that define that particular artist we are studying, and
what is true of De Kooning need have nothing to do
with what is true of anyone else. The concept of
expression makes such a view possible, relativizing
art, as it does, to individual artists. The history of art
is just the lives of the artists, one after another.

It is striking that the history of science is thought
of somewhat along these lines today—not, as in the
optimism of the nineteenth century, as a linear,
inevitable progression toward an end state of total
cognitive representation, but as a discontinuous
sequence of phases between which there is a radical
incommensurability. It is almost as though the
semantics of scientific terms were like the semantics
of terms like "pain," where each user is referring to
something different and speaking in a private
idiom—so that to the degree that we understand one
another at all, we do so on our own terms. Thus
"mass" means something different in each phase of

science, in part because it is redefined with each theory that employs it, so that synonymy between theory and theory is ruled out. But even if we stop short of this extreme lexical radicalism, the mere structure of history might insure some degree of incommensurability. Imagine the history of art reversed, so that it begins with Picasso and Matisse, passes through Impressionism and the Baroque, suffers a decline with Giotto, only to reach its pinnacle with the original of the *Apollo Belvedere,* beyond which it would be impossible to imagine a further advance. Strictly speaking, the works in question *could* have been produced in that order. But they could not have the interpretation, nor hence the structure, we perceive them as having under the present chronology. Picasso, only for example, is constantly referring to the history of art he systematically deconstructs, and so presupposes those past works. And something of the same sort is true of science. Even if scientists are not as conscious of their history as artists are, in truth there are intertheoretic references which assure a degree of incommensurability, if only because we know Galileo and he could not have known us, and to the degree that our uses refer to his, the terms we use cannot have the same meanings his did. So there is an important respect in which we *have* to understand the past in our *own* terms, and there can in consequence be no uniform usage from phase to phase.

There have been philosophies of history which have made these incommensurabilities central, if not for precisely the reasons I have sketched. I am thinking just now of Spengler, who dissolved what had been assumed to be the linear history of the West into three distinct and self-contained historical periods, Classical, Magian, and Faustian, each with its own vocabulary of cultural forms, between which no commensurability of meaning could be assumed. The classical temple, the domed basilica, the vaulted cathedral are less three moments in a linear history than three distinct expressions in the medium of architecture of distinct underlying cultural spirits. In some absolute sense the three periods succeed one another, but only in the way in which one generation succeeds another, with the specific analogy to be drawn that each generation reaches and expresses its maturity in its own way. Each of them defines a dif-

ferent world, and it is the worlds that are incommensurable. Spengler's book was notoriously titled *The Decline of the West,* and it was reckoned exceedingly pessimistic when it first appeared, in part because of the biological metaphors Spengler employed, which required each of his civilizations to go through its own cycle of youth, maturity, decline, and death. So the future of *our* art is very dim, if we accept his premises, but—and how optimistic he after all was— a new cycle will begin, with its own peaks, and we can no more imagine it than *we* could have been imagined from an earlier cycle. So *art* will have a future, it is only that *our* art will not. *Ours* is a form of life that has grown old. So you could look on Spengler as saying something dark or something bright, depending upon how you feel about your own culture within the framework of the severe relativism it, as indeed all the views I have been discussing in this section, presupposes.

And the reason I am stressing this relativism here is that the question I began with, whether art has a future, clearly is antirelativistic in that it really does presuppose a linear history in some sense. This has an absolutely profound philosophical implication, in that it requires an internal connection between the way we define art and the way we think of the history of art. Only, for instance, if we first think of art as representation can we then think of art as having the sort of history which fulfills the progressive model. If, on the other hand, we think of art as simply being expression, or the communication of feelings, as Croce did, well, it just can't have a history of that sort and the question of the end of art can have no application, just because the concept of expression goes with that sort of incommensurability in which one thing just comes after another thing. So that even if it is a fact that artists express feelings, well, this is only a fact, and cannot be the essence of art *if* art has the kind of history within which the question of its coming to an end makes sense. That art is the business of perceptual equivalence is consistent with its having that sort of history, but then, as we saw, it is insufficiently general as a definition of art. So what emerges from this dialectic is that if we are to think of art as having an end, we need a conception of art history which is linear, but a theory of art which is general enough to include representations other than the sort illusionistic painting exemplifies best: literary representations, for example, and even music.

Now Hegel's theory meets all these demands. His thought requires that there be genuine historical continuity, and indeed a kind of progress. The progress in question is not that of an increasingly refined technology of perceptual equivalence. Rather, there is a kind of *cognitive* progress, where it is understood that art progressively approaches that kind of cognition. When the cognition is achieved, there really is no longer any point to or need for art. Art is a transitional stage in the coming of a certain kind of knowledge. The question then is what sort of cognition this can be, and the answer, disappointing as it must sound at first, is the knowledge of what art is. Just as we saw is required, there is an internal connection between the nature and the history of art. History ends with the advent of self-consciousness, or better, self-knowledge. I suppose in a way our personal histories have that structure, or at least our educational histories do, in that they end with maturity, where maturity is understood as knowing—and accepting—what or even who we are. Art ends with the advent of its own philosophy. I shall now tell this last story by returning to the history of past perceptual art.

The success of the Expression Theory of art is also the failure of the Expression Theory of art. Its success consisted in the fact that it was able to explain all of art in a uniform way—i.e., as the expression of feelings. Its failure consisted in the fact that it has only one way of explaining all of art. When discontinuities first appeared as puzzling phenomena in the progressive history of representation, it was a genuine insight that perhaps artists were trying to express rather than primarily to represent. But after about 1906, the history of art simply seemed to be the history of discontinuities. To be sure, this could be accommodated to the theory. Each of us has his or her own feelings, so it is to be expected that these will be expressed in individual ways, and even in incommensurable ways. Most of us, of course, express our feelings in very similar ways, and there are forms of expression which must in fact be understood in evolutionary, not to say physiological, terms: we are

built to express feelings in ways we all recognize. But then the theory is that these are artists and artists are defined in part through the uniqueness of their feelings. The artist is different from the rest of us. But the trouble with this plausible if romantic account lay in the fact that each new movement, from Fauvism down, let alone the Post-Impressionism from which that derived, seemed to require some kind of *theoretical* understanding to which the language and the psychology of emotions seemed less and less adequate.

Just think of the dazzling succession of art movements in our century: Fauvism, the Cubisms, Futurism, Vorticism, Synchronism, Abstractionism, Surrealism, Dada, Expressionism, Abstract Expressionism, Pop, Op, Minimalism, Post-Minimalism, Conceptualism, Photorealism, Abstract Realism, Neo-Expressionism—simply to list some of the more familiar ones. Fauvism lasted about two years, and there was a time when a whole period of art history seemed destined to endure about five months, or half a season. Creativity at that time seemed more to consist in making a period than in making a work. The imperatives of art were virtually historical imperatives—Make an art-historical period!—and success consisted in producing an accepted innovation. If you were successful, you had the monopoly on producing works no one else could, since no one else had made the period with which you and perhaps a few collaborators were from now on to be identified. With this went a certain financial security, inasmuch as museums, wedded to historical structure and the kind of completeness which went with having examples from each period, would want an example from you if you were a suitable period. As innovative an artist as De Kooning was never especially allowed to evolve, and De Chirico, who understood these mechanisms exactly, painted de chiricos throughout his life, since that's what the market wanted. Who would want a Utrillo that looked like Mondrian, or a Marie Laurencin that looked like Grace Hartigan, or a Modigliani like Franz Kline? And each period required a certain amount of quite complex theory in order that the often very minimal objects could be transacted onto the plane of art. In the face of this deep interplay between historical location and theoretical enfranchisement, the appeal to feeling and expression seemed just less and less convincing. Even today we hardly know what Cubism was really about, but I am certain that there is a great deal more to it than Braque and Picasso ventilating their surprisingly congruent feelings toward guitars.

The Expression Theory, while too thin by far to account for this rich profusion of artistic styles and genres, has nevertheless the great merit of having approached works of art as constituting a natural kind, surface variations notwithstanding, and to have responded in the spirit of science to what has been a brooding question since Plato—namely, What is Art? The question became urgent in the twentieth century, when the received model collapsed, though that was not even a good model when no one could tell that it was not. But the inadequacy of the theory became year by year—or, if I may, period by period—more apparent as each movement raised the question afresh, offering itself as a possible final answer. The question indeed accompanied each new artform as the Cogito, according to a great thesis of Kant's, accompanies each judgment, as though each judgment raises about itself the question of What is Thought? And it began to seem as though the whole main point of art in our century was to pursue the question of its own identity while rejecting all available answers as insufficiently general. It was as though, to paraphrase a famous formula of Kant, art were something conceptuable without satisfying any specific concept.

It is this way of looking at things which suggests another model of art history altogether, a model narratively exemplified by the *Bildungsroman,* the novel of self-education which climaxes in the self's recognition of the self. This is a genre recently and, I think, not inappropriately to be mainly found in feminist literature, where the question the heroine raises, for reader and for herself, is at once who is she and what is it to be a woman. The great philosophical work which has this form is Hegel's astonishing *Phenomenology of Spirit,* a work whose hero is the spirit of the world—whom Hegel names *Geist*—the stages of whose development toward self-knowledge, and toward self-realization through self-knowledge, Hegel traces dialectically. Art is one of these stages—indeed, one of the nearly final stages of spirit's return

to spirit through spirit—but it is a stage which must be gone through in the painful ascent toward the final redeeming cognition.

The culmination of Geist's quest and destiny is, as it happens, philosophy, according to Hegel's scheme, largely because philosophy is essentially reflexive, in the sense that the question of what it is is part of what it is, its own nature being one of its major problems: Indeed, the history of philosophy may be read as the story of philosophy's mistaken identities, and of its failures in seeing through and to itself. It is possible to read Hegel as claiming that art's philosophical history consists in its being absorbed ultimately into its own philosophy, demonstrating then that self-theoretization is a genuine possibility and guarantee that there is something whose identity consists in self-understanding. So the great drama of history, which in Hegel is a divine comedy of the mind, can end in a moment of final self-enlightenment, where the enlightenment consists in itself. The historical importance of art then lies in the fact that it makes philosophy of art possible and important. Now if we look at the art of our recent past in these terms, grandiose as they are, what we see is something which depends more and more upon theory for its existence as art, so that theory is not something external to a world it seeks to understand, so that in understanding its object it has to understand itself. But there is another feature exhibited by these late productions which is that the objects approach zero as their theory approaches infinity, so that virtually all there is at the end *is* theory, art having finally become vaporized in a dazzle of pure thought about itself, and remaining, as it were, solely as the object of its own theoretical consciousness.

If something like this view has the remotest chance of being plausible, it is possible to suppose that art had come to an end. Of course, there will go on being art-making. But art-makers, living in what I like to call the post-historical period of art, will bring into existence works which lack the historical importance or meaning we have for a very long time come to expect. The historical stage of art is done with when it is known what art is and means. The artists have made the way open for philosophy, and the moment has arrived at which the task must be transferred finally into the hands of philosophers. Let me conclude by spelling this out in a way which might make it acceptable.

"The end of history" is a phrase which carries ominous overtones at a time when we hold it in our power to end everything, to expel mankind explosively from being. Apocalypse has always been a possible vision, but has seldom seemed so close to actuality as it is today. When there is nothing left to make history—i.e., no more human beings—there will be no more history. But the great meta-historians of the nineteenth century, with their essentially religious readings of history, had rather something more benign in mind, even if, in the case of Karl Marx, violence was to be the engine of this benign culmination. For these thinkers, history was some kind of necessary agony through which the end of history was somehow to be earned, and the end of history then meant the end of that agony. History comes to an end, but not mankind—as the story comes to an end, but not the characters, who live on, happily ever after, doing whatever they do in their post-narrational insignificance. Whatever they do and whatever now happens to them is not part of the story lived through them, as though they were the vehicle and it the subject.

Here is a pertinent summation by that profound and influential commentator on Hegel, Alexandre Kojève:

> In point of fact, the end of human time, or History—that is, the definitive annihilation of Man, properly speaking, or of the free and historical individual—means quite simply the cessation of action in the full sense of the term. Practically, this means the disappearance of wars and bloodly revolutions. And also the disappearance of Philosophy. For since Man no longer changes essentially, there is no reason to change the (true) principles which are at the basis of his understanding of the world and himself. But all the rest can be preserved indefinitely: art, love, play, etc.: in short, everything that makes man *happy.*

And Marx, in a famous passage upon which there can be little doubt that Kojève based his, describes the life of man when all the contradictions that define history, and which are expressed socially as the class

wars so ominously specified in *The Communist Manifesto,* have worked themselves out through the agony of history, so that society is now classless and there is nothing left to generate more history, and man is deposited on the promised shores of utopia, a paradise of nonalienation and nonspecialization. There, Marx tells us, I can be a hunter in the morning and a fisher in the afternoon and a critical critic in the evening. Post-historical life, for Hegel as for Marx, will have the form of a kind of philosophical *Club mediterranée,* or what used to be known as heaven, where there is nothing left for us to do but—in the phrase of our adolescents—hang out. Or, to take another image, this time from Plato, where, at the end of his *Republic,* he depicts a choosing situation, in which men, purged in the afterlife and ready to reenter the world, have arrayed before them the variety of lives from which they may pick one: and the canny Odysseus chooses a life of quiet obscurity, the sort of life most people live most of the time, the simple dumb existence of the sitcom, village life, domestic life, the kind of life lamented, in a painful episode, by Achilles in the underworld. Only, in Marx and in Hegel, there is no history to rumble beyond the distant horizons. The storms have abated forever. And now we can do what we like, heeding that imperative that is no imperative at all: *Fay çe que voudras*—"Do whatever you want."

The End of History coincides, and is indeed identical, with what Hegel speaks of as the advent of Absolute Knowledge. Knowledge is absolute when there is no gap between knowledge and its object, or knowledge is its own object, hence subject and object at once. The closing paragraph of the *Phenomenology* suitably characterizes the philosophical closure of the subject it treats of, by saying that it "consists in perfectly knowing itself, in knowing what it is." Nothing is now outside knowledge, nor opaque to the light of cognitive intuition. Such a conception of knowledge is, I believe, fatally flawed. But if anything comes close to exemplifying it, art in our times does—for the object in which the artwork consists is so irradiated by theoretical consciousness that the division between object and subject is all but overcome, and it little matters whether art is philosophy in action or philosophy is art in thought. "It is no doubt the case," Hegel writes in his *Philosophy of the Fine Arts,* "that art can be utilized as a mere pastime and entertainment, either in the embellishment of our surroundings, the imprinting of a life-enhancing surface to the external conditions of our life, or the emphasis placed by decoration on other subjects." Some such function must be what Kojève has in mind when he speaks of art as among the things that will make men happy in the posthistorical time. It is a kind of play. But this kind of art, Hegel contends, is not really free, "since subservient to other objects." Art is truly free, he goes on to say, only when "it has established itself in a sphere it shares with religion and philosophy, becoming thereby one mode more and form through which . . . the spiritual truths of widest range are brought home to consciousness." All this and, being Hegel, a good bit more having been said, he concludes, dismally or not I leave it to the reader to determine, "Art is and remains for us a thing of the past." And: "On the side of its highest possibilities [art] has lost its genuine truth and life, and is rather transported to our world of *ideas* than is able to maintain its former necessity and its superior place in reality." So a "science of art," or *Kunstwissenschaft*— by which certainly Hegel meant nothing remotely like art history as practiced as an academic discipline today, but rather instead a sort of cultural philosophy of the sort he himself was working out—a "science of art is a far more urgent necessity in our own times than in times in which art sufficed by itself alone to give full satisfaction." And further on in this utterly amazing passage he says, "We are invited by art to contemplate it reflectively . . . in order to ascertain scientifically its nature." And this is hardly something art history as we know it attempts to do, though I am certain that the present rather anemic discipline grew out of something as robust in its conception as Hegel meant for it to be. But it is also possible that art history has the form we know because art as we knew it is finished.

Well.

As Marx might say, you can be an abstractionist in the morning, a photorealist in the afternoon, a minimal minimalist in the evening. Or you can cut out paper dolls or do what you damned please. The age of pluralism is upon us. It does not matter any longer what you do, which is what pluralism means. When one direction is as good as another direction, there is no concept of direction any longer to apply. Decoration, self-expression, entertainment are, of course, abiding human needs. There will always be a service for art to perform, if artists are content with that. Freedom ends in its own fulfillment. A subservient art has always been with us. The institutions of the artworld—galleries, collectors, exhibitions, journalism—which are predicated upon history and hence marking what is new, will bit by bit wither away. How happy happiness will make us is difficult to foretell, but just think of the difference the rage for gourmet cooking has made in common American life. On the other hand, it has been an immense privilege to have lived in history.

Glaring Omissions in Traditional Theories of Art

~

PEG ZEGLIN BRAND

Peg Zeglin Brand is assistant professor of philosophy and gender studies at Indiana University, Bloomington. She has edited a number of books on aesthetics, including *Beauty Matters.*

Within current philosophical aesthetics, various theories of "art" continue to be proposed in spite of mid-century misgivings and against the backdrop of early Greek origins rooted in the term *techne* (meaning "craft" and not "art"). When Wittgenstein questioned the very enterprise of defining as the purview and purpose of philosophy, he broke the historical chain—dating back to Plato and Aristotle—that sought to identify the essence of that uniquely human activity now collectively labeled "art." The common perception that philosophical aesthetics began at some undetermined point in time and progressed triumphantly and predictably toward some goal until its recent demise (Arthur Danto's "end" of art; Victor Burgin's "end" of art theory) is a myth.[1] It invariably portrayed Wittgenstein's influence on the field—evidenced in the writings of Morris Weitz and others—as an irreparable and cataclysmic break in the chain. The resistance of Weitz to "any attempt to state the defining properties of art" constituted a severing of stasis in the ongoing theorizing about art; a break in the narrative of "art"; a collapse of the long-standing institution. In no uncertain terms, Weitz argued that "theory—in the requisite classical sense—is *never* forthcoming in art."[2] If this pronouncement had been accepted as true, there would have been no post-Wittgensteinian proliferation of theories about art. But there has been, and analytic aesthetics has been quick to revise its picture of past philosophizing about

art and Wittengenstein's role in it. The break in the chain was reinterpreted as a temporary aberration quickly repaired.

Now, at the end of the twentieth century, we find ourselves not only theorizing about art but also classifying those theories into categories. We live in an age of functional, procedural, historical, and intentional theories of art whereby the former define "art" in terms of the unique function it fulfills while the latter cast the creation of art in terms of its accordance with certain rules and procedures. Many theories are also labeled "contextual" since, unlike old-fashioned functional accounts, they utilize an analysis of the art-historical context of the work.

Why are there so many theories? And why particularly—in contrast to fields such as literary theory, feminist art criticism, and subdisciplines of philosophy that have generated influential feminist theories in ethics, epistemology, and philosophy of science—has no feminist theory of art gained prominence in philosophical aesthetics? Why, in light of nearly thirty years of feminist theorizing on art, do gender and race still fail to play a significant role even in recent contextual theories, poised as they are to lead us into the next millennium?

This chapter will investigate the role of feminist theorizing in relation to traditional aesthetics. Section 1 will explore women's art as it has evolved into a separate category of feminist expression and will

Reprinted from *Theories of Art Today,* ed. Noel Carroll (Madison: University of Wisconsin Press, 2000), by permission of the publisher.

ask the question "Is there a theory of feminist art?" Noting that feminist artworks have arisen within the context of a patriarchal artworld dominated for thousands of years by male artists, critics, theorists, and philosophers, the second section will look at the history of that context as it impacts philosophical theory by pinpointing the narrow range of paradigms used in defining "art." I will test the plausibility of Danto's vision of a posthistorical, pluralistic future in which "everything is possible": a future that unfortunately rests upon the same foundation as the past concept of "art."[3] The third section will ask, in contrast to the question posed in the first section, what constitutes a feminist theory of art and where might it lead in terms of the future of philosophical theorizing. I will consider Stephen Davies' suggestion that the future of theorizing about art lies in an extension of Dickie's institutional theory: one that relies upon the democratic structure of the institution of art.[4] I will review a sociological approach proposed by Janet Wolff as one way of answering some of the questions posed by Davies, and finally, I will suggest some guidelines for an unconventional feminist theory of art.[5]

IS THERE A THEORY OF FEMINIST ART?

There is art about women and there is feminist art. In addition, some art is created by male artists while some is created by women. Feminist art is nearly always produced by women; one is hard-pressed to think of work by a male artist that has come to be called "feminist" in common parlance. It is a mistake, of course, to think that just because a work of art is produced by a woman, it is necessarily feminist. It is anachronistic, though not totally inappropriate, to call a work "feminist" when it was created before the 1960s and 1970s American and British feminist political movements. It is controversial to call a work "feminist" when its creator flatly denies it. (Consider the case of Georgia O'Keeffe.) Controversy, however, can fuel good marketing; much of the mystique and popularity of some current artists—Cindy Sherman, Kiki Smith, and Sue Williams—can be attributed to the deliberate use of ambiguity that allows viewers to interpret them as either feminist or not. For example, Arthur Danto has claimed that Cindy

Sherman's early black and white film stills "serve as a fulcrum for raising the deepest questions of what it meant to be a woman in America in the late twentieth century."[6] Critic Jeff Perrone assesses her later works differently:

> Sherman poses herself in Playboy like centerfolds, . . . I think some people (men) like it so much because some critics and collectors (men) like a little blonde served up in juicy color. That her photographs are ostensibly about female representation in popular culture seems beside the point.[7]

Gender plays a role in art that is neither subliminal nor secondary to aesthetic concerns, affecting not only the interpretation but also the evaluation of Sherman's work. It plays a crucial role in theorizing about her art. What I hope to show is that this role has been largely ignored in philosophical theorizing about art in general, beginning, as it typically does, with Greek culture as the first and primary example of art.

Since Wittengenstein and Weitz, many theories of art have been proposed that include an art context as the necessary factor distinguishing ordinary objects from their indiscernible art counterparts. Authors of procedural definitions have posted conditions (or rules) that theorize a framework—an "artworld" or an institution of art—by which the distinction can be discerned. Those rules purport to capture the established practices (or conventions) of an ongoing art tradition that have been observed in a neutral, objective way. What is really captured, however, is the history of "art" in (only) the Western world, as perceived by certain people, as they have been privileged to see it and promote it to others. Only certain people have appropriated the authority needed to sanction (only) certain artifacts as art. Beginning with patriarchal Greco-Roman cultures, proceeding through the Renaissance, and evolving into the twentieth century, the world of art has narrowed to an artworld whose conventions have been established and perpetuated by a relatively elite group. The roles of artist, critic, philosopher, and historian have been populated by white males who have successfully controlled the institution of the artworld. What has come down to us is an art of exclusion.[8] Eighteenth-century philosophers set the parameters of aesthetics; nineteenth-century critics and historians opened museums and wrote the history of art. "Art" is broader than their combined efforts would indicate. (Unless, as Davies suggests, there can be more than one artworld.)[9] The glaring omissions in traditional theories of art are the accomplishments and perspectives of women, persons of color, and cultures that predate and overshadow a narrowly circumscribed European-American artworld context. In other words, when artists are named in traditional theories of art, women are usually omitted. Consider one glaring example: the role of women in the history of art.

The history of women artists is only beginning to be amply documented in essays, catalogues, and books, including some carefully gender-balanced art history texts. The pervasive practice of representing women in art is an indication of their important social role, but it is still unclear how far back the roles of women as creators extends. Looking back, we come across evidence of the persistence of goddess worship from the Paleolithic to the Neolithic periods (40,000–8,000 B.C.E.) in the form of "a series of conventionalized images" that spanned twenty thousand years.[10] Thirty thousand miniature sculptures of clay, marble, bone, copper, or gold that represent the female body have been excavated from a total of three thousand sites in southeastern Europe. One image made famous in art history texts is the small limestone figure originally called the "Venus of Willendorf" and subsequently renamed "Woman from Willendorf," which dates from c. 22,000–21,000 B.C.E.[11] These revolutionary findings, initiated by Marija Gimbutas, proved that the culture called Old Europe (pre-Indo-European culture of Europe from between 6500 and 3500 B.C.E.) was characterized by a dominance of women in a matrifocal and probably matrilineal society that was egalitarian, peaceful, and focused on the worship of a goddess who exclusively incarnated the creative principle as source and giver of all.[12] However, the proto-Indo-European culture that replaced it between 4500 and 2500 B.C.E. was patriarchal, hierarchical, and war-oriented.[13] It subsequently replaced the strong and powerful female deities with predominantly male ones. The longstanding tradition of depicting women in art constituted the earliest convention in artistic creativity, as cultural artifacts focused exclusively on women,

their procreative powers, and their dominance within the culture.

In a similar manner, the first written text that survives is of Sumerian origin, dating from the third millennium B.C.E. It is a sacred narrative that tells the cycle of the goddess Inanna, a story focusing on a female protagonist that predates male Greek epic heroes by nearly two thousand years.[14] It is the product of a culture in which women held important legal rights such as owning property and engaging in business. Written in pictographic cuneiform, dozens of carved stone images have been discovered that illustrate the text. Inanna is the main character represented, usually with numerous worshipers in attendance. Cycladic art from the Aegean Islands (2500 B.C.E.) also predates ancient Greek art and consists of images of women. They are the most common form of religious art found in Aegean graves, sacred hilltop sites, and palace shrines, and may have represented goddesses, priestesses, or female worshipers.

In these cases in which representations of women are clearly predominant, we cannot know who created them, but it is possible that women partook in the creative production in these eras. Even recent theories about the creation of Greek art created in a patriarchal culture maintain that women participated in the studios and workshops of various mediums including sculpture, painting, and pottery making.[15] Whether or not women participated in the actual creation of the thousands of artifacts predating Greek art, these objects show us that the origins of art are steeped in cultural practices that included women as subject matter. Gender now plays an important role in revisionist histories of art (like Stokstad's). They have not, however, been utilized as aesthetic paradigms. Aesthetics has been content to remain tied to the conception of a patriarchal artworld conceivably begun in ancient Greece that included only male artists.

The various roles women played in pre-Greek art were not an isolated occurrence in the history of art. Rather, there is a continuum of women who functioned in the role of artist. Because they ignored the medieval norm of anonymity, we know of women manuscript illuminators: Ende (c. 975), Claricia (who promoted herself in a self-portrait and signature of the bottom part of the letter *Q* on a page of a twelfth-century German psalter), and Hildegard of

Bingen (1098–1179), who was not only an abbess of significant repute but also a composer, author, and illustrator of spiritual visions experienced in her sixty years of religious life.

Sofonisba Anguissola was the first woman to gain recognition in the Renaissance, often exchanging her delicate drawings of intimate family settings with Michelangelo. Bologna was a city that boasted a number of women scholars as well as two dozen women painters, including the renowned Lavinia Fontana, who eventually become an official painter of the papal court and a favorite artist of the Habsburgs. As a daughter who apprenticed in her father's studio, Lavinia prefigured a number of artists such as the Baroque Italian painter Artemisia Gentileschi, also a painter of religious scenes. In Holland, Judith Leyster gained repute as a portrait painter. So did her successors Anna Maria Sibylla Merian, a painter of flowers, fruits, birds, and insects, and Rachel Ruysch, primarily a flower painter. The eighteenth century witnessed the achievements of a number of significant women. Elizabeth Godfrey was a renowned London silversmith. Angelica Kauffmann was a history painter who in 1768 became one of only two women among the founding members of the Royal British Academy of Painting and Sculpture. (She and Mary Moser were deliberately excluded from Johann Zoffany's famous painting, *Academicians of the Royal Academy* of 1771–72, represented instead as busts set on a wall shelf.) Rosalba Carriera, honorary member of Rome's Academy of Saint Luke and member of the Royal British Academy, was known for introducing pastels as a portraiture medium to French artists of the Rococo era. Marie-Louise-Élisabeth Vigée-Lebrun was probably the most famous woman artist of the era. As court painter to Marie-Antoinette she was forced to flee the country during the Revolution, but continued painting successfully in Russia and throughout Europe, completing eight hundred portraits in her long career. Her contemporary, Adelaide Labille-Guiard, joined her in being elected in 1783 to the Royal Academy. By then, Marie Thérèse Reboul and Anne Vallayer-Coster were already members.

The proliferation of women in the nineteenth century included sculptors Harriet Hosmer (of mixed race, she lived in France which offered a more receptive audience to her work), Anne Whitney, Edmonia Lewis, and Camille Claudel (model and mistress of Auguste Rodin), the photographer Julia Margaret Cameron, the painter Rosa Bonheur, and the more familiar Berthe Morisot and Mary Cassatt. The twentieth century brought an explosion in numbers and a variety of artistic styles. Some twentieth-century women artists include Paula Modersohn-Becker, Suzanne Valadon, Käthe Kollwitz, Natalya Goncharova, Louise Nevelson, Helen Frankenthaler, Elaine de Kooning (wife of the late Willem), Lee Krasner (wife of Jackson Pollock), Surrealists Dorothea Tanning and Leonora Carrington, Louise Bourgeois, Alice Neel, Florine Stettheimer, Georgia O'Keeffe, Isabel Bishop, Marisol, Hannah Höch, Frida Kahlo, Dorothea Lange, Diane Arbus, Eva Hesse, performance artists Ana Mendieta, Carolee Schneemann, Hannah Wilke, and contemporary artists Judy Chicago, Miriam Schapiro, Susan Rothenberg, Audrey Flack, Nancy Spero, Sherry Levine, Jenny Holzer, Barbara Kruger, Cindy Sherman, Rosemarie Troeckel, Kiki Smith, Sue Williams, Sue Coe, Gladys Nilsson, Adrian Piper, Faith Ringgold, Lorna Simpson, Carrie Mae Weems, and filmmakers Yvonne Rainer, Trinh T. Minh-ha, and Julie Dash.

These artists make up a continuum, a history: one we presume is integral to the canonical history of art (once presumed to be objectively established and promoted). As already noted, these women rarely, if ever, surface in philosophical discussions about the nature and theories of art. Philosophers unfamiliar with them often rationalize their omission by saying, "If women were any good, they would have been included in standard histories of art." It was not until the 1980s that women regained a foothold in the history of art, and have come to be included in greater numbers in basic texts ever since. Even so, many feminist theorists have come up with their own alternative theories to explain what women create and why they have been excluded from the canon and central sources of recognition and funding for so long.[16] In effect, they have developed their own feminist theories of art. Allow me to explain a few examples of recent feminist scholarship documenting reasons why women have come to achieve only a small measure of recognition and success within art theorizing.

In 1971 Linda Nochlin prompted an entire realm of new scholarship based on an interest in gender by asking the question "Why have there been no great women artists?"[17] She initiated the exploration of accolades which consistently eluded women in the arts. She began investigations into the underpinnings of art-historical rankings and art-critical evaluations. Her work resulted in uncovering the social, economic, and political dimensions of life that precluded women's full participation in the arts through the centuries. She disclosed the conditions by which women were consistently nurtured to be less than creative, autonomous, and independent beings. For example, under the law, women were denied the rights of full citizenship: legal representation, the right to inherit, the right to vote. Often the rationale was based on well-entrenched but unchallenged philosophies by which the status of women in the sixteenth through the nineteenth centuries deviated little from Aristotle's categorization of them as deformed males. They were seen as less rational, less virtuous, and, in line with early and medieval Christian theology, antithetical to the higher pursuits of the mind and spirit.[18] They were the repository of bodily based passions and uncontrollable emotions. Eve was considered the personification of these evils; she was not only secondary to Adam (i.e., man in general) but also the source of his downfall. As less than fully rational, woman was less than fully human. With theories that advanced levels of human nature determined by sex, color, and class, women were consistently assigned an inferior status. It is no surprise that basic rights to education were denied and that when female artists, writers, and musicians appeared, they were considered anomalies and excluded by philosophers from the ranks of "great art."[19]

For these reasons, feminist scholars have considered it futile to assess the productivity of women in terms of male-defined criteria. They have been suspicious of the most basic concepts of art history and art criticism, such as "genius" and "masterpiece" (the latter doubly fraught with sexist and racist overtones), and have questioned the standard parameters of interpretation and judgments of value.[20] They have sought to implement other modes of inquiry in order to try to understand the lack of esteem which women's art has suffered. Theorists Griselda Pollock and Roszika Parker extended the analysis of women artists to issues of class, citing the sexist ideology of early art historians who purposely failed to include women in the official history of art as it came to be recorded.[21] They also unsuccessfully attempted to find a term equivalent to "old masters" as evidenced by their title, *Old Mistresses: Women, Art, and Ideology*.

Most important, feminists have come to designate a particular type of art as "feminist art." The ensuing debate has been lively. Norma Broude and Mary D. Garrard's critical collection of essays, *The Power of Feminist Art*, chronicles the first twenty-five years of feminist art, including a variety of approaches to "defining" feminist art.[22] For instance, artist Judy Chicago suggests,

> True feminist art embodies a value system based on the opportunity for empowerment for everyone, rather than the notion of striving for power over others, which is the patriarchal paradigm.[23]

Critic Lucy Lippard considers feminist art an ideology, a way of life.[24] But according to Linda Nochlin, "There is no such thing as feminist art in general." Mary Kelly concurs, "There is no such thing as feminist art, only art informed by different feminism." In spite of theoretical suspicions, even young women artists admit the influence of feminism on their work. Ann Hamilton (born in 1956) writes: "You can't separate your life from feminism. How can you know what your life would be like without that kind of context?"[25] At the very least, a characterization of feminist art includes an artist's intention to portray a politically based ideology of gender representation and gender equality. Thus, feminist art is typically defined by work from the 1960s to the present. As stated earlier, it would be anachronistic and mistaken to call earlier works by women "feminist." Prehistoric, Greek, Renaissance, and other works may have been created by women, but they are not considered feminist.

Thus, there have been many feminist theories about women's art without there being one defining theory of feminist art. Nor will there be one forth-coming. It is a mistake to transpose philosophical goals of defining "art" to feminist investigations. As Rita Felski has argued, "feminist criticism does not need *an* (autonomous) aesthetic."[26] It is crucial to recognize that the lack of such a theory does not indicate a significant failure on the part of theorists. It is not that feminists writing about art seek a defining theory that universally, once and for all, defines "art" and sets the parameters for its interpretation and evaluation. Rather, the resistance to one overall theory comes from within feminism itself. As in feminist theorizing in ethics, epistemology, and the philosophy of science, no one theory dominates. Feminist scholarship seeks to avoid essentialism and to allow for a proliferation of views. In their recognition of pluralist critical approaches, feminists naturally fail to agree with each other. Philosophers, of course, disagree as well, but their agenda is radically different. They are still enmeshed in the traditional enterprise of finding the best, most inclusive, universal definition of "art." It is significant to note that the age of pluralism has only recently been acknowledged by Arthur Danto.[27] Feminist and other postmodern theorists have been actively engaged in establishing an age of pluralism for decades. Feminist art has been explained in terms of context since it began in the 1960s. Any theory of feminist art that differentiates it from *non*feminist art necessarily takes the context of the artworld, its past history, and its continuing conventions and institutions into account. In fact, given its political nature (Lippard once called feminist art "propaganda"), one might say that there can be no theory of feminist art that is not contextual in nature. Given this predisposal of feminist theories toward contextuality, how do standard contextual philosophical theories fare?

PHILOSOPHICAL THEORIES AND DEFINITIONS OF ART

Several issues bear emphasizing when we look back at the history of writing about art in terms of its internal dynamic, complex interactions as well as its interconnections with philosophical aesthetics. At times, one seems to predate and determine the other, while at other times they work in tandem. Artistic and historical criteria for evaluating art did not arise in a vacuum, completely separate and outside philosophical interests. Likewise, the philosophy of art was not immune from overwhelming influences of certain types of art held in high regard. This was especially true during the time in which art history was being "written" in the nineteenth century, with the rise of museums and the demarcation of High Art from low. It is perhaps no coincidence that Hegel's historical theory of art was a product of this time. At no time in these theoretical developments—of museums, art history, philosophical aesthetics—were women artists or theorists allowed to play a real role. One would hope that such insularity was short-lived. But even in the twentieth century, especially with regard to the dominant philosophical theories of art, women's input has been negligible.

The entire history of art has been based on paradigms. It is the history of the "great masters," works of genius, and "masterpieces." The history is clearly traceable back to the Greeks, highlighted with the names of such sculptors as Polykleitos and Praxiteles. In spite of the Renaissance writer Vasari's citing several women in his renowned *Lives of the Artists,* male artists have dominated the established historicizing of art as a scholarly field and academic discipline. Pressure from feminist art historians has forced the canon to become more inclusive, bringing recognition to other artists as well: more examples by artists of color, new explanations of American Indian artifacts and culture, and entire reconceptualizations of the way art history had been previously cast. For instance, the classification of certain peoples as "primitive" has been rethought; the roots of African art have been traced back to the zenith of Egyptian civilization; the art of Asian and Pacific cultures has gained in stature; the collective label of "other" is no longer attached to any culture different from the predominant Western; and a general dissection of the history-by-paradigm approach has become standard practice in light of charges of elitism, sexism, racism, and homophobia. The history of art has come under scrutiny as has its foundation of aesthetic criteria—criteria established by white males of an upper-class eighteenth-century European society who ushered in the birth of modern aesthetics.

Philosophers, who rarely argue for the artistic status of a work of art that has not already been deemed a paradigm by art critics or art historians, continue to rely upon antiquated versions of art history. Thus, philosophical theorizing is nearly three decades behind in updating its paradigms. Given this fact, it is no surprise to read volumes of writings in aesthetics and find no references to women artists. If one rereads Plato on imitation, beauty is the ideal, but one can only surmise as to whether women—who were allowed a role in the Republic in waging war and governance—would also be allowed to participate in the arts. In reviewing Aristotle on tragedy, we are reminded that it was inappropriate for a female character to be manly or clever due to her inferiority. In addition, "art" defined as imitation ironically excluded women from performing women's roles on stage! When eighteenth-century empiricists introduced gender into aesthetic discourse, nature and art became feminine (the beautiful) or masculine (the sublime).[28] Does it come as any surprise that the sublime was ranked above the beautiful? Woman's role was as passive exemplar of beauty: good only for being looked at. Some well-known theories of art were promulgated by several of the most notorious misogynists in the history of philosophy, namely, Schopenhauer and Nietzsche. Hegel, in keeping with Aristotle, claimed that "womankind" is constituted through suppression. This does not mean that their theories of art were necessarily misogynistic, but it certainly insured that their base of artistic examples excluded women as artists on a par with men.

Given these philosophical convictions, women were denied active roles in the establishing of the philosophical foundations of aesthetics, denied recognition as artists in the production of art, and excluded from establishing the criteria for canonizing art-historical styles and personae.[29] Aesthetics was gendered masculine from the beginning. These are strong charges in light of philosophy's claims to pursue criteria for definition and evaluation that are purportedly universal and objective. What feminist scholars have tried to show (and I will continue to argue below) is that any theory purporting to be universal but based on biased criteria with a limited range of applicability is inherently flawed.

Aesthetic theorists placed significant emphasis on the notion of disinterestedness, setting the stage for the advent of aesthetic attitude theories and isolationist theories that precluded contextual data from being relevant to the aesthetic experiencing of art. Information about the artists' origins and intentions was considered irrelevant, and the theories of Stolnitz and Beardsley, among others, sought to isolate art from its sociohistorical context at all costs.[30] Consistent with their predecessors, twentieth-century aestheticians appropriated their paradigms from the same art history as did previous philosophers. In order to meet the challenge of explaining Duchamp's *Fountain,* Warhol's *Brillo Box,* and other conceptual art—in conjunction with Wittgenstein's anti-essentialism—theories arose that took sociological (institutions of art) and art-historical contexts into consideration. Two main leaders in this move were Arthur Danto and George Dickie. Their writings contained the germ of theories subsequently proposed by Lucian Krukowski, Jerrold Levinson, Noël Carroll, and Marcia Eaton.

According to Stephen Davies' *Definitions of Art,* theories of art divide into three categories: functional, procedural, and historical/intentional. Even within contemporary theorizing about art, however, the range of paradigms he cites is grossly skewed to white male artists. The problem with these theories is not just that women have been left out of the written and conceptual histories of art, nor that they still fail to function within art history, art criticism, and aesthetics as paradigms of "art" or "good art." Rather it's that theorizing about art—as guided by this narrow range of paradigms—is incomplete and conceptually inadequate. It cannot encompass all art because the stipulated precedents from history and criticism preclude the broader spectrum of what counts as human expression and creativity. This explains continual challenges to existing theories: What about the case of driftwood? Salvador Dali's pile of rocks? Aboriginal art? Naive art? Graffiti art? Digital art?

Let us look at some of the language used to stipulate the narrow range of paradigms and the way such paradigms are established. In Dickie's two versions (and related writings) of the Institutional Theory, no woman artist is cited although the definitions appear relatively gender-neutral. In the first definition, a work of art is an artifact that has been bestowed upon it the status of art by someone qualified within the ongoing institution of art.[31] For Dickie, this means the continuum of practices—conventions—that constitute the ongoing practice, or institution, of art. Davies designates Dickie's theory as inadequate and "ahistorical" since it stipulates roles that members of the artworld hold without providing any particulars of those roles. In other words, Dickie fails

> to characterize the roles that generate the structure of that institution—their boundaries, their limitations, the circumstances under which they change, the conditions for their occupancy, and so on.[32]

Thus Dickie has failed to amplify the details of art history which function as the basis of his theory, thereby leaving open to speculation the specifics of who has occupied those roles in the past, who occupies them now, and who will come to occupy them in the future. (More on this in the third section.) That is, in spite of Dickie's oversimplified claim that anyone "could" be an artist within the artworld, some reflection on the sociohistorical restrictions on women such as those described by Parker, Pollock, and Nochlin (see section 1) would prompt us to question his generalization.

The revised version of the institutional theory, although clearer, still falls short for Davies, who seeks more information about the authority of persons in the artworld by which they may confer the status of arthood.[33] Feminists have asked the same type of question for years, though not in the same terminology. They, too, have challenged the authority of the philosophers of taste of the eighteenth century, the historians of art of the nineteenth century, the art critics and theorists of the twentieth century. It appears that philosophers have come rather late to the fundamental questions that challenge the variety of procedures by which definitions of "art" have come to be codified. Given this state of things, the procedural approach may be suspect in all its manifestations.

Let's take another example. In *After the End of Art: Contemporary Art and the Pale of History,* Arthur

Danto discusses the "experts" who accorded the status of art to Warhol's *Brillo Box* and Duchamp's *Fountain:*

> The experts really were experts in the same way in which astronomers are experts on whether something is a star. They saw that these works had meanings which their indiscernible counterparts lacked, and they saw as well the way these works embodied those meanings.[34]

Who were these experts? The art critics, we presume, empowered by the artworld (on Danto's theory) and authorized by the institution of art (on Dickie's theory). Who deemed them expert? It is unclear, although the analogy to astronomy implies that these are persons educated and experienced in knowing about art, reminiscent of Hume's qualified person of taste.

The fact that artworks by women fail to be cited as paradigms and women critics fail to be considered "expert" explains why the paradigms remain less than fully representative of the artworld population. This is particularly interesting, given Danto's recent adjustment of his "admittedly somewhat reckless claim" concerning the death of art.[35] In prior writings, Danto claimed that art, in its linear progression (à la Hegel), had reached its end—or had at least reached the point at which it "had nearly turned into philosophy." He has subsequently reconsidered and now defines the present moment in art as "open" and at "the conjunction of essentialism and historicism."

> As we seek to grasp the essence of art—or to speak less portentously, of an adequate philosophical definition of art— our task is immensely facilitated by the recognition that the extension of the term "work of art" is now altogether open, so that in effect we live in a time when everything is possible for artists.[36]

Still borrowing from Hegel, he claims that freedom defines our posthistorical period of art; it stipulates our "modalities of history":

> The sense in which everything is possible is that in which there are no *a priori* constraints on what a

work of visual art can look like, so that anything visible can be a visual work. This is part of what it really means to live at the end of art history.[37]

This should come as good news for women artists who worked outside the "pale of history" (i.e., raced pale/white) for so long and for feminist theorists who developed alternative theories of art that deviated from the canonical norm. If we are truly living at the end of art history, several possibilities lie before us.

One is to consider ourselves at a moment in time when we can say good riddance to the old exclusivity of art history and welcome to the new. But it's not clear what Danto foresees as the new history nor how it will come to be generated. He cites Wolfflin "with his keen sense of historical modalities—of possibility and impossibility" as his guide, but his examples reflect the narrowness of staunch conservative art historians like Kenneth Clark and Robert Hughes.[38] In Danto's vision of the future, the range of possibilities of art still extend no further than Grünewald, Dürer, Terborch, Bernini, Botticelli, Lorenzo di Credi, Caravaggio, Pinturicchio, Courbet, Giotto, Cervantes, Guercino, Feuerbach, Manet, Poussin, the Bolognese "masters," Praxiteles, Van Meegeren, Vermeer, Rubens, Rembrandt, the "postmodern masterpiece" of the American painter Russell Connor and the "masterpiece" of the "true heroes of the post-historical period," the "post-historical masters" Komar and Melamid.[39] It appears that art paradigms in a posthistorical period are no different in terms of gender from ones from a historical period. Danto may simply answer this charge by claiming that women artists implicitly form part of the canon of art, but his negligence in citing them *as paradigms* might lead us to view his response as ad hoc and inadequate. If women artists, critics, and theorists are part of the posthistorical age of pluralism, why are they not mentioned?

More pointedly, given that Connor's work consists of jointly parodying Rubens's *Rape of the Daughters of Leucippus* and Picasso's *Demoiselles d'Avignon*—in which the women being carried off by the two horsemen are imitations of Picasso's women (already an appropriation of African art)—how do we interpret Danto's judgment of this as a "masterpiece"

much less as comic? Defining what is funny can be delicately gender- and race-specific.[40] It is questionable to some feminists whether any rape scene can count as an artistic "masterpiece," much less whether a parodied rape scene can ever be considered "comic"—even if appropriation is fashionable and sometimes funny in the 1990s. . . .

A FEMINIST THEORY OF ART

Perhaps a simple remedy for the narrowness of philosophical aesthetics is simply to "add women and stir." But to do so is to misunderstand the role of gender in transforming the mainstream, the canon, and the tradition, and to misperceive the possibility of turning theories of feminist art into more complex feminist theories of art. Consider a quote from Arthur Danto regarding the political activities of the subversive art-world group known as the Guerilla Girls.

> The group has been exceedingly radical in its means and in its spirit. It is genuinely collaborative, to the point that the anonymity of its members is a fiercely held secret: appearing in gorilla masks is a metaphor for that. And the art of this superordinate entity is certainly a form of direct action: its members plaster the walls of Soho with brilliant, biting posters. But the message of the posters is that not enough women are represented in museums, in major shows, in important galleries. So it envisages artistic success in the traditional, let us say, using their concept, white male terms. Its means are radical and deconstructive, but its goals are altogether conservative.[41]

Commenting on the "somewhat paradoxical character of the Guerilla Girls," Danto exemplifies a typical misunderstanding of the feminist agenda. The Guerilla Girls have come to symbolize the embodiment of feminist political activity; as strategizers, they are united, determined, and skillful.[42] They are out in force, operating openly in the artworld: planting a banana on a public podium or posting an announcement decrying the oppressive gender politics at the Whitney. They are not only attempting to balance the institutional scales so that gender equity might be achieved in the artworld but they are also attempting to radically alter the artworld itself.

Danto seriously understates their case in terms of both intentionality and political achievement. In asking why they strive for artistic success in traditional, conservative, white male terms, Danto is really asking why they don't just create their own alternative artworld or why they aren't more feminist. The irony is that as women seek the attention, respect, and praise of art critics, often the foothold gained is diminished by what gets said about them. They succeed in securing critical attention while being simultaneously undermined. Their goals are dismissed as "altogether conservative," and their motivation is reduced to a desire to be accepted on "white male terms."

On the contrary, most feminists do not want to break into the artworld as it now exists: traditional, hierarchical, conservative, and founded on "white male terms." Their goals are to be included in museums as those museums start to welcome a variety of works in a true spirit of openness; they want major shows and important galleries to value their work for how it redefines or discards "masterpiece" and "genius." They seek to move beyond the pale of art history by creating the next critical era: one that values artworks *because* they diverge from the white, male viewpoint and traditional aesthetic norms of evaluation. (Not only when they acquiesce and uplift, as in the case of Sherman.) A truly new age would include women and artists of color using radical and deconstructive means toward the end of altering (perhaps abolishing) the artworld.[43] In philosophical terms, this would mean the influx of feminist theories of art into aesthetics.

What might such theories look like? One suggested direction, as mentioned earlier, is the institutional theory of art.[44] Davies distrusts Dickie's theory for its lack of clarification about the "artists" who have the authority to confer the status of arthood by virtue of their occupying a role within the artworld to which that authority attaches. He questions how a person comes to acquire such authority at a particular time and not others, and how the artworld "persists through time."

> Dickie needs to say something about the history of art not in order to explain why artworks are as they are now, but rather, to explain why the Artworld is as

it is, and hence to explain why the process by which art status can be achieved and the restrictions on who might effectively use this process are as they are.[45]

A quick glance back at Danto reveals that "most if not all people" are able to make something into art. For Dickie to hold the same belief would not be inconsistent with the conditions of his theory. Davies introduces a new term to Dickie's theory, "democratic," intended to characterize the nature of the role of artist in history. According to Davies:

> Dickie should describe the structure of the Artworld, showing how different roles within the institution attract to themselves different amounts or kinds of authority. To that story he should add an account of the organic, historical nature of the institution in order to explain how it might come to have its present "democratic" structure.[46]

Although I recognize the cogency of Davies' (and others') critique of the vagueness of the institutional theory, I beg to differ with his account. The artworld has never been "democratic." This is true for Davies' examples of the fifteenth century when hobby painters could not be artists, as well as the twentieth century. For instance, I would wager that no woman could have produced *Fountain.* That is, even if some woman, for example, Meret Oppenheim or Hannah Höch, had dated and signed a man's urinal, it would never have merited the same attention or acclaim as Duchamp's. (Similarly for *L.H.O.O.Q.* and other masculine Duchampian gestures.) Although Davies dismisses the historian's and social anthropologist's approach, they might be exactly what is needed.

It should be noted at this point that traditional aesthetics has never been eager to undertake a sociological approach to art. Recall Marcia Eaton's warning and dismissal of sociological accounts of art like that of marxist aesthetics:

> One of the problems with Marxism (and other sociologies of art) is that it assumes a connection between art and social features that has yet to be shown to exist. That is, it presupposes the existence of lawlike connections between social factors and artistic creation.[47]

Given the skepticism about the empirical verification of such connections, Eaton dismisses any such approach as "aesthetic sociology":

> Marxism identifies artworks with their contexts and hence does not allow us to see what is special about them. There is a sense in which Marxist aesthetics ceases to be aesthetics at all.[48]

But maintaining strictures about what counts as "aesthetics" is precisely what impedes progress in pursuing clarification of the social factors surrounding the creation and distribution of art. All contextual theories, including Eaton's, are based precisely on such connections; such connections constitute the foundation of all contextual theories of art. Eaton confirms this when she states that "outside the context of social and cultural practices and conventions, 'art' does not make sense."[49]

What is needed is something like a feminist account of the artworld that has looked seriously at the way the roles of the institution have been meted out to a particular subpopulation across the centuries. If women and persons of color have consistently been denied access to these roles, the artworld cannot call itself democratic. If they continue to be denied, the artworld will never be democratic. The authority by which the artworld proceeds remains institutionally intact. The hierarchy, the privileging of power, and the denial of access remain institutionalized (in the most negative sense of the term): frozen in place. There is no way out other than radical departure from the ongoing social practices. The radical restructuring advocated by the Guerilla Girls and other feminists is precisely what is needed.

For thirty years, feminists have been involved with the process of fleshing out what a variety of such theories might include. German, French, British, and American feminists have debated the integral parts of a variety of approaches to theorizing about art. As far back as the 1970s, Gisela Ecker proposed the following:

> Feminist aesthetic theory must insist that all investigations into art have to be *thoroughly genderised*. . . . A truly genderised perspective would mean that the sex—male or female—of both the

artist and the critic is taken into account. This also implies their relation to gender-values in the institutions and within the theories they apply.[50]

Many other theorists have supported this view.

Given the suggestions of Stephen Davies, one promising approach is provided by Janet Wolff, who argues for a new aesthetic based in a sociological study of the arts: one that addresses not only issues of gender but also class and the influence of political or moral ideals on the ways "art" comes to be defined and artworks valued. In *The Social Production of Art,* she states,

> Understanding art as socially produced necessarily involves illuminating some of the ways in which various forms, genres, styles, etc. come to have value ascribed to them by certain groups in particular contexts.[51]

In other words, Wolff promotes an investigation into "the ways these categories and divisions are historically created and sustained": precisely what Davies called for in the hopes of elucidating philosophical contextual theories such as Dickie's. Wolff provides accounts of the social structure of the institutions of the artworld that indicate how the rise of art criticism, art markets, and the codification of the history of art have come to affect what subsequently assumed "neutral, objective" status within philosophical theory. She argues that artistic production has little to do with "genius" and is much more like other forms of production and human agency, especially in terms of the influence of economic factors. Rejecting a traditional sociological analysis of the concept of "genius," Wolff argues,

> It has *never* been true, and it is not true today, that the artist has worked in isolation from social and political constraints of a direct or indirect kind.[52]

Therefore, she debunks the philosophical notion of the Ur-artist and instead pursues the various strands that make up the social production of art, including the roles of artist, the patronage system, and the "mediators" ("gatekeepers").

In a more recent work, *Aesthetics and the Sociol-*

ogy of Art, Wolff locates herself between opposing camps: one that denies sociology a role in the analysis of aesthetic value, and the opposite view of reductionists who collapse aesthetic value into social or political value. Although she fails to incorporate the contextual theories of Danto and Dickie into her discussion, she notes that philosophers have "abandoned the field of pure philosophy" by incorporating "the contingent and the social into their analyses":

> The sociological nature of the institutional theory of art is self-evident, for the theory relies on the social roles and institutions in which art is produced and accredited.[53]

Her suggestions, although brief, are directed to the further delineation of a sociological aesthetics, somewhat similar to that promoted by Rita Felski:

> A feminist aesthetic theory, then, must take into account this institutionalized status of art as exemplified in existing ideological and discursive frameworks.[54]

Davies' final suggestions do not sufficiently move such an agenda forward. His call for a proceduralist approach dismisses the functionalist approach by which art is defined and gauged by individuals' reactions to a particular stimulus. To dismiss the functionalist approach is to deny the importance of the diversity of reactions art can inspire. He returns briefly to these matters when he states that the primary function of art is to provide enjoyment and that art can have "far-reaching social benefits" as well. But his claim that "Good artworks, properly approached and understood, afford enjoyment" still invokes a standard of propriety mired in the past. Consider his confirmation of this look backward:

> Standards for the proper approach to artworks are governed by interpersonal conventions of the Artworld [which are] grounded in the history of the practices of the Artworld and are not established by stipulation.[55]

On the contrary, conventions are often established by stipulation: by certain persons, in particular roles,

within broader contexts. It is a mistake to think that the social contexts of those who have been allowed to set the standards, establish the practices, and establish the conventions are not relevant and that only history counts. What is enjoyable can also be generalized into what is good. This is the resurfacing of Hume's problem of the standard of taste. But what counts as enjoyable for the African or the Indian appreciator has not become part of the standards of the artworld as institutionalized in the Western world. The democratization of enjoyment has not played a role in the history of art. Members, in a variety of roles within the artworld, have simply refused to allow it.

Finally, Davies claims that intentionality is necessary for something to become an artwork. But he stipulates artists' intentions as follows: the art maker must intend her product "to be viewed in one or another of the ways in which art has been correctly viewed in the past." Again, the past sets the precedent. Even the success of originality depends on the agent's having a "recognized, established position of prominence within the Artworld."[56] On this view most women, feminists, persons of color are automatically excluded. To stipulate prominence in the artworld as a prerequisite for having the authority to create art begs the question. I suggest a return to a more functionalist account, particularly along the following lines.

Given the conventions of the tradition already in place within philosophical aesthetics, an unconventional feminist theory of art would include the following:

1. A recognition that the past history of art, criticism, theory, and philosophy has been dominated by a particular subpopulation with a particular taste and a particular agenda. The artworld has been undemocratic from the start and still continues to be.
2. A recognition that the roles of authority within the artworld have had no basis in objective criteria and that value judgments issued by such "experts" are subjective and idiosyncratic.
3. A recognition that the Hegelian approach to the linearity of "art" is flawed; it fails to recog-

nize "art" from a variety of cultures and across a significant length of time, art that may not fit the narrowing criterion of originality.

4. A recognition that sexist and racist assumptions have permeated philosophical aesthetics as instituted in the eighteenth century and continued into the nineteenth and twentieth centuries.

5. A recognition that Ur-roles have been filled in ways that the artworld has failed to recognize.

6. A recognition that gender and race are essential components of the context in which an artwork is created and thus cannot be excluded from consideration in procedural (historical, intentional) definitions of "art."

Far from essentializing a feminist theory of art, these suggestions serve as a starting point for further discussion between philosophers and feminist theorists. The undisclosed conventions of the artworld are only fully coming to light as recent scholarship develops. Suggestions 1–6 stand as markers of acknowledgment: demands for "recognition" (or recognizing) of the "interpersonal conventions" called for by Davies. (1) is a general statement calling attention to the demographics of the vast majority of art practitioners who have established and dominated an undemocratic artworld. (2) admonishes the figures who have institutionalized artworld roles of authority predicated upon the presumption of objective, universal criteria. (3) undermines the pervasiveness of a strict, linear concept of "art" that fails to recognize its more complex repetitious and cyclical nature; this conception depended heavily upon the insistance on originality as an artistic criterion, so that whatever is "new" counts as valuable and thus progressive. (4) singles out the legacy of philosophers, especially as they have contributed to the foundations of art criticism and art history, as well as their practice of deriving aesthetic criteria from those institutions and scholarly disciplines. (5) attempts to complicate the philosophical notion of the Ur-work by inviting reflection upon actual archeological evidence, much of which has only tangentially been considered part of the continuum of "art." Toward that end it might be helpful to expand the functions usually attributed to

early/Ur-works: beyond the magical, religious, and spiritual. Finally, (6) promotes a more inclusive mode of organizing the components of future contextual theories of art. A corollary might emphasize the various types of theories of feminist art and sociological aesthetics that have already arisen apart from the analytic tradition. Perhaps a reconsideration of art in terms of gender, race, class, ethnicity, and sexual orientation would add a new dimension to functional accounts of art that might be used in consort with procedural definitions.

Thus, the glaring omissions in traditional theories of art can be corrected. Feminist theories of art can serve as models for expanding the range of paradigms within aesthetics and challenging ingrained cliches. As Hilde Hein reminds us,

> Feminism creates new ways of thinking, new meanings, and new categories of critical reflection; it is not merely an extension of old concepts to new domains.[57]

Perhaps, even within the most historically bound philosophies of art, its time has come.

NOTES

1. See Arthur C. Danto, *The Transfiguration of the Commonplace* (Cambridge: Harvard University Press, 1981); and Victor Burgin, *The End of Art Theory: Criticism and Postmodernity* (London: Macmillan, 1986).

2. Morris Weitz, "The Role of Theory in Aesthetics," *Journal of Aesthetics and Art Criticism* 15 (1956): 27–35.

3. Arthur C. Danto, *After the End of Art: Contemporary Art and the Pale of History* (Princeton: Princeton University Press, 1997).

4. Stephen Davies, *Definitions of Art* (Ithaca, N.Y.: Cornell University Press, 1991).

5. Janet Wolff, *The Social Production of Art,* 2d ed. (New York: New York University Press, 1993); Wolff, *Aesthetics and the Sociology of Art,* 2d ed. (Ann Arbor: University of Michigan Press, 1993).

6. Danto, *After the End of Art,* 148.

7. Jeff Perrone, "Unfinished Business: 1982 New York Overview," *Images and Issues* (January/February 1983): 39.

8. This, in fact, is the title of a text by Albert Boime, *The Art of Exclusion: Representing Blacks in the Nineteenth Century* (Washington, D.C.: Smithsonian Institution

Press, 1990). I intend the term more broadly, that is, to refer to more than just the nineteenth century.

9. Davies, *Definitions of Art,* 97.

10. Marija Gimbutas, *The Goddesses and Gods of Old Europe* (Berkeley: University of California Press, 1982), 10.

11. Marilyn Stokstad, *Art History* (New York: Harry N. Abrams, 1995), 39.

12. Males (men and animals) represented "spontaneous and life-stimulating—but not life-generating—powers." Gimbutus, *Goddesses and Gods,* 9.

13. A recent essay gives evidence that disputes this; see Lawrence Osborne, "The Women Warriors," *Lingua Franca* 7 (1998): 50–57.

14. Diane Wolkstein and Samuel Noah Kramer, *Inanna, Queen of Heaven and Earth* (New York: Harper & Row, 1983), xvi.

15. Stokstad notes that several women are mentioned in the ancient writings of Pliny the Elder. See *Art History,* 207.

16. As of 1995, over 50 percent of artists in the United States are women; however, 85 percent of artists who are invited to participate in gallery and museum shows are male. (When shows are blindly juried, the ratio is nearly half and half.) See Rebecca Phillips Abbott, *Women in the Arts* 13 (1995): 2. According to the National Museum of Women in the Arts in Washington, D.C., updated statistics for the 1997–98 season show only 7 out of 45 solo exhibitions at major U.S. museums went to women (again, only 15 percent).

17. The essay is reprinted in Linda Nochlin, *Women, Art, and Power and Other Essays* (New York: Harper and Row, 1988).

18. See Genevieve Lloyd, *The Man of Reason: "Male" and "Female" in Western Philosophy,* 2d ed. (Minneapolis: University of Minnesota Press, 1984, 1993); and Nancy Tuana, *The Less Noble Sex: Scientific, Religious, and Philosophical Conceptions of Woman's Nature* (Bloomington: Indiana University Press, 1993).

19. Recall that many of the women listed were members of the Royal Academy in their day, successful artists, and court painters. It is art history and philosophy that have subsequently omitted them from their histories.

20. See Christine Battersby, *Gender and Genius: Towards a Feminist Aesthetics* (London: Women's Press, 1989; Bloomington: Indiana University Press, 1990); or Barbara Herrnstein Smith, *Contingencies of Value: Alternative Perspectives for Critical Theory* (Cambridge: Harvard University Press, 1988).

21. Griselda Pollock and Roszika Parker, *Old Mistresses: Women, Art, and Ideology* (New York: Pantheon Books, 1981).

22. Norma Broude and Mary D. Garrard, eds., *The Power of Feminist Art: The American Movement of the 1970s, History and Impact* (New York: Abrams, 1994).

23. Ibid., 73.

24. Ibid., 150.

25. Carey Lovelace, "Weighing in on Feminism," *ARTnews* 96 (1997): 142.

26. Rita Felski, "Why Feminism Doesn't Need an Aesthetic (And Why It Can't Ignore Aesthetics)," in *Feminism and Tradition in Aesthetics,* ed. Peg Zeglin Brand and Carolyn Korsmeyer (University Park: Pennsylvania State University Press, 1995), 431.

27. Danto, *After the End of Art,* 197.

28. Edmund Burke, *A Philosophical Enquiry into the Origin of Our Ideas of the Sublime and Beautiful,* ed. J. T. Boulton (Notre Dame: University of Notre Dame Press, 1958).

29. Susanne Langer should not be considered as representing a significant counterexample to this trend. Apart from her popularity with music educators, she is rarely taught in aesthetics classes or included in aesthetics anthologies.

30. See Peg Zeglin Brand, "Feminism in Context: A Role for Feminist Theory in Aesthetic Evaluation," in *Contemporary Philosophy of Art: Readings in Analytic Aesthetics,* ed. John W. Bender and H. Gene Blocker (Englewood Cliffs, N.J.: Prentice Hall, 1993), 106–21.

31. George Dickie, *Art and the Aesthetic: An Institutional Analysis* (Ithaca, N.Y.: Cornell University Press, 1974).

32. Davies, *Definitions of Art,* 94.

33. George Dickie, *The Art Circle: A Theory of Art* (New York: Haven, 1984).

34. Danto, *After the End of Art,* 195.

35. Ibid.

36. Ibid., 197.

37. Ibid., 198.

38. Ibid., 199.

39. Ibid., 199–210.

40. See my forthcoming *Parodies as Politics,* which discusses feminist theories of humor in comparison to traditional theories written by Plato, Aristotle, Hobbes, Hutcheson, Kant, Schopenhauer, Kierkegaard, Bergson, Freud, and others.

41. Danto, *After the End of Art,* 147.

42. See their website at www.guerrillagirls.com.

43. One example of the new diversified approach is Phoebe Farris-Dufrene, *Voices of Color: Art and Society in the Americas* (Atlantic Highlands, N.J.: Humanities Press, 1997).

44. In an extension of Dickie's theories on evaluation, I have argued for a more workable framework for understanding the type of critical statements traditionally used to devalue works by female artists. See "Evaluating Art: A Feminist Case for Dickie's Matrix System," in *Institutions of Art: Reconsiderations of George Dickie's Philosophy,* ed. Robert J. Yanal (University Park: Pennsylvania State University Press, 1994), 87–107.

45. Davies, *Definitions of Art,* 95.

46. Ibid., 97.

47. Marcia Muelder Eaton, *Basic Issues in Aesthetics* (Belmont, Calif.: Wadsworth, 1988), 87–88.

48. Ibid., 88.

49. Ibid., 96.

50. Gisela Ecker, *Feminist Aesthetics,* trans. Harriet Anderson (Boston: Beacon Press, 1985), 22.

51. Wolff, *Social Production of Art,* 7.

52. Ibid., 27.

53. Wolff, *Aesthetics and the Sociology of Art,* 79.

54. Rita Felski, *Beyond Feminist Aesthetics: Feminist Literature and Social Change* (Cambridge: Harvard University Press, 1989), 158.

55. Davies, *Definitions of Art,* 220.

56. Ibid., 221.

57. Hilde Hein, "The Role of Feminist Aesthetics in Feminist Theory," in *Feminism and Tradition in Aesthetics,* 446.

Of the Standard of Taste

DAVID HUME

David Hume (1711–1776) was a Scottish empiricist philosopher, historian, and essayist. His works include *A Treatise of Human Nature, An Inquiry Concerning Human Understanding,* and numerous essays on issues ranging from the passions to politics to economics.

The great variety of Taste, as well as of opinion, which prevails in the world, is too obvious not to have fallen under every one's observation. Men of the most confined knowledge are able to remark a difference of taste in the narrow circle of their acquaintance, even where the persons have been educated under the same government, and have early imbibed the same prejudices. But those, who can enlarge their view to contemplate distant nations and remote ages, are still more surprized at the great inconsistence and contrariety. We are apt to call *barbarous* whatever departs widely from our own taste and apprehension: But soon find the epithet of reproach retorted on us. And the highest arrogance and self-conceit is at last startled, on observing an equal assurance on all sides, and scruples, amidst such a contest of sentiment, to pronounce positively in its own favour.

As this variety of taste is obvious to the most careless enquirer; so will it be found, on examination, to be still greater in reality than in appearance. The sentiments of men often differ with regard to beauty and deformity of all kinds, even while their general discourse is the same. There are certain terms in every language, which import blame, and others praise; and all men, who use the same tongue, must agree in their application of them. Every voice is united in applauding elegance, propriety, simplicity, spirit in writing; and in blaming fustian, affectation, coldness, and a false brilliancy: But when critics come to particulars, this seeming unanimity vanishes; and it is found, that

From David Hume, *Essay XXIII: Of the Standard of Taste.*

they had affixed a very different meaning to their expressions. In all matters of opinion and science, the case is opposite: The difference among men is there oftener found to lie in generals than in particulars; and to be less in reality than in appearance. An explanation of the terms commonly ends the controversy; and the disputants are surprized to find, that they had been quarrelling, while at bottom they agreed in their judgment.

Those who found morality on sentiment, more than on reason, are inclined to comprehend ethics under the former observation, and to maintain, that, in all questions, which regard conduct and manners, the difference among men is really greater than at first sight it appears. It is indeed obvious, that writers of all nations and all ages concur in applauding justice, humanity, magnanimity, prudence, veracity; and in blaming the opposite qualities. Even poets and other authors, whose compositions are chiefly calculated to please the imagination, are yet found from HOMER down to FENELON, to inculcate the same moral precepts, and to bestow their applause and blame on the same virtues and vices. This great unanimity is usually ascribed to the influence of plain reason; which, in all these cases, maintains similar sentiments in all men, and prevents those controversies, to which the abstract sciences are so much exposed. So far as the unanimity is real, this account may be admitted as satisfactory: But we must also allow that some part of the seeming harmony in morals may be accounted for from the very nature of language. The word *virtue,* with its equivalent in every tongue, implies praise; as that of *vice* does blame: And no one, without the most obvious and grossest impropriety, could affix reproach to a term, which in general acceptation is understood in a good sense; or bestow applause, where the idiom requires disapprobation. HOMER'S general precepts, where he delivers any such, will never be controverted; but it is obvious, that, when he draws particular pictures of manners, and represents heroism in ACHILLES and prudence in ULYSSES, he intermixes a much greater degree of ferocity in the former, and of cunning and fraud in the latter, than FENELON would admit of. The sage ULYSSES in the GREEK poet seems to delight in lies and fictions, and often employs them without any

necessity or even advantage: But his more scrupulous son, in the FRENCH epic writer, exposes himself to the most imminent perils, rather than depart from the most exact line of truth and veracity.

The admirers and followers of the ALCORAN insist on the excellent moral precepts interspersed throughout that wild and absurd performance. But it is to be supposed, that the ARABIC words, which correspond to the ENGLISH, equity, justice, temperance, meekness, charity, were such as, from the constant use of that tongue, must always be taken in a good sense; and it would have argued the greatest ignorance, not of morals, but of language, to have mentioned them with any epithets, besides those of applause and approbation. But would we know, whether the pretended prophet had really attained a just sentiment of morals? Let us attend to his narration; and we shall soon find, that he bestows praise on such instances of treachery, inhumanity, cruelty, revenge, bigotry, as are utterly incompatible with civilized society. No steady rule of right seems there to be attended to; and every action is blamed or praised, so far only as it is beneficial or hurtful to the true believers.

The merit of delivering true general precepts in ethics is indeed very small. Whoever recommends any moral virtues, really does no more than is implied in the terms themselves. That people, who invented the word *charity,* and used it in a good sense, inculcated more clearly and much more efficaciously, the precept, *be charitable,* than any pretended legislator or prophet, who should insert such a *maxim* in his writings. Of all expressions, those, which, together with their other meaning, imply a degree either of blame or approbation, are the least liable to be perverted or mistaken.

It is natural for us to seek a *Standard of Taste;* a rule, by which the various sentiments of men may be reconciled; at least, a decision, afforded, confirming one sentiment, and condemning another.

There is a species of philosophy, which cuts off all hopes of success in such an attempt, and represents the impossibility of ever attaining any standard of taste. The difference, it is said, is very wide between judgment and sentiment. All sentiment is right; because sentiment has a reference to nothing beyond itself, and is always real, wherever a man is conscious of it. But all determinations of the understanding are not right; because they have a reference to something beyond themselves, to wit, real matter of fact; and are not always conformable to that standard. Among a thousand different opinions which different men may entertain of the same subject, there is one, and but one, that is just and true; and the only difficulty is to fix and ascertain it. On the contrary, a thousand different sentiments, excited by the same object, are all right: Because no sentiment represents what is really in the object. It only marks a certain conformity or relation between the object and the organs or faculties of the mind; and if that conformity did not really exist, the sentiment could never possibly have being. Beauty is no quality in things themselves: It exists merely in the mind which contemplates them; and each mind perceives a different beauty. One person may even perceive deformity, where another is sensible of beauty; and every individual ought to acquiesce in his own sentiment, without pretending to regulate those of others. To seek the real beauty, or real deformity, is as fruitless an enquiry, as to pretend to ascertain the real sweet or real bitter. According to the disposition of the organs, the same object may be both sweet and bitter; and the proverb has justly determined it to be fruitless to dispute concerning tastes. It is very natural, and even quite necessary, to extend this axiom to mental, as well as bodily taste; and thus common sense, which is so often at variance with philosophy, especially with the sceptical kind, is found, in one instance at least, to agree in pronouncing the same decision.

But though this axiom, by passing into a proverb, seems to have attained the sanction of common sense; there is certainly a species of common sense which opposes it, at least serves to modify and restrain it. Whoever would assert an equality of genius and elegance between OGILBY and MILTON, or BUNYAN and ADDISON, would be thought to defend no less an extravagance, than if he had maintained a mole-hill to be as high as TENERIFFE, or a pond as extensive as the ocean. Though there may be found persons, who give the preference to the former authors; no one pays attention to such a taste; and we pronounce without scruple the sentiment of these pretended critics to be absurd and ridiculous. The

principle of the natural equality of tastes is then totally forgot, and while we admit it on some occasions, where the objects seem near an equality, it appears an extravagant paradox, or rather a palpable absurdity, where objects so disproportioned are compared together.

It is evident that none of the rules of composition are fixed by reasonings a priori, or can be esteemed abstract conclusions of the understanding, from comparing those habitudes and relations of ideas, which are eternal and immutable. Their foundation is the same with that of all the practical sciences, experience; nor are they any thing but general observations, concerning what has been universally found to please in all countries and in all ages. Many of the beauties of poetry and even of eloquence are founded on falsehood and fiction, on hyperboles, metaphors, and an abuse or perversion of terms from their natural meaning. To check the sallies of the imagination, and to reduce every expression to geometrical truth and exactness, would be the most contrary to the laws of criticism; because it would produce a work, which, by universal experience, has been found the most insipid and disagreeable. But though poetry can never submit to exact truth, it must be confined by rules of art, discovered to the author either by genius or observation. If some negligent or irregular writers have pleased, they have not pleased by their transgressions of rule or order, but in spite of these transgressions: They have possessed other beauties, which were conformable to just criticism; and the force of these beauties has been able to overpower censure, and give the mind a satisfaction superior to the disgust arising from the blemishes. ARIOSTO pleases; but not by his monstrous and improbable fictions, by his bizarre mixture of the serious and comic styles, by the want of coherence in his stories, or by the continual interruptions of his narration. He charms by the force and clearness of his expression, by the readiness and variety of his inventions, and by his natural pictures of the passions, especially those of the gay and amorous kind: And however his faults may diminish our satisfaction, they are not able entirely to destroy it. Did our pleasure really arise from those parts of his poem, which we denominate faults, this would be no objection to criticism in general: It would only be an objection to those particular rules of criticism, which would establish such circumstances to be faults, and would represent them as universally blameable. If they are found to please, they cannot be faults; let the pleasure, which they produce, be ever so unexpected and unaccountable.

But though all the general rules of art are founded only on experience and on the observation of the common sentiments of human nature, we must not imagine, that, on every occasion, the feelings of men will be conformable to these rules. Those finer emotions of the mind are of a very tender and delicate nature, and require the concurrence of many favourable circumstances to make them play with facility and exactness, according to their general and established principles. The least exterior hindrance to such small springs, or the least internal disorder, disturbs their motion, and confounds the operation of the whole machine. When we would make an experiment of this nature, and would try the force of any beauty or deformity, we must choose with care a proper time and place, and bring the fancy to a suitable situation and disposition. A perfect serenity of mind, a recollection of thought, a due attention to the object; if any of these circumstances be wanting, our experiment will be fallacious, and we shall be unable to judge of the catholic and universal beauty. The relation, which nature has placed between the form and the sentiment, will at least be more obscure; and it will require greater accuracy to trace and discern it. We shall be able to ascertain its influence not so much from the operation of each particular beauty, as from the durable admiration, which attends those works, that have survived all the caprices of mode and fashion, all the mistakes of ignorance and envy.

The same HOMER, who pleased at ATHENS and ROME two thousand years ago, is still admired at PARIS and at LONDON. All the changes of climate, government, religion, and language, have not been able to obscure his glory. Authority or prejudice may give a temporary vogue to a bad poet or orator; but his reputation will never be durable or general. When his compositions are examined by posterity or by foreigners, the enchantment is dissipated, and his faults appear in their true colours. On the contrary, a real genius, the longer his works endure, and the more

wide they are spread, the more sincere is the admiration which he meets with. Envy and jealousy have too much place in a narrow circle; and even familiar acquaintance with his person may diminish the applause due to his performances: But when these obstructions are removed, the beauties, which are naturally fitted to excite agreeable sentiments, immediately display their energy; and while the world endures, they maintain their authority over the minds of men.

It appears then, that, amidst all the variety and caprice of taste, there are certain general principles of approbation or blame, whose influence a careful eye may trace in all operations of the mind. Some particular forms or qualities, from the original structure of the internal fabric, are calculated to please, and others to displease; and if they fail of their effect in any particular instance, it is from some apparent defect or imperfection in the organ. A man in a fever would not insist on his palate as able to decide concerning flavours; nor would one, affected with the jaundice, pretend to give a verdict with regard to colours. In each creature, there is a sound and a defective state; and the former alone can be supposed to afford us a true standard of taste and sentiment. If, in the sound state of the organ, there be an entire or a considerable uniformity of sentiment among men, we may thence derive an idea of the perfect beauty; in like manner as the appearance of objects in day-light, to the eye of a man in health, is denominated their true and real colour, even while colour is allowed to be merely a phantasm of the senses.

Many and frequent are the defects in the internal organs, which prevent or weaken the influence of those general principles, on which depends our sentiment of beauty or deformity. Though some objects, by the structure of the mind, be naturally calculated to give pleasure, it is not to be expected, that in every individual the pleasure will be equally felt. Particular incidents and situations occur, which either throw a false light on the objects, or hinder the true from conveying to the imagination the proper sentiment and perception.

One obvious cause, why many feel not the proper sentiment of beauty, is the want of that *delicacy* of imagination, which is requisite to convey a sensibility of those finer emotions. This delicacy every one pretends to: Every one talks of it; and would reduce every kind of taste or sentiment to its standard. But as our intention in this essay is to mingle some light of the understanding with the feelings of sentiment, it will be proper to give a more accurate definition of delicacy, than has hitherto been attempted. And not to draw our philosophy from too profound a source, we shall have recourse to a noted story in DON QUIXOTE.

It is with good reason, says SANCHO to the squire with the great nose, that I pretend to have a judgment in wine: This is a quality hereditary in our family. Two of my kinsmen were once called to give their opinion of a hogshead, which was supposed to be excellent, being old and of a good vintage. One of them tastes it; considers it; and after mature reflection pronounces the wine to be good, were it not for a small taste of leather, which he perceived in it. The other, after using the same precautions, gives also his verdict in favour of the wine; but with the reserve of a taste of iron, which he could easily distinguish. You cannot imagine how much they were both ridiculed for their judgment. But who laughed in the end? On emptying the hogshead, there was found at the bottom, an old key with a leathern thong tied to it.

The great resemblance between mental and bodily taste will easily teach us to apply this story. Though it be certain, that beauty and deformity, more than sweet and bitter, are not qualities in objects, but belong entirely to the sentiment, internal or external; it must be allowed, that there are certain qualities in objects, which are fitted by nature to produce those particular feelings. Now as these qualities may be found in a small degree, or may be mixed and confounded with each other, it often happens, that the taste is not affected with such minute qualities, or is not able to distinguish all the particular flavours, amidst the disorder, in which they are presented. Where the organs are so fine, as to allow nothing to escape them; and at the same time so exact as to perceive every ingredient in the composition: This we call delicacy of taste, whether we employ these terms in the literal or metaphorical sense. Here then the general rules of beauty are of use; being drawn from established models, and from the observation of what pleases or displeases, when presented singly and in a

high degree: And if the same qualities, in a continued composition and in a smaller degree, affect not the organs with a sensible delight or uneasiness, we exclude the person from all pretensions to this delicacy. To produce these general rules or avowed patterns of composition is like finding the key with the leathern thong; which justified the verdict of SANCHO'S kinsmen, and confounded those pretended judges who had condemned them. Though the hogshead had never been emptied, the taste of the one was still equally delicate, and that of the other equally dull and languid: But it would have been more difficult to have proved the superiority of the former, to the conviction of every by-stander. In like manner, though the beauties of writing had never been methodized, or reduced to general principles; though no excellent models had ever been acknowledged; the different degrees of taste would still have subsisted, and the judgment of one man been preferable to that of another; but it would not have been so easy to silence the bad critic, who might always insist upon his particular sentiment, and refuse to submit to his antagonist. But when we show him an avowed principle of art; when we illustrate this principle by examples, whose operation, from his own particular taste, he acknowledges to be conformable to the principle; when we prove, that the same principle may be applied to the present case, where he did not perceive or feel its influence: He must conclude, upon the whole, that the fault lies in himself, and that he wants the delicacy, which is requisite to make him sensible of every beauty and every blemish, in any composition or discourse.

It is acknowledged to be the perfection of every sense or faculty, to perceive with exactness its most minute objects, and allow nothing to escape its notice and observation. The smaller the objects are, which become sensible to the eye, the finer is that organ, and the more elaborate its make and composition. A good palate is not tried by strong flavours; but by a mixture of small ingredients, where we are still sensible of each part, notwithstanding its minuteness and its confusion with the rest. In like manner, a quick and acute perception of beauty and deformity must be the perfection of our mental taste; nor can a man be satisfied with himself while he suspects, that any excellence or blemish in a discourse has passed him unobserved. In this case, the perfection of the man, and the perfection of the sense or feeling, are found to be united. A very delicate palate, on many occasions, may be a great inconvenience both to a man himself and to his friends: But a delicate taste of wit or beauty must always be a desirable quality; because it is the source of all the finest and most innocent enjoyments, of which human nature is susceptible. In this decision the sentiments of all mankind are agreed. Wherever you can ascertain a delicacy of taste, it is sure to meet with approbation; and the best way of ascertaining it is to appeal to those models and principles, which have been established by the uniform consent and experience of nations and ages.

But though there be naturally a wide difference in point of delicacy between one person and another, nothing tends further to encrease and improve this talent, than *practice* in a particular art, and the frequent survey or contemplation of a particular species of beauty. When objects of any kind are first presented to the eye or imagination, the sentiment, which attends them, is obscure and confused; and the mind is, in a great measure, incapable of pronouncing concerning their merits or defects. The taste cannot perceive the several excellencies of the performance; much less distinguish the particular character of each excellency, and ascertain its quality and degree. If it pronounce the whole in general to be beautiful or deformed, it is the utmost that can be expected; and even this judgment, a person, so unpractised, will be apt to deliver with great hesitation and reserve. But allow him to acquire experience in those objects, his feeling becomes more exact and nice: He not only perceives the beauties and defects of each part, but marks the distinguishing species of each quality, and assigns it suitable praise or blame. A clear and distinct sentiment attends him though the whole survey of the objects; and he discerns that very degree and kind of approbation or displeasure, which each part is naturally fitted to produce. The mist dissipates, which seemed formerly to hang over the object: The organ acquires greater perfection in its operations; and can pronounce, without danger of mistake, concerning the merits of every performance. In a word, the same address and dexterity, which

practice gives to the execution of any work, is also acquired by the same means, in the judging of it.

So advantageous is practice to the discernment of beauty, that, before we can give judgment on any work of importance, it will even be requisite, that that very individual performance be more than once perused by us, and be surveyed in different lights with attention and deliberation. There is a flutter or hurry of thought which attends the first perusal of any piece, and which confounds the genuine sentiment of beauty. The relation of the parts is not discerned: The true characters of style are little distinguished: The several perfections and defects seem wrapped up in a species of confusion, and present themselves indistinctly to the imagination. Not to mention, that there is a species of beauty, which, as it is florid and superficial, pleases at first; but being found incompatible with a just expression either of reason or passion, soon palls upon the taste, and is then rejected with disdain, at least rated at a much lower value.

It is impossible to continue in the practice of contemplating any order of beauty, without being frequently obliged to form *comparisons* between the several species and degrees of excellence, and estimating their proportion to each other. A man, who has had no opportunity of comparing the different kinds of beauty, is indeed totally unqualified to pronounce an opinion with regard to any object presented to him. By comparison alone we fix the epithets of praise or blame, and learn how to assign the due degree of each. The coarsest daubing contains a certain lustre of colours and exactness of imitation, which are so far beauties, and would affect the mind of a peasant or Indian with the highest admiration. The most vulgar ballads are not entirely destitute of harmony or nature; and none but a person, familiarized to superior beauties, would pronounce their numbers harsh, or narration uninteresting. A great inferiority of beauty gives pain to a person conversant in the highest excellence of the kind, and is for that reason pronounced a deformity: As the most finished object, with which we are acquainted, is naturally supposed to have reached the pinnacle of perfection, and to be entitled to the highest applause. One accustomed to see, and examine, and weigh the several performances, admired in different ages and nations, can alone rate the merits of a work exhibited to his view, and assign its proper rank among the productions of genius.

But to enable a critic the more fully to execute this undertaking, he must preserve his mind free from all *prejudice,* and allow nothing to enter into his consideration, but the very object which is submitted to his examination. We may observe, that every work of art, in order to produce its due effect on the mind, must be surveyed in a certain point of view, and cannot be fully relishcd by persons, whose situation, real or imaginary, is not conformable to that which is required by the performance. An orator addresses himself to a particular audience, and must have a regard to their particular genius, interests, opinions, passions, and prejudices; otherwise he hopes in vain to govern their resolutions, and inflame their affections. Should they even have entertained some prepossessions against him, however unreasonable, he must not overlook this disadvantage; but, before he enters upon the subject, must endeavour to conciliate their affection, and acquire their good graces. A critic of a different age or nation, who should peruse this discourse, must have all these circumstances in his eye, and must place himself in the same situation as the audience, in order to form a true judgment of the oration. In like manner, when any work is addressed to the public, though I should have a friendship or enmity with the author, I must depart from this situation; and considering myself as a man in general, forget, if possible, my individual being and my peculiar circumstances. A person influenced by prejudice, complies not with this condition; but obstinately maintains his natural position, without placing himself in that point of view, which the performance supposes. If the work be addressed to persons of a different age or nation, he makes no allowance for their peculiar views and prejudices; but, full of the manners of his own age and country, rashly condemns what seemed admirable in the eyes of those for whom alone the discourse was calculated. If the work be executed for the public, he never sufficiently enlarges his comprehension, or forgets his interest as a friend or enemy, as a rival or commentator. By this means, his sentiments are perverted; nor have the same beauties and blemishes the same influence upon him, as if he had imposed a proper violence on his imagination, and had forgotten himself for a moment. So far his taste evidently departs from the true standard; and of consequence loses all credit and authority.

It is well known, that in all questions, submitted to the understanding, prejudice is destructive of sound judgment, and perverts all operations of the intellectual faculties: It is no less contrary to good taste; nor has it less influence to corrupt our sentiment of beauty. It belongs to *good sense* to check its influence in both cases; and in this respect, as well as in many others, reason, if not an essential part of taste, is at least requisite to the operations of this latter faculty. In all the nobler productions of genius, there is a mutual relation and correspondence of parts; nor can either the beauties or blemishes be perceived by him, whose thought is not capacious enough to comprehend all those parts, and compare them with each other, in order to perceive the consistence and uniformity of the whole. Every work of art has also a certain end or purpose, for which it is calculated; and is to be deemed more or less perfect, as it is more or less fitted to attain this end. The object of eloquence is to persuade, of history to instruct, of poetry to please by means of the passions and the imagination. These ends we must carry constantly in our view, when we peruse any performance; and we must be able to judge how far the means employed are adapted to their respective purposes. Besides, every kind of composition, even the most poetical, is nothing but a chain of propositions and reasonings; not always, indeed, the justest and most exact, but still plausible and specious, however disguised by the colouring of the imagination. The persons introduced in tragedy and epic poetry, must be represented as reasoning, and thinking, and concluding, and acting, suitably to their character and circumstances; and without judgment, as well as taste and invention, a poet can never hope to succeed in so delicate an undertaking. Not to mention, that the same excellence of faculties which contributes to the improvement of reason, the same clearness of conception, the same exactness of distinction, the same vivacity of apprehension, are essential to the operations of true taste, and are its infallible concomitants. It seldom, or never happens, that a man of sense, who has experience in any art, cannot judge of its beauty; and it is no less rare to meet with a man who has a just taste without a sound understanding.

Thus, though the principles of taste be universal, and nearly, if not entirely the same in all men; yet few are qualified to give judgment on any work of art, or establish their own sentiment as the standard of beauty. The organs of internal sensation are seldom so perfect as to allow the general principles their full play, and produce a feeling correspondent to those principles. They either labour under some defect, or are vitiated by some disorder; and by that means, excite a sentiment, which may be pronounced erroneous. When the critic has no delicacy, he judges without any distinction, and is only affected by the grosser and more palpable qualities of the object: The finer touches pass unnoticed and disregarded. Where he is not aided by practice, his verdict is attended with confusion and hesitation. Where no comparison has been employed, the most frivolous beauties, such as rather merit the name of defects, are the object of his admiration. Where he lies under the influence of prejudice, all his natural sentiments are perverted. Where good sense is wanting, he is not qualified to discern the beauties of design and reasoning, which are the highest and most excellent. Under some or other of these imperfections, the generality of men labour; and hence a true judge in the finer arts is observed, even during the most polished ages, to be so rare a character: Strong sense, united to delicate sentiment, improved by practice, perfected by comparison, and cleared of all prejudice, can alone entitle critics to this valuable character; and the joint verdict of such, wherever they are to be found, is the true standard of taste and beauty.

But where are such critics to be found? By what marks are they to be known? How distinguish them from pretenders? These questions are embarrassing; and seem to throw us back into the same uncertainty, from which, during the course of this essay, we have endeavoured to extricate ourselves.

But if we consider the matter aright, these are questions of fact, not of sentiment. Whether any particular person be endowed with good sense and a delicate imagination, free from prejudice, may often be the subject of dispute, and be liable to great discus-

sion and enquiry: But that such a character is valuable and estimable will be agreed in by all mankind. Where these doubts occur, men can do no more than in other disputable questions, which are submitted to the understanding: They must produce the best arguments, that their invention suggests to them; they must acknowledge a true and decisive standard to exist somewhere, to wit, real existence and matter of fact; and they must have indulgence to such as differ from them in their appeals to this standard. It is sufficient for our present purpose, if we have proved, that the taste of all individuals is not upon an equal footing, and that some men in general, however difficult to be particularly pitched upon, will be acknowledged by universal sentiment to have a preference above others.

But in reality the difficulty of finding, even in particulars, the standard of taste, is not so great as it is represented. Though in speculation, we may readily avow a certain criterion in science and deny it in sentiment, the matter is found in practice to be much more hard to ascertain in the former case than in the latter. Theories of abstract philosophy, systems of profound theology, have prevailed during one age: In a successive period, these have been universally exploded: Their absurdity has been detected: Other theories and systems have supplied their place, which again gave place to their successors: And nothing has been experienced more liable to the revolutions of chance and fashion than these pretended decisions of science. The case is not the same with the beauties of eloquence and poetry. Just expressions of passion and nature are sure, after a little time, to gain public applause, which they maintain for ever. ARISTOTLE, and PLATO, and EPICURUS, and DESCARTES, may successively yield to each other: But TERENCE and VIRGIL maintain an universal, undisputed empire over the minds of men. The abstract philosophy of CICERO has lost its credit: The vehemence of his oratory is still the object of our admiration.

Though men of delicate taste be rare, they are easily to be distinguished in society, by the soundness of their understanding and the superiority of their faculties above the rest of mankind. The ascendant, which they acquire, gives a prevalence to that lively approbation, with which they receive any productions of genius, and renders it generally predominant. Many men, when left to themselves, have but a faint and dubious perception of beauty, who yet are capable of relishing any fine stroke, which is pointed out to them. Every convert to the admiration of the real poet or orator is the cause of some new conversion. And though prejudices may prevail for a time, they never unite in celebrating any rival to the true genius, but yield at last to the force of nature and just sentiment. Thus, though a civilized nation may easily be mistaken in the choice of their admired philosopher, they never have been found long to err, in their affection for a favourite epic or tragic author.

But notwithstanding all our endeavours to fix a standard of taste, and reconcile the discordant apprehensions of men, there still remain two sources of variation, which are not sufficient indeed to confound all the boundaries of beauty and deformity, but will often serve to produce a difference in the degrees of our approbation or blame. The one is the different humours of particular men; the other, the particular manners and opinions of our age and country. The general principles of taste are uniform in human nature: Where men vary in their judgments, some defect or perversion in the faculties may commonly be remarked; proceeding either from prejudice, from want of practice, or want of delicacy; and there is just reason for approving one taste, and condemning another. But where there is such a diversity in the internal frame or external situation as is entirely blameless on both sides, and leaves no room to give one the preference above the other; in that case a certain degree of diversity in judgment is unavoidable, and we seek in vain for a standard, by which we can reconcile the contrary sentiments.

A young man, whose passions are warm, will be more sensibly touched with amorous and tender images, than a man more advanced in years, who takes pleasure in wise, philosophical reflections concerning the conduct of life and moderation of the passions. At twenty, OVID may be the favourite author; HORACE at forty; and perhaps TACITUS at fifty. Vainly would we, in such cases, endeavour to enter into the sentiments of others, and divest ourselves of those propensities, which are natural to us. We choose our favourite author as we do our friend, from a con-

formity of humour and disposition. Mirth or passion, sentiment or reflection; whichever of these most predominates in our temper, it gives us a peculiar sympathy with the writer who resembles us.

One person is more pleased with the sublime; another with the tender; a third with raillery. One has a strong sensibility to blemishes, and is extremely studious of correctness: Another has a more lively feeling of beauties, and pardons twenty absurdities and defects for one elevated or pathetic° stroke. The ear of this man is entirely turned towards conciseness and energy; that man is delighted with a copious, rich, and harmonious expression. Simplicity is affected by one; ornament by another. Comedy, tragedy, satire, odes, have each its partizans, who prefer that particular species of writing to all others. It is plainly an error in a critic, to confine his approbation to one species or style of writing, and condemn all the rest. But it is almost impossible not to feel a predilection for that which suits our particular turn and disposition. Such preferences are innocent and unavoidable, and can never reasonably be the object of dispute, because there is no standard, by which they can be decided.

For a like reason, we are more pleased, in the course of our reading, with pictures and characters, that resemble objects which are found in our own age or country, than with those which describe a different set of customs. It is not without some effort, that we reconcile ourselves to the simplicity of ancient manners, and behold princesses carrying water from the spring, and kings and heroes dressing their own victuals. We may allow in general, that the representation of such manners is no fault in the author, nor deformity in the piece; but we are not so sensibly touched with them. For this reason, comedy is not easily transferred from one age or nation to another. A FRENCHMAN or ENGLISHMAN is not pleased with the ANDRIA of TERENCE, or CLITIA of MACHIAVEL; where the fine lady, upon whom all the play turns, never once appears to the spectators, but is always kept behind the scenes, suitably to the reserved humour of the ancient GREEKS and modern ITALIANS. A man of learning and reflection can make allowance for these peculiarities of manners; but a common audience can never divest themselves so far of their usual ideas and sentiments, as to relish pictures which no wise resemble them.

But here there occurs a reflection, which may, perhaps, be useful in examining the celebrated controversy concerning ancient and modern learning; where we often find the one side excusing any seeming absurdity in the ancients from the manners of the age, and the other refusing to admit this excuse, or at least, admitting it only as an apology for the author, not for the performance. In my opinion, the proper boundaries in this subject have seldom been fixed between the contending parties. Where any innocent peculiarities of manners are represented, such as those above mentioned, they ought certainly to be admitted; and a man, who is shocked with them, gives an evident proof of false delicacy and refinement. The poet's *monument more durable than brass,* must fall to the ground like common brick or clay, were men to make no allowance for the continual revolutions of manners and customs, and would admit of nothing but what was suitable to the prevailing fashion. Must we throw aside the pictures of our ancestors, because of their ruffs° and fardingales?° But where the ideas of morality and decency alter from one age to another, and where vicious manners are described, without being marked with the proper characters of blame and disapprobation; this must be allowed to disfigure the poem, and to be a real deformity. I cannot, nor is it proper I should, enter into such sentiments; and however I may excuse the poet, on account of the manners of his age, I never can relish the composition. The want of humanity and of decency, so conspicuous in the characters drawn by several of the ancient poets, even sometimes by HOMER and the GREEK tragedians, diminishes considerably the merit of their noble performances, and gives modern authors an advantage over them. We are not interested in the fortunes and sentiments of such rough heroes: We are displeased to find the limits of vice and virtue so much confounded: And whatever indulgence we may give to the writer on account of his prejudices, we cannot prevail on ourselves to enter into his sentiments, or bear an affection to characters, which we plainly discover to be blameable.

The case is not the same with moral principles, as with speculative opinions of any kind. These are in continual flux and revolution. The son embraces a different system from the father. Nay, there scarcely is any man, who can boast of great constancy and uniformity in this particular. Whatever speculative errors may be found in the polite writings of any age or country, they detract but little from the value of those compositions. There needs but a certain turn of thought or imagination to make us enter into all the opinions, which then prevailed, and relish the sentiments or conclusions derived from them. But a very violent effort is requisite to change our judgment of manners, and excite sentiments of approbation or blame, love or hatred, different from those to which the mind from long custom has been familiarized. And where a man is confident of the rectitude of that moral standard, by which he judges, he is justly jealous of it, and will not pervert the sentiments of his heart for a moment, in complaisance° to any writer whatsoever.

Of all speculative errors, those, which regard religion, are the most excusable in compositions of genius; nor is it ever permitted to judge of the civility or wisdom of any people, or even of single persons, by the grossness or refinement of their theological principles. The same good sense, that directs men in the ordinary occurrences of life, is not hearkened to in religious matters, which are supposed to be placed altogether above the cognizance of human reason. On this account, all the absurdities of the pagan system of theology must be overlooked by every critic, who would pretend to form a just notion of ancient poetry; and our posterity, in their turn, must have the same indulgence to their forefathers. No religious principles can ever be imputed as a fault to any poet, while they remain merely principles, and take not such strong possession of his heart, as to lay him under the imputation of *bigotry* or *superstition.* Where that happens, they confound the sentiments of morality, and alter the natural boundaries of vice and virtue. They are therefore eternal blemishes, according to the principle abovementioned; nor are the prejudices and false opinions of the age sufficient to justify them.

It is essential to the ROMAN catholic religion to inspire a violent hatred of every other worship, and to represent all pagans, mahometans, and heretics as the objects of divine wrath and vengeance. Such sentiments, though they are in reality very blameable, are considered as virtues by the zealots of that communion, and are represented in their tragedies and epic poems as a kind of divine heroism. This bigotry has disfigured two very fine tragedies of the FRENCH theatre, POLIEUCTE and ATHALIA; where an intemperate zeal for particular modes of worship is set off with all the pomp imaginable, and forms the predominant character of the heroes. "What is this," says the sublime JOAD to JOSABET, finding her in discourse with MATHAN, the priest of BAAL, "Does the daughter of DAVID speak to this traitor? Are you not afraid, lest the earth should open and pour forth flames to devour you both? Or lest these holy walls should fall and crush you together? What is his purpose? Why comes that enemy of God hither to poison the air, which we breathe, with his horrid presence?" Such sentiments are received with great applause on the theatre of PARIS; but at LONDON the spectators would be full as

much pleased to hear ACHILLES tell AGAMEMNON, that he was a dog in his forehead, and a deer in his heart, or JUPITER threaten JUNO with a sound drubbing, if she will not be quiet.

RELIGIOUS principles are also a blemish in any polite composition, when they rise up to superstition, and intrude themselves into every sentiment, however remote from any connection with religion. It is no excuse for the poet, that the customs of his country had burthened life with so many religious ceremonies and observances, that no part of it was exempt from that yoke. It must for ever be ridiculous in PETRARCH to compare his mistress, LAURA, to JESUS CHRIST. Nor is it less ridiculous in that agreeable libertine, BOCCACE, very seriously to give thanks to GOD ALMIGHTY and the ladies, for their assistance in defending him against his enemies.

Critique of Judgment

IMMANUEL KANT

Immanuel Kant (1724–1804) was one of the greatest philosophers in the Western tradition. His three critiques explore the grounds and limits of human reason, action, and judgment.

FIRST BOOK • ANALYTIC OF THE BEAUTIFUL

First Moment • Of the Judgment of Taste[1] According to Quality

§ 1.   The Judgment of Taste Is Æsthetical

In order to distinguish whether anything is beautiful or not, we refer the representation not by the Understanding to the Object for cognition, but by the Imagination (perhaps in conjunction with the Understanding) to the subject, and its feeling of pleasure or pain. The judgment of taste is therefore not a judgment of

cognition, and is consequently not logical but æsthetical, by which we understand that whose determining ground can be *no other than subjective*. Every reference of representations, even that of sensations, may be objective (and then it signifies the real [element] of an empirical representation); save only the reference to the feeling of pleasure and pain, by which nothing in the Object is signified, but through which there is a feeling in the subject, as it is affected by the representation.

To apprehend a regular, purposive building by means of one's cognitive faculty (whether in a clear or a confused way of representation) is something

Translated by J. H. Bernard.

quite different from being conscious of this representation as connected with the sensation of satisfaction. Here the representation is altogether referred to the subject and to its feeling of life, under the name of the feeling of pleasure or pain. This establishes a quite separate faculty of distinction and of judgment, adding nothing to cognition, but only comparing the given representation in the subject with the whole faculty of representations, of which the mind is conscious in the feeling of its state. Given representations in a judgment can be empirical (consequently, æsthetical); but the judgment which is formed by means of them is logical, provided they are referred in the judgment to the Object. Conversely, if the given representations are rational, but are referred in a judgment simply to the subject (to its feeling), the judgment is so far always æsthetical.

§ 2.   *The Satisfaction Which Determines the Judgment of Taste Is Disinterested*

The satisfaction which we combine with the representation of the existence of an object is called interest. Such satisfaction always has reference to the faculty of desire, either as its determining ground or as necessarily connected with its determining ground. Now when the question is if a thing is beautiful, we do not want to know whether anything depends or can depend on the existence of the thing either for myself or for any one else, but how we judge it by mere observation (intuition or reflection). If any one asks me if I find that palace beautiful which I see before me, I may answer: I do not like things of that kind which are made merely to be stared at. Or I can answer like that Iroquois *Sachem* who was pleased in Paris by nothing more than by the cook-shops. Or again after the manner of *Rousseau* I may rebuke the vanity of the great who waste the sweat of the people on such superfluous things. In fine I could easily convince myself that if I found myself on an uninhabited island without the hope of ever again coming among men, and could conjure up just such a splendid building by my mere wish, I should not even give myself the trouble if I had a sufficiently comfortable hut. This may all be admitted and approved; but we are not now talking of this. We wish only to know if this mere representation of the object is accompanied in

me with satisfaction, however indifferent I may be as regards the existence of the object of this representation. We easily see that in saying it is *beautiful* and in showing that I have taste, I am concerned, not with that in which I depend on the existence of the object, but with that which I make out of this representation in myself. Every one must admit that a judgment about beauty, in which the least interest mingles, is very partial and is not a pure judgment of taste. We must not be in the least prejudiced in favour of the existence of the things, but be quite indifferent in this respect, in order to play the judge in things of taste.

We cannot, however, better elucidate this proposition, which is of capital importance, than by contrasting the pure disinterested[2] satisfaction in judgments of taste, with that which is bound up with an interest, especially if we can at the same time be certain that there are no other kinds of interest than those which are to be now specified.

§ 3.   *The Satisfaction in the* Pleasant *Is Bound Up with Interest*

That which pleases the senses in sensation is PLEASANT. Here the opportunity presents itself of censuring a very common confusion of the double sense which the word sensation can have, and of calling attention to it. All satisfaction (it is said or thought) is itself sensation (of a pleasure). Consequently everything that pleases is pleasant because it pleases (and according to its different degrees or its relations to other pleasant sensations it is *agreeable, lovely, delightful, enjoyable,* etc.) But if this be admitted, then impressions of Sense which determine the inclination, fundamental propositions of Reason which determine the Will, mere reflective forms of intuition which determine the Judgment, are quite the same, as regards the effect upon the feeling of pleasure. For this would be pleasantness in the sensation of one's state, and since in the end all the operations of our faculties must issue in the practical and unite in it as their goal, we could suppose no other way of estimating things and their worth than that which consists in the gratification that they promise. It is of no consequence at all how this is attained, and since then the choice of means alone could make a difference, men could indeed blame one another for stupidity and indiscretion, but never for baseness and wickedness. For thus they all, each according to his own way of seeing things, seek one goal, that is, gratification.

If a determination of the feeling of pleasure or pain is called sensation, this expression signifies something quite different from what I mean when I call the representation of a thing (by sense, as a receptivity belonging to the cognitive faculty) sensation. For in the latter case the representation is referred to the Object, in the former simply to the subject, and is available for no cognition whatever, not even for that by which the subject *cognises* itself.

In the above elucidation we understand by the word sensation, an objective representation of sense; and in order to avoid misinterpretation, we shall call that, which must always remain merely subjective and can constitute absolutely no representation of an object, by the ordinary term "feeling." The green colour of the meadows belongs to *objective* sensation, as a perception of an object of sense; the pleasantness of this belongs to *subjective* sensation by which no object is represented, i.e. to feeling, by which the object is considered as an Object of satisfaction (which does not furnish a cognition of it).

Now that a judgment about an object, by which I describe it as pleasant, expresses an interest in it, is plain from the fact that by sensation it excites a desire for objects of that kind; consequently the satisfaction presupposes not the mere judgment about it, but the relation of its existence to my state, so far as this is affected by such an Object. Hence we do not merely say of the pleasant, *it pleases;* but, *it gratifies.* I give to it no mere assent, but inclination is aroused by it; and in the case of what is pleasant in the most lively fashion, there is no judgment at all upon the character of the Object, for those [persons] who always lay themselves out for enjoyment (for that is the word describing intense gratification) would fain dispense with all judgment.

§ 4. *The Satisfaction in the* Good *Is Bound Up with Interest*

Whatever by means of Reason pleases through the mere concept is GOOD. That which pleases only as a means we call *good for something* (the useful); but that which pleases for itself is *good in itself.* In both

there is always involved the concept of a purpose, and consequently the relation of Reason to the (at least possible) volition, and thus a satisfaction in the *presence* of an Object or an action, i.e. some kind of interest.

In order to find anything good, I must always know what sort of a thing the object ought to be, i.e. I must have a concept of it. But there is no need of this, to find a thing beautiful. Flowers, free delineations, outlines intertwined with one another without design and called [conventional] foliage, have no meaning, depend on no definite concept, and yet they please. The satisfaction in the beautiful must depend on the reflection upon an object, leading to any concept (however indefinite); and it is thus distinguished from the pleasant which rests entirely upon sensation.

It is true, the Pleasant seems in many cases to be the same as the Good. Thus people are accustomed to say that all gratification (especially if it lasts) is good in itself; which is very much the same as to say that lasting pleasure and the good are the same. But we can soon see that this is merely a confusion of words; for the concepts which properly belong to these expressions can in no way be interchanged. The pleasant, which, as such, represents the object simply in relation to Sense, must first be brought by the concept of a purpose under principles of Reason, in order to call it good, as an object of the Will. But that there is [involved] a quite different relation to satisfaction in calling that which gratifies at the same time *good,* may be seen from the fact that in the case of the good the question always is, whether it is mediately or immediately good (useful or good in itself); but on the contrary in the case of the pleasant there can be no question about this at all, for the word always signifies something which pleases immediately. (The same is applicable to what I call beautiful.)

Even in common speech men distinguish the Pleasant from the Good. Of a dish which stimulates the taste by spices and other condiments we say unhesitatingly that it is pleasant, though it is at the same time admitted not to be good; for though it immediately *delights* the senses, yet mediately, i.e. considered by Reason which looks to the after results, it displeases. Even in the judging of health we may notice this distinction. It is immediately pleasant to every one possessing it (at least negatively, i.e. as the absence of all bodily pains). But in order to say that it is good, it must be considered by Reason with reference to purposes; viz., that it is a state which makes us fit for all our business. Finally in respect of happiness every one believes himself entitled to describe the greatest sum of the pleasantness of life (as regards both their number and their duration) as a true, even as the highest, good. However Reason is opposed to this. Pleasantness is enjoyment. And if we were concerned with this alone, it would be foolish to be scrupulous as regards the means which procure it for us, or [to care] whether it is obtained passively by the bounty of nature or by our own activity and work. But Reason can never be persuaded that the existence of a man who merely lives for *enjoyment* (however busy he may be in this point of view), has a worth in itself; even if he at the same time is conducive as a means to the best enjoyment of others, and shares in all their gratifications by sympathy. Only what he does, without reference to enjoyment, in full freedom and independently of what nature can procure for him passively, gives an [absolute] worth to his presence [in the world] as the existence of a person; and happiness, with the whole abundance of its pleasures, is far from being an unconditioned good.[3]

However, notwithstanding all this difference between the pleasant and the good, they both agree in this that they are always bound up with an interest in their object; so are not only the pleasant (§ 3), and the mediate good (the useful) which is pleasing as a means towards pleasantness somewhere, but also that which is good absolutely and in every aspect, viz., moral good, which brings with it the highest interest. For the good is the Object of will (i.e. of a faculty of desire determined by Reason). But to wish for something, and to have a satisfaction in its existence, i.e. to take an interest in it, are identical.

§ 5. *Comparison of the Three Specifically Different Kinds of Satisfaction*

The pleasant and the good have both a reference to the faculty of desire; and they bring with them—the former a satisfaction pathologically conditioned (by impulses, *stimuli*)—the latter a pure practical satisfaction, which is determined not merely by the repre-

sentation of the object, but also by the represented connection of the subject with the existence of the object. [It is not merely the object that pleases, but also its existence.] On the other hand, the judgment of taste is merely *contemplative;* i.e. it is a judgment which, indifferent as regards the existence of an object, compares its character with the feeling of pleasure and pain. But this contemplation itself is not directed to concepts; for the judgment of taste is not a cognitive judgment (either theoretical or practical), and thus is not *based* on concepts, nor has it concepts as its *purpose.*

The Pleasant, the Beautiful, and the Good, designate then, three different relations of representations to the feeling of pleasure and pain, in reference to which we distinguish from each other objects or methods of representing them. And the expressions corresponding to each, by which we mark our complacency in them, are not the same. That which GRATIFIES a man is called *pleasant;* that which merely PLEASES him is *beautiful;* that which is ESTEEMED [or *approved*] by him, i.e. that to which he accords an objective worth, is *good.* Pleasantness concerns irrational animals also; but Beauty only concerns men, i.e. animal, but still rational, beings—not merely *quâ* rational (e.g. spirits), but quâ animal also; and the Good concerns every rational being in general. This is a proposition which can only be completely established and explained in the sequel. We may say that of all these three kinds of satisfaction, that of taste in the Beautiful is alone a disinterested and *free* satisfaction; for no interest, either of Sense or of Reason, here forces our assent. Hence we may say of satisfaction that it is related in the three aforesaid cases to *inclination,* to *favour,* or to *respect.* Now *favour* is the only free satisfaction. An object of inclination, and one that is proposed to our desire by a law of Reason, leave us no freedom in forming for ourselves anywhere an object of pleasure. All interest presupposes or generates a want; and, as the determining ground of assent, it leaves the judgment about the object no longer free.

As regards the interest of inclination in the case of the Pleasant, every one says that hunger is the best sauce, and everything that is eatable is relished by people with a healthy appetite; and thus a satisfaction of this sort shows no choice directed by taste. It is only when the want is appeased that we can distinguish which of many men has or has not taste. In the same way there may be manners (conduct) without virtue, politeness without goodwill, decorum without modesty, etc. For where the moral law speaks there is no longer, objectively, a free choice as regards what is to be done; and to display taste in its fulfilment (or in judging of another's fulfilment of it) is something quite different from manifesting the moral attitude of thought. For this involves a command and generates a want, whilst moral taste only plays with the objects of satisfaction, without attaching itself to one of them.

EXPLANATION OF THE BEAUTIFUL RESULTING FROM THE FIRST MOMENT

Taste is the faculty of judging of an object or a method of representing it by an *entirely disinterested* satisfaction or dissatisfaction. The object of such satisfaction is called *beautiful*.

Second Moment • *Of the Judgment of Taste, viz., According to Quantity*

§ 6. *The Beautiful Is That Which Apart from Concepts Is Represented as the Object of a Universal Satisfaction*

This explanation of the beautiful can be derived from the preceding explanation of it as the object of an entirely disinterested satisfaction. For the fact of which every one is conscious, that the satisfaction is for him quite disinterested, implies in his judgment a ground of satisfaction for all men. For since it does not rest on any inclination of the subject (nor upon any other premeditated interest), but since the person who judges feels himself quite *free* as regards the satisfaction which he attaches to the object, he cannot find the ground of this satisfaction in any private conditions connected with his own subject; and hence it must be regarded as grounded on what he can presuppose in every other person. Consequently he must believe that he has reason for attributing a similar satisfaction to every one. He will therefore speak of the beautiful, as if beauty were a characteristic of the object and the judgment logical (constituting a cognition of the Object by means of concepts of it);

although it is only æsthetical and involves merely a reference of the representation of the object to the subject. For it has this similarity to a logical judgment that we can presuppose its validity for all men. But this universality cannot arise from concepts; for from concepts there is no transition to the feeling of pleasure or pain (except in pure practical laws, which bring an interest with them such as is not bound up with the pure judgment of taste). Consequently the judgment of taste, accompanied with the consciousness of separation from all interest, must claim validity for every man, without this universality depending on Objects. That is, there must be bound up with it a title to subjective universality.

§ 7. *Comparison of the Beautiful with the Pleasant and the Good by Means of the Above Characteristic*

As regards the Pleasant every one is content that his judgment, which he bases upon private feeling, and by which he says of an object that it pleases him, should be limited merely to his own person. Thus he is quite contented that if he says "Canary wine is pleasant," another man may correct his expression and remind him that he ought to say "It is pleasant *to me*." And this is the case not only as regards the taste of the tongue, the palate, and the throat, but for whatever is pleasant to any one's eyes and ears. To one violet colour is soft and lovely, to another it is washed out and dead. One man likes the tone of wind instruments, another that of strings. To strive here with the design of reproving as incorrect another man's judgment which is different from our own, as if the judgments were logically opposed, would be folly. As regards the pleasant therefore the fundamental proposition is valid, *every one has his own taste* (the taste of Sense).

The case is quite different with the Beautiful. It would (on the contrary) be laughable if a man who imagined anything to his own taste, thought to justify himself by saying: "This object (the house we see, the coat that person wears, the concert we hear, the poem submitted to our judgment) is beautiful *for me*." For he must not call it *beautiful* if it merely pleases him. Many things may have for him charm and pleasantness; no one troubles himself at that; but if he gives out anything as beautiful, he supposes in others the same satisfaction—he judges not merely for himself, but for every one, and speaks of beauty as if it were a property of things. Hence he says "the *thing* is beautiful"; and he does not count on the agreement of others with this his judgment of satisfaction, because he has found this agreement several times before, but he *demands* it of them. He blames them if they judge otherwise and he denies them taste, which he nevertheless requires from them. Here then we cannot say that each man has his own particular taste. For this would be as much as to say that there is no taste whatever; i.e. no æsthetical judgment, which can make a rightful claim upon every one's assent.

At the same time we find as regards the Pleasant that there is an agreement among men in their judgments upon it, in regard to which we deny Taste to some and attribute it to others; by this not meaning one of our organic senses, but a faculty of judging in respect of the pleasant generally. Thus we say of a man who knows how to entertain his guests with pleasures (of enjoyment for all the senses), so that they are all pleased, "he has taste." But here the universality is only taken comparatively; and there emerge rules which are only *general* (like all empirical ones), and not *universal;* which latter the judgment of Taste upon the beautiful undertakes or lays claim to. It is a judgment in reference to sociability, so far as this rests on empirical rules. In respect of the Good it is true that judgments make rightful claim to validity for every one; but the Good is represented only *by means of a concept* as the Object of a universal satisfaction, which is the case neither with the Pleasant nor with the Beautiful.

§ 8. *The Universality of the Satisfaction Is Represented in a Judgment of Taste Only as Subjective*

This particular determination of the universality of an æsthetical judgment, which is to be met with in a judgment of taste, is noteworthy, not indeed for the logician, but for the transcendental philosopher. It requires no small trouble to discover its origin, but we thus detect a property of our cognitive faculty which without this analysis would remain unknown.

First, we must be fully convinced of the fact that in a judgment of taste (about the Beautiful) the satisfaction in the object is imputed to *every one,* without being based on a concept (for then it would be the Good). Further, this claim to universal validity so essentially belongs to a judgment by which we describe anything as *beautiful,* that if this were not thought in it, it would never come into our thoughts to use the expression at all, but everything which pleases without a concept would be counted as pleasant. In respect of the latter every one has his own opinion; and no one assumes in another, agreement with his judgment of taste, which is always the case in a judgment of taste about beauty. I may call the first the taste of Sense, the second the taste of Reflection; so far as the first lays down mere private judgments, and the second judgments supposed to be generally valid (public), but in both cases æsthetical (not practical) judgments about an object merely in respect of the relation of its representation to the feeling of pleasure and pain. Now here is something strange. As regards the taste of Sense not only does experience show that its judgment (of pleasure or pain connected with anything) is not valid universally, but every one is content not to impute agreement with it to others (although actually there is often found a very extended concurrence in these judgments). On the other hand, the taste of Reflection has its claim to the universal validity of its judgments (about the beautiful) rejected often enough, as experience teaches; although it may find it possible (as it actually does) to represent judgments which can demand this universal agreement. In fact it imputes this to every one for each of its judgments of taste, without the persons that judge disputing as to the possibility of such a claim; although in particular cases they cannot agree as to the correct application of this faculty.

Here we must, in the first place, remark that a universality which does not rest on concepts of Objects (not even on empirical ones) is not logical but æsthetical, i.e. it involves no objective quantity of the judgment but only that which is subjective. For this I use the expression *general validity* which signifies the validity of the reference of a representation not to the cognitive faculty, but to the feeling of pleasure and pain for every subject. (We can avail ourselves also of the same expression for the logical quantity of the judgment, if only we prefix *objective* to "universal validity," to distinguish it from that which is merely subjective and æsthetical.)

A judgment with *objective universal validity* is also always valid subjectively; i.e. if the judgment holds for everything contained under a given concept, it holds also for every one who represents an object by means of this concept. But from a *subjective universal validity,* i.e. æsthetical and resting on no concept, we cannot infer that which is logical; because that kind of judgment does not extend to the Object. But therefore the æsthetical universality which is ascribed to a judgment must be of a particular kind, because it does not unite the predicate of beauty with the concept of the *Object,* considered in its whole logical sphere, and yet extends it to the whole sphere of judging persons.

In respect of logical quantity all judgments of taste are *singular* judgments. For because I must refer the object immediately to my feeling of pleasure and pain, and that not by means of concepts, they cannot have the quantity of objective generally valid judgments. Nevertheless if the singular representation of the Object of the judgment of taste in accordance with the conditions determining the latter, were transformed by comparison into a concept, a logically universal judgment could result therefrom. E.g. I describe by a judgment of taste the rose, that I see, as beautiful. But the judgment which results from the comparison of several singular judgments, "Roses in general are beautiful" is no longer described simply as æsthetical, but as a logical judgment based on an æsthetical one. Again the judgment "The rose is pleasant" (to use) is, although æsthetical and singular, not a judgment of Taste but of Sense. It is distinguished from the former by the fact that the judgment of Taste carries with it an *æsthetical quantity* of universality, i.e. of validity for every one; which cannot be found in a judgment about the Pleasant. It is only judgments about the Good which—although they also determine satisfaction in an object,—have logical and not merely æsthetical universality; for they are valid of the Object, as cognitive of it, and thus are valid for every one.

If we judge Objects merely according to concepts, then all representation of beauty is lost. Thus there can be no rule according to which any one is to be forced to recognise anything as beautiful. We cannot press [upon others] by the aid of any reasons or fundamental propositions our judgment that a coat, a house, or a flower is beautiful. People wish to submit the Object to their own eyes, as if the satisfaction in it depended on sensation; and yet if we then call the object beautiful, we believe that we speak with a universal voice, and we claim the assent of every one, although on the contrary all private sensation can only decide for the observer himself and his satisfaction.

We may see now that in the judgment of taste nothing is postulated but such a *universal voice,* in respect of the satisfaction without the intervention of concepts; and thus the *possibility* of an æsthetical judgment that can, at the same time, be regarded as valid for every one. The judgment of taste itself does not *postulate* the agreement of every one (for that can only be done by a logically universal judgment because it can adduce reasons); it only *imputes* this agreement to every one, as a case of the rule in respect of which it expects, not confirmation by concepts, but assent from others. The universal voice is, therefore, only an Idea (we do not yet inquire upon what it rests). It may be uncertain whether or not the man, who believes that he is laying down a judgment of taste, is, as a matter of fact, judging in conformity with that Idea; but that he refers his judgment thereto, and, consequently, that it is intended to be a judgment of taste, he announces by the expression "beauty." He can be quite certain of this for himself by the mere consciousness of the separating off everything belonging to the Pleasant and the Good from the satisfaction which is left; and this is all for which he promises himself the agreement of every one—a claim which would be justifiable under these conditions, provided only he did not often make mistakes, and thus lay down an erroneous judgment of taste. . . . .

EXPLANATION OF THE BEAUTIFUL RESULTING FROM THE SECOND MOMENT

The *beautiful* is that which pleases universally without [requiring] a concept. . . .

Fourth Moment • Of the Judgment of Taste, According to the Modality of the Satisfaction in the Object

§ 18.   What the Modality in a Judgment of Taste Is

I can say of every representation that it is at least *possible* that (as a cognition) it should be bound up with a pleasure. Of a representation that I call *pleasant* I say that it *actually* excites pleasure in me. But the *beautiful* we think as having a *necessary* reference to satisfaction. Now this necessity is of a peculiar kind. It is not a theoretical objective necessity; in which case it would be cognised *a priori* that every one *will feel* this satisfaction in the object called beautiful by me. It is not a practical necessity; in which case, by concepts of a pure rational will serving as a rule for freely acting beings, the satisfaction is the necessary result of an objective law and only indicates that we absolutely (without any further design) ought to act in a certain way. But the necessity which is thought in an æsthetical judgment can only be called *exemplary;* i.e., a necessity of the assent of *all* to a judgment which is regarded as the example of a universal rule that we cannot state. Since an æsthetical judgment is not an objective cognitive judgment, this necessity cannot be derived from definite concepts, and is therefore not apodictic. Still less can it be inferred from the universality of experience (of a complete agreement of judgments as to the beauty of a certain object). For not only would experience hardly furnish sufficiently numerous vouchers for this; but also, on empirical judgments we can base no concept of the necessity of these judgments.

§ 19.   The Subjective Necessity, Which We Ascribe to the Judgment of Taste, Is Conditioned

The judgment of taste requires the agreement of every one; and he who describes anything as beautiful claims that every one *ought* to give his approval to the object in question and also describe it as beautiful. The *ought* in the æsthetical judgment is therefore pronounced in accordance with all the data which are required for judging and yet is only conditioned. We ask for the agreement of every one else, because we

have for it a ground that is common to all; and we could count on this agreement, provided we were always sure that the case was correctly subsumed under that ground as rule of assent.

§ 20.   The Condition of Necessity Which a Judgment of Taste Asserts Is the Idea of a Common Sense

If judgments of taste (like cognitive judgments) had a definite objective principle, then the person who lays them down in accordance with this latter would claim an unconditioned necessity for his judgment. If they were devoid of all principle, like those of the mere taste of sense, we would not allow them in thought any necessity whatever. Hence they must have a subjective principle which determines what pleases or displeases only by feeling and not by concepts, but yet with universal validity. But such a principle could only be regarded as a *common sense,* which is essentially different from common Understanding which people sometimes call common Sense (*sensus communis*); for the latter does not judge by feeling but always by concepts, although ordinarily only as by obscurely represented principles.

Hence it is only under the presupposition that there is a common sense (by which we do not understand an external sense, but the effect resulting from the free play of our cognitive powers)—it is only under this presupposition, I say, that the judgment of taste can be laid down.

§ 21.   Have We Ground for Presupposing a Common Sense?

Cognitions and judgments must, along with the conviction that accompanies them, admit of universal communicability; for otherwise there would be no harmony between them and the Object, and they would be collectively a mere subjective play of the representative powers, exactly as scepticism desires. But if cognitions are to admit of communicability, so must also the state of mind,—i.e. the accordance of the cognitive powers with a cognition generally, and that proportion of them which is suitable for a representation (by which an object is given to us) in order that a cognition may be made out of it—admit of universal communicability. For without this as the subjective condition of cognition, cognition as an effect could not arise. This actually always takes place when a given object by means of Sense excites the Imagination to collect the manifold, and the Imagination in its turn excites the Understanding to bring about a unity of this collective process in concepts. But this accordance of the cognitive powers has a different proportion according to the variety of the Objects which are given. However, it must be such that this internal relation, by which one mental faculty is excited by another, shall be generally the most beneficial for both faculties in respect of cognition (of given objects); and this accordance can only be determined by feeling (not according to concepts). Since now this accordance itself must admit of universal communicability, and consequently also our feeling of it (in a given representation), and since the universal communicability of a feeling presupposes a common sense, we have grounds for assuming this latter. And this common sense is assumed without relying on psychological observations, but simply as the necessary condition of the universal communicability of our knowledge, which is presupposed in every Logic and in every principle of knowledge that is not sceptical.

§ 22.   The Necessity of the Universal Agreement that Is Thought in a Judgment of Taste Is a Subjective Necessity, Which Is Represented as Objective Under the Presupposition of a Common Sense

In all judgments by which we describe anything as beautiful, we allow no one to be of another opinion; without however grounding our judgment on concepts but only on our feeling, which we therefore place at its basis not as a private, but as a common, feeling. Now this common sense cannot be grounded on experience; for it aims at justifying judgments which contain an *ought*. It does not say that every one *will* agree with my judgment, but that he *ought*. And so common sense, as an example of whose judgment I here put forward my judgment of taste and on account of which I attribute to the latter an *exemplary* validity, is a mere ideal norm, under the supposition of which I have a right to make into a rule for every

one a judgment that accords therewith, as well as the satisfaction in an Object expressed in such judgment. For the principle, which concerns the agreement of different judging persons, although only subjective, is yet assumed as subjectively universal (an Idea necessary for every one); and thus can claim universal assent (as if it were objective) provided we are sure that we have correctly subsumed [the particulars] under it.

This indeterminate norm of a common sense is actually presupposed by us; as is shown by our claim to lay down judgments of taste. Whether there is in fact such a common sense, as a constitutive principle of the possibility of experience, or whether a yet higher principle of Reason makes it only into a regulative principle for producing in us a common sense for higher purposes: whether therefore Taste is an original and natural faculty, or only the Idea of an artificial one yet to be acquired, so that a judgment of taste with its assumption of a universal assent in fact, is only a requirement of Reason for producing such harmony of sentiment; whether the ought, i.e. the objective necessity of the confluence of the feeling of any one man with that of every other, only signifies the possibility of arriving at this accord, and the judgment of taste only affords an example of the application of this principle: these questions we have neither the wish nor the power to investigate as yet; we have now only to resolve the faculty of taste into its elements in order to unite them at last in the Idea of a common sense.

EXPLANATION OF THE BEAUTIFUL RESULTING FROM THE FOURTH MOMENT

The *beautiful* is that which without any concept is cognised as the object of a *necessary* satisfaction.

NOTES

1. The definition of taste which is laid down here is that it is the faculty of judging of the beautiful. But the analysis of judgments of taste must show what is required in order to call an object beautiful. The moments, to which this Judgment has regard in its reflection, I have sought in accordance with the guidance of the logical functions of

judgment (for in a judgment of taste a reference to the Understanding is always involved). I have considered the moment of quality first, because the æsthetical judgment upon the beautiful first pays attention to it.

2. A judgment upon an object of satisfaction may be quite *disinterested*, but yet very *interesting*, i.e. not based upon an interest, but bringing an interest with it; of this kind are all pure moral judgments. Judgments of taste,

however, do not in themselves establish any interest. Only in society is it *interesting* to have taste: the reason of this will be shown in the sequel.

3. An obligation to enjoyment is a manifest absurdity. Thus the obligation to all actions which have merely enjoyment for their aim can only be a pretended one; however spiritually it may be conceived (or decked out), even if it is a mystical, or so-called heavenly, enjoyment.

Categories of Art

~

KENDALL L. WALTON

Kendall L. Walton is the James B. and Grace J. Nelson Professor of Philosophy at the University of Michigan, Ann Arbor. His work has explored connections between theoretical issues about the arts and issues in the philosophy of mind, metaphysics and the philosophy of language. Walton has written extensively on pictorial representation, fiction, and music and is the author of *Mimesis as Make-Believe: On the Foundations of the Representational Arts*.

I.   INTRODUCTION

False judgments enter art history if we judge from the impression which pictures of different epochs, placed side by side, make on us. . . . They speak a different language.[1]

Paintings and sculptures are to be looked at; sonatas and songs are to be heard. What is important about these works of art, as works of art, is what can be seen or heard in them.[2] Inspired partly by apparent commonplaces such as these, many recent aesthetic theorists have attempted to purge from criticism of works of art supposedly extraneous excursions into matters not (or not "directly") available to inspection of the works, and to focus attention on the works themselves. Circumstances connected with a work's origin, in particular, are frequently held to have no essential bearing on an assessment of its aesthetic nature—for example, who created the work, how,

and when; the artist's intentions and expectations concerning it, his philosophical views, psychological state, and love life; the artistic traditions and intellectual atmosphere of his society. Once produced (it is argued) the work must stand or fall on its own; it must be judged for what it is, regardless of how it came to be as it is. . . .

The view sketched above can easily seem very persuasive. But the tendency of critics to discuss the histories of works of art in the course of justifying aesthetic judgments about them has been remarkably persistent. This is partly because hints derived from facts about a work's history, however dispensable they may be "in principle," are often crucially important in practice. (One might simply not think to listen for a recurring series of intervals in a piece of music, until he learns that the composer meant the work to be structured around it.) No doubt it is partly due also to genuine confusions on the part of critics. But I will

Reprinted from *The Philosophical Review*, 79 (1970).

argue that (some) facts about the origins of works of art have an *essential* role in criticism, that aesthetic judgments rest on them in an absolutely fundamental way. For this reason, and for another as well, the view that works of art should be judged simply by what can be perceived in them is seriously misleading, though there is something right in the idea that what matters aesthetically about a painting or a sonata is just how it looks or sounds.

II. STANDARD, VARIABLE, AND CONTRA-STANDARD PROPERTIES

I will continue to call tension, mystery, energy, coherence, balance, serenity, sentimentality, pallidness, disunity, grotesqueness, and so forth, as well as colors and shapes, pitches and timbres *properties* of works of art, though "property" is to be construed broadly enough not to beg any important questions. I will also, following Sibley, call properties of the former sort "aesthetic" properties, but purely for reasons of convenience I will include in this category "representational" and "resemblance" properties, which Sibley excludes—for example, the property of representing or being a picture of Napoleon, that of depicting an old man (as) stooping over a fire, that of resembling, or merely suggesting, a human face, claws (the petals of Van Gogh's sunflowers), or (in music) footsteps or conversation. It is not essential for my purposes to delimit with any exactness the class of aesthetic properties (if indeed any such delimitation is possible), for I am more interested in discussing particular examples of such properties than in making generalizations about the class as a whole. It will be obvious, however, that what I say about the examples I deal with is also applicable to a great many other properties we would want to call aesthetic.

Sibley points out that a work's aesthetic properties depend on its nonaesthetic properties; the former are "emergent" or "*Gestalt*" properties based on the latter.[3] I take this to be true of all the examples of aesthetic properties we will be dealing with, including representational and resemblance ones. It is because of the configuration of colors and shapes on a painting, perhaps in particular its dark colors and diagonal composition, that it has a sense of mystery and ten-

sion, if it does. The colors and shapes of a portrait are responsible for its resembling an old man and (perhaps with its title) its depicting an old man. The coherence or unity of a piece of music (for example, Beethoven's *Fifth Symphony*) may be largely due to the frequent recurrence of a rhythmic motive, and the regular meter of a song plus the absence of harmonic modulation and of large intervals in the voice part may make it serene or peaceful.

Moreover, a work *seems* or *appears* to us to have certain aesthetic properties because we observe in it, or it appears to us to have, certain nonaesthetic features (though it may not be necessary to notice consciously all the relevant nonaesthetic features). A painting depicting an old man may not look like an old man to someone who is color-blind, or when it is seen from an extreme angle or in bad lighting conditions so that its colors or shapes are distorted or obscured. Beethoven's *Fifth Symphony* performed in such a sloppy manner that many occurrences of the four-note rhythmic motive do not sound similar may seem incoherent or disunified.

I will argue, however, that a work's aesthetic properties depend not only on its nonaesthetic ones, but also on which of its nonaesthetic properties are "standard," which "variable," and which "contra-standard," in senses to be explained. I will approach this thesis by way of the psychological point that what aesthetic properties a work seems to us to have depends not only on what nonaesthetic features we perceive in it, but also on which of them are standard, which variable, and which contra-standard *for us* (in a sense also to be explained). . . .

A feature of a work of art is *standard* with respect to a (perceptually distinguishable) category just in case it is among those in virtue of which works in that category belong to that category—that is, just in case the lack of that feature would disqualify, or tend to disqualify, a work from that category. A feature is *variable* with respect to a category just in case it has nothing to do with works' belonging to that category; the possession or lack of the feature is irrelevant to whether a work qualifies for the category. Finally, a *contra-standard* feature with respect to a category is the absence of a standard feature with respect to that category—that is, a feature whose presence tends to *disqualify* works as members of the category. Needless to say, it will not be clear in *all* cases whether a feature of a work is standard, variable, or contra-standard relative to a given category, since the criteria for classifying works of art are far from precise. But clear examples are abundant. The flatness of a painting and the motionlessness of its markings are standard, and its particular shapes and colors are variable, relative to the category of painting. A protruding three-dimensional object or an electrically driven twitching of the canvas would be contra-standard relative to this category. The straight lines in stick-figure drawings and squarish shapes in cubist paintings are standard with respect to those categories respectively, though they are variable with respect to the categories of drawing and painting. The exposition-development-recapitulation form of a classical sonata is standard, and its thematic material is variable, relative to the category of sonatas. . . .

It will be useful to point out some of the *causes* of our perceiving works in certain categories. (*a*) In which categories we perceive a work depends in part, of course, on what other works we are familiar with. The more works of a certain sort we have experienced, the more likely it is that we will perceive a particular work in that category. (*b*) What we have heard critics and others say about works we have experienced, how they have categorized them, and what resemblances they have pointed out to us is also important. If no one has ever explained to me what is distinctive about Schubert's style (as opposed to the styles of, say, Schumann, Mendelssohn, Beethoven, Brahms, Hugo Wolf), or even pointed out that there is such a distinctive style, I may never have learned to hear the Schubertian *Gestalt* quality, even if I have heard many of Schubert's works, and so I may not hear his works as Schubertian. (*c*) How we are introduced to the particular work in question may be involved. If a Cézanne painting is exhibited in a collection of French Impressionist works, or if before seeing it we are told that it is French Impressionist, we are more likely to see it as French Impressionist than if it is exhibited in a random collection and we are not told anything about it beforehand.

I will say that a feature of a work is standard for a particular person on a particular occasion when, and

only when, it is standard relative to some category in which he perceives it, and is not contra-standard relative to any category in which he perceives it. A feature is variable for a person on an occasion just when it is variable relative to *all* of the categories in which he perceives it. And a feature is contra-standard for a person on an occasion just when it is contra-standard relative to *any* of the categories in which he perceives it.[4]

III. A POINT ABOUT PERCEPTION

I turn now to my psychological thesis that what aesthetic properties a work seems to have, what aesthetic effect it has on us, how it strikes us aesthetically often depends (in part) on which of its features are standard, which variable, and which contra-standard for us. I offer a series of examples in support of this thesis.

(*a*) Representational and resemblance properties provide perhaps the most obvious illustration of this thesis. Many works of art look like or resemble other objects—people, buildings, mountains, bowls of fruit, and so forth. Rembrandt's "Titus Reading" looks like a boy, and in particular like Rembrandt's son; Picasso's "Les Demoiselles d'Avignon" looks like five women, four standing and one sitting (though not *especially* like any particular women). A portrait may even be said to be a *perfect* likeness of the sitter, or to capture his image *exactly*.

An important consideration in determining whether a work *depicts* or *represents* a particular object, or an object of a certain sort (for example, Rembrandt's son, or simply *a* boy), in the sense of being a picture, sculpture, or whatever of it[5] is whether the work resembles that object, or objects of that kind. A significant degree of resemblance is, I suggest, a necessary condition in most contexts for such representation or depiction,[6] though the resemblance need not be obvious at first glance. If we are unable to see a similarity between a painting purportedly of a woman and women, I think we would have to suppose either that there is such a similarity which we have not yet discovered (as one might fail to see a face in a maze of lines), or that it simply is not a picture of a woman. Resemblance is of course not a *sufficient* condition for representation, since a portrait (containing only one figure) might resemble both the sitter and his twin brother equally but is not a portrait of both of them. (The title might determine which of them it depicts.)[7]

It takes only a touch of perversity, however, to find much of our talk about resemblances between works of art and other things preposterous. Paintings and people are *very* different sorts of things. Paintings are pieces of canvas supporting splotches of paint, while people are live, three-dimensional, flesh-and-blood animals. Moreover, except rarely and under special conditions of observation (probably including bad lighting) paintings and people *look* very different. Paintings look like pieces of canvas (or anyway flat surfaces) covered with paint and people look like flesh-and-blood animals. There is practically no danger of confusing them. How, then, can anyone seriously hold that a portrait resembles the sitter to any significant extent, let alone that it is a perfect likeness of him? Yet it remains true that many paintings strike us as resembling people, sometimes very much or even exactly—despite the fact that they look so very different!

To resolve this paradox we must recognize that the resemblances we perceive between, for example, portraits and people, those that are relevant in determining what works of art depict or represent, are resemblances of a somewhat special sort, tied up with the categories in which we perceive such works. The properties of a work which are standard for us are ordinarily irrelevant to what we take it to look like or resemble in the relevant sense, and hence to what we take it to depict or represent. The properties of a portrait which make it *so* different from, so easily distinguishable from, a person—such as its flatness and its *painted* look—are standard for us. Hence these properties just do not count with regard to what (or whom) it looks like. It is only the properties which are variable for us, the colors and shapes on the work's surface, that make it look to us like what it does. And these are the ones which are taken as relevant in determining what (if anything) the work represents.[8]

Other examples will reinforce this point. A marble bust of a Roman emperor seems to us to resemble a man with, say, an aquiline nose, a wrinkled brow, and an expression of grim determination, and we take it to represent a man with, or as having, those characteristics. But why don't we say that it resembles and represents a perpetually motionless man, of uniform (marble) color, who is severed at the chest? It is similar to such a man, it seems, and much more so than to a normally colored, mobile, and whole man. But we are not struck by the former similarity when we see the bust, obvious though it is on reflection. The bust's uniform color, motionlessness, and abrupt ending at the chest are standard properties relative to the category of busts, and since we see it as a bust they are standard for us. Similarly, black-and-white drawings do not look to us like colorless scenes and we do not take them to depict things as being colorless, nor do we regard stick-figure drawings as resembling and depicting only very thin people. A cubist work might look like a person with a cubical head to someone not familiar with the cubist style. But the standardness of such cubical shapes for people who see it as a cubist work prevents them from making that comparison.

The shapes of a painting or a still photograph of a high jumper in action are motionless, but these pictures do not look to us like a high jumper frozen in midair. Indeed, depending on features of the pictures which are variable for us (for example, the exact positions of the figures, swirling brush strokes in the painting, slight blurrings of the photographic image) the athlete may seem in a frenzy of activity; the pictures may convey a vivid sense of movement. But if static images exactly like those of the two pictures occur in a motion picture, and we see it as a motion picture, they probably would strike us as resembling a static athlete. This is because the immobility of the images is standard relative to the category of still pictures and variable relative to that of motion pictures. (Since we are so familiar with still pictures it might be difficult to see the static images as motion pictures for very long, rather than as [filmed] still pictures. But we could not help seeing them that way if we had no acquaintance at all with the medium of still pictures.) My point here is brought out by the tremendous aesthetic difference we are likely to experience between a film of a dancer moving *very* slowly and a still picture of him, even if "objectively" the two images are very nearly identical. We might well find the former studied, calm, deliberate, laborious, and the latter dynamic, energetic, flowing, or frenzied.

In general, then, what we regard a work as resembling, and as representing, depends on the properties of the work which are variable, and not on those which are standard for us.[9] The latter properties serve to determine what *kind* of a representation the work is, rather than what it represents or resembles. We take them for granted, as it were, in representations of that kind. This principle helps to explain also how clouds can look like elephants, how diatonic orchestral music can suggest a conversation or a person crying or laughing, and how a twelve-year-old boy can look like his middle-aged father. . . .

(*b*) The importance of the distinction between standard and variable properties is by no means limited to cases involving representation or resemblance. Imagine a society which does not have an established medium of painting, but does produce a kind of work of art called *guernicas*. *Guernicas* are like versions of Picasso's "Guernica" done in various bas-relief dimensions. All of them are surfaces with the colors and shapes of Picasso's "Guernica," but the surfaces are molded to protrude from the wall like relief maps of different kinds of terrain. Some *guernicas* have rolling surfaces, others are sharp and jagged, still others contain several relatively flat planes at various angles to each other, and so forth. Picasso's "Guernica" would be counted as a *guernica* in this society—a perfectly flat one—rather than as a painting. Its flatness is variable and the figures on its surface are standard relative to the category of *guernicas*. Thus the flatness, which is standard for us, would be variable for members of the other society (if they should come across "Guernica") and the figures on the surface, which are variable for us, would be standard for them. This would make for a profound difference between our aesthetic reaction to "Guernica" and theirs. It seems violent, dynamic, vital, disturbing to us. But I imagine it would strike them as cold, stark, lifeless, or serene and restful, or perhaps bland, dull, boring—but in any case *not* violent, dynamic, and vital. We do not pay attention to or take note of "Guernica"'s flatness; this is a feature we take for granted in paintings, as it were. But for the other society this is "Guernica"'s most striking and noteworthy characteristic—what is *expressive* about it. Conversely, "Guernica"'s color patches, which we

find noteworthy and expressive, are insignificant to them. . . .

(*c*) Because of the very fact that features standard for us do not seem striking or noteworthy, that they are somehow expected or taken for granted, they can contribute to a work a sense of order, inevitability, stability, correctness. This is perhaps most notably true of large-scale structural properties in the time arts. The exposition-development-recapitulation form (including the typical key and thematic relationships) of the first movements of classical sonatas, symphonies, and string quartets is standard with respect to the category of works in sonata-allegro form, and standard for listeners, including most of us, who hear them as belonging to that category. So proceeding along the lines of sonata-allegro form seems *right* to us; to our ears that is how sonatas are *supposed* to behave. We feel that we know where we are and where we are going throughout the work—more so, I suggest, than we would if we were not familiar with sonata-allegro form, if following the strictures of that form were variable rather than standard for us.[10] Properties standard for us do not always have this sort of unifying effect, however. The fact that a piano sonata contains only piano sounds, or uses the Western system of harmony throughout, does not make it seem unified to us. The reason, I think, is that these properties are *too* standard for us in a sense that needs explicating (cf. note 10). Nevertheless, sonata form is unifying partly because it is standard rather than variable for us.

(*d*) That a work (or part of it) has a certain determinate characteristic (for example, of size, speed, length, volume) is often variable relative to a particular category, when it is nevertheless standard for that category that the variable characteristic falls within a certain range. In such cases the aesthetic effect of the determinate variable property may be colored by the standard limits of the range. Hence these limits function as an aesthetic catalyst, even if not as an active ingredient.

Piano music is frequently marked *sostenuto, cantabile, legato,* or *lyrical*. But how can the pianist possibly carry out such instructions? Piano tones diminish in volume drastically immediately after the key is struck, becoming inaudible relatively promptly, and there is no way the player can prevent this. If a singer or violinist should produce sounds even approaching a piano's in suddenness of demise, they would be nerve-wrackingly sharp and percussive— anything but *cantabile* or lyrical! Yet piano music *can* be *cantabile, legato,* or lyrical nevertheless; sometimes it is extraordinarily so (for example, a good performance of the *Adagio Cantabile* movement of Beethoven's *Pathétique* sonata). What makes this possible is the very fact that the drastic diminution of piano tones cannot be prevented, and hence never is. It is a standard feature for piano music. A pianist can, however, by a variety of devices, control a tone's rate of diminution and length within the limits dictated by the nature of the instrument.[11] Piano tones may thus be *more or less* sustained within these limits, and *how* sustained they are, how quickly or slowly they diminish and how long they last, within the range of possibilities, is variable for piano music. A piano passage that sounds lyrical or *cantabile* to us is one in which the individual tones are *relatively* sustained, given the capabilities of the instrument. Such a passage sounds lyrical only because piano music is limited as it is, and we hear it as piano music; that is, the limitations are standard properties for us. The character of the passage is determined not merely by the "absolute" nature of the sounds, but by that in relation to the standard property of what piano tones can be like.[12]

This principle helps to explain the lack of energy and brilliance that we sometimes find even in very fast passages of electronic music. The energy and brilliance of a fast violin or piano passage derives not merely from the absolute speed of the music (together with accents, rhythmic characteristics, and so forth), but from the fact that it is fast *for that particular medium.* In electronic music different pitches can succeed one another at any frequency up to and including that at which they are no longer separately distinguishable. Because of this it is difficult to make electronic music *sound* fast (energetic, violent). For when we have heard enough electronic music to be aware of the possibilities we do not feel that the speed of a passage approaches a limit, no matter how fast it is.[13] . . .

(*e*) Properties standard for a certain category which do not derive from physical limitations of the medium can be regarded as results of more or less conventional "rules" for producing works in the given category (for example, the "rules" of sixteenth-century counterpoint, or those for twelve-tone music). These rules may combine to create a dilemma for the artist which, if he is talented, he may resolve ingeniously and gracefully. The result may be a work with an aesthetic character very different from what it would have had if it had not been for those rules. Suppose that the first movement of a sonata in G major modulates to C-sharp major by the end of the development section. A rule of sonata form decrees that it must return to G for the recapitulation. But the keys of G and C-sharp are as unrelated as any two keys can be; it is difficult to modulate smoothly and quickly from one to the other. Suppose also that while the sonata is in C-sharp there are signs that, given other rules of sonata form, indicate that the recapitulation is imminent (for example, motivic hints of the return, an emotional climax, or a cadenza). Listeners who hear it as a work in sonata form are likely to have a distinct feeling of unease, tension, uncertainty, as the time for the recapitulation approaches. If the composer with a stroke of ingenuity accomplishes the necessary modulation quickly, efficiently, and naturally, this will give them a feeling of relief—one might say of deliverance. The movement to C-sharp (which may have seemed alien and brashly adventurous) will have proven to be quite appropriate, and the entire sequence will in retrospect have a sense of correctness and perfection about it. Our impression of it is likely, I think, to be very much like our impression of a "beautiful" or "elegant" proof in mathematics. (Indeed the composer's task in this example is not unlike that of producing such a proof.)

But suppose that the rule for sonatas were that the recapitulation must be *either* in the original key *or* in the key one half-step below it. Thus in the example above the recapitulation could have been in F-sharp major rather than G major. This possibility removes the sense of tension from the occurrence of C-sharp major in the development section, for a modulation from C-sharp to F-sharp is as easy as any modulation is (since C-sharp is the dominant of F-sharp). Of course, there would also be no special *release* of tension when the modulation to G is effected, there being no tension to be released. In fact, that modulation probably would be rather surprising, since the permissible modulation to F-sharp would be much more natural.

Thus the effect that the sonata has on us depends on which of its properties are dictated by "rules," which ones are standard relative to the category of sonatas and hence standard for us.

(*f*) I turn now to features which are contra-standard for us—that is, ones which have a tendency to disqualify a work from a category in which we nevertheless perceive it. We are likely to find such features shocking, or disconcerting, or startling, or upsetting, just because they are contra-standard for us. Their presence may be so obtrusive that they obscure the work's variable properties. Three-dimensional objects protruding from a canvas and movement in a sculpture are contra-standard relative to the categories of painting and (traditional) sculpture respectively. These features are contra-standard for us, and probably shocking, if despite them we perceive the works possessing them in the mentioned categories. The monochromatic paintings of Yves Klein are disturbing to us (at least at first) for this reason: we see them as paintings, though they contain the feature contra-standard for paintings of being one solid color. Notice that we find other similarly monochromatic surfaces—for example, walls of living rooms—not in the least disturbing, and indeed quite unnoteworthy.

If we are exposed frequently to works containing a certain kind of feature which is contra-standard for us, we ordinarily adjust our categories to accommodate it, making it contra-standard for us no longer. The first painting with a three-dimensional object glued to it was no doubt shocking. But now that the technique has become commonplace we are not shocked. This is because we no longer see these works as *paintings,* but rather as members of either (*a*) a new category— *collages*—in which case the offending feature has become standard rather than contra-standard for us, or (*b*) an expanded category which includes paintings both with and without attached objects, in which case that feature is variable for us.

But it is not just the rarity, unusualness, or unexpectedness of a feature that makes it shocking. If a work differs *too* significantly from the norms of a certain category we do not perceive it in that category and

hence the difference is not contra-standard for us, even if we have not previously experienced works differing from that category in that way. A sculpture which is constantly and vigorously in motion would be so obviously and radically different from traditional sculptures that we probably would not perceive it as one even if it is the first moving sculpture we have come across. We would either perceive it as a *kinetic* sculpture, or simply remain confused. In contrast, a sculptured bust which is traditional in every respect except that one ear twitches slightly every thirty seconds would be perceived as an ordinary sculpture. So the twitching ear would be contra-standard for us and would be considerably more unsettling than the much greater movement of the other kinetic sculpture. Similarly, a very small colored area of an otherwise entirely black-and-white drawing would be very disconcerting. But if enough additional color is added to it we will see it as a colored rather than a black-and-white drawing, and the shock will vanish. . . .

It should be clear from the above examples that how a work affects us aesthetically—what aesthetic properties it seems to us to have and what ones we are inclined to attribute to it—depends in a variety of important ways on which of its features are standard, which variable, and which contra-standard for us. Moreover, this is obviously not an isolated or exceptional phenomenon, but a pervasive characteristic of aesthetic perception. I should emphasize that my purpose has not been to establish general principles about how each of the three sorts of properties affects us. How any particular feature affects us depends also on many variables I have not discussed. The important point is that in many cases whether a feature is standard, variable, or contra-standard for us has a great deal to do with what effect it has on us. We must now begin to assess the theoretical consequences of this.

IV.   TRUTH AND FALSITY

The fact that what aesthetic properties a thing seems to have may depend on what categories it is perceived in raises a question about how to determine what aesthetic properties it really does have. If "Guernica" appears dynamic when seen as a painting, and not dynamic when seen as a *guernica,* is it dynamic or not? Can one way of seeing it be ruled correct, and the other incorrect? One way of approaching this problem is to deny that the apparently conflicting aesthetic judgments of people who perceive a work in different categories actually do conflict.[14]

Judgments that works of art have certain aesthetic properties, it might be suggested, implicitly involve reference to some particular set of categories. Thus our claim that "Guernica" is dynamic really amounts to the claim that it is (as we might say) dynamic *as a painting,* or for people who see it as a painting. The judgment that it is not dynamic made by people who see it as a *guernica* amounts simply to the judgment that it is not dynamic *as a guernica.* Interpreted in these ways, the two judgments are of course quite compatible. Terms like "large" and "small" provide a convenient model for this interpretation. An elephant might be both small as an elephant and large as a mini-elephant, and hence it might be called truly either "large" or "small," depending on which category is implicitly referred to.

I think that aesthetic judgments are in *some* contexts amenable to such category-relative interpretations, especially aesthetic judgments about natural objects (clouds, mountains, sunsets) rather than works of art. (It will be evident that the alternative account suggested below is not readily applicable to most judgments about natural objects.) But most of our aesthetic judgments can be forced into this mold only at the cost of distorting them beyond recognition.

My main objection is that category-relative interpretations do not allow aesthetic judgments to be mistaken often enough. It would certainly be natural to consider a person who calls "Guernica" stark, cold, or dull, because he sees it as a *guernica,* to be *mistaken:* he misunderstands the work because he is looking at it in the wrong way. Similarly, one who asserts that a good performance of the *Adagio Cantabile* of Beethoven's *Pathétique* is percussive, or that a Roman bust looks like a unicolored, immobile man severed at the chest and depicts him as such, is simply wrong, even if his judgment is a result of his perceiving the work in different categories from those in which we perceive it. Moreover, we do not accord a status any more privileged to our own aesthetic judgments. We are likely to regard, for example, cubist paintings, serial music, or Chinese music as formless, incoherent, or disturbing on our first contact with these forms largely because, I suggest, we would not be perceiving the works as cubist paintings, serial music, or Chinese music. But after becoming familiar with these kinds of art we would probably *retract* our previous judgments, admit that they were mistaken. It would be quite inappropriate to protest that what we meant previously was merely that the works were formless or disturbing for the categories in which we then perceived them, while admitting that they are not for the categories of cubist paintings, or serial, or Chinese music. The conflict between apparently incompatible aesthetic judgments made while perceiving a work in different categories does not simply evaporate when the difference of categories is pointed out, as does the conflict between the claims that an animal is large and that it is small, when it is made clear that the person making the first claim regarded it as a mini-elephant and the one making the second regarded it as an elephant. The latter judgments do not (necessarily) reflect a real disagreement about the size of the animal, but the former do reflect a real disagreement about the aesthetic nature of the work.

Thus it seems that, at least in some cases, it is *correct* to perceive a work in certain categories, and *incorrect* to perceive it in certain others; that is, our judgments of it when we perceive it in the former are likely to be true, and those we make when perceiving it in the latter false. This provides us with absolute senses of "standard," "variable," and "contra-standard": features of a work are standard, variable, or contra-standard absolutely just in case they are standard, variable, or contra-standard (respectively) for people who perceive the work correctly. (Thus an absolutely standard feature is standard relative to some category in which the work is correctly perceived and contra-standard relative to none, an absolutely variable feature is variable relative to all such categories, and an absolutely contra-standard feature is contra-standard relative to at least one such category.)

How is it to be determined in which categories a work is correctly perceived? There is certainly no very precise or well-defined procedure to be followed. Different criteria are emphasized by different people and in different situations. But there are several fairly definite considerations which typically figure in critical discussions and fit our intuitions reasonably well. I suggest that the following circumstances count toward its being correct to perceive a work, *W,* in a given category, *C:*

(*i*) The presence in *W* of a relatively large number of features standard with respect to *C.* The correct way of perceiving a work is likely to be that in which it has a minimum of contra-standard features for us. I take the relevance of this consideration to be obvious. It cannot be correct to perceive Rembrandt's "Titus Reading" as a kinetic sculpture, if this is possible, just because that work has too few of the features which make kinetic sculptures kinetic sculptures. But of course this does not get us very far, for "Guernica," for example, qualifies equally well on this count for being perceived as a painting and as a *guernica.*

(*ii*) The fact, if it is one, that *W* is better, or more interesting or pleasing aesthetically, or more worth experiencing when perceived in *C* than it is when perceived in alternative ways. The correct way of perceiving a work is likely to be the way in which it comes off best.

(*iii*) The fact, if it is one, that the artist who produced *W* intended or expected it to be perceived in *C,* or thought of it as a *C.*

(*iv*) The fact, if it is one, that *C* is well established in and recognized by the society in which *W* was produced. A category is well established in and recognized by a society if the members of the society are familiar with works in that category, consider a work's membership in it a fact worth mentioning, exhibit works of that category together, and so forth—that is, roughly if that category figures importantly in their way of classifying works of art. The categories of impressionist painting and Brahmsian music are well established and recognized in our society; those of *guernicas,* paintings with diagonal composition containing green crosses, and pieces of music containing between four and eight F-sharps and at least seventeen quarter notes every eight bars are not. The categories in which a work is correctly perceived, according to this condition, are generally the ones in which the artist's contemporaries did perceive or would have perceived it. . . .

. . . What can be said in support of the relevance of conditions (*ii*), (*iii*), and (*iv*)? In the examples mentioned above, the categories in which we consider a work correctly perceived seem to meet (to the best of our knowledge) each of these three conditions. I would suppose that "Guernica" is better seen as a painting than it would be seen as a *guernica* (though this would be hard to prove). In any case, Picasso certainly intended it to be seen as a painting rather than a *guernica,* and the category of paintings is, and that of *guernicas* is not, well established in his (that is, our) society. But this of course does not show that (*ii*), (*iii*), and (*iv*) *each* is relevant. It tends to indicate only that one or other of them, or some combination, is relevant. The difficulty of assessing each of the three conditions individually is complicated by the fact that by and large they can be expected to coincide, to yield identical conclusions. Since an artist usually intends his works for his contemporaries he is likely to intend them to be perceived in categories established in and recognized by his society. Moreover, it is reasonable to expect works to come off better when perceived in the intended categories than when perceived in others. An artist tries to produce works which are well worth experiencing when perceived in the intended way and, unless we have reason to think he is totally incompetent, there is some presumption that he succeeded at least to some extent. But it is more or less a matter of chance whether the work comes off well when perceived in some unintended way. The convergence of the three conditions, however, at the same time diminishes the *practical* importance of justifying them individually, since in most cases we can decide how to judge particular works of art without doing so. But the theoretical question remains.

I will begin with (*ii*). If we are faced with a choice between two ways of perceiving a work, and the work is very much better perceived in one way than it is perceived in the other, I think that, at least in the absence of contrary considerations, we would be strongly inclined to settle on the former way of perceiving it as the *correct* way. The process of trying to determine what is in a work consists partly in casting around among otherwise plausible ways of perceiving it for one in which the work is good. We feel we are coming to a correct understanding of a work when we begin to like or enjoy it; we are finding what is really there when it seems to be worth experiencing.

But if (*ii*) is relevant, it is quite clearly not the *only* relevant consideration. Take any work of art we can agree is of fourth- or fifth- or tenth-rate quality. It is quite possible that if this work were perceived in some far-fetched set of categories that someone might dream up, it would appear to be first-rate, a masterpiece. Finding such *ad hoc* categories obviously would require talent and ingenuity on the order of that necessary to produce a masterpiece in the first place. But we can sketch how one might begin searching for them. (*a*) If the mediocre work suffers from some disturbingly prominent feature that distracts from whatever merits the work has, this feature might be toned down by choosing categories with respect to which it is standard, rather than variable or contra-standard. When the work is perceived in the new way the offending feature may be no more distracting than the flatness of a painting is to us. (*b*) If the work suffers from an overabundance of clichés it might be livened up by choosing categories with respect to which the clichés are variable or contra-standard rather than standard. (*c*) If it needs ingenuity we might devise a set of rules in terms of which the work finds itself in a dilemma and then ingeniously escapes from it, and build these rules into a set of categories. Surely, however, if there are categories waiting to be discovered which would transform a mediocre work into a masterpiece, it does not follow that the work really is a hitherto unrecognized masterpiece. The fact that when perceived in such categories it would appear exciting, ingenious, and so forth, rather than grating, cliché-ridden, pedestrian, does not make it so. It *cannot* be correct, I suggest, to perceive a work in categories which are totally foreign to the artist and his society, even if it comes across as a masterpiece in them.[15]

This brings us to the historical conditions (*iii*) and (*iv*). I see no way of avoiding the conclusion that one or the other of them at least is relevant in determining in what categories a work is correctly perceived. I consider both relevant, but will not argue here for the independent relevance of (*iv*). (*iii*) merits special attention in light of the recent prevalence of disputes about the importance of artists' intentions. To test the relevance of (*iii*) we must consider a case in which (*iii*) and (*iv*) diverge. One such instance occurred during the early days of the twelve-tone movement in music. Schoenberg no doubt intended even his earliest twelve-tone works to be heard as such. But this category was certainly not then well established or recognized in his society: virtually none of his contemporaries (except close associates such as Berg and Webern), even musically sophisticated ones, would have (or could have) heard these works in that category. But it seems to me that even the very first twelve-tone compositions are correctly heard as such, that the judgments one who hears them otherwise would make of them (for example, that they are chaotic, formless) are mistaken. I think this would be so even if Schoenberg had been working entirely alone, if *none* of his contemporaries had any inkling of the twelve-tone system. No doubt the first twelve-tone compositions are much better when heard in the category of twelve-tone works than when they are heard in any other way people might be likely to hear them. But as we have seen this cannot *by itself* account for the correctness of hearing them in the former way. The only other feature of the situation which could be relevant, so far as I can see, is Schoenberg's intention.

The above example is unusual in that Schoenberg was extraordinarily self-conscious about what he was doing, having explicitly formulated rules—that is, specified standard properties—for twelve-tone composition. Artists are of course not often so self-conscious, even when producing revolutionary works of art. Their intentions as to which categories their works are to be perceived in are not nearly as clear as Schoenberg's were, and often they change their minds considerably during the process of creation. In such cases (as well as ones in which the artists' intentions are unknown) the question of what categories a work is correctly perceived in is, I think, left by default to condition (*iv*), together with (*i*) and (*ii*). But it seems to me that in almost all cases at least one of the historical conditions, (*iii*) and (*iv*), is of crucial importance.

My account of the rules governing decisions about what categories works are correctly perceived in leaves a lot undone. There are bound to be a large number of undecidable cases on my criteria. Artists' intentions are frequently unclear, variable, or undiscoverable. Many works belong to categories which are borderline cases of being well established in the artists' societies (perhaps, for example, the categories of rococo music—for instance, C.P.E. Bach—of music in the style of early Mozart, and of very thin metal sculptured figures of the kind that Giacometti made). Many works fall between well-established categories (for example, between impressionist and cubist paintings), possessing *some* of the standard features relative to each, and so neither clearly qualify nor clearly fail to qualify on the basis of condition (*i*) to be perceived in either. There is, in addition, the question of what relative weights to accord the various conditions when they conflict.

It would be a mistake, however, to try to tighten up much further the rules for deciding how works are correctly perceived. To do so would be simply to legislate gratuitously, since the intuitions and precedents we have to go on are highly variable and often confused. But it is important to notice just where these intuitions and precedents are inconclusive, for doing so will expose the sources of many critical disputes. One such dispute might well arise concerning Giacometti's thin metal sculptures. To a critic who sees them simply as sculptures, or sculptures of people, they look frail, emaciated, wispy, or wiry. But that is not how they would strike a critic who sees them in the category of thin metal sculptures of that sort (just as stick figures do not strike us as wispy or emaciated). He would be impressed not by the thinness of the sculptures, but by the expressive nature of the positions of their limbs, and so forth, and so no doubt would attribute very different aesthetic properties to them. Which of the two ways of seeing these works is correct is, I suspect, undecidable. It is not clear whether enough such works have been made and have been regarded sufficiently often as constituting a category for that category to be deemed well established in Giacometti's society. And I doubt whether any of the other conditions settle the issue conclusively. So perhaps the dispute between the two critics is essentially unresolvable. The most that we can do is to point out just what sort of a difference of perception underlies the dispute, and why it is unresolvable.

The occurrence of such impasses is by no means something to be regretted. Works may be fascinating precisely because of shifts between equally permissible ways of perceiving them. And the enormous richness of some works is due in part to the variety of permissible, and worthwhile, ways of perceiving them. But it should be emphasized that even when my criteria do not clearly specify a *single* set of categories in which a work is correctly perceived, there are bound to be possible ways of perceiving it (which we may or may not have thought of) that they definitely rule out.

The question posed at the outset of this section was how to determine what aesthetic properties a work has, given that which ones it seems to have depends on what categories it is perceived in, on which of its properties are standard, which variable, and which contra-standard for us. I have sketched in rough outline rules for deciding in what categories a work is *correctly* perceived (and hence which of its features are absolutely standard, variable, and contra-standard). The aesthetic properties it actually possesses are those that are to be found in it when it is perceived correctly.[16]

V. CONCLUSION

I return now to the issues raised in Section I. (I will adopt for the remainder of this paper the simplifying assumption that there is only one correct way of perceiving any work. Nothing important depends on this.) If a work's aesthetic properties are those that are to be found in it when it is perceived correctly, and the correct way to perceive it is determined partly by historical facts about the artist's intention and/or his society, no examination of the work itself, however thorough, will by itself reveal those properties.[17] If we are confronted by a work about whose origins we know absolutely nothing (for example, one lifted from the dust at an as yet unexcavated archaeological site on Mars), we would simply not be in a position to judge it aesthetically. We could not possibly tell by staring at it, no matter how intently and intelligently, whether it is coherent, or serene, or dynamic, for by staring we cannot tell whether it is to be seen as a sculpture, a *guernica,* or some other exotic or mundane kind of work of art. (We could attribute aesthetic properties to it in the way we do to natural objects, which of course does not involve consideration of historical facts about artists or their societies. . . . But to do this would not be to treat the object as a *work* of art.)

It should be emphasized that the relevant historical facts are not merely useful aids to aesthetic judgment; they do not simply provide hints concerning what might be found in the work. Rather they help to *determine* what aesthetic properties a work has; they, together with the work's nonaesthetic features, *make* it coherent, serene, or whatever. If the origin of a work which is coherent and serene had been different in crucial respects, the work would not have had these qualities; we would not merely have lacked a means for *discovering* them. And of two works which differ *only* in respect of their origins—that is, which are perceptually indistinguishable—one might be coherent or serene, and the other not. Thus, since artists' intentions are among the relevant historical considerations, the "intentional fallacy" is not a fallacy at all. I have of course made no claims about the relevance of artists' intentions as to the aesthetic properties that their works should have, and these intentions are among those most discussed in writings on aesthetics. I am willing to agree that whether an artist intended his work to be coherent or serene has nothing essential to do with whether it is coherent or serene. But this must not be allowed to seduce us into thinking that *no* intentions are relevant.

Aesthetic properties, then, are not to be found in works themselves in the straightforward way that colors and shapes or pitches and rhythms are. But I do not mean to deny that we perceive aesthetic properties in works of art. I see the serenity of a painting, and hear the coherence of a sonata, despite the fact that the presence of these qualities in the works depends partly on circumstances of their origin, which I cannot (now) perceive. Jones's marital status is part of what makes him a bachelor, if he is one, and we cannot tell his marital status just by looking at him, though we can thus ascertain his sex. Hence, I

suppose, his bachelorhood is not a property we can be said to perceive in him. But the aesthetic properties of a work do not depend on historical facts about it in anything like the way Jones's bachelorhood depends on his marital status. The point is not that the historical facts (or in what categories the work is correctly perceived, or which of its properties are absolutely standard, variable, and contra-standard) function as *grounds* in any ordinary sense for aesthetic judgments. By themselves they do not, in general, count either for or against the presence of any particular aesthetic property. And they are not part of a larger body of information (also including data about the work derived from an examination of it) from which conclusions about the work's aesthetic properties are to be deduced or inferred. We must learn to *perceive* the work in the correct categories, as determined in part by the historical facts, and judge it by what we then perceive in it. The historical facts help to determine whether a painting is, for example, serene *only* (as far as my arguments go) by affecting what way of perceiving the painting must reveal this quality if it is truly attributable to the work.

We must not, however, expect to judge a work simply by setting ourselves to perceive it correctly, once it is determined what the correct way of perceiving it is. For one cannot, in general, perceive a work in a given set of categories simply by setting himself to do it. I could not possibly, merely by an act of will, see "Guernica" as a *guernica* rather than a painting, or hear a succession of street sounds in any arbitrary category one might dream up, even if the category has been explained to me in detail. (Nor can I imagine except in a rather vague way what it would be like, for example, to see "Guernica" as a *guernica.*) One cannot merely decide to respond appropriately to a work—to be shocked or unnerved or surprised by its (absolutely) contra-standard features, to find its standard features familiar or mundane, and to react to its variable features in other ways—once he knows the correct categories. Perceiving a work in a certain category or set of categories is a skill that must be acquired by training, and exposure to a great many other works of the category or categories in question is ordinarily, I believe, an essential part of this training. (But an effort of will may facilitate the training, and once the skill is acquired one may be able to decide at will whether or not to perceive it in that or those categories.) This has important consequences concerning how best to approach works of art of kinds that are new to us—contemporary works in new idioms, works from foreign cultures, or newly resurrected works from the ancient past. It is no use just immersing ourselves in a particular work, even with the knowledge of what categories it is correctly perceived in, for that alone will not enable us to perceive it in those categories. We must become familiar with a considerable variety of works of similar sorts.

When dealing with works of more familiar kinds it is not generally necessary to undertake deliberately the task of training ourselves to be able to perceive them in the correct categories (expect perhaps when those categories include relatively subtle ones). But this is almost always, I think, only because we have been trained unwittingly. Even the ability to see paintings as paintings had to be acquired, it seems to me, by repeated exposure to a great many paintings. The critic must thus go beyond the work before him in order to judge it aesthetically, not only to discover what the correct categories are, but also to be able to perceive it in them. The latter does not require consideration of historical facts, or consideration of facts at all, but it requires directing one's attention nonetheless to things other than the work in question.

Probably no one would deny that *some* sort of perceptual training is necessary, in many if not all instances, for apprehending a work's serenity or coherence, or other aesthetic properties. And of course it is not only *aesthetic* properties whose apprehension by the senses requires training. But the kind of training required in the aesthetic cases (and perhaps some others as well) has not been properly appreciated. In order to learn how to recognize gulls of various kinds, or the sex of chicks, or a certain person's handwriting, one must usually have gulls of those kinds, or chicks of the two sexes, or examples of that person's handwriting pointed out to him, practice recognizing them himself, and be corrected when he makes mistakes. But the training important for discovering the serenity or coherence of a work of art that I have been discussing is not of this sort (though this sort of training might be important as well).

Acquiring the ability to perceive a serene or coherent work in the correct categories is not a matter of having had serene or coherent things pointed out to one, or having practiced recognizing them. What is important is not (or not merely) experience with other serene and coherent things, but experience with other things of the appropriate categories.

Much of the argument in this paper has been directed against the seemingly common-sense notion that aesthetic judgments about works of art are to be based solely on what can be perceived in them, how they look or sound. That notion is seriously misleading, I claim, on two quite different counts. I do not deny that paintings and sonatas are to be judged solely on what can be seen or heard in them—when they are perceived correctly. But examining a work with the senses can by itself reveal neither how it is correct to perceive it, nor how to perceive it that way.

NOTES

1. Heinrich Wölfflin, *Principles of Art History,* trans. by M. D. Hottinger (7th ed.; New York, 1929), p. 228.

2. "[W]e should all agree, I think, . . . that any quality that cannot even in principle be heard in it [a musical composition] does not belong to it as music." Monroe Beardsley, *Aesthetics: Problems in the Philosophy of Criticism* (New York, 1958), pp. 31–32.

3. "Aesthetic and Nonaesthetic," *Philosophical Review,* LXXII (1965).

4. In order to avoid excessive complexity and length, I am ignoring some considerations that might be important at a later stage of investigation. In particular, I think it would be important at some point to distinguish between different *degrees* or *levels* of standardness, variableness, and contra-standardness for a person; to speak, e.g., of features being *more* or *less* standard for him. At least two distinct sorts of grounds for such differences of degree should be recognized. (*a*) Distinctions between perceiving a work in a certain category to a greater and lesser extent should be allowed for, with corresponding differences of degree in the standardness for the perceiver of properties relative to that category. (*b*) A feature which is standard relative to more, and/or more specific, categories in which a person perceives the work should thereby count as more standard for him. Thus, if we see something as a painting and also as a French Impressionist painting, features standard relative

to both categories are more standard for us than features standard relative only to the latter.

5. This excludes, e.g., the sense of "represent" in which a picture might represent justice or courage, and probably other senses as well.

6. This does not hold for the special case of photography. A photograph is a photograph of a woman no matter what it looks like, I take it, if a woman was in front of the lens when it was produced.

7. Nelson Goodman denies that resemblance is necessary for representation—and obviously not merely because of isolated or marginal examples of non-resembling representations (p. 5). I cannot treat his arguments here, but rather than reject en masse the common-sense beliefs that pictures do resemble significantly what they depict and that they depict what they do partly because of such resemblances, if Goodman advocates rejecting them, I prefer to recognize a sense of "resemblance" in which these beliefs are true. My disagreement with him is perhaps less sharp than it appears since, as will be evident, I am quite willing to grant that the relevant resemblances are "conventional." Cf. Goodman, *Languages of Art* (Indianapolis, 1968), p. 39, n. 31.

8. The connection between features variable for us and what the work looks like is by no means a straightforward or simple one, however. It may involve "rules" which are more or less "conventional" (e.g., the "laws" of perspective). Cf. E. H. Gombrich, *Art and Illusion* (New York, 1960) and Nelson Goodman, op cit.

9. There is at least one group of exceptions to this. Obviously features of a work which are standard for us because they are standard relative to some *representational* category which we see it in—e.g., the category of nudes, still lifes, or landscapes—do help determine what the work looks like to us and what we take it to depict.

10. The presence of clichés in a work sometimes allows it to contain drastically disorderly elements without becoming chaotic or incoherent. Cf. Anton Ehrenzweig, *The Hidden Order of Art* (London, 1967), pp. 114–116.

11. The timing of the release of the key affects the tone's length. Use of the sustaining pedal can lessen slightly a tone's diminuendo by reinforcing its overtones with sympathetic vibrations from other strings. The rate of diminuendo is affected somewhat more drastically by the force with which the key is struck. The more forcefully it is struck the greater is the tone's relative diminuendo. (Obviously the rate of diminuendo cannot be controlled in this way independently of the tone's initial volume.) The successive tones of a melody can be made to overlap so that each tone's sharp attack is partially obscured by the lingering end of the preceding tone. A melodic tone may also be reinforced after it begins by sympathetic vibrations from harmonically related accompanying figures, contributed by the composer.

12. "[T]he musical media we know thus far derive their whole character and their usefulness as musical media precisely from their limitations." Roger Sessions, "Problems and Issues Facing the Composer Today," in Paul Henry Lang, *Problems of Modern Music* (New York, 1960), p. 31.

13. One way to make electronic music sound fast would be to make it sound like some traditional instrument, thereby trading on the limitations of that instrument.

14. I am ruling out the view that the notions of truth and falsity are not applicable to aesthetic judgments, on the ground that it would force us to reject so much of our normal discourse and common-sense intuitions about art that theoretical aesthetics, conceived as attempting to understand the institution of art, would hardly have left a recognizable subject matter to investigate. (Cf. the quotation from Wölfflin, above.)

15. To say that it is incorrect (in my sense) to perceive a work in certain categories is not necessarily to claim that one *ought not* to perceive it that way. I heartily recommend perceiving mediocre works in categories that make perceiving them worthwhile whenever possible. The point is that one is not likely to *judge* the work correctly when he perceives it incorrectly.

16. This is a considerable oversimplification. If there are two equally correct ways of perceiving a work, and it appears to have a certain aesthetic property perceived in one but not the other of them, does it actually possess this property or not? There is no easy general answer. Probably in some such cases the question is undecidable. But I think we would sometimes be willing to say that a work is, e.g., touching or serene if it seems so when perceived in one correct way (or, more hesitantly, that there is "something very touching, or serene, about it"), while allowing that it does not seem so when perceived in another way which we do not want to rule incorrect. In some cases works have aesthetic properties (e.g., intriguing, subtle, alive, interesting, deep) which are not apparent on perceiving it in any single acceptable way, but which depend on the multiplicity of acceptable ways of perceiving it and relations between them. None of these complications relieves the critic of the responsibility for determining in what way or ways it is correct to perceive a work.

17. But this, plus a general knowledge of what sorts of works were produced when and by whom, might.

The Very Idea of Art

~

TED COHEN

Ted Cohen is professor of philosophy at the University of Chicago. He has published articles on 18th-century aesthetics, television, photography, metaphor, and humor and is the author of *Jokes: Philosophical Thoughts on Joking Matters*.

WHAT'S SPECIAL ABOUT PHOTOGRAPHY?[1]

Writing about photography—theoretical, critical, practical, and historical writing—is hamstrung. Some of this writing is good, but virtually all of it suffers from some variety of unconfidence about the nature of the subject. Even in the writing of those who think they know very well just what photography is, there is an almost truculent insistence on the author's particular version of the deep truths about the nature of the medium. The essential character of photography has been alleged to debar it from any status as fine art, or from the possession of any significant style, or from the capacity for any but gross and pedestrian representational values. The arguments for such allegations are often implicit, but even in the case of explicit versions I cannot see why anyone believes any of these arguments to be sound. Many of them incorporate premises which are ambiguous at best and probably false, and nearly all of the arguments are invalid, so that it doesn't matter how things stand with the premises. For instance, this argument and counter can be found throughout a wide range of the literature:

Photography is fundamentally mechanical and automatic.
Therefore, photography is not an art, not a serious, fine art.

And the counter:

Photography is a true fine art.
Therefore, photography is not mechanical.

It takes little acumen to note that the argument is radically incomplete, at best. It isn't clear what "mechanical" or "automatic" means, and in particular it isn't clear what sense of either word might obtain so that anything mechanical or automatic in that sense could not be art. Put this baldly the arguments do not appear in any literature I know, but in scores of pages of the literature this is all the argument that is even implicitly present.

In the "theoretical" literature on photography the question of whether photography is, after all, an *art* is customarily related to the question of whether photography is just another way of making pictures or is a *special* way of making pictures. Neither question seems to me very clear, and even less clear is the relation between the two questions. One idea seems to be that unless there is something special in photographic pictures, those pictures must be inferior versions of pictures whose superior versions are the products of painting and drawing. I find it difficult to follow these arguments because I am unable to get a good grip on the idea that there might be *another* way of making pictures which is not a *special* way. An auxiliary idea is that photography begins as just another way of making pictures and is therefore initially a *craft*,

Reprinted from *The Monist, 71* (1988), by permission of the journal.

awaiting a chance to become *art,* as it will when the *special* character of photographic picture-making comes to the fore.

These ideas are present in writing about photography since at least as early as 1845. I will not discuss this literature at any length, although I aim to capture arguments to be found there. I would like to lay these arguments to rest, and I do not think it will help to become entangled in their various specific formulations. I believe that the questions of what photography *is* and of whether it is *art* have been unclear from the start. Photography itself has always been what it is: it had no need to evolve into something else. What needs some evolution is the way in which we think about photography, and I would like to make a modest contribution to that project. The task of appreciating the history of writing about photography is another project, and that project is already off to an excellent beginning in the work of Joel Snyder.[2] My aim is to provide a general assessment of what seem to be the leading arguments, and beyond that I will have a look at the putative insights which underlie them. I will do this mostly by way of analogies. There is no issue which this paper is likely to settle. My ambition is the modest one of unpacking some of the insights and temptations of those who think there is something extraordinary in photography, something of philosophical or aesthetic interest.

I

The single most pervasive conviction about photographs is that they stand in some peculiar relation to the world, a relation not shared by other pictures. We might try to put this by saying that a photograph must be *of* something. This is not clear enough, however, even for getting started, because it is ambiguous. If "being a photograph of" means being a picture of, and any picture of *I* guarantees the existence of *I,* then the statement that every photograph must be of something is false. On the other hand, if "being a photograph of" means being a causal sequel to something's reflection or emission of light, then the statement that every photograph must be of something is true—but this is an odd sense of "photograph of" which is not congruent with the normal sense of "pic-

ture of" or of "photograph of." A photograph certainly guarantees the existence of a light source, but that much follows trivially from the meaning of the word "photograph."

The conviction that photographs hold a special relation to the world seems most often to amount to the idea that a photograph is a *fossil.* Perhaps this idea is defensible, but fossils are not, in general, pictures. The amplified idea, perhaps, is that a photograph is a picture of whatever it is a fossil of. I would not like to defend this formulation, because of cases like this:

> You have a family photograph showing several people on the beach. In the upper right there is dark speck. As a matter of fact, although no one could determine this by looking at the photograph, that speck is there because Uncle Fritz was frolicking in the waves far off shore at the instant the shutter snapped (and, as another matter of fact, the photographer didn't even notice him).

Do you think this photograph is a *picture* of Uncle Fritz? I am not sure, and I'm not entirely comfortable even with the assertion that it is, or contains, a *photograph* of him. What makes me uncomfortable is the knowledge that this photograph might look exactly the same if Uncle Fritz had been out to lunch but a piece of dirt had been on the camera lens or if a speck of lint had been on the enlarger's lens or if a stray shaft of light had struck the undeveloped photographic paper. And yet in the photograph as we are imagining it, there is no doubt that the speck is a fossil of Fritz; as a matter of relatively simple causation, it is there in the photograph because Uncle Fritz was there in the waves.

We need a better idea than that a photograph is a picture of whatever it is a fossil of. A promising idea is that it is a fossil of whatever it happens to be a picture of. There is no doubt that the speck is a fossil of Fritz. Whether it is a photograph of him now depends upon whether it is a picture of him, and that is a question to be decided independently, and in any case this example and ones like it cease to be troublesome. It is an idea like this, I believe, which has led Kendall Walton to assert that photographs are "transparent," by which he means that in them we see—literally—

what they depict. In a photograph of Ken you see Ken. I see less in this idea than Walton does but I am not sure that he is wrong.

When discussing Ken Walton's work it is good to have some symbols in hand, and I think we could use some now anyway. P is a photograph. L is the light source used to make P. O is the subject of P: it is the object depicted by P. One might now say that by definition P "gives us" L. There is no *a priori* assurance, definitional or otherwise, that L is identical with O. (Thus Roland Barthes is simply wrong about a photograph's transmission of literal reality.)

No doubt in many cases P is such that $L = O$. Note, however, that this is a contingent fact which can not be told from examination of P alone, even if that examination somehow reveals that P is a photograph. When Ken Walton asserts that what is depicted in a photograph is seen by those who see the photograph (thus is the camera what he calls an "aid to vision"), this assertion must be qualified to apply only to photographs of which it's true that $L = O$.[3] Thus qualified, the assertion is acceptable, at least to me, and I think it says something about the metaphysics of some photographic pictures. I have yet to see the epistemological or aesthetical consequences.

Let me meander in search of consequences by simply supposing that in a particular case it is known or strongly believed that $L = O$. How does that affect one's sense of the photograph? How should it?

An Analogy

Perhaps a photograph is like a natural child, while other pictures are like adopted children. An adopted child may resemble a parent, and to some extent this may be due to its acquisition of mannerisms, posture, etc. which do come from the adoptive parents. And a natural child may not resemble the parent, or it may resemble it only with regard to this set of acquired, environmental features. But if it does resemble the parent, then we think that the resemblance is the result of genetic influence—a kind of basic, direct causation. So with photographs. A photograph may not resemble its subject, and a non-photographic picture may resemble its subject; but when a photograph does resemble its subject we think that the resemblance is the result of some basic, direct causation.

We look for parents in their children. We look for subjects in their photographs. If we find parents in their adopted children, or subjects in non-photographic pictures, we attribute this to artifice. If we find them in natural children or photographs, we attribute this to nature. I do not doubt that we do this. I wonder whether we are sensible to do it. Some cases, and they are not atypical, are mixed and complex. When I was a child, people remarked that I looked like my father when seen walking down the street, and the same thing has been said about my son and me. The noted similarity has many components. There are size, shape of body, relative length of limbs, for instance, but there are also posture and manner of walking. This manner incorporates speed, gait, placement of heel and toe, and motion of arms, while the posture includes the angle of head and torso. Some of these characteristics would be shared by my son, probably, if he were adopted and had spent as many years walking with me, but some would not. And some would be partial. For instance if my son's neck and torso were larger—if, say, I had adopted the child of a football player, a defensive lineman—then he would likely acquire a semblance of my walking posture but not a complete one. As things stand, some of my son's walking similarity seems due to genetics and some to habits acquired in his association with me. To these two constituents, the first apparently more directly and simply natural than the other, although the other is not "unnatural," might have been added characteristics developed in him by my explicit artifice. I might, for instance, have ordered him to walk in a certain way or suggested that he assume an erect posture. In the end, if you say that he looks like me, you will not have an easy time analyzing the similarity into discrete, simple parts, some natural and some not.

You will not have a much easier time explaining the resemblance of a photograph to its subject. The fact that the photograph shows a man with close-set, brooding eyes may be due to the fact that the subject has such eyes, but it may also be due to the angle from which the photographer shot, the play of light around the forehead, nose, and eyes—and this light display may have been wrought largely in the darkroom. Certainly a photographer can shoot a picture of me which resembles me so little that you won't pick me out. Why deny, then, that when his picture does resemble me, at least some measure of the resemblance is due to how he made the picture?

Then let us not deny it; let us suppose that all characteristics of the photograph, including those which have to do with its status as a representation and a resembler, are there, at least in part—and probably in very large part—because of the efforts of the photographer.

We should, however, note another thing as well. Earlier I said that I do not doubt that when we find parents in their children or subjects in their photographs, we attribute this to something more or other than artifice—call it "nature." I also said that I do not know just why we make this attribution. My remarks about parents and children were meant to show that when we do it we do it rather clumsily and out of a kind of prejudice, and that it is unclear what we are saying when we credit nature with my daughter's resemblance to her mother. But we do say it, we do do it. I do it. I admit it. I want to find the implicit content when I say it.

I am looking at a photograph. In it I see my son and his bicycle, among other things. This fact, that I see my son and his Motobecane in there, is due to the fact that *he and the bike were there* when the shot was taken. This is not a priori. The fact needn't have been a fact. There are other ways in which a photographic picture which looks much like this one might have been made. And my boy and his bike might have been there, and a photograph have been made which looked so little like this one that you couldn't see the boy and bike in it. So the fact of their being there is not an a priori fact, not a necessary fact, and certainly not a fact you could discern with certainty merely by gazing at this photograph. But it is a fact. And the knowledge that it is a fact informs my view of this photograph every instant. It is this quality, this flavor, this phenomenology of viewing photographs which leads people to say that when we look at photographs we look—really look—into the world's past. It may be one of the things that lead Ken Walton to say that we look at the things themselves. It leads us, at least some of us, some times, to prefer to look at a photograph than any other kind of picture.

This may sound like voodoo. (This may *be* voodoo.[4]) But try to keep the epistemology out of it. Maybe I am wrong about the photograph. Maybe it wasn't taken in the summer of 1984. Maybe it's not Amos: it's his twin or a robot or a picture of him. Can I prove that it's him? No. So what? When I look at my daughter, sometimes, it makes all the difference that I know she is my daughter. I know she is my natural daughter, in fact. Can I prove it? Maybe she's the milkman's. Maybe, as she is wont to insist when she is disgusted, she was stolen at birth from a better family and brought to us, and maybe I don't know this. So I look at her as my natural daughter and I am wrong to do so. I can't prove that she is my daughter. So what?

One has faith in photographs, so to speak. It can be misplaced. When photographs are introduced in court, competent attorneys insist on documentation of the provenance of the pictures. They know that a photograph itself, alone, doesn't prove anything. And sometimes, in court and elsewhere, a man might have to try to prove, as they say, beyond a reasonable doubt, that a girl is his daughter. The fact that the man and the girl look alike and have been together virtually all her life—those things themselves, alone, don't prove fatherhood.

Fatherhood is not carried out in court, however, nor are photographs characteristically appreciated there. To see this photograph, of my son and his wheels, as if it were merely contingently, incidentally, insignificantly connected to the fact that once he and it were there, on Dorchester Avenue, is a possible achievement, I suppose. It is, however, an arch aestheticization, a diminution, I think.

Another kind of diminution is achieved by those who view this as the only relevant fact, as if it were trivial that the film was Kodak's MP 5247, ASA 200, that the *f* stop was 8 and the shutter speed 1/250 of a second, and the rest of those things. Drop those things out and *you* are practicing voodoo. If those things weren't as they were, you wouldn't see him in the photograph as you do.

What follows from this? Nothing, I think, in this sense: nothing follows about the character of photography or its aesthetics. There is nothing in this to suggest that photographs are devoid of art; but there is nothing to suggest that their capacity to support nostalgia and their use as a tool against skepticism are illegitimate. The relation of photographs to the world is in some respects more natural than the comparable relation of other pictures. I have said what I can about those respects, and I conclude this section by observing that nothing whatever is implied about whether photographs are art, or have style, or can be expressive, or are in those respects different from other pictures.

II

The alleged special relation of photographs to the world is, allegedly, related to the alleged mechanical or automatic character of photography. What about this machinery? The machine in question, I suppose, is the camera, although the not infrequent reference to things like "optical and chemical" properties suggests that darkroom apparatus involved in developing and printing is to be included. There are two, separate points, and I will take them quickly in turn. The first concerns the fact that there is a machine in the works, the second has to do with the fact that this machine is somehow automatic.

The first point, despite the extent to which it dominates much thinking about photography, has remarkably little substance. It often seems to amount to an obsession with the fact of the camera, with the fact that it is a *machine*. This fact cannot by itself be especially pertinent, because machines are parts of a number of arts. When my son is cleaning and repairing his French horn the parts of this incredible apparatus cover the dining room floor. He plays the horn well, and he has a commendable knowledge of how the thing works. I would guess that his knowledge is comparable in scope to a photographer's knowledge of how his machine works. The difference, some would say, is that the camera is an *automatic* kind of machine and the horn is not that kind of machine. What does that mean? That cameras work all by themselves? They can be made to work by themselves, after a fashion; but if you outfitted the horn with an altered mouthpiece and set it out in a blizzard then it would work by itself. Responding to praise of

his performance at the organ, Bach is reported to have said this:

> There is nothing remarkable about it. All one has to do is hit the right notes at the right time, and the instrument plays itself.[5]

A charming remark, but not meant to be taken seriously; and the idea of setting up the French horn in a blizzard is just foolish. Still, I don't see exactly how it is more foolish than the idea that the camera is automatic—when this automatism is cited as an inherently unartistic or uncreative core in photography. With a camera, I suppose one might say, all one has to do is set the aperture and shutter mechanisms, point the thing the right way, hit the shutter button at the right time, and the instrument will play itself, just like Bach's organ.

The significant difference has to do with the results: the camera delivers a picture (at least sometimes), and it might do this, as it were, almost "by chance." Neither a pipe organ nor a French horn is likely to deliver a tune by chance. Let us try to get a grip on this idea that a camera is an automatic picture-making machine. Then we can try to understand why this fact about the camera seems to some to diminish the artistic capacities of photography, and finally I can say why this fact does not do this but does render photographs a special kind of picture.

It is undeniable that photography is automatically in possession of a capacity for a kind of gross, generic representation. By that I mean that with a camera virtually anyone can make easily detected likenesses of things and people. Not many of us can do this without a camera, especially when the task is to make a likeness of a person. In this respect one might say that photographs are infinitely "easier" to make than are other kinds of pictures. But it is only in this respect, and negative consequences for the artistic potential of photographs would follow, if at all, only if they were easier in all other respects. Some people write as if they were.

One way to make a picture which looks like a tall man is to turn your camera on a tall man (and pay some attention to what else shows up in your picture). One way to make a picture which looks like a tall, sad man is to turn your camera on a tall man looking sad. Some writers write as if they thought that were the only way to get sadness into a photograph, indeed as if the only way any of the oft-cited, little-understood values of plastic art—the expression of feeling and emotion, the celebration of life or God or whatever—as if the only way any of that could get into a photograph is by way of the photographer's finding those expressions, celebrations, etc. in the world and turning his camera on them. That idea is so misguided and so wrong that the only interest it yields is wonder at how it can arise. I personally believe it arises either from (1) an abysmal ignorance of the most elementary facts concerning how photographs are made, or (2) a steady diet of examples in each of which something like a family-album snapshot is compared with something like a Velazquez or a Rembrandt. Or it arises from the ignorance plus the stacked examples, perhaps because the ignorance leads one to choose just such pairs of examples.

A photograph might be profoundly sad and yet show a happy-looking person, or the other way round. A photograph might be "about" the isolation of a person from others, the insignificance of people, the triumph of the will, the eternal newness of America, the impossibility of the marriage contract. Of course it might, it could be about any of those things. And the photographer's problem in making such a photograph would be exactly the same as any picture-maker's, except, of course, that he has to address the problem in terms of the resources of photography, which are not the same as those of oil painting, but they do not make his task easier, nor do they make it impossible.

The picture we seem to be stuck with is this. Suppose M [a maker] makes something, X. Suppose L [a looker] looks at X. The question is, how does the relation of M to X compare with the relation of L to X? There seem to be two extreme cases, one in which the relations have to be the same, and one in which they cannot be the same. We are tempted to believe that photography is an instance of the first case, and painting an example of the second. In the second case M must have had a pre-conception of X in order to make X, and therefore his relation to it is different from that

of L, who has no conception of X until he sees it. (This pre-conception is what, in the *Critique of Judgment*, Kant calls a *Zweck*.) That is to say, for instance, that the painter has to know what he's going to do before he does it. This contrasts with the first case, where photography is supposed to belong, in which M needs no prior conceptualizing but makes do with a camera, something to point it at, and some light to reflect off whatever he's pointing at. He need have no efficacious conception, and so his photograph can be his occasion for the conception just as it is L's. (This is why it seems unremarkable when a photographer *discovers* what is in his own picture.)

This way of thinking of things leaves very little room for artistry on the part of the photographer. There certainly are photographs like this, ones about which, had you noticed where the camera was aimed, you would have as good an idea as the photographer how the picture would look. But if the photographer is able, and especially if he is very good, you won't know how his picture will look, not even if you look through the viewfinder. Or, to put it better, the things you do know are precisely not the things that will matter most.

The things you do know about what the photograph is likely to look like are, on the whole, exactly those things that will appear because of photography's automatic capacity for what I am calling gross depiction—the achievement of easily recognized likenesses. My idea is that this achievement dislocates the value of representation, especially relative to its value in other kinds of pictures. It is an old idea that photography freed painting from the burden of representing. I think this old idea is backwards. It is photography which is freed of this burden, just because it is no *burden* in photography. Contrary to Susan Sontag, for instance, I think that one's informed attention when looking at photographs tends to go elsewhere than to what is (grossly) depicted.

Another Analogy

Representation, in this sense of gross depiction, is something like pitch in the performance of music. With photographs this kind of representation has, roughly, the importance that pitch has in piano playing. It is sensible and important to attend to pitch when hearing people sing or when listening to strings, winds, and brasses play. Mastery of pitch is very important in the successful use of these instruments. But unless you object to the way a piano was tuned before the performance, there is no comparable way to dwell on achievements of pitch control when listening to a piano sonata. Pitch is, we might say, an *automatic* achievement of the piano. It is also a kind of limitation. Those shadings sharp and flat which mark a good string player, those adjustments which the good horn player makes to preserve the harmonics of the ensemble, are beyond the power of a pianist because of the *mechanical* character of the instrument. It is ridiculous to suggest that piano playing could not be good music, or that it could not incorporate features of style. It is possible, however, to imagine someone so misguided in his understanding of the piano and piano music that he found it inherently inartistic. I put it to you that this is how some writers seem to have found photography because of the automatic, mechanical character of the camera. Just as some people regard photographs as debased paintings made with the aid of an automatic tool, whose one interesting feature is that they record faithfully, so someone might regard piano playing as a debased form of string ensemble playing done with a clumsy string-sounder, whose one interesting feature was constancy of intonation. 'Absurd' is too soft a word for such an idea. The fact that pianos produce correct pitches and do so automatically is neither a guarantee of nor a barier to the artistic possibilities of piano music. The fact that cameras produce likenesses and do so automatically is neither a guarantee of nor a barrier to the artistic possibilities of photography.[6]

III

Neither the intimate relation of photographs to reality (such as that relation may be), nor the mechanical character of the camera is a bar to art in photography. It follows that there is no need for those who find photography artistic to deny either of these things. And it would be a mistake to do so. In the first place, as difficult as it is to describe the intimate relation, and as annoying as it is to be forced to say what's different in photography's automatism that would distinguish it from any other art's machinery, these are special, unique features of photography. In the second place, these features endow photographs with special interests which may or may not have to do with *Art*. There is nothing which prevents a single object's being a work of art and also engaging you in some respect which may seem to have nothing to do with that, and I dare say there is nothing wrong with that. Let me give you one very small example, from another art—literature.

It is a small passage. To follow it you need to know only that the first-person narrator is Anna, Janet is her daughter, and Marie is a friend of Janet's.

> Janet says, tell me a story. "There was once a little girl called Janet," I begin, and she smiles with pleasure. I tell how this little girl went to school on a rainy day, did lessons, played with the other children, quarrelled with her friend. . . . "No, mummy, I didn't, that was yesterday. I *love* Marie for ever and ever." So I change the story so that Janet loves Marie for ever and ever. Janet eats dreamily, conveying her spoon back and forth to her mouth, listening while I create her day, give it form.

The section goes on a bit, with the development of a wonderful negotiation between Anna and Janet over just how the story is to be told, over just what parts of the story must conform to Janet's day and what parts of Janet's day will be made to match the story; but we will not go into that. What is the point of Anna's telling this story to Janet? Well, it helps the child end her day; it helps her give in to bed, sleep, and the night. That is a sublime achievement. Anna says that the story creates Janet's day, gives it form. I do not know that it is easier to make the parts of one's life into a *day* than it is to make one's things into a *world;* so let us credit Anna with a real success. Her story has real value. Is the story also a work of art? I doubt that you would like to say so, and so let us turn to the larger story, of which this is a very small section. It is Doris Lessing's *The Golden Notebook*. That story is a work of art. It also creates a day, many days, a big part of someone's life, and it does it by (or in) giving it form. Whose life? Anna's. (But Anna *is* Doris Lessing, or at least she is nearly.) The value of

The Golden Notebook for Anna is the same as the value of Anna's little story for Janet. Now in the larger case, perhaps the value to Anna (and to any reader who can feel herself to be Anna) has become integral to the fact that the book is art, or the fact that it's good art. I don't know that it has. I only know that personal, intimate attachments to works are identifiable separately from the artistry of those works even if in some cases they merge.

Take my photograph of my son. Like Anna's story to Janet, this picture is no work of art, or at least it is not one of consequence. It is, however, of considerable value to me; and I dearly hope that someday it will touch him as what it is, or was meant to be, my attempt to make sense for him and me of the day of a city boy and his bike in the summer—an attempt to create his day.

Only a photograph could do this for us, because, unlike a painting, it signals that he was there and I was there and we were together making this photograph. Photographs can do such things for us. They can also be art. Perhaps in some cases their artistry incorporates this value of intimacy in the past preserved, this sense of the object and the photographer united in this picture. I think this of some things by Atget and some by Walker Evans. In those pictures I sense the choice of the photographer, the selection of something with which to unite. But this is all very flighty (as my friendly critic Joel Snyder would say, I have left the ground). Let me conclude, therefore, by concluding that there is nothing whatever in the nature of photography which disqualifies it as art, and by speculating that there are things in its nature which make it—some of the time—one of the kinds of art it can be.

NOTES

1. This paper began as a response to an excellent paper by Professor Cynthia Freeland, for a symposium at eastern-division meetings of the American Philosophical Association. I am grateful to her for having shown me that there is a good, difficult topic here. And I am grateful beyond adequate expression to Professor Joel Snyder who, first, has taught me virtually all I know about photography, and, second, has discussed and argued these questions with me at great length, refusing my extravagances but hearing them out sympathetically.

2. The best guide I know to this literature is "Photography, Vision and Representation" by Joel Snyder and Neil Walsh Allen, in *Critical Inquiry,* v. 2, n. 1, 1975. Early arguments to the effect that a photograph is essentially only another kind of picture can be found in William Henry Fox Talbot, *The Pencil of Nature* (London, 1845), and Peter Henry Emerson, *Naturalistic Photography* (London, 1889). (Snyder has told me that Ermerson later changed his opinions and makes the argument in question only in the first edition of the book.)

Arguments to the effect that photographs have a special nature are relatively more recent. They can be found, for instance, in Edward Weston, "Seeing Photographically," in *The Complete Photographer,* v. 9, n. 49 (New York, 1943); Beaumont Newhall, *The History of Photography,* (New York: 1964); and John Szarkowski, *The Photographer's Eye* (New York, 1967). (The last two texts were published by the Museum of Modern Art.).

3. Perhaps Walton would insist that the photograph is of *L,* even if *L* is not identical with *O,* or perhaps he would say that it is a characteristic feature of photographs that they invariably do depict *L.* I do not know his most recent thinking on these matters, and in any case I do not mean to be tangling with him here.

Two criteria come to mind for use in determining whether *P* depicts something, *L,* for instance. One is resemblance, if it can be explained well enough to settle the question of whether *P* resembles *L.* The other is some Goodman-like set of conditions for determining, as a matter of formal semantics, what *P* refers to, supposing it to be settled that *P* is the kind of symbol which can depict. On either ground, it seems clear to me that *P* does not depict Uncle Fritz. If one continues to maintain that *P* does depict Uncle Fritz (and any other light source whose light is realized in *P*), it seems to me that one must be doing so solely on the basis of this causal connection, and a consequence will be that the representational capacity of photographs will be entirely different from that of non-photographic pictures. If in our treatment of photographs—I mean how we look at them and try to make sense of them—we behave as we do when treating other pictures, at least with regard to determining what they depict, then we should be unwilling to suppose that they secure their depictions in any radically different way. If one persists in thinking that they do work in this different way, operating on the basis of one necessary and sufficient condition, namely the causal efficacy of a light source, then perhaps one should just abandon the idea that photographs are representational at all. Roger Scruton has taken this position. Perhaps Walton would agree, although for different reasons, for if he believes that in a photograph of Ken I see Ken literally, then why bother with the idea that I see a representation of Ken? It is only in peculiar and logically obnoxious cases that *X* represents *Y* and also is identical with *Y*. It might be more comfortable to think that photographs are (pictorially) representational and their frequent—even standard—causal relation to their depictions is an additional feature.

4. I owe this term to Joel Snyder. I first heard it in this technical employment when Snyder responded to the observation that photographs must themselves be close to the things they picture just as the shroud of Turin is thought to be nearer to Jesus himself than is any conceivable painting or drawing. It was also Snyder who got me to take note of what the word 'photograph' means.

5. Quoted by J. F. Köhler, as reported in *The Bach Reader,* rev. ed., edited by Hans T. David and Arthur Mendel (New York, 1966 and 1945). My thanks to Professor Peter Kivy who recalled that Bach had said something like this and put me on to it, and to Professor Ellen Harris who lent me the book and gave me guidance, and to myself who spent most of a summer looking in the book for this remark.

6. Of course neither the piano nor the camera does its trick all by itself. It must be prepared, by the performer or by someone else. I wish to compare the performer who sits down to a tuned piano with a photographer who picks up a ready-to-shoot camera. You are free to imagine the tuner to be simply a person who has tools for tightening and loosening strings, with either a good ear, a tuning fork, or an electronic pitch-checker, or you may think of him as someone who knows in detail how the thing works and builds the whole piano from scratch as well as tuning it. You may think of the photographer's helper as someone who focuses the lens and sets the aperture and shutter (or perhaps you prefer to think of it as a whiz-bang, super-automated camera which does all that on its own), or you may think of him as someone who really knows how the thing works and even builds it from scratch. The parallel remains.